Lecture Notes in Computer Science 10586

Commenced Publication in 1973
Founding and Former Series Editors:
Gerhard Goos, Juris Hartmanis, and Jan van Leeuwen

Editorial Board

More information about this series at http://www.springer.com/series/7409

Sergio F. Ochoa · Pritpal Singh
José Bravo (Eds.)

Ubiquitous Computing and Ambient Intelligence

11th International Conference, UCAmI 2017
Philadelphia, PA, USA, November 7–10, 2017
Proceedings

 Springer

Editors
Sergio F. Ochoa
University of Santiago Chile
Santiago
Chile

José Bravo
University of Castilla La Mancha
Ciudad Real
Spain

Pritpal Singh
Villanova University
Villanova, PA
USA

ISSN 0302-9743   ISSN 1611-3349 (electronic)
Lecture Notes in Computer Science
ISBN 978-3-319-67584-8   ISBN 978-3-319-67585-5 (eBook)
DOI 10.1007/978-3-319-67585-5

Library of Congress Control Number: 2017954895

LNCS Sublibrary: SL3 – Information Systems and Applications, incl. Internet/Web, and HCI

This Springer imprint is published by Springer Nature
The registered company is Springer International Publishing AG
The registered company address is: Gewerbestrasse 11, 6330 Cham, Switzerland

Preface

The UCAmI Conference brings together the fields of ubiquitous computing (UC) and ambient intelligence (AmI). The first one is defined as the integration of human factors, computer science, engineering, and social sciences, and the second one refers to sensitive electronic environments responsive to the presence of people. This year we celebrated the 11th International Conference on Ubiquitous Computing and Ambient Intelligence (UCAmI 2017) in Philadelphia, USA, during November 7–10, 2017. In this conference edition the contributions were submitted to six tracks and two special sessions. The tracks were *Ambient-Assisted Living, Human–Computer Interaction, Ambient Intelligence for Health, Internet of Things and Smart Cities, Ad-hoc and Sensor Networks, and Sustainability*; and the special sessions were focused on *Socio-Cognitive and Affective Computing*, and *AmI Systems and Machine Learning*.

A total of 100 submissions were received and 60 of them were accepted as full papers to be presented during the conference. The reviews of every submission were managed by the chairs of the corresponding tracks. All submissions were reviewed by at least three members of the Program Committee. The reviewers' comments and recommendations were taken into consideration while selecting submissions for inclusion in the proceedings, and were communicated to the authors. Authors whose manuscripts were accepted were asked to address the reviewers' comments. Next we briefly introduce each conference track and special session.

The *Ambient-Assisted Living* (AAL) track, chaired by Ian Cleland and Jesus Fontecha, selected contributions that highlight the role of AmI in the design of innovative solutions that empower and enrich people's capabilities. This role is facilitated through digitally augmented environments that sense, adapt, and react to human habits, needs, gestures, and emotions. This potential to create more effective, pre-emptive interactions is the core of what makes AmI of interest for developing and deploying solutions for many real-life problems, most notably within ambient-assisted living. Within this context, this edition of the AAL track focused on the "development and testing of ICT-based solutions in real-life situations, which enable and support sustainable care models for older adults." The accepted articles in this track cover several topics including promotion of self-care, improving activity classification in a smart home, and monitoring of social activities.

The *Human–Computer Interaction* (HCI) track, chaired by Francisco J. Gutierrez and Alberto L. Morán, presents novel proposals in the way the people interact with computer and vice versa. Building upon the research and practice traditions of ubiquitous computing, pervasive computing, and context awareness, AmI represents a new generation of user-centered computing environments that aim at finding new ways of integrating information technology in everyday life. More recently, AmI systems have largely increased in complexity and diversity, with advances in diverse domains, including smart homes, ambient-assisted living, e-health, and IoT. However, there are still many open research problems and challenges to be explored. Particularly, we need to further our understanding on the role of "human" in the interaction with these systems. The aim of this track was to bring together experts, academics, and practitioners from a wide range of disciplines to present and discuss state-of-the-art research and development, up-to-date issues, and HCI challenges in the field of AmI.

The track entitled *Ambient Intelligence for Health* (AmIHealth), chaired by Ramón Hervás and Oresti Baños, presented several contributions that intend to improve people's quality of life. The AmiHealth track addressed this topic from a holistic point of view, covering a wide variety of research challenges including wellness promotion and coaching, disease monitoring, knowledge and data analytics for health, adaptive and smart interfaces for special needs, among many others. New paradigms are emerging from the aforementioned topics, such as e-health, i-health, and m-health that involve, respectively, the digital society, intelligent systems, and mobile computing, providing technological solutions to effectively impact in people's life.

The track entitled *Internet of Things (IoT) and Smart Cities*, chaired by Macarena Espinilla and Shuai Zhang, focused on showing how IoT and smart cities technologies make an impact on our communities and everyday lives. The track selected exciting contributions from researchers and teams, most of which are multidisciplinary. They range from research and innovation in multiple IoT services for supporting interoperability and integration, to addressing security and privacy challenges. Furthermore, this track also addressed multiple applications of IoT within the field of smart cities, such as tourism, urban transportation, agricultural activities, and industry 4.0.

The track entitled *Ad-hoc and Sensor Networks*, chaired by Gabriel Urzaiz, presents novel research works on this topic. Computer networks continues to be a very active research field, constituting a basis for most of the existing and emerging technologies for implementing the IoT paradigm. In recent years, emphasis has been placed on mobility, energy-efficiency, heterogeneity, network security, and infrastructureless architectures. Papers in this track range from protocols and architectures, to middleware, sensors and communication issues. This track also addressed energy-efficiency considerations, enabling applications to impact not only on the sustainability of the solutions, but also on the social and economic aspects of our lives.

The track on *Sustainability*, chaired by Pritpal ("Pali") Singh, selected articles focused on achieving a more sustainable world. Ubiquitous computing uses information and communication technologies, sensors, and other means to improve quality of life, efficiency of operation and services, and reduced environmental impact of different processes. Application areas covered in this track included employing ubiquitous computing and ambient intelligence for better predicting household electrical energy demand under different weather conditions, reducing the energy consumption of buildings, and predicting the onset of frost to mitigate crop damage due to changing weather conditions.

The special session entitled *AmI Systems and Machine Learning* was chaired by José L. Montaña and Rafael Duque-Medina, and co-chaired by Cristina Tirnauca, Sergio Salomón, Santiago Ontañón, and Avelino J. González. This special session considers articles that address the challenge of providing low-level-type intelligence in the absence of artificial intelligence (AI). This challenge has been rapidly solved with emerging software machine learning (ML) applications that provide a balanced combination of ubiquitous technologies and AI methodologies. This session brings together those investigators who are active in all fields of ML and AI research. Their research work can help AmI systems in a variety of activities, such as interpreting the environment's state, modeling, simulating, and representing entities in the environment, representing the information and knowledge associated with the environment, planning decisions or actions, learning about the environment and associated aspects interacting with humans.

The special session entitled *Socio-Cognitive and Affective Computing* was chaired by Antonio Fernández-Caballero, and co-chaired by Pascual González, José Manuel Pastor, Elena Navarro and Arturo Martínez-Rodrigo. Socio-cognitive and affective computing systems should be able to adapt their behavior according to the physiological computing paradigm. This special session on socio-cognitive and affective computing aims at integrating these various albeit complementary fields. Proposals of researchers who use signals from the brain and/or body to infer people's intentions and psychological state in smart computing systems are welcome. Designing this kind of system requires combining knowledge and methods of ubiquitous and pervasive computing, as well as physiological data measurement and processing, with those of socio-cognitive and affective computing. The special session provided a meeting point for UCAmI 2017 attendees with a current or developing interest in the topics. The selected papers had a special focus on multidisciplinary approaches and multimodality.

We would like to thank all the authors who submitted their work to UCAmI 2017, the chairs of the conference tracks and special sessions for the great effort in making this edition successful, and also the reviewers for providing detailed and constructive reviews.

Furthermore, in an effort to increase the visibility of the contributions of this conference, selected papers were invited to be submitted as extended versions in the following journals: *Sensors, Frontiers in Human Neuroscience, Journal of Ambient Intelligence and Humanized Computing*, and *Applied Sciences*. We would like to thank the distinguished editors of these journals for providing us with these opportunities.

Finally, we would like to especially thank the organizers, Villanova University and MAmI Research Lab, for the huge effort and dedication toward making UCAmI 2017 a high-quality event and a meeting point for this research community.

November 2017

Sergio Ochoa
Pritpal Singh
José Bravo

Organization

General Chair

Jose Bravo   University of Castilla-La Mancha, Spain

Local Organizing Chair

Pritpal Singh   Villanova University, USA

PC Chairs

Sergio Ochoa   University of Chile, Chile
Xiaofang Wang   Villanova University, USA

Publicity Chairs

Jesús Fontecha   University of Castilla-La Mancha, Spain
Vladimir Villarreal   Technological University of Panamá, Panamá

Steering Committee

Xavier Alaman, Spain
Jose Bravo, Spain
Jesús Favela, México
Juan Manuel García, Spain
Luis Guerrero, Costa Rica
Ramón Hervás, Spain
Rui Jose, Portugal
Diego López-De-Ipiña, Spain
Chris Nugent, UK
Sergio F. Ochoa, Chile
Gabriel Urzáiz, México
Vladimir Villarreal, Panamá

Organization Committee

Stephen Suffian, USA
Javier Urquizo, USA
Iván González, Spain
Tania Mondéjar, Spain
Elitania Jiménez, Spain

Carlos Gutiérrez, Spain
Esperanza Johnson, Spain
Raúl Campos, Spain
María Martínez, Spain
Carlos Dafonte, Spain

Track Chairs

AAL (IWAAL)

Jesús Fontecha, Spain
Ian Cleland, UK

Ad-hoc Sensor Networks

Gabriel Urzáiz, Mexico

Health (AmIHEALTH)

Ramón Hervás, Spain
Oresti Baños, Netherlands

Human-Computer Interaction

Alberto Morán, México
Francisco Gutiérrez, Chile

IoT and Smart Cities

Macarena Espinilla, Spain
Shuai Zhang, UK

Sustainability

Pritpal Singh, USA

Special Session Chairs

Socio-Cognitive and Affective Computing

Antonio Fernández-Caballero, Spain

AmI Systems and Machine Learning

José L. Montaña, Spain

Program Committee

Bessam Abdulrazak	Université de Sherbrooke, Canada
Xavier Alamán	UAM, Spain
Ramón Alcarria	UPM, Spain
Jan Alexandersson	DFKI GmbH, Germany
Rosa Arriaga	Georgia Institute of Technology, USA
Mohamed Bakhouya	International University of Rabat, Morocco
Oresti Banos	University of Twente, The Netherlands
Jean-Paul Barthès	UTC, France
Paolo Bellavista	University of Bologna, Italy
Fatima Boujarwah	Kuwait University, Kuwait
Jose Bravo	University of Castilla La Mancha, Spain
Willem-Paul Brinkman	Delft University of Technology, The Netherlands
Mike Burmester	Florida State University, USA
Pino Caballero-Gil	University of La Laguna, Spain
Giorgio Carpino	University Campus Bio-Medico of Rome, Italy
José Carlos Castillo	Carlos III University of Madrid, Spain
Filippo Cavallo	The BioRobotics Institute, Italy
Sophie Chabridon	Institut TELECOM, France
Wei Chen	Fudan University, China
Ian Cleland	University of Ulster, UK
Diane Cook	Washington State University, USA
Ray Cornejo	Northwestern, USA
Domenico Cotroneo	University of Naples Federico II, Italy
Michael P. Craven	University of Nottingham, UK
Fabio De Felice	Università degli Studi di Cassino, Italy
Félix de La Paz	Universidad Nacional de Educación a Distancia, Spain
Stefan Decker	RWTH Aachen, Germany
Flavia Delicato	Federal University of Rio de Janeiro, Brazil
Giuseppe Depietro	ICARCNR (Italian National Council of Research), Italy
Rafa Duque	University of Cantabria, Spain
Rachael Dutton	Accord Group, UK
Macarena Espinilla	University of Jaen, Spain
Christopher Fabian	UNICEF, USA
Jesus Favela	CICESE, Mexico
Antonio Fernández-Caballero	University of Castilla La Mancha, Spain
Carlo Ferrari	University of Padova, Italy
José Manuel Ferrández	Universidad Politecnica Cartagena, Spain
Giuseppe Fico	Universidad Politécnica de Madrid, Spain
Laura Fiorini	The BioRobotics Institute, Italy
Jesus Fontecha	University of Castilla La Mancha, Spain

Andrea Gaggioli	Catholic University of Milan, Italy
Juan Manuel Garcia-Chamizo	University of Alicante, Spain
Carmelo R. García	University of Las Palmas de Gran Canaria, Spain
Juan Manuel Garcia-Chamizo	University of Alicante, Spain
Pascual Gonzalez	University of Castilla La Mancha, Spain
Victor Gonzalez	Instituto Tecnológico Autónomo de México, Mexico
Dan Grigoras	University College Cork, Ireland
Luis Guerrero	University of Costa Rica, Costa Rica
Antonio Guerrieri	University of Calabria, Italy
Francisco Gutierrez	University of Chile, Chile
Jan Havlik	Czech Technical University in Prague, Czech Republic
Valeria Herskovic	Pontificia Universidad Católica de Chile, Chile
Ramon Hervas	University of Castilla La Mancha, Spain
Jesse Hoey	University of Waterloo, Canada
Wijnand Ijsselsteijn	Eindhoven University of Technology, The Netherlands
Martin Jaekel	ZHAW Zurich University of Applied Sciences, Switzerland
Javier Jaén	Polytechnic University of Valencia, Spain
Alan Jovic	University of Zagreb, Croatia
Amal Kabalan	Bucknell University, USA
Martin Kampel	Vienna University of Technology, Austria
Wolfgang Kastner	TU Vienna, Austria
Abdelmajid Khelil	Landshut University, Germany
Ernst Leiss	University of Houston, USA
Lenka Lhotska	Czech Technical University in Prague, Czech Republic
Vincenzo Loia	Università degli Studi di Salerno, Italy
Tun Lu	Fudan University, China
Jens Lundström	Högskolan i Halmstad, Sweden
Wolfram Luther	University of Duisburg-Essen, Germany
María T. López	University of Castilla la Mancha, Spain
Diego López-De-Ipiña	University of Deusto, Spain
Ratko Magjarevic	University of Zagreb, Croatia
Rafael Martinez Tomas	Universidad Nacional de Educación a Distancia, Spain
Arturo Martínez-Rodrigo	University of Castilla la Mancha, Spain
Oscar Mayora	CREATE-NET, Italy
Paolo Melillo	Second University of Naples, Italy
Vittorio Miori	ISTI-CNR, Italy
Jose Luis Montaña	University of Cantabria, Spain
Alberto Moran	UABC, Mexico
Francisco Moya	University of Castilla la Mancha, Spain
Tatsuo Nakajima	Waseda University, Japan
Elena Navarro	University of Castilla la Mancha, Spain

Additional Reviewers

Brewer, Robin
Cibrian, Franceli L.
Crespo, Jonathan
Fiorini, Laura
Ghayvat, Hemant
González Díaz, Iván
Gutiérrez López de La Franca, Carlos
Labella Romero, Álvaro
Limosani, Raffaele

Luo, Chunbo
Martínez Mimbrera, Francisco Jesús
Moschetti, Alessandra
Navarro, Rene
Ponce Diaz, Victor Manuel
Raich, Philipp
Tröger, Johannes
Wurzenberger, Markus

Contents

HEALTH (AmIHEALTH)

Ambient Assisted Living (IWAAL)

Ad-hoc and Sensor Networks

Human-Computer Interaction (HCI)

Sustainability

Special Session on Socio-Cognitive and Affective Computing

Special Session on AmI Systems and Machine Learning

Internet of Things (IoT) and Smart Cities

Multi-layer Security Mechanism for Networked Embedded Devices

Christopher Mansour$^{(\boxtimes)}$ and Danai Chasaki

Villanova University, Villanova, PA 19085, USA
cmansour@villanova.edu

Abstract. Networked embedded systems are impacting the way we interact with the world around us. They are at the core of the advancements in information and communication technologies which have been driving the fourth generation revolution in today's industry and networks. This technology allows for better integrated communications, integrated local and global control, supervision and maintenance. Billions of smart devices are being implemented - from smart TVs and cars to other smart health monitors and wearable technologies and this resulted in the development of smart interconnected environments. The core vision of the aforementioned smart interconnected environment is the realization of a reliable and secure two way communication between smart devices. However, the high level of heterogeneity, coupled with the wide scale of smart embedded systems, has magnified the security threats. Traditional security countermeasures and privacy cannot be enforced directly on such systems due to their limited computing capabilities and their diverse set of hardware architectures. In this paper we are proposing a multi-level security approach for smart interconnected environments/networks. We address the security at three main pillars: application level, system level, and network level.

1 Introduction

The increasing deployment of smart devices and its different applications in our daily lives raises privacy and security concerns at unprecedented scale. A simple search in the literature about the security requirements and challenges for such interconnected devices will result in the following main security requirements: Confidentiality, Authentication, Availability, Privacy, and Trust.

In [4,7,8,11,14] the authors address the confidentiality and authentication security requirements for the so call Internet of Things which is a nomenclature reflecting several varieties of smart interconnected devices. In [14], the authors presented intelligent Service Security Application Protocol that combines cross-platform communications with encryption, signature, and authentication, to improve application development capabilities. In [4], the authors introduced the first fully implemented two-way authentication security scheme.

In [1–3,10,12] the authors address the privacy security requirement for smart devices. In [1], the authors proposed data tagging techniques from the information flow control to allow the systems to reason about flows of data and preserve

© Springer International Publishing AG 2017
S.F. Ochoa et al. (Eds.): UCAmI 2017, LNCS 10586, pp. 3–14, 2017.
DOI: 10.1007/978-3-319-67585-5_1

privacy of individuals. In [2], the authors proposed a user-controlled privacy-preserved access control protocol which is based on context-aware k-anonymity privacy policies to protect the privacy of smart interconnected devices.

In [5,6] the authors address the trust security requirement for smart interconnected devices. In [5], Martinez et al. present an architecture that decouples the identification and location by using identities to identify the network nodes and moving from a host-to-host to a fine-grained process-to-process view of the network. In [6], Liu et al. propose a WSN-oriented key agreement protocol to achieve privacy and trust.

Most of the aforementioned work that is found in literature have tried to address the security requirements for Internet of Things which are also important to the network of interconnected smart devices. Their approaches were basically per-requirement solution. However, non of the previous work proposed a complete multi-layer security framework which not only address such security requirements combined but even detect any faulty behavior as well. In this paper we are proposing a multi-level security approach for smart interconnected environments/networks that helps in detecting any malicious activity threatening most of the aforementioned security requirements.

2   Smart Device Components

The smart devices are at the core of a smart networked embedded system. Each smart device is generally application specific and has its own computing abilities that allows it to perform certain operations and communicate with other devices to exchange information. Figure 1 presents a graphical representation of the components that can be available in a smart device, and the following is a description of such components.

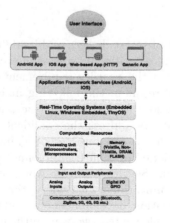

Fig. 1. Smart device generic architecture

2.1   Power Component

Every smart device, as any other device, needs a power source. The power source can be an immediate power supply, a battery or even solar. The power component will include a certain controller that can manage the power consumption and be aware of the energy requirements.

2.2   Memory Component

In order for a smart device to be able to perform certain computations and behave in a certain way, it has to include an internal memory that stores the correct operations to be executed. This memory is split up into many different use cases: processor memory, cache, volatile memory, and non-volatile memory. It is an extremely important feature in every smart device. It is used to store the firmware that helps in performing certain operations and data manipulations. For example, modern audio devices have a specific erasable programmable read-only memory (EPROM) to store the firmware necessary to perform audio processing, such EPROM is important in order to later update the firmware to include more codecs for audio processing. Another example, is the boot sequence of a router and the underlying software that has the necessary functionalities to start the router is also stored on an EPROM memory.

2.3   Processing Component

In order to perform computations and other specific functionalities, a smart device includes an embedded processing component. This processing component will serve as the primary execution environment for the specific applications. This processing unit will run a specific operating system, discussed in a following subsection, which hosts the applications that require to run. A smart device might also include more than one processing unit; for instance, a smart mobile device will include an ARM processor to run the operating system and user applications, and another processor which performs digital signal processing for audio and image specific applications. The processing power and capabilities can vary depending on the nature of the smart device and the required functionalities. This is evident in today's mobile phone industries where phones are being supplied with more powerful and functionally capable processors in order to meet the demand of services required by the end user.

2.4   Communications Interface

In order to exchange information between one another, smart devices need efficient communication interfaces. There are a variety of physical communication interfaces that may be used ranging from wired digital and analog connections such as Ethernet, USB (Universal Serial Bus), Profinet, to wireless connections including IEEE 802.11, Bluetooth, ZigBee, GPRS, 3G, 4G, 5G, transceivers, etc.

2.5   Real Time Operating System

The operating system in smart devices runs on top of the processing components, such as microprocessors, providing access to shared resources including memory and other device peripherals such as: communication interfaces, input/output ports etc. The operating system inside the smart device provides interfaces abstracting the underlying hardware and allowing users and developers to write specific applications to specify the functionality of the smart device. The operating systems in smart devices are real-time operating systems because they deal with real-time applications. They need to guarantee a high level of consistency concerning the amount of time it takes to accept and complete an application's task. An example of a real time operating system includes Embedded Linux and Windows Embedded.

2.6   Application Software

Most consumers are familiar with application software that provide functionality on a computer. Smart embedded device's software however is often less visible but has the same complexity. Unlike application software, software on smart devices has fixed hardware requirements and capabilities. An addition of third-party hardware or software is strictly controlled. Software in smart devices needs to include all the drivers required to drive the peripherals, and the latter are written for the specific hardware. The software is highly dependent on the CPU and specific chips chosen. Today's modern smart embedded devices have enough processing capabilities and memory to perform complex and sophisticated tasks. This fact in addition to the development of the Linux kernel and its wide deployment in smart devices have contributed to the development of different sophisticated and complex application frameworks such as Android and IOS. The linux kernel on the smart device will manage the resources and other peripheral drivers, and the application framework on top of that provides the necessary interface between the kernel and the user applications. This allowed the developers to create a plethora of useful applications on smart devices using high level programming languages.

3   Security Model

The monitoring framework we are proposing follows the following security model:

- Resiliency: there should not exist any single point of failure in a network of interconnected smart devices. The network should be able to adjust itself to any device replacement or failure.
- Data Authentication: interconnected smart devices should be trusted and authenticated and the same applies to the applications installed on the smart devices
- User's Privacy: information being exchanged between smart devices should not be disclosed, and only service providers (device manufacturers) will have the necessary access to update the systems and to enhance the services.

– Data integrity: a network of smart devices should be able to guarantee that an adversary cannot modify data in the transaction without the system detecting the change
– Any attempts to modify smart device functionalities should be detected and lead to an alert and device disconnection

In the context of our security model, we assume that an attacker is able to perform the following actions:

– Attempt to control sensor nodes, or smart devices in the smart network of interconnected devices
– Perform passive eavesdropping trying to listen on ongoing communications and extract information
– Exert a Denial of Service attack to degrade the performance of the network
– Replay attack in which the adversary can capture some request messages and replays them later to extract some sensitive information
– Modify the application on some smart devices trying to gain access to the network, or even sniff packets outside the network

4   Application Level Security

Due to the fact that smart interconnected devices are being increasingly deployed in many different environments, they have become targets for malicious activities. For instance, attackers might aim to modify the binary code of the applications running on such embedded devices to either modify the correct functionality of the device or to snoop and sniff information being exchanged, which is a clear attack against privacy and integrity. Such activities harness the weaknesses available in the third party applications and the fact that smart embedded devices lack the necessary mechanism to evaluate the authenticity and trustworthiness of such applications.

The application level security framework aims to ensure the security of the applications being installed on the embedded devices. It aims to establish trust between the application being installed and the underlying smart device itself. The framework we are proposing consists of two main parts, a unique hashing algorithm inside the software applications to be installed, and a Physical Unclonable Function (PUF) on the device. Recent work [9] have shown that the SRAM memory modules available on most embedded smart devices can be used as a PUF instance. Hence, each embedded smart device will generate a unique device dependent secret. Additionally, the work provided by Horne et al. [1] shows the ability to implement an optimum hash function with an acceptable speed and size.

Figure 2 represents the architecture of our framework. In prior to the application installation, the application permissions are checked by the orchestrator in order to verify that the application is allowed to perform any operations that would not adversely impact other applications, the operating system, or the user. This includes reading or writing the user's attributes and parameters, reading or writing another application's data, performing network access, keeping the device awake, and so on. Once such permissions are granted, a unique bit stream will be extracted from the target device and used by the hashing algorithm provided by the application to generate a unique hash of certain parameters and attributes available within the application itself. Such parameters may include initialization values of certain settings that cannot be changed and that are stored in the text section of the application code stack.

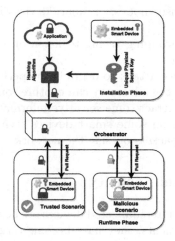

Fig. 2. Proposed application security framework

The generated unique value will then be stored securely by the orchestrator. At any time during runtime, the orchestrator will poll periodically the interconnected devices, extract the unique secret from their PUF, reevaluate the hash of the code running on the corresponding device and check its integrity. If the integrity is satisfied, the operation of the device continues normally. However, if the integrity is not valid, the device/application combination is flagged. Such security framework will tie a previously evaluated application to a device and prevents any attempts to modify the application binary code or to install malicious applications, not checked by the orchestrator, on the device.

4.1   System Level Security

The use of counterfeit smart devices inside the smart environments is particularly dangerous and poses a real problem. Counterfeit devices inside a smart environment might lead to the injection of faulty and malicious data that can corrupt services and threatens the integrity and trustworthiness of the information being exchanged. A counterfeit malicious device can be the single point of entry to the network giving the attacker an easy access to the network. Malicious code can be carefully inserted between legitimate lines of code in order to be executed later allowing attackers to gain access to systems and disclose information. Even a software bug existing in the firmware running on such smart devices can lead to a disastrous outcome, e.g. Dyn DNS DDoS attack [13].

In order to prevent such attacks and malicious activities from occurring, and in order to ensure a resilient network of smart devices, we propose a new modern reliable security framework. This framework acts at the system level and helps monitor and detect counterfeit and malicious devices existing in a smart network of interconnected devices. In our security framework, we monitor the system calls, libraries and other processing characteristics being used by such smart devices at the kernel level in order to extract information and detect any counterfeit devices or undergoing malicious activities. Such system characteristics can be system calls, CPU status, wakeups/sec, and power consumption.

Figure 3 presents our security framework. The system will consist of a main orchestrator which will order a monitor to communicate with other interconnected devices and periodically, based on a predefined period, poll each and every smart device connected to the network. The monitor will request system call traces, CPU status, wakeups/sec and power consumption information to be echoed back in a specific format. Such information will be statistically correlated later by the orchestrator with benchmark information retrieved from trusted entities for non-malicious devices, and the results are provided to a decision module. The decision module will compare the results with a predetermined threshold and detect the existence of a counterfeit or a malicious device. The Orchestrator will alert the network administrator or users and flag the malicious device.

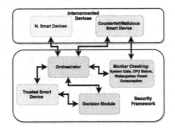

Fig. 3. Proposed security framework

4.2 Network Level Security

Smart interconnected devices today come in different varieties and processing abilities. They also have unique characteristics and traffic patterns that can differentiate them from one another. Different devices use different protocols and thus different headers format, different packet size etc. For example, smart devices used in surveillance will most of the time be in sleep mode only sending small amounts of traffic to notify the rest of the network that it is still functioning; on the other hand when it is triggered by motion then the traffic will come in bursts. Thus, traffic resulting from such smart devices might be as follows: a sustained low rate of traffic to establish its online status during sleep-mode, and bursts of communications traffic when they are active or triggered. The rate of which packets are exchanged to establish online status changes between devices, and the same condition applies for the burst size where different devices have different burst sizes. Hence, such traffic patterns and packet attributes may be used as a unique characteristics for different smart interconnected devices. Therefore, we propose a security framework that leverages such unique characteristics in order to detect any malicious faulty device or malicious activities.

Inter-arrival Time. One of the main characteristics that can be used and monitored at the network level is the packet inter-arrival rate. A key question that we try to implement and answer is what inferences can be made about the operation of smart devices by merely observing its input and output operation. We argue that observing the inter-arrival time of packets, that is the time between a specific packet entering and leaving the smart device, can provide sufficient information to detect some failures due to soft errors and due to attacks.This can also help in determining whether the device has been compromised in order to induce any attack on the network of interconnected device.

Figure 4 represents the monitor architecture. Packets arriving at the smart device are time stamped by the monitor, and the corresponding throughput is calculated. Outgoing packets coming out of the smart device are also monitored in order to infer the processing time and delay in addition to the output throughput. Such information will be read and analyzed by a decision module which will infer the status of the smart device. The decision module will use the aforementioned KL-divergence statistical method to estimate the difference between the measured delay and throughput with the benchmark information provided by the smart device manufacturer. If the difference exceeded a carefully chosen threshold, then an abnormal behavior is detect. In the latter scenario, the device is disconnected and flagged.

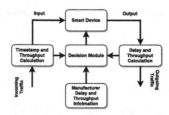

Fig. 4. Packet inter-arrival network monitor

Packet Count IO Monitor. Another characteristic that can be used to determine any malicious activity at the network level is the Input/Output Packet count. Hence, another I/O monitoring system can be implemented in order to detect any malicious activity affecting an interconnected smart environment. The I/O monitor we are proposing correlates the flow of outgoing packets to the flow of incoming packets. By tracking such information, the monitor can determine when conditions occur that are considered unusual from a networking perspective. These conditions may not be detected by any other monitoring system on the device since it may be caused by the device itself. Examples of such conditions include the dropping of incoming packets that is not due to congestion and the transmission of large numbers of packets that is not triggered by incoming packets. For example, the scenario where a smart device in sleep mode starts transmitting packets that are more than the expected online status packets, should be detected as a malicious activity. Another scenario that should raise a flag is when within a specific time window a single incoming packet causes a huge amount of unexpected traffic to be generated by the device, hence, such an incident is clearly an attack changing the device to a bot participating in a Denial-of-Service attack. Therefore, an I/O packet monitoring becomes a necessity in order to detect such behaviors.

Implementing an I/O monitor can easily be achieved. The smart devices come with an abundance amount of memory and logic resources (microcontrollers, Raspberry pi's etc.). Thus we use logic resources that are already present to design two counters, one attached to the input queue interface keeping track of the incoming packets, and the other one connected to the output queues, counting the outgoing packets within a specific time window.

Traffic Characteristics and Signatures. A network of interconnected smart devices will use several standardized protocols such as: ZigBee, 6LoWPAN, Z-Wave etc. Thus, the packet header characteristics are well known, as well as the ports of communications between the devices and the packet size. Additionally, each protocol has its own unique traffic characteristics and traces. Therefore, based on such information, a specific trace can be extracted for each type of flow as well as a specific signature can be extracted for each different type of packets in order to differentiate between flow characteristics and communication traffic. Hence, we can design two types of network level monitoring that deals with traffic characteristics.

Furthermore, most of the scenarios in the interconnected smart systems follow a polling scheme which is based on request/response communications. Hence, there should not be any response from a device that has not been polled, that is has not received any request. Thus, if a response carrying data is available on the network, and it does not correspond to an existing request, then this should automatically determine the existence of a malicious activity on the network. Therefore, analyzing the trace of network in real time and extracting certain traffic characteristics will definitely help in detecting such malicious activity.

Assuming a scenario of smart devices communicating using ZigBee protocol, the traffic characteristics will also depend on the type of devices and their
functionality. A sample ZigBee authentication/join trace between two devices is
represented in Fig. 5.

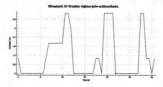

Fig. 5. ZigBee authenticate/join sample trace

One type of network level traffic monitor is a monitor that will perform, for
a certain sliding time window, real-time analysis on the traffic traces and check
whether they meet the expected trace. The architecture of the monitor is represented in Fig. 6. For example, in the scenario of smart interconnected devices
using ZigBee, the monitor will check during a specific time window whether the
traffic matches the expected normal traffic represented in Fig. 5. If there is a
match within a predetermined threshold, then this is a normal activity, however, if the threshold is crossed, then the monitor detects a malicious activity on
the network.

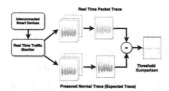

Fig. 6. Traffic characteristics network monitor

Another type of network level traffic monitoring is to use pre-analysis and
machine learning algorithms to study the behavior of different types of flows
and extract fixed packet header fields. For example, a smart device using ZigBee
protocol that have a maximum physical layer packet size of 127 octets will leave
on average 50–70 bytes of payload. Thus knowing this information from spec
sheets and pre-deployment analysis will help in extracting specific unique traffic
signatures within the same protocol. Such signatures can be used later in order
to perform real-time matching between incoming packets and the saved analyzed
signatures.

The signatures are considered as regular expressions whose natural representation is a finite automata. The latter can be implemented as a deterministic

finite automata (DFA) or non-deterministic finite automata (NFA). The implementation depends on the trade-off between correct detection and matching on one side and time and memory space on the other side. Due to the fact that we are using smart devices with available memory storage, (storage is cheap and being provided on many devices), DFA technique sounds reasonable because it can perform $O(1)$ matching even if it can take more memory resources.

The monitor we propose to design will use an advanced type of memory, the Ternary Content Addressable Memory (TCAM). The TCAM memory consists of a set of entries where the top entry has the smallest index. Each entry is a bit vector storing a certain string pattern. Hence, given an input string, the input string will be compared against all the entries in parallel and reports the entry which has the maximum match. The lookup time is deterministic for any input. We are proposing to use TCAM due to its intrinsic parallel search capabilities.

We propose to store the packet signatures extracted during pre-deployment phase in the TCAM. We note that this can be pre-initialized with previously known malicious packet signatures as well. During run-time, a packet analyzer in our monitor will extract the signature and supplies it to the matching module designed using TCAM. If a match happens, then this packet has a signature which matched a malicious one and thus should be dropped. Another approach may also exist, that is to store the signatures that we only consider benign. Hence, packets in the latter approach are only allowed if they match the signatures. The concept of the monitor we are proposing is presented in Fig. 7.

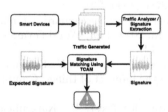

Fig. 7. Signature network level monitoring

5   Conclusion

In this paper we are proposing a multi-level security approach for smart interconnected environments/networks. We address the security at three main pillars: the application level, the system level, and the network level. We address the application level security by the design of a framework which consists of a unique hashing algorithm inside the software applications to be installed, and a Physical Unclonable Function (PUF) on the device. Additionally, the system level security is addressed by the design of a framework that monitors the system calls, libraries and other processing characteristics being used by smart devices at the kernel level in order to extract information and detect any counterfeit devices or those undergoing malicious activities. Finally, we address the network level security by designing a framework that leverages the unique characteristics of the network traffic in order to detect any malicious faulty devices or malicious activities. We believe that this multi-layer security framework can help secure networked embedded systems and a smart network of interconnected devices.

References

1. Cao, J., Carminati, B., Ferrari, E., Tan, K.L.: CASTLE: continuously anonymizing data streams. IEEE Trans. Depend. Secur. Comput **8**(3), 337–352 (2011)
2. Evans, D., Eyers, D.M.: Efficient data tagging for managing privacy in the internet of things. In: 2012 IEEE International Conference on Green Computing and Communications (GreenCom), pp. 244–248. IEEE (2012)
3. Huang, X., Fu, R., Chen, B., Zhang, T., Roscoe, A.: User interactive internet of things privacy preserved access control. In: 2012 International Conference on Internet Technology and Secured Transactions, pp. 597–602. IEEE (2012)
4. Kothmayr, T., Schmitt, C., Hu, W., Brünig, M., Carle, G.: DTLS based security and two-way authentication for the internet of things. Ad Hoc Netw. **11**(8), 2710–2723 (2013)
5. Liu, T., Guan, Y.W., Yan, Y.Q., Liu, L., Deng, Q.C.: A WSN-oriented key agreement protocol in internet of things. In: Applied Mechanics and Materials. vol. 401, pp. 1792–1795. Trans Tech Publications (2013)
6. Martinez-Julia, P., Skarmeta, A.F.: Beyond the separation of identifier and locator: building an identity-based overlay network architecture for the future internet. Comput. Netw. **57**(10), 2280–2300 (2013)
7. Piro, G., Boggia, G., Grieco, L.A.: A standard compliant security framework for IEEE 802.15.4 networks. In: 2014 IEEE World Forum on Internet of Things (WF-IoT), pp. 27–30. IEEE (2014)
8. Roman, R., Alcaraz, C., Lopez, J., Sklavos, N.: Key management systems for sensor networks in the context of the internet of things. Comput. Electr. Eng. **37**(2), 147–159 (2011)
9. Schaller, A., Arul, T., van der Leest, V., Katzenbeisser, S.: Lightweight anticounterfeiting solution for low-end commodity hardware using inherent PUFs. In: Holz, T., Ioannidis, S. (eds.) Trust 2014. LNCS, vol. 8564, pp. 83–100. Springer, Cham (2014). doi:10.1007/978-3-319-08593-7_6
10. Wang, Y., Wen, Q.: A privacy enhanced DNS scheme for the internet of things. In: IET International Conference on Communication Technology and Application (ICCTA 2011), pp. 699–702. IET (2011)
11. Evans, D., Eyers, D.M.: Efficient data tagging for managing privacy in the internet of things. Chin. J. Comput. **34**(8), 1351–1364 (2011)
12. Yang, J., Fang, B.: Security model and key technologies for the internet of things. J. China Univ. Posts Telecommun. **18**, 109–112 (2011)
13. York, K.: Dyn statement on 10/21/2016 DDoS attack (2016). http://dyn.com/blog/dyn-statement-on-10212016-DdoS-attack/
14. Zhao, Y.L.: Research on data security technology in internet of things. In: Applied Mechanics and Materials, vol. 433, pp. 1752–1755. Trans Tech Publications (2013)

Smart Cities in Latin America

Realities and Technical Readiness

Marta Calderón[✉], Gustavo López, and Gabriela Marín

Universidad de Costa Rica, San Pedro, Costa Rica
marta.calderon@ecci.ucr.ac.cr,
{gustavo.lopez_h,gabriela.marin}@ucr.ac.cr

Abstract. In almost every forum around the world, country leaders are discussing the necessity of creating smart cities. However, even the term "smart city" is diffuse nowadays. Some countries want their cities to become smarter and others want to create smart cities from scratch. Several mappings have been developed around the world to locate the smartest cities. We believe that, since Latin American and Caribbean countries are exploring in the creation of smart cities, a proper mapping and plan is necessary to assure that the efforts in creating smart cities are not a waste. Using a literature review and a survey, we try to determine the state of smart cities development and its technical readiness in the Region.

Keywords: Smart city · IoT technologies · Technical readiness

1 Introduction

Even though several international forums are discussing heavily on the topic, the definition of smart cities is still diffuse [1]. On its basis, smart cities represent an urban development model that utilizes human, collective, and technological capital for the development of urban agglomerations.

Smart cities development should be conceived as a multidisciplinary task that includes socio-economic, governance, and multi-stakeholder aspects [2]. Moreover, it is driven by advances in technology and urban development. Smart cities use information and communication technologies (ICT) to enhance quality of services, reduce resource consumption, and improve communication between citizens and government (to make them efficient, sustainable and attractive to residents and businesses) [3].

Problems associated with urban agglomerations have usually been solved by means of creativity, human capital, cooperation (sometimes bargaining) among relevant stakeholders, and bright scientific ideas: in a nutshell, 'smart' solutions. The label 'smart city' should therefore point to clever solutions allowing modern cities to thrive through quantitative and qualitative improvement in productivity [4].

European and North American cities dominate the list of the 50 smartest cities in the world according to [5]. Buenos Aires, Argentina, is the top Latin American ranked city, occupying the 83rd position on the IESE Cities in Motion Index 2017 [5].

© Springer International Publishing AG 2017
S.F. Ochoa et al. (Eds.): UCAmI 2017, LNCS 10586, pp. 15–26, 2017.
DOI: 10.1007/978-3-319-67585-5_2

We believe that, since Latin American and Caribbean (LAC) countries are exploring in the creation of smart cities, a proper mapping and plan is necessary to assure that the efforts in creating smart cities are not a waste. In this paper, we try to determine the state of smart cities development and its technical readiness in the LAC region.

The structure of this paper is as follows. Section 2 describes Smart Cities and its dimensions. Section 3 describes the quality of life in Latin American and the Caribbean (LAC) cities. Section 4 shows evidence of smart cities in LAC. Section 5 describes the methodological approach followed on this research Sect. 6 presents the results of the survey conducted and Sect. 7 our conclusions.

2   Smart Cities Definition

There are several definitions of smart cities. However, for the purpose of this paper a city would be considered "smart" if it applies ICT based solutions to problems in these six dimensions: governance, quality of life and essential services, transportation (mobility), economy, people, and environmental issues.

The *governance* dimension considers all forms of social coordination and patterns of rule. ICT solutions are applied in this domain to provide citizens with easy access to government services, enable information-based decision-making and increase transparency [6].

As for the *quality of life* or *living* dimension, a smart city must of course consider ICT-enabled life styles and consumption. It should stimulate healthy regimes for its population and assure safety, provide quality housing and accommodations. It would be expected of a smart city to provide decent cultural and education facilities and to have touristic attractiveness. Finally, a high degree of social cohesion would be expected, although this might not be the result of this dimension alone [7].

The *mobility* or transportation dimension includes integrated transport and logistics systems (i.e., interconnected trams, buses, trains, metros, taxis, among others). Moreover, smart cities should provide accessible and efficient ways for pedestrians and other vehicles to mobilize (e.g., smart traffic lights and signals). Besides, non-motorized means of transportation should be prioritized.

In the *economical* dimension, a smart city will be expected to have e-business and e-commerce support, ICT-driven manufacturing, delivery of services and innovation.

The essence of a city is its *people*. In the people dimension, a smart city should provide inclusive education and training that fosters creativity and innovation. Access and use of communication technologies should also be supplied [8].

Finally, in the *environment* dimension, renewable energy, smart electric grids, green buildings, efficient use of resources and several other strategies must be addressed and worked on to consider a city environmentally smart [9]. Table 1 shows a summary of cities indicators of "smartness" proposed by Cohen [10] for the six dimensions previously mentioned.

Table 1. Summary of cities indicators of "smartness" (source: Smart City Index [10])

Dimension	Working areas
Government	Online services/Infrastructure/Open government
Living	Culture and well-being/Safety/Health/Technology infrastructure
Mobility	Efficient transport/Multimodal access/Technology infrastructure
Economy	Entrepreneurship & innovation/Productivity/Local and global connection
People	Inclusion/Education/Creativity
Environment	Smart buildings/Source management/Sustainable urban planning

3   Quality of Life in Latin American and the Caribbean Cities

LAC is the region with the largest proportion of the population concentrated in megacities, that is, cities with more than 10 million inhabitants [11]. In 2016, 12.7% of the total population of the region lived in 5 megacities, but this percentage will rise to 14.3 when Bogotá reaches this city category, estimated to happen in 2030 [11].

Cities drive LAC economies, but disparities are a constant. Informal labor plays a very important role in LAC economies, but at the same time contribute to inequality [12]. Cities in LAC are the most unequal in the world, which undermines urban prosperity and can affect personal security and safety [12, 13].

Public security remains as the weakest point of LAC urban life [14, 15]. This region has one of the world´s highest rates of victimization (robbery). Lack of security and personal safety limits "freedom, mobility, productivity and public interactions" [13], which decreases quality of life. Therefore, the financial burden of crime is high, ascending, in some cases, up to 25% of the gross domestic product (GDP) of the country, for example, in Colombia and El Salvador.

Quantity and quality of dwelling houses is not sufficient to warranty adequate conditions to LAC city inhabitants [13]. Access to electricity is practically universal in urban areas (95%). Access to running water is high (85%), but the region is very heterogeneous because some cities have serious shortages and others do not face this problem [14]. Cell phones and fixed lines are widespread in LAC cities [13]. The cell phone sector contributes significantly to the region´s public finances and economy.

Problems in LAC cities are: persistent deficit in dwelling of quality, insecurity, traffic congestion, lack of public space, and severe economic segregation [14].

LAC cities are expanding their area at a higher rate than the increase of their population [12]. This is unsustainable in the long term and causes physical and social fragmentation. The region needs to develop territorial policies for making better use of the available space and preventing environmental disasters due to degradation of the ecosystem [12].

Despite health services, roads, air quality, water quality, and traffic flow are deficient, when LAC citizens were asked about their degree of satisfaction with the city they live in, these aspects did not have significant impact in their quality of life [14]. Particularly interesting is the traffic congestion issue. LAC has the highest motorization rate of all developing regions, with the consequence of less use of public transport [13]. Lack of security and physical expansion of cities are two of the triggers of high motorization. Traffic congestion is the most important infrastructure deficiency in LAC cities [13].

Governments do no pay attention to the creation and maintenance of public spaces, such as parks. Shopping malls are the new socialization spaces [12].

LAC cities face environmental problems [13]. Sanitation is not adequate in many cities. Waste management is a major problem in some of them [12]. The environmental situation creates health and environmental hazards.

Urban governance is a topic that requires attention. There is a significant progress in democratization and decentralization, but it does not mean that resources and capabilities have been transferred to local governments [12]. More active citizen participation has to be encouraged in order to strengthen more transparent governance processes. A taxation culture has to be established, so that local governments can work with effectiveness, efficiency, and equality [16].

E-government must become a priority for local governments. Successful experiences in Colombia, Uruguay and Panama show that political support of the project, qualification of human resources, and availability of financial resources are key factors [16]. All governments in LAC face the challenge of providing high broadband connectivity to remain competitive.

Perceived impediments to the prosperity of LAC cities are, on descending order of importance: poor governance and weak institutions, high incidence of slums and poverty, high levels of crime, corruption, high cost of doing business, inadequate infrastructure, and low levels of human capital [13]. LAC cities face these great challenges to become smart. However, these impediments can also constitute opportunities to improve quality of life, which could be addressed through "smart" initiatives driven by ICTs.

4   Latin-American and the Caribbean Smart Cities

According to our literature review, the number of cities with smart initiatives in LAC is relatively very low compared with the number of large cities (more than one million inhabitants) in the region. They constitute only one percent of all smart cities in the world [17]. According to [18], the eight smartest cities in LAC are:

1. Santiago (Chile)	5. Rio de Janeiro (Brazil)
2. Mexico City (Mcxico)	6. Curitiba (Brazil)
3. Bogotá (Colombia)	7. Medellín (Colombia)
4. Buenos Aires (Argentina)	8. Montevideo (Uruguay)

These cities have developed very diverse projects. Most of them have focused on transport (e.g.: public bicycles and bus corridors). Environment, more efficient energy use, and security are some of the aspects that have also been addressed. Other cities in the region that have started at least one "smart" initiative are Lima (Perú), Quito (Ecuador), Monterrey (México), Panama City (Panama), Santo Domingo (Dominican

Republic), Sao Paulo (Brazil), Paraná (Brazil), Juarez (Mexico) and Nassau (Bahamas) [17, 18]. LAC cities characterized as smart still face great challenges and have a long way before they become truly smart cities.

Mexico is developing the project called IQ Smart City for building the first smart city of the country, Ciudad Maderas [19]. The idea was proposed to the local government by the cluster of information and communication technologies of the State of Querétaro. The project includes building a smart energy grid. Juan Carlos Coronado, director of the project, believes that thinking about a large city becoming smart requires a larger investment in infrastructure than building a new relatively small smart city. The Ciudad Maderas project could be replicated in LAC.

The case of Ciudad Maderas illustrates what Lucas Lanza says *"The challenge for a city to turn "smart" ... is a process that requires developing a capacity to reach agreements and a global consensus about the best interfaces between public and private actors and a balance between technology and politics"* [20].

Some urban developments in LAC are still oriented to creating isolated communities, a tendency during the last decades with the goal of achieving security. For example, Ciudad Cayalá, near Guatemala City, is a private real estate development that includes dwelling and commerce facilities for high income class residents and is surrounded by a wall [21]. Though Ciudad Cayalá could be considered a smart city because of the use of technology, it does not lead to the inclusion of all urban social groups.

LAC is a heterogeneous region. No rules can be applied to all cities. Each LAC city wanting to become smart has to analyze its weaknesses and establish priorities, since financial resources are limited. Understanding citizen concerns and needs is crucial for success.

5   Methodological Approach

In this paper, we propose a methodological approach to discover and assess the realities and technical readiness for Smart Cities in LAC. This proposal is driven by the fact that several smart cities in LAC are being proposed; however, most of them lack (or at least there is no academic evidence) of a proper assessment of the current status of "smartness" in the main cities or proposed cities in the region. We believe that technical readiness and a diagnosis are necessary to reassure that smart cities will be successful both within themselves and interconnecting among them.

The desk research approach has been applied in several projects with the goal of mapping smart cities. Our proposal does not escape from this reality since the first step was to **conduct a literature review** including academic sources, national reports and plans. Unfortunately, this documentation is not always available in all LAC countries or it is not updated. During a brief review, we found that the main sources of information easily findable about smart cities in LAC were news or media reports (most of them lacking a systematic approach).

A review of smart cities, initiatives and projects was conducted. For the purpose of this paper, a city becomes smart if a series of initiatives (different dimensions) are carried, and an initiative is composed of projects (same dimension). Information at this level was not found in literature or web browsing. Therefore, a deeper search in LAC countries national archives and smart cities proposals should be performed.

Parallel to the literature review, an updated *assessment of the smartness of cities* in their current state became necessary. A *cross-sectional study* could allow the identification of patterns when comparing cities characteristics and their level of smartness in the region. To assure that the smartness of cities is measured systematically, a the *Smart City Index Master Indicators Survey* [10] has been proposed by the literature as *evaluating instrument*.

We designed an on-line survey using Lime Survey, and used its categories, to try to assess the level of smartness in the LAC region. The survey included:

- Information on the city the interviewee lives in (name, type of city, and size, based on the categorization proposed by Doxiadis Konstantinos [22].
- Data of the interviewee: his/her area of your expertise and knowledge on the concept of smart cities and on the following technologies used
  - interaction with the environment
    - sensors, actuators
    - Internet of Things (IoT) service architecture
  - data storage
    - open data, ontologies, taxonomies, and data integration
    - cloud computing
  - decision making
    - data analytics, data visualization, and big data
    - domain specific modeling
    - crowdsourcing and collaborative decision making
- Data on the interviewee´s perception on the city´s state of smartness, and on the potential benefits of and the viability of becoming smart, for each of the specific Smart City dimensions presented in Table 1.
- An open question for comments participants wanted to make about the topic.

An online questionnaire was designed mainly with closed questions to ease its analysis. It was distributed using the institutional representatives and divulgation mailing lists of CLEI (Latin American Center for Informatics Studies) augmented by the Central American mailing list of WITFOR 2016 (World Information Technology Forum). People receiving the questionnaire link were invited to share the survey among colleagues. Anonymity was offered and an open space for suggestions or general comments was provided.

6   Results

The following subsections describe the demographic data on participants and results obtained about Smart City technical readiness and smartness of LAC cities, as reported by participants.

6.1 Demographic Data of the Survey

The questionnaire remained open until the last week of April 2017. We received 154 complete valid responses.

Figure 1 shows the distribution of respondents per country. Although it is not evenly distributed amongst LAC countries, most countries are represented, except small and insular countries in the Caribbean. Participants' areas of expertise are Computer Science (76%), Electrical Engineering (13%), other engineering (7%), and other 4%.

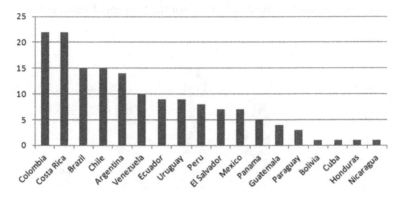

Fig. 1. Number of responses per Country

Respondents were asked to typify the smart city situation of the city they lived in. Figure 2 categorizes the response frequency per size of city. Almost half of the responses correspond to metropolis (26%) and large cities (23%). Moreover, many of the largest cities are also represented, conurbation (15%) and megapolis (8%). Smaller urban areas are also represented by cities (15%), large towns (10%) and towns (3%).

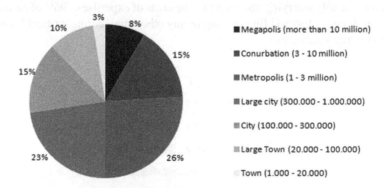

Fig. 2. Percentage of responses per city size

Responses were also categorized by type of city. The resulting distributing was 41.9% Capital city of the country, 48.4% Capital of province or department, and 9.7% other type of cities. Responses were tabulated by city size and by type of city. Results by city size are considered more interesting and therefore are reported in Sect. 6.3 using this categorization.

6.2 Smart City Technical Readiness as Reported by Respondents

As can be seen in Fig. 3, the understanding of the Smart City concept is normally distributed among respondents. One third of the respondents report they have very good or excellent knowledge; one third report having good knowledge; and finally, one third report having poor or fair technical knowledge of the concept of smart cities.

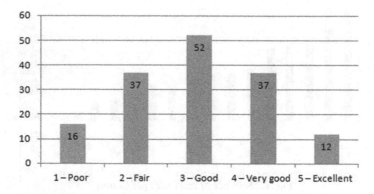

Fig. 3. General knowledge of the concept of Smart Cities of respondents

Figure 4 displays the average level of knowledge reported by respondents on the different technologies used to develop smart city applications. Although small differences exist, the level of average technical expertise is low. It ranges from 2.82 to 3.26, which correspond only to **good**, corresponding to the same scale used in Fig. 3. This situation is especially worrying knowing that the areas of expertise of 96% of participants is Computer Science, Electric Engineering or any other engineering, critical knowledge fields for creating smart cities.

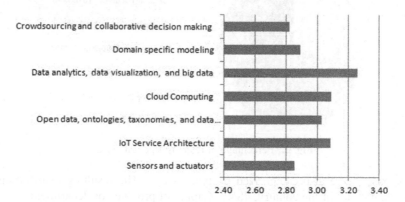

Fig. 4. Average specific knowledge of respondents

The distribution of technical knowledge on specific technologies can be seen on Fig. 5. There are not significant differences among the distribution of knowledge level reported on the seven different technologies. It is worth highlighting that only a small percentage of respondents consider themselves as experts on the subject.

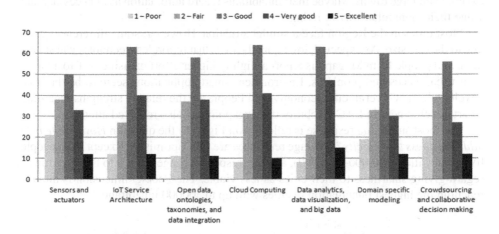

Fig. 5. Distribution of specific knowledge of respondents

6.3 Smartness of LAC Cities

Figure 6 demonstrates the exiting gap between the level of smartness of LAC cities (considerably low), and the perceived potential benefits from the six dimensions of

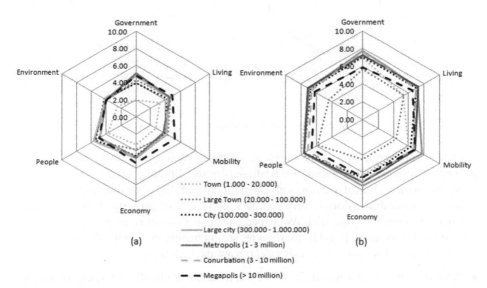

Fig. 6. City degree of smartness (a) and perceived degree of benefits from implementing the six dimensions of Smart Cities (b)

Smart Cities (deemed considerably high). *How Smart is your city?* In each dimension was graded by respondents on a range from 1 to 10. All average grades are below 6 and very few average grades surpass the middle grade of 5. On the other hand, benefits of adding smartness to the city range much higher, with average grades between 6 and 8, except from large towns. Maybe their inhabitants regard automation as unnecessary and value their more relax way of living.

Most cities in the Region face a similar situation. However, some differences exist due to the city size. As expected, towns are the ones that report less technological smartness, and people from Megapolis report a slightly higher effort on using ICT to address their urban needs and problems. Environment smart applications seem to be the least developed, and Government, Economy, and People are the relative strengths regarding smart development in LAC. Mobility on Megapolis has also received attention.

The most surprising response is reflected on Fig. 7, to the question *How viable is to add smartness to your city?* Average responses are very optimistic. Except from people living on Cities (100.000–300.000), average responses range from 6 to 8. Large towns regard giving smartness to their cities as less viable. The People dimension is the one reaching the highest punctuation in cities with up to 300000 inhabitants.

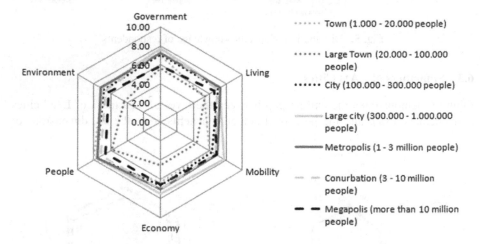

Fig. 7. Degree of viability of implementing the six Smart City dimensions

The viability question is the only one in which participants could decide if they wanted to respond. This decision was driven by the difficulty of the question, since deciding on the technical, economical, and political viability of developing smart applications for most dimensions is very complex. Only 10% of participants felt they could not answer the viability question. We expected a higher rate of *no response*. We suspect most participants answered this question regarding mainly on technical viability.

Some interesting insights of this research are the following:

- *"Adding smart features to a city is not just a matter of installing services or devices, it has to be an integral process. People's needs have to be identified, modeled, understood and then solutions have to be designed and prototypes have to be built."*

- *"the main difficult obstacle for smart cities is to reach an efficient articulation between the main actors in city management (local government, academia and industry)"*

Another interesting finding in the responses is that, in several cities there are isolated smart city initiatives. However, the lack of a governmental approach prevents the growing of these initiatives.

Finally, some respondents think that university cities and small cities could be used as laboratory settings because there is less resistance to change.

7 Conclusions

Smart cities are a hot topic nowadays and can provide several benefits to the inhabitants of cities around the world. This paper presented the results of a regional survey assessing the viability and technical difficulties of developing smart cities. The goal of this research was to understand the realities and expectations of smart cities in Latin America.

One hundred fifty-five (155) experts in technical areas answered an online survey. Towns and cities ranging from thousands to millions of inhabitants were considered. Morcover, six dimensions of smartness were considered: government, living, mobility, economy, people, and environment.

The perceived level of smartness of cities was average, around 4.5 in a scale (1–10). However, the potential benefits of becoming smart are evident, 8.2 in a scale (1–10), and the perceived level of viability was 6.9 in a scale (1–10).

Despite being so positive about viability, some participants highlighted that the establishment of smart cities is an integral process that requires more than technology. According to participants, a national policy on technological development and articulation of different actors, including the government, industry and people, are necessary in order to implement smart solutions.

LAC cities are growing continuously, and their urban and quality of life problems are also growing fast, especially on the most populated cities. Solutions are more than ever needed. It is our duty to evaluate and propose alternative solutions and accompany our local and federal governments to implement more smartness into our surroundings. Helping get our international academic communities together to address this challenge may be the best result of the research endeavor.

Acknowledgement. We thank the 155 participants who answered our questionnaire.

References

1. Angelidou, M.: Smart cities: a conjuncture of four forces. Cities **47**, 95–106 (2015)
2. Manville, C., Cochrane, G., Cave, J., Millard, J., Pederson, J., Thaarup, R., Liebe, A., Wissner, M., Massink, R., Kotterink, B.: Mapping Smart Cities in the EU. European Parliament, Washington, DC (2014)
3. Deakin, M.: Smart Cities - Governing, Modelling and Analysing the Transition. Taylor & Francis, New York (2013)

4. Caragliu, A., Del Bo, C., Nijkamp, P.: Smart cities in Europe. In: Central European Conference in Regional Science, pp. 45–59 (2009)
5. Berrone, P., Ricart, J.E.: IESE Cities in Motion 2017 (2017)
6. Bevir, M.: Governance: A Very Short Introduction. Oxford University Press, Oxford (2012)
7. Shapiro, J.M.: Smart cities: quality of life, productivity, and the growth effects of human capital. Rev. Econ. Stat. **88**, 324–335 (2006)
8. Twinomurinzi, H.: The role of ICT in sustainable and responsible development: E-skilling. In: IFIP Advances in Information and Communication Technology, pp. 90–99 (2012)
9. Suryawanshi, K., Narkhede, S.: Green ICT for sustainable development: a higher education perspective. In: Procedia Computer Science, pp. 701–707. Elsevier Masson SAS, Moulineaux (2015)
10. Cohen, B.: Smart City Index Master Indicators Survey (2014)
11. UN-HABITAT: The World´s Cities in 2016. http://wcr.unhabitat.org/main-report/
12. UN-HABITAT: State of Latin America and the Caribbean Cities 2012: Towards a New Urban Transition. UN-HABITAT, Nairobi (2012)
13. López, E., Arimah, B.C., Mboup, G., Halfani, M., Oyeyinka, O.O.: State of the World's Cities (2013)
14. Lora, E.: Latin American cities: their origins, achievements, and problems. In: The Quality of Life in Latin American Cities: Markets and Perception (2010)
15. Powel, A., Sanguinetti, P.: Measuring quality of life in Latin America's urban neighborhoods: a summary of results from the city case studies. In: The Quality of Life in Latin American Cities: Markets and Perception, p. 200 (2010)
16. Porrúa, M.A.: E-Government in Latin America: a review of the success in Colombia, Uruguay, and Panama. In: The Global Information Technology Report 2013, pp. 127–136 (2013)
17. Cocchia, A.: Smart and digital city: a systematic literature review. In: Dameri, R.P., Rosenthal-Sabroux, C. (eds.) Smart City. PI, pp. 13–43. Springer, Cham (2014). doi: 10.1007/978-3-319-06160-3_2
18. Cohen, B.: The 8 Smartest Cities in Latin America. http://www.fastcoexist.com/3022533/the-8-smartest-cities-in-latin-america
19. Pérez, I.: Proyectan la primera ciudad inteligente de México. http://conacytprensa.mx/index.php/tecnologia/tic/3189-proyectan-primera-ciudad-inteligente-de-mexico
20. Lanza, L.: Smart Cities: size does not matter. https://m2m.telefonica.com/blog/smart-cities-size-does-not-matter
21. Cayalá: Cayalá. http://www.cayala.com.gt/
22. Doxiades, K.A.: Ekistics: An Introduction to the Science of Human Settlements. Hutchinson, London (1968)

Combining Fog Architectures and Distributed Event-Based Systems for Mobile Sensor Location Certification

Fátima Castro-Jul[1]([✉]), Denis Conan[2], Sophie Chabridon[2],
Rebeca P. Díaz Redondo[1], Ana Fernández Vilas[1], and Chantal Taconet[2]

[1] I&C Lab, AtlantTIC Research Center, Universidade de Vigo, Vigo, Spain
{fatima,rebeca,avilas}@det.uvigo.es
[2] SAMOVAR, Télécom SudParis, CNRS, Université Paris-Saclay, Évry, France
{denis.conan,sophie.chabridon,chantal.taconet}@telecom-sudparis.eu

Abstract. Event filtering is of paramount importance in large-scale urban sensing, where an enormous quantity of data is generated. Multiple criteria can be considered for filtering, location being one of the most valuable ones. Obtaining high-quality (trustworthy, accurate) location information helps to contextualize the event content and provides trust both on the source producer and on the publication itself. However, IoT-based urban services rely often on cloud architectures, which have no means to support location certification. To meet the need for location certification support in urban distributed event-based systems (DEBS), we propose three different fog architectures targeted at scenarios with mobile event producers.

Keywords: Participatory sensing · Smart city · Internet of Things

1 Introduction

The Smart City paradigm envisions a city where information technologies enhance citizens quality of life by improving urban services. The Internet of Things (IoT) plays a major role in building smart cities since it enables the interconnection of different devices, vehicles or any kind of objects. Additionally, Distributed Event-based Systems (DEBS) [1] have become a popular interaction paradigm for IoT-based smart city services [2]. These systems support event filtering and producer mobility. The former is essential in large-scale urban sensing, due to the tremendous quantity of data produced. The latter is a promising alternative to building a costly fixed sensing and communication infrastructure to cover the whole city.

Location is one of the main criteria to categorize and filter urban events. Providing spatial context in event distribution allows consumers to subscribe only to their geographical areas of interest. Moreover, even when the event is not location-dependent, receiving information on the producers' whereabouts

© Springer International Publishing AG 2017
S.F. Ochoa et al. (Eds.): UCAmI 2017, LNCS 10586, pp. 27–33, 2017.
DOI: 10.1007/978-3-319-67585-5_3

increases trust in the event content. Implementing location evaluation mechanisms is a non-trivial task in cloud architectures. However, it becomes simpler when part of the data processing is moved to the edges of the network, using a fog architecture.

Fog computing is a promising yet still unexploited possibility to build urban DEBS that provide sensor location certification. To analyze their potential, we have designed three architectures based on fog computing that combine proximity and cloud communication. Our contribution is targeted at providing proximity-based location verification on the edges of the network while employing an architecture that enables communication over a wide-spread area. The aim is to support the quality assessment of publications by relying on proximity-based communication. Thus, we leverage our previous works on quality of context information in DEBS [3] and on distributed proximity-based collaboration with peer devices [4].

This paper is structured as follows. First, we present an overview of related work (Sect. 2). Then, we detail our proposal (Sects. 3 and 4). Finally, we conclude and present our ongoing work in Sect. 5.

2   Related Work

The importance of mobile event producers has considerably grown over the last ten years, due to the emergence of participatory sensing [5] and mobile crowd-sensing systems [6, 7]. These systems rely on collaborative data gathering and can be implemented using different architectures. When data is collected in a centralized manner, a cloud entity is in charge of receiving all the sensor readings and analyzing them. In this case, a blind confidence is placed in the locations claimed by data producers. In order to enhance trust in the provided location, a possible solution is to switch to a proximity-based totally ad hoc network that ensures producers' communication directly with consumers in their very area [4]. This is a good solution for small and densely populated urban areas but it becomes expensive when producers and their subscribed consumers are far away from each other. An alternative is to migrate part of the data processing from the cloud to the edges of the network, using a fog computing architecture. Fog computing [8] has become a useful paradigm for IoT architectures since it provides heterogeneity and fast mobility support [9], low latency and scalability [10]. [11] targets better localized accuracy through location-based customization but does not verify the trustworthiness of location information. To the best of our knowledge, the potential of fog architectures to support location certification schemes has remained unexploited.

3   DEBS with Location Certification Support

Our DEBS is targeted at participatory sensing scenarios with high producer mobility and periodic publications of sensed data. We can think of, for instance, a participatory noise measurement system that relies on citizens smartphones.

Using a DEBS architecture, event distribution is not limited to the close producer's neighborhood but extends outside the city boundaries and beyond. Consumers subscribe by providing filters that specify the publications they are interested in. Publications are routed from producers to consumers by an overlay network of brokers.

Our goal is to improve publication quality by increasing trust on the publication's source location. As a result, we focus our attention on producers' mobility, and for the sake of simplicity we assume the broker and consumer structure to be fixed. A producer is connected to at most one broker, namely its access broker. When producers move, they may disconnect and reconnect to a different broker.

Location information may be included in every publication: it consists of an explicit representation using coordinates, or of the identifier of a specific area or neighborhood. When the location can be verified, the publication is enriched with a location certificate. The location is added by the producer and may be verified either by the producer or the broker but it is always the broker, assumed to be trustworthy, that decides whether to provide the certificate (Algorithm 1). Consumers choose whether they ask the DEBS to filter out uncertified location.

Algorithm 1. At broker B, handle a publication

1: **procedure** HANDLEPUBLICATION(Producer X, Publication n)
2:     **if** B is the access broker of X **then**
3:         $locOk \leftarrow$ VerifyLocation(n)   // verify location information included in n
4:         **if** $locOk$ **then**
5:             ProvideLocationCertificate(n)   // add to n a location certificate
6:     Forward n to interested neighbor brokers and local consumers

---

A publication is certified if the location claim has been verified. The verification consists in assessing the location information using either extra information provided by the producer to support the location claim or the collaboration of other peers in the area. In both cases, the verification relies on proximity-based communication. Proximity-based communication connects devices that are placed closely, at a distance from each other that allows them to be reached using a wireless short-range communication technology, such as Bluetooth or ad hoc WiFi. If a producer that claims to be in a certain area cannot be reached by other devices known to be there, we can conclude that it is not providing its actual location. Following these principles, we foresee three different DEBS architectures supporting location verification and detailed in Sect. 4.

4 Fog-Based Architectures

In traditional DEBS cloud architectures, clients (producers and consumers) are connected through an overlay of brokers that are hosted in a cloud. An access broker may serve clients from different locations (Fig. 1a). It has no knowledge

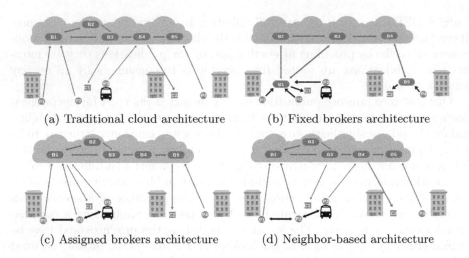

   (a) Traditional cloud architecture   (b) Fixed brokers architecture

   (c) Assigned brokers architecture   (d) Neighbor-based architecture

Fig. 1. Fog-based architectures

about the clients' location and no way to verify whether they are claiming false locations. As an alternative, we introduce three different fog architectures for a DEBS with location verification support. The different combinations of cloud and short-range communication determine how the location verification process is performed.

4.1 Fixed Brokers Architecture

This architecture considers two levels of brokers: border brokers that are in the vicinity (e.g., B1, B5 in Fig. 1b) and inner brokers that are hosted in the cloud (e.g., B2, B3, B4). Border brokers are placed all over the city covering different areas; they are fixed, thus being assigned an immutable location. Clients in the same area are connected to the same access broker using a short-range transmission technology that ensures the veracity of the clients' location. As a result, location verification is straightforward. The access broker will certify the location of every publication whose location attribute coincides with the broker location (Algorithm 2).

A mobile producer may have to disconnect temporary. Publications created by disconnected producers are stored in a local queue, to be issued to the new access broker when reconnecting. If the location is different from the new access broker's location, they are distributed but not considered for location certification because a broker can not certify a location different from its own.

4.2 Assigned Brokers Architecture

Even though a hybrid architecture is a cheaper alternative to deploying a purely fixed sensor network architecture, its cost is still high. As a result, we have designed

Algorithm 2. Verify location information (Fixed brokers architecture)

1: **procedure** VERIFYLOCATION(Publication n)
2:     **return** (location included in n "equals" access broker's location)

a second architecture, which still exploits location verification through proximity-based communication but gives up the requirements for a fixed infrastructure. By considering location-based network partitions, we maximize the probability of having all the clients in an area connected to the same broker (Fig. 1c). Thus, they can still be in charge of producers' location verification even though they cannot communicate with them using a short-range transmission technology. Producers obtain the IP address of their access brokers by providing their location to a discovery service. Producers include in their publications a set of other producers in the area with whom they have established a short-range communication link and who are connected to the same broker (*neigh*). If nearly all[1] of the producers included in the set are registered as local producers of the same access broker, the location is confirmed (Algorithm 3). Producers claiming a false location are not able to provide a valid set of neighbors.

Algorithm 3. Verify location information (Assigned brokers architecture)

1: **procedure** VERIFYLOCATIONINFORMATION(Publication n)
2:     **return** (location included in n "equals" access broker's location $\land$ "most of"
        the producers $\in$ *neigh* are local producers)

4.3   Neighbor-Based Architecture

Unlike the two previous architectures, brokers are not assigned to specific areas and location verification takes place between peer neighbor producers. Producers can be connected to any access broker, which may be different from the one their close neighbors are connected to (Fig. 1d). By exchanging short-range messages, they are always aware of who their neighbors are. When a producer is going to send a publication, it triggers a consensus process between its neighbors. In this process, neighbor producers propose location values and decide on one of them, which will be included in the publication. Since we are dealing with a dynamic scenario where it may be difficult to decide due to variations in the number of neighbors, we consider abortable consensus [12,13]: the result of the consensus is either a location value or *aborted*. If no location value can be reached by consensus, the producer includes its own proposed location value in the notification. Then, the publication sent to the broker includes, in addition to the location, an indication about the consensus result (*successful* or *aborted*). The broker does not take part in the verification process and certifies every publication that includes an indication of successful consensus (Algorithm 4).

---

[1] To tolerate disconnections and overlapping.

Remark that changing the access broker does not necessarily imply a change of producers' location and does not invalidate a location certification.

Algorithm 4. Verify location information (Neighbor-based architecture)

1: **procedure** VERIFYLOCATIONINFORMATION(Publication n)
2:      **return** (indication of consensus in n equals *successful*)

---

5   Conclusion and Ongoing Work

This paper presents three different fog architectures, targeted at location certification support in DEBS for IoT urban services. They combine cloud and proximity-based communication, which enables them to provide first-hand location verification.

We are currently working on the evaluation of the architectures. We plan to employ network simulations based on pedestrian traces generated in real urban maps. The assessment will be focused on the appropriate location verification and on the ability to handle producer's mobility in highly dynamic urban scenarios.

Acknowledgments. This work is funded by: the European Regional Development Fund (ERDF) and the Galician Regional Government under agreement for funding the Atlantic Research Center for Information and Communication Technologies (Atlant-TIC), the Spanish Ministry of Economy and Competitiveness under the National Science Program (TEC2014-54335-C4-3-R) and a predoctoral grant financed by the Galician Regional Government (Consellería de Cultura, Educación e Ordenación Universitaria) and the European Social Fund.

References

1. Eugster, P., Felber, P., Guerraoui, R., Kermarrec, A.-M.: The many faces of publish/subscribe. ACM Comput. Surv. **35**, 114–131 (2003)
2. Antonic, A., Roankovic, K., Marjanovic, M., Pripuic, K., et al.: A mobile crowdsensing ecosystem enabled by a cloud-based publish/subscribe middleware. In: FiCloud 2014, pp. 107–114, IEEE (2014)
3. Lim, L., Marie, P., Conan, D., Chabridon, S., Desprats, T., Manzoor, A.: Enhancing context data distribution for the internet of things using QoC-awareness and attribute-based access control. Ann. Telecommun. **71**(3), 121–132 (2016)
4. Castro-Jul, F., Díaz-Redondo, R.P., Fernández-Vilas, A.: Have you also seen that? Collaborative alert assessment in ad hoc participatory sensing. In: García, C.R., Caballero-Gil, P., Burmester, M., Quesada-Arencibia, A. (eds.) UCAmI/IWAAL/AmIHEALTH -2016. LNCS, vol. 10070, pp. 125–130. Springer, Cham (2016). doi:10.1007/978-3-319-48799-1_15
5. Burke, J., Estrin, D., Hansen, M., Parker, A., Ramanathan, N., Reddy, S., Srivastava, M.: Participatory sensing. Center for Embedded Network Sensing (2006)

6. Ganti, R.K., Ye, F., Lei, H.: Mobile crowdsensing: current state and future challenges. IEEE Commun. Mag. **49**(11), 32–39 (2011)
7. Guo, B., Yu, Z., Zhou, X., Zhang, D.: From participatory sensing to mobile crowd sensing. In: PERCOM 2014, pp. 593–598. IEEE (2014)
8. Bonomi, F., Milito, R., Zhu, J., Addepalli, S.: Fog computing and its role in the internet of things. In: MCC 2012, pp. 13–16. ACM (2012)
9. Yannuzzi, M., Milito, R., Serral-Gracià, R., Montero, D., Nemirovsky, M.: Key ingredients in an IoT recipe: fog computing, cloud computing, and more fog computing. In: CAMAD 2014, pp. 325–329. IEEE (2014)
10. Hong, K., Lillethun, D., Ramachandran, U., Ottenwälder, B., Koldehofe, B.: Mobile fog: a programming model for large-scale applications on the internet of things. In: ACM SIGCOMM, MCC 2013, pp. 15–20. ACM (2013)
11. Munir, A., Kansakar, P., Khan, S.U.: IFCIoT: integrated fog cloud IoT architectural paradigm for future internet of things. CoRR (2017). http://arxiv.org/abs/org/abs/1701.08474
12. Guerraoui, R., Rodrigues, L.: Introduction to Reliable Distributed Programming. Springer, Heidelberg (2006). doi:10.1007/3-540-28846-5
13. Chen, W.: Abortable consensus and its application to probabilistic atomic broadcast. Technical report MSR-TR-2006-135, Microsoft Research (2006)

IOT Service Recommendation Strategy
Based on Attribute Relevance

Pingquan Wang[1,2(✉)], Hong Luo[2], and Yan Sun[2]

[1] Beijing University of Posts and Telecommunications, Beijing, China
pingquanw@l63.com
[2] Huhhot University for Nationalities, Huhhot, China
{luoh, sunyan}@bupt.edu.cn

Abstract. In this article, we research on the service recommendation strategy in the IoT. The user attribute similarity and the attribute correlation of user and device service are computed, and the recommendation system is recommended based on the calculation results. In order to solve the cold start problem, we propose the tensor linear regression model. The experiment results show the recommendation strategy was effective.

Keywords: IoT · Service recommendation · Attribute relevance · Tensor · Cold start

1 Introduction

As the society gradually enters the aging society, more and more elderly people suffer from angiocardiopathy, hypertension, trouble walking and other diseases, and their daily life needs to receive special care and rehabilitation treatment. The smart rehabilitation wards which are designed for the elder emerged, in which there are special facilities to assist the elderly in their daily life, such as intelligent temperature control facilities, intelligent lighting facilities, walking aids, etc. However, because of the decline in learning comprehension of the elderly, they will find it difficult to use these highly intelligent facilities in the new living environment. In order to solve these problems, this paper studied and designed the service recommendation strategy for the IoT.

In the Internet of things (IoT), lots of smart facilities are connected with the Internet. These facilities will provide value-added and user- friendly services and they will be widely applied to health care, intelligent transportation system, intelligent agriculture, smart home and smart city [1]. However, at present, there are only a few service recommendation strategies for the IoT. The traditional service recommendation is mainly aiming at the Internet, and provides the corresponding products for the users according to their previous evaluations, access records or preferences, for example the content filtering algorithm, the collaborative filtering algorithm and the hybrid system algorithm. However, in the IoT, the traditional service recommendation method is very difficult to use effectively, which is due to two reasons as follows. For one thing, the users seldom assess the service after using the corresponding IOT device services, so we can't use the previous users' evaluations to recommend the service. For another, the

© Springer International Publishing AG 2017
S.F. Ochoa et al. (Eds.): UCAmI 2017, LNCS 10586, pp. 34–43, 2017.
DOI: 10.1007/978-3-319-67585-5_4

service includes more attribute information, such as the location of the service, the owners, access control permission, social relations, etc., which are difficult to use effectively with the traditional service recommendation methods.

The main contribution of this paper included the following three aspects: Firstly, it was the first time in the IoT that the service content based on the healthy living habits had been recommended to other users according to the similarities of the user attributes. Secondly, this paper presented the user - attribute similarity matrix and classified the user attributes into the must-same attribute sets and similar attribute sets, then decided the two users' similarities by the cosine similarity method, and lastly recommended the corresponding services to the users with high similarity. Thirdly, this paper described the device service attributes of the IoT by the method of Tensor and recommended the services to the cold-start users based on Tensor linear regression mode.

2   Related Works

The IoT had such a large quantity of services, making it difficult for the users to find the appropriate service content. Therefore, it is necessary to design the service recommendation strategy for the IoT.

Now there is still not enough service recommendation methods specially for the IoT. In the [2], as far as many socialized tag existed in the IoT are concerned, the paper put forward an undirected tripartite graph recommendation algorithm based on the weight, but it just presented the relevant theory without verification in the experimental or real IoT. In the [3], the paper came up with the service recommendation strategy of the location awareness in the intelligent space. However, in the smart space, the same activity scene is often common, while the service offered by each smart space is quite different. At present, the researches service recommendation are mostly in the internet environment. The commonly used methods include the filtering algorithm based on the users as well as the filtering algorithm based on the items. However, the IoT environment is different from the traditional Internet. Most services of the IoT exist in the form of the device service, and they have more user attributes. Therefore, it is necessary to design the service recommendation strategy for the IoT environment.

3   The Recommendation Strategy of the IoT Based on the Similarity of the User Attributes

An investigation has showed that healthy living habits are good for the rehabilitation of the patient [4, 5]. In the [6], the article helped improve the hypertension symptoms by assisting the users in forming healthy living habits. As is shown in Fig. 1, a healthy living habit of a user is composed of a series of equipment operation sequences.

In the smart space, as is shown in the figure above, the users' living habits can be collected by the sensor or video equipment and these habit characteristics can be used as the IoT service rules. In the [7], these users' habits expressed as semantic context and were derived among the rules through the ontology and the semantic web rules language (SWRL). In such space as the intelligent ward, some healthy living habits of

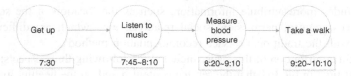

Fig. 1. User's habit characteristic

the recovered patients can be recommended to the new patients so as to help them do the rehabilitation exercises. By comparing the similarities of the attributes of the new patients with the user attributes in the application service of the IoT, the corresponding service content is recommended to the new users. The user attributes usually include their own attributes and social attributes. For example, name, age, location, etc., are used to describe the inherent information of the users, which are called their own attributes. The users' departments, job levels, roles given by the outside world to show their identities are called the social attributes. This $\mu_t = \{\mu_{t_1}, \mu_{t_2}, \ldots, \mu_{t_n}\}$ paper described the user attributes as and established the following user - attribute matrix.

$$
\begin{array}{c}
\mu_{t_1}\, \mu_{t_2}\, \mu_{t_3}\, \cdots\, \mu_{t_m} \\
\begin{array}{c}
S \\
U_1 \\
U_2 \\
\cdots \\
U_n
\end{array}
\left[
\begin{array}{ccccc}
1 & 1 & 0 & \ldots & 0 \\
0 & 0 & 1 & \ldots & 1 \\
1 & 0 & 1 & \ldots & 1 \\
\multicolumn{5}{c}{\cdots\cdots\cdots\cdots\cdots} \\
0 & 1 & 0 & \ldots & 0
\end{array}
\right]
\end{array}
$$

In the matrix, S stands for the new users of the smart space, U_i stands for the owner of the habit rules which form the internet of thing service, and $U_1 \ldots U_n$ stand for n healthy habit rules, which respectively come from n users. μ_{t_i} stands for the types of attributes owned by the users. For example, in such space as the smart rehabilitation wards, the user attributes include their age, gender, the disease types, the disease conditions, etc. If the user has a certain attribute, the corresponding attribute value of the matrix is 1. If not, then the corresponding attribute value is 0.

This paper further classified the user attributes into two types. One type was defined as *must-same* attribute type, which was described as $\Re$ in the paper. For example, in such special environment as the smart ward, only if there were certain same attribute types between the two users, was the corresponding service content recommended to the users, for example, they suffered from the same symptoms. Another type was defined as the similar attribute type, which was described as M in this paper. For example, the age of the two users was in a certain range, so their age attributes were thought to be similar.

We described the *must-same* attribute set of the new user S as $\Re(s)$, described the *must-same* attribute set of the user u_j as $\Re(u_j)$, described the *similar* attribute set of the user S as $M(s)$, and described the *similar* attribute set of the user u_j as $M(u_j)$. Then the similarities of the attributes between the two users were calculated in the form of the cosine similarity, as Eq. (1).

$$q_{ij} = \frac{\lambda |M(u_j) \cap M(s)|}{\sqrt{|M(u_j)||M(s)|}} \tag{1}$$

λ represents the consistency parameter of the must-same attribute set, whose value is shown as Eq. (2)

$$\lambda = \begin{Bmatrix} 1 & \text{if} & \Re(s) = \Re(u_j) \\ 0 & \text{if} & \Re(s) \neq \Re(u_j) \end{Bmatrix} \tag{2}$$

From the Formula (2), we can see that the similarity between the two users will be 0 if the must-same attributes of the users are different, showing that the two users have essential differences. we define the $\wp$ as the threshold, when $q_{ij} \geq \wp$, showing that the two users are very similar. At this time, the service content of the users' healthy living habit can be recommended to the new user of the smart room.

4   The Recommendation Strategy of IoT Based on the Attribute Correlation of User and Device Service

When the attributes of a new user have no relation with those of users of the service habits in the smart room, the above way based on the user attribute similarities can't be used to recommend the service. For example, in the above formula (1), if λ is zero, maybe the two users have great difference in the state of their illnesses. When the new user enters an environment like the smart ward, he won't know which intelligent service to use because of the lack of knowledge about the environment. The paper called this kind of problem as the cold start problem of the intelligent service recommendation. In this case, according to the correlation between the new user' attributes and the device service attributes, the paper will recommend the corresponding device service, that is to say the paper will regard the recommendation score of the device service as how the user attributes and the attributes of the device service are related, and predict the recommendation score by finding the correlation degree between the three vectors, namely the user attributes, the attributes of the device service and the prediction score. The attributes of the IoT device service usually include the attributes of the device as well as the corresponding device service attributes of the device, the attributes of the device usually include the manufacturer and type of the device, and the service attributes of the device usually include the information of the service owners and the service department, etc.

In order to better describe the relation of the three attributes, this paper constructed the linear regression model based on Tensor as was shown in Fig. 2 and called the method as Tensor based service recommendation strategy, or Tensor - AR for short. In this model, the calculation of the grade R for the device service is based on three sections, respectively the user attributes, the attributes of the device service and the

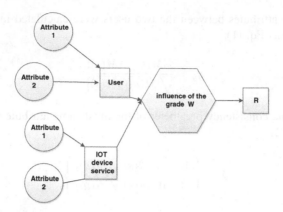

Fig. 2. The linear regression model based on Tensor

influence of the grade from the user attributes and service attributes w. In order to better describe the relation of the three sections, this paper described the user attributes and the attributes of the device service by Tensor.

The definition of the user attributes and the attributes of the device service based on Tensor is as follows: The vector space $U^{(1)}$ stands for the user attributes and the vector space $U^{(2)}$ represents the attributes of the device service. The space of their outer product (also called tensor product). $U^{(1)} \otimes U^{(2)}$ includes all the vector space $\sum ku^{(1)} \otimes u^{(2)}$ of the linear combination of $u^{(1)} \otimes u^{(2)}$ of which $u^{(1)} \in U^{(1)}, u^{(2)} \in U^{(2)}, k \in R.$ $\otimes$ meets the attributes of multi-linear, shown in formulas (3) and (4):

$$(\alpha u_1^{(1)} + \beta u_1^{(1)}) \otimes u^{(2)} = au_1^{(1)} \otimes u^{(2)} + \beta u_1^{(1)} \otimes u^{(2)} \tag{3}$$

$$u^{(1)} \otimes (\alpha u_1^{(2)} + \beta u_2^{(2)}) = au^{(1)} \otimes u_1^{(2)} + \beta u^{(1)} \otimes u_2^{(2)} \tag{4}$$

$\alpha, \beta \in R$, and we defined the element $X \in U^{(1)} \otimes U^{(2)}$ as two-order tensor. Based on Tensor definition of the user attributes and the device service attributes, we defined the bilinear relation among the user attribute vector $u^{(1)}$, the device service attribute vector $u^{(2)}$ and the prediction grade R. The concrete description is shown in formula (5):

$$R = W^T (U^{(1)} \otimes U^{(2)})$$
$$= \sum_{a=1}^{C} \sum_{b=1}^{D} u_a^{(1)} u_b^{(2)} w_{ab} \tag{5}$$

$U^{(1)}$ represents the user's attribute vector, $U^{(2)}$ represents the attribute vector of the device service, C and D respectively represent the number of the user attributes and the number of the device service attributes, a and b respectively stand for the user attribute and the property of the subscript of the device service, $u_a^{(1)}$ shows the a_{th} attribute value of the user, $u_b^{(2)}$ means the b_{th} attribute value of the device service, and w_{ab} stands for the weight, which is independent of the user properties and the device service attribute characteristics, showing the correlation between the user attribute $u_a^{(1)}$ and the attribute of the device service $u_b^{(2)}$. The matrix W is consists of the entity w_{ab}, w^T stands for the transpose of the matrix, and $U^{(1)} \otimes U^{(2)}$ is the tensor product of the vector $U^{(1)}$ and the vector $U^{(2)}$.

According to the bilinear relation among the user attribute's vector $U^{(1)}$, the vector of the device service attribute $U^{(2)}$ and the prediction grade R, this paper calculated the prediction grade of a device service, based on which the user's recommendation list will be realized.

5 Experiment

In order to verify the proposed theory, we constructed three intelligent environments, respectively the hospital's rehabilitation wards, conference rooms and laboratories. In these environments, we arranged different types of intelligent devices. The details of the intelligent space were shown in Table 1. Besides, this paper constructed a ZigBee network in the intelligent environment to transmit various data collected by the sensors, and these data were stored in the MySQL database after data preprocessing. This paper implemented the service recommendation algorithm based on the user-device service attribute described by Tensor in the JAVA language.

Table 1. Intelligent space

Testbed			
Environment characteristic	Rehabilitation wards, adjuvant therapy	New meeting room, Public meeting room.	Laboratory, new students join it every year
User characteristics	Patients in recovering, age between 35 to 70, 60 people	Employees, age between 20~60, 35 people	Student, age between 20~35, 35people
Smart device	Curtain, TV, temperature humidity sensor, smart band, etc.	Projector, air conditioning, curtain, etc.	Light sensor, smart switch, etc.

5.1 The Validation of the Recommendation Strategy Based on the Similarities of the User Attributes

In order to verify the effectiveness of the proposed recommendation strategy based on the similarities of the user attributes, the paper selected a room like the rehabilitation ward, in which there are often some patients living or recovering. The paper used the method of [7], gaining the attributes of two recovered patients as well as their healthy living habits shown in Table 2.

Table 2. The characteristics of the user habits

ID	Patient attribute	Habit character
001	Case: primary hypertension, hypertensive heart disease, gender: man, age: 60	Get up at 7:30, listen music between7:45 and 8:10, blood pressure gauge between 8:00 and 8:10, take medicine between 8:15 and 8:25, wander between 9:20 and 10:10
002	Case:type 2 diabetes, gender: woman, age: 35	Get up at 7:00, blood glucose at 7:20, wander between 7:30 and 8:00, listen music between 8:10 and 9:00

Afterwards, the recommendation system would recommend the service with the corresponding habit characteristics to 60 new patients based on the users' characteristics, who were divided into primary hypertension patients and type 2 diabetic patients, and each of them was divided into 30 to 45 years old, between 45 and 60 years old, and between 60 and 75 years old. Then the results would be analyzed by questionnaires, which are from both patients and their doctors.

The users are the important participants of the recommendation system, so their satisfaction is the most important indicator of the evaluating recommendation system. However, the user satisfaction can't be calculated off-line. On the contrary, it can only be gained through the user survey or the on-line experiment. Surveying the users to gain the user satisfaction is mainly through the form of questionnaires, and the users' satisfaction with the recommendation system is divided into different levels. This paper designed the following questionnaire for the rehabilitation patients: 1. The recommended service is what I really want. 2. I have seen most of the recommended services, and I think some of them are of benefit to my rehabilitation. 3. I have no idea why these services are recommended, as they are of no help to my rehabilitation. In addition, the paper also designed the corresponding hierarchical questionnaire for the corresponding attending doctors. 1. All the recommended services are beneficial to the rehabilitation of the patient. 2. Some of the recommended services are beneficial to the rehabilitation of the patient. 3. The recommended services are of no help to the rehabilitation of the patient.

Tables 3 and 4 are questionnaires about the habit recommendation results for patient 001 and patient 002. From Table 3, we can see the habits of the patient 001 are recommended to 30 people, 76.6% of whom are very satisfied with the recommended results. Besides, in the doctor questionnaires, 87.6% of them show that the recommended services are good for the rehabilitation of the patients. From Table 4, we can

Table 3. The habit recommendation results of the patient 001

Age group	Patient questionnaire			Doctor questionnaire		
	1#	2#	3#	1#	2#	3#
30–45	6	2	2	8	2	0
45–60	8	2	0	9	1	0
60–75	9	1	0	9	1	0
Total (%)	76.6%	16.6%	6.6%	87.6%	13.3%	0%

Table 4. The habit recommendation results of the patient 002

Age group	Patient questionnaire			Doctor questionnaire		
	1#	2#	3#	1#	2#	3#
30–45	9	1	0	10	0	0
45–60	8	1	1	9	1	0
60–75	8	2	0	8	1	1
Total (%)	83.30%	13.30%	3%	90%	6.60%	3.30%

see the habits of the patient 002 are also recommended to 30 people, 83.3% of whom show their satisfaction, and 87.6% of the doctors indicate that the recommended services are of benefit to the rehabilitation of the patients. According to the above two questionnaires, we can see that the recommendation strategy of the IoT application service based on the similarities of the user attributes got a good recommendation result from both the patients and the doctors.

5.2 The Service Recommendation Strategy Based on the Device Service Attributes Described by Tensor

In order to verify the service recommendation strategy based on the attributes of the user-device service described by Tensor (Tensor-AR), the paper selected 35 new users from the intelligent rehabilitation wards, conference rooms and the laboratory. These users' attributes are quite different from the other users, and on such condition λ is zero in Eq. (1). Afterwards, by recommending to the users through the recommendation system and observing the changing situation of the corresponding mean absolute error, the paper compared two typical service recommendation methods, namely SRMTC put forward by [8] and the CF-DNC collaborative filtering recommendation algorithm based on the double neighbor selection strategy [9]. At present, most of the references use the mean absolute error MAE as a standard to measure the recommendation quality and evaluate the accuracy of the service recommendation [10].

In the conference room as shown in Fig. 3, we could find that with the increase of the number of the observers, the mean absolute errors gained by the three algorithms would reduce gradually. In addition, the mean absolute error curve of Tensor-AR was at a minimum, while the mean absolute error curve of CF-DNC was at the peak, the same results could get from Figs. 4 and 5, which showed that the recommendation strategy of the Internet service based on the user-device service attributes had a good recommendation result in different scenes. Comparing the mean absolute errors of the three scenes, we found that the mean absolute error in the Fig. 5 was lower than that in the other two scenes as shown in Figs. 3 and 4. Analyzing the three scenes further, we found that more user attributes and the attributes of the sensing devices would be gained in the intelligent wards so that the recommendation accuracy was improved effectively.

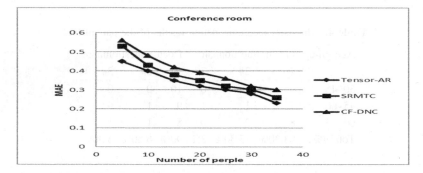

Fig. 3. The mean absolute error in the conference room

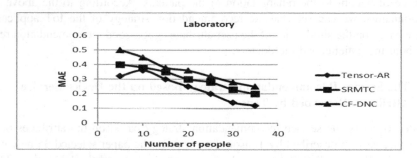

Fig. 4. The mean absolute error in the laboratory

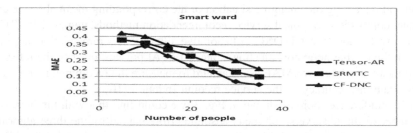

Fig. 5. The mean absolute error in the smart ward

6 Conclusion

This paper studied the service recommendation strategy of the IoT based on the similarities of the user attributes as well as the service recommendation strategy of the user-device service attributes based on what Tensor had described. The corresponding theory was validated in the real experimental environment. In the following work, the author will continue to study other recommendation methods of the IoT.

Acknowledgement. This work is partly supported by the National Natural Science Foundation of China under Grants 61272520, 61370196, 61532012; Scientific Studies Program of Higher Education of Inner Mongolia Municipality (NJZY237).

References

1. Atzori, L., Iera, A., Morabito, G.: The IoT: a survey. Comput. Netw. **54**(15), 2787–2805 (2010)
2. Mashal, I., Chung, T.Y., Alsaryrah O.: Toward service recommendation in IoT. pp. 328–31 (2015)
3. Ko, H,G., Kim, T., Kim, B.: Place-aware opportunistic service recommendation scheme in a smart space with IoT. In: Consumer Communications and Networking Conference (2014)
4. Martelli, M.F., Zasler, N.D., Pickett, T.C.: A habit retraining model for neurobehavioral rehabilitation. Arch. Clin. Neuropsychol. **15**(8), 662–669 (2000)
5. Reynolds, C.R.: Arch. Clin. Neuropsychol. (4):359 (2008)
6. Lijie, C.: Influence of changing bad living habits on blood pressure control of hypertension patients. Chin. J. Clin. Rehabil. (2003)
7. Wang, P., Luo, H., Sun, Y., (eds.): A habit-based SWRL generation and reasoning approach in smart home. In: IEEE International Conference on Parallel and Distributed Systems (2015)
8. Wang, H.Y., Yang, W.B., Wang, S.C., Li, S.-R.: A service recommendation method based on trustworthy community. Chin. J. Comput. **37**, 301–311 (2014)
9. O'Donovan, J., Smyth, B., (eds.). Trust in recommender systems. In: International Conference on Intelligent User Interfaces, pp. 10–13 (2005)
10. Jia, D., Zhang, F.: A collaborative filtering recommendation algorithm based on double neighbor choosing strategy. J. Comput. Res. Dev. **50**(5), 1076–1084 (2013)

Methodology for Analyzing the Travel Time Variability in Public Road Transport

Teresa Cristóbal(✉), Gabino Padrón, Alexis Quesada-Arencibia,
Francisco Alayón, and Carmelo R. García

Institute for Cybernetics, Universidad de Las Palmas de Gran Canaria,
Las Palmas de Gran Canaria, Spain
teresa.cristobalb@alu.ulpgc.es,
{gabino.padron,alexis.quesada,fracncisco.alayon,
ruben.garcia}@ulpgc.es

Abstract. The quality of the time travel prediction is a key factor in the transport of people and goods. This prediction is used in different facets related to management and planning of the transport activity, having special influence in the service quality in public transport. In this paper a methodology to analyse the factors which affect to travel time prediction in routes of road public transport is presented. This methodology uses vehicles GPS data to identify the causes of the travel time variability, georeferencing these causes. The infrastructure elements required, data used and the processing techniques are explained. The methodology was applied to analyse the travel time of a line of a public transport company, presenting the results of this test.

Keywords: Intelligent transport systems · Automatic. public transport planning · Automatic vehicle location · GPS data

1 Introduction

The transport systems play an important role in the economic and social development of the societies. This fact implies a massive use of these systems, especially road transport system, producing environmental degradation, traffic congestion and increment the accidents risk. For example, it is estimated that over 40% of the world population spends at least an hour a day travelling by road [1] and according to statistics, every year 250,000 people in the European Union [2] are seriously injured as a result of traffic accidents. An effective policy to reduce the impact of these problems consists of the use of reliable and safe public transport systems.

In public transport, the service reliability is a main element to provide an efficient and convenient transport service. According to Peek [3], there are five factors which affect to the transport user opinion about the service quality: in first place the safety and the reliability, in second place the travel time and finally, in third place, the comfort and the experience. A methodology to identify the causes which produce systematic delays and variability in the travel time in the routes of a public transport network is presented in this paper. The data used by this methodology are provided by different sources

© Springer International Publishing AG 2017
S.F. Ochoa et al. (Eds.): UCAmI 2017, LNCS 10586, pp. 44–49, 2017.
DOI: 10.1007/978-3-319-67585-5_5

available in the transport infrastructure, playing a main role the GPS positioning and the mobile data communication of the vehicles. The proposed methodology specifies how to fusion these data, which can be massive, and the required processes to identify the factors which affect to the durability and variability of the travel time in a line service of public transport.

In addition to this introductory section, this paper is structured in four more sections. The next section is dedicated to present related works about the travel time prediction. The Methodology is explained in the third section, exposing the data and infrastructure required and the techniques used. The fourth section is dedicated to present the results obtained in the tests executed in a public transport company. The last section is dedicated to present the conclusions.

2   Related Works

The travel time prediction is a classic problem in transport. This prediction plays a main role in the information systems of both, public and private transport. There are two kinds of time travel prediction; the short-term prediction and the long-term prediction. Based on the techniques used to solve short-term travel time prediction problem, the approaches to this problem are classified in four groups. In the first group, Khosravi [4] and Zaki [5] use multi-level neuronal networks and Baptista [6] uses a classification and regression method based on k-nearest neighbors algorithm. In the second group of methods, Lin [7] uses Markov models and Shalaby [8] uses Kalman filters. A third group consists of approaches based on traffic models, making the predictions considering the traffic density estimations, the work of Dong [9] is an example of this kind of technique.

The duration of the long-distance travel is a parameter necessary for operations scheduling, affecting to its reliability. Despite the importance of this type of prediction, in the bibliography there are not many references about this topic. Mendes-Moreira [10] use several techniques based on regression vectors, projection pursuit regression and Random Forest decision trees

3   Methodolgy Description

Different types of activities in public transport require to make travel time estimations, for example: service scheduling, operations control, traveler information, etc. The travel time of a public transport line, TT, can be expressed as:

$$TT = \sum_{n=0}^{N-1} \left(DW_n + RT_n \right) \qquad (1)$$

In the expression of TT, the sub-index n represents the segment of route between two consecutive bus stops of the sequence of the line. The term DW_n represents to dwell time in the bus stop P_n, being this time a function of the number of passenger that embarking and disembarking at P_n. The term RT_n represents the non-stop running time between the bus stop P_n and P_{n+1}, that is the route segment n. This time depend on traffic conditions, road conditions, driving style, etc. The commercial speed of a vehicle making a line service is a function of the speed of the vehicle in the different segments of the line and the velocity of boarding and disembarkation process of the travellers in the different bus stops of the line. The aim of this work is to define a methodology for detecting systematically the causes which produce an increase of the travel time or variability on this time.

The hypothesis that justifies this methodology can be expressed in the following way: using the vehicles positioning data, it is possible to identify the causes that systematically produce the increment of the non-stop running time, RT Hereinafter, or the variability of this time. Additionally, once these causes are identified, it is possible to analyse possible actions to reduce its impact.

From technological point of view, see Fig. 1, the methodology is supported by two main elements commonly available in the infrastructures of road transit systems. The first of these elements is the vehicle GPS positioning system and the data communication system deployed in the transport network (vehicles, stations, garages, etc.), by this system the vehicle positioning data, provided by the Automatic Vehicle Location System (AVL), are transferred to the central data repository for processing, based on the methodology. The set of all positioning records obtained by AVL is represented by {RAVL}.

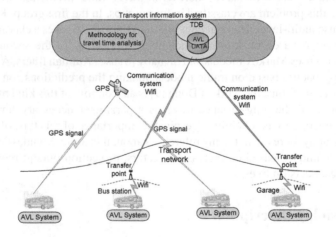

Fig. 1. General vision of the infrastructure used

The aim is to know the causes which systematically produce increments or variations of RT during the line services. Additionally, these causes must be georeferenced, in order to study if it is possible to develop actions to minimize the impact in RT. The main goal is that vehicles travel time is uniform, facilitating its prediction in the different segments of the line. Figure 2 shows a blocks diagram of the proposed methodology. The initial specifications of the methodology are the line, L, and the time period, T, used to analyze the line L. The processing steps of the methodology are four. The First step is the tracking module; its goal is to select the data records provided by AVL system that must be processed to analyze the line L during the period T, this set is represented by the $\{RAVL\}_{L,T}$. Using the data set provide by the previous step, the second phase is a filtering process, its goal is to make an integral data set, represented by $\{QAVL\}_{L,T}$. In the third step, the arrival time of each bus stop for each line service of L is obtained and with these data the RT value for each segment of the line is calculated, the set of RT values of the line is represented by $\{RT_n\}_{L,T}$. The last step is to identify the segments of the line L where RT has a high variability, analyzing each segment to identify the causes of this variability and georerefecing these causes.

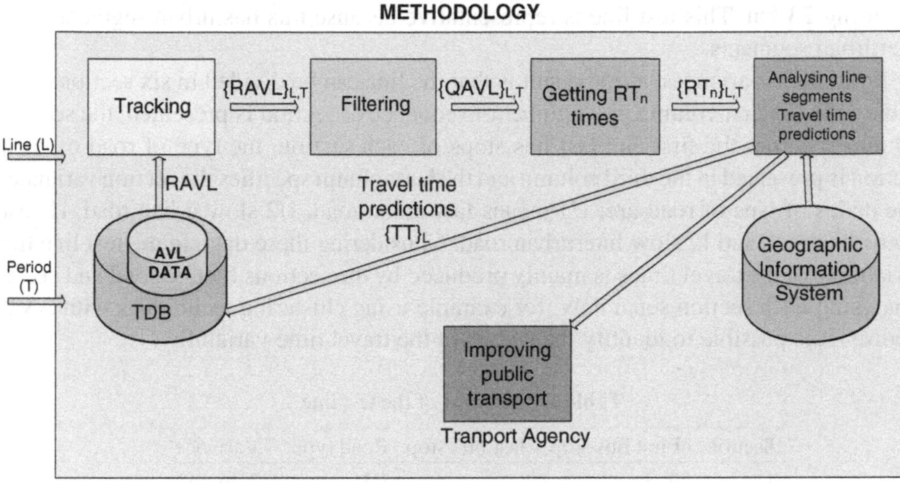

Fig. 2. Methodology

Starting from the initial specifications, L and T, the aim of this tracking phase is to select the data set from data registers provided by AVL systems. Considering the initial specifications, L and T, the records provided by AVL that are useful for analyzing the line L during the period T are those which were acquired in any vehicle of the fleet making a service line of the line L during the period T. $\{RAVL\}_{L,T}$ represents this set of useful positioning records that will be selected in this phase. To achieve this initial selection of data record, it is necessary use the Transport Database (TDB).

Data integrity must be ensured to guarantee the reliability of the study; this is the purpose of filtering phase of the methodology. Data integrity means that there are no wrong data and that dataset is complete. In the methodology, this integrity is achieved by executing two filtering rules. The first filtering rule eliminates from the $\{RAV\}_{L,T}$ those records containing position data that are not good quality The second filtering rules removes those records that are not part of a sequence of position readings that represent a complete and consistent expedition of the line L. $\{QAVL\}_{L,T}$ represents the reliable data provided by this phase.

The next methodology phase gets the times RT_n of each service line of the line L. To get the RT_n, the records set $\{QAVL\}_{L,T}$ are sorted by the time instant of the positioning reading, to get a complete and coherent representation of each service line of the line L.

4   Results and Discussion

The proposed methodology was tested in the public transport company Salcai-Utinsa S.A. This corporation works in Gran Canaria Island (Canary Islands, Spain), has a fleet of 345 vehicles, operating 127 different lines and transporting 19,284,378 passengers in the year 2015. The results presented were obtained applying the methodology to a line of this company, during 6 months of the year 2015. This test line has 30 bus stops and travelling 23 km. This test line is representative because this has urban segments and interurban segments.

From these variances, a first result is that the line can be divided in six sections, see Table 1. In the first column, the number of sequence of section is presented, the second column specifies the first and last bus stops of each section, the type of road of each section is presented in the third column and the last column specifies the section variance. The codes of type of road are: U1 means fast urban road, U2 slow urban road, I1 fast interurban road and I2 slow interurban road. Considering these data, in the test line the variability of the travel times is mainly produced by the sections first, second and sixth. Analysing each section separately, for example using clustering techniques with AVL records, it is possible to identify the causes of the travel time variability.

Table 1. Sections of the test line

Section	First bus stop – last bus stop	Road type	Variance
1	0–3	U1	7.46
2	3–7	U2	3.35
3	7–14	I1	0.85
4	14–21	I2	1.08
5	21–27	U2	0.72
6	27–30	U2	4.26

5   Conclusions

Travel time prediction is a classic problem in the transporting field. This time is a key factor, used in different facets of public transport: services scheduling, real time operation control, traveller information, etc. In this paper, a methodology to identify systematically the causes of the variability of travel time of public transport buses has been presented. Additionally, combined use of the methodology and information systems such as geographical information systems, different actions can be studied to reduce the travel time or the variability of this time. The results of this test have permitted to identify the causes that produce variability in the travel time in an urban section of this line. Also, these results permit to propose possible actions to reduce this variability. This methodology can be expanded to include the use of the data provided by the on-boarded payment systems to estimate the dwell time during of the buses.

References

1. Zhang, J., Wang, F., Wang, K., Lin, W., Xu, X., Chen, Ch.: Data-driven intelligent transportation systems: a survey. IEEE Trans. Intell. Transp. Syst. **4**, 1624–1639 (2011). doi: 10.1109/TITS.2011.2158001
2. European Commission. http://europa.eu/rapid/press-release_IP-13-236_en.htm. Accessed 1 May 2017
3. Peek, G., van Hagen, M.: Creating synergy in and around stations: three strategies for adding value. J. Transp. Res. Board **1793**, 1–6 (2002). doi:10.3141/1793-01
4. Khosravi, A., Mazloumi, E., Nahavandi, S., Creighton, D., Van Lint, J.: Prediction intervals to account for uncertainties in travel time prediction. IEEE Trans. Intell. Transp. Syst. **12**, 537–547 (2011). doi:10.1109/TITS.2011.2106209
5. Zaki, M., Ashour, I., Zorkany, M., Hesham, B.: Online bus arrival time prediction using hybrid neural network and Kalman filter techniques. Int. J. Mod. Eng. Res. **3**(4), 2035–2041 (2013)
6. Baptista, A., Bouillet, E., Pompey, P.: Towards an uncertainty aware short-term travel time prediction using GPS bus data: Case study in Dublin. In: Proceedings 15th Int. IEEE ITSC, pp. 1620–1625. doi:10.1109/ITSC.2012.6338633 (2012)
7. Lin, W., Bertini, R.: Modeling schedule recovery processes in transit operations for bus arrival time prediction. J. Adv. Transp. **38**, 347–365 (2004). doi:10.1109/ITSC.2002.1041332
8. Shalaby, A., Farhan, A.: Bus travel time prediction model for dynamic operations control and passenger information systems. In: TRB 82nd Annual Meeting (2003)
9. Dong, J., Zou, L., Zhang, Y.: Mixed model for prediction of bus arrival times. In: Proceedings 2013 IEEE Congress on Evolutionary Computation (CEC), pp. 2918–2923. doi:10.1109/CEC.2013.6557924 (2013)
10. Mendes-Moreira, J., Jorge, A., de Sousa, J., Soares, C.: Comparing state-of-the-art regression methods for long term travel time prediction. Intell. Data Anal. **16**, 427–449 (2012). doi: 10.3233/IDA-2012-0532

Scheduler for Automatic Management of Maintenance Jobs in Large-Size Systems: A Case Study Applied to Smart City

Rafael J. Valdivieso-Sarabia[1]([✉]), Oscar Marín-Alonso[1], Fernando G. Guerrero-Gómez[1], Francisco J. Ferrández-Pastor[2], Jerónimo Mora-Pascual[2], and Juan M. García-Chamizo[2]

[1] Nouss Intelligence S.L., Pza San Cristobal 14, 03002 Alicante, Spain
{rvaldivieso,omarin,fguerrero}@nouss.eu
[2] Department of Computer Technology, University of Alicante,
Carretera San Vicente del Raspeig s/n, 03690 Alicante, Spain
{fjferran,jeronimo,juanma}@dtic.ua.es

Abstract. Maintenance of systems such as infrastructure, services and equipment on city context requires a complex management process in order to provide quality services, comply with regulations and extend lifespan of urban equipment and infrastructure without neglecting the proper use of resources to execute maintenance jobs. Cities can generate hundreds or thousands of maintenance jobs during a particular time period. These jobs can be generated automatically by equipment or can be reported by citizens/users. This work introduces a scheduling architecture for automatic management of maintenance jobs. The proposal is able to handle preventive and corrective maintenance jobs looking for available human and instrumental resources during the common time period required by the job to be executed. The scheduler uses intelligent strategies to satisfy constraints of each job in order to get a scheduling according to the criterion of the manager of maintenance. A case study is applied to smart city.

Keywords: Scheduler · Automatic · Resources · Smart maintenance · Multidimensional constraints · CMMS

1 Introduction

Cities can be considered as complex systems that evolve during time. The Smart City (SC) approach tries to solve problems originated mainly from large population, communications, transport, services and infrastructure using information, communication and control technologies (ICCT) to automate jobs, recollect data and connect different systems in order to get knowledge that can be applied to improve services and urban infrastructure.

The maintenance of urban infrastructure is a key point to provide services like water, electric and gas supply, public lighting, roads, garbage collection, vehicles and bicycle parking, public transport, healthcare. Large-size cities by population can generate hundreds of thousands of maintenance jobs to be carried out during a particular time

© Springer International Publishing AG 2017
S.F. Ochoa et al. (Eds.): UCAmI 2017, LNCS 10586, pp. 50–55, 2017.
DOI: 10.1007/978-3-319-67585-5_6

period, e.g. a day, week, and month. Maintenance jobs can be generated automatically by electronic equipment, e.g. parking meters when it runs out of paper, or manually by citizens or users who reports an error or malfunction of a particular service or infrastructure.

The management of maintenance jobs takes hard work of the team leader or manager. Manager has to authorize all the manual maintenance jobs. Jobs, which are generated automatically, are authorized by default. Then, all the authorized jobs have to be scheduled in a time period and the required resources has to be assigned taking into account constraints of each job. Resources and time allocation for each job is a non-trivial task and it requires to consult managers of all the areas involved in scheduling.

This paper proposes a scheduler for automatic management of maintenance jobs that makes resources and time allocation automatic using intelligent strategy to satisfy constraints in order to get a scheduling according to the user criterion. Following section describes the background of automatic scheduling systems. Third section describes the automatic scheduler of maintenance jobs. Fourth section presents a case of study applied to a large-size city and the automatic scheduling results. Finally, conclusion discusses about the results presented and future work.

2   Related Work

Traditionally, three types of basic maintenance management has been identified as corrective, preventive and predictive [1]. Maintenance taxonomy has been defined in [1, 2]. The most common management strategy of maintenance jobs in cities is composed by preventive, corrective and predictive.

There are well-known algorithms for automatic scheduling of process in multi-core computers, where the operative system assigns the required resources to each process guaranteeing concurrent execution avoiding resource starvation [3–5]. Scheduling of tasks in cloud platforms is described in [6]. These techniques cannot be used in the context of maintenance jobs due to the nature of process that are executed on multi-core processor. All the processes that require the processor to be executed get access to the processor during a determined number of cycles. After that following process gain access to processor, i.e. processes can be divided in order to execute each fragment. Maintenance jobs cannot be divided in n fragments, which each one requires a few milliseconds, because each job must be executed continuously. Maybe, due to the particular nature of painting job, it could be defined by the manager as divisible with a minimum time of 1 h fragment. In this scenario neither can be used previous techniques because the size of each fragment is significantly greater than the milliseconds used by the scheduler of the operative system.

Following techniques are focused on scheduling applied into maintenance context. Moradi et al. in [7] present a bi-objective optimization research on integrated fixed time interval preventive maintenance. This work is focused in optimize only two variables. Real scenario like cities requires considering higher number of variables to optimize. The use of a fixed time interval represents a static approach that does not permit to take advantage of dynamical conditions. Only the preventive maintenance is considered to be scheduled but in real scenario like cities corrective maintenance is required and preventive maintenance is not always required.

The work presented in [8] is focused to solve the automatic test task scheduling problem (TTSP) with the objectives of minimizing the maximal test completion time (makespan) and the mean workload of the instruments. The problem solved is NP-hard and it is based on genetic algorithm in order to get a continuous multi-objective optimization problem [9]. This proposal cannot be applied under realistic conditions in a large city because it is focused on test scenarios i.e. in mobile phone terminal manufacturing, and the multi-objective optimization problem requires long time to get the best solution.

A single-machine-based optimization model of production scheduling and preventive maintenance under group production is introduced in [10]. This model is focused on generate preventive maintenance according to the state of the system to keep in good conditions in order to reduce maintenance cost and required time. It considers failure rate threshold and minimal repair based on machine's age is performed considering unexpected failure. This proposal is not focused on automatic resource and time allocation of the maintenance jobs to be executed.

3   Automatic Scheduler for Maintenance Jobs

The scheduling process begins when the manager of maintenance job defines the scheduling period that is going to be scheduled, e.g. the next week. The input of the automatic scheduler for maintenance jobs is the preventive jobs pool and the corrective job pool. This pool contains all the jobs that are able to be carried on in the scheduling period. The preventive job pool is automatically generated based on contracts with outsourcing companies and the maintenance jobs established by regulation organizations. Corrective job pool is composed by automatically generated jobs from devices that identify a failure or a breakdown situation and jobs generated from the reports sent by citizen or users of the system. These reports should be approved by the manager of the maintenance service during the task of corrective job approval, who determines if a report is transformed into a corrective job. The preventive and corrective job pools are submitted to the automatic scheduler.

The output of the automatic scheduler is a job scheduling of all the jobs. In large-size organizations the global scheduling must be validated by all the managers of each area. Each manager can validate the scheduling or can make a statement in order to suggest a change in a set of jobs. This confirmation and argument task is complex to carry out in large-size organizations because a lot of managers must be orchestrated through a validation flow. Each manager has a time period for validate or make suggestions, if the time period for the manager is finished and any suggestion has been made, then the scheduling is considered validated and the validation time for the following manager begins. This flow is done when all the managers are checked. The output of the confirmation and argument task is the job scheduling confirmed that contains all the scheduling jobs. Next, the splitting task classifies all the jobs by human resources in order to notify each worker their individual jobs scheduling for each day through their mobile phone. The complete process is illustrated in Fig. 1.

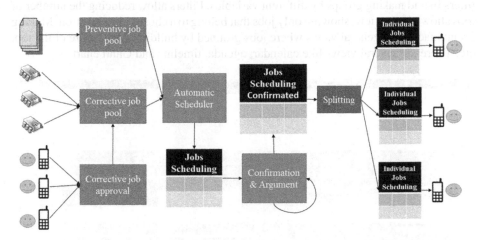

Fig. 1. Data flow from automatically generated preventive and corrective jobs to the individual job scheduling for each worker in the organization.

4   A Case Study Applied to City

A large-size city is described in order to illustrate a scenario where the proposed solution is ready to be deployed. The metropolitan area of the city has a population of 5 million people, the city area is around 100 km^2 and a population density of 16,000 pop/km^2. The city meet the need of manage around 3700 jobs by week. The maintenance management system is deployed over following organizational units: Sport area, Zoo, Theme park, Public parking garages and Parking meters.

The complexity of scheduling service is based on: the number of maintenance jobs to be scheduled, the time period when the jobs have to be scheduled and the number of resources required by each job. Each job requires an average of 3.89 resources.

From 3700 maintenance jobs introduced as input to the scheduler server, 3624 jobs has been successfully scheduled, nearly 98%. 76 remaining jobs cannot be scheduled automatically because there were not available resources that meets with the constraints defined for these jobs. If the manager has to schedule some of the remaining jobs, some scheduled jobs have to be deleted from the schedule in order to get resources free. These free resources can be assigned to the remaining jobs. Other action is to mark jobs that can be divided in order to fill in gaps in the schedule. None of the jobs has been automatically divided because these jobs have been defined indivisible.

Figure 2 shows a partial view of the main schedule. It contains 14 jobs automatically scheduled in a single day from 9:00 to 14:00 and 15:00 to 18:00. This scheduler view can show a day view, week view, month view, agenda view, timeline view and Gantt view. The view contains some gaps. These gaps are from two situations. First, there were not enough resources to carry out jobs during the gap. The second one, duration of jobs is larger than gap duration, so if the job cannot be divided, the job cannot be scheduled in this gap. In order to facilitate jobs visualization, controls allows applying filters in and making groups by different variables. Filters allow reducing the number of jobs shown in the view, showing only jobs that belong to a chosen classification. Making groups facilitates general views where jobs grouped by buildings, the nature of the job, etc. There are several views like calendar, agenda, timeline and Gantt chart.

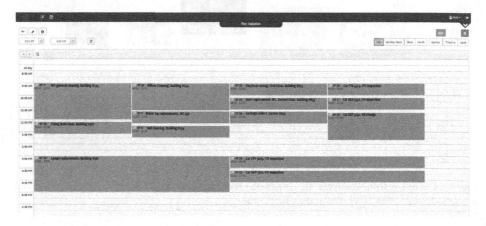

Fig. 2. Partial view of the schedule with some maintenance jobs in a single day, from 9:00 to 14:00 and 15:00 to 18:00

5   Conclusion

A scheduler for automatic management of maintenance jobs in large-size systems has been proposed. This proposal has been applied into a smart city where maintenance jobs are automatically generated by equipment and can be reported by citizens. The proposal is able to handle preventive and corrective maintenance jobs looking for available human and instrumental resources during the common time period required by the job to be done. The scheduler uses intelligent strategies to satisfy constraints of each job in order to get a productive scheduling according to the criterion of the manager of maintenance. The proposal has been studied in a large-size city by population, which requires to schedule around 3700 jobs every week. Results shows 98% of jobs automatically scheduled. A graphical user interface of the scheduler view is presented and allows to the maintenance manager to validate and to make changes.

Future work is focused on improve latency of the intelligent strategy applied to schedule jobs because database access punishes latency. Moreover, new criterion for change the behaviour of the scheduler services has to be defined in order to give more flexibility to the managers.

References

1. Khazraei, K., Deuse, J.: A strategic standpoint on maintenance taxonomy. J. Facil. Manag, **9**(2), 96–113 (2011). doi:10.1108/14725961111128452
2. Javed, K., Gouriveau, R., Zerhouni, N.: State of the art and taxonomy of prognostics approaches, trends of prognostics applications and open issues towards maturity at different technology readiness levels. Mech. Syst. Signal Process. **94**, 214–236 (2017). ISSN 0888-3270
3. Kwok, Y.-K., Ahmad, I.: Static scheduling algorithms for allocating directed task graphs to multiprocessors. ACM Comput. Surv. **31**(4), 406–471 (1999)
4. Augonnet, C., Thibault, S., Namyst, R., Wacrenier, P.A.: StarPU: a unified platform for task scheduling on heterogeneous multicore architectures. Concurr. Comput. Pract. Exp. **23**(2), 187–198 (2011)
5. Zhang, W., Xie, H., Cao, B., Cheng, A.M.K.: Energy-aware real-time task scheduling for heterogeneous multiprocessors with particle swarm optimization algorithm. Prob. Eng. Math. (2014). doi:10.1155/2014/287475
6. Zhang, F., Cao, J., Li, K., Khan, S.U., Hwang, K.: Multi-objective scheduling of many tasks in cloud platforms. Future Gener. Comput. Syst. **37**, 309–320 (2014). doi:10.1016/j.future. 2013.09.006. ISSN 0167-739X
7. Moradi, E., Fatemi Ghomi, S.M.T., Zandieh, M.: Bi-objective optimization research on integrated fixed time interval preventive maintenance and production for scheduling flexible job-shop problem. Expert Syst. Appl. **38**(6), 7169–7178 (2011). doi:10.1016/j.eswa. 2010.12.043. ISSN 0957-4174
8. Lu, H., Niu, R., Liu, J., Zhu, Z.: A chaotic non-dominated sorting genetic algorithm for the multi-objective automatic test task scheduling problem. Appl. Soft Comput. **13**(5), 2790–2802 (2013). doi:10.1016/j.asoc.2012.10.001. ISSN 1568-4946
9. Deb, K., Sindhya, K., Hakanen, J.: Multi-objective optimization. Decis. Sci. Theory Pract., 145–184 (2016). doi:10.1201/9781315183176-4. ISBN: 978-1-4665-6430-5
10. Liao, W., Zhang, X., Jiang, M.: An optimization model integrated production scheduling and preventive maintenance for group production. In: 2016 IEEE International Conference on Industrial Engineering and Engineering Management (IEEM), Bali, pp. 936–940 (2016). doi: 10.1109/IEEM.2016.7798015

User-Centered Design of Agriculture Automation Systems Using Internet of Things Paradigm

Francisco-Javier Ferrández-Pastor[(✉)], Juan-Manuel García-Chamizo,
Mario Nieto Hidalgo, and José Mora-Martínez

University of Alicante, Ctra San Vicente del Raspeig,
s/n, 03690 San Vicente del Raspeig, Alicante, Spain
fjferran@dtic.ua.es

Abstract. During the past decades, new advances in agriculture automation systems have gained more and more importance and capabilities. In parallel, Internet of Things represents the pervasive presence of a variety of objects (devices, sensors, actuators, mobile phones), which are able to interact with each other, cooperate and create new interfaces (human-machine and machine-machine), to reach common goals. Automation on agriculture systems, or precision agriculture, uses control and communication paradigms to develop new systems: devices, sensors and actuators are interoperable. This technologies (software and hardware) improves the capacity of agricultural installations and agronomists take advantage of new services. This paper presents a research on user-centered design integrated with Internet of Things paradigm. A model-driven development of interactive interfaces that can be adapted and modified by the agronomists in their own agriculturals production is proposed. Additionally, control rules and human-computer interfaces are co-designed by agronomist to adapt the needs of each type of crop and other local and temporal condition (climate, water, energy, nutrients, soil).

Keywords: User-centered design · Model-driven design · Precision Agriculture · Interactive user interfaces · Internet of Things

1 Introduction

In the past few years, new trends have emerged in the agricultural sector. Developments in the field of software design, WSN (Wireless Sensor Networks) and the miniaturization of the sensor boards offer new resources. Precision Agriculture (PA), or automation in agriculture scenarios [3, 6, 21] uses these new technologies. But even though there has been considerable progresses in different technological areas, only a small number of them are focused on the design and implementation of specialized systems for agricultural environments [16]. Traditionally, information technologies are available but they have not been widely introduced

© Springer International Publishing AG 2017
S.F. Ochoa et al. (Eds.): UCAmI 2017, LNCS 10586, pp. 56–66, 2017.
DOI: 10.1007/978-3-319-67585-5_7

in agricultural scenarios: expensive systems and difficulties in installing, controlling, and maintaining are the main barriers. In this regard, new models and platforms particularly directed to remove these barriers are needed. This work proposes a solution based on two main ideas: design centered in agricultural worker (adaptation of user-centered design models) and Internet of Thinks (Iot) resources use (integration of hardware-software paradigms). The model proposed is specialized in agricultural processes, based in six subsystems: crop, soil, water, nutrients, climate and energy management.

2   Related Work

Sensors, actuators and machinery perform work that automate tasks to optimize production. These devices use specialised hardware integrated in Human Computer Interactions (HCI). To design appropriate solutions users must interact intuitively, control efficiently, maintain easily and to modify according to the needs of the process. Low-cost of infrastructure is another important requirement. The approach of this work consider that user-centered design models and IoT paradigms provide the tools to implement advanced solutions with this requirements.

User-Centered Design Models. User-centered design (UCD) describe a design process where end-users influence the process of how the design takes shape. There is several ways in which the user (agricultural specialist) can be involved in the process. This term describes a set of methods to create models on which design adapted solutions. The user-centered design process works against subjective assumptions about user behaviour. It requires proof that the design decisions are effective. If user-centered design is done correctly, applications becomes an outcome of actively engaging users. Therefore, any design decisions that were made by observing and listening to them will not be based on whims or personal preferences. User experience (UX) is one of the many focuses of UCD. It includes the user's entire experience with the product, including physical and emotional reactions. UCD is not subjective and often relies on data to support design decisions [15]. According to [18] user centred design is a development method that guarantees your product, software or web site will be easy to use. The International Usability Standard, ISO 13407, specifies the principles that underlie user centred design:

The design is based upon an explicit understanding of users, tasks and environments. Users are involved throughout design and development. The process is iterative. The design is driven and refined by user-centred evaluation. The design addresses the whole user experience. The design team includes multidisciplinary skills and perspectives.

User-centered design (UCD) is a project approach that puts the intended users of a site at the centre of its design and development. It does this by talking directly to the user at key points in the project to make sure the site will deliver upon their requirements. The stages are carried out in an iterative fashion, with the cycle being repeated until the project's usability objectives have been attained. This makes it critical that the participants in these methods accurately reflect the profile of your actual users. ISO 13407 outlines four essential activities in a user-centred design project [17]: Requirements gathering, Requirements specification, Design and Evaluation.

Internet of Things. Continuous technological advances have allowed the development of devices with wireless communication capabilities, installed at any location, smaller, efficient, autonomous and more powerful [5]; which communicate the collected data to processing stations. This is important since many network applications require hundreds or even thousand of sensor nodes, often deployed in remote and inaccessible areas. Therefore, a wireless sensor has not only a sensing component, but also on-board processing, communication, and storage capabilities. With these enhancements, a sensor node is often not only responsible for data collection but also for in-network analysis correlation, and fuses its own sensor data from other sensor nodes. When many sensors monitor large physical environments cooperatively, they form a WSN [11]. Sensor nodes communicate not only with each other but also with a base station, allowing them to disseminate their data to remote processing, visualization, analysis and storage systems [7]. There is no universal definition for the IoT, the core concept is that everyday objects can be equipped with identifying, sensing, networking and processing capabilities that will allow them to communicate with one another and with other devices and services over the Internet to achieve some useful objective. Global network supporting ubiquitous computing [4] and context-awareness among devices [10] are achieved using IoT networks; these requirements are key in ambience intelligence services [19]. The IoT offers a great market opportunity for equipment manufacturers, Internet service providers and application developers. The IoT smart objects are expected to reach 212 billion entities deployed globally by the end of 2020. By 2022, M2M traffic flows are expected to constitute up to 45% of the whole Internet traffic [9]. From the pool of proposed models, the basic model is a 3-layer architecture [13,20], consisting of the Application, Network, and Perception Layers. Some other models have been proposed that add more abstraction to the IoT architecture [1,2].

3   Agricultural Platform Design: User-Centered Model, Things-Driven Rules and Design Patterns

In this first work participatory designs and interview method are proposed. In Fig. 1 two kind of users are identified in the first design stage (agronomist or agriculture user expert and ICT technician). Each of them have thoughts and knowledge related to their experience. UCD process must these consider these two issues. Expert users in agriculture are interviewed to define main processes to control. All these issues are related with ICT expert in a participatory design. The results of this first approach are the things required to design services and

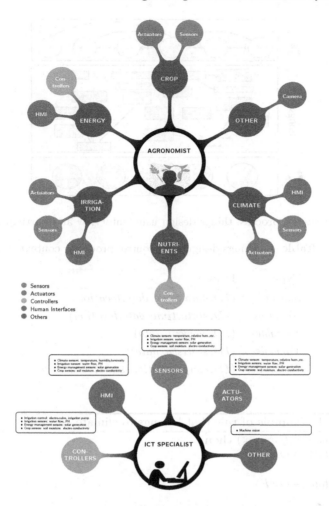

Fig. 1. User-centered process: identify needs using interview and participatory design

control. In Fig. 2 a first set of sensors, actuators and controllers are proposed considering a basic greenhouse production. This set of objects will be considers like *things* in the next stage. In this description a *thing* is formed by an object/entity and a context with data associated. Each *thing* has a n-tuple data structure $(d_1, \ldots, d_n)$. Some example of *things* the table are showed in Table 1. Expert users design control rules using the different things defined (Algorithm 1). These control rules are part of control processes (climate, soil, irrigation, crop, energy or image) that are distributed in different embedded systems connected to the network (intranet/internet).

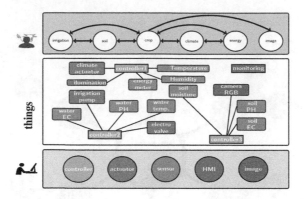

Fig. 2. User-centered process: things design using interview and participatory design

Table 1. Things designed in control processes context

Type	Data
Sensor	$(ID, data, time, date, location)$
Actuator	$(ID, state, time, date, location)$
Variable$_1$	$(ID, current\_data)$
Variable$_2$	$(ID, statistic\_data)$
Controller	$(ID, configuration, state, time, date)$

Algorithm 1. Example of rule that belongs to climate control

---

if $(sensor.data < temp_{min})$ **then**
  $(timer.state \rightarrow ON)$
else
  $(timer.state \rightarrow OFF)$
end if
if $(timer.estate$ *is* ON *during* $time_{max})$ **then**
  $(heater.state \rightarrow ON)$
end if

Design patterns are conceptual solutions to commonly encountered problems that can be applied in a variety of different situations. Applications based in pattern design are widely accepted, well-known and easily recognizable. Different pattern design can be used in design process. Basic and advanced patterns are selected in analysis and design stages. Basic design pattern are: state-machine, event driven user interfaces, producer-consumer, client-server, publisher-subscriber. Advanced pattern is object-oriented programming. Each has its unique functionality and is used in different situations:

– The design pattern used in control rules designed by agronomist and implemented by ICT technicians is **state-machine (SM)** algorithm. SM executes a sequence of events, but the order is determined programmatically.
– **Producer-consumer (PC)** pattern is used to collect and store data over a period of time in order to analyse specific trends or record the data-based events/actions of a system, network or IT environment. The PC pattern decouple processes that produce and consume data at different rates.
– **Publisher-subscriber (PS)** pattern is a communication model used by network nodes (devices, controllers,...) to share data in distributed networks. PS is a messaging pattern.
– Intranet and internet applications use **client-server (CS)** pattern. The CS model is a distributed application structure that partitions tasks or workloads between the providers of a resource or service, called servers, and service requesters, called clients.
– Finally **event-driven (ED)** is the model used to build user interfaces (human machine interfaces HMI). Events are actions performed by users.

Using adequate design pattern model all things (sensors, actuators, etc.) are interoperable and can be used by all algorithms implemented on the network nodes. Each process algorithm is integrated in a controller device that can use data of sensors installed in others devices. The following shows an example of a part of climate algorithm that is designed by agricultural expert using a combination of things ICT technician convert and complete this design in a finite-state machine algorithm that can be installed on any network controller device. Expert users can work together in the design of control processes and can propose new services using *things* as support for new developments. A *thing* has a representation in local and cloud environment. Depending on its nature each *thing* can be modified in local and/or cloud environment. Communication, analytic, storage and smart services are developed in the cloud. Local control and edge computing

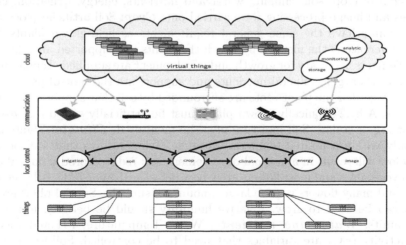

Fig. 3. Communication architecture used in design process

are developed in local environment. Expert users must design where the *things* are located, and how can write or read them. The necessary support to design on this context are showed in Fig. 3, where an architecture developed in [8] offers all basic requirements (accessibility, communication, interoperability) demanded.

The design proposed follows user-centered model and uses IoT paradigms combining design patterns to implement control algorithms, communication protocols, human interfaces and cloud services. The *thing* concept is therefore present in all services and processes and it extend information processing. Expert rules based in information unit (*things*) extend the applications functionality. IoT paradigm offers support to develop new services and improvements to the agricultural processes.

4   Prototype

A greenhouse using artificial soil (coco coir) is introduced to test the process designed. Soil artificial culture is the technique of growing plants in soil-less condition with their roots immersed in nutrient solution. Soil-less culture is the fastest growing sector of agriculture, and it could be impetus to food production in the future. The industry is expected to grow exponentially also in future, as conditions of soil growing becoming difficult. The application of a soil-less culture system using artificial substrates would result in efficient and effective use of water and fertilizers and minimize the use of chemicals for pest and disease control. Plants grown in soil less culture has consistently superior quality, high yield, rapid harvest, and high nutrient content [12].

4.1   Identify Requirements and Analysis

In the first stage of UCD the analysis carried out by the agronomist and ICT technician of crop, soil, climate, water and nutrients, energy, irrigation, cloud services and image processing were carried out: **Crop**: Soil artificial (coco coil) grown plants have the same general requirements as field-grown plants. The major difference is the method by which the plants are supported and the inorganic elements necessary for growth and development are supplied: Temperature, light, water, oxygen, mineral nutrients and support are the control parameters. **Soil**: In a garden the plant roots are surrounded by soil that supports the growing plant. A hydroponically grown plant must be artificially supported, usually with string or stakes. Soil moisture must be monitored. **Climate**: Plants grow well only within a limited temperature range. Temperatures that are too high or too low will result in abnormal development and reduced production. Warm-season vegetables and most flowers grow best between 15 and 25 °C. All vegetable plants and many flowers require large amounts of sunlight. Special plant-growth lamps can be used to grow. Relative humidity should be between upper and lower limits. **Water and nutrients**: Water Temperature, PH and Electro-Conductivity (EC) are variables that need to be controlled. Soil-less growing requires complete and effective hydroponic nutrient solutions. Liquid nutrients (nitrogen, phosphorus, potassium) are prepared by agronomist. *Energy*: Monitoring energy consumption and controlling photovoltaic generation enables powering devices only when needed. The energy balance of the activity (processes and things) must be analysed. *Irrigation*: A controlled (time and flow) irrigation is necessary. If the aggregate is not kept sufficiently moist, the plant roots will dry out and some will die. *Cloud services*. Storage, analytic and user interfaces must be designed. Tables and graphs with statistical data show data in real time. IoT resources store principal data. Subsequent analysis generate information about the growing process *Image processing*: RGB sensors capture images daily that can be processed to analyse the evolution of production. Expert users can design different kind of processes using image captured.

Sensors (temperature, moisture, PH, Electro Conductivity, water flow, luminosity, etc.), actuators (light, heater, pump), energy management (solar, harvesting), Sensor Network architecture and IoT protocols are selected by agronomist and ICT experts.

Network Communication. Publisher-Subscriber Model. MQTT protocol is proposed as communication paradigm between local sensor/actuator devices. Some of the features that makes it especially suitable for this project are:

MQTT is a publish-subscribe messaging protocol developed for resource-constrained devices, a model already in use by enterprises worldwide, and can work with legacy systems. All messages have a topic path composed of words separated by slashes. The bandwidth requirements are extremely low, and the nature of the protocol makes it very energy-efficient. Three Quality of Service (QoS) levels provide reliable operations.

MQTT uses an open message protocol that enables the transfer of telemetry-style data (i.e. measurements collected in remote locations) in the form of messages from devices and sensors, along unreliable or constrained networks, to a server (BROKER). Messages are simple, a compact binary packet payload (compressed headers, much less verbose than HTTP), and it makes a good fit for simple push messaging scenarios such as temperature updates or mobile notifications. It also works well connecting constrained or smaller devices and sensors to a web service, for example. The Publish/Subscribe model used in MQTT and many other M2M systems is mapped to resource observers (Fig. 4 and Table 2).

Processes Control. Rules and State-Machine model. Algorithms like 1 shows processes and rules based in *things*. In the participatory design, developers and users work together to design an initial prototype. Rules are designed by agriculture expert users and state machine are developed by ICT users and validated by all. Any controller is able to query and be queried by other nodes. In addition, any controller may play the role of a base station (skin node) capable of transmitting its information to remote processing places using a gateway device. Sensor Network local nodes can use and process local data, with a gateway these nodes have a global accessibility and they offer extended services on an IoT scenario. Local and global access over the same node (sensor/device/actuator) has

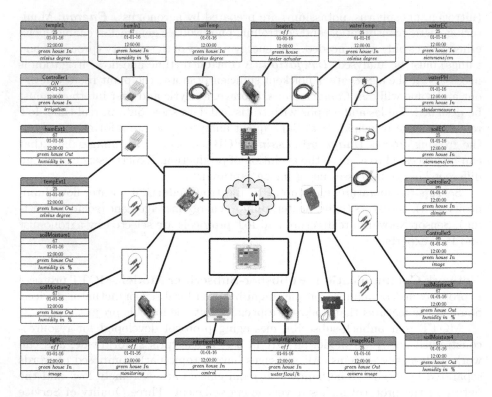

Fig. 4. Experimental prototype design: things and their physical objects. All sensors/actuators (things) are interoperable and can be connected to different controllers (nodes)

Table 2. Design of processes and things in experimental prototype

Processes and things design	
Crop	sensor/things: $\{growing\ crop\ images\}$ agricultural-processes: $\{image\ analysis\}$
Soil	sensor/things: $\{soil\ moisture,\ soil\ temperature\}$ agricultural-processes: $\{nutrients\ composition\ control\}$
Climate	sensor/things: $\{temperat.,\ luminosity,\ humidity\}$ actuator/things: $\{heater,\ lamp,\ humidifier\}$ agricultural-processes: $\{light,\ climate\ control\}$
Water nutrients	sensor/things: $\{PH, EC, irrigation flow\}$ actuator/things: $\{electrovalve,\ water\ pump\}$ agricultural-processes: $\{irrigation,\ PH\ and\ EC\ control\}$
energy	sensor/things: $\{energy\ meter\ sensors\}$ actuator/things: $\{switch,\ photovoltaic\ panel\}$ agricultural-processes: $\{energy\ management\}$
Irrigation	things: $\{tables, graphs, variables, events\}$ cloud-processes: $\{user\ interfaces,\ data\ storage,\ statistical\ calculations,\ analytics\}$
Cloud service	things: $\{tables, graphs, variables, events\}$ cloud-processes: $\{user\ interfaces,\ data\ storage,\ statistical\ calculations,\ analytics\}$

different possibilities and benefits. Whereas a local data processing is necessary in basic process control (security, system start-stop, etc.), global processing (analytic) can be used in pattern detection and information generation. In this sense, the proposed platform uses both technologies combined: different USN over a local network area (intranet) connected to cloud-IoT services (internet). A computing layer in local area, called *edge computing*, will serve as interface between control processes and cloud-services [8].

Human Machine Inteface. Event-Driven Model. Decisions regarding interface design can be influenced by a variety of factors. The main objective in User-Centered Design is understand users and involving them in the design process. The user research was conducted with the following methods [14]:

Contextual Inquiry. The goal of contextual inquiry is to understand agronomist and their work environment. *Design concept walk-through.* The goal of design concept walk-through is to identify preliminary operator responses to new design concepts and new features. *Participatory design.* The goal of participatory design is to discover agronomist perspective of important data and information. *Observation.* The goal of observation is to understand what happens in natural settings and identify any discrepancies in use HMI.

5 Conclusions

The results of all these steps make it possible to achieve and *context of use.* The context of use of HMI can be summarized as the following aspects: First, agronomist does not have experience in these innovations. Second, agronomist work is make it in mobility. Last, agricultural activities (sensor calibration, automated operating rules, analytics) is realised using friendly interfaces. Based on the understanding of the context of the use, a design philosophy and a set of guidelines were established and refined. The goal of HMI is to enable following experience for agronomist. The goal is to develop an HMI: **simple** (where agronomist recognize and understand information with ease and speed); **intuitive** (to anticipate and recognize issues quickly, and respond instantly); **complete** (provides all the necessary components) and **flexible** (when agronomist interact the way they want). User-centered model and Internet of Things paradigm provide technological support to design, implement and maintain. These systems become more flexible, adapted to local needs, friendly for combing data from multiple sensors to improve timely detection and diagnosis of crop status.

References

1. White papar: IOT PLATFORMS The central backbone for the Internet of Things. IoT Analytics GmbH (2015)
2. Atzori, L., Iera, A., Morabito, G.: The internet of things: a survey. Comput. Netw. **54**(15), 2787–2805 (2010)

3. Baggio, A.: Wireless sensor networks in precision agriculture. In: ACM Workshop on Real-World Wireless Sensor Networks (REALWSN 2005), Stockholm, Sweden. Citeseer (2005)
4. Bandyopadhyay, S., Sengupta, M., Maiti, S., Dutta, S.: Role of middleware for internet of things: a study. Int. J. Comput. Sci. Eng. Surv. **2**(3), 94–105 (2011)
5. Becker, T., Kluge, M., Schalk, J., Tiplady, K., Paget, C., Hilleringmann, U., Otterpohl, T.: Autonomous sensor nodes for aircraft structural health monitoring. IEEE Sens. J. **9**(11), 1589–1595 (2009)
6. Burrell, J., Brooke, T., Beckwith, R.: Vineyard computing: sensor networks in agricultural production. IEEE Pervasive Comput. **3**(1), 38–45 (2004)
7. Dargie, W.W., Poellabauer, C.: Fundamentals of Wireless Sensor Networks: Theory and Practice. Wiley, Hoboken (2010)
8. Ferrández-Pastor, F.J., García-Chamizo, J.M., Nieto-Hidalgo, M., Mora-Pascual, J., Mora-Martínez, J.: Developing ubiquitous sensor network platform using internet of things: application in precision agriculture. Sensors **16**(7), 1141 (2016)
9. Gantz, J., Reinsel, D.: The digital universe in 2020: Big data, bigger digital shadows, and biggest growth in the far east. IDC Go-to-Market Services (2012)
10. Garrido, P.C., Miraz, G.M., Ruiz, I.L., Gómez-Nieto, M.Á.: A model for the development of NFC context-awareness applications on internet of things. In: 2010 Second International Workshop on Near Field Communication (NFC), pp. 9–14. IEEE (2010)
11. Hu, J., Shen, L., Yang, Y., Lv, R.: Design and implementation of wireless sensor and actor network for precision agriculture. In: 2010 IEEE International Conference on Wireless Communications, Networking and Information Security (WCNIS), pp. 571–575. IEEE (2010)
12. Hussain, A., Iqbal, K., Aziem, S., Mahato, P., Negi, A.K.: A review on the science of growing crops without soil (soilless culture)-a novel alternative for growing crops. Int. J. Agric. Crop Sci. **7**(11), 833 (2014)
13. Khan, R., Khan, S.U., Zaheer, R., Khan, S.: Future internet: the internet of things architecture, possible applications and key challenges. In: 2012 10th International Conference on Frontiers of Information Technology (FIT), pp. 257–260. IEEE (2012)
14. Kim, S.Y., Van Wormer, J.: Human-machine interface (HMI) design for power generation plant operators: applying user-centered design approach. International Society of Automation, GE Power and Water (2014)
15. Lowdermilk, T.: What is centered-user design? In: Editor, F., Meditor, A. (eds.) The Book Title, pp. 13–15. O'Reilly Media (2013)
16. McBratney, A., Whelan, B., Ancev, T., Bouma, J.: Future directions of precision agriculture. Precis. Agric. **6**(1), 7–23 (2005)
17. Teoh, C.: User-centred design (UCD) - 6 methods (2009). Accessed October 2016
18. Userfocus: What is user centred design? (2015). Accessed 23 Sep 2016
19. Whitmore, A., Agarwal, A., Da Xu, L.: The internet of things-a survey of topics and trends. Inf. Syst. Front. **17**(2), 261–274 (2015)
20. Yang, Z., Yue, Y., Yang, Y., Peng, Y., Wang, X., Liu, W.: Study and application on the architecture and key technologies for IOT. In: 2011 International Conference on Multimedia Technology (ICMT), pp. 747–751. IEEE (2011)
21. Zhang, W., Kantor, G., Singh, S.: Demo abstract: integrated wireless sensor/actuator networks in an agricultural application. In: ACM SenSys, vol. 4 (2004)

Study of Dynamic Factors in Indoor Positioning for Harsh Environments

Gabriel de Blasio[1]([✉]), Alexis Quesada-Arencibia[1], Carmelo R. García[1], Jezabel Miriam Molina-Gil[2], and Cándido Caballero-Gil[2]

[1] Instituto Universitario de Ciencias y Tecnologías Cibernéticas,
ULPGC, Las Palmas de Gran Canaria, Spain
{gabriel.deblasio,alexis.quesada,ruben.garcia}@ulpgc.es
[2] Universidad de La Laguna, Santa Cruz de Tenerife, Spain
jmmolina@ull.edu.es, ccabgil@ull.es

Abstract. This paper presents a study of the impact of dynamic factors on indoor positioning. A positioning system is presented that provides advanced information services based on two subsystems: Wi-Fi and Bluetooth Low Energy (BLE). The first subsystem was intended to position users with not very high levels of accuracy and precision, but not too far from reality, and the second one was intended to position users with greater precision. It is designed for use in stations and terminals of public transportation systems in which the conditions are "hostile" or unfavourable. Experimental results demonstrate that, using different devices for both offline and online phase, RSS differences, Euclidean distance and comparing fingerprints with Weighted k-Nearest Neighbours (WKNN) algorithm, the system is able to position users with reasonable values of accuracy and precision: for Wi-Fi, with only 3 samples, depending on the orientation and compared with 3 neighbours, an average accuracy between 4.15 and 4.58 m and a precision in the range 4–7 m or less 90% of the time were obtained; for BLE, best accuracy results were obtained by comparison with 2 neighbours, giving a position error of 1.59 m and a CDF value of 2.83 m or less 90% of the time.

1 Introduction

Fingerprinting-based indoor positioning is a widely employed method, mainly because: (a) it is easy to implement, (b) use existing wireless infrastructure making it a low-cost option for which received signal strength (RSS) data are easily obtained, (c) the computational complexity is low, and (d) gives reasonable accuracy and precision values [13]. However, "dynamic factors", such as changes in the environment and hardware structure, presence of people, user's devices heterogeneity, etc. are the main drawbacks of this method, initially affecting the signal strength, and finally, affecting positioning accuracy and precision [8, 14, 21]. The challenge of this work is to minimize the dynamic factors effects, mainly on public transportation environments, where those factors vary according to the time, day or time of year. The ultimate aim is to provide a service to assist

© Springer International Publishing AG 2017
S.F. Ochoa et al. (Eds.): UCAmI 2017, LNCS 10586, pp. 67–78, 2017.
DOI: 10.1007/978-3-319-67585-5_8

people with special needs, such as people with visual impairments or cognitive problems, who may feel disoriented in public spaces that are new to them. The proposed system obtains the user's position through the combined use of WLAN and BLE technologies at the bus station used for this study. In addition to indoor positioning, BLE beacons are specially interesting for stations of public transportation systems because it can be used for other advanced information services such as bus station guide, ticketing or line information.

The main contributions of this system are: first, it provides a real implementation of a positioning system in an environment that is not favourable to the use of these technologies; second, it does not require any additional deployment of the available WLAN infrastructure, using the elements already installed in the bus stations; third, it studies the behaviour of different positioning methods, proposed by different authors, using these technologies to monitor their behaviour in environments with changing conditions (variations in the number of persons in the station according to the time of day, variations in environmental conditions, such as humidity, the location of the Wi-Fi access points (AP) and Bluetooth beacons at points that are not optimal for positioning purposes and signal strength variance between diverse devices), and finally, it studies the impact in the positioning of the number of samples taken in the online phase.

This article is divided into five sections. In the following section we will describe the studies relevant to the proposed system. In the Sect. 3 we describe the testbed where we performed the different tests that were carried out using the Wi-Fi and BLE infrastructure. In the Sect. 4, we will show in each case the results that are obtained with those tests. Finally, the conclusions and future lines of work are presented in the Sect. 5.

2   Related Works

We begin mentioning some general studies like those of Liu et al. [21], which offers a broad overview of existing wireless indoor positioning solutions and attempts to classify different techniques and systems. Honkavirta et al. [14] outlined positioning methods that use scene analysis, as did He et al. [13], although the latter focused on more recent developments. Mautz [22] reviews many indoor positioning approaches and describes the measuring principles of each. Brena et al. [6] provide a technological perspective of indoor positioning systems, comprising a wide range of technologies and approaches.

With respect to systems focused on WLAN or BLE technologies or a combination of both, Bahl et al. [2], proposed the pioneer system RADAR, a radio-frequency (RF) based system for locating and tracking users inside buildings, which is the basis of many later works. Kaemarungsi et al. [16] conducted an interesting and exhaustive study of the statistical properties of RSS reported by IEEE 802.11b wireless network interface cards for position location by scene analysis. Hossain et al. [15] derive analytically a robust location fingerprint definition, the Signal Strength Difference (SSD), and verify its performance experimentally using a number of different mobile devices with heterogeneous hardware, considering in their experiments both Wi-Fi and Bluetooth devices. King et al. [18] presented a detailed analysis of the deployment, calibration, and measurement factors that cause positioning errors for indoor positioning systems based on 802.11 wireless networks. Kjærgaard [19] studied the problem of location fingerprinting with heterogeneous IEEE 802.11 wireless clients. Torres-Sospedra et al. [25] observed that for Wi-Fi fingerprinting, most studies use Euclidean distance and raw data, and therefore carried out a study of the best distance function, the best way to represent the data, and the effect of applying thresholding techniques. Faragher et al. [11] conducted a detailed scene analysis study using proximity and k-Nearest Neighbours (KNN) algorithm with the aggregation of the 3 BLE advertising channels; they also provide quantitative comparison with WiFi fingerprinting. Zhuang et al. [26] used an algorithm that combines a polynomial regression model, BLE fingerprinting with channel separation, outlier detection, and Kalman filtering. Kajioka [17] demonstrated the viability of positioning through the received signal strength of BLE beacons. Baniukevic et al. [3] developed an algorithm that prevents positioning errors caused by reference positions that are similar by separating these positions into different smaller radio maps through the deployment of Bluetooth beacons at particular locations. Metola et al. [23] compared two different positioning algorithms using Bluetooth and WLAN: the first is based on the construction of a fusion map using the Wi-Fi and Bluetooth RSS values; in the second algorithm, the position is determined independently by each technology and the results are subsequently combined.

A particularly notable application of indoor positioning systems is the provision of assistance for people with special needs. Au et al. [1] proposed an indoor tracking and navigation system based on RSS measurements in a WLAN. Moder et al. [24] presents the possibility of indoor positioning for visually impaired people with cheap, universally available signals and sensors already present in today's smartphones. Ge [12] implemented two BLE-based indoor positioning systems and a specific interface. The first system achieves a positioning accuracy of 1.83 m; the second system uses a proximity algorithm, and a specific user interface was tailor-made for blind and visually impaired users of these two systems. Castillo-Cara et al. [7] presented a prototype of an indoor mobility assistant for visually impaired users. The system uses the RSS provided by BLE beacons strategically placed to identify different areas of a building, using also the pedometer and gyroscope of a smartphone.

The final area of related studies concerns positioning system proposals for indoor public spaces on public transport networks. In such indoor environments —bus, metro or train stations, shopping centres, etc.— there may be a lot of noise produced by the presence of many people or by humidity. We may mention the study conducted by Ladd [20], in which the system design begins with the observation that the determination of position from complex, noisy and non-Gaussian signals is a well-studied problem in the field of robotics; a robust position estimation to within a metre is achieved in an experimental context. De Blasio et al. [4] presents a study on a positioning system that provides advanced information services based on Wi-Fi and Bluetooth Low Energy designed for use in stations and terminals of public transportation systems. Dickinson [9] introduced a framework for the positioning of users in a large wholesale shopping store, presenting results obtained using different methods of positioning and using RSS measurements.

3   Deployment Environment

The scenario in which the positioning system will be tested is a local bus station, the same used in previous works [4,5]. Users access the station and then move to bus stops zones. The system must position users in one of the two bus stops zones and then provide them with a service (information about a bus line, etc.). Wi-Fi technology will be used first as a rough positioning system to approach users towards bus stops, where BLE technology come into play later as a fine grain positioning system and as a provider of advanced services. It should be noted that the station is located very close to the sea, so ambient humidity is a factor to consider.

From the above scenario, and taking into account the fact that the station only have 3 detectable Wi-Fi APs that have already been deployed, it is necessary to deploy BLE beacons to meet two objectives: Signals reach all zones with sufficient intensity, and particularly, to bus stops zones, correctly positioning users (avoiding positioning errors that will lead users to danger zones) and that users are provided with the desired advanced services.

Within the bus station described above, a $40\,m \times 8\,m$ rectangular central section was chosen as the testbed (see Fig. 1(a)). This area is a representative example of the complete scenario, and possibly the zone of the station with the greatest difficulty for positioning due to the continuous transit of users and buses in the surrounding areas. Figures 1(a) and (b) shows the section (marked with a red rectangle) and the chosen origin of coordinates, O, as the reference for the coordinates of the points in the database. Wi-Fi APs, BLE beacons and columns are marked as yellow squares and blue and black dots respectively.

To create the database of Wi-Fi reference points, and considering that the accuracy that we will require from this positioning system is low, we chose a grid of 20 cells, each measuring $4\,m \times 4\,m$ (see Fig. 2(a) and (b)), with the reference points aligned on two parallel lines (which we have labelled as lines 1 and 2), and each reference point in the centre of each cell. Line 1 is closer to bus stops, while line 2 is further away. The testbed therefore has an area of $320\,m^2$. Wi-Fi APs are aligned along reference points line 1 (see Fig. 2(a)) and practically in line of sight (LOS) conditions.

To construct the BLE database, a structure similar to that described above was chosen, but taking into account the fact that the accuracy required for the BLE positioning system is greater: we therefore chose a grid of 42 cells, each measuring $1\,m \times 1\,m$.

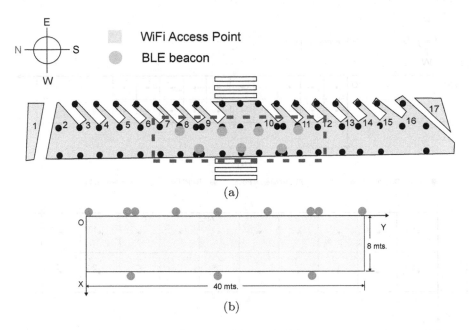

Fig. 1. Testbed: schematic view (highlighted in red); (b) dimensions and axes of chosen coordinates. (Color figure online)

4   Performance Evaluation

The distance metric used was the Euclidean metric, and the algorithm employed to compare the fingerprints was Weighted k-Nearest Neighbours (WKNN). For this study, the positioning accuracy is expressed by the mean error and its precision by the cumulative probability function (CDF), which is expressed in practice in percentile format [21].

In the offline phase, with an ASUS N56J laptop and Wi-Fi scanner software (Vistumbler), 15 samples were taken at each reference point (1 sample every 2 s) for each access point and each orientation (N, E, S, W). By means of a laser pointer and for each reference point, the coordinates (x, y) were taken with respect to the origin of coordinates, O, of the grid. In the online phase: the same laptop used in the offline phase was used to record 15 samples (1 sample every 2 s); an iPhone 7 mobile phone with Airport app was used to record 15 samples (1 sample every 2–3 s). All measurements were done in 10 random points of the grid (see Fig. 2(b)) and for each orientation, their coordinates also being recorded with the laser pointer.

4.1   Wi-Fi Analysis

From the original database of reference points, another two databases were built: in the first one (which we call *WDBmean*), the mean RSS values for all orientation were obtained, and then, the mean value from all four orientations was

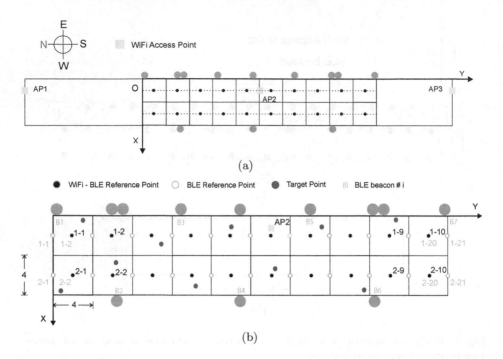

Fig. 2. Grid chosen in the testbed: (a) in relation to the 3 Wi-Fi APs; (b) detail showing the reference points of the Wi-Fi and BLE databases, the arrangement of the BLE beacons and target points.

obtained; in the second one (which we call *WDBmax*), the maximum value of the mean RSS values for all four orientation was obtained [2]. For each entry in the new database, the signal strength difference every AP pair was calculated [10, 15]. With 10 randomly selected target points on the grid, N RSS samples were recorded for each AP and orientation at consecutive time points and their mean value calculated, being the signal strength difference for every AP pair also calculated. From there, the Euclidean distance (in RSS space and RSS differences space) between each reference fingerprint and each target fingerprint (by orientation) was calculated, i.e. each north-facing target fingerprint was compared with the mean RSS of reference fingerprints for all orientations, etc. The purpose of this test was to simulate a real scenario, that is to say: (a) to simulate the positioning of users with different devices which are specifically facing in one of the 4 possible directions in real time (these data could be ascertained through the device compass); (b) to simulate the impact of the number of online samples in position accuracy and precision, because the number of samples determines the time required to calculate a reliable position estimate [18].

As a result of these tests, the following observations were made:

(a) The best results are obtained with *WDBmax* database, RSS differences and using different devices for the offline-online phases (laptop-iPhone).

Table 1. Accuracy of Wi-Fi test using RSS differences: mean errors (in metres) for 3 online samples, k = 3 neighbours and different orientation values

N	E	S	W
4.58	4.46	4.15	4.17

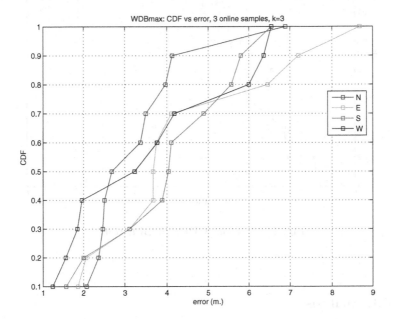

Fig. 3. Precision of Wi-Fi test for all 4 orientations (3 online samples, k = 3 neighbours).

(b) With 3 samples and k = 3 neighbours accuracy results of the order of the dimension of a cell in the grid are obtained.

(c) There are some directions that present better accuracy-precision than others.

Accuracy and precision results of the test are shown in Table 1 and Fig. 3. As we might expect, those values are strongly dependent of orientation, and it can be observed that with only 3 samples, values of accuracy are obtained that would place a user in the desired cell or in one immediately nearby. With respect to precision, and depending on the orientation, those results would place a user 90% of the times in the 4–7 m range, that is, in the desired cell or in the immediate.

Table 2. Accuracy of BLE test: mean error (in metres) for different k-values

k	1	2	3	4
Error	2.38	1.59	2.16	2.15

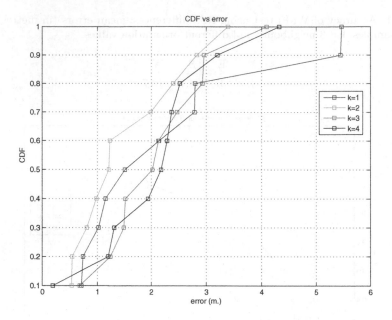

Fig. 4. Precision (CDF) for BLE test.

4.2   BLE Analysis

The empirical approach followed was similar to that followed with Wi-Fi. In this case, however, it was chosen a grid of 42 cells, each measuring 1 m × 1 m and 7 BLE beacons were deployed (see Figs. 1 and 2). The configuration of each beacon was: only UID frame for Eddystone protocol was set, an advertising interval of 500 ms and an output power of 0 dBm. The density of beacons is not ideally suited to the purposes of our study (to position a user at the desired stop and offer advanced services) but it may give us an idea of a higher level of positioning error for this technology and in this environment. In the offline phase, with a Samsung Galaxy S5 mobile device and BEACON SCANNER application, 1 sample per second was taken at each reference point for 30 s and for each beacon. The scanning was performed in aggregate mode, i.e. without individually distinguishing BLE advertising channels 37, 38 and 39, therefore, in this case it was not possible to carry out a study of the impact of the number of samples because it is not guaranteed that each fingerprint contains one reading on each of the channels [11].

From the original database a new database was created in which the mean RSS values were obtained for each beacon (*BDBmean*). In the online phase, 10 target points were used, the same points that had been used for Wi-Fi positioning. Two mobile phones were used: the same for the offline phase and a Samsung S7 Edge. A procedure was carried out for the databases similar to the reference fingerprints procedure. From there, the distance (in RSS space and RSS differences space) between each reference fingerprint and each target fingerprint was calculated using the Euclidean distance metric, where the fingerprint comparison implemented was the WKNN algorithm. As a result of these tests, the following observations were made:

(a) The best results are obtained with RSS differences and using different devices for the offline-online phases (Samsung Galaxy S5-Samsung S7 Edge).
(b) With k = 2 neighbours accuracy results near the dimension of a cell in the grid are obtained.

The accuracy and precision results of the BLE test are shown in Table 2 and Fig. 4. A value of accuracy of 1.59 m is obtained for k = 2 neighbours: that would place a user in the desired cell or in one immediately nearby. With respect to precision, a CDF value of 2.83 m or less was obtained.

5   Conclusions and Future Works

In this paper, we have presented a positioning system based on two subsystems: Wi-Fi and Bluetooth Low Energy. As the user enters in the station, the first subsystem come into play and was intended to position users with not very high levels of accuracy and precision, but not too far from reality; the second subsystem come into play as the user approaches bus stops and was intended to position users with greater precision, as well as to provide advanced information services at the destination point. For each test done, the Euclidean distance metric was used and the fingerprint comparison algorithm applied was WKNN. In the Wi-Fi tests, measurements were taken at reference points spaced every 4 m, the mean and the maximum value of the mean RSS for all four orientations were taken for reference points and the signal strength difference every AP pair was also calculated. In the online phase, the Euclidean distance (in RSS and RSS differences space) between each reference fingerprint and each target fingerprint (by orientation) was calculated using the same device of the offline phase and also a different device. Depending on orientation, and compared with 3 neighbours, an average accuracy between 4.15 and 4.58 m and a precision in the range 4–7 m or less 90% of the time was obtained. We observed a strong dependence of orientation in accuracy and precision results, probably due to the dynamic factors mentioned before and the arrangement of the access points with respect to the person measuring the data, who screens the signal coming from these access points. With regard to the BLE tests, measurements were taken at reference points spaced every 1 m. The data collection was carried out in aggregate mode; the mean RSS values for every beacon was taken both in offline and online phase and the Euclidean distance (in RSS space and RSS differences space) between each reference fingerprint and each target fingerprint. Best accuracy results were obtained using RSS differences and by comparison with 2 neighbours, with a position error of 1.59 m. Regarding precision, a CDF value of 2.83 m or less 90% of the time for k = 2 neighbours.

Therefore, considering that, (1) under dynamic factors mentioned before, (2) under conditions that are not optimal for Wi-Fi positioning, and (3) with few samples collected in the offline and online phase and values that were not processed, we may conclude that acceptable values of accuracy and precision are obtained that would place a user in the desired cell, or in the immediately adjacent cell, in the worst case, on a high percentage of occasions, as was originally required. In addition, we can conclude that for BLE positioning, excellent accuracy and precision values are achieved, so this method would position a user with even greater precision than Wi-Fi positioning. We understand that, for the conditions in which this system was deployed, the error values obtained for both positioning systems, but mainly for Wi-Fi, reflect upper bounds and could be improved, making this system a strong candidate for deployment in other similar environments. To this end, and as future lines of action, we may mention the following: a greater deployment of BLE transmitters, use of grids with reference points with smaller spacing, data collection campaigns with greater numbers of samples, reduction of their duration, pre-processing of data and search filtering in the reference point database, use of a greater number of heterogeneous devices for the offline and online data collection phases, studies of probabilistic positioning algorithms and comparison of the results obtained with other distance metrics that may be suitable for this type of environment.

References

1. Au, A.W.S., Feng, C., Valaee, S., Reyes, S., Sorour, S., Markowitz, S.N., Gold, D., Gordon, K., Eizenman, M.: Indoor tracking and navigation using received signal strength and compressive sensing on a mobile device. IEEE Trans. Mob. Comput. **12**(10), 2050–2062 (2013)
2. Bahl, P., Padmanabhan, V.N.: RADAR: an in-building RF-based user location and tracking system. In: Proceedings IEEE INFOCOM, the Conference on Computer Communications, Nineteenth Annual Joint Conference of the IEEE Computer and Communications Societies, Reaching the Promised Land of Communications, Tel Aviv, Israel, 26–30 March, pp. 775–784 (2000)
3. Baniukevic, A., Jensen, C.S., Lu, H.: Hybrid indoor positioning with Wi-Fi and Bluetooth: architecture and performance. In: 2013 IEEE 14th International Conference on Mobile Data Management, Milan, Italy, 3–6 June 2013, vol. 1, pp. 207–216 (2013)
4. de Blasio, G., Quesada-Arencibia, A., García, C.R., Molina-Gil, J.M., Caballero-Gil, C.: Study on an indoor positioning system for harsh environments based on Wi-Fi and Bluetooth low energy. Sensors **17**(6), 1299 (2017)
5. de Blasio, G., Quesada-Arencibia, A., García-Rodríguez, C.R., Molina-Gil, J.M., Caballero-Gil, C.: Ubiquitous signaling system for public road transport network. In: García, C.R., Caballero-Gil, P., Burmester, M., Quesada-Arencibia, A. (eds.) UCAmI/IWAAL/AmIHEALTH -2016. LNCS, vol. 10070, pp. 445–457. Springer, Cham (2016). doi:10.1007/978-3-319-48799-1_49
6. Brena, R.F., García-Vázquez, J., Galván-Tejada, C.E., Rodríguez, D.M., Rosales Jr., C.V., J.F.: Evolution of indoor positioning technologies: a survey. J. Sens. **2017**, 2630413:1–2630413:21 (2017)

7. Castillo-Cara, M., Huaranga-Junco, E., Mondragón-Ruiz, G., Salazar, A., Barbosa, L.O., Antúnez, E.A.: Ray: smart indoor/outdoor routes for the blind using Bluetooth 4.0 BLE. Procedia Comput. Sci. **83**, 690–694 (2016)
8. Chapre, Y., Ignjatovic, A., Seneviratne, A., Jha, S.: Csi-mimo: indoor Wi-Fi fingerprinting system. In: 39th Annual IEEE Conference on Local Computer Networks, pp. 202–209, September 2014
9. Dickinson, P., Cielniak, G., Szymanezyk, O., Mannion, M.: Indoor positioning of shoppers using a network of Bluetooth Low Energy beacons. In: 2016 International Conference on Indoor Positioning and Indoor Navigation (IPIN), pp. 1–8, October 2016
10. Dong, F., Chen, Y., Liu, J., Ning, Q., Piao, S.: A calibration-free localization solution for handling signal strength variance. In: Proceedings of the 2nd International Conference on Mobile Entity Localization and Tracking in GPS-less Environments, pp. 79–90 (2009)
11. Faragher, R., Harle, R.: Location fingerprinting with Bluetooth Low Energy beacons. IEEE J. Sel. Areas Commun. **33**(11), 2418–2428 (2015)
12. Ge, T.: Indoor positioning system based on Bluetooth Low Energy for blind or visually impaired users. Master's thesis, KTH Royal Institute of Technology, School of Information and Communication Technology (ICT), Department of Communication Systems, October 2015
13. He, S., Chan, S.: Wi-Fi fingerprint-based indoor positioning: recent advances and comparisons. IEEE Commun. Surv. Tut. **18**, 466–490 (2016)
14. Honkavirta, V., Perälä, T., All-Löytty, S., Piché, R.: A comparative survey of WLAN location fingerprinting methods. In: Proceedings of the 6th Workshop on Positioning, Navigation and Communication, Hannover, Germany, 19 March 2009, pp. 243–251 (2009)
15. Hossain, A.K.M.M., Jin, Y., Soh, W.S., Van, H.N.: SSD: a robust RF location fingerprint addressing mobile devices' heterogeneity. IEEE Trans. Mob. Comput. **12**(1), 65–77 (2013)
16. Kaemarungsi, K., Krishnamurthy, P.: Properties of indoor received signal strength for WLAN location fingerprinting. In: Proceedings of the First Annual International Conference on Mobile and Ubiquitous Systems: Networking and Services, Boston, MA, USA, 22–25 August 2004, pp. 14–23 (2004)
17. Kajioka, S., Mori, T., Uchiya, T., Takumi, I., Matsuo, H.: Experiment of indoor position presumption based on RSSI of Bluetooth LE beacon. In: IEEE 3rd Global Conference on Consumer Electronics, Tokyo, Japan, 7–10 October 2014, pp. 337–339 (2014)
18. King, T., Haenselmann, T., Effelsberg, W.: Deployment, calibration, and measurement factors for position errors in 802.11-based indoor positioning systems. In: Hightower, J., Schiele, B., Strang, T. (eds.) LoCA 2007. LNCS, vol. 4718, pp. 17–34. Springer, Heidelberg (2007). doi:10.1007/978-3-540-75160-1_2
19. Kjaergaard, M.: Indoor location fingerprinting with heterogeneous clients. Pervasive Mob. Comput. **7**, 31–43 (2011)
20. Ladd, A.M., Bekris, K., Rudys, A., Kavraki, L., Wallach, D.: Robotics-based location sensing using wireless ethernet. Wirel. Netw. **11**, 189–204 (2005)
21. Liu, H., Darabi, H., Banerjee, P.P., Liu, J.: Survey of wireless indoor positioning techniques and systems. IEEE Trans. Syst. Man Cybern. Part C **37**(6), 1067–1080 (2007)
22. Mautz, R.: Indoor positioning technologies. Master's thesis, Institute of Geodesy and Photogrammetry, Department of Civil, Environmental and Geomatic Engineering, ETH Zurich, February 2012

23. Metola, E., Aparicio, S., Tarrío, P., Casar, J.R.: Comparison of localization methods using calibrated and simulated fingerprints for indoor systems based on Bluetooth and WLAN technologies. In: Proceedings MADRINET 10 (2009)
24. Moder, T., Hafner, P., Wieser, W.: Indoor positioning for visually impaired people based on smartphones. In: Proceedings of the 14th International Conference Computers Helping People with Special Needs, Paris, France, 9–11 July 2014, pp. 441–444 (2014)
25. Torres-Sospedra, J., Montoliu, R., Trilles, S., Belmonte, O., Huerta, J.: Comprehensive analysis of distance and similarity measures for Wi-Fi fingerprinting indoor positioning systems. Expert Syst. Appl. **42**, 9263–9278 (2015)
26. Zhuang, Y., Yang, J., Li, J., Qi, L., El-Sheimy, N.: Smartphone-based indoor localization with Bluetooth Low Energy beacons. Sensors **16**, 596 (2011)

A Secure, Out-of-Band, Mechanism to Manage Internet of Things Devices

Joseph Rafferty[1(✉)], Jonathan Synnott[1], Andrew Ennis[1], Ian Cleland[1], Chris Nugent[1], and Michael Little[2]

[1] School of Computing and Mathematics, Ulster University, Coleraine, Northern Ireland, UK
{j.rafferty,j.synnott,a.ennis,i.cleland,cd.nugent}@ulster.ac.uk
[2] RF Proximity LTD, The Innovation Center, Northern Ireland Science Park, Belfast, UK
michael@iotiger.net

Abstract. Adoption of the pervasive and ubiquitous computing paradigm is increasing. One application of this paradigm is Ambient Assistive Living where ICT-based assistive services are deployed in an environment. In this study, a Smart Home in a Box (SHIB) has been devised as an AAL solution. This SHIB relies upon Internet of Things (IoT) devices, such as thermal vision sensors, within an environment to function. Each SHIB deployment consists of IoT devices taken from a common pool of devices. The exact device manifest of each SHIB deployment will change as dictated by end-user requirements. Additionally, this pool will grow and expand when devices are removed or added from previous SHIB deployments. To efficiently manage this pool of devices, and SHIB deployments, a remote management solution is required. Current remote management solutions have a range of deficiencies that render them unsuitable for use with the current SHIB platform. To address these deficiencies, a secure mechanism to manage the IoT devices has been devised. This paper presents this mechanism and evaluates its applicability to SHIB deployments. The evaluation focused on assessing the security of the mechanism and the viability of its Low-Power Wireless Wide-Area Network-based communications. This evaluation showed that the proposed solution was reliable and suitable for the intended deployment scenario. An extended evaluation and system improvements have been identified and proposed within future work.

Keywords: Security · Internet of things · Low-power wireless wide-area network · Encryption · Management · Out of band management · LoRa · LoRaWAN

1 Introduction

Pervasive and ubiquitous computing is a paradigm which is realized through embedding sensing, networked communication, actuation and computational services within environments [1, 2]. This computing paradigm offers several applications including; environmental monitoring, use of internet connected appliances and providing Ambient Assistive Living (AAL) services, to name but a few [3–6].

© Springer International Publishing AG 2017
S.F. Ochoa et al. (Eds.): UCAmI 2017, LNCS 10586, pp. 79–90, 2017.
DOI: 10.1007/978-3-319-67585-5_9

Recently, there has been an increase in the adoption of this paradigm though the proliferation of smart devices, networked connectivity, cloud computing and Internet of Things (IoT) devices [3–5].

IoT devices, can include smartphones and tablet computers that users may carry on their person. Networked connectivity includes mobile networks, dedicated Radio Frequency (RF) based solutions, wireless personal area networks, long range wireless area networks and Wi-Fi. Cloud computing provides offsite computational and data storage capacity - augmenting functionality of environmentally deployed devices. IoT devices include local sensing, actuation and computational elements which are deployed to an environment.

AAL is an approach to providing assistive services for persons within an environment [7, 8]. AAL services have a broad range of functionality ranging from simple to complex scenarios. Simple AAL scenarios include use of IoT sensors to enable detection of dangers in the home, such as smoke, and relaying alerts to parties to act upon them [9]. Complex AAL scenarios include the use of advanced sensing to monitor inhabitant behavior and issue alerts when behaviors of interest have occurred [6].

In this study, an AAL platform has been developed with the goal of providing a modular, reusable, dynamically configurable, Smart Home in a Box (SHIB) solution.

An aim of this SHIB is to enable technology assistance to at risk individuals in their own home. Specifically, the goal of this SHIB is to supplement, augment and replace traditional support, such as that provided by domiciliary care staff. This will reduce costs of providing care while simultaneously increasing levels of support.

This SHIB has a number of deployment scenarios broadly classified as permanent or temporary. Permanent deployments will monitor individuals on a long-term basis to support living with ailments such as Alzheimer's disease, until a change in housing circumstance or care needs occurs. Temporary installations will monitor individuals during times of interest, such as when recuperating from surgery or when suffering from a temporary ailment that requires monitoring.

This SHIB solution has two main elements; (1) locally deployed sensing and networking components and (2) cloud based computational and alert generation components. The specific sensors provided to end users may vary as dictated by their care needs. Such variation requires that SHIB deployments are reconfigured on a case by case basis, reusing previously deployed sensors to increase return on investment.

One of the goals of this SHIB is to enable end users to deploy it within their environment with minimal of effort. Such seamless reconfiguration reduces the overall cost of operating SHIB installations by allowing variations of the SHIB to be rapidly redeployed where it is most effective, as needs evolve.

Current approaches to managing IoT devices have several flaws and weaknesses that either represent a security risk or are unsuitable for managing a consumer SHIB solution. To this end, a secure and novel IoT management platform that addresses the shortcomings of contemporary approaches is required. The primary goals of this management platform are to; facilitate reconfiguration of devices for redeployment, issue commands remotely and enable modification of firmware. Devising and implementing such a management platform is the primary focus of this study.

The remaining Sections of this paper are organized as follows; Sect. 2 provides an overview of related work, Sect. 3 presents a description of a devised and implemented IoT management platform, Sect. 4 provides an evaluation of the approach and Sect. 5 provides a conclusion and discussion on future work.

2 Related Work

Typically, IoT devices require management once deployed to an environment, this may include tasks such as re-configuration or updating a device's firmware. Currently, this management may occur over a variety of communication technologies, such as an IP-based network or custom RF solutions [10].

IP-based networks may use a variety of transmission mediums including cable, and wireless [10]. This IP-based management may occur in an in-band or out-of-band manner. In-band management involves providing management interfaces through a channel that may be shared with other communication. Out-of-band management employs a dedicated channel for management functions.

Previously, both in-band and out-of-band IoT device management over IP based networks have had significant and severe issues related to security. These issues have several root causes including: use of the common IP network, implementation flaws in externally contactable services, adoption of password based authentication mechanism and use of compromised or inappropriate public-private key pairs.

IoT devices that use the common IP network, or that have components that are routable through the common IP network, hold an inherent flaw related to access controls on that network. Specifically, access to the common IP network is weakly audited and easily accessed by malicious actors. This ease of accessibility and weak auditing enables several abilities that malicious actors find desirable, including:

- enabling Denial of Service attacks upon IP connected devices [11]
- exploitation of management interfaces on IP connected devices [12–14]
- interference with, and manipulation of, communications [15]
- masquerading as legitimate device administrators when credentials and certificates are compromised [16, 17]
- detection and fingerprinting devices to identify potential targets [11]

IoT devices typically host management services that respond to inbound communication. Implementation flaws in such services provide an attack vector that may be exploited, this is a major factor in the viability of remote exploits [12–14].

Providing authenticated access for management of IoT devices is typically achieved using credential based authentication or public/private certificate-pairs. Weak or compromised credentials can enable access to an entire class of devices [16, 17]. Certificate pairs offer stronger authentication; however, they may not necessarily be generated on a per-device basis, meaning that a compromise of one private certificate can provide management access to an entire class of device [17]. Additionally, certificate-pairs offer lower protection than symmetric encryption keys at any given bit size and require significantly more computational resources to function [18]. IoT devices typically have constrained computational resources and so will typically use lower strength certificate-pairs, weakening security. The use of Elliptic Curve Digital Signature Algorithm (ECDSA) keys has been proposed for use in devices that have low computational resources. ECDSA is, however, a relatively immature, and unproven, approach to encryption and has been compromised on a number of recent occasions [19, 20].

Additionally, IP based management requires a correctly configured connection to operate. This may not be possible especially if an IP connection needs to be configured or an IP related firmware bug needs to be addressed.

Custom RF based management solutions may require specialized, expensive, hardware, use protocols which operate to varying levels of security, offer limited interoperability and typically do not offer coverage of a large geographical area or formal peering arrangements to increase communications area [21–24].

It is possible to use wireless telecoms networks, such as 3G, as signal carriers in a custom RF solution. These networks currently offer limited security due to their protocols [25] and as such have suffered several high-profile attacks [26]. Additionally, network operators typically incorporate man in the middle access for government oversight [27] and to enable internal operational support.

To address these deficiencies a novel solution to manage IoT device has been devised and implemented. This solution uses a combination of strong, proven, cryptography and a hybrid communications model incorporating IP and Low Power Wireless Wide Area Network (LPWWAN) based communication.

3 A Secure, Out-of-Band, Mechanism to Manage IoT Devices

The devised and implemented solution employs a hybrid communication model employing IP and LPWWAN technologies. IP based technologies are used for high bandwidth communication from IoT devices, within SHIB deployments, to central cloud-based resources. LPWWAN technologies enable low bandwidth communications for device management. In this implementation LoRaWAN [28] was the selected LPWWAN as is it key to several large scale efforts, including one covering the intended deployment area of this SHIB solution [29]. A general overview of this hybrid communication model is presented in Fig. 1.

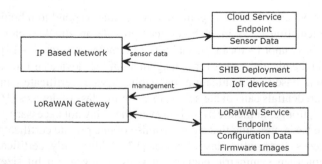

Fig. 1. An overview of the hybrid communications employed by the devised out-of-band management solution.

In this communication model, sensor data will be transmitted through IP based networks, enabling high-bandwidth communications. Management tasks, such as configuration of; local Wi-Fi parameters, device parameters, controlling enabled features and updating firmware will occur though LoRaWAN. Specifically, IoT devices will use a LoRaWAN gateway to communicate with a backend server. Further information on this communication model is presented in Sect. 3.1.

3.1   Hybrid Communication Incorporating IP Networks and LoRaWAN

LoRaWAN was selected as the LPWWAN in this solution as it facilitates long range communications from base stations, has extremely low power consumption and is central to a number of geographically large deployments. LoRaWAN enables devices to communicate with base stations with a maximum range of 15–30 km. Bandwidth provided may range from 0.3 kbps to 50 kbps, as dictated by environmental factors.

Notably, LoRaWAN has been selected as the backbone of an international effort to provide IoT connectivity to the entire island of Ireland through the Pervasive Nation study [29]. This wide area of coverage will enable management of SHIB installations in this study, across all potential deployment areas. Use of this communication model reduces the available attack surface of IoT devices while simultaneously facilitating management.

Specifically, using a LoRaWAN as the out-of-band management channel and restricting IP based data to transmission to an endpoint only reduces the applicability of most IP based exploits. In addition, the communications and access model employed by LoRaWAN brings several additional strengths, further augmenting security.

LoRaWAN employs a level of transport layer security by default. Specifically, it supports cryptographic signing of communications and encrypted transit of data. LoRaWAN requires that devices must initiate communication to a specific service. These services may have unique identifiers and encryption keys helping to protect against spoofing of communication, resisting man in the middle attacks.

LoRaWAN networks are not as open and accessible as the common IP networks. Instead they require actors to be granted appropriate access rights. This benefits security by having centralized control that may provide auditing of how actors use these networks. This access control offers the opportunity to deny malicious actors and ensure that potential users are vetted. This greatly reduces the potential for malicious attacks to be launched on IoT devices connected to LoRaWAN networks. LoRaWAN provides basic transport layer encryption enabling basic security for management of IoT devices. Nevertheless, this security is insufficient to offer robust protection against attacks that may be launched on the service side of the LoRaWAN gateway. These attacks may involve compromising server hosting the service host or hijacking the link between the service and gateway. Additionally, use of a single and common set of encryption keys provides a single point of failure in providing trustworthy and protected communications. To address these deficiencies, an additional mechanism of providing trust and encrypted traffic must be implemented. This mechanism of trust and privacy was introduced as an element of a purpose-built, application layer, message format for transportation of management payloads. This message format enables adoption of stronger encryption and trust assurance than LoRaWAN offers – contributing to ensure future security. An additional benefit of this message format is removal of reliance on vendor specific transmission encryption and message signing, enabling this management solution to be adopted with other LPWWAN systems. The message format devised and implemented is detailed in in Sect. 3.2.

3.2   A Message Format Enabling Secure Management of IoT Devices

The devised trusted command message enables strong privacy and strong assurance of trust, through proven cryptographic techniques. In addition, generic functionality is facilitated though a flexible, JavaScript Object Notation (JSON) based, data structure.

Strong privacy has been provided through use of the Rijndael/the Advanced Encryption Standard (AES) [30] to protect communications. AES is one of the strongest, proven, encryption standards that is publicly available [31].

AES offers three available key lengths that may be used; 128-bit, 192-bit and 256-bit. 256-bit keys offer the strongest protection available, followed by 192 and then 128. It has been shown 128-bit keys offer protection that is computationally infeasible to bypass within the next 15 years [32]. Nevertheless, AES using 256-bit keys is the current National Security Administration standard for protecting top secret documents and communications [33], as such it will be adopted in this approach to provide future proofing. Also, AES offers several operational modes which dictate how data is encrypted using the algorithm.

AES operational modes have a significant effect on the strength of the cypher text produced. Contemporary operational modes that are suitable for communication include Electronic Code Book (EBC), Cipher Feedback (CFB), Output Feedback (OFB), Counter (CTR), Offset Codebook Mode (OCB) and Cipher Block Chaining (CBC) [34]. OCB is the strongest AES operational mode [34], however, it is patent encumbered and computationally expensive. AES in CBC mode is the next strongest mode [35] and when combined with a strong keyed Hash Message Authentication Code (HMAC) it can offer cryptograph strength which is equivalent to, or exceeds, AES in OBC mode [36]. In addition, AES in CBC mode requires relatively low computational resources to be implemented, increasing it suitability for IoT devices where constrained resources are available [37, 38]. Furthermore, many CPU based security engines have native support for this encryption scheme, reducing computational resources and time required to encrypt/decrypt communications [39].

In addition to providing communication privacy, through AES-CBC, trust needs to be incorporated. A mechanism of trust ensures that management payloads originate from an authentic and assured source. This prevents spoofing of management payloads and ensures that only actors with the necessary rights may issue valid management payloads. One strong and proven way of providing this trust is through use of a HMAC [36, 40] to verify the integrity and authenticity of a management payload.

A HMAC uses a hashing function and a key to produce a unique signature for a specific block of data. This process is expressed in (1) [41] where K is the secret/shared key, m is the message to be authenticated, $\oplus$ is an exclusive or operation, $\parallel$ is a concatenation, *ipad* is inner padding and *opad* is outer padding.

$$HMAC(K, m) = H((K \oplus opad) \,||\, H((K \oplus ipad) \,||\, m)) \tag{1}$$

The trust and integrity offered by a HMAC process is intrinsically dependent on the hashing function that has been adopted. When employing a sufficiently strong hashing function a HMAC offers high levels of trust and integrity. In this case SHA-512 has been selected due to its proven strength and resistance to attacks [42].

In this message format a unique signature is generated for a block of encrypted data and recorded in the trusted command message. In this instance, each management command message is encrypted on a management server using a per-device primary device key. A HMAC is subsequently calculated from this encrypted data and a secondary device key. This HMAC is then recorded in the trusted command message.

In all cases, these keys are derived from 512-bit cryptographic nonces that were generated using a high-quality source of entropy during the initial device enrollment process, outlined in Sect. 3.3. This encryption and signing process offering trust and privacy in this trusted command message is presented in Fig. 2.

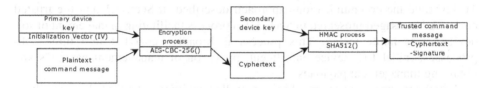

Fig. 2. An overview of the encryption and signing process that enables trust and privacy within this message format.

The trusted command message is encoded into JSON which contains three key-value pairs. These key value pairs are presented in Table 1.

Table 1. The format of the trusted command message, as encoded in JSON.

Key-value pair	Data type	Description
Command type	Integer	An enumeration representing the type of message command contained within the Encrypted Payload. A trusted representation of this is encoded in the first 4 bytes of the payload meaning that this may be removed from the message for privacy. This removal would be at the expense of management/prioritization of commands. Current enumerations are: 0: configuration update, such as Wi-Fi settings 1: system command, such as device reset 2: firmware update
Encrypted payload	String	The encrypted payload – containing the core of the management payload
Hashed MAC	String	The Hashed MAC signature, providing trust

An example trusted command message is presented in Fig. 3. This message was used to successfully reconfigure Wi-Fi settings, SSID and WPA Key, on a prototype sensor.

```
{
    "commandType":0,
    "encryptedPayload":
    "9512bb204fea154633df9caa7a183c872162193ac15386c768f4f4c25227527e74eed361ae
    fa9c25b5905539c85079863e6bc775646c3d455c90c6daead801c62453eafd98b212bdb824b
    43daef80809ff30046407828ff2b170c340b2cf4d1d0e1642800900d941b22f0543192d4411
    743bc63477c063bb9c089ff906dc649131685f0d5258c6ce773b32c0cbcf42e",
    "hmac":"af9151a9c287e6358e7b58514e668de2384849078dcf266c42a17fc51301ddcd"
}
```

Fig. 3. An example of the trusted command message produced by this approach.

To provide secure management functionality, this trusted command message must be incorporated into a secure management process. This is presented in Sect. 3.3.

3.3   A Process Facilitating Secure Management of IoT Devices

To leverage the communications approach described in Sect. 3.1 and the trusted command messaged presented in Sect. 3.2, a process facilitating management of IoT devices was implemented. This process is broadly separated into three sub-processes, initial IoT device enrollment, provision of management payloads and obtaining management payloads.

Initial enrollment is performed in a controlled environment after IoT devices have been tested and loaded with an initial firmware. Following this, the device would be attached to a secure Initialization Network (InitNet). Once attached to an InitNet, a server will automatically generate several per device encryption parameters. These parameters include three 512-bit cryptographic nonces; these are used to derive the primary device key, secondary device key and Initialization Vector (IV) for the AES-CBC-256 cypher. These cryptographic nonces are generated from a high-quality source of entropy.

These per-device encryption parameters are securely stored in a database for future communication with that IoT device. Following this, these encryption parameters are stored on the IoT device, in addition to any LoRaWAN parameters. At this stage, the IoT device may be managed when a management payload is issued.

The process of provisioning of management payload is performed though a web service. This service currently offers three functional modes; specify a new configuration, perform a remote command and upload a firmware. Once a management payload has been specified, a device or group of devices may be selected as a configuration target. On selection of the configuration target a per-device flag is set to transmit this management payload on the next communication with that device. These management payloads will be transferred in order of specification.

The process of obtaining the management payload is facilitated via LoRaWAN. Communications on LoRaWAN are request based, requiring that communication is initiated by client/IoT devices. This communication model adds to security by not requiring a service to run on the IoT device. Such a service would increase its surface for attacks. On receipt of a request, the configuration server checks to see if there are any flagged management payload. If there is a flag set, then the management server encrypts the plaintext command message using its copy of that device's primary key and IV. This encrypted representation is then converted to a Base64 representation and set as the *encryptedPayload* of the trusted command message. The HMAC is then calculated from the *encryptedPayload* of the trusted command message using the server copy of that device's secondary key. This HMAC is then stored in the JSON message, along with the *encryptedPayload*. This complete trusted command message is then returned to the IoT device and the flag for that management payload is cleared.

On receipt of the trusted command message the IoT device uses its local copy of its secondary key to generate a reference/trusted HMAC. This reference/trusted HMAC is then compared with the supplied version in the trusted command message. If this comparison is identical then the message is trustworthy. If the HMAC comparison fails then the message is not trusted and discarded. The *encryptedPayload* of trustworthy messages are decrypted using the IoT device copy of the primary device key. The decrypted version of the payload is then handled by the device and applied as desired.

In this mechanism IoT devices are currently designed to contact the update server via LoRaWAN on a device reboot, at a set interval of 12 h and after processing a management payload. Checking for further management payloads after processing a management payload facilitates a sequence payloads to be applied in quick succession.

4 Evaluation

Evaluation of this approach focused on two aspects; functionality of the management mechanism and the area of communication provided by a single LoRaWAN gateway.

To evaluate the functionality of the management mechanism 80 updates were issued to a target IoT device; 40 of these were correctly signed/encrypted and the remaining 40 were incorrectly signed/encrypted. 10 of the incorrect updates had the encrypted Payload modified; 10 had the HMAC modified; 10 were signed with another device's secondary key and 10 were encrypted with another device's primary key. In all cases the incorrectly signed/encrypted messages were rejected and the correctly signed/encrypted messages were enacted.

To evaluate the communication area of a single LoRaWAN gateway two aspects were considered; the claimed maximum coverage range and the intended deployment area for the SHIB. The intended deployment area for the SHIB is the Belfast Urban Area (BUA). To this end, a LoRaWAN connected GPS logger was used to log the area covered by a LoRaWAN gateway. This logger was placed in a car that was driven from a location north of the BUA to a location 1 km south of the BUA. During this journey, the locate and transmit button was pressed periodically. This locate and transmit function does not cache records and will only be reviewed if there is a LoRaWAN connection. Additionally, many samples occurred in the BUA; across buildings, built-up streets and retail outlets. All 314 GPS readings that were transmitted were correctly received by a LoRaWAN gateway. These readings showed that the gateway has a communications range of at least 18.2 km, farther than the claimed lower maximum range of 15 km, with this gateway providing communication across the entire BUA. The projected area covered by that LoRaWAN gateway, as determined by GPS logging, is presented in Fig. 4.

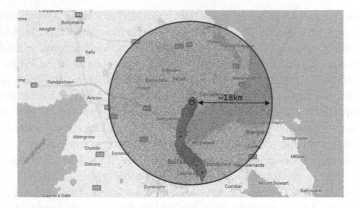

Fig. 4. The projected area of coverage for a single LoRaWAN gateway, as determined by point-mapping connectivity of a LoRaWAN GPS receiver.

From the evaluation, it can be determined that the management mechanism proposed is suitable for its intended purposes, as demonstrated by the functionality of the encryption process and transmissible range. Further discussion is presented in Sect. 5.

5 Conclusion

This study introduces a novel, secure, out-of-band mechanism to manage IoT devices via a hybrid communications model. The hybrid communications model uses IP based networking for one-way transmission of data from IoT devices to web services and LoRaWAN, a LPWWAN, for traffic from management services to IoT devices. The communications model was combined with a secure trusted command message format and associated processes. The trusted command message and associated processes employ strong, proven, cryptographic techniques. This cryptography enables management payloads to be sent from a management server to IoT devices in a manner that ensures privacy and trust subsequently providing security.

This management mechanism addresses a range of the deficiencies of current IoT device management solutions and provides a secure and capable management mechanism. During an evaluation, this mechanism was shown to operate reliably and across a large geographic area, covering the intended deployment area of the devised SHIB.

Future work will deploy several SHIB installations across the BUA. Subsequently, the utility of this management platform and the suitability of the LoRaWAN platform will be evaluated. Additional security may also be incorporated through integration of a Hardware Security Module within the management platform.

Acknowledgments. Invest Northern Ireland is acknowledged for supporting this project under the Competence Centre Programs Grant RD0513853 – Connected Health Innovation Centre. Pervasive Nation is acknowledged for providing access to their LoRaWAN infrastructure and offering support during this project.

References

1. Weiser, M.: The computer for the 21st century. Sci. Am. **265**, 94–104 (1991)
2. Satyanarayanan, M.: Pervasive computing: vision and challenges. IEEE Pers. Commun. **8**, 10–17 (2001)
3. Lee, I.: An exploratory study of the impact of the internet of things (IoT) on business model innovation: building smart enterprises at fortune 500 companies. Int. J. Inf. Syst. Soc. Change **7**, 1–15 (2016)
4. Riggins, F.J., Wamba, S.F.: Research directions on the adoption, usage, and impact of the internet of things through the use of big data analytics. In: 2015 48th Hawaii International Conference on System Sciences (HICSS), pp. 1531–1540 (2015)
5. Bradley, J., Reberger, C., Dixit, A., Gupta, V.: Internet of everything: a \$4.6 trillion public-sector opportunity. Cisco White Paper (2013)
6. Rafferty, J., Nugent, C.D., Liu, J.: From Activity Recognition to Intention Recognition for Assisted Living Within Smart Homes, pp. 1–12 (2017)
7. Roy, N., Misra, A., Cook, D.: Ambient and smartphone sensor assisted ADL recognition in multi-inhabitant smart environments. J. Ambient Intell. Humanized Comput. **7**(1), 1–19 (2015)
8. European Commission: The Ambient Assisted Living (AAL) Joint Programme. http://ec.europa.eu/information_society/activities/einclusion/docs/ageing/aal_overview.pdf
9. Tozlu, S., Senel, M., Mao, W., Keshavarzian, A.: Wi-Fi enabled sensors for internet of things: a practical approach. IEEE Commun. Mag. **50**, 134–143 (2012)
10. Al-Fuqaha, A., Guizani, M., Mohammadi, M., Aledhari, M., Ayyash, M.: Internet of things: a survey on enabling technologies, protocols, and applications. IEEE Commun. Surv. Tutor. **17**, 2347–2376 (2015)
11. Bertino, E., Islam, N.: Botnets and internet of things security. Computer **50**, 76–79 (2017)
12. Shah, M., Soni, V., Shah, H., Desai, M.: TCP/IP network protocols—security threats, flaws and defense methods. In: 2016 3rd International Conference On Computing for Sustainable Global Development, pp. 2693–2699 (2016)
13. Bruno, L., Graziano, M., Balzarotti, D., Francillon, A.: Through the looking-glass, and what eve found there. In: WOOT (2014)
14. CVE-2017-5689. http://cve.mitre.org/cgi-bin/cvename.cgi?name=CVE-2017-5689
15. Conti, M., Dragoni, N., Lesyk, V.: A survey of man in the middle attacks. IEEE Commun. Surv. Tutor. **18**, 2027–2051 (2016)
16. CVE-2017-7925. http://cve.mitre.org/cgi-bin/cvename.cgi?name=CVE-2017-7925
17. Zhang, Z.-K., Cho, M.C.Y., Shieh, S.: Emerging security threats and countermeasures in IoT. In: Proceedings of the 10th ACM Symposium on Information, Computer and Communications Security - ASIA CCS 2015, pp. 1–6. ACM Press, New York, USA (2015)
18. Smart, N.P.: Certificates, key transport and key agreement. Cryptography Made Simple. ISC, pp. 369–399. Springer, Cham (2016). doi:10.1007/978-3-319-21936-3_18
19. Dubeuf, J., Hely, D., Beroulle, V.: ECDSA passive attacks, leakage sources, and common design mistakes. ACM Trans. Des. Autom. Electron. Syst. **21**, 1–24 (2016)
20. Schneier, B., Fredrikson, M., Kohno, T., Ristenpart, T.: Surreptitiously weakening cryptographic systems. IACR Cryptol. ePrint Arch. (2015)
21. Centenaro, M., Vangelista, L., Zanella, A., Zorzi, M.: Long-range communications in unlicensed bands: the rising stars in the IoT and smart city scenarios. IEEE Wirel. Commun. **23**, 60–67 (2016)

22. Andreev, S., Galinina, O., Pyattaev, A., Gerasimenko, M., Tirronen, T., Torsner, J., Sachs, J., Dohler, M., Koucheryavy, Y.: Understanding the IoT connectivity landscape: a contemporary M2 M radio technology roadmap. IEEE Commun. Mag. **53**, 32–40 (2015)
23. Khan, Z., Lehtomaki, J.J., Iellamo, S.I., Vuohtoniemi, R., Hossain, E., Han, Z.: IoT Connectivity in radar bands: a shared access model based on spectrum measurements. IEEE Commun. Mag. **55**, 88–96 (2017)
24. Ijaz, A., Zhang, L., Grau, M., Mohamed, A., Vural, S., Quddus, A.U., Imran, M.A., Foh, C.H., Tafazolli, R.: Enabling massive IoT in 5G and beyond systems: PHY radio frame design considerations. IEEE Access **4**, 3322–3339 (2016)
25. Welch, B.: Exploiting the weaknesses of SS7. Netw. Secur. **2017**, 17–19 (2017)
26. SS7 routing protocol vulnerability let thieves drain 2FA-protected bank accounts|Ars Technica UK, https://arstechnica.co.uk/security/2017/05/thieves-drain-2fa-protected-bank-accounts-by-abusing-ss7-routing-protocol/
27. Regulation of Investigatory Powers Act, UK (2000)
28. Alliance, L.: A technical overview of LoRa and LoRaWAN. White Paper, November (2015)
29. Pervasive Nation. https://connectcentre.ie/pervasive-nation/
30. Daemen, J., Rijmen, V.: The Rijndael Block Cipher: AES Proposal (2003)
31. Kumar, P., Rawat, S., Choudhury, T., Pradhan, S.: A performance based comparison of various symmetric cryptographic algorithms in run-time scenario. In: International Conference on System Modeling & Advancement in Research Trends (SMART), pp. 37–41 (2016)
32. Ågren, M.: On some symmetric lightweight cryptographic designs (2012)
33. Bajaj, R.D., Gokhale, M., Tech Vlsi, M.: Design and simulation of AES algorithm for cryptography. Int. J. Eng. Sci. Comput. (2016)
34. Ertaul, L., Sravya, K.L., Sanka, N.: Implementation of authenticated encryption algorithm offset code book (OCB). In: Proceedings of the International Conference on Wireless Networks (ICWN), p. 78 (2016)
35. Vaidehi, M., Rabi, B.J.: Design and analysis of AES-CBC mode for high security applications. In: 2014 2nd International Conference on Current Trends in Engineering and Technology (ICCTET), pp. 499–502 (2014)
36. Paterson, K., Foley, J., McGrew, D.: Authenticated Encryption with AES-CBC and HMAC-SHA (2014)
37. System, method, and computer program product for optimizing data encryption and decryption by implementing asymmetric AES-CBC channels (2013)
38. Feldhofer, M., Wolkerstorfer, J., Rijmen, V.: AES implementation on a grain of sand. IEE Proc. Inf. Secur. **152**, 13 (2005)
39. Saito, T., Yasuda, K., Ishikawa, T., Hosoi, R., Takahashi, K., Chen, Y., Zalasinski, M.: Estimating CPU features by browser fingerprinting. In: 2016 10th International Conference on Innovative Mobile and Internet Services in Ubiquitous Computing (IMIS), pp. 587–592. IEEE (2016)
40. Bellare, M.: New proofs for NMAC and HMAC: security without collision resistance. J. Cryptol. **28**, 844–878 (2015)
41. Krawczyk, H., Canetti, R., Bellare, M.: HMAC: Keyed-hashing for message authentication.
42. Bharati, P.V., Mahalakshmi, T.S.: A Combinational Approach for securing the data in cloud storage using HMAC-SHA512 and Information Secured Algorithm (ISA). Int. J. Appl. Eng. Res. **11**, 973–4562 (2016)

Secure System Communication to Emergencies for Victims Management Through Identity Based Signcryption Scheme

Alexandra Rivero-García$^{(\boxtimes)}$, Candelaria Hernández-Goya$^{(\boxtimes)}$,
Iván Santos-González$^{(\boxtimes)}$, and Pino Caballero-Gil$^{(\boxtimes)}$

Departamento de Ingeniería Informática y de Sistemas,
Universidad de La Laguna, Tenerife, Spain
{ariverog,mchgoya,jsantosg,pcaballe}@ull.es

Abstract. In this proposal an optimized system designed to help the greatest number of injured people in emergency situations is described, using the shortest possible time and cost. It is composed of a mobile application (assigned to medical staff and helpers), a web service and Near Field Communication wristbands assigned to victims. The mobile application is devoted to providing medical staff with the geolocation of victims as well as with an assistant indicating the best route to follow in order to take care of them based on the severity of their conditions and based on a triage method. Resolution of the routes is solved based on a classical problem, a Travelling Salesman Problem, using a k-partition algorithm to divide the huge number of victims in different clusters. Thus, each doctor has a specific area to assist victims. Besides, doctors can use a functionality of the application to contact their peers through a chat when additional help is needed. An IDentity-Based Signcryption is used for communication confidentiality, authenticity and integrity, both among peers, and between server and medical staff.

Keywords: ID-Based Signcryption · mHealth · Android · NFC

1 Introduction

This paper presents a platform for improving logistics of medical staff in emergency situations in a distributed way. In particular, it is based on data obtained from a triage application developed in [1], where a mobile system for victim classification in emergency situations was implemented. The definition of triage can be described as follows. A simple, complete, objective and fast process to obtain an initial clinical assessment of people with the objective of evaluating their immediate survival capacities and prioritizing them according their severity is a triage. In order to achieve the classification, all triage systems distinguish two steps. The first triage or simple triage is used for the generation of a classification based on the severity of injuries of the victims evaluating their survival skills in some seconds. The second triage is where medical staff analyses each

© Springer International Publishing AG 2017
S.F. Ochoa et al. (Eds.): UCAmI 2017, LNCS 10586, pp. 91–96, 2017.
DOI: 10.1007/978-3-319-67585-5_10

patient's state: bruises, wounds and injuries. Simple Triage and Rapid Treatment Algorithm (START) [2] method is used as first triage, specifically the JUMP-START [3] which has a child triage. Its output is the victim's classification based on coloured tags, where each colour defines the priority of the victim: black, dead or irrecoverable victims; red, victims requiring immediate care; yellow, victims requiring urgent care but who can wait for treatment from half an hour to one hour; green, victims who are not seriously injured. They can wait for treatment more than an hour. Here the use of Near Field Communication (NFC) [4] is proposed to deal with the triage result. NFC stickers are used to save triage results based on the generation of a JSON Web Token (JWT) scheme. Furthermore, the route to attend victims for each doctor is shown through a map in their smartphones based on the priorities of victims and they can share information peer-to-peer with their colleagues in the affected area. All these communications are protected through an IDentity-based (ID-based) cryptography, specifically a ID-Based Signcryption scheme (IBSC).

2 Proposed System

This work is a tool that can help to improve the management of patients and medical staff communication and organization. The main objective is to generate a tool to save as many time as possible in emergency situations. Therefore, doctors have their mobile phones a communication way by a BLE chat and a map that helps them in every moment to decide the route to patients. This route is based on the severity of the injuries. This colour result is stored on tags. In this case NFC tags, specifically NFC stickers are used to save the triage result. The triage result is stored in the NFC stickers through a JWT, where in the header the medical staff add the used algorithm (HS256) and in the payload the data related with the triage result, the medical ID and a previous shared emergency code generated for each emergency situation. The result of the JSON Web Token generated is the information stored in the NFC sticker, see Fig. 1.

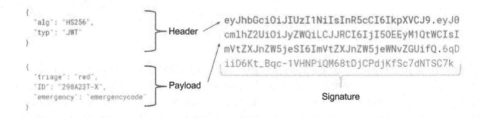

Fig. 1. JSON web token

When the first triage is finished, is time to the second stage. In this step the victims' locations given by the first triage is essential being the starting point. A graph of each colour is generated based on the victim's location in a map. Victims represent nodes and the routes to reach them are de edges.

3 Route Generation of Healthcare Workers

In the generation of doctors' routes, first of all, an undirected graph is created from the points defined during the first triage. There are as many points as patients on the map, these are the vertices of our graph. The edges will be defined undirected between the vertices. This distance between points will be the cost of the edge. Each edge has a cost. This cost is the distance between two nodes calculated through the Haversine Formula [5]. The system generates one graph for each triage colour, the main objective is treating patients based on their injuries. Specifically a graph based on the Delaunay Triangulation [6] is created.

Initially, the system divides into clusters the red graph. At the end, there are as many subgraphs as doctors in the emergency area. Specifically our system generates a $k - partition$ based on [7], where k is the number of doctors. The system assigns to each doctor, depending on the location, the node that is the highest priority and closest to the coloration performed. That is, the nearest doctor is distributed for each partition, excluding the doctors already assigned.

Then the system generates the path of each sub-graph. This is the problem known as the Travelling Salesman Problem (TSP) [8] and we solve this through the Nearest Neighbour approach, because this is one of the rules of all triage systems. Thus, a graph of routes is generated for each doctor, based on the combination of different sub-graphs that are produced with patients of the same priority level.

4 Medical Staff Communication with Signcryption Scheme

The application has enabled a communication between medical staff. It is a bluetooth chat, and with this when a doctor or nurse requires additional help from peers he/she can make a question to a specific person or to nearby people. Everybody share their own ID (it is a public information) through beacon mode. Medical staff can share information with only one person through a ID-Based Signcryption and with multiple users through ID-Based Multi-Receiver Signcryption Scheme, that provides private and authenticated delivery of information between two parties or more in an efficient way with a composition of an encryption scheme with a signature scheme [9]. The Private Key Generator (PKG) is a server in charge of generating health staff private keys. The identifier of medical staff is the number of registered medical practitioners and for nurses the same (ID).

Considering two cycling groups $(G, +)$ and $(V, \cdot)$ of the same prime order q. P is a generator of G and there is a bilinear map paring $\hat{e} : G \times G \to V$ satisfying the following conditions: bilinear, non-degenerate and there exists an algorithm to compute $\hat{e}(P, Q), \forall P, Q \in G$. Some hash functions denoted as follows are also needed: $H_1 : \{0,1\}^* \to G^*, H_2 : \{0,1\}^* \to \mathbb{Z}_q^*, H_3 : \mathbb{Z}_q^* \to \{0,1\}^n, H_4 : \{0,1\}^n \to \{0,1\}^{|m|}, H_5 : G \times G \times \{0,1\}^n \times \mathbb{Z}_q^* \times \mathbb{Z}_q^* \times ... \times \mathbb{Z}_q^* \to \mathbb{Z}_q^*$, where the size of the

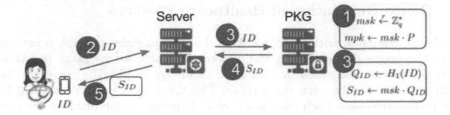

Fig. 2. Initialization step

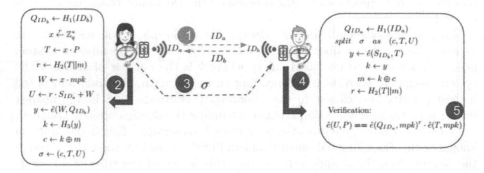

Fig. 3. Single signcryption/unsigncryption

message is defined by n. The signcryption scheme used is a combination between the ID-Based Signcryption Scheme proposed in [10] and ID-Based Signcryption Scheme for Multiple Receivers. Some basic notation used: $x \leftarrow rS$ stands for an element x randomly selected from a set S, $x \leftarrow y$ denotes the assignation of the value y to x and $\|$ is used for concatenation. The steps needed for the signcryption scheme are the following:

- **Initialization:** The initial parameters are established and the server generates the master public key (mpk) and the master secret key (msk). Then, the secret key for each member of the medical staff based on their ID is generated. The public key $Q_{ID} \in G$ and the secret key $S_{ID} \in G$ are calculated taking into account the msk. It should be pointed out that this key exchange between server and the doctor is performed using the stream cipher SNOW3G [11] under the session key obtained through an Elliptic Curve Diffie-Hellman (ECDH) [12] (See Fig. 2).

- **Single communication.** All the messages $m \in \{0,1\}^n$ will be encrypted and signed. The receiver's public key is generated taking into account ID_b and then the message is signed with S_{ID_a} and encrypted with Q_{ID_b} giving as result σ (with three components: c, T, U). On the other hand, the receiver has to verify the message, if it is successful m is returned, otherwise $\perp$ is returned (See Fig. 3).

- **Multiple receiver communication:** If there are n receivers, the system has $ID_1, ID_2, ..., ID_n$. The sender is ID_a. All the broadcast messages $m \in \{0, 1\}^n$ will be encrypted and signed. The receivers' public keys are generated taking into account all the identifications. Each receiver decrypt the message and $m \in \{0, 1\}^n$ is returned if everything is right (See Fig. 4).

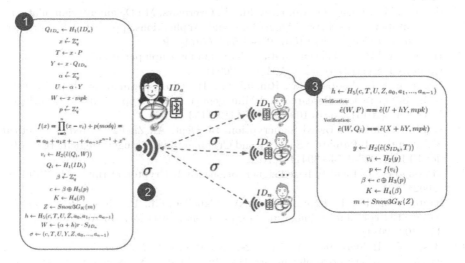

Fig. 4. Multiple receiver signcryption/unsigncryption

5 Conclusions and Future Work

In this work, a system has been presented to may to improve logistics and attention of casualties in extreme situations. The priority is to serve the greatest number of injuries using the shortest possible time and cost. The tool consists on a mobile application, NFC tags and a web service. Specifically the system create a graph based on the Delaunay Triangulation and uses a $k - partition$ to divide it in clusters. The system has an emergency support tool to contact peers through a BLE chat when doctors require additional support with a ID-Based Signcryption. A first approach has been implemented. More functionalities can be added to the server, such as statistics, a real-time map with events, etc.

Acknowledgments. Research supported by TESIS2015010102, TESIS2015010106, RTC-2014-1648-8, TEC2014-54110-R, MTM-2015-69138-REDT and DIG02-INSITU.

References

1. Rivero-García, A., Hernández-Goya, C., Santos-González, I., Caballero-Gil, P.: Fasttriaje: A mobile system for victim classification in emergency situations (2014)
2. Kahn, C.A., Schultz, C.H., Miller, K.T., Anderson, C.L.: Does start triage work? an outcomes assessment after a disaster. Ann. Emerg. Med. **54**(3), 424–430 (2009)

3. Romig, L.E.: Pediatric triage. A system to jumpstart your triage of young patients at MCIs. JEMS J. Emerg. Med. Serv. **27**(7), 52–58 (2002)
4. Want, R.: Near field communication. IEEE Pervasive Comput. **10**(3), 4–7 (2011)
5. Chopde, N.R., Nichat, M.: Landmark based shortest path detection by using A* and Haversine formula. Int. J. Innov. Res. Comput. Commun. Eng. **1**(2), 298–302 (2013)
6. de Berg, M., Cheong, O., van Kreveld, M., Overmars, M.: Delaunay triangulations. Computational Geometry: Algorithms and Applications, pp. 191–218. Springer, Heidelberg (2008). doi:10.1007/978-3-540-77974-2_9
7. Hespanha, J.P.: An efficient matlab algorithm for graph partitioning. University of California, Santa Barbara, CA, USA (2004)
8. Hoffman, K.L., Padberg, M., Rinaldi, G.: Traveling salesman problem. Encyclopedia of Operations Research and Management Science, pp. 1573–1578. Springer, New York (2013). doi:10.1007/978-1-4419-1153-7_1068
9. Boyen, X.: Identity-Based Signcryption. In: Dent, A., Zheng, Y. (eds.) Practical Signcryption. Information Security and Cryptography. Springer, Heidelberg (2010). doi:10.1007/978-3-540-89411-7_10
10. Malone-Lee, J.: Identity-based signcryption. IACR Cryptol. ePrint Arch. **2002**, 98 (2002)
11. Santos-González, I., Rivero-García, A., Caballero-Gil, P., Hernández-Goya, C.: Alternative communication system for emergency situations. In: WEBIST (2), pp. 397–402 (2014)
12. Bos, J.W., Halderman, J.A., Heninger, N., Moore, J., Naehrig, M., Wustrow, E.: Elliptic curve cryptography in practice. In: Christin, N., Safavi-Naini, R. (eds.) FC 2014. LNCS, vol. 8437, pp. 157–175. Springer, Heidelberg (2014). doi:10.1007/978-3-662-45472-5_11

SensorCentral: A Research Oriented, Device Agnostic, Sensor Data Platform

Joseph Rafferty[✉], Jonathan Synnott, Andrew Ennis, Chris Nugent,
Ian McChesney, and Ian Cleland

School of Computing and Mathematics, Ulster University, Coleraine, Northern Ireland, UK
{j.rafferty,j.synnott,a.ennis,cd.nugent,ir.mcchesney,
i.cleland}@ulster.ac.uk

Abstract. Increasingly research interests within the area of pervasive and ubiquitous computing, such as activity recognition, rely upon storage and retrieval of sensor data. Due to the increase in volume, velocity and variation of such sensor data its storage and retrieval has become a big data problem. There are a number of current platforms that are intended to store large amount of sensor data, however, they lack research oriented features. To address these deficiencies this study introduces a research oriented, device agnostic sensor, data platform called *SensorCentral*. This platform incorporates several research oriented features such as offering annotation interfaces, metric generation, exporting experimental datasets, machine learning services, rule based classification, forwarding live sensor records to other systems and quick sensor configuration. The current main installation of this platform has been in place for over 18 months, has been successfully associated with 6 sensor classes from 13 vendors and currently holds over 500 million records. Future work will involve offering this platform to other researchers and incorporating direct integration with the Open Data Initiative enabling better collaboration with other researchers on an international scale.

Keywords: Big data · Sensor data · Internet of things · Scalable storage · Machine learning · Open data initiative · Research tools · Data science

1 Introduction

Increasingly a number of research interests within the area of pervasive and ubiquitous computing are reliant on sensor data [1–3]. These interests include activity recognition, management of road traffic, assessment of pollution levels, population movement pattern analysis and weather prediction.

The sensor data that is to be stored and leveraged may be heterogenous, spanning a *variety* of sensor data types from numerous devices that may be produced by many vendors. Additionally, such sensor data would, ideally, be produced at the highest sample rate possible, to provide a more complete dataset providing more informed research outputs. An example of such a high *velocity* stream of sensor data would be sampling the temperature reading produced by a sensor every 1 s. Finally, there is consensus [1–3] in the relevant research communities that having the greatest volume

© Springer International Publishing AG 2017
S.F. Ochoa et al. (Eds.): UCAmI 2017, LNCS 10586, pp. 97–108, 2017.
DOI: 10.1007/978-3-319-67585-5_11

of sensor possible generally leads to better informed outcomes and higher quality solutions. Such a *volume* may be produced by *variety* of sensors which sample their state at a high *velocity*.

In the scenario of pollution assessment within a city, sensor data may include: (1) temperature, (2) humidity, (3) air pollution determined by the concentration of particulates of interest, (4) levels of light and (5) volume of road traffic as indicated by inductance sensors. To obtain this data a large number of varying sensors would be placed across a city and sampled at the highest possible rate.

Storage and exploitation of this sensor data is classified as a big data problem as the three key characteristics of a big data problem are present. These characteristics are *variety* of data, *volume* of data and *velocity* of data – summarized as the three V's [4, 5].

Currently there are a number of databases and platforms that are designed to assist with the storage and exploitation of such data. However, these have some deficiencies when applied to the realm of research. Specifically, these solutions do not offer research oriented features such as, (1) definition of experiments, (2) exporting experimental records into a research oriented data format, (3) providing functions to forward sensor records to independent experimental systems, (4) integrated machine learning services/ reasoning and (5) sensor agnostic function.

In order to address these deficiencies a research oriented sensor platform has been created, this has been called *SensorCentral*. This platform offers a multitude of features that would benefit research communities. This paper presents this devised solution and is structured as follows: Sect. 2 contains an overview of related works, Sect. 3 presents the developed platform, Sect. 4 provides an overview of some of the current uses of the platform and Sect. 6 provides a conclusion and some information on future work.

2   Related Work

Several platforms for storing and querying sensor data currently exist. However, they have some deficiencies related to the ability to scale and handle big data and have limited research oriented functionality [5–8]. Specifically, researchers within a candidate research group require features that complement their efforts. These include the ability to forward live sensor data to independent systems, simple annotation interfaces, the ability to specify functions that enable exporting experimental metadata and related sensor records, reasoning functionality and analysis services.

Sowe *et al.* [7] proposed a sensor data platform that would enable storage of a large volume of heterogenous sensor data. This platform offered some interfaces that enables external research oriented tools to access the data contained within. Data was to be stored within MongoDB and MySQL databases. However, this platform was not tested with any significant amount of traffic and does not provide real time/low latency analysis.

Cheng *et al.* [9] produced a platform that is designed to store sensor data for smart cities. This platform was intended to store sensor data from a city that has over 180,000 inhabitants. Data was stored within CouchDB and Hadoop offering scalable storage. However, the platform does not support low latency reasoning/analytics or sensor agnostic function.

Bonomi *et al.* [10] proposed a 'fog computing' approach to storing, querying and processing sensor data. This approach would support real-time reasoning/analytics, in addition to the scalable storage. However, the approach silos sensor information reducing the ability to query the complete data set.

Lee *et al.* [11] produced a 'universal sensor platform' for modelling and providing real time analytics on sensors related to railway systems. This platform was scalable but does not offer sensor agnostic function as it is intended to operate with specific sensors related to enabling a smart railway.

Cecchinel *et al.* [12] proposed an architecture to store a large volume of sensor data that is produced at a high velocity. This platform is sensor agnostic and uses MongoDB as its primary sensor storage database.

Thingspeak [13] is a commercial, cloud-based, sensor data platform. This platform provides sensor agnostic function through a REpresentational State Transfer (REST) or Message Queue Telemetry Transport interfaces (MQTT). This platform offers a high latency analysis functions through a web-embedded, reduced functionality, instance of MatLAB. This platform facilitates scheduling of MATLAB scripts to provide some automated analysis.

Beebottle [14] is a commercial, cloud-based, data platform that supports sensor data. This platform supports communication through MQTT, REST and WebSockets. This platform does not provide any analysis functionality.

None of the previously existing sensor data platforms have incorporated any of the desired research oriented features mandated by the members of the candidate research group. In order to address the deficiencies, present in previous sensor data platforms a solution that is sensor agnostic, scalable and offers research oriented features was devised and developed. This solution is presented in Sect. 3.

3   A Research Oriented, Device Agnostic, Sensor Data Platform

The developed solution is a scalable sensor data platform which is designed to provide device agnostic integration thus supporting a multitude of sensor devices, from differing manufacturers. Currently the platform has been integrated with 6 classes of sensors from 13 different vendors. These sensors include thermal vision sensors, smart floors, contact sensors, pressure sensors and power usage monitors. Additionally, a number of research-oriented features are incorporated. These features include:

- machine learning tools – both supervised and unsupervised
- annotation tools – through a web interface and a NFC based solution supported by a companion app [15]
- facility to group sensors in arbitrary/flexible ways – such as by room or experiment
- forwarding sensor data to external systems – such as a prototypical experiment
- simple reconfiguration of sensors
- the ability to export experimental records to enable sharing datasets to the research community

This platform supports a fully modular web frontend enabling visualization of sensor data, assisting with research outputs and informing direction. Finally, the platform has been developed to be high performance, operate with low latency and be scalable. The architecture of the platform is presented in Sect. 3.1.

3.1 Platform Architecture

The developed architecture has several components, these are:

1. A storage engine for storing sensor and non-sensor data. This is a high performance and scalable storage engine based upon MongoDB and InfluxDB. More details about this storage engine and the rationale behind it is provided in Sect. 3.2.
2. A REST based web service endpoint. This enables communications with environmental components such as sensor listeners, web-based User Interfaces (UI) and smartphone apps. This endpoint is Java based and hosted though the scalable Tomcat web service host.
3. Sensor listeners to gather data from sensors and forward it to the REST endpoint of the platform. These can be written in any programming language that supports communications with the sensor and HTTP communications. Currently these have been written in C, C#, Python and Java.
4. A modular Web UI to configure experiments, visualize metrics, manage sensors and annotate experiments. This interface is developed in AngularJS [16] and incorporates an extensible architecture enabling modular development of features.
5. A metric generation framework that can process raw sensor data into windows of metrics. This framework is currently exposed though the REST endpoint and requires some custom logic to be implemented in order to function efficiently.
6. A machine learning core [17] to process windows of metrics in a supervised or unsupervised manner. This machine learning core is based upon the Neuroph framework [18]. This is licensed under an open source license that does not require works incorporating the framework to be published under an open source license. Neuroph may be incorporated into the Weka tool [19] to prototype solutions using a graphical interface.
7. A rule engine [17] to classify windows of metrics. Rules are specified in the Web UI and when they are encountered their triggering is recorded in the storage engine. The rule engine supports the following operators: *greater than, less than, equal to*. Additionally, a negation operator is supported.
8. A sensor forwarder – to forward sensor records to independent systems, such as experimental prototype systems. These records are forwarded though REST calls or web sockets. The forwarding rules are specified though the Web UI and can be targeted at individual sensors or a grouping specified in the Web UI. The facility to forward sensor records to a number of platforms maximizes the research potential of individual experiments by allowing simultaneous development or comparison of individual solutions given a single live stream of sensor data.
9. Smartphone applications for configuring sensors and annotating datasets. These apps require Near Field Communication (NFC) [20] tags to be deployed to an

environment and to be affixed to or near sensor devices. Further information is provided in Sect. 3.4.

10. A record exporter enabling researchers to export full records of experimental instances and associated sensor data into self-contained datasets. Currently export to a single custom JavaScript Object Notation (JSON) document is supported, however, direct export to the Open Data Initiative (ODI) [21] is planned.

The architecture of this platform is presented in Fig. 1.

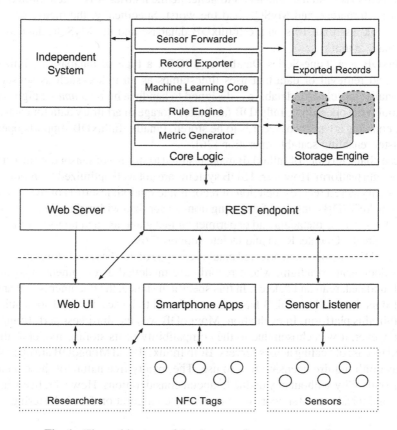

Fig. 1. The architecture of the developed sensor data platform.

3.2   Storage Engine

Core to the design of this platform is the storage engine employed, this storage engine adopted two database systems as determined by evaluation of a number of candidates. The two selected database systems are InfluxDB [22] and MongoDB [23].

These databases were chosen after a comparative performance analysis was carried out. This analysis compared the performance of a number of databases including: HBase, InfluxDB, MongoDB, MS SQL, MySQL and Oracle DB. It is notable that Hadoop was ruled out within the initial selection as its design goals do not prioritize low latency queries, due to its model of data locality [24]. Similarly, graph databases were determined to be unsuitable due to the storage model adopted and notable performance issues inherent [25].

The strategy for performance testing focused on the time taken to generate metrics from raw sensor data. The raw sensor data was generated through sampling two thermal vision sensors over the course of two days. These sensors sample information at 10 Hz, producing 3,163,174 samples across the two days. This dataset was subsequently loaded into each database and the time taken to generate the metrics was tested. InfluxDB had the best performance and MySQL had the worst. Specifically, the metric generation process took less than 10 s on the InfluxDB database and the MySQL database took longer than 23 min.

InfluxDB is a Time-Series DataBase (TSDB), a type of database optimized for storage and retrieval of data that uses timestamps as an index, such as sensor data. Additionally, this class of database is designed to handle a high *volume* of high *velocity* sequential write operations. InfluxDB facilitates storage of arbitrary data for each stored record, enabling a *variety* of records to be stored. Finally, InfluxDB supports operation in a cluster, enabling scalable operation [26].

These characteristics of InfluxDB make it suited to storage of sensor data in a purpose built big data platform. However, TSDB systems are not well optimized for modification of previously stored records, deletion of records and random insertion of records. These failings make TSDBs unsuited for storing non-sensor data within this platform, such as user profiles, sensor metadata and experimental metadata, as such non-sensor data will need full Create, Update, Read and Delete support [26].

MongoDB is a document oriented database, a type of database that stores information using a document paradigm, where records are modelled as documents that may be created, updated, read and deleted. In this specific instance, the documents that are used are in JSON format. MongoDB has been developed to be scalable and so is suited for use within this platform. In evaluation, MongoDB was the third best performing database, however, it was chosen due to the compatibility of its storage model to this use case and its ease of scaling across servers. Both InfluxDB and MongoDB are open source and thus don't require licensing fees to use. The royalty free nature of these databases enables scalability without any undue financial considerations. However, licensing fees may be paid for advanced support and automatic, 'configuration-free', clustering support [22, 23].

3.3   Device Agnostic Sensor Support

Device agnostic sensor support is a key tenet of the platform. This is facilitated in two ways: (1) having a nomenclature for each sensor device and (2) supporting a generic message format for sensor data.

A nomenclature incorporating a unique naming strategy for each sensor ensures that the data produced by sensors do not conflict with other sensors. Sensor manufacturers typically provide unique identifiers for their sensors. However, sensors from the same vendor but in a different class may conflict, such as a passive infrared movement detector having the same sensor identifier as a contact switch. Additionally, due to lack of coordination between different sensor manufacturers, there can be no guarantee of cross-manufacturer sensors identifiers being unique.

In order to cater for potential conflicts, it can be assumed that identifiers are only unique for sensors within each class produced by a manufacturer. Therefore, it is necessary to include this fact within the adopted nomenclature to produce Universally Unique IDentifiers (UUID). These UUIDs will incorporate the sensor identifier and then append the sensor class and manufacturer ID. An example of this is a contact switch sensor produced by Nexa corporation. This sensor has an ID of *19457978,* contact sensors are registered as device class *3* in the platform and the Nexa corporation is registered in the system as manufacturer *10*. The combination of these factors yields a UUID of *19457978_3_10*. Typically, these UUIDs are generated by sensor listeners written to communicate with the platform. These sensor listeners read sensor data, convert it to the platform's message format for sensor data and supply necessary metadata. This message format is JSON, enabling operability with the REST endpoint of the platform. The keys-value pairs of the JSON in the sensor message format is presented in Table 1.

Table 1. The message format for sensor data within the platform.

Key-value pair	Data type	Description
Event Code	Long	An enumeration representing the sensor state being transmitted. This could be 0 for off, 1 for on or 101 to refer to blob JSON. This is defined by the sensor listener and can be registered to the platform to serve as a reference
Sensor Class	Long	The registered class of a sensor, such as a contact sensor
Device Manufacturer	Long	The registered class of the sensor device manufacturer
Sensor UUID	String	The UUID of the sensor that generated the data
Timestamp	Long	The 'UNIX time' timestamp of the sensor reading, as determined by the listening device. This can be overwritten with a timestamp generated by the platform
Blob JSON	String	A string containing sensor specific data, such as a frame of thermal vision data

3.4   Sensor Management, Experimental Support and Annotation

The developed platform has several inbuilt features to ease research efforts. Many of these features were previously detailed in Sect. 3.1, however, some would benefit from more detailed explanation. These are sensor setup and reconfiguration, and experiment support and annotation mechanisms.

3.5   Sensor Setup and Configuration

Sensor setup is facilitated in through three primary mechanisms: sensor listeners, via the Web UI and NFC based management. When a sensor is initially discovered by a sensor listener, the listener may attempt to enroll it via a specific function of the REST interface. This function will process the metadata for that sensor and enroll it to the metadata records, if it does not already exist, otherwise, the registration request will be ignored. This provides a zero-configuration option for enrollment of sensors which may subsequently be modified through the Web UI. This Web UI also enables sensors to be enrolled manually by specification of necessary parameters. The Web UI that may be used to modify enrolled sensors or enroll new sensors is presented in Fig. 2.

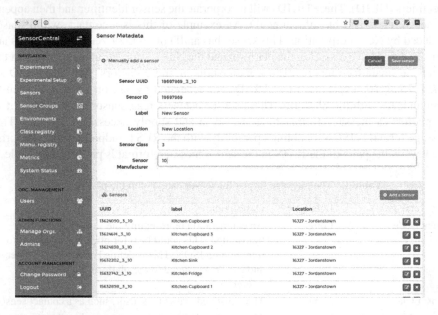

Fig. 2. The Web UI the platform offers enabling management of sensors. The enrollment of a new sensor is shown.

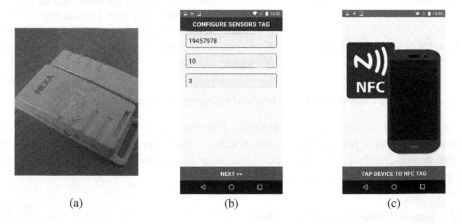

(a)   (b)   (c)

Fig. 3. Management of sensors in the platform through NFC tags. (a) depicts a contact sensor with a NFC tag affixed, (b) presents the tag configuration interface to enroll the sensor, (c) presents the prompt advising the user to tap the smartphone to the NFC tag to finish the configuration.

Finally, sensors may be managed and enrolled through use of a smartphone in combination with NFC tags. To enroll sensors, a NFC tag is affixed to, or placed close, them. Once the NFC tag is in place, a sensor management app installed onto a smartphone allows registration of the sensor ID, class and manufacturer. Figure 3 shows enrollment of a sensor. Once this has been registered to the NFC tag then it can subsequently read by the management app and may be reconfigured, Fig. 4 shows this management.

(a)

(b)

Fig. 4. Management of sensors in the platform through NFC tags. (a) presents the reconfiguration interface of the app after a NFC tag was tapped and (b) depicts the confirmation of a successful update operation.

The ability to quickly enroll and reconfigure sensors provides researchers with an avenue to quickly setup experiments, thus increasing efficiency.

4   Experimental Support and Annotation Mechanisms

The platform has features to support experiments and annotation. To support experiments, sensor groups, experimental setup and experiments may be defined. Sensors may be grouped into logical units such as rooms. Once defined, sensor groups may be incorporated into experimental setups alongside any written experimental protocol, ethics information, number of participants and any other metadata that is unlikely to change when instances of the experiment are run. Once the experimental setup is defined, it can be used within an experimental instance, this allows specification of further information such as date/time of experiment, the location of the experiment and details about the subject(s). Once created, the experimental instance can be used to annotate the start and end of experiments, through the Web UI. After the end of an experiment is annotated it is possible to provide a post-experiment report.

Through combining a list of sensors and experimental metadata it is possible to export full records of an experiment in order to collaborate with other researchers or facilitate replication of results. Currently exports produce a JSON document containing a list of sensor events, sensor metadata, experimental setup and metadata for experimental instance. The information provided in this JSON document is compatible with the ontological structure devised for data interchange within the ODI project [21].

Additionally, events of interest during an experiment may be annotated through the use of NFC tags that are placed within an environment and registered as annotation interfaces through a dedicated smartphone application. Once registered the meaning of these tags may be specified through the experimental setup. If the annotation application interacts with a NFC tag set up for annotation, it will record this event within the TSDB. Further information on this annotation mechanism is available in [15].

5   Use Cases

This platform has been in use for over 18 months and is central to more than 10 projects. The current active installation currently holds over 500 million sensor records. The substantial number of sensor records has not degraded the performance of the platform. These projects may use a subset of the functionality offered or all features.

One notable study has been where thermal vision sensors are used to monitor inhabitants of an environment, classify their behavior and generate alerts for behaviors of interest [17]. This behavioral alerting is performed via rules or supervised machine learning that is trained through annotations generated from interaction with NFC tags. This study relies upon all functionality of the project barring the data export feature.

Another study [27] uses this platform to store sensor data from accelerometers that are attached to variable seated-standing desks. This sensor data is used to determine the state of the standing desk, seated or standing, and if there are any vibrations characteristic of typing. This is used to characterize the use of such desks to provide metrics to give insight into adoption and utility of standing desks.

An additional study [28] has incorporated this platform to allow visualization and capturing of sensor actuations within an environment. Additionally, this study has developed to allow exporting of sensor activations in the platform to a data format devised by the ODI to facilitate meaningful exports of experimental data to facilitate collaboration within the research community.

Finally, an ongoing study incorporates all features of the platform to provide an assistive Smart Home solution to provide in home assistive services. These services include behavioral monitoring, alert generation and tracking the progression of conditions such as Alzheimer's Disease. This study is mid-phase but will ultimately supply the Smart Home solution to several care facility providers, across four trials in order to provide care for dozens of individuals.

This platform is central to a number of sensor based research efforts within the research group it has been initially developed in. Currently, discussions are underway to deploy this platform to other universities and research groups.

6   Conclusion

This study has produced a research oriented sensor data platform. This platform can integrate with sensors in a device agnostic manner, providing a central storage and processing platform. Currently 6 sensor classes from 13 vendors have been integrated.

Several research oriented features, such as offering annotations through a Web UI or companion app, metric generation, one-click exports of experimental datasets, machine learning services, rule based classification, forwarding live sensor records to independent systems and quick sensor configuration are incorporated to provide a flexible and efficient platform for research communities.

The solution has been proven through deployment within a research group for over 18 months. In this time, the platform has been incorporated into over 10 projects with the current active installation storing more than 500 million sensor records.

Future works will focus on providing use of this solution to the wider research community, initially through offering a service instance hosted by the parent research group with the aim of eventually open sourcing the codebase. Negotiations focused on deploying this platform with external universities are ongoing. Additionally, modifications will be made to integrate this platform into the ODI to offer simple exporting of experimental datasets to the wider research community.

Acknowledgments. Invest Northern Ireland is acknowledged for supporting this project under the Competence Centre Programs Grant RD0513853 – Connected Health Innovation Centre.

References

1. López-de-Ipiña, D., Chen, L., Jara, A., Mannens, E., Li, Y.: Internet of things, linked data, and citizen participation as enablers of smarter cities. Int. J. Distrib. Sens. Netw. **12**, 2595847 (2016)
2. Brush, A.J., Hong, J., Scott, J.: Pervasive Computing Moves in. IEEE Pervasive Comput. **15**, 14–15 (2016)
3. Patterson, D., Kautz, H., Fox, D., Liao, L.: Pervasive Computing in the Home and Community. CRC Press, Boca Raton (2007)
4. Kaisler, S., Armour, F., Espinosa, J.A., Money, W.: Big data: issues and challenges moving forward. In: 2013 46th Hawaii International Conference on System sciences. pp. 995–1004. IEEE (2013)
5. Sagiroglu, S., Sinanc, D.: Big data: a review. In: 2013 International Conference on Collaboration Technologies and Systems (CTS). pp. 42–47. IEEE (2013)
6. Aggarwal, C.C.: Managing and Mining Sensor Data. Springer, New York (2013). doi: 10.1007/978-1-4614-6309-2
7. Sowe, S.K., Kimata, T., Dong, M., Zettsu, K.: Managing heterogeneous sensor data on a big data platform: IoT services for Data-Intensive Science. In: 2014 IEEE 38th International Computer Software and Applications Conference Workshops, pp. 295–300. IEEE (2014)
8. Chen, M., Mao, S., Liu, Y.: Big data: A Survey. Mob. Networks Appl. **19**, 171–209 (2014)
9. Cheng, B., Longo, S., Cirillo, F., Bauer, M., Kovacs, E.: Building a big data platform for smart cities: experience and lessons from Santander. In: 2015 IEEE International Congress on Big Data. pp. 592–599. IEEE (2015)

10. Bonomi, F., Milito, R., Natarajan, P., Zhu, J.: Fog Computing: A Platform for Internet of Things and Analytics. Springer, Cham (2014). doi:10.1007/978-3-319-05029-4_7
11. Lee, T., Tso, M.: A universal sensor data platform modelled for realtime asset condition surveillance and big data analytics for railway systems: developing a "Smart Railway" mastermind for the betterment of reliability, availability, maintainbility and safety of railway systems and passenger service. In: 2016 IEEE Sensors. pp. 1–3. IEEE (2016)
12. Cecchinel, C., Jimenez, M., Mosser, S., Riveill, M.: An architecture to support the collection of big data in the internet of things. In: 2014 IEEE World Congress on Services. pp. 442–449. IEEE (2014)
13. IoT Analytics - ThingSpeak, https://thingspeak.com/
14. Beebotte, https://beebotte.com/
15. Rafferty, J., Synnott, J., Nugent, C., Morrison, G., Tamburini, E.: NFC Based dataset annotation within a behavioral alerting platform. In: 2017 IEEE International Conference on Pervasive Computing and Communications Workshops (PerCom Workshops). pp. 146–151. IEEE (2017)
16. Angular JS—Superheroic JavaScript MVW Framework, https://angularjs.org/
17. Rafferty, J., Synnott, J., Nugent, C.: A Hybrid Rule and Machine Learning Based Generic Alerting Platform for Smart Environments. In: 2016 38th Annual International Conference of the IEEE on Engineering in Medicine and Biology Society (EMBC), IEE (2016)
18. Neuroph, http://neuroph.sourceforge.net/
19. Frank, E., Hall, M.A., Witten, I.H.: The WEKA workbench. Online Appendix for "Data Mining: Practical Machine Learning Tools and Techniques". Morgan Kaufmann. 4th edn. (2016)
20. Bravo, J., López-De-Ipiña, D., Fuentes, C.: Enabling NFC technology for supporting chronic diseases: a proposal for alzheimer caregivers. Ambient Intell. 5355, 109–125 (2008)
21. Nugent, C., Synnott, J., Gabrielli, C., Zhang, S., Espinilla, M., Calzada, A., Lundstrom, J., Cleland, I., Synnes, K., Hallberg, J., Spinsante, S., Barrios, M.A.O.: In: 2016 IEEE International Conference on Improving the Quality of User Generated Data Sets for Activity Recognition. Presented at the IEEE (2016)
22. InfluxData (InfluxDB) - Open Source Time Series Database for Monitoring Metrics and Events, https://www.influxdata.com/
23. MongoDB for GIANT Ideas | MongoDB, https://www.mongodb.com/
24. Basha, S.K.J., Kumar, P.A., Babu, S.G.: Storage and processing speed for knowledge from enhanced cloud computing with Hadoop frame work: a survey. IJSRSET 2, 126–132 (2016)
25. Holzschuher, F., Peinl, R.: Querying a graph database – language selection and performance considerations. J. Comput. Syst. Sci. 82, 45–68 (2016)
26. Leighton, B., Cox, S.J.D., Car, N.J., Stenson, M.P., Vleeshouwer, J., Hodge, J.: A Best of Both Worlds Approach to Complex, Efficient, Time Series Data Delivery. Springer, Cham (2015). doi:10.1007/978-3-319-15994-2_37
27. Mair, J., Cleland, I., Nugent, C., Rafferty, J., Sant'Anna, A.: Sensorized workplaces for monitoring sedentary behavior. In: 2016 IEEE 38th International Conference on Engineering. in Medicine and Biology Sociery (EMBC), IEEE. (2016)
28. Synnott, J., Nugent, C., Zhang, S., Calzada, A., Cleland, I., Espinilla, M., Quero, J.M., Lundstrom, J.: Environment Simulation for the Promotion of the Open Data Initiative. In: 2016 IEEE International Conference on Smart Computing (SMARTCOMP), pp. 1–6. IEEE (2016)

Prosumerization Approach to Semantic Ambient Intelligence Platforms

Diego Martín[1]([✉]), Borja Bordel[1], Ramón Alcarria[2], Álvaro Sánchez-Picot[1],
Diego Sánchez de Rivera[1], and Tomás Robles[1]

[1] ETSI Telecommunications, Technical University of Madrid,
Av. Complutense 30, 28040 Madrid, Spain
{diego.martin.de.andres,tomas.robles}@upm.es, bbordel@dit.upm.es,
alvaro.spicot@gmail.com, diego.sanchezderiveracordoba@gmail.com
[2] ETSI Topography, Geodetics and Cartography, Technical University of Madrid,
Camino de la Arboleda s/n, 28031 Madrid, Spain
ramon.alcarria@upm.es

Abstract. Service creation and customization are expensive tasks that require specialists. In many cases these simple services could be implemented by domain experts with no programming abilities. This research work proposes the application of a prosumer model to facilitate access to information and creation of new knowledge to domain experts without experience in the use of semantic AmI platforms. This paper presents a prosumer tool called *DataQuest* to gather and analyze data from an AmI platform based on ontologies using simple services. An empirical study was carried out in order to demonstrate that, based on the defined prosumer model; a domain expert can create services with acceptable quality for a given domain. The authors performed a case study where 24 people used the prosumer tool to create simple services over a prosumer infrastructure for retrieving and analyzing data from a semantic AmI platform; the aim of this study consists of analyzing the quality of the services built and studying the effort needed to build prosumer services compared with traditional development.

Keywords: Prosumer · End-user development · Domain experts · AmI platforms · IoT ontologies · Empirical study

1 Introduction

The Internet of Things (IoT) enables efficient and seamless interconnectivity between a huge number of devices, empowering data consumers to access information and creating services over that information in an abstract way, and regardless of the heterogeneity of the underlying devices. The ontologies are a useful technique used to gather heterogeneous devices and access to their data in an agnostic way offering models and linked data sets; then, a gap between hardware infrastructure and high-level final applications appears.

© Springer International Publishing AG 2017
S.F. Ochoa et al. (Eds.): UCAmI 2017, LNCS 10586, pp. 109–120, 2017.
DOI: 10.1007/978-3-319-67585-5_12

These linked data sets offer data gathered from all the deployment regardless of underlying hardware technology.

Usually the ontology designed for interoperability is a composition of other more specific ontologies such as IoT-Lite, M3-Lite taxonomy, SSN and DUL; but it doesn't define classes and elements about data quality and data transmission provided by devices and deployments. This information, however, can be very useful for data consumers when they need to create data services on the platform. For example, a researcher using the platform needs to create a service to get the temperature from several deployments but only from specific AmI elements that guarantee a temporal availability over a specific value (e.g. sending data 95% of the time). In addition, the creation of services in a specific platform can be difficult for non-experts users. Taking the above example, the researcher has knowledge about his/her domain of expertise but has no knowledge about creating services using the platform.

In order to guide this research work three research questions were stated:

- **RQ1:** What is the quality of the services developed by prosumers?
- **RQ2:** Who are more efficient: prosumers or expert developers?

A case study was carried out by the authors in order to test our proposal showed in this paper; where 24 domain experts and six experts developers create some services running on the AmI heterogeneous platform. The validation consisted of studying the capacity of non-expert users to develop useful services for them and their community, comparing it with the development of the same services by experts in software development. The obtained results confirm that the solution proposed in this paper is feasible. Results are in a very preliminary version. However, they are very promising, as they allow us to find weaknesses in the proposal with the aim of improving the solution and the proposal validation in future experiments (Fig. 1).

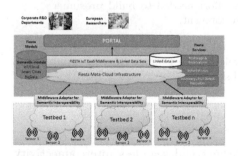

Fig. 1. Heterogeneous AmI platform based on ontologies.

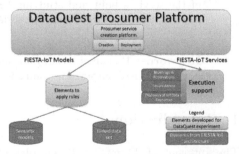

Fig. 2. DataQuest architecture (Color figure online)

2   Related Work

This research work proposal consists of gathering and analyzing data from AmI platforms based on ontologies, enabling users without technical knowledge to create simple services. This section presents a brief review of the state of the art where three main research areas were taken into account:

AmI Platforms Based on Ontologies. The ambient intelligence scenarios are characterized by heterogeneity [4]. Each vertical sector, such as Smart Cities, Transportation, Healthcare, energy, etc. uses domain specific technology solutions that cannot easily interoperate with one another. These specific solutions promote the creation of clusters of technology and data silos which cannot be exploited in other domains. There are several solutions to take advantage of the data among different specific developments or deployments [1]. One of the most used techniques are the semantic technologies, more specifically the ontologies, allowing the description of objects, setting all the data generated by the elements displayed in an AmI scenario, sharing and integrating information, as well as the inference of new knowledge [6].

User Involvement in Service Co-creation. Co-creation is defined by Prahalad and Ramaswamy [10] as a business strategy that emphasizes the generation and on-going realization of mutual firm-customer value. Thus, new forms of interaction between firms and customers are defined to create Value, as a combination of resources and services. Vargo and Lusch [13] proposed the Service-Dominant Logic to explain how a person who receives a service recognizes the value of the received service. S-D Logic determines service value as "the comparative appreciation of reciprocal skills or services that are exchanged to obtain utility". Prosumer service creation produces several benefits for companies and customers. Companies benefit from customer satisfaction: Golinelli [3] concludes in his work that value cannot be seen from a partial perspective of corporate benefit, but rather as the synergistic results of cooperative processes that generate satisfaction and benefits for every entity.

Frameworks Enabling Service Prosumerization. Some works deal with the concept of end-user development and prosumer and the difficulty of offering tools according to their experience. Among the service creation tools that provide different creation strategies [8,9] we studied some semi-automatic solutions that require additional investment from end-users [12]. We highlighted the tools that consist of component interconnection such as mashup tools, which facilitate the definition of execution sequences of services by end-users. There are several research works proposing visual frameworks where domain experts can be involved in the development life cycle. For example, DiaSuite toolkit [2] offers a domain-specific design language and a specific compiler for this language. Another example is the OPEN framework [5], a programming environment for rapid prototyping based on ontologies of context-aware applications which helps creating semantic rules in order to trigger predefined actions.

Conclusions. The AmI scenarios are complex (among other reasons) due to the number of elements involved in those deployments and their heterogeneity; and a very powerful solution to be able to make these deployments interoperable in an agnostic way is to use an ontology that groups information among domains, allowing to infer new knowledge. However end users who want to use the ontology-based platforms are specialists in their own domains but they are not specialists in ontology query techniques [11] such as SPARQL if they want to use the platform querying data or inferring new knowledge. The creation of services harnessing the full power offered by a semantic AmI platform can be easily and visually performed by users with no special skills about its architecture if a Prosumer Platform is offered to them; where they can create, deploy and share services which run over the semantic platform.

3   Approach to Semantic Ambient Intelligence Platforms Prosumerization

In this section it is proposed a Prosumer framework for easy service creation by end users with no experience creating and deploying services over a semantic AmI platform taking advantage of knowledge from several AmI deployments domains. This Prosumer platform will enable the creation of services where any person with no knowledge about ontologies, models, service composition or AmI architecture; can create visually functional services for running them over a semantic AmI platform regardless of the testbeds that are bellow, and allowing services portability across platforms. This Prosumer framework offers the services creation and deployment, and also the design of service templates allowing services portability from one environment to another in just a click, optimizing the performances of services running, as well as the data consumed itself by each service. This platform will allow the consumption and use of data from the a semantic AmI platform in a much more accessible and flexible way for end users; making it a "deployment-Agnostic query" system. We called this Prosumer framework *"Dataquest"*. This research work and development is being conducted by the FIESTA-IoT[1] from the European Horizon 2020 Programme.

3.1   FIESTA-IoT

FIESTA-IoT (Federated Interoperable Semantic IoT Testbeds and Applications) is a research project from the European Horizon 2020 Programme which its main aim is to share and reuse data form diverse IoT deployments in a flexible way. FIESTA-IoT integrates several IoT platforms, deployments (also called testbeds), it open up new chances in the research, development and deployment of research works that take advantage of data and capabilities. FIESTA-IoT aggregates four core deployments which are SmartSantander[2] (a large-scale Smart

---

[1] http://fiesta-iot.eu/.
[2] http://www.smartsantander.eu/.

City deployment), SmartICS[3] (a smart environment, based on an indoor sensors nodes deployment), SoundCity[4] (a large-scale crowd-sensing testbed) and KETI[5] (a indoor and outdoor building smart environment deployment). The project FIESTA-IoT proposes an ontology that aims to achieve semantic interoperability among heterogeneous deployments, allowing to seamlessly support the federation of testbeds using semantic-based technologies [6].

For this research, we are going to focus on a very small part of the ontology proposed by FIESTA-IoT; considering the following elements: deployments, devices, and observations. The data model used in this research; where a deployment is an aggregation of devices, and a devices have many observations.

3.2   DataQuest

DataQuest is a web portal where a non-expert in FIESTA-IoT architecture nor experts in the AmI platform architecture can easily develop services over the FIESTA-IoT platform also taking advantage about the information and data offered by the FIESTA-IoT ontology. User participation is a new trend today. Participants in this environment evolve from content consumers, who use the FIESTA-IoT platform to find for important information for their work and research and also to produce new knowledge and create services, making them available to other users. Figure 2 shows in red the elements developed in this research work, while blue elements show the assets where our proposal will be supported from FIESTA-IoT architecture. Our research exploits semantic technologies not only for the provision of interoperability among federated testbeds but also due to the potential of these technologies in the derivation of further higher-level knowledge. DataQuest offers a visual web front-end programmed using HTML5, CSS3 and JavaScript; in order to facilitate end users the creation and deployment their own services in a simple way. DataQuest has two different operating environments: service creation and service provision environment; both are based on ECA [7] (event, condition, action) rules. But in our previous research [8] we demonstrated that "condition" elements generated confusion and modeling problems for users. We have decided to remove this element and the rules are composed by two elements: an Event as an occurrence triggering the action.

Using the service creation tool, a prosumer can create a service joining an event with an action visually as shown in Fig. 3. A prosumer can create two kinds of services:

– services for information gathering and aggregation (Fig. 3).
– and services to alert when a device obtains a specific data.

At the moment we have designed a closed set of events that can trigger an action, this set of events will be increased as DataQuest requirements increase.

---

[3] https://www.surrey.ac.uk/ics/.
[4] https://mimove.inria.fr/soundcity/.
[5] http://www.keti.re.kr/.

These events depend on information obtained in real time through the FIESTA-IoT query system, that is, the set of deployments, devices and observations that DataQuest offers to its users are obtained on running time by asking SPARQL questions to the queries systems of FIESTA-IoT. A user can configure an event when the FIESTA-IoT ontology provides information about the creation or deletion of a specific deployment, when a device is created or deleted within a deployment, or when a device provides new observations within a specific deployment.

The actions developed for DataQuest, like the set of events, are a closed set but can be added more as requirements grow. An action can be:

- An alert, being able to report with an email or SMS when a device has reached a specific value or has exceeded a threshold or when a deployment or device appears or disappears from the ontology.
- A subscription to the values that a specific device generates, to receive that information in a simpler and aggregated form in a set of values.
- Statistical values on the observations of a particular device in a specific period, such as the mean, median, standard deviation, etc.

Each of the rules are transformed into a SPARQL query with a specific execution frequency. This query (and its execution frequency) is sent to the "FIESTA-IoT service execution support system", which returns the results of the SPARQL query with the indicated frequency to DataQuest "service provision environment".

The service provision environment consists of an visual web application dashboard (see Fig. 4) where a prosumer can start, pause, stop, resume, modify and delete rules running over the "FIESTA-IoT service execution support system". We also call it DataQuest engine, since it is a server that is responsible for the execution of each of the rules created and to attend to the requests with the results of SPARQL queries from "FIESTA-IoT service execution support system".

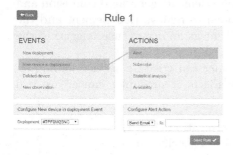

Fig. 3. Screenshot of Prosumer rule creation for alert

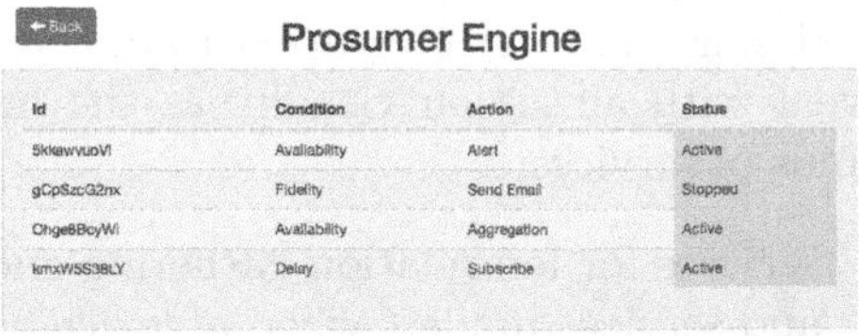

Fig. 4. Screenshot of Prosumer Engine controlling all the rules created

4 Experimental Validation

In order to guide this research work we will use the three research questions presented in the introduction. An experimental validation was carried out in order to address these research questions. During the experimentation step, it was proposed to prosumers the creation of four different services to solve four specific problems using DataQuest. The quality of the services created by the prosumers using DataQuest were analyzed and several specialists made estimations of the cost needed (in terms of time) to develop such services by a software development organization.

4.1 Context

Twenty-four people (hereafter, participants) at Technical University of Madrid carried out the empirical study using DataQuest. These people are first year telecommunications engineering students and were collaborating with the GISAI group at Technical University of Madrid; creating four different services. To evaluate whether prosumers were efficient creating the services, the experts reviewed each services created by the participants, testing them in a simulated environment created for this experiment. A full factorial experimental design was followed where all 24 participants created four services.

4.2 Planning

The experiment was divided into three phases:

- *Training phase*: The participants were trained in the principles of service creation using a prosumer environment using DataQuest. The training sessions consisted of 2 h of theory at the beginning of the experiment execution and personal interviews to solve specific issues raised by the participants during the services creation.
- *Service creation phase*: During this phase, each participant had to create four services for solving the four problems proposed by the experts; these services were:
    - Subscribe to all observations generated by a device with a daily frequency.
    - Calculate the median of all observations generated by a device with a daily frequency.
    - Create an alert that sends an email when a device ceases to exist in the FIESTA-IoT system.
    - Create an alert that sends an sms when a new deployment appears on the FIESTA-IoT system.

    These services were created in random order by each of the participants.
- *Services evaluation phase*: All the services created by the participants were evaluated by the experts who assigned a quality score to each one. In this phase the participants also assessed DataQuest by means of a survey.

4.3   Data Collection

To address the first research question it was necessary to conduct a study on the quality of the services created by the prosumers. The experts managing the experiment evaluated all the services created using DataQuest and assessed the quality of the services elements used by the participants to build each service. The quality evaluations were performed after the services prepared by the participants were delivered.

– The time spent by participants to create the services. The experts carrying out the experiment analyzed the log files created by DataQuest when the participants created the services with a semiautomatic tool in order to determine the building time of each service.
– The estimated time required to create the services by a software development organization. These estimations were made by a group of six experts; four of them belong to an software development oriented SME and with wide experience in estimating projects using agile methodologies, such as SCRUM and XP. The other two experts who made the estimations are two of the authors of this work, who have experience in cost estimation in software engineering and estimations techniques like COCOMO or COSYSMO.

The data collected to address the third research objective were the subjective satisfaction evaluation of the participants obtained through an anonymous survey filled up at the services evaluation phase by the participants.

5   Result

This section presents and discusses the results obtained in the experimental validation and will be presented according to the research questions proposed in this work.

Analysis of the Quality of the Services Developed by Prosumers. Table 1 summarizes the average quality of the services built by the prosumers during "service creation phase", ranked from 0 to 5.

The results obtained indicate that the global quality of services built were good but depended on the difficulty of the requirements for each service. In the case of the third and fourth services, low quality scores were obtained. The questions that obtained the best scores for quality were those that measure the quality of the feedback reported by the tool when an action occurs, and the ability to solve the problem posed by the requirements of the service. The reason for these good scores for the variable "Quality of feedback" was that the messages are intended to be read by a human. Thus, nearly all the messages in natural language were understood and evaluated as positive. The reason for positive values for the variable that measures problem resolution by the service was that most of the services solve the problem. It should be borne in mind that products created by prosumers may have more errors than those developed by professional experts.

Table 1. Summary of the quality of the service built

	First service		Second service		Third service		Fourth service		Total	
	Mean	SD	Mean	SD	Mean	SD	Mean	SD	Mean	SD
Problem resolution	3.72	1.47	2.56	1.78	3.31	1.38	1.73	1.72	2.93	1.75
Service accuracy	3.16	1.42	1.99	1.39	2.59	1.21	1.24	1.3	2.24	1.49
Test results	2.68	1.25	1.65	1.23	2.27	1.53	0.91	1.15	1.88	1.44
Quality of feedback	4.14	1.39	2.86	1.95	4.15	1.06	1.76	1.92	3.23	1.89
Quality aggregate	3.34	1.28	2.21	1.51	3.14	1.23	1.33	1.32	2.5	1.54

Figure 5 shows the distributions of the quality aggregate scores for the total and for each service quality. The first service obtained the best scores for quality, with more than 90.90% of the services above 5 and a narrow value for the standard deviation; meaning that the quality is very predictable and it is easy to obtain in a prosumer environment.

The second and third services obtained very similar values for the mean, but although the third service obtained a slightly higher mean of 70.83%, the second one obtained 100% of the scores above 5. As shown in Fig. 5 the standard deviation for the second service is very narrow (0.98), while the standard deviation for the third one is very wide (2.45). This means that quality for the second service is more predictable than the first service; the quality is easily obtained with a prosumer environment whenever the difficulty is accessible to the prosumers. The fourth service got lower scores on quality, only 46.66% of the services exceeded 5 points. The quality scores were very low for this service because it is the most difficult to build. As stated above, in a prosumer environment, the prosumers can achieve high quality products as long as it is not too difficult for them.

Analysis of Who is More Efficient: Prosumers or Expert Developers.
A study of the time required to build a service using a prosumer environment was carried out, analyzing the time spent by the prosumers using DataQuest and comparing it with estimations made by code development experts in a

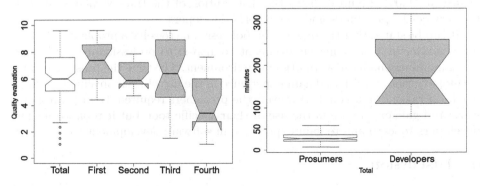

Fig. 5. Distributions of services quality   **Fig. 6.** Distributions of time spent in creating the services

traditional environment; both met the same requirements. A summary of the time (measured in minutes) required to build and develop services is shown in Table 2. The values of the mean, median and standard deviations for services building time are shown for both groups. As explained in Sect. 4.3, the prosumers received two hours of training; this training time has not been taken into consideration to measure services building time, nor was the time taken by the expert developers for the taking of requirements, analysis and design. In other words, the time measured for the prosumers was the time taken to build each service while the time measured for developers was the estimation of the time they would take to develop the services.

Table 2. Summary of the time spent in creating the services

	Prosumers			Developers		
	Mean	Median	SD	Mean	Median	SD
Time to build first service	19	18	6.09	195	200	102.47
Time to build second service	25.92	25.5	6.36	190	170	88.32
Time to build third service	30.58	30.5	7.59	177.5	185	96.05
Time to build fourth service	37.37	38	9.84	202.5	190	104.04
Time to build all services	28.22	27	10.08	191.25	170	88.08

The prosumers took considerably less time to build services. Moreover, the building time increases slightly depending on the difficulty of the service. However, the development time that developers took remains practically constant in the four services, and the same happens with the standard deviation. This means that the difficulty affects the prosumers as they are not professional developers, while a slight increase in the difficulty of the services does not require more time for developers. A Mann-Whitney U test was conducted to confirm that the prosumers take less time to build a service. The results are positive and support the previous assertion. The results of the test were within the expected significance, $\rho < 0.001$. Figure 6 shows the distribution of the time spent in creating the services by prosumers and the experts developers.

It can be stated that the prosumers took less time to solve a problem by building a service in a prosumer environment compared to professionals developing the same functionality in a traditional environment. The time the prosumers and developers took to learn and gain experience in the use of their specific tools has not been taken into account. However, the prosumers required 2 h of training to learn and gain experience in the use of their specific tool, but it took longer for developers to learn and to gain experience in software development tools.

6   Discussion

In this research work we present DataQuest, this framework constitutes a new approach for creating and managing services for new functionalities built by prosumers, enabling end-users to take advantage of this new kind of development. With this approach users and prosumers can create and control simple services for extract, analysis information from semantic AmI scenarios. This section will be also guided by the three research questions stated in this work.

Quality of the Services Developed in the Prosumer Environment. The statistical study carried out in the experimental validation indicates that the quality of the services in general is good but it depends on the difficulty of the requirements of the problem to solve using the prosumer environment. In this way prosumers can create their own services but always taking into account that the prosumer environment must be clear and easy to configure. Simpler services have been those who have obtained better quality scores, however the most complex ones have not been easily implemented by prosumers. This was the first time that participants faced the creation of prosumer services; we believe that with practice and more training they will create better services and more complex. DataQuest is a very useful tool but is still undergoing testing and improvements. We believe, following comments from participants of the experiment; if a more intuitive tool is offered, the results in the quality of the services developed will be better. This would be very interesting issue to be studied as a future work. In terms of quality we can conclude that a prosumer environment is not as flexible as developing the functionality by experts but is more efficient, this issue is analyzed in the next point.

Who is More Efficient: Prosumers of Expert Developers? The results obtained during the validation of DataQuest platform indicate that the time spent by prosumers is considerably less than the time needed by a professional developer or an SME to implement the same functionality. In terms of average time spent in building the four services, prosumers take more than six times less than a professional developers. This work does not take into account the correspondence of time spent with costs because it is very difficult to estimate, but it is reasonable to think that this approach may save time and money. One issue that should be studied is the cost of developing and maintaining a prosumer platform like DataQuest, since obviously the development of a prosumer platform is costly at first.

This research work can conclude that prosumer environments are a reliable solution where end-users and domain experts can evolve to prosumers enabling them to create their own functionality in a platform where they are experts; allowing the reduction of development costs; always taking into account that the problems they can solve must be simple and that a prosumer service does not offer the same flexibility of professional development.

Acknowledgement. The research leading to these results has received funding from FIESTA-IoT 1st Open Call and the Ministry of Economy and Competitiveness through SEMOLA project (TEC2015-68284- R).

References

1. Barnaghi, P., Wang, W., Henson, C., Taylor, K.: Semantics for the internet of things: early progress and back to the future. Int. J. Semant. Web Inf. Syst. (IJSWIS) **8**(1), 1–21 (2012)
2. Bertran, B., Bruneau, J., Cassou, D., Loriant, N., Balland, E., Consel, C.: Diasuite: a tool suite to develop sense/compute/control applications. Sci. Comput. Program. **79**, 39–51 (2014)
3. Golinelli, G.M., Barile, S., Spohrer, J., Bassano, C.: The evolving dynamics of service co-creation in a viable systems perspective. In: Toulon-Verona Conference "Excellence in Services" (2015)
4. Gubbi, J., Buyya, R., Marusic, S., Palaniswami, M.: Internet of Things (IoT): a vision, architectural elements, and future directions. Future Gener. Comput. Syst. **29**(7), 1645–1660 (2013)
5. Guo, B., Zhang, D., Imai, M.: Toward a cooperative programming framework for context-aware applications. Pers. Ubiquit. Comput. **15**(3), 221–233 (2011)
6. Gyrard, A., Serrano, M., Atemezing, G.A.: Semantic web methodologies, best practices and ontology engineering applied to internet of things. In: 2015 IEEE 2nd World Forum on Internet of Things (WF-IoT), pp. 412–417. IEEE (2015)
7. Martín, D., López-de Ipiña, D., Alzua-Sorzabal, A., Lamsfus, C., Torres-Manzanera, E.: A methodology and a web platform for the collaborative development of context-aware systems. Sensors **13**(5), 6032–6053 (2013)
8. Martin, D., Alcarria, R., Robles, T., Morales, A.: A systematic approach for service prosumerization in IoT scenarios. In: 2013 Seventh International Conference on Innovative Mobile and Internet Services in Ubiquitous Computing (IMIS), pp. 494–499. IEEE (2013)
9. Martín, D., Alcarria, R., Robles, T., Sánchez-Picot, Á.: Prosumer framework for knowledge management based on prosumer service patterns. Int. J. Software Eng. Knowl. Eng. **26**(07), 1145–1173 (2016)
10. Prahalad, C.K., Ramaswamy, V.: The co-creation connection. Strategy and Business, pp. 50–61 (2002)
11. Robles, T.S., Alcarria, R., Morales, A., Martín, D.: Supporting variability dependencies for rule-based service compositions in prosumer environments. Int. J. Web Grid Serv. **11**(1), 57–77 (2015)
12. Soriano, J., Lizcano, D., Hierro, J.J., Reyes, M., Schroth, C., Janner, T.: Enhancing user-service interaction through a global user-centric approach to SOA. In: Fourth International Conference on Networking and Services, ICNS 2008, pp. 194–203. IEEE (2008)
13. Vargo, S.L., Lusch, R.F.: Evolving to a new dominant logic for marketing. J. Mark. **68**(1), 1–17 (2004)

Modeling the Origin-Destination Matrix with Incomplete Information

Rodrigo René Cura[1,2($\boxtimes$)], Romina Stickar[1], Claudio Delrieux[1,3], Fernando Tohmé[3], Leo Ordinez[1], and Damián Barry[1]

[1] LINVI - UNPSJB, Bvd. Brown, 3051 Puerto Madryn, Argentina
romistickar@gmail.com, cad@uns.edu.ar, leo.ordinez@gmail.com,
demian.barry@gmail.com
[2] IPCSH - CENPAT - CONICET, Bvd. Brown, 2915 Puerto Madryn, Argentina
rodrigo.renecura@gmail.com
[3] UNS - CONICET, Av. Alem, 1253 Bahía Blanca, Argentina
ftohme@gmail.com
http://www.madryn.unp.edu.ar/, http://www.cenpat-conicet.gob.ar/ipcsh/,
http://www.uns.edu.ar/

Abstract. Different methods exist for the estimation of trips in public transportation systems based on automatized fare collection data. Some of the widely adopted estimation strategies are based on the traceability of passenger transfers. They may be effective in large cities, but fall short for trip estimation of single-routes, which are mostly the case in small-to-medium cities. We present a model to estimate the Origin-Destination Matrix, independent of transfers and passenger identification, using only boarding and alighting counts. The model is based on a system of linear diophantine equations, together with a method that computes the general solution and reduces the evaluation space, achieving useful estimations in polynomial time.

Keywords: Transportation · Origin-Destination Matrix · Dynamic estimation

1 Motivation

Transportation is perhaps the most important factor in urban planning, and therefore an adequate assessment of public transportation systems is essential for a comprehensive city organization. However, this assessment presents difficulties, in particular related to the estimation of current and future mobility requirements. Urban growth is usually not accompanied by a sensible reconfiguration of public transportation infrastructure, which in turn leads to a significant decrease in the actual and perceived quality of transportation services [1]. Large cities have public transportation networks combining different kinds of transportation means, for instance subways, buses and trains. The widespread use of card-based fare collection systems produces relevant information that can be

© Springer International Publishing AG 2017
S.F. Ochoa et al. (Eds.): UCAmI 2017, LNCS 10586, pp. 121–127, 2017.
DOI: 10.1007/978-3-319-67585-5_13

mined to estimate urban mobility patterns. For example, if a user consistently uses the same card along a period of time, useful transportation parameters like daily uses, waiting times, as well as transfer times and places can be easily gathered. This information, collected in massive amounts, together with reasonable assumptions, provides detailed parameters to assess the efficiency of the transportation network as a whole, as well as to spot specific bottlenecks and suggest policies to handle contingencies [2–4]. Another source of information is based on sensors that count how many passengers board or alight a given cart, and thus provide direct information on the amount of passengers at any given point of the route. A key element in this analysis is the information about round-trips, since transportation in working days is used mostly by workers, students, and people subject to fixed schedules. On the other hand, one-way only information is of little or no use at all. Unfortunately, this is the only information available in small towns, where no subway infrastructure is available, and therefore buses are the major (or only) public transportation system. In this case, users do not transfer between different bus lines, and therefore round-trip assumptions are harder to figure out. Then, the only feasible means of assessing the use of the transportation network is tracking the amount of passengers along the routes, and then estimating the origin-destination matrix. Since most of the literature is focused on the transportation models of large cities, this latter perspective is seldom considered, and very few prior work on this topic can be gathered.

In this paper we develop a model to estimate an origin-destination matrix based only on counting the boarding and alighting of passengers at each stop, without requiring individual per-passenger tracking. The structure of the paper is as follows. In Sect. 2 we review related works. In 3 we state the formal definition of the model of the system. Next, in 4 we present a strategy for finding the space of solutions. Finally, in 5 we summarize the results and briefly describe future lines of research.

2   Related Work

Urban transportation systems research has gained momentum in the last couple of decades, given the availability of huge amounts of data collected through the use of different kinds of smart cards. Cards offer an opportunity for measuring and analysing different aspects of transportation dynamics and their related social, economical and urban planning implications. In [4] the authors make a contribution to closing the gap between the availability of data and its useful exploitation. An important aspect highlighted in that article, and also in [5], is the difficulties involved in the estimation of alightings based on smart card data, given that usually these systems register only boardings. In [5] the authors build a mathematical model aimed to determine the alightings of passengers based on the same assumptions as in [6], in which the main focus is to find routine roundtrips as chains of multiple single-route trips. This technique is further improved in [2], where the authors present a method for the construction of a Origin-Destination Matrix (OD Matrix) for the Transantiago multimodal transport system, by optimizing different objective functions, mainly related to waiting and interarrival times. Finally, Nagy [7] states a series of assumptions for the construction of the OD matrix, stating that without these assumptions the models are imprecise.

The aforementioned research relies on the correct identification of *transfers*, and for this it is critical to track the behavior of individual passengers. Consequently, these strategies are dependant on identifying the ownership of smart cards, an information which is not always available. Moreover, the literature conceives commutes as chains of several direct trips. This is a valid assumption in large cities with complex interconnected networks, but it is not the case of small and medium size cities, where multi-route trips are not usual. The latter cases have not yet been thoroughly discussed in the literature. The main contribution of this paper is the development of a model focusing on small-to-medium cities, based only on passenger counts instead of specific data on boardings and alightings.

3   The Model

A bus route R can be identified with the class $\{s_k\}_{k=1,\ldots,\mathcal{N}}$, where each s_k is a bus stop, and $\mathcal{N}$ the number of stops. The class of possible trips in the route is $T = \{(s_i, s_j) \mid i < j\}$. Each pair (s_i, s_j) indicates, respectively, the boarding and alighting stops. The number of boarding and alighting passengers is given by $F = \{f_B, f_A\}$, where $f_B : R \to \mathbb{R}^+$ and $f_A : R \to \mathbb{R}^+$ are the information functions that provide the number of up and down passengers, respectively, at each particular stop.

This information structure can be captured in a directed weighted graph of the form $G = \langle R, T, w \rangle$ where w is an unknown function such that $w : T \to \mathbb{R}^+$ and $w(t)$ is the number of passengers that go from s_i to s_j given $t = (s_i, s_j)$. Our goal is to find an estimation of w, $\widehat{w}$, given the information summarized in F. The estimation approximates a matrix of the form $M_w = [w(t)]_{\mathcal{N} \times \mathcal{N}}$, where each cell $w_{i,j}$ of M_w indicates the value of $w(t)$ for $t = (s_i, s_j)$. We call the matrix M_w *OD Matrix*, while we seek to find $\widehat{M_w} = [\widehat{w}(t)]_{\mathcal{N} \times \mathcal{N}}$, the *Estimated OD Matrix*.

Let $\mathcal{K}$ be the bus capacity and $P(k)$ the number of passengers on-board after leaving s_k. It is clear that

$$P(k) = \begin{cases} f_B(k) & \text{if } k = 1 \\ P(k-1) + f_B(k) - f_A(k) & \text{if } 1 < k < \mathcal{N} \\ 0 & \text{if } k = \mathcal{N} \end{cases} \quad (1)$$

Note that the functions $f_B(k)$, $f_A(k)$ and $P(k)$ satisfy the following conditions:

- $0 \leq P(k) \leq \mathcal{K}$ for all k.
- $0 \leq f_B(k) \leq \mathcal{K}$ for all k, and $f_B(\mathcal{N}) = 0$. No passengers board on the last stop.
- $0 \leq f_A(k) \leq P(k-1)$ for all k, given that it is not possible to alight more passengers than those on-board after s_k. Also, $f_A(1) = 0$ and $f_A(\mathcal{N}) = P(\mathcal{N}-$

1). The last restriction establishes that all passengers leave the bus at the last stop.

Observation 1. $f_B(k) \leq \mathcal{K} + f_A(k) - P(k-1)$. *That is, on one hand, the number of passengers that board the bus cannot exceed the available space in the bus, and on the other, no more than the on-board passengers can alight.*

Linear equations for f_B: To find $\hat{w}$ the first step is to establish how the function f_B is related to the values of M_w. Formally, for each $k = 1, \ldots, \mathcal{N}$

$$f_B(k) = \sum_{w_{i,j} \in \varPhi(k)} w_{i,j} \quad \text{where} \quad \varPhi(k) = \{w_{i,j} \mid i = k \land j > k\}. \tag{2}$$

Notice that $|\cup_{k=1}^{\mathcal{N}} \varPhi(k)| = \frac{\mathcal{N}(\mathcal{N}-1)}{2}$. Then, $\cup_{k=1}^{\mathcal{N}} \varPhi(k)$ can be endowed with a lexicographic order: $(i,j) \preceq (i',j')$ iff $(i < i')$ or, if $i = i'$, $j < j'$). This order is linear and thus there exists a one-to-one function flat : $\{1, \ldots, \frac{\mathcal{N}(\mathcal{N}-1)}{2}\} \to \langle \cup_{k=1}^{\mathcal{N}} \varPhi(k), \preceq \rangle$. Then, for any $h \in \{1, \ldots, \frac{\mathcal{N}(\mathcal{N}-1)}{2}\}$, flat$(h) = (i,j)$, such that (i,j) is the h-th element in $\cup_{k=1}^{\mathcal{N}} \varPhi(k)$. Then, given $V = [v_{k,h}]$, a matrix of size $\mathcal{N} \times \frac{\mathcal{N}(\mathcal{N}-1)}{2}$, (2) can be expressed as a system of linear equations of the form:

$$V\mathbf{x} = [f_B(k)]_{\mathcal{N} \times 1} \quad \text{with} \quad v_{k,h} = \begin{cases} 1 \; if \; w_{\text{flat}(h)} \in \varPhi(k) \\ 0 \; otherwise. \end{cases} \tag{3}$$

Linear equation system for f_A: Similarly, the relation of f_A with M_w is given by:

$$f_A(k) = \sum_{w_{i,j} \in \varXi(k)} w_{i,j} \quad \text{where} \quad \varXi(k) = \{w_{i,j} \mid i < k \land j = k\}, \tag{4}$$

Given $U = [u_{k,h}]$, also a matrix of size $\mathcal{N} \times \frac{\mathcal{N}(\mathcal{N}-1)}{2}$ and defining flat$':\{1, \ldots, \frac{\mathcal{N}(\mathcal{N}-1)}{2}\} \to \langle \cup_{k=1}^{\mathcal{N}} \varXi(k), \preceq \rangle$ (where $\preceq$ is a linear ordering, defined lexicographically, of $\cup_{k=1}^{\mathcal{N}} \varXi(k)$) (4) can be expressed as a system of linear equations of the form:

$$U\mathbf{x} = [f_A(k)]_{\mathcal{N} \times 1} \quad \text{with} \quad u_{k,h} = \begin{cases} 1 \; if \; w_{\text{flat}'(h)} \in \varXi(k) \\ 0 \; otherwise. \end{cases} \tag{5}$$

A general model: A general system of linear equations for the entire model combines the aforementioned systems, as follows:

$$\left[\frac{V}{U} \right] \mathbf{x} = \left[\frac{[f_B(k)]}{[f_A(k)]} \right]. \tag{6}$$

A sequence of simplifying steps yields:

$$A\mathbf{x} = \mathbf{b} \quad \text{with} \quad \mathbf{b} = \left[\frac{[f_B(k_1)]}{[f_A(k_2)]} \right]. \tag{7}$$

where A is obtained from $\left[\frac{V}{U} \right]$ eliminating the null and redundant rows. The arguments on the right-hand side of (7) vary with $k_1 = 2, \ldots, \mathcal{N} - 1$ and $k_2 =$

$1, \ldots, \mathcal{N} - 1$. A is a block matrix of size $(2\mathcal{N} - 3) \times \frac{\mathcal{N}(\mathcal{N}-1)}{2}$, and $\mathbf{b}$ is a column matrix with $2\mathcal{N}-3$ rows. Since the rank of the system is $2\mathcal{N}-3$ but the number of variables is $\frac{\mathcal{N}(\mathcal{N}-1)}{2}$, the system is consistent but underdetermined. In particular, we know that M_w is a particular solution of the general system.

4   Finding Solutions

Our goal now is to establish a strategy to select one of the solutions of the system and derive $\widehat{M_w} \simeq M_w$. A general solution of the system can be found applying a process summarized in [8]. If $\mathbb{Z}$ denotes the ring of integers, $M_{n,m}(\mathbb{Z}), 1 \leq n \leq m$, is the ring of all $n \times m$ integer matrices, while $SL_r(\mathbb{Z})$ is the set of all square $r \times r$ matrices with integer entries and determinant 1 or -1 (*unimodular* matrices). By $D = diag(d_1, d_2, \ldots, d_n) \in M_{n,m}(\mathbb{Z})$ we denote the diagonal matrix that has an integer d_i in the (i, i) entry, $i = 1, \ldots, n$, and zeros elsewhere. Then we have the following:

Theorem 1. *Let $A \in M_{n,m}(\mathbb{Z})$. There exists $L \in SL_n(\mathbb{Z})$ and $R \in SL_m(\mathbb{Z})$ such that*

$$LAR = D = diag(d_1, d_2, \ldots, d_s, 0, \ldots, 0),$$

where $d_i > 0$, $i = 1, \ldots, s$, and d_i is divisible by d_{i+1} for $i = 1, \ldots, (s - 1)$.

The matrix D can be found using elementary operations on rows and columns of A, and matrices L and R obtain by composing these operations. Though matrices L and R in Theorem 1 may vary, the matrix D is uniquely defined by A and it is called the *Smith normal form* of A. Given $A\mathbf{x} = \mathbf{b}$, we can rewrite it as $D\mathbf{y} = \mathbf{c}$ with $R\mathbf{y} = \mathbf{x}$, $LAR = D$ and $\mathbf{c} = L\mathbf{b}$. A general solution of $D\mathbf{y} = \mathbf{c}$ can be given in the form $\mathbf{y} = (y_1, \ldots, y_s, t_1, \ldots, t_{(m-s)})$, where $y_i = c_i/d_i, i = 1, \ldots, s$, where $t_1, \ldots, t_{(m-s)}$ are free integer parameters. Then the general solution of $A\mathbf{x} = \mathbf{b}$ is just $R\mathbf{y}$.

For computing solutions, recall from (7) that in the model defined here $A \in M_{n,m}(\{0, 1\})$, then $d_i = 1$ for $i = 1, \ldots, s$; it also ensues that $s = n$. Let $\mathbf{x}_p, \mathbf{y}_p$ and $\mathbf{t}_p$ be particular cases of $\mathbf{x}, \mathbf{y}$ and $\mathbf{t}$ respectively. From Theorem 1 we have $\mathbf{y}_p = \begin{bmatrix} \mathbf{c} \\ \mathbf{t}_p \end{bmatrix}$ and $\mathbf{x}_p = R\mathbf{y}_p$. Since $\mathbf{c}$ is fixed for all p, we can define a stepwise computation of $\mathbf{x}_p$ starting from a partition of R such that $R = [R_1 \mid R_2]$ with $R_1 \in M_{m,n}(\mathbb{Z})$ and $R_2 \in M_{m,(m-n)}(\mathbb{Z})$. Therefore, given that $\mathbf{c} = L\mathbf{b}$

$$\mathbf{x}_p = R_1 L\mathbf{b} + R_2 \mathbf{t}_p \tag{8}$$

Since $\mathbf{b}$ is the input data, we have to compute $R_1 L\mathbf{b}$ once in order to generate a set of $\mathbf{x}_p$'s, by giving values $\mathbf{t}_p$ with $p \in [1, \ldots, \mathcal{P}]$, calculating $R_2\mathbf{t}_p$ and adding. To sum up, since L and R depend only on the number of stops $\mathcal{N}$ of the target route, we have to carry out the following computation steps: (1) Compute L, R once per route; (2) Compute $R_1 L\mathbf{b}$ once per input data $\mathbf{b}$; (3) Compute $R_2\mathbf{t}_p$ once per p. While step 2 may require a large number of iterations, step 3 is the critical one. Let us start analyzing the former. The complexity of finding the complete solution set for one input vector $\mathbf{b}$ is the complexity of multiplying $R_2 \mathbf{t}_p$, $\mathcal{P}$ times.

To determine the complexity of step 3, let us note that the complexity of matrix multiplication is in our case, according to the typical textbook algorithm, $O(m\ (m-n)\ 1)$. Since $n = 2\mathcal{N} - 3$ and $m = \frac{\mathcal{N}(\mathcal{N}-1)}{2}$, with the proper reduction we obtain that the complexity of step 3 is $O(\mathcal{N}^4)$, and then the time to find $\mathbf{x}_p$ for all p is $O(\mathcal{N}^4 \mathcal{P})$. The number $\mathcal{P}$ depends on $\mathcal{N}$ and $\mathcal{K}$, and in the worst case $\mathcal{P} = (\mathcal{K}+1)^{(m-n)}$. That is, the number of steps becomes exponential. According to this, we will state restrictions over $\mathbf{t}_p$ that reduce the whole problem to a *Quadratic Programming* problem and thus, tractable.

Now, the question is how to bound the values of $\mathbf{t}$ in order to generate $\mathbf{x}_p$'s that satisfy the conditions derived by fixing the capacity $\mathcal{K}$ presented in Sect. 3.

Definition 1 (Bounds of t). *Given that* $0 \le x_i \le \mathcal{K}$ *for all* $x_i \in \mathbf{x}_p$. *Let* $q_i \in R_1 L\mathbf{b}, r_{i,j} \in R_2$, $t_j \in \mathbf{t}_p$ *and* $x_i = q_i + \sum_j r_{i,j} t_j$ *then* $0 \le q_i + \sum_j r_{i,j} t_j \le \mathcal{K}$. $\square$

Then, the solution of the problem is obtained as a solution to a quadratic programming problem under the aforementioned constraints. A set of feasible candidates is

$$S = \{\mathbf{t} \in \mathbb{Z}^m \mid \mathbf{0} \le R_1 L\mathbf{b} + R_2 \mathbf{t} \le \mathcal{K}^m\},$$

and, given the actual solution $\mathbf{x}_r \in \mathbf{x}$, the target function is

$$\min\ (\mathbf{x}_r - \mathbf{x}_p)^2.$$

$\mathbf{x}_r$ is unknown and therefore the goal function cannot be evaluated with the information presented here. But, it is known that the $\mathbf{x}_p$ that minimizes the goal function must be one of the vertices of the convex polytope defined by S (or on a linear combination of vertices of S).

5   Conclusions and Further Work

We estimate the Origin-Destination matrix based only on passengers counts. A refinement yields an elegant way to plug assumptions in the model, obtained from external data sources or expert opinions. The next step is to verify the model with real data and real assumptions, and study in depth the natural constraints on the system and the routes. Finally, the model can yield an estimation of the alighting counts, which as said, is not usually available for this kind of transportation system. In any case, further experimentation and evaluation is needed to make this model a useful tool for the analysis and design of small and medium public transportation systems.

References

1. De Dios Ortúzar, J., Willumsen, L.G: Modelos de transporte. Vasa (2008)

2. Munizaga, M.A., Palma, C.: Estimation of a disaggregate multimodal public transport Origin-Destination matrix from passive smartcard data from Santiago, Chile. Transp. Res. Part C Emerg. Technol. **24**, 9–18 (2012)
3. Munizaga, M., Devillaine, F., Navarrete, C., Silva, D.: Validating travel behavior estimated from smartcard data. Transp. Res. Part C Emerg. Technol. **44**, 70–79 (2014)
4. Pelletier, M.-P., Trépanier, M., Morency, C.: Smart card data use in public transit: a literature review. Transp. Res. Part C Emerg. Technol. **19**(4), 557–568 (2011)
5. Trépanier, M., Tranchant, N., Chapleau, R.: Individual trip destination estimation in a transit smart card automated fare collection system. J. Intell. Transp. Syst. Technol. Plann. Oper. **11**(1), 1–14 (2007)
6. Barry, J., Newhouser, R., Rahbee, A., Sayeda, S.: Origin and destination estimation in new york city with automated fare system data. Transp. Res. Rec. J. Transp. Res. Board **1817**, 183–187 (2002)
7. Nagy, V.: Theoretical method for building OD matrix from AFC data. Trans. Res. Procedia **14**, 1802–1808 (2016)
8. Lazebnik, F.: On systems of linear Diophantine equations. Math. Mag. **69**(4), 261–266 (1996)

Decision-Making Intelligent System for Passenger of Urban Transports

Pedro Wences[1(✉)], Alicia Martinez[1], Hugo Estrada[2], and Miguel Gonzalez[3]

[1] National Technology of Mexico/CENIDET, Cuernavaca, Mexico
{wences,amartinez}@cenidet.edu.mx
[2] Center for Research and Innovation in Information Technologies and Communication,
Mexico City, Mexico
hugo.estrada@infotec.mx
[3] Monterrey Institute of Technology and Higher Education, Monterrey, Mexico
mgonza@itesm.mx

Abstract. Smart transportation systems have now been implemented in many cities. The implementation of these systems requires having a solid infrastructure and specialized devices. However, the implementation of these systems does not consider the infrastructure of other countries. As result, its implementation can be costly. Specifically, in Mexico, Urban Passenger Transport has few transportation units to meet the demand of the population. Also, these do not provide precise information of arrival times of buses. In this research work, we present a software system that combats the inconveniences of public transportation in Mexico, providing information in real time that will allow the passengers to make informed or correct decisions regarding their journey. The information provided to the passengers will be the availability of seats and the arrival times of the buses.

Keywords: Arrival time · Urban passenger transport · Whereabouts · Decision-making · Passenger counter

1   Introduction

Intelligent transport systems [1] have been implemented in many cities; Generally, these make use of the infrastructure of the country, which has allowed its rapid implementation. However, in many remote provinces there is no solid infrastructure or economic resources to implement such intelligent transport systems.

Therefore, transportation problems can be very different from one city to another, as well as how to solve them. For example, public transport in highly developed countries does not exist the problem of insufficiency of transport units. In addition, there is a good administration of such units. In this sense, the main problem in Mexico is the bad administration of the corporations that handle the Urban Passenger Transport service, followed by enormous amount of people who make use of this service. Thus, the public transport in Mexico faces the following problems [2, 3]:

© Springer International Publishing AG 2017
S.F. Ochoa et al. (Eds.): UCAmI 2017, LNCS 10586, pp. 128–139, 2017.
DOI: 10.1007/978-3-319-67585-5_14

- Transport units in poor conditions.
- Insufficiency in the number of units to fulfill the demand of users.
- Lack of accurate real-time information about location of public buses.

Despite these problems, the passengers continue using the Urban Passenger Transport, because in several cases they cannot buy their own car, and to travel in this service is cheaper. Other factors that influence the passengers to choose the bus are: the route, the availability of seats, the price, the periodicity, the comfort, etc.

At present, the situation of transport in Mexico is very uncertain for passengers because there are no intelligent systems that help mobility and decision making. For example, when a tired user waits to board a bus very full, without him knowing that in a few minutes another empty bus would arrive.

In this research work, we present a decision-making intelligent system [4, 5] for passenger of urban transports. This proposal allows passengers making decisions about their travel, their time of wait, and comfort in the transport service. The system consists of three components (Traveler information services, Accurate tracking system, Smart model to predict arrival time) of the intelligent transport systems, which are used to calculate and display to passengers the availability of seats and the arrival times of the buses, due this information changes constantly. The intelligent system must be implemented in a smartphone, which obtains the GPS position of public transport drivers, and calculates the arrival time and seating availability of next bus. This last is possible, because we have developed a low-cost device that counts the amount passengers traveling in the bus.

The paper is organized as follows: Sect. 2 presents the related work; Sect. 3 shows the system design, Sect. 4 shows our System Automatic: Context Time app which implements our proposal, Sect. 5 shows Test and results obtained, and finally, Sect. 6 presents the conclusions, and future work.

2 Related Work

Many efforts have been made to improve ground communication routes, for example: road maintenance, bridge construction, tunnels, signals, radars, RSU, etc. However, very little information has been made available to users, so a large number of intelligent transport systems have been developed that make information useful for user decision making. In this section, we present a review of the literature related to intelligent transportation systems that provide information to public transport users.

In the city of Southampton, a smart transport system was implemented in which QR code posters were printed and placed in 44 bus stops. The purpose of printing the posters is that users can scan these codes with their Smartphone to be redirected to a web page that will display the times of arrival of the buses [6].

Yu and Lam [7] propose a model to predict bus arrival times with different routes. They use several methods for predicting arrival times: support vector machine (SVM), artificial neural network (ANN), k nearest neighbor algorithm (k-NN) and linear regression (LR). In other works such as that of Li and Gao [8] a mixed model is proposed. This model uses KNN, K-means, KF and Markov chain (KKM) for predicting arrival times. In the work of Zhou and Zheng [9] use participatory detection of passengers, the system collects the identifiers of nearby cell towers and sends that information to a server. Another work is the one of Wang and Zuo [10], in which they propose an approach to predict the time of arrival of the buses, Wang and Zuo use a Radial Basis Function Neural Network Model (RBFNN) and a real-time tuning method. Finally, in the research of Edison and Ferris [11] a case study is presented that addresses the perception of waiting time of the passengers that use a system in real time against those that do not use any system in real time. The Edison work examines the *OneBusAway* transit information system that provides real-time countdown information for the next bus for King County (KCM) users in Seattle.

As stated in this section, there are several investigations in the area of intelligent transportation applied to public transport. In most cases their objective is to provide information so that passengers can make informed decisions. For this reason, we propose a system that monitors and processes information on the context of buses to provide passengers, owners and drivers services for decision making in public transport.

3   System Design

Currently, Mexican Urban Passenger Transport does not have enough information to allows users or passengers to know the arrival times of the waiting transport units or if they have available seats. In this section, we describe the major components of the system design. The Fig. 1 shows our solution methodology. This methodology is composing of four main phases. The entire context information is stored in a database.

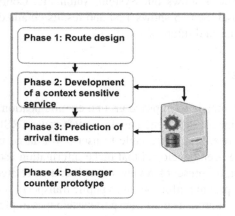

Fig. 1.   Proposed solution methodology.

3.1   Route Design

Urban Passenger Transport in normal conditions always follows a fixed route, and also establishes buses stops that the people use to have access to the service.

Generally, an urban passenger transport route is rarely symmetrical. Thus, in a few cases a bus leaves from point A to point B, and returns following exactly the same route. For this reason, we have considered that a route is composed of two journeys: one journey starting from point A to point B and another journey is when starting from point B to return to original point A. To carry out the route design, two routes must be created with their corresponding bus stops each one. These routes can be seen as directional graphs; where whereabouts are represented as nodes, and the distances between one node and another are represented as segments or edges.

In the first phase of our proposed methodology it was necessary developing a method to establish the public transport routes. This module uses the Google maps API and extends it for the definition of each whereabouts of urban passenger transport. This extension is done as follows:

1. The map of Google Maps is displayed; this map makes use of the class *"Support-MapFragment"*. On this map, the geographical location where the users want to design a route is indicated. The stroke of the route uses the *"moveCamera"* method.
2. The system obtains the Global Position system (GPS) coordinates (latitude, longitude) where a whereabouts is established.
3. The variability of the latitude and longitude must be defined and analyzed (except for the first whereabouts). This is done in order to determine the arrival times of the urban passenger transport.
4. Once the variability is defined, then the whereabouts are identified assigning a position in the route and a name.
5. The defined whereabouts are drawn on the map.

It is important to point out that design of the route of the system is very important. The system will present better results with a well defining route. Care must be taken when establishing a route because generally a route is not completely straight, that is contains curves. Figure 2 shows a route well designed and a route poorly designed.

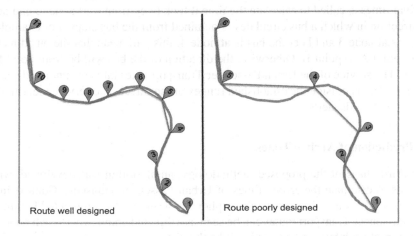

Fig. 2. Example of a route well designed and a route poorly designed.

3.2   Development of a Context-Sensitive Service

The concept of context awareness [12] is very relevant in current research on ubiquitous computing systems [13] and environmental intelligence [14, 15], and it implies giving this systems awareness of the environment in which they are executed. That is, turning them into context-sensitive services.

In the second phase of our proposed methodology "Context processing" a service that allows constant monitoring of the situation of the Urban Passenger Transport is defined. The monitoring is carried out with a smartphone and a passenger counter; it has called *"USoniCont"*. Whereas the smartphone constantly obtains the GPS position, the device *USoniCont* updates the status of the Urban Passenger Transport obtaining the number of people traveling on a bus. The obtained data are compiled in a class java denominated Bus and transformed to a JSON object. This JSON object is continuously sent over the Internet (using the Smartphone resources) to the server. This service detects in which edge of the graph a bus is located, when the Bus ends and starts on each edge, and also the direction in which the bus circulates.

The detection of the edge in which the bus is located and the previous edge is carried out as follows:

1. An edge is composed of two nodes, representing two bus stops. These have a GPS position on the map. Each time the service receives the context data, it determines the edge in which the bus is located, validating if the GPS position of the bus is located between some interval ($Node_{Start}$ – $Nodo_{End}$) of the edges of a route.
2. Also, the detection of the current edge of the bus allows detecting the end of the previous edge. That is, when the edge in which the bus is circulating is detected, it is validated if it is the first time that the service receives data from the same edge. If it is the first time, it means that recently the bus entered a new edge and therefore ended the previous edge.

When the service detects that an edge has been traversed, the algorithm of prediction of arrival times is called to calculate the time it took to go from start node to end node. The direction in which a bus circulates is obtained from the bus stops. For example, if the bus is at node 3 and later the bus is at node 4, this will mean that the bus direction is from point A to point B. Otherwise, the direction of the bus will be from point B to point A. The service of the Urban Passenger Transport takes into account the detection of GPS positions outside the established ranges of the travel. The service identifies the situation and sends alerts.

3.3   Prediction of Arrival Times

In the third phase of the proposed methodology, an algorithm was developed, which allows us to calculate the arrival times of Urban Passenger Transport. Context information is sent through the driver's Smartphone to a server. As commented before, the Urban Passenger Transport routes can be seen as a directed graph, where each node will be the stop of each bus, and an edge will be the distance between two stops or nodes.

Our proposed algorithm is detailed two sections. The first refers to the processing of context information, while the second is when the algorithm processes user queries. The first section of algorithm is carried out as follows:

1. The context sensitive service executes the algorithm sending two parameters, which are the current edge and the edge to calculate.
2. The algorithm performs the update in the database. The data updated are: the edge in which the bus is circulating and the direction of the route.
3. The algorithm verifies the edge to calculate E_3 (Called E_c). Figure 3 shows the edge E_3 that must be calculated, once that it is traversed.

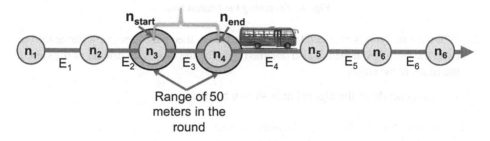

Range of 50 meters in the round

Fig. 3. Time to travel an edge by urban passenger transport unit, and detection of the initial and final nodes.

4. The travel time of the E_c edge (tE_c) is calculated by searching the database for the time the bus passed through the initial and final nodes (n_s and n_e). However, the GPS position of the stops varies with respect to the GPS position of the bus. This is because, the bus is not exactly in the GPS position of the bus stops or because the context data was not sent at the precise moment when the bus passed by the bus stops. For this reason, the algorithm searches the database for 50 m around the stops (to see Fig. 3).
5. A subtraction is carried out to calculate the time of travel of the bus by an edge. The formula used is as follows: $tE_c = tn_e - tn_s.$
6. The value obtained (tE_c) is averaged with the value of the database (tE_{db}). Greater weight should be given to the new value (because it presents the current traffic conditions) and lower weight to the value stored in the database. We use the formula: $tE_{db} = (tE_c * 0.6) + (tE_{db} * 0.4)$. The values 0.6 and 0.4 are given depending on whether traffic conditions increase or decrease in a short time.
7. Finally, the calculated edge is updated in the database.

The second section of algorithm is carried out as follows:

1. The algorithm is executed to respond to requests from users. The users must define a journey, the direction and a stop of journey.
2. The Urban Passenger Transport units closest to the point of consultation are obtained. Looking for the bus that is circulating in the edge before the point of consultation. If a bus is not found on the given edge, the algorithm continues to search the edges after the query node. Figure 4 shows this point.

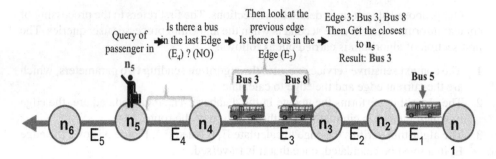

Fig. 4. Searching the nearest bus.

3. When the next bus is obtained from consulted node, then the edges that separate the bus from the consulted node are also obtained. Finally, the algorithm calculates the sum of the times of the edges.

The pseudocode of the algorithm is shown below:

```
IF requestBus == requestReceived THEN
  directionBus = getDirectionBus();
  new_edge = getEdgeBus(getPositionGPSBus(),
directionBus);
  current_edge = new_edge;
  WHILE (edge_current == new_edge) DO
      new_edge = getEdgeBus (getPositionGPSBus());
  END_WHILE
  timeEdge = calculateTimeEdge(directionBus, current_edge
);
  timeBD = getTimeEdgeBD(directionBus, current_edge );
  timeBD = (timeEdge *0.6) + (timeBD*0.4);
  setTimeEdgeBD(timeBD, directionBus, current_edge );
  current_edge = new_edge;

END_IF

IF requestUser == requestReceived THEN
  nextBus = getNextBus(JSON_User.stop);
  listEdges = getEdges(nextBus, JSON_User.stop)
  WHILE (edge: listEdges) DO
    arrivalTime = arrivalTime + edge.getTime();
  END_ WHILE
  returnArrivalTime(arrivalTime);
END_IF
```

3.4   Passenger Counter: USoniCont

Public transport is a service that has a high demand for the population. Currently in Mexico there is no information available to the population for decision-making regarding the occupation of public urban transport units. In this section, we describe the design of a passenger counter device, that we have called "USoniCont". This device allows register when a passenger boards the bus, or when the passenger gets off of bus. Also, this allows passengers to know seat availability of a bus. The values show will be: good, regular and low availability of seats.

3.4.1   Design of the People Counter

We propose a device low-cost passenger counter, which allow us to count the number of passengers that board or get off of a bus. Thus, this device allows our application to show passengers in real time the availability of seats of the buses.

Our passengers counter is composed of two ultrasonic sensors, a Bluetooth module and an Arduino nano board. The ultrasonic sensors were aligned side by side with a separation of 15 cm; the information obtained from the sensors is processed on the Arduino board. The sensors were configured for measuring a maximum distance; equivalent to the distance that measures the width of the door of the bus. USoniCont counts passengers as they pass sensors 1 and 2. As a result, the sensors measurement is less than the width of the door.

USoniCont works as follows when a person boards a bus:

When the person passes through the sensor 1 the distance measurement of said sensor will be less than the maximum distance established (in this case 80 cm), creating a waiting cycle. From that moment, the counter is waiting for the user to pass through the sensor 2.

If the passenger crosses sensor 2 before the timeout period, the counter will record that action as ascent. If sensor 2 is not crossed, the counter will start its normal cycle. Figure 5 incise a, shows the ascent of a passenger. The operation is similar when a person descends from the bus with the difference that in this case the passenger first passes through the sensor 2 and then through the sensor 1. Figure 5 incise b, shows the descent of a passenger.

a) Ascent   b) Descent

Fig. 5.   (a) Position of sensors to count the *ascent* of a passenger; (b) Position of sensors to count the *descent* of a passenger

The passenger counter sends the "ascent" and "descent" events via Bluetooth. The events are received and processed by the driver's smartphone. The algorithm adds 1 value when the event is "ascent" and subtracts −1 when the event is "descent". The states of availability in the app are: good, regular and low availability of seats.

4   System Automatic: Context Time App

In this section, we present the system developed from the design presented in Sect. 3. This system has been called Context Time. This allows optimizing public transport, through different services that are provided to passengers, drivers and owners (concessionaire), or managers of unit of transport.

The system ContextTime is composed of three applications. They are executed from the smartphone of each user. For example, the owners (concessionaire) must register the route that exists in the Urban Passenger Transport using the first application: the Management Urban Passenger Transport App. In addition, owners must register and assign drivers and buses to a route.

The second Application: Monitoring Drivers Context Information App is the driver´s application, which carries out the monitoring of the transport unit and the journey of the bus. This app will send to the server all the information of the context. The third application Passenger Transport App allows consult at any time the arrival time of a transport unit to a bus stop.

4.1   Management Urban Passenger Transport App

The Urban Passenger Transport App is the application of the manager. The main functionalities of this application are the following:

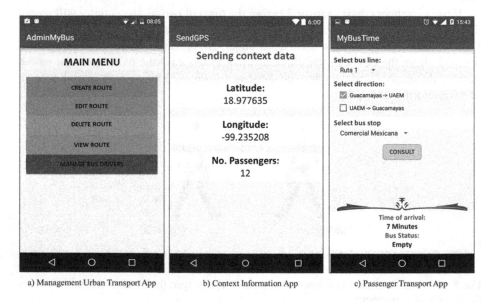

a) Management Urban Transport App   b) Context Information App   c) Passenger Transport App

Fig. 6. Developed apps for passengers transport

Manage Routes: In this module, the user can register the name of the route and to set the bus stops. Also, the manager can modify a route, eliminate a route and can view the transport units.

Manage Drivers: This module is responsible for registering, modifying, deleting or showing the drivers that make up the management. In this module establishes the passenger capacity of the transport unit, (to see Fig. 6, incise a).

4.2 Monitoring Drivers Context Information App

The second application Monitoring Drivers Context Information allows to monitor, collect and send all the information of the context of each transport unit that circulates in the journey of a route to the database, (to see Fig. 6, incise b). The main function of this application is the following:

Sending the Context Information: This module periodically sends to the server the GPS position, the Seating Availability, the unit number and the route in which the transport unit travels.

4.3 Passenger Transport App

The third application, Passenger Transport App permits consult at any time the arrival time of a bus to a specific bus stop. This application must be installed in the smartphones of the users of Urban Passenger Transport.

The main function of this application is *Visualization of arrival times*: this module allows the user to specify the characteristics of his query. The app will show the arrival time of next bus, and its state of availability of seats, (to see Fig. 6, incise c). The information provided by the app to the users allows them to choice if she/he could board the next bus. This will depend if the bus has available seats; or if they should wait a lot or little time for the next bus.

5   Test and Results

In this section, the tests and results of proposed approach are presented. These were done as follows: We designed a route with 27 stops. From this route we selected five stops, one person measured the actual time that the bus took to reach the consulted whereabouts. We create a table to compare the estimated time of arrival with the developed application. Table 1 shows the results obtained in this test in seconds and their percentage accuracy.

We used Root Mean Square Error (RMSE) and Mean Absolute Percentage Error (MAPE) to measure the performance of the algorithm calculating arrival times. The results obtained were the following: RMSE = ± 94 and MAPE = 6.19%.

In addition, we perform another test to analyze the operation of our USoniCont counter from the people who board and/or descend from the public transport units (see Table 2). For this test, the USoniCont device was installed in a transport unit and 5 trips were performed. Along the way, the persons who boarded the transport unit were counted manually, as well as the number of times the accountant correctly identified the ascents and descents of the passengers.

Table 1. Results obtained of real time and arrival time of app and their percentage accuracy.

Bus stops	Real time (s)	Arrival time of app (s)	Accuracy
Bus stop 1	160	148	92.5%
Bus stop 2	719	697	96.9%
Bus stop 3	1329	1221	91.9%
Bus stop 4	701	647	92.3%
Bus stop 5	350	334	95.4%

Table 2. Comparing passengers who boarded the bus and those counted by USoniCont.

# Trip	People who got on the bus	USoniCont passenger ascent	USoniCont passenger descent	Passenger ascent	Passenger descent
1	108	99	97	91.7%	89.8%
2	114	104	100	91.2%	87.7%
3	97	87	92	89.7%	94.8%
4	110	107	98	97.3%	89.1%
5	122	108	106	88.5%	86.9%

The passenger counter does not have 100% accuracy due to the passengers' walking speed, for this reason, three availability states have been created to deal with this inconvenience.

6   Conclusions and Future Work

This research work presented a system that allows us obtaining the times of arrival of the Urban Transport and the Seat availability. Three applications were developed: Management Urban Passenger Transport App, Monitoring Drivers Context Information App and Passenger Transport App.

Currently we are working in the execution of more complete tests that will allow improving the proposed algorithm. Additionally, we are working on the development of a module to consult the routes of the concessionaires and generate the optimal route and the instructions to arrive from point A to point B. This type of work promotes the improvement of the public transport by improving the experience of the people who use this means of transport. This intends to avoid the excessive use of private transport, also helping reduce levels of pollution, traffic, noise, etc. This will be a contribution to improve the quality of life of the people living in cities.

Acknowledgments. This research work has been partially funded by European Commission and CONACYT, through the SmartSDK project.

References

1. ITS Canada: Intelligent transportation, ITS Canada (2012). https://www.itscanada.ca/it/
2. Villanueva, E.Á.: Planeación para la administración de una flotilla de autobuses de transporte público, Instituto Politécnico Nacional (2015)
3. Notimex: Los problemas de usuarios de transporte público, inseguridad, saturación y largos trayectos (2014). http://www.animalpolitico.com/2014/05/inseguridad-saturacion-y-largos-trayectos-los-problemas-de-usuarios-de-transporte-publico/. Accessed 02 May 2017
4. Alessio Ishizaka, P.N.: Multi-criteria Decision Analysis: Methods and Software. Wiley, Hoboken (2013)
5. Chernoff, H., Moses, L.: Elementary Decision Theory. Dover, New York (1987)
6. Gammer, N., Cherrett, T., Gutteridge, C.: Disseminating real-time bus arrival information via QRcode tagged bus stops: a case study of user take-up and reaction in Southampton, UK. J. Transp. Geogr. **34**, 254–261 (2014)
7. Yu, B., Lam, W.H.K., Lam, M.: Bus arrival time prediction at bus stop with multiple routes. Transp. Res. C. **19**(6), 1157–1170 (2011)
8. Li, J., Gao, J., Yang, Y., Wei, H.: Bus arrival time prediction based on mixed model. China. Commun. **14**, 38–47 (2015)
9. Zhou, P., Zheng, Y., Li, M.: "How long to wait? predicting bus arrival time with mobile phone based participatory sensing. In: Proceeding of 10th International Conference on Mobile Systems, Applications, and Services - MobiSys 2012, vol. 13, pp. 379–392 (2012)
10. Wang, L., Zuo, Z., Fu, J.: Bus arrival time prediction using RBF neural networks adjusted by online data. Procedia Soc. Behav. Sci. **138**, 67–75 (2014)
11. Edison, K., Ferris, B., Borning, A., Rutherford, G.S., Layton, D.: Where is my bus ? Impact of mobile real-time information on the perceived and actual wait time of transit riders. Transp. Res. A. **45**(8), 839–848 (2011)
12. Emmanouilidis, C., Koutsiamanis, R.-A.: Mobile guides: taxonomy of architectures, context awareness, technologies and applications. J. Netw. Comput. Appl. **36**(1), 103–125 (2013)
13. Perera, C., Member, S., Zaslavsky, A., Christen, P., Georgakopoulos, D.: Context aware computing for the internet of things : a survey. IEEE. Commun. Surv. Tutor. **16**(1), 414–454 (2014)
14. Cook, D.J., Augusto, J.C.: Ambient intelligence: technologies, applications, and opportunities. Pervasive. Mob. Comput. **5**(4), 277–298 (2009)
15. Synott, G., Chen, J., Nugent, L., Moore, C.D.: Flexible and customizable visualization of data generated within intelligent environments. Annu. Int. Conf. IEEE Eng. Med. Biol. Soc. (2012). doi:10.1109/EMBC.2012.6347317

A Dictionary Based Protocol over LoRa (Long Range) Technology for Applications in Internet of Things

Félix Sasián[1], Diego Gachet[2(✉)], Manuel de Buenaga[2], and Fernando Aparicio[2]

[1] Desing3 SL, Recinto Interior Zona Franca Nave 1-A1, Cádiz, Spain
felix.sasian@desing3.com
[2] Universidad Europea de Madrid, 28670 Villaviciosa de Odón, Spain
{diego.gachet,buenaga,fernando.aparicio}@universidadeuropea.es

Abstract. Internet of the things (IoT) is a new scenario that aims to integrate into the global network "things" or devices such as sensors or embedded electronics equipment, sharing information and enabling interaction with them from anywhere. A very important aspect in IoT applications is the communication protocols used by sensors for sending and exchange information. Traditional protocols used so far do not have the scope and ability to manage a growing up computational elements used in modern IoT applications. New communications schemes based on spread spectrum and Long Range (LoRa) coverage, offer new horizons for design and implement low power and long-range sensor networks. In this paper, we describe a new, robust and lightweight communication protocol implemented over the physical layer of LoRa, providing effectiveness and low power consumption suitable for IoT applications. A coverage analysis in both urban and rural environments confirms the success in the selection of this technology and opens new challenges for developing useful applications in several domains as for example smart cities, smart-health, smart factory, remote monitoring, precision agriculture, energy management and remote monitoring and control.

Keywords: Internet of Things · Cloud computing · Wireless protocol · LoRa technology · Smart city · Sensors · Big data

1 Introduction

Internet of Things along with cloud computing and big data makes up the main technological pillars nowadays. IoT forms an integral part of the basis for the digitization of our society and economy, where objects and people are interconnected through communication and computer networks, sharing information about the environment around them. The role of technologies, applications and services in the framework of IoT is growing. A representative study by Gartner [1] estimates that in 2020, there will be 26 trillion devices with an internet connection, and those IoT products and services suppliers will generate an incremental revenue exceeding $300 billion. Most of this revenue will come from services, resulting in $1.9 trillion in global economic value-add through sales into diverse end markets. Also, according to another recent study by the

© Springer International Publishing AG 2017
S.F. Ochoa et al. (Eds.): UCAmI 2017, LNCS 10586, pp. 140–148, 2017.
DOI: 10.1007/978-3-319-67585-5_15

European Commission, the value of the IoT market in the EU is expected to exceed one trillion euros in 2020 [2].

The areas of application and new services under IoT are multiple, including industrial applications, smart cities, healthy aging, smart agriculture, smart energy, wearables and smart accessories among others. There is a relevant relationship between IoT and Smart Cities, in which citizens, companies, transport and a wide spectrum of services and urban objects increase their level of interconnection by providing value and making cities more sustainable. The definition of a Smart City remains controversial. While the overall concept is generally perceived as an ideal fusion of sustainability with advanced technology, there is still some confusion regarding the place that the term "intelligent" deals among "sustainable", "strong" and "resilient" [3]. Authors in [4], provide a first operational definition of Smart Cities, grouping 74 indicators in six categories.

The European Union (EU) is investing a great amount of resources in developing a strategy for a "smart" urban growth for their metropolitan regions. Consequently, EU has developed a series of actions included in the Digital Agenda for Europe. In fact, the Horizon 2020 is the biggest EU Research and Innovation programme of the European Commission giving the opportunity to private and public actors, as well as the researchers, to propose projects related to the Smart Cities involving of course the use of IoT Technologies.

The purpose of this paper, is to describe a technological approach related to the development of a new low weight and robust data communications protocol over the LoRa (Long Range) physical layer. This layer can be used for the Internet of Things (IoT) applications and specifically in the context of Smart Cities.

2   Related Work

There is a crucial role of data communications in the applications developed for Internet of Things, especially for those related to the wireless communication technology [5]. If we are considering the necessity of sensing the whole environment, it is clear that a huge set of heterogeneous sensors need to communicate among them and with others devices. The problem is that at present there are a wide range of technologies to be used but there is no a defined standard yet. In this sense a further relevant IETF (Internet Engineering Task Force) Working Group named Routing Over Low power and Lossy networks (ROLL) has recently written the RPL (IPv6 Routing Protocol for Low-Power and Lossy Networks) draft. This will be the basis for routing data over low power and lossy networks including 6LoWPAN, which still need many contributions to reach a full solution and to reduce the uncertainty in their implementation.

LoRa WAN [6] is a specification for LPWAN (Low Power WAN) network that provides bi-directional communication and, it is focused on battery-powered devices. It is supported by the LoRa Alliance, a non-profit organization made up of several companies that collaborate in the development of a common protocol. LoRa WAN is a good choice to develop IoT applications with excellent range and energy consumption, and it offers free access to the source code. However, the use of LoRa involves implementing the complete specification, regardless of the needs that a particular application requires.

Moreover, at present, this specification is not yet established as a reference in the market, and other competitors are developing and offering various alternatives using LoRa's physical layer.

A good comparison of communication technologies used in the context of IoT and with focus on Smart Cities can be found in [7]. Using as example the intelligent management of solid urban waste, some interesting information can be extracted from that analysis in the sense that there are some important variables to be considered for developing IoT applications. For example, the scope, consumption, range and specially the ownership of the communication networks. This last aspect can often be decisive, because in most cases these technologies are protected by patents and ultimately involve the payment of royalties for developing new deployments.

The current picture of existing technological solutions for application in wireless sensor networks is wide. It makes possible to perform a multicriteria selection that suits to the "smart" ecosystem needs. Due to the requirements of low battery consumption, embedded sensors are preferred in the nodes themselves, and with the capability to communicate with very low data rate. This is especially important in applications like e-health, tele-monitoring, smart healthcare or wellbeing monitoring [8]. On the other hand, GPS/GPRS networks work with a great bandwidth, but has a high installation cost, high-energy consumption and, the most important aspect, the prize of connection.

With LoRa technology in mind, this paper proposes a new lightweight, flexible and secure protocol, based on the concept of a "dictionary". This DBP (Dictionary Based Protocol) is developed over the physical layer of a LoRa network. It has the advantage of allowing the exchange of information in a simple and efficient way to the nodes, from small local networks with few components, to large networks of thousands of participants.

3   Development of a Dictionary Based Protocol

LoRa technology describes and implements only the physical layer (PHY) in a network, the new protocol proposed in this paper can be used on top of this layer. This protocol is based on the concept of "dictionary", in which each component of the network can exchange information contained in their own dictionary with other members without having to establish any previous relationship between them. An advantage for implementing this protocol over LoRa is the existence of a specific communication processor, to manage a network with a density of 10–50000 nodes.

The implementation of specific functionalities allows to optimize the performance, including 50 parallel demodulation paths, that, together, and with the orthogonal modulation scheme permits a level of coexistence in the network unattainable with solutions based on FSK (Frequency Shift Keying) or OOK (On-Off Keying). The implementation of DBP (Dictionary Based Protocol) over LoRa transceivers allows the use of this technology in situations where a long range (even over 10 km) and networks with large numbers of nodes are needed. Independently of the protocol's characteristics, and having in mind the change towards different topologies, the recommended model is a star type of network as it is shown in Fig. 1. This network is composed by several gateways and a fixed number of final nodes.

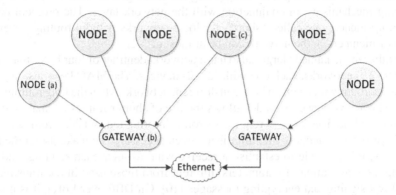

Fig. 1. Topology for DBP network over LORA.

3.1 Physical Layer

The physical layer is used by the transceiver to synchronize the communication and ensure its viability. It is implemented using the Semtech LoRa chipset [9]. Messages are in "explicit mode", in which the length of the data is not always fixed and is not known in advance. The frame of a LoRa package begins with the preamble, followed by the sync byte and a header that includes the length of the message and a CRC header (Cyclic Redundant Check). The detail of a complete DBP packet is shown in Fig. 2.

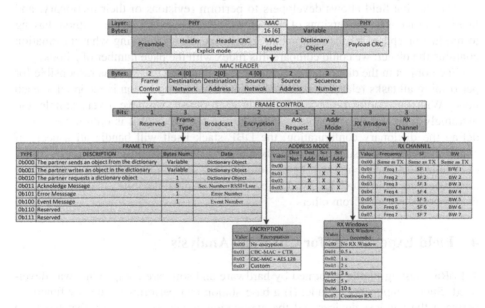

Fig. 2. DBP protocol packet detail.

3.2   MAC Layer

It is in charge of delimiting and recognizing the messages, as well as, providing the addressing mechanisms, in conjunction with the network layer. The protocol defines two routing modes, one called "short", for local networks without routing, where the number of members in the network can be at most (2^{16}-2).

The other mode named "large" also has a network identifier of four bytes that allows to deploy (2^{32}) networks, each one with (2^{16}-2) devices. The MAC layer also provides the message routing mechanism between different networks when the long routing mode is used. This network access model allows the use of shorter frames in small networks where the end devices do not require to route information outside from their own network, or where a network identifier is not even necessary. To make use of the LoRa capabilities, it is possible to establish a receive window after each sending, and even receiving a configuration of parameters different from those used in the transmission. DBP allows signing and encrypting messages [10]. On DBP over LoRa, it is possible to use XTEA, AES or another proprietary algorithm to perform the encryption.

3.3   The Dictionary

The dictionary is an ordered set of objects, addressed by an 8-bit index and no more than 100 bytes of information. In addition, each object has a 1-byte field that defines the Type, a 1-byte field that defines the Version, and a 1-byte field that indicates the size of the data. With this information of type, version, index and size, the interlocutor is able to interpret the data contained in the message since the information is not fragmented (a message is a unit of complete information).

The version field allows developers to perform revisions of their dictionary, and facilitates that different versions of the same type can coexist together without having to modify or update all the equipment. The index allows knowing what information contains the object; we could compare this index with the page number of a book.

Each object in the dictionary is configured so that the DBP stack is responsible for performing all tasks related to communication. This configuration is recorded at each node. With this configuration capability in each object, we have a very simple and extremely powerful, and flexible system. To use the protocol it is only necessary to define the dictionary configuration, the DBP stack itself will handle all aspects of communication with a single call from the main loop in the user program. The possibility of defining which function will be executed before sending the data after a request or after receiving valid data for a given object provides a great flexibility that differentiates the proposed protocol from others.

4   Field Experiments for Coverage Analysis

A LoRa's testing platform formed by hardware and software components was developed. Such components include: (i) a base station that performs a gateway functions between the wireless devices and the application server; (ii) a station that has been installed over a communications tower located 40 m high by using a 3G modem; several end devices or nodes, which are powered by batteries and implemented through a small microcontroller, these nodes are equipped with LoRa technology transceivers.

Also, with the aim of collecting data, representing and analyzing the received information it was developed a terminal application programmed in C# language running on Windows platform.

As shown in Fig. 3, the base station is based on a IC880A-USB (SX1301 + 2× SX1557) Card. Figure 3(a); a Raspberry PI with a control application based on Linux, as show in Figs. 3(b) and 4(c), an ISM band base antenna with a gain of 5 dBi. Figure 3(d) represents this component installed inside the testing cabinet and a 3G Teltronika RUT500 Router, which is also shown in Fig. 3(b). The SX1301 management software is implemented on Linux (although it was also developed a Windows version).

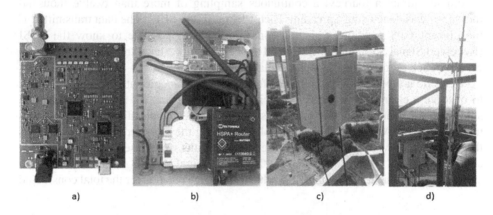

a)   b)   c)   d)

Fig. 3. Gateway based on SX1301.

Fig. 4. Geographical coordinates of the base station: 36°32'03.4"N 6°10'01.8"W

This software is based on the public information given by the manufacturer and a Raspberry PI card connected via a USB port to facilitate a rapid implementation of the software and to easily carry out its execution. Moreover, in order to have a more stable application, the use of a 32-bit microcontroller connected through a SPI port is recommended. The end nodes are based on the PIC24f32KA302 microcontroller, which is specifically designed for ultra-low power consumption, being powered by two AAA size batteries. A certain number of these nodes use a whip antenna with a gain of +3 dBi, whereas others contain an internal ceramic antenna of +0 dBi gain.

5   Results and Discussion

Up to now, it is not possible to have reliable data on the real coverage of a LoRa LPWAN based network. However, it is possible to find in the literature some tests based on point-to-point fixed geographical locations used for this purpose. It is clear, therefore, that the development of the proposed hardware prototypes and the DBP protocol is an important contribution to this field. The prototype has been used to perform a full analysis of coverage in both, urban and rural environments.

As noted above, to carry out the tests, the base station was installed on a 40 m telecommunications tower located in the city of Puerto Real, with a total height over sea level of 94 m as shown in Fig. 4. For final nodes, we have installed two transmitters on a vehicle, during a journey; a continuous sampling of more than twelve thousand messages was done using Spreading Factor from SF7 to SF12. The data transmitted is the current GPS position, with this configuration was possible to know the RSSI (Received Signal Strength Indicator) and the LSNR (Low Signal to Noise Ratio) measured for each of traveled geographical places.

If we do a superposition of all the information on a Google satellite map, it is easy to observe a clear view about the capacity of the LoRa link for any point inside the studied geographical area. Our group has developed a C# application for data analysis using GMap.net API [10]. The values collected using the proposed prototype confirms the initial data given by the manufacturer; these results were based on "line of sight" applications on a 10 km radius and in "No line of sight" with 3 km radius. Figure 5 shows a geographical map with real results of the range reached for the total considered

Fig. 5. Map of real coverage obtained as result of test in urban and rural areas around Cádiz with Spreading Factor SF = 11

sampling points in the test done in rural and urban zones. It is important to note the value of RSSI = -100 dBM on the town of Medina Sidonia 22 km away from the base station.

6 Conclusions

This paper presents a new protocol for wireless network implemented on LoRa technology, the main characteristic is that is based on the concept of a dictionary. In other words this implies that the nodes exchange information like object previously defined in their own dictionary. This concept simplifies the design and the implementation of small and big scale wireless networks from a few to thousand nodes. The protocol also implements the necessary mechanism for signing and encrypting of communications. The results obtained in the coverage tests show that the LoRa based protocol is a viable alternative to be used for developing IoT applications specially having in mind new Smart Cities market, it is clear that the protocol could be used in applications like street lighting control, water and waste control, or like smart factory, etc.

The LoRa network can be deployed with an initial low cost because a gateway can control an urban or rural area up to 10 km of radius, if it is installed in an adequate geographical area. It is important the availability of a isocoberture map for identify shadow zones. The features mentioned for the new protocol combined with the low cost, scalability, flexibility and public availability of LoRa specifications make the proposed prototype a valid solution for new developments of wireless-sensors network applications.

Acknowledgments. This work is still being developed through the support of Desing3 S.L Company. Some aspects of this project were studied through funds granted by the Spanish Ministry of Economy and Competitiveness under project iPHealth (TIN-2013-47153-C3-1). The authors wish to acknowledge Dr. Ricardo Terón for their invaluable comments and Mr. Angel Ruiz-Mateos for their help in the installation of the gateway and the antenna.

References

1. Gartner Says the Internet of Things Installed Base will Grow to 26 Billion Units by 2020 (2013). http://www.gartner.com/newsroom/id/2636073
2. Staff Working Document: Advancing the Internet of Things in Europe (2016). https://ec.europa.eu/digital-single-market/en/news/staff-working-document-advancing-internet-things-europe
3. UN-Habitat. The city resilience profiling programme, CRPP (2012). http://unhabitat.org/urban-initiatives/initiatives-programmes/city-resilience-profiling-programme. Accessed 20 Nov 2016
4. Giffinger, R.: Smart cities. Ranking of European medium-sized cities. October. 16: 13–18 (2007)
5. Atzori, L., Lera, A., Morabito, G.: The internet of things: a survey. Comput. Netw. 54(15) (2010). Elsevier
6. Semtech. LoRa Technology (2015). http://www.semtech.com/wireless-rf/lora.html. Accessed 10 Nov 2016

148   F. Sasián et al.

7. Hannan, M.A., Abdulla Al Mamun, M., Hussain, A., Basri, H., Begum, R.A.: A review on technologies and their usage in solid waste monitoring and management systems: issues and challenges. Waste. Manag. **43**, 509–523 (2015)
8. Páez, D.G., de Buenaga Rodríguez, M., Sánz, E.P., Villalba, M.T., Gil, R.M.: Big data processing using wearable devices for wellbeing and healthy activities promotion. In: Cleland, I., Guerrero, L., Bravo, J. (eds.) IWAAL 2015. LNCS, vol. 9455, pp. 196–205. Springer, Cham (2015). doi:10.1007/978-3-319-26410-3_19
9. Semtech, Sx1272/73. Datasheet (2015). http://www.semtech.com/images/datasheet/sx1272.pdf. Accessed 12 May 2015
10. Sasián, F., Theron, R., Gachet, D.: Protocolo para comunicación inalámbrica en instalaciones de energías renovables. RIAI **13**(3), 310–321 (2016)
11. Margelis, G., Piechocki, R., Kaleshi, D., Thomas, P.: Low throughput networks for the IoT: lessons learned from industrial implementations. In: Proceedings 2015 IEEE World Forum on Internet of Things (WF-IoT) (2015)
12. Gomez, C., Paradells, J.: Urban automation networks: current and emerging solutions for sensed data collection and actuation in smart cities. Sensors **15**(9), 22874–22898 (2015)

Improving Tourist Experience Through an IoT Application Based on FatBeacons

Moisés Lodeiro-Santiago$^{(\boxtimes)}$, Pino Caballero-Gil, Cándido Caballero-Gil,
and Félix Herrera Priano

Departamento de Ingeniería Informática y de Sistemas,
Universidad de La Laguna, Tenerife, Spain
{mlodeirs,pcaballe,ccabgil,fpriano}@ull.edu.es

Abstract. This paper describes the use of a new extension of the Bluetooth connection protocol, called FatBeacon, which faces the problem of
obtaining information where no Internet connection is available. Rather
than advertising a URL to load a web page, the FatBeacon protocol has
the ability to broadcast any basic web contents actually hosted on the
device. In particular, FatBeacons are here used to improve the tourist
experience in places with no Internet coverage through a new application
of the Internet of Things (IoT). Thanks to the fact that the web content is emitted by the own FatBeacon, any smartphone with Bluetooth
Low Energy (BLE) can be used to receive touristic information, even
in uncovered areas, such as rural or mountain destinations. This work
does not only show the applicability of the new FatBeacon protocol, but
it also presents a performance comparison of different BLE technologies
used for similar touristic applications.

Keywords: Bluetooth Low Energy · FatBeacon · IoT · Tourism · Point
Of Interest

1 Introduction

Tourism has become one of the major economic activities in most countries
around the world. Tourism offers have changed a lot in recent years mainly due
to the increase in the interest of tourists in new outdoor activities. A proof of
that is searching terms like "Rural tourism" have increased notably in contrast
to the classic "Sunshine and beach tourism" [1] to the point of overcoming it
(see Fig. 1). Tourism has been also affected in recent years due to the widespread
of many new technologies. That is why, even in rural tourism, it is frequently
common to combine it with activities that demand a certain use of technology. In
particular, the potential of Internet of things (IoT) in tourism has been proven
through many different applications and proposals.

Point Of Interest (POI) is the name given to places such as natural landmarks, historic monuments, museums and other places geolocated at a specific
position considered of a high interest for tourists. In many cases, tourists can

© Springer International Publishing AG 2017
S.F. Ochoa et al. (Eds.): UCAmI 2017, LNCS 10586, pp. 149–160, 2017.
DOI: 10.1007/978-3-319-67585-5_16

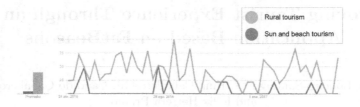

Fig. 1. Comparison between searching terms

not find basic information about the place, or about possible cultural or gastronomic activities that can be done there. In recent years the POIs have been technified, using for example Bluetooth technology in autonomous beacons. As described in Sect. 3, those Bluetooth beacons are continuously broadcasting a Uniform Resource Locator (URL) pointing to a web page. Android devices that have a Bluetooth 4.0 version or higher will receive this signal with the contained URL and will automatically proceed to download the content of this URL [2]. The main disadvantage and problem of this kind of technology is that it requires an Internet connection in the terminal. This requirement is a real problem in many cases because although in cities it is common to have coverage 2, 3 and 4G, there are many remote places where no Internet connection is available.

This paper proposes an IoT-based application of the new protocol presented in the summer of 2016, known as FatBeacon. This new protocol allows the broadcast of web content (not to be confused with a URL) that may contain HTML, CSS, JavaScript and other resources like images, vectors, etc. The main advantage of this new protocol is that the end user does not need to have an Internet connection to be able to see the content on its mobile terminal.

Bluetooth is nowadays a well-known technology thanks to its many different applications. Its use has been enhanced through several improvements in the corresponding protocols. Especially in recent years, with its integration into beacons, Bluetooth has been proposed as a solution to optimize resource allocation and indoor location [3] or in combination with technologies such as unmanned aerial vehicles (commonly known as drones) for the location of missing people [4]. It has also been used in the smart-city concept [5], which has been aroused in the last years, to broadcast information of POIs, products, shops, etc. Until today, all applications and projects have made use of Bluetooth technology for POIs as a sensor dependent on other technologies, such as the Internet, to obtain information, as shown in [6]. The new FatBeacon protocol has the advantage of allowing connectivity in areas without Internet signal. However, it has disadvantages such as high power consumption and low battery life. However, these problems can be reduced or mitigated using other power energy like solar cells.

Until now, there was no application that allowed to obtain information from any POI without making use of an Internet connection [7]. The use of Bluetooth technologies to solve localisation problems has been widespread for this purpose. There is a lot of references similar to this kind of works like [8,9] where BLE beacon are used to locate people and objects inside buildings (where it is common for guides to manage and inform tourists). Our proposal is focused on the use of outdoor beacons where it is not common to find guides. On the other hand, there are other similar solutions in the exterior to locate points of interest like [10] where beacon beacons are used as POI but an Internet connection is necessary to obtain the information. On the contrary our system works without an Internet connection.

This paper considers the solution to this problem using the new FatBeacon protocol applied for this purpose. In addition, it provides a comparison of different beacon protocols by measuring their performance.

The present paper is organised as follows. Section 2 describes the network coverage issue. A brief overview of Bluetooth technology is presented in Sect. 3. In Sect. 4, a case study and a detailed proof of concept are presented. Finally, in Sect. 5, the work is closed with some conclusions and future lines.

2 Preliminaries

The use of mobile networks is becoming more common. In fact it is already considered almost vital in the daily life of a common user. This type of network is deployed by establishing telephone antennas located at strategic points to attempt to cover a maximized radio and mobile coverage area. At present, connection bands are divided into 2G, 3G, 4G and even in the near future (2018), the use of 5G connections will be in regular use. The range of coverage of data networks is usually inversely proportional to their speed. For example, the 2G connection has low speed, compared to the other connections, but has a fairly wide coverage.

The majority of users who have an Internet connection on their mobile phones use them to obtain information about places, restaurants, social networks, etc. However, in hiking tourism, this type of information, such as weather, track status, local flora and fauna, recommendations or activities related to trekking, is not available in many cases. The FatBeacon protocol is used here to help solve this problem.

As an example, we now consider the case of the Spanish community of Santa Cruz de Tenerife, where many outdoor activities are offered for hikers [11] in different varieties of trails approved and enabled for their use. Some of them are even enabled for people with reduced mobility. At present, the trails (see Fig. 2b) are classified as follows:

- Green: These are local trails, less than 10 km, approved and verified by the issuing authority.
- Yellow: These are short distance trails, with a length between 10 and 50 km, but generally with quite a few slopes.
- Red: These trails are long-haul, over 50 km, so they are designed to make them in several days.

Figure 2a shows that a large part of the area is not covered even by the wider range (2G). This implies that approximately 40% of the island is inaccessible to

Internet connections. Figure 2c shows an overlap of the trails layer over the 2G map layer (see Fig. 2a). Working with this composition and using a technique of difference of layers of the image where if there is a point in the layer A that is present in the layer B, that point is painted a certain colour, as seen in Fig. 2d, it is possible to graphically visualize the total area of trails that have 2G coverage, and which of them do not have it. In this case, we can see the red colour indicating the number of trails (60% of the trails section) that is not covered coverage. On the other hand, 40% does have, at best, mobile data coverage.

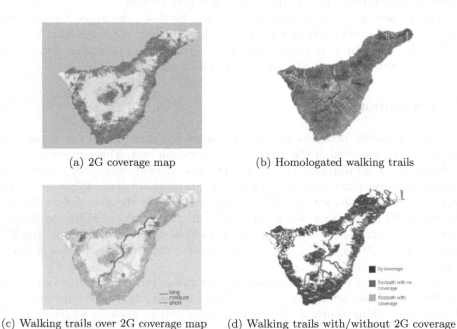

(a) 2G coverage map   (b) Homologated walking trails

(c) Walking trails over 2G coverage map   (d) Walking trails with/without 2G coverage

Fig. 2. Example of trail routes and signal coverage. (Color figure online)

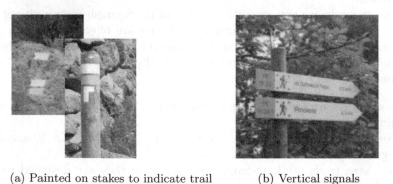

(a) Painted on stakes to indicate trail   (b) Vertical signals

Fig. 3. Guide signals

The signs that a tourist can find along the trail are those that can be seen in Fig. 2 (among others). For example, we can find logs with the colours of the trails or vertical signs that can give us a notion or guide of the site. These types of signs often deteriorate due to various climatic conditions or due to bandy acts.

3   FatBeacon-Based Implementation

BLE devices that operate on batteries and offer specific functionality are generally referred to as beacons. These devices emit a spherical BLE signal that, depending on the used protocol, can broadcast different contents, although in the majority of cases it emits a web address URL. Apart from the URL, there are other parameters that are emitted in each packet, such as the transmission power (TX power), which is a fixed emission value. This value determines the approximate emission range of each beacon and the battery consumption. The emission range has a direct relationship with the TX value so that a higher TX value implies that the signal will be emitted strongest and will reach a longer distance. However, this implies a greater consumption of battery, which with a lower level of TX would not happen. The emission frequency is the period between two consecutive transmissions. This can also affect battery consumption, since a higher frequency means more battery consumption. Frequency times are generally expressed in milliseconds (ms), so that a low value (higher emission frequency) could be 100 ms (10 times of emission in one second) while a high frequency (500 ms for example) would imply the emission of two transmissions per second. Mainly the beacon's life (in battery consumption) depends on these two values, so that the more it requires emission, the faster the battery will be spent. Generally, beacons are powered by lithium batteries such as CR2032 because they take up little space and have enough strength to power up the internal circuit. There are also models powered by a sunlight panel [12] (among others) that also has a charge accumulator to be able to work at night with the energy obtained during the day.

As explained, the BLE signal is emitted using a data transmission protocol. Currently, the best-known protocols are the protocols: iBeacon [13] developed by Apple [14], AltBeacon [15] designed by Radius Networks, and Eddystone [16] created by Google. The main difference between these three protocols and the new FatBeacon protocol (also created by Google) is that the latter can be used to broadcast much more content, making use of a connection by the Bluetooth from the transmitter to the receiver. This protocol is still in an experimental state. The detection operation is identical to the other presented protocols (such as Eddystone), except that, together with the packages with different parameters, an internal HTML content is emitted. The main advantage of this is that it makes the user being independent of an Internet connection (and related to it, independent of any antenna coverage).

The main disadvantage of emitting HTML content through this new protocol is that the stream emitted must be atomic (indivisible). Usually, when creating a web page the common thing is having the styles, JavaScript scripts, images and HTML code separately in order to have a cleaner code and to have the resources separately. In this case, to transmit HTML content using FatBeacon it is necessary that everything is inside the HTML. This is solved by including CSS and JavaScript scripts in the document's `<head>...</head>` header. In the case of images, icons and other resources that have to be included in the web, a previous base64 encoding is necessary for their inclusion as a string next to the `<img src="data:image/format;base64,/9j/2306AQS..."/>` image tag.

In the following example (see Fig. 4) a diagram is shown divided into two parts (Fig. 4a and b). This scheme differentiates the way that the beacons are normally used and how the new FatBeacon protocol works (left and right respectively). The first image shows how a beacon emits a web address (URL) that a smartphone receives through Bluetooth. Automatically, the smartphone, making use of an Internet connection, (mostly using 2G, 3G or 4G networks) downloads the content of the web and shows a notification on the screen. In the second image, where the FatBeacon protocol is used, steps 2 and 3 of Fig. 4 do not exist. This is because, with the new FatBeacon protocol, web content (HTML content) is emitted directly by using a Bluetooth connection instead of downloading the contents from a web server.

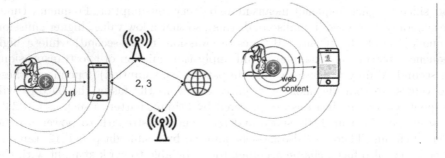

(a) Actual use of BLE Beacons

(b) New use of BLE Beacons using Fat-Beacon protocol

Fig. 4. Differences between Eddystone and FatBeacon protocols

In the following, some results are shown of some comparative tests to compare the efficiency of the new protocol related to the others. Likewise, a comparison of load times for different connection types, different sizes and different distances is also made to determine a degree of correlation between the test and results. The way to obtain the different speeds for BLE 4 has been empirical, making use of two mobile devices, one as emitter and the other one as receiver (because there are currently no physical devices that implement the protocol FatBeacon). For this, as an emitter, a Samsung Galaxy S7 (model SM-G930F) has been chosen. As receiver, a Xiaomi Mi 5s smart-phone (model 3G/64 GB) has been used. About the software, a custom version of the official Google Physical Web application (available to the public in [17]) has been used.

The changes made with respect to the original have been:

- Modify the `BluetoothSite.java` adding the following variables `private long start_time = 0;` and `private long end_time = 0;`.
- In the `connect` function was added `start_time = System.nanoTime();`
- In the `close` method, it was added `end_time = System.nanotime();` and `double difference = (end_time - start_time)/1e6;` at the end of the function (with a `System.out.println(difference)` to check the result).

The file where the HTML content was stored was also modified to fit the following sizes (in kilobytes): 10, 20, 40, 100 and 200. Having this when running the application (having the receiver smart-phone connected to the emulation terminal) it is possible to see the time it took to transfer data using FatBeacon from one terminal to the another one.

Other transfer speeds (BLE5 [18], 2G and 3G [19]) have been extracted from the speed specifications of each type of connection and considering that 1 byte = 8 bits, what means that if the speed is 1 Mbit/s then, the real ratio is 0,125 MB/s.

The resulting download times, taken by each kind of connection and sizes, are shown in the next Table 1.

Table 1. Download speeds for different protocols and sizes (in second/s)

	BLE 4	BLE 5[a]	2G[b]	3G[b]
10 kb	5.21	1.30	5	0
20 kb	8.82	2.20	11	0
40 kb	7.43	1.85	23	0
100 kb	15.18	3.79	58	2
200 kb	28.14	7.03	107	4

[a]Based on the BLE5 specifications
[b]Based on 3GPP specifications and without considering the TCP connection delay

The connection times for BLE 4 have been extracted from Table 2 performed in a related way (empirical) maintaining a distance between the transmitter and receiver of 1 m. For each size of web page, five measurements were made. Then, discarding the best and the worst result, a mean of the remaining values was performed. When performing this experiment, a rare case was that the first result of each size was the worst, which could indicate that the RAM load of the web is done on the fly keeping it for the succeeding results.

Table 2. Times at 1 m

1m	10 kb	20 kb	40 kb	100 kb	200 kb
1	4.0498	6.1178	4.3513	12.5816	15.8346
2	4.4163	7.5264	7.2030	12.7050	23.4155
3	5.2194	8.8279	7.4392	15.1869	28.1433
4	6.8424	12.0863	8.6729	18.4735	33.7344
5	7.3336	14.4279	10.35.77	74.8106	87.9002
Median	5.5219	8.8279	7.7492	15.1869	28.1433

According to the results shown in Table 2, the correlation index (0.9468) between size and speed indicates that a very strong dependence exists between size and speed of transmission.

In order to determine whether the transfer time depends on the distance, another empirical experiment was done, establishing a static web page size (40 kb approximately) and a variable distance. The experiment was performed for each test, in a straight line without obstacles through and without factors that could attenuate the strength of the signal such as solar rays, wind, etc. resulting in the values shown in Table 3 (where the results are ordered from best to worst for each distance).

Table 3. Checking that the transfer time depends on the distance

40 kb	1 m	5 m	10 m	15 m
1 best result	4.351	4.237	6.283	7.769
2	7.203	4.539	6.668	8.001
3	7.439	6.718	7.117	8.075
4	8.673	7.614	8.668	10.235
5 worst result	10.358	10.246	30.187	10.784
Median (discarding the best and the worst result)	7.439	6.718	7.117	8.075

In the case shown in Table 3, the correlation index (0.6851) indicates that exist a relationship between the distance and the speed.

Another great advantage of using a Bluetooth protocol in comparison with other connections, such as 2G, is that the battery consumption is quite lower, such as it is shown in the screen-shots of Fig. 5. Keep in mind that these data can change according to the user profile.

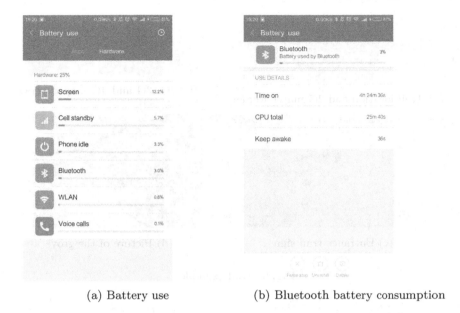

(a) Battery use   (b) Bluetooth battery consumption

Fig. 5. Bluetooth battery consumption

4   Case Study

As presented in Sect. 2, one of the main problems with information on the fly is mobile coverage in many areas. In particular, in this case of use, the hypothesis of not having a connection at the entrance of a path covered by trees has been adopted. In normal situations in this trail, there could be a connection 2G as maximum (see Fig. 6a and b), if it is interposed any kind of vegetation or obstacles (trees, for example) the 2G connection turns into inexistent.

In this case, the practical tests were carried out on the "Sendero de los Sentidos" [20] in the island of Tenerife, in Spain. This trail is very popular among visitors that come to Tenerife due to its low level of physical requirement, its accessibility (it is possible to arrive by car at the entry), access to people with reduced mobility, its diversity in flora and sensory experiences that are offered (see Fig. 6c). A feature of this trail is that its path is covered by trees (see Fig. 6d) so, any mobile coverage in the area is almost nonexistent.

After validating that the coverage was non-existent in the area, it was decided to disable connections referring to Internet data and Wi-Fi (to save battery). At the beginning of the trail, the emitter was placed emitting a 40 kb (approximately) web content. When a user approaches a reasonable distance, the receiver picks up the signal emitted by the transmitter showing a notification in the panel of the smart-phone (see Fig. 7a). When the user clicks on the notification, a message of loading content appears to later open the web browser with the content emitted by the sender (see Fig. 7b).

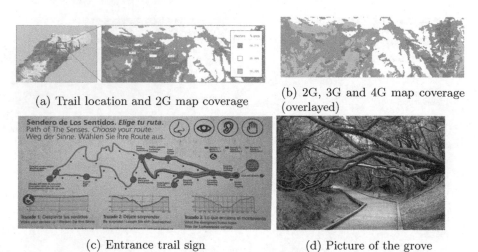

(a) Trail location and 2G map coverage

(b) 2G, 3G and 4G map coverage (overlayed)

(c) Entrance trail sign

(d) Picture of the grove

Fig. 6. Trail example

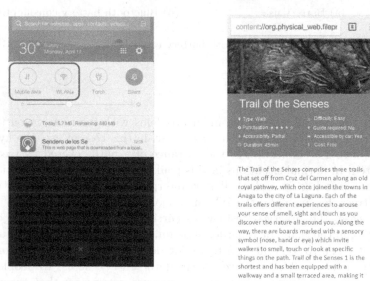

(a) Content notification emitted by a beacon

(b) Web content emitted by a beacon

Fig. 7. BLE FatBeacon emission

5   Conclusions

In this paper, the new protocol (still in pre-release phases) FatBeacon has been presented as an alternative that does not require any data connection to download a beacon web information. In addition, a comparison has been made between said technology and other known BLE protocols, such as Eddystone, iBeacon or

AltBeacon. This new protocol offers the possibility of sending static HTML content through a Bluetooth connection so that people do not need to have data connectivity on their smartphones or an Internet connection to receive information from isolated POIs. This work shows a study of the efficiency of battery consumption of a device with Bluetooth Low Energy compared to others (like WiFi and data connection). In addition to this, empirical data of the efficiency of the new FatBeacon protocol is shown for different factors, such as distances, web page sizes, etc. and has been compared with other BLE protocols such as BLE5. In this comparison, other forms of data transfer (having Internet) have been contrasted, considering different speeds like 2G, 3G and higher versions of Bluetooth as the integrated 5 in its low energy version. The main conclusion of the experiments presented in this paper is the great utility of this new protocol and the advantages that it offers in front of its predecessors due to its versatility, low consumption and low cost of deployment. As future work, a wider comparison among BLE protocols will be made. Furthermore, the idea of creating a physical device based on components such as Arduino powered by a solar panel, which is able to broadcast by FatBeacon web content to offer tourist information in smart cities and isolated environments.

Acknowledgments. Research supported by the Spanish Ministry of Economy and Competitiveness, the FEDER Fund, and the CajaCanarias Foundation, under Projects TEC2014-54110-R, RTC-2014-1648-8, MTM2015-69138-REDT and DIG02-INSITU.

References

1. Google trends - tourism (2016). https://goo.gl/fSxWSL
2. Choi, M., Park, W.K., Lee, I.: Smart office energy management system using bluetooth low energy based beacons and a mobile app. In: 2015 IEEE International Conference on Consumer Electronics (ICCE), pp. 501–502, January 2015
3. Alvarez-Díaz, N., Caballero-Gil, P., Reboso-Morales, H., Martın-Fernández, F.: Optimizing resource allocation and indoor location using bluetooth low energy (2016)
4. Lodeiro-Santiago, M., Santos-González, I., Caballero-Gil, P.: UAV-Based rescue system for emergency situations. In: García, C.R., Caballero-Gil, P., Burmester, M., Quesada-Arencibia, A. (eds.) UCAmI/IWAAL/AmIHEALTH 2016. LNCS, vol. 10070, pp. 163–173. Springer, Cham (2016). doi:10.1007/978-3-319-48799-1_20
5. Kim, H.-C., Kim, Y.-S.: Smart tourism information system using location-based technology. Int. J. Softw. Eng. Appl. **10**(11), 11–24 (2016)
6. Shibata, Y., Sasaki, K.: Tourist information system based on beacon and augumented reality technologies. In: 2016 19th International Conference on Network-Based Information Systems (NBiS), pp. 410–413. IEEE (2016)
7. Ruta, M., Ieva, S., Loseto, G., Di Sciascio, E.: From the physical web to the physical semantic web: knowledge discovery in the internet of things. In: UBICOMM 2016, The Tenth International Conference on Mobile Ubiquitous Computing, Systems, Services and Technologies (2016)
8. Fujihara, A., Yanagizawa, T.: Proposing an extended ibeacon system for indoor route guidance. In: 2015 International Conference on Intelligent Networking and Collaborative Systems, pp. 31–37, September 2015

9. Zhuang, Y., Yang, J., Li, Y., Qi, L., El-Sheimy, N.: Smartphone-based indoor localization with bluetooth low energy beacons. Sensors (Switzerland) **16**(5), 596 (2016)
10. Lee, H.-E., Choi, H.-S.: Improvements of the Korean tourism application, visit Korea, for foreigners-based on beacon functions. Int. J. Softw. Eng. Appl. **10**(4), 103–116 (2016)
11. Secretos naturales culturales de la isla al alcande de todos (online). http://www.diariodeavisos.com/2013/09/secretos-naturales-culturales-isla-al-alcance-todos/
12. Cyalkit-e02 solar-powered ble sensor beacon (online). https://goo.gl/E7fnkG
13. ibeacon apple (online). https://developer.apple.com/ibeacon/
14. Newman, N.: Apple ibeacon technology briefing. J. Direct Data Digit. Market. Pract. **15**(3), 222–225 (2014)
15. Altbeacon protocol (online). http://altbeacon.org/
16. Eddystone protocol (online). https://developers.google.com/beacons/
17. Google physical-web (online). https://github.com/google/physical-web
18. Bluetooth 5 specifications (online). https://goo.gl/Oy5zLK
19. 3g pp the mobile broadband standard. http://www.3gpp.org/
20. Sendero de los sentidos 1/3 (online). https://goo.gl/BA3P9R

Protecting Industry 4.0 Systems Against the Malicious Effects of Cyber-Physical Attacks

Borja Bordel$^{(\boxtimes)}$, Ramón Alcarria, Diego Sánchez-de-Rivera, and Tomás Robles

Universidad Politécnica de Madrid, Madrid, Spain
bbordel@dit.upm.es,
{ramon.alcarria,tomas.robles}@upm.es,
diego.sanchezderiveracordoba@gmail.com

Abstract. Industry 4.0 refers a new industrial paradigm based on Cyber-Physical Systems principles. In these new, complex and highly interdependent systems, the traditional definition of "cyber-attack" is not enough to represent all the situations may occur. Furthermore, traditional security policies and defense strategies are not designed to be effective in scenarios mixing cyber and physical elements. In this context, this work presents a new idea about what cyber-physical attacks are, and a technological solution to protect and compensate the malicious effects of these attacks in Industry 4.0 systems. The proposal is based on a specific description language (CP-ADL) for cyber-physical attacks, and a mathematical framework allowing a decision making about the most adequate defense strategy. Finally, and experimental validation is provided, showing with our proposal the impact of cyber-physical attacks is highly reduced.

Keywords: Cyber-physical attacks · Industry 4.0 · Process execution · CP-ADL · Security

1 Introduction

The emerging term Industry 4.0 was coined for the first time at the Hannover Fair during the presentation of the "Industry 4.0" initiative in Germany [1]. In general words, Industry 4.0 refers a new industrial scenario where a new type of systems consisting of the intersection of the physical and the cyber world (the so-called Cyber-Physical Systems-CPS-) is employed.

Traditional industrial systems are focused on control, so standard security policies consist of feedback loops with the objective of compensating the malicious effects of cyber-attacks [2, 3]. However, CPS present some special characteristics (such as the pervasiveness and the hybrid design) which make them vulnerable to a new and more general type of attacks known as cyber-physical attacks [4]. In these attacks, changes (accidental or not) in both (the physical and the cyber space) may appear, but due to the highly interdependency of components in CPS, the effects may influence any other part of the system, and thousands of components could be the final objective of the attack [4]. The genuine approach of cyber-physical attacks is acting on the weakest elements in the system (usually sensors deployed in a public space) in such a way that these

© Springer International Publishing AG 2017
S.F. Ochoa et al. (Eds.): UCAmI 2017, LNCS 10586, pp. 161–171, 2017.
DOI: 10.1007/978-3-319-67585-5_17

elements (which have full access to the system) cause a fail in the critical components (as every element in the system is integrated with the others). For example, vandalism, weather damages and, of course, traditional cyber-attacks, may be considered as cyber-physical attacks. CPS, moreover, may be deployed together with critical infrastructures (such as smart grids), so disconnecting the system or waiting until the attack finishes are not valid solutions.

The problem associated with these new attacks is their amplitude: there is an infinite amount of ways to perform a successful cyber-physical attack. Thus, depending on the attacked element, the aggression method and the final objective of the attack, protecting policies must be different. In a simple example, if control components are affected, traditional security policies for control systems should be applied; on the contrary if the data analytics layer is implicated, the attacks could be addressed as a computer virus. In this context, once detected a cyber-physical attack is taken place, it is necessary to infer the type of attack being performed in order to protect the system adequately. However, information about a running attack is obtained as time passes, while the effects in the system are getting worse.

Therefore the objective of this paper is to provide a solution in order to infer the type of cyber-physical attack that an Industry 4.0 system is suffering, as well as a decision making framework to determine if a certain security or protection policy must be applied or if it is more profitable to wait for more information about the attack. Our proposal is based on a specific description language (CP-ADL) for cyber-physical attacks, on the use of XML patterns and templates and on a mathematical framework using the game theory.

The rest of the paper is organized as follows. Section 2 describes the state of the art on Industry 4.0 and CPS security solutions. Section 3 describes the proposed solution. Section 4 explains the simulation scenario used as experimental validation. Finally, Sect. 5 presents the results of the experimental validation and Sect. 6 concludes the paper.

2 State of the Art

Security is one of the most popular research topics nowadays. The use of technological systems to digitalize critical infrastructures has cause an increase in the number of works about that issue. The emerging Industry 4.0 systems are also part of this trend.

Different works may be found. On the one hand, works about security in new generation smart grids have been proposed. Most of them are focused on the design of enhanced control loops [3, 5], but cyber-attacks taxonomies have been also described [6, 7]. Proposals about protection schemes for CPS applied to smart grids [2] and other systems under cyber-physical attacks [8] have been also described. On the other hand, security solutions for networked control systems and industrial applications have been also investigated [4].

The problem of all these proposals is that they are focused on attacks which introduce perturbations or known malicious signals in the system, so security and protection solutions are fixed and rigid. In consequence, these proposals reduce their usability if new or slightly different attacks are performed.

In addition, works about how traditional security solutions (i.e. firewalls, computer shields, etc.) could be applied to CPS and Industry 4.0 scenarios have been recently described [9]. However, this approach only covers partially the problems and vulnerabilities associated with cyber-physical attacks, so more general solutions are required. General reviews about the problems associated with security in these new scenarios have been also reported. Works about critical industrial scenarios [18], Industry 4.0 systems [19] and CPS [20] may be found.

Finally, the concept of cyber-physical attack has been investigated. Abstract taxonomies and description languages have been proposed [10]. These instruments are very useful to classify and infer the use of certain types of cyber-physical attacks.

3   A Protection Solution for Industry 4.0 Systems

A cyber-physical attack may be described using only six different fields [10] (see Fig. 1). Below a brief explanation of each field is provided:

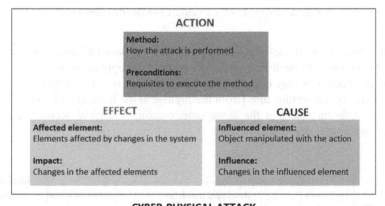

Fig. 1. Description of cyber-physical attacks

- Method: It represents the procedure employed to affect the system.
- Preconditions: They list the requirements to be present in the system so the method is a successful way of attacking the system. Together with the "method" this list made up the "action" of the cyber-physical attack.
- Influenced element: It refers the elements which have been manipulated through the described action.
- Influence: The produced changes in the influenced element. Together with the "influenced element", it describes the "cause" of the cyber-physical attack.
- Affected element: A list of the elements which have been affected by the changes in the system (usually it is the objective of the attack).
- Impact: A description of the changes in the system. Together with the "affected element", it describes the "effect" of the cyber-physical attack.

In this context, a cyber-physical attack may be modeled by means of a XML document, describing the value of each one of the previously identified fields. CP-ADL is a description language [10] focused on this objective (see Fig. 2).

```
<Action>
    <Method>
        <Category>
            //Physical, cyber or hybrid
        </Category>
        <Description>
            //Free text
        </Description>
    </Method>
    <Precondition>
        <Category> … </Category>
        <Description>
            …
        </Description>
    </Precondition >
    …
</Action>
```

```
<Cause>
    <InfluencedElement>
        <Category> … </Category>
        <Name> … </Name>
    </InfluencedElement>
    <Influence>
        …
    </Influence>
</Cause>
<Effect>
    <AffectedElement>
        …
    </AffectedElement>
    <Impact>
        …
    </Impact>
</Effect>
```

Fig. 2. Example of a generic CP-ADL description

Then, considering this description language, it is proposed a functional architecture in order to support a protection system for Industry 4.0 applications (see Fig. 3). The proposed architecture is very horizontal and general, so it may be integrated at different levels in Industry 4.0 architecture (from the highest to the lowest) and, even, it may be included in different places at the same time, creating a vertical security solution of connected horizontal deployments.

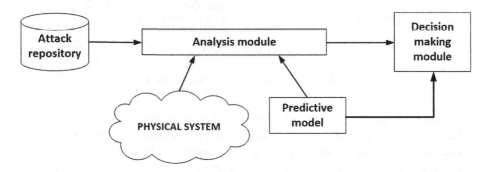

Fig. 3. Functional architecture

In this architecture, different components may be identified. A *Predictive model* represents the system's state in a certain moment and at some future instants. This model may be updated through a hybrid simulator and interpolation techniques [11]. This information is provided to an *Analysis module*, where these data are compared to the real state of the components in the system. Results of the comparison process are employed to infer if the system is under a cyber-physical attack. In order to do that, a collection of templates describing different cyber-physical attacks (and the security and protection policies associated with these attacks) is included in a *Template repository*. A distance function is employed to determine the set of templates (i.e. attacks) which are closer to the observations made about the system (a pattern recognition process is, in that way, performed). Finally, this set of patterns is used by a *Decision making module* to select the protection method to be applied (if decided it is necessary to perform some actions).

Mathematically, the process is described as follows.

An Industry 4.0 system $\mathfrak{T}$ is described in a certain instant $t = T_0$ as a collection of $N(T_0)$ components c_i whose state is represented through a set of M_i parameters p_j. See (1).

$$\begin{aligned}
\mathfrak{T}(t = T_0) &= \{c_i(T_0), \quad i = 1, \ldots, N(T_0)\} \\
&= \{\{p_j(T_0), j = 1, \ldots, M_i\}_i, \quad i = 1, \ldots, N(T_0)\}
\end{aligned} \tag{1}$$

Two different representations of the system are obtained, then, at each moment: on the one hand, the state calculated by the *Predictive model* $\mathfrak{T}_p$ and, on the other hand, the state obtained from the real deployment $\mathfrak{T}_r$. The difference between both representations ε is obtained in order to evaluate whether any component in the system is affected by a cyber-physical attack (2). This difference is calculated for each component ε_{c_i} and for the global system through a deformation estimation process [12]. If the deformation in the state of any component is higher than the maximum allowed threshold ε_{th_i}, then, that component is considered affected (3).

$$\varepsilon = \|F(\mathfrak{T}_p, \mathfrak{T}_r)\| \tag{2}$$

$$\varepsilon_{c_i} > \varepsilon_{th_i} \tag{3}$$

Where $F(\cdot, \cdot)$ is a strain tensor (i.e. the Jacobian matrix of the application which transforms $\mathfrak{T}_p$ into $\mathfrak{T}_r$) and the operator "norm" $\|\cdot\|$ represents the module of a matrix.

Then, the list of affected components is employed to instantiate a XML template t containing the information about the potential cyber-physical attack the system is suffering (4). The Cyber-Physical Attack Description language (CP-ADL) is employed. Usually, only the fields related to the "effect" of the attack could be described, although depending on the available information sometimes is possible to determine the "cause" as well.

$$t = XML(\varepsilon_{c_i}, \mathfrak{T}_p, \mathfrak{T}_r) \tag{4}$$

In a standard case, information collected at the first instant $t = T_0$ is not enough to determine without any doubt which attack is being taken place or if, in fact, an attack is being performed. Thus, a statistical procedure is needed, so the set of the most probable options have to be calculated. In order to do that, it is considered the collection of templates $\mathbb{T}$ stored in the *Template repository*. Each one of these templates describes a cyber-physical attack, and it has associated a certain protection policy, adequate for such attack.

The set of most probable attacks $\mathcal{A}$ is then obtained by means of a Dynamic time warping (DTW) pattern recognition process [15], which may be understood as an enhanced distance in a generalized space (5). The basic idea is to calculate the proximity of the performed observations to every cyber-attack template.

$$\mathcal{A} = dtw(\mathbb{T}, t) \tag{5}$$

If the DTW algorithm is too heavy to be executed in the scenario under study, a generalized distance could be also employed, such as d_1 or d_∞ (which, at the end, compute the number of coincidences between two templates) [16]. Finally, the set $\mathcal{A}$ may be composed by the attacks whose distance to the instantiated template t is lower than a certain limit; or may be forced to present a specific cardinality.

At this stage, different strategies (one for each cyber-physical attack contained in $\mathcal{A}$) may be followed (6) by the system manager (i.e. different protection policies could be applied or no action could be performed), and each one of these strategies produces different benefits/problems (i.e. different payoffs) in the system (7).

$$S_{admin} = \left\{ s_1^{admin}, \ldots, s_q^{admin} \right\} \tag{6}$$

$$U_{admin} = \left\{ u_{s_1^{admin}}, \ldots, u_{s_q^{admin}} \right\} \tag{7}$$

These payoffs will be directly proportional to the compensation of the malicious effects of the cyber-physical attack produced by the protection policy under study. Moreover, the attacker may be running any of the cyber-physical attacks considered in $\mathcal{A}$, or, even, any other non-considered attack. Sometimes, besides, no attack is running (then, the attacker has one strategy more to choose than the system manager). Thus, the attacker may follow also different strategies (8), each one giving different payoffs (directly proportional to the malicious effects caused in the system) (9).

$$S_{attack} = \left\{ s_1^{attack}, \ldots, s_{q+1}^{attack} \right\} \tag{8}$$

$$U_{attack} = \left\{ u_{s_1^{attack}}, \ldots, u_{s_{q+1}^{attack}} \right\} \tag{9}$$

In that way, a game can be defined, considering the attacker and the system administrator as players of the game (10). The game G is dynamic and the number of considered rounds should be proportional to the observation period. For a standard configuration [17] three rounds should be considered. In this context, the intervention order in the game would be: Attacker-Manager-Attacker. Figure 4 represents the game in an extensive way.

$$G = [S, U] = \left\{ S_{admin}, S_{attack}; U_{admin}, U_{attack} \right\} \tag{10}$$

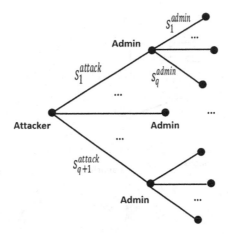

Fig. 4. Proposed dynamic game

Considering the first player who selects first a strategy is the attacker, three different tactics may be followed:

- Minimum effect: In this tactic, the manager selects the strategy which reduces as much as possible the payoff of the attacker. In this approach, the attacker usually tries to change the strategy to obtain a higher payoff.
- Satisfaction and control: In this tactic, it is selected the strategy which gives a highest payoff to the attacker. Thus, its objectives are fulfilled and the manager can be focused on controlling the malicious effects as much as possible. It is a very stable approach but very risky, especially if some effects become uncontrolled.
- Optimum: The system manager selects the strategy that generates a Nash equilibrium [13] (so the game does not advance as no individual incentive is possible). However, this strategy is only successful if the attacker is a rational entity.

Once, following any of the proposed tactics, a protection policy is selected, it is applied (or not, if decided waiting for more information). At this moment, the described process is restarted in order to re-evaluate the system performance and the effects of the selected security solution.

4 Experimental Validation

In this Section we propose a first validation of the proposed solution by means of a simulation environment. The experimental validation consisted of a simulated scenario based on the NS3 simulator.

The proposed Industry 4.0 (Fig. 5) scenario consisted of different production systems of electronic devices and components. In particular three different types were considered: manufacture of diodes, manufacture of capacitors and manufacture of logic gates. Details about the components which are included in each one of the production systems are provided in the literature [14].

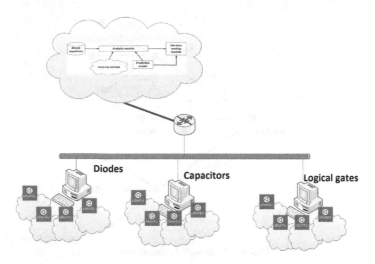

Fig. 5. Simulation scenario

Moreover, the proposed architecture was implemented in the top layer, in order to protect the system against cyber-physical attacks. With this approach, attack detection is slower but the scope of the applied protection policies turns wider. In order to implement the described solution in the components of the simulated scenario, each node in the NS3 simulator was provided with a tap bridge (or ghost node). These bridges are able to connect an internal NS3 component with an external entity, which allows implementing in a very easy way complex algorithms and other proprietary solutions for which there are no C++ libraries (the programming language of the NS3 simulator). In particular, elements in the functional architecture were connected with virtual Linux machines based on the KVM technology (so they may be automatically deployed using the *libvirt* interface).

The simulation was programmed to introduce a cyber-physical attack in a random way, selecting the type of attack from a previously created catalogue.

Two different experiments were performed in this scenario. During the first experiment it was evaluated the number of attacks which were successfully addressed. Different tactics were considered in order to compare the obtained performance. Moreover, information about the protection procedure was obtained, so the causes of failures were also studied. During the second experiment, the required time to protect the system in an adequate way was measured.

5 Results

Results of the first experiment are showed on Fig. 6. As can be seen, the proposed framework allows protecting successfully the system against cyber-physical attacks in more than 90% of cases. The tactic which produces the best results is "satisfaction and control", as it is the approach which forces the system to employ the most general and ambitious security policy (as the reduction in the malicious effects, in the first step, is considered to be minimum).

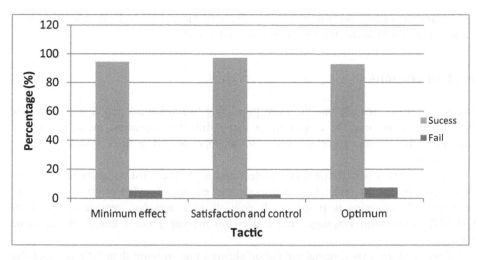

Fig. 6. Results of the first experiment

An study about the causes of failure showed that (in general), optimum tactic fails because the attacker is not a rational entity (for example, it cannot change its behavior depending on the applied security policy). On the other hand, the minimum effect tactic fails as predictions must be very precise to reach that situation and this is quite complicated if a fast response is desired.

Results of the second experiment are showed on Fig. 7. As the interesting information is the comparison among the different tactics, but not the particular time values, time scale is normalized using the maximum value.

As can be seen, the time required to implement and protect the system using the "satisfaction and control" tactic is the lowest. It is a very easy approach to execute, as no effort to control the appearance of new malicious effects is provided. On the contrary, the "minimum effect" approach is a very complicated tactic, as it requires a

Fig. 7. Results of the second experiment

procedure to compensate the malicious effects of the cyber-physical attack and protection policies to avoid the appearance of new effects.

6 Conclusions

Industry 4.0 systems are one the most promising technological paradigms. This new type of solutions may be employed in many different scenarios, including critical infrastructures. In this context, security to be implemented in these systems is a key topic in research.

In this work a new framework to select and apply the most adequate security and protection policy in order to compensate the effects of cyber-physical attacks in Industry 4.0 scenarios is proposed. It consists of a template repository based on CP-ADL description language, and a decision making process based on the game theory.

Results of the experimental validation showed that in more than 90% of cases the proposed framework allows protecting Industry 4.0 systems against cyber-physical attacks. "Satisfaction and control" approach is the most successful tactic. Moreover, it is the fastest tactic to implement.

Acknowledgments. Borja Bordel has received funding from the Ministry of Education through the FPU program (grant number FPU15/03977). Additionally, the research leading to these results has received funding from the Ministry of Economy and Competitiveness through SEMOLA project (TEC2015-68284-R) and from the Autonomous Region of Madrid through MOSI-AGIL-CM project (grant P2013/ICE-3019, co-funded by EU Structural Funds FSE and FEDER).

References

1. Dujin, A., Geissler, C., Horstkötter, D.: Industry 4.0: The new industrial revolution. Roland Berger Strategy Consultants, Munich (2014)
2. Mo, Y., Kim, T.H.J., Brancik, K., Dickinson, D., Lee, H., Perrig, A., Sinopoli, B.: Cyber–physical security of a smart grid infrastructure. Proc. IEEE **100**(1), 195–209 (2012)
3. Sridhar, S., Hahn, A., Govindarasu, M.: Cyber–physical system security for the electric power grid. Proc. IEEE **100**(1), 210–224 (2012)
4. Pasqualetti, F., Dörfler, F., Bullo, F.: Cyber-physical attacks in power networks: Models, fundamental limitations and monitor design. In: 2011 50th IEEE Conference on Decision and Control and European Control Conference (CDC-ECC), pp. 2195–2201, December 2011
5. Hahn, A., Ashok, A., Sridhar, S., Govindarasu, M.: Cyber-physical security testbeds: architecture, application, and evaluation for smart grid. IEEE Trans. Smart Grid **4**(2), 847–855 (2013)
6. Zhu, B., Sastry, S.: SCADA-specific intrusion detection/prevention systems: a survey and taxonomy. In: Proceedings of the 1st Workshop on Secure Control Systems (SCS), vol. 11, April 2010

7. Zhu, B., Joseph, A., Sastry, S.: A taxonomy of cyber attacks on SCADA systems. In: 2011 International Conference on Internet of Things (iThings/CPSCom) and 4th International Conference on Cyber, Physical and Social Computing, pp. 380–388, October 2011
8. Clark, R.M., Hakim, S.: Cyber-Physical Security. Springer, Switzerland (2017)
9. Genge, B., Nai Fovino, I., Siaterlis, C., Masera, M.: Analyzing cyber-physical attacks on networked industrial control systems. In: Butts, J., Shenoi, S. (eds.) ICCIP 2011. IAICT, vol. 367, pp. 167–183. Springer, Heidelberg (2011). doi:10.1007/978-3-642-24864-1_12
10. Yampolskiy, M., Horváth, P., Koutsoukos, X.D., Xue, Y., Sztipanovits, J.: A language for describing attacks on cyber-physical systems. Int. J. Crit. Infrastruct. Prot. 8, 40–52 (2015)
11. Bordel Sánchez, B., Alcarria, R., De Rivera, D.S., Sánchez-Picot, A.: Predictive algorithms for mobility and device lifecycle management in Cyber-physical Systems. EURASIP J. Wirel. Commun. Netw. 2016(1), 228 (2016)
12. Bordel, B., Alcarria, R., Jara, A.: Process execution in humanized Cyber-physical systems: soft processes. In: 2017 12th Iberian Conference on Information Systems and Technologies (CISTI), pp. 1–7, June 2017
13. Fudenberg, D., Tirole, J.: Game Theory (1991)
14. Bordel, B., Alcarria, R., Sanchez, D., Sánchez, A.: Enhancing process control in industry 4.0 scenarios using cyber-physical systems. J. Wirel. Mob. Netw. Ubiquit. Comput. Dependable Appl. 7, 41–64 (2016)
15. Berndt, D.J., Clifford, J.: Using dynamic time warping to find patterns in time series. In: KDD workshop, vol. 10, No. 16, pp. 359–370. Innovative Information Science & Technology Research Group, South Korea, July 1994. http://isyou.info/jowua/papers/jowua-v7n4-3.pdf. ISSN: 2093-5374 (printed), ISSN: 2093-5382 (online)
16. Munkres, J.R.: Topology. Prentice Hall, Upper Saddle River (2000)
17. Alcarria, R., de Andrés, D.M., Bordel, B., de Rivera, D.S., Sánchez-Picot, Á., Robles, T.: A service-oriented monitoring system based on rule evaluation for Home Automation. In: 2017 IEEE International Conference on Consumer Electronics (ICCE), pp. 329–330. IEEE, January 2017
18. Uchenna, P., Ani, D., Hongmei, M., Tiwari, H.A.: Review of cybersecurity issues in industrial critical infrastructure: manufacturing in perspective. J. Cyber Secur. Technol. 1(1), 32–74 (2017)
19. Waslo, R.: Industry 4.0 and Cybersecurity - Managing Risk in an Age of Connected Production. Deloitte University Press, Washington (2017)
20. Cardenas, A., Amin, S., Sinopoli, B., Giani, A., Perrig, A., Sastry, S.: Challenges for securing cyber physical systems. In: Workshop on Future Directions in Cyber-Physical Systems Security, p. 5, July 2009

Fuzzy-Based Approach of Concept Alignment

María de Lourdes Martínez-Villaseñor[1,2(✉)]
and Miguel González-Mendoza[2]

[1] Universidad Panamericana, Facultad de Ingeniería,
Augusto Rodin 498, México, 03920 Ciudad de México, Mexico
lmartine@up.edu.mx
[2] Tecnológico de Monterrey, Campus Estado de México,
Carretera Lago de Guadalupe Km 2.5, Atizapán de Zaragoza,
Edo. de México, México, Mexico
mgonza@itesm.mx

Abstract. The need to share and reuse information has grown in the new era of Internet of things and ubiquitous computing. Researchers in ontology and schema matching use mapping approaches in order to achieve interoperability between heterogeneous sources. The use of multiple similarity measures that take into account lexical, structural and semantic properties of the concepts is often found in schema matching for the purpose of data integration, sharing and reusing. Mappings identified by automatic or semi-automatic tools can never be certain. In this paper, we present a fuzzy-based approach to combine different similarity measures to deal with scenarios where ambiguity of terms hinder the process of alignment and add uncertainty to the match.

Keywords: Concept alignment · Uncertainty · Fuzzy logic

1 Introduction

In ubiquitous environments new applications and devices appear as potential information consumers and suppliers. The need to share and reuse information has grown in the new era of Internet of things and ubiquitous computing. Wide research has been done in ontology [1] and schema matching [2], however, achieving interoperability between heterogeneous sources is still an open issue due to high dynamicity and variety of the stakeholders.

The calculation of the similarities between to concepts is the primary operation in the process of concept alignment that enables schema matching for the purpose of data integration, sharing and reusing. One can never be sure that mappings identified by automatic or semi-automatic tools are correct [3]. Human effort is usually needed to determine the right matches between concepts or to correct semi-automatic or automatic concept alignments. Schema mappings are inherently uncertain [4]. Alignment systems turn out to be uncertain when concept are neither completely similar nor dissimilar [5]. It is necessary to deal with this uncertainty.

In this paper, we propose to use a fuzzy-based approach [6] in order to combine different similarity measures in as an improvement of the concept of process alignment

© Springer International Publishing AG 2017
S.F. Ochoa et al. (Eds.): UCAmI 2017, LNCS 10586, pp. 172–180, 2017.
DOI: 10.1007/978-3-319-67585-5_18

presented in [7, 8]. This is the first step to deal with uncertainty in schema matching process. In the process of concept alignment homonyms are frequently found; some strings are used in many schemas with different meaning. An automatic alignment can find several exact matches or none. In this work, we focus in these cases where ambiguity of terms hinder the process of alignment and add uncertainty to the match.

The rest of the paper is organized as follows. A brief overview of uncertainty in schema matching is presented in Sect. 2. Our fuzzy-based concept alignment is presented in Sect. 3. Experiments and results are shown in Sect. 4. Conclusions are given in Sect. 5.

2 Uncertainty in Schema Matching

Schema matching is an important operation that provides correspondences between concepts of various heterogeneous sources like relational databases, XML-schemas, catalogs, directories etc. [4]. An excellent review in schema matching is presented in [9]. Data integration of heterogeneous sources has become relevant in the last decades for health, E-business, and Semantic Web domains among others. The process of finding schema mappings is inherently uncertain [4]; mappings identified by automatic or semi-automatic tools can never be 100% certain [3]. Dong et al. [10] state that data integration systems must handle uncertainty at three levels: uncertain schema mapping, uncertain data, and uncertain queries. Regarding uncertain schema mapping, the authors argue that sometimes users are not skilled enough to provide precise mappings, or the scale of the data makes it impossible to generate and maintain precise mappings.

In [4], the authors consider the problem of uncertainty modeling and management in schema matching process. They present various aspects of uncertainty in schema matching starting with basic notions of probability theory and fuzzy set theory for representing uncertainty of the matching process. They propose a model for uncertainty in schema matching, and matcher ensembles and Top-k schema matching strategies to reduce the uncertainty in the process.

Some authors manage uncertainty in Schema Matching process using probabilistic mappings [4, 10, 11]. They associated probabilities to tuples and semantic mappings in order to rank and obtain the best results for data integration and data exchange. Dong et al. [10] define probabilistic schema mapping as "a set of possible (ordinary) mappings between a source schema and a target schema, where each possible mapping has an associated probability".

Agreste et al. [12] provide a review and classification of XML Matchers, and discussed the challenge of uncertainty management in XML Matchers.

Fernandez et al. [13] presented a system for ontology alignment using fuzzy logic techniques to combine similarity measures between entities of different sensor ontologies. Jan et al. [5] proposed an ontology alignment system using a combination of string, linguistic and structural matchers to find similarities between entities. They used Rough Sets to deal with uncertainties in unmapped entities.

3 Fuzzy–Based Concept Alignment

From the state of the art in ontology and schema matching, we learn that it is necessary to use different type of similarities, and processes that refine the element based overall similarity considering structural and internal context of the concepts in order to align to entities. Nevertheless, it is very difficult to find an automatic exact match between two concepts given the inherent uncertainty of the alignment process. We propose a fuzzy approach to merge different similarity measures as the first step to deal with this uncertainty.

3.1 Process of Concept Alignment

A process of concept alignment is necessary, as we stated above, in many applications such as data integration, sharing and/or reusing. The process of concept alignment should contemplate approximate matching, because it not only considers exact match or disjoint (black or white); the matching can consider semantic relaxation suggesting possible answers to requests also including neighbors (hypernyms, hyponyms, meronyms) when no exact match is available. It can also be partial because finding a match of all concepts of the source schema with a target schema is not necessary or possible for all case scenarios. Some source documents have concepts that are only useful for the provider, or have concepts with high matching difficulty. Typically, schema matching is performed on *"design-time"* to address semantic heterogeneity, but ubiquitous web applications may require *"run-time"* matching operations. New stakeholders appear, and changes to current stakeholders participating in the interoperability process can be discovered at run-time. In order to cope with this dynamicity, a continuous *"design-time"* and *"run-time"* matching strategy can be acceptable (Shvaiko et al. 2006).In this work, we consider the cardinality of the output alignment is 1:1 so one concept on the source is aligned with only one concept on the target. The type of relation is *equivalent* (=), *related* ($\subseteq, \supseteq, \cap$) or *independent*: ($\perp$). The ultimate goal of the concept alignment is to enable data integration, sharing and/or reusing.

A concept scheme is considered as *(C, H_C, V_C)* where C is a set of concepts arranged in a subsumption hierarchy H_C. V_C is the set of corresponding concept values.

Each concept c_s in a set of concept source C_S is defined by: a label *string1:string2* where *string1* is optional and *string2* is mandatory, and subclass relationships. When namespaces, other than default, are specified in the source document *string1* is used. The attribute or element identifier corresponds to *string2* and it is typically described as a simple or compound word in natural language. Subclass relationships set up a link with other concepts in the source document. The hierarchical structure H_s must be described as a *skos:ConceptScheme*.

A concept on the target side C_T is described by set of labels included in the target *skos:Concept* consisting of lexical labeling, notation and documentation SKOS properties.

The proposed automatic process of concept alignment uses a two-tier matching strategy to find semantic mappings between two schemas as a variation of the process presented in [7, 8]. First an element level matching step finds a set of concept candidates for alignment for each concept in the source concept scheme. Next, the method looks for structure similarity to disambiguate the meaning of the word analyzing its context, this means analyzing the structure and meaning of the neighbor concepts in the same source document.

3.2 Concept Alignment Similarities

In order to determine the similarity between concept c_s in C_S and concept c_t in C_T we combine three matching techniques:

The inclusion of each of these three similarity measures has a purpose. Similarity based in Dice coefficient [11] $sim_{Dice}(c_s, c_t) \in [0, 1])$ has the purpose of finding if concept c_s in X and a concept c_t in U have a high lexical similarity. Dice coefficient is a simple and normalized similarity measure [14] that can show if the two concept labels are similar at string level. Equation (1) calculates the longest common substring (LCS) distance similarity $(d_{lcs}(c_s, c_t) \in [0, 1])$ which tries to find if one label is subsumed in the other. The semantic similarity $(sim_{wordnet}(c_s, c_t) \in [0, 1])$ is based in Wu and Palmer path lengths method [15] using WordNet [16] as an external resource and tries to find the semantic similarity of the labels. Similarity in concepts other than English can be also included if the proper lexical resource is available.

$$d_{lcs}(c_s, c_t) = \frac{Lenght(LCS(c_s, c_t))}{\min(Lenght(c_s), Lenght(c_t))} \qquad (1)$$

In the next section, we propose to use a fuzzy-based approach in order to combine different similarity measures with fuzzy logic.

3.3 Fuzzy-Based Approach to Combine Similarity Measures

In the process of concept alignment, it is commonly found that two entities are neither completely similar nor dissimilar. It is necessary to deal with this uncertainty. In this paper, we propose to use a Fuzzy-based approach in order to combine different similarity measures with fuzzy logic instead of using the highest of the three similarity measures is considered to determine relation R presented in previous work [7, 8].

We define each of the similarity measures with trapezoid membership functions and linguistic term sets [17]{*low, medium, high*} as presented in Fig. 1.

The result of the combination of three similarity measures is considered to determine relation R in the triple $<c_s, c_t, R >$ of a mapping element according of the following criteria:

1. *Equivalent* (=): Two concept elements c_s and c_t are *equivalent* iff $sim_0(c_s, c_t) \geq t_e$.
2. *Related* ($\subseteq, \supseteq, \cap$): Two concept elements c_s and c_t are *related* iff $0.9 > sim_0(c_s, c_t) \geq t_r$.
3. *Independent* ($\perp$): Two concept elements c_s and c_t are *independent* iff $t_r > sim_0(c_s, c_t)$.

where $t_e = 0.9$ and $t_r = 0.6$. This means that in order to consider a concept to be equivalent (skos:closeMatch or skos:exactMatch) the combined similarity measure between the concepts must at least be 0.9. Similarly, in order to consider a concept

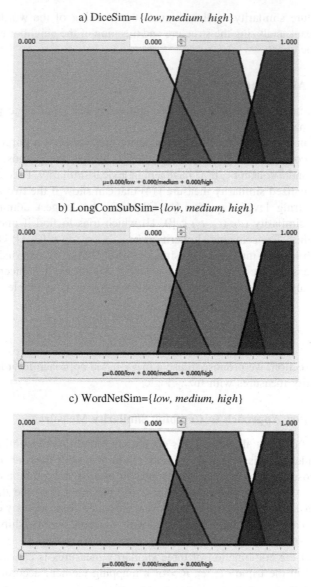

Fig. 1. Linguistic terms set and membership functions (a) String similarity; (b) Longest common substring similarity; (c) Semantic similarity

related (skos:related) the combined similarity measure between two concepts must at least be .6.

Figure 2 shows the output variable *Similarity*, its linguistic term sets {*independent, related, equivalent*}, and the Gaussian membership functions.

We used minimum for the conjunction and fuzzy aggregation, which are useful for selecting only the best results of competing alignments [18]. Mamdani [19] type rule

Similarity={*independent, related, equivalent*}

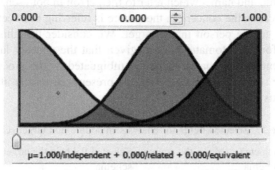

Fig. 2. Linguistic terms set and membership functions of output variable Similarity

inference is used in this approach given that the rule base is easier to design, interpret, and debug using linguistic variables.

We selected the centroid method to defuzzify the output variable, and maximum operator to accumulate the activated terms.

The inference rules are designed trying to capture the common sense of a human expert who would prioritize the semantic meaning similarity to the string similarity given that many homonyms can be found when aligning concepts. Labels are not always meaningful or used frequently with different interpretations. The fuzzy rules are shown in Fig. 3.

if DiceSim is high and LongComSubSim is high and WordNetSim is high then Similarity is equivalent
if (DiceSim is high and LongComSubSim is medium) or (DiceSim is medium and LongComSubSim is high) then Similarity is equivalent
if DiceSim is high and LongComSubSim is high then Similarity is equivalent
if WordNetSim is high then Similarity is equivalent
if DiceSim is high then Similarity is equivalent
if DiceSim is medium and LongComSubSim is medium and WordNetSim is medium then Similarity is related
if (DiceSim is medium and LongComSubSim is medium) or (DiceSim is medium and WordNetSim is medium) then Similarity is related
if DiceSim is low and LongComSubSim is low and WordNetSim is low then Similarity is independent
if (DiceSim is low and LongComSubSim is medium) or (DiceSim is medium and LongComSubSim is low) and WordNetSim is low then Similarity is independent

Fig. 3. Fuzzy rules

4   Experiment and Results

The goal of experimentation is to assess the performance of our Fuzzy-based process of concept alignment in the cases where ambiguity of terms hinder the process of alignment and add uncertainty to the match. For our experiment, we selected to find the possible semantic mappings between an XML document of the job-application of LinkedIn [20] and the core fields of Facebook profile [21]. LinkedIn schema has 62 concepts and Facebook has 14 core fields. We focus only in core fields given that they are less likely to change. Facebook states that core fields will remain available and unchanged for at least two years from the launch of that version. LinkedIn's application is considered the source schema and Facebook's profile the target schema.

In a previous expert analysis of the 62 fields of the source schema, we found twelve concepts shown in Table 1 in which we want to focus on this experiment. From this partial alignment, a human expert would expect the process to find three exact matches: first-name, last-name and name, which refer to the person in both schemas. Email is not an exact match because the concept in the source is referring to a recommender and in the concept refers to the person in the target. We consider that this example is particularly difficult for an automatic process given that the concept labels are repeated referring to different objects that must be disambiguated by the process. Although the 62 concepts in the source where processed, we present our results in the twelve fields selected in previous analysis.

Table 1. Selected fields for analysis in source and target schema

Selected fields in the source schema		Selected fields in the target schema	
Refers to a	Concept label	Refers to a	Concept label
job	name		
person	first-name	person	first-name
	last-name		last-name
	name		name
company	name		email
skill	name		
	school-name		
language	name		
certification	name		
recommender	first-name		
	last-name		
	email-address		

We used *precision*, *recall*, and *accuracy* to evaluate the quality of the generated mappings by the process of concept alignment. For this experiment exact match relations found correctly are considered true positives (TP).

Wrong exact matches are listed as false positives (FP). When the process does not find a relevant exact match it is registered as false negative (FN). Properly discarded concepts were recorded as true negative (TN).

The confusion matrix resulting from the analysis of the source fields shown in Table 1 is presented in Table 2.

Table 2. Resulting confusion matrix of the matching process between *partial LinkedIn* and *Facebook Core*

		Expected matches	
		positive	negative
Process of concept alignment outcome	positive	TP=1	FP=3
	negative	FN=2	TN=5

Person's *name* exact match was correctly found by the process, but first-name and last-name mappings were not found. It is important to notice that the object of referral (person) is not explicitly expressed in the hierarchy of the target. Wrong close matches were found for the name referring to the company, *school-name*, and *email-address*. In these cases, the process was not able to disambiguate the meaning in the structural-level matching. Nevertheless, the semantic mappings were considered close match instead of exact match due to the fuzzy approach. Five name homonyms were correctly found.

For this experiment considering only the tough matching cases, *precision* is 25%, *recall* 33.3% and *accuracy* 50%.

5   Conclusions and Future Work

We presented a process of concept alignment using a fuzzy-based approach to combine different similarity measures to deal with scenarios where ambiguity of terms hinder the process of alignment and add uncertainty to the match. The performance of our Fuzzy-based process of concept alignment was tested with the schema matching process between LinkedIn's job application and Facebook's core profile. Although the 62 concepts in the source where processed, we present our results in the twelve toughest concepts which present more ambiguity. The results are encouraging given that the majority of homonyms were disambiguated, but more work has to be done to improve the precision, recall and accuracy. This work is the first approach towards a process of concept alignment that can deal with the inherent uncertainty of schema matching. We recognize the enormous impact that uncertainty can have in a wide range of real-world applications based on schema matching. In ubiquitous environments data integration and exchange must be done in a highly dynamic scenario where autonomous data suppliers and consumers constantly change.

References

1. Shvaiko, P., Euzenat, J., Matching, O.: State of the art and future challenges. IEEE Transact. Knowl. Data Eng. **25**(1), 158–176 (2013). doi:10.1109/TKDE.2011.253
2. Bellahsene, Z., Bonifati, A., Rahm, E.: Schema Matching and Mapping. Springer, Heidelberg (2011)
3. Rizopoulos, N.: Schema matching and schema merging based on uncertain semantic mappings. Dissertation, Ph.D. thesis, Imperial College London (2010)
4. Gal, A.: Uncertain schema matching. Synth. Lect. Data Manag. **3**(1), 1–97 (2011)
5. Jan, S. et al.: Ontology alignment using rough sets. In: Proceedings of the 2011 Eighth International Conference on Fuzzy Systems and Knowledge Discovery (FSKD), pp. 2683–2686. IEEE (2011)
6. Zadeh, L.A.: Fuzzy sets. Inf. Cont. **8**, 338–353 (1965)
7. de Lourdes Guadalupe Martínez-Villaseñor, M., González-Mendoza, M.: Process of concept alignment for interoperability between heterogeneous sources. In: Batyrshin, I., González Mendoza, M. (eds.) MICAI 2012. LNCS, vol. 7629, pp. 311–320. Springer, Heidelberg (2013). doi:10.1007/978-3-642-37807-2_27

8. Martinez-Villaseñor, M.L., González-Mendoza, M.: An enhanced process of concept alignment for dealing with overweight and obesity. J. UCS **19**(9), 1315–1333 (2013)
9. Shvaiko, P., Euzenat, J.: A survey of schema-based matching approaches. J. Data Seman. IV **3730**, 146–171 (2005)
10. Dong, X.L., Halevy, A.: Data integration with uncertainty. VLDB J. **18**(2), 469–500 (2009)
11. Dong, X.L., Srivastava, D.: Big data integration. Synth. Lect. Data Manag. **7**(1), 1–198 (2015)
12. Agreste, S., et al.: XML matchers: approaches and challenges. Knowl.-Based Syst. **66**, 190–209 (2014)
13. Fernández, S., et al.: Ontology alignment architecture for semantic sensor web integration. Sensors **13**(9), 12581–12604 (2013)
14. Dice, L.R.: Measures of the amount of ecologic association between species. Ecology **26**, 297–302 (1945)
15. Wu, Z., Palmer, M.: Verb semantics and lexical selection. In: Proceedings of the 32nd Annual Meeting of the Association for Computational Linguistics, Las Cruces, NM, USA, pp. 133–138 (1994)
16. Fellbaum, C.: WordNet and Wordnets. In: Brown, K. (ed.) Encyclopedia of Language and Linguistics, pp. 665–670. Elsevier, Oxford (2005)
17. Zadeh, L.A.: The concept of a linguistic variable and its applications to approximate reasoning. Inf. Sci. **8**(3), 199–249 (1975)
18. Euzenat, J.: Algebras of ontology alignment relations. In: Sheth, A., Staab, S., Dean, M., Paolucci, M., Maynard, D., Finin, T., Thirunarayan, K. (eds.) ISWC 2008. LNCS, vol. 5318, pp. 387–402. Springer, Heidelberg (2008). doi:10.1007/978-3-540-88564-1_25
19. Mamdani, E.H.: Application of fuzzy logic to approximate reasoning using linguistic synthesis. In: Proceedings of the Sixth International Symposium on Multiple-Valued Logic, pp. 196–202. IEEE Computer Society Press (1976)
20. LinkedIn Corporation (2017). https://developer.linkedin.com/docs/fields. Accessed 2017, Consulted 2014
21. Facebook for developers (2017). https://developers.facebook.com/docs/graph-api/reference/v2.2/user. Consulted May 2017

A Location-Based Service to Support Collaboration and Strategic Control in a Real Estate Broker

Christian A. Cancino$^{(\boxtimes)}$ (iD) and Gustavo N. Zurita (iD)

Department of Management Control and Information Systems,
Faculty of Economics and Business, University of Chile,
8330015 Santiago, Chile
{cancino, gzurita}@fen.uchile.cl

Abstract. Increasingly more companies support their strategies and value propositions offering their clients some services that require physical mobility and teamwork by their staff. This article proposes a type of Location-based Services system called Geomanagement, which supports the fulfilment of business strategy for a real estate broker agency, based on mobility and collaborative work of their employees. Geomanagement application acts as a valuable support to explore real estate and potential client information in each showing appointment, to share information among realtors and to help new and old realtors in developing teamwork skills while they are in movement. Clients also value the great contribution of Geomanagement regarding the collaboration between realtors. This study demonstrates the effectiveness of Geomanagement by generating value in, an uncommon scenario, as is a real state broker agency. We show that the implementation of Geomanagement increases both collaboration among realtors, and strategic control of managers and heads. Strengthening the link between collaboration and management control systems supported by Geomanagement, turned out to be crucial in business strategy follow-up and monitoring.

Keywords: Location-based systems · Collaboration · Management control systems

1 Introduction

Increasingly more companies sustain their added value offered to their clients, based on: (a) the execution of processes that require mobility by their staff [1]; (b) physical location information management [2]; (c) the transfer of information in real time [3]; and (d) collaborative processes and tasks support from their staff [4].

In general, Location-based Services (LBS) purposes are broadly defined as applications that provide an information service related to and dependent on the location of the mobile user [1]. According to [2], the potential for LBS is evident from powerful and ubiquitous mobile and wireless devices, which are growing in popularity. The most common LBS usage scenarios found in the literature are: emergency caller location identification [3]; vehicle fleet management [4, 5]; mobile yellow pages [6, 7]; route

© Springer International Publishing AG 2017
S.F. Ochoa et al. (Eds.): UCAmI 2017, LNCS 10586, pp. 181–193, 2017.
DOI: 10.1007/978-3-319-67585-5_19

finding [8, 9]; roadside assistance [10]; search and rescue missions [11]; marketing promotions and client notification [12, 13]; and identification in the neighborhood store [2, 14]. Research around LBS can be viewed from different perspectives, although less frequent from a business or strategic viewpoint [14], as we can see in this study.

This article proposes a type of LBS system, which supports the fulfilment of business strategy, and collaborative work, to a real estate broker. The aim of this article is to explore the influence and benefits that a LBS has on the business strategy of a business, with the goal to specifically generate added value for its clients and manage the performance of its employees. Specifically, the LBS system-type proposed, named here on Geomanagement, aims to give collaborative support to real estate agency staff, dedicated to selling and leasing property, whose entrepreneurial business strategy sets a value proposition to its clients based on: (a) "*personalized service*", and (b) "*quality information*". This implies that resources should be allocated so that all the information on the status information with respect to the lease or sale of a property be managed in real time among the different actors of the organization – realtors, heads of departments and the general manager – improving company response times, not only to respond to its clients, but also to increase the rotation of property sales and leasing. In this usage scenario, physical location management of the properties for sale or lease, transfer and exchange of information in real time, and support for collaborative work among staff, are crucial.

Our research hypothesis is that using Geomanagement at a small real estate broker agency, generates positive effects on the fulfillment of the "personalized service" and "quality information" value proposition offered to clients, where collaboration, location information, and mobility management are part of the business model on which its performance depends.

Therefore, Geomanagement was designed, implemented, and launched, as a type of LBS application that supports the activities and tasks of the personnel of the company indicated; and whose utility was assessed based on questionnaires and in depth interviews applied to its staff and clients, in terms of how much Geomanagement supports the value proposition offered to clients.

The results found suggest that Geomanagement can doubly support a business strategy. On the one hand, it supports compliance and monitoring of the business strategy of the business through geolocation information management, which benefits heads of division and managers by reducing the asymmetry of information regarding the real activities of field staff. On the other hand, Geomanagement also supports the exchange and transfer of information, supporting collaborative activities that field staff require, with the aim of delivering quality and real-time client information.

2   Related Work

The term LBS appeared at the end of the 1990s, and is used for applications that leverage the user's physical location to provide an enhanced service or experience [16]. Since then, different definitions and usage scenarios have emerged that are important to highlight.

There are several definitions of LBS [3]: (a) LBS are applications that depend on the location of the user's device [15, 17]; (b) LBS pertain to any service that considers the geographic location of an entity [18]; and (c) LBS is a service for mobile users, where the awareness of current, past or future location forms an integral part of the service [19]. According to [2], LBS can be defined as services that depend on and are enhanced by positional information from mobile devices; and also extend spatial and temporal information processing capability to end users via Internet and wireless communication [20–23].

Table 1. Types of LBS, their usage environments and main features.

Types of LBS	Scenario of use	Main purposes and characteristics
Information and directory services	Dynamic yellow pages	Provide a wide range of localized information: landmarks, restaurants, petrol stations, ATM locations
	Personalized recommender for places in location-based online Social Network services	Users can check their nearby location information depending on where they are
Tracking and navigation services	Tracking of children, older adult or lost pets	Helps to avoid elders, children, or pets from getting lost, LBS provides a tracking assistance to users
	Tracking stolen vehicles or assets tracking	Helps to track loved things, users can also track their property, goods, or cars at any time and place
	Voice-enabled route description.	Route guidance based on map services that help users know where they are located
Emergency services	Roadside assistance	Time of roadside assistance may be reduced greatly by a tracking service
	Search and rescue missions	Guide rescuers in locating a destination efficiently and accurately; especially in the case of emergency alert services
	Police and fire response; E911; Emergency medical ambulance	LBS can guide policemen and firefighters to identify location in the case of emergency calls
Location-based advertising	Wireless coupon presentation; Client notification and identification in neighborhood store	Potential clients can receive coupons, sales information or advertisements from nearby stores
	Marketing promotions and alerts, targeted & customized ads	Promote products or services, because of the participative, interactive, open and transparent nature of social media

Source: Based on the typology of [2]

Table 1 shows a taxonomy defined by four types of services in which it is possible to group LBS: information or directory services; tracking and navigation services; emergency services; and location-based advertising.

In the first group of applications, *Information and directory services*, a study shows that, by using the location data based on GPS and users' comments at various locations, it is possible to discover interesting locations and possible activities that can be performed there for recommendations [6]. Some systems, based on an individual user's current location, retrieve important surrounding locations and their contexts for recommendations [24].

In the second group of applications, *tracking and navigation services*, studies reveal that a people location system involving a people locator with GPS capabilities in communication with a wireless network so a user interface accessible on a common computer network or by telephone is provided. These location systems include access to the user interface via a computer on the common computer network or via a telecommunications network [25–27].

In the third group of applications, *emergency services*, the literature shows mobile alerts, notifications and location-based emergency warning systems evolving from traditional short message service (SMS) notifications and cell broadcasting to more advanced location-based services. Current research explores the major issues faced by governments, businesses and society at large, toward the realization of a fully fledged system for personal mobile devices [11, 28].

Finally, with *location based advertising aplications* group, businesses can quickly contact potential clients. Augmented reality coupled with LBS has immense potential for mobile marketing in social networking scenarios [2]. According to [29], personal profiling has been regarded as a way to enrich and enhance LBS and supply people with the information that they are likely to need.

Regarding the taxonomy exposed in [2], it is important to highlight that it is difficult to find companies using LBS to support the monitoring and control of their business strategies in the series of studies analysed. It is also difficult to identify cases which explain collaboration among individuals who work in the same company, but not together, either by not sharing the same geographical location or by doing so asynchronously. In this context we believe that it is possible to extend the classification of applications shown in Table 1, which is the objective of our work.

New LBS applications can be developed to support collaboration between personnel inside organizations, and also to increase strategic control of managers and heads of areas regarding their personnel. This would support the value proposition compliance for clients, with the fulfilment of a company's strategic objectives and its long-term growth.

Can LBS support the fulfilment of the business value proposition and thus improve strategic control in an organization?

To answer this question, in this research we will develop a LBS application to support the monitoring and control of a company's strategy that provides real estate services. In this context, it is necessary to rely on the cooperation of workers engaged in mobile environments, to be able to meet a clearly defined value proposition. Questionnaires and in-depth interviews with workers, the company executive team and its clients, are applied to identify the results of its implementation.

3 The Real Estate Broker Agency and Its Value Proposition

As previously mentioned, the usage scenario corresponds to a small company, founded in 2008, which is involved in the real estate business of selling and leasing properties in Chile. It currently operates with two branches located in Santiago, and in its organizational structure, its operation with little personnel is noticeable, which in turn demands great collaboration among them and technological support to maintain its operations. The company personnel consist of eight realtors who permanently work in movement and in the field, plus the head of the sales team who remains at the branch performing the monitoring processes dealing with property sales or leasing, including business deals (Front office). A Chief Operating Officer, whose function is to control documentation and client service when property sales or leasing is defined, is also involved (Back office). Both the head of the commercial team and the chief operating officer report to the General Manager of the company (its owner), who in turn is also in charge of the guidelines and strategy of the company.

In order to explain its business strategy and to monitor the fulfilment of its objectives, the company uses the Balanced Scorecard (BSC) as a strategic control tool, which allows assessing the compliance of its monthly goals. In Fig. 1, the strategy map of the company is observed, which was developed in the year 2012 and is currently valid. In this *strategy map*, the *financial perspective* shows that the company expected to maximize an ultimate goal, expressed as the monthly income of the company. To do this, it generates a series of measurements at the system level, resources prospects, processes and clients, with which it hopes to induce positive results at the global level. From the *client perspective*, it can be observed that the value proposition seeks to provide services with "personalized service" and "quality information". Thus, it is based on property sales and lease management, a process that depends directly on resources: personnel, information systems, and properties.

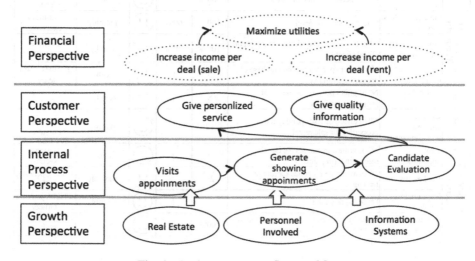

Fig. 1. Real estate agency Strategy Map

As in every BSC, four prospects presented in the *Strategy Map* are measurable through a series of performance indicators associated with the objectives pursued by the company. In Table 2, it is possible to see the BSC of the company. To understand Table 2, we will analyse a couple of objectives and their relevant indicators. One of the objectives of the relevant level of processes is to generate showing appointments, either for lease or sale of properties, the company set a goal of five *effective visits* per day to show properties. Table 2 shows that in the case of effective visits for properties for sale the goal of five visits, is being fulfilled. Therefore, BSC is associated with a positive sign of goal achievement. Regarding a second important objective, *effective visits* of leasing do not meet the daily goal.

In order to comply with the indicators in Table 2 in this usage scenario, in general it is required that the Geomanagement application is able to support: (a) the mobility of its realtors to present properties on-site to clients that are for sale or lease – complying with the added value of *personalized information* for our clients; (b) managing the information required by their clients in places where the properties are shown, or generating and/or requesting the information identified as relevant by realtors as a result of these visits, and transferring it in a collaborative way and in real time to the rest of the staff (realtors, business team leader, and Chief Operating Officer) thus complying with the added value of *quality information* for our clients.

Table 2. Balanced Scorecard of the real estate agency

	Strategy objetives	Management indicators	Goal	current		assessment	Responsable
Financial Perspective	Maximize utilities	EBITDA	2.5MM	1.5MM	😐	monthly	General manger
	Increase income per deal	Commision for sold properties	100%	70%	😐	monthly	Business team leader
		Commision for rental properties	100%	95%	🙂	monthly	Business team leader
Clients Perspective	Give personlized service	Client satisfaction level	100%	60%	☹️	monthly	Business executive
	Give quality information	Clients who recieve administration report /Total clients	100%	70%	😐	weelky	Business executive
Processes Perspective	Candidate Evaluation	Nº of offers per day for the purchase of properties available	5	1	😐	weelky	Business team leader
		Nº of offers per day for the rental of properties available	8	4	☹️	weelky	Business team leader
	Generate showing appoinments	Nº of effective visits per day for properties for sale/rental	12	11	🙂	weelky	Business executive
	Visits appoinments	Nº of visits agreements per day for sales/rental properties	2	2	🙂	daily	Business executive
Resources Perspective	Real estate	Nº of available propeties for sale or leasing	20	15	😐	monthly	Chief Operating Officer
	Personnel involved	Nº of 'weekly talks'	2	2	🙂	monthly	Chief Operating Officer
	Information system	Availibility of real estate administration system	100%	100%	🙂	monthly	Chief Operating Officer

3.1   Design and Description of Geomanagement Requirements

Specifically, Geomanagement (see main interface in Fig. 2) supports the objectives of the processes described in Table 2: scheduled visits per property sale and lease i.e., those processes for which indicators must operate with a daily monitoring frequency. Geomanagement works on any browser with Internet access and can therefore operate on desktop computers or mobile devices. In a series of meetings with the company Manager, business team leader, Chief of operations and 8 realtors; five relevant Geomanagement requirements were identified and defined; expecting that it can support the monitoring and control of the company's strategy, which are described below.

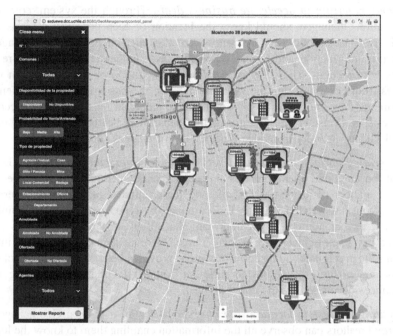

Fig. 2. Main interface of Geomagement in view of all the properties that are available to schedule visits. Icons indicate the type of property, its value, if it is for sale or lease, and the level of interest generated by the property. Left side: the filter properties options are type, probability of sale, etc.

R1. Reducing the asymmetry of information of the departments. Considering weakness problems in controlling the genuine efforts of sales executives [30], with respect to what was observed by head of sales and operations, it is necessary to control the attendance of realtors at each visit for a potential lease or sale of a property. In many situations bosses have doubts regarding staff punctuality; which is solved by validating the attendance of a realtor, by tracking mobile devices that realtors use via GPS and which is shown in Geomanagement. Knowing where the company staff is located, allows improving its control capacity.

R2. Responding in real time to client inquiries. According to the value proposition of the company to deliver a *personalized service* with *quality information*, the system manages registration, follow up and answers to all the questions and concerns that a client may have about a property for lease or sale. In order to do so, the system is required to save records of all consultations, regardless of the number of visits to a property by a client, coordinating the efforts of the various realtors involved. Through Geomanagement, realtors can jointly collaborate, because for each visit they can record the perceptions that they have of those interested in properties, and hence maximize the personalized service of future visits by clients by maintaining a single record which is accessible in real time, even if another realtor is assisting the client.

R3. Timely reporting to accelerate business deals. Through the system, commercial and operations managers should know the location of each property in terms of the probability of success of closing a business deal after each client visit. Geomanagement records this information and is accessible for any commercial realtor who resumes business with a client. Thus, the expectation or likelihood of success that an realtor perceives from a client during the visit, the number of visits from the same client, and all comments showing interest which realtors can generate regarding the expectations of their clients. Considering this information, department heads could directly contact potential clients, in order to reduce the duration of business deals.

R4. Generating periodic reports to assess business management. Through Geoman-agement, business and operations managers can generate periodic reports that evaluate inter alia: number of properties for sale and lease, number of successful operations, number of business deals by agent, by 'comuna', by type of property, by number of operations, etc. In addition, it is important that all of the above indicators can be recovered for a particular date or date range. Geomanagement, by managing and retrieving the previously indicated information, provides better strategic control of the business, and assigns properties to different commercial realtors according to the performances developed by the company staff.

R5. Locating real estate location and characteristics on a map. n Geomanagement, commercial realtors can observe all the information enabling them to know the location of the properties to be able to show them on a map, their main characteristics, history of inquiries performed by different clients about a specific property, as well as the history of questions and answers given to a client by different commercial realtors, if available. The application must allow finding the location of a property on a map, with immediate feedback if it is a house or apartment, if it is furnished or unfurnished, the number of other interested clients, i.e. information that allows hastening the process of doing business, and that meets the information requirements of the clients, see Fig. 2.

4   Evaluation Methodology of Requirements Compliance

In this section we describe the measurement of Geomanagement performance as a management and strategic control mechanism, and also in helping to facilitate the supply of reliable and timely information to the different actors in the company.

4.1   Geomanagement Testing and Use

Geomanagement testing encompassed a 6-month period, from January to June of 2016, in which there were eighty visits concentrated in fourteen of the available properties. The process began with an explanation and demonstration to realtors and heads of departments of the company regarding the main aspects of the system, its operation and the information that could be obtained from its use. Subsequently, user profiles were created for every manager and realtor, who were supplied with a manual, and oriented to the Scorecard use. Afterwards we entered the property data; owner identification, realtor responsible, type of property, sale/lease, square meters, value, detail and address. This last element is considered indispensable for geolocation. Every Monday, the realtors scheduled showing appointments for the rest of the week. After data submissions were registered in the system, managers could see properties in the Scorecard which had been visited and client interest. Additionally, they could see the details of each visit, which showed date and time of the start and end of the visit, responsible realtor, client, if he appeared or not, client doubts and the answers that the realtor gave him.

Finally, the Manager has the possibility of generating a report according to different filters. For example, by property number, 'comuna' (neighborhood), property availability, probability of sale or lease, type of property, if it is furnished, if it is on offer, and by realtor. The generated report showed the data of all the properties that met the characteristics that the Manager selected, among which was the number of visits that the property had had and the perception of sale or lease.

5   Survey Results of the Geo-Management Evaluation

Using structured surveys applied to the system users (business realtors or field staff) and department heads (managers, Business team leader and Chief Operating Officer), we will analyse whether the Geomanagement application provides better support for the visiting activities regarding real estate sale and lease. In the case of the two surveys developed (for field staff and managers) a Likert scale was used (see Tables 3 and 4), with values between 1 and 5, to define a valuation of the answers to the following questions:

The company managers indicated that there are almost always problems identifying the most attractive properties for clients. However, Geomanagement allowed respondents to appreciate obtaining information in real time about potential clients and providing them with "personalized service". 100% of respondents completely agreed that

Table 3. Questionnaire about Geomanagement System to business leaders*

(a) How do you value using the Geomanagement system supporting the attributes of "personalized service and quality information" in the company?	A1	A2	A3	A4	A5	Score
(a1) How do you think clients rated their team's work on the new Geomanagement?	4	5	4	4	5	4,4
(a2) How much did your sales force collaborate with the new Geomanagement?	4	4	4	3	4	3,8
(a3) How did operational processes improve with the new Geomanagement?	4	5	4	3	4	4,0
(a4) How much do you value the LBS for strategic control?	4	5	4	3	5	4,2

*The answers to the questions to business leaders are the average data of the answer given by five senior executives of the company that manage the organization under a strategic view.

Table 4. Questionnaire about Geomanagement system to business realtors*

(b) How do you value using the Geomanagement system supporting your business activities of sales or rental in the company?	A1	A2	A3	A4	A5	A6	A7	A8	Score
(b1) How does LBS improve the relationship with clients?	4	5	4	5	5	5	4	5	4,6
(b2) How does LBS use improve collaboration with other realtors?	5	5	5	5	5	5	5	5	5,0
(b3) How does LBS improve quality information for clients?	4	5	5	5	5	4	5	5	4,8
(b4) How does the LBS improve the personalized service for clients?	4	5	4	5	3	4	4	4	4,1

*The answers to the questions to business realtors are the average data of the answered by eight sales realtors that develop their activity directly assisting the customers.

the system would help new managers who were not able to manage the characteristics of real estate. Moreover, all the managers acknowledged agreeing that the information provided by Geomanagement would be useful to keep track of their realtors and provide better information to interest groups, complying with the "quality information" value proposition (Table 5).

Table 5. Balanced Scorecard of the real estate agency after the LBS

		Strategy objetives	Management indicators	Goal	current	assessment		Responsable
Financial Perspective		Maximize utilities	EBITDA	2.5MM	2.6MM	☺	monthly	General manger
		Increase income per deal	Commision for sold properties	100%	95%	☺	monthly	Business team leader
			Commision for rental properties	100%	95%	☺	monthly	Business team leader
Clients Perspective		Give personlized service	Client satisfaction level	100%	60%	☺	monthly	Business executive
		Give quality information	Clients who recieve administration report /Total clients	100%	96%	☺	weelky	Business executive
Processes Perspective		Candidate Evaluation	N° of offers per day for the purchase of properties available	4	3	☺	weelky	Business team leader
			N° of offers per day for the rental of properties available	8	7	☺	weelky	Business team leader
		Generate showing appoinments	N° of effective visits per day for properties for sale/rental	12	11	☺	weelky	Business executive
		Visits appoinments	N° of visits agreements per day for sales/rental properties	2	2	☺	daily	Business executive
Resources Perspective		Real estate	N° of available propeties for sale or leasing	20	15	☹	monthly	Chief Operating Officer
		Personnel involved	N° of 'weekly talks'	2	2	☺	monthly	Chief Operating Officer
		Information system	Availibility of real estate administration system	100%	100%	☺	monthly	Chief Operating Officer

6   LBS Performance Management

In general, after the use of Geomanagement, it was possible to observe an improvement in the fulfillment of the goals and objectives proposed in the control panel of the company. The proposed Geomanagement complies with being a tool that not only supports the operational management of the business, but also strategic control, supporting the fulfilment of its value proposition.

7   Conclusions

Specifically, the results of this study show that Geomanagement such as the one applied in this study can be a useful tool for monitoring strategy and enhancing collaboration among peers. The implemented Geomanagement acts as a valuable resource to view property and potential client data in each showing appointment, to transfer information between realtors and to help new and old realtors in developing their work. The same users value the great contribution of Geomanagement to enhance collaboration between colleagues. In our understanding a contribution of this study is showing the use of LBS-systems support in contexts other than the traditionally studied (vehicle fleet management, mobile yellow pages, route finding, roadside assistance, search and rescue missions, among others) such as supporting business strategy follow-up, and certainly, supporting collaboration among colleagues that together fulfill a business's value proposition.

The limitations of this study are related with expanding the use of Geomanagement implemented in larger organizations, to see if all the expected benefits of the system are achieved. In addition, another limitation is a longer-term assessment, in order to consider potential improvements to the system that may arise from the permanent use of Geomanagement by different users.

References

1. Petrova, K., Wang, B.: Location-based services deployment and demand: a roadmap model. Electron. Commer. Res. **11**(1), 5–29 (2011)
2. Dhar, S., Varshney, U.: Challenges and business models for mobile location-based services and advertising. Commun. ACM **54**(5), 121–128 (2011)
3. Chen, P.-T., Lin, Y.-S.: Mobile location-based services: an empirical study of user preferences. Int. J. Inf. Educ. Technol. **1**(5), 416 (2011)
4. Maurya, K., Singh, M., Jain, N.: Real time vehicle tracking system using GSM and GPS technology: an anti-theft tracking system. Int. J. Electron. Comput. Sci. Eng. IJECSE **1**(03), 1103–1107 (2012). ISSN: 2277-1956
5. Almomani, I.M., et al.: Ubiquitous GPS vehicle tracking and management system. In: 2011 IEEE Jordan Conference on Applied Electrical Engineering and Computing Technologies (AEECT). IEEE (2011)
6. Zheng, V.W., et al.: Collaborative location and activity recommendations with gps history data. In: Proceedings of the 19th International Conference on World Wide Web. ACM (2010)
7. Chow, C.-Y., Mokbel, M.F., Liu, X.: Spatial cloaking for anonymous location-based services in mobile peer-to-peer environments. GeoInformatica **15**(2), 351–380 (2011)
8. Rehrl, K., Häusler, E., Leitinger, S.: Comparing the effectiveness of gps-enhanced voice guidance for pedestrians with metric- and landmark-based instruction sets. In: Fabrikant, S. I., Reichenbacher, T., van Kreveld, M., Schlieder, C. (eds.) GIScience 2010. LNCS, vol. 6292, pp. 189–203. Springer, Heidelberg (2010). doi:10.1007/978-3-642-15300-6_14
9. Sarjakoski, L.T., et al.: Analysis of verbal route descriptions and landmarks for hiking. Pers. Ubiquit. Comput. **16**(8), 1001–1011 (2012)
10. Yang, B., Fang, L.: Automated extraction of 3-D railway tracks from mobile laser scanning point clouds. IEEE J. Sel. Top. Appl. Earth Observ. Remote Sens. **7**(12), 4750–4761 (2014)
11. Rahdar, R., Stracener, J.T., Olinick, E.V.: A systems engineering approach to improving the accuracy of mobile station location estimation. IEEE Syst. J. **8**(1), 14–22 (2014)
12. Chen, S.Z.: Social media: an unmissable opportunity for Chinese enterprises. Mod. Econ. Inf. **6**, 2 (2012)
13. Zhou, L., Wang, T.: Social media: a new vehicle for city marketing in China. Cities **37**, 27–32 (2014)
14. Wilson, M.W.: Location-based services, conspicuous mobility, and the location-aware future. Geoforum **43**(6), 1266–1275 (2012)
15. Liang, T.-P., et al.: Adoption of mobile technology in business: a fit-viability model. Ind. Manag. Data Syst. **107**(8), 1154–1169 (2007)
16. Kosta, E., et al.: Legal considerations on privacy-enhancing location based services using PRIME technology. Comput. Law Secur. Rev. **24**(2), 139–146 (2008)

17. Liang, C.W., et al.: Open location-based services: LBS toolbar as example. ICL Tech. J. **123**, 35–41 (2008)
18. Junglas, I.A., Watson, R.T.: Location-based services. Commun. ACM **51**(3), 65–69 (2008)
19. Kühn, P.J.: Location-based services in mobile communication infrastructures. AEU-Int. J. Electron. Commun. **58**(3), 159–164 (2004)
20. Giaglis, G., Kourouthanassis, P., Tsamakos, A.: Towards a classification framework for mobile location services. In: Mobile Commerce: Technology, Theory and Application, pp. 67–85 (2003)
21. Zeimpekis, V., Giaglis, G.M., Lekakos, G.: A taxonomy of indoor and outdoor positioning techniques for mobile location services. ACM SIGecom Exch. **3**(4), 19–27 (2002)
22. Heinonen, K., Pura, M.: Classifying mobile services (2006)
23. Schumann, M., Narzt, W.: Business model development for a mobile context-aware service. In: Bled eConference (2013)
24. Chow, C.-Y., Mokbel, M.F., He, T.: A privacy-preserving location monitoring system for wireless sensor networks. IEEE Trans. Mob. Comput. **10**(1), 94–107 (2011)
25. Soper, D.: Is human mobility tracking a good idea? Commun. ACM **55**(4), 35–37 (2012)
26. Zickuhr, K., Madden, M.: Older Adults and Internet Use. Pew Internet & American Life Project, Washington, DC (2012)
27. Thomas, L., et al.: Location tracking: views from the older adult population. Age Ageing **42** (6), 758–763 (2013)
28. Aloudat, A., Michael, K.: The socio-ethical considerations surrounding government mandated location-based services during emergencies: an Australian case study. In: Quigley, M. (ed.) ICT Ethics and Security in the 21st Century: New Developments and Applications. ISI Global, Hershey (2010)
29. Shiode, N., et al.: The impact and penetration of location-based services (2002)
30. Anthony, R., Govindarajan, V.: Management Control Systems. McGraw-Hill, North Tazewell (2008)

A Proposal for a Distributed Computational Framework in IoT Context

Higinio Mora[✉], María Teresa Signes-Pont, David Gil-Méndez,
and Francisco Javier Ferrández-Pastor

Department of Computer Science Technology and Computation,
University of Alicante, Alicante, Spain
hmora@ua.es, {teresa,dgil,fjferran}@dtic.ua.es

Abstract. The new internet of things paradigm allows for small devices with sensing, processing and communication capabilities to be designed, which enable the development of sensors, embedded devices and other 'things' ready to understand the environment. In this paper, a distributed model and an architecture for internet of things paradigm is proposed to perform complex computational tasks and run advanced applications. This novel computing system defines a network design with different levels which combines sensing and processing capabilities based on the Mobile Cloud Computing paradigm.

Keywords: Mobile cloud computing · Internet of things · Embedded systems · Computer modelling · Novel computing systems

1 Introduction

The development of the Internet of Things (IoT) paradigm and communication technologies allow the deployment of new applications for sensing the environment and designing new ways of actuating. This progress has enabled the provision of advanced services for improving the quality of life of citizens and making better use of resources. In this way, new concepts have been created which apply IoT to benefit different areas of society and industry such as for instance, ambient assisted living [1], smart cities [2] or smart logistics [3]. In these scenarios, new data management issues arise for integrating environmental sensor data efficiently and handling data from different sources [4].

Recent applications have been developed around the aforementioned concepts where sensing and processing capabilities of the 'things' play an important role. This 'things' are usually embedded systems and/or mobile devices such as smart watches, phones, wearables, etc.). However, the design of advanced applications for IoT environments remains a challenge. Handling with simultaneous data flows and/or processing complex mathematical functions could overflow the computing capabilities of the embedded systems and mobile devices.

This drawback could be overcome by the deployment of a centralized system that performs the hard processing, although some bottlenecks and delays may result from

© Springer International Publishing AG 2017
S.F. Ochoa et al. (Eds.): UCAmI 2017, LNCS 10586, pp. 194–200, 2017.
DOI: 10.1007/978-3-319-67585-5_20

the communications among the things and the centralized system, especially when multimedia data takes place. For example, from video and image acquisition devices.

In this work, a distributed architecture for Internet of Things' environments has been proposed to overcome the previous problems. The **aim of this proposal** is to optimize the use of computing resources in a IoT environment. To that end, the framework may be able to obtain data from sensors, perform complex computational tasks and run advanced applications. The **working hypothesis** of this work is that the conception and development of processing models based on schemes of cloud computing can supply the necessary processing power for running applications when they run on embedded devices with limited performance. The auxiliary use of cloud computing infrastructure on demand will provide flexibility in order to execute the necessary tasks and mechanisms to support the service quality maintenance, even with devices and sensors with low computing capability. The **main contribution** of this paper is the proposal of a distributed model that combines sensing and processing at different levels of the network based on the Mobile Cloud Computing (MCC) paradigm.

The remaining part of the paper is organized as follows: Sect. 2 describes the basic background of the distributed computing for IoT; Sect. 3 defines a distributed computational model, and finally, Sect. 4 draws the relevant conclusions and presents future work.

2 Background of IoT Distributed Computing

Distributed computing is a field of computer science studying distributed systems. The components of a distributed system are located on networked computers, communicating and coordinating their actions by means of exchanging messages to meet a common goal [5].

The IoT environments are highly distributed architectures and they can be considered as very weakly-coupled computer systems. Usually, the connected devices are heterogeneous and present a dynamic behavior. Intensive research is carried out to adapt the job-based scheduling methods to embedded devices and types of applications involved in the IoT environments to fully utilize the nodes and to achieve performance improvements [6–9].

In addition to the existing variety of embedded systems, the mobile devices play an important role in development of IoT solutions. Mobile devices have evolved considerably in recent years as a result of improvements in mobile technology, mobile networking and mobile computing. Examples are increased processing power of mobile devices, novel forms of user interaction and new connectivity protocols. These hardware improvements have motivated the increase in the range and availability of mobile applications, especially those that can perform off-screen processing, reducing battery consumption. These processing features are commonly adopted by apps such as music players and activity trackers that are widespread in the smartphone user community.

The main challenges of distributing applications among these systems are those related to modelling and design tasks, interconnection and interoperability of heterogeneous devices, security issues, QoS, scheduling and control of the system [10, 11]. There are a lot of research focused on all these topics. On this last matter, the problem is defined as resource provisioning in highly distributed systems.

MCC is one of the main processing strategies adopted by software developer communities over recent years. This paradigm combines cloud computing, mobile computing and wireless networks to bring rich computational resources to mobile users, network operators, as well as cloud computing providers [12, 13]. The use of cloud computing means that the intensification of processing needs and server-side backups imply an increase in costs of the server-side resources required to certify the reliability of all this processing. Nowadays it is a fact that a great number of people are living in a smart society. These people use mobile applications or 'apps' for mailing, newspapers, social networks, instant messaging, health, fitness and other areas. All these apps are within the scope of MCC. Moreover, these apps are available across different devices such as smartphones and wearables, and data synchronization is necessary to ensure data consistency. The distribution of the processing between devices of the IoT and cloud computing resources seems to be a promising way to increase the capabilities of the system and to achieve greater overall performance. The efficiently dynamic allocation of tasks is a very important and difficult topic on IoT environments.

3   Distributed Computational Framework

The primary objective of the proposed distributed system is to take advantage of the deployed infrastructure of things and the cloud computing resources to reduce computing costs and improve overall performance. The main idea is to share the application's workload between the server-side and the rest of things with computing capabilities such as smartphones, wearables and tablets. Thus, in accordance with our proposal, these kinds of devices perform more processing tasks than the server-side layer. In addition, cloud computing is available to use if needed. In the case of the asynchronous synchronization needs between cloud server computing and the different devices, our system develops a push notification based approach.

In this section, a model of computation suitable for IoT applications is defined according to that idea. The proposal focuses on distributed applications that can be represented by a directed graph $= \{, \}$ where:

- is the vertex set and represents the set of application tasks required for data acquisition, processing, storing and actuating. The IoT application can be broken down into a list of tasks: $= \{t1, t2, ..., tn\}$
- is the edge set and represents the data flows exchanged between the tasks. The data flows set the precedence between the tasks and the volume of exchanged data. $F(i, j) \in$ defines the volume of data exchanged between the tasks i and j.

In accordance with the proposed model, the devices $\mathbb{D}$ involved in the IoT applications are defined as follows:

- Let S be the set of sensor devices. These devices do not have computing capabilities themselves. Their work consists in sensing and communicating the data to other devices or the cloud.

- Let P be the set of available computing platforms. This set includes the things that have processing capabilities. The devices of the P set can also acquire the data and process it.
- Let C be the set of cloud computing resources. In this set the remote servers where the processing load is outsourced are located.

That is: $\mathbb{D} = \{S\} \bigcup \{P\} \bigcup \{C\}$

The elements of those sets are interconnected creating the IoT communication network. The architecture model distributes tasks $\{T\}$ across the available devices $\mathbb{D}$ according to their particular capabilities and the application constraints. Figure 1 illustrates this idea.

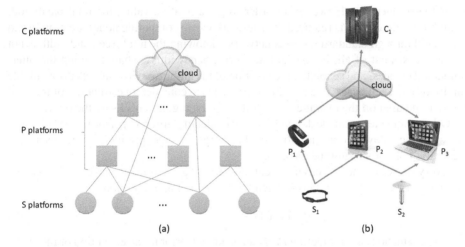

Fig. 1. IoT communication network. (a) General scheme; (b) Example case

As shown in Fig. 1, the computing platforms are usually connected to the cloud server through wireless communication protocols. The wireless local area networking (Wifi) is usually present in tablets devices, mobile phones or laptops. Moreover, this technology is being incorporated in modern other devices such as health bracelets or smart watches to provide better communication performance.

To distribute resources in an efficient way and meet the application requirements, the resource utilization must be properly characterized. For this reason, L is defined as a vector domain of relevant features modelling the behavior of the computing load on each device. For applications such as the ones this work focuses on, L could be defined as a domain of vectors with two components in the range [0,1], with the following semantics.

$$\mathbb{L} = \text{Response\_time} \times \text{Transfer\_rate} \tag{1}$$

The 'Response_time' of a computer is defined proportionally to the execution time required by a selected benchmark task in the computer (0 and 1 are mapped to situations where the processor is practically idle and unacceptably busy, respectively). The benchmark task does not communicate through the network, so it does not take into account network latencies, but only local resources, mostly being the processor.

The 'Transfer_rate' is defined as the portion of available bandwidth used to process a task. This portion includes the input and the output data of the task. The method for quantifying 'Transfer_rate' will take into account the characteristics of the interconnecting network.

In general, the set of devices P and S are connected to a Local Area Network (LAN) in a wireless way. Thus, these devices can form a wireless local area network (WLAN) among them. The maximum number of supported devices or stations connected to a WLAN depends on the data rate of the connection since they have to share the available bandwidth. The current transfer rate can be known for each device by simply monitoring the network interface. However, in order to get a relative value, the total bandwidth available for the device is required. In a network where computing nodes are mobile and connected through standard wireless networks, knowing the total free bandwidth is not an easy task. First of all, in standard networks, bandwidth is shared among the interconnected devices, and secondly, the position of the mobile devices affects the available bandwidth. In such cases, one feasible approach is to consider an estimation of the total bandwidth based on the average values retrieved on regular checks by the devices.

Other components can be defined in order to identify different performance behavior. For example, 'Power_consumption' of the things, 'Usage_pricing' of the resources, 'Security_risk' of sharing the data, etc.

Every device of the IoT environment, $d_i \in D$, has a performance level, which can be characterized by a function Perf defined by the following expression:

$$\text{Perf}: \mathbb{D} \to \mathbb{L} \tag{2}$$

The evaluation of the function *Perf* can be known prior to the execution of the application or can be dynamic over time. For example, a smartphone device will show high values for Response_time if it is busy with user activity. In this case, the performance function must be updated periodically to make the right decisions. Other devices could have stable performance levels due to their dedicated use or their capacity for absorbing new tasks. The static data can be stored in a Look-Up Table for fast evaluation.

Once the computational load is characterized with normalized and relative values, each device of the IoT environment shows its ability to run tasks in for the application in a homogeneous and comparable way.

In order to successfully design and configure a distributed application making the most of this framework, a method is proposed. Table 1 gives a general overview of the inputs and outputs for each design stage. As can be appreciated, the design of distributed applications under the proposed model consists of three main steps: (1) task and data flow break down; (2) resource planning and (3) deployment and empirical adjustments.

Table 1. Distributed application design methodology

Design stages	Inputs	Outputs
1. Tasks and dataflows break down	Implementations State_of_the_art techniques Application requirements Working environment constraints	Data flow diagram
2. Resource planning	Cloud market Network architecture IoT environment	IoT environment configuration: sensors, wearables, mobile devices, cloud servers, etc.
3. Deployment and calibration of the system	Configuration set up. Test	Distributed architecture for IoT environment

4 Conclusions and Future Work

The computing requirements for monitoring and advanced analysing of the data acquired by IoT environments usually overcomes the capabilities of the sensors and even the mobile computers. In this work, a distributed architecture that combines sensing and processing at different levels of the network to share the computing load among the available devices has been proposed to address this challenge. The IoT environments composed of wearables and other biosensors may benefit of this architecture by allowing the processing of advanced applications with real-time constraints in a collaborative way.

The main advantages and novelties of the proposed system are that it enables real-time monitoring and analysis of all acquired data. In addition, it provides flexibility to the application execution by using resources from cloud computing services, but also from other available computers when recommended for reducing costs or better availability.

Further work must be invested in building a proper predictive model of the available resources, aimed at providing valuable information for increasing the effectiveness of the scheduler component. System resilience is another interesting issue that should be further developed. The proposed framework could support a fallback policy, to be activated when central control is not available or accessible. This point could be expanded by adding a service discovery mechanism, allowing computers to autonomously take suboptimal decisions based on local information coming from neighboring devices.

References

1. Zhu, N., et al.: Bridging e-health and the internet of things: the SPHERE project. IEEE Intell. Syst. **30**(4), 39–46 (2015)
2. Mora-Mora, H., Gilart-Iglesias, V., Gil, D., Sirvent-Llamas, A.: A computational architecture based on RFID sensors for traceability in smart cities. Sensors **15**, 13591–13626 (2015)
3. Qin, G., Wang, L., Li, Q.: Resource symmetric dispatch model for internet of things on advanced logistics. Symmetry **8**(4), 20 (2016)

4. Pérez-Delhoyo, R., et al.: Improving urban accessibility: a methodology for urban dynamics analysis in smart, sustainable and inclusive cities. Int. J. Sust. Dev. Plan. **12**(3), 357–367 (2017)
5. Arslan, M.Y., Singh, I., Singh, S., Madhyastha, H.V., Sundaresan, K., Krishnamurthy, S.V.: CWC: a distributed computing infrastructure using smartphones. IEEE Trans. Mob. Comput. **14**(8), 1587–1600 (2015)
6. Keller, C., Schlegel, T.: Model based and service oriented interaction for ubiquitous environments. In: ACM International Joint Conference on Pervasive and Ubiquitous Computing, pp. 429–434 (2016)
7. Narman, H.S., Hossain, M.S., Atiquzzaman, M., et al.: Scheduling internet of things applications in cloud computing. Ann. Telecommun. **72**, 79 (2017)
8. Haferkamp, M., Sliwa, B., Ide, C., Wietfeld, C.: Payload-size and deadline-aware scheduling for time-critical cyber physical systems. In: Wireless Days (2017)
9. Li, L., Li, S., Zhao, S.: QoS-aware scheduling of services-oriented internet of things. IEEE Trans. Ind. Inf. **10**(2), 1497–1505 (2014)
10. Gil, D., et al.: Internet of things: a review of surveys based on context aware intelligent services. Sensors **16**(7), 1069 (2016)
11. Colom, J.F., et al.: Collaborative building of behavioural models based on internet of things. Comput. Electr. Eng. **58**, 385–396 (2016)
12. Dinh, H.T., Lee, C., Niyato, D., Wang, P.: A survey of mobile cloud computing: architecture, applications, and approaches. Wirel. Commun. Mob. Comput. **3**(18), 1587–1611 (2013)
13. Mora, H., Mendez, D.G., López, J.F.C., Pont, M.T.S.: Flexible frame-work for real-time embedded systems based on mobile cloud computing paradigm. Mob. Inf. Syst. (2015). doi: 10.1155/2015/652462

Data Structures Modelling for Citizen Tracking Based Applications in Smart Cities

Alejandro Sirvent-Llamas[1], Higinio Mora[1], Virgilio Gilart-Iglesias[1(✉)],
María Dolores Andújar-Montoya[2], Raquel Pérez-del Hoyo[2],
and Alberto de Ramón-Fernandez[1]

[1] Department of Computer Science Technology and Computation,
University of Alicante, 03690 Alicante, Spain
{asirvent,hmora,vgilart,aderamon}@dtic.ua.es
[2] Department of Building and Urbanism, University of Alicante, 03690 Alicante, Spain
{lola.andujar,perezdelhoyo}@ua.es

Abstract. Internet of Things is a promising paradigm for designing context-aware systems. The information provided can be used for understanding the environment and providing intelligent services to the citizen. There are several studies on the information acquisition of Smart Cities. This work is focused on citizens' traceability technologies and the data structures involved in representing and querying this information. A location and route data structure is proposed for handling data from different sources and devices, and meet the requirements of citizens' flow management in Smart Cities.

Keywords: Smart sensor network · Smart City · Computational Architectures · Internet of Things

1 Introduction

Smart Cities and Internet of Things (IoT) are currently very intensive research areas. These topics are related to make an efficient use of resources in cities [1] and offer better services to citizens [2]. As general rule, the design of intelligent services requires to know the environment in which the service is provided in order to customize it to the final user and to the particular conditions at each moment. This feature leads to context-aware systems, where the systems are able to know relevant aspects of their physical surrounding and adapt their behavior accordingly. That paradigm has open new research areas such as intelligent environments, pervasive & ubiquitous computing and ambient intelligence [3].

IoT provides the technology for make reality real context-aware systems [4]. This work falls within this topic and it is built on previous works for making context aware systems for track and trace citizens in Smart Cities using the IoT paradigm [5, 6]. A need is emerging in cities about the new sources of information on what is happening in the city: traffic, pollution, flows of citizen movements, etc. But one having those data through several sensor networks, the real challenge lies in understanding of the impact that information has on city behavior.

© Springer International Publishing AG 2017
S.F. Ochoa et al. (Eds.): UCAmI 2017, LNCS 10586, pp. 201–206, 2017.
DOI: 10.1007/978-3-319-67585-5_21

The particular aims of this research are focused on modelling the data structures for handling locations and routes of citizens. The purposes are to find a canonical structure that unify the different representations of the citizens' locations and the routes they follow. This format may store data from several sources, devices and technologies, and allow making queries under different search filters. It would then be possible to understand citizens' daily mobility patterns for planning and management of urban facilities and intelligent services.

This paper is organised into sections as follows: Sect. 2 provides a brief review of related works; in Sect. 3, the data structure model is introduced, and finally, conclusion remarks are presented in Sect. 4.

2 Related Work

Currently, there are many available technologies for acquiring user location. There are studies where Global Position System (GPS) technology is used for positioning and tracking. With GPS, It is easy establish the position on the world map. Thus it is the most used for orientation purposes by drivers and pedestrians since it has become quite available [7]. In addition, it is now integrated into many devices such as mobile phones or other ubiquitous devices.

This kind of mobile devices provide other interesting communication technology for enabling user positioning. The Global System for Mobile Communications (GSM) technology can also be used to perform large-scale tracking and tracing of users [8].

The communication technologies Bluetooth [9] and Wireless local area networking (Wifi) can also be used for position acquisition by triangulation [10].

Another case, could be the RFID/NFC technology, which we have every time implanted in our daily life since, currently, large manufacturers and distributors tag their articles using this technology. The research works and proposals for this technology work in controlled environments, and then, when the users access a system are given a tag to carry around the working environment. Many studies have been conducted for track and trace indoors and outdoors [11, 12].

At this time, all the previous technologies are able to generate positioning data. As mentioned, a great advantage is that most technologies are embedded in devices of daily use, which most people have and carry with them. A possible working scenario where several technologies are combined is shown below in Fig. 1.

However, the data acquired from these devices with different technologies need to be integrated in a unique way.

Usually, the data provided by GPS device comes in GPX (GPS Exchange Format) format. This is a light-weight XML structure for the interchange of GPS data [13]. Other formats are also used to export the location data to Geographic Information Systems. This is the case of the Keyhole Markup Language (KML) extensively used by Google Earth application [14]. In addition, other sources can be in CSV or TXT plain format depending on the vendor-specific schemes.

Fig. 1. Scenario of capture of information of different technologies.

The previous formats represent both single locations and routes. The single location is usually represented by Lat/Lon, elevation, timestamp, speed and course. The routes are a set of single locations to help navigation systems compute routes dynamically.

Moreover, there are another issues related to the data fields. For example, GPS time typically is reported in Universal Time Coordinated (UTC) and it does not automatically adjusts for timezone or daylight savings.

3   Architecture of the Generalization Model

The storage structure is a fundamental aspect to take into account when designing a data acquisition system and we will have to take into account a series of factors that we will detail below.

In order to create the structure, we have to take into account the following considerations: on the one hand we must be able to know, once the reading has been done, what technology was used to read the position. This will be important because there are technologies with minimal errors of positioning, however, other technologies introduce higher error level. It may also be necessary in a later treatment of the data to achieve completeness information with any technology; To determine that in certain environments the readings made are mostly of a certain technology, for example GSM, it can help to know that in that environment only individuals with smartphones and not RFID tags, for example. It is interesting to know that to obtain a positioning data in GSM we have performed a triangulation.

We must therefore create a global structure, regardless of the acquisition technology, achieving complete and reliable information. For this reason, the information model has been created taking into account the following data:

Positioning Data (readingPosition): Here we must have information about the position where the reading has been made, for this we will use the latitude and longitude, obtained at the time of reading the reading station, this will determine the latitude and length. With a margin of error determined by the technology and the reading device, hence the need to store the type of technology used also at the time of reading. It will be represented by two *float (latitude, length)*.

Identification of the Device/Card (idReading): Depending on the device used, we will store one or other information, in the case of RFID Tags, we will only store the EPC of the card, in case of GPS/Wifi/Bluetooth technology we will store the MAC address of the device, in summary, we must put an unique id of the device read, which, for any technology of the raised, is possible to obtain. It will be represented by an *integer*.

Power Used (powerEmploy): It will be interesting to know if the value can be obtained by the reading station through which the reading has been made for the RFID case, or the signal strength for Wifi, etc. This value may be interesting in later studies to determine if an increase of reading stations is necessary for a greater capacity of readings, or the increase of the Wi-Fi signal, to avoid loss of readings, for example. It will be represented by a *float*.

Identification of the Reading Station (idStationReading): we need to store a reading station identifier in charge of reading, as well as the type of reading station (Type of technology: GPS/Wifi/RFID…); In case more than one reading station is necessary to read (a triangle, for example to locate a GPS device), we must store all the stations that have intervened in said reading. It will be represented by an *integer*.

Date and Time (dateTimeReading): is one of the most important values to be stored, since it will intervene in any subsequent calculation of possible tracking, being necessary to be able to distinguish previous or later readings in time; For our system to be reliable all the readers must be synchronized with a minimum margin of error, for this we will apply a method of synchronization of clocks, being NTP [6], which allows a correct synchronization, is perfect Tested and presents acceptable margins of errors, which, although not the most optimal, are sufficient for our system. It will be represented by a *TimeStamp*.

Technology used (readingTechnology): a very important aspect to store, since later on when making inquiries about traceability, depending on the type of technology used to perform the reading, we can determine possible mistakes, to know the accuracy of reading, habits of the individual who carry the device/tag read in the environment to be analyzed, as well as other possible aspects. It will be represented by a *string* that indicate the technology employed (RFID, GPS, GSM, Wifi, Bluetooth…)

Once the needs are defined, we have defined the storage structure. In our case, we will define a vector-like structure where we will store the different fields previously defined as shown below.

The basic entity where we will store the locations will be defined by the following tuple:

R = {readingPosition, idReading, powerEmploy, isStationReading, dateTimeReading, readingTechnology}.

And where we will have a set of readings:

$$RN = \{R1 \dots Rn\}$$

On the other hand, we need to store in another entity the network topology of deployed reader stations. That entity will be determined by:

Data of Positioning of the Reader (positioningStation): This value determinates the exact position of the reader, to locate it we will make use of latitude and longitude. This value can be analyzed later to determine if its position is the correct one or to modify it (depending on the power with which the readings are made), or to add more readers or other possible actions. It will be represented by two *float (latitude, length)*.

Identification of the Reading Station (stationId): Identifier of the reading station. It will be represented by an *integer*.

Technology Used (technologyStation): technology used by the reading station, to carry out the readings. It will be represented by a *string* that indicate the technology employed (RFID, GPS, GSM, Wifi, Bluetooth…)

The basic entity where we will store the reading stations will be defined by the following tuple:

$$S = \{positioningStation, stationId, technologyStation\}.$$

Where the set of reading stations, will be determined by:

$$SN = \{S1, S2 \dots Sn\}.$$

With these two tuples defined (tuple readings and tuple reading stations), we will store all the readings made by the reading stations, as well as the positions of these, including all the necessary data to later analyze different scenarios of traceability, Or other possibilities where such information can be exploited.

4 Conclusions

A study has been carried out in which it has been verified that although there are numerous studies within the field of intelligent cities, where the acquisition of information through different technologies is approached through the use of devices available to citizens, there was no common structure to be able to store the information collected for later exploitation. With this objective a structure has been proposed on the one hand to store certain parameters of the reading stations, common to the different technologies proposed, as well as another storage structure where to store the readings made using different technologies. It has been proposed the model for the use of the most used technologies for the different jobs (RFID, NFC, Wifi, Bluetooth, GSM, GPS), being extended to possible extensions of technologies that a future could be used for the acquisition of data in a Smart City.

References

1. Neirotti, P., de Marco, A., Cagliano, A.C., Mangano, G., Scorrano, F.: Current trends in Smart City initiatives: some stylised facts. Cities 38, 25–36 (2014)
2. Gil, D., Ferrández, A., Mora-Mora, H., Peral, J.: Internet of Things: a review of surveys based on context aware intelligent services. Sensors 16(7), 1069 (2016)
3. Alegre, A., Augusto, J.C., Clark, T.: Engineering context-aware systems and applications: a survey. J. Syst. Softw. 117, 55–83 (2016). doi:10.1016/j.jss.2016.02.010
4. Perera, C., Zaslavsky, A., Christen, P., Georgakopoulos, D.: Context aware computing for the Internet of Things: a survey. IEEE Commun. Surv. Tutor. 16(1), 414–454 (2014). doi: 10.1109/SURV.2013.042313.00197
5. Mora, H., Gilart-Iglesias, V., Gil, D., Sirvent-Llamas, A.: A computational architecture based on RFID sensors for traceability in Smart Cities. Sensors 15(6), 13591–13626 (2015). doi: 10.3390/s150613591
6. Mora, H., Gilart-Iglesias, V., Pérez-delHoyo, R., Andújar-Montoya, M.D., Compañ-Gabucio, H.J.: Interactive cloud system for the analysis of accessibility in Smart Cities. Int. J. Des. Nat. Ecodyn. 11(3), 447–458 (2016)
7. Bajaj, R., Ranaweera, S.L., Agrawal, D.P.: GPS location-tracking technology. Computer 35, 92–94 (2002)
8. Al Rashed, M.A., Oumar, O.A., Singh, D.: A real time GSM/GPS based tracking system based on GSM mobile phone. Int. Conf. Future Gener. Commun. Technol. (FGCT) (2013). doi:10.1109/FGCT.2013.6767186
9. Versichelea, M., et al.: Pattern mining in tourist attraction visits through association rule learning on Bluetooth tracking data: a case study of Ghent, Belgium. Tour. Manage. 44, 67–81 (2014)
10. Sapiezynski, P., et al.: Tracking human mobility using WiFi signals. PLoS ONE 10(7), e0130824 (2015)
11. Ni, L.M., Zhang, D., Souryal, M.R.: RFID-based localization and tracking technologies. IEEE Wirel. Commun. 18, 45–51 (2011)
12. Gilart-Iglesias, V., Mora, H., Pérez-delHoyo, R., García-Mayor, C.: A computational method based on radio frequency technologies for the analysis of accessibility of disabled people in sustainable cities. Sustainability 7(11), 14935–14963 (2015)
13. GPX: The GPS exchange format (2017). http://www.topografix.com/gpx.asp. Accessed 01 May 2017
14. Du, Y., Yu, C., Liu, J.: A study of GIS development based on KML and Google Earth. In: International Joint Conference on INC, IMS and IDC (2009)

System Model for a Continuous Improvement of Road Mass Transit

Teresa Cristóbal, Gabino Padrón, Alexis Quesada-Arencibia, Francisco Alayón,
and Carmelo R. García(✉)

Institute for Cybernetics, Universidad de Las Palmas de Gran Canaria,
Las Palmas de Gran Canaria, Spain
teresa.cristobalb@alu.ulpgc.es,
{gabino.padron,alexis.quesada,fracncisco.alayon,
ruben.garcia}@ulpgc.es, rgarcia@dis.ulpgc.es

Abstract. The quality of service has a main relevance in mass transit systems, being the reliability a key factor for this quality. A system model for the continuous transport data acquisition and computing of these data to improve the quality of service of road mass transit systems is presented in this contribution. This proposal has been conceived to provide services adapted to the needs of the travellers by a continuous monitoring of the transport activity. The data obtained by buses on boarded systems have a special relevance in the proposed model, specially the data provided by the on boarded sensors, such as GPS positioning system. The system model has been applied to analyse the reliability of the operation scheduling of a road mass transit operator, and the results of this test are presented in this paper.

Keywords: Intelligent transport systems · Automatic public transport planning · GPS data

1 Introduction

Transport systems have a relevant role in the modern society because they permit the mobility of people and goods, facilitating the integration and the economic and social development of the people. For this reason, public authorities assume the development of efficient transport systems as a priority goal. Therefore, nowadays the use of transport systems is massive, especially private road transport, for example according to the International Energy Agency the number of vehicles running on our roads is 870 million and the prediction for the next 25 years is 1700 million of vehicles [1]. The consequences are well known: environmental degradation, traffic congestion and a significant increment in the risk of accidents. For example, the World Health Organization [2] estimates that around 3 million people die annually due to outdoor air pollution and every year 250,000 people in the European Union [3] are seriously injured as a result of traffic accidents. An effective policy to reduce the impact of these problems consists of using of public transport systems.

© Springer International Publishing AG 2017
S.F. Ochoa et al. (Eds.): UCAmI 2017, LNCS 10586, pp. 207–212, 2017.
DOI: 10.1007/978-3-319-67585-5_22

The quality of service has a main relevance in public transport systems, being a key factor for this quality the reliability. In the case of road mass transit systems, to achieve a high level of reliability is a challenge because the transport activity on the roads is affected by variable factors which are external to the public transport operators, for example: accidents, weather, traffic density, etc. A system model for the continuous transport data acquisition and computing of these data to improve the quality of service is presented in this contribution.

In addition to this introductory section, this paper is structured in four more sections. The next section is dedicated to present related works. The system is explained in the third section, exposing the data and infrastructure required and the techniques. The fourth section is dedicated to present some results obtained applying this system. The last section is dedicated to present the conclusions.

2 Related Works

The development of efficient and reliable road mass transit system is a challenge for transport agency and scientific community. According to Ceder [4], to provide an efficient public transport service, it is necessary to optimize the design of the network transport, the scheduling of the operations and the resources assignment to perform these operations. To achieve a high level of reliability it is necessary to register all the operations made by the vehicles and to calculate the different metrics used to measure the reliability of the operations scheduling, Nakanishi [5] proposes different criteria and metrics to perform this evaluation. The reliability is a main property of the quality of service because high level of reliability increases the demand and consequently the profitability of transport activity, but from the point of view of the transport user, this property is relevant because low level of reliability affects to this perception about the convenience and the comfort, Strathman [6]. However, the road mass transit operators must face unforeseen situations that make difficult to fulfill their services scheduling, being necessary to execute real time actions to restore the service normality or to minimize the deviation with respect to the scheduling [7].

To have all the data required to execute the different strategies and techniques for improving the public transport, various transports mass transit agencies have used automatic data collection systems to track the vehicles activity. These systems can be classified in two categories: automatic counter passengers systems (APC) that track the movements of the passengers in the vehicles and automatic vehicle location systems (AVL) that track the vehicle position. These systems have a common structure configured by three main onboard elements: positioning system, sensors and communication system [8]. Works that illustrate the use of this type of data for improving the road public transport are the contribution of Zhao [9], who used GPS data to determine optimal slack time for planning schedule-based services and the work of Derevitskiy [10], who studied traffic conditions in the transport network using GPS data.

3   System Model Proposal

The aim of the proposed system model is to provide a framework for systematically controlling and improving the efficiency and quality of service of the road mass transit. To achieve this goal, it is necessary to evaluate systematically metrics that measure the level of optimization of the transport network and the operation scheduling, the reliability of the operations scheduling and the convenience of the transport service from the point of view of the transport user. The model working principles are based on the general principles of the modern architectures of intelligent transport systems, see Fig. 1.

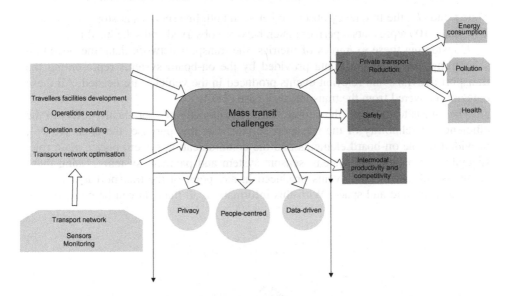

Fig. 1   General vision of the working principles of the system model

As mentioned in the previous section, in road mass transit there are different criteria for evaluating the quality of service. Normally, the urban public transport is scheduled by frequency and long distance public transport is scheduled by timetable, for this reason the regularity is a criterion used to evaluate the reliability in urban public transport and the punctuality the criterion for long distance public transport. Next, to identify the data required to evaluate and improve the quality of service some examples of parameters are presented. In these examples of metrics, l represents a route of public transport, l_i a service line of the route l and p a bus stop of the line l.

To evaluate the reliability of the operation scheduling, for long distance the punctuality of the line service, the RTV metric is used. For a line l, the metric RTV is calculated by the following expression:

$$RTV_{li} = n^{-1} \times \sum_{p=0}^{n} \frac{|OT_{li,p} - ST_{li,p}|}{OT_{li,p}}.$$

(1)

$OT_{li,p}$ is the observed passing time through stop p and $ST_{li,p}$ the scheduled passing time through that stop, when operating the line service l_i.

For line services operating by frequency, the proposed criterion is regularity. To evaluate regularity, a basic metric used is the Headway Ratio (HR):

$$HR_{li,k}^p = \left(\frac{H_{li,k}^p}{f_{li,k}^p}\right) \times 100 \tag{2}$$

Where $f_{li,k}^p$ is the scheduled frequency between two line services l_i, l_{i+1} at stop p on route r and $H_{li,k}^p$ the frequency observed between both line services at stop p on route r. The factor 100 represents a perfect match between observed and scheduled time.

Considering these examples of metrics, the transport network data, the operation scheduling, the timetables, data provided by the on-board systems representing the transport activities and relevant events produced in the vehicles are needed. All these data are recovered from the transport data base (TDB).

The aim is to know all the causes that systematically or sporadically affect to the efficiency or reliability of the transport service. For this purpose, the data, {RAV}, provided by the on-board elements and the communication system play a main role, specially the positioning system, sensors system and payment systems. Using these elements, all the relevant events produced in any point of the transport network are referenced in time and space. With this information, all the data can be merged with

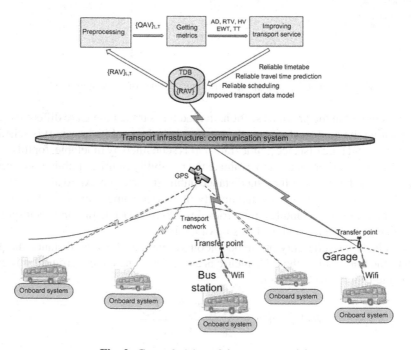

Fig. 2 General vision of the system model

external data of the transport activity to perform advanced techniques such as big data, data mining, machine learning, etc. Figure 2 shows a general vision of the system model integrating the proposed methodology. The first step is the preprocessing phase; its goal is to select the data provided by the transport infrastructure that must be taken into account to analyze a quality or an efficiency parameter during the period T, the output data of this phase is represented by $\{QRA\}_{L,T}$. Using the selected data, the second phase is a computing process to obtain the metrics required for the analysis. For the last step, it is required to identify the causes that affect the efficiency or reliability of the transport activity, executing actions to improve it.

4   Use Case

The proposed system model has been applied to analyze the efficiency and quality of service of the road mass transit in Gran Canaria island (Canary Islands, Spain). To perform the analysis, the more important interurban public transport operator in the Island, Global Salcai-Utinsa S.A., collaborated in the study. In the case of interurban transport, the most important criteria of efficiency and reliability is the punctuality. Low levels of punctuality imply low reliability that produces an inefficient assignment of resources (vehicles and drivers), reducing the profitability of the transport activity, even affecting to the safety of the service. A public transport operator's schedule consists of a set of scheduling units. For each scheduling unit consists of a set of operations to be carried by a vehicle and driver. The operations may be of different types, but for the purposes of monitoring efficiency, duration of line service operations is the most important element.

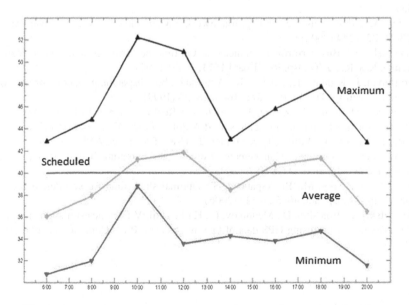

Fig. 3 Graphical representation of the results of the line services duration.

A study of the line service duration of a route is presented. The route has 30 bus stops, it is 23 kilometres long. The vehicles involved in the line services of this route during 3 months provided the data used for the study. Specifically, the positioning records acquired each second by the vehicle GPS. Figure 3 shows these results in a graphical way, the hour of the start time of the line service is represented in the horizontal axis and the line service duration is represented in the vertical axis.

5   Conclusions

The improvement of the mass transit system is a main goal for transport authorities, being technology a useful tool to achieve this goal. In this contribution, a system model for the systematic public road transport data acquisition and processing has been presented. The proposed model permits to get massive transport data and metrics associated with the road mass transit quality of service, merging different type of data: geographical, operation scheduling, production, etc. The proposal has been applied to analyze the interurban mass transit of the Gran Canaria Island, presenting as a case of use the results obtained to study the reliability of the operation scheduling of line services of interurban routes.

References

1. Word Energey Outlook 2012. International Energy Agency, p. 89, Paris, (2012)
2. World Health Organization. http://www.who.int/mediacentre/news/releases/2016/air-pollution-estimates/en/. Accessed 1 May 2017
3. European Commission. http://europa.eu/rapid/press-release_IP-13-236_en.htm. Accessed 1 May 2017
4. Ceder, A.: Urban transit scheduling: framework, review and examples. J. Urban Plan. Dev. **128**(4), 225–244 (2002)
5. Nakanishi, Y.: Bus performance indicators: On-time performance and service regularity. Transp. Res. Rec J. Transp. Res. Board **1571**, 1–13 (1997)
6. Strathman, J., Kimpel, T., Dueker, K.: Automated bus dispatching, operations control and service reliability. Transp. Res. Rec. **1666**, 28–36 (1999)
7. Dessouky, M., Hall, R., Zhang, L., Singh, A.: Real-time control of buses for schedule coordination at a terminal. Transp. Res. Part A Policy Pract. **37**(2), 145–164 (2003)
8. Furth, P., Hemily, B., Muller, T., Strathman, J.: Uses of Archived AVLAPC Data to Improve Transit Performance and Management: Review and Potential, Transportation Research Board, Ed. Washington, D.C., USA (2003)
9. Zhao, J., Dessouky, M., Bukkapatnam, S.: Optimal slack time for schedule-based transit operations. Transp. Sci. **40**, 529–539 (2006)
10. Derevitskiy, I., Voloshin, D., Mednikov, L., Karbovskii, V.: Traffic estimation on full graph of transport network using GPS data of bus movements. Proc. Comput. Sci. **101**, 207–216 (2016)

Analysis of Distance and Similarity Metrics in Indoor Positioning Based on Bluetooth Low Energy

Gabriel de Blasio, Alexis Quesada-Arencibia[✉], Carmelo R. García,
Roberto Moreno-Díaz Jr., and Jose Carlos Rodríguez-Rodríguez

Instituto Universitario de Ciencias y Tecnologías Cibernéticas, IUCTC,
ULPGC, Las Palmas de Gran Canaria, Spain
{gabriel.deblasio,alexis.quesada,ruben.garcia,
roberto.morenodiaz}@ulpgc.es, jcarlos@ciber.ulpgc.es

Abstract. In this work, we provide an analysis of BLE channel-separate fingerprinting using different distance and similarity measures. In a 168 m^2 testbed, 12 beacons with Eddystone and iBeacon protocols set were deployed, taking into account the orientation of users and considering 10 distance/similarity measures. We have observed that there is an orientation that offers the best positioning performance with the combination of iBeacon protocol, channel 38 and Mahalanobis distance. Taking 8 samples in the online phase, accuracy values obtained are in the range 1.28 m–1.88 m, and precision values are within 1.90 m–3.76 m or less, 90% of the time and depending which orientation the observer is facing.

1 Introduction

The commitment to the use of Bluetooth Low Energy, BLE, technology in indoor positioning is no longer a coincidence, especially when the Bluetooth Special Interest Group, BSIG, has recently launched the Bluetooth 5.0 protocol, which offers 4× range, 2× speed and 8× broadcasting message capacity [3]. It is a fact that indoor positioning using BLE technology offers many advantages with respect to the Wi-Fi positioning: beacons that are portable and battery-powered, easily deployable at low cost, with small size, light weight and low energy consumption, widely supported by mobile devices, and finally, better accuracy and precision [6,15]. On the other hand, the choice of the appropriate distance/similarity measure in indoor positioning is essential as it may affect data analysis and the interpretation of results.

In this work we make the main following contributions: (a) we provide a deep analysis of BLE protocols and advertising channels performance taking into account user orientation and using different distance and similarity measures; (b) both in the offline and online phases, data collection has been carried out in conditions very close to reality.

This paper is organized into six sections. The following section reviews the related work. In the Sect. 3 we will describe the Materials and Methods used in

© Springer International Publishing AG 2017
S.F. Ochoa et al. (Eds.): UCAmI 2017, LNCS 10586, pp. 213–224, 2017.
DOI: 10.1007/978-3-319-67585-5_23

the experiments. The experiments and theirs results are described and analysed in the Sect. 4. Section 5 discusses the results. Finally, the conclusions and future lines of work are presented in the sixth section.

2   Related Works

We will start with a list of surveys on distance and similarity metrics to continue with works where a particular distance metric is used.

Cha [5] reviewed and categorized various distance and similarity measures applicable to compare two probability density functions. Torres-Sospedra et al. [13] present a comprehensive study using 51 distance metrics and 4 alternatives to represent the raw data for Wi-Fi fingerprinting. In Moghtadaiee's et al. work [11] deterministic fingerprinting algorithms based on the nearest neighbor algorithm are analysed; the positioning performance using Manhattan, Euclidean and Chebyshev distance in terms of the probability of error are compared analytically and the results are confirmed by simulations and real Wi-Fi experiments. In Caso's et al. work [4] a comprehensive review of WKNN WiFi fingerprinting-based indoor positioning algorithms is presented; the role of the similarity metric between reference points fingerprints and online readings is investigated, by considering both flat WKNN algorithms and two-step algorithms based on affinity propagation.

Faragher's et al. work [6] is one of the first experimental tests of fine-grained BLE positioning using fingerprinting and a detailed study into the key parameters for accurate indoor positioning using the BLE radio signals; the distance metric used is the Euclidean to generate a score for each cell in the grid, and then that score is weighted using a Gaussian kernel to generate a probability. Peng et al. [12] proposed an Iterative Weighted KNN localization method based on the RSSI of BLE; Euclidean distance and Cosine similarity are combined to measure the similarity of two RSSI vectors. Zhuang et al. [15] used an algorithm that combines a polynomial regression model, fingerprinting with BLE channel separation, outlier detection, and Kalman filtering; the Euclidean distance based WKNN algorithm is used. Ishida et al. [9] proposed a BLE-based fingerprinting localization scheme; employing channel-specific features to location fingerprint and using a ℓ_1 norm for distance calculation, the system improves the localization accuracy. Fard et al. [7] used RSSI values returned by iBeacons to estimate the distance from the beacon transmitters at a coarse granularity; the distance in the signal space employed is a weighted average signal difference for each beacon, where the weight is the combined number of non-zero entries for that beacon. Hossain et al. [8] considered both Wi-Fi and Bluetooth devices, defining a robust location fingerprint based on the signal strength difference to avoid hardware heterogeneity and presenting results using K-Nearest Neighbor and Bayesian Inference. De Blasio et al. [2] presents a study of a positioning system for harsh environments that provides advanced information services based on Wi-Fi and BLE technologies; the main distance metric used was the Euclidean distance but the Mahalanobis distance was also used in one test for BLE.

3   Materials and Methods

In scene analysis or fingerprinting technique, a position is characterised by the signal pattern detected from each BLE beacon. In order to estimate the position of a user, in the so called *offline phase*, it is necessary to construct a fingerprint database for a set of reference points of known positions [1]. In that database, each reference element, or fingerprint, consists of the coordinates of the reference point, the received signal strength (RSS) of each beacon, the orientation in which these RSS readings have been taken, etc. In the so called *online phase*, users in an unknown position initially obtain the RSS values for the different beacons (target fingerprint) and by means of some algorithm, such as Weighted k-Nearest Neighbor, WKNN, users compare these RSS values with those stored in the database, to ultimately obtain the coordinates of their location.

For deterministic algorithms, the position of the user may be determined using distance/similarity metrics. The process starts comparing the fingerprints stored in the offline phase with the measurements taken in the online phase: the user is located at the coordinates for which the reference fingerprint is at the minimum distance in the signal space of the target fingerprint.

In the offline phase, 12 iBKS105 beacons were deployed, and a laptop Asus N56J with a Nordic Semiconductor nRF51 BLE dongle was used to obtain the RSS measures. The software employed were *ble-sniffer win-1.0.1-1111* and *Wireshark 1.10.14*. In the online phase, the same laptop, dongle and software were used.

3.1   WKNN

WKNN is the algorithm employed in this paper to compare the fingerprints: this algorithm is an improvement of the classic algorithms, Nearest Neighbor, NN, and k-Nearest Neighbor, KNN. Reference points obtained in the offline phase which are close to test points, obtained in the online phase, should get a higher weight than reference points which are far away. Estimated coordinates (x_e, y_e) of test points are calculated using the formula:

$$(x_e, y_e) = \frac{\sum_{i=1}^{k}(x_i, y_i) \cdot w_i}{\sum_{i=1}^{k} w_i}, \qquad w_i = \frac{1}{d_i} \tag{1}$$

where (x_e, y_e), (x_i, y_i) are respectively the estimated coordinates of the target points and the coordinates of the k reference points and w_i are the weights for each distance, d_i.

3.2   Distance and Similarity Measures

Given two RSS vectors, P, Q, with p elements, we will use some of the following distance/similarity equations in our analysis [5,13]. We will use:

The Euclidean distance from the Minkowski family, L_p, that also includes City Block (or Manhattan or Taxi-cab), Minkowski and Chebyshev distances:

$$d_{Eucl}(P,Q) = \sqrt{\sum_{i=1}^{d}(P_i - Q_i)^2} \tag{2}$$

The Sørensen distance from the L_1 family that also includes Gower, Soergel, Kulczynski, Canberra, and Lorentzian distances:

$$d_{S\phi re}(P,Q) = \frac{\sum_{i=1}^{d}|P_i - Q_i|}{\sum_{i=1}^{d}(P_i + Q_i)} \tag{3}$$

The Wave Hedges distance from the intersection family, that also includes Intersection, Czekanowski, Motyka and Tanimoto distances; Kulczynski and Ruzicka similarities:

$$d_{Wave}(P,Q) = \frac{|P_i - Q_i|}{max(P_i, Q_i)} \tag{4}$$

The Cosine similarity from the Inner product family, that also includes Inner Product, Harmonic mean and Kumar-Hassebrook similarities; Jaccard and Dice distances:

$$d_{Cos}(P,Q) = \frac{\sum_{i=1}^{d}P_iQ_i}{\sqrt{\sum_{i=1}^{d}P_i^2}\sqrt{\sum_{i=1}^{d}Q_i^2}} \tag{5}$$

The Pearson χ^2 distance from the Squared L_2 family that also includes Squared Euclidean, Neyman χ^2, Squared χ^2, Probabilistic Symmetric χ^2, Divergence, Clark, and Additive Symmetric χ^2 distances:

$$d_{Pear}(P,Q) = \sum_{i=1}^{d}\frac{(P_i - Q_i)^2}{Q_i} \tag{6}$$

The Fidelity similarity from the Fidelity or Squared-chord family that also includes Bhattacharyya, Hellinger, Matusita and Squared-chord distances:

$$d_{Fide}(P,Q) = \sum_{i=1}^{d}\sqrt{P_iQ_i} \tag{7}$$

The Jeffreys distance from the Shannon's Entropy family that also includes Kullback-Leibler, K divergence, Topsøe, Jensen-Shannon and Jensen difference distances:

$$d_{Jeff}(P,Q) = \sum_{i=1}^{d}(P_i - Q_i)\,ln\frac{P_i}{Q_i} \tag{8}$$

The Taneja distance from the Combinations family that also includes Kumar-Johnson and Avg distances:

$$d_{Tane}(P,Q) = \sum_{i=1}^{d}\left(\frac{P_i + Q_i}{2}\right)ln\frac{P_i + Q_i}{2\sqrt{P_iQ_i}} \tag{9}$$

In addition to the above distances/similarities, we will use the Mahalanobis and Normalized-Euclidean distances, whose formulae are respectively:

$$d_{Maha}(P,Q) = \sqrt{(P-Q)C^{-1}(P-Q)^t} \tag{10}$$

$$d_{Norm}(P,Q) = \sqrt{\sum_{i=1}^{p}\frac{(P_i - Q_i)^2}{\sigma_i^2}} \tag{11}$$

where C is the covariance matrix and σ_i is the standard deviation.

4 Experiments and Results

4.1 Experimental Setup

To evaluate the performance of different distance and similarity metrics mentioned in Sect. 3.2, we conducted several experiments in a $168\,m^2$ testbed, shown in Fig. 1(a). The testbed chosen was the main corridor of the IUCTC building, which is squared-shaped of 17 m long and 3 m wide. 12 BLE beacons (blue dots in Fig. 1(b)) were deployed in columns at a height of 2.1 m with Eddystone and iBeacon protocols set. It was chosen a grid of 112 cells, each measuring 1 m × 1 m (black dots in Fig. 1(b)), which implies an average beacon deployment of 1 beacon per $14\,m^2$ and an average of 1.5 fingerprint per m^2. For these tests, the configuration of each beacon was:

- Eddystone protocol: only UID frame was set, an advertising interval of 500 ms and an output power of 0 dBm.
- for iBeacon: an advertising interval of 500 ms and an output power of 0 dBm.

In the offline phase, 60 s of samples (120 samples) were taken for each reference point, orientation (N, E, S, W), protocol (iBeacon and Eddystone) and 3 advertising BLE channels (37, 38 and 39). By means of a laser pointer with a range of up to 200 m and a precision of 1.0 mm, and for each reference point, the coordinates (x, y) were taken with respect to the coordinate source, O, of the

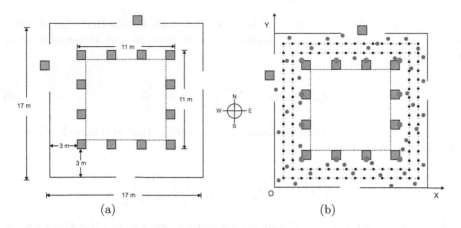

Fig. 1. Schematic view of the testbed: (a) dimensions; (b) axes of chosen coordinates with reference and test points. (Color figure online)

grid. Once the reference fingerprints had been recorded, a database which we call *RP-max* was constructed: the mean RSS value for each orientation and beacon was calculated and then the maximum of those mean RSS values was selected. In the online phase, the same laptop and dongle used in the offline phase were used to record 40 target points randomly situated in the grid (see Fig. 1(b)). Only 8 samples (4 s) were taken for each orientation, protocol and BLE channels and their coordinates also being recorded with the laser pointer. For each test point, orientation, protocol and BLE channels, the mean and maximum values of the 8 samples were calculated. We shall call those RSS values *TP-mean* and *TP-max* respectively. The purpose of taking into account orientation in the online phase is to simulate the positioning of a user who is specifically facing in one of the four possible directions in real time [2]. These data could be ascertained through the device compass. In both the offline and online phases: (a) Measures were taken with little presence of people, and (b) At all measurement points and for some instants of time, no signal was received from some beacons: in those cases an arbitrary weak RSS value of −101 dBm was assigned.

In this paper, positioning accuracy is expressed by the mean error and its precision by the cumulative probability function, CDF, which is expressed in practice in percentile format [10]. For the sake of space, we present in the next sections only some accuracy and precision results, indicating if those are or not general results for all possible cases.

4.2   Accuracy Results

Accuracy vs. Number of Neighbours, K. Comparing RSS values in the *RP-max* database with those in the *TP-mean* and *TP-max*, it is observed that the value of k that produces the best accuracy depends on the protocol, channel, orientation and distance/similarity metric considered. We will use values of $k = 3$

Table 1. Accuracies (in metres) obtained for $k = 3$ and $k = 5$ neighbours using iBeacon protocol and channel 38 with Mahalanobis distance, if TP-mean and TP-max RSS values are used

k	TP-mean				TP-max			
	N	E	W	S	N	E	W	S
3	1.97	1.45	1.78	1.77	1.72	1.28	1.48	1.45
5	2.00	1.38	1.83	1.83	1.66	1.35	1.69	1.64

or $k = 5$ that in general offers good accuracy results and usually around the 10% of the best accuracy values.

TP-mean vs. TP-max. Comparing RSS values in the *RP-max* database with those in the *TP-mean* and *TP-max*, the second observation we made was that best accuracies are obtained using *TP-max*. This fact can be observed in Table 1 for a particular protocol (iBeacon), BLE channel (38), distance (Mahalanobis) and $k = 3$ and $k = 5$ neighbours. Similar results were observed in other cases.

Protocol, Channel and Orientation Performance. Taking into account *RP-max* and *TP-max* databases, we present in Tables 2 and 3 accuracy results for six different distances and two orientations of the observer in the online

Table 2. iBeacon vs. Eddystone accuracy (in metres) for 6 different distances, k = 3 neighbours and North orientation

iBeacon																	
ch.37						ch.38						ch.39					
Eu	Ne	M	C	Sø	Wa	Eu	Ne	M	C	Sø	Wa	Eu	Ne	M	C	Sø	Wa
1.91	1.86	1.86	1.94	2.31	2.45	1.71	1.74	1.72	1.72	1.93	1.82	1.86	1.90	1.93	1.87	2.16	2.01
Eddystone																	
ch.37						ch.38						ch.39					
Eu	Ne	M	C	Sø	Wa	Eu	Ne	M	C	Sø	Wa	Eu	Ne	M	C	Sø	Wa
1.79	2.10	1.66	2.23	2.55	2.60	2.12	2.02	2.04	2.06	2.34	2.36	2.05	1.95	1.88	1.99	2.19	2.29

Table 3. iBeacon vs. Eddystone accuracy (in metres) for 6 different distances, k = 3 neighbours and East orientation

iBeacon																	
ch.37						ch.38						ch.39					
Eu	Ne	M	C	Sø	Wa	Eu	Ne	M	C	Sø	Wa	Eu	Ne	M	C	Sø	Wa
1.51	1.50	1.50	1.53	1.65	1.62	1.45	1.32	1.28	1.43	1.34	1.33	1.59	1.64	1.58	1.62	1.83	1.72
Eddystone																	
ch.37						ch.38						ch.39					
Eu	Ne	M	C	Sø	Wa	Eu	Ne	M	C	Sø	Wa	Eu	Ne	M	C	Sø	Wa
1.51	1.45	1.40	1.60	1.59	1.71	1.51	1.46	1.51	1.51	1.55	1.59	1.64	1.67	1.61	1.69	1.72	1.75

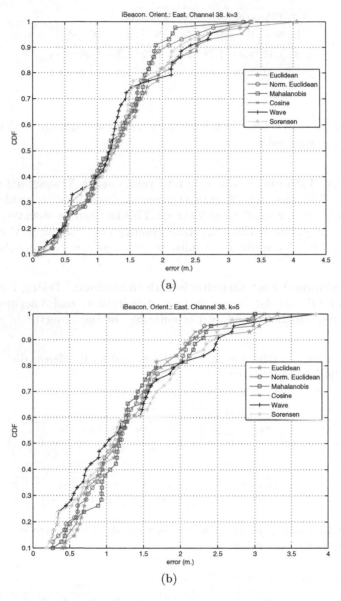

(a)

(b)

Fig. 2. Precisions for six different distances, iBeacon protocol, channel 38 and East orientation with: (a) $k = 3$ neighbours; (b) $k = 5$ neighbours

phase. We have selected the following distances: *Eu*-Euclidean, *Ne*-Normalized Euclidean, *M*-Mahalanobis, *C*-Cosine, *Sø*-Sørensen, *Wa*-Wave Hedges. With the other distances metrics mentioned in Sect. 3.2, worse results of accuracy were obtained.

Comparing Tables 2 and 3 it can be observed that:

(a) There is a remarkable difference in accuracy between orientation North and East: East orientation outperforms in all cases North orientation. The same result occurs with orientation East with respect to South and West.
(b) For a given orientation and considering channel 38, iBeacon accuracy outperforms Eddystone accuracy for the same distance metric. The same result occurs with orientation South and West. For channels 37 and 39 something similar occurs but to a lesser extent.
(c) For a given orientation and iBeacon protocol, accuracy obtained with channel 38 outperforms accuracy obtained channels 37 and 39 with the same protocol and same distance metric. This is not always true for Eddystone protocol.
(d) For a given protocol, channel and orientation, Mahalanobis, Normalized Euclidean, Euclidean and Cosine distance in general offer the best accuracy results with respect to the other distances studied.

4.3 Precision Results

As stated in Sect. 4.2, in general iBeacon protocol with channel 38 and orientation East and $k = 3$ or $k = 5$ neighbours, combined with Mahalanobis, Normalized-Euclidean, Euclidean or Cosine distance produces the best accuracy results. Figure 2(a) show precision performance for those distances and two more (Wave-Hedges and Sørensen) for comparative reasons.

As it can be seen in Fig. 2, Mahalanobis distance clearly performs better than the others five distances with $k = 3$ neighbours because its CDF graph reaches

Table 4. Accuracy and precision (in metres) for some BLE indoor positioning systems

System	Accuracy	Precision
Faragher [6]	N/A	295% within 2.6 m (1 beacon per 30 m^2)–4.8 m (1 beacon per 100 m^2)
Cinefra	0.71 m–2.52 m (office env.)	72% within 1.70 m (1 beacon per 8 m^2)
	0.84 m–3.95 m (home env.)	64% within 1.70 m (1 beacon per 32 m^2)
Indoo.rs	N/A	95% within 5.0 m
Peng [12]	2.52 m–4.48 m (office env.)	90% within 4.12 m (1 beacon per 21 m^2)
de Blasio [2]	1.47 m–2.15 m (harsh env.)	90% within 1.81 m–3.58 m (1 beacon per 45.7 m^2)
Zhuang [15]	N/A	90% within 2.56 m (1 beacon per 9 m^2)–3.88 m (1 beacon per 18 m^2)

Table 5. Minimum and maximum accuracy (in metres) for all distances considered, taking values of k between 1 and 5, iBeacon-Eddystone protocols, 3 channels and combining all orientations

| | Accuracy | | | | | |
| | iBeacon | | | Eddystone | | |
	37	38	39	37	38	39
M	1.39–2.12	1.28–1.88	1.51–2.14	1.37–2.31	1.47–2.24	1.47–2.16
Ne	1.38–2.12	1.25–1.96	1.46–2.30	1.40–2.52	1.37–2.17	1.54–2.09
Eu	1.47–2.40	1.37–2.18	1.52–2.34	1.44–2.31	1.50–2.20	1.56–2.19
C	1.53–2.37	1.32–2.03	1.45–2.36	1.57–2.69	1.36–2.15	1.49–2.14
Wa	1.47–2.90	1.33–2.13	1.64–2.40	1.56–3.05	1.54–2.46	1.70–2.43
Sø	1.37–2.82	1.34–2.13	1.58–2.52	1.57–3.20	1.50–2.43	1.68–2.50
F	2.34–3.22	2.00–3.37	2.07–3.46	2.30–3.45	2.16–3.06	1.82–3.31
J	1.52–2.42	1.71–2.24	1.78–2.59	1.68–2.68	1.67–2.36	1.75–2.30
P	2.35–3.22	2.00–3.37	2.07–3.46	2.29–3.45	2.16–3.06	1.82–3.31
T	1.52–2.77	1.73–2.47	1.84–2.75	1.78–2.56	1.70–2.31	1.72–2.34

Table 6. Minimum and maximum precision (in metres, CDF: 90%) for all distances considered, taking values of k between 1 and 5, iBeacon-Eddystone protocols, 3 channels and combining all orientations

| | Precision | | | | | |
| | iBeacon | | | Eddystone | | |
	37	38	39	37	38	39
M	2.24–3.67	1.90–3.76	2.33–4.50	1.97–4.95	2.20–4.15	2.36–4.26
Ne	2.23–3.88	1.94–4.02	2.14–3.76	2.12–4.56	2.30–3.80	2.61–4.50
Eu	2.55–4.43	2.19–4.50	2.45–4.50	2.10–4.75	2.31–4.78	2.47–4.12
C	2.59–4.43	2.14–4.08	2.30–3.76	2.39–4.87	2.12–4.74	2.37–4.50
Wa	2.35–5.23	2.43–3.64	2.82–4.56	2.48–5.12	2.51–4.69	3.06–4.48
Sø	2.18–4.54	2.28–3.81	2.79–4.74	2.37–5.71	2.20–4.60	2.95–4.48
F	3.93–6.50	3.92–6.53	3.57–8.00	4.28–7.33	3.62–6.44	3.22–8.00
J	2.59–4.76	2.55–4.48	3.04–4.65	2.68–5.00	2.94–4.59	2.76–4.35
P	3.89–6.50	4.00–6.53	3.58–8.00	4.26–7.33	3.57–6.44	3.22–8.00
T	2.44–5.40	2.72–4.88	3.27–5.57	2.65–5.18	2.94–4.74	2.77–4.50

high probability values faster [10]. For $k = 5$ Mahalanobis, Normalized-Euclidean and Sørensen are the distances that performs better reaching high probability values faster, but this time the values are closer together than in previous case.

5   Discussion

In Table 4, accuracy and precision for some BLE indoor positioning systems are shown [14]. Tables 5, 6 and Figs. 2(a), (b) show minimum and maximum accuracy and precision values obtained in this work for all the distances considered comparing *RP-max* and *TP-max*. As it was mentioned in Sect. 4.2, Mahalanobis distance show the best performance both in accuracy and precision.

For iBeacon protocol, channel 38 and Mahalanobis distance, we have obtained accuracy values in the range 1.28 m–1.88 m, and precision values 90% of the time within 1.90 m–3.76 m depending which orientation the observer is facing. Comparing this values with those obtained with other positioning systems (see Table 4), we observe that our values are in the same range.

6   Conclusions and Future Works

In this work, we provide an analysis of BLE channel-separate fingerprinting using 10 distance/similarity measures. We conducted several tests in a 168 m² testbed with 12 BLE beacons deployed in columns at a height of 2.1 m with Eddystone and iBeacon protocols set, both with an advertising interval of 500 ms and an output power of 0 dBm. A grid of 112 cells was chosen each measuring 1 m × 1 m. As a result of our tests, and with only 8 samples in the online phase, we have observed that: (a) East orientation outperforms in all cases other orientations; (b) Regardless of orientation, iBeacon accuracy with channel 38 outperforms Eddystone accuracy for the same distance metric: with channels 37 and 39 something similar occurs but to a lesser extent; (c) For a given orientation and iBeacon protocol, accuracy obtained with channel 38 outperforms accuracy obtained with channels 37 and 39 and the same protocol and distance metric: this is not always true for Eddystone protocol; (d) For a given protocol, channel and orientation, from all the distance/metrics studied, Mahalanobis, Normalized Euclidean, Euclidean and Cosine distance in general offer the best accuracy results.

We conclude that in the selected testbed, while not all the beacons were in line of sight conditions all the time, the combination of iBeacon protocol, channel 38 and Mahalanobis distance, offers the best positioning performance. We have obtained accuracy values, for the mentioned combination, in the range 1.28 m–1.88 m, and precision values 90% of the time within 1.90 m–3.76 m depending on which orientation the observer is facing: those values are in the same range of those obtained in other works. As future lines of action, we may mention the following: test other testbeds and deployments of BLE transmitters to compare accuracy and precision results, use of heterogeneous devices for the offline and online data collection phases and study other probabilistic positioning algorithms.

References

1. Bahl, P., Padmanabhan, V.N.: RADAR: an in-building RF-based user location and tracking system. In: Proceedings of IEEE INFOCOM, the Conference on Computer Communications, Nineteenth Annual Joint Conference of the IEEE Computer and Communications Societies, Reaching the Promised Land of Communications, Tel Aviv, Israel, pp. 775–784, 26–30 March 2000
2. de Blasio, G., Quesada-Arencibia, A., García, C.R., Molina-Gil, J.M., Caballero-Gil, C.: Study on an indoor positioning system for harsh environments based on Wi-Fi and bluetooth low energy. Sensors **17**(6), 27692–27720 (2017)
3. Bluetooth Special Interest Group: Bluetooth 5—Bluetooth technology website.   https://www.bluetooth.com/specifications/bluetooth-core-specification/bluetooth5/. Accessed 1 Mar 2017
4. Caso, G., de Nardis, L., di Benedetto, M.G.: A mixed approach to similarity metric selection in affinity propagation-based WiFi fingerprinting indoor positioning. Sensors **15**(11), 27692–27720 (2015). http://www.mdpi.com/1424-8220/15/11/27692
5. Cha, S.H.: Comprehensive survey on distance/similarity measures between probability density functions. Int. J. Math. Models Methods Appl. Sci. **1**(4), 300–307 (2007)
6. Faragher, R., Harle, R.: Location fingerprinting with Bluetooth low energy beacons. IEEE J. Sel. Areas Commun. **33**(11), 2418–2428 (2015)
7. Fard, H.K., Chen, Y., Son, K.K.: Indoor positioning of mobile devices with agile iBeacon deployment. In: CCECE, pp. 275–279. IEEE (2015)
8. Hossain, A.K.M.M., Jin, Y., Soh, W.S., Van, H.N.: SSD: a robust RF location fingerprint addressing mobile devices' heterogeneity. IEEE Trans. Mob. Comput. **12**(1), 65–77 (2013)
9. Ishida, S., Takashima, Y., Tagashira, S., Fukuda, A.: Proposal of separate channel fingerprinting using Bluetooth low energy. In: 2016 5th IIAI International Congress on Advanced Applied Informatics (IIAI-AAI), pp. 230–233, July 2016
10. Liu, H., Darabi, H., Banerjee, P.P., Liu, J.: Survey of wireless indoor positioning techniques and systems. IEEE Trans. Syst. Man Cybern. Part C **37**(6), 1067–1080 (2007)
11. Moghtadaiee, V., Dempster, A.G.: Determining the best vector distance measure for use in location fingerprinting. Pervasive Mob. Comput. **23**, 59–79 (2015)
12. Peng, Y., Fan, W., Dong, X., Zhang, X.: An iterative weighted KNN (IW-KNN) based indoor localization method in bluetooth low energy (BLE) environment. In: 2016 International IEEE Conferences on Ubiquitous Intelligence Computing, Advanced and Trusted Computing, Scalable Computing and Communications, Cloud and Big Data Computing, Internet of People, and Smart World Congress (UIC/ATC/ScalCom/CBDCom/IoP/SmartWorld), pp. 794–800, July 2016
13. Torres-Sospedra, J., Montoliu, R., Trilles, S., Belmonte, O., Huerta, J.: Comprehensive analysis of distance and similarity measures for Wi-Fi fingerprinting indoor positioning systems. Expert Syst. Appl. **42**, 9263–9278 (2015)
14. Čabarkapa, D., Grujić, I., Pavlović, P.: Comparative analysis of the Bluetooth low-energy indoor positioning systems. In: 2015 12th International Conference on Telecommunication in Modern Satellite, Cable and Broadcasting Services (TELSIKS), pp. 76–79, October 2015
15. Zhuang, Y., Yang, J., Li, J., Qi, L., El-Sheimy, N.: Smartphone-based indoor localization with Bluetooth low energy beacons. Sensors **16**, 596 (2011)

HEALTH (AmIHEALTH)

Usability and Acceptance of a Mobile and Cloud-Based Platform for Supporting Diabetes Self-management

Jesús Fontecha[1]([✉]), Iván González[1], M. Estrella Saucedo[2], M. José Sánchez[2], and José Bravo[1]

[1] MAmI Research Lab, University of Castilla-La Mancha, Ciudad Real, Spain
{jesus.fontecha,ivan.gdiaz,jose.bravo}@uclm.es
[2] HGUCR, Ciudad Real, Spain
{mesaucedo,majosef}@sescam.jccm.es

Abstract. Millions of people are suffering from Diabetes Mellitus today. This amount is expected to increase over the next few years due to multiple factors, not only genetic ones, but also because of our sedentary lifestyle according to the World Health Organization.

This work presents a cloud-based system which consists of a web platform, a mobile application and a set of services to facilitate a centralised study of the most relevant parameters involved in diabetes self-care. The system was evaluated by a group of diabetic patients in which 75% of them showed their satisfaction using this system for diabetes self-control. Also, the acceptance level between user and system was studied by means of an usability analysis focused on several evaluation techniques.

Keywords: Diabetes · mHealth · Monitoring · System acceptance · Usability

1 Introduction

Diabetes is a metabolic and chronic disease which occurs when pancreas is unable to produce insulin correctly, causing hyperglycemia (increase of blood sugar level). Insulin is a hormone that absorbs glucose from the bloodstream and converts it into energy for the body's cells. There are several types of Diabetes due to the different hormonal behavior, although two are the most known. In Diabetes Type I, pancreas does not produce insulin, or insulin does not work properly (Diabetes Type II). Likewise, diabetic patients suffer periods of hypoglycemia (low levels of blood sugar) which should be treated carefully.

Diabetes Type I usually appears during childhood requiring a permanent treatment with insulin, since it is not produced by the body itself. While Diabetes Type II causes a deficit in insuline production by the pancreas, being necessary a partial insuline treatment. However, there are other less common types of diabetes as it was mentioned before.

© Springer International Publishing AG 2017
S.F. Ochoa et al. (Eds.): UCAmI 2017, LNCS 10586, pp. 227–239, 2017.
DOI: 10.1007/978-3-319-67585-5_24

Nowadays, hundreds of millions of people suffer from diabetes, affecting 15% of the population according to World Health Organisation (WHO) information. Diabetes Type II is the most widespread (about 95% of the diabetic population) and it is usually related to lifestyle. Promotion of healthy habits could decrease the number of type II diabetic patients. It is expected that in the next decades the number of people affected by some type of diabetes will increase considerably.

The costs associated with treatment and hospitalization due to Diabetes and its health complications are around millions of euros. The quality of care, habits of the patient, treatment and education about Diabetes are considered the main domains of action for improvement patient life quality. Diabetes self-care consists of an appropriate monitoring and management of several parameters related to glucose levels, diet and physical activity, in order to avoid periods of hypoglycemia and hyperglycemia, ensuring that glucose levels are kept under control (within an optimal range).

In this work, we present a cloud-based platform consisting of an Android mobile application, a responsive web application and a RESTful API to interact with several cloud services. These software components were developed to support diabetic patients in monitoring and managing aspects related to glucose levels and insulin dose, nutritional intake, and physical activity. Then, we have carried out an evaluation of usability and user experience to determine how improvements in the developed applications (and generally in this type of systems) influence on patient's adherence to the treatment for copying with diabetes.

2   Related Work

Recently, the use of new technologies and devices for disease monitoring and management has increased exponentially. Smartphone is the most extended device able to provide mechanisms to address monitoring tasks on chronic diseases with little cost and accessible to everyone. There are many mobile applications and systems focused on self-caring of diabetic patients. Control of glucose levels is the most important feature of these applications, although a healthy lifestyle has also a positive impact on the disease. In this case, diet and physical exercise are domains to be considered. In the literature, there are many works focused on using cloud-based technologies and mobile applications in self-management of chronic diseases such as Diabetes. In these sense, Smartphones provide a powerful tool to deploy new solutions in self-control and management domain [1]. Lanzola [2] highlights the role of remote and continuous monitoring of chronic patients in mHealth environments. Adherence of patients to treatments and systems by means of self-management are key points for a successful solution [3]. Georgsson [4] presents the importance in the use and application of usability standards to ensure success of mHealth systems. Acceptance and mass use of these systems in our society can prevent new diseases, reduce hospitalizations, and costs derived from a poor disease control. Hartz [5] shows how the use of mobile technologies that help in Diabetes self-control has a positive impact on the prevention of other diseases (in this case cardiovascular). Also, Castelnuovo [6] studied the use of mHealth systems in the joint treatment of diseases such as Diabetes and Obesity.

In this work, we have carried out an usability assessment focused on context and interaction aspects from the developed system for diabetes self-control. Unfortunately, there are few studies focused on usability of mHealth applications, and many less focused on diabetes self-management [7]. Some related works employ a single mechanism to acquire data from user interactions [8] (usually through a questionnaire). While, other studies perform qualitative usability analysis but from unstructured points of view and with poor methodological rigor on collected data [9], making it impossible to reproduce in future studies. Due to these reasons, in this work we have used a hybrid usability study for usability data acquisition and evaluation from diabetic users. The analysis of these data is carried out by two different methods: "*Framework Analysis*" (FA) [10] and "Usability Problem Taxonomy" (UPT) of Keenan et al. [11].

FA method consists of a flexible framework to analyse qualitative data. Its main objective is to facilitate the study of descriptive data sources producing reliable qualitative results. This method has been used in sociology, however, in the last years, it is being applied in medical care studies with large qualitative datasets [12]. FA method is especially useful for organising, simplifying and interpreting qualitative data.

On the other hand, UPT provides a scheme to classify usability issues. These problems are analyzed from a "task-artifact" perspective, proposed by Carroll et al. [13].

3   Cloud-Based Platform

Improvement of life quality and autonomy of diabetic patients is possible by using current technologies and devices. In this sense, we have developed a system to monitor and manage the following factors in a centralised way:

- **Blood glucose level**, and also maximum and minimum reference values to determine a control range.
- **Physical activity**. It includes type of activity (walk, run), duration, calories burned and geolocation data.
- **Nutritional params**. From the consumed food, the system gathers information about type of food, amount and some values of nutritional composition (proteins, fats, carbohydrates and glycemic index).
- **Insuline administration**. It includes type and dose of insuline.
- **Patient data**. General information about the patient is stored by the system, including date of diabetic debut, height and weight.

We have called this system DiMo as an acronym of "Diabetes Monitoring". Figure 1 shows the general diagram of DiMo system. This system is divided into three main software components: (a) A library of web services based on REST protocol [14] which interacts with a cloud storage, (b) A mobile application

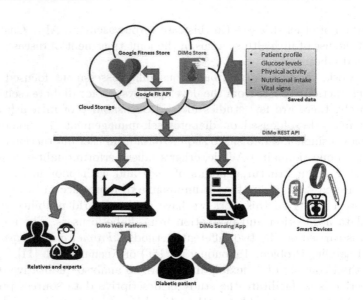

Fig. 1. Overview of DiMo system. Interactions between software components, devices, and users.

to gather and visualise params information from diabetic patients, and (c) a web platform to study in detail all considered params, both individually and correlated.

The system works with the information processed synchronously due to the cloud approach, maintaining interoperability between developed applications. In addition, OAuth[1] protocol has been implemented in all system applications to facilitate secure access to users' information, through their Google accounts.

3.1 DiMo Store and RESTful API

Information from diabetic users in DiMo system is saved into two different stores as follows:

– *Google Fitness Store.* We took advantage of the benefits provided by Google to save values from some parameters (physical and nutritional data). Temporal and evolutionary data are easily managed by means of Google Fit API[2].
– *DiMo Store.* The system has a complementary cloud storage based on MongoDB technology[3] to save data from glucose, personal profile, clinical reports and system settings.

DiMo applications communicate with the cloud storage through a library of web services called DiMo RESTful API. This software component acts as a bridge

---

[1] https://oauth.net
[2] https://developers.google.com/fit/.
[3] https://www.mongodb.com/.

between DiMo applications and the cloud storage options. DiMo RESTful API interacts with DiMo Store directly and with Google Fitness Store by means of Google Fit services, in a transparent way for developers. Storing and retrieving data, as well as running some algorithms are its outstanding features. Also, third-party applications could enrich DiMo system using DiMo RESTful API specification to save and retrieve data from the cloud storage, so that a DiMo ecosystem with more applications would be possible in a short term.

3.2   DiMo Sensing App

Self-management of diabetes is carried out by an Android application called DiMo Sensing App. This mobile application is responsible for gathering all data to be saved and processed by the system. In addition, DiMo Sensing App provides the user several simple mechanisms to visualise the information graphically showing single or correlated charts regarding values of params over time. Collected information from the application corresponds to blood glucose measurements, doses of insuline administered, physical activity performed, food intake and other information from user profile. Figure 2 shows three screenshots of DiMo Sensing App running on a mobile phone.

(a)   (b)   (c)

Fig. 2. Screenshots of DiMo sensing app. (a) Dashboard. It shows a summary of the last 72 h about the main monitored aspects: Physical activity, glucose levels and nutritional intake, (b) Adding measurements. Some parameter values can be taken by the user and manually added to the system, (c) Correlated charts. A set of correlated charts filtering by dates can be shown to the user such as glucose levels and calories consumed.

This mobile application has the ability of communicating with wireless smart devices like glucometers, scales or bracelets. Also, it can use the own Smartphone sensors to detect, for example, physical activity. Our first prototype gathers data from two physical activities, walk and run, automatically by using built-in accelerometer sensor of the Smartphone. While, data from glucose, food intake and insuline doses must be entered manually in the app.

Management of glucose ranges, setting patient profile and configuration of alerts and medical appointments are other actions also covered by DiMo Sensing app.

3.3   DiMo Web Platform

A responsive web application called DiMo Web Platform was also developed as another software component of DiMo system. With this application, built using Ember[4] framework, diabetic patients are knowing details about evolution of their disease, from all the information acquired by DiMo Sensing App and saved into the cloud storage. All the information is structured in blocks with a complete set of charts. Thus, user can view charts about blood glucose, physical activity performed, burned and consumed calories among others, as well as correlated charts to analyse the influence between groups of parameters. For example, diabetic users could know, at a glance, how certain types of food influence in their glucose levels, or what happens with this when they practise exercise. Figure 3 shows two screenshots from DiMo Web Platform.

Fig. 3. Screenshots of DiMo web Platform. (a) Dashboard. It shows a summary of the last 72 h about the main monitored aspects: Physical activity, glucose levels and nutritional intake. User can access to detailed views from each aspect, (b) Statistics & correlated charts. Detailed charts with modifiable date filters make it possible to analyse parameters in depth.

Both, DiMo Sensing App and DiMo Web Platform use RESTful API transparently, keeping data synchronisation with the cloud storage.

Furthermore, this web application provides a tool to generate user reports. This feature allows to save locally (not only in the cloud) information about evolution of parameters such as glucose, carbohydrates or physical activity among others, previously filtered by dates and selected by the user. Likewise, these reports can be exported to complement the traditional patient follow-up by clinicians and experts.

---

[4] https://emberjs.com/.

4 Usability Evaluation

DiMo System was assessed for a group of ten diabetic patients (five women and five men, aged between 17 and 59), with the following inclusion criteria: (1) they suffer from Diabetes Type I, (2) they have not any type of cognitive impairment, (3) they have basic knowledge of computers, internet and have used a Smartphone, (4) they have a minimum age of 12 years, and (5) they do not have prior knowledge of DiMo project. We have used a hybrid analysis to evaluate usability and user experience aspects from DiMo Sensing App and DiMo Web Platform.

4.1 Hybrid Approach for Data Acquisition and Evaluation

Usability data acquisition was carried out through two different methods as part of a hybrid proposal. This hybrid approach combines a post-questionnaire completed by patients after a whole week using DiMo applications, and a evaluation test based on *"Think Aloud"* technique [15]. This mechanism is originally applied in psychology, encouraging users to speak aloud during system interactions, expressing their reactions and thoughts while they complete a set of proposed tasks. Finally, these two data acquisition mechanisms, that have a user-centered approach, are complemented with a usability heuristic inspection methodology (based on the ten criteria of Nielsen Usability [16]). In our case, an expert panel has examined DiMo System in depth, identifying possible usability issues. All the information from these sources of data acquisition and evaluation is processed together in a structured manner by means of FA [10] and UPT [11] methods.

"Think Aloud" protocol. Four participants (two men and two women) used DiMo Sensing App and DiMo Web App in a laboratory environment. In this case, their system interactions on a set of representative tasks, were recorded through video capture software and voice recorder, as well as a set of additional notes collected by the expert. The application of *Think Aloud* technique ensures the minimal intervention of the expert and a wide knowledge about decisions taken by subjects from their interactions. The cognitive task of the subjects is not interrupted, only encouraging them to think aloud. This protocol is able to identify about 80–85% of usability problems [17].

Post-evaluation questionnaire. In this case, the whole group of subjects completed a questionnaire after a week using DiMo Sensing App and DiMo Web App in their daily lives. This questionnaire was created through Google Forms[5] services and it was sent to participants by email. It had 26 questions, 24 with multiple answer (but single choice by the user) and 2 open questions (for free text by the user). Likewise, the test was divided into three sections: (1) general information about diabetic patient, (2) questions about use of DiMo Sensing App and (3) DiMo Web App.

---

[5] https://docs.google.com/forms/.

Heuristic evaluation. An expert panel formed by two people with extensive knowledge in user interface design and a clinician have analysed all components and elements of DiMo Sensing App and DiMo Web App. During this evaluation process, the experts contrasted the properties of all dialog elements from DiMo applications with respect to the list of heuristics of usable interfaces proposed by Nielsen [18].

4.2 Application of Framework Analysis and Usability Problem Taxonomy

As mentioned in Sect. 2, UPT classification contains two component categories: (1) "artifact" to define usability issues regarding interaction with user interface, and (2) "task" focused on usability problems that appear during the completeness of a particular task.

UPT is integrated in FA framework, so that FA allows synthesize and structure usability issues previously detected in DiMo Sensing App and DiMo Web Platform, and UPT provides a classification according to their components. The final result, as output of a last stage, is a structured description of usability problems valuable for in-depth analysis. The whole process can be divided into the following five stages [10]:

1. *Familiarization with collected data.* Data from the storage sources were extensively studied by experts in charge of the evaluation.
2. *Identification of usability problems and analysis methods.* Using inductive method on previous data, all identified problems were grouped removing duplicities between them. This stage provided a list of consolidated problems which were classified using deductive reasoning as indicated in the UPT taxonomy.
3. *Classification of usability problems.* Identified problems were classify according to UTP [11]. Also, all issues were grouped according to their severity (from 1-not serious to 4-critical) by using the method created by Travis [19]. All repeated problems are removed and the rest of issues categorized.
4. *Data structuring and adding charts.* From classification of identified problems, information is structured in table format and several charts and statistics are created to facilitate usability problems analysis.
5. *Result interpretation.* A final list of usability problems is created taking into account most prevalent problems, nature of problems, and most critical problems to users.

4.3 Results

The group of diabetic patients who evaluated DiMo applications consisted of ten patients (five men and five women). Table 1 shows a summary about the main characteristics of these selected users. This first analysis provided general information of users and their relationship with mobile and web technologies.

Table 1. Characteristics from descriptive analysis of subjects

Characteristics	Values	%
Gender	M	50
	F	50
Age	17–39 years	70
	40–59 years	30
Education level	Secondary education	30
	Higher education	70
Occupation	Employee	60
	Student	40
Diabetic debut	From 0 to 12 years	40
	From 13 to 17	10
	>= 18 years	50
Computer and internet skills	High	70
	Medium	30
Smartphone skills	High	60
	Medium	40
Computer & Internet use	Everyday	90
	Several times a week	10
Smartphone use (not for calling)	Everyday	90
	Sometimes	10
Do you enjoy using your computer?	Totally agree	60
	Agree	30
	Disagree	10

Thus, 70% of diabetic participants were between 17 and 39 years of age, and 70% have higher education. The date of diabetic debut of participants exceeds 18 years in half of the cases. Besides, most of the subjects use technological devices usually. At least, 60% of them have an extensive knowledge of Smartphone and computers, and 90% use the internet everyday.

An action protocol was created to guide users in the use of DiMo applications. First, two experts explained, during twenty minutes, the project and all the features of DiMo Sensing App and DiMo Web Platform; this initial training is essential to avoid variability factor [20]. Secondly, four participants carried out an usability evaluation of DiMo applications individually; in this, "Think Aloud" method was used from a set of tasks proposed by experts in the lab environment. Third, all subjects used both DiMo applications for a week autonomously in their everyday life; after this, participants completed a post-evaluation questionnaire.

In this evaluation, 80% of subjects said they would use DiMo applications for diabetes self-management. 10% of participants introduced data in the system several times per day, 40% inserted data once a day, another 40% of users claimed not to perform daily data insertions, and finally, a 10% stopped using DiMo applications in the last days of the experiment. However, most of participants agreed on the benefits of such systems for Diabetes self-control.

These results show the importance of user-system acceptance. As part of our evaluation, 109 usability problems were identified by using the hybrid acquisition methods. 43 usability issues come from the heuristic evaluation performed by the experts (16 problems from DiMo Sensing App and 27 from DiMo Web Platform). The user-centered "Think Aloud" acquisition mechanism identified 40 problems (26 in DiMo Sensing App and 14 in DiMo Web Platform). And finally, post-questionnaire evaluation resulted in 26 usability problems (20 from DiMo Sensing App and 6 from DiMo Web Platform). These problems were analysed and classified by means of FA and UPT methods, obtaining a list of 28 consolidated problems for both DiMo applications.

Figure 4a shows a Venn diagram of consolidated problems from DiMo Sensing App. The number of problems identified from each acquisition method is very similar (15 with Think Aloud and questionnaire, and 13 with heuristic evaluation). As we can see, 5 problems are common and were identified using the three acquisition methods. Both, Think Aloud and post-questionnaire have in common 9 problems (32%), heuristic evaluation has in common 5 problems with Think Aloud (18%), and 6 problems with post-evaluation questionnaire (21%). Besides, the percentage of unique usability issues detected in each method are: 25% in heuristic evaluation (7 problems), 21% in Think Aloud (6), and 18% in post-evaluation questionnaire (5). Figure 4b shows Venn diagram of DiMo Web Platform consolidated problems. In this case, heuristic evaluation covered a wider spectrum of usability issues (71%), and Think Aloud identified 12 problems (43%). In contrast, post-evaluation questionnaire only identified 18% of usability problems. As unique issues, post-evaluation questionnaire identified only one problem, heuristic evaluation provides 13 unique problems (46%), and 7 the Think Aloud method (25%).

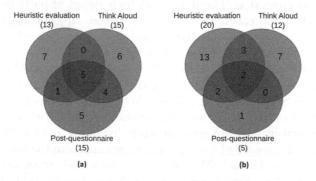

Fig. 4. Venn diagrams of DiMo consolidated usability problems. (a) DiMo Sensing App, (b) DiMo Web Platform.

Consolidated usability problems whose severity is in the range of moderate and critical levels, (>2) according to Travis [19], and/or with high recurrence rates are listed. In DiMo Sensing App, there are 5 serious issues (=3) related to *"Presentation and Design of Statistical Panels"*. *"Insertion Controls"* gather 7 problems with an average severity of 3.5. In addition, there are a number of isolated critical problems associated with the *"Lack of Feedback after Insertions"*, *"Lack of Freedom to edit or delete added data"*, *"Ambiguous titles in Panels and Sections"* and *"Issues recording Physical Activity"*. In DiMo Web Platform, there are 10 problems related to the *"Presentation and Design of Statistical and Correlation Panels"* dealing with severities slightly higher than 2 (moderate). Views related to *"Future Appointments"* have 4 usability problems with a severity level close to 3 (serious). Furthermore, as in DiMo Sensing App, isolated critical problems related to *"Sections and Panels titles"* and the *"Lack of Feedback in Statistical Panels"* must be highlighted in DiMo Web Platform.

These results are very valuable to address a refinement of DiMo applications with the aim of improving system acceptance an therefore treatment adherence, and also promoting the widespread use of this type of tools for continuous monitoring and management.

5   Conclusions

In this paper we have presented a system for Diabetes management which consists of three software components: (1) a RESTful services library (DiMo RESTful API), (2) a mobile app (DiMo Sensing App), and (3) a web platform (DiMo Web Platform). With DiMo Sensing App, diabetic patients can monitor and manage the most relevant aspects of Diabetes including: glucose levels, insuline doses, physical activity and nutritional intake, some of them in a natural and transparent way. While, patients use DiMo Web Platform to carry out an evolutionary analysis of all parameters handled and acquired by DiMo Sensing App, and thus contribute to proper self-management of the disease. DiMo RESTful API ensure the interoperability between apps.

Both applications, DiMo Sensing App and DiMo Web Platform were evaluated on a group of diabetic patients from usability and system acceptance viewpoint. Results of this evaluation highlighted the power of including this type of systems and technologies for chronic diseases monitoring and management; however, usability problems have a negative impact on system acceptance causing users to stop using the applications. We have addressed an evaluation process of DiMo applications based on a hybrid approach for data acquisition and evaluation, making use of a heuristic evaluation, "Think Aloud" mechanism, and a post-evaluation questionnaire. Then, data were analysed through FA and UPT methods to find out and classify usability problems. An in-depth analysis of these usability issues revealed several shortcomings and concluded that a refinement of the system would increase the degree of acceptance, favoring a widespread and continuous use, and consequently improving user treatment adherence.

Acknowledgments. This work has been funded by MAPFRE Foundation and supported by the Plan Propio de Investigación program of Castilla-La Mancha University. Authors gratefully acknowledge the participation and collaboration of the whole group of diabetic users in the evaluation process.

References

1. Shah, V., Garg, S.: Managing diabetes in the digital age. Clin. Diabetes Endocrinol. **1**, 16 (2015)
2. Lanzola, G., Losiouk, E., Favero, S.D., Facchinetti, A., Galderisi, A., Quaglini, S., Magni, L., Cobelli, C.: Remote blood glucose monitoring in mHealth scenarios: a review. Sensors **16**(12), 2–16 (2016)
3. Hood, M., Wilson, R., Corsica, J., Bradley, L., Chirinos, D., Vivo, A.: What do we know about mobile applications for diabetes management? a review of reviews. J. Behav. Med. **39**(6), 981–994 (2016)
4. Georgsson, M., Staggers, N.: Quantifying usability: an evaluation of a diabetes mhealth system on effectiveness, efficiency, and satisfaction metrics with associated user characteristics. J. Am. Med. Inf. Assoc. **23**(1), 5–11 (2016)
5. Hartz, J., Yingling, L., Powel-Wiley, T.: Use of mobile technology in the prevention and management of diabetes mellitus. Curr. Cardiol. Rep. **18**(12), 130 (2016)
6. Castelnuovo, G., Mauri, G., Waki, K.: mHeatlh and eHealth for obesity and types 2 and 1 diabetes. J. Diabetes Res. **2016**, 1 (2016)
7. El-Gayar, O., Timsina, P., Nawar, N., Eid, W.: Mobile applications for diabetes self-management: status and potential. J. Diabetes Sci. Technol. **7**(1), 247–262 (2013)
8. Zapata, B., Fernandez-Aleman, J., Idri, A., Toval, A.: Empirical studies on usability of mHealth apps: a systematic literature review. J. Med. Syst. **39**(2), 1 (2015)
9. Lyles, C., Sarkar, U., Osborn, C.: Getting a technology-based diabetes intervention ready for prime time: a review of usability testing studies. Curr. Diabetes Rep. **14**(10), 534 (2014)
10. Ritchie, J., Spencer, L.: Qualitative data analysis for applied policy research. In: Bryman, A., Burgess, R. (eds.) Analyzing Qualitative Data, pp. 173–194. Routledge, London (1994)
11. Keenan, S., Hartson, H., Kafura, D., Schulman, R.: The usability problem taxonomy: a framework for classification and analysis. Empir. Soft. Eng. **4**(1), 71–104 (1999)
12. Gale, N., Heath, G., Cameron, E., Rashid, S., Redwood, S.: Using the framework method for the analysis of qualitative data in multi-disciplinary health research. BMC Med. Res. Methodol. **13**, 117 (2013)
13. Carroll, J., Kellog, W., Rosson, M.: The task-artifact cycle. In: Carroll, J. (ed.) Designing Interaction, pp. 74–102. Cambridge University Press, New York (1991)
14. Richardson, L., Ruby, S.: RESTful Web Services. O'Reilly Media, Sebastopol (2008)
15. Ericsson, K., Simon, H.: Protocol Analysis: Verbal Reports as Data (Revised Edition). The MIT Press, Cambridge (1993)
16. Nielsen, J.: Usability inspection methods. In: CHI 1994 Conference Companion on Human Factors in Computing Systems, pp. 413–414 (1994)
17. Virzi, R.: Refining the test phase of usability evaluation: how many subjects is enough? Hum. Factors **34**(4), 457–468 (1992)

18. Nielsen, J., Molich, R.: Heuristic evaluation of user interfaces. In: Proceedings of the SIGCHI Conference on Human Factors in Computing Systems. ACM (1990)
19. Travis, D.: How to prioritise usability problems, October 2009
20. Karsh, B., Weinger, M., Abbott, P., Wears, R.: Health information technology: fallacies and sober realities. J. Am. Med. Inf. Assoc. **17**(6), 617–623 (2010)

A Web and Mobile Applications for Self-control of Patient Blood Pressure Through Mobiles and Biometrics Devices

Vladimir Villarreal^(✉), Mel Nielsen, and Manuel Samudio

GITCE Research Lab, Technological University of Panama, David, Chiriquí, Panama
{vladimir.villarreal,mel.nielsen,manuel.samudio}@utp.ac.pa

Abstract. In this article, we want to present a platform that allows the integration of different applications for the follow-up of patients with chronic diseases. We are developing two elements: the first one, is a mobile application that allows the capture and processing of vital sign for patient with high blood pressure (hypertension). This application allows to store the patient data obtained, the show historical and trends of the stored measures, a list of foods to consume, alerts and recommendations according to ranges of measures obtained. The second one, is a web application, this application allows the doctor and patients relatives to have updated information of the disease behavior through the measures obtained, food consumed, and others. Through this web application, we can also generate statistics about average measures in a given time, by age, by region, by specific date.

Keywords: Blood pressure · Mobile applications · Web applications · Mobile health

1 Introduction

Hypertension is a public health problem and affects millions of people worldwide, it is an asymptomatic disease and easy to detect, if not treated early can lead to serious or fatal complications. In 2010, a global disease burden study revealed that nine million people died because of hypertension, making this cardiovascular problem the world's leading health risk factor [1].

The President of the Panamanian Heart Foundation, Dr. Bey Mario Lombana, said that out of every three adults, one is hypertensive. "33% of the adult population suffers high blood pressure. Of these people, there is a third party who does not know that they are suffering, have not been detected, "he says and warns that is what the world statistics reflects. "Panama, has its 'numbers', which are not the best," said Lombana [2]. This proportion, according to information from the Ministry of Health contained in its official website, increases with age: one in ten people between 20 and 40 years old, and five in ten from 50 to 60 years.

These figures are similar to those of the PREFREC study conducted in 2010 by the Gorgas Memorial Institute for Health Studies and the Ministry of Health, which indicate that 28.4% of the study participants reported a history of hypertension due to diagnosis Physician and 24.1% had blood pressure values classified as hypertension [3].

© Springer International Publishing AG 2017
S.F. Ochoa et al. (Eds.): UCAmI 2017, LNCS 10586, pp. 240–249, 2017.
DOI: 10.1007/978-3-319-67585-5_25

As a consequence of this disease patients become dependent on medicines and medical care. The research and development of this project seeks to improve the quality of life of each patient with hypertension that depends on constant measurements and frequent check-ups; In addition to making use of mobile technologies to reach the largest population possible to help early detection of this disease. A web and mobile platform is being implemented to manage patient data in the country's health center.

2   Related Works

The care of the dependents today is in charge of their own relatives. However, according to the changes that have been presented by society, working hours, fewer days at home and lack of organization in families make this little formal model is unsustainable in the medium term. When patients are in a care setting, they are often isolated from their social environment; A situation that greatly complicates monitoring, or complicates the patient's privacy. The monitoring of people who are at risk, is done through equipment that is not mobile, or their transportation becomes complicated.

Another problem is the lack of staff in residential complexes to attend to all patients in an active way, since usually, in order to reduce costs, the ratio between the number of patients and medical staff is very high, and this penalizes attention to patients. The solutions of medical control through technologies, facilitates the remote and mobile monitoring of each of the patients, obtaining that the patient gains in quality of life [4].

Some solutions have tried to answer the problem of medical follow-up of patients, on the one hand [5] proposed a system that provides sanitary control of patients reducing the possibilities of hospitalization. The problem with this proposal was that the patient had to interact frequently with the mobile device. Our proposal seeks to minimize this interaction with technology, avoiding intrusion into the daily life of the patient.

In addition [6] presents an important tool to evaluate the health of patients suffering from chronic diseases and affecting their mobility such as multiple sclerosis (MS), Parkinson's disease and muscular dystrophy through evaluation when walking. Our proposal maintains the behavior in the background suggested by Ryder, that is to say that the application of patient monitoring is executed without interfering with the daily use that is given to the mobile device. This makes the functionality transparent to the user and minimizing the interaction.

Other proposals such as [7, 8].The integration of the Web in the process of patient follow-up, which limits the patient's free mobility.

3   Patient's Data Manager Platform

We are working on the development of a technological platform that allows the tracking of patients through mobile devices, web system and biometric devices. This platform allows to integrate diverse mobile applications for the self-control of diseases like blood pressure, nutrition, diabetes, among others.

In Fig. 1, the elements that integrate the platform are shown. The platform must allow the connection of biometric devices through Bluetooth technology, WiFi, among others.

These devices are responsible for capturing patient or user data. This information is stored on the mobile device (Smartphone, Tablet, Computer) through a remote database hosted on a central server.

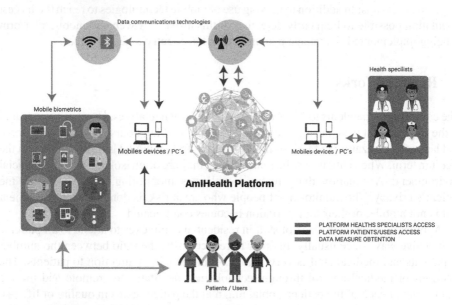

Fig. 1. Schema of proposal for Health Platform.

The information obtained from patients can be reviewed and consulted by medical specialists, through a web application, where you can observe the history of measurements, food consumed, recommendations generated.

Through the creation of this application will offer technological solutions that allow patients better and more timely monitoring and control of their disease, offering constant answers in the right time and facilitating doctor-patient communication.

In addition to facilitating patient self-monitoring, the platform allows the generation of average blood pressure statistics by day, month, year. It is also possible to obtain statistics of average tension by age range, geographical location, most consumed foods, among others.

The Fig. 2 shows the database schema of the health platform for a basic user registry for patients. The users table contains all the general data of a user who can be assigned the role of patient, doctor or administrator. When a patient registers in the platform, he must enter his general data in addition to his ethnicity, weight, height and waist.

Once the patient has activated his account can proceed to register his blood pressure measurements. The table of measures contains the patient's identification number, systolic pressure, diastolic pressure and pulse. The patient will be able to see his measurements over time. Also, the system classifies the patient's blood pressure using the 2013 guidelines on hypertension of the European Society of Hypertension (ESH) and the European Society of Cardiology (ESC).

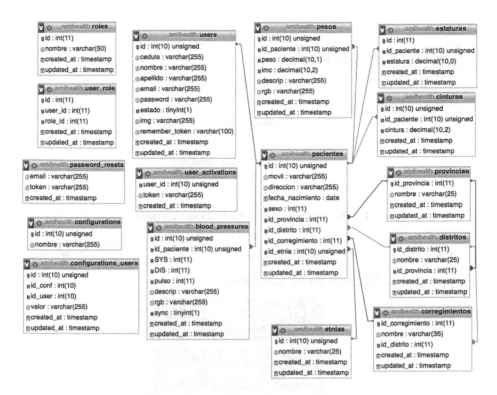

Fig. 2. Health platform Database Schema.

3.1 A Web Applications for Patient's Follow-Up

Doctors and relative patient can see the information related to the patient blood pressure. We are developing a web application for the control and historical information about patient or group of patients.

In Fig. 3 shows the view of a new blood pressure measurement. The patient should enter manually the values of the systolic and diastolic pressure, these values must be given in mmHg and the value of the pulse in Bpm.

As you can see in the Fig. 4, all patient measurements are shown in a list. This allows the patient to see how their measurements have been classified by the platform. In addition, it allows you to edit or delete measurements, if they have not been taken correctly (Fig. 5).

The same approach was used in the weights module, here the patient can add a new weight measure, list them all, and see the weight trends in a graph. When a new weight is added, the system calculates your Body Mass Index (BMI) using the World Health Organization (WHO) classification of nutritional status according to the BMI.

Figure 6 is the patient's dashboard which shows the most recent blood pressure and weight measurements per week, month, or year, and graphs them in a way that is simple and easy for the patient to understand. Also, it has a sidebar that shows the different

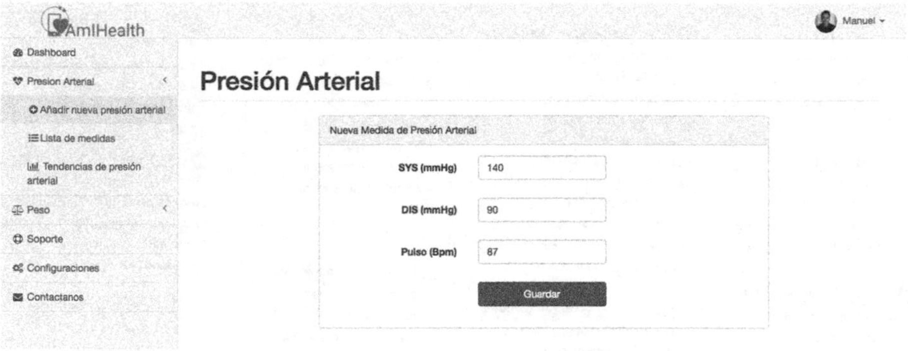

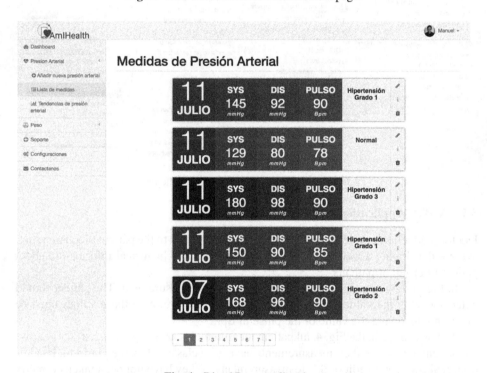

Fig. 3. New Blood Pressure Measurement page.

Fig. 4. Blood Pressure list view.

actions that the patient can do, such as adding a new blood pressure measurement, a new weight, see the blood pressure and weight trends, and a list of the last measurements.

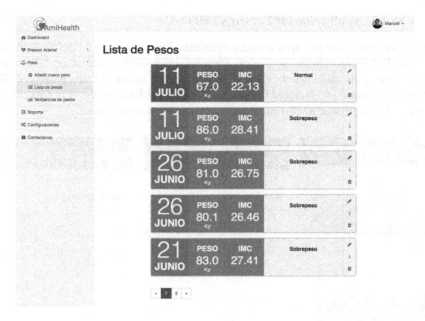

Fig. 5. Weights list view.

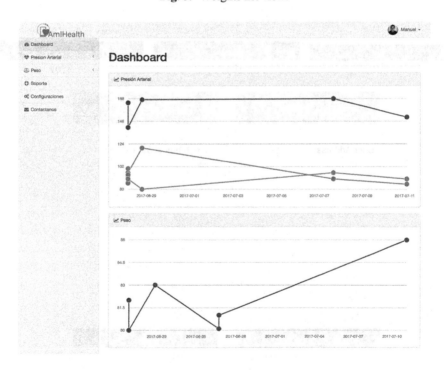

Fig. 6. Dashboard page.

3.2 A Mobile Application for Patient's Follow-Up

We are developing a mobile application for patients. The patient can be store information about the last measurement, activities, personal information, and other. The access session in the application is very easy. All patient needs an email and a password. This information is related with stored information for the platform access (Fig. 7a). Also, if you are a new user/patient, you can register the personal information.

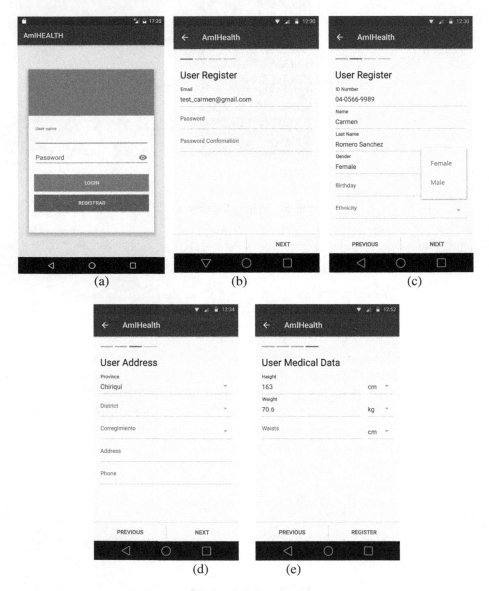

Fig. 7. (a) Access for users, (b) New user's registration, (c) General data for new users, (d) New users address registration, (e) Height and Weight registration.

3.3   User's Registration

The user's registration is compounded by four registration fragment. This registration fragment obtains information about basic patient data, password, address and others.

In Fig. 7b, we begin the new user's registration with a valid email. The email is a unique id for each patient. The password is compounded by minimum six characters, with a one lower case, one upper case, and one number. In Fig. 7c the application asks about the patient id, name, last name, gender, birthday (with this information the applications obtain the age) and the ethnic.

Next, in Fig. 7d, we add information about the patient address (province, district, corregimiento and specific address), this information is very important to generate future statistics for area. The Fig. 7e, we show a fragment for information about patient height, weight and waist measurement.

This information is necessary to calculate and store the user obesity level. For patient with high blood pressure is very important the information about obesity as a risk facts for the patient.

It is the last fragment in the new users/patient registration. When all data submitted is correct, the platform sends an email for the user verification.

When the patient is registered, it can access to the High Blood Pressure (HBP) measure module (Fig. 8a) This Android Activity is compounded for a tab bar through two fragments: the first one, shows graphic views for the blood pressure (weekly) last measure, the next blood pressure measurement and the next medication intake.

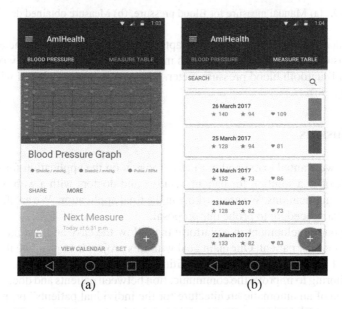

Fig. 8. HBP measure module (a). Graphic View, (b). Tab View.

The second one, shows (Fig. 8b) a tab view for all measurement in order (the last in, first out), also in the bottom of the screen we have a *datetimepicker* for searching information by date. This module has a bottom for new measure (Fig. 9a).

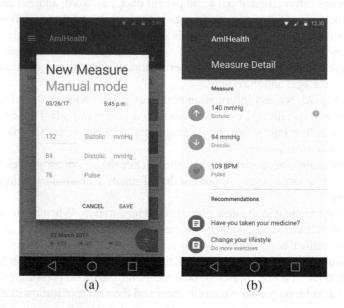

(a)   (b)

Fig. 9. (a) Manual measure for Blood pressure, (b) Measure obtained details.

The manual blood pressure measure capture interface has three elements: systolic pressure, diastolic pressure and pulse. This information is stored manually or automatically with a Bluetooth blood pressure meter. The new measure is stored with the date and time (Fig. 9b).

4   Conclusions

In this work, we wanted to expand our field of vision on the application for high blood pressure. We offer a solution for patient, relative and doctors with a web solution and mobile phone applications. We are working in the final application. We are development the assessment procedure to probe our proposal.

We base our development in a platform that allow the easy and fast integration for new applications for patient. Our main goal with this project is to promote the easy day-by-day life of people with a chronic condition. This architecture provides continuous patient monitoring to improve the communication between patients and doctors allowing the generation of an automatic architecture for the individual patients" profiles of each patient, self-control, and education modules for their chronic diseases. This has been developed for the mobile monitoring of patients via biometric devices and a mobile phone.

Acknowledgments. The first author is member of the National Research Investigator award (SNI) from the SENACYT as a National Research. This article is presented as part of a project ITE15-001 financed by SENACYT and development by Technological University of Panama, Columbus University and Universidad Cooperativa de Colombia.

References

1. Minsa.gob.pa: Día Mundial de la hipertensión arterial (HTA). http://www.minsa.gob.pa/noticia/dia-mundial-de-la-hipertension-arterial-hta (2016). Last access 18 Sept 2016
2. La Estrella de Panamá: Un 33% de población adulta en Panamá sufre de hipertensión arterial. http://laestrella.com.pa/vida-de-hoy/salud/94-millones-personas-mueren-cada-hipertension-arterial/23807287 (2014). Last access 18 Sept 2016
3. Saludpanama.com: Hipertensión arterial: el asesino silencioso. http://www.saludpanama.com/hipertension-arterial-el-asesino-silencioso (2016). Last access18 Sept 2016
4. González, V., Jose, A.: Aplicación para la monitorización remota de pacientes, p. 139. Universidad de Valladolid, Dep. de Ingeniería Técnica de Informática de Sistemas. PFC, Valladolid (2009)
5. BOSCH.: Health buddy system. http://www.bosch-telehealth.com (2011). Last access 2012
6. Ryder, J., Longstaff, B., et al.: Ambulation: a tool for monitoring mobility patterns over time using mobile phones. Computational Science and Engineering. CSE 2009 (2009)
7. Wan-Young, C., Seung-Chul, L., et al.: WSN based mobile u-healthcare system with ECG, blood pressure measurement function. In: 30th Annual International Conference of the IEEE on Engineering in Medicine and Biology Society. EMBS 2008 (2008)
8. Paradiso, R., Alonso, A., et al.: Remote health monitoring with wearable non-invasive mobile system: the Healthwear project. In: 30th Annual International Conference of the IEEE on Engineering in Medicine and Biology Society. EMBS 2008 (2008)

Proposal for Monitoring the Stress Through the Sensing of Environmental Variables in a Workplace

Alberto de Ramón-Fernández, Daniel Ruiz-Fernández[✉], Diego Marcos-Jorquera, Virgilio Gilart-Iglesias, and Antonio Soriano-Payá

Department of Computer Technology, University of Alicante, Alicante, Spain
{aderamon,druiz,dmarcos,vgilart,asoriano}@dtic.ua.es

Abstract. Occupational stress has become a problem that increasingly affects the health of workers. Suffering stress continuously can lead to more serious behavioural disorders such as anxiety or depression. Our work focuses in the proposal of a system which can monitor the stress thanks to subjective information from the workers and objective data from the environment. The information can be consulted by a specialist, and thus, assist the worker in a personalised way and help in the detection and prevention of acute stress cases.

Keywords: Occupational stress · Environmental factors · Monitoring system

1 Introduction

The growing popularity of the term of stress makes clear the concern that provoke in our society nowadays. It has also led to some confusion of the concept and mistaken beliefs. So, what is stress really? Since the first time in 1936, the researcher Hans Selye defined stress as "the non-specific response of the body to any demand for change" different definitions have emerged over time. Among the more recent ones we find that of Roger in 1998 who described stress as a "pre-occupation with the negative emotion following the event". The American Psychological Association (APA), classifies different types of stress according to their duration: acute stress, acute episodic stress and chronic stress [1], the latter being the most common form of stress.

Regarding the impact on the society, statistics show that stress levels have been increasing every year and are affecting more people over the years. According to an APA study, american adults continue to report high levels of stress and many reports that their stress has increased over the past years. Of all the causes, the occupational stress is the cause that affects a greater number of people. Occupational stress is the response people may have when presented with work demands and pressures that are not matched to their knowledge and abilities and which challenge their ability to cope [2]. According to the American Institute of Stress, 80% of american workers feel stress on the job and nearly half say they need help in learning how to manage stress. At this point, it seemed logical wonder if there is any objective way of measuring the level of stress. Thomas Holmes and Richard Hae, in 1973, were the first to establish a scale of stress after evaluating thousands of people who asked about their life experiences [3].

© Springer International Publishing AG 2017
S.F. Ochoa et al. (Eds.): UCAmI 2017, LNCS 10586, pp. 250–255, 2017.
DOI: 10.1007/978-3-319-67585-5_26

Each of these lived experiences corresponded to a number called "unit of vital change" (UCV). The higher the score, the more likely was the probability of becoming ill of stress. Since then, numerous evaluation and scoring systems have been appearing over time [4].

This study describes a proposal of a monitoring system for the people who suffers stress during their workday. Through Web Service or mobile application, a person can report his mood and evaluate his level of stress daily. Moreover, through the work environmental sensing, we can analyse how other factors such as noise or excessive flow of people in an office during a working day can affect the worker's behaviour.

2 Related Work

Stress implies a physical and mental deterioration for those who suffer it. There is, therefore, the need to be able to control stress in real time over extended periods. With this purpose, researchers have been contributing different systems of evaluation and monitoring of the level of stress. The easiest and most practical is through questionnaires related to feelings, stressful situations lived previously or future events. Each answer is associated with a score. The final score along with other indicators such as age, gender, etc. serve the specialist to classifier the level of stress according to a scale. The main drawback of this method is the subjective way to estimate the perceived stress scale.

Other way to assess stress is based on the study of voice. Voice pitch (represented by the fundamental frequency) is a subjective feature that correlates with the way the voice is perceived as higher or lower. Different studies have shown that the changes experienced by the fundamental frequency are strongly related to the emotional load [5].

The newest form of stress monitoring is based on the development of wearable systems using multiple sensors. This method involves the ambient sensing of the worker to capture the greatest number of variables related to suffer stress. The information recorded by the different sensors is received by a microcontroller coupled to the body and sent via Bluetooth to a mobile device that will act as gateway to a data centre where the information is processed. There are numerous sensors used to detect stress signals or indicators. One of them is heart rate variability (HRV) that is the physiological phenomenon of variation in the time interval between heart-beats. It is measured by a chest strap and this measure has been shown to have a very good correlation with stress level [6]. Moreover, other studies have introduced a respiration sensor and an accelerometer in the chest strap to consider the respiration [7] and the acceleration of the body in every moment [6]. Other commonly used indicator is EDA (electrodermal activity) also known as GSR (galvanic skin response) [8]. Muscle tension measured through the electromyographical (EMG) activity of the trapezius muscle is another parameter that has recently been taken into account by researchers for assessing stress [7]. It is estimated that the tension in this muscle increases in stressful situations. There are other physiological markers as blood volume pressure [9], skin temperature [8, 9], or pupil diameter [9] that experience significant changes in situations of tension. However, the main drawback of all the described sensors is that the person must wear them permanently coupled to their body, becoming something annoying and creating the sensation of being permanently subject to study.

So far, none of the studies mentioned are focused on the measurement of two of the main sources of stress mentioned above: environmental stress and occupational stress or work stress. To this end, and avoiding the uncomfortable and excessive monitoring of the worker, this study **proposes a** system of occupational stress monitoring through environmental sensing of the workplace. Moreover, the system allows communication between specialist and worker, improving the attention received and performing a continuous evaluation, overcoming an important limitation that exists in current systems.

3   System Developed

Our study presents a proposal to evaluate environmental factors that affect the level of stress of a worker in his job. To do this, it has been proposed to collect in a work centre the noise level, the flow of people existing throughout the working day, the number of times the user/worker leaves his workplace and the assessment of his level of stress. Regarding with the noise level, the World Health Organization (WHO), considers 65 db as the desirable upper limit. According to studies of environmental noise in Europe, 80 million people are exposed daily to noise levels above 65 db and 170 million are at levels between 55–65 db [10]. Among the consequences derived from workplace noise are annoyance, hypertension, disturbance of psychosocial well-being, and psychiatric disorders [11].

The working architecture of our proposed system is made up of 3 areas: workplace/ office, data centre and specialist/psychologist area as shown in Fig. 1.

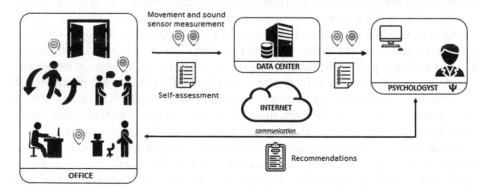

Fig. 1. Proposed system for stress monitoring

The information provided to the system from the workplace will be sending from two main sources: an automatic data sending through the environment sensors and a manual data input by the users referred to their level of stress (auto-assessment test) and mental state. The hardware architecture of our proposed system is composed of five elements: two motion sensors, a noise pollution sensor, a computational platform and an add-on board. The *Grove Loudness Sensor* will be responsible for measuring the noise pollution of the place. On the other hand, the *Grove PIR Motion Sensor* will be placed on the workplace entrance door serves to measure the number of people accessing or leaving it during the working day. A second motion sensor placed on the user's workspace will measure the number of times the workers momentarily leaves their workstation. To get information, each sensor will be individually connected to a single-board computer (SBC) called *Raspberry Pi 3*, which will be used as computational platform. *Raspberry Pi 3* includes integrated wireless LAN and Bluetooth, and allows the collecting and sending of data via wireless connection to the data centre for its treatment and management without the need to connect any other peripherals. The *GrovePi board* is an add-on board that is coupled to the *Raspberry Pi 3* and enables it to interface with *Grove* sensors avoiding soldering the sensor directly to the *Raspberry Pi 3*. All the information will be collected and stored in the Data Centre, where will be processed properly to provide useful information to both worker and specialist. Thus, the system could send alerts to warn the workers of excessive noise, not having performed the stress test or not having reported their mood. It also will generate a historical profile of the worker, where all the study variables are related to the level of stress generated, and can establish trends, behaviour patterns, etc. All this information will be available via the web for the psychologist/specialist being able to propose recommendations, personalize a treatment or make an appointment with the worker. Moreover, the system will allow real time user-specialist communication through messages to improve the psychological support received by the worker during episodes of work stress. In addition, the specialist can help to prevent the worker when the first signs of suffer stress are detected, preventing it from becoming a more acute case and reducing the high cost that involves the long-term sick leave caused by stress.

Our system aims at evaluating the occupational stress of the worker in a non-invasive way, without having to carry permanently coupled sensors. Thus, the workers do not feel subject of study at any time and can evaluate their level of stress quickly and easily.

4   User Interface

In addition to the automatic data sending through the environment sensors, the monitoring system designed has simple user interfaces that will allow the introduction and consultation of data in an easy and intuitive way through the web or the mobile application. The users could perform an auto-assessment of the level of stress perceived by performing a simple test of 20 questions and provide information related to his mood to the system. These questions are oriented to indicate how the workers feels (calm, upset, worried...) and to what degree (not at all, somewhat, moderately or very much). Each response is associated with a score and the stress level is calculated according to a scale with the total score of the test. They can also record their daily mood through an emoticon interface (see Fig. 2). Each emoticon represents a mood (very lively, normal mood, discouraged, very discouraged) and clicking on any of them the information will be collected in the system. All this information could be consulted via web at any time by the psychologists/specialists who is overseeing the worker. They could evaluate the worker's tests, analyse graphs that relate the environmental factors to the mood and consult historical data (Fig. 2). This information will be helpful for an ongoing worker evaluation. Through messages via web, the specialist could be in touch with the user, with the purpose of suggesting recommendations, possible anti-stress treatments or proposing an appointment for clinical consultation.

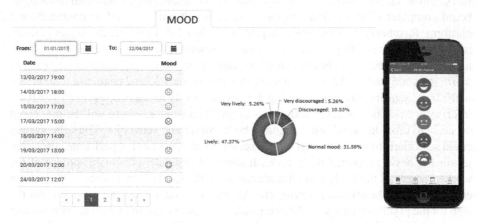

Fig. 2.   Web interface for mood monitoring and mobile interface for mood input

5   Conclusions

At present, it is well known that occupational stress is one of the main problems for the health of workers and the accurate operation of the entities for which they work. Research results show that the type of work that produces the most stress is one in which demands and pressures exceed the worker's knowledge and skills. In addition, we must add aspects related to the environment that surrounds us and that in many cases sharpens this feeling of stress in the worker. The purpose of this study is analysing how work environment can affect the worker negatively by increasing his level of stress. Thus, the system, through the ambient sensing of the workspace, could measure variables such as noise, flow of people, or times that a worker leaves his workplace during a working day. This, combined with the worker's self-assessment, will allow a direct relationship between the variables monitored and the level of perceived stress. By this method, we avoid that the person must be permanently connected with sensors for the measurement of physiological variables as it happens in most of the studies evaluated.

On the other hand, as a novel approach, the designed system will store and provide the data for the specialist in charge of the worker. Based on the information provided by the system, it could be possible evaluate the worker on a continuous basis and suggest recommendations that fit better for each person. In this way, we improve the care received by the workers, and can be used to predict or warn about recurrent episodes of stress that can lead to more serious behavioural disorders such as anxiety or depression.

Conflict of Interest   The authors declare no conflict of interest in this article.

Acknowledgements. This work has been granted by the Ministerio de Economía y Competitividad of the Spanish Government (ref. TIN2014-53067-C3-1-R) and cofinanced by FEDER.

References

1. American psychological association. stress: the different kinds of stress. http://www.apa.org/helpcenter/stress-kinds.aspx
2. Workers, P.: Protecting Workers' Work World Health
3. Holmes, T.H., Rahe, R.H.: The social readjustment rating scale. J. Psychosom. Res. **11**, 213–218 (1967)
4. Cohen, S., Kamarck, T., Mermelstein, R., Health, J., Behavior, S., Dec, N.: A global measure of perceived stress. J. Health Soc. Behav. **24**, 385–396 (2008)
5. Sandulescu, V., Andrews, S., Ellis, D., Dobrescu, R., Martinez-Mozos, O.: Mobile app for stress monitoring using voice features. In: 2015 E-Health Bioengineering Conference EHB 2015, pp. 2–5 (2016)
6. Tartarisco, G., Baldus, G., Corda, D., Raso, R., Arnao, A., Ferro, M., Gaggioli, A., Pioggia, G.: Personal Health System architecture for stress monitoring and support to clinical decisions. Comput. Commun. **35**, 1296–1305 (2012)
7. Choi, J., Ahmed, B., Gutierrez-Osuna, R.: Development and evaluation of an ambulatory stress monitor based on wearable sensors. IEEE Trans. Inf. Technol. Biomed. **16**, 279–286 (2012)
8. Lebepe, F., Niezen, G., Hancke, G.P., Ramotsoela, T.D.: Wearable stress monitoring system using multiple sensors. In: 2016 IEEE 14th International Conference on (Industrial Informatics INDIN), pp. 895–898 (2016)
9. Zhai, A.B.: Stress detection in computer users through non-invasive monitoring of physiological signals. Biomed. Sci. Instrum. **42**, 495–500 (2006)
10. Pillar, E., Ireland, S.P.: European Commission-Green Paper of the European Communities, pp. 1–23 (2009)
11. Kirchner, D.B., Evenson, E., Dobie, R.A., Rabinowitz, P., Crawford, J., Kopke, R., Hudson, T.W.: Occupational noise-induced hearing loss: ACOEM task force on occupational hearing loss. J. Occup. Environ. Med. **54**, 106–108 (2012)

The Differences Between Children with Autism and Typically Developed Children in Using a Hand-Eye-Coordination Video Game

Athar Mahmoudi-Nejad[1], Hadi Moradi[1,2(✉)], and Hamid-Reza Pouretemad[3]

[1] School of ECE, University of Tehran, North Karegar Street, Tehran, Iran
{athar.mahmudi,moradih}@ut.ac.ir
[2] Intelligent Systems Research Institute, SKKU, Suwon, South Korea
[3] Shahid Beheshti University, Tehran, Iran
pouretemad.h@gmail.com

Abstract. Several evidences showed poor motor coordination in individuals with autism. Thus, in this paper, we present a touch-based hand-eye coordination video game which shows clear difference between children with autism and typically developed children. The game is tested on five children with autism and seven typically developed children. These groups presented totally different patterns from each other; hence they can be distinguished with only two features in the game environment. This promising result encourages us to use this video game for initial screening of hand-eye coordination problem, especially in children with autism, which can be used everywhere without any costs.

Keywords: Autism spectrum disorders · Autism screening · Touch-based game · Hand-eye-coordination

1 Introduction

Autism spectrum disorder (ASD) is a lifelong mental disability that affects the development process of early-aged children. ASD is defined by diagnostic criteria of DSM-V [1] as a disorder that includes difficulties in social communication, social interaction, and restricted, repetitive patterns of behavior. These deficits can be used by experts to screen these children. For instance, social deficits and behavioral patterns may be used to recognize children with autism [2]. However, it becomes difficult in areas with no access to an expert. Furthermore, the signs of deficits may not clearly show themselves at a level to be observed by parents and caregivers. On the other hand, the early detection and identification of this disorder is essential, since it is usually followed by early interventions that may cause improvement and decrease out-of-control behaviors [3]. Consequently, it is important to develop intelligent and automatic methods to detect possible deficits at early stages of children's developmental process to consult experts and start intervention, if needed.

That is why we have started developing several different systems for automatic screening of children with autism. One of these systems is based on a hand-eye

© Springer International Publishing AG 2017
S.F. Ochoa et al. (Eds.): UCAmI 2017, LNCS 10586, pp. 256–264, 2017.
DOI: 10.1007/978-3-319-67585-5_27

coordination game since research on children with ASD suggests that their motor skills deficits exceed their other ability deficits [4] and across a varied range of behaviors [5]. The game has been tested on several Typically Developed (TD) and autistic children showing clear difference between these two groups.

2 Related Work

There are several clinical and manual methods for screening autism. Some of them are questionnaire-based, such as Checklist for Autism in Toddlers (CHAT) [6], Social communication Questionnaire (SCQ) [7], Autism Spectrum Screening Questionnaire (ASSQ) [8], and Social Responsiveness Scale [9].

There have been many attempts to develop systems and methods to automatically perform initial screening as early as possible. For instance, Scassellati [10] investigated the detection of gaze direction and realized autistic adolescents, in comparison to TD children, focus more on mouth rather than eyes when they see a face image.

Ebrahimi et al. [11] accoumplished distinguishing the different walking pattern, i.e. tiptoe walking, of children with autism from normal waking pattern of TD children. They collected body skeleton data using Microsoft Kinect^{TM} and achieved the accuracy of 86%.

Scassellati [10] tracked the position of children in a room by a stereo camera and observed different amount of time that children with autism spent near adults in comparison to TD children. In addition, they figured out that children with autism kept different distance to others, compared to TD children, while interacting with them.

Ekhtiari et al. [12] developed an intelligent toy car and observed different playing pattern of 25 children with autism in compare to 25 TD peers with 87% accuracy. It is equiped with a 3-axis accelerometer to collect data while it is used by a child. Five features, extracted from data, are used for classification.

Motlagh et al. [13] investigated the differences in the voice of children with autism from TD children. They showed that there are features, such as temporal, harmonic, perceptual and spectral voice features, that can be used to distinguish children with autism from TD children.

To the best of our knowledge, there are only two studies that used machine learning to find motor patterns in order to distinguish between children with autism and their TD peers. Crippa et al. [14] developed a scenario in which children had to reach and grab a ball and put it into the hole of the square box. They used markers and infrared camera to record data. They have reached the maximum accuracy of 96.7% using linear SVM method. The main difficulty of this approach is in using markers on the body of subjects. Furthermore, it needs complex vision processing to analyze the motion of subject. The other work is by Ebrahimi et al. [11] which was discussed earlier.

Anzulewicz et al. [15] employed two serious games on a tablet to collect interaction data with these games. In the first game, a player should divide fruit among 4 characters. In the second one, a player should choose an object or animal, trace the shape and then color it. Features were derived from touch screen and inertial sensors of the tablet. They tested 37 autistic and 45 TD children aged 3–6 years. They could screen with 93% of accuracy using Regularized Greedy Forest on 262 features. They considered the pressure on the tablet's screen and the tilt of the tablet. They did not consider the movement of the hand/figure on the screen which is very rich in fine movement information.

Our approach is similar to Anzulewicz approach. However, our approach does not require inertial sensors which makes the approach applicable on typical smartphones or tablets.

There are several manual tests to assess fine movement using paper and pencil such as Movement Assessment Battery for Children-2 Checklist (MABC-2) [17], Peabody Developmental Motor Scales [18], Beery-Buktenica [19], and Developmental Test of Visual Perception (DTVP2) [20]. The advantage of the proposed video game-based method, in comparison to the paper and pencil methods, is that we can measure time. Thus, the speed and acceleration of motion can be calculated which are very important in hand-eye coordination.

3   Method

3.1   Development and Design

The game is developed with Game Maker[1] which is a rapid application development tool currently used worldwide. It uses an object-oriented, event-driven approach. The program produces cross-platform and stand-alone games that can be distributed freely [16].

In our game environment, a player should control a bee character to its hive based on a given trajectory of flowers using his/her index finger (Fig. 1). The score of a player represents as a honey jar which is actually shows the accuracy of following the trajectory. At the end of each level, the player's overall performance is shown with three stars in four levels, i.e. poor performance with no stars, low performance with one star, mid performance with two stars, and good performance with three stars. When a child cannot follow a defined trajectory, auditory, visual, and haptic feedbacks will be given.

The game trajectories have four difficulty levels: easy, medium, hard and very hard, which are shown in Fig. 1. Easy levels are straight lines in different orientation and direction, medium levels are simple curved and broken lines, hard levels have multiple curved and broken lines, and very hard levels are complicated lines such as spiral. Each level has eight sub-levels and users should pass them twice, so 16 sub-levels exist in each level. These trajectories appear sequentially based on their difficulty and the player should follow them using his/her index finger on the touch screen platform, e.g. tablet or smartphone. In should be noted that these trajectories are designed based on available hand-eye coordination assessments or therapy.

---

[1]   http://www.gamemaker.nl/.

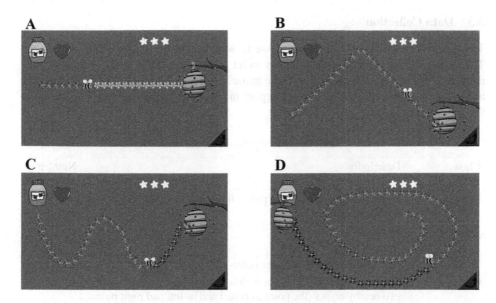

Fig. 1. A, B, C and D show examples of level easy (straight line), medium (broken and curve line), hard (mix line) and very hard (complicated line) which are the sections of our game respectively.

3.2 Participants

Five children aged 4–7 years old clinically diagnosed with Autism, all male were considered as the "Autism" group. Seven TD children age-matched, 3 female and 4 male, were included in the "control" group. The privacy considerations and ethical issues were enforced in our experiment design and process (Table 1).

Table 1. The participants and their statistics.

		Age	Gender	Number of attempts	Number of attempts for easy level
TD	N1	4	F	77	17
	N2	6	F	184	117
	N3	5	M	55	19
	N4	8	F	192	182
	N5	6	M	127	32
	N6	5	M	94	38
	N7	7	M	169	48
Autistic	A1	4	M	389	293
	A2	5	M	172	172
	A3	7	M	218	158
	A4	6	M	717	597
	A5	5	M	188	146

3.3   Data Collection

The parents/therapists can allow the game to send the game statistics into our server. This is one of our ethical design factors to let parents leave the study whenever they decide. The collected information are: the game score, time of play, the position of touch as points, and time. A brief statistical report in the game environment is available for the parents/therapists.

Table 2. List of point-based features

Class	Description	Number of feature(s)
Distance	Distance between two near points in x and y direction and Euclidean distance	3
Velocity	Distance/Time	3
Acceleration	Velocity/Time	3
Time	Delta time between two near points	1
Curvature	The angle between two lines which pass through one point and its two nearby points (the point as center and its left and right points, hence it calculated based on three near points)	1
Error	The distance of each point from the nearest flower	1

3.4   Data Analysis

Since most of the children with autism cannot pass easy level, the data of easy level are considered and other data are ignored in both ASD and TD children in order to have similar data in both groups. Different features such as score, errors, hand speed, acceleration, and motion curvature are extracted from data. Table 3 shows the complete list of extracted features from data.

Table 3. List of general features

Feature name	Description	Number of feature(s)
Room name	Name of sub-level which is 1 to 32 (4 levels with 8 sub-levels)	1
Duration	Amount of time that spent in a sub-level	1
Grabbed bee	Ratio of the points that player touched the bee to all touched points on the screen	1
Score	Score in the game	1
Score ratio	Ratio of score to the amount of flower in the sub-level	1
Flower state ratio	Ratio of win(green)/neutral/fail(red) flower in the attempt to all flowers	3
Up the path ratio	Ratio of the points which are at one side of the path to all the points	1

3.5 Feature Selection

Forty five features have been extracted from data which are listed in Tables 2 and 3. There are two categories of features: point-based and progress-based. There are 12 classes of point-based features that are driven from the touched points of a player. They are mostly calculated using two adjacent points. Calculating "curvature", however, needs two adjacent lines, hence three tandem points are considered. The "error" is obtained by calculating the distance of each point from the specified path of flowers. The minimum, maximum, and average of each point-based feature are also considered among the features. Progress-based features are the specifications of each attempt such as score.

Forward feature selection is used to choose the best set of features. One layer neural network with 20 neurons and linear Support Vector Machine (SVM) are used with 10-fold-cross-validation. Selected features by neural network were: Avg_distance_X, Avg_Velocity, Avg_Curvature, and Score. And features selected by SVM were: Min_Distance_X, Avg_Distance_Y, Min_time, Min_Velocity_Y, Avg_Velocity, Max_Velocity, Max_Accelaration_Y, Avg_Curvature, and Score. As it can be seen they have three features in common: Avg_Velocity, Avg_Curvature, and Score.

4   Result and Discussion

Each child played easy level many times and the mean of each feature for all attempts have been calculated as a feature for each person. Therefore, there are 45 values for each child. As it can be seen in Fig. 2, the velocity-score and curvature-score features can distinguish children with autism from typically developed ones clearly. The blue and red marks in Fig. 2 represent TD and ASD children respectively. As it can be seen, although different algorithms like simple neural network or logistic regression can be

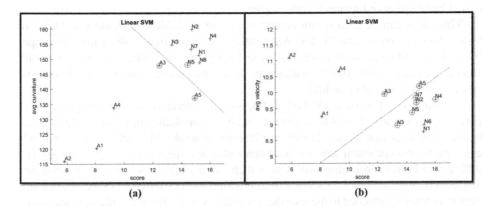

Fig. 2. Support vector machine result on (a) score and average curvature (b) score and average velocity – blue points are typically developed children and red ones are children with autism (Color figure online)

used, in this paper we used Support Vector Machine (SVM) in order to separate data of these two classes.

This game has four level of difficulty, but children with autism rarely reached the level 3 and 4. This shows the lower performance of these children compared to TD children. This result is consistent with previously reported findings, i.e. the children with autism have substantial motor coordination deficits [5]. We also observed that these children have low accuracy in following a given trajectory, which is also shown in their lower score (Fig. 2(a)).

This study indicated a significant difference in the fine movement of children with autism and TD peers. These motor patterns were derived from tablet and smartphones, which are available everywhere and at any time. This method of screening does not need experts or clinical environment, and it is easy to use and cost effective. In addition, it can be easily used by children because they are usually very interested in video games.

5   Conclusion

In this study, we designed and developed a touchscreen-based video game which heavily relies on hand-eye-coordination. The results of using the game by ASD and TD children were investigated. The data of the game is sent to a server and is processed in order to extract several features. After extracting 45 features and examining them, we concluded that by using only two features, we can clearly distinguish between ASD and TD children. Or it is better to say that we distinguish between TD children and non-TD children. This result is consistent with other researches that showed poor hand-eye-coordination in ASD children.

The benefit of this study, compared to recent studies, is that it is low cost and does not need any special tool or device, so it can be used anytime and everywhere. In addition, it does not need any marker to be worn by subject which may annoy them. There also exist several features, such as velocity and acceleration, that can be collected and used for further analysis and investigations, while these are not available in the pen and pencil hand eye coordination tests/therapies.

This game can be used for automatic screening of children with autism. Thus, we tested the game on several TD and ASD children to determine its discrimination capability. It should be noted that we did not test the game on children under 4 years old. Hence, we cannot claim that it could screen before parents or experts. In the future, the game should be tested on toddlers.

Although our proposed method distinguished several ASD and TD participants perfectly, this study should be applied to a larger population in order to validate the results with more confidence. However, obtaining several ASD participants with hand-eye coordination problem who has not been forbidden interacting with technology is a difficult and time-consuming task. Using technological devices, such as smartphones and tablets, are prohibited for some children with autism by therapist or expert, because they may become attached to these devices which lowers their communication and social interaction. In addition, as a study shows, male autistic children are more than female (about 4 out of 5 are male) [2], so unfortunately all of our autistic participants are male.

As mentioned before, we have tested the game just on typically developed and children with autism. Thus, we cannot claim to use it for screening children with autism and typically developed one. But, we can claim that it can distinguish between typically developed and abnormal children. Therefore, one of our future tasks is to test the game on other abnormalities such as Down syndrome, Parkinson's disease, and developmental coordination disorders.

This game can also be used for other hand-eye-coordination researches and tasks. The game is developed such that it can be played by two players on a local wireless network so parents and therapists can adjust the level of the difficulty of the game as they needed. Furthermore, it worth studying this two-player mode and determine its effect in creating more social interaction between parents and children with autism.

Acknowledgement. This research is supported by the Cognitive Sciences and Technologies Council (COGC). We would like to thank the Center for Treatment of Autism Disorder (CTAD) for supporting this study.

References

1. Bell, C.C.: DSM-IV: diagnostic and statistical manual of mental disorders (1994)
2. Report, M.W.: Prevalence of autism spectrum disorder among children aged 8 years—autism and developmental disabilities monitoring network, 11 sites, United States, 2010. MMWR. Surveill. Summ. **63**, 1–21 (2014)
3. Robins, D.L., Fein, D., Barton, M.L., Green, J.A.: The modified checklist for autism in toddlers: an initial study investigating the early detection of autism and pervasive developmental disorders. J. Autism Dev. Disord. **31**, 131–144 (2001)
4. Piek, J.P., Dick, M.J.: Sensory-motor deficits in children with developmental coordination disorder, attention deficit hyperactivity disorder and autistic disorder. Hum. Mov. Sci. **23**, 475–488 (2004)
5. Fournier, K.A., Hass, C.J., Naik, S.K., Lodha, N., Cauraugh, J.H.: Motor coordination in autism spectrum disorders: a synthesis and meta-analysis. J. Autism Dev. Disord. **40**, 1227–1240 (2010)
6. A screening instrument for autism at 18 months of age: A 6-year follow-up study
7. Pickles, A.: Autism screening questionnaire: diagnostic validity (1999)
8. Ehlers, S., Gillberg, C., Wing, L.: A screening questionnaire for asperger syndrome and other high-functioning autism spectrum disorders in school age children (2015)
9. Constantino, J.N., Davis, S.A., Todd, R.D., Schindler, M.K., Gross, M.M., Brophy, S.L., Metzger, L.M., Shoushtari, C.S., Splinter, R., Reich, W.: Validation of a brief quantitative measure of autistic traits: comparison of the social responsiveness scale with the autism diagnostic interview-revised. J. Autism Dev. Disord. **33**, 427–433 (2003)
10. Scassellati, B.: Quantitative metrics of social response for autism diagnosis. Proc. - IEEE Int. Work. Robot Hum. Interact. Commun. 2005, 585–590 (2005)
11. Ebrahimi, M., Feghi, M., Moradi, H., Mirian, M., Pouretemad, H.: Distinguishing tip-toe walking from normal walking using skeleton data gathered by 3D sensors. In: 2015 3rd RSI International Conference on Robot. Mechatronics (ICROM), pp. 450–455 (2015)
12. Ekhtiari, S., Moradi, H., Pouretemad, H., Araabi, B.: Early autism screening using an intelligent toy. In: The 5th International Congress of Child and Adolescent Psychiatry (2012)

13. Motlagh, S.H.R.E., Moradi, H., Pouretemad, H.: Using general sound descriptors for early autism detection. In: 2013 9th Asian Control Conference on ASCC 2013 (2013)
14. Crippa, A., Salvatore, C., Perego, P., Forti, S., Nobile, M., Molteni, M., Castiglioni, I.: Use of machine learning to identify children with autism and their motor abnormalities. J. Autism Dev. Disord. **45**, 2146–2156 (2015)
15. Anzulewicz, A., Sobota, K., Delafield-Butt, J.T.: Toward the Autism Motor Signature: Gesture patterns during smart tablet gameplay identify children with autism. Nat. Publ. Gr. 1–13 (2016)
16. Overmars, M.: Teaching computer science through game design. Computer **37**, 81–83 (2004)
17. Schoemaker, M.M., Niemeijer, A.S., Flapper, B.C.T., Smits-Engelsman, B.C.M.: Validity and reliability of the movement assessment battery for children-2 checklist for children with and without motor impairments. Dev. Med. Child Neurol. **54**, 368–375 (2012)
18. Wang, H.-H., Liao, H.-F., Hsieh, C.-L.: Reliability, sensitivity to change, and responsiveness of the peabody developmental motor scales-for children with cerebral palsy. Phys. Ther. **86**, 1351–1359 (2006)
19. Preda, C.: Test of visual-motor integration: construct validity in a comparison with the Beery-Buktenica Developmental Test of Visual-Motor Integration. Percept. Mot. Skills **84**, 1439–1443 (1997)
20. Brown, T., Rodger, S., Davis, A.: Factor structure of the four motor-free scales of the developmental test of visual perception, 2nd Edition (DTVP–2). Am. J. Occup. Ther. **62**, 502–513 (2008)

Classification of Pathologies Using a Vision Based Feature Extraction

Mario Nieto-Hidalgo[(✉)] and Juan Manuel García-Chamizo

Department of Computing Technology, University of Alicante,
Campus San Vicente del Raspeig, Alicante, Spain
{mnieto,juanma}@dtic.ua.es
http://www.dtic.ua.es

Abstract. A lot of studies linking gait to different pathologies exists. However, few have addressed the automatic classification of such pathologies through computer vision. In this paper, a method to classify different gait pathologies is proposed. Using a smartphone camera, a sagittal view of the subject's gait is recorded. This record is processed by a computer vision algorithm that extract different gait parameters. These parameters are then used to perform a classification between 5 types of gait: normal, diplegic, hemiplegic, neuropathic and parkinsonian. Using a standard smartphone camera allows to simplify the data capturing step making this method suitable for Ambient Assisted Living. The experiments performed show an accuracy rate of 74% with a hierarchical classifier using Support Vector Machine combining Gait Energy Images and legs angle time series. The accuracy is improved to an 80% by applying data augmentation techniques during test, i.e., obtaining one sample per gait cycle and then combining the results to provide a more robust classification of the entire record.

Keywords: Gait analysis · Computer vision · Machine learning · Parkinson · Diplegia · Hemiplegia · Neuropathy

1 Introduction

The main objective of this work is to assess the suitability of a set of gait features based on computer vision to classify different gait pathologies. Physical activity is one of the main component involved in some syndromes evaluation like frailty [3,18], parkinson [6], neuropathy [21], hemiplegia [2] and diplegia [16]. Gait is identified as a high cognitive task in which attention, planning, memory and other cognitive processes are involved [4,11].

Through gait analysis, quantification of measurable information of gait and its interpretation [8,20], different syndromes and pathologies can be diagnosed. This process is carried out by specialist and is based on estimations through visual inspection of gait.

In this work we propose a feature set that could classify different gait pathologies and, thus, aid the specialists providing them with tool specialised in gait pathologies diagnosis.

© Springer International Publishing AG 2017
S.F. Ochoa et al. (Eds.): UCAmI 2017, LNCS 10586, pp. 265–274, 2017.
DOI: 10.1007/978-3-319-67585-5_28

In our previous contribution [12,14] we proposed a method to obtain gait features using computer vision with smartphone cameras and a classifier able to determine if the gait was normal or not obtained more than 90% accuracy.

This paper is organised as follows. Section 2 describe related works. Section 3 presents the features used in the task of classifying different pathologies. Section 4 provides the experimentation performed and the obtained results. Finally Sect. 5 provides the conclusion.

2 Related Works

There are a great variety of proposals for human identification using gait analysis, however, few proposals exist for different gait pathologies classification.

Meyer et al. [10] proposed a method to classify gait between walking, hopping, running and limping, they track the head and trunk position and train some Hidden Markov Models (HMM). They obtained 62.2% accuracy rate between those four gait patterns.

To classify between normal and abnormal gait, Bauckhage et al. [1] proposed a homeomorphisms between 2D lattices and binary shapes to obtain a vector space where the silhouette is encoded. They performed successive bounding box splittings to obtain different lattices, then Support Vector Machine (SVM) was used for classification obtaining around 80% accuracy rate. For the same purpose, Wang [19] proposed a method based on optical flow to calculate a histogram of silhouette-masked flows, then an eigenspace transformation is performed. They compare with a normal gait template to calculate a deviation with which they obtain 90% accuracy rate.

An approach for parkinsonian gait recognition is presented by Khan et al. [5]. They use the silhouette to obtain the bounding box and fit a human model to find head, torso and legs segments. The skeleton is obtained by computing the mean points of each body segment. Following, they obtain legs movement and the posture inclination while the person is walking to get a particular score that it is compared with a normal gait model in order to get a similarity score. This approach provides 100% accuracy to detect parkinsonian gait through legs angle and posture inclination because there is a sufficient difference between normal and parkinsonian gait. To distinguish other gait types of pathological gait this approach could be insufficient but it provides a first approach. Similarly, Krishnan et al. [7] use lean and ramp angles to detect abnormalities such us postural instability and heel strike instability with satisfactory results.

3 Feature Selection

Although our previously proposed method [13,14] for gait feature extraction can work with both sagittal and frontal gait images, in this work we focus only in the sagittal ones as those provide more information for the classifier to discriminate the different classes.

For the purpose of classifying different gait pathologies we propose the use of leg angle time series as this feature was the most successful in our previous works classifying normal and abnormal gait patterns [14] were more than 90% accuracy was obtained. Leg-angle is obtained by computing the angle formed by the hip and each foot. In addition, we want to also assess the power of the Gait Energy Image (GEI) for classification. Using the heel strike (HS) we segment the gait sequence and obtain a GEI [9] for each cycle. A GEI is obtained by averaging all the silhouettes of the cycle aligned by the center of gravity of its bounding box. We compute a GEI for each cycle to obtain more samples to train and thus requiring HS to segment the cycle. The process to obtain HS can be avoided if we average all the silhouettes of a sequence simplifying the acquisition of the input, but we obtain one for each cycle to obtain a large amount of samples. We compute each GEI as described in Eq. 1.

$$GEI_i = \frac{1}{h_{i+2} - h_i} \sum_{k=h_i}^{h_{i+2}} s_k \tag{1}$$

Where s_k is the silhouette of frame k and $i = \{1, 2, \ldots, n-2\}$ the corresponding HS of the set of HS detected for the recording sample.

The main issue of GEI is the amount of dimensions it has to compare. For instance, we are using 50×50 pixels, that means we have to compare 2500 components for each sample. A large amount of pixels are empty so there are some pixels that are not necessary to compare so an optimization can be performed. We use Principal Components Analysis (PCA) to select the n main eigenvectors of all the training samples and then project all the samples into this new eigenspace. Now we only compare the n principal components instead of 2500 using SVM. This method is similar to the eigenfaces proposed by Turk and Pentland [17] and it is also applied by Man and Bhanu [9] for person identification using GEI.

Each recorded gait sample provides an average of 4 gait cycles. The training process usually needs a large amount of samples to obtain enough information

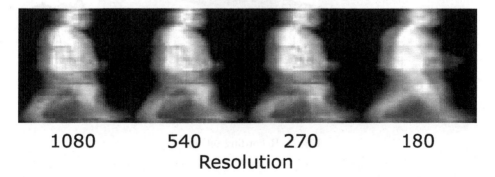

1080   540   270   180
Resolution

Fig. 1. This figure shows the different synthetic samples obtained from the original (left).

to perform a classification. That means we would have to record a great number of gait sequences to obtain a sufficient amount of samples. To solve this issue we propose the use of synthetic samples to increase the size of the training set.

For such purpose we use the multiresolution approach proposed in [15]. This method uses different resolutions to compute the silhouette providing a new synthetic sample for each subsampled resolution. By obtaining these samples, we provide robustness against scale variations.

This method transforms the original samples in new synthetic samples by adding artefacts that could be produced in reality. By using this method, we obtain 4 times more samples as shown in Fig. 1.

4   Experiments

For experimentation purposes, we recorded a dataset of subjects walking. We use healthy subjects feigning different pathologies due to having trouble finding real patient. However, we consider the feigned pathologies to be sufficient for our goal, which is to test if the proposed classifiers are capable of classifying between different pathologies. The data set is composed of samples of subjects walking over an 8 m hall. We set a camera perpendicular to gait direction at 4 m distance to record a side view of the person (around four steps). Figure 2 shows the set previously described.

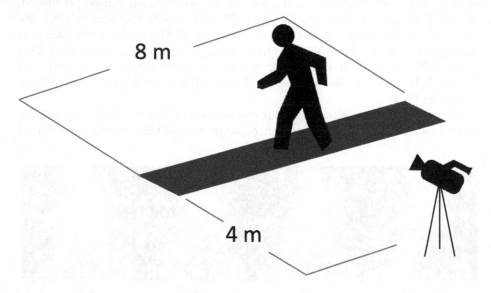

Fig. 2. Recording set up.

Table 1. Confusion matrix of legs-angle with DTW and KNN

		Actual				
		Normal	Diplegic	Hemiplegic	Neuropathic	Parkinsonian
Predicted	Normal	89,13%	0,00%	2,35%	18,45%	0,00%
	Diplegic	6,52%	47,27%	47,06%	4,85%	6,83%
	Hemiplegic	2,17%	14,55%	32,94%	7,77%	0,00%
	Neuropathic	2,17%	0,00%	12,94%	62,14%	0,00%
	Parkinsonian	0,00%	38,18%	4,71%	6,80%	93,17%

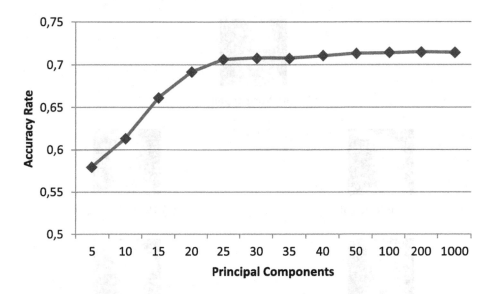

Fig. 3. Classification with different number of principal components

To perform the experiment we use this dataset with side view samples of five subjects feigning four different pathologies and normal gait. We recorded three samples of each subject and gait class which provided a total of 75 samples. The selected gait pathologies were diplegic, hemiplegic, neuropathic and parkinsonian.

We processed the new dataset with the HSTOD algorithm [14] to obtain the HS to separate each gait cycle. We first tried the legs-angle time series with K-Nearest Neighbors (KNN) and Dynamic Time Warping (DTW) as distance function like in previous experiments [14]. Results, shown in Table 1, were not good as diplegic and hemiplegic are frequently confused and neuropathic is confused with normal gait because the pattern is similar between those classes and, thus, the DTW score is low. Normal gait and parkinsonian were successfully classified confirming the results of Khan et al. [5]. We then tried the GEI approach. For each gait cycle, a GEI is obtained as described in the previous section.

Figure 4 shows a GEI of each class. To assess the accuracy of the classifier we use 5-fold cross-validation using for each fold all the samples of one subject as test and the other subjects as training including synthetic samples in this case as well. This ensures that the subject silhouette has not been learned by the classifier. We apply PCA to reduce the dimensionality of the input images. Several classifications using SVM were performed with a different number of principal components as shown in Fig. 3. That allowed to determine that the optimal value is 50 which is the value where the curve stabilises. Therefore, 50 is the value used in the subsequent experiments.

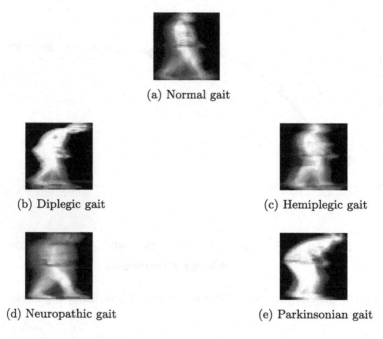

(a) Normal gait

(b) Diplegic gait   (c) Hemiplegic gait

(d) Neuropathic gait   (e) Parkinsonian gait

Fig. 4. GEI image of each of the 5 different classes.

The confusion matrix in Table 2 shows an accuracy of 71.17%. It also show that hemiplegic and neuropathic gait are frequently confused between each other. Also diplegic is confused with parkinsonian, the other way around as well but in a lesser degree. Therefore, a new classifier capable of classifying neuropathic and hemiplegic and another for classifying parkinsonian and diplegic is needed. The fact that the couples hemiplegic-neuropathic and diplegic-parkinsonian are well distinguished provides a way of developing a hierarchical classifier, the first level classifies between normal, hemiplegic-neuropathic and diplegic-parkinsonian. Then in the next level two binary classifiers should deal with each couple. Observing Figs. 4b and e it can be seen the similarity between those two silhouettes. In the same way, Figs. 4c and d are also similar to each other.

Table 2. Confusion matrix of PCA with GEI and SVM

		Actual				
		Normal	Diplegic	Hemiplegic	Neuropathic	Parkinsonian
Predicted	Normal	89,13%	11,82%	3,53%	9,71%	0,00%
	Diplegic	0,00%	40,00%	1,18%	4,85%	7,45%
	Hemiplegic	2,17%	9,09%	62,35%	13,59%	0,00%
	Neuropathic	8,70%	1,82%	32,94%	71,84%	0,00%
	Parkinsonian	0,00%	37,27%	0,00%	0,00%	92,55%

That is the reason why the classifier is not capable of properly distinguish both couples using GEI.

Both couples cannot be classified with the first classifier because their shape is very similar. To differentiate hemiplegic from neuropathic we use the legs-angle time series because the results of Table 1 show that those two pathologies are well distinguished with legs-angle. In the case of diplegic and parkinsonian, we did not find a suitable classifier to deal with the problem, however, frontal view could provide a way to differentiate them. After applying the reclassification of hemiplegic-neuropathic, the resultant confusion matrix is as shown in Table 3 where the accuracy is slightly improved to reach 74.66%. This accuracy can be improved to 80.33% if for each GEI of each recording sample (there is one GEI images per gait cycle) we output the mode class, i.e., the class that is predicted in most cycles of the recording sample. E.g. assuming we have a recording sample which contains 5 gait cycles, we process each cycle with the classifier and obtains that parkinsonian is the output of 3 of the 5 cycles, then we assume that the whole recording sample output is parkinsonian (the class of most cycles). Diplegic is confused with parkinsonian in both GEI and legs-angle classifiers. As an example, removing diplegic from the dataset we obtain 86.52% accuracy reaching a 95% applying the mode as shown in Table 4.

Table 3. Confusion matrix of PCA with GEI and SVM after applying reclassification of hemiplegic-neuropathic with legs angle time series and KNN.

		Actual				
		Normal	Diplegic	Hemiplegic	Neuropathic	Parkinsonian
Predicted	Normal	89,13%	11,82%	3,53%	9,71%	0,00%
	Diplegic	0,00%	40,00%	1,18%	4,85%	7,45%
	Hemiplegic	2,17%	10,00%	78,82%	12,62%	0,00%
	Neuropathic	8,70%	0,91%	16,47%	72,82%	0,00%
	Parkinsonian	0,00%	37,27%	0,00%	0,00%	92,55%

Table 4. Confusion matrix of PCA with GEI and SVM after applying reclassification of hemiplegic-neuropathic with legs angle time series and KNN and removing diplegic gait.

		Actual			
		Normal	Hemiplegic	Neuropathic	Parkinsonian
Predicted	Normal	82,61%	2,35%	0,97%	0,00%
	Hemiplegic	4,35%	80,00%	15,53%	0,00%
	Neuropathic	13,04%	16,47%	83,50%	0,00%
	Parkinsonian	0,00%	1,18%	0,00%	100,00%

5   Conclusion

Using our feature extraction method based on computer vision we selected legs-angle time series and GEI as features to perform classification of different pathologies. The experiments performed with the recorded dataset show that both legs-angle and GEI features are capable of classify normal and abnormal gait patterns, however, legs-angle confuses hemiplegic with diplegic and neuropathic with normal gait because the pattern is very similar obtaining a low DTW score, while GEI confuses diplegic with parkinsonian and hemiplegic with neuropathic because the GEI silhouettes are very similar for those classes. The results are improved by combining both classifiers obtaining an accuracy of 74% by first classifying between normal, hemiplegic-neuropathic and diplegic-parkinsonian and then reclassifying both couples to improve the results. However, diplegic and parkinsonian are still not properly distinguished by the second level of the classifier.

As future work we will try to find a suitable feature set to classify between diplegic and parkinsonian to improve the results. We will also test the power of Convolutional Neural Network with the GEI because these neural network has proven to have great potential when applied to image classification as is our case.

Acknowledgements. This research is part of the FRASE MINECO project (TIN2013-47152-C3-2-R) funded by the Ministry of Economy and Competitiveness of Spain.

References

1. Bauckhage, C., Tsotsos, J.K., Bunn, F.E.: Automatic detection of abnormal gait. Image Vis. Comput. **27**(1), 108–115 (2009)
2. Boudarham, J., Roche, N., Pradon, D., Bonnyaud, C., Bensmail, D., Zory, R.: Variations in kinematics during clinical gait analysis in stroke patients. PLoS ONE **8**(6), e66421 (2013)

3. Fried, L.P., Tangen, C.M., Walston, J., Newman, A.B., Hirsch, C., Gottdiener, J., Seeman, T., Tracy, R., Kop, W.J., Burke, G., et al.: Frailty in older adults evidence for a phenotype. J. Gerontol. Ser. A: Biol. Sci. Med. Sci. **56**(3), M146–M157 (2001)
4. Hausdorff, J.M., Yogev, G., Springer, S., Simon, E.S., Giladi, N.: Walking is more like catching than tapping: gait in the elderly as a complex cognitive task. Exp. Brain Res. **164**(4), 541–548 (2005)
5. Khan, T., Westin, J., Dougherty, M.: Motion cue analysis for parkinsonian gait recognition. Open Biomed. Eng. J. **7**, 1 (2013)
6. Klucken, J., Barth, J., Kugler, P., Schlachetzki, J., Henze, T., Marxreiter, F., Kohl, Z., Steidl, R., Hornegger, J., Eskofier, B., et al.: Unbiased and mobile gait analysis detects motor impairment in parkinson's disease. PLoS ONE **8**(2), e56956 (2013)
7. Krishnan, R., Sivarathinabala, M., Abirami, S.: Abnormal gait detection using lean and ramp angle features. In: Behera, H.S., Mohapatra, D.P. (eds.) Computational Intelligence in Data Mining—Volume 1. AISC, vol. 410, pp. 325–335. Springer, New Delhi (2016). doi:10.1007/978-81-322-2734-2_33
8. Mahoney, F.I.: Functional evaluation: the barthel index. Maryland State Med. J. **14**, 61–65 (1965)
9. Man, J., Bhanu, B.: Individual recognition using gait energy image. IEEE Trans. Pattern Anal. Mach. Intell. **28**(2), 316–322 (2006)
10. Meyer, D., Pösl, J., Niemann, H.: Gait classification with HMMs for trajectories of body parts extracted by mixture densities. In: BMVC, pp. 1–10. Citeseer (1998)
11. Mulder, T., Zijlstra, W., Geurts, A.: Assessment of motor recovery and decline. Gait & Posture **16**(2), 198–210 (2002)
12. Nieto-Hidalgo, M., Ferrández-Pastor, F.J., Valdivieso-Sarabia, R.J., Mora-Pascual, J., García-Chamizo, J.M.: Vision based extraction of dynamic gait features focused on feet movement using RGB camera. In: Bravo, J., Hervás, R., Villarreal, V. (eds.) AmIHEALTH 2015. LNCS, vol. 9456, pp. 155–166. Springer, Cham (2015). doi:10.1007/978-3-319-26508-7_16
13. Nieto-Hidalgo, M., Ferrández-Pastor, F.J., Valdivieso-Sarabia, R.J., Mora-Pascual, J., García-Chamizo, J.M.: Vision based gait analysis for frontal view gait sequences using RGB camera. In: García, C.R., Caballero-Gil, P., Burmester, M., Quesada-Arencibia, A. (eds.) UCAmI 2016. LNCS, vol. 10069, pp. 26–37. Springer, Cham (2016). doi:10.1007/978-3-319-48746-5_3
14. Nieto-Hidalgo, M., Ferrández-Pastor, F.J., Valdivieso-Sarabia, R.J., Mora-Pascual, J., García-Chamizo, J.M.: A vision based proposal for classification of normal and abnormal gait using RGB camera. J. Biomed. Inform. **63**, 82–89 (2016)
15. Nieto-Hidalgo, M., García-Chamizo, J.M.: Real time gait analysis using RGB camera. In: García, C.R., Caballero-Gil, P., Burmester, M., Quesada-Arencibia, A. (eds.) UCAmI 2016. LNCS, vol. 10069, pp. 111–120. Springer, Cham (2016). doi:10.1007/978-3-319-48746-5_12
16. Piccinini, L., Cimolin, V., D'Angelo, M.G., Turconi, A.C., Crivellini, M., Galli, M.: 3d gait analysis in patients with hereditary spastic paraparesis and spastic diplegia: a kinematic, kinetic and emg comparison. Eur. J. Paediatr. Neurol. **15**(2), 138–145 (2011)
17. Turk, M., Pentland, A.: Eigenfaces for recognition. J. Cogn. Neurosci. **3**(1), 71–86 (1991)
18. Waltson, J., Fried, L.: Frailty and the old man. Med. Clin. North Am. **83**(5), 1173–1194 (1999)
19. Wang, L.: Abnormal walking gait analysis using silhouette-masked flow histograms. In: 18th International Conference on Pattern Recognition, ICPR 2006, vol. 3, pp. 473–476. IEEE (2006)

20. Whittle, M.W.: Gait Analysis: An Introduction. Butterworth-Heinemann, London (2014)
21. Wuehr, M., Schniepp, R., Schlick, C., Huth, S., Pradhan, C., Dieterich, M., Brandt, T., Jahn, K.: Sensory loss and walking speed related factors for gait alterations in patients with peripheral neuropathy. Gait & Posture 39(3), 852–858 (2014)

Evaluation of Fall and Seizure Detection with Smartphone and Smartwatch Devices

Veno Bojanovsky[1(✉)], Shane Byrne[1], Philip Kirwan[1], Ian Cleland[2], and Chris Nugent[2]

[1] Responder Technologies, Blue Cow Technologies, Unit 21, Block 1, Broomhall Business Park, Rathnew, A67 H221, County Wicklow, Ireland
{veno,shane,philip}@responder.ie
[2] Computer Science Research Institute and School of Computing and Mathematics, Ulster University, Newtownabbey BT37 0QB, County Antrim, Northern Ireland, UK
{cd.nugent,i.cleland}@ulster.ac.uk

Abstract. Epilepsy and falls incur a great social and economic cost globally. Automatically detecting their occurrence would help mitigate the myriad of issues that arise from not receiving assistance after such an event. Despite existing research showing the potential advantages in using the ever-improving sensor technology incorporated within commercially available smartphone and smartwatch devices for human activity recognition, most available solutions for fall and seizure detection are still offered with dedicated hardware, which is often more expensive and less practical. This paper presents a comparison and evaluation of algorithms for detecting convulsions and falls, separately and combined, using smartphone and smartwatch devices. With a dataset of ordinary activities and simulated falls and convulsions, recorded by 15 test subjects, we found the devices a viable option for the successful detection of the activities, achieving accuracy rates between 89.7% and 98.5% with C4.5 decision tree algorithms.

1 Introduction

Epilepsy and falls come at great economic and social cost [1–6]. The following subsections provide an overview of the prevalence and impact of epilepsy and falls, and the state of the art of solutions currently in place to provide healthcare support.

1.1 Societal Impact of Epilepsy

Epilepsy is the second most common neurological disorder, affecting approximately 1% of the world population [1]. It is identified by the occurrence of at least two unprovoked seizures more than 24 h apart, or one unprovoked seizure in individuals with other factors associated with a high likelihood of a persistently lowered seizure threshold [7]. The seizures are characterized as brief episodes of involuntary movement that may involve a part of the body (partial) or the entire body (generalized).

Some of the many types of epileptic seizures [8], such as the most recognizable – the generalized tonic-clonic seizure (GTCS), carry an increased risk for injuries and for death from drowning, car accidents, falls, sudden unexpected death in epilepsy (SUDEP)

© Springer International Publishing AG 2017
S.F. Ochoa et al. (Eds.): UCAmI 2017, LNCS 10586, pp. 275–286, 2017.
DOI: 10.1007/978-3-319-67585-5_29

[9] and status epilepticus [10], especially when left unattended. As mentioned, some epilepsy types may cause a fall during a seizure due to loss of muscle control and consciousness [11] and carry all the subsequent risks involved with falls.

1.2 Societal Impact of Falls

Falls are commonly defined as "inadvertently coming to rest on the ground, floor or other lower level, excluding intentional change in position to rest in furniture, wall or other objects" [12]. Even though they are often underreported [13], falls are one of the leading the leading causes of medically consulted injuries [14] (which may lead to disability [16] and institutionalization [14]) and death in people aged 65 or over [15].

A consequence of falling, called the "long lie", poses additional risks. It is defined as remaining on the ground or floor for more than an hour after a fall, and is associated with high mortality rates among the elderly [13].

An initial fall or seizure event can lead to a spiral of decline [17], causing disability, sedentary behavior, decreased mobility and independence, amplified by fear of subsequent falls, and thus increasing the risk of their recurrence [13]. These issues are growing in importance [12, 18–20] due to population aging [21]. It was noted that reducing the risks of the described health issues must begin with their reliable detection [8, 17], which involves notifying others to assist the individual in need.

1.3 Seizure and Fall Detection

Seizure and fall detection are generally performed separately. The gold standard for seizure detection in a clinical setting utilizes video-electroencephalography (video-EEG) monitoring [22, 23]. Whilst accurate, this is costly and impractical for use in everyday life, due to its greatly limited range and physical constraints, requiring test subjects to wear intrusive sensors on their scalp. Commercial products for seizure or fall detection mostly come as dedicated hardware solutions, with varying degrees of practicality, accuracy and affordability for consumers. For instance, many commercially available fall detection solutions have to be worn around the neck and require mobile subscriptions without offering the versatility of a smartphone. Adoption rates may be negatively affected due to social stigma, as is the case with hearing aids [24].

There are reports of highly accurate seizure detection systems using dedicated wrist-worn devices that have been helped by using electrodermal activity (EDA) sensors [22, 25, 26], which are currently unavailable in mainstream wearable devices.

As Klapuri [8] suggested, this paper considers a solution combining fall and seizure detection. Using only motion sensors, this would improve detection of seizures that do not exhibit a "vibratory" phase [27], and result in falls, which is a frequent consequence of some types of epileptic seizures [8]. Fall detection can achieve high detection rates using simple threshold-based algorithms (TBAs) [28–31], therefore the added functionality would not add significant complexity.

Given that the marketplace seems to lack a widely accepted solution that provides the aforementioned functionalities [9], this paper assesses the viability of using smartphone and smartwatch devices for detecting epileptic convulsions and falls. Similar research has identified issues [32] with achieving both high accuracy and low power consumption [33], hence within this current research they were placed in primary focus.

The remainder of this paper is structured as follows: Existing solutions and the research direction for the current work are presented within the *Background* Section. Following this, the *Methodology* Section describes the tools used and approaches taken for the data collection, feature extraction and classification. The results are then presented and discussed. Finally, conclusions for the study are drawn.

2 Background

Relevant research generally utilizes dedicated hardware solutions and software solutions on widespread multimedia devices (smartphones and smartwatches). The former run the activity recognition software, along with some additional services that act as extensions of the core activity detection, while the latter can offer the same services with increased practicality, less possibility of social discomfort and the versatility of the device's other features, albeit lacking some additional specialized sensors. Mainstream smartphones also regularly feature a GPS module, which is useful for providing assistance once an alarming event is detected, through provisioning of location-based information. Moreover, to owners of smartphone and smartwatch devices, acquiring software solutions comes at a lower cost.

Currently, dedicated hardware solutions appear to be more common, however, the proportion of mainstream devices has increased in relevant research in recent years [9]. This indicates that the increasingly sophisticated sensors in mainstream devices, paired with their ubiquity and unobtrusiveness [34], have made them a valid and practical option for Human Activity Recognition (HAR).

Recent work by Khan *et al.* presented HAR with detection rates of 87% [32] and 92.4% [34], recorded with smartphone devices by 40 and 30 test subjects, respectively. The presented solutions achieved high accuracy, particularly considering the high number of classes, while making them lightweight at the same time. Low power consumption was achieved by keeping the data-windows short (3 and 3.5 s), the sampling frequencies low (20 Hz), and utilizing time-domain autoregressive (AR) features, kernel discriminant analysis (KDA) for dimensionality reduction, and artificial neural networks (ANNs) and support vector machines (SVMs) for classification. These were chosen for their combination of high accuracy and lower power consumption compared to most HAR solutions not running on mobile or wearable devices.

The accuracy in the described work [32, 34] was adversely affected by the increased complexity from the large number of classes used (six [32] and fifteen [34]). This showed potential for greater detection rates if less classes were used, and diminishing power consumption if using less sensors, shorter data-windows and lower sampling frequencies, which helped inform the approach taken in this research.

2.1   Seizure Detection

Research focusing on seizure detection using only movement sensors reported promising results, while noting that detecting only convulsive movement for seizure detection [8] would compromise accuracy for seizures that do not exhibit convulsive behavior, however, may still be detectable via falls.

2.2   Fall Detection

It has been reported that it is feasible to develop a lightweight fall detection system using a triaxial accelerometer worn at the waist, with simple TBAs, achieving sensitivity and specificity rates in excess of 95% [28–31]. There is, however, rarely mention of which activities of daily living (ADLs) were recorded for the datasets used, nor are there comments on balancing the data, which would help to better assess the approaches.

Wrist-worn sensors were reported to be less appropriate for fall detection [8], with sensitivity ranging from 45 to 100% [35]. This would follow as a consequence of inconsistent possible arm movement during falls. Fall detection should be reliable when the sensors receive direct impact from the fall, however it may be less reliable when one reaches out during a fall, trying to grip something to steady themselves, or in the case of a lateral fall, with the device on the side opposite of the impact.

2.3   Research Direction

Although Khan *et al.* [34] demonstrated HAR with high accuracy and low power consumption, it was adversely affected by the inclusion of high-level activities (such as watching television, having a meeting), requiring the use of additional sensors (such as a microphone), adding complexity and intrusiveness. Existing research [28] demonstrated lightweight fall detection to be accurate for sensors in a smartphone located near the waist area, while using movement sensors on the wrist was shown to provide accurate detection of GTCSs [10].

The aim of this paper is to assess the viability of using smartphone and smartwatch movement sensor data for lightweight detection of epileptic convulsions and falls with reliable accuracy. The reliability is ensured by including a set of balanced activities, further described in the following Sections. Such a system would allow assistance when a fall or seizure occurs, helping avoid issues such as the long lie, status epilepticus and SUDEP. It would also help individuals maintain their independence and confidence by providing reassurance.

As not all seizure types can be detected with movement sensors, the seizures covered include those exhibiting detectable motor function activity [7], such as GTCS, which are detectable by their "vibratory" phase [27]. Additionally, seizure types that can be detected as falls, commonly grouped as static seizures or drop attacks [8, 36] are also covered. To the best of our knowledge, other research has not combined seizure detection with falls in this manner, hence we evaluated the viability of this approach.

3 Methodology

The approach guiding this research aimed to achieve high detection accuracies with the least computationally demanding methods. Fall detection, in addition to detection of convulsions, are developed and tested separately and combined, to evaluate accuracies for each case. This is performed separately for smartphone and smartwatch devices. The following sub-sections outline the approach adopted.

3.1 Data Collection

Developing the fall and seizure detection systems for this research required recording a representative dataset with healthy individuals performing or simulating activities whilst wearing smartphone and smartwatch devices. The choice and performance of the included activities were informed by existing research (the corresponding sources are noted in the descriptions within Table 1).

Table 1. Classification of recorded activity groups.

Activity group	Description
Stationary	Inactive behavior (resting, sitting, standing, etc.)
Dynamic	Active behavior (various forms of ambulation, regular usage of the device, etc.)
Convulsive-like	Movements relatively similar to convulsions (brushing teeth, exercising, writing, etc.) [8]
Fall-like	Movements relatively similar to falling (sitting down, placing the smartphone in one's pocket, etc.)
Convulsion simulation	Simulation of the "vibratory" phase of a GTCS [8, 27, 40]
Fall simulation	Simulations of falls (10 different types were performed, including simulations of accidental falls and falls due to seizures, grouped as forward, backward and lateral falls) [17, 28]

For the smartphone device, placement was restricted to trouser pockets, to reduce complexity without significantly hindering usability. As the conventional location for carrying smartphone devices, it was also deemed adequate in other research [37]. For improved data reliability, it was ensured that the smartwatch is not worn too loosely.

Similar research has predominantly used Android devices [38, 39], while this current work utilized the underrepresented iOS devices (Apple iPhone 6 and Apple Watch), however the results should be similarly applicable in both. The activities and their respective durations were chosen to help generate robust detection algorithms.

The activity groups considered are presented in Table 1, where there are three different classifications considered: *CF* (Convulsions and Falls) includes all activity groups, *C* (Convulsions) includes all activity groups aside from *Fall-like* and *Fall Simulation* activities, and *F* (Falls) includes all activity groups aside from *Convulsion-like* and *Convulsion Simulation* activities. Each of the three classification cases contains only two classes – ADL and Alarm. The first four activity groups from Table 1 always belong to the ADL class, while the final two belong to the Alarm class.

Durations of the activity groups presented in Table 1 were chosen to best ensure equivalent amounts of data samples for both classes in every instance. For example, when training and testing the binary classification between *Fall Simulation* and *ADL* activities, the number of data samples was equivalent in both classes. The balancing, more closely described in Sect. 3.2 *Data Processing*, was performed separately for training and testing the algorithms to produce the most accurate fall and seizure detection algorithms, with reliable accuracy.

3.2   Data Processing

The data were processed with Python scripts that generated a range of time-domain attributes from accelerometry, gyroscope and orientation data, the three dimensions of each being combined into one measure, the Signal Magnitude Vector (SMV), the square root of the sum of squares of all three dimensions. This makes the attributes independent of orientation, and was considered beneficial in other research [28, 39]. We also applied the *diff* method of Python's *NumPy* library to generate attributes containing the differences between neighboring elements of the SMVs. The six SMV data sources for which attributes were generated include three from accelerometry data (directly with and without the gravity component, and with the *diff* version of the latter), two from gyroscope data (directly, and with the *diff* version) and one from only the *diff* version of orientation data.

The generated attributes for the individual SMVs' data-windows include simple statistical features and features customized to better describe the data behavior for relevant classes. The latter include measures for data-window amplitude (absolute, averaged over the four maximum and minimum values), comparisons of amplitudes in data-window subsections, maximum positive and negative differences between neighboring elements (and the amplitude from these), their median, direction changes surpassing different thresholds, local maxima before and after the maximum value, variations on expressing amplitude (divisions, multiplications and subtractions with other amplitude measures, standard deviations, entropy, etc.) and vibratory movements (direction changes multiplied with amplitude), averages and standard deviations of local maxima. The number of attributes used was 48 per each of the six SMVs, or 288 in total.

After generating the attributes, they were reformatted and transferred to the WEKA classification software, where the data samples were randomized using the *Randomize* tool. To ensure equal numbers of data samples in the classes, the data were subsequently balanced. This was performed by over-sampling using *SMOTE* (from 39.4% to 69.8%) and under-sampling using the *SpreadSubsample* tool.

To illustrate the importance of balancing and investigating metrics other than accuracy, we will use an example lacking them. If one were to train the system on more realistic behavior, they would record relatively few falls, compared to other activities. If they recorded 20 min of ADL and 12 fall simulations, the system could classify every sample, including the falls, as *ADLs*, while showing a misleadingly high 95% accuracy. This is a drastic example showing the importance of balancing data and reporting other measures besides accuracy, and it is why we have presented a number of metrics in Table 3, within the Sect. 4.2 *Performance Metrics* Section.

3.3 Test Subjects

The individuals that participated in data collection for this research provided informed consent, and the data collection received approval from relevant ethical boards at the Ulster University. The participants were trained to properly perform the activities, while ensuring the safety of participants was preserved, similar to relevant research [27, 28]. In cases where comfort or safety were at odds with the accuracy of simulations, the activities were performed safely, with the assumption that the performed simulations would still feature movement data mostly different from normal ADLs and add realistic variability to the dataset.

For determining the accuracy, a mean of three-fold validation was used, with folds containing data from discrete groups of test subjects. This was performed separately for the six classification cases – *CF* (Convulsions and Falls), *C* (Convulsions) and *F* (Falls), for smartphone and for smartwatch devices. Overall, the dataset included data from fifteen test subjects. Ten of the test subjects performed convulsion simulations and fall simulations, recording approximately 800 simulated falls, and an equivalent amount of convulsion simulation data samples. The average age of the test subjects was 28 years, ranging from 18 to 37 years. The dataset skewed male, with only 20% of test subjects being female.

3.4 Classification

Given that the goal of this research was to determine whether a medically relevant event (fall or seizure) has occurred, it is not necessary to discriminate between sub-activities within a class (falls from convulsions, or sitting from walking). Reducing the complexity to a binary classification problem allowed using simpler tools without a great loss in accuracy.

Given the large number of attributes generated, it is necessary to reduce these to only the attributes containing relevant information. This was determined using the *CfsSubsetEval* attribute selection tool in WEKA, with the bi-directional *BestFirst* search method. *CfsSubsetEval* was chosen in lieu of more complex methods used in other research [32, 34, 37, 38], as initial results suggested accuracy would remain high without increasing the computational complexity. This step reduced the number of attributes from 288 to between 13 and 31 for the six relevant classification cases, greatly simplifying the resultant decision trees. The attributes that were included after the attribute selection step varied for each of the eighteen tested folds. In general, the classifications for detecting convulsions heavily featured threshold-crossings measurements and some cross-correlations and averages, while fall classifications relied on local maxima and measurements of amplitude differences between subsections of a data-window.

4 Results

We compared the results obtained for 4, 6 and 8 s data-windows, informed by relevant research [32]. A sliding window with a size 50% of the data-window was used in all cases. This was chosen to improve fall detection in cases where the fall would have occurred near the margins of a data-window. It was determined that there were no significant gains in accuracy for larger data-windows, hence final results were generated using 4 s data-windows in all cases. This was in line with expectations due to the nature of fall and convulsion simulation activities, which would not gain much information from expanded data-windows.

Results obtained with 10, 25 and 50 Hz sampling frequencies were also compared. It was determined that for fall simulation activities, greater sampling frequency did not significantly improve accuracy for values in the compared range. For activities featuring convulsion simulations, a sampling frequency of 25 Hz generated significantly better results than 10 Hz, particularly for the smartwatch device. This was expected, as convulsive activities exhibit a greater deal of information in higher frequency of movement. The results generated with a 25 Hz sampling frequency were not significantly worse than those for 50 Hz. These results are at first somewhat surprising, compared to other research [32]. Nevertheless, as the classes in this research contain specific and more distinguishable movements than in the mentioned work, it follows that this approach would allow for using lower sampling frequencies.

4.1 Classification Algorithms

Table 2 presents a comparison of accuracy rates for a range of popular classification algorithms, primarily informed by Wu *et al.* [41]. These include the Adaptive Boosting (*AB*), C4.5 Decision Tree (*DT*), k-Nearest Neighbors (*k-NN*), Naïve Bayes (*NB*), Neural Networks (*NN*), Random Forest (*RF*) and Support Vector Machine (*SVM*) algorithms. The implementations for each of these classifiers were generated via WEKA with default settings used in each case.

Table 2. Accuracy rates (presented in percentages) for the six binary classification cases– *CF* (Convulsions and Falls), *C* (Convulsions) and *F* (Falls) recorded separately with smartphone and smartwatch devices.

	Smartphone			Smartwatch		
	CF (25 Hz)	C (25 Hz)	F (10 Hz)	CF (25 Hz)	C (25 Hz)	F (10 Hz)
AB	91.9	94.1	96.7	92.7	97.6	97.5
DT	89.7	94.9	96.4	94.5	96.1	98.5
k-NN	87.6	94.8	95.8	89.4	96.5	96.2
NB	84.4	94.9	91.9	93.4	96.6	95.4
NN	88.4	94.8	96.7	96.3	94.8	96.1
RF	92.7	97.2	97.7	96.6	97.5	98.5
SVM	91.8	97.8	96.8	94.9	97.5	97.0

4.2 Performance Metrics

As it is a simple and consistently accurate algorithm, Table 3 contains a better view of the results generated with the C4.5 decision trees. The results are presented with a number of metrics, most of which are recommended and described by Casilari *et al.* [38]

as necessary for adequately assessing performance: False Positive Rate (FPR), Precision (PPV), False Discovery Rate (FDR), False Omission Rate (FOR), Negative Predictive Value (NPV). Also presented are the Area Under the receiver operating characteristic Curve (AUC) and the kappa statistic – a measure that accounts for agreement occurring by chance. These metrics provide a robust view of accuracy.

Table 3. Performance metrics (presented in percentages) for the six binary classification cases– CF (Convulsions and Falls), C (Convulsions) and F (Falls) recorded separately with smartphone and smartwatch devices; using the resulting C4.5 classification algorithms.

	Smartphone			Smartwatch		
	CF (25 Hz)	C (25 Hz)	F (10 Hz)	CF (25 Hz)	C (25 Hz)	F (10 Hz)
Accuracy	89.7	94.9	96.4	94.5	96.1	98.5
Specificity	92.4	93.9	96.8	94.4	96.8	98.2
Sensitivity	87.0	95.9	96.1	94.5	95.5	98.8
FPR	7.6	6.1	3.2	5.6	3.2	1.8
PPV	91.8	94.1	96.7	94.5	96.9	98.2
FDR	8.2	5.9	3.3	5.5	3.1	1.8
FOR	11.8	4.1	3.8	5.5	4.4	1.2
NPV	88.2	95.9	96.2	94.5	95.6	98.8
F-score	89.2	95.0	96.4	94.5	96.1	98.5
AUC	79.4	89.9	92.8	89.0	92.3	97.0
Kappa	88.6	95.0	96.5	93.8	95.1	98.6

5 Discussion

Empirical leave-one-out testing revealed that the results have significant variability, with some test subjects having significantly lower accuracy rates than others. This is likely a consequence of additional safety measures, used for recording fall and convulsion simulation activities of some test subjects, diminishing the veracity of some of the recordings. It is also interpreted as correct simulation of the activities with the expected movements being diminished or obstructed, such as it would happen in real life situations, a consequence of using one device. This indicates a combination of devices would be beneficial, however, this would require an additional layer of logic, the development of which exceeds the scope of this paper.

The results in Table 2 show high detection rates for falls using the smartwatch device. This is somewhat higher than in other research [28, 36]. As the test subjects recorded a great variety of falls, the results indicate greater applicability of smartwatch devices for fall detection than previously reported, when the described methods are used. Smartphones produced accurate results consistent with other research [29–31]. Convulsion detection accuracy is similar to existing hardware solutions [26], however, conclusively confirming the results and determining the viability of combining falls and seizures requires data from real epilepsy patients.

Using smartphone and smartwatch devices has the downside of lacking the choice of the embedded sensors. For instance, older smartphone devices might not feature accelerometers with optimal characteristics for detecting falls. Moreover, accurate heart-rate and EDA sensors are not commonly found in smartwatch devices, even though their inclusion would be beneficial for detecting alarming states [22, 25]. Nevertheless, with the increasing quantity and quality of sensors in modern devices, this is becoming less of an issue. Furthermore, growing usage of these devices for fall and seizure detection would provide incentives for hardware manufacturers to add sensors more suitable for detecting medically significant states.

6   Conclusions

We compared accuracy rates for detecting convulsions and falls, separately and combined. This was done for mainstream smartphone and smartwatch devices. The results indicate the viability of the devices for providing highly accurate detection (from 89.7 to 98.5% with C4.5 decision trees, as shown in Table 2).

Developing and realizing an online solution would help provide assistance and reassurance to a portion of the population at risk from suffering a fall or some types of epilepsy. Real-time classification on the device would help further verify the reported accuracy of the results, in addition to allowing for precise measurement of the effect on battery life.

A limitation of the current study is the lack of data from epilepsy patients, and including it would be an improvement for further research. Additionally, although smartphones have been identified as suitable for the task of activity detection, there has been little research in solutions combining smartphone and smartwatch data, which would enhance detection accuracy and expand the number of cases when detection is viable by functioning when only one device is worn. This happens frequently, as people do not always wear all of their devices simultaneously. Thus, a future goal should include developing a fall and seizure detection system with a smartphone and smartwatch working together to increase robustness.

In conclusion, our results indicate that achieving accurate fall and convulsion detection systems using smartphone and smartwatch devices is a viable and practical alternative to existing solutions.

Acknowledgments.   The work described in this paper was supported by InterTradeIreland FUSION project FU4223 between Blue Cow Technologies Ltd t/a Showoff and Ulster University. Invest Northern Ireland is acknowledged for partially supporting this project under the Competence Centre Programs Grant RD0513853 – Connected Health Innovation Centre. The authors thank all subjects for contributing to the dataset.

References

1. World Health Organizations (WHO): Global Burden of Epilepsy and the need for Coordinated Action at the Country Level to Address its Health, Social and Public Knowledge Implications. IOM, Geneva (2014)
2. Begley, C.E., Famulari, M., Annegers, J.F., et al.: The cost of epilepsy in the United States: an estimate from population-based clinical and survey data. Epilepsia **41**(3), 342–351 (2000)

3. Pitkänen, A., Schwartzkroin, P., Moshé, S.: Models of Seizures and Epilepsy, 1st edn. Elsevier Science, Academic Press, London (2005)
4. Bergen, G., Stevens, M.R., Burns, E.R., Centers for Disease Control and Prevention: Falls and fall injuries among adults aged ≥ 65 years – United States, 2014. Morb. Mortal. Wkly Rep. **65**(37), 993–998 (2016)
5. Carey, D., Laffoy, M.: Hospitalisations due to falls in older persons. Irish Med. J. **98**(6), 179–181 (2005)
6. Roudsari, B., et al.: The acute medical care costs of fall-related injuries among the U.S. older adults. Injury **36**(11), 1316–1322 (2005)
7. Fisher, R.S., Acevedo, C., Arzimanoglou, A., Bogacz, A., et al.: A practical clinical definition of epilepsy: ILAE official report. Epilepsia **55**(4), 475–482 (2014)
8. Klapuri, J.: Epileptic seizure detection using a wrist-worn triaxial accelerometer [dissertation]. University of Helsinki, Finland (2013)
9. Van de Vel, A., Cuppens, K., Bonroy, B., et al.: Non-EEG seizure detection systems and potential SUDEP prevention: state of the art – review and update. Seizure **41**, 141–153 (2016)
10. Al-Mufti, F., Claassen, J.: Neurocritical care: status epilepticus review. Crit. Care Clinics **30**(4), 751–764 (2014)
11. Yavuz, G.R., Kocak, M.E., Ergun, G., Alemdar, H., Yalcin, H., Incel, O.D., et al.: A smartphone based fall detector with online location support. In: PhotoSense 2010. Proceedings of the First International Workshop on Sensing for App Phones, Zürich (Switzerland), 2 Nov 2010
12. Kalache, A., Fu, D., Yoshida, S.: WHO global report on falls prevention in older age. World Health Organization, Geneva (2007)
13. Lord, S.R., Sherrington, C., Menz, H.B.: Falls in older people – risk factors and strategies for prevention. Cambridge University Press, Cambridge (2001)
14. Adams, P.F., Kirzinger, W.K., Martinez, M.E.: Summary health statistics for the U.S. population: National Health Interview Survey, 2011. NCHS. Vital Health Stat. **10**(255), 26–29 (2012)
15. Rubenstein, L.Z.: Falls in older people: epidemiology, risk factors and strategies for prevention. Age Ageing **35**(S2), 37–41 (2006)
16. Sadigh, S., Reimers, A., Andersson, R., et al.: Fall and fall-related injuries among the elderly: a survey of residential-care facilities in a Swedish municipality. J. Community Health **29**, 129 (2004)
17. Doughty, K., Lewis, R., McIntosh, A.: The design of a practical and reliable fall detector for community and institutional applications. J. Telemed. Telecare **6**(Suppl 1), 150–154 (2000)
18. Kramarow, E., Chen, L.-H., Hedegaard, H., Warner, M.: Deaths from unintentional injury among adults aged 65 and over: United States, 2000–2013. NCHS data brief, no 199. National Center for Health Statistics (NCHS), Centers for Disease Control and Prevention (CDC) (2015)
19. The 2015 Aging Report: Economic and budgetary projects for the 28 EU Member states. European Commission. European Publications, Brussels (2015)
20. Hu, G., Baker, S.P.: An explanation for the recent increase in the fall death rate among older Americans: a subgroup analysis. Public Health Rep. **127**, 275–281 (2012)
21. United Nations (UN), Department of Economic and Social Affairs (DESA), Population Division (2015). World Population Aging 2015. (ST/ESA/SER.A/390)
22. Onorati, F., Regalia, G., Caborni, C., Picard, R.W.: Improvement of a convulsive seizure detector relying on accelerometer and electrodermal activity collected continuously by a wristband. In: Epilepsy Pipeline Conference 2016

23. Conradsen, I., Wolf, P., Sams, T., Sorensen, H.B.D., Beniczky, S.: Patterns of muscle activation during generalized tonic-clonic epileptic seizures. Epilepsia **52**(11), 2125–2132 (2011)
24. Kochkin, S.: MarkeTrak VII: Obstacles to adult non-user adoption of hearing aids. Hear. J. **60**(4), 24–50 (2007)
25. Caborni, C., Onorati, F., Regalia, G., Migliorini, M., Picard, R.W.: A wristband assessment of accelerometry and autonomic activity of epileptic patients. In: Proceedings of Partners Against Mortality in Epilepsy (PAME), Washington D.C. (2016)
26. Regalia, G., Onorati, F., Migliorini, M., Picard, R.W.: An improved wrist-worn convulsive seizure detector based on accelerometry and electrodermal activity sensors. American Epilepsy Society annual meeting 2015. Abs no. 3096
27. Conradsen, I., Moldovan, M., Jennum, P., Wolf, P., Farina, D., Beniczky, S.: Dynamics of muscle activation during tonic-clonic seizures. Epilepsy Res. **104**, 84–93 (2013)
28. Kangas, M., Lindgren, P., Jämsa, T.: Comparison of low-complexity fall detection algorithms for body attached accelerometers. Gait Posture **28**(2), 285–291 (2008)
29. Wu, F., Zhao, H., Zhao, Y., Zhong, H.: Development of a wearable-sensor-based fall detection system. Int. J. Telemed. Appl. **2015**, (2015). Article ID 576364
30. Mao, L., Liang, D., Ning, Y., et al.: Pre-impact and impact detection of falls using built-in tri-accelerometer of smartphone. Health Inf. Sci. **8423**, 167–174 (2014)
31. Chaudhuri, S., Thompson, H., Demiris, G.: Fall detection devices and their use with older adults: a systemic review. J. Geriatr. Phys. Ther. **37**(4), 178–196 (2014)
32. Khan, A.M., Siddiqi, M.H., Lee, S.W.: Exploratory data analysis of acceleration signals to select light-weight and accurate features for real-time activity recognition on smartphones. Sensors **13**(10), 13099–13122 (2013)
33. Majumder, A.J.A., Zerin, I., Ahamed, S.I., Smith, R.O.A.: Multi-sensor approach for fall risk prediction and prevention in elderly. ACM SIGAPP Appl. Comput. Rev. **14**, 41–52 (2014)
34. Khan, A.M., Tufail, A., Khattak, A.M., Laine, T.H.: Activity recognition on smartphones via sensor-fusion and KDA-based SVMs. Int. J. Distrib. Sens. Netw. **2014**, 1–14 (2014). Article ID 503291
35. Degen, T., Jaeckel, H., Rufer, M., Wyss, S.: Speedy: a fall detector in a wrist watch. In: Proceedings of the 7th IEEE International Symposium on Wearable Computers, p. 184. IEEE Computer Society (2003)
36. Milošević, M., Van de Vel, A., Cuppens, K., Bonroy, B., Ceulemans, B., Lagae, L., et al.: Feature selection methods for accelerometry-based seizure detection in children. Med. Biol. Eng. Compu. **55**(1), 151–165 (2016)
37. He, Z., Jin, L.: Activity recognition from acceleration data based on discrete consine [sic] transform and SVM. In: Proceedings of the IEEE International Conference on Systems, Man and Cybernetics (SMC), pp. 5041–5044 (2009)
38. Casilari, E., Luque, R., Morón, M.-J.: Analysis of android device-based solutions for fall detection. Sensors **15**(8), 17827–17894 (2015)
39. Rasheed, M.B., Javaid, N., Khan, Z.A., Qasim, U.: Evaluation of human activity recognition and fall detection and using Android phone. In: Proceedings of the IEEE 29th International Conference on the Advanced Information Networking and Applications (AINA) (2015)
40. Struska, J.: Tonic Clonic/Grand Mal Seizure. https://www.youtube.com/watch?v=Nds2U4CzvC4. Accessed 6 April 2017
41. Wu, X.D., Kumar, V., Quinlan, J.R., Ghosh, J., Yang, Q., Motoda, H., McLachlan, G.J., Ng, A., Liu, B., Yu, P.S., et al.: Top 10 algorithms in data mining. Knowl. Inf. Syst. **14**(1), 1–37 (2008)

Tip-Toe Walking Detection Using CPG Parameters from Skeleton Data Gathered by Kinect

Rasool Taban[1], Atoosa Parsa[1], and Hadi Moradi[1,2(✉)]

[1] Advanced Robotics and Intelligent Systems Laboratory, School of ECE,
College of Engineering, University of Tehran, Tehran, Iran
{rasooltaban,a.parsa,moradih}@ut.ac.ir
[2] Intelligent Systems Research Institute, SKKU, Suwon, South Korea

Abstract. Distinguishing tip-toe walking from normal walking, in human locomotion patterns, becomes important in applications such as Autism disorder identification. In this paper, we propose a novel approach for tip-toe walking detection based on the walk's Central Pattern Generator (CPG) parameters. In the proposed approach, the tip-toe walking is modeled by a CPG. Then, the motions of subjects are recorded and skeleton data are extracted using the first-generation Microsoft Kinect sensor. The CPG parameters of these motions are determined and compared to the given patterns to distinguish between tip-toe walking and normal walking. The accuracy of classification is promising while further data will improve the accuracy rate.

Keywords: Central pattern generator · Gait recognition · Activity recognition · Tip-toe walking detection · Skeletal tracking · Autism Spectrum Disorder

1 Introduction

Nowadays, off the shelf intelligent sensors play a great role in human's daily life. Because of their wide availability they can be used in various tasks such as human behavior perception and activity recognition [1–6]. Activity recognition, as a field of human behavior recognition, has been of great interest in the last three decades. This field has many applications, from surveillance and healthcare systems to human-computer interaction and Internet of Things [7–10]. From these sensors, the vision-based sensors have been used widely for activity recognition due to rich and huge information that they provide. In the last decade, RGB-Depth sensors, as a subcategory of vision-based sensors, have been widely used by many researchers due to their low cost and rich development tool kits. Microsoft Kinect [11] is one of the most famous RGB-Depth sensors in educational researches because of its affordable price, good accuracy, and Software Development Kit (SDK) available for research and development.

One of the areas which these systems can be used is gait recognition, in which the locomotion pattern is detected. Gait recognition can be used for screening abnormality in movement or can be used for improving/correcting movements. One of the

© Springer International Publishing AG 2017
S.F. Ochoa et al. (Eds.): UCAmI 2017, LNCS 10586, pp. 287–298, 2017.
DOI: 10.1007/978-3-319-67585-5_30

abnormalities in movements is related to children with Autism, who fall into Autism Spectrum Disorder (ASD) which is a kind of cognitive disability with symptoms shown in communication and social difficulties and repetitive patterns of behavior [12]. One of the most common habits in individuals with ASD is tip-toe walking that can be used as a feature to distinguish individuals with ASD from normal children. In other words, if we can detect tip-toe walking with high accuracy then we can use that to determine whether a person has Autism or not.

In general, activity recognition is used in different tasks such as person identification and helping old people in their daily life [6, 13, 14]. For instance, Sung et al. [4] tried to recognize 12 different activities using Microsoft Kinect in different environments. The final goal of that research was making personal assistant robots capable of operating in different situations. Zhang et al. [5] proposed a system for tracking old people using Microsoft Kinect. They tried to detect abnormal activities which are dangerous for them, especially activities which are related to falling. Their system could detect 5 different activities using skeleton joints features. Those activities are standing, falling from standing, falling from sitting, sitting on the chair, and sitting on the floor.

One of the areas in activity recognition is the gait recognition, in which a specific motion or a pattern in motion is recognized. The common approach for gait recognition is the feature extraction from raw data, which comes from RGB-Depth sensor. Then, the classification step with these features is applicable [15]. One of the issues in this approach is the noise involved in the features extracted from a motion. In this paper, we introduce a new gait modeling approach based on Central Pattern Generator (CPG) [16, 17]. CPG is a bio-inspired approach to produce periodic locomotion signals, inspired from animals [18], and using those signals to produce rhythmic motions for robots. Here, we utilize this idea to extract features from human's walking patterns in the form of CPG. In other words, gaits, such as tip-toe walking, are modeled by CPG and these models are used to compare a given gait to the available ones to classify it. Figure 1 shows a comparison of the structure of the gait recognition system including the common approaches and our proposed one.

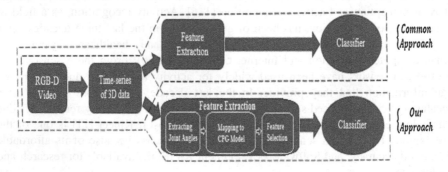

Fig. 1. Structure of the gate recognition system with common approach vs. our approach

In the rest of the paper, first we explain our method which consists of the CPG specifications, feature extraction, and classification details. Next, in Sect. 3 we describe the test configuration that has been used for this purpose. Last two sections are the results and conclusion parts.

2 Methodology

2.1 Central Pattern Generator

Since locomotion is a basic ability for real world creatures, it has a great significance in building robotic creatures too. Exploring new control methodologies for legged locomotion has been of great interest, especially in the recent decades. Inspired from the process underlying the generation of coordinated rhythmic behaviors both in invertebrate and vertebrate animals, CPG has been introduced as a new paradigm for controlling autonomous robots.

Considering a legged robot, the first step towards a successful locomotion is to find suitable trajectories for each of the individual joints in a robot's legs. CPGs are used to produce periodic stable trajectories for robot's active joints. The idea is based on encoding rhythmic trajectories as limit cycles of a nonlinear dynamical system [18]. Similar to a dynamical system paradigm, in which an oscillator is a system with a single stable limit cycle, here, the system is made of a set of coupled oscillators. Because of the properties such as stability, tolerance to perturbations, and online modulation using small parameter changes, CPGs have been applied widely to the biped and quadruped robots [19].

In [20] a system of coupled adaptive oscillators is presented that can learn any periodic input signal. The oscillators are adaptive frequency Hopf oscillators, which can learn the frequency of the input signal. Figure 2, shows the structure of such a network. The dynamical equations governing each oscillator's behavior and equations of the CPG are given in [20].

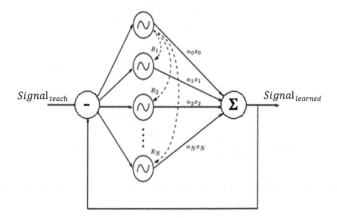

Fig. 2. Structure of the network of coupled adaptive Hopf oscillators [20]

To explain our proposed approach, a short introduction to CPG is given. Each oscillator has five state variables representing its internal dynamics. Adaptation is an intrinsic property of this oscillator and the evolution rule is designed such that imposing a periodic input will cause the system's internal state to converge to one of the frequency components of the input signal.

As can be seen in Fig. 2, to generate each target signal, i.e. desired signal to be generated, a set of oscillators are trained and combined. Each oscillator i can be formulated as follows:

$$y_i = a_i \cdot \sin(\omega_i \cdot t + \phi_i) \tag{1}$$

in which α_i represents the oscillator's amplitude, ω_i is the frequency of the oscillator, and φ_i is its phase difference with oscillator 0, i.e. the base oscillator. The input to this system is the target signal while the output signal is the signal that is learned as the summation of weighted sinusoidals. The process of learning is to adjust these three parameters such that the error between the target and the output signal is minimized.

It should be mentioned that, in this way any periodic input will be simulated as a combination of several sinusoidals with different amplitudes and frequencies. The main innovation is that the dynamical system behind this procedure is a network of coupled oscillators with properties such as stability, tolerance to perturbations, and modulation of amplitude and frequency to the changed input signal.

When considering the problem of controlling a biped robot, a structure of coupling between each of these oscillators, utilized at each active joint, is used. For example Fig. 3 shows the structure used in [20]. This is because, practically, the signals used for actuating each joint are not completely independent of others.

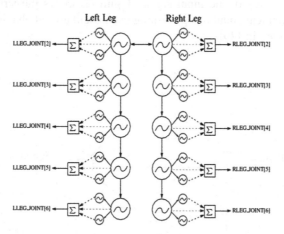

Fig. 3. Structure of the CPG for a bipedal gait. The input signal is given to each oscillator [20]

Choosing the number of oscillators for each joint trajectory is a trivial task, as the system has to adapt to main frequencies of the input signal. We will investigate the effect of this in the results section.

2.2 Classifying Semblables

As mentioned in the previous section, the idea behind CPG is to create similar movement to a motion using a combination of oscillators. In other words, CPG can be used to create similar motion to a desired motion. Thus, the produced motion is a formalized motion with high similarity to the desired motion. Consequently, it would be easier to work on this formalized version of the motion rather than working on the original noisy one. Thus, we propose the Semblable Classification in which the signals are classified based on the generated CPG version of them instead of classifying the original input signal. In this paper, we test the proposed approach on classifying tip-toe walking from normal walking. The CPG parameters of normal walking and tip-toe walking are used to extract features which are useful for distinguishing between these two walking patterns.

2.3 Motivation

Most of the methods developed for gait recognition are based on direct feature extraction. However, it is intuitive to find a space where features are more discriminative for our desired task. For instance, explicit features such as leg's joints' trajectories, step size, and Cartesian positions might not be useful to distinguish tip-toe from normal walking. Our novelty here is to move to another abstract space using the CPG model, where in that space there are features that are better discriminators for gait classification. As introduced before, CPGs are a network of coupled oscillators, inspired from the locomotion of animals, used to produce cyclic motions for robotic gaits. Here we consider the inverse problem, and find the CPG parameters supposing that the joint angle trajectories are the result of a CPG model. A mapping by the CPG model and using those parameters in this abstract higher space would lead to better results in gait recognition. It should be mentioned that in the process of moving to another space, i.e. the CPG space, the noises and less important information would be removed to ease the classification process.

2.4 Feature Extraction

Data used in this study is gathered using the first-generation Microsoft Kinect's 3D sensor. It benefits skeletal tracker algorithms to estimate 20 joints of a subject's body. These 3D points in the Cartesian space are filtered and used to design CPG for the walking patterns. In our first study [15], we considered the angles of the legs as features for walking classification task to detect tip-toe from normal patterns. Six angles were considered, three for each leg as is shown in Fig. 4. θ_1 and θ_4 are the angles between the vertical line and the thigh links, i.e. the link between the hip center and the knee. θ_2 and θ_5 are considered to be the angles between stalk links, i.e. the link between knee

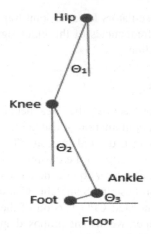

Fig. 4. This figure shows θ_1 through θ_3 from the side view of one leg

and the ankle, and the vertical line. Similarly, θ_3 and θ_6 are the angles between foot and the horizontal line parallel to the ground.

In this study, these 6 angles are considered to train the CPG for the lower part of a subject's body to model the walking pattern. For each angle different number of oscillators are considered with 3 parameters, i.e. α as the amplitude of sinusoid, ω as the frequency, and φ as the phase difference. Consequently, if, for example, we consider 3 oscillators for each angle, then we have 27 parameters for each leg.

In conclusion, in our proposed methodology, the structure of the CPG network, the number of oscillators and their coupling will be fixed. Then using the angle data extracted from subjects by Kinect sensor, we train the CPG network to find the best parameter set for each type of walking. In the next step, we use these parameters to classify new walking patterns into normal or tip-toe walking pattern.

2.5 Classification

We use different classifiers to distinguish tip-toe walkers from normal walkers and investigate the performance of each classifier and choose the best one. The classifiers that are used in this study are K-Nearest Neighbors (K-NN) as the simplest and basic classifier, Linear Support Vector Machine (SVM), Multi-layered perceptron (MLP) as a General Function Approximator (GFA), and Random Forest (RF). Linear SVM is used due to its advantages and frequent uses in different tasks and RF is selected as one of the best ensemble solutions. K-fold cross validation was applied with K = 5. Each classifier was executed 100 times to check that whether the success or failure has not been obtained by chance. Data was shuffled for each classification iteration to check the robustness of different methods.

We can describe our whole system as below:

1. Record RGB-D video from many subjects and crop the best part of each one as cleaned video.

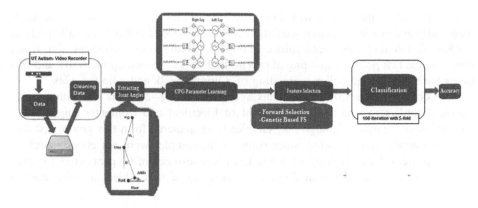

Fig. 5. The system's structure

2. Extract joint angles from cleaned videos as data.
3. Feed data to CPG network and learn the parameters.
4. Select best features from CPG parameters.
5. Examine the accuracy of different classifiers to distinguish tip-toe walkers from normal walkers.

The complete system structure is shown in Fig. 5.

3 Experiment and Test Configuration

Because there is no dataset available for this task, we implemented a platform that uses Microsoft Kinect as its main sensor to collect 3D data from subjects. The Graphical User Interface (GUI) of this platform is presented in Fig. 6. Each subject is asked to

Fig. 6. Screenshot of the system developed to gather data from individuals. The left video stream shows the raw RGB data, the middle one shows the skeleton overlapped on the raw image and the right video stream shows the extracted skeleton.

walk on front of the Kinect with two different policies. The first policy is to walk diagonally and in a linear path toward the Kinect. The second policy is to walk freely in the Kinect's field of view. Each subject is required to do this task six times, four times based on the first policy, consisting of two normal walks and two tip-toe walks and two times based on second policy, consisting of a normal walk and a tip-toe walk.

We collected data from 75 students aged between 18–26 years old with no particular disorders in walking at the school of Electrical and Computer Engineering, University of Tehran. Although 300 samples were gathered from this group, just 207 cleaned samples were selected, since some of the samples were not good enough to detect tip-toe walking even by a human. Data is time-series of 60 parameters for each person. These 60 parameters are 20 joints' data points of each subject in 3-dimensional space.

4   Simulation and Results

As we see the system structure in Fig. 5. First the extracted joint angles are fed to CPG network without joint coupling and obtain the CPG parameters. The CPG parameters are used to determine the best features using two different feature selection method (evolutionary feature selection method based on Genetic Algorithm and Forward feature selection). Then these features are used for classification.

We use RapidMiner Studio 7.3.0 for feature extraction and k-fold classification tasks. The average accuracy of each classifier is shown in Tables 1 and 2. As it can be seen, the results are not very good while the results after considering the joint couplings are better. That is actually expected since the joints work dependently while a subject

Table 1. Average Accuracy of Classifiers on 100 Executions With Joint Coupling

Oscillator	Classifier			
	KNN	Linear SVM	RF	MLP
1	65.14	66.80	62.28	71.95
2	74.52	77.93	66.66	79.70
3	74.56	72.86	65.03	75.36
4	70.41	70.21	66.01	72.00

Table 2. Specificity of Classifiers on 100 Executions With Joint Coupling

Oscillator	Classifier			
	KNN	Linear SVM	RF	MLP
1	0.67	0.71	0.88	0.80
2	0.76	0.82	0.89	0.85
3	0.82	0.73	0.86	0.79
4	0.73	0.73	0.89	0.71

move. As it can be seen, the results have improved in a range of 5–10 percent compared to the case in which the joints coupling was not considered. To see if the data for both legs are needed, we performed the above process considering one leg only and both legs. The result shows a little improvement when both legs are processed. Thus, we decided to perform the feature extraction and classification on both legs.

Table 3. Average Accuracy of Classifiers on 100 Executions Without Joint Coupling

Oscillator	Classifier			
	KNN	Linear SVM	RF	MLP
1	70.17	66.67	62.93	70.72
2	66.01	65.17	62.83	75.07
3	68.54	69.82	66.23	71.49
4	70.65	68.95	65.43	70.25

Table 4. Sensitivity of Classifiers on 100 Executions With Joint Coupling

Oscillator	Classifier			
	KNN	Linear SVM	RF	MLP
1	0.61	0.55	0.26	0.59
2	0.71	0.73	0.42	0.73
3	0.63	0.71	0.45	0.71
4	0.67	0.67	0.42	0.73

Table 5. Specificity of Classifiers on 100 Executions Without Joint Coupling

Oscillator	Classifier			
	KNN	Linear SVM	RF	MLP
1	0.63	0.65	0.83	0.74
2	0.67	0.82	0.83	0.82
3	0.73	0.85	0.83	0.77
4	0.76	0.82	0.91	0.76

Table 6. Sensitivity of Classifiers on 100 Executions Without Joint Coupling

Oscillator	Classifier			
	KNN	Linear SVM	RF	MLP
1	0.76	0.67	0.34	0.70
2	0.65	0.42	0.32	0.65
3	0.59	0.48	0.42	0.63
4	0.63	0.51	0.30	0.63

For better comparison between results, sensitivity and specificity for every condition are shown in Tables 3, 4, 5 and 6. Tables 3 and 4 are sensitivity and specificity results of data with coupling. Tables 5 and 6 are sensitivity and specificity results of data without coupling.

To further evaluate the classification process and its accuracy, the classifier type and the number of oscillators used at each joint were analyzed. In the following sections we consider each of these cases and analyze the results in more detail.

4.1   Type of Classifier

The type of classifier plays a significant role in the classification's accuracy. KNN with k = 5, linear kernel for SVM classifier, RF with 50 trees, and MLP with 1 hidden layer. In our study, MLP has the best accuracy in both joint coupling strategies because of the good number of samples. As shown in Tables 3 and 4, MLP has the best sensitivity result with rate of 73% and good specificity result with rate of 85%. On the other hand, Linear SVM and KNN lead to better results than Random Forest. Linear SVM seems to be a good classifier for this problem specially in coupled joints approach, because it is well-suited for binary classification problem and linearity of its kernel makes the computation easier than other two classifiers. When we subtilize the sensitivity and specificity results, we can see Linear SVM is nearly strong as MLP specially when we consider joint coupling. Random Forest weaker result derived from less number of features for learning, if we notice sensitivity and specificity results, we can see the best specificity result that shows, this approach is very powerful to recognize normal walking but very poor in tip-toe walking recognition.

4.2   Number of Oscillators

The number of oscillators affects the accuracy of CPG's estimated parameters. We tested 1, 2, 3, and 4 oscillators per joint, with 18, 36, 54, and 72 features respectively, to evaluate the effect of the number of oscillators. As it is shown in Tables 1 and 2, increasing the number of oscillators does not lead to better classification rate. Because our training signal is time-limited, the error signal, which is the difference between learning and learned signal, cannot be decreased below a certain point, so the output is not fully mapped to the target signal. Furthermore, more number of oscillators led us to overfitting to learning signal and decreases the average accuracy; even so, less number of oscillators especially 1 oscillator per joint cannot learn input signal with high accuracy because of multi sinusoidal input signal. Nevertheless, we can find best accuracy with 2 oscillators per joints.

5   Conclusion

In this paper, we introduced an approach to distinguish tip-toe walking from normal walking using semblable CPGs rather than the original walking patterns. This approach can be used in applications such as autism screening and games. In this approach we use inverse problem of CPG to extract 3 basic parameter of CPG. Parameters are extracted from time-series data of subject's legs' angles. Extracted parameters fed as input data to different classifiers. The system has been tested on 75 normal people's data that consist of two different walking patterns. With comparison of obtained results, MLP has better performance than three other classifiers. But more samples are needed to conclude confidently. It was also shown that the correlation between the joint angles cannot be ignored system it would decrease the accuracy of classification. The experiment shows about 20% increase in the classification when joints are considered coupled.

In the next step, we would perform input signal extrapolation to solve short duration problem of input signals. Furthermore, more data would be collected to improve the classification accuracy.

We also hope to test our approach on children with autism to make sure the goal of the project, i.e. screening of the children with autism, can be achieved.

Acknowledgments. This research is partially funded by Cognitive Sciences and Technologies Council (COGC) of Iran. Special thanks to Dr. Babak Nadjar Araabi and Dr. Hamid Reza Pour Etemad and Centre for the Treatment of Autistic Disorders (CTAD) for their help. We want to thank all members of Advanced Robotics and Intelligent Systems (ARIS) Lab for their generous help.

References

1. Pantic, M., Pentland, A., Nijholt, A., Huang, T.S.: Human computing and machine understanding of human behavior: a survey. In: Huang, T.S., Nijholt, A., Pantic, M., Pentland, A. (eds.) Artifical Intelligence for Human Computing. LNCS, vol. 4451, pp. 47–71. Springer, Heidelberg (2007). doi:10.1007/978-3-540-72348-6_3
2. Brdiczka, O., Langet, M., Maisonnasse, J., Crowley, J.L.: Detecting human behavior models from multimodal observation in a smart home. IEEE Trans. Autom. Sci. Eng. **6**, 588–597 (2009)
3. Pentland, A.: Looking at people: sensing for ubiquitous and wearable computing. IEEE Trans. Pattern Anal. Mach. Intell. **22**, 107–119 (2000)
4. Sung, J., Ponce, C., Selman, B., Saxena, A.: Human activity detection from RGBD images. In: IEEE International Conference on Robotics and Automation, pp. 842–849 (2011)
5. Zhang, C., Tian, Y.: RGB-D camera-based daily living activity recognition. J. Comput. Vis. Image Process. **2**, 12 (2012)
6. Yang, X., Tian, Y.: Effective 3D action recognition using Eigenjoints. J. Vis. Commun. Image Represent. **25**, 2–11 (2014)
7. Steele, R., Lo, A., Secombe, C., Wong, Y.K.: Elderly persons' perception and acceptance of using wireless sensor networks to assist healthcare. Int. J. Med. Inform. **78**, 788–801 (2009)
8. Atzori, L., Iera, A., Morabito, G.: The internet of things: a survey. Comput. Netw. **54**, 2787–2805 (2010)
9. León, O., Hernández-Serrano, J., Soriano, M.: Internet of things. Int. J. Commun. Syst. **23**, 633–652 (2010)
10. Weber, R.H., Weber, R.: Internet of Things. Springer, Heidelberg (2010). doi:10.1007/978-3-642-11710-7
11. Zhang, Z.: Microsoft kinect sensor and its effect. IEEE Multimed. **19**, 4–10 (2012)

12. Bell, C.C.: DSM-IV: diagnostic and statistical manual of mental disorders. JAMA **272**, 828–829 (1994)
13. Zhang, H., Parker, L.E.: 4-Dimensional local spatio-temporal features for human activity recognition. In: IEEE International Conference on Intelligent Robots and Systems (IROS), pp. 2044–2049 (2011)
14. Popa, M., Kemal Koc, A., Rothkrantz, L.J.M., Shan, C., Wiggers, P.: Kinect sensing of shopping related actions. In: Wichert, R., Van Laerhoven, K., Gelissen, J. (eds.) AmI 2011. CCIS, vol. 277, pp. 91–100. Springer, Heidelberg (2012). doi:10.1007/978-3-642-31479-7_16
15. Ebrahimi, M., Feghi, M., Moradi, H., Mirian, M., Pouretemad, H.: Distinguishing tip-toe walking from normal walking using skeleton data gathered by 3D sensors, pp. 1–6 (2015)
16. Bucher, D., Haspel, G., Golowasch, J., Nadim, F., Bucher, D., Haspel, G., Golowasch, J., Nadim, F.: Central pattern generators. Encyclopedia of Life Sciences, pp. 1–12. Wiley, Chichester, UK (2015)
17. Grillner, S., Wallen, P.: Central pattern generators for locomotion, with special reference to vertebrates. Annu. Rev. Neurosci (2003). doi:10.1146/annurev.ne.08.030185.001313
18. Ijspeert, A.J.: Central pattern generators for locomotion control in animals and robots: a review. Neural Netw. **21**, 642–653 (2008)
19. Righetti, L., Ijspeert, A.J.: Pattern generators with sensory feedback for the control of quadruped locomotion. In: Proceedings - IEEE International Conference on Robotics and Automation, pp. 819–824 (2008)
20. Righetti, L., Ijspeert, A.J.: Programmable central pattern generators: an application to biped locomotion control. In: Proceedings IEEE ICRA, pp. 1585–1590 (2006)

Couplable Components for Data Processing in Mobile Sensing Campaigns

Daniel Maya-Zapata, Iván R. Félix, Luis A. Castro[✉], Luis-Felipe Rodríguez, and Manuel Domitsu

Sonora Institute of Technology (ITSON), Ciudad Obregon, Mexico
daniel_maya94@hotmail.com, rogelio.felix@gmail.com,
luis.castro@acm.org,
{luis.rodriguez,manuel.domitsu}@itson.edu.mx

Abstract. In mobile sensing, modern phones allow scientists obtain the information about the participants and their surroundings. At times, obtaining raw sensor data from mobile devices demands their collection through sensing campaigns. Often, processing these data requires data processing components in the mobile device. Some of the data processing components pertain to mathematical functions that can be reused to form other functions. These types of functions are usually crafted at a design stage by the programmers. In this work, we present a novel way in which components can be coupled at the design of the sensing campaign, without the need to redeploy the app. That is, scientists can couple two existing data processing components into a new, high-level component. The results of this paper can facilitate code re-use, code maintenance, and flexibility to a mobile sensing campaign.

Keywords: Mobile phone sensing · Sensing platform · Data processing components · Couplable components

1 Introduction

When doing research, acquiring data from experiments or fieldwork could take a considerable amount of effort depending on what is needed. Mobile phones have become one of the preferred tools to collect data about users' behavior and their surroundings through sensing campaigns. A sensing campaign is a planned enterprise for collecting data from end users, typically through a research protocol. A sensing campaign defines what data are to be captured and when. That is, what sensors are needed, how and when these sensors will be used, and if there are going to be some processing of the collected data in the mobile device.

Mobile sensing has been used in different domains. For instance in health, they have promoted wellbeing [1, 2], and monitored the quality of the sleep [3]; in psychology to gather personality traits [4]; in urbanity to help create maps of noise pollution [4], map potholes or problematic traffic areas [5], and finally, in human computer interaction to create better ways to interact with the smartphone [6, 7]. Most of the works mentioned earlier usually construct a mobile software tool to fulfill the sensing campaign to be

© Springer International Publishing AG 2017
S.F. Ochoa et al. (Eds.): UCAmI 2017, LNCS 10586, pp. 299–304, 2017.
DOI: 10.1007/978-3-319-67585-5_31

deployed. These developed tools can be hardly reused in a different sensing campaign without modifying their very essence.

There are some works that have aimed at enabling scientists to obtain data from mobile phones without developing a software tool from scratch every time. One of them is AndWellness [8], developed for obtaining data from end users through surveys that are launched based on a schedule or on a reduced set of events that AndWellness is able to detect. Also, MyExperience [9], a platform that presented a more elaborated architecture, through which you can select from a set of available sensors to obtain data, monitor the gathered data by triggers to detect particulars events, and take actions based on detected events. Finally, Funf [10] and AWARE framework [11] aim at easing development of sensing tools by providing pre-programed routines that allows a developer to easily access a sensor or send the collected data to remote repositories. In this work, we present a mechanism to couple components in a sensing campaign, which can facilitate code reuse and maintenance in sensing campaigns.

2 Problem Statement

Most current platforms for sensing campaigns place particular emphasis on collecting raw data from sensors for server-side processing or offline analysis in the lab. However, it is important to have on-device data analysis for several reasons, including privacy, data annotation and anonymization, or reducing network traffic. Often times, scientists use algorithms for pre-processing or processing data. In many cases, there are algorithms that make use of other known algorithms. Formally, these algorithms can be represented as functions f, g and h. If $f:A \rightarrow B$ and $g:B \rightarrow C$, we define h as a composite function, which is denoted by:

$$h:A \rightarrow C, \; by \, h(a) = g(f(a)), \; for \; each \, a \in A$$

In most sensing platforms, scientists re-use existing functions from previous works. Having all these functions in separate components makes it easier to maintain. Moreover, some functions are used throughout several application domains (e.g., Fourier transform, step counter), so they can be re-used by several scientists. These types of functions, which we call low-level functions, hardly ever change, and relate to mathematical functions underlying complex computations. There are, however, other functions that may be much more complex in terms of the sensors they use, the information they need, and the computations they need. These functions, which we refer to them as high-level functions, can use several sensors or even some of the aforementioned low-level functions. Programmatically speaking, however, connecting these functions at runtime requires standard definitions of those components so that they can send one's output to another's input.

Therefore, there is a need for a mechanism that can be used to effortlessly connect two components during the design of the sensing campaign. In a conventional approach, this is carried out during design stage, by a programmer, who needs to code, compile, debug, and finally build the project. This means that this process has to be carried out offline and further updates of the application need to be pushed to the end user participating in the sensing campaign. Finally, having a composite function *h* requires assessing whether *f* and *g* functions are compatible. That is, we need to know if the output of the function *f* can be understood as valid arguments (i.e., input) to the function *g*. Again, programmatically speaking, depending on the language, this can be carried out during design stage by the programmer or during runtime (by throwing an exception). Therefore, it is desirable to have a compatibility assessment during the design of the campaign, not by the programmer, but by the scientist herself.

3   Couplable Components Paradigm in Mobile Sensing Campaigns

This work draws on a mobile phone sensing platform called InCense [12, 13]. InCense was conceived as a means wherein scientists interested in analyzing behavior data from populations could create sensing campaigns. In [13], a component-based model for mobile sensing is proposed, which facilitates on-device analytics. This model relies on on-device analytics for data pre-processing, and provides a way to incorporate new processing components into the mobile phone sensing platform.

The component-based model is based on the idea of having loosely-coupled components within the mobile phone app. In doing so, the components can be individually and remotely updated without directly modifying the mobile phone app source code, meaning that participants will not be bothered with frequent app updates. The couplable components paradigm uses two main types of components which we called low and high-level components. Low-level components are those functions that hardly ever change, and can be the building blocks of components of a higher level of abstraction. Also, high-level components necessarily involve the use of low-level components. This paradigm is based on the following premises: (a) Low-level components can be re-used in other high-level components, (b) Low-level components can be coupled in an effortlessly fashion, (c) High-level components can be readily used by others, and (d) the graphical user interface (GUI) must identify component compatibility.

For this to work out, the component structure has to be known. The component-based model is based on a standard definition of a component called component schema (see [13]). This schema is used to establish the required elements of a component for generating a code that can be seamlessly integrated into the InCense client (i.e., mobile phone app) at runtime. Because components need to connect to each other, then the schema is used to match among those compatible components through the InputDataType and OuputDataType definitions. This, in turn, is used to obtain high-level components, out of low-level components.

A RESTful web service provides a list of all the component schemas defined in the server. Following Fig. 1, in the *Work Area*, the components listed on the left (i.e., menu) can be dragged and dropped, where the scientist can compose new high-level components based on low-level components. All of the components that are linked in the *Work Area* make up the new high-level component. In the background, the InCense platform connects the existing components into a high-level component. High-level components are not necessarily made of source code, but rather they are a JSON-based mechanism that internally redirects the execution of the components, and also directs the outputs to the corresponding inputs.

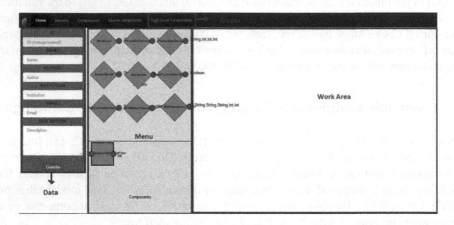

Fig. 1. Graphical User Interface of the scientist for coupling high-level components

Based on the list of components schema retrieved from the web service, the GUI reflects those components that are compatible with each other by displaying a different color (see Fig. 2). The input and output of each component is visually displayed for the scientist to see before creating a connection between them.

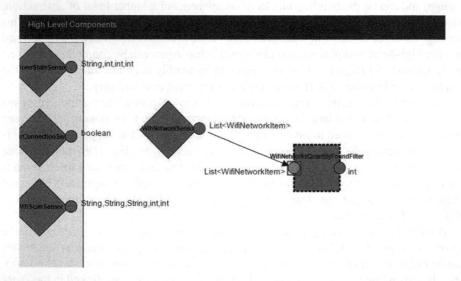

Fig. 2. When coupling components, component compatibility can be visually verified

To illustrate how this couplable components work, consider the example presented in Fig. 3, in which there is a *Socialization Component* that takes the audio signal from the *audio sensor* (i.e., microphone), and then decides whether there is human voice in the audio excerpt. Apart from the audio coming from the microphone, there is one that extracts the *Audio Signal Features*. Then, based on those features, there is a *Human Voice Classifier* that makes the actual classification of the audio into the following classes: 0 for No Human Voice, 1 for #1 human voice, 2 for #2 human voice, and so on. Depending on the number of voices detected in the audio excerpt, the *Socialization Component* decides how sociable the individual is. Following Fig. 3, one of the most important features is that the boxes are independently created functions, and that they are treated as black boxes, meaning that we only care for the inputs needed and the outputs generated. Although the source code can be in fact inspected, this is only needed for debugging or code optimization purposes.

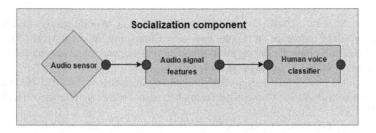

Fig. 3. Socialization component high-level component

4   Closing Remarks

In this work, we presented the couplable components paradigm for mobile sensing campaigns. Compared to the conventional approach, the work presented in this paper has several advantages: functions can be independently created by third parties, increase in code re-use, faster and easier code maintenance, and scientist involvement in component creation. In a traditional mobile sensing approach, programmers do most of the work beforehand, and later changes to code may lead to redeploying the application, and pushing it to the participants of the sensing campaign. Also, in the latter, the design of the sensing campaign usually goes hand in hand with coding, which may be too rigid for sensing campaigns usually demand adjustments during execution.

Compared with the traditional approaches, the approach presented in this paper is much more flexible as it allows the scientist to create high-level components based on existing functions. As of now, InCense only supports two levels: low and high levels, but some functions can be so complex that they can be formed by more than two levels. Also, with this approach, the design of the components can be separated from coding, enabling the scientist to create new high-level components. In addition, code maintenance is much more efficient since an update to an existing function has to be carried out only once, rather than updating all the components that use that algorithm.

Although the current component compatibility feature can be somewhat inefficient, this can be enhanced if colors or different shapes are used in the connectors, having compatible connectors use the same color/shape combination. This can be fine for a reduced number of components, but as the number grows, finding an available combination can be difficult. For now, we decided to rely on match verification once the output connector is being dropped onto the input connector of the next component. A better way to show the compatibility between two components is needed. As future work, we are considering creating multi-level components that can be used to create much more complex sensing campaigns by dragging and dropping components on a GUI.

Acknowledgements. This work was partially funded by the Instituto Tecnológico de Sonora through grant #PROFAPI_2016_0041.

References

1. Consolvo, S., et al.: Activity sensing in the wild: a field trial of ubifit garden. In: Proceedings of the SIGCHI Conference on Human Factors in Computing Systems. ACM (2008)
2. Lane, N.D., et al.: Bewell: sensing sleep, physical activities and social interactions to promote wellbeing. Mob. Netw. Appl. **19**(3), 345–359 (2014)
3. Chen, Z., et al.: Unobtrusive sleep monitoring using smartphones. In: 2013 7th International Conference on Pervasive Computing Technologies for Healthcare (PervasiveHealth). IEEE (2013)
4. Chittaranjan, G., Blom, J., Gatica-Perez, D.: Who's who with big-five: analyzing and classifying personality traits with smartphones. In: 2011 15th Annual International Symposium on Wearable Computers (ISWC). IEEE (2011)
5. Mohan, P., Padmanabhan, V.N., Ramjee, R.: Nericell: rich monitoring of road and traffic conditions using mobile smartphones. In: Proceedings of the 6th ACM Conference on Embedded Network Sensor Systems. ACM (2008)
6. Campbell, A., et al.: NeuroPhone: brain-mobile phone interface using a wireless EEG headset. In: Proceedings of the Second ACM SIGCOMM Workshop on Networking, Systems, and Applications on Mobile Handhelds. ACM (2010)
7. Miluzzo, E., Wang, T., Campbell, A.T.: EyePhone: activating mobile phones with your eyes. In: Proceedings of the Second ACM SIGCOMM Workshop on Networking, Systems, and Applications on Mobile Handhelds. ACM (2010)
8. Hicks, J., et al.: AndWellness: an open mobile system for activity and experience sampling. In: Wireless Health 2010. ACM (2010)
9. Froehlich, J., et al.: MyExperience: a system for in situ tracing and capturing of user feedback on mobile phones. In: Proceedings of the 5th International Conference on Mobile Systems, Applications and Services. ACM (2007)
10. Xue, Q.L., et al.: Life-space constriction, development of frailty, and the competing risk of mortality: the Women's Health and Aging Study I. Am. J. Epidemiol. **167**, 240–248 (2008)
11. Ferreira, D., Kostakos, V., Dey, A.K.: AWARE: mobile context instrumentation framework. Front. ICT **2**, 6 (2015)
12. Castro, L.A., et al.: Behavioral data gathering for assessing functional status and health in older adults using mobile phones. Pers. Ubiquit. Comput. **19**(2), 379–391 (2015)
13. Félix, I.R., Castro, L.A., Rodríguez, L.F., Ruíz, E.C.: Component-based model for on-device pre-processing in mobile phone sensing campaigns. In: García, C., Caballero-Gil, P., Burmester, M., Quesada-Arencibia, A. (eds.) Ubiquitous Computing and Ambient Intelligence. UCAmI 2016. LNCS, vol. 10069. Springer, Cham (2016). doi: 10.1007/978-3-319-48746-5_20

Affective Avatar Interactions: Towards Recognizing Emotions in Verbal Interaction

Esperanza Johnson[1(✉)], Ramón Hervás[1(✉)], Carlos Gutiérrez-López-Franca[1],
Tania Mondéjar[1,2], and José Bravo[1]

[1] MAmI Research Lab, University of Castilla-La Mancha, Paseo de la Universidad 4, Ciudad Real, Spain
{MEsperanza.Johnson,Ramon.Hlucas,Carlos.Gutierrez,
jose.bravo}@uclm.es, Tania.mondejar@esmile.es
[2] eSmile, Psychology for Children and Adolescents, Calle Toledo 79 1°E, Ciudad Real, Spain
http://mami.uclm.es

Abstract. In current times, virtual agents, also known as avatars, are being used for many different tasks, from helping guide a user experience, to aiding in the diagnosis and treatment of different health issues, both physical and mental. In past work, we have explored the use of an affective avatar that responds to tactile interaction with a pc–tablet, the response from the users and the possible uses for aiding the diagnosis and treatment of Social Communications Disorders. In this paper, we present our proposal as a work in progress, based on our previous work with an affective avatar, but adding verbal interaction. We will also discuss what future work we have thought of doing with this particular interaction of the model.

Keywords: Cognitive computing · Affective computing · Affective avatar · IBM Watson

1 Introduction

In recent times, we have seen an emergence of technologies that use avatars to give support to the diagnosis and treatment of different health issues. While many of these proposals are quite interesting, a lot of them focus more on helping or guiding the people with their physical ailments. For the cases of mental health, there are several options that we have found to be interesting, but they are not focused on the same solution we are trying to provide.

As it is, in this paper we are focusing on that void, with the capabilities of a software to recognize and show emotion. In this particular case, we will focus more on the recognition of the basic emotional states a user can present, and we will have our avatar mirror those emotions with facial expressions. With this, we aim to engage the user on an emotional level when interacting with the avatar. The goal of this is to engage their emotions to improve their emotional management, as well as to promote empathy in their interactions with others.

In this paper we will present the works we have studied in Sect. 2, with Sect. 3 dedicated towards our intention for the new functionalities that our avatar will have. Section 4 is dedicated to explaining the experiment we will carry out, and how it ties in

© Springer International Publishing AG 2017
S.F. Ochoa et al. (Eds.): UCAmI 2017, LNCS 10586, pp. 305–310, 2017.
DOI: 10.1007/978-3-319-67585-5_32

with our previous work, as well as the expectations we have for the results of the experiment itself. Finally, we will end with Sect. 5, which will cover the conclusions and the future work we intent to do.

2 Related Work

To better understand what has been done, and what we can contribute with our work, we explored other work that relates to what we are trying to achieve. In those terms, we focused our search of related work on avatars, as well as avatars related to the area of health, and software that detects emotion from the user.

Related work in the area of avatars and health include the creation of a multimodal affective user interface (MAUI) [1] to capture the user's emotional physiological signals using wearable technology, and whose avatar mirrors the user's facial expressions. There was also work related to building an on-demand avatar-based health intervention [2], with an avatar that showed emotions, and acted as the recipient of health-related consultations. Another example of avatars for health is an eCounsellor that simulates facial animations and advice of a professional psychologist to support undergraduate students in stress management during their exams [3].

On the area of emotion recognition, we have seen different approaches that range from emotion recognition using facial expressions, speech and multimodal information [4], a framework for emotion recognition from speech [5] and speech emotion recognition using Fourier parameters [6].

While all of these works have an interesting approach, they cover different aspects of a person's needs; from an avatar showing emotion and responding to emotional cues from users to make them feel more comfortable, to simply gathering data. From this point of view, our avatar differs from these works by having its emotional response be an integral part of the proposal instead of an aspect to give more realism to the avatar, or to make the user feel more comfortable. On the front of emotion recognition, we are not using facial recognition to infer the emotional state of the user, and we are not using a tone analyzer in the traditional sense of the word. What we are using is an API from IBM Watson™ which analyzes the words that are being said by the user, and extracts data such as the conveyed emotion (IBM Watson Tone Analyzer).

We will now proceed to describe our intention for the next phase in our work, followed by the experiment to perform, and our intentions and expectations for it.

3 Emotion Recognition Through Voice

Taking into account our previous proposal with tactile interaction, we felt it was an interesting and necessary approach to integrate verbal interaction as well. Given this decision, there were several options that could be taken, as exemplified in Sect. 2 by some of the studied works. One of the important points of the verbal interaction was that it should not be just a simple Speech-To-Text from the user to the avatar, and then a verbal response from the avatar to the user. This is due to our previous statement that the emotions in our avatar were an integral part of it, hence our decision that said verbal interaction should also have a component of emotion recognition.

Due to this, we were left with some of the options that were exemplified in Sect. 2; which were the classical emotion recognition through facial expressions (in its many variations), or emotion recognition through the analysis of the tone, which falls under the area of signal analysis. When studying our options, we came across the technology developed by IBM, called IBM Watson, which has several services that can be used as APIs. One of those APIs is called Tone Analyzer, which does not analyze the pitch or the variations of the voice of the user, but uses the text of what the user says, and analyzes the contents of the text, assigning different values to the sentences. These values are categorized in three clearly differentiated sets: emotions, language style and social tendencies. Each of those sets can take different values, with the set of emotions having the similar values to Paul Ekman's basic emotions, which are joy, sadness, fear, anger and disgust, without the surprised emotion being among the values that can be assigned. Each emotion is given a value between 0 and 1, with a value of <0.5 indicating that it is likely not present, >0.5 that it is likely present, and a value greater than 0.75 being that it is very likely present. With this information, our proposal is to use IBM Watson Speech-To-Text, so that it will feed that text to IBM Watson Tone Analyzer, which in turn will give us all the information we have previously mentioned. At this current point of the proposal, we will be focusing on the output for the set of emotions. Depending on the value given out of the possible five, it will be classed as a positive or negative, and the changes in the avatar will be influenced depending on the type of interaction the system has classed the words of the user to be.

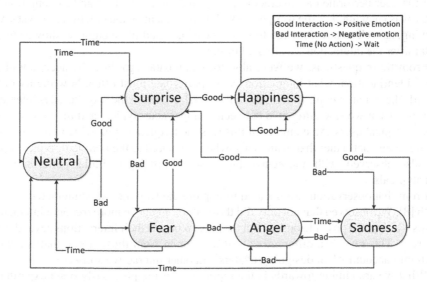

Fig. 1. The state machine that represents the transition between states according to the emotion detected and how it translates into a positive or negative interaction.

According to the type of interaction, the avatar will react positively to positive emotions (classed as good interaction), and negatively to negative emotions (classed as bad interaction). This kind of process can be seen in Fig. 1 below.

Having seen how we would proceed to incorporate verbal interaction into the avatar, and how the avatar itself would react to said interaction, we will now proceed to the final section of this paper. In it we will discuss our intentions in terms of the application we hope to do with this system.

4   Experiment Design and Expectation

After exploring what we are going to be implementing into our avatar, in this section we will discuss the experiment we are currently performing with the avatar (which is still in progress), as well as the results we are expecting given past experiments with the previous iteration of our avatar.

In a previous work [7], we performed two experiments, with two different groups of people, and proceeded to analyze the results of both groups individually and also comparatively. There was a group of 30 neurotypical users, which are those users without any cognitive issue or disability, and a group of 20 non-neurotypical users. Both groups were subdivided into different cohorts, where the neurotypicals were subdivided by age, and the non-neurotypicals were subdivided according to their cognitive issue (in this case, Down's syndrome and Intellectual Disability).

For everyone involved in the experiment, we asked the same questions and extracted the same data. The experiment consisted in showing the avatar in its starting point (showing the emotion neutral) and, due to the nature of the experiment, the users could only perform one of three possible interactions: caress, poke (both tactile) or wait. Each time the user performed an interaction, we noted the interaction and the emotion the avatar was showing. For the user, we asked them to identify the emotion the avatar was showing, as well as how they felt towards the avatar, and if the emotion showed by the avatar after the interaction was logical or not.

From those questions, we were able to obtain data regarding the accuracy of the users' identification, what interactions were performed most often, how the users felt towards the avatar overall, validation of the model, etc. From the way the users interacted with the avatar we saw difference between younger neurotypical and the older cohorts of neurotypical users. An example of this was the frequency with which younger users choose to interact rather than wait. This, when compared to the non-neurotypical users, was also observed, with non-neurotypical users following a similar patter as young neurotypicals.

From that observation, we decided to explore the way the users interacted more in depth [8]. We observed that not only did those users engage in more frequent interaction, versus waiting as a possible option, but they also repeated their interactions several times in a row. This reveals a different way of interacting from those users, that should be taken into account when designing avatars and other interactive software.

What we are aiming towards is the replication of the previously done experiment, but instead of using tactile interaction, it would be performed with verbal interaction.

This means that the user would only be able to communicate with the avatar through voice, as they would do in any regular conversation with another person. From their words, we would use IBM Watson's Speech-To-Text API to input their words into Watson's Tone Analyzer API, which would give us the emotional tone of their words. This information would be fed to our avatar's code, which would classify the emotions that we have been provided as positive or negative, and then consider them as a positive or negative interaction with the avatar, as it could be seen before in Fig. 1. The way the avatar would work on a global level can be seen in Fig. 2 below.

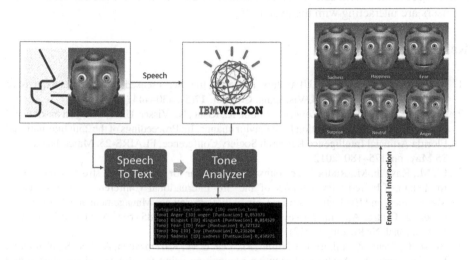

Fig. 2. Flow of the interaction with the avatar, and the processes that lead to the change in its facial expression.

With this replication we will analyze the results given by the experiment in an individual manner, as we did in previous work. But the replication of the experiment with the same format will also serve to see if the affective interaction differs when the interaction is verbal, versus tactile.

5 Conclusions and Future Work

From our previous work, and the related work that we have studied, we can conclude that the work with avatars, and affective avatars, is something that is novel and thus, still open to many different applications. In our particular case, we can conclude that the natural progression of our work implied implementing more types of interaction. Given the types of interaction that usually come into play when people interact among themselves, it was only logical to follow up the work and studies done with tactile interaction with verbal interaction.

Considering this, our future work would not only consist on implementing this model, but performing tests with it. Due to the nature of our previous work, which studied the way users interacted and reacted to the avatar, we would perform the same test. This would be done to study how the users interact with the avatar when the interaction is verbal, and we would also perform a comparative study, to observe if there is any difference between the interaction when it is tactile and when it is verbal.

We would also perform these tests with neurotypical and non-neurotypical users, to maximize the comparisons, not just between tactile and verbal interaction, but among the different users and cohorts as well.

This system would later be combined with others, such as activity recognition [9] to better observe the interaction of users at a different level, as well as EEG correlates when the users are interacting with the avatar [10].

References

1. Nasoz, F., Lisetti, C.L.: MAUI avatars: mirroring the user's sensed emotions via expressive multi-ethnic facial avatars. J. Vis. Lang. Comput. **17**(5), 430–444 (2006)
2. Lisetti, C., Yasavur, U., De Leon, C., Amini, R., Rishe, N., Visser, U.: Building an on-demand avatar-based health intervention for behavior change. In: Proceedings of the 25th International Florida Artificial Intelligence Research Society Conference, FLAIRS-25, Marco Island, 23–25 May, pp. 175–180 (2012)
3. Li, M., Kavakli, M., Rudra, T.: eCounsellor: an avatar for student exam stress management. In: Erkan, T.E. (ed.) Proceedings of the 3rd International Conference on Information Management and Evaluation: Atilim University Performance Management and Applications Research Centre, Ankara, Turkey, 16–17 April 2012, pp. 185–193. Academic Publishing International, Nr Reading (2012)
4. Busso, C., Deng, Z., Yildirim, S., Bulut, M., Lee, C.M., Kazemzadeh, A., Lee, S., Neumann, U., Narayanan, S.: Analysis of emotion recognition using facial expressions, speech and multimodal information. In: Proceedings of the 6th International Conference on Multimodal Interfaces, pp. 205–211. ACM, New York (2004)
5. Vogt, Thurid, André, Elisabeth, Bee, Nikolaus: EmoVoice — A Framework for Online Recognition of Emotions from Voice. In: André, Elisabeth, Dybkjær, Laila, Minker, Wolfgang, Neumann, Heiko, Pieraccini, Roberto, Weber, Michael (eds.) PIT 2008. LNCS, vol. 5078, pp. 188–199. Springer, Heidelberg (2008). doi:10.1007/978-3-540-69369-7_21
6. Wang, K., An, N., Li, B.N., Zhang, Y., Li, L.: Speech emotion recognition using Fourier parameters. IEEE Trans. Affect. Comput. **6**(1), 69–75 (2015)
7. Johnson, E., Hervás, R., de la Gutiérrez-López Franca, C., Mondéjar, T., Ochoa, S.F., Favela, J.: Assessing empathy and managing emotions through interactions with an affective avatar. Health Inf. J. (2016). doi:10.1177/1460458216661864
8. Johnson, E., Hervás, R., Gutiérrez-López-Franca, C., Mondéjar, T., Bravo, J.: Analyzing and predicting empathy in neurotypical and non-neurotypical users with an affective avatar. Mob. Inf. Syst. (2017). doi:10.1155/2017/7932529
9. de la Franca, C.G.L., Hervás, R., Johnson, E., Mondéjar, T., Bravo, J.: Extended body-angles algorithm to recognize activities within intelligent environments. J. Ambient Intell. Hum. Comput. (2017). doi:10.1007/s12652-017-0463-y
10. Mondéjar, T., Hervás, R., Johnson, E., Gutierrez, C., Latorre, J.M.: Correlation between videogame mechanics and executive functions through EEG analysis. J. Biomed. Inf. **63**, 131–140 (2016). doi:10.1016/j.jbi.2016.08.006

Towards Job Stress Recognition Based on Behavior and Physiological Features

Wendy Sanchez[1], Alicia Martinez[1(✉)], and Miguel Gonzalez[2]

[1] National Technology of Mexico/CENIDET, Cuernavaca, Mexico
{wendy.sanchez11c,amartinez}@cenidet.edu.mx
[2] Monterrey Institute of Technology and Higher Education, Monterrey, Mexico
mgonza@itesm.mx

Abstract. Nowadays, job stress is very common and it has a high cost in terms of employees' health, absenteeism and lower performance. It is so big the impact of this psychological disease that the WHO recognizes it as one of the great epidemics of modern life. This paper presents a job stress predictive model from monitoring employees' behavior and physiological features. The monitoring was carried out through their job computer and a wrist-worn sensor. The proposed model obtained an accuracy of 94%, a precision of 0.943, a recall and a F-Measure of 0.914. Also, the results obtained of the evaluation of the selected model are presented.

Keywords: Job stress recognition · Predictive model · Monitoring application · Behavior features · Physiological features

1 Introduction

In many countries, the number of people suffering job stress has increased as a consequence of the accelerated rhythm in the actual life [1]. It is so big the impact of this psychological disease that the WHO recognizes it as one of the great epidemics of modern life [1]. Job stress is very common and it has a high cost in terms of employees' health, absenteeism and lower performance [2].

Job stress is a group of emotional, physiological, cognitive and behavioral reactions of an employee which appear in demanding situations in means of content, organization and work environment [3]. The employees feel the job demands exceed their capabilities to keep them under control [3, 4]. These demands are not only related to high workload or long working hours, but also to high perceived stress, low social support from colleagues and managers, or to the individual characteristics of each one like the education and competitiveness. If the employee is not able to recover, long-term damage may result in the development of depression, gastric ulcers, or increased sensitivity to infections.

Currently, technological progress has enabled monitoring of wide aspects of human behavior, including capability of recognizing activities and inferring behavior patterns. As a result, job stress could be recognized through a continuous monitoring of employees during office work towards positive behavior change and their health management.

© Springer International Publishing AG 2017
S.F. Ochoa et al. (Eds.): UCAmI 2017, LNCS 10586, pp. 311–322, 2017.
DOI: 10.1007/978-3-319-67585-5_33

The aim of our research is the automatic recognition of job stress from monitoring employees' behavior and physiological features. The monitoring is done through their job computer and a Fitbit® wrist-worn sensor. This paper presents a job stress predictive model. The paper is structured as follows: Sect. 2 describes the related works for job stress recognition. In Sect. 3, the methodology used is presented. In Sect. 4, a monitoring application called LaborCheck application is presented. Section 5 shows the process to get the proposed job stress predictive model. Section 6 shows the evaluation of the proposed model; and finally, Sect. 7 presents the conclusions and future work.

2   Related Works

A substantial amount of research on stress recognition focused on physiological measurements to detect stress. In particular, several methods have been based on physiological signals, such as heart rate [5, 6], corporal temperature [7], skin galvanic response [8], respiration rate [9, 10], ambulatory activity respiration [11], subcutaneous cortisol [12] and electro-encephalic activity [13]. These measurements are done through corporal sensors that are in contact with the person's skin. Despite their high reliability in stress detection, technologies based on this approach present considerable weaknesses because they need to be carried at all times in order to allow continuous monitoring.

Other researches have used mobile phone usage patterns, such as calls, SMSs and e-mails [8, 16], app usage, location, screen on/off [9], social interactions [14–16] and accelerometer data [17, 18]. Also, stress have been detected through measurement of press force on certain objects such as keyboard [23], mouse [8], office chair [24] and car steering-wheel [12], interactions with technological devices [25] and ambient and environment temperature [7, 14]. Some other researches have focused in measurement of human-computer interactions to detect stress such as web sites visited, switching between windows, keyboard and mouse usage [19–22].

Our research focuses on job stress automatic recognition through the combination of employees' behavior and physiological features in order to get a better precision. The monitoring is carried out through their job computers and a Fitbit® wrist-worn sensor.

3   Methodology

Job stress is a group of emotional, physiological, cognitive and behavioral reactions of an employee which appear in demanding situations in means of content, organization and work environment [3]. The aim of our research is the automatic recognition of job stress of employees who use a computer as their work tool. Therefore, employees' app usage was monitored in their real work environment through their computers. Also, physiological features were monitored through a Fitbit® wrist-worn sensor.

Our solution methodology is shown in Fig. 1 This methodology is composed of two phases. In the first phase, an application called LaborCheck was developed. This application collects the employees' behavior and physiological features. In the second phase of our methodology, the job stress predictive model is generated. A data collection in a real work environment was carried out. In order to generate the predictive model, the data collected was pre-processed and then, classifier algorithms were applied. In the following sections, these phases are explained in more detail.

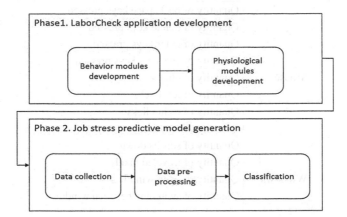

Fig. 1. Our solution methodology used for job stress recognition

4 LaborCheck Application Development

LaborCheck is an application that ubiquitously collects the employees' behavior and physiological features. The first phase of our methodology is the development of Labor-Check application that is compose of two processes: behavior monitoring and physiological monitoring.

4.1 Behavior Monitoring Process

In this process, the behavior monitoring application was developed. This application ubiquitously collects employees' computer data such as keyboard, mouse and windows usage in their real work environment. Also, the application captures employees' stress self-reported survey. All behavior features monitored are shown in Table 1.

The behavior monitoring application must be installed on Windows OS and it is compatible with the Windows 7, Windows 8 and Windows 10 versions. Once the installation is completed, the application automatically starts the continuous monitoring even when the computer is restarted or logged off. Every minute, data collected is temporary stored in a local database. After 20 min, data is send to the server database through a web service. In order to obtain the employee stress level of the morning and of the afternoon, every 210 min a stress self-reported survey appears.

Table 1. Behavior features

Modality	Features
Keyboard	Quantity of keys pressed
	Quantity of backspace keys pressed
	Quantity of delete keys pressed
	Quantity of enter keys pressed
	Quantity of spacebar keys pressed
Mouse	Quantity of clicks
	Quantity of left clicks
	Quantity of right clicks
	Quantity of scrolls up
	Quantity of scrolls down
	Quantity of traveled pixels
Windows	Quantity of open windows
	Quantity of switching between windows

The employees have to select their perceived stress level in a scale from one to five where level one means no stress and level five means extremely stressed. The stress self-reported survey is shown in Fig. 2.

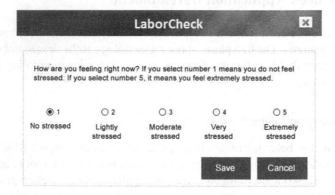

Fig. 2. Stress self-reported survey

4.2 Physiological Monitoring Process

In this process, the physiological monitoring application was developed. This application ubiquitously collects employees' physiological data such as physic activity, heart rate and sleep data during all day and night. The physiological data is collected through a Fitbit® wrist-worn sensor. All physiological features monitored are shown in Table 2.

Table 2. Physiological features

Modality	Features
Physic activity	Quantity of steps
	Quantity of floors
	Distance traveled
Heart rate	Heart rate
Sleep	Quantity of minutes of sleep
	Quantity of minutes of deep sleep
	Quantity of minutes of light sleep
	Quantity of minutes awaken
	Sleep efficiency

The physiological monitoring application works as follows. The Fitbit® wrist-worn sensor stores physiological data locally. Afterwards, it synchronizes with Fitbit® server through the official Fitbit® app. Daily, the physiological monitoring application pulls out the data through a Fitbit® API app, and stores them in the server database. The employee should use the wrist-worn sensor during all day in order to monitor the heart rate date minute by minute and all night to monitor the sleep data.

5   Predictive Model

Machine learning's algorithms search natural patterns in data to generate knowledge that help in making decisions. The aim of machine learning is generating a model for predicting in presence of uncertainty. A learning algorithm takes an input dataset with its respective outputs to generate a model capable to produce reasonable predictions in new data. The second phase of our methodology is the generation of a job stress predictive model. The procedure was carried out as follows:

5.1   Data Collection

Data collection was done through a continuous monitoring of 41 participants of three different companies in their job environment for a period of five labor days. The participants were 37% male and 63% female; their ages were 59% from 20 to 30, 24% from 31 to 40 and 17% from 41 and older; and 61% were single and 39% were married. Their job positions were software developers, system analysts, project leaders, and office bosses. They have the following profile: (i) Employees whose work is focused mainly on a computer, (ii) Ages from twenty and older, (iii) Employees who have a computer and also, they have permission from the companies to install our LaborCheck application, (iv) The employee's computer should have the Windows operating system installed. The materials used in data collection were the following:

– The LaborCheck application monitors behavior and physiological features.
– The wrist-worn sensor Fitbit®. The monitoring was carried out with thirteen Fitbit® Charge HR wrist-worn sensors.

- Official Fitbit® app to synchronize data.
- Demographic and job information questionnaire. The information collected though this questionnaire was: gender, marital status, number of children, height, weight, age, if they were sick, level of education, date of entry to work, date of entry to their currently job position, number of dependents, official time of entry and exit of work.
- A web site that contains information about the research, the links to download Labor-Check application and the questionnaire.
- An informed consent, which specifies data collected, the participants' rights and the privacy notice of their data.

The process of data collection was carried out as follows:

1. At the beginning the experiment. We personally contacted different employees of three different companies, who agreed to participate in this research work. A meeting in the companies was carried out with the participating employees. We explain the details of the experiment and the profile that each participant should have. The LaborCheck application was installed on their work computers and the Fitbit® app on their cell phones. They were given a wrist-worn Fitbit® sensor. Participants answered the questionnaire and signed the informed consent.
2. During the experiment. Employees would work normally with their computers. Additionally, they must answer the stress self-report survey. It will would appear two to three times during the day. Participants should wear Fitbit® wrist-worn sensor all day and all night, except when bathing. The sensor must be synchronized daily and charged every two days outside working hours.
3. End of the experiment. Uninstallation of the LaborCheck application and the Fitbit® app from the participants' cell phones was carried out. Participants returned the wrist-worn Fitbit® sensor.

5.2 Data Pre-processing

Today's real-world databases are highly susceptible to noisy, missing, and inconsistent data due to their typically huge size and their likely origin from multiple, heterogeneous sources. Low-quality data will lead to low-quality mining results. Data preprocessing techniques can improve the accuracy and efficiency of mining algorithms involving distance measurements [26]. Before analyzing the data, a pre-processing was performed to obtain a higher quality database.

From the data collected, time windows of 210 min were created associating a level of stress. Thus, 300 instances of all participants were obtained. We classified stress levels as follows: (i) the self-reports levels one and two were classified at the low level, (ii) the self-reports levels three were classified at the medium level and (iii) the self-reports levels four and five were classified at the high level. Table 3 shows the number of records for each stress level classified.

The information of the database was analyzed manually. When there were several missing features in an instance, this was not considered for analysis. For example, data from three participants were not considered because no data on sleep quality were recorded in any of the days of the experiment.

Table 3. Number of records for each stress level

Stress level	Number of records
Low	198
Medium	75
High	27

However, when there were only one or two missing data, these were completed with the average value of the 210 min monitored. Additionally, we generate new features based on the information collected. For example, we obtained the Body Mass Index (BMI) of the participant based on their weight and height. The employees' seniority in their work and in their current job position was also calculated from the dates of entry of their work and their current position. A position ranking was done according to the hierarchical level in the organization chart of the companies. Features from numerical to Boolean were also transformed, such as the number of children, illnesses and number of dependents. The number of official hours worked by each employee and the number of overtime worked on each day of the experiment was calculated. Other features were created such as the day of the week and whether the self-report occurred in the morning (7 am–12 pm), late (12 pm–6 pm) or evening (after 6 pm). In the case of numerical features, each instance contains the sum, average, and standard deviation of each feature.

The data was compiled into one dataset (DS01) containing all the features monitored, the demographic and company data plus the output class the level of job stress. Data that did not vary between 210 min were analyzed separately. Table 4 shows all the features contained in the dataset DS01.

Table 4. Features contained in the dataset DS01

Modality	Features
Demographic	Gender, marital status, number of children, height, weight, IMC, illnesses, age and level of education
Company	Seniority in the work in months and years, seniority in the current job position in months and years, job position category, number of dependents, official time of entry and exit of work, number of hours worked, number of overtime worked, self-report in the morning, afternoon or night and day of the week
Behavior	Total, average and standard deviation of keys pressed, backspace keys, delete keys, enter keys, spacebar keys, number of clicks, number of left clicks, number of right clicks, number of scrolls up, number of scrolls down, number of pixels traveled, number of open windows and number of switches between windows
Physiological	Average and standard deviation of heart rate, number of steps, number of floors, distance traveled, total minutes of sleep, total minutes of deep sleep, total minutes of light sleep, total minutes awaken, sleep efficiency

5.3 Feature Selection

Feature selection is the process of identifying and removing as much irrelevant and redundant information as possible. As a result, there was an improvement in the process's predictive performance, a decrease in its elapsed time, and a reduction in its storage needs. At the same time, a better view and understanding of the data was obtained. Most machine learning algorithms are designed to learn which are the most appropriate attributes to use for making their decisions. The dataset was assessed using Chi-Squared [27] and Ranker methods for evaluation of attributes, Correlation-based Feature Selection and Greedy Stepwise [28] for evaluation of the sets of attributes and Greedy Stepwise method and J48 classification algorithm for the evaluation of the Wrapper attribute sets [29]. The attributes selected by these methods were considered as relevant attributes, and they are gender, illnesses, age, seniority in current job position, time of entry to work, day of the week, standard deviation of the number of scrolls up, standard deviation of the number of open windows, minutes of light sleep and minutes awaken. All the tests were performed with a 10-fold cross validation as the standard evaluation technique [30]. We create another dataset (DS02) that contains only the relevant features.

5.4 Dataset Balancing

A database consists of a set of features and a set of instances. Each instance has a class. A database is not balanced if its classes are not equally represented [31]. In the classification, the unbalance of classes can cause a bias toward the majority class. Disease databases are generally unbalanced because the proportion of healthy people is higher than ill people [32]. Prediction of disease requires high coverage in the minority class, while maintaining high accuracy in the majority class. Likewise, it is necessary to build classifiers with a good performance in the minority class. In the classification, the unbalance of classes can cause bias toward the majority class.

Our database presented an imbalance in its classes. In order to handle the imbalance, the Resample technique was applied to dataset DS02. Resample technique is included in the toolkit WEKA version 3.8.1 [33]. This technique increases or decreases the number of instances by creating a copy of the instances randomly. WEKA offers some options to configure the Resampling technique. The option *"biasToUniformClass = 1"* enable the class balance. The option *"sampleSizePercent"* enable select the increasing or decreasing percentage of the number of instances. We applied a 170%. As a result, the dataset was balanced with 105 instances each class. A third-class balanced dataset (DS03) was created.

5.5 Classification

A classifier algorithm is a machine learning algorithm which founds the relation between unknown objects and a set of correctly labeled objects in order to correctly classify the unknown objects [34]. The classification procedure used was the comparison of metrics obtained with a set of classifier algorithms to select the best performance model [35]. The classifier algorithms used are: ZeroR (ZR)which was the baseline; Naive Bayes (NB) [36]; Simple Logistics (SL) [37]; Support Vector Machine (SVM) [38] with the polynomic function [39]; k-Nearest-Neighbor (kNN) [40]; AdaBoost (AB) [41]; J48 and Random Tree (RT). A stratified ten times ten-fold cross-validation technique was used because it is the standard evaluation technique in situations where only limited data is available [30]. The three subsets (DS01, DS02 and DS03) were evaluated by means of accuracy (percentage correctly classified among all employees), precision (percentage correctly classified as stressed among all classified as stressed), recall (percentage correctly classified as stressed among all really stressed) and F-measure (combined measure between precision and recall). The performance results are shown in Table 5.

Table 5. Classifier algorithms performance results

Dataset	Accuracy	Precision	Recall	F-Measure	Classifier
DS01	67%	0.674	0.672	0.673	IBk
DS02	65%	0.63	0.652	0.638	AB
DS03	94%	0.943	0.941	0.941	AB

The model generated from dataset DS03 with AB classifier was selected because obtained the best performance with an accuracy of 94%, a precision of 0.943 and a recall and F-measure of 0.941.

6 Evaluation

In order to evaluate the selected model, an experiment with 16 new employees was conducted. The participants met the same profile requirements as in the previous phase. The data was collected in the same way as in the first data collection. LaborCheck application, the Fitbit® wrist-worn sensor and the questionnaire were used. Also, time windows of 210 min were created and a low, medium and high stress levels were associated. 153 instances were obtained and compiled in a testset (TS01) which was evaluated with the selected model. The model correctly classified 106 participants obtaining an accuracy of 71%, a precision of 0.743, a recall of 0.714 and F-measure of 0.724.

7 Conclusions and Future Works

Job stress is very common and it has a high cost in terms of employees' health, absenteeism and lower performance [2]. It is so big the impact of this psychological disease that the WHO recognizes it as one of the great epidemics of modern life [1]. Job stress could be recognized through a continuous monitoring of employees during office work. The aim of our research was the automatic recognition of job stress from monitoring employees' behavior and physiological features. An application called LaborCheck was developed which is capable to monitor employees. Data from 41 participants in their real work environment was collected through LaborCheck and a Fitbit® wrist-worn sensor. A 300-instances dataset (DS01) was obtained. Relevant features were identified (DS02) and balancing techniques (DS03) were applied to the dataset. Predictive models were generated implementing a range of classifier algorithms. The model generated from dataset DS03 with AB classifier was selected because obtained the best performance with an accuracy of 94%, a precision of 0.943 and a recall and F-measure of 0.941. In order to evaluate the selected model, an experiment with 16 new employees was conducted. The model correctly classified 106 participants obtaining an accuracy of 71%, a precision of 0.743, a recall of 0.714 and F-measure of 0.724.

The evaluation showed a good level of accuracy. The differences between the two accuracies could be due the different job positions of the participants or the hierarchical level in the organization chart. Whereby, we are considering a deeper analysis in order to discover differences between gender, age or job position. Also, we are considering to develop an application capable to prevent stress episodes through the implementation of the selected predictive model.

Acknowledgments. This research work has been partially funded by European Commission and CONACYT, through the SmartSDK project.

References

1. Leka, S., Griffiths, A., Cox, T.: Work Organization and stress: systematic problem approaches for employers, managers and trade union representatives, Paris, France (2004)
2. Aquino Lopes, R., Cardoso, A., Afonso Lamounier, E., Jose Lopes, E., Notargiacomo Mustaro, P.: Digital games for coping with occupational stress. IEEE Latin Am. Trans. **13**(12), 3907–3912 (2015)
3. World Health Organization: Sensibilizando sobre el Estrés Laboral en los Países en Desarrollo
4. Blaug, R., Kenyon, A., Lekhi, R.: Stress at Work: A Report Prepared for The Work Foundation's Principal Partners. The Work Foundation, London (2007)
5. Plarre, K., Raij, A., Hossain, S.M., Ali, A.A., Nakajima, M., Absi, M., Ertin, E., Kamarck, T., Kumar, S., Scott, M., Siewiorek, D., Smailagic, A., Wittmers, L.E.: Continuous inference of psychological stress from sensory measurements collected in the natural environment. In: Information Processing in Sensor Networks (IPSN), pp. 97–108 (2011)
6. Bakker, J., Pechenizkiy, M., Sidorova, N.: What's your current stress level? Detection of stress patterns from gsr sensor data. Paper presented at IEEE 11th International Conference on Data Mining Working, no. 1, pp. 573–580 (2011)
7. Raij, A., Blitz, P., Ali, A.A., Fisk, S., French, B., Mitra, S., Nakajima, M., Nguyen, M.H., Plarre, K., Rahman, M., Shah, S., Shi, Y., Stohs, N., Absi, M., Ertin, E., Kamarck, T., Kumar, S., Scott, M., Siewiorek, D., Smailagic, A.: mStress: supporting continuous collection of objective and subjective measures of psychosocial stress on mobile devices. Technical report No. CS-10-004, University of Memphis (2010)
8. Hernandez, J., Paredes, P., Roseway, A., Czerwinski, M.: Under pressure: sensing stress of computer users. In: ACM SIGCHI Conference on Human Factors in Computing Systems, pp. 51–60 (2014)
9. Sano, A., Picard, R.W.: Stress recognition using wearable sensors and mobile phones. In: Humaine Association Conference on Affective Computing and Intelligent Interaction, pp. 671–676 (2013)
10. Hernandez, J., Morris, Rob R., Picard, Rosalind W.: Call center stress recognition with person-specific models. In: D'Mello, S., Graesser, A., Schuller, B., Martin, J.-C. (eds.) ACII 2011. LNCS, vol. 6974, pp. 125–134. Springer, Heidelberg (2011). doi: 10.1007/978-3-642-24600-5_16

11. Majoe, D., Bonhof, P., Kaegi-trachsel, T., Gutknecht, J., Widmer, L.: Stress and sleep quality estimation from a smart wearable sensor. In: Pervasive Computing and Applications (ICPCA), pp. 14–19 (2010)
12. Hernandez, J., Benavides, X., Maes, P., McDuff, D., Amores, J., Picard, R.W.: AutoEmotive: bringing empathy to the driving experience to manage stress. In: Designing Interactive Systems, pp. 53–56 (2014)
13. Sharma, N., Gedeon, T.: Modeling stress recognition in typical virtual environments. In: Proceedings of the ICTs for improving Patients Rehabilitation Research Techniques, pp. 17–24 (2013)
14. Bogomolov, A., Lepri, B., Ferron, M., Pianesi, F., Pentland, A.S.: Pervasive stress recognition for sustainable living, pp. 345–350 (2014)
15. Maxhuni, A., Hernandez-Leal, P., Sucar, L.E., Osmani, V., Morales, E.F., Mayora, O.: Stress modelling and prediction in presence of scarce data. J. Biomed. Inform. **63**, 344–356 (2016)
16. Ferdous, R., Osmani, V., Beltran, J., Mayora, O.: Investigating correlation between verbal interactions and perceived stress. In: Engineering in Medicine and Biology Society (EMBS) (2015)
17. Garcia-Ceja, E., Osmani, V., Mayora, O.: Automatic stress detection in working environments from smartphones' accelerometer data: a first step. IEEE J. Biomed. Heal. Informatics **20**(4), 1053–1060 (2015)
18. Maxhuni, A., Hernandez-leal, P., Morales, E., Enrique, L., Osmani, V., Mayora, O.: Using Intermediate Models and Knowledge Learning to Improve Stress Prediction, vol. 179. Springer, New York (2017)
19. Karunaratne, I., Atukorale, A.S., Perera, H.: The relationship between psychological distress and human computer interaction parameters: linear or non-linear? Lect. Notes Electr. Eng. **312**, 471–478 (2015)
20. Pimenta, A., Carneiro, D., Neves, J., Novais, P.: A neural network to classify fatigue from human-computer interaction. Neurocomputing **172**, 413–426 (2016)
21. Liao, W., Zhang, W., Zhu, Z., Ji, Q.: A real-time human stress monitoring system using dynamic bayesian network. Paper presented at 2005 IEEE Computer Society Conference on Computer Vision and Pattern Recognition, vol. 3, p. 70 (2005)
22. Khan, I.A., Brinkman, W.P., Hierons, R.: Towards estimating computer users' mood from interaction behaviour with keyboard and mouse. Front. Comput. Sci. **7**(6), 943–954 (2013)
23. Karunaratne, I., Atukorale, A.S., Perera, H.: Surveillance of human-computer interactions: a way forward to detection of users' psychological distress. In: Humanities, Science and Engineering (CHUSER), pp. 491–496 (2011)
24. Arnrich, B., Setz, C., La Marca, R., Troster, G., Ehlert, U.: What does your chair know about your stress level? IEEE Trans. Inf. Technol. Biomed. **14**(2), 207–214 (2010)
25. Carneiro, D., Castillo, J.C., Novais, P., Fernández-Caballero, A., Neves, J.: Multimodal behavioral analysis for non-invasive stress detection. Exp. Syst. Appl. **39**(18), 13376–13389 (2012)
26. Han, J., Kamber, M., Pei, J.: Data Mining. Concepts and Techniques, 3rd edn. Morgan Kaufmann, Burlington (2012)
27. Moore, D.S.: Estadística aplicada básica. Antoni Bosch editor (2005)
28. Hall, M.A.: Correlation-Based Feature Selection for Machine Learning. The University of Waikato, Hamilton (1999)
29. Kohavi, R., John, G.H.: Wrappers for feature subset selection. Artif. Intell. **97**(1–2), 273–324 (1997)
30. Witten, I.H., Frank, E., Hall, M.: Data Mining: Practical Machine Learning Tools and Techniques, 3rd ed. Burlington, US (2011)

31. Chawla, N.V., Bowyer, K.W., Hall, L.O., Kegelmeyer, W.P.: SMOTE: synthetic minority over-sampling technique. J. Artif. Intell. Res. **16**, 321–357 (2002)
32. More, A.: Survey of resampling techniques for improving classification performance in unbalanced datasets. Computing Research Repository (CoRR). arXiv:1608.06048 (2016)
33. Hall, M., Frank, E., Holmes, G., Pfahringer, B., Reutemann, P., Witten, I.H.: The WEKA data mining software: an update. In: SIGKDD Explorations, vol. 11, no. 1 (2009)
34. Loyola, O., Medina, M.A., García, M.: Inducing decision trees based on a cluster quality index. IEEE Latin Am. Trans. **13**(4), 1141–1147 (2015)
35. Univaso, P., Ale, J.M., Gurlekian, J.A.: Data mining applied to forensic speaker identification. IEEE Latin Am. Trans. **13**(4), 1098–1111 (2015)
36. John, G.H., Langley, P.: Estimating continuous distributions in Bayesian classifiers. Paper presented at the UAI 1995 Eleventh Conference on Uncertainty in Artificial Intelligence, pp. 338–345, (1995)
37. Landwehr, N., Hall, M., Frank, E.: Logistic model trees. Mach. Learn. **59**(1–2), 161–205 (2005)
38. Platt, J.C.: Fast training of support vector machines using sequential minimal optimization. In: Schölkopf, B., Burges, C.J.C., Smola, A.J. (eds.) Advances in Kernel Methods: Support Vector Learning, pp. 185–208. MIT Press, Cambridge (1999)
39. Schölkopf, B., Smola, A.J.: Learning with Kernels: Support Vector Machines, Regularization, Optimization, and Beyond. MIT Press, Cambridge (2002)
40. Aha, D.W., Kibler, D., Albert, M.K.: Instance-based learning algorithms. Mach. Learn. **6**(1), 37–66 (1991)
41. Freund, Y., Schapire, R.E.: Experiments with a new boosting algorithm. In: Thirteen International Conference on Machine Learning, pp. 148–156 (1996)

Applying Computer Simulation Modelling to Minimizing Appointment Lead-Time in Elderly Outpatient Clinics: A Case Study

Miguel Ortíz-Barrios[1](✉), Pedro López-Meza[2], and Genett Jimenez-Delgado[2]

[1] Department of Industrial Management, Agroindustry and Operations,
Universidad de la Costa CUC, Barranquilla, Colombia
mortiz1@cuc.edu.co
[2] Department of Industrial Processes Engineering, Institución Universitaria ITSA,
Soledad, Colombia
{plopezmeza,gjimenez}@itsa.edu.co

Abstract. Appointment lead-time is a pivotal parameter in elderly outpatient clinics. In this regard, delayed medical care may represent complications in the elderly population and the development of more severe diseases. However, healthcare managers are not skilled in methods effectively reducing waiting times. Therefore, this paper presents the computer simulation modelling to tackle this problem. In this regard, the real-world system was initially simulated and then, three improvement scenarios were designed and validated operationally and financially. The results evidenced that Scenario 2 was the best choice since it provided a low investment per reduced day and a significant reduction (47.1%) regarding the probability of waiting for more than 8 days per appointment. With this proposal, the quality of medical care in elderly population can be meaningfully increased and decision-making process can be effectively supported.

Keywords: Discrete event simulation (DES) · Outpatient clinics · Appointment lead-time · Healthcare · Elderly

1 Introduction

The constant growth in the population increases the demand for better planning and management of the healthcare services. This implies providing medical care with high-quality standards which are relevant when preventing more complex diseases and symptoms [1]. Nevertheless, the hospital managers usually apply conventional methods not considering the interactions between departments in terms of clinic capacity, patient demand, clinical policies and patient behavior. Additionally, they face increasing pressure to control costs while delivering effective medical care [2]. Therefore, it is necessary to assist healthcare professionals in tackling this particular problem satisfactorily.

In this regard, one of the services most affected by interactions between departments is outpatient clinics. Herein, the pivotal process parameter is appointment lead-time. In this regard, long appointment delays are found to cause clinical ramifications, increase patient no-shows [3] and patient dissatisfaction [4]. This evidences that the degree to

© Springer International Publishing AG 2017
S.F. Ochoa et al. (Eds.): UCAmI 2017, LNCS 10586, pp. 323–329, 2017.
DOI: 10.1007/978-3-319-67585-5_34

which patients are satisfied with the medical received is highly associated to the appointment lead-time. This variable tends to be longer when the hospital's capacity cannot catch up with the increasing demand [5] which makes healthcare providers less attractive to patients.

Additionally, outpatient clinics are full of uncertainties that should not be ignored by the decision makers [5]. These failures may cause extra patient waiting time and negatively influence on other performance measures [6]. This is even more relevant in the elderly patients who experience increased rates of complications when taking so long to get a doctor's appointment [7]. This is the case of several outpatient departments in most developing countries where elderly population tends to develop long-term and more severe complications. To address this problem, simulation modelling approaches have been widely applied as described in Sect. 2. However, applications on elderly outpatient clinics are largely limited and should be consequently studied to design effective solutions that must be clinically validated and adhered to standards. In an effort to cover this gap, this paper reports on the main results derived from the application of Discrete-event simulation (DES) to design strategies reducing appointment lead-time in an elderly outpatient clinic. We focused on two aspects related to appointment lead-time: the capacity required to meet the norm of seeing the patients within 8 days and the evaluation of strategies to minimize this lead-time (e.g. improved appointment scheduling, capacity planning, and allocation of doctors to shifts). In this case, DES provided an opportunity to alleviate the burden faced as a result of the long appointment lead-times. The remainder of this paper is organized as follows: In Sect. 2, a literature review on DES applications for healthcare is presented. In Sect. 3, a case study in the internal medicine service and the results are described and analysed. Finally, Sect. 4 presents conclusions and future work.

2   A Brief Literature Review

The scientific literature has reported several academic works and real-life applications regarding the simulation modelling in healthcare. At the level of the state of art, the classification of the existing literature on simulation and modeling of healthcare services is highlighted by analyzing the use of simulation techniques when addressing the appointment lead-time problem in both outpatient and inpatient services [8]. In this regard, simulation approaches are a very useful tool for decision making in healthcare management and become more effective when combining with other operative research techniques, such as the estimation of objective functions and the use of optimization techniques to improve the effectiveness of healthcare services [9]. Through the simulation, different process variables affecting healthcare services can be considered (e.g. equipment and workforce) [10]. This is very useful when defining optimal operating conditions in clinics, hospitals and health centers and it is even more important in vital services where the access time is crucial to provide more effective medical care [11]. In this respect, DES is a fundamental technique to reduce patient waiting time [14, 15]. Specifically, [13] developed a computer simulation study to improve the quality of care in an emergency service. In this work, a sensitivity analysis was carried out to evaluate the impact of medical staff and equipment on service quality and flow control in the emergency department. This framework was also used to effectively allocate resources in medical services [12, 18]. On the other hand and considering the most recent studies, DES has been employed as a tool to support decision-making process in different outpatient services of hospitals [16], e.g. internal medicine department [17] and gynecology-obstetrics [1]. However, this problem has not been addressed in elderly outpatient clinic. In light of this, this paper presents a case study where DES was applied to improve the appointment lead-time in an elderly outpatient clinics. In this case, a simulation model was created to represent the real system and then improvement scenarios were proposed to reduce the lead-time. In this respect, the scenarios were financially and operationally assessed to finally select the best option for both patients and clinics. The novelty of this study lies in the use of DES to design and validate improvement scenarios for minimizing the appointment lead-time in these kinds of clinics. This is underpinned by the study performed in [19] where it is evidenced that little work has been done to evaluate the impact of improvement strategies and then the "evidence base is small and poorly developed"

3 An Illustrative Example: Modelling the Elderly Outpatient Clinics

A case study of an elderly outpatient clinic from healthcare sector is presented to validate the effectiveness of the proposed approach. This system operates from 8:00 to 17:00 from Monday to Friday and two appointment types (first-time and control). Medical consultation is in charge of three doctors who have different schedules. Doctors 1 and 2 treat elderly patients from 10:30 to 14:00 (Mondays–Thursdays and Tuesdays–Wednesdays respectively), whilst Doctor 3 attends them from 8:30 to 12:00 (Fridays).

This service is regulated by the Ministry of Health and Social Protection. In this respect, the upper specification limit for average appointment lead-time has been set as 8 days/appointment. This information was considered in a simulation model that was designed with the support of Arena 15 ® software in order to reduce the current appointment lead-time of the clinic. A Mann-Whitney Test was performed to determine if the simulated model was equivalent to the real-world system. In this respect, a P-value equal to 0.4292 (alpha level = 0.05), W = 139 and CI [−1.895; 6.239] demonstrated that the model was statistically equal to the outpatient clinic under study. Then, the current average appointment lead-time was calculated. On average an elderly patient has to wait for 9.78 days with a standard deviation of 4.45. This means that there is a probability of 55.17% that an elderly patient waits for more than 8 days between the request date and consultation time. In addition, DPM = 551719 which denotes that 551719 appointments out of 1 million will have a lead-time higher than 8 days. In an effort to address this problem, three improvement scenarios were created in conjunction with the medical staff from the clinic. Each scenario was assessed through the simulation model before implementation (refer to Fig. 1).

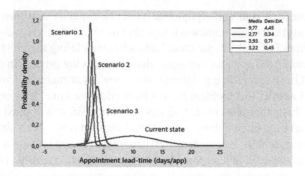

Fig. 1. Comparative analysis between current state and Scenario 1, Scenario 2 and Scenario 3

Scenario 1 proposes hiring 1 additional doctor with this schedule: Monday to Friday from 8:30 to 18:00. On the other hand, Scenario 2 suggests adding 1 doctor with this schedule configuration: Friday from 8:30 to 15:00 Finally, Scenario 3 recommends changing the schedule of Doctor 3 to a night shift (Monday to Wednesday from 19:00 to 22:00). After simulating these scenarios, the results showed that all the proposals are satisfying due to they provide a reduced average appointment lead-time. In this respect, a Mann–Whitney test was carried out for each comparison (refer to Table 1).

Table 1. P-values, W statistics and confidence intervals for comparisons between real system and proposed scenarios

Improvement Scenario	P-value	W	CI (95%)
Scenario 1	0	469	[2.981; 10.113]
Scenario 2	0	845	[2.125; 8.862]
Scenario 3	0	343	[2.518; 9.983]

Considering the aforementioned results, the scenarios were compared in terms of average appointment lead-time (refer to Table 2). It is seen that the scenario 1 provides the best operational performance due to its reduced variability and satisfying mean. Nonetheless, it is also necessary to evaluate these proposals financially. Thus, two indicators were designed: IAALTD and IVC (refer to Eqs. 1–2) where VC_i and VC_f are the initial and final variation coefficients (refer to Table 2).

$$IAALTD = \frac{Investment}{Initialaverageappointmentlead - time - Finalaverageappointmentlead - time} \quad (1)$$

$$IVC = \frac{Investment}{VC_i - VC_f} \quad (2)$$

Table 2. Financial and operational evaluation of proposed scenarios

Scenario	Investment – I (COP)	Average appointment lead-time (AALT)	Standard deviation (days)– SD	IAALTD (COP/ day)	IVC
1	11.200.000	2.77	0.32	1597717.5	32990977.4
2	2.100.000	3.92	0.97	358361.7	10117495.7
3	3.600.000	3.23	0.42	549618.3	11077629.8

Based on the results provided by Table 2, the best option is Scenario 2 with the lowest IAALTD (358361.7 COP/day). This denotes that it is necessary to invest 358361.7 COP per each reduced day in average appointment lead-time. Additionally, when calculating IVC, Scenario 2 was also found to be the most beneficial choice (IVC = 10117495.7 COP). This indicator considers both mean and standard deviation which increases the confidence level of the conclusions provided by this study. This represents a probability of 8.07% (DPM = 80762) that an elderly patient waits for more than 8 days between the request date and consultation time.

4 Conclusions and Future Work

In this paper, we have validated the effectiveness of computer simulation modelling to improve average appointment lead-time in an elderly outpatient clinic. The results evidenced that, considering the current system, 55.17% of the appointments scheduled in this clinic will have a lead-time higher than 8 days. Therefore, three proposals were simulated and assessed with the aid of Arena 15 ® software and knowledge provided by the healthcare managers of the clinic. In this case, all the proposals were found to be operationally satisfactory due to they provide a reduced lead-time compared to the real-world system. This is relevant to avoid mistakes and cost overruns during the implementation process of improvement philosophy. Additionally, these scenarios were both technically and financially evaluated by calculating IAALTD and IVC. In this regard, scenario 2 was found to be the best choice with 358361.7 COP/day and 10117495.7 COP respectively. Besides, the probability of waiting for more than 8 days can be significantly reduced to 8.07% (DPMO = 80762). This scenario will contribute to meaningfully decrease the disease complexity in the elderly population and reduce complications by providing earlier medical care. The proposed approach can be replicated in other outpatient environments with high level of effectiveness for both patients and healthcare managers. However, the interactions, system configurations and government regulations may be different; thus, future work will include exploring new applications on outpatient clinics related to cancer and mental diseases where these parameters may change and some other considerations must be deemed to fully represent the system.

References

1. Ortíz Barrios, M.A., McClean, S., Nugent, C.D., Castillo, A.: Reducing appointment lead-time in an outpatient department of gynecology and obstetrics through discrete-event simulation: a case study. Springer, Cham (2016)
2. LaGanga, L.R., Lawrence, S.R.: Clinic overbooking to improve patient access and increase provider productivity. Decis. Sci. **38**(2), 251–276 (2007)
3. Giachetti, R.E.: A simulation study of interventions to reduce appointment lead-time and patient no-show rate. In: Simulation Conference, 2008. WSC 2008, Winter pp. 1463–1468, IEEE
4. Rohleder, T.R., Lewkonia, P., Bischak, D.P., Duffy, P., Hendijani, R.: Using simulation modeling to improve patient flow at an outpatient orthopedic clinic. Health Care Manag. Sci. **14**(2), 135–145 (2011)
5. Zhu, Z., Heng, B.H., Teow, K.L.: Analysis of factors causing long patient waiting time and clinic overtime in outpatient clinics. J. Med. Syst. **36**(2), 707–713 (2012)
6. Barrios, M.O., Jiménez, H.F.: Reduction of average lead time in outpatient service of obstetrics through six sigma methodology. Ambient intelligence for health, pp. 293–302. Springer, London (2015)
7. Oche, M.O., Adamu, H.: Determinants of patient waiting time in the general outpatient department of a tertiary health institution in north Western Nigeria. Ann. Med. Health Sci. Res. **3**(4), 588–592 (2013)
8. Brailsford, S., Harper, P., Patel, B., Pitt, M.: An analysis of the academic literature on simulation and modeling in health care. J. Simul. **3**, 130–140 (2009)
9. De Angelis, V., Felici, G., Impelluso, P.: Integrating simulation and optimization in health care centre management. Eur. J. Oper. Res. **150**, 101–114 (2003)
10. Coelli, F., Ferreira, R., Almeida, R., Pereira, W.: Computer simulation and discrete-event models in the analysis of a mammography clinic patient flow. Comput. Methods Programs Biomed. **87**, 201–207 (2007)
11. Elkhuizen, S., Das, S., Bakker, P., Hontelez, J.: Using computer simulation to reduce access time for outpatient departments. Qual. Saf. Health Care **16**, 382–386 (2007)
12. Villamizar, J., Coelli, F., Pereira, W., Almeida, R.: Discrete-event computer simulation methods in the optimization of a physiotherapy clinic. Physiotherapy **97**, 71–77 (2011)
13. Zeng, Z., Ma, X., Hu, Y., Li, J., Bryant, D.: A simulation study to improve quality of care in the emergency department of a community hospital. J. Emerg. Nurs. **38**, 322–328 (2012)
14. Mocarzel, B., Shelton, D., Uyan, B., Pérez, E., Jimenez, J., DePagter, L.: Modeling and simulation of patient admission services in a multi-specialty outpatient clinic. In: Proceedings of the 2013 Winter Simulation Conference, pp. 2309–2319 (2013)
15. Viana, J., Brailsford, S.C., Harindra, V., Harper, P.R.: Combining discrete-event simulation and system dynamics in a healthcare setting: a composite model for Chlamydia infection. Eur. J. Oper. Res. **237**, 196–206 (2014)
16. Ben-Tovim, D., Filar, J., Hakendorf, P., Qin, S., Thompson, C., Ward, D.: Hospital event simulation model: arrivals to discharge-design, development and application. Simul. Model. Pract. Theory **68**, 80–94 (2016)
17. Ortiz, M.A., López-Meza, P.: Using computer simulation to improve patient flow at an outpatient internal medicine department. In: García, Carmelo R., Caballero-Gil, P., Burmester, M., Quesada-Arencibia, A. (eds.) UCAmI 2016. LNCS, vol. 10069, pp. 294–299. Springer, Cham (2016). doi:10.1007/978-3-319-48746-5_30

18. Herazo-Padilla, N., Montoya-Torres, J.R., Muñoz-Villamizar, A., Isaza, S.N., Polo, L.R.: Coupling ant colony optimization and discrete-event simulation to solve a stochastic location-routing problem. In: Proceedings of the 2013 Winter Simulation Conference: Simulation: Making Decisions in a Complex World, pp. 3352–3362. IEEE Press (2013)
19. Mohiuddin, S., Busby, J., Savović, J., Richards, A., Northstone, K., Hollingworth, W., Donovan, J., Vasilakis, C.: Patient flow within UK emergency departments: a systematic review of the use of computer simulation modelling methods. BMJ Open 7(5), e015007 (2017)

Evaluation of a Multisensory Stimulation Tool: Effect of Auditory, Olfactory and Visual Stimuli for Scenario Identification and Memory Evocation

Raúl Casillas[✉], Alberto L. Morán, and Victoria Meza-Kubo

Facultad de Ciencias, Universidad Autónoma de Baja California, Ensenada, Mexico
{rcasillas,alberto.moran,mmeza}@uabc.edu.mx

Abstract. In this paper we present the results of the evaluation of a low-level prototype implementing the concept of Personal Spaces for Multisensory Stimulation (PS4MS). A wizard of Oz evaluation was conducted in terms of the identification of the scenarios presented and the evocation of memories through the stimuli provided to study participants. Evaluation results provide evidence regarding: (i) that participants were able to recognize the scenarios 97.11% of the times and evoke memories 73.26% of the times using the tool, based on the provided olfactory, auditory and visual stimuli; (ii) understanding that although visual stimuli were determinant for scenario recognition, olfactory stimuli were perceived by participants as the most important for memory evocation; and (iii) understanding that the familiarity of the scenario is key both for scenario identification and for the evocation of memories in the participants. This results encourage us to continue working on the construction and evaluation of a high-level version of our PS4MS prototype, which will include tactile (haptic) stimuli in addition to the stimuli already provided.

Keywords: Multisensory stimulation · Evocation of memories · Computer support · Rehabilitation

1   Introduction

According to the WHO [1], a disability occurs when the interaction between a person and personal and/or environmental factors is not adequate, which may be due to illness. According to recent INEGI data [2], in Mexico, people with some form of disability are 7.1 million, which represents 6% of the total population.

In this paper we focus on cognitive impairment, which is due to a decrease in higher mental functions such as intelligence, language and learning, as well as motor functions [3]. The rehabilitation of patients with this type of disability is carried out with a structured set of therapeutic activities designed to train the individual's ability to think, use judgment and make decisions. One of the most used methods for cognitive rehabilitation is Multisensory Stimulation [4], which is a therapeutic specialty that is based on the principles of sensory integration; through the use of multisensory stimuli the central nervous system is directly stimulated favoring the development of cognitive processes such as attention, memory and language.

© Springer International Publishing AG 2017
S.F. Ochoa et al. (Eds.): UCAmI 2017, LNCS 10586, pp. 330–339, 2017.
DOI: 10.1007/978-3-319-67585-5_35

According to [5], one of the main tools to provide multisensory stimulation therapy are Multisensory Stimulation (MS) rooms, which consist of a room with materials specifically designed so that users are exposed to controlled stimuli, to favor their level of sensory integration, thus facilitating basic learning and fostering more meaningful relationships. However, in [6, 7] it is shown that it is not strictly necessary to dedicate a whole room to provide multisensory therapy, as it can be provided in smaller spaces that include the elements necessary to perform a therapy session.

According to the information obtained from interviews with specialists in MS therapy and after having observed therapy sessions in a MS room, three scenarios can be highlighted:

1. MS therapy has worked to evoke memories in people who have suffered a stroke, which has supported their recovery.
2. Patients should usually be taken to where the room is located to attend the therapy session, which may involve considerable distances.
3. In MS rooms each patient is treated in a mutually exclusive manner, as the stimuli of one's therapy could interfere with the stimuli of the other's therapy; for this reason a significant part of the available equipment can remain idle.

Considering these limitations, we identified the possibility of creating Personal Spaces for Multi-sensory Stimulation (PS4MS) that would allow to: (i) provide therapy to more than one patient at a time, and (2) be taken to a patient if s/he can not go or can not be taken to the MS room.

Since the PS4MS concept does not currently exist in the literature, a definition for it is proposed from concepts such as personal and peripersonal spaces [8, 9], and body schema and multisensory integration [10]. Thus, a PS4MS is defined as: the physical space that surrounds a person within 1 m of distance, where s/he can receive multiple auditory, visual, olfactory and tactile stimuli in a clear way.

The objective of the present work is to conceptualize, construct and evaluate a prototype of PS4MS as a tool that allows the integration of sensory information to iden-tify scenarios and to evoke memories in people (reminiscence), and to analyze if any of the stimulated senses stands out about the others to evoke memories in people. In addi-tion, it seeks to determine the type of scenarios that should be used to evoke these memories effectively in people. It is intended that the findings of this research could guide developers who need to create technological tools that seek to support the tasks of multisensory stimulation therapy.

2   Background

Starting from the objective of this work, literature defines the concept of reminiscence, as the process of remembering personal events or past experiences that are memorable for a person [11].

Information and Communication Technologies (ICTs) are a potential medium to support the provision of different types of therapy, including Reminiscence Therapy (RT). RT is a non-pharmacological intervention involving the incitement of past memories, often with artifacts such as old photographs or music for therapeutic benefits, which include facilitating social interaction or increasing self-esteem [12]

RT support systems found in the literature can be classified into two main categories, those designed for: (1) individual reminiscence, in order to incite autobiographical memories to the subjects and, (2) group reminiscence, which supports sharing autobiographical memories with colleagues. In addition, it can be emphasized that the main means used by these systems are photographs and music. The following describes a number of RT support systems classified by the purpose for which they were created and the technology they use.

Mitigate Motor and Sensory Deficiencies: MINWii [13], is a reminiscence game that employs a Wii Remote as input device, performs a signal filter to accommodate the motor deficiencies of users not be able to play the game; CIRCA [14], employs a touch screen to allow users with some degree of dementia to manipulate reminiscence materials.

Compensate for Attention Deficit: MyBrainBook [15] is an online platform that aims to record information about the person with dementia in order to produce a care plan that is created jointly between the person with dementia and their families, and that is easily shared with professionals; MemoryLane [16], is a desktop application to support people with mild dementia through the creation of digital life histories to which the context of the place where the images were taken is added. REMPAD [17], is an online system designed to facilitate group RT for people with Alzheimer's and other dementias, it uses intelligent classifiers to recommend Internet accessible videos (e.g. YouTube) based on the profile, interests, and hobbies of group participants.

In addition, other projects that present systems architectures were found, such as [18], which aims to provide remote RT; to deploy daily activities of users with dementia [19]; and finally, [20] presents an architecture to deploy multimedia systems to compensate for the feeling of loneliness in older adults.

It is noteworthy that, of the projects analyzed so far, none of them uses olfactory stimuli for RT, although Proust [21] described an olfactory memory in which the smell and taste of a French muffin triggers a far memory of childhood. In the study conducted in this work, we included olfactory stimuli to analyze participants' behavior as activator of memories in conjunction with visual and auditory stimuli.

3 Methodology

In order to reach the objective established in this work, we attempted to immerse the subject in three different scenarios using sounds, aromas and video, as a way to evoke some past situation; the scenarios that were chosen according to the specific mores for the inhabitants of the locality were: (1) preparing a cup of coffee may be more common in many countries and is part of the daily life of Mexican families; (2) cutting and eating guavas from a tree was chosen because in the region many people have guava trees in their homes and it is common to find them; and (3) preparing strawberries with cream, was chosen because in the southern part of the state this fruit is produced in abundance and it is a dessert typical of the region. For convenience we selected these scenarios that have characteristic sounds, aromas and images, and that involved preparing or eating a meal, although others were considered.

Instruments Used. To carry out the experiment we used a low fidelity prototype, and the Wizard of Oz technique. Additionally, we used real fragrances contained in jars, actual ambient sounds and videos where real subjects performed the activities of the scenario presented. The aromas were released manually and the audio and videos were played on a laptop also manually.

Participants. In this preliminary study, subjects were 35 university students, 14 women and 21 men, with a mean age of 21.85 years (SD = 2.09), 21 studied in a local public university and 14 in a local technological institute.

Independent Variables. The proposed scenarios:

- Preparing a cup of coffee.
- Cutting and eating guavas from a tree.
- Preparing strawberries with cream.

3.1 Dependent Variables.

- Scenario identification.
- Effectiveness of the scenario to evoke memories.

Hypotheses. In order to determine if a scenario is better than the others to allow participants to identify it and evoque memories in them, we selected one of the scenarios at random and compared to the other two.

Hypothesis 1: The scenario that will be identified the most is the preparation of a cup of coffee.

Hypothesis 2: The most effective scenario to evoke memories in the subjects is the preparation of a cup of coffee.

Procedure The study was conducted within subjects, one subject at a time, each with an average time of 13 min. Before starting, they were asked for demographic data, later, each subject was asked to wear a mask to prevent their sight, which was removed when they should receive visual stimuli. Each scenario was divided into three stages, each lasting 30 s: in the first stage a single stimulus was provided, in the second two stimuli were provided and in the third stage the three stimuli were provided. It should be noted that the visual stimuli (video) was presented always in the third stage, as according to [22] looking at an image for 0.33 s will provide enough information to interpret it, even if it is not something representative for the subject. At the end of each stage, the subject was asked if s/he was able to identify the scenario that was presented to him/her. At the conclusion of the reproduction of each scenario, the subject was asked as to whether s/he evoked some memory and what stimulus s/he felt was more effective in evoking that memory.

4 Results

The objective of the experiment was to determine the feasibility of evoking memories to participants through multisensory stimulation, so that they could bring to their mind significant memories with a specific stimulus or a combination of them, as well as to identify which scenario performed better to evoke memories.

Hypothesis 1: *The scenario that will be identified the most is the preparation of a cup of coffee.*

From the results obtained for the identification of the three scenarios presented, both the preparation of a cup of coffee and the preparation of strawberries with cream were identified by 97.14% (34/35) of the subjects, while the one of cutting and eating guavas from a tree was identified by 92.28% (33/35) of subjects. A Kruskal-Wallis H test was performed to determine if the results were significant and to statistically verify if any of the scenarios were identified more than the other two.

According to the results of this test, no significant differences were observed (K-W statistic = 0.5149, p = 0.7730) to affirm that the scenarios were not equally identifiable by the subjects; preparation of a cup of coffee scenario had a mean = 1971 and a standard deviation = 0.169, cutting and eating guavas from a tree an average = 1943 and standard deviation = 0.2355 and, preparation of strawberries with cream had a mean = 1971 and a standard deviation = 0.169. Thus, it can be said that people may identify the scenarios presented to them, and that there is no significant difference between the means of the three scenarios reproduced, to assert that the scenario of the preparation of a cup of coffee is identified the most, therefore *hypothesis 1 is rejected.*

Hypothesis 2: *The most effective scenario to evoke memories in the subjects is the preparation of a cup of coffee.*

The results obtained in the evocation of memories from the three scenarios presented were: the preparation of a cup of coffee evoked some memories to 85.7% (30/35) of the subjects, the cutting and to eating guavas from a tree evoked some memories to 68.5% (24/35) of them, and the preparation of strawberries with cream evoked some memories to 57.1% (20/35) of the subjects. A Kruskal-Wallis H test was performed to determine if the results are significant and verifying, statistically, if one of the scenarios is superior to the others to evoke memories on them. Based on the test results, there were significant differences in the effectiveness of the three scenarios to evoke memories in the subjects (K-W statistic = 6891, p = 0.0319). It was also observed (Fig. 1) that the most effective scenario to evoke memories was the one on preparing a cup of coffee (Mean = 1857, Std Dev = 0.355), followed by cutting and eating guavas from a tree (Mean = 1.686, Std Dev = 0.471) and lastly the one on the preparation of strawberries with cream (Mean = 1.571, Std Dev = 0.5021).

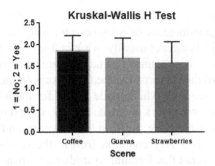

Fig. 1. Results from the Kruskal-Wallis H test to evoke memories; for the test, the coding 1 = NO and 2 = YES were taken into account.

Based on the data presented above, it can be said that it is possible to evoke memories in the subjects through the recreation of scenarios, and that there is a significant difference between the means of the different scenarios presented. The scenario of the preparation of a cup of coffee evoked memories to more subjects than the other two scenarios, therefore, *hypothesis 2 is accepted.*

5 Discussion

In this experiment three different scenarios were presented aiming at evoking memories to the participants of the study. Although the three scenarios were equally identifiable by them – participants were able to identify the scenarios 101 times out of the 105 instances presented (with a mean very close to 2, see Fig. 2), this was not the same for their effectiveness at evoking memories, as only in 74 cases out of 105 scenarios presented, they evoked a memory to the participant.

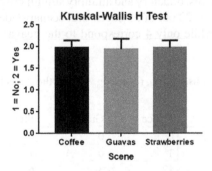

Fig. 2. Results from the Kruskal-Wallis H test for the identification of scenarios; for the test, the coding 1 = NO and 2 = YES were taken into account

Familiarity of the Scenario for Identification A possible explanation for the difference of scenario identification by participants vs. memory evocation on participants, based on the memories that the subjects described, may be that this is due to how familiar the scenarios are to them. For example, the preparation of the cup of coffee reminded them of their parents, grandparents or relatives preparing and drinking coffee, even though some of the subjects did not usually drink coffee. As for the cutting and eating guavas from a tree scenario, it is not unusual that there are guava trees in the local gardens and backyards, but not all the subjects like the fruit. Some of them even mentioned that they did not know it (2 subjects), which made it hard for them to identify the scenario and, even more, to evoke memories about it. Finally, the preparation of strawberries with cream scenario was in the same situation as the cutting and eating guavas from the tree, because although it is a very common fruit in the southern area of the region, preparing them this way is not that familiar to study participants.

From these results it can be established that, in order to evoke memories in people, the selected scenarios should be familiar to participants; thus, the selection of a scenario should be made according to the profile and customs of each subject, or better yet, tailor-made for each of them, to ensure that it is significant to them, and thus help them remembering a significant past situation of their life.

Scenario Identification Also, we analyzed which stimulus aided the most to identify the scenario. We looked at this from the perspective of an observer (observation data). Table 1 shows that the observer noticed that (i) a single stimulus (either auditory or olfactory) usually provides not enough information as to identify the scenario - only in 2 cases out of 101 identifications, participants were able to identify (i.e. guess) the scenario (1 coffee, 1 strawberries) with the olfactory stimulus and none with the auditory stimulus; (ii) two stimuli (both auditory or olfactory) provide enough information as to identify the scenario – in 39 cases out of 101 participants were able to identify the scenario (22 coffee, 4 guavas, 13 strawberries); and (iii) including the visual stimulus in addition to auditory and olfactory stimuli provides most information as to identify the scenario – in 60 cases out of the 101 participants were able to identify the scenario (11 coffee, 29 guavas, 20 strawberries). Also, it can be seen in Table 1, that when the scenario is familiar to the participants, olfactory and auditory stimuli provide enough information as to identify the scenario (22 out of 39 successful scenario identifications correspond to the coffee scenario, while only 4 correspond to the guavas scenario and 13 to the strawberries scenario).

Table 1. Data obtained by observation, regarding whether the subject identified the scenario by the end of each stage

Stimuli	Coffee	Guavas	Strawberries	Total
Auditory	0	0	0	0
Olfactory	1	0	1	2
Auditory+Olfactory	12	3	6	21
Olfactory+Auditory	10	1	7	18
Auditory+Olfactory+Visual	6	13	10	29
Olfactory+Auditory+Visual	5	16	10	31
Total	34	33	34	101

Memory Evocation Finally, we analyzed which stimulus or combination of stimuli was perceived by participants as aiding them most to evoke memories. The data was obtained by self-report from participants, whom were asked the question "What stimulus (or combination of them) do you consider to have supported you the most in evoking your memory?". The results obtained are presented in Fig. 3. The individual stimuli and the combinations mentioned by the subjects are presented in the lower part of the graph. It should be noted that in only 74 out of the 105 instances of scenarios presented participants responded on evoking a memory.

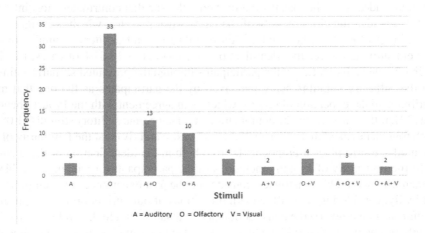

Fig. 3. Stimulus and stimuli combinations that participants considered to aid them most to evoke a memory

As can be seen in Fig. 3, participants considered that the most important stimulus to aid them on evoking a memory is the olfactory (33 out of 74 times), followed by the combination of olfactory and auditory stimulus, for which participants considered that it aided them to evoke a memory 23 out of 74 times. Also, for the remaining 18 instances, 15 times participants considered that the visual stimuli (alone or in any combination with the other stimuli) aided them to evoke a memory.

These data provide evidence of the importance that study participants gave to olfactory stimuli as reminiscent of memories, which is in accordance with the Proust phenomenon [23]; it emphasizes that aromas are more important to evoke memories (reminiscence) than any other stimulus. Also, it can be emphasized that the sounds are an important element in the task of remembering and if they are used in conjunction with the olfactory stimuli (aromas) it results in a greater potential to evoke memories in people [24]. This contrasts with scenario identification, where the visual stimulus was the most prominent.

6 Conclusions and Future Work

In this paper we present the results of the evaluation of a low level prototype of the proposed concept of Personal Spaces for Multisensory Stimulation (PS4MS). A scenario-based assessment was conducted in terms of the identification of the scenarios presented and the evocation of memories through the stimuli presented to the participants. The results of the evaluation provide evidence that: (i) it is feasible for the participants to identify the scenarios presented through the auditory, olfactory and visual stimuli provided, with the visual stimulus being the one that contributes most information for this identification (59.40% of the cases when present), which is in agreement with [22]; (ii) likewise, the combination of olfactory and auditory stimuli provided sufficient information for the identification of scenarios in 38.61% of cases; (iii) it is possible to evoke memories in the participants through the presented scenarios/stimuli, with the olfactory stimulus being perceived by the participants as the one that most contributes to the evocation (44.59%), which is in agreement with the Proust phenomenon [23], followed again by the combination of olfactory and auditory stimuli (31.08%), which together evoked memories in 75.56% of cases; and (iv) that the familiarity of the presented scenario plays a preponderant role both in the identification of the scenario and in the possibility of evoking memories in the participant, for which, in a PS4MS, the scenarios should be constructed considering the past experiences of each subject.

Finally, considering two of the main limitations of our current prototype, our lines of future work include (i) the construction and evaluation of a high-level version of the PS4MS prototype, which will include tactile (haptic) stimulus as well as olfactory, auditory and visual stimuli; and (ii) its evaluation with actual end users from particular MS target populations (e.g. older adults and stroke survivors).

References

1. Thomas, C.: How is disability understood? An examination of sociological approaches. Disabil. Soc. **19**(6), 569–583 (2004)
2. INEGI (México).: La discapacidad en México, datos al 2014. In: Instituto Nacional de Estadística y Geografía—INEGI, México (2016)
3. Braddock, D., Rizzolo, M.C., Thompson, M., Bell, R.: Emerging technologies and cognitive disability. J. Spec. Educ. Technol. **19**(4), 49–56 (2004)
4. Baillon, S., Van Diepen, E., Prettyman, R.: Multi-sensory therapy in psychiatric care. Adv. Psychiatr. Treat. **8**(6), 444–450 (2002)
5. Vlaskamp, C., De Geeter, K.I., Huijsmans, L.M., Smit, I.H.: Passive activities: the effectiveness of multisensory environments on the level of activity of individuals with profound multiple disabilities. J. Appl. Res. Intellect. Disabil. **16**(2), 135–143 (2003)
6. Baker, R., Holloway, J., Holtkamp, C., Larsson, A., Hartman, L.C., Pearce, R., Owens, M.: Effects of multi-sensory stimulation for people with dementia. J. Adv. Nurs. **43**(5), 465–477 (2003)
7. Martin, N.T., Gaffan, E.A., Williams, T.: Behavioural effects of long-term multi-sensory stimulation. Br. J. Clin. Psychol. **37**(1), 69–82 (1998)
8. Cardinali, L., Brozzoli, C., Farne, A.: Peripersonal space and body schema: two labels for the same concept? Brain Topogr. **21**(3–4), 252–260 (2009)

9. Rizzolatti, G., Scandolara, C., Matelli, M., Gentilucci, M.: Afferent properties of periarcuate neurons in macaque monkeys II. Visual responses. Behav. Brain Res. **2**(2), 147–163 (1981)
10. Maravita, A., Spence, C., Driver, J.: Multisensory integration and the body schema: close to hand and within reach. Curr. Biol. **13**(13), R531–R539 (2003)
11. Butler, R.: The life review: an interpretation of reminiscence in the aged. Psychiatry **26**(1), 65–76 (1963)
12. Lazar, A., Thompson, H., Demiris, G.: A systematic review of the use of technology for reminiscence therapy. Health Educ. Behav. **41**, 51S–61S (2014)
13. Benveniste, S., Jouvelot, P., Péquignot, R.: The MINWii Project: renarcissization of patients suffering from Alzheimer's disease through video game-based music therapy. In: International Conference on Entertainment Computing, pp. 79–90. Springer, Berlin, Heidelberg (2010)
14. Astell, A.J., Ellis, M.P., Bernardi, L., Alm, N., Dye, R., Gowans, G., Campbell, J.: Using a touch screen computer to support relationships between people with dementia and caregivers. Interact. Comput. **22**(4), 267–275 (2010)
15. Savitch, N.: My Brain Book: A Case Study on Responsible Research and Innovation in Information and Communications Technology for Ageing People. Health Innovation Network South London (2015). http://www.hin-southlondon.org/system/resources/resources/000/000/081/original/ResponsibleIndustry_CaseStudy_02_savitch_FINAL.pdf? 1425984274. Recuperado 20 de Febrero de 2017
16. Kikhia, B., Bengtsson, J. E., Synnes, K., Hallberg, J.: Creating digital life stories through activity recognition with image filtering. In: International Conference on Smart Homes and Health Telematics, pp. 203–210. Springer, Berlin, Heidelberg (2010)
17. Yang, Y., Caprani, N., Bermingham, A., O'Rourke, J., Collins, R., Gurrin, C., Smeaton, A. F.: Design and field evaluation of REMPAD: a recommender system supporting group reminiscence therapy. Evol. Ambient Intell. 13–22 (2013)
18. Hamada, T., Kuwahara, N., Morimoto, K., Yasuda, K., Akira, U., Abe, S.: Preliminary study on remote assistance for people with dementia at home by using multi-media contents. Univers. Access Hum.–Comput. Interact. Addressing Divers. (2009). doi: 10.1007/978-3-642-02707-9_26
19. Kikhia, B., Hallberg, J., Bengtsson, J.E., Savenstedt, S., Synnes, K.: Building digital life stories for memory support. Int. J. Comput. in Healthc. **1**(2), 161–176 (2010)
20. Caprani, N., Dwyer, N., Harrison, K., O'Brien, K.: Remember when: development of an interactive reminiscence device. In: CHI'05 Extended Abstracts on Human Factors in Computing Systems, pp. 2070–2073. ACM (2005)
21. Shanahan, L. K., Gottfried, J. A.: Scents and reminiscence: olfactory influences on memory consolidation in the sleeping human brain. In: Cognitive Neuroscience of Memory Consolidation, pp. 335–346. Springer, Berlin (2017)
22. Potter, M.C.: Meaning in visual search. Science **187**(4180), 965–966 (1975)
23. Chu, S., Downes, J.J.: Odour-evoked autobiographical memories: psychological investigations of Proustian phenomena. Chem. Senses **25**(1), 111–116 (2000)
24. Toffolo, M.B., Smeets, M.A., Van Den Hout, M.A.: Proust revisited: odours as triggers of aversive memories. Cogn. Emot. **26**(1), 83–92 (2012)

Automatic Mapping of Motivational Text Messages into Ontological Entities for Smart Coaching Applications

Claudia Villalonga[1]([✉]), Harm op den Akker[2], Hermie Hermens[2,3],
Luis Javier Herrera[1], Hector Pomares[1], Ignacio Rojas[1], Olga Valenzuela[4],
and Oresti Banos[3]

[1] Research Center for Information and Communications Technologies,
University of Granada, Granada, Spain
{cvillalonga,jherrera,hector,irojas}@ugr.es
[2] Roessingh Research and Development, Telemedicine Group,
Enschede, The Netherlands
{H.opdenAkker,h.hermens}@rrd.nl
[3] Center for Telematics and Information Technology, University of Twente,
Telemedicine Group, Enschede, The Netherlands
{h.j.hermens,o.banoslegran}@utwente.nl
[4] Department of Applied Mathematics, University of Granada, Granada, Spain
olgavc@ugr.es

Abstract. Unwholesome lifestyles can reduce lifespan by several years
or even decades. Therefore, raising awareness and promoting healthier behaviors prove essential to revert this dramatic panorama. Virtual
coaching systems are at the forefront of digital solutions to educate people and procure a more effective health self-management. Despite their
increasing popularity, virtual coaching systems are still regarded as entertainment applications with an arguable efficacy for changing behaviors,
since messages can be perceived to be boring, unpersonalized and can
become repetitive over time. In fact, messages tend to be quite general,
repetitive and rarely tailored to the specific needs, preferences and conditions of each user. In the light of these limitations, this work aims
at help building a new generation of methods for automatically generating user-tailored motivational messages. While the creation of messages is addressed in a previous work, in this paper the authors rather
present a method to automatically extract the semantics of motivational
messages and to create the ontological representation of these messages.
The method uses first natural language processing to perform a linguistic analysis of the message. The extracted information is then mapped
to the concepts of the motivational messages ontology. The proposed
method could boost the quantity and diversity of messages by automatically mining and parsing existing messages from the internet or other
digitised sources, which can be later tailored according to the specific
needs and particularities of each user.

Keywords: Ontology · Natural language processing · Motivational
messages · Smart coaching

© Springer International Publishing AG 2017
S.F. Ochoa et al. (Eds.): UCAmI 2017, LNCS 10586, pp. 340–351, 2017.
DOI: 10.1007/978-3-319-67585-5_36

1   Introduction

Daily life in modern industrialized societies is characterized by high rates of sedentary behavior, and a general lack of everyday physical activity. As a result, people living in developed nations face serious health challenges related to sedentary lifestyles and diseases arising from the lack of activity thereof [14]. This worrisome situation makes it crucial to find new ways to improve health so that people can live longer and age well. While research has traditionally focused on biomedical science and advances in clinical practices, recent efforts have made significant strides in finding novel ways to promote behavioral changes to improve health outcomes. In fact, avoiding unhealthy habits is currently a major epidemiological priority. To achieve this goal, innovative approaches that automatically and autonomously coach people in healthier behaviors are essential in leading to lasting, beneficial behavioral changes.

All people around the globe, from children to older adults, are or will be in need of health coaching solutions at some point in their lives. Virtual coaching solutions are therefore called upon to possibly be the only means to cope with such an enormous group of target users. As a matter of fact, virtual coaching is no longer a sci-fi concept and its use is increasing over time [5,13,19,23]. However, the effectiveness of these systems while changing and promoting healthier behaviours is at stake. One main limiting factor has to do with the frequent use of generic and impersonal motivational messages [17], which hardly hold in people's mind. In order to increase the effectiveness of these messages more personalized strategies are required [4,10].

Creating tailored motivational messages for coaching is difficult, costly and time consuming. Dedicated experts, such as the ones providing health counseling services, have to normally elaborate custom-made recommendations based on each individual characteristics, preferences and behaviors. In order to automate this process systems need to fully comprehend the content of existing motivational messages, available from the internet or other digitized sources, which can be later tailored according to the specific needs and particularities of each user. This understanding of messages may be achieved through the use of ontologies, which are semantic models enabling the automatic interpretation of the information encapsulated in the motivational messages.

The two main challenges for the automatic generation of tailored messages are: (1) using the semantics of existing messages to create new tailored messages and (2) automatically extracting the semantics of existing messages. The first challenge is addressed by the authors in an earlier work [20]. Therefore, this paper focuses on the latter challenge and presents a new method to automatically extract the semantics of motivational messages and to create the ontological representation of the messages. The method uses natural language processing to perform a linguistic analysis of the message. The extracted information is mapped to the concepts of the motivational messages ontology.

2   State of the Art

The generation of personalized advisory messages can be supported by the use of ontologies. In fact, there exist some solutions using ontologies for the creation of motivational messages. For example, an ontology-based method is defined as part of an eHealth service to produce customized recommendations [9]. The main message components and their structure are modeled in the proposed ontology which also describes the user general information, their abilities, interests and preferences. Furthermore, ontologies have also been used in the physical activity domain to model multimodal contexts [21] and to generate dynamic feedback. The appropriate feedback is derived from the ontology in [24] by pruning irrelevant branches based on context information. Predefined feedback messages, which could be delivered to the user, are modeled in this ontology. The selection process is adapted by deriving the probabilities about user preferences for certain message types. Finally, an ontology modeling the messages intention is used in [4], a practical framework for the automatic generation of real-time tailored messages in behavior change applications.

Ontologies have already been used to model motivational messages. However, these models only describe the structure of the message and its intention but not its actual content. Modeling the message content is quite important for the automatic selection of the most suitable messages to be delivered by the smart coach. In our previous work [20], we have proposed an ontological approach to comprehensively model motivational messages used by smart coaches in the domain of physical activity. The ontology describes the main characteristics of motivational messages, including the message metadata such as its length, type or composition but also information about the message content, e.g. place or object required to perform the recommended action. Apart from the ontology, our previous work describes the ontological querying method used by the smart coach to retrieve the most adequate message depending on the user's status, preferences and context.

Ontology learning has been used in many works to extract semantic information from unstructured data like text and semi-structured data like XML. For example, in [12] the authors make a comprehensive review of the available techniques for ontology learning from semi-structured and unstructured data and in [25] the authors focus on ontology learning from text. In the state-of-the-art research, natural language processing techniques are used in combination with statistical analysis or machine learning techniques to identify the grammar dependencies and to parse the discovered relation between syntactic entities in the text. Furthermore, ontology learning is not only a field of theoretical research, but several tools to perform ontology learning based on natural language processing techniques have been made available online; for example, Text2Onto [7], OntoLT [6], OntoLern [16] or Flax Clade PoC [2]. The main problem of using these available tools to extract the semantics of motivational text messages and to create the ontological representation of these messages is that they require long texts in order to apply the statistical analysis. Therefore, these tools are not suitable for detecting information out of short motivational messages which contain limited information. As such, a new method based on natural language processing has been developed.

3   Method

A method to automatically extract the semantics of motivational text messages and to create the ontological representation of these messages is here presented. The input to this method are plain text motivational messages created by a domain expert or retrieved from the internet or any other available digitized source. The output of this method is the ontological representation of the motivational messages, which could be used by smart coaches for translating behavioral findings into realizable actions.

The proposed method is composed of four different steps: (1) linguistic analysis of the text message using natural language processing techniques, (2) generation of the ontological representation of the message, (3) creation of new messages based on splitting complex messages, and (4) creation of new messages based on the knowledge modeled in the ontology.

3.1   Linguistic Analysis of the Message

The motivational messages are analyzed using natural language processing techniques in order to identify the content of the text message. The most important information that needs to be extracted from the motivational messages for physical activity coaching is the action described in the text messages, the location and the time in which this action takes place and the elements which might be required for the action to be executed.

The grammatical structure of the sentence is detected using a probabilistic natural language parser, which uses the knowledge gained from hand-parsed sentences to automatically parse any new sentences. This parser groups words that go together in phrases and detects which words are the verb, the subject or the object of the sentence. Furthermore, the parser provides the grammatical relations among words and the structure of the phrases in a tree representation. Detecting the predicate of the sentence is helpful in the recognition of the action that is recommended in the motivational message. The direct object that accompanies the verb is also part of the description of the action as it is an element required for the action to be executed. The temporal modifier of the predicate specifies a time; thus, it determines the time in which the action described in the motivational message takes place. The place modifier of the predicate specifies a the location in which the action described in the motivational message takes place.

In the linguistic analysis, not only is the grammatical structure of the sentence detected but also the part of speech. Using a log-linear part-of-speech tagger, each word in the sentence is assigned a tag about the part of speech to which it belongs, e.g., noun, verb or adjective. Part-of-speech information can be relevant to identify the main word of a phrase that has been recognized using the probabilistic natural language parser. For example, in case a direct object has three words, the part of speech analysis allows to determine that the word which is a noun is the head of the phrase.

Finally, recognizing the named entities in a sentence is also an essential part of the linguistic analysis. Using a linear chain conditional random field sequence model, it is possible to label the words in the sentence which are names of things, such as person, location, date and time. Identifying the named entities of the type location allows to determine where the action in the motivational message takes place. Similarly, the named entities of the type time indicate when the action in the motivational message takes place.

3.2 Generation of the Ontological Representation

The message, which has been linguistically analyzed in the previous step, is mapped into the concepts of the motivational messages ontology presented in [20]. This ontology describes several aspects of the motivational messages, such as its intention, its components and its content. Therefore, it defines classes like *Message*, *MessageComponent*, *Action*, *Time*, *Place* or *Element*. For more information about the ontology and how it has been designed please refer to [20].

An instance of the class *Message* is created to model the semantics of the motivational message. For each sentence in the message a new instance of the class *MessageComponent* is created. These instances of the class *MessageComponent* are linked via the property *hasComponent* to the instance of the class *Message*, i.e. to the actual message from which they are part. Once the structure of the message has been created, the actual content of the message is modeled. First, the plain text of the sentence is asserted as the value of the data property *hasContent* for the instance of the class *MessageComponent*. The main verb of the sentence and head of the predicate, detected by analyzing the grammatical structure of the sentence and the part of speech, is used as the action presented in the message. Therefore, it is mapped into the corresponding instance of the class *Action* and linked to the instance of the class *MessageComponent* via the property *hasAction*. Furthermore, if there are coordinated verbs to the main verb, these verbs are also mapped into the corresponding instance of the class *Action* and also linked to the instance of the class *MessageComponent*.

Apart from the action itself, the message contains some other information that further describes the action. The time in which the action takes place, identified as a temporal modifier of the predicate or as a named entity of type time, is assigned the corresponding instance of the class *Time* and linked to the instance of the class *MessageComponent* via the property *hasTime*. The place where the actions occurs, identified as a place modifier of the predicate or as a named entity of type location, is mapped into the corresponding instance of the class *Place* and linked to the instance of the class *MessageComponent* via the property *hasPlace*. The noun which is the head of the direct object of the sentence is mapped into the element required to perform the action. Thus, this object is mapped into the corresponding instance of the class *Element* and linked to the instance of the class *MessageComponent* via the property *hasRequiredElement*.

If there are coordinated nouns to the head of the direct object, these nouns are also mapped into the corresponding instance of the class *Element* and also linked to the instance of the class *MessageComponent*. Finally, in case the action presented in the message is negated, this is represented in the ontology as asserting to true the value of the data property *hasNegatedAction*.

3.3 Creation of New Messages Based on Splitting Complex Messages

The splitting method automatically creates simpler messages out of complex ones; thus, increasing the variety of motivational messages available for the virtual coaches. A motivational message which contains multiple different concepts is split into several messages which contain a single concept. In fact, the splitting method could be applied in different scenarios, for example, when multiple coordinated verbs conform the predicate of the sentence or when a direct object is composed of several coordinated nouns.

In case the predicate of the sentence contains several verbs joined via a coordinating conjunction, i.e., the message component describes several actions combined via a conjunction such us "and", "or" or "but", the message is split into as many messages as the number of verbs in the original message, and each newly created message only contains a single action. Therefore, a new instance of the class *Message* is created for each of the split messages and a new instance of the class *MessageComponent* is associated to it. Then, each action, which is already mapped into the instance of the class *Action*, is linked to the corresponding instance of the class *MessageComponent* via the property *hasAction*.

In case the direct object of the sentence is composed of several nouns linked via a coordinating conjunction, i.e., the message has a single action but several elements in the direct object, the message is split into as many messages as the number of nouns in the original direct object, and each newly created message contains an action with a single element in the direct object. Therefore, a new instance of the class *Message* is created for each of the split messages and a new instance of the class *MessageComponent* is associated to it. Then, the action mapped into the instance of the class *Action* is linked via the property *hasAction* to all the instances of the class *MessageComponent*. Finally, each element of the direct object, which is mapped to the instance of the class *Element*, is linked to the corresponding instance of the class *MessageComponent* via the property *hasRequieredElement*.

3.4 Creation of New Messages Based on the Knowledge Modeled in the Ontology

New messages can be derived from existing ones using the motivational messages ontology [20]. The domain knowledge modeled in the ontology, which describes the time and the location where the actions take place, is vital to derive new messages and make them more diverse. For example, the information about the multiple locations in which an action can take place is used to determine alternatives locations for the same action. Therefore, a motivational message which recommends an action that takes place in a given location could be cloned and generate a new message which proposes the execution of the same action but in another alternative location. In the proposed method, a new instance of the class *Message* is created for each of the possible alternative locations and a new instance of the class *MessageComponent* is associated to it. Then, the action in the original sentence, which is mapped into the instance of the class *Action*, is linked via the property *hasAction* to all the instances of the class *MessageComponent*. Finally, for each of the possible locations, the actual instance of the class *Place* is linked to the corresponding instance of the class *MessageComponent* via the property *hasPlace*.

4   Implementation

The presented method to automatically extract the semantics of motivational text messages and to create the ontological representation of these messages has been implemented in Java. Several existing open source tools and APIs have been utilized to facilitate the development of this method. The linguistic analysis of the text message is implemented using Stanford CoreNLP [15], a set of open source tools for natural language processing. The generation of the ontological representation is developed using Apache Jena (v2.11.2) [1], a semantic web framework which includes some APIs for handling RDF [8], OWL [22], and SPARQL [11].

For the linguistic analysis of the motivational messages, the parser provided by the Stanford CoreNLP software is configured to annotate the text in several different ways: obtaining the tokens, splitting the different sentences, recognizing the part of speech, identifying the lemma for each word, recognizing the named entities, and detecting the grammatical structure of the sentence. The parser generates a semantic graph which contains the grammatical relations between the phrases in the sentence, the part-of-speech tags (POS tags) for each word and the lemmas associated to these words. Furthermore, the parser also provides the list of named entity tags (NER tags) for each word in the sentence.

Once the motivational message has been linguistically analyzed, the relevant information is extracted and mapped into the concepts of the motivational message ontology; thus, creating the ontological representation of the message. First, the element identified as "ROOT" of the semantic graph and which has a POS tag named "VB" (verb) is mapped into the member of the class *Action* which has as name the lemma of the element. If the "ROOT" has some relation of type "cc" (coordination) and a relation of type "conj" (conjunct) to an element which has a POS tag named "VB", then this element, which is a coordinated verb, is mapped into the member of the class *Action* which has as name the lemma of the element. In case any of the verbs were phrasal verbs, they would have a grammatical relation of type "prt" (phrasal verb particle) to the particle. Thus, this element would also be taken into consideration and the actual verb plus the particle would be mapped into the ontology. All the mapped instances of the class *Action* are linked to the instance of the class *MessageComponent* via the property *hasAction*. Moreover, if the "ROOT" has a relation of type "neg" (negation modifier), i.e., the verb is negated in the sentence, the property *hasNegatedAction* for the member of the class *MessageComponent* is asserted to take the value *xsd:true* which is a datatype of the W3C XML Schema Definition Language (XSD) [18].

Apart from mapping the action itself, the element required to perform an action is also mapped into the ontology. In case the "ROOT" of the semantic graph having a POS tag named "VB" has also a grammatical relation of type "dobj" (direct object) to an element which has a POS tag named "NN" (noun singular), "NNS" (noun plural), "NNP" (proper noun singular) or "NNPS" (proper noun plural), then this element is mapped into the member of the class *Element* which has as name the lemma of the element. Moreover, if this element has some relation of type "cc" (coordination) and a relation of type "conj" (conjunct) to an element which has a POS tag named "NN", "NNS", "NNP" or "NNPS", then this element, which is a coordinated direct object, is mapped into the member of the class *Element* which has as name the lemma of the element. All the mapped instances of the class *Element* are linked to the instance of the class *MessageComponent* via the property *hasRequiredElement*.

Finally, the other elements of the message which further describe the action are also mapped into the ontology. If the list of named entity tags contains a NER tag named "TIME", then the element which has been assigned this tag represents the time in which the action takes place and it is mapped into the member of the class *Time* which has as name the lemma of the element. Similarly, if the list of named entity tags contains a NER tag named "PLACE", then the element which has been assigned this tag represents the location in which the action takes place and it is mapped into the member of the class *Place* which has as name the lemma of the element.

5   Use Case

The functioning of the proposed method is here described via a use case. Let us consider that a domain expert has created the following motivational message "You should walk the dog to the park early in the morning". Then the method is applied and its outcome is presented in Fig. 1.

In the first step the linguistic analysis of the message is performed. The grammatical relations among words can be observed in the first block of text in Fig. 1. For example "dobj(walk/VB-3, dog/NN-5)" indicates that the noun "dog" is the direct object of the verb "walk".

In the second step the ontological representation of the message is created. The relevant information obtained in the linguistic analysis is identified to create the ontological representation. Therefore, the instance m_01 of the class *Message* and the instance mc_01 of the class *MessageComponent* are created, and m_01 is linked to mc_01 via the property *hasComponent*. The action walking, which is the element identified as "ROOT" of the semantic graph and which has a POS

Fig. 1. Outcome of applying the method to automatically extract the semantics of the motivational message "You should walk the dog to the park early in the morning" and to create the ontological representation of this message.

tag named "VB", specifically "walk/VB-3", is mapped into the individual *walk* which is a member of the class *Action* and linked to the individual *mc_01* via the property *hasAction*. Moreover, the element "walk/VB-3" has a grammatical relation of type "dobj" to the element "dog/NN-5". Therefore, this element is mapped into the individual *dog* which is a member of the class *Animal*, a subclass of the class *Element*, and linked to the individual *mc_01* via the property *hasRequiredElement*. Finally, the time and place which further describe the action are also mapped into the ontology. The list of named entity tags contains a NER tag named "TIME" for the element "morning/NN-12"; thus, this element is mapped into the individual *morning* of the class *Time* and linked to the individual *mc_01* via the property *hasTime*. The list of named entity tags also contains a NER tag named "PLACE" for the element "park/NN-8"; thus, this element is mapped into the individual *park* of the class *Place* and linked to the individual *mc_01* via the property *hasPlace*. The resulting ontological representation of the motivational message can be observed in the last block of text in Fig. 1. Furthermore, a graphical representation of the message component *mc_01*, obtained using the open source ontology editor Protégé [3], is shown in Fig. 2.

Fig. 2. Instance of the message component *mc_01* which has been created to capture the semantics of the motivational message "You should walk the dog to the park early in the morning".

The third and the forth step of the method, i.e., the creation of new messages based on splitting complex messages or based on the knowledge modeled in the ontology, do not produce any output for the message "You should walk the dog to the park early in the morning" since this message describes a single action and there is no domain knowledge in the ontology regarding the locations of this action.

6   Conclusions

This paper has presented a new approach for automatically extracting the semantics of motivational messages and creating the ontological representation of these messages. The method builds on natural language processing techniques to elaborate a linguistic analysis of the message body. The extracted information is then mapped to the concepts defined in the ontology of motivational messages. Some uses cases have been further presented in order to showcase the end-to-end process and its main outcomes.

The proposed method is intended to serve as a cornerstone element in the automatic generation of tailored coaching messages. In fact, the method is expected to significantly increase the quantity and diversity of messages by automatically mining and parsing existing messages from the internet or other digitized sources, which can be later personalized to each user needs and characteristics. This method allows domain experts, i.e. coaching experts, to simply add their coaching message suggestions to the database, while not having to be concerned with the technical underlying concepts of the coaching system. Automatically extracted relevant concepts can be used by an automated system to provide tailoring through simple filtering methods or mapping of user characteristics with the ontology domain concepts. Future work aims at contrasting this hypothesis and also testing a virtual coaching system building on this concept in the wild and for large cohort of people.

Acknowledgments. This work was supported by Project TIN2015-71873-R (Spanish Ministry of Economy and Competitiveness -MINECO- and the European Regional Development Fund -ERDF).

References

1. Apache Jena: https://jena.apache.org/. Accessed 13 July 2017
2. Flax clade poc: https://github.com/flaxsearch/clade
3. Protégé: http://protege.stanford.edu/. Accessed 13 July 2017
4. op den Akker, H., Cabrita, M., op den Akker, R., Jones, V.M., Hermens, H.J.: Tailored motivational message generation: a model and practical framework for real-time physical activity coaching. J. Biomed. Inf. **55**, 104–115 (2015). http://www.sciencedirect.com/science/article/pii/S1532046415000489
5. Banos, O., Bilal Amin, M., Ali Khan, W., Afzal, M., Hussain, M., Kang, B.H., Lee, S.: The mining minds digital health and wellness framework. Biomed. Eng. Online **15**(1), 165–186 (2016). http://dx.doi.org/10.1186/s12938-016-0179-9
6. Buitelaar, P., Olejnik, D., Sintek, M.: A protg plug-in for ontology extraction from text based on linguistic analysis. In: The Semantic Web: Research and Applications. Proceedings of the 1st European Semantic Web Symposium (ESWS04). pp. 31–44. Springer (2004)
7. Cimiano, P., Völker, J.: Text2Onto. In: Montoyo, A., Muñoz, R., Métais, E. (eds.) NLDB 2005. LNCS, vol. 3513, pp. 227–238. Springer, Heidelberg (2005). doi:10.1007/11428817_21
8. Cyganiak, R., Wood, D., Lanthaler, M.: RDF 1.1 Concepts and Abstract Syntax. W3C Recommendation. https://www.w3.org/TR/rdf11-concepts/. Accessed 25 Feb 2014
9. Erriquez, E., Grasso, F.: Generation of personalised advisory messages: an ontology based approach. In: 2008 21st IEEE International Symposium on Computer-Based Medical Systems, pp. 437–442 (2008)
10. Gerdes, M., Martinez, S.G., Tjondronegoro, D.: Conceptualization of a personalized ecoach for wellness promotion. In: 11th EAI International Conference on Pervasive Computing Technologies for Healthcare (2017)
11. Harris, S., Seaborne, A.: SPARQL 1.1 (SPARQL Query Language for RDF). W3C Recommendation. http://www.w3.org/TR/sparql11-query/. Accessed 21 Mar 2013
12. Hazman, M., El-Beltagy, S.R., Rafea, A.: Article: a survey of ontology learning approaches. Int. J. Comput. Appl. **22**(8), 36–43 (2011)
13. Kitsiou, S., Thomas, M., Marai, G.E., Maglaveras, N., Kondos, G., Arena, R., Gerber, B.: Development of an innovative mhealth platform for remote physical activity monitoring and health coaching of cardiac rehabilitation patients. In: 2017 IEEE EMBS International Conference on Biomedical & Health Informatics (BHI), pp. 133–136. IEEE (2017)
14. Malina, R.M., Little, B.B.: Physical activity: the present in the context of the past. Am. J. Hum. Biol. **20**(4), 373–391 (2008)

15. Manning, C.D., Surdeanu, M., Bauer, J., Finkel, J., Bethard, S.J., McClosky, D.: The Stanford CoreNLP natural language processingtoolkit. In: Association for Computational Linguistics (ACL) System Demonstrations, pp. 55–60 (2014). http://www.aclweb.org/anthology/P/P14/P14-5010

16. Missikoff, M., Navigli, R., Velardi, P.: Integrated approach to web ontology learning and engineering. IEEE Comput. **35**(11), 60–63 (2002). https://doi.org/10.1109/MC.2002.1046976

17. Mollee, J., Middelweerd, A., Velde, S.T., Klein, M.: Evaluation of a personalized coaching system for physical activity: user appreciation and adherence. In: 11th EAI International Conference on Pervasive Computing Technologies for Healthcare (2017)

18. Peterson, D., Gao, S., Malhotra, A., Sperberg-McQueen, C.M., Thompson, H.S.: W3C XML Schema Definition Language (XSD) 1.1 Part 2: Datatypes. W3C Recommendation. http://www.w3.org/TR/xmlschema11-2/. Accessed 5 Apr 2012

19. Stephens, J., Allen, J.K., Himmelfarb, C.R.D.: Smart coaching to promote physical activity, diet change, and cardiovascular health. J. Cardiovasc. Nurs. **26**(4), 282 (2011)

20. Villalonga, C., op den Akker, H., Hermens, H., Herrera, L.J., Pomares, H., Rojas, I., Valenzuela, O., Banos, O.: Ontological modeling of motivational messages for physical activity coaching. In: 11th EAI International Conference on Pervasive Computing Technologies for Healthcare (2017)

21. Villalonga, C., Razzaq, M.A., Khan, W.A., Pomares, H., Rojas, I., Lee, S., Banos, O.: Ontology-based high-level context inference for human behavior identification. Sensors **16**(10), 1617 (2016). http://www.mdpi.com/1424-8220/16/10/1617

22. W3C OWL Working Group : OWL 2 Web Ontology Language: Document Overview, 2nd edn. W3C Recommendation. http://www.w3.org/TR/owl2-overview/. Accessed 11 Dec 2012

23. Watson, A., Bickmore, T., Cange, A., Kulshreshtha, A., Kvedar, J.: An internet-based virtual coach to promote physical activity adherence in overweight adults: randomized controlled trial. J. Med. Internet Res. **14**(1), 1–12 (2012)

24. Wieringa, W., Akker, H., Jones, V.M., Akker, R., Hermens, Hermie J.: Ontology-based generation of dynamic feedback on physical activity. In: Peleg, M., Lavrač, N., Combi, C. (eds.) AIME 2011. LNCS (LNAI), vol. 6747, pp. 55–59. Springer, Heidelberg (2011). doi:10.1007/978-3-642-22218-4_7

25. Wong, W., Liu, W., Bennamoun, M.: Ontology learning from text: a look back and into the future. ACM Comput. Surv. **44**(4), 20: 1–20: 36. http://doi.acm.org/10.1145/2333112.2333115

Discrete-Event Simulation to Reduce Waiting Time in Accident and Emergency Departments: A Case Study in a District General Clinic

Nixon Nuñez-Perez[1], Miguel Ortíz-Barrios[1(✉)], Sally McClean[2], Katherinne Salas-Navarro[1], Genett Jimenez-Delgado[3], and Anyeliz Castillo-Zea[1]

[1] Department of Industrial Management, Agroindustry and Operations, Universidad de La Costa CUC, Barranquilla, Colombia
{nnunez2,mortiz1,ksalas2,acastillo20}@cuc.edu.co
[2] School of Computing and Information Engineering, University of Ulster, Coleraine, Co. Londonderry BT52 1SA, UK
si.mcclean@ulster.ac.uk
[3] Department of Industrial Processes Engineering, Institución Universitaria ITSA, Soledad, Colombia
gjimenez@itsa.edu.co

Abstract. Waiting time is a crucial performance metric in A&E departments. In this regard, longer waiting times are related to low patient satisfaction, high mortality rates and more severe physical health complications. To analyze patient flow in these departments, discrete-event simulation (DES) has been used; however, its application has not been extended to evaluate the impact of improvement strategies. Therefore, this paper aims to design and pretest operational strategies for better ED care delivery using DES. First, input data analysis is carried out. Afterward, the DES model is developed and validated to establish whether it is statistically comparable with the real-world. Then, performance indicators of the current system are computed and analyzed. Finally, improvement strategies are proposed and evaluated by simulation modelling and statistical tests. A case study of an A&E department from a district general clinic is presented to validate the proposed framework. In particular, we will validate the effectiveness of introducing a triage system (Scenario 3), a strategy that is not currently adopted by the clinic. Results demonstrate that waiting times could be meaningfully diminished based on the proposed approaches within this paper.

Keywords: Discrete event simulation (DES) · Accident and emergency (A&E) · Emergency departments (EDs) · Healthcare

1 Introduction

Accident and Emergency (A&E) and Emergency Departments (EDs) have been experiencing increasing demands worldwide, with healthcare often facing financial difficulties and departments expanding their range of responsibilities to include, for example, uninsured patients, or arrivals during times and in places where community health and

© Springer International Publishing AG 2017
S.F. Ochoa et al. (Eds.): UCAmI 2017, LNCS 10586, pp. 352–363, 2017.
DOI: 10.1007/978-3-319-67585-5_37

social services are unavailable. A&Es also play a key role in public health surveillance and disaster response; as a result there has been an increasing need for departments to become more efficient as evidenced by various standards and targets. For example, the UK National Health Service (NHS) has had a target of 95 per cent of patients being seen in under 4 h for over a decade, yet the NHS Director (Sir Bruce Keogh) has recently announced that this the problem of long waits in A&E should now be addressed by improving services in the community, evidencing the need for urgent improvement and novel strategies.

In recent years, the use of discrete event simulation (DES) to support healthcare evaluation has gained increasing prominence [1–3]. Reasons for A&E departments featuring so prominently may include the relatively short timescales required for treatment and corresponding data collection as well as the comparatively self-contained nature of the department [4, 5]. Moreover, as a showcase of the healthcare system, treating large numbers of patients, these departments attract a lot of interest from the public, commentators and policy makers.

Other techniques have also been used in modelling the healthcare environment. For example, [6] use systems dynamics to demonstrate the interaction between the A&E department and the rest of the hospital. Also, [7] used a stochastic dynamic model that consisted of a noisy measurement and first-order autoregressive (AR) stochastic dynamic process, for modelling the throughput of emergency departments using available time-series data from a London hospital. Such approaches, which link the performance of A&E departments to the arrival mechanism as well as the rest of the hospital system, resonate well with simulation models of A&E which seek to develop new strategies for managing the queues and resource utilization.

Nonetheless, while there is an extensive research literature on simulation and modelling of A&E, little work has been done as yet on the impact of such strategies. In fact, a recent British Medical Journal paper [8] carried out a systematic review of the use of discrete event simulation for patient behavior in UK emergency departments and concluded that while "computer simulation can provide a means to pretest changes to ED care delivery before implementation in a safe and efficient manner" the "evidence base is small and poorly developed" and there are also additional issues which should be addressed.

In this paper, we model the A&E Department of a District General Clinic, motivated initially by a desire to set up a baseline against which a number of streamlining strategies could be assessed. The novelty lies in the application of DES to reduce waiting times in a clinic that is dedicated to people suffering from accidents. In addition, once we have developed the model, improvement strategies can be evaluated. In particular, we will validate the effectiveness of introducing a triage system, a strategy that is not currently adopted by the clinic. We also will endeavor to address issues identified by [8], particularly with regard to establishing a baseline which can then be used to evaluate proposed improvement strategies. The novelty also resides in the fact that this is a unit for accidents only and the results might be thus different.

The remainder of this paper is organized as follows: in Sect. 2, a brief literature review relating to improvement strategies for A&E improvement is presented; Sect. 3 illustrates the proposed methodology; Sect. 4 describes and analyzes the results of a case study from a clinic that deals solely with accidents. Finally, Sect. 5 presents the conclusions and future work emanating from this study.

2 A Recent Literature Review

The use of mathematical models and optimization methods as mechanisms of characterization, analysis, evaluation and selection of alternatives, has an increasingly significant importance in health care decision-making [9], especially in process improvement, customer satisfaction and economic evaluation of services and technologies for diagnosis and health care, where the simulation plays a key role to achieve these goals.

Simulation is defined as the act of representing a real system so that certain key characteristics or behaviors can be effectively described [10]. Considering the above-mentioned definition, the simulation can be carried out from the real or computational perspective. In this regard, an increasingly used alternative to address this problem is DES models. In this respect, DES assists in the development and experimentation of computational models representing complex systems, with the objective of characterizing their behavior [11], as well as analyzing scenarios for the improvement of current systems performance before implementation. In the scientific literature, there are different studies related to the application of DES in different healthcare areas and processes, including its combinations with other modelling techniques. In this sense, we have highlighted scientific studies analyzed the existing literature on the use of the simulation and modeling of processes in health care, from a multidimensional perspective [1]. In this respect, several articles were found to be related to the use of simulation tools for performance improvement in different areas and health processes, such as mammography [12], reduction of planning time and service waiting times in radiation therapy [13], characterization of overall capacity, length of stay, waiting times and service times in physiotherapy [14], and reduction of waiting times in several outpatient specialties [15, 16]. There are also projects carried out in highly complex processes such as gynecology and obstetrics, aiming at improving appointment times, contributing to patient satisfaction and reducing the rate of maternal and infant mortality [17]. Another example of DES application in complex services can be found in [18] where this technique was used to establish strategies for timely planning and care in a stroke unit.

Additionally, DES has been used to analyzing key performance indicators such as resource utilization [19], the design of facilities and healthcare networks [20], reduction of appointment lead-times [17, 21]; reduction of access time to health care services [22, 23], delay minimization in outpatient clinics [24], and improvement in patient waiting times [15, 25]. In the aforementioned works, operational inefficiencies have been identified and significant improvements have been achieved using DES technique.

We also identified that DES can be combined with other techniques e.g. linear programming [19, 21]; systems dynamics [26], Lean methodology [27, 28], queuing theory [29] and agent-based modeling [30]. Regarding the research field of this work, which is oriented to DES applications in A&E and EDs, only a few studies are available. For instance, an analysis of patient flow within emergency departments (ED) was performed in a hospital located in the UK [8]. Another application can be found in [31, 32] where DES was performed to improve the care quality in the emergency department of a community hospital in Lexington and Ireland respectively. On the other hand, in [5], the maximization of expectations (EM) algorithm was used to simulate the performance of EDs. Also, in [7], a study was also carried out in an emergency department located in the United Kingdom via the application of DES to characterize, analyze and improve the length of stay by considering the operational standards demanded by the government. Likewise, in [33] a DES model was developed to analyze the patient flow in an ED in Hong Kong to improve its current performance and evaluate the impact of possible changes in the system. Other interesting work can be found in [34, 35].

However, considering the literature review presented in [35] and the findings derived from this study, little work has been done as yet on the impact of improvement strategies in EDs via using simulation. This is in spite of DES providing a means to evaluate changes to ED care delivery before implementation in an effective manner. Therefore, this work represents a reference source for both ED and A&E managers when assessing possible improvement scenarios reducing patient waiting time. Additionally, related works about the problem of waiting time in accidents and emergency departments are predominantly centered in the UK health care infrastructure and Hong Kong; in this respect the case study presented in this paper was developed in a colombian clinic; thus, new outcomes may be achieved.

3   Methodology

Within our modelling framework, it is necessary to ensure that the simulation model is statistically equivalent to the real-world system. In this respect, data assumptions should be rigorously validated and processes must be effectively characterized. In addition, if the model does not provide a good representation of the A&E department, further analysis cannot be carried out and thus, improvement strategies cannot be properly created and pretested. A methodology comprised of five stages has been developed with the foresight to be applied in other A&E departments (refer to Fig. 1).

Fig. 1. Methodological framework to reduce waiting times in A&E departments

Our framework starts with the system description (Stage 1) where the healthcare professionals and other medical staff are asked to give information related to the identification of processes, patient flow and stakeholders in order to be described by flow and SIPOC diagrams. Then, in Stage 2, data (process variables and parameters) are identified, collected and analyzed by using intra-variable tests, homogeneity test and tests for goodness-of-fit [36]. This is important to provide more realistic models incorporating variability in accordance with the real-world system. Afterward, the DES model is created with the aid of a simulation software package (Stage 3). The animation provided by the software facilitates engagement with the healthcare managers and underpins the decision-making process in relation to the resource utilization, performance analysis and the identification of bottlenecks [37]. After this, the model should be rigorously validated through statistical tests in order to determine whether it is equivalent ($\alpha = 0.05$) to the real-world system (Stage 4). Finally, the improvement scenarios should be clearly stated with the support of the healthcare staff and validated via using DES models (Stage 5). This is relevant to pretest the changes to ED care delivery before implementation in a safe and efficient manner as stated in [8].

4   Modeling the A&E Department: A Case Study in a District General Clinic

A case study of an A&E department from a district general clinic has been explored. The model describes the journey of patients from arrival time to discharge. Our simulation model was based on a 3-year prospective dataset extracted from the User Information System (UIS) and consisting of all patients admitted between 1 January 2014 and 31 December 2016. This system operates 24 h per day, 365 days per year. In this department, a discrete distribution was fitted to the arrival process: 92.33% (1 patient/arrival), 6.84% (2 patients/arrival), 0.69% (3 patients/arrival) and 0.14% (4 patients/arrival). Then, an intra-variable independence test was performed to establish whether the variable "time between arrivals" was random. To evaluate this, a run test was carried out with $\alpha = 0.05$. The results evidenced with p-value = 0.921 that this variable could be modelled with a probability distribution. Afterward, the "time between arrivals" variable was proved to be modelled with an exponential distribution ($\beta = 18.8$ min). For the goodness-of-fit of this distribution, the chi-squared test ($\chi^2 = 15.5$, d.f. = 4, p < 0.005) provided good support for the exponential assumption.

On the other hand, the department does not currently adopt the triage system. In this regard, patients are classified into two categories: "poor clinical condition" and "minor complications" In the period, there were 33% admitted who had been categorized with a poor clinical condition and 67% with minor complications. Within this system, a homogeneity test (Kruskal-Wallis) was performed to establish whether the distribution of times between arrivals should be modelled separately according to the patient category. In this case, with a p-value = 0.2172 (greater than alpha level = 0.05), the datasets were found to be homogeneous and could be characterized by a single probability distribution.

Medical care is provided by ten doctors who have different schedules. The current schedules of these doctors are described in Table 1. In this regard, there are four types of shifts: Night (N), Mixed 1 (M1), Mixed 2 (M2) and Shared (S).

Table 1. Schedules of doctors attending in the A&E department

Resource – Doctor	Schedule
Doctor 1	Night (N)
Doctor 2	
Doctor 3	
Doctor 4	Mixed 1 (M1)
Doctor 5	
Doctor 6	
Doctor 7	Mixed 2 (M2)
Doctor 8	
Doctor 9	
Doctor 10	Shared (S)

Regarding the length of stay (LOS) in A&E department, a run test was also performed. In this respect, with a p-value = 1.000, this variable was found to be randomly distributed. After this, sub-groups of patients were identified which are not homogeneous (p-value = 0.3630) with respect to the distribution of LOS. These pipelines were stratified based on whether the patient was admitted to A&E with minor complications or poor clinical condition. For the goodness-of-fit of LOS distribution, the Kolmogorov-Smirnov (K-S) test (p-value = 0) provided good support for the uniform assumption in both patient categories: Poor clinical condition (a = 10 min, b = 45 min) and minor complications (a = 10 min, b = 15 min). After staying in this department, five types of destination discharges could occur: Hospitalization, Surgery, Intensive Care Unit (UCI), Home or Death. In this sense, according to the data provided by UIS, the discharge distribution shows that: 15.3% are discharged to UCI, 20% are remitted to Hospitalization Department, and 18.1% to Surgery Unit, 46.4% are discharged to home and 0.2% to the "Dead Room". The model does not consider the final destination discharges of patients since they depend on the performance of other services.

This service is regulated by the Ministry of Health and Social Protection. In this respect, the upper specification limit (USL) for average waiting time in A&E has been

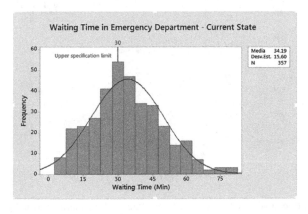

Fig. 2. Current performance of the A&E department in terms of patient waiting time

established as 30 min/admission. This information was considered in the simulation model that was designed with the support of Arena 15® software in order to reduce the current waiting time of the A&E department. A Mann–Whitney Test was performed to determine if the simulated model was equivalent to the real-world system. In this regard, a P-value equal to 0.079 (alpha level = 0.05) and W = 4590 demonstrated that the model was statistically equal to the real-world system. Afterward, the current mean waiting time was calculated. On average, a patient has to wait for 34.19 min with a standard deviation of 15.6 min (refer to Fig. 2).

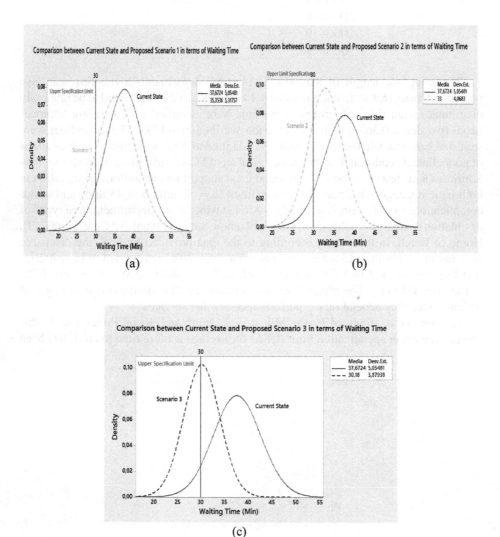

Fig. 3. Comparative analysis between current state and Scenario 1 (a), Scenario 2 (b) and Scenario 3 (c)

This means that there is a probability of 96.15% that an admitted patient waits for more than 30 min between the arrival time and the start of medical care. In addition, DPM = 961518 which denotes that 961,518 patients out of 1 million will have to wait for more than 30 min. In an effort to face this problem, three improvement scenarios were designed with the support of the A&E healthcare managers. Each scenario was evaluated via a simulation model before implementation (refer to Fig. 3a–c).

After pretesting these scenarios, the results demonstrated that two of the proposals are promising since they provide a reduced waiting time. In this regard, a Mann–Whitney test was carried to compare the current state of the system and each improvement scenario (Table 2). The results have been presented in Table 3.

Table 2. Schedules of practitioners in triage systems

Resource – General Practitioner/Doctor	Schedule
Practitioner 1	Night
Practitioner 2	
Practitioner 3	Shared
Practitioner 4	Mixed 1
Practitioner 5	
Practitioner 6	Mixed 2
Practitioner 7	Weekend
Practitioner 8	
Doctor 11	Mixed 1
Doctor 12	
Doctor 13	Weekend
Doctor 14	

Table 3. P-values, W statistics and confidence intervals for comparisons between real system and proposed scenarios

Improvement scenario	p-value	W	CI (95%)
Scenario 1	0.055	604.5	[−0.541; 5.250]
Scenario 2	0.0025	607	[1.429; 7.329]
Scenario 3	0	666	[4.356; 10.062]

Taking into account the aforementioned results, the improvement scenarios were compared in terms of waiting time via applying box-and-whiskers plots (refer to Fig. 4). It can be appreciated that the proposed scenario 3 provides the best operational performance due to its reduced variation. This is beneficial to increase the customer satisfaction since the main patient complaint is having to wait too long. Furthermore, it reduces the increased suffering for those in pain and the need of more complex healthcare services.

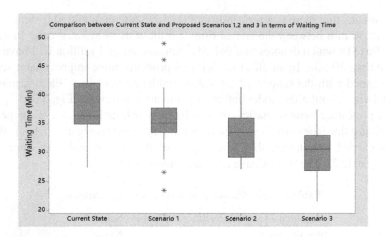

Fig. 4. Box-and-whiskers plots for comparisons between improvement scenarios

5   Conclusions and Future Work

In this paper, we have validated the effectiveness of discrete-event simulation to improve patient waiting time in an A&E department from a district general clinic. The results demonstrated that considering the current system, 96.15% of the admitted patients in this department will have a waiting time higher than 30 min. Therefore, three proposals were simulated and evaluated with the aid of Arena 15® software, Minitab 16 and knowledge provided by the healthcare managers of the A&E department. In this case, two of the proposals were identified to be operationally effective since they provide a reduced waiting time compared to the real-world system. In particular, the best scenario (Scenario 3) allowed managers to decrease average waiting times from 37.67 min to 30.18 min and the standard deviation from 5.05 min to 3.87 min. This represents an earlier diagnosis and treatment which is beneficial for patients.

On the other hand, healthcare managers can pretest changes to ED care delivery before implementation in an effective manner using DES technique. This is relevant to avoid mistakes, misunderstandings and cost overruns during the implementation process of these changes. Nonetheless, it is necessary to work closely with clinicians and other healthcare professionals to ensure that the models are equivalent to the real-world system. Additionally, collecting suitable and high-quality data is a pivotal aspect when modelling healthcare systems that provide a good representation of the processes variability.

Our case study enriches the existing literature and contributes to the evidence base related to the use of DES techniques when pretesting changes to ED delivery care. However, we plan in future work to develop financial evaluations of each improvement scenario in order to deploy more detailed and informative simulation models. In addition, our work will also consider interactions with other healthcare services (e.g. hospitalization and surgery care) to effectively support integrated planning processes for both hospitals and government.

References

1. Brailsford, S., Harper, P., Patel, B., Pitt, M.: An analysis of the academic literature on simulation and modelling in health care. J. Simul. **3**(3), 130–140 (2009)
2. Fletcher, A., Worthington, D.: What is a 'generic' hospital model?—a comparison of 'generic' and 'specific' hospital models of emergency patient flows. Health Care Manag. Sci. **12**(4), 374–391 (2009)
3. Gillespie, J., McClean, S., Garg, L., Barton, M., Scotney, B., Fullerton, K.: A multi-phase DES modelling framework for patient-centred care. J. Oper. Res. Soc. **67**(10), 1239–1249 (2016)
4. Neil, N.: Transparently, with Validation. Med. Decis. Mak. **2012**(32), 660–662 (2012)
5. Wang, Z., Eatock, J., McClean, S., Liu, D., Liu, X., Young, T.: Modeling throughput of emergency departments via time series: an expectation maximization algorithm. ACM Trans. Manag. Inf. Syst. **4**(4), 16 (2013)
6. Lane, D.C., Monefeldt, C., Rosenhead, J.V.: Looking in the wrong place for healthcare improvements: a system dynamics study of an accident and emergency department. J. Oper. Res. Soc. **51**(5), 518–531 (2000)
7. Eatock, J., Clarke, M., Picton, C., Young, T.: Meeting the four-hour deadline in an A&E department. J Health Organ. Manag. **25**(6), 606–624 (2011)
8. Mohiuddin, S., Busby, J., Savović, J., Richards, A., Northstone, K., Hollingworth, W., Donovan, J.L., Vasilakis, C.: Patient flow within UK emergency departments: a systematic review of the use of computer simulation modelling methods. BMJ Open **7**(5), e015007 (2017)
9. The Discrete Event Simulation as a Fundamental technique in making high impact decisions. http://www.vaticgroup.com/perspectiva-logistica/ediciones-anteriores/simulacion-de-eventos-discretos/
10. Rodríguez, J., Serrano, D., Monleón, T., Caroc, J.: Discrete-event simulation models in the economic evaluation of health technologies and health products. Gac. Sanit. **22**(2), 151–161 (2008)
11. Gómez, A., Quintana, N., Ávila, J.: Discrete event simulation and line of balance diagram, applied to the improvement of the foundation construction process. Ing. y Cienc. **11**(21), 157–175 (2015)
12. Coelli, F., Ferreira, R., Almeida, R., Pereira, W.: Computer simulation and discrete-event models in the analysis of a mammography clinic patient flow. Comput. Methods Progr. Biomed. **87**, 201–207 (2007)
13. Werker, G., Sauré, A., French, J., Shechter, S.: The use of discrete-event simulation modelling to improve radiation therapy planning processes. Radiother. Oncol. **92**, 76–82 (2009)
14. Villamizar, J., Coelli, F., Pereira, W., Almeida, R.: Discrete-event computer simulation methods in the optimization of a physiotherapy clinic. Physiotherapy **97**, 71–77 (2011)
15. Ortiz, M.A., López-Meza, P.: Using computer simulation to improve patient flow at an outpatient internal medicine department. In: García, Carmelo R., Caballero-Gil, P., Burmester, M., Quesada-Arencibia, A. (eds.) UCAmI 2016. LNCS, vol. 10069, pp. 294–299. Springer, Cham (2016). doi:10.1007/978-3-319-48746-5_30
16. Mocarzel, B., Shelton, D., Uyan, B., Pérez, E., Jimenez, J., DePagter, L.: Modeling and simulation of patient admission services in a multi-specialty outpatient clinic. In: Proceedings of the 2013 Winter Simulation Conference, pp. 2309–2319 (2013)

17. Ortiz, M.A., McClean, S., Nugent, C., Castillo, A.: Reducing appointment lead-time in an outpatient department of gynecology and obstetrics through discrete-event simulation: a case study. In: García, C.R., Caballero-Gil, P., Burmester, M., Quesada-Arencibia, A. (eds.) UCAmI 2016. LNCS, vol. 10069, pp. 274–285. Springer, Cham (2016). doi: 10.1007/978-3-319-48746-5_28

18. Pitt, M., Monks, T., Crowe, S., Vasilakis, C.: Systems modelling and simulation in health service design, delivery and decision making. BMJ Qual. Saf. **25**, 1–8 (2015)

19. De Angelis, V., Felici, G., Impelluso, P.: Integrating simulation and optimization in health care centre management. Eur. J. Oper. Res. **150**, 101–114 (2003)

20. Swisher, J., Jacobson, S., Jun, B., Balci, O.: Modeling and analyzing a physician clinic environment using discrete-event (visual) simulation. Comput. Oper. Res. **28**, 105–125 (2001)

21. Granja, C., Almada-Lobo, B., Janela, F., Seabra, J., Mendes, A.: An optimization based on simulation approach to the patient admission scheduling problem using a linear programing algorithm. J. Biomed. Inform. **52**, 427–437 (2014)

22. Elkhuizen, S., Das, S., Bakker, P., Hontelez, J.: Using computer simulation to reduce access time for outpatient departments. Qual. Saf. Health Care **16**, 382–386 (2007)

23. Van Sambeek, J., Joustra, P., Das, S., Bakker, P., Maas, M.: Reducing MRI access times by tackling the appointment-scheduling strategy. BMJ Qual. Saf. **20**(12), 1075–1080 (2015)

24. Araidah, A., Boran, O., Wahsheh, A.: Reducing delay in healthcare delivery at outpatients clinics using discrete event simulation. Int. J. Simul. Model **4**, 185–195 (2012)

25. Aeenparast, A., Tabibi, S., Shahanaghi, K., Aryanejhad, M.: Reducing outpatient waiting time: a simulation modeling approach. Iran. Red Crescent Med. J. **15**(9), 865–869 (2013)

26. Viana, J., Brailsford, S.C., Harindra, V., Harper, P.R.: Combining discrete-event simulation and system dynamics in a healthcare setting: a composite model for Chlamydia infection. Eur. J. Oper. Res. **237**, 196–206 (2014)

27. Robinson, S., Radnorb, Z., Burgessc, N., Worthington, C.: SimLean: utilising simulation in the implementation of lean in healthcare. Eur. J. Oper. Res. **219**, 188–197 (2012)

28. Nasiri, S.: Lean thinking and queue modelling in healthcare. Lancaster University Management School, Lancastar (2009)

29. Bahadori, M., Mohammadnejhad, S., Ravangard, R., Teymourzadeh, E.: Using queuing theory and simulation model to optimize hospital pharmacy performance. Iran. Red Crescent Med. J. **16**(3), 1–7 (2014)

30. Marshall, D., Burgos-Liz, L., Ijzerman, M., Osgood, N., Padula, W., Higashi, M., Wong, P., Pasupathy, K., Crown, W.: Applying dynamic simulation modeling methods in health care delivery research—the simulate checklist: report of the ISPOR simulation modeling emerging good practices task force. Value Health **18**, 5–16 (2015)

31. Zeng, Z., Ma, X., Hu, Y., Li, J., Bryant, D.: A simulation study to improve quality of care in the emergency department of a community hospital. J. Emerg. Nurs. **38**, 322–328 (2012)

32. Abo-Hamad, W., Arisha, A.: Simulation-based framework to improve patient experience in an emergency department. Eur. J. Oper. Res. **224**, 154–166 (2013)

33. Rado, O., Lupia, B., Leung, J.M.Y., Kuo, Y.H., Graham, C.A.: Using simulation to analyze patient flows in a hospital emergency department. Springer Proc. Math. Stat. **61**, 289–301 (2014)

34. Gul, M., Guneri, A.: Simulation modelling of a patient surge in an emergency department under disaster conditions. Croat. Oper. Res. Rev. **6**, 429–443 (2015)

35. Mandahawi, N., Al-Shihabi, S., Abdallah, A., Alfarah, Y.: Reducing waiting time at an emergency department using design for Six Sigma and discrete event simulation. Int. J. Six Sigma Compet. Adv. **6**(1), 91–104 (2010)

36. Comas, A.S., Palacio, A.T., Mendoza, S.T., Rodado, D.N.: Aplicación del diseño de experimentos taguchi para la identificación de factores de influencias en tiempos de impresión 3D con modelado por deposición fundida. Int. J. Manag. Sci. Oper. Res. 1(1), 43–48 (2016)
37. Barrios, M.A.O., Caballero, J.E., Sánchez, F.S.: A methodology for the creation of integrated service networks in outpatient internal medicine. Ambient Intelligence for Health. Springer, Cham (2015). doi:10.1007/978-3-319-26508-7_24

A Support System for Cardiopulmonary Resuscitation Technique Using Wearable Devices

Daniel Ruiz-Fernández$^{(\boxtimes)}$, Diego Marcos-Jorquera,
Alberto de Ramón-Fernández, Víctor Vives-Boix, Virgilio Gilart-Iglesias,
and Antonio Soriano-Payá

Department of Computer Technology, University of Alicante, Alicante, Spain
{druiz,dmarcos,aderamon,vvives,vgilart,soriano}@dtic.ua.es

Abstract. Cardiopulmonary resuscitation is an emergency procedure that can save the life of a person, which combines manual chest compressions on the sternum and insufflations. The depth of the compressions and the cadence at which they are performed are two key factors for the effectiveness of the technique. This study presents a novel support system for cardiopulmonary resuscitation, helping the rescuer to perform the compressions with a correct cadence. To do this, a wearable device adapts to the initial pace of the rescuer, leading him gradually to reach the appropriate cadence.

Keywords: Smartwatch · Wearable device · Assistance · Adaptive · Fuzzy logic · Cardiopulmonary resuscitation · Chest compression

1 Introduction

Cardiac arrest - an electrical malfunction in the heart that causes an irregular heartbeat (arrhythmia) and disrupts the flow of blood to the brain, lungs and other organs - is a leading cause of death. Cardiopulmonary resuscitation (CPR) is an emergency procedure that can save the person's life. It has to be done when a person's breathing has stopped and their heart has stopped beating. CPR techniques combine rescue breathing and chest compressions. There are several risk factors that can increase the chance of suffering an out-of-hospital cardiac arrest among those are age, body mass index, high cholesterol and triglycerides level, smoking, high blood pressure, diabetes, etc. [1]. In the US alone, occur more than 350.000 out-of-hospital cardiac arrests. Almost 90 percent of people who suffer out-of-hospital cardiac arrests die. CPR, especially if performed in the first few minutes, can double or triple a person's chance of survival [2].

However, cardiopulmonary resuscitation is a technique prone to execution errors because is often performed in non-controlled environments or stressful situations. Although many organizations are responsible for offering free CPR instruction, many people who need to know the technique do not take the enough time to learn the procedure. Moreover, in many cases, the training is not aimed at the right people, who are those who live daily with the person at risk of

S.F. Ochoa et al. (Eds.): UCAmI 2017, LNCS 10586, pp. 364–369, 2017.
DOI: 10.1007/978-3-319-67585-5_38

suffering cardiac arrest. In addition, the most commonly taught technique is difficult to perform for at least ten minutes for the vast majority of people, either because they do not have enough strength to achieve the compression of the sternum or just because they do not know how to perform the technique correctly. Finally, the pace and number of compressions to be performed is a key factor and it is often done incorrectly, with an inappropriate pace. That is why American Heart Association (AHA) experts have established a series of recommendations to improve this practice, including minimizing interruptions of chest compressions. This is because the compressions generate the blood flow and this must be delivered 80% of the time in which the patient has no pulse and it is recommended to perform from 100 to 120 compressions per minute for an adult patient, combined with 2 insufflations for each 30 compressions. The insufflations should be about 1 second, making sure that the sternum elevation occurs. Chest pressures should allow the sternum to descend from 5 to 6 cm in adults and children over 8 and 3–4 cm in children under 8 years.

These recommendations highlight the importance of a correct performing cardiac massage to ensure the quality of CPR, emphasizing on the strength and rate at which the compressions should be performed. Our study presents a system to assist the chest compression technique in cardiopulmonary resuscitation through a wearable device. The assistant device provides usability, verbal instructions and vibrations for a correctly execution of the CPR technique.

2   State of the Art

In recent years, the interest in knowing first aid techniques and how to perform resuscitation maneuvers has been progressively increased. This is due to the efforts of public associations related to health to promote programs that allow training in CPR. Thanks to the technological contribution have also arisen different mobile applications oriented to teach and guide the rescuer during the resuscitation maneuver. Some of these applications just describe a step-by-step guide to be used during the maneuver.

This is the case of the CPR11 mobile app described in [3], a simple application that describes in 11 brief videos an action guide to identify sudden cardiac arrest and starting resuscitation maneuvers in the first two minutes. However, the app cannot measure if the rescuer is performing as instructed by the video, which represents an important disadvantage.

This limitation has been overcome in the app developed by Srither et al. [4]. It is a mobile application that allows training in CPR. The user places the hands in the suitable position to make the compressions holding the mobile between both hands. A beep indicates the rescuer when to perform the compression. Thanks to the accelerometer of the phone, the application manages to detect the pace and depth of the compressions, and warns the user with different types of beeps when doing them correctly or incorrectly. Also, the app can locate the nearby automated external defibrillators (AEDs). The main limitation observed is that the position of the mobile makes difficult place the hands correctly.

A more sophisticated system is proposed in [5]. It is a smart backboard that provides a real time feedback for chest compression during CPR. It uses two accelerometers connected to the backboard by a bus cable. One is placed in the center of the backboard and the other is inserted in a hand pad, which the rescuer will use to perform the compressions on the sternum. In the same hand pad a force sensor is integrated to detect whether the decompression is performed correctly or not. The information provided by the sensors is collected by a small microprocessor, and through a LED output display it informs in real time whether the compressions are being performed correctly. The colors: yellow, green and red, indicate respectively the depth range. An audible metronome is also integrated to the backboard to ensure that the appropriate rate of chest compressions is delivered. Although this system provides useful information for performing CPR, it is more complex and expensive than those described above, making it difficult for domestic use.

3   Design

In the current literature we found multiple weaknesses in cardiopulmonary resuscitation assistance with digital devices: (1) it physically interferes in the CPR procedure (smartphone between both hands during chest compressions), (2) it requires manually interaction with the assistance device, (3) it mostly depends on a screen display and (4) it is not adaptive for each rescuer. In this paper we propose a novel system that solves these weaknesses.

Physical interference during cardiopulmonary resuscitation can be critical. The technique for chest compression in CPR requires the use of both hands for proper performance [6]. The dominant hand has to be placed over the center of the patient's chest, specifically in the lower half of the sternum. The heel of this hand is positioned in the midline and aligned with the long axis of the sternum, thus focusing the compressive force on the sternum and decreasing the chance of rib fractures. The non-dominant hand is placed hand on top of the first hand, so that both hands are overlapped and parallel. The fingers should be raised from the patient's ribs to minimize force over them. In addition to fractured ribs, a correct compression on the upper abdomen can also prevent iatrogenic injury, an injury caused by an involuntary medical act. For this reason, we discard the use of a smartphone as a device for CPR assistance.

Manually interaction and screen display dependance can also hinder a correctly execution of the CPR technique. In addition, current assistant devices just consider compressions to be in range (100–120 beats per minute) and do not adapt its assistance to the rescuer physical capacity. That is, a situation where the rescuer need to compress the chest faster or slower can produce stress or helplessness and subsequently cause a bad execution of the technique.

Thus, in this work we propose the use of a wearable device in the wrist to assist chest compressions, since it does not interfere in the placement of the hands and allows a correct use of the technique. These devices are provided with the same elements needed to aid the rescuer, as they can vibrate or speak

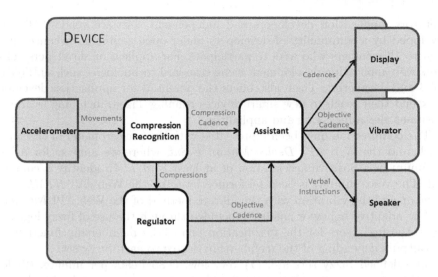

Fig. 1. Device architecture

to notify the cadence of compression. Thus, we propose a non-invasive solution without training requirements and that is able to support anyone in a situation of cardiorespiratory arrest. The device architecture is shown in Fig. 1.

The accelerometer module represents the input of our system, where movements in chest compressions are read as accelerations vectors. The compression recognition module is responsible for analyzing these movements and detecting compressions. The regulator module has as objective to set the suitable cadence in function of the observed cadence by the compression recognition module. In this module can be included artificial intelligence algorithms for the adaptive behavior and the flexibility and adaptability of our proposal is considered. The assistant module reads both compression and objective cadence and provides the rescuer the suitable instructions to carry out the CPR procedure. For that, this module uses three output peripherals of the device: a display to show all the information, a vibrator to lead the objective cadence and a speaker to provide verbal instructions. The vibrator and the speaker provide unattended assistance, so the display screen could be merely informative and no dependant for the correct use of the technique.

4 Prototype

In this work, in order to validate our proposal an entire functional prototype has been developed. For this prototype, the *Samsung Gear S3 frontier* smartwatch has been selected as hardware platform because it has all the peripherals included in our proposal. This smartwatch is a Tizen based wearable and one of the most complete and advanced smartwatches in the current market. Tizen is an open operating system built from scratch to meet the needs of all participants of the mobile and connected device ecosystem, including device manufacturers, mobile operators, application developers and independent software vendors. Tizen is developed by a community of developers under open source governance and is open to all members who wish to participate. For application developers, Tizen offers web application development using standard technologies such as HTML5, CSS3 and JavaScript. Tizen also offers the potential for application developers to extend their reach to new smart devices running Tizen, including wearables, consumer electronics, cars and appliances.

The compression have been represented with the accelerometer of the smartwatch and the Web API *Device Motion Event*, where we analyze for a local maximum of a positive acceleration of at least 8 m/s^2 to identify a compression. The voice support is been performed by using the Web API *HTML Audio Element* and the vibration with the vibrate method of the Web API *Navigator*.

The adaptive behavior has been included through the use of fuzzy logic. We define the fuzzy sets for the fuzzification phase, the membership function and the outputs depending of the membership degree to each fuzzy set.

The defined fuzzy sets are: (1) very low, 0–85 beats per minute, (2) low, 75–105 beat per minute, (3) normal, 95–125 beats per minute and (4) high, more than 130 beats per minute. The membership function depends on the cadence taking into account just the last ten compressions (cad_{10}). Functions for each defined fuzzy set are:

$$f_{mem}(very\_low) = \begin{cases} 1, & \text{if } cad_{10} \leq 70 \\ \frac{85-cad_{10}}{15}, & \text{if } 70 < cad_{10} < 85 \\ 0, & \text{in other case} \end{cases}$$

$$f_{mem}(low) = \begin{cases} 1 - \frac{90-cad_{10}}{15}, & \text{if } 75 < cad_{10} < 90 \\ \frac{105-cad_{10}}{15}, & \text{if } 90 \leq cad_{10} < 105 \\ 0, & \text{in other case} \end{cases}$$

$$f_{mem}(normal) = \begin{cases} 1 - \frac{110-cad_{10}}{15}, & \text{if } 95 < cad_{10} < 110 \\ \frac{125-cad_{10}}{15}, & \text{if } 110 \leq cad_{10} < 125 \\ 0, & \text{in other case} \end{cases}$$

$$f_{mem}(high) = \begin{cases} 1, & \text{if } cad_{10} \geq 130 \\ \frac{150-cad_{10}}{15}, & \text{if } 115 < cad_{10} < 130 \\ 0, & \text{in other case} \end{cases}$$

Finally, we define the outputs according to the fuzzy set and the degree of belonging to a set. The resulting output is:

$$f_{output} = cad_{10} \left[\frac{70}{60} \cdot f_{mem}(very\_low) + \frac{110}{100} \cdot f_{mem}(low) + \right.$$
$$\left. 110 \cdot f_{mem}(normal) + \frac{110}{120} \cdot f_{mem}(high) \right]$$

5   Conclusions

During the cardiac massage, the cadence of the chest compressions represents a key factor for correctly performing cardiopulmonary resuscitation technique. The use of a smartwatch is a more useful tool than a smartphone for CPR, so it can facilitate a correct hand position, thus avoiding ribs fractures or internally thoracic injuries. In this paper we have been developed an application that assists a rescuer in an emergency situation of a cardiopulmonary resuscitation by using the smartwatch vibrator, the speaker and the display screen to keep a correct cadence between 100 and 120 beats per minute. In addition, we include a novel adaptive process in the rescuers assistance that allows them to gradually reach this beat range through the use of fuzzy logic.

Conflict of Interest

The authors declare no conflict of interest.

Acknowledgments. This work has been granted by the Ministerio de Economía y Competitividad of the Spanish Government (ref. TIN2014-53067-C3-1-R) and cofinanced by FEDER.

References

1. Thorgeirsson, G., Thorgeirsson, G., Sigvaldason, H., Witteman, J.: Risk factors for out-of-hospital cardiac arrest: The Reykjavik Study. Eur. Heart J. **26**(15), 1499–1505 (2005)
2. America Heart Association: CPR Facts and Stats. http://cpr.heart.org/
3. Serratosa, L.J., Kramer, E.B., Pereira, H.D., Dvorak, J., Ripoll, P.L.: CPR 11: a mobile application that can help in saving lives (Mobile App User Guide). Bri. J. Sports Med. **50**(13), 823–824 (2016)
4. Elliot Srither, D., Lateef, F.: A novel CPR training method using a smartphone app. J. Acute Dis. **5**(6), 517–520 (2016)
5. Gohier, F., Dellimore, K., Scheffer, C.: Development of a smart backboard system for real-time feedback during CPR chest compression on a soft back support surface. In: Proceedings of the Annual International Conference of the IEEE Engineering in Medicine and Biology Society, EMBS pp. 346–349. (2013)
6. Rajab, T.K., Pozner, C.N., Conrad, C., Cohn, L.H., Schmitto, J.D.: Technique for chest compressions in adult CPR. World J. Emerg. Surg. WJES **6**(41) (2011)

Impact of Missing Clinical Data for the Monitoring of Patients with Chronic Diseases

Víctor Vives-Boix, Daniel Ruiz-Fernández[⊠], Diego Marcos-Jorquera, and Virgilio Gilart-Iglesias

Department of Computer Technology, University of Alicante, Alicante, Spain
{vvives,druiz,dmarcos,vgilart}@dtic.ua.es

Abstract. Missing data is a common problem in clinical datasets due to the large amount of information generated that must be handled, mostly in places where data is entered manually by staff or patients or when sensors or devices for data collection are faulty or damaged. In this work we compare different supervised learning algorithms with an incomplete chronic kidney disease dataset. The aim of this comparison is to select an algorithm to use with missing data from hypertensive patients. In this way, we want to be able to prevent or diagnose chronic kidney disease in hypertensive patients, while we are monitoring their lifestyle through a clinical process improvement based on personalised recommendations using multiple physiological and environmental variables.

Keywords: Missing data · Supervised learning · Chronic disease · Patient monitoring · High blood pressure · Chronic kidney disease

1 Introduction

In the early years of artificial intelligence in medicine, several decision support systems were developed to assist physicians in clinical diagnosis by providing a second expert opinion during consultation. The intelligence of these early systems was based on simple rules and associations from input data, mainly using control structures, so it did not provide enough support to physicians in the decision-making process. However, the emergence of new artificial intelligence fields, such as machine learning, has enabled clinical decision support systems (CDSS) to become a powerful tool to enhance and support physicians [1].

At present, machine learning algorithms in combination with the large amount of data generated by modern medicine can become critical in the decision-making process and the subsequent solution of complex problems. These algorithms are able to acquire a knowledge model from a database and use it to perform predictions with a high success rate. Even so, in this field still exist unsolved problems that hinder the performance of an accurate conclusion, such as the knowledge discovery when the input dataset is incomplete. The appearance of missing data is a common problem in clinical datasets due to the large

© Springer International Publishing AG 2017
S.F. Ochoa et al. (Eds.): UCAmI 2017, LNCS 10586, pp. 370–377, 2017.
DOI: 10.1007/978-3-319-67585-5_39

amount of information being handled, especially in places where data entry is done by manual procedures or when devices for data collection are defective or damaged [2].

Both problems, manual data entry and devices errors, motivate this paper, which arises as a need from a previous work in which we use several process management strategies to improve health care for patients with chronic diseases. This prior work was specifically performed for patients with hypertension [3] and Crohn's disease [4], but in this paper we focus on kidney chronic disease because of its direct relationship with hypertension.

In [5], Judd concludes that high blood pressure may be the earliest sign of kidney dysfunction and that proper management of hypertension reduces both cardiovascular and kidney outcomes. In addition, part of our previous work consists in the use of artificial intelligence techniques for the development of a CDSS in order to achieve personalised lifestyle recommendations based on multiple variables [6]. This information, in the form of physiological and environmental, is collected through the use of several sensors and devices and by manually entering data into our web platform or through the use of our mobile application.

Moreover, imputation methods as a solution for missing clinical data can alter the training of a neural network towards unwanted behaviour. Data imputation, according to the current literature, is performed in most cases using deletion methods and statistical procedures such as mean or regression. This generated information does not correspond to real data, which can cause an incorrect monitoring of patients.

In this paper we show how missing clinical data can affect different supervised learning algorithms using hypertension variables as entry dataset for chronic kidney disease diagnosis. The algorithms performance is estimated using the following metrics: sensitivity, specificity, precision and F1 score.

The paper is organised as follows. Section 2 contains a brief explanation about missing data and a review of the related technical literature. Dataset and used algorithms are described in Sect. 3. Experimental results and discussion about the obtained performances are shown in Sect. 4. Finally, Sect. 5 contains a summary of conclusions and future work.

2 Background

2.1 Missing Data

The proper way to handle incomplete information depends, in most cases, on knowing the reason why data is lost. Little and Rubin in [7] identify three mechanisms that represent the different ways that information can be lost: missing completely at random (MCAR), missing at random (MAR) and not missing at random (NMAR). Missing completely at random (MCAR) means that the probability of missing data is not related to any observed or unobserved variable. That is, the probability of missing data is the same for individuals in different treatment groups and those with differential disease severity or response to treatment. On the other hand, it is known as missing at random (MAR) when the missing data probability is related to observed variables but not to unobserved variables. Last, missing not at random (MNAR) means that the probability of missing data depends only on the unobserved data.

The MAR and MCAR mechanisms are also called ignorable because in both cases it is allowed to ignore the reason because the values has been lost, thus simplifying the subsequent analysis. These distributions are merely conceptual and it is normal that they appear together in an event. However, when the database is taken as a starting point in the analysis and not in the process of data collection, is not possible to determine how the values are lost.

The most accepted strategies in the treatment of missing values are traditional strategies such us deletion methods and imputation methods based on statistical procedures. Deletion is often an option when the percentage of missing values is small and statistical methods are commonly used due to its simplicity. In both cases it supposes a greater loss of information, especially when working with clinical data.

2.2 Literature Review

In this paper we assume that information is missing completely at random (MCAR) in the experimental phase of our mentioned previous work, since MCAR can include lost data, accidental omission of an answer, accidental breaking of a device or a sensor and personnel errors [8]. Missing data can be handled in several ways: deletion methods, statistical procedures, maximum likelihood and even machine learning. However, when you are dealing with missing clinical data the options are greatly reduced and just a few methods can be really useful.

On the one hand, in [9] is concluded that there is no way to adequately test the robustness of the assumptions about missing data when an analysis is performed. They also concluded that this happens because the handling of missing data requires a scientifically defensible study coupled with a sensitivity analysis to assess robustness so as not to produce unjustified assumptions.

On the other hand, and more recently, in [10] is shown multiple imputation as a flexible method for handling missing data in clinical research, but it is also said that methods like multiple imputation and maximum likelihood estimation typically require a MAR mechanism. In addition, in [11] is also considered multiple imputation to handle missing data in clinical epidemiological research. They also conclude that imputation methods applied under the MCAR assumption can be handled, but they can provide unbiased estimates.

Last, in [12] it is illustrated some applications of Monte-Carlo simulation methods for handling missing data issues for longitudinal clinical trials. They also proposed a Bayesian Markov chain Monte-Carlo method which provides more appropriate variance estimate than conventional multiple imputation. However, they also concluded that missing data can be unavoidable in many clinical trials.

For all these reasons, in this work we pretend analyse different supervised learning algorithms performance without preprocessing input data with any imputation method. The objective in which this paper is framed is to monitor patients with chronic diseases in real time, so we can perform daily lifestyle recommendations based on their preferences and some physical and environmental variables. This work not only allow us to monitor hypertensive patients, but also make use of this data to prevent or diagnose chronic kidney disease.

3   Method

3.1   Dataset

The dataset used in this study is the chronic kidney disease dataset from UCI Machine Learning repository [13]. This selection was made because the attributes matches with almost all variables acquired with our CDSS. This CDSS is currently used by a group of patients with hypertension or Crohn's disease, so the aim of using this dataset is to select a supervised learning algorithm for the subsequent analysis after the experimental phase.

The dataset is composed by 400 instances, with 25 attributes and missing values (see Table 1). All the information is blood related, such as blood pressure, blood cells or blood glucose, among others. Much of this information can be collected through monitoring devices or by drawing blood. In this way it would be possible to monitor hypertensive patients or with high blood pressure to try to diagnose other related diseases. Current data are intended to diagnose whether or not a patient has chronic kidney disease.

3.2   Algorithms

In this work we have perform a first trial with three supervised learning algorithms that are frequently used in clinical decision support systems: (1) a multilayer perceptron (MLP), (2) a radial basis function network (RBFN) and (3) a bayesian network (BN). Moreover, these algorithms were also selected because of their capability to work with incomplete information as entry. The algorithms implementation was performed using the Waikato Environment for Knowledge Analysis (WEKA) developed under GPL license at the University of Waikato (New Zealand). The training was performed using the cross validation method in all cases and we did not use any preprocessing method before that.

In addition, we have performed a second trial by using principal component analysis (PCA), a main linear technique for dimensionality reduction that performs a linear mapping of the data to a lower-dimensional space in such a way that the variance of the data in the low-dimensional representation is maximised. In practice, the covariance (and sometimes the correlation) matrix of the data is constructed and the eigenvectors on this matrix are computed.

Last, we have performed a statistical procedure for preprocessing the dataset, where all missing value have been replaced for nominal and numeric attributes with the modes and means from the rest of the data. Statistical procedures are often used as a fast solution for preprocessing data and avoid incomplete datasets. However, imputation of clinical data implies adding unrealistic information, being a solution that can alter the accuracy of a patient's diagnosis and thus being unviable for healthcare. Even so, this study has been carried out to verify the impact that such amount of missing values may have.

Table 1. Chronic kidney disease dataset information

Attribute	Category	Measure	Missing data
Age	Numerical	age in years	9 (2%)
Blood pressure	Numerical	mm/Hg	12 (3%)
Specific gravity	Nominal	1.005, 1.010, 1.015, 1.025	47 (12%)
Albumin	Nominal	0, 1, 2, 3, 4, 5	46 (12%)
Sugar	Nominal	0, 1, 2, 3, 4, 5	49 (12%)
Red blood cells	Nominal	normal, abnormal	152 (38%)
Pus cell	Nominal	normal, abnormal	65 (16%)
Pus cell clumps	Nominal	present, notpresent	4 (1%)
Bacteria	Nominal	present, notpresent	4 (1%)
Blood glucose random	Numerical	mgs/dl	44 (11%)
Blood urea	Numerical	mgs/dl	19 (52%)
Serum creatinine	Numerical	mgs/dl	17 (4%)
Sodium	Numerical	mEq/L	87 (22%)
Potassium	Numerical	mEq/L	88 (22%)
Haemoglobin	Numerical	gms	52 (13%)
Packed cell volume	Numerical	-	71 (18%)
White blood cell count	Numerical	cells/cumm	106 (27%)
Red blood cell count	Numerical	millions/cumm	131 (33%)
Hypertension	Nominal	yes, no	2 (1%)
Diabetes mellitus	Nominal	yes, no	2 (1%)
Coronary artery disease	Nominal	yes, no	2 (1%)
Appetite	Nominal	good, poor	1 (1%)
Pedal oedema	Nominal	yes, no	1 (1%)
Anaemia	Nominal	yes, no	1 (1%)
Class	Nominal	ckd, notckd	0 (0%)

4   Results

Algorithms performance has been measured using the following metrics: (1) sensitivity (also recall): measures the proportion of positives that are correctly identified as such; (2) specificity (or true negative rate): measures the proportion of negatives that are correctly identified as such; (3) precision (or positive predictive value): the fraction of relevant instances among the retrieved instances; and (4) F1 Score: the harmonic mean of precision and sensitivity. We have performed two trials, a first trial without a preprocessing method and a second with a principal component analysis before training each network. Both of them have been performed with any imputation method.

Table 2. Algorithms results comparison

Algorithm	Sensitivity	Specificity	F1 Score	Precision
MLP	**0.998**	**0.998**	**0.998**	**0.998**
RBFN	0.985	0.991	0.985	0.985
BN	0.988	0.992	0.988	0.988

Table 3. Algorithms results comparison after principal component analysis.

Algorithm	Sensitivity	Specificity	F1 Score	Precision
MLP	0.978	0.978	0.978	0.978
RBFN	**0.990**	**0.991**	**0.990**	**0.990**
BN	0.985	0.986	0.985	0.985

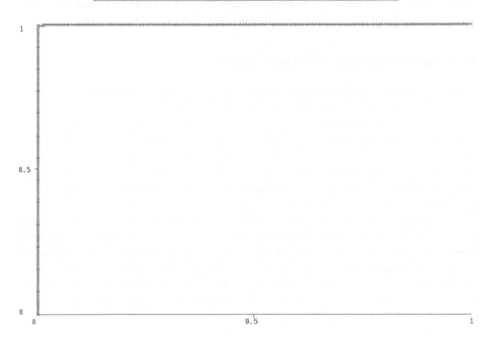

Fig. 1. Area under ROC curve = 0.9999, where the X axis is the false positive rate and the Y axis the true positive rate.

In the first trial, without dimensionality reduction, multilayer perceptron outperforms the rest of algorithms (see Table 2) with a sensitivity of 0.998, a specificity of 0.998 and a precision of 0.998. Second trial, applying previously principal component analysis, shows a better performance in the radial basis function network with a sensitivity of 0.990, a specificity of 0.991 and a precision of 0.990 (see Table 3). However, it does not show a better performance than the

Table 4. Algorithms results comparison with preprocessed missing values

Algorithm	Sensitivity	Specificity	F1 Score	Precision
MLP	0.978	0.984	0.978	0.978
RBFN	**0.988**	**0.992**	**0.988**	**0.989**
BN	0.985	0.980	0.985	0.985

multilayer perceptron in the first trial. The MLP area under the ROC curve can be seen in Fig. 1 with a diagnosis almost perfect (0.9999).

Last, a comparison with a preprocessed dataset have been performed in order to observe how the results differ from each other (see Table 4). It can be observed that, although slightly improving the performance of the RBF, performance of the MLP is considerably reduced. Therefore, the MLP not only improves performance, but ensures that the dataset has completely true data.

5   Conclusions and Future Work

According to the obtained results, all tested algorithms perform well using an incomplete dataset with blood related information. However, it is the multilayer perceptron which performs better rates of precision, sensitivity and specificity. In addition, it is also observed that the radial basis function network performs better when a principal components analysis is applied before training (trial 2), but it is still not enough to outperform the previous multilayer perceptron results (trial 1). The bayesian network also provides good metrics to the problem posed in both trials, but always with a lower performance than the rest.

In conclusion, we are going to try all three algorithms after the experimental phase, still in process, in our clinical decision support system for monitoring chronic diseases. We are optimistic that this work will be a great addition to the recently developed system and that it will provide a very useful feature for all patients who are currently using it. As future work, we want to analyse the percentage of missing values when the experimentation finishes, as well as repeat this work with real data and see how it works.

Conflict of Interest

The authors declare no conflict of interest.

Acknowledgments. This work has been granted by the Ministerio de Economía y Competitividad of the Spanish Government (ref. TIN2014-53067-C3-1-R) and cofinanced by the European Regional Development Fund.

References

1. Berner, E.S., LA Lande, T.J.: Overview of clinical decision support systems. In: Berner, E.S. (ed.) Clinical Decision Support Systems: Theory and Practice. HI, pp. 1–17. Springer, Cham (2016). doi:10.1007/978-3-319-31913-1_1
2. Weitschek, E., Felici, G., Bertolazzi, P.: Clinical data mining: problems, pitfalls and solutions. In: 2013 24th International Workshop on Database and Expert Systems Applications, pp. 90–94. IEEE, August 2013
3. Ramírez-Navarro, J., Gilart-Iglesias, V., Soriano-Paya, A., Ruiz-Fernandez, D., Marcos-Jorquera, D., Vives-Boix, V.: Management of the hypertension: an architecture based on BPM integration. In: García, C.R., Caballero-Gil, P., Burmester, M., Quesada-Arencibia, A. (eds.) UCAmI 2016. LNCS, vol. 10069, pp. 146–155. Springer, Cham (2016). doi:10.1007/978-3-319-48746-5_15
4. de Ramón-Fernández, A., Marcos-Jorquera, D., Soriano-Payá, A., Gilart-Iglesias, V., Ruiz-Fernández, D., Ramirez-Navarro, J.: Business process management for the crohn's disease clinical process. In: García, C.R., Caballero-Gil, P., Burmester, M., Quesada-Arencibia, A. (eds.) UCAmI 2016. LNCS, vol. 10069, pp. 74–79. Springer, Cham (2016). doi:10.1007/978-3-319-48746-5_8
5. Judd, E., Calhoun, D.A.: Management of hypertension in CKD: beyond the guidelines. Adv. chronic kidney dis. **22**(2), 116–22 (2015)
6. Vives-Boix, V., Ruiz-Fernández, D., Soriano-Payá, A., Marcos-Jorquera, D., Gilart-Iglesias, V., de Ramón-Fernández, A.: Personalised support system for hypertensive patients based on genetic algorithms. In: García, C.R., Caballero-Gil, P., Burmester, M., Quesada-Arencibia, A. (eds.) UCAmI 2016. LNCS, vol. 10069, pp. 67–73. Springer, Cham (2016). doi:10.1007/978-3-319-48746-5_7
7. Little, R.J.A., Rubin, D.B.: Statistical Analysis with Missing Data. Wiley, Hoboken, NJ, USA (2002)
8. Ibrahim, J.G., Chu, H., Chen, M.H.: Missing data in clinical studies: issues and methods. J. clin. oncol. off. J. Am. Soc. Clin. Oncol. **30**(26), 3297–303 (2012)
9. Little, R.J., D'Agostino, R., Cohen, M.L., Dickersin, K., Emerson, S.S., Farrar, J.T., Frangakis, C., Hogan, J.W., Molenberghs, G., Murphy, S.A., Neaton, J.D., Rotnitzky, A., Scharfstein, D., Shih, W.J., Siegel, J.P., Stern, H.: The prevention and treatment of missing data in clinical trials. New Engl. J. Med. **367**(14), 1355–60 (2012)
10. Enders, C.K.: Multiple imputation as a flexible tool for missing data handling in clinical research. Behav. Res. Ther. **98**, 4–18 (2016)
11. Pedersen, A.B., Mikkelsen, E.M., Cronin-Fenton, D., Kristensen, N.R., Pham, T.M., Pedersen, L., Petersen, I.: Missing data and multiple imputation in clinical epidemiological research. Clin. Epidemiol **9**, 157–166 (2017)
12. Liu, G.F., Kost, J.: Applications of simulation for missing data issues in longitudinal clinical trials. In: Chen, D.-G.D., Chen, J.D. (eds.) Monte-Carlo Simulation-Based Statistical Modeling. IBSS, pp. 211–232. Springer, Singapore (2017). doi:10.1007/978-981-10-3307-0_11
13. Lichman, M.: UCI machine learning repository (2013)

Ambient Assisted Living (IWAAL)

Improving Activity Classification Using Ontologies to Expand Features in Smart Environments

Alberto Salguero[1](✉) and Macarena Espinilla[2]

[1] Universidad de Cádiz, Cádiz, Spain
alberto.salguero@uca.es
[2] Universidad de Jaén, Jaén, Spain
mestevez@ujaen.es

Abstract. Activity recognition is a promising field of research aiming to develop solutions within smart environments to provide relevant solutions on ambient assisted living, among others. The process of activity recognition aims to recognize the actions and goals of one or more person in a environment with a set of sensors are deployed, basing on the sensor data stream that capture a series of observations of actions and environmental conditions. This contributions presents the initial results from a new methodology that considers the use of ontologies to expand the set of feature vector, which is computed by using the sensor data stream, that is used in the process of activity recognition by data-driven approaches. The obtained results indicates that the use of extended feature vectors provided by the use of ontology offers a better accuracy regarding the original feature vectors used in the process of activity recognition with different data-driven approaches.

Keywords: Activity recognition · Smart environments · Ontology · Data-driven approaches · Knowledge-driven approaches

1 Introduction

Sensor-based activity recognition [2] is a very relevant process at the core of smart environments. This type of activity recognition is focused on recognizing the actions of one or more persons within the smart environment based on a series of observations of sub-actions and environmental conditions over a period of finite time. It can be deemed as a complex process that involves the following steps: (i) select and deploy the appropriate sensors to be attached to objects within the smart environment; (ii) collect, store and pre-process the sensor related data and, finally, (iii) to classify activities from the sensor data through the use of activity models.

The sensor-based activity recognition is particular suitable to deal with activities that involve a number of objects within an environment, or instrumental activities of daily living (ADL) [9]. Approaches used for sensor-based activity

© Springer International Publishing AG 2017
S.F. Ochoa et al. (Eds.): UCAmI 2017, LNCS 10586, pp. 381–393, 2017.
DOI: 10.1007/978-3-319-67585-5_40

recognition have been divided into two main categories: Data-Driven (DDA) and Knowledge-Driven (KDA) approaches [2].

The former, DDA, are based on machine learning techniques in which a preexistent dataset of user behaviors is required. A training process is carried out, usually, to build an activity model which is followed by a testing processes to evaluate the generalization of the model in classifying unseen activities [10]. The advantages of the DDA are the capabilities of handling uncertainty and temporal information. However, these approaches require large datasets for training and learning, and suffer from the data scarcity or the cold start problem.

There are repositories which contain several ADL datasets in smart environments. One of the most well-known repositories is CASAS[1] [6]. In the context, it is interesting to mention the Open Data Initiative (ODI) [11] for Activity Recognition consortium that aims to create a structured approach to provide annotated datasets in an accessible format.

With KDA, an activity model is built through the incorporation of rich prior domain knowledge gleaned from the application domain, using knowledge engineering and knowledge management techniques [3,5]. KDA has the advantages of being semantically clear, logically elegant, and easy to get started. Nonetheless, they are weak to deal with uncertainty and temporal information as well as the activity models can be considered as static and incomplete.

In the context of KDAs, ontologies for activity recognition have provided success results. In this kind of approach, interpretable activity models are built in order to match different object names with a term in an ontology that is related to a particular activity.

Some hybrid approaches have been developed [4,12] that take advantage of the main benefits provided by DDAs and the use of an ontology. Thereby, ontological ADL models capture and encode rich domain knowledge and heuristics in a machine understandable and processable way.

This contribution of our current work proposes to use an ontology in order to extend the feature vectors to enrich these vectors through inferred knowledge in the ontology, improving the accuracy of classifiers based on DDAs used in the recognition of activities against the unextended feature vectors.

An evaluation is undertaken with a popular dataset to consider the effects of the extension of feature vectors in terms of overall accuracy for activity recognition based on sensor data gleaned from smart environments.

The remainder of the paper is structured as follows: Sect. 2 reviews some notions about ontologies that are needed to understand our proposal. Section 3 proposes the methodology to extended the set of feature vectors by means of an ontology. Section 4 presents an empirical study that analyzes our proposed methodology of extended feature vector in terms of accuracy based on a popular dataset by using the ontology. Finally, in Sect. 5, conclusions and future work are presented.

---

[1] http://ailab.wsu.edu/casas/datasets/ (last checked on April 19, 2017).

2   Review of Ontologies

In this section some relevant concepts related to ontologies are reviewed in order to understand our proposed methodology. Ontologies are used to provide structured vocabularies that explain the relations among terms, allowing an unambiguous interpretation of their meaning. Ontologies are formed by concepts (or classes) which are, usually, organized in hierarchies [1,14], being the ontologies more complex than taxonomies because they not only consider *type-of* relations, but they also consider other relations, including *part-of* or domain-specific relations [8].

A formal language for working with ontologies is OWL [7,13], which is developed by the World Wide Web Consortium (W3C). The design of OWL is greatly influenced by Description Logics (DL), particularly in the formalism of semantics, the choice of language constructs and the integration of data types and data values.

In an ontology, the symbol $\top$ stands for the *top* concept of the hierarchy, all being concepts subsets of $\top$. The *subsumption* relation is usually expressed using the symbol $A \sqsubseteq B$, meaning that the concept A is a subset of the concept B. Concepts can also be specified as logical combinations of other concepts. The semantic of operators for combining concepts is shown in Table 1, where $C, C_1, C_2 \sqsubseteq \top$, R is a relation among concepts, Δ_I is the domain of individuals in the model and I is an interpretation function.

Table 1. Semantic of OWL logical operators

	DL syntax	Manchester syntax	Semantics
$\mathcal{I}$	$C_1 \sqcap C_2$	C_1 and C_2	$(C_1 \sqcap C_2)^I = (C_1^I \cap C_2^I)$
$\mathcal{U}$	$C_1 \sqcup C_2$	C_1 or C_2	$(C_1 \sqcup C_2)^I = (C_1^I \cup C_2^I)$
$\mathcal{C}$	$\neg C$	not C	$(\neg C)^I = \Delta_I \setminus C^I$
$\mathcal{S}$	$\exists R.C$	R some C	$(\exists R.C)^I = \{x \mid \exists y.\langle x,y \rangle \in R^I \wedge y \in C^I\}$
$\mathcal{A}$	$\forall R.C$	R only C	$(\forall R.C)^I = \{x \mid \forall y.\langle x,y \rangle \in R^I \to y \in C^I\}$
$\mathcal{X}$	$\leq nR.C$	R max n C	$(\geq nR.C)^I = \{x \mid card\ \{y.\langle x,y \rangle \in R^I \wedge y \in C^I\} \leq n\}$
$\mathcal{M}$	$\geq nR.C$	R min n C	$(\leq nR.C)^I = \{x \mid card\ \{y.\langle x,y \rangle \in R^I \wedge y \in C^I\} \geq n\}$

3   Methodology

This section describes the proposed methodology, which is made up of several independent applications. The purpose of the methodology is to add relevant features to the dataset to improve the accuracy of the classifiers in DDA by means an ontology.

3.1   An Ontology for the Description of Activities

To describe the activities in [15] an ontology has been developed in OWL. The ontology defines two basic concepts, *Activity* and *Event*, which respectively represent all the activities in the dataset and the activation of the sensors during these activities. Fourteen new subclasses of the *Event* class have been defined, each of them representing the activation during the activity of each of the sensors in the dataset[2]. The class *Frontdoor_set*, for example, represents the set of events corresponding to the activation of the sensor in the front door.

To relate sensors events to the activities we have defined four properties, shown in Fig. 1. The properties *startsWith* and *endsWith* relate a particular activity to the first and the last events that occur during that activity, respectively. Both properties have been defined as functional, since an activity can only begin and end with a unique event. They have been declared as sub-properties of the *hasItem* property, which relates an activity to the events that have occurred during that activity. The property *hasItem* has been defined as inverse functional, since an event may occurs just in one activity. The class description *hasItem some Frontdoor_set*, for example, represents all those activities during which the front door sensor has been fired.

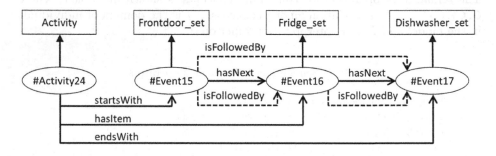

Fig. 1. Ontology example.

The order among events produced in an activity is maintained through the *hasNext* property. This property has been defined as functional and inverse functional, since an event can only be immediately followed or preceded by a single event. It has also been declared as an asymmetric and irreflexive property, since an event that happens after another event cannot happen before the former one, nor after itself. This property allows us to describe activities as chains of events. The class description *startsWith some (Frondoor_set and hasNext some (Fridge_set and hasNext some Dishwasher_set))*, for example, represents the activities that begin with the activation of the sensor of the front door, which

---

[2] For simplicity, only the activation of the sensors has been taken into account for the experiment in Sect. 4.2. However, it is also possible to consider the deactivations of the sensors by just enabling a flag in the application developed for loading the dataset in the ontology.

is immediately followed by the activation of the fridge sensor and then by the dishwasher sensor, immediately. The activity #*Activity24* in Fig. 1 is an example of activity described by the above class description.

The *hasNext* property has been declared as a subproperty of the *isFollowedBy* transitive property, which relates an event to all events that happen after it in an activity. Events related through the latter property do not have to occur consecutively in the activity. The class description *hasItem some (Frontdoor_set and isFollowedBy some Dishwasher_set)* is another way of describing the activity #*Activity24* of the example in Fig. 1.

Due to the high formalization of ontologies, it is not necessary to make all relations in the dataset explicit. Many of them may be inferred by the reasoner. Knowing that #*Event15 hasNext #Event16*, the reasoner may infer that #*Event15 isFollowedBy #Event16*, since *hasNext* $\sqsubseteq$ *isFollowedBy*. In addition, if #*Event16 hasNext #Event17*, the reasoner may easily infer that #*Event15 isFollowedBy #Event17*, since the property *isFollowedBy* has been declared as transitive (Fig. 2).

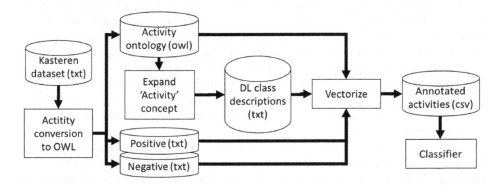

Fig. 2. Functional architecture.

3.2   Extended Features Generation

In this section we explain how the features are generated from the information in the ontology. Basically, the idea consists on the combination of the entities in the ontology (concepts and relations), by means of logic operators, to generate new class descriptions that may be useful for the classification of the activities. Eventually, a class description that describes certain kind of activities may be found and selected as a new feature for the classifiers. The process is repeated until sufficient number of new relevant features are found. All the components of the methodology proposed in this work and how the information flows among them are explained in this section.

The system starts from a dataset with a set of labeled activities. First of all it is necessary to convert the dataset information into an ontology. In the experiment described in Sect. 4.2 an application has been developed to convert the information in [15] into an ontology following the rules in Sect. 3.1. In this first step two text files are also generated that contain: (a) the list of individuals in the ontology of the kind of activity to be recognized by the classifier (positives), and (b) the rest of individuals (negatives). These lists of individuals will be used to generate the input data for the classifier in a later step.

Next, it is necessary to expand the definition of the *Activity* concept in the ontology. The expansion process consists on generating new class descriptions that represent different patterns of activities, without taking into account the specific type of activity that is going to be recognized by the classifier. More specifically, the *OWLExpand* program takes the concept to be expanded (*Activity*) as an argument and uses a given set of classes, properties and operators to construct new class descriptions in DL. All the concepts in the ontology that at least describe some individual in the ontology have been taken as the set of classes L. All properties defined in the ontology have been taken as the set of properties P. The set of operators O is specified by the user and consists on a subset of all operators that can be used to combine class descriptions (see Sect. 2).

The expansion process begins by combining all the concepts in L by means of O operators. The complement operator ($\mathcal{C}$) results in class expressions of the form *not* c_i, where $c_i \in L$. Class expressions such as *not Cupboard_set* or *not Activity* are produced using the complement operator, for example.

All class descriptions in L are combined with themselves in the case of operators that require two class descriptions, resulting in expressions of the form $c_i \ o_k \ c_j$, where $c_i, c_j \in L$, $i \neq j$ and $o_k \in \{and, or\}$. In this process, expressions such as *Event and Cupboard_set* or *Cupboard_set or HallBedroom_Door_set* are generated, for example.

There are operators that require a property to form valid class descriptions. They are the existential quantifiers and the universal quantifier. In this case, the expansion process combines all class descriptions in L with all properties in the ontology, producing expressions of the form $p_i \ o_k \ c_j$, where $p_i \in P$, $o_k \in \{some, all\}$ and $c_j \in L$. *startsWith some HallBedroom_Door_set* or *isFollowedBy all Cupboard_set* are examples of expressions generated by existential and universal quantifiers. These class expressions represent all those individuals that begin with the firing of the HallBedroom_Door sensor and all those individuals that are only followed by Cupboard sensor activations, respectively.

The last type of operator that implements the *OWLExpand* application is the cardinality constraints. These operators limit the number of individuals to which an individual may be related among a given property. The class descriptions generated with this operators have the form $p_i \ or_k \ n \ c_j$, where $p_i \in P$, $o_k \in \{min, max, exact\}$, $c_j \in L$ and $n \in N$. Expressions such as *isFollowedBy min 4 Event* or *isFollowedBy exact 2 Cupboard_set* are generated, for example, representing the set of individuals followed by at least four sensor activations and the set of individuals followed by exactly two activations of the *Cupboard* sensor, respectively. The number of constraints to be generated is virtually infinite since $n \in N$. It is the user who must specify the values for n. For example, $n \in \{2, 3\}$ in the experiment of Sect. 4.2.

All the expressions generated are added to L and the process is repeated again. However, not all of the expressions generated are relevant. Some of them are simply unsatisfiable. A class expression such as *hasItem some Activity*, for example, is unsatisfiable since the range of the property *hasItem* is the *Event* concept, which is defined to be disjoint with the concept *Activity*. There cannot be an individual in the ontology which meets such restriction. For the same reason, expressions like *hasItem some startsWith some HallBedroom_Door_set* are also unsatisfiable, since the domain of the *startsWith* property is the concept *Activity*. Only satisfiable class expressions are added to L.

On the other hand, not all class expressions in L describe activities. With the help of the reasoner, a new set $V \subseteq L$ is created, which contains all the class expressions in L that describe activities. These are the expressions that the program *OWLExpand* produces as result, in a text file.

The *OWLVectorize* application takes the class expressions generated in the previous step as input and produces a table with k rows and n binary columns, where k is the number of annotated activities in the dataset and n is the number of class descriptions generated in the expansion process. Each of the rows is therefore a vector $F^k = \{f_1^k, ..., f_j^k, ..., f_n^k, f_{n+1}^k\}$. Each of the n generated class expressions corresponds to a feature $f_j^k \in F^k$. $F_j^k = 1$ if the activity k is an instance of the class description j. $F_j^k = 0$ otherwise. $F_{n+1}^k = 1$ if the activity k is an instance of the kind of activity to be recognized by the classifier (positive). $F_{n+1}^k = 0$ otherwise. The list of annotated individuals generated at the beginning of the process is used for this purpose. An example of the results obtained by this application is shown in Table 2.

Table 2. Example of resultant data

Activity	startsWith some HallBedroom_Door_set	hasItem min 2 Hall-Bedroom_door_set	Positive
1	1	0	1
2	0	1	0
3	1	1	1
4	0	0	1

4   Experiment

In this contribution, a popular activity recognition dataset [15] of a smart environment is used to evaluate the performance of our proposal. In this section we first describe the dataset and the experiment. Then, we compare the results obtained by classifiers using the classical approach and classifiers using the methodology proposed in this work.

4.1 From the Sensor Data Stream to Feature Vectors

The dataset [15] used in the experiment to evaluate our proposal is composed by binary temporal data from a number of sensors, which monitored the ADLs carried out in a home setting by a single inhabitant. This dataset was collected in the house of a 26-year-old male who lived alone in a three-room apartment. This dataset contains 245 activities that are annotated in the stream of state-change sensors generated by 14 binary sensors (Fig. 3).

```
2015-02-20 18:22:32 D01 CLOSE Begin_1        Feature vectors
2015-02-20 18:22:46 D01 OPEN
2015-02-20 18:22:53 D01 CLOSE
2015-02-20 18:23:07 D05 OPEN     D01 D02 D03 D04 D05 D06 D07 D08 KT M01 M02 PH TV WT1 Activity
2015-02-20 18:23:20 D05 CLOSE     1   0   0   0   1   0   0   0   0   0   0   0  0   1     1
2015-02-20 18:23:27 WT1 OPEN      0   1   0   0   0   0   0   0   0   0   1   0  0   0     5
2015-02-20 18:23:36 WT1 CLOSE     1   0   0   1   0   1   0   1   0   1   0   0  0   0     7
2015-02-20 18:24:35 D01 OPEN      0   1   0   0   0   0   0   0   0   0   1   0  1   0     8
2015-02-20 18:24:41 D01 CLOSE End_1  1 0 0 1 1 0 0 0 0 0 0 0 1     9
                                  1   0   0   0   1   1   0   0   1   0   0   0  0   1     2
                                  0   1   0   0   0   0   0   0   0   0   1   0  0   0     5
                                  1   0   0   1   0   1   0   1   0   1   0   0  0   0     7
                                  0   1   0   0   0   0   0   0   0   0   1   0  1   0     8
```

Fig. 3. Partial sensor data stream of a dataset and its computed feature vector

Each sensor is located in one of 14 different places within a home setting: microwave, hall-toilet door, hall-bathroom door, cups' cupboard, fridge, plates' cupboard, front door, dishwasher, toilet flush, freezer, pans' cupboard, washing machine, groceries' cupboard and hall-bedroom door. Sensors were left unattended, collecting data for 28 days in the apartment. Activities were annotated by the subject himself using a Bluetooth headset.

Seven different activities are annotated, namely: going to bed, using toilet, preparing breakfast, preparing dinner, getting a drink, taking a shower and leaving the house.

Usually, feature vectors of the dataset are computed from the temporal dataset, the sensor data stream is discretized into a set of time windows, denoting each time window by W^k that is limited by each activity. The set of activities are denoted by $A = \{a_1, ..., a_i, ..., a_{AN}\}$, being AN the number of activities of the dataset.

Each feature vector is denoted by F^k and has $N_S + 1$ components, being N_S the number of sensors in the dataset denoted by $S = \{s_1, ..., s_j, ..., s_{N_S}\}$. Therefore, each computed feature vector in the dataset is defined by the following equation:

$$F^k = \{f_1^k, ..., f_j^k, ..., f_{N_S}^k, f_{N_S+1}^k\}$$

being $f_j^k; j = \{1, ..., N_S\}$ a binary value that indicates if the sensor s_i was fired at least once, 1, or was not fired 0 in this time window W^k. The last component $f_{N_S+1}^k \in A$ indicates the activity carried out in the time window W^k.

4.2 Experiment Description

In order to evaluate the quality of the methodology proposed in this work an experiment has been carried out, in which the dataset in [15] have been used.

The objective of the experiment is to determine whether or not a particular activity has been performed based on the sensors that have been fired during a specific period of time. To simplify the experiment, the time intervals always correspond to the annotated activities in the dataset.

The results obtained by four classifiers that use a classic DDA to solve this problem have been taken as reference to measure the efficiency of our proposal. For this purpose an application that identifies the sensors that have been fired during each of the activities has been built. The application generates a file in Weka format, following the structure presented in Sect. 4.1. This file contains an instance for each activity and as many features as sensors in the dataset. All the features are binary and specify if the sensor has been fired during the activity or not. Finally, it includes a class attribute, also binary, that indicates if it is the activity that the classifier is learning to identify or not. Each experiment consists, therefore, in determining which combination of sensors are fired for a particular activity, such as 'take shower', for example.

By using the Weka data mining software, we have generated C4.5[3], Sequential Minimal Optimization (SMO), Voted perceptron (VP) and Decision Table (DT) classifiers for all the activities in the dataset. The most difficult activities to be identified are 'go to bed' and 'use toilet', with 94.67% and 91.97% accuracy, respectively. These are the activities chosen to test the performance of the proposed system in this work.

Starting from the ontology proposed in Sect. 3.1, to which the information contained in [15] has been added, the *OWLExpand* program is used to generate new class descriptions automatically. All new class descriptions describe the *Activity* concept. Three subsets of operators have been used to generate three different sets of new class descriptions. For the first one, all available operators ($\mathcal{ACIXMSU}$) have been used. The complement, minimum cardinality and the existential quantifier operators ($\mathcal{CMS}$) have been used for the second one and only the existential quantifier ($\mathcal{S}$) has been used for the latter. In addition, versions with 50, 100, 150 and 200 class expressions have been generated for each of these sets.

All files with new class descriptions are evaluated by the *OWLVectorize* application and a new file in Weka format is generated for each of them. The same four types of classifiers that were employed to evaluate the performance of the classifiers using the classical approach have been used to evaluate the accuracy of the classifiers based on the new approach. Results are discussed in the next section.

4.3 Results

The accuracy obtained by all the different classifiers generated in the previous section for the 'go to bed' and 'use toilet' activities are shown in the Tables 3 and 4, respectively. The first column indicates the approach used to generate

---

[3] The Weka implementation of the C4.5 classifier is called J48.

Table 3. 'Go to bed' classification accuracy

Dataset	$|\mathcal{F}|$	C4.5	SMO	VP	DT
Classic	14	93,87	94,67	91,72	94,67
$\mathcal{ACIXMSU}$	50	90,65	91,04	90,37	90,23
$\mathcal{ACIXMSU}$	100	98,66	98,51	96,48	**98,79**
$\mathcal{ACIXMSU}$	150	98,66	98,78	97,02	98,79
$\mathcal{ACIXMSU}$	200	98,66	98,37	93,63	98,79
$\mathcal{CMS}$	50	90,65	91,04	90,37	90,23
$\mathcal{CMS}$	100	98,24	**99,06**	96,06	98,38
$\mathcal{CMS}$	150	98,24	98,38	94,16	98,38
$\mathcal{CMS}$	200	98,24	98,38	92,81	98,38
$\mathcal{S}$	50	98,52	98,38	93,88	98,79
$\mathcal{S}$	100	98,52	**98,92**	92,13	98,79
$\mathcal{S}$	150	98,11	98,24	96,21	98,11
$\mathcal{S}$	200	98,11	98,38	96,73	98,11
$\mathcal{S}$	300	98,11	98,24	94,70	98,11
$\mathcal{S}$	400	98,11	98,38	94,58	98,11
$\mathcal{S}$	500	98,11	98,66	95,39	98,11

Table 4. 'Use toiled' classification accuracy

Dataset	$|\mathcal{F}|$	C4.5	SMO	VP	DT
Classic	14	91,97	91,16	89,39	90,09
$\mathcal{ACIXMSU}$	50	86,53	87,33	84,88	85,03
$\mathcal{ACIXMSU}$	100	95,77	**96,86**	93,72	94,8
$\mathcal{ACIXMSU}$	150	95,77	96,16	92,9	94,8
$\mathcal{ACIXMSU}$	200	95,77	96,3	91,94	95,07
$\mathcal{CMS}$	50	86,53	87,33	84,88	85,03
$\mathcal{CMS}$	100	95,77	95,76	90,33	94,53
$\mathcal{CMS}$	150	95,22	96,16	90,19	93,71
$\mathcal{CMS}$	200	95,22	**96,29**	89,79	93,71
$\mathcal{S}$	50	96,32	96,32	91,28	95,76
$\mathcal{S}$	100	95,62	**97,67**	90,87	94,81
$\mathcal{S}$	150	97,26	97,53	92,76	94,96
$\mathcal{S}$	200	97,26	97,26	91,55	94,96
$\mathcal{S}$	300	97,26	97,53	90,59	94,96
$\mathcal{S}$	400	97,26	96,72	90,46	94,96
$\mathcal{S}$	500	97,26	96,45	89,53	94,96

the $|\mathcal{F}|$ features for the classifier, in the second column. The remaining columns indicate the accuracy of the corresponding classifier, in percentage values.

The first row contains the data related to the classifiers constructed using the classical approach. This approach yields a precision of 94.67% for the best case of the activity 'go to bed'. In spite of being a very high value, most of the classifiers created with the approach proposed in this work surpassed that value. The worst results are obtained for classifiers using the new approach, but just when the number of features (class descriptions) generated is insufficient.

Regarding the accuracy of the classifiers with respect to the set of operators used, it is noteworthy that there is no significant difference. The best values obtained for $\mathcal{ACIXMSU}$, $\mathcal{CMS}$ and $\mathcal{S}$ have been 98.79, 99.06 and 98.92%, respectively. All these values have been obtained for one hundred or more features. However, there is a significant difference in the time required to evaluate the class descriptions generated from the different sets of operators. The total time required for the generation and evaluation of the different characteristics varies between 2.07 and 1577.28 s. The best precision for the activity 'go to bed' is obtained for the classifier $\mathcal{CMS}$, using a total of 233.84 s to obtain an accuracy of 99.06%. However, it takes only 2.60 s to get an accuracy of 98.92% for the classifier that only uses the existential quantifier as the operator to generate the class expressions ($\mathcal{S}$).

The class expressions generated by the $\mathcal{S}$ classifier include, for example,

$$hasItem \ some \ (isFollowedBy \ some \ Hall\text{-}Toilet\_door\_set) \tag{1}$$
$$startsWith \ some \ (hasNext \ some \ Hall\text{-}Bathroom\_door\_set) \tag{2}$$

which represent activities in which there is a sensor that is fired before the *Hall-Toilet_door* sensor (1) and activities in which the *Hall-Bathroom_door* is the second sensor that has been fired (2).

A very similar behavior is observed in the case of the activity 'use toilet'. As shown in Table 4, the accuracy of the classifiers using the methodology proposed in this work increases significantly when one hundred or more features are generated. It goes from an accuracy of 91.92% with the best case of DT to an accuracy of 97.67% when only the existential quantifier (S) is used as the operator to generate new class expressions.

Finally, it should be noted that the classifier based on neural networks (VP) is the classifier that worst responded to the feature expansion process proposed in this work. The improvement in the case of the activity 'use toilet' is insignificant. In any case, one of the advantages offered by the system proposed in this work is the possibility of identifying the relevant features for the classifiers. However, the classifier based on neural networks is the only classifier of the four employed in the test that does not allow the identification of these features, because it is a 'black box' classifier.

Table 5 summarizes the results discussed above and also includes the results obtained for other two activities in the dataset. Again, we have selected the other two activities in the dataset for which the classifiers using the classic approach obtain worst results, shown in the second column. It is worth to note the so high accuracy values that the classifiers using the classic approach obtain for these two new activities selected. The third column shows the accuracy of the best classifier that uses the proposed approach. The difference between those values is shown in fifth column and, finally, the last column indicates the percentage of gain achieved by the classifier with respect to the maximum possible gain. As it can be seen, the classifiers based on the proposal presented in this paper improve the accuracy obtained by the classifiers using the classic approach in all cases. The average classification accuracy for the classifiers using the classic approach is 95.57. The average classification accuracy for the classifiers using the proposed approach is 98.98. This mean that the classifiers using the proposed approach have trimmed down the difference with respect to the perfect classifiers a 79.00%.

Table 5. Global classification accuracy

Activity	Classic	Proposal	Gain	% Gain
Go to bed	94.67	99.06	4.39	82.36
Prepare dinner	97.68	99.60	1.92	82.76
Take shower	97.96	99.59	1.63	79.90
Use toilet	91.97	97.67	5.70	70.98
Average	95.57	98.98	3.41	79.00

5   Conclusion and Future Work

This contribution has been focused on a new methodology that uses ontology for the purpose of binary sensor-based activity recognition with DDA in order to increase the accuracy in the classification process when a single activity is carried out by a single person. To do so, the set of feature vector computed by the dataset are extended with the inferred knowledge from the ontology. An evaluation has been carried out with the following four popular classifiers: C4.5, Sequential Minimal Optimization, Voted perceptron and Decision Table. Results from the evaluation demonstrated the ability of the ontology to extend the vector features to provide an increase of the performance in all evaluated classifiers. Our future work is addressed on evaluating the proposed methodology by means a dataset with a greater number of sensors and activities.

Acknowledgments. This project has received funding from the European Unions Horizon 2020 research and innovation programme under the Marie Sklodowska-Curie grant agreement No. 734355 together the Spanish government by research project TIN2015-66524-P.

References

1. Chandrasekaran, B., Josephson, J., Benjamins, V.: What are ontologies, and why do we need them? IEEE Intell. Syst. Appl. **14**(1), 20–26 (1999)
2. Chen, L., Hoey, J., Nugent, C., Cook, D., Yu, Z.: Sensor-based activity recognition. IEEE Trans. Syst. Man Cybern. Part C Appl. Rev. **42**(6), 790–808 (2012)
3. Chen, L., Nugent, C.: Ontology-based activity recognition in intelligent pervasive environments. Int. J. Web Inf. Syst. **5**(4), 410–430 (2009)
4. Chen, L., Nugent, C., Okeyo, G.: An ontology-based hybrid approach to activity modeling for smart homes. IEEE Trans. Hum. Mach. Syst. **44**(1), 92–105 (2014)
5. Chen, L., Nugent, C., Wang, H.: A knowledge-driven approach to activity recognition in smart homes. IEEE Trans. Knowl. Data Eng. **24**(6), 961–974 (2012)
6. Cook, D., Schmitter-Edgecombe, M., Crandall, A., Sanders, C., Thomas, B.: Collecting and disseminating smart home sensor data in the CASAS project. In: Proceedings of the CHI Workshop on Developing Shared Home Behavior Datasets to Advance HCI and Ubiquitous Computing Research (2009)
7. Horrocks, I., Patel-Schneider, P., Van Harmelen, F.: From SHIQ and RDF to OWL: the making of a web ontology language. Web Semant. **1**(1), 7–26 (2003)
8. Knijff, J., Frasincar, F., Hogenboom, F.: Domain taxonomy learning from text: the subsumption method versus hierarchical clustering. Data Knowl. Eng. **83**, 54–69 (2013)
9. Korhonen, I., Parkka, J., Van Gils, M.: Health monitoring in the home of the future. IEEE Eng. Med. Biol. Mag. **22**(3), 66–73 (2003)
10. Li, C., Lin, M., Yang, L., Ding, C.: Integrating the enriched feature with machine learning algorithms for human movement and fall detection. J. Supercomput. **67**(3), 854–865 (2014)
11. Nugent, C., Synnott, J., Santanna, A., Espinilla, M., Cleland, I., Banos, O., Lundström, J., Hallberg, J., Calzada, A.: An initiative for the creation of open datasets within the pervasive healthcare, pp. 180–183 (2016)

12. Rafferty, J., Chen, L., Nugent, C., Liu, J.: Goal lifecycles and ontological models for intention based assistive living within smart environments. Comput. Syst. Sci. Eng. **30**(1), 7–18 (2015)
13. Sirin, E., Parsia, B., Grau, B., Kalyanpur, A., Katz, Y.: Pellet: a practical OWL-DL reasoner. Web Semant. **5**(2), 51–53 (2007)
14. Uschold, M., Gruninger, M.: Ontologies: principles, methods and applications. Knowl. Eng. Rev. **11**(2), 93–136 (1996)
15. Van Kasteren, T., Noulas, A., Englebienne, G., Kröse, B.: Accurate activity recognition in a home setting, pp. 1–9 (2008)

Inter-activity Behaviour Modelling Using Long Short-Term Memory Networks

Aitor Almeida[✉] and Gorka Azkune

DeustoTech-Deusto Foundation, University of Deusto,
Av. Universidades 24, 48007 Bilbao, Spain
{aitor.almeida,gorka.azkune}@deusto.es

Abstract. As the average age of the urban population increases, cities must adapt to improve the quality of life of their citizens. The City4Age H2020 project is working on the early detection of the risks related to Mild Cognitive Impairment and Frailty and on providing meaningful interventions that prevent those risks. As part of the risk detection process we have developed a multilevel conceptual model that describes the user behaviour using *actions, activities, intra-activity behaviour* and *inter-activity behaviour*. Using that conceptual model we have created a deep learning architecture based on Long Short-Term Memory Networks that models the *inter-activity behaviour*. The presented architecture offers a probabilistic model that allows to predict the users next *actions* and to identify anomalous user behaviours.

1 Introduction

City4Age[1] is a H2020 research and innovation project with the aim of enabling age-friendly cities. The project aims to create an innovative framework on ICT tools and services that can be deployed by European cities in order to enhance the early detection of risk related to frailty and MCI, and provide personalized interventions that can help the elderly population to improve their daily life by promoting positive behaviour changes. As part of the tools created for the framework, we have developed a series of algorithms for activity recognition and behaviour modelling. The recognized activities and the behaviour variations are then used to ascertain the frailty and MCI risks levels of the users. In the past we have worked on creating single-home activity recognition algorithms [1,2], but in the case of City4Age we have created algorithms that take into account both the large scale scenarios of the project and the variation on the behaviours of the users.

In this paper we present a conceptual classification of the user behaviour in intelligent environments according with the different levels of granularity used to describe it (Sect. 2). Using that classification we also describe the algorithm developed to automatically model the Inter-Activity Behaviour (Sect. 2). This algorithm uses Long Short-Term Memory Networks (LSTMs) [3] to create a

---

[1] http://www.city4ageproject.eu/.

© Springer International Publishing AG 2017
S.F. Ochoa et al. (Eds.): UCAmI 2017, LNCS 10586, pp. 394–399, 2017.
DOI: 10.1007/978-3-319-67585-5_41

probabilistic model of user behaviour that can predict the next user action and detect unexpected behaviours. Our evaluation (Sect. 3) analyses different architectures for the creation of an statistical model of user behaviour.

2 Actions, Activities and Behaviours

User behaviours are comprised of a large collection of defining elements, making it a complex structure. In order to properly describe it, we have defined a series of concepts based on the ones proposed in [4] to describe it: *Actions*, *Activities* and *Behaviours*. *Actions* describe the most simple conscious movements, while *behaviours* describe the most complex conduct. The different elements of the user behaviour are: (1) *Actions*, which are temporally short and conscious muscular movements done by the users (e.g. taking a cup, opening the fridge...); (2) *Activities*, which are temporally longer, but finite, and are composed by several *actions* (e.g. preparing dinner, taking a shower, watching a movie...) and (3) *Behaviours*, that describe how the user performs those *activities* at different times. We have identified two types of *behaviours*. The *Intra-Activity Behaviours* describe how a single *activity* is performed by a user at different times (e.g. while the user is preparing dinner, sometimes a user may gather all the ingredients before starting, while in other occasions he may take them as they are needed). The *Inter-Activity Behaviours* describe how the user chains different *activities* (e.g. on Mondays after having breakfast she leaves the house to go to work, but in the weekends she goes to the main room).

Traditionally in activity recognition or behaviour modelling tasks, the inputs (when using *actions*) have being represented as IDs, strings or one-hot vectors. The problem with this type of representations is that they do not contain any information about the action meaning. Using a one-hot vector alone, is not possible to compute how similar two actions are and that information is not available for the model that will use the *actions*. A similar problem occurs in the area of Natural Language Processing (NLP) with the representation of words. The solution to this is to use embeddings [5] to represent the words, and we have used the same approach for the *actions*. While one-hot vectors are sparse and the features of the model increase with the *action* dictionary size, embeddings are dense and more computationally efficient, with the number of features being constant, independent from the number of *action* types. Most significantly for our model, embeddings provide semantic meaning to the representation of the actions. Each *action* is represented as a point in a multidimensional plane, which place them at a distance of the other *actions*, thus providing relations of similitude and significance between them. In our model we use the word2vec to represent each action with a vector of 50 float values, due to the small number of *action* instances compared with the number of words that are usually used in NLP tasks. Instead of providing the values directly to our model we have included an Embedding layer in it. In this layer we store the procedural information on how to transform an *action* ID to its embedding. Adding this layer allows us to train it with the rest of the model and in that way to fine tune the embedding values to the current task, improving the general accuracy of the model.

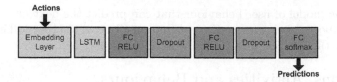

Fig. 1. Network for Behaviour Modelling. FC denotes fully connected networks.

In order to create a probabilistic model for behaviour prediction, we have used a deep neural network architecture (see Fig. 1) based on recurrent neural networks, specifically on Long Short-Term Memory Networks [3]. LSTM networks are universal, in the sense that they can theoretically compute anything that a computer can, given enough network units. These types of networks are specially well suited for modelling problems in which temporal relations are relevant and where the time gaps between the events are of unknown size, which is the case for the behaviour modelling. The first layer of our network is the embeddings layer, which receives the action IDs and transforms them into embeddings with semantic meaning. This layer is configured as trainable i.e. is able to learn during the training process. The action embeddings go to a LSTM layer with a size of 512 network units. After the LSTM layer we use two blocks of densely connected layers with Rectified Linear Unit activations (ReLU) [6]. Each of these layers has a size of 1024 network units. After the ReLU activation we use dropout regularizations [7] with a value of 0.8, in order to prevent the overfitting of the fully connected layers. Finally we use a third fully connected layer with a softmax activation function to obtain the next action predictions.

3   Evaluation

In order to validate our algorithm, we used the dataset[2] published by Kasteren et al. This dataset includes sensor data for 28 days was collected for a total of 2120 sensor events and 245 activity instances. The dataset was split into a training set (80% of the dataset) and a validation set (20% of the dataset) of continuous days for the experiments. Each of the experiments has been trained for 1000 epochs, with a batch size of 128, using Categorical Cross Entropy as the loss function and Adam [8] as the optimizer. After the 1000 epochs we selected the best model using the validation accuracy as the fitness metric. The *action* embeddings were calculated using the full Kasteren dataset and using the word2vec [5] algorithm and the embedding layer was configured as trainable. To validate the results of the architecture we have performed three types of experiments: (1) Architecture experiments: where we evaluate different architectures, varying the number of LSTM and fully connected dense layers; (2) Sequence length experiments: where we evaluate the effects of altering the input *action* sequence length and (3)Time experiments: where we evaluate the effects of taking into account the timestamps of the input *actions* (See Table 1).

---

[2] https://sites.google.com/site/tim0306/datasets.

Table 1. Architecture (A), sequence (S) and time (T) experiments. *Dropout* is the value of the dropout regularizations. *LSTM #* is the number of LSTM layers in the architecture. *LSTM size* is the size of the LSTM layers. *Dense #* is the number of fully connected layers with a ReLU activation (all the architectures have a final fully connected layer with a softmax activation). *Dense size* is the size of the fully connected layers with a ReLU activation. *Sequence length* is the length of the input *action* sequence. *Time* states if time have been taken into account in the model and the fusion strategy [9] used.

ID	Dropout	LSTM #	LSTM size	Dense #	Dense size	Sequence length	Time
A1	0.4	1 (Standard)	512	1	1024	5	No
A2	0.8	1 (Standard)	512	1	1024	5	No
A3	0.8	1 (Standard)	512	2	1024	5	No
A4	0.8	2 (Standard)	512	2	1024	5	No
A5	0.2	1 (Standard)	512	5	50	5	No
A6	0.8	1 (Bidirectional)	512	2	1024	5	No
S1	0.8	1 (Standard)	512	2	1024	2	No
S2	0.8	1 (Standard)	512	2	1024	1	No
S3	0.8	1 (Standard)	512	2	1024	4	No
S4	0.8	1 (Standard)	512	2	1024	6	No
S5	0.8	1 (Standard)	512	2	1024	10	No
S6	0.8	1 (Standard)	512	2	1024	30	No
T1	0.8	1 (Standard)	512	2	1024	5	Yes (late fusion)
T2	0.8	1 (Standard)	512	2	1024	5	Yes (early fusion)
T3	0.8	1 (Standard)	512	2	1024	5	Yes (slow fusion)

To properly validate the predicting capabilities of the proposed architectures we evaluated how they perform providing different numbers of predictions (from 1 to 5 predictions). To do this took the 1, 2, 3, 4 and 5 best predictions and checked if the next action of the ground-truth was amongst them. In this case, accuracy is defined as dividing the sum of true positives and negatives by the sum of total positives and negatives. Table 2 shows the obtained results. In the case of the architecture experiments adding more LSTM layers (A4) or more, smaller, densely connected layers (A5) reduced the overall accuracy of the model no matter the number of predictions. The usage of bidirectional LSTMs (A6) was also detrimental. Generally higher dropout regularization values (A2 and A3) produced better results. Overall the A3 configuration offered the best results across the board. For the sequence length experiments, the best results were achieved using sequences with a length of 4 (S3) or 5 (A3) *actions*. In this specific case, the optimal sequence length was closely related with each deployment, being determined by the average action length of the activities in each scenario. This value should be adjusted in each specific case in order to achieve the best results and can not be generalized. Finally for the time experiments the evaluation shows

Table 2. Accuracy for the different experiments.

ID	1 prediction	2 predictions	3 predictions	4 predictions	5 predictions
A1	0.4487	0.6367	0.7094	0.7948	0.8461
A2	0.4530	0.6239	0.7222	0.7692	0.8504
A3	**0.4744**	0.6282	0.7179	0.7905	**0.8589**
A4	0.4444	0.5940	0.6965	0.7735	0.8247
A5	0.4402	0.5982	0.7136	0.7820	0.8418
A6	0.4487	0.6068	0.7136	0.7905	0.8376
S1	0.4553	0.5957	0.7021	0.8	0.8553
S2	0.4255	0.6255	0.7021	**0.8085**	0.8382
S3	0.4658	**0.6452**	**0.7264**	0.7948	0.8504
S4	0.4700	0.6196	0.6965	0.7692	0.8461
S5	0.4592	0.6351	0.7210	0.7896	0.8369
S6	0.4192	0.5589	0.6593	0.7554	0.8122
T1	0.4487	0.6239	0.7094	0.7692	0.8076
T2	0.4487	0.6111	0.7008	0.7692	0.8247
T3	0.3846	0.5940	0.7051	0.7564	0.8076

that none of the proposed options to take into account the timestamps (T1, T2 and T3) improved the results. When comparing them with an architecture with a similar configuration and no timestamps (A3), the results are clearly worse. Our initial intuition was that taking into account the timestamps would help to model the temporal patterns in the actions, but the results show that this information is not so relevant for the behaviour modelling task. We expect that the temporal data will be much more relevant in the activity recognition task, specially when discriminating between activity patterns with similar actions that happen at different periods (prepare breakfast versus prepare dinner).

4   Conclusions and Future Work

In this paper we have proposed a multilevel conceptual model that describes the user behaviour using *actions*, *activities*, *intra-activity behaviour* and *inter-activity behaviour*. Using that conceptual model we have presented a Deep Learning architecture based on Long Short-Term Memory Networks that models the *inter-activity behaviour*. Our architecture offers a probabilistic model that allows to predict the users next *actions* and to identify anomalous user behaviours. We have evaluated several architectures, analysing how each one of them behaves for a different number of *action* predictions. As future work we plan to continue studying how the temporal and spatial information could be integrated in the architecture to improve the statistical model. We would like to explore other deep learning architectures, for example using Convolutional Neural Networks instead of LSTMs. We also plan to develop architectures that will cover other aspects of the proposed multilevel conceptual model, starting with the activity recognition task.

Acknowledgment. This work has been supported by the European Commission under the City4Age project grant agreement (number 689731). We gratefully acknowledge the support of NVIDIA Corporation with the donation of the Titan X Pascal GPU used for this research.

References

1. Azkune, G., Almeida, A., López-de-Ipiña, D., Chen, L.: Extending knowledge-driven activity models through data-driven learning techniques. Expert Syst. Appl. **42**(6), 3115–3128 (2015)
2. Bilbao, A., Almeida, A., López-de-Ipiña, D.: Promotion of active ageing combining sensor and social network data. J. Biomed. Inform. **64**, 108–115 (2016)
3. Hochreiter, S., Schmidhuber, J.: Long short-term memory. Neural Comput. **9**(8), 1735–1780 (1997)
4. Chaaraoui, A.A., Climent-Prez, P., Flrez-Revuelta, F.: A review on vision techniques applied to human behaviour analysis for ambient-assisted living. Expert Syst. Appl. **39**(12), 10873–10888 (2012)
5. Mikolov, T., Sutskever, I., Chen, K., Corrado, G.S. Dean, J.: Distributed representations of words and phrases and their compositionality. In: Advances in Neural Information Processing Systems, pp. 3111–3119 (2013)
6. Glorot, X., Bordes, A., Bengio, Y.: Deep Sparse Rectifier Neural Networks. In: Aistats, vol. 15, no. 106, p. 275, April 2011
7. Srivastava, N., Hinton, G.E., Krizhevsky, A., Sutskever, I., Salakhutdinov, R.: Dropout: a simple way to prevent neural networks from overfitting. J, Mach. Learn. Res. **15**(1), 1929–1958 (2014)
8. Kingma, D., Ba, J.: A method for stochastic optimization (2014). arXiv:1412.6980
9. Karpathy, A., Toderici, G., Shetty, S., Leung, T., Sukthankar, R., Fei-Fei, L.: Large-scale video classification with convolutional neural networks. In: Proceedings of the IEEE Conference on Computer Vision and Pattern Recognition, pp. 1725–1732 (2014)

Exploring an Open Data Initiative Ontology for Shareable Smart Environment Experimental Datasets

Ian McChesney[(✉)], Chris Nugent, Joseph Rafferty, and Jonathan Synnott

School of Computing and Mathematics, Ulster University, Newtownabbey, Northern Ireland, UK
{ir.mcchesney,cd.nugent,j.rafferty,j.synnott}@ulster.ac.uk

Abstract. The Open Data Initiative (ODI) has previously been proposed as a framework for the collection, annotation, management and sharing of data gathered through research in pervasive health and smart environment systems. It includes the provision of open access protocols for the conduct of experiments and a standard format for the exchange of datasets. In this paper we formalize the structure of the ODI repository through development of an ontology which seeks to unify the representation of ODI objects, experimental protocols, and event logs. An XML-based standards approach to storing event logs, using eXtensible Event Stream (XES) enables data sharing, manipulation and ontology integration. Typical usage scenarios are presented based on published experimental data to validate the concepts of the presented work. Related SPARQL queries are used to illustrate the outputs which can be derived. Based on these initial results, we outline a system architecture for prototyping further ODI related work.

Keywords: Activity recognition · Pervasive health · Smart environments · Open data · Repository · Ontology · XES

1 Introduction

Within the pervasive healthcare community, the Open Data Initiative (ODI) has been proposed to facilitate the sharing of annotated data sets [1]. The ODI framework includes a common protocol for data collection, a common format for data exchange, and a data repository and related tools to underpin research within the domain of activity recognition.

The motivation behind the ODI is to support collaboration, data exchange and accelerated reporting of results in the expanding field of activity recognition in smart environments [2]. The research community currently uses a range of established data sets, for example the van Kasteren [3] and WSU CASAS datasets [4]. Experimental data in this area is produced in a variety of formats, using protocols and sensing technologies that can vary from one experiment to the next. Such heterogeneity in the datasets is an inherent feature of the field, however, the ability to organize and annotate these datasets in a way which facilitates their discovery, adaptation and reuse, would greatly benefit the research community.

© Springer International Publishing AG 2017
S.F. Ochoa et al. (Eds.): UCAmI 2017, LNCS 10586, pp. 400–412, 2017.
DOI: 10.1007/978-3-319-67585-5_42

Previous work on the ODI framework has involved the development of homeML, a standard vocabulary for describing experiments and an XML template for data storage [5]. In this paper we build on this work, extending the ODI framework to incorporate the eXtensible Event Stream (XES) standard for event data storage [6] and an ontological model, replacing homeML, for describing experiment metadata.

The ontological modelling approach to the ODI arose from consideration of the following options for integration between homeML/ODI concepts and the semantic modelling capabilities of XES. These options are visualized in Fig. 1 and summarized below:

- Option 1: Fully embed homeML/ODI data in the XES event stream. This would require the pre-processing of raw smart environment event logs into an enhanced log in which every event has a set of attributes which fully describe the activity context and its environment.
- Option 2: Separating events from homeML into XES. The events are represented in XES and the experiment metadata is stored in an XML format such as the current homeML structure.
- Option 3: Developing a homeML-XES extension. In XES, a domain-specific extension can be created which defines standard attributes for a particular application. A "smart environment" extension could effectively implement the set of attributes which are currently defined as part of homeML.
- Option 4: Representation of homeML/ODI data using an XES-ontology combination. With the XES ability to relate event data to a semantic model of other objects in the domain, this leads to the possibility of an ontology representation for all of the experiment metadata, with XES being used to define only the event log. An ontological representation for experiment metadata (a subset of which is currently modelled by homeML) would facilitate the description of an experiment in a natural and flexible way and enable the unique identification of objects and relationships therein.

The remainder of the paper elaborates on option 4 and is organized as follows. First, a discussion of related work is presented in Sect. 2. Section 3 then presents user requirements for the ODI framework in the form of four usage scenarios which encapsulate a range of problems the framework should be able to address. Section 4 outlines the ODI modelling framework in terms of an ontology to facilitate storage, reasoning and retrieval of experiment metadata and the formatting requirements for event data in XES. Section 5 describes our initial experimental setup using Protégé, populated with a range of data from published experiments. Based on interactions with this system, Sect. 6 discusses the results attained. Section 7 presents future work and concluding remarks.

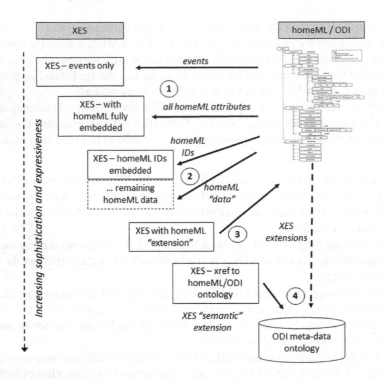

Fig. 1. Options 1-4 for homeML/ODI and XES integration

2 Related Work

Previous work in activity recognition in smart environments has made use of the notion of ontologies in relation to both context modelling for smart homes [7] and ontological models to support recognition of activities of daily living (ADL) [8–11].

In the wider context of pervasive computing, a number of upper level ontologies have been proposed for knowledge sharing and reuse [12]. SOUPA (Standard Ontologies for Ubiquitous and Pervasive Applications) [13] aims to support the developers of pervasive computing applications by providing a shared ontology for describing core concepts in a pervasive system such as person, action, policy, time, space and event. CONON (Context Ontology) [14] is an ontology devised for use in context aware computing. It identifies the core, underpinning concepts for modelling a domain such as location, user, activity and computational entity. Ye et al. [15] describe another top-level ontology specifically for smart environments which seeks to provide a meta-structure for describing and reasoning about objects in an existing domain ontology.

The application of ontology concepts to more specific smart environment applications includes SOCOM (multi-Sensor Oriented COntext Model) [16] and SensorML [17]. SOCOM is an example of an ontology specifically focused on sensors in a context aware system. The ontology provides constructs for modelling both physical and logical sensors.

Previous work has been undertaken which seeks to harmonize smart environment datasets to enable exchange and reuse. For example, Helal et al. [19] have developed an XML-based Sensory Dataset Description Language with the aim of sharing pervasive space research datasets. Their markup specification is based on an analysis of existing publicly available data sets, such as CASAS [4]. In addition, their work seeks to provide algorithms for repurposing existing data sets for use in other research contexts. In contrast to the approach in [19], in developing our ODI framework we have utilized the existing published standard of XES [6] as the XML markup specification for recording events.

Ontological modelling of experimental datasets has been adopted as a sharing mechanism in other domains. For example, in biology, the exchange of datasets was faced with problems similar to that of the current ADL community as described above. Our approach has similarities to [20] which describes a tool for the integration of biomedical datasets across repositories and for the annotation and indexing of these to facilitate dataset discovery. The Open Biomedical Annotator [21] adopts a similar approach of a tool which offers an ontological vocabulary for dataset annotation. [22] describes an approach whereby datasets from multiple experiments in DNA analysis can be integrated for visual analysis based on the underlying ontology structures used for genome investigation.

3   Usage Scenarios

Our approach to developing an ontology for the ODI framework has been informed by the principles of ontological engineering [23, 24]. As an initial step in requirements definition, we sought to determine the scope of the ODI ontology by considering the types of query it should be able to address. These competency questions were framed in the context of four usage scenarios covering the range of requirements a researcher might have when interacting with the ODI repository. These scenarios are outlined below:

ODI Scenario 1 – Consider a researcher who wishes to gain access to existing datasets. This scenario concerns a researcher developing a new approach for activity recognition. At their research group they have limited resources to generate and collect data and they have not been able to find a suitable dataset online to assist with their research. They are in need of a specific dataset to both assist with training and evaluation of their activity recognition approach.

Once accessing the ODI repository they have an initial requirement to view all datasets available. They then have the need to check which activities have been recorded, how many instances there are per activity class and what is the balance of the dataset in terms of spread of classes across instances. They will also have a general requirement to know about numbers of participants and the protocols used for collecting the data, however, this information is not essential.

For the purposes of disseminating their findings, the ability to benchmark their activity recognition performance against other systems which have used identical data would be of significant benefit.

Finally and perhaps most importantly, they will need to know about the format of the data. This will be important to allow them to re-purpose the data for training and testing with their own approach.

ODI Scenario 2 – Consider a researcher who wishes to share their dataset with other researchers working within the field of activity recognition.
In this scenario we have a researcher who wishes to increase the awareness of their research and the datasets which they have collected. Once entering the ODI online repository, and in the spirit of sharing their data, they are interested in knowing how they can make available their dataset for the purposes of experiment replication, transfer learning or benchmarking.

To be able to share their data they are faced with a number of requirements before their work can be validated and made widely available. They must share the protocol for their data collection. They must share the details of the technology used. They must also share the details of the ethics associated with their research and confirm, if applicable, that their data can be openly shared within the research community. A description of the data is also required to profile the activity labels, number of instances and any missing values. Any publications directly related to the collection and processing of their data should also be shared with a version of the published works, complying with open access. Finally, details of the format used to store the data needs to be shared.

ODI Scenario 3 – Consider a researcher who wants to replicate an experiment.
This scenario concerns a researcher wishing to generate data and make it available through the ODI. To avoid duplication of effort whilst at the same time maximizing the impact on the research community, the researcher decides they wish to follow the same protocol as others who have already collected data and make this available through the ODI.

Upon accessing the ODI website the researcher wishes to know which datasets have been collected and which activity classes have been recorded. Upon finding the dataset which best matches the potential dataset that they wish to record they subsequently require details of the technology platform used, the protocol used to collect the data and any ethical implications to be considered whilst completing the data collection process. Finally, the format of how the data should be stored will also be required by the researcher. Once the data has been collected it can then be used to augment the dataset(s) currently available through the ODI which have adhered to the same protocol/technology/format as the researcher has with their experiments.

ODI Scenario 4 – Consider a researcher who wishes to benchmark their activity recognition algorithm.
Here we have a researcher who has developed their own unique approach to activity recognition. In an effort to gauge the effectiveness of the work the researcher wishes to benchmark their approach against other known approaches in the domain through processing an unseen and unlabeled dataset.

Once arriving at the ODI website the researcher will wish to find details relating to how to benchmark their approach. They will require information relating to the format of the data and how they should present their results following processing of the data.

They will also require details of how they can submit their results file to the ODI repository and log this against their approach to ensure the research community can view its performance. Other researchers who have previously submitted datasets can be notified of new datasets and benchmarks.

4   The ODI Ontology

Using Protégé [25] and the OWL 2 concepts of Individuals, Properties and Classes [26], and guided by the above usage scenarios, an ontology representation of the ODI metadata has been constructed as presented in Fig. 2 (Class Hierarchy section).

Fig. 2. Protégé extract showing Instance data for experiment IESimApril2016 [27]

A typical experiment uploaded to the ODI repository will involve the collection of sensor generated data arising from the actions of inhabitants (experiment participants), completing a range of ADLs across a range of locations such as kitchen, living room and bedroom. The level 1 ontology classes represent these primary objects, the metadata for the experiment.

– An `Experiment` has both data properties and object properties. Data properties include experiment start date/time and end date/time. Object properties model its relationship to other objects in the ontology. For example, we say that an `Experiment` follows some `Protocol` which describes the experimental setup and methodology. An `Experiment` has some `Ethical Issue`, describing the ethical considerations addressed in the experiment, and any ethical approval obtained and conditions applied. An `Experiment` consists of some `Activity`, enabling a description of the activity types which were being measured during the experiment run.

– Regarding `Activity` types, the ontology distinguishes between single participant activities (activities in locations where there is only one participant e.g. an elderly person living alone) and multi participant activities (those in locations where there are multiple participants e.g. children playing in a group setting). The various activity types which the experiment relates to are described as Individuals (instances) for any given experiment, e.g. Going To Bed or Making Breakfast.

– A `Location` in each experiment can have information such as location description (e.g. kitchen, bathroom, living room, bedroom) and a bitmap of the location layout. Locations involved in the experiment are described as instances for any given experiment.

– `Inhabitants` (participants) who took part can be recorded with respect to data properties such as age, care plan and any medical condition pertinent to the experiment. The ontology can also record the type of activities the inhabitant might be expected to perform.

– When describing an experiment, it is necessary to record information about the `Devices` used. This will relate to the sensor devices used, either fixed location or mobile. For a fixed location device, data properties such as coordinates can be stored. A location `Device` is linked to the `Location` class through object property *hasLocation*. For a mobile device, data properties include device placement, size and weight. Information about any data storage equipment used in the experiment can also be stored.

5   ODI Exploratory Setup Using Protégé and XES

Our first approach to exploring these concepts has been to set up a prototype dataset directly in Protégé, populating the ontology with Individuals representing experiments and their associated information. By way of example, we refer to three published experiments, referred to here as IESimApril2016, Kasteren2008 and CASAS01. These are described in references [27, 3, 4] respectively.

Based on a literal reading of the experiments as described in these papers, we have identified the descriptive data which might be stored in the ontology if the experiments were to be uploaded to the ODI by the researchers. Table 1 presents an excerpt of data for IESimApril2016 and Fig. 2 presents its representation in the ODI ontology, validated by the primary researcher from the IESimApril2016 study.

Table 1. Sample data from experiement IESimApril2016 [27]

Class	Instance
Activity → SingleParticipantActivity	Go to Bed, Get Dressed, Use Telephone, Use Toilet, Watch TV, Prepare Breakfast, Take Shower, Leave House, Get Cold Drink, Get Hot Drink, Prepare Dinner
Device → Location Device	(IESim) Contact Sensor, Pressure Sensor, Bed Sensor, Shower Sensor, Sink Sensor.
Ethical Issue	Simulated Environment
Experiment	IESimApril2016
Experimenter	John Smith
Inhabitant	IESimApril2016_P1... IESimApril2016_P8
Location	IESimApril2016-Shower, -Toilet, -Bedroom, -Hall, -LivingRoom, -Kitchen
Log	http://www.example.com/IESimApril2016.xes
Medical Condition	None
Protocol	ExperimentProtocol.docx

Note that in Table 1 the Log is identified as being available at some URL. In the ontology, the `Log` class has the object property *belongsTo* exactly 1 `Experiment`, providing the semantic reference between the two objects. In the XES file (discussed below, Fig. 4) the XES Semantic Extension is used to link the event log to the IESimApril2016 ontology.

By populating the Protégé ontology with sample data for each of the three experiments, we can begin to test some of the queries arising from the usage scenarios described in Sect. 3. For example, typical queries might include: What experiments are contained in the repository? Which ADLs have been considered within the experiments? Which experiments involve recording events in a kitchen?

The ontology schema and data can be queried using SPARQL, a W3C defined query language for RDF (Resource Description Framework) graphs. A SPARQL query typically consists of a set of triple patterns, with components of the pattern containing values or variables matching against the RDF graph representation of the ontology [28].

Figure 3 presents the SPARQL query for resolving the query to show all experiments involving a kitchen. The WHERE line showing `?e ?x ?k` is retrieving *hasLocation* relationships (`?x`) for all experiments, and the `FILTER` line is selecting those which contain the text "`kitc`" (for kitchen). The results are as shown in Fig. 3. The prefixes define shorthand representations of namespaces which can be used in the query. In this example, `odi:` refers to the Protégé implementation of the ODI repository. The remaining namespaces are standard entries in a SPARQL query.

```
PREFIX odi: <http://webprotege.stanford.edu/project/86mAzIFOMQ
PREFIX rdf: <http://www.w3.org/1999/02/22-rdf-syntax-ns#>
PREFIX owl: <http://www.w3.org/2002/07/owl#>
PREFIX rdfs: <http://www.w3.org/2000/01/rdf-schema#>
PREFIX xsd: <http://www.w3.org/2001/XMLSchema#>
SELECT DISTINCT ?e ?k
    WHERE { ?x rdfs:label "hasLocation"^^xsd:string .
            ?e ?x ?k .
            ?k rdf:type owl:NamedIndividual .
            FILTER regex (str(?k), "kitc", "i") .
    }
===
e, k
CASAS01, Kitchen
Kasteren2008, Kitchen
IESimApril2016, IESimApril2016-Kitchen
===
```

Fig. 3. SPARQL query to show all experiments using a kitchen within the ODI repository

Whereas SPARQL is used to query the experiment metadata as stored in the ontology, the linked dataset itself is stored separately, as an XES event log. Figure 4 presents an extract of a raw event log for experiment data generated using the IESimApril2016 smart environment (lines 1–3), and an extract of the corresponding XES event log (lines 5–24).

```
1   id,time,sensor_id,name,description
2   4158,"2016-04-05 13:13:12",100,"Hall-Bedroom Door",Go-to-Bed
3   4159,"2016-04-05 13:13:16",100,"Hall-Bedroom Door",
4   ...
5   <?xml version="1.0" encoding="UTF-8" ?>
6   <log xes.version="1.0" xes.features="nested-attributes">
7     <extension name="Semantic" prefix="semantic"
8       uri="http://www.xes-standard.org/semantic.xesext"/>
9     # ...
10    <string key="semantic:modelReference"
11      value="http://example.com/idString#IESimApril2016.xes" />
12    # ...
13    <trace>
14      <event>
15        <int key="sensor_id" value="100"/>
16        <date key="time:timestamp" value="2016-04-05T13:13:12"/>
17        <string key="concept:name" value="4158"/>
18        <string key="lifecycle:transition" value="complete"/>
19        <string key="description" value="Go-to-Bed"/>
20        <string key="name" value="Hall-Bedroom Door"/>
21      </event>
22      # ...
23    </trace>
24  </log>
```

Fig. 4. XES event log extract for IESimApril2016 – note lines 6,13,14 and 7,10

This XES file can be generated from the raw event log using the OpenXES library [29] or a smart environment experiment can generate the event data natively according to the XES specification. This example conveys the XES element structure of log (line 6), trace (line 13), and event (line 14). Use of the XES Semantic Extension (defined in line 7, instantiated in line 10) enables this event log file to be linked to the Log object in the IESimApril2016 ODI ontological model. Use of the semantic:modelReference attribute is not limited to the log element. Any trace and /or event element in the XES file can be given further semantics through linking a modelReference tag to a uniform resource identifier of an associated ontology object.

6   Discussion

Having used the exploratory configuration of the ODI framework to define and query a range of datasets, a number of issues and open questions arise.

A common problem in ontological engineering is, with respect to the class hierarchy, knowing when to stop representing a concept as a class and when to define it as an instance. For example, we have taken the decision that an activity can be either a single or multi participant activity. We could define further subclasses for a single participant activity such as get dressed, go to bed, prepare drink. Prepare drink could in turn be specialized as prepare cold drink and prepare hot drink. Nevertheless, we have taken the decision to represent particular activities as instances, allowing the experimenter to describe activities using their own labels. Similar decisions apply to other objects in the class hierarchy and this is an issue to be reviewed during subsequent formal evaluation.

One particular issue in determining the granularity of the class hierarchy is its ability to facilitate transfer learning in experimental activity recognition. The ability to distinguish between characteristics of the experimental setting - characteristics such as sensor types, location features, and completeness of annotations – is essential to the meaningful application of transfer learning algorithms [30]. The ODI ontology captures these characteristics but formal evaluation of the framework will take account of their usefulness for transfer learning and online learning.

A feature of the ODI repository is the ability of an experimenter to lookup the protocol followed in any given experiment. At one level, the protocol can be described in a single file (such as a Word document). Alternatively, there is a case for further specialization of the protocol class to describe the sections it might contain, as they could be of relevance to a researcher enquiring of the repository.

It is anticipated that, over time, the preferred method of event log formatting will be XES. In the smart environment research community at this time, other formats are much more common. The ODI will be designed to work with these, requiring the experimenter to include a README.TXT file as necessary. One advantage of pursuing the XES format is that a set of standard tools can be developed for preprocessing of event log files. For example, it would be possible to analyze the file to identify how many activity types and activity instances there are in an experiment, or how many distinct sensors have been used. This can be used to cross-validate against the metadata which the experimenter will upload for the experiment and as a pre-processing step for transfer learning.

Operation of the ODI repository in a live environment will require considerable attention to authentication and to vetting of candidate data sets. It is of the utmost importance that the material which it hosts is validated and of suitable quality for dissemination and as a basis for future experiments.

7 Conclusions and Future Work

The exploratory setup using Protégé has been of value in identifying the modelling and practical problems to be addressed in achieving a viable ODI repository. This setup will continue to be used for investigative work. Nevertheless, a high-level system design is in the process of being developed which will enable the ontology and event logs to be deployed in a laboratory test environment to be evaluated by smart environment researchers. The aim is to develop a lean prototype version of the ODI as on online repository, to include the ability to upload datasets and to provide a visual query builder using, for example, AngularJS. A REST endpoint will be established for the prototype to talk to. Distributed database options will be evaluated such as MongoDB and Ceph Storage, with the ability to link to the ODI ontology via UIDs. Options such as Stardog are being considered for the ontology server itself.

With a prototype system in place, evaluation experiments will be set up for researchers from a range of smart environment research groups to use the ODI repository and its web frontend to upload and retrieve datasets. This will inform the necessary refinements for further ODI development.

Acknowledgements. Invest Northern Ireland is acknowledged for partially supporting this project under the Competence Centre Programme Grant RD0513853 - Connected Health Innovation Centre. This work was conducted using the Protégé resource, which is supported by grant GM10331601 from the National Institute of General Medical Sciences of the United States National Institutes of Health.

References

1. Nugent, C., Synnott, J., Santanna, A., Espinilla, M., Cleland, I., Banos, L., Lundström, J., Hallberg, J. Calzada, A.: An initiative for the creation of open datasets within the pervasive healthcare. In: 10th EAI Int. Conf. on Pervasive Computing Technologies for Healthcare, Cancun, Mexico, pp. 16–19 (2016)
2. Chen, L., Hoey, J., Nugent, C., Cook, D., Yu, Z.: Sensor-based activity recognition. IEEE Trans. Syst. Man Cybern. Part C (Applications and Reviews) **42**(6), 790–808 (2012)
3. van Kasteren, T., Noulas, A., Englebienne, G., Kröse, B.: Accurate activity recognition in a home setting. In: ACM 10th Int. Conf. on Ubiquitous Computing, pp. 1–9. ACM Press (2008)
4. Cook, D., Schmitter-Edgecombe, M.: Assessing the quality of activities in a smart environment. Methods Inf. Med. **48**(5), 480 (2009)
5. McDonald, H., Nugent, C., Hallberg, J., Finlay, D., Moore, G., Synnes, K.: The homeML suite: shareable datasets for smart home environments. Health Technol. **3**(2), 177–193 (2013)
6. IEEE Standard for eXtensible Event Stream (XES) for Achieving Interoperability in Event Logs and Event Streams, IEEE Std 1849–2016, (2016)

7. Chen, L., Nugent, C., Mulvenna, M., Finlay, D., Hong, X., Poland, M.: A logical framework for behaviour reasoning and assistance in a smart home. Int. J. Assistive Robot. Mechatron. **9**(4), 20–42 (2008)
8. Chen, L., Nugent, C., Wang, H.: A knowledge-driven approach to activity recognition in smart homes. IEEE Trans. Knowl. Data Eng. **24**(6), 961–974 (2012)
9. Bae, I.H.: An ontology-based approach to ADL recognition in smart homes. Future Gener. Comput. Syst. **33**, 32–41 (2014)
10. Chen, L., Nugent, C., Okeyo, G.: An ontology-based hybrid approach to activity modeling for smart homes. IEEE Trans. Human-Mach. Syst. **44**(1), 92–105 (2014)
11. Rafferty, J., Nugent, C., Liu, J., Chen, L.: From activity recognition to intention recognition for assisted living within smart homes. IEEE Trans. Human-Mach. Syst. (2017) http://ieeexplore.ieee.org/document/7807210/
12. Ye, J., Coyle, L., Dobson, S., Nixon, P.: Ontology-based models in pervasive computing systems. Knowl. Eng. Rev. **22**(4), 315–347 (2007)
13. Chen, H., Perich F., Finin, T. Joshi, A.: Soupa: Standard ontology for ubiquitous and pervasive applications. In: 1st IEEE Intl. Conf. on Mobile and Ubiquitous Systems: Networking and Services, MOBIQUITOUS 2004, pp. 258–267. IEEE Press (2004)
14. Wang, X., Zhang, D., Gu, T., Pung, H.: Ontology based context modeling and reasoning using OWL. In: 2nd IEEE Conf. Pervasive Computing and Communications Workshops, pp. 18–22. IEEE Press (2004)
15. Ye, J., Stevenson, G., Dobson, S.: A top-level ontology for smart environments. Pervasive and Mobile Computing **7**(3), 359–378 (2011)
16. Rong, T., Gu, J., Zhong, Z., Chen, P.: SOCOM: Multi-sensor oriented context model based on ontologies. In 8th International Conference on Intelligent Environments (IE), pp. 236–242. IEEE Press (2012)
17. Botts, M., Robin, A.: OpenGIS sensor model language (SensorML) implementation specification. OpenGIS Implement. Specif. OGC 7, no. 000 (2007)
18. Compton, M., Barnaghi, P., Bermudez, L., GarcíA-Castro, R., Corcho, O., Cox, S., Graybeal, J.: The SSN ontology of the W3C semantic sensor network incubator group. Web semantics: science, services and agents on the World Wide Web **17**, 25–32 (2012)
19. Helal, A., Mendez-Vazquez, A., Hossain, S.: Specification and synthesis of sensory datasets in pervasive spaces. In IEEE Symposium on Computers and Communications, ISCC 2009. pp. 920–925. IEEE Press (2009)
20. Shah, N.H., Jonquet, C., Chiang, A.P., Butte, A.J., Chen, R., Musen, M.A.: Ontology-driven indexing of public datasets for translational bioinformatics. BMC Bioinform. **10**(2), S1 (2008)
21. Jonquet, C., Shah, N.H., Musen, M.A.: The open biomedical annotator. In Summit on Translational Bioinformatics, pp. 56–60. (2009)
22. Usadel, B., Nagel, A., Steinhauser, D., Gibon, Y., Bläsing, O.E., Redestig, H., Sreenivasulu, N., Krall, L., Hannah, M.A., Poree, F., Fernie, A.R.: PageMan: an interactive ontology tool to generate, display, and annotate overview graphs for profiling experiments. BMC Bioinformatics **7**(1), 535–543 (2006)
23. Noy, N., McGuinness, D.: Ontology development 101: A guide to creating your first ontology (2001)
24. Pinto, H., Martins, J.: Ontologies: How can they be built? Knowl. Inf. Syst. **6**(4), 441–464 (2004)
25. Musen, M.A.: The Protégé project: a look back and a look forward. AI Matters **1**(4), 4–12 (2015)
26. W3C: OWL 2 Web Ontology Language Document Overview (Second Edition) (2012). https://www.w3.org/TR/owl2-overview/

27. Synnott, J., Nugent, C., Zhang, S., Calzada, A., Cleland, I., Espinilla, M., Quero, J., Lundstrom, J.: Environment simulation for the promotion of the open data initiative. In IEEE Int. Conf. Smart Computing (SMARTCOMP), pp 1–6. IEEE Press (2016)
28. W3C: SPARQL Query Language for RDF (2008) https://www.w3.org/TR/rdf-sparql-query/,
29. Günther, C.W., Verbeek, E.: OpenXES Developer Guide. University of Technology, Eindhoven **61** (2009)
30. Cook, D., Feuz, K.D., Krishnan, N.C.: Transfer learning for activity recognition: a survey. Knowl. Inf. Syst. **36**(3), 537–556 (2013)

A Dataset of Routine Daily Activities in an Instrumented Home

Julien Cumin[1,2(✉)], Grégoire Lefebvre[1], Fano Ramparany[1],
and James L. Crowley[2]

[1] Orange Labs, Meylan, France
{julien1.cumin,gregoire.lefebvre,fano.ramparany}@orange.com
[2] Univ. Grenoble Alpes, Inria, CNRS,
Grenoble INP, LIG, 38000 Grenoble, France
james.crowley@inria.fr

Abstract. We present a new dataset, called Orange4Home, of activities of daily living of one inhabitant in a smart home environment. We collected data from 236 heterogeneous sensors in a fully integrated instrumented apartment. Data collection spanned 4 consecutive weeks of working days for a total of around 180 h of recording. 20 classes of varied activities were labeled *in situ*. We report the methodology adopted to establish a representative, challenging dataset, as well as present the apartment and sensors used to collect this data.

Keywords: Dataset · Activities of daily living · Smart home

1 Introduction

Development, evaluation and comparison of machine learning approaches for activity recognition in smart home environments all require realistic data labeled with ground truth. Acquiring labeled data of activities in a smart home is challenging and costly for a number of reason. For one thing, few instrumented smart homes exist. Furthermore, providing accurate ground truth is costly and tedious. Giving a meaning to data collected by many heterogeneous sensors in an instrumented environment is difficult. For example, finding whether an occupant is currently cooking or not (which might impact the service that the system wants to provide to the occupant), using only low-level sensors such as door openings, luminosity, ambient noise, etc. is challenging. In addition, The range of possible activities is highly variable, and there are no guarantees that activities of an individual in a specific home are representative of the entire population of inhabitants or homes. Thus, establishing a representative dataset of activities in smart homes requires both technical work on instrumenting a home and an important effort to accurately label activities.

In this paper, we present a new labeled dataset, named *Orange4Home*[1], of activities of daily living (ADL) of an occupant in an instrumented smart home

---

[1] http://amiqual4home.inria.fr/orange4home.

© Springer International Publishing AG 2017
S.F. Ochoa et al. (Eds.): UCAmI 2017, LNCS 10586, pp. 413–425, 2017.
DOI: 10.1007/978-3-319-67585-5_43

environment. The Amiqual4Home smart home environment is a fully equipped furnished 87 m^2 apartment, that has been instrumented with 236 data sources, which capture information about use of electrical equipment, water consumption, operation of doors, etc. The facility was constructed to serve as a resource for research in smart home services. We used this facility to acquire data about human daily activities, over a period of 20 working days. Labels for 20 classes of activity were noted *in situ* by the occupant, representative of the performed activities. This data is designed to be used for supervised offline activity recognition [4], supervised online activity recognition [6], unsupervised activity discovery [2], activity prediction [5], as well as other applications.

We report in Sect. 2 related datasets of activities in the home. We present in Sect. 3 the methodology adopted to establish a realistic dataset of labeled activities, and in Sect. 4 the technical aspects of the experiment. We conclude in Sect. 5 on future uses of this dataset.

2   Related Work

The dataset presented in this work complements the already significant number of existing datasets of ADL, such as the Opportunity dataset, the Transfer Learning dataset, and other datasets of ADL.

Opportunity [7] is a dataset where activities of 4 different occupants are recorded using a high number of both environmental (i.e. fixed in the home) sensors and body-worn (i.e. placed on the occupant) sensors. This dataset provides 3 levels of labeling of activities, from atomic arm gestures to high level activities such as eating a sandwich. However, the *Opportunity* dataset was recorded in a single experimental environment of only 1 room, which lessens its representativeness of real, inhabited homes. Moreover, nearly half of the sensors used are body-worn sensors, which is not realistic for smart home systems aimed at the general population, which is what we are interested in in this work. Finally, the sequence of activities captured in this dataset are very limited in time (about half an hour).

The *Transfer Learning dataset* [9] is another dataset of activities of daily living, recorded in 3 different real homes inhabited by 3 different persons. Labeling was done *in situ* by the occupant for a period of 13/18/25 days respectively, depending on the home. This dataset unfortunately contains the labeling of only 8 classes of activities (not including an *"Other"* activity), which may be too limited to be representative of all significant activities of a home. Moreover, only 23/21/14 sensors respectively were present in each home, which is possibly too little to realistically represent the complexity of future smart home systems.

ARAS [1] is a dataset of activities of daily living recorded in two real houses for a full month. This dataset contains the labels of 27 different activity classes labeled *in situ* by the inhabitant to a good degree of accuracy. Each house was equiped with 20 binary sensors, which is unfortunately restrictive in terms of algorithmic evaluation: it is not possible to use this dataset to experiment on algorithms that deal with heterogeneous data, nor is it possible to study sensors redundancy due to the small number of sensors.

A dataset by Tapia et al. presented in [8] provides the recordings of 77/84 sensors respectively in 2 real homes, inhabited by 2 different persons, for a period of 14 consecutive days. 33 different activities are labeled, each being part of categories of activities. This dataset was recorded with the intent of evaluating recognition of activities useful to healthcare applications, such as care to elderly people, which makes its representativeness of systems aimed at the general population debatable. Moreover, the authors of this work report significant difficulties in *in situ* labeling of activities, which was too coercive for both occupants, leading to imprecise or missing labels which had to be fixed by hand after the experiments.

The MavPad 2005 dataset [10] is a dataset recorded in a student apartment instrumented with 76 sensors of various kinds (light, temperature, humidity, motion, doors, water leak, smoke and CO_2), for a duration of 7 weeks during which one occupant was present in the home. This dataset is unfortunately not labeled with activities, which limits its usefulness to applications such as sensor events prediction, while not being usable for activity-related problems.

In this work, we aim at recording a dataset of activities which combines the positive points of these state-of-the-art datasets into one: our dataset provides the recordings of a high number of heterogeneous sensors scattered seamlessly in a real home, labeled *in situ* with a significant number of representative classes of activities performed by one occupant for a duration of 20 days.

3   Methodology

3.1   Goals of the Experiment

Based on the positive and negative points of state-of-the-art datasets of activities in the home, presented in Sect. 2, we based our methodology for recording the Orange4Home dataset on the following goals that we intend to reach:

1. label accurately all 4 main context information of the home for the entirety of the experiment;
2. record realistic routines of daily living of the general public (i.e. not of a specific population such as elderly people);
3. record data in a realistic environment, which is as close to a real home as possible;
4. record data in a pervasively instrumented environment, where as many objects as possible are instrumented, with as many different types of sensors as possible;
5. record data on a sufficiently long time scale such that the dataset is usable to test activity prediction approaches.

To fulfill goal 1, we need to provide information of *identity, time-of-day, place* and *activity* [4]. The Orange4Home dataset contains all 4 information, as there is only one occupant (identity is thus unique), all events are timestamped, and both place and activity are labeled *in situ* by the occupant (see Sect. 4.3).

The experiment spanned 4 consecutive weeks of working days, in order to fulfill goal 5.

We present in Sect. 4.1 the instrumented apartment used as the recording environment to fulfill goal 3, and in Sect. 4.2 the sensors and data types recorded during the experiment to fulfill goal 4.

To fulfill goal 2, we need to establish a home occupancy scenario, which will guide the choices of routines the occupants need to perform. We present this scenario in Sect. 3.2.

3.2 Home Occupancy Scenario

In this experiment, we imagine that the home is a coworking apartment in which the subject of the experiment, Bob, comes to work alone every working day, from around 08:00 to 17:00. This apartment is a pervasive environment filled with sensors of various kinds, which transmit their data to a centralized system in charge of the home.

Bob is interested in having personalized services in this coworking environment, based on his activities. As such, he will label his routines for a duration of 20 days (i.e. 4 weeks of working days). Since this is Bob's coworking apartment, his activities will not only be work-related, but also lunch and leisure related.

Bob does not live in the home outside of working hours, since this is a coworking environment. Therefore, data outside these hours is not provided.

3.3 Activities in Orange4Home

As mentionned in Sect. 3.1, identity, time-of-day, places and activities are key information of context. Identity is both the identity in the literal sense of an occupant, but also their social role in the home. Time-of-day can be any semantic temporal information such as a part of the year, whether it's a week day or not, etc. Places is a geographical location in the home which holds a specific function for the occupant, such as the bathroom or the kitchen. An activity is a set of tasks (or operations), a task being a set of actions [3].

Selecting the actual sets of labels used in the dataset for identity, time-of-day and place values is rather direct: names, timestamps and rooms of the home, respectively, are sufficient, since we can extract semantic labels from those values (e.g. all semantic labels for time-of-day can be obtained from a timestamp). It is less clear what set of labels should be used for activities. For example, in the *Opportunity* dataset [7], there are 3 *levels* of activity labeling, from complex activities like "*Sandwich time*" to atomic gestures like "*Interact with the bottle with the left arm*" (which match the activities, tasks and actions hierarchy).

In this dataset, we only label activities. Actions do not carry any functional meaning and are therefore not useful labels to characterize context in the home. Tasks, like activities, do carry functional meaning, but we believe that contextual information provided by tasks is too limited for general-purpose context-aware services (but could be useful for specific applications). Furthermore, tasks and actions are too numerous and possibly too short-lived to be effectively and accurately labeled, be it from an occupant in a real-world setting, but also in an experimental setting of data collection.

The activities we aim to record are those that are quite frequent, and fairly recurrent in time. They must also fit the scenario established in Sect. 3.2. We present below the list of activities, grouped by places (see Figs. 3 and 4) in which they can occur:

- **Entrance** *Entering, Leaving*;
- **Kitchen** *Preparing, Cooking, Washing the dishes*;
- **Living Room** *Eating, Watching TV, Computing*;
- **Toilet** *Using the toilet*;
- **Staircase** *Going up, Going down*;
- **Walkway** (no activity specific to this place);
- **Bathroom** *Using the sink, Using the toilet, Showering*;
- **Office** *Computing, Watching TV*;
- **Bedroom** *Dressing, Reading, Napping*;
- **Common to all places** *Cleaning.*

We have established this list of activities based on the existing places and appliances available in the apartment, such that all realistic and common classes of activities that are usually performed in a coworking home are represented in the dataset. We have also tried to balance classes such that no place contains the majority of classes.

As we can see, some activities can occur in multiple different places (e.g. *Watching TV* in both the Living Room and the Office, *Using the toilet* in both the Toilet and the Bathroom, etc.). It is very common for occupants to be able to perform certain activities in multiple different places, which is not a possibility often captured in state-of-the-art datasets of ADL. Our experiment is set in a real home, in which forbidding those situations would not be realistic; allowing that some activity classes can happen in different places also adds complexity to the dataset, making it more challenging as a benchmark for ADL-related algorithmic problems.

There is no trivial link between activity and sensor data in the general case. Activities can vary in duration and in the way they are performed by the occupant. For example, the activity *Preparing* will be heavily dependent on what the occupant is intending to cook: differences in which cupboards are opened and in what order can for example appear. The occupant can also do mistakes or change their mind on what they want to do in this activity, adding more sensor events.

3.4   Occupant's Routine in Orange4Home

The experiment ran from January 30th 2017 to February 24th 2017, during working days: 08:00 to 17:00 on average, from Monday to Friday.

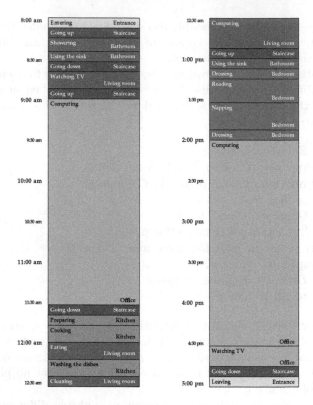

Fig. 1. Standard day routine. Activity is indicated on the left side, and the place in which they are performed on the right side.

Since the occupant is not normally working in this apartment, imposing a specific routine to the occupant is a necessity. Indeed, with very limited familiarity with the home, and with only 20 working days of experiment, an occupant might have the tendency to limit their activities to those they do in their own home and workplace, or with appliances that they are familiar with (although a mock experiment for a single day was performed prior to the real experiment so that the occupant gained more familiarity with the home). Moreover, imposing a routine on the user allows us to make sure that all activities are sufficiently represented in the dataset (so that it is for example usable with supervised machine learning techniques) and that sequences of activities are sufficiently frequent so that the dataset can be used to experiment activity prediction approaches.

The planning has been established around a standard day routine, presented on Fig. 1. This standard day routine has been carefully established with the following goals in mind:

- this routine must contain all activity classes (except for *Using the toilet* which is unpredictable);
- this routine must span an entire working day;

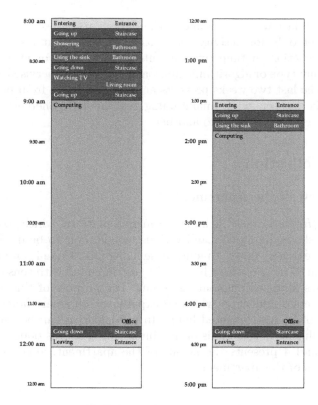

Fig. 2. Routine for February 21st, 2017. Activity is indicated on the left side, and the place in which they are performed on the right side.

– this routine must fit our coworking scenario presented in Sect. 3.2.

The standard day routine chosen therefore includes the occupant showering, using the sink and watching TV news in the morning, cooking and eating their food in the apartment, spending leisure time after lunch on their computer, reading and napping, and spending the rest of their time during the morning and the afternoon working on their computer in the Office.

This routine is strictly followed during the first two weeks (with leniency on the times at which activities start and end, and with slight differences on Fridays), and minor to major changes (such as interversion, omission, shortening, etc. of activities) to this daily routine are applied to establish the planning for the last two weeks. For example, we present on Fig. 2 the daily routine followed on Tuesday of the fourth week (February 21st, 2017). We can see fairly significant deviations from the standard daily routine this day: the occupant leaves the home at lunch time, the occupant does not perform any of the leisure activities during the lunch break, but instead goes back to work upon reentering the home (after the activity *Using the sink*).

This way, the dataset contains a routine of sufficiently recurring activities in the first 2 weeks, while also containing minor to major variations on that routine in the 2 last weeks; this allows the dataset to be used as a challenging benchmark, not only for activity recognition problems but also for problems of activity prediction in time (over minutes, hours, days or even weeks time scales), with any type of algorithmic approach including supervised models. The variations in the last two weeks prevents activity prediction from being a trivial task with this dataset, while maintaining realism and coherency in the way routines evolve from one week to another.

4 Data Collection

4.1 Overview of the Apartment

The *Amiqual4Home* project[2] is an experimental platform which comprises prototyping workshops, living labs and various mobile tools to be used in ambient intelligence research projects. Among those living labs, there is an instrumented apartment[3]: an $87\,\mathrm{m}^2$ two-story home fully instrumented with sensors and actuators of various kinds throughout its rooms. The purpose of this apartment is to provide an environment in which to experiment on smart home systems in a real setting of an instrumented home. In particular, it can be used to record sensors' data during long periods of inhabited times, as was done in this work.

Figures 3 and 4 presents the layout of the apartment, annotated with the names of places of the apartment.

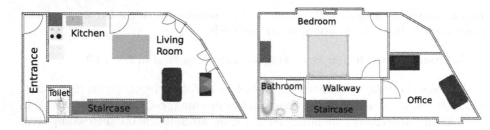

Fig. 3. Ground floor of the apartment   **Fig. 4.** First floor of the apartment

4.2 Sensors and Data Collection

The apartment has been furnished with the explicit goal of being an experimental apartment; as such, it is instrumented with many fully integrated sensors that are either not visible or not a hindrance to the occupant, as opposed to sensors installed in a standard apartment. The extensive list of sensors provides many different kinds of data, such as doors or cupboards opening, ambient noise,

[2] https://amiqual4home.inria.fr/.
[3] http://amiqual4home.inria.fr/tools/smart-home.

temperature, CO_2 levels, presence, switches being pressed, electrical information about appliances, hot and cold water consumption, luminosity, heaters information, weather information, etc. Moreover, all sensors are associated to the room they are installed in (or to the entire apartment, if it is a global information about the home). A total of 236 different data sources are present in the dataset.

OpenHAB[4] is used to collect data from all those sensors during the experiment. A MySQL[5] database is used to persist the data collected by openHAB. Videos from cameras placed on the ceiling of most rooms were also recorded to serve as ground truth; they were used to correct the few labeling mistakes made during the experiment, but are not provided in this dataset.

We present in Table 1 the number of sensors in each place of Orange4Home and for each of the 4 main types of data produced by sensors: binary (door opening, presence, switches, etc.), integers (total cold water consumption, appliance power, humidity, etc.), real numbers (luminosity, voltage, CO_2 levels, noise levels, etc.) and categorical data (weather, heater modes, AC modes, wind direction, etc.). We can see that there are large variations in the number of sensors per place, and on the types of sensors per place, which is expected because each place has a different use and thus different objects that need to be instrumented. We can also observe that all 4 types of data are well-represented, making Orange4Home a dataset of truly heterogeneous sensors.

Table 1. Number of sensors per place and per type of data in Orange4Home.

Place	Data type				
	Binary	Integer	Real number	Categorical	Total
Entrance	3	1	2	3	9
Kitchen	13	21	18	0	52
Living room	16	6	8	7	37
Toilet	3	1	1	0	5
Staircase	3	0	0	0	3
Walkway	9	0	1	0	10
Bathroom	9	6	8	3	26
Office	9	3	3	5	20
Bedroom	17	4	6	7	34
Global	1	13	20	6	40
Total	83	55	67	31	236

----

[4] https://www.openhab.org.
[5] https://www.mysql.com.

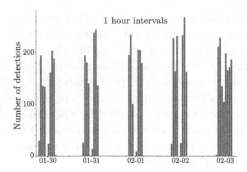
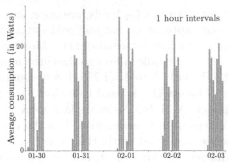

Fig. 5. Presence in the Office during the first week (each box is a 1 h interval).

Fig. 6. Power consumption of the computer in the Office during the first week (each box is a 1 h interval).

We present on Figs. 5 and 6 the number of presence detections and the power consumption of the computer in the Office during the first 5 days of experiment. We can observe that both sensors provide valuable information for activity recognition: both sensors capture correctly that something is happening in the Office on mornings and afternoons, while nothing happens during the lunch break (there are data during the lunch break on Friday because the lunch break on Friday is shorter, and thus does not cover an entire hour interval). We expect that data from all sensors is sufficiently rich to capture all activity classes performed during this experiment.

There are no body-worn sensors in this dataset. We indeed believe that body-worn sensors are not a realistic data source to use in a smart home system intended for the general public, where data collection should be as seamless as possible (as opposed, for example, to healthcare or wellness systems, where trading seamlessness for more health-related data sources is desirable). Smartphones could be an example of realistic body-worn data sources; however they are not necessarily always carried or even owned by an occupant, and are thus not included in this dataset.

4.3 *In Situ* Labeling

Labeling of activities was performed in real time by the occupant, using an Android application on a smartphone that the occupant carried throughout the home. This application sent events of virtual sensors (one for labels and one for comments) to OpenHAB's APIs through WiFi.

This application allows the occupant to select the room they are in, and then selected the activity they will perform (the set of activities being restricted to those that can happen in the selected place). The occupant can then press the *"START"* button before beginning their activity, and the *"STOP"* button (which appears in a modal window) once the activity ended. The application also allows the occupant to send comments through the *"ERROR"* button. This was used to comment any unexpected event (such as the occupant pressing "*STOP*" later than the actual end of the activity), in order to greatly simplify the task of fixing labeling issues (which there were very few of) after the experiment.

Table 2. Number of instances of each class of activity.

Place	Activity	Number of instances	Total
Entrance	Entering	21	42
	Leaving	21	
Kitchen	Preparing	19	
	Cooking	19	61
	Washing the dishes	19	
	Cleaning	4	
Living room	Eating	19	
	Watching TV	18	71
	Computing	15	
	Cleaning	19	
Toilet	Using the toilet	8	8
Staircase	Going up	57	114
	Going down	57	
Bathroom	Using the sink	38	
	Using the toilet	9	70
	Showering	19	
	Cleaning	4	
Office	Computing	46	
	Watching TV	14	64
	Cleaning	4	
Bedroom	Dressing	30	
	Reading	15	63
	Napping	15	
	Cleaning	3	
	Total		493

We present in Table 2 the number of instances of each class of activity that was labeled during the 20 working days of data collection. We can observe that some activity classes are way more numerous than others (e.g. *Computing* in Office compared to *Cleaning* in Bathroom), which is also a reality in a real home setting. No activities other than those presented in Table 2 were performed (the occupant could select an activity named *Other* in the labeling application, but this was never needed). 493 instances of activities were performed in total during roughly 180 h of experiment, for a total of 21 MB of data (in a MySQL database dump format).

4.4 Postprocesses

Electrical consumption data for the connected plugs of the computer and the TV, in both the living room and the office (5 plugs in total), have been simulated for the first day (30th of January) of the experiment, using averaged data from other days of the experiment. Those plugs were indeed non-functional this day. Data from those plugs were also filtered to remove sporadic outliers most likely induced by intrinsic problems with the plugs.

Events are persisted at most every second for a sensor; therefore, if two events happened during the same second (such as pressing and releasing a switch), the first one was persisted one second earlier than the second event.

Apart from the previous two points, no other postprocesses were applied to the data. In particular, we report no missing sensor values for the entirety of the experiment, thanks to the constant and extensive work done in maintaining the experimental apartment for the sake of the Amiqual4Home project.

5 Conclusions

We presented in this paper a dataset of labeled activities of daily-living of an occupant in a fully-integrated, instrumented smart home. This dataset spans 20 working days of realistic routines and contains 236 heterogeneous data sources capturing an extensive amount of events happening in the home. Experimenting in a home that the occupant is not used to forced us to carefully craft routines of activities (the process of which we have reported here) such that the occupant feels comfortable and confident enough to act as if they were in their own home.

We believe this dataset can be used as a realistic benchmark for various different kinds of algorithmic problems we are facing in smart homes: activity recognition, activity segmentation, etc. In particular, the length of the experiment as well as the established routine and its variability makes this dataset a good benchmark for activity prediction in smart homes for different time scales.

Acknowledgments. We thank Nicolas Bonnefond and Stan Borkowski for their technical and organizational help. This work benefited from the support of the French State through the *Agence Nationale de la Recherche* under the Future Investments program referenced ANR-11-EQPX-0002.

References

1. Alemdar, H., Ertan, H., Incel, O.D., Ersoy, C.: Aras human activity datasets in multiple homes with multiple residents. In: 7th International Conference on Pervasive Computing Technologies for Healthcare, pp. 232–235 (2013)
2. Cook, D.J., Krishnan, N.C., Rashidi, P.: Activity discovery and activity recognition: a new partnership. IEEE Trans. Cybern. **43**(3), 820–828 (2013)
3. Crowley, J.L., Coutaz, J., Rey, G., Reignier, P.: Perceptual components for context aware computing. In: Borriello, G., Holmquist, L.E. (eds.) UbiComp 2002. LNCS, vol. 2498, pp. 117–134. Springer, Heidelberg (2002). doi:10.1007/3-540-45809-3_9
4. Cumin, J., Lefebvre, G., Ramparany, F., Crowley, J.L.: Human activity recognition using place-based decision fusion in smart homes. In: Brézillon, P., Turner, R., Penco, C. (eds.) CONTEXT 2017. LNCS, vol. 10257, pp. 137–150. Springer, Cham (2017). doi:10.1007/978-3-319-57837-8_11
5. Li, K., Fu, Y.: Prediction of human activity by discovering temporal sequence patterns. IEEE Trans. Pattern Anal. Mach. Intell. **36**(8), 1644–1657 (2014)
6. Ordóñez, F.J., Roggen, D.: Deep convolutional and LSTM recurrent neural networks for multimodal wearable activity recognition. Sensors **16**(1), 115 (2016)
7. Roggen, D., Calatroni, A., Rossi, M., Holleczek, T., Förster, K., Tröster, G., Lukowicz, P., Bannach, D., Pirkl, G., Ferscha, A., et al.: Collecting complex activity datasets in highly rich networked sensor environments. In: 2010 Seventh International Conference on Networked Sensing Systems (INSS), pp. 233–240. IEEE (2010)
8. Tapia, E.M., Intille, S.S., Larson, K.: Activity recognition in the home using simple and ubiquitous sensors. In: Ferscha, A., Mattern, F. (eds.) Pervasive 2004. LNCS, vol. 3001, pp. 158–175. Springer, Heidelberg (2004). doi:10.1007/978-3-540-24646-6_10
9. van Kasteren, T.L.M., Englebienne, G., Kröse, B.J.A.: Transferring knowledge of activity recognition across sensor networks. In: Floréen, P., Krüger, A., Spasojevic, M. (eds.) Pervasive 2010. LNCS, vol. 6030, pp. 283–300. Springer, Heidelberg (2010). doi:10.1007/978-3-642-12654-3_17
10. Youngblood, G.M., Cook, D.J.: Data mining for hierarchical model creation. IEEE Trans. Syst. Man Cybern. **37**(4), 561–572 (2007)

A Context-Aware System
for Ambient Assisted Living

Alessandra De Paola(✉), Pierluca Ferraro, Salvatore Gaglio, Giuseppe Lo Re,
Marco Morana, Marco Ortolani, and Daniele Peri

DIID Department, University of Palermo, Palermo, Italy
{alessandra.depaola,pierluca.ferraro,salvatore.gaglio,giuseppe.lore,
marco.morana,marco.ortolani,daniele.peri}@unipa.it

Abstract. In the near future, the world's population will be characterized by an increasing average age, and consequently, the number of
people requiring for a special household assistance will dramatically rise.
In this scenario, smart homes will significantly help users to increase their
quality of life, while maintaining a great level of autonomy. This paper
presents a system for Ambient Assisted Living (AAL) capable of understanding context and user's behavior by exploiting data gathered by a
pervasive sensor network. The knowledge inferred by adopting a Bayesian
knowledge extraction approach is exploited to disambiguate the collected
observations, making the AAL system able to detect and predict anomalies in user's behavior or health condition, in order to send appropriate
alerts to family members and caregivers. Experimental results performed
on a simulated smart home prove the effectiveness of the proposed system.

Keywords: Ambient Assisted Living · Multi-sensor data fusion ·
Dynamic Bayesian Networks · Context awareness · Rule-based reasoning

1 Motivations and Related Work

Nowadays, the world's elderly population is rapidly increasing. Recent studies
carried out by the World Health Organization report that, by 2020, people aged
60 years and older will outnumber children younger than 5 years, and that there
will be more than two billions of elderly people by 2050 [28]. The rising average
age of the world's population implies an increase of chronic diseases and requests
for specialized assistance.

In such scenario, smart homes might significantly improve elderly and disabled people's quality of life and safety, by helping them live independently and
comfortably with the aid of intelligent devices pervasively deployed in the environment. Such vision is in line with the paradigm of Ambient Assisted Living
(AAL) [23], a specialization of Ambient Intelligence (AmI) which aims to design
intelligent pervasive systems to provide optimal environmental conditions for
elders or disabled people.

© Springer International Publishing AG 2017
S.F. Ochoa et al. (Eds.): UCAmI 2017, LNCS 10586, pp. 426–438, 2017.
DOI: 10.1007/978-3-319-67585-5_44

Understanding user's behavior is one of the key functionalities of these systems, since the detection or prediction of anomalies and dangerous situations can trigger specific actions, e.g., controlling the smart home automation system, sending appropriate alarms to the users or to their family and caregivers [4]. Moreover, the smart home can warn users if they are skipping their usual activities, such as having lunch at the right time or taking medicines, reminding them of the most probable activity to perform in a particular context. This is especially useful for patients suffering from dementia [20,25]. Obviously, in a smart home, special users will also take advantage of all usual benefits of AmI systems, which unobtrusively modify the environment to improve users' comfort and satisfy their needs, whilst reducing energy consumption [11].

To achieve such high-level goals, unobtrusive sensors (e.g., motion and door sensors, or bluetooth beacons to locate users) and actuators can be pervasively deployed in the smart home to monitor and modify ambient properties such as temperature, humidity and lighting. In the specific case of AAL, wearable sensors such as accelerometers and gyroscopes embedded in smart watches, smartphones, wristbands, or RGB-D sensors [5,13] can also be used to recognize relevant physical activities, e.g., sitting down or standing up, as well as to automatically detect falls [19]. Moreover, if the user suffers from specific health conditions, continuous monitoring of vital signs can be achieved by exploiting specialized devices [21,26]. A survey on AAL tools can be found in [23].

The large amount of raw data collected from all these heterogeneous sensors requires an efficient and accurate information fusion process to infer user's activity, current situation and potential anomalies. To this end, multi-sensor data fusion algorithms have been widely adopted to merge data coming from heterogeneous sources [6,16]. in particular, probabilistic techniques such as Dynamic Bayesian Networks (DBNs) are able to explicitly model the unavoidable uncertainty derived from sensor noise and malfunctioning [8]. DBNs have been described in many works for different applications, such as user presence detection [9,10], target tracking [29], and fire detection [1].

As demonstrated by a large body of research on the topic [2,14,22], raw measures acquired by ad hoc sensor can be enriched by considering context information that can be exploited to further increase the inference accuracy. This is especially useful in AAL scenarios in order to distinguish among ambiguous situations. For example, an increase in body temperature and blood pressure might be normal if the user is exercising, or might indicate an anomaly if the user is laying down on the bed in distress [24]. Given the frequency of ambiguous situations in a real world setting, and the importance of minimizing false positives and false negatives, accurately determining the user's context is paramount to develop a functional AAL system which can effectively assist elderly people [24].

In this work we present a multi-layered architecture for a complete AAL system, capable of understanding the current situation and detecting anomalies in users' behavior and health condition, as well as planning the best course of actions to help them avoiding dangerous situations and living safely in their own home. Our system is based on a context-aware, multi-sensor data fusion module able to infer users' activities and describe the environment through high level concepts. Context information is correlated with vital signs data coming from specialized sensors to unambiguously determine if the user is in distress. A rule-based reasoner has been designed to plan the best sequence of actions to perform, so as to ensure the safety and well-being of the monitored users.

The remainder of this paper is organized as follows. Section 2 introduces the multi-layered architecture of the proposed system, focusing on the activity recognition and reasoning modules. Section 3 describes how mixing sensor data and context attributes can be exploited to increase the accuracy of the system. Section 4 presents the experimental setting and the evaluation results. Finally, Sect. 5 draws our conclusions with directions for future work.

2   Multi-layer Architecture

The AAL system we propose here is based on a multi-layer architecture (Fig. 1) designed to collect raw data from heterogeneous sensors and aggregate them with increasing levels of abstraction, so as to unambiguously understand the current situation of the user (e.g., normal, abnormal, emergency). The inferred high level knowledge is exploited by a symbolic reasoner that plans the best sequence of actions to perform.

Modules at the lowest levels of the architecture are responsible for managing the sensory infrastructure. The *Sensor Manager* module sends control messages to sensors and collects raw data needed by the higher levels of the architecture. Data stream is analyzed by the *Pre-processing* module which detects outliers, filtering out unreliable data, in order to improve the accuracy of the system.

One of the most relevant component of the AAL system is the *Activity Recognition* module, that adopts a probabilistic approach based on Dynamic Bayesian Networks (DBN) to deal with uncertain sensory data. Low-level context information (e.g., time and location) and sensory data are used to recognize the activity

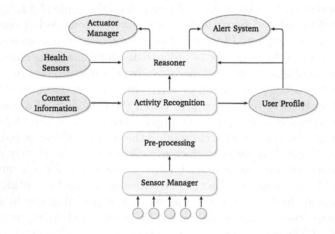

Fig. 1. Multi-layered architecture of the proposed system.

performed by the user, so producing high-level context information related to the currently performed activities. The knowledge inferred by the Activity Recognition module is used to build a user profile, which represents the historical user behavior through a DBN.

At the topmost level of the AAL system, the rule-based symbolic *Reasoner* infers the user's condition by merging data coming from specialized health sensors, the user's activity as detected by the Activity Recognition module, and the user's profile historical data. The Reasoner is also responsible for planning the best sequence of actions to perform in order to guarantee the user's safety and well-being, even through the generation of automatic and manual alerts. When the user's condition is considered anomalous, the Reasoner triggers the *Alert system*, which sends appropriate alerts to users and their caregivers. Moreover, the user is able to manually ask for a suggestion about the next activity to perform; such functionality is particularly useful for users affected by dementia. The Reasoner also triggers the *Actuator Manager*, which coordinates sensors and actuators, modifying the state of the environment by controlling heating, ventilation, air conditioning (HVAC) and lighting systems, in line with the paradigm of AmI.

The following sections provide an in-depth description of the most complex modules, i.e., the Activity Recognition module and the Reasoner.

2.1   Activity Recognition Module

The Activity Recognition module is one of the core modules of the system. It performs a multi-sensor data-fusion process by exploiting a Dynamic Bayesian Network (DBN) to handle dynamic phenomena and to deal with the unavoidable inaccuracy of sensors. DBNs are a generalization of Hidden Markov Models (HMMs), which allows the adoption of general topologies. They model the time flow as a sequence of slices, where each slice represents the state of the observed phenomena at a given time. Each slice is composed of an arbitrary number of state nodes, which represent the knowledge to be inferred, and a set of evidence nodes, which represent known information.

The DBN adopted by the Activity Recognition module is shown in Fig. 2. The hidden variable X_t represents the observed phenomena, i.e., the activity performed by the user at any time slice t. To update its belief, the system exploits

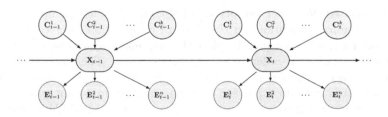

Fig. 2. Structure of the DBN used for inferring the activity performed by the user.

evidence nodes, which are composed of a set of sensor nodes, $\boldsymbol{E}_t = (E_t^1, \ldots, E_t^n)$, and a set of context nodes, $\boldsymbol{C}_t = (C_t^1, \ldots, C_t^k)$ in the time slice t. Context nodes provide further information by exploiting readily available context attributes, such as time and location. The role of context information in our system will be analyzed in detail in Sect. 3.

The proposed DBN is fully characterized by its structure and its *sensor* and *state transition* models. The *sensor model*, defined as the probability distribution $P(\boldsymbol{E}_t|X_t)$, expresses the correlation between sensor readings and the value of the state variable. The *state transition model*, defined as $P(X_t|X_{t-1}, \boldsymbol{C}_t)$, is the probability distribution indicating how likely is each value of the state variable, given its previous value and all available context information. The DBN performs inference by maintaining and updating its *belief* about a specific system state, x_t, in the time slice t, as follows:

$$Bel(x_t) = P(x_t|\boldsymbol{E}_{1:t}, \boldsymbol{C}_{1:t}). \tag{1}$$

Equation (1) can be expressed by the following recursive equation:

$$Bel(x_t) = \eta \cdot \prod_{e_t^i} P(e_t^i|x_t) \cdot \sum_{x_{t-1}} P(x_t|x_{t-1}, \boldsymbol{C}_t) \cdot Bel(x_{t-1}), \tag{2}$$

where η is a normalizing constant. The derivation of Eq. (2) is given in [8] and is omitted here due to space limitations. According to Eq. (2), the Activity Recognition module can update its belief about the user's activity by storing only the last two slices of the DBN. Time and space complexity of the inference process are thus independent of the sequence length. The conditional probability tables which define sensor and state transition models can be learned in different ways, depending on the available training data, e.g., sample statistics, Expectation Maximization algorithm or gradient ascent [17].

2.2 Rule-Based Reasoner

The classic monitor-analyze-plan-execute cycle implemented by most AmI systems is particularly useful for designing adaptive systems that operate in dynamic scenarios [15]. Such paradigm requires continuous monitoring of the surrounding environment, and allows the system to quickly react in case of emergency.

The proposed *Reasoner* adopts a rule-based approach to infer the user's health and comfort condition, on the basis of information received from lower-levels modules, and consequently plan the sequence of actions to perform in the current situation in order to satisfy user's needs. The Reasoner has been implemented using the rule-based inference engine Jess (Java Expert System Shell) [12]. Jess exploits a pattern matching algorithm to query a knowledge base and act according to logical rules, expressed with a LISP-like programming language. Each Jess rule has the "if $<conditions>$ then $<actions>$" form, and it is executed when all of the specified conditions are satisfied.

One of the most relevant properties at the basis of the Reasoner behavior is named *user-condition*. It describes the inferred condition of the user, and can take three possible values, namely *normal*, *anomaly*, and *emergency*. Depending on the value of the *user-condition* property, the system changes its alert level, and consequently, dynamically modifies the type and amount of sensory information used in the data fusion process, together with the recipients, the frequency and the level of detail of alert messages. A *normal* condition indicates that the user is healthy and no anomalies or emergencies were detected; the system enters a power saving mode, turning off unused sensors and focusing on discreetly monitoring the user, guaranteeing his comfort, and sending sporadic alert messages. An *anomaly* occurs when the readings from specialized health sensors are slightly out of the norm, or when the user is skipping his usual activities (e.g., taking medicines at the right time). In such cases, the system requires increased accuracy to ascertain the gravity of the situation and, if the anomaly persists, it starts sending alerts. Finally, the system enters in *emergency* mode when it detects a serious or prolonged anomaly, by analyzing both vital signs and information from the *Activity Recognition* module.

In the following, a small subset of the rules exploited by the system are described to illustrate how the system infers the *user-condition* property and modifies its own behavior dynamically. The first rule puts the system into the *anomaly* condition if the user's blood pressure is out of the norm and the user is laying on the bed:

defrule anomalyHighBloodPressure:
> **if** (*blood pressure* is "high") **and** (*activity* is "laying on bed") **then**
>   *user-condition* ← "anomaly"

It is worth noticing that the same blood pressure reading is normal if the user is exercising, as shown by the following rule:

defrule normalHighBloodPressure:
> **if** (*blood pressure* is "high") **and** (*activity* is "exercising") **then**
>   *user-condition* ← "normal"

In this case the high blood pressure can be explained by the stress of doing physical exercise. The system correctly disambiguates the sensory readings and infers that the *user-condition* is *normal*.

Finally, the following rule is triggered when the system detects a medical *emergency* and the user is laying on the floor in distress:

defrule emergencyHeartRate:
> **if** (*heart rate* is "very high") **and** (*activity* is "laying on the floor") **then**
>   *user-condition* ← "emergency"
>   send alerts to family members, caregivers and medical staff

The system recognizes the seriousness of the emergency and immediately sends appropriate alerts to the involved people and medical staff.

It is worth noticing that the user can also force the system to enter in *anomaly* state, by explicitly asking for assistance, or in *emergency* state by indicating a state of distress.

3   Context-Awareness

In the architecture proposed here, context information is exploited at multiple levels. The multi-level nature of the system allows and encourages reuse of information acquired or inferred by lower-level modules. In such architecture, higher-level modules exploit context information in a transparent way, totally decoupled from the implementation of lower levels. For example, knowledge about the activity performed by the user can be exploited by high level components, even neglecting the algorithm adopted by the *Activity Recognition* module, that can be considered as a smart *virtual sensor* responsible for perceiving the activity performed by the user. Such abstraction mechanism can be applied to all modules below the *Reasoner*, as depicted in Fig. 3, which suggests an alternative view of the proposed architecture, highlighting the data flow between the modules of the AAL system. To be more specific, knowledge flows from low to high levels, starting from raw data acquired by physical sensors, up to a high-level description of the user's condition and the environment.

In the application scenario of AAL, physical sensors representing the input of the knowledge extraction process can be classified in three categories: ambient sensors, personal (or inertial) sensors, and specialized health sensors. Ambient sensors, such as lighting, temperature, motion and door sensors, are pervasively deployed in the smart home and constitute the main input of the *Activity Recognition* module. Information coming from these sensors can be fused to infer the user's location with room-level granularity, so feeding a *virtual location* sensor which produces part of the context information exploited by higher-level modules.

Personal sensors, e.g., accelerometers and gyroscopes, might be embedded in smartphones, smart watches or smart wristbands, and thus follow users wherever they go. The fusion of their readings can be seen as a *virtual posture* sensor capable of detecting if the user is sitting, standing up, or laying on the floor or on the bed.

Besides location and posture, the set of context information is enriched with simple time-related information (e.g., the time of day, the month, or the day).

Context information and ambient sensory readings are the input of the *virtual activity* sensor, whose output is in turn combined with historical user data to infer the *user context*, which is a high-level description of what the user is doing and why. An example of user context is *"the user is correctly taking her morning medicines after breakfast"*. Inferring such detailed information is possible by correctly recognizing the sequence of actions performed by the user (e.g., having breakfast followed by taking medicines) and comparing it to the user's daily schedule, which may include taking specific medicines after breakfast. Then, to effectively determine the *user condition*, the output of the *virtual activity* sensor and the inferred *user condition* are fused with data coming from specialized health sensors, which measure vital signs such as heart rate and blood pressure. Finally, this symbolic description is leveraged by the Reasoner module, as described in Sect. 2.2.

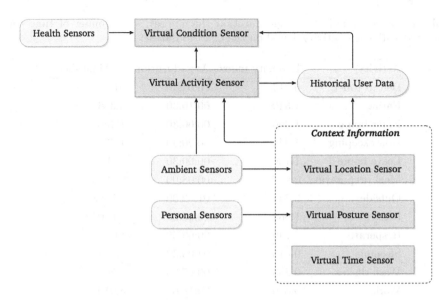

Fig. 3. Data flow through modules of the proposed architecture.

4   Experimental Analysis

Experimental Setting. The proposed system is evaluated in a simulated smart home, where several sensor devices are pervasively deployed in all rooms. Sensor traces were obtained from the Aruba dataset of the Washington State University's CASAS Smart Home Project [3].

Such data was collected over a period of seven months in a smart home, with eight rooms and a single resident, by means of 31 motion sensors, 5 temperature sensors, and 3 door sensors. The original data has been preprocessed by grouping sensor events into time windows of 30 s, counting the number of activations of each sensor in each window. Temperature data has been discarded, given its low correlation with the user's activities, as previously shown in [8].

The Aruba dataset is annotated with 11 activities of daily living, namely *eating, meal preparation, wash dishes, sleeping, bed to toilet, housekeeping, relax, work, enter home, leave home,* and *resperate* (i.e., using a device for the treatment of high blood pressure). Two other activities have been added to the dataset as a preprocessing step, i.e., *outside* and *other*. The former covers the periods when the user is not at home (intervals between *leave home* and *enter home*), while the latter groups sensor events not belonging to known activities, as proposed by [18].

Impact of Location-Related Context Information. The first set of experiments presented here aims to prove the relevance of location-related context information, which is extrapolated from ambient sensors and grouped in a *Virtual Location Sensor*, as described in Sect. 3. In particular, we extensively studied different features of the most common daily living activities performed in a

Table 1. Diversity index, average duration (hh:mm:ss), and number of time slices associated with each activity, based on the CASAS dataset [3].

Activity	Diversity index	Avg. duration	# Time slices
Bed to toilet	0.713	00:02:30	912
Eating	1.340	00:10:30	5,366
Enter home	1.296	00:00:30	173
Housekeeping	1.942	00:20:30	1,373
Leave home	1.156	00:00:30	173
Meal preparation	0.997	00:08:00	25,246
Outside	0.734	01:50:00	89,498
Relax	1.064	00:36:00	197,072
Resperate	0.749	00:09:00	110
Sleeping	0.615	04:03:30	192,433
Wash dishes	0.853	00:07:30	978
Work	0.800	00:18:00	6,010
Other	1.895	00:12:30	114,244

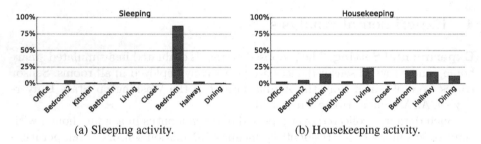

(a) Sleeping activity.   (b) Housekeeping activity.

Fig. 4. Rooms where the activities with the lowest (a) and highest (b) *diversity index* are performed.

smart home in the application scenario of AAL. Our findings are summarized in Table 1, which reports the diversity index, average duration, and number of time slices associated with each activity in the considered setting. The diversity index is a measure that reflects how evenly the activities are carried out in different functional areas of the smart home. In particular, we divided the smart house in rooms, assigning each sensor to one of them. Then, we analyzed the ground truth of each activity to identify those performed exclusively in a single room, and those carried out in different locations.

We adopted the Shannon-Wiener index, i.e., the classical Shannon entropy [27], to evaluate the diversity index of activities. Accordingly to such metric, an activity that is performed in a well-defined location, such as *sleeping*, has a low diversity index, while activities carried out in numerous rooms of the smart house, such as *housekeeping* and *other*, have a high diversity index.

To better illustrate this aspect, we selected the activity with the lowest diversity index (i.e., *sleeping*), and the one with the highest index (i.e., *housekeeping*). Figure 4 shows the rooms where the *sleeping* and *housekeeping* activities were performed. As expected, *housekeeping* is carried on in almost all rooms, whilst *sleeping* is concentrated in the bedroom. As it turns out, many activities present low diversity indices (in fact, more than half of them are less than 1) being performed in very specific locations, like *sleeping*. Thus, adding context information related to the current user's position greatly improve the accuracy of the system, as will be shown in the following.

Location information is easily obtainable in a reliable way by exploiting cheap motion sensors. Simply knowing the room where each sensor is deployed is enough to infer the room the user is in as the one where more motion sensors are active in the current time window. If the smart home has a single resident, this simple counting operation is enough to guarantee a highly reliable virtual location sensor with room-level granularity, as confirmed by the experiments we performed. If the smart home is occupied by multiple residents, more advanced techniques involving the use of bluetooth beacons or RFID chips can be exploited to identify and locate each user.

Impact of Other Context Information. Evaluating the accuracy of the *Activity Recognition* module is paramount to assess the whole system behavior, since if the system fails to correctly infer the activity performed by the user, higher level modules are unable to work reliably. We verified that context information is useful to improve the accuracy of such module.

As expected, it can be observed that the activities with a high diversity index are difficult to be correctly recognized, while regular activities, such as *sleeping*, are classified more accurately. Similar remarks apply to the average duration and the number of occurrences reported in Table 1: it is more difficult to classify activities that are short, or that occur very rarely.

Table 1 also highlights that most activities have similar average durations (with some obvious exceptions), and thus this attribute is not useful to better disambiguate between them. However, this kind of information can be extremely valuable for energy optimization systems, as described in [8].

As regards the *Virtual Time Sensor*, we found out that the most impactful attribute is the period of day (i.e., morning, afternoon, evening, or night), which greatly influences the activities performed by users. Surprisingly, other time-related attributes, such as month or day of week, are less impactful, and sometimes even harmful for accuracy.

Activity Recognition Evaluation. Finally, the whole system has been evaluated. It is worth noticing that, since the Reasoner has a deterministic behavior, its accuracy is directly dependent on the accuracy of the Activity Recognition module.

In order to evaluate system performances, we adopted a set of well known metrics, namely *accuracy*, *precision* (or positive predictive value) and *recall* (or sensitivity) which provide more details on fidelity and completeness of the system, and *F-score* which represents the harmonic mean of precision and recall.

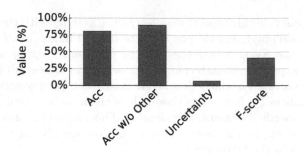

Fig. 5. Accuracy, accuracy ignoring the *other* activity, normalized uncertainty, and F-score of the proposed system.

All experiments have been performed by using the cross-validation method. The dataset was partitioned into ten parts, nine of which were used for learning the DBN parameters, whilst the tenth was used for evaluating the system; this process was repeated ten times by changing the test set and averaging the results.

Figure 5 shows the accuracy, average uncertainty, precision, recall, and F-score obtained by exploiting both the virtual time and location sensors. Choosing the right combination of context attributes is fundamental to improve the accuracy of activity recognition systems, as it can modify such results by up to 12% [7]. For this reason, great attention has been paid to selecting optimal context attributes in the application scenario of AAL. Figure 5 shows that the system achieves a remarkable average accuracy of 0.805, by choosing the best combination of context information available. This result is especially good because it includes the *other* activity which is particularly difficult to recognize. If we don't consider this ambiguous activity, the accuracy of the system reaches 0.897, with an increase of almost ten percent. Finally, the uncertainty of the system, defined as the classic Shannon entropy, is satisfactorily low, with a reported value of 0.294 over a maximum of 3.7.

5   Conclusions

In this paper, we proposed a context-aware system for Ambient Assisted Living, which aims to improve elderly and disabled people's quality of life by helping them living safely and independently in their own home. The proposed multi-layered architecture allows to understand the current situation and detect anomalies and emergencies in user's health conditions and behavior.

A context-aware multi-sensor data fusion module infers users' activities with remarkable accuracy, as shown in the experimental section. Context information is exploited at various levels to improve the inference accuracy and disambiguate between different situations. At the highest level, a rule-based inference engine plans the best course of actions when the user needs help, by assessing the gravity of the situation and sending alerts to specialized people that can rapidly assist the user. Even though all the parts of the proposed architecture have been individually tested, an overall evaluation of the whole AAL system, as well as a comparison with other state of the art approaches, is still in progress and will be presented in a future work. Currently, the rules exploited by the *Reasoner* are manually defined by a domain expert. In the future, we are interested in automatically learn such rules, making the system even more adaptive.

Finally, as suggested in the experimental section, multi-user scenarios would be both extremely challenging and interesting to study as the next step in developing a complete AAL system. The biggest challenge in this area comes from the fact that users' activities can influence each other, and thus personalized users' models are needed to effectively handle multiple users living in the same smart apartment.

Acknowledgment. This work is partially supported by the grant DM. 46965 LATO CIPE2.

References

1. Cheng, N., Wu, Q.: A decision-making method for fire detection data fusion based on Bayesian approach. In: Proceeding of 4th International Conference on Digital Manufacturing and Automation (ICDMA), pp. 21–23. IEEE (2013)
2. Cho, K., Hwang, I., Kang, S., Kim, B., Lee, J., Lee, S., Park, S., Song, J., Rhee, Y.: HiCon: a hierarchical context monitoring and composition framework for next-generation context-aware services. IEEE Netw. **22**(4), 34–42 (2008)
3. Cook, D.J.: Learning setting-generalized activity models for smart spaces. IEEE Intell. Syst. **2010**(99), 1 (2010)
4. Cook, D.J., Youngblood, M., Das, S.K.: A Multi-agent approach to controlling a smart environment. In: Augusto, J.C., Nugent, C.D. (eds.) Designing Smart Homes: The Role of Artificial Intelligence. LNCS, vol. 4008, pp. 165–182. Springer, Heidelberg (2006). doi:10.1007/11788485_10
5. Cottone, P., Lo Re, G., Maida, G., Morana, M.: Motion sensors for activity recognition in an ambient-intelligence scenario. In: 2013 IEEE International Conference on Pervasive Computing and Communications Workshops, PerCom Workshops 2013, pp. 646–651 (2013)
6. De Paola, A., La Cascia, M., Lo Re, G., Morana, M., Ortolani, M.: Mimicking biological mechanisms for sensory information fusion. Biol. Inspired Cogn. Architect. **3**, 27–38 (2013)
7. De Paola, A., Ferraro, P., Gaglio, S., Lo Re, G.: Context-awareness for multisensor data fusion in smart environments. In: Adorni, G., Cagnoni, S., Gori, M., Maratea, M. (eds.) AI*IA 2016. LNCS, vol. 10037, pp. 377–391. Springer, Cham (2016). doi:10.1007/978-3-319-49130-1_28
8. De Paola, A., Ferraro, P., Gaglio, S., Lo Re, G., Das, S.: An adaptive bayesian system for context-aware data fusion in smart environments. IEEE Trans. Mob. Comput. **16**, 1502–1515 (2016)
9. De Paola, A., Gaglio, S., Lo Re, G., Ortolani, M.: Multi-sensor fusion through adaptive Bayesian networks. In: Pirrone, R., Sorbello, F. (eds.) AI*IA 2011. LNCS, vol. 6934, pp. 360–371. Springer, Heidelberg (2011). doi:10.1007/978-3-642-23954-0_33
10. De Paola, A., La Cascia, M., Lo Re, G., Morana, M., Ortolani, M.: User detection through multi-sensor fusion in an Am I scenario. In: Proceeding of 15th International Conference on Information Fusion (FUSION), pp. 2502–2509. IEEE (2012)

11. De Paola, A., Lo Re, G., Morana, M., Ortolani, M.: Smartbuildings: an AmI system for energy efficiency. In: Sustainable Internet and ICT for Sustainability (SustainIT), pp. 1–7. IEEE (2015)
12. Friedman, E.: Jess in Action: Rule-Based Systems in Java. Manning Publications Co., Greenwich (2003)
13. Gaglio, S., Lo Re, G., Morana, M.: Human activity recognition process Using 3-D posture data. IEEE Trans. Hum. Mach. Syst. **45**(5), 586–597 (2015)
14. Huebscher, M.C., McCann, J.A.: Adaptive middleware for context-aware applications in smart-homes. In: Proceeding of 2nd Workshop on Middleware for Pervasive and Ad-Hoc Computing, pp. 111–116. ACM (2004)
15. Kephart, J., Chess, D.: The vision of autonomic computing. Computer **36**(1), 41–50 (2003)
16. Khaleghi, B., Khamis, A., Karray, F.O., Razavi, S.N.: Multisensor data fusion: a review of the state-of-the-art. Inf. Fus. **14**(1), 28–44 (2013)
17. Koller, D., Friedman, N.: Probabilistic Graphical Models: Principles and Techniques. MIT press, Cambridge (2009)
18. Krishnan, N.C., Cook, D.J.: Activity recognition on streaming sensor data. Pervasive Mob. Comput. **10**, 138–154 (2012)
19. Lombardi, A., Ferri, M., Rescio, G., Grassi, M., Malcovati, P.: Wearable wireless accelerometer with embedded fall-detection logic for multi-sensor ambient assisted living applications. In: Sensors, pp. 1967–1970. IEEE (2009)
20. Lotfi, A., Langensiepen, C., Mahmoud, S.M., Akhlaghinia, M.J.: Smart homes for the elderly dementia sufferers: identification and prediction of abnormal behaviour. J. Ambient Intell. Hum. Comput. **3**(3), 205–218 (2012)
21. Ni, Q., García Hernando, A.B., de la Cruz, I.P.: The elderly's independent living in smart homes: A characterization of activities and sensing infrastructure survey to facilitate services development. Sensors **15**(5), 11312–11362 (2015)
22. Padovitz, A., Loke, S.W., Zaslavsky, A., Burg, B., Bartolini, C.: an approach to data fusion for context awareness. In: Dey, A., Kokinov, B., Leake, D., Turner, R. (eds.) CONTEXT 2005. LNCS, vol. 3554, pp. 353–367. Springer, Heidelberg (2005). doi:10.1007/11508373_27
23. Rashidi, P., Mihailidis, A.: A survey on ambient-assisted living tools for older adults. IEEE J. Biomed. Health Inform. **17**(3), 579–590 (2013)
24. Roy, N., Das, S.K., Julien, C.: Resolving and mediating ambiguous contexts in pervasive environments. Smart Healthcare Applications and Services: Developments and Practices, pp. 122–147 (2011)
25. Roy, N., Pallapa, G., Das, S.K.: A middleware framework for ambiguous context mediation in smart healthcare application. In: Proceeding of 3rd IEEE International Conference on Wireless and Mobile Computing, Networking and Communications (WiMOB), pp. 72–79. IEEE (2007)
26. Sardini, E., Serpelloni, M.: T-shirt for vital parameter monitoring. In: Baldini, F., et al. (eds.) Sensors. Lecture Notes in Electrical Engineering, pp. 201–205. Springer, New York (2014)
27. Shannon, C.E.: A mathematical theory of communication. ACM SIGMOBILE Mob. Comput. Commun. Rev. **5**(1), 3–55 (2001)
28. Suzman, R., Beard, J.R., Boerma, T., Chatterji, S.: Health in an ageing world - what do we know? Lancet **385**(9967), 484–486 (2015)
29. Zhang, Y., Ji, Q.: Active and dynamic information fusion for multisensor systems with dynamic Bayesian networks. IEEE Trans. Syst. Man Cybern. Part B Cybern. **36**(2), 467–472 (2006)

Hierarchical Task Recognition and Planning in Smart Homes with Partial Observability

Dan Wang$^{(\boxtimes)}$ and Jesse Hoey

David R. Cheriton School of Computer Science, University of Waterloo,
200 University Avenue West, Waterloo, ON N2L 3G1, Canada
d97wang@uwaterloo.ca, jhoey@cs.uwaterloo.ca

Abstract. This paper proposes a goal recognition and planning algorithm, HTN-GRP-PO, to enable intelligent assistant agents to recognize older adults' goals and reason about desired further steps. It will be used in a larger system aimed to help older adults with cognitive impairments to accomplish activities of daily living independently. The algorithm addresses issues including partial observability due to unreliable or missing sensors, concurrent goals, and incorrectly executed steps. The algorithm has a Hierarchical Task Network basis, which enables it to deal with partially ordered subtasks and alternative plans. We test on simulated cases of different difficulties. The algorithm works very well on simple cases, with accuracy close to 100%. Even for the hardest cases, the performance is acceptable when sensor reliabilities are above 0.95.

Keywords: Hierarchical task network · Goal recognition · Partial observability · Cognitive impairments

1 Introduction

Nowadays, more and more older adults suffer from cognitive impairments, which cause difficulties in activities of daily living (ADLs) [3]. Developing intelligent assistant agents (IAAs) in smart homes to guide them on ADLs becomes urgent. IAAs are intelligent real-time reminders, prompting the older adult whenever he/she is confused in ADLs. IAAs should at least gather sensor signals, be aware of situations [2], recognize ongoing goals, and present effective assistances [9].

Due to limitations of sensors and privacy concerns, not all attributes of physical objects can be measured. Thus IAAs should cope with partial observability due to missing or unreliable sensors. Older adults with cognitive impairments commonly execute ADLs with irrational, repeated and disordered steps. IAAs are required to identify these improper behaviors and present help. Geib et al. [5] discussed several critical considerations of goal recognition for older adults, including multiple concurrent goals, actions used for multiple effects, and failure to observe. According to Hoey et al. [8], smart home assistance should be as passive as possible, so as to maintain feelings of independence.

An IAA helping older adults with cognitive impairments on their ADLs should address the following aspects: (1) Tolerate partial observability caused

© Springer International Publishing AG 2017
S.F. Ochoa et al. (Eds.): UCAmI 2017, LNCS 10586, pp. 439–452, 2017.
DOI: 10.1007/978-3-319-67585-5_45

by missing and unreliable sensors; (2) Recognize concurrent goals; (3) Detect improper steps and rectify the older adult from mistakes; and (4) Present hints or prompts of various detail levels, such as desired next steps or higher level tasks. The proposed **HTN-GRP-PO** algorithm[1] addresses these issues. It adopts the hierarchical paradigm as defined in Hierarchical Task Network (HTN) planning [4]. With HTN, the goal recognition process to recognize ongoing goals and the planning process to generate feasible next steps (or tasks) are combined together. Partially ordered subtasks, alternative ways to achieve a goal, and preconditions of tasks and steps are considered thanks to the expressive power of HTN. When the algorithm is running, it tracks the ongoing goals, updates beliefs based on new observations, reports wrong steps, and presents prompts with different details. Issues like unreliable or missing sensors, concurrent goals, and wrong steps make the problem more difficult, and decrease the performance of the algorithm.

The paper is arranged as follows. Section 2 discusses related works. Section 3 defines the problem, Sect. 4 details the HTN-GRP-PO algorithm, Sect. 5 reports on simulations *in silico*, and Sect. 6 concludes the work.

2 Related Works

Kautz et al. defined goal recognition as finding possible top level tasks (goals) to explain a set of observed steps [10]. The definition of goal recognition indicates its hierarchical nature. In [1], goal recognition is classified as either single layer or hierarchical. For single layer approaches, the reasoning process matches the raw data observations directly to goals. The inference from data to goals, without considering intermediate level tasks, makes status tracking not feasible. So a non-hierarchical method is inappropriate for the IAA in this work.

Hierarchical approaches recognize the highest level goals and inner level subgoals. A milestone in goal recognition is the conceptual framework published by Kautz and Allen [10]. They proposed the hierarchy format to represent top level tasks and low level steps, and the concept of decomposition. Advantages of hierarchical approaches are summarized in [1], including the suitability for recognizing high level tasks with complex structures, interactions with humans and incorporating prior knowledge into the representation. HTN-based and ontology-based hierarchical approaches are two main streams relating to this work.

HTN, a terminology in planning, is firstly proposed by Sacerdoti and Earl in 1975 [15]. The seminal work by Goldman et al. [7] proposed HTN for goal recognition. Their framework is called PHATT (Probabilistic Hostile Agent Task Tracker), which can deal with partially ordered subtasks, overloaded steps, contextual influence on choices of steps and goals, and observation failures. An additional module is added to PHATT to identify abandoned goals in [5]. Follow-up work [6] summarized previous works and integrated PHATT with a constraint reasoning module for parametrized actions and temporal constraints.

---

[1] "Hierarchical Task Network based Goal Recognition and Planning with Partial Observability".

The PHATT framework is very powerful, but assumes full observability of steps, which is impossible in reality.

Ontology-based approaches highlight the modeling of activities and behaviors with rich semantics. They characterized activities into atomic, simple, and composite ones [13]. Composite activities are formulated using both ontological and temporal modeling formalisms. In [14], two types of composite activities (concurrent and interleaved) and sequential activities are handled. They use ontological reasoning for simple activity recognition and rule-based temporal inference to recognize composite activities. To reason about temporal constraints among subtasks of a composite task, Okeyo et al. [12] proposed a hybrid ontological and temporal approach to model composite activities. Their work focused on temporal constraints, not addressing partial observability.

Our algorithm is a HTN-based approach, where knowledge base is expressed in methods and operators using similar formats described in SHOP2 [11]. It adopts the plan execution concept in [7]. However, our algorithm explicitly considers partial observation of steps and the feasibility of pending steps (or tasks). The algorithm integrates goal recognition in planning by utilizing HTN. It can not only recognize what the older adults is trying to do, but also what are the proper next steps and tasks in order to achieve the recognized goals.

3   Problem Description

Helping older adults with cognitive impairments to implement ADLs needs to recognize ongoing goals and to present prompts for next steps, which is a combination of goal recognition and planning. The definition of the goal recognition and planning problem in this work is given in Definition 1.

Definition 1 (Goal Recognition and Planning Problem). *It is a tuple*

$$P^{rp} = (bs, obs, G, prior, D, PROB, PS),$$

where bs is belief state, obs is sensor readings, G is a set of goals, prior is the prior probabilities of goals in G. PROB is a distribution showing the goal recognition result, PS is the planning result with multiple levels, showing the next tasks and steps in order to achieve PROB together with probabilities. Its step level is PS_{step}. $D = (O, M)$ is the knowledge base (methods and operators).

Table 1 (left) shows method *prepare-hot-water*. *mName* is the task name that *m* can be applied to. A method having multiple branches with each has *precondition* and *subtasks* indicates multiple ways to accomplish a task. *parent* specifies methods whose *subtasks* contains *mName*. *startStep* are the beginning steps of a goal. It is present only when *m* stands for a goal. Table 1 (right) is an operator which can be applied to step *turn-on-faucet-1*. *effect* contains fluents which become true after executing the step. It has similar format to that of *precondition*. *parent* specifies all methods whose *subtasks* contains *oName*.

The problem in this work is classified into eight categories (Table 2) based on three properties: the number of goals that the executed steps account for,

Table 1. Method (left) and Operator (right) example

$nName$	prepare-hot-water
$precondition$	{[(kettle-1, has-water, yes), (kettle-1, switch, off), (kettle-1, water-hot, not)]}
$subtasks$	{[kettle-1-heat-water: {pre: [], dec:[]}]}
$parent$	[make-coffee, make-tea]
$startStep$	NA (not a goal)

$oName$	turn-on-faucet-1
$precondition$	(faucet-1, state, off)
$effect$	[(faucet-1, state, on)]
$parent$	[wash-hand, kettle-1-add-water]

Table 2. Problem categories

Sensor config.	Single goal		Multiple foals	
	Correct step	Wrong step	Correct step	Wrong step
Reliability	**p1**	**p2**	**p3**	**p4**
Missing sensor	**p5**	**p6**	**p7**	**p8**

present wrong steps or not, with unreliable sensor or missing sensor. In the "Sensor Config." column, "Reliability" means that every sensor has a reliability. "Missing Sensor" means that some sensors are missing and the agent knows about which ones are missing. As one can imagine, **p1** is the easiest problem category, while **p8** is the hardest one.

4   Algorithm

4.1   Terminologies

Changes of sensor measurements at a time point will trigger an algorithm **iteration**. An iteration reasons about the new bs and the new $PROB$ and PS result by adding the observations from the just happened step. Simultaneous steps are not considered in this work. An example iteration, shown in Table 3, changes P_0^{rp} to P_1^{rp}. Note G, $prior$, and D are neglected because of no change. PS_1 has several levels to provide help in different details. Only the step level (level 0) and a task level (level 1) are shown to save space. obs is not the outcome but the trigger of an iteration. The iteration in Table 3 is triggered by obs_1. Similarly, obs_2 will trigger the next iteration.

The proposed algorithm lies on explanations. Typically, a goal recognition result should explain observations so far. Multiple explanations exist when considering partial observability. The recognition result would be a distribution over possible explanations. To obtain next steps or tasks hint, ongoing statuses of goals should be tracked. Based on those considerations, Definition 2 shows the structure used to explain observations so far in this work.

Table 3. The outcome of an algorithm iteration

P_0^{rp}		P_1^{rp}	
Variable	Value	Variable	Value
bs_0	(*faucet-1, state*, {*off*: 0.999, *on*: 0.001})	bs_1	(*faucet-1, state*, {**off**: 0.0001, **on**: 0.9999})
obs_1	[(*faucet-1*, {*state, on*})]	obs_2	[(*hand-1*, {*soapy: yes, dry: no*})]
$PROB_0$	*wash-hand*: 0.333, *make-coffee*: 0.333, *make-tea*: 0.333	$PROB_1$	*wash-hand*: 0.3574, *make-coffee*: 0.3213, *make-tea*: 0.3213
PS_0	level-0: *turn-on-faucet-1*: 0.666, *switch-on-kettle-1*: 0.333	PS_1	level-0: *use-soap*: 0.357, *add-water-kettle-1*: 0.643 level-1: clean-hand:0.357, prepare-hot-water:0.643

Table 4. Explanations after the Iteration shown in Table 3

Variable	$expla_1$	$expla_2$	$expla_3$
prob	0.3574	0.3213	0.3213
forest	[*goalN*$_1$], in Table 5	[*goalN*$_2$]	[*goalN*$_3$]
pendingStep	[*use-soap*]	[*add-water-kettle-1*]	[*add-water-kettle-1*]
startGoal	*wash-hand*: **True**, *make-tea*: *False*, *make-coffee*: *False*	*wash-hand*: *False*, *make-tea*: **True**, *make-coffee*: *False*	*wash-hand*: *False*, *make-tea*: *False*, *make-coffee*: **True**

Definition 2 (Explanation). *An explanation, expla $\in$ ExplaSet, is a tuple*

$$expla = (prob, forest\ [\ ], pendingStep\ [\ ], startGoal\{\}),$$

*where prob tells to which degree we can rely on this explanation. forest is a list, with each element recording the **ongoing status** of a goal. pendingStep is the next steps suggested by the explanation to proceed towards ongoing goals. startGoal records goals that are ongoing in this explanation.*

Each iteration computes $PROB$ and PS based on explanations (see Definition 2), which are stored in $ExplaSet$. Multiple explanations might exist to explain a given observation series. The iteration in Table 3 gets $ExplaSet$ containing $expla_1$, $expla_2$ and

Table 5. $goalN_1$ for $expla_1$ in Table 4

Variable	Value
goalName	*wash-hand*
tree	*tree*$_1$, in Fig. 1
expandProb	1.0
pendingGoalNet	[*decompGN*$_1$] in Fig. 1
completeness	*False*
executeSequence	{*turn-on-faucet-1*, (*faucet-1, state, on*)}

$expla_3$, with each a complete explanation for $obs = \{obs_1\}$. They are shown

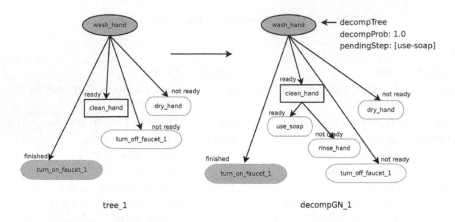

Fig. 1. $tree_1$ and $decompGN_1$ in $goalN_1$

in Table 4. $expla_1$ believes that *wash-hand* is ongoing and the supposed next step is *use-soap*. $goalN_1$ records the ongoing status of *wash-hand*. Table 5 and Fig. 1 explains the **goal network**. *tree* is a hierarchical task network reflecting the ongoing status of the goal $goalName$. For example, $tree_1$ in Fig. 1 shows that *turn-on-faucet-1* for *wash-hand* has been finished. $expandProb$ tells the probability of this way being chosen. $pendingGoalNet$ is the results of decomposing *tree*, which is a list. Each element in $pendingGoalNet$ is a feasible way to proceed towards $goalName$ from the status in *tree*. Figure 1 tells *use-soap* proceeds from $tree_1$ towards *wash-hand*. Only $decompGN_1$ is derived means that there is only one way to decompose *clean-hand* which explains $decompProb = 1.0$.

In summary, an iteration reasons with **Explanation**s, which are stored in **Explanation Set**. A **goal network** in an explanation's $forest$ explains the ongoing status of a goal. More than one goal networks in $forest$ indicate concurrent goals. A **decomposed goal network** in a goal network's $pendingGoalNet$ stands for a specific way to proceed towards the corresponding goal.

4.2 The HTN-GRP-PO Algorithm

Figure 2 is the algorithm flow chart, with the iteration in Table 3 as the example. Inputs and outputs of each module are included. **Compute** PS_{step} **Posterior** is the step recognition process adopting Bayesian inference as shown in Eqs. 1 and 2. Its output is $(PS_{step})_{posterior}$. Equation 1 is applied to every step in $(PS_0)_{step}$. Note that 0.999 is used in Eq. 2 because when the precondition of st_t is not satisfied, it is usually impossible to happen. $p(st_t)$ in Eq. 1 takes the corresponding probability in $(PS_0)_{step}$. Equation 3 explains wrong steps detection. Comprehensive experiment results show that if $otherHappenProb$ is bigger than **0.75**, a wrong step happens.

Update bs also adopts Bayesian inference. Because the "wrong step" branch is dropped, $(PS_{step})_{posterior}$ is normalized to get $(PS_{step})'_{prior}$ which become

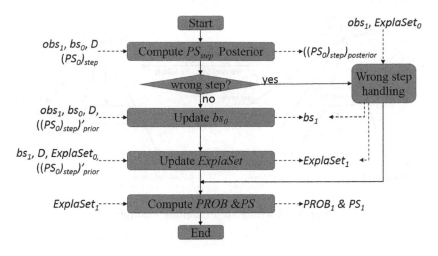

Fig. 2. An algorithm iteration

the new priors of steps. The algorithm applies Eqs. 4 and 2 to every attribute related to the current iteration. Given an attribute, the sum over s_{t-1} in Eq. 4 enumerates all possible values of the attribute.

$$p(st_t|obs_t) = \frac{p(st_t, obs_t)}{p(obs_t)} \propto p(st_t, obs_t) = \sum_{s_t} \sum_{s_{t-1}} p(st_t, s_t, s_{t-1}, obs_t)$$
$$= \sum_{s_t} \sum_{s_{t-1}} p(s_t|s_{t-1}, st_t) \times p(obs_t|s_t) \times p(s_{t-1}) \times p(st_t) \tag{1}$$

$$p(s_t|s_{t-1}, st_t) = \begin{cases} 0.999, \text{ if } st_t(precondition) \subset s_{t-1} \text{ and } \theta(st_t, s_{t-1}) \subset s_t \\ 0.001, \text{ otherwise} \end{cases} \tag{2}$$

$$otherHappenProb = 1 - \sum_{st \in PS_{step}} (PS_{step})_{posterior}(st) \tag{3}$$

$$p(s_t|obs_t) = \sum_{s_{t-1}} \sum_{st'_t \in (PS_{step})'_{prior}} p(s_t|s_{t-1}, st'_t) \times p(obs_t|s'_t) \times p(s_{t-1}) \times p(st'_t)$$
$$\tag{4}$$

$$new\_expla(prob) = st_{prob} \times goalNet(expandProb) \times expla(prob) \tag{5}$$

Update ExplaSet. Given a step $st \in (PS_{step})'_{prior}$, each explanation $expla \in ExplaSet_0$ will be updated to several new ones, which are stored in $ExplaSet_1$. It includes two procedures: recognition and decomposition. The **recognition** procedure adopts a new $goalNet$ to represent the new ongoing status of the corresponding goal and computes the new explanation probability using Eq. 5. The creation of the new $goalNets$ has two cases.

Case 1, st starts a new goal. Thus there is no $goalNet_{base}$ for creating the new one. A bottom up procedure is used to create a new $goalNet$ from scratch.

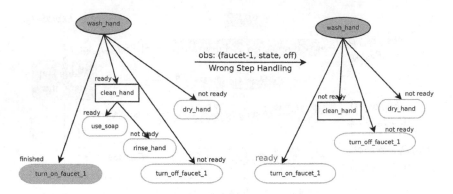

Fig. 3. A wrong step handling example

For example, with $st = turn\text{-}on\text{-}faucet\text{-}1$, when creating $goalN_1$ for $expla_1$ in Table 4, the bottom up procedure creates $tree_1$ as shown in Table 1. Note that case 1 enables the algorithm handle concurrent goals. Case 2, st continues an ongoing goal. In this case, a proper decomposed goal network is chosen from the given $goalNet(pendingGoalNet)$ as the new $goalNet$. For example, given $expla_1$ in Table 4 and $st = use\text{-}soap$, $decompGN_1$ (Fig. 1, right) will replace $goalN_1$, becoming the new $goalNet$ in the new explanation.

The **decomposition** procedure creates $pendingGoalNet$ for a $goalNet$. In Table 5, $goalN_1(pendingGoalNet)$ is obtained through the decomposition procedure. The decomposition result is shown in the right part of Fig. 1. When applying methods for decomposition, the probability that a precondition is satisfied is computed and accumulated to derive $decompProb$, which indicates to which degree the corresponding decomposition path is feasible in bs. The decomposition process that ends every leaf in $tree$ is either a node standing for a step or a node standing for a task satisfying $node(data)(readiness) == False$.

Wrong Step Handling. This module rectifies existing explanations so as to restore from the wrong step. Figure 3 is an visualization example. Assume that $expla$ contains ongoing status of $wash\text{-}hand$ as shown in the left tree of Fig. 3. So the desired next step is $use\text{-}soap$. However, a wrong step is reported during the computation of $(PS_{step})_{posterior}$. The observation indicates that the effect of step $turn\text{-}on\text{-}faucet\text{-}1$ has been destroyed by the wrong step. The wrong step handling module rectifies the ongoing status of $wash\text{-}hand$ to the point as shown in the right tree of Fig. 3. Consequently, the algorithm will remind the the older adult to do $turn\text{-}on\text{-}faucet\text{-}1$ again.

Compute $PROB$ and PS. This module purely depends on the latest $ExplaSet$. The probability of goal g in $PROB$ is the sum of probabilities of explanations whose $startGoal$ contains g. The probability of a task t(or step st) in PS is the sum of probabilities of explanations whose $forest$ contains a node standing for t (or st) with $completeness$ being false while $readiness$ being true.

5   Experimental Simulations

5.1   Knowledge Base, Sensors, and Simulator

Scenario. Helen is an older adult with mild Alzheimer's disease. She has problems doing three daily tasks in the kitchen: washing hands, making a cup of tea, and making a cup of coffee. Her caregiver reports her common mistakes. When washing hands, she might forget to use soap or turn the faucet off, or repeatedly rinse her hands. Similar issues happen when making a cup of tea or coffee. The caregiver hopes an IAA can help her complete those tasks independently.

The **Knowledge Base** has three goals : *wash-hand*, *make-tea* and *make-coffee*. Although M and O are individual pieces, they implicitly indicate a hierarchical plan graph, as shown in Fig. 4. Root nodes stand for goals G. Leaf nodes are the lowest level steps. Other internal nodes are inner level tasks. Each goal or task node corresponds to a method in M. Each step node corresponds to a step in O. To save space, details of M and O are not given.

According to the knowledge base, 18 virtual binary **sensors** (Table 6) are set up for the sake of simulation. Sensor reliability has four values, [0.99, 0.95, 0.9, 0.8]. We use ID to refer an sensor. *obj* and *att* determines which attribute the sensor is monitor. The **simulator** simulates real environment state changes and step executions. No real human are involved in the experiment, however, our study is applicable to cases in reality. Given an input step, the simulator firstly updates real state according to the effects of the step, and then changes sensor measurements based on the simulated real state and sensor reliability.

5.2   Test Cases and Evaluation Criteria

Each test case is a list of steps in the order of execution. It accounts for one single goal or multiple goals. Noisy wrong steps can exist in the list. The algorithm reasons about $PROB$ and PS for each step. The ground truth of each step's

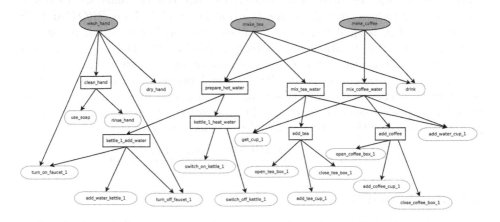

Fig. 4. The hierarchical task network for experiment

Table 6. Sensors used in the experiment (initial values are in **boldface**)

ID	Obj	Att	Value	ID	Obj	Att	Value
1	hand-1	soapy	**no**, yes	10	kettle-1	water-hot	**no**, yes
2	hand-1	dirty	**yes**, no	11	cup-1	location	**cabinet**, table
3	hand-1	dry	**yes**, no	12	cup-1	has-water	**no**, yes
4	faucet-1	state	**on**, off	13	cup-1	has-tea	**no**, yes
5	faucet-1	location	**kitchen**, washroom	14	cup-1	has-coffee	**no**, yes
6	person-1	location	**kitchen**, washroom	15	tea-box-1	location	**table**, cabinet
7	person-1	ability	**0.6**, [0–1]	16	tea-box-1	open	**no**, yes
8	kettle-1	has-water	**no**, yes	17	coffee-box-1	location	**table**, cabinet
9	kettle-1	switch	**off**, on	18	coffee-box-1	open	**no**, yes

Table 7. Test cases for problem categories

Sensor config.	Single goal		Multiple goals	
	Correct step	Wrong step	Correct step	Wrong step
Reliability	Case 1–3	Case 6–9	Case 4–5	Case 10–11
Missing sensor	Case 1–3	Case 6–9	Case 4–5	Case 10–11

$PROB$ and PS in a test case can be obtained from the knowledge base shown in Fig. 4. Table 7 presents test cases for each problem category. All test cases are based on the knowledge base in Sect. 5.1. Table 8 selects one case for each category to show.

An iteration computes $PROB$ and PS after each step. Given a step, $PROB$ is correct if the ongoing goal has the highest probability. PS can be partially correct since it involves different levels. To simplify evaluation, we measure PS in a strict way. PS is correct only when its lowest step level is correct, which guarantees a complete correct PS. Note that recognizing the older adult's intent and providing proper hints are both important for an IAA. Thus $PROB$ and PS are considered with equal weights. Assume that the number of steps in a test case is N, the number of iterations with correct $PROB$ is $PROB_C$, and the number of iterations with correct PS is PS_C. The performance is computed using Eq. 6. Thanks to the strict criterion on PS, the real performance of the algorithm is better than the computed performance. Each test case is run 20 times and the average performance is computed. The algorithm removes explanations with probability smaller than **0.001** to avoid too much calculation.

$$Performance = \frac{0.5 \times PROB_C + 0.5 \times PS_C}{N} \times 100\% \qquad (6)$$

5.3   Results and Discussion

The average accuracies of all the test cases with changing reliabilities is presented in Table 9, for which we conclude: (1) The performances positively correlate with

Table 8. Example test case for each category (wrong steps have <u>underlines</u>; steps for *wash-hand* in case 5&10 are **boldface**)

Case 1 *wash-hand*	Case 5 *wash-hand, make-coffee*	Case 10 *wash-hand, make-coffee*
turn-on-faucet-1	turn-on-faucet-1	**turn-on-faucet-1**
use-soap	add-water-kettle-1	**use-soap**
rinse-hand	turn-off-faucet-1	**rinse-hand**
turn-off-faucet-1	switch-on-kettle-1	<u>**rinse-hand**</u>
dry-hand	**turn-on-faucet-1**	**turn-off-faucet-1**
Case 8 *wash-hand*	**use-soap**	turn-on-faucet-1
	rinse-hand	**dry-hand**
turn-on-faucet-1	**turn-off-faucet-1**	add-water-kettle-1
use-soap	**dry-hand**	turn-off-faucet-1
use-soap	switch-off-kettle-1	switch-on-kettle-1
<u>turn-off-faucet-1</u>	get-cup-1	switch-off-kettle-1
turn-on-faucet-1	open-coffee-box-1	get-cup-1
use-soap	add-coffee-cup-1	open-coffee-box-1
rinse-hand	close-coffee-box-1	add-water-cup-1
<u>rinse-hand</u>	add-water-cup-1	<u>close-coffee-box-1</u>
dry-hand	drink	open-coffee-box-1
turn-off-faucet-1		add-coffee-cup-1
		close-coffee-box-1
		drink

sensor reliabilities. When sensor reliabilities reduce, the average accuracies deteriorate as well. (2) The easiest problem category **p1**, which targets problems with single goal and correct steps, has the best performance. The average accuracies are very high even when sensor reliabilities are only 0.8. (3) The hardest problem category **p4**, which targets problems with multiple goals and wrong steps, has the worst performance. The accuracies are acceptable only when sensor reliabilities are above 0.95. This result is reasonable since the algorithm has to deal with noisy sensors, multiple goals and wrong steps. (4) The other two categories, **p2** and **p3**, have similar performances, which are acceptable when sensor reliabilities are above 0.9. The results in Table 9 demonstrate the proposed algorithm's capacity to solve the goal recognition and planning problem described in Definition 1. Our algorithm can efficiently handle issues including partial observability, wrong steps, unordered steps, and simultaneous goals.

The influence of sensor reliabilities on $PROB$**.** Figure 5 shows the $PROB$ of case 10. Wrong steps are marked with *. The convergence of $PROB$ is correlated with sensor reliability. The probabilities of ongoing goals outweigh those of non-happening goals after the second or third steps. The probabilities of goal *make-tea* and *make-coffee* align with each other until step *get-cup-1* because they have the same step sequence before *get-cup-1* (refer Fig. 4). A goal's probability

Table 9. Average performances on test cases (sensor reliabilities, in bold)

Case num.	0.99	0.95	0.90	0.80
Case 1	100%	97%	95%	93%
Case 2	100%	99%	99%	97%
Case 3	100%	100%	98%	98%
Case 4	99%	99%	90%	79%
Case 5	100%	99%	93%	86%
Case 6	100%	98%	93%	**44%**
Case 7	100%	99%	98%	96%
Case 8	100%	96%	94%	**59%**
Case 9	100%	92%	83%	**62%**
Case 10	100%	90%	70%	66%
Case 11	100%	94%	79%	69%

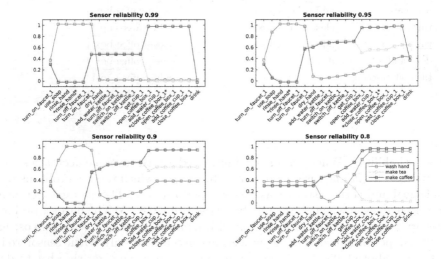

Fig. 5. The *PROB* output for Case 10 (*wash-hand*, *make-coffee*)

drops to 0.0 when it is finished. The horizontally straight lines in plots with sensor reliability 0.9 and 0.8 means the algorithm gets lost and does not update the explanations any more. The algorithm usually get lost when wrong sensor measurements, improper priors, and wrong steps happen together.

A missing sensor is the same as a sensor having reliability 0.5. The algorithm deals with known missing sensors by regarding their reliabilities as 0.5. Experiments with missing sensors suggest how to set up sensors. (1) Sensors related to start steps of goals should not be missing. (2) If a step related to multiple sensors, one of the sensors is missing can be tolerated. (3) A sensor relates to many steps should not be missing. (4) If the older adult repeatedly makes mistakes on some steps, the related sensors should not be missing.

6   Conclusion

This proposed HTN-GRP-PO algorithm is a HTN framework based goal recognition and planning process. The recognition and planning procedures are highly coupled. The HTN framework reduces the search space for goal recognition. The planning procedure generates the desired next steps to proceed towards ongoing goals. It addresses issues including partial observability due to unreliable or missing sensors, concurrent goals, and incorrectly executed steps. The algorithm is tested on cases with different difficulties. An interesting future direction is extending the algorithm to handle step duration and shared steps.

Acknowledgments. We thank the support of AGE-WELL NCE Inc., the Canadian Consortium on Neurodegeneration and Aging, and of the Alzheimers Association (grant number ETAC-14-321494).

References

1. Aggarwal, J.K., Ryoo, M.S.: Human activity analysis: a review. ACM Comput. Surv. (CSUR) **43**(3), 16 (2011)
2. Cook, D.J., Hagras, H., Callaghan, V., Helal, A.: Making our environments intelligent. Pervasive Mob. Comput. **5**(5), 556–557 (2009)
3. Desrichard, O., Köpetz, C.: A threat in the elder: the impact of task-instructions, self-efficacy and performance expectations on memory performance in the elderly. Eur. J. Soc. Psychol. **35**(4), 537–552 (2005)
4. Erol, K., Hendler, J., Nau, D.S.: HTN planning: complexity and expressivity. In: AAAI, vol. 94, pp. 1123–1128 (1994)
5. Geib, C.W.: Problems with intent recognition for elder care. In: Proceedings of the AAAI 2002 Workshop Automation as Caregiver, pp. 13–17 (2002)
6. Geib, C.W., Goldman, R.P.: A probabilistic plan recognition algorithm based on plan tree grammars. Artif. Intell. **173**(11), 1101–1132 (2009)
7. Goldman, R.P., Geib, C.W., Miller, C.A.: A new model of plan recognition. In: Proceedings of the Fifteenth Conference on Uncertainty in Artificial Intelligence, pp. 245–254. Morgan Kaufmann Publishers Inc. (1999)
8. Hoey, J., Poupart, P., von Bertoldi, A., Craig, T., Boutilier, C., Mihailidis, A.: Automated handwashing assistance for persons with dementia using video and a partially observable Markov decision process. Comput. Vis. Image Underst. **114**(5), 503–519 (2010)
9. Hwang, A., Hoey, J.: DIY smart home: narrowing the gap between users and technology. In: Proceedings of the Interactive Machine Learning Workshop, 2013 International Conference on Intelligent User Interfaces (2013)
10. Kautz, H.A., Allen, J.F.: Generalized plan recognition. In: AAAI, vol. 86, p. 5 (1986)
11. Nau, D.S., Au, T.-C., Ilghami, O., Kuter, U., Murdock, J.W., Wu, D., Yaman, F.: SHOP2: an HTN planning system. J. Artif. Intell. Res. (JAIR) **20**, 379–404 (2003)

12. Okeyo, G., Chen, L., Wang, H.: Combining ontological and temporal formalisms for composite activity modelling and recognition in smart homes. Future Gener. Comput. Syst. **39**, 29–43 (2014)
13. Okeyo, G., Chen, L., Wang, H., Sterritt, R.: A hybrid ontological and temporal approach for composite activity modelling. In: 2012 IEEE 11th International Conference on Trust, Security and Privacy in Computing and Communications (TrustCom), pp. 1763–1770. IEEE (2012)
14. Okeyo, G., Chen, L., Wang, H., Sterritt, R.: A knowledge-driven approach to composite activity recognition in smart environments. In: Bravo, J., López-de-Ipiña, D., Moya, F. (eds.) UCAmI 2012. LNCS, vol. 7656, pp. 322–329. Springer, Heidelberg (2012). doi:10.1007/978-3-642-35377-2_44
15. Sacerdoti, E.D.: A structure for plans and behavior. Technical report, DTIC Document (1975)

A Holistic Technology-Based Solution for Prevention and Management of Diabetic Foot Complications

Ian Cleland[1(✉)], Joseph Rafferty[1], Jonathan Synnott[1], Jill Cundell[2], Adele Boyd[1],
Chris Nugent[1], Priyanka Chaurasia[1], Gareth Morrison[3], Godfrey Madill[4],
Leeann Monk-Ozgul[5], and Stephen Burns[6]

[1] Computer Science Research Institute and School of Computing and Mathematics,
Ulster University, Newtownabbey BT37 0QB, Co. Antrim, Northern Ireland
{i.cleland,j.rafferty,j.synnott,a.boyd,cd.nugent,
p.chaurasia}@ulster.ac.uk
[2] Institute of Nursing and Health Research, Ulster University,
Newtownabbey BT37 0QB, Northern Ireland
jh.cundell@ulster.ac.uk
[3] Lava Group, 17 Falcon Road, Belfast, BT12 6RD, UK
g.morrison@thelavagroup.co.uk
[4] Prosthetics Forum Northern Ireland, Belfast BT9 7JB, Northern Ireland
godfreymadill@gmail.com
[5] Elemental Software, Holywell Trust, 10-12 Bishop Street, Derry BT48 6PW, Northern Ireland
leeann@elementalsoftware.co
[6] PillPacPlus, Unit 9, 20 Antrim Road, Ballymena BT42 2BJ, Northern Ireland
stephen@pillpacplus.com

Abstract. It has been estimated, on a global scale, that a limb is lost every 20 s due to diabetes. Effective treatment has, however, been shown to reduce the risk of amputations and foot ulcers. Self-management and the provision of effective foot care in the clinic and at home, is viewed as instrumental in providing appropriate care for people with diabetes. This in turn can reduce the costs associated with treating and managing diabetes and its associated complications. This paper presents a usability evaluation of a smartphone based solution for the management of diabetic foot disease. The solution combines novel thermal imaging with tailored educational content and gamification elements in an attempt to improve self-management of the condition. The solution was evaluated in a workshop setting by 7 participants. Overall, the participants felt the proposed solution would be a very worthwhile endeavor. They rated the usability and utility at an acceptable level (SUS 69.1/100). Notable suggested improvements focused on how educational content was formatted and searched in addition to the physical support provided to facilitate imaging of the feet.

Keywords: Self-management · Diabetic foot disease · Thermal imaging · m-health

© Springer International Publishing AG 2017
S.F. Ochoa et al. (Eds.): UCAmI 2017, LNCS 10586, pp. 453–465, 2017.
DOI: 10.1007/978-3-319-67585-5_46

1 Introduction

By 2035 it is estimated that around 600 million people worldwide will have diabetes mellitus [1]. This increase threatens to bring huge financial instability to healthcare systems, including the National Health Services. The management of diabetes currently costs the National Health Service in the UK £10 billion each year [2]. If not properly managed and treated diabetes can lead to serious complications such as heart disease, stroke, blindness, kidney failure and amputation [1]. Among these complications, Diabetic Foot Disease (DFD), is one of the most debilitating, posing a substantial health and societal burden on patients and healthcare systems. Each year around 1 million people lose at least part of a leg as a consequence of DFD [3]. This equates to an amputation every 20 s worldwide [3]. People with diabetes are 15 times more likely to need an amputation than those without the condition [4]. Diabetic foot ulcers are the most prevalent problem, with a yearly incidence of around 2–4% in developed countries [1]. Typically, 25% of patients who present to a multi-disciplinary clinic with neuropathy will develop a foot ulcer. Of these foot ulcers, around 50% will become infected and 20% of these infected ulcers will lead to varying degrees of amputation [5]. New products and services that improve these statistics will have a major impact on the quality of life in addition to reducing the financial burden that DFD places on healthcare systems.

Self-management is viewed as instrumental in providing appropriate care for people with diabetes while, simultaneously, reducing the costs associated with treating and managing diabetes and its associated complications [6]. Self-management focuses on providing the individual with the skills and knowledge to stay healthy and prevent costly complications. For DFD, self-management activities may include, effective footcare, healthy eating, being physically active, monitoring of blood sugar, compliance with medications, good problem-solving skills, healthy coping skills and risk-reduction behaviors. Effective treatment reduces the risk of foot ulcers and amputations.

For prevention and care specific to DFD, it is recommended that patients check their feet daily [7]. Signs of foot ulceration may include: redness, pain, loss of sensation, callus or thickened skin around the ulcer. In addition to every day self-checks, the National Institute for Health and Care Excellence (NICE) recommends attending at least an annual foot review with a clinician to identify and treat ulceration quickly and effectively [7]. These checks aim to identify changes in foot health e.g. neuropathy, peripheral arterial disease or infection and advise the person of their risk status as per Diabetes UK's risk stratification. Nevertheless, a considerable number of people with diabetes are receiving inadequate care during annual foot checks, increasing their risk of amputation, according to research carried out by Diabetes UK [5]. In an online survey of almost 6700 people with diabetes, approximately one third said they were not informed about their level of risk regarding foot problems during the check. The same proportion said they were not given advice about their foot care. [8] There is therefore a need to provide better education and tools for people with diabetes and primary care providers to provide adequate and effective foot care both at home and in the clinic.

This paper presents the design and usability evaluation of a self-management solution for the prevention and management of DFD. Specifically, the solution combines emerging thermal imaging technology for the identification of early signs of ulceration, with a smartphone application to deliver educational information pertinent to effective prevention and management of diabetic foot conditions. This is achieved through intelligent data analytics. The paper is structured as follows: firstly, a review of technology solutions for the management of DFD is presented. Following this an overview of the proposed solution for management and prevention along with the evaluation methodology is provided. The results of the usability evaluation are then presented and discussed.

2 Background

A patient's awareness of their risk and of the protective measures they can take is important in preventing diabetes-related foot ulceration, as has been evidenced in recent Cochrane database reviews [9–11]. Moreover, in its published Standards of Medical Care in Diabetes, the American Diabetes Association recommends self-monitoring of foot health and family involvement as useful strategies for improving diabetes healthcare outcomes [12]. A large element of this is the ability to carry out a thorough foot examination and identify signs of a foot infection.

In the UK, diabetes foot surveillance is mainly performed by the primary care health professionals and forms a part of their Quality and Outcomes Framework (QOF) programme [13]. Nevertheless, the 2010 National Health Survey diabetes-led patient survey showed that over 50% of people with diabetes claimed not to recollect having had their feet examined or being given any advice related to foot care [13]. This disparity suggests that an examination had either not been performed and/or the patients had not been engaged in the purpose and the findings of the foot examination. Home examinations, via a number of methods, have been proposed in order to thwart this disparity [12]. Various solutions exist that aim to detect DFD, nevertheless, the current in practice approach of manual inspection of the foot is still the most common method of detecting DFD. The following sections describe diagnostic tests and devices for identifying early signs of DFD.

2.1 Devices for Diagnosis

Pressure perception, using a 10-g monofilament instrument, is the most commonly used screening test to identify loss of protective sensation in primary care as it is a relatively simple procedure and an abnormal result has been found to be associated with a 7.7-fold increased ulceration risk [14]. It could potentially be used by non-professionals such as relatives, as it is quick to perform; however, it requires some training and supplying a device for each patient to be screened [12]. Pressure has been and remains to be an important indicator of ulceration [5–8]. In-shoe pressure, unfortunately, is a difficult and expensive parameter to measure. Pressure-sensing devices are available such as the Tekscan F-scan [15], however, these are expensive, have a relatively short product life span and are not be suitable for everyday use [16].

Temperature, is very closely associated with pressure and is considered as a more reliable measurement [17]. This is mainly due, to the availability of hardware with thermistors providing highly accurate measurement in a small form. Less attention has, however, been directed towards foot plantar temperatures as an indicator of ulcer risk as compared to pressure [17]. Studies have shown that there is a relationship between increased temperature and foot complications in diabetes [17]. Increased temperature may be present up to a week before a foot ulcer occurs. In such an early stage of the disease, patients seldom feel pain because of neuropathic sensory loss, indicating that increased temperature can be a useful predictive sign of foot ulceration and sub-clinical inflammation of the feet. Infrared (IR) thermometers are commonly used to assess temperature differences in the feet caused by DFD [17].

The use of handheld dermal IR thermometers in the home environment has been validated by randomized controlled trials for the prevention of recurrent diabetic foot ulceration. Three randomized controlled trials tested patient monitoring of foot skin temperature as an indicator of an impending ulcer [18–20]. These studies found a significant reduction in new foot ulcers with use of a temperature monitoring device. This technology, however, requires, the temperature to be measured manually on specific spots on the foot. This makes it subjective, and it is difficult to obtain the temperature distribution of the whole foot. Furthermore, this technology misses the opportunity for automatic detection of DFD [21].

Another method, which is less ambulatory, is the use of liquid crystal thermography in such products as Thermoscale, Tempstat and SpectraSole Pro 1000 [23]. TempStat uses specialized liquid crystal technology (LCT) to monitor the temperature on the bottom of the feet [23]. TempStat has been approved by the U.S. Food and Drug Administration to identify areas of inflammation. Some limitations to LCT include low sensitivity, low image resolution and pressure sensitivity, in addition to the disadvantage of a very demanding device handling during contact of the crystals with examined body area [21]. Compared with LCT, IR camera systems have the advantage of being noncontact, which prevents unwanted pressures and the transmission of pathological organisms. The temperatures of noncontact foot regions, such as the medial arch, can be easily measured with IR camera systems. Additionally, it is capable of measuring the dorsal side of the foot as well. As such, IR camera systems show a greater potential for telemedical applications [21]. Moreover, the authors have provided evidence that detection of temperature differences are independent of the quality of the IR camera used and that it can be achieved without image processing algorithms [22]. Nevertheless, LCT offers the possibility of both static and dynamic measurements on the plantar aspect of the foot [23]. It was concluded that the IR camera is the most usable and cost-effective thermography option for the prevention of diabetic foot complications [23]. They also proposed that the use of such devices over the next 5 years in a patient centered fashion may not only aid in the early detection and avoidance of foot complications, however, also contribute to patient education, encouraging a healthier lifestyle [23]. A number of companies supply IR cameras for thermography, however, to date no products targeted specifically at the DFD market are commercially available.

2.2   The Role of Education

In addition to daily foot examination, education has an important part to play in the prevention of DFD. Lack of education leads to unawareness of diabetic foot problems and their prevention. Interestingly, one study demonstrated that 90% of screened diabetic patients had poor knowledge about their disease and 96.3% had poor awareness about its control [18]. Education has been recognized as a fundamental aspect of diabetes treatment for all age groups [24–26]. This is particularly the case for older patients, however, it has been suggested that diabetic education would be most effective if it is tailored to the particular needs of older learners [24]. This includes individualized self-management plans and advice, and should also consider the particular health characteristics of older adults. Educational provision should be adaptable to conditions such as visual and hearing impairments and cognitive and physical abilities [24, 26]. Several apps are now available for smartphones which provide stratified educational content. Recently the College of Podiatry, in collaboration with the special advisory group Foot in Diabetes UK and the British Association of Prosthetists and Orthotists, have created two apps to enable increased knowledge around the problems that can occur for those with DFD. One is for health care professionals who undertake diabetic foot screenings, the other is for people with diabetes to ensure they are empowered to prevent problems with their feet. These apps provide risk categorization to groups of high, moderate and low risk and provide relevant information and advice on self-care and assessment. Whilst these apps provide excellent educational resources tailored to the user, they do not include tools to aid in assessment of feet at home as previously detailed.

Whilst more contemporary methods, such as pressure/temperature insoles, do provide the flexibility to measure continuously, many insoles are currently cumbersome to use, having external power and processing units and users must remember to charge them and transfer them from shoe to shoe. Also, the data generated is not intuitive to interpret and can require clinical knowledge to do so. Furthermore, none of the solutions currently available provide educational information, which is an important part of any self-management programme. The solution developed and evaluated within this work, seeks to fill these gaps in the market by providing a non-intrusive and automatic method of detecting DFD. The project seeks to utilize thermal imaging technology to implement an ambulatory, non-invasive method of automatically detecting early signs of DFD and providing the user with the knowledge to effectively address these issues. Additionally, the solution will tackle prevention of DFD though promotion of healthy lifestyle, education and prompting the individual to check their feet regularly. Such monitoring and education, if more widespread and frequent, can potentially reduce amputation rates and thus reduce associated costs attributed to diabetic related amputation. The following Sections provide an overview of the proposed solution.

3   Solution to Prevent and Manage DFD

The developed solution has two main components, a mobile application and an associated thermal camera, and an analysis platform - a cloud-based service that hosts a web interface. This thermal camera has been validated within previous research for the purposes of hotspot detection (temperature difference of >2 °C is defined as a hotspot) [27]. The mobile app captures thermal vision data and raw RGB images. These are then uploaded, though a service, to the backend database. The backend stores this data in database and processes it to extract metrics to automatically identify hotspots. The Web-API of the local login scenario uses the standardized Open Authentication (OAuth) mechanism to authenticate the request and to manage data flow according to authorization credentials. The architecture of the developed solution is presented in Fig. 1. Thermal images are captured by the thermal sensor and the associated mobile app. These images are processed locally for hotspot detection before being uploaded to the backend via a rest endpoint. These images are combined with a personalized profile and patient history information to generate a personalized profile for tracking and processing the thermal images. This profile is generated through the application of machine learning techniques. A Web User Interface (UI) allows professional caregivers to view images and update patient profiles and educational content.

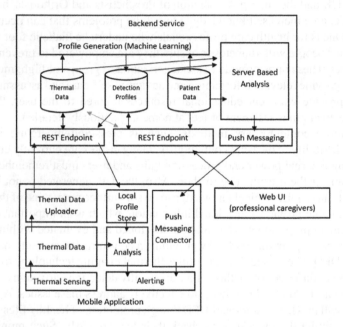

Fig. 1. Overview of the thermal imaging architecture developed for the management of DFD.

The educational app, delivers tailored educational facts and suggestions to aid in selfcare of DFD. Educational content is delivered in two modes. The first is a short fact and suggestion pair that is pushed to the user on a daily basis. These daily facts are short, evidence backed, statements with which a user can leverage to manage, prevent or reduce their risk of developing DFD. Educational content is also available through educational resources/articles, which can be multimodal, containing text, images or video content. These articles relate to self-management, prevention and care. Educational content is stratified based on risk category in a similar fashion to other applications. Both the educational resources and daily facts can be managed and populated through a content management system. This allows non-technical users to update and amend educational content based on clinical or research insight. In addition to the delivery of educational content and capture/review of thermal imaging, the mobile app also allows the user to rate educational content and update user profile information. An overview of the educational app is provided in Fig. 2.

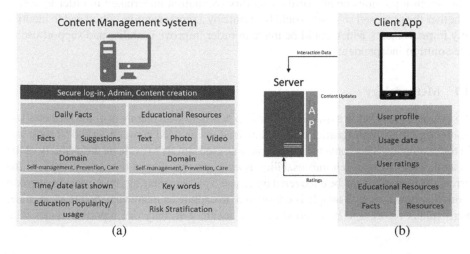

(a)   (b)

Fig. 2. Overview of educational client app and content management system. The client app (a) allows for interaction with the user to view and rate educational content. The content management system (b) provides the ability for a non-technical user to create and tailor educational content and facts.

In addition to the thermal imaging analysis and educational components of the app, a number of gamification elements have been included. The aim of these is to motivate the user to sustain engagement with the solution and develop self-management habits through behavior change. Figure 3 below shows the interface for the mobile app.

(a)   (b)   (c)   (d)

Fig. 3. Screenshots illustrating the various functions of the app including (a) thermal scanning of feet, (b) daily facts, (c) educational resources and (d) gamification.

4   Usability Evaluation

This section provides details of the usability evaluation undertaken in order to assess whether the proposed solution would be usable by a representative cohort and to identify any improvements which could be made in order improve usability and support use of the solution independently.

4.1   Methodology

To evaluate the solution a usability workshop was held with members of the Diabetes UK voluntary group. Seven participants (3 female, 4 male), aged between 30 and 67 took part in the evaluation. This convenience sample was used simply to evaluate the usability of the system. Previous research into usability assessments has shown that around 80% of the errors in an interface can be uncovered using just 5 participants [28, 29] A varied age group from this representative sample is considered, to capture as many view points as possible. Participants reported to be in good general health, with only one reporting issues with

Table 1. Task list completed by workshop participants in order to showcase functionality of the app.

	Task description	Task purpose
1	Complete the following steps • Launch app on mobile phone device • Review the home screen and identify what options are available • Rate the daily fact on the home screen. • Navigate to the educational content and review each of the available information sources under self-management • Navigate to the *"Your Progress"* section of the app and review the recent badges • Tap to find out more information about the available badges • Access the app menu and navigate back to the app home screen	To demonstrate overall function of app and highlight specific features and to obtain user opinion on usefulness of features and to obtain service user opinion on accessibility of educational materials
2	• Access the *"Scan your feet"* section and use the *"show me how"* instructions to find out how to attach the camera to the mobile device • Turn on the thermal camera • Use the app to capture a thermal image • Use the Thermal camera to try to capture an image of one foot at a time • Use the thermal camera to try and capture an image of both feet simultaneously	To assess the practical issues around using the camera to capture thermal images of the feet

mobility and dexterity. Only one of the participants had a history of previous diabetic foot infection. All users owned a smartphone (5/7 Android, 2/7 iOS) and reported to be familiar with smartphone apps.

After a brief introduction to the project and an overview of the solution, participants were invited to undertake two tasks that showcased the features of the app thus enabling users to evaluate usability. Tasks where split into two components, as presented in Table 1. Task 1 focused on the usability and gamification aspects and asked users to review both how the content was presented in addition to the literacy of the content itself. Task 2 asked participants to review instructions of how to use the thermal camera and then to take an image of their feet. Participants were asked to scan one foot at a time and then both feet simultaneously, if able to.

Following completion of the tasks, participants were asked to complete an evaluation questionnaire. This questionnaire had 3 sections: (1) usability of the app and (2) standard System Usability Scale (SUS) and (3) usage of the thermal camera and scanning of the feet. The questionnaire asked them to rate various aspects about the app including; look and feel, ease of use, ease of navigation and the utility of the app. Participants were also asked about how easy it would be to learn to use the app and how long that learning would take, how easy it was to use and attach the camera and how easy it was to scan both and/or one foot independently. Finally, participants were also asked to provide comments on what they felt was good or bad about the app and any improvements they would recommend. In addition to these customized questions about the app, the usability was measured using the System Usability Scale (SUS) [30]. This validated metric provides a reliable tool for measuring usability. It consists of a 10-item questionnaire with five response items; from Strongly Agree to Strongly Disagree. The SUS is scored out of 100 with an acceptable score being greater or equal to 70 [31]. In addition to the usability of the app, participants were also asked to comment on the set-up process for the camera and the practical issues of imaging one's feet. Results from the usability assessment are presented in the following section.

5   Results

In terms of the smartphone application, participants reported that it was generally very easy to use and thought the concept of combining thermal imaging and education content 'very worthwhile'. In general participants found the app responsive (mean - 3.57/5) easy to use (mean - 3.57/5) and easy to navigate (mean - 3.57/5). Participants also felt that it would be easy (mean - 3.7/5) and quick to learn to use the app with most users stating they could do so within a few hours (5 reported hours, 2 reported minutes). When asked to consider how useful the app had been in improving their knowledge of diabetic foot conditions, users reported very useful (mean - 4.14/5). Full results are reported in Fig. 4.

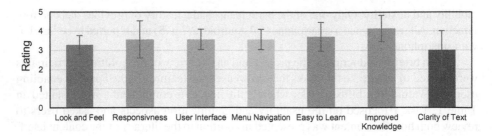

Fig. 4. General usability results from the questionnaire for app look and feel, responsiveness, user interface design, menu navigation, ease of learning, ability to improve knowledge and clarity of text. Error bars represent standard deviation.

The SUS scores echoed the same results as the general usability questions. Results for the SUS are represented with a single score ranging between 0 and 100. Scores below 50 indicate poor design; scores between 50 and 70 indicate an acceptable design; scores between 70 and 85 indicate a good design; and scores above 85 indicate an excellent design [31]. Over all the app and thermal imager received an SUS score of 69.1/100, placing it in the acceptable range of design, however, a number of changes could be made to improve this, as presented later within this section. Average scores with standard deviation for each question in the SUS are presented in Fig. 5.

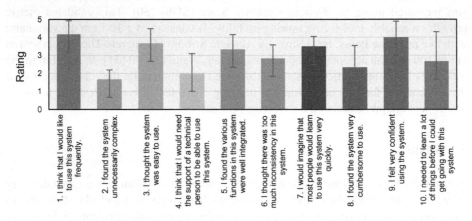

Fig. 5. Average rating given to each question in the System Usability Scale (SUS). Error bars represent standard deviation. Each question was rated on a scale of 1–5 with 1 being strongly disagree and 5 being strongly agree.

When considering the use of the thermal camera, participants reported that the camera was simple to use (mean 4.42/5). Participants also reported that the instructions provided showing how to use the app/camera, turn on the camera and launch the app were clear and easy to understand (mean 4.85/5). When asked to consider how easy it was to capture an image of both feet simultaneously, only 3 of 7 participants could do so, and provided a rating of 2.67/5. The other participants were unable to complete the task. Six of the 7 participants could scan one foot at a time, with one participant citing poor flexibility as a limiting factor. Participants rated scanning one foot as 3.83/5 showing that whilst possible, some help would be required to facilitate this on a daily basis. Participants noted that capturing an image of the feet may be easier if they had assistance from a carer or family member. All the participants agreed that they would be comfortable to ask a family member to scan their feet on a regular basis, though one participant highlighted the increase in carer burden associated with this.

When considering how the app could be improved, participants commented on the vast amount of text in the educational content. This content was repurposed from wed-based educational resources and therefore contained large bodies of text. Participants commented that this could be improved by summarizing the main points and providing more images. They also mentioned the need for better searching capabilities within the app to find content that they were looking for. This included key word searching and bookmarking sections so that text could be skipped and move to the section of interest. A similar comment was mentioned for video content, where participants wished to skip to sections of the video that they were interested in without watching the whole video. This could be further improved by stratifying the educational content based on the user's risk level and their health literacy.

In general participants felt the solution functioned well and would be a useful tool in managing their feet and avoiding complications. Participants felt the solution would need to be fully embraced by clinicians to be adopted fully into the foot care pathway.

6   Conclusion

This paper describes a holistic solution for the prevention and management of DFD. The solution combines a thermal imaging solution with tailored educational content to provide the tools and knowledge required for a user to better manage and prevent deterioration of their condition. In an initial usability evaluation, the solution has been assessed in a workshop setting by 7 members of a representative cohort. General usability ratings and scores from the SUS have proven promising, however, there is room for improvement, particularly in terms of how educational content is delivered and the support necessary to capture clear and reliable images of the participant's feet. Additionally, the workshop has highlighted the need to engage with clinicians to have the solution adopted into the care pathway. To assess whether this solution is effective in improving foot care and capturing early signs of DFD, the solution will need to be evaluated longitudinally. Future work will therefore aim to evaluate the solution longitudinally in a home setting to assess its impact on prevention, self-care and knowledge of diabetic foot complications. Additionally, we will seek to engage with clinicians to gain insight into how this solution could be integrated further within a foot care pathway.

Acknowledgment. Invest Northern Ireland is acknowledged for supporting this project under the Competence Centre Programme Grant RD0513853 - Connected Health Innovation Center. The authors would like to thank Diabetes UK for organising the workshop and the participants who attended and provided valuable feedback.

References

1. Bakker, K., Apelqvist, J., Lipsky, B.A., Van Netten, J.J., Schaper, N.C.: The 2015 IWGDF guidance documents on prevention and management of foot problems in diabetes: development of an evidence-based global consensus. Diabetes/Metab. Res. Rev. **32**(S1), 2–6 (2016)
2. Health and Social Care Information Centre. National diabetes audit - 2011–12 (2012). http://www.hscic.gov.uk/catalogue/PUB12421. Accessed March 2012
3. Bakker, K., Schaper, N.C.: The development of global consensus guidelines on the management and prevention of the diabetic foot 2011. Diabetes/Metab. Res. Rev. **28**(S1), 116–118 (2012)
4. Diabetes UK: More than 135 diabetes amputations every week. https://www.diabetes.org.uk/About_us/News/More-than-135-diabetes-amputations-every-week/. Accessed 16 Sept 2015
5. Putting Feet First: commissioning specialist services for the management and prevention of diabetic foot disease in hospitals. Diabetes UK (2009)
6. Ellis, P., Senior, C.: Diabetes education: the big missed opportunity in diabetes care. Diabetes UK (2015)
7. NICE clinical guideline (CG19): Diabetic foot problems: prevention and management (2016)
8. Diabetes UK online footcare survey (2014). https://www.diabetes.org.uk/About_us/News/Poor-diabetes-foot-checks/Footcare-survey-results/. Accessed Sept 2015
9. Schillinger, D., Grumbach, K., Piette, J., Wang, F., Osmond, D., Daher, C., Bindman, A.B.: Association of health literacy with diabetes outcomes. JAMA **288**(4), 475–482 (2002)
10. Duke, S.A., Colagiuri, S., Colagiuri, R.: Individual patient education for people with type 2 diabetes mellitus. Cochrane Database Syst. Rev. **1**, CD005268 (2009)
11. Dorresteijn, J.A., Kriegsman, D.M., Assendelft, W.J., Valk, G.D.: Patient education for preventing diabetic foot ulceration. Cochrane Database Syst. Rev. **5**, CD001488 (2010)
12. American Diabetes Association: Standards of medical care in diabetes—2013. Diabetes Care **36**, S11–S66 (2013)
13. Sharma, S., Kerry, C., Atkins, H., Rayman, G.: The Ipswich Touch Test: a simple and novel method to screen patients with diabetes at home for increased risk of foot ulceration. Diabet. Med. **31**(9), 1100–1103 (2014)
14. Square, T., Lane, B.: Patient experience of diabetes services (2013)
15. Lung, C.W., Hsiao-Wecksler, E.T., Burns, S., Lin, F., Jan, Y.K.: Quantifying dynamic changes in plantar pressure gradient in diabetics with peripheral neuropathy. Front. Bioeng. Biotechnol. **4**, 54 (2016)
16. Taborri, J., Palermo, E., Rossi, S., Cappa, P.: Gait partitioning methods: a systematic review. Sensors **16**(1), 66 (2016)
17. Bus, S.A., Netten, J.J., Lavery, L.A., Monteiro-Soares, M., Rasmussen, A., Jubiz, Y., Price, P.E.: IWGDF guidance on the prevention of foot ulcers in at-risk patients with diabetes. Diabetes/Metab. Res. Rev. **32**(S1), 16–24 (2016)
18. Liu, C., van Netten, J.J., Van Baal, J.G., Bus, S.A., van Der Heijden, F.: Automatic detection of diabetic foot complications with infrared thermography by asymmetric analysis. J. Biomed. Opt. **20**(2), 026003 (2015)
19. Lavery, L.A., Higgins, K.R., Lanctot, D.R., Constantinides, G.P., Zamorano, R.G., Athanasiou, K.A., et al.: Preventing diabetic foot ulcer recurrence in high-risk patients use of temperature monitoring as a self-assessment tool. Diabetes Care **30**, 14–20 (2007)
20. Armstrong, D.G., Holtz-Neiderer, K., Wendel, C., Mohler, M.J., Kimbriel, H.R., Lavery, L.A.: Skin temperature monitoring reduces the risk for diabetic foot ulceration in high-risk patients. Am. J. Med. **120**, 1042 (2007)

21. Jung, Y., et al.: Ground reaction force estimation using an insole-type pressure mat and joint kinematics during walking. J. Biomech. **47**(11), 2693–2699 (2014)
22. Lavery, L.A., Higgins, K.R., Lanctot, D.R., Constantinides, G.P., Zamorano, R.G., et al.: Home monitoring of foot skin temperatures to prevent ulceration. Diabetes Care **27**, 2642–2647 (2004)
23. Frykberg, R.G., Tallis, A., Tierney, E.: Diabetic foot self examination with the Tempstat as an integral component of a comprehensive prevention program. J. Diabet. Foot Complic. **1**(1), 13–18 (2009)
24. Quinn, C.W., Bond, R., Nugent, C.: Ontological modelling and rule-based reasoning for the provision of personalized patient education. Expert Syst. (2015)
25. International Diabetes Federation: Managing older people with type 2 diabetes global guideline. http://www.idf.org/guidelines/managing-older-people-type-2-diabetes. Accessed 24 Nov 2015
26. Mcdowell, J., Brown, F., Matthews, D. (eds.): Diabetes: A Handbook for the Primary Healthcare Team, 2nd edn. Churchill Livingstone, Edinburgh (2007)
27. Rafferty J., Cleland I., Nugent C., Armstrong, K., Madill, G.: An evaluation of contactless thermal sensing elements for use in a technology based diabetic foot disease detection solution. In: IEEE Engineering in Medicine and Biology Society Conference, Orlando, Florida, USA, pp. 4379–4382. IEEE, EMBC'16 (2016)
28. Nielsen, J.: Estimating the number of subjects needed for a thinking aloud test. Int. J. Hum. Comput. Stud. **41**, 385–397 (1994)
29. Nielsen, J., Molich, R.: HE of user interface. In: CHI '90 Conference Proceedings. ACM, pp. 249–256 (1990)
30. Brooke, J.: SUS-A quick and dirty usability scale. Usability Eval. Ind. **189**(194), 4–7 (1996)
31. Bangor, A., Kortum, P., Miller, J.: Determining what individual SUS scores mean: Adding an adjective rating scale. J. Usability Stud. **4**(3), 114–123 (2009)

A Smart Cabinet and Voice Assistant to Support Independence in Older Adults

Andrew Ennis[1(✉)], Joseph Rafferty[1], Jonathan Synnott[1], Ian Cleland[1], Chris Nugent[1],
Andrea Selby[2], Sharon McIlroy[2], Ambre Berthelot[3], and Giovanni Masci[4]

[1] Computer Science Research Institute and School of Computing and Mathematics,
Ulster University, Newtownabbey BT37 0QB, Co. Antrim, Northern Ireland
{a.ennis,j.rafferty,j.synnott,i.cleland,cd.nugent}@ulster.ac.uk
[2] Kirk House Care Home, 110 Kings Rd, Belfast BT5 7BX, Northern Ireland
{aselby,smcilroy}@belfastcentralmission.org
[3] Faculté des Siences et Techniques, Université de Limoges, Limoges, France
ambre.berthelot@club-internet.fr
[4] Dipartimento di Ingegneria dell'Informazione,
Università Politecnica delle Marche, Ancona, Italy
s1056247@studenti.univpm.it

Abstract. With the growing change to a more aged population and greater strain on our health care services, due to higher costs and demand, there is a growing need to develop solutions to help solve this health care crisis. Generally older people prefer to keep their independence as they age, which gives them a better quality of life. Independent living can be achieved both within care homes and at home, and with the assistance of technology this can be achieved more easily. In this study a Smart Home in a Box (SHIB) solution has been developed to support Ambient Assistive Living (AAL). This paper presents a solution for an interface to interact and be notified by the SHIB platform. A usability evaluation of the developed solution is also presented in the paper. This evaluation asked 8 people consisting of management staff and a Family and Relatives group from a care home, to determine how older people would feel about a solution like this. Overall the participants of the usability evaluation felt the developed solution would benefit older people living at home.

Keywords: Smart cabinet · Smart mirror · Voice assistant · Ambient assisted living · Intelligent environments

1 Introduction

It is estimated that by 2050, 20% of the world's population is expected be over the age of 80 and by 2030 older people will outnumber children aged 0–9 years, by 100 million [1]. With a more aged population, there will be greater strain on healthcare services, due to higher costs and demand, which will ultimately degrade the quality of care provided. In addition, many older people prefer to keep their independence as they age, whether this be within a care home or at their own home. Enabling older people to continue to live an independent life, can help to alleviate many of the problems faced by health care

© Springer International Publishing AG 2017
S.F. Ochoa et al. (Eds.): UCAmI 2017, LNCS 10586, pp. 466–472, 2017.
DOI: 10.1007/978-3-319-67585-5_47

services. A significant level of research interest has developed due to the forecasted strain on health care services and older people wanting to live independently [2]. Much of the research has been carried out in the area of Ambient Assistive Living (AAL), to support individuals with daily tasks and goal completion [3]. A Smart Home in a Box (SHIB) platform has been developed, to provide support to individuals within their own home and assist care home providers to better assist their patients. The SHIB platform aims to create a platform that can be deployed and setup by non-technical people, and in addition can be rapidly redeployed to an alternative location, when needed. There has been a great deal of research into developing smarter and more intelligent homes [4] and research has looked at using smart mirrors for interactive interfaces for smart homes [5, 6] and also goal motivation for fitness [7]. Further research has also considered the use of virtual assistants to support elderly care home residents [8]. The virtual assistant used was in the form of a visual avatar, presented on a screen. Generally, the avatar worked well with the study group of older people. The authors reported, however, that the avatar made the older people feel dependent, losing cognitive functions, or reminded them that they are not as active as they used to be [8]. With the rise of artificial intelligence, a range of commercial voice assistants, such as Amazon's Echo (AE), Microsoft's Cortana, and Google Home, have now provided a more intuitive way to interact with smart homes simply by using voice. The remainder of this paper is structured as follows: Sect. 2 details the developed solution; Sect. 3 details a usability evaluation of the developed solution; Sect. 4 presents the conclusions and discussion for future work.

2   Developed Solution

The developed solution within this work provides an unobtrusive assistant within a bathroom environment, however, this technology can also be located elsewhere, such as the kitchen. A general overview of the solution is presented in Fig. 1. The solution consists of a custom-built cabinet containing a smart mirror and medication tracking shelves. An Amazon Echo (AE) is connected to allow the user to interact vocally with the solution. The solution hides the technology from the user, such as, when the smart mirror is off it looks just like an ordinary mirror. Nevertheless, text, images and video can be displayed and made visible through the mirror. This is possible using a two-way mirror in front of the monitor, as shown in Fig. 2b. The display is powered by a Raspberry Pi, running a UWP (Universal Windows Platform) hosted web app, on top of Windows

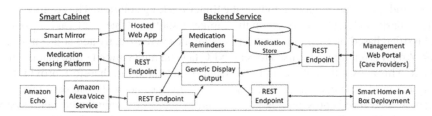

Fig. 1. An overview of the system architecture, showing the interaction between the smart cabinet, backend service, Amazon Echo server, and SHIB service.

10 IoT. The hosted web app interacts via REST to the backend server, which handles what is to be displayed, commands, medication sensing commands and the SHIB commands.

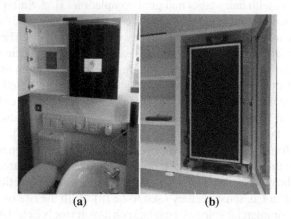

(a)   (b)

Fig. 2. Smart cabinet installed in bathroom lab. **(a)** Smart cabinet and Amazon Echo in bathroom test lab, showing instructions of how to take medication. Alexa is also verbally saying the instructions. **(b)** Smart mirror display, with mirror glass removed and display turned off due to inactivity.

The AE was chosen because it is available on the market and is low cost. AE does, however, have a number of limitations, in particular it cannot proactivly speak. This means that it is not possible to vocally prompt the user, however, we can use the display to do this, which might be a less distressing approach, for an older person, than the AE suddenly speaking. A tailored platform for the voice assistant is currently being investigated to overcome the limitations of the AE. This paper considers the application scenario to assist an older person with taking their medication, in a bathroom environment as shown in Fig. 2a. The smart cabinet is linked into the SHIB deployment, so metrics, alerts, suggestions, remote care giver assistance can all be displayed. Live and historic metrics from a user's smart weight scales or other smart devices can also be displayed.

2.1   Proposed Cabinet Tracking Solution

In this study, we also propose a low-cost cabinet tracking solution. The solution uses a switch matrix to detect objects set on the cabinet's shelves. Objects of varying size can be classified based on the number of micro-switches that are activated adjacent to each other. An NFC reader is also used to scan NFC tags on medication before placing in the cabinet. This allows the cabinet to know what objects are in it, therefore providing the older person advice about the medication, such as dosage and medication last taken. The system architecture is presented in Fig. 3a, and integrates through the backend system, as shown in Fig. 1. When a new medication is placed in the cabinet, the NFC tag is first scanned which tells the smart cabinet what it is. The object is then placed on a shelf and the system detects its location. A person can then ask the AE, "where is my medication?". The smart cabinet will show the older person which shelf it is on and where on the shelf, with the use of LED indicators. Figure 3b shows the early stage prototype of the switch matrix and NFC reader, connected to a Raspberry Pi.

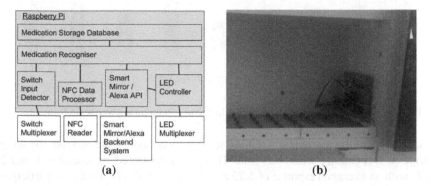

(a)   (b)

Fig. 3. Architecture and prototype of medication tracking solution. **(a)** Object and medication tracking system architecture. **(b)** Prototype switch matrix installed in the smart cabinet. The switch matrix cover is not shown here.

3 Usability Evaluation

To evaluate the developed solution an evaluation workshop was held, with a group of 8 people consisting of care home staff and members of a Family and Relatives group from Kirk House, a local care home, to determine how elderly people would feel about using a solution like this. The various features of the solution were demonstrated to the group and all participants were invited to use and interact with the solution. Each person in the group was then asked to complete a usability questionnaire. Table 1 provides an overview of the questions from the survey that had an answer scale from 1 (very bad) to 7 (very good). Figure 4 shows the results of each of these questions. Further open

Table 1. Survey questions with an answer scale of 1 to 7, 1 = very bad, 7 = very good.

Number	Question
1	How easy do you feel the system is to use?
2	How Accurate do you feel Amazon Alexa is at recognising what was said?
3	How useful do you think this system would be to an elderly person?
4	How natural do you think an elderly person would find this system to interact with?
5	How intrusive would you feel a system like this would be in your home?
6	How comfortable would you feel interacting with this system, in your home?
7	How useful do you think this system would be when you are older?
8	How natural do you think you would find this system to interact with when you are older?

questions were asked to gather user's opinions on various aspects of the solution, as discussed below.

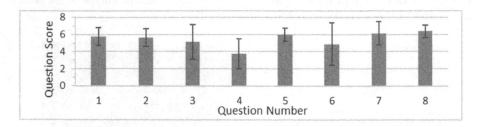

Fig. 4. Responses to questions detailed in Table 1, with an answer scale from 1 to 7.

Generally, all the participants felt the solution was easy to use and that the AE was accurate at recognizing what was said. This is demonstrated by question 1 and 2 in Fig. 4, with an average response of 5.75 and 5.63, respectively. From the participant's responses, it shows they felt that the solution would be useful to an older person with an average score of 5.14, as shown by question 3 in Fig. 4. In the open questions, one carer highlighted that if the older person suffered from dementia, then the mirror and the voice would cause distress to them. With advances in voice syntheses [9, 10], it could be possible to have it speak in a familiar voice, therefor not causing distress. The issue of the mirror, could be solved by removing the mirror and simply have an ordinary monitor, possibly placed within a picture frame. The participants found the solution easy to use for older people, with an average score of 3.75. They also said they did not find the solution to be intrusive, with an average score of 6.0, however, 2 participants said they would from the solution intrusive. Question 7 and 8 also highlighted the participants found the solution easy to use and would be useful for them. Figure 5a, presents the participants answers to the question "Do you feel an elderly person would be confused by the mirror?". As shown, the general answer was that an elderly person would be confused by the mirror. It was commented, however, that this would mainly be the case if the elderly person had dementia, as the mirror would cause distress to them. The participants responded with an indecisive answer regarding if an elderly person would be confused by the AE voice, as shown in Fig. 5b. The participants again mentioned that older people with dementia would be distressed by the voice. Also, one participant said that a "local" accent or familiar voice could help with dementia patients.

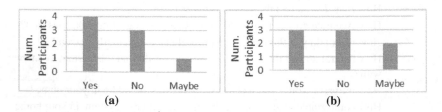

Fig. 5. Question responses, **(a)** "Do you feel an elderly person would be confused by the mirror?" **(b)** "Do you fell an elderly person would be confused by the voice of Amazon Alexa?"

The participants were asked to rank the importance of the four application areas of the solution (1–4). With rank 1 having the most benefit and 4 having the least benefit. Figure 6 shows the results of this question and the most voted application area was for a medication reminders assistant with 5 participants voting rank 1. An assistant to enable interactions and reporting to a remote caregiver was the second most rated application area, with rank 1 and 2 receiving 3 votes each. The least voted application area was an activity assistant within the kitchen, with rank 4 receiving 4 votes.

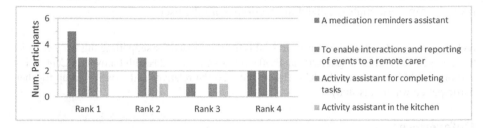

Fig. 6. Responses to question "Can you rank the following application areas in the order you think would have the most benefits?" Application areas are detailed in the chart legend.

Some of the other comments made by the participants provided insightful application areas and uses. Such as to monitor the elderly person's bathroom patterns, to determine if they are waking up at night to use the bathroom. This could be achieved using sound level monitoring to detect if the bathroom is being used. This metric can feedback into our SHIB deployment to pre-empt a potential fall within the bathroom and ensure the staff can respond quick when a fall does happen. Another area, is the elderly person can self-report various symptoms in an intuitive and interactive way. The various symptom questionnaires can be pushed to the smart cabinet by the care provider, through the SHIB deployment, for the older person to complete via voice responses. Another application area that was suggested, was for reassurance to the elderly person. Since our solution is connected to all the other SHIB devices, the elderly person can tell our solution they are going to bed. Our system can then do a health check of the home and reassure the person that all the doors and windows are locked and that all the appliances in the home are switched off. Or if there are appliances still turned on, the system can turn them off for the elderly person.

4   Conclusions

This paper has described a solution to assist older people to live independently within their home, or care home. The solution combines commercial voice assistants with an unobtrusive smart bathroom cabinet, to enable an older person to very easily ask for assistance. In addition a solution to track objects within the smart cabinet, has been proposed, which can enable the smart cabinet to aid an older person on how to take their medication, or use a toothbrush for example. An initial usability evaluation has been carried out with 8 members of a families and relatives group and care management staff of Kirk House care home. The general usability scores from the evaluation have proven positive, however, they have highlighted further areas of research. From this study, we have highlighted several limitations in using the commercial off the shelf voice assistants. In particular, the most apparent limitation is that Amazon's Alexa cannot proactively speak, in other words the user must initiate the conversation. Future work will investigate the limitations of Amazon's Alexa to enable proactive conversations. Future work will also address the feedback from the evaluation and look to integrate further contextualization to understand who and when someone is at the smart cabinet and then provide improved contextualized interactions with the user.

Acknowledgments. Invest Northern Ireland is acknowledged for supporting this project under the Competence Centre Programs Grant RD0513853 – Connected Health Innovation Centre. The authors would like to thank the Kirk House staff and the relatives and families group for their participation within this study.

References

1. ONU: "World population, ageing," Suggest. Cit. United Nations, Dep. Econ. Soc. Aff. Popul. Div. (2015). World Popul. Ageing, vol. United Nat, no. (ST/ESA/SER.A/390, p. 164 (2015)
2. Rashidi, P., Mihailidis, A.: A survey on ambient-assisted living tools for older adults. IEEE J. Biomed. Heal. Inf. **17**(3), 579–590 (2013)
3. Rafferty, J., Nugent, C., Liu, J., Chen, L.: A mechanism for nominating video clips to provide assistance for instrumental activities of daily living. In: Cleland, I., Guerrero, L., Bravo, J. (eds.) IWAAL 2015. LNCS, vol. 9455, pp. 65–76. Springer, Cham (2015). doi: 10.1007/978-3-319-26410-3_7
4. Helal, S., Mann, W., El-Zabadani, H., King, J., Kaddoura, Y., Jansen, E.: The Gator tech smart house: a programmable pervasive space. Computer (Long Beach, Calif.) **38**(3), 50–60 (2005)
5. Saeed, F., Khan, D.M., Saher, N., Shahzad, F., Ammer, N.: SMART MIRROR: a novel framework for interactive display. In: International Conference on Circuit, Power Computing Technologies [ICCPCT], vol. 26, no. 5, pp. 2089–2095 (2014)
6. Yue, P., Jing, L.: A study on intelligent housekeeper of smart home system. In: Proceedings of the 9th International Conference on Measuring Technology and Mechatronics Automation, 2017, pp. 124–127 (2017)
7. Besserer, D., Bäurlem, J., Nikic, A., Honold, F., Schüssel, F., Weber, M.: FitMirror: a smart mirror for positive affect in everyday user morning routines. In: Proceedings of the Workshop on Multimodal Analyses enabling Artificial Agents in Human-Machine Interaction, pp. 48–55 (2016)
8. König, A., Malhotra, A., Hoey, J., Francis, L.E.: Designing personalized prompts for a virtual assistant to support elderly care home residents. In: Proceedings of the 10th EAI International Conference on Pervasive Computing Technologies Healthcare, pp. 278–282 (2016)
9. CandyVoice: Candy Voice (2017). https://candyvoice.com/. Accessed 10 May 2017
10. Lyrebird: LYREBIRD (2017). https://lyrebird.ai/. Accessed 10 May 2017

Fuzzy Fog Computing: A Linguistic Approach for Knowledge Inference in Wearable Devices

Javier Medina[1]($\boxtimes$), Macarena Espinilla[1], Daniel Zafra[1], Luis Martínez[1], and Christopher Nugent[2]

[1] Department of Computer Science, University of Jaen, Jaén, Spain
jmquero@ujaen.es
[2] School of Computing and Mathematics, Ulster University, Jordanstown, UK

Abstract. Fog Computing has emerged as a new paradigm where the processing of data and collaborative services are embedded within smart objects, which cooperate between them to reach common goals. In this work, a rule-based Inference Engine based on fuzzy linguistic approach is integrated in the smart devices. The linguistic representation of local and remote sensors is defined by protoforms, which configure the antecedents of the rules in the Inference Engine. A case study where two inhabitants with a wearable device conduct activities in a Smart Lab is presented. Each wearable device infers the daily activities within the wearable devices by means of the rule-based Inference Engine.

Keywords: Fog computing sensors · Linguistic terms · Rule-based inference engine · Wearable devices

1 Introduction

Since last years, Ambient Intelligence (AmI) [1] and the Ubiquitous Computing (UC) [2] have developed new computing paradigms integrating intelligence systems in the sensor and environments for an ambient assisted living [3]. These trends have enabled analyzing daily human activities from computer sciences by means of pervasive and mobile computing [4]. In this way, activity recognition has resulted a challenging research topic because of supervising elderly people to stay with the best quality of life as long as possible in their sustainable, healthy and manufacturing homes [5], whose percentage of population over 65 up to 15% [6].

Currently, recent paradigms, such as Edge Computing [7] or Fog Computing [8] edges the data and services within the devices where data are collected *providing virtualized resources and engaged location-based services to the edge of the mobile networks* [9]. This new perspective translates the focus on Internet of Things (IoT) [10], from Cloud Computing with centralized processing [11], to collaborative networks where the smart objects *interact with each other and cooperate with their neighbors to reach common goals* [12,13]. In concrete, Fog Computing has involved a great impact between ambient devices [14] and wearable devices [15].

© Springer International Publishing AG 2017
S.F. Ochoa et al. (Eds.): UCAmI 2017, LNCS 10586, pp. 473–485, 2017.
DOI: 10.1007/978-3-319-67585-5_48

In order to integrate intelligence systems in smart objects and smart environments by means of Fog Computing, several key aspects have to be handled:

- Real time ubiquitous computing. The adequate distribution of services between smart objects is crucial to provide sensitivity to real time [16] where the most important part of information processing is distributed in different central processing units [17].
- Knowledge representation of data streams from heterogeneous sensors. A wide range of heterogeneous sensors are deployed in smart objects being necessary: (i) standard structural models, such as SensorML [18], developed by Open Geospatial Consortium, (ii) semantic model ontologies, such as the W3C Semantic Sensor Networks (SSN) specifications [19] or (iii) *ad hoc* proposals which provide scientist interoperability [20].
- Collaborative knowledge generation. Fog Computing requires by information processing of sensors to generate richer and higher-level information [21] in the devices where data are collected. This issue requires that raw data from sensors have to be analyzed, summarized and merged with other sensor information by means of context-aware computing [22].

Based on these issues, in this work, we describe a straightforward approach for the fusion and reasoning of knowledge within smart objects using a formal linguistic representation from the stream of data generated within the environment. In order to illustrate the usefulness and effectiveness of our proposal for integrating a fuzzy linguistic representation in Fog Computing, we present a case study where two inhabitants with a wearable device conduct activities in a Smart Lab and the inference of daily activities is computed within the wearable devices using a linguistic representation of local sensors.

The remainder of the paper is structured as follows: in Sect. 2, the proposed approach for distributing and inferring fuzzy linguistic terms in smart objects is presented; in Sect. 3, a case study of daily living activities in an intelligent environment is presented and the approach for ambient and wearable sensors is evaluated. Finally, in Sect. 4, conclusions and future works are pointed out.

1.1   Background

In this work we introduce an intuitive linguistic representation of data streams by means of *protoforms* based on an extension of temporal linguistic terms [23,24]. Protoforms were proposed by Zadeh [25] as useful knowledge model for reasoning [26], summarization [27] and aggregation [28] of data under uncertainty. The managing of uncertainty and vagueness in intelligent environments has been described as a key issue to obtain an high performance and results [29], in particular for Activity Recognition [30].

On the other hand, in Fog Computing, the Real-Time distribution of collaborative information and knowledge is required [31] to provide a scalable approach in which the heterogeneous sensors are distributed to dynamic subscribers in real-time. In this contribution the smart objects are defined as both sources and targets of information using a Publish-Subscribe model [32]. In concrete, the smart objects interact with each others describing their sensor streams by means of protoforms.

Finally, a rule-based Inference Engine based on the fuzzy linguistic approach [33] is integrated in the smart objects, such as wearable devices, to generate higher-level information. The antecedents of the rules are defined by protoforms under a linguistic representation of local and remote data streams. This inference model is close related to the Mamdani inference method [34], although the degree of terms are replaced by the degree of protoforms. The rules can be defined and configured by means of remote services enabling devices being remotely programmed.

2 Approach for Generating and Distributing Protoforms in Real-Time Collaborative Environments

The main contribution of this paper is to provide a straightforward approach for generating and distributing protoforms in real-time collaborative environments. The approach is based on the definition of intuitive protoforms for representing sensor streams and the integration of a fuzzy Inference Engine within smart objects.

In Fig. 1, the generation of protoforms, distribution under a Real-Time Publish-Subscribe model and the inference engine using a fuzzy linguistic approach are shown. The components are further detailed in next sections.

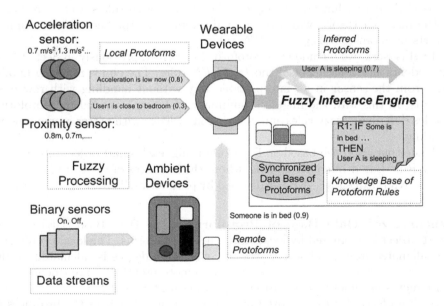

Fig. 1. Architecture of components. Wearable and ambient data streams are translated to protoforms, which are distributed in real-time to be processed in rule-based inference engines of wearable devices.

2.1 Protoforms of Sensor Streams

In this section, we resume a previous work [23], where a linguistic summary of sensor streams were proposed using *protoforms*. Based on our linguistic approach, each sensor data stream s^j is composed of a set of measures $s^j = \{m_i^j\}$, where each measure is represented by $m_i^j = \{v_i^j, t_i^j\}$. v_i^j represents the raw value that measures the sensor. For each sensor data stream s^j, we associate a fuzzy linguistic terms V_r to describe the measures of the sensor. Second, we associate fuzzy linguistic terms T_k with the temporal component of the data stream, defined by the distance $\Delta t_i^j = t^* - t_i^j, t^* > t_i^j$ from a reference point of time t^* to the timestamp of the measurement t_i. Third, we aggregate both terms computing the relevance of a linguistic value term $V_k(v)$ in a fuzzy temporal term $T_k(t)$ using the t-norm and co-norm operators:

$$V_r \cup T_k(s^j) = \bigcup_{m_i^j \in s^j} V_r \cap T_k(m_i^j) \in [0,1] \tag{1}$$

The linguistic terms T_k and V_k which are instanced in the sensor stream s^j represent a protoform in the shape of: s^j is T_k V_r. For example, the protoform instance: *Motion is now low*.

2.2 Fuzzy Inference Engine with Distributed Protoforms Within Smart Objects

In this section, we describe a Fuzzy Inference Engine with Distributed Protoforms (FIEDP) within Smart Objects. The fuzzy based-rule systems are based on the fuzzy set theory, which traditionally represents the knowledge of human experts by means of fuzzy *IF-THEN* rules.

In this work, we include the protoforms, described previously in Sect. 2.1, as antecedents and consequent of the *IF-THEN* rules. The aim is inferring knowledge from the sensor in an interpretable way without handling with raw data streams. In this way, the linguistic summary of sensor provided by protoforms enables describing fuzzy rules and inferring knowledge with better human understanding.

Under our approach based on Fog Computing, each smart object integrates a Fuzzy Rule-Based Inference Engine, where the instances of the Data Base (DB) and the Knowledge Base (KB) are defined by protoforms. The are shown in Fig. 1.

Synchronized Data Base of Protoforms. The Data Base (DB) of each smart object is composed by local and remote protoforms. The local protoforms are calculated from local sensor streams, where the degree is calculated by the approach described in Sect. 2.1, whilst the remote protoforms are calculated as consequents in remote smart objects regarding next Sect. 2.2.

A *Protoform Service* deployed in each smart object defines the instances of the local protoforms. The local protoforms enable us configuring different linguistic summaries for each local sensor stream. These protoforms can be subscribed by other smart objects, in order to obtain a linguistic representation of a remote sensor. So, every time that a given data stream updates a new measure, the Fuzzy Rule Based Inference Engine: (i) updates the Data Base calculating the degree of the local protoform, and (ii) sends an event with new degree to the remote subscribers.

Knowledge Base of Protoform Rules. The Knowledge Base (KB) for each smart object is composed of rules of protoforms. The antecedents A_{i_j} of each rule R_i correspond on local or remote protoforms integrated in the Data Base.

$$R_j : IF A_1 \ldots and A_n THEN C_j$$

where A_i is a protoform related to the linguistic terms of a sensor in the shape of s^j is T_k V_r, based on the description of Sect. 2.1.

The consequents C_i is defined as a new inferred protoform, whose degree is calculated by concatenating the antecedents $A_{i_1} \ldots and A_{i_n}$ using fuzzy conjunctive operators (t-norm) $\cap$ and aggregating the same consequents using fuzzy disjunctive operators (t-conorm) $\cup$:

$$\mu_{C_j} = \bigcup_{R_j \in R} \bigcap_{A_i \in R_j} (\mu A_i), \forall A_i, C_j \in R_j$$

A *Rule Subscription Service* deployed in each smart object allows adding or removing instances of rules. Each rule enables us defining new shaped-protoform consequents and distributing the inferred degrees to the subscriber in real time. In this way, the subscribers can keep a real-time synchronization of remote protoforms collected in their Data Bases.

Finally, the Fuzzy Rule Based Inference Engine updates the degrees of inferred protoform consequents for each rule when an antecedent in the Data Base is triggered. This occurs when: (i) the local data stream updates a new measure for local protoforms, or (ii) a degree of a shaped-protoform consequent from a remote subscription is received.

3   Case Study

In this section, a description of a scene of daily activities is carried out by two inhabitants in a Smart Lab. Inhabitants wear a wearable device and the Smart Lab integrate several ambient sensor in several smart objects. The description of inhabitant and ambient sensors is modeled under the fuzzy linguistic approach using protoforms. Moreover, the wearable devices integrate the proposed Fuzzy Inference Engine receiving remote protoforms, which are connected under a subscription model to ambient objects. The aim of this case study is evaluating the capabilities of wearable devices for inferring the daily activity of each inhabitant in real time.

The case study was carried out in the smart lab of the ACETIC (Center for Advanced Studies in Information Technology and Communication) of University of Jaen[1].

At the scene:

(1) Inhabitant A in the bed, wakes up and brushes his teeth.
(2) Inhabitant A goes to the kitchen, prepares breakfast with the kettle and cereal and sits in the kitchen to have breakfast.
(3) While inhabitant A is eating, inhabitant B enters through the door and prepares a cold drink using the fridge and glasses.
(4) Inhabitant B goes to the living room to watch TV.
(5) Inhabitant A, finishes the breakfast and introduces the dishes in the dishwasher.
(6) Inhabitant B, goes to the living room to watch the TV together with inhabitant B.

The video of the scene is located in the next URL[2].

3.1 Sensors

In order to describe the daily activity carried out by the two inhabitants, we have integrated several ambient sensors to convert traditional objects into smart object:

- Motion Cookies. They are movement sensors located in objects, which notify of a specific patter movement, such as brushing teeth or diking a water, to a base station called Mother Sense by means of Z-Wave protocol. Receiving the pattern events is enabled by means of a REST-oriented API. Three cookies have been installed within two cups and a toothbrush respectively.
- Pressure sensor. A pressure sensor is installed at the sofa and bed, which notifies to a base station by means of Z-Wave protocol.
- Bluetooth Beacons. Six Bluetooth Beacons, in concrete Estimote sensors, are located in the sofa, bathroom, bed and glasses respectively. They enable wearable devices with Low Bluetooth Energy calculating the distance and proximity from inhabitants to the rooms and objects.

The wearable devices of an inhabitants are smart watches with Android Wear, specifically the model LG Urban Watch. In this case scene, we have integrated two sensors from the smart watches:

- Accelerometer sensor. It measures the linear acceleration in m/s^2 representing the inhabitant motion.
- Bluetooth Low Energy (BLE). It enables smart watches obtain the proximity in dBm based on the RSSI signal to a Bluetooth Beacon, as well as the estimated distance in meters.

---

[1] http://ceatic.ujaen.es/.
[2] http://sinbad2.ujaen.es/video/smartwatch.mp4.

3.2 Protoforms for Sensor and Rule Definition

At the case scene, we have defined several protoforms to describe the sensor streams from ambient objects and smart watches using a linguistic approach.

First, to instance the protoforms, an expert defines the variables and linguistic terms related to each sensor stream, which is shown in Table 1. On the first hand, to translate the data from sensor of accelerometer and BLE from wearable devices to linguistic terms, we have defined their membership functions using *trapezoidal function*. It is a common representation to define a membership function in continuous domains, which is achieved by a 4-tuple $TS(a,b,c,d)$ where b and c indicate the point in which the membership value is 1, with a and d indicating the left and right limits of the definition domain of the membership function. On the second hand, the ambient devices (mother and z-wave base) translate binary data from crisp sensor (cookies and pressure of sofa and bed) to protoforms using a easygoing transformation $\{on, off\} \rightarrow \{0, 1\}$. The fuzzy temporal term for calculating the degree of protoforms regarding with Sect. 2.1 has been modeled by the short-term *now* with the trapezoidal function $\mu_{T_k(\Delta t)} = TS(0, 0, 2, 4)$ defined in seconds. We note that to simplify, we have missed *now* in the description of all protoforms.

Second, the protoforms are distributed under subscription model under a publish model. The distribution of changes of the degree have been implemented with an Object Oriented Middleware, ZeroC Ice [32], which provides a compressive framework for using subscriptions and sending data through channels of real-time events. Based on the principles of Fog Computing related on this work, the events from ambient devices and objects have been spread to smart watches in real time. So, in the scene, the events from cookies and binary sensors are received in their base stations, which have been integrated in the middleware to spread the events to smart watches using the TCP protocol by WiFi connection.

Table 1. Translation of sensor streams to protoforms

Protoform	Sensor/Device	Term V_r	Domain	μ_{V_r}
The motion of inhabitant [A|B] is relevant	*accelerometer/ wearable*	*relevant*	$[0,2]$ m/s^2	$TS(0,0, 0.25.2)$
Inhabitant [A|B] is close to [cup|sofa|bathroom|bed]	*BLE/wearable*		$[0,10]$ m	$[0,10]$ m	$TS(0,0, 2,5)$
Toothbrush is brushing	*Cookie/Mother Base*	*brushing*	$\{on, off\}$	$\{0, 1\}$
Cup is drunk	*Cookie/Mother Base*	*drunk*	$\{on, off\}$	$\{0, 1\}$
Someone is in sofa	*Binary sensor/Z-Wave base*	*in*	$\{on, off\}$	$\{0, 1\}$
Someone is in bed	*Binary sensor/Z-Wave base*	*in*	$\{on, off\}$	$\{0, 1\}$

Third, a Fuzzy Inference Engine is deployed in each smart watch. Based on the daily activities carried out by inhabitants at this case scene, the Knowledge Base has been composed by the next rules:

(1) *IF motion of inhabitant is relevant AND cup is now drunk AND inhabitant is close to cup THEN inhabitant is drinking*
(2) *IF motion of inhabitant is now relevant AND inhabitant is close to bathroom AND toothbrush is brushing THEN inhabitant is brushing teeth*
(3) *IF NOT motion of inhabitant is relevant AND inhabitant is close to bed AND someone is in bed THEN inhabitant is sleeping*
(4) *IF NOT motion of inhabitant is relevant AND inhabitant is close to sofa AND someone is in sofa THEN inhabitant is in sofa*

3.3   Results

In this section, we present the time-line related to each inhabitant by means of the smart watch and the inference of activities in the scene.

First, in Fig. 2, three time-lines with the degree of protoforms for each ambient and wearable sensor are shown. Although the degrees of local protoforms of inhabitant may seem chaotic, they describe the basic antecedents to infer activities in the Inference Engine in each smart watch.

Second, in Fig. 3, two time-lines with the degree of inferred protoforms for both inhabitants and ground-truth activities are shown. They represent *the point of view* at the scene of each inhabitant A and B. For example, the fact that the inhabitant B is sleeping is related to the low motion, proximity to bed and pressure sensor of bed. Later, brushing teeth of inhabitant B is inferred by the cookie sensor from toothbrush as well as the strong movement and the proximity to bathroom. Inhabitant A appears in the scene while inhabitant B is having breakfast. Inhabitant A enters into kitchen and takes the cup A for drinking. The proximity related to the cups A and B allows Inference Engine detecting which one is drinking from each cup. When inhabitant A sits down on sofa and drinks, it is inferred by the activation of ambient sensors of the cup and the sofa together with the proximity to the sofa. Finally, when inhabitant B sits down on the sofa too, and at the same time inhabitant A drinks, the inferred actions of drinking is detected by both smart watches due to the proximity to the cup and relevant movement of both, although with a higher degree in the correct inhabitant A.

3.4   Limitations of the Work

The main limitation of the work is related to the current weak-spots of smart watches. Keeping alive a permanent WiFi connection for receiving ambient events in real-time is not trivial. They have been programatically strained to not closing the network connectivity, which is the default internal policy of the smart watches for reducing battery consumption. So, in real environments, keeping real-time connectivity could not be sensible for long time.

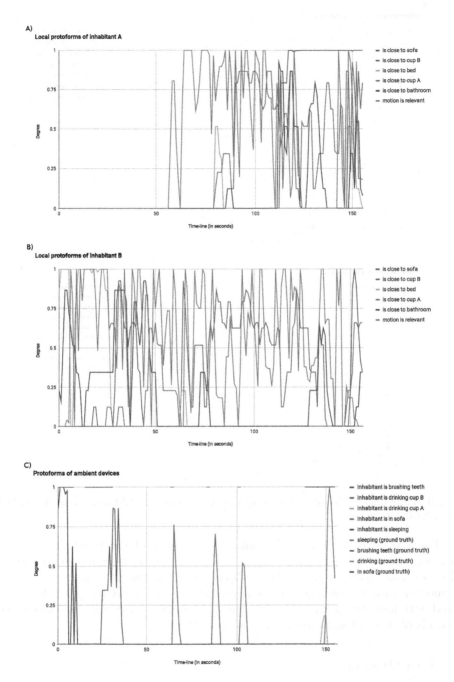

Fig. 2. Time-lines with the degree of protoforms for the sensor streams regarding with (A) inhabitant A, (B) inhabitant B and (C) ambient sensors in in the scene

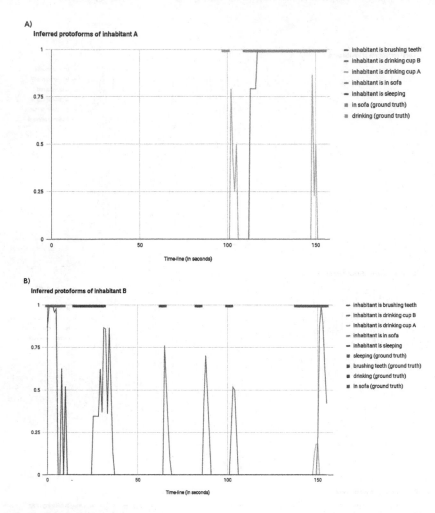

Fig. 3. Time-lines with the degree of inferred protoforms for (A) inhabitant A and (B) inhabitant B.

The second issue is the delay and discontinuity of the proximity of BLE beacons. The need for some seconds to be aware of the proximity with rooms. Moreover, in regard to proximity to objects, we also note that locating beacons in moving objects, such as cups, has provided a better accuracy for detecting hand activities, but accuracy is affected while walking and it is necessary some seconds of motionless to recover the measurement.

4   Conclusions

In this work, we have described a fuzzy linguistic approach for handling Fog Computing in wearable devices, which provide a new perspective and accuracy in activity recognition.

For that, we have extended the use of protoforms of previous works [23, 24], where linguistic expressions for describing data streams were proposed, with a Fuzzy Inference Engine integrated within wearable devices. It has provided a new perspective based on Fog Computing, where the inference of activities is deployed within wearable devices. So, the intelligence of recognizing activities has been focused on the devices of user, keeping the privacy of processing the personal sensor streams away from cloud services.

On the case scene presented in results, we have deployed proximity beacons both in room and smart objects detecting the proximity of inhabitants when interacting with objects. However, improvements in movement and accuracy are needs in next generation of devices to guaranty a higher detection of a closer proximity in real-time. Moreover, real-time distribution of ambient events to smart watches has been developed with WiFi under TCP protocol. In real environments, the connectivity by Bluetooth Low Energy instead of WiFi could provide a better battery life of smart watches. Next generation of middleware for IoT should deal with this problem.

In future works, we will focus on describing a longer dataset of daily activities in smart environments using wearable devices in order to provide a better accuracy in Multioccupant Activity Recognition.

Acknowledgments. This contribution has been supported by European Unions Horizon 2020 research and innovation programme under the Marie Sklodowska-Curie grant agreement No 734355 together the Spanish government by research project TIN2015-66524-P.

References

1. Zelkha, E., Epstein, B., Birrell, S., Dodsworth, C.: From devices to ambient intelligence. In: Digital Living Room Conference, vol. 6, June 1998
2. Weiser, M.: The computer for the 21st century. Sci. Am. **265**(3), 94–104 (1991)
3. Yin, J., Tian, G., Feng, Z., Li, J.: Human activity recognition based on multiple order temporal information. Comput. Electr. Eng. **40**(5), 1538–1551 (2014)
4. Varshney, U.: Pervasive healthcare and wireless health monitoring. Mob. Netw. Appl. **12**(2–3), 113–127 (2007)
5. Branger, J., Pang, Z.: From automated home to sustainable, healthy and manufacturing home a new story enabled by the internet-of-things and industry 4.0. J. Manag. Anal. **2**(4), 314–332 (2015)
6. United Nations, Department of Economic and Social Affairs, Population Division (2013). World Population Ageing 2013. ST/ESA/SER.A/348
7. Garcia Lopez, P., Montresor, A., Epema, D., Datta, A., Higashino, T., Iamnitchi, A., Barcellos, M., Felber, P., Riviere, E.: Edge-centric computing: vision and challenges. ACM SIGCOMM Comput. Commun. Rev. **45**(5), 37–42 (2015)
8. Bonomi, F., Milito, R., Zhu, J., Addepalli, S.: Fog computing and its role in the internet of things. In: Proceedings of the 1st edition of the MCC Workshop on Mobile Cloud Computing, pp. 13–16. ACM, August 2012
9. Luan, T.H., Gao, L., Li, Z., Xiang, Y., Wei, G., Sun, L.: Focusing on mobile users at the edge. arXiv preprint arXiv:1502.01815 (2015)

10. Kopetz, H.: Internet of things. In: Kopetz, H. (ed.) Real-Time Systems, pp. 307–323. Springer, USA (2011)
11. Chen, L.W., Ho, Y.F., Kuo, W. T., Tsai, M.F.: Intelligent file transfer for smart handheld devices based on mobile cloud computing. Int. J. Commun. Syst. (2015)
12. Atzori, L., Iera, A., Morabito, G.: The internet of things: a survey. Comput. Netw. **54**(15), 2787–2805 (2010)
13. Kortuem, G., Kawsar, F., Sundramoorthy, V., Fitton, D.: Smart objects as building blocks for the internet of things. IEEE Internet Comput. **14**(1), 44–51 (2010)
14. Kim, J.E., Boulos, G., Yackovich, J., Barth, T., Beckel, C., Mosse, D.: Seamless integration of heterogeneous devices and access control in smart homes. In: 2012 8th International Conference on Intelligent Environments (IE), pp. 206–213. IEEE, June 2012
15. Lara, O.D., Labrador, M.A.: A survey on human activity recognition using wearable sensors. IEEE Commun. Surv. Tutor. **15**(3), 1192–1209 (2013)
16. Balan, R.K., Satyanarayanan, M., Park, S.Y., Okoshi, T.: Tactics-based remote execution for mobile computing. In: Proceedings of the 1st International Conference on Mobile Systems, Applications and Services, pp. 273–286. ACM, May 2003
17. Verissimo, P., Rodrigues, L.: Distributed Systems for System Architects, vol. 1. Springer Science & Business Media, Heidelberg (2012)
18. Botts, M., Robin, A.: OpenGIS sensor model language (SensorML) implementation specification. OpenGIS Implementation Specification OGC, 07–000 (2007)
19. Compton, M., Barnaghi, P., Bermudez, L., Garcia-Castro, R., Corcho, O., Cox, S., Graybeal, J., Hauswirth, M., Henson, C., Herzog, A., Huang, V., Taylor, K.: The SSN ontology of the W3C semantic sensor network incubator group. Web Semant. Sci. Serv. Agents World Wide Web **17**, 25–32 (2012)
20. Nugent, C.D., Finlay, D.D., Davies, R.J., Wang, H.Y., Zheng, H., Hallberg, J., Synnes, K., Mulvenna, M.D.: homeML - an open standard for the exchange of data within smart environments. In: Okadome, T., Yamazaki, T., Makhtari, M. (eds.) ICOST 2007. LNCS, vol. 4541, pp. 121–129. Springer, Heidelberg (2007). doi:10.1007/978-3-540-73035-4_13
21. Haefner, K.: Evolution of Information Processing Systems: An Interdisciplinary Approach for a New Understanding of Nature and Society. Springer Publishing Company, Incorporated, Heidelberg (2011)
22. Perera, C., Zaslavsky, A., Christen, P., Georgakopoulos, D.: Context aware computing for the internet of things: a survey. IEEE Commun. Surv. Tutor. **16**(1), 414–454 (2014)
23. Medina, J., Martinez, L., Espinilla, M.: Subscribing to fuzzy temporal aggregation of heterogeneous sensor streams in real-time distributed environments. Int. J. Commun. Syst. **30**(5) (2017)
24. Medina, J., Espinilla, M., Nugent, C.: Real-time fuzzy linguistic analysis of anomalies from medical monitoring devices on data streams. In: Proceedings of the 10th EAI International Conference on Pervasive Computing Technologies for Healthcare, pp. 300–303. ICST (Institute for Computer Sciences, Social-Informatics and Telecommunications Engineering), May 2016
25. Zadeh, L.A.: Generalized theory of uncertainty (GTU)—principal concepts and ideas. Comput. Stat. Data Anal. **51**(1), 15–46 (2006)
26. Zadeh, L.A.: A prototype-centered approach to adding deduction capability to search engines-the concept of protoform. In: 2002 Annual Meeting of the North American Fuzzy Information Processing Society, Proceedings NAFIPS, pp. 523–525. IEEE (2002)

27. Kacprzyk, J., Zadrony, S.: Linguistic database summaries and their protoforms: towards natural language based knowledge discovery tools. Inf. Sci. **173**(4), 281–304 (2005)
28. Yager, R.R.: On linguistic summaries of data. In: Piatetsky-Shapiro, G., Frawley, B. (eds.) Knowledge Discovery in Databases, pp. 347–363. MIT, Cambridge (1991)
29. Kim, E., Helal, S., Nugent, C., Beattie, M.: Analyzing activity recognition uncertainties in smart home environments. ACM Trans. Intell. Syst. Technol. (TIST) **6**(4), 52 (2015)
30. Krishnan, N.C., Cook, D.J.: Activity recognition on streaming sensor data. Pervasive Mob. Comput. **10**, 138–154 (2014)
31. Shi, H., Chen, N., Deters, R.: Combining mobile and fog computing: using CoAP to link mobile device clouds with fog computing. In: 2015 IEEE International Conference on Data Science and Data Intensive Systems (DSDIS), pp. 564–571. IEEE (2015)
32. Henning, M.: A new approach to object-oriented middleware. IEEE Internet Comput. **8**(1), 66–75 (2004)
33. Nalepa, G.J., Bobek, S.: Rule-based solution for context-aware reasoning on mobile devices. Comput. Sci. Inf. Syst. **11**(1), 171–193 (2014)
34. Mamdani, E.H., Assilian, S.: An experiment in linguistic synthesis with a fuzzy logic controller. International journal of man-machine studies **7**(1), 1–13 (1975)

InMyDay: A Digital Diary to Promote Self-care Among Elders

Marcelo Fernández[1], Iyubanit Rodríguez[2]⊙, Pedro O. Rossel[1]⊙,
Carolina Fuentes[3], and Valeria Herskovic[2](⊠)⊙

[1] Department of Computer Science, Universidad Católica de la Santísima
Concepción, Concepción, Chile
`mafernandeze@ing.ucsc.cl, prossel@ucsc.cl`

[2] Department of Computer Science, Pontificia Universidad Católica de Chile,
Santiago, Chile
`{iyubanit,vherskovic}@uc.cl`

[3] School of Computer Science, University of Nottingham, Nottingham, UK
`carolina.fuentes@nottingham.ac.uk`

Abstract. Diaries allow users to record personal events and experiences, and are frequently used to collect participant data in user studies. Digital diaries have several benefits over traditional paper-based diaries, reducing respondents' burden, administrative costs, and improving navigation. However, for elderly users, there are several challenges in the use of a digital diary: they may have cognitive and motor impairments, and fewer digital skills than other populations. We implemented a digital diary called *InMyDay*, specifically designed for elderly users. The goal of this diary is to promote self-care and self-reflection, by allowing users to register their activities and emotions. Ten elderly users tested the diary for five days, recording entries related to their days and how they felt. All of the participants used the diary every day and after the experiment, nine declared that they would use such an application at least once a week. We found that the diary promoted reflection, that users felt that this allowed them a moment of self-care during their day, and that they felt this was especially important for them as elderly people. Future work will focus on increasing the number of participants and emotions that may be reported and exploring new mechanisms of interaction.

1 Introduction

The world is aging; there will be approximately 2 billion people over 60 years of age by 2050 [1]. The additional burden this will cause on healthcare systems may be offset somewhat by the use of technology in home settings. Technology may be used to monitor, manage and motivate elderly patients in their own care [2]. Self-care is defined as "the ability of individuals, families and communities to promote health, prevent disease, and maintain health and to cope with illness and disability with or without the support of a health-care provider" [3]. Self-care requires self-reflection and it involves strategies that help promote or maintain physical, mental, emotional and spiritual health [4].

© Springer International Publishing AG 2017
S.F. Ochoa et al. (Eds.): UCAmI 2017, LNCS 10586, pp. 486–497, 2017.
DOI: 10.1007/978-3-319-67585-5_49

Technologies for the self-care for elders have been proposed, helping monitor their activities [5] and their health, and remain independent in their own residences [6]. Additionally, health monitoring allows users to reflect on the collected data [6]. However, older adults are not usually involved in the design process of health and wellness applications [7], and their physical and neuro-degenerative limitations [8] may make it necessary to create and design technologies to suit their specific needs.

Diaries are books in which users may record personal events and experiences [9]. Diaries may be used to collect participant data (e.g. in user studies). However, motor problems in some elderly users impede writing, and carrying out challenging tasks interferes with journaling [10]. The use of digital diaries can reduce respondents' burden, administration costs and help the user to more efficiently navigate their digital memories [11]. However, the digital skills required to successfully record information in a digital diary may not be present in some elderly users, and their physical and cognitive limitations may further challenge their use of such a diary.

Therefore, the main research question guiding this research was: *does a digital diary allow older adults to record their activities and reflect on their emotional state?* This paper presents *InMyDay*, a digital diary for self-reporting emotions and daily activities for older adults. The diary was designed iteratively and refined using heuristics specific for elderly adults. To evaluate its use, we recruited 10 adults (over 60 years old), who each used the diary for 5 days and then participated in an interview.

This paper is organized as follows. First, we discuss related work, considering technology that supports self-care and self-reflection. Then, we describe the design and implementation of our prototype. Section 4 describes our methodology, then Sect. 5 describes the results and Sect. 6 shows the discussion. Finally, Sect. 7 presents our conclusions and discusses possible avenues of future work.

2   Related Work

Diary studies, or diary methods, are used to capture information about user experiences in their natural context [12]. For example, diary studies, used in combination with focus groups, have been found to provide a comprehensive view of elders' information [13]. Diaries have been used to record daily activities (e.g. [14]), diseases (e.g. pain [15]), and emotional state (e.g. [16]).

Diaries may be implemented through pen-and-paper, augmented paper or through technological means [12]. Web and mobile application versions have been found to provide better data quality than paper [11], as well as other benefits such as signaling, timestamps, flexibility in question presentation, data entry, management and accuracy, and taking into account the participant's schedule [12]. However, computer literacy, and the need of training for use, are limitations which still endure [12]. Elderly users have been found to prefer touchscreens over RFID-based interaction in a digital agenda [17]. A recent study found elderly users were found to be able to successfully use a digital diary; even though they took a longer time to complete tasks (than on a paper form) and lengthy training may be needed to use the application [18]. However, few diaries have been proposed for the elderly, and generally, older users are not the target of design of mobile applications [19].

Some applications have been proposed to promote specific behaviors. For example, a diary application to control food intake stimulated self-control, behavior change and learning [20]. A reminder system for elderly adults found the importance of establishing a link between the reminder on paper and the reminder system, and then, imitating reminder strategies of users [21]. Diary applications have also been proposed for elderly users with specific impairments, e.g. an audio-based interface for users with visual impairments [22].

One of the challenges of applications that help the self-expression of older adults is that they should include support for reflection, interaction and review of activities [23]. This paper presents the design and evaluation of a digital diary that aims to allow elderly users to reflect on their activities and emotions, keeping a record of them for self-reflection.

3   InMyDay: Design and Implementation of the Digital Diary Application

We designed and implemented a digital diary for tablet devices called "InMy-Day", that allows self-reporting of emotional state and daily activities. The application stores daily entries in a pre-defined format, and these entries can be viewed again by the users. The application was implemented for the Android system, with local data storage.

The diary was adapted from a pen-and-paper version, which consisted of several pages with pre-defined questions about self-care and emotions, e.g. *Did I take care of myself today?*, with options such as: *Food intake: I ate/I did not eat*, and space for participants to explain their choices.

First, we implemented a direct replica of the paper version (Fig. 1(a) and (b)), for a Samsung Galaxy tablet device, trying to preserve as much of the original paper version as possible.

This first digital version incorporated a few features, such as creating an entry for a new day, reviewing past entries, viewing the next/previous pages, and saving the entry (Fig. 1(c)). We reviewed this application using heuristic evaluation, which is a usability assessment method that uses experts in usability to find problems in a system using usability principles [24]. We chose to use heuristics specifically designed to evaluate applications for older adults [25]. One expert conducted the evaluation, finding several problems (e.g. font could not be resized, no auditory response for certain cases, use of high-contrast combination of font and background, no feedback about the success or failure of the save task). The evaluation resulted in several changes: (1) font size and type and interface colors were changed to improve contrast, (2) icons were changed/improved and text was added to explain them, (3) a tutorial was added, (4) improvements in date selection, (5) diary pages were rearranged to improve readability, (6) error

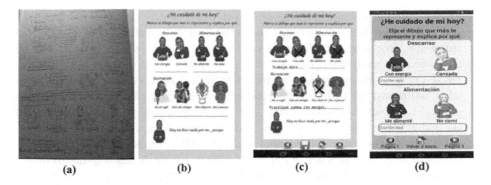

Fig. 1. (a) Initial mockup of diary. (b) Final diary in paper format. (c) InMyDay, first version. (d) InMyDay, final version.

messages were improved, (7) save/delete functions were simplified. The resulting interface is shown in Figs. 1(d) and 2. This interface was evaluated again using heuristic evaluation, finding no further usability problems.

Fig. 2. Final version of *InMyDay* diary application.

4   Methodology

4.1   Data Collection

We collected participant responses from three standard questionnaires, selected to measure digital skills (DIGCOMP), anxiety and depression (GADS) and the usability of the application (SUS). Each instrument is described below:

1. System usability scale (SUS) is a Likert Scale which includes 10 questions and it is quick way to measure the overall usability of the system [26]. In this scale, scores over 80 indicate very good usability, while scores below 60 indicate poor usability [27].
2. DIGCOMP is an instrument to measure digital competences (set of knowledge, skills and attitudes needed today to be functional in a digital environment). Users are categorized into one of four possible groups, according to their digital skill levels: *none, low, basic* or *above basic* [28].
3. Goldberg Anxiety and Depression Scale (GADS) consists of two sub-scales: one of anxiety and another of depression; each sub-scale has 9 items to determine whether or not there is a mental disorder [29].

Information from the use of the diary application was recorded and used for analysis. Participants were interviewed, and the audio from these interviews was recorded and transcribed.

4.2 Participants

Our participants were 10 people (7 women, 3 men) over 60 years (average age: 65, SD: 4.12). Six were married and four were single. None of the participants lived on their own. Each participant signed an inform consent form for participating in the experiment.

Table 1. Description of study participants.

P	Age	G	Occupation	Impairment			Digital skills	Goldberg scale	
				Visual	Auditory	Motor		Anxiety	Depression
P1	68	F	Housewife	•			None		
P2	61	F	Craftswoman	•			Basic	•	•
P3	61	M	Teacher	•	•		Basic	•	•
P4	60	F	Teacher	•	•	•	Above basic	•	•
P5	72	F	Housewife	•	•	•	None		•
P6	66	M	Retired	•	•	•	Above basic	•	•
P7	66	F	Merchant	•			Basic	•	•
P8	63	F	Merchant	•			Above basic	•	
P9	70	M	Retired				Low	•	•
P10	60	F	House cleaner			•	Basic	•	•

Table 1 summarizes our study participants, displaying the age, occupation and gender of each, as well as whether they had visual, auditory or motor impairments (marked as •), their level of digital skills according to the DIGCOMP questionnaire, and whether they had anxiety and/or depression according to the GADS questionnaire (marked as •). Most participants had vision problems, and 7 out of 10 had depression or anxiety.

4.3   Experiment

To evaluate the prototype, each participant used the digital diary for five days, using the tablet device provided by the researchers. First, one researcher gave a brief introduction about the study and its purpose and the participants completed the DIGCOMP test and GADS survey. Then, the diary application was explained and each participant was given the tablet with the application installed and ready to use. The participant interacted with the application during five days in his/her house, with no researcher intervention (see Fig. 3a). On the sixth day, the researcher conducted a brief semi-structured interview to assess user experiences. Finally, participants completed the SUS questionnaire (see Fig. 3b). The evaluation was conducted between December 2016 and January 2017.

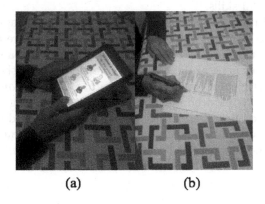

(a)   (b)

Fig. 3. (a) Participant trying out the digital diary application. (b) User filling out evaluation questionnaires.

4.4   Analysis

Interviews and information obtained from diary entries were analyzed using thematic analysis. The thematic map allowed us to see the topics emerge from interviews [30]. Some quotes from participants are provided in the results (translated from Spanish).

5   Results

5.1   InMyDay Usability Evaluation

The average SUS score given to the application was 63.5, which is neither poor nor good. However, we grouped the participants according to their digital skills, to analyze the average SUS score per group. Table 2 shows that, as digital skill levels increase, SUS score increased; i.e., the digital diary is more usable for

Table 2. Participants by digital skills and SUS score.

Digital skills	SUS
None	46.25
Low	57.5
Basic	64.38
Above basic	73.83
Average	**63.5**

people with higher digital competences. Although this is a natural phenomenon, we do believe this means that usability must be improved, especially considering users with low digital skills.

Two main usability problems were mentioned by participants: first, choosing a date (see Fig. 4(a)), because the dates on the calendar were too close to each other, and second, typing in the diary was considered to be a slow process (see Fig. 4(b)), because of general difficulty with keyboards and the size of the keyboard, e.g. one participant stated: *"When writing, I took a long time and could not find the keys"*. People who mentioned difficulty in typing had on average a 43.3 SUS score, and those that mentioned keyboard size had 62.5, while those that did not mention any specific problems gave the application a 82.5 score. We found significant differences between groups *Keyboard typing* and *None* using Student's t-test (level of significance = 0.05).

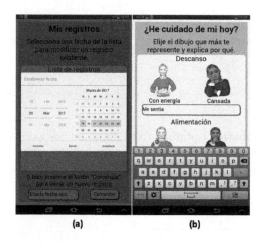

Fig. 4. (a) Choose the date problem. (b) Keyboard typing problem.

Regarding the usefulness of each of the pages of the diary, one section was the least useful. This page listed four emotions which they users could fill out to describe their day (*I laughed because..../I cried because.../I was scared because.../I was angry because...*). Four users commented that the number of options per section should be increased (e.g. *"I thought some options were missing in some pages"*)

All of the participants filled an entry for each of the five days they had the diary. However, as this was what they were asked to do and they may have been filling the diary out of obligation, we asked them in the final interview how often they would use the digital diary if they were able to keep the device. Three participants responded that they would write everyday, three that they would write two times a week or more, three that they would write once a week, and one was unsure. One said: *"I would try to use it every day, because it is very important for us older people"*.

5.2 Supporting Reflective Processes Through Elicitation of Emotions and Activities of Older Adults

All participants mentioned that the digital diary allowed them to reflect on their emotions, specifically mentioning that they reflected more about the activities that they had done and their emotions *"...you made me think about me and dedicate time to myself, which is something I never do... time is for those that surround me"*.

The users effectively wrote about their emotions in the diary. Most entries were about being "happy", especially related to sharing anecdotes, jokes, stories or being with loved ones (e.g. one response was *"I goofed around with my friends at the station"*). However, the participants also shared other types of emotions, such as being scared (*"I thought I had made a serious mistake at work"* or angry (*"Sometimes I get angry when I lose in a card game"*). Five women indicated that they felt alone during the day, two of them on multiple days.

Participants also registered their daily activities, ranging from household chores such as cooking, cleaning and shopping in the mornings, resting, shopping and napping during the afternoons, and watching movies, talking and resting in the evening. Participants who were employed mostly reported being at work and afterwords resting and watching movies or TV in the evenings. The final questions in the diary asked users to reflect on their days (questions "What was the best thing that happened today?" and "These are the final reflections on my day"), and users provided their thoughts and reflections, suggesting self-reflection was happening. Only 10% of responses to the first question were blank, and 22% left the second question blank, suggesting that concrete questions may have better response rates. Users' answers ranged from very brief and noncommittal (e.g. *"Good day"*, *"Typical day"*, *"I think nothing out of the ordinary happened"*) to reflective (*"I would like to go to the countryside and rest"*, *"I can't run around as much anymore"*) and profound (*"It was a tiring day and it reinforced that I don't want to work anymore"*, *"Tiring day but I could manage it when I thought that retirement is not too far away"* - these last two quotes are from two different participants' diaries).

6 Discussion

We created a digital diary with fixed questions and a limited number of emotions that could be reported. Participants used the diary, registering their activities and reflecting on their emotions. Some of the questions prompted reflection more than others, and it seems that asking a concrete question (such as "What was the best thing that happened today?") promoted more participation than more open questions (such as "These are the final reflections on my day"). Participants would have liked more options for reporting emotions, as they felt constrained by the few emotions that the diary held. A model of emotions could be incorporated into a next version of the diary (e.g. [31]). However, more options have to be included carefully, so as not to broaden the diary too much, provoking open questions that users do not feel inspired to answer.

We found responses that were superficial or noncommittal, as well as more profound reflections. Naturally, the participants knew that their diaries would be read by researchers, so many might have held back on expressing their feelings in more depth. However, all but one of the participants would like to write in such a diary at least once a week, so a more private setting for a digital diary may produce deeper reflection.

As a user experience research tool, we found that older adults are able to use digital diaries such as this one, and that special consideration must be taken with the size of the keyboards and the text on the screen. Previous research has shown successful interactions for older adults when paper and digital systems are linked [21]. In our case, the task was completely digital and users had the most difficulty with the tasks that were not easily comparable to paper tasks (e.g. choosing a date on a calendar). An avenue of further exploration of these issues would be to consider older adults using a digital stylus pen to input information, to provide a better reference to the physical world.

The Goldberg Anxiety and Depression Scale was applied in order to correlate its results with the diary data. However, only two participants did not have depression or anxiety, so it was not possible to find relationships between the reported data and these conditions. Although some studies have found that the prevalence of depressive symptoms is lower in older people [32], our study had a high percentage of participants with depression or anxiety.

Our proposal and preliminary evaluation have some limitations that we would like to acknowledge. First, the use of the diary did not focus on a specific context, so it was not possible to determine the motivation of use. Second, the sample of the study is small, so it is not possible to generalize our findings to the general population. Third, we used one set of heuristics to create the diary, but there are several other guidelines for designing interactive systems for elderly persons (e.g. [33,34]), and the variability of impairments that elderly people suffer may make it necessary to design diaries with specific heuristics to cater to these impairments.

7 Conclusion

This paper presented a digital diary for elderly adults to self-report their emotions, and an evaluation of this diary with 10 elderly adults (over 60 years old) in Chile. The digital diary allows to record the emotional state and the activities carried out on a daily basis.

We found that the older adults used the diary to reflect on their emotions, registering positive as well as negative emotions. Several users also provided deep reflections, and since all but one of the participants would like to write in such a diary at least once a week, we believe a more private setting for a digital diary may produce deeper reflection.

The next steps in this research will be to improve the diary, incorporating more possible emotions while maintaining its simplicity and directed questions, and exploring new mechanisms of interaction, such as stylus pens, which may be more familiar to elderly users due to their direct link with their physical counterparts, or voice dictation, which may help users with decreased motor skills. We will also increase the number of participants in future evaluations, to be able to understand users more thoroughly.

Acknowledgments. The artwork was provided by artist Marcela Donoso (http://www.marceladonoso.cl). This project was supported partially by CONICYT-PCHA/Doctorado Nacional/2014-63140077, CONICIT and MICIT Costa Rica PhD scholarship grant, Universidad de Costa Rica and CONICYT/FONDECYT N°1150365 (Chile).

References

1. World Health Organization: The worlds population is rapidly ageing (2017)
2. Coughlin, J.F., Pope, J.E., Ben, R., Leedle, J.: Old age, new technology, and future innovations in disease management and home health care. Home Health Care Manag. Pract. **18**(3), 196–207 (2006)
3. World Health Organization: Self-care in the context of primary health care. Technical report, Report of the Regional Consultation (2009)
4. Mills, J., Chapman, M.: Compassion and self-compassion in medicine: self-care for the caregiver. Aust. Med. J. **9**(8), 87–91 (2016)
5. La, T.T., Valera, A.C., Tan, H.P., Koh, C.: Online detection of behavioral change using unobtrusive eldercare monitoring system. In: Proceedings of the 11th International Conference on Queueing Theory and Network Applications, QTNA 2016, pp. 16:1–16:8. ACM (2016)
6. Caldeira, C., Bietz, M., Vidauri, M., Chen, Y.: Senior care for aging in place: balancing assistance and independence. In: Proceedings of the 2017 ACM Conference on Computer Supported Cooperative Work and Social Computing, CSCW 2017, pp. 1605–1617. ACM (2017)
7. Davidson, J.L., Jensen, C.: What health topics older adults want to track: a participatory design study. In: Proceedings of the 15th International ACM SIGACCESS Conference on Computers and Accessibility, pp. 26:1–26:8. ACM (2013)

8. Li, Q., Luximon, Y.: Older adults and digital technology: a study of user perception and usage behavior. In: Goonetilleke, R., Karwowski, W. (eds.) Advances in Physical Ergonomics and Human Factors. AISC, vol. 489, pp. 155–163. Springer, Cham (2016). doi:10.1007/978-3-319-41694-6_16

9. Ståhl, A., Höök, K., Svensson, M., Taylor, A.S., Combetto, M.: Experiencing the affective diary. Pers. Ubiquit. Comput. **13**(5), 365–378 (2009)

10. Dickinson, A., Arnott, J.L., Prior, S.: Methods for human-computer interaction research with older people. Behav. Inf. Technol. **26**(4), 343–352 (2007)

11. Chatzitheochari, S., Fisher, K., Gilbert, E., Calderwood, L., Huskinson, T., Cleary, A., Gershuny, J.: Using new technologies for time diary data collection: instrument design and data quality findings from a mixed-mode pilot survey. Soc. Indic. Res. (2017). doi:10.1007/s11205-017-1569-5

12. Bolger, N., Davis, A., Rafaeli, E.: Diary methods: capturing life as it is lived. Annu. Rev. Psychol. **54**, 579–616 (2003)

13. Koopman-Boyden, P., Richardson, M.: An evaluation of mixed methods (diaries and focus groups) when working with older people. Int. J. Soc. Res. Methodol. **16**(5), 389–401 (2013)

14. Vrotsou, K., Bergqvist, M., Cooper, M., Ellegård, K.: PODD: a portable diary data collection system. In: Proceedings of the 2014 International Working Conference on Advanced Visual Interfaces (AVI 2014), pp. 381–382. ACM (2014)

15. Lind, L., Karlsson, D., Fridlund, B.: Patients' use of digital pens for pain assessment in advanced palliative home healthcare. Int. J. Med. Inform. **77**(2), 129–136 (2008)

16. Morris, M.E., Kathawala, Q., Leen, T.K., Gorenstein, E.E., Guilak, F., Labhard, M., Deleeuw, W.: Mobile therapy: case study evaluations of a cell phone application for emotional self-awareness. J. Med. Internet Res. **12**(2), e10 (2010)

17. Iglesias, R., de Segura, N.G., Iturburu, M.: The elderly interacting with a digital agenda through an RFID pen and a touch screen. In: Proceedings of the 1st ACM SIGMM International Workshop on Media Studies and Implementations that Help Improving Access to Disabled Users (MSIADU 2009), pp. 63–70. ACM (2009)

18. Courbet, L., Bauchet, J., Rialle, V.: Evaluation of a digital diary for old people living in a retirement. Gerontechnology **15**, 76s (2016)

19. García-Peñalvo, F.J., Conde, M.Á., Matellán-Olivera, V.: Mobile apps for older users – the development of a mobile apps repository for older people. In: Zaphiris, P., Ioannou, A. (eds.) LCT 2014. LNCS, vol. 8524, pp. 117–126. Springer, Cham (2014). doi:10.1007/978-3-319-07485-6_12

20. Hakobyan, L., Lumsden, J., Shaw, R., O'Sullivan, D.: A longitudinal evaluation of the acceptability and impact of a diet diary app. for older adults with age-related macular degeneration. In: Proceedings of the 18th International Conference on Human-Computer Interaction with Mobile Devices and Services, MobileHCI 2016, pp. 124–134. ACM (2016)

21. Williamson, J.R., McGee-Lennon, M., Freeman, E., Brewster, S.: Designing a smartpen reminder system for older adults. In: Proceedings of the CHI 2013 Extended Abstracts on Human Factors in Computing Systems, pp. 73–78. ACM (2013)

22. Brewer, R.N., Cartwright, M., Karp, A., Pardo, B., Piper, A.M.: An approach to audio-only editing for visually impaired seniors. In: Proceedings of the 18th International ACM SIGACCESS Conference on Computers and Accessibility. ASSETS 2016, pp. 307–308. ACM (2016)

23. Brewer, R., Piper, A.M.: "Tell It Like It Really Is": a case of online content creation and sharing among older adult bloggers. In: Proceedings of the 2016 CHI Conference on Human Factors in Computing Systems, pp. 5529–5542. ACM (2016)

24. Nielsen, J.: Finding usability problems through heuristic evaluation. In: Proceedings of the SIGCHI Conference on Human Factors in Computing Systems, CHI 1992, pp. 373–380. ACM (1992)
25. Silva, P.A., Holden, K., Jordan, P.: Towards a list of heuristics to evaluate smartphone apps targeted at older adults: a study with apps that aim at promoting healthand well-being. In: Proceedings of the 48th Hawaii International Conference on System Sciences (HICSS 2015), pp. 3237–3246. IEEE (2015)
26. Brooke, J.: SUS-a quick and dirty usability scale. Usabil. Eval. Ind. **189**(194), 4–7 (1996)
27. Tullis, T., Albert, W.: Measuring the User Experience: Collecting, Analyzing, and Presenting Usability Metrics. Morgan Kaufmann Publishers Inc., San Francisco (2008)
28. Ferrari, A.: Digital competence in practice: an analysis of frameworks. Technical report, Research Centre of the European Commission (2012)
29. Goldberg, D., Bridges, K., Duncan-Jones, P., Grayson, D.: Detecting anxiety and depression in general medical settings. Br. Med. J. **297**(6653), 897–899 (1988)
30. Braun, V., Clarke, V.: Using thematic analysis in psychology. Qual. Res. Psychol. **3**(2), 77–101 (2006)
31. Russell, J.A.: A circumplex model of affect. J. Pers. Soc. Psychol. **39**(6), 1161–1178 (1980)
32. Christensen, H., Jorm, A.F., Mackinnon, A.J., Korten, A.E., Jacomb, P.A., Henderson, A.S., Rodgers, B.: Age differences in depression and anxiety symptoms: a structural equation modelling analysis of data from a general population sample. Psychol. Med. **29**, 325–39 (1999)
33. Jian, C., Shi, H., Schafmeister, F., Rachuy, C., Sasse, N., Schmidt, H., Hoemberg, V., von Steinbüchel, N.: Touch and speech: multimodal interaction for elderly persons. In: Gabriel, J., Schier, J., Van Huffel, S., Conchon, E., Correia, C., Fred, A., Gamboa, H. (eds.) BIOSTEC 2012. CCIS, vol. 357, pp. 385–400. Springer, Heidelberg (2013). doi:10.1007/978-3-642-38256-7_26
34. Nunes, F., Silva, P.A., Cevada, J., Barros, A.C., Teixeira, L.: User interface design guidelines for smartphone applications for people with Parkinson's disease. Univ. Access Inf. Soc. **15**(4), 659–679 (2015)

Human Activity Recognition Using Radial Basis Function Neural Network Trained via a Minimization of Localized Generalization Error

Shuai Zhang[1]([⊠]), Wing W.Y. Ng[2]([⊠]), Jianjun Zhang[2], and Chris D. Nugent[1]

[1] School of Computing and Mathematics, Ulster University, Newtownabbey BT37 0QB, Co. Antrim, Northern Ireland, UK
{s.zhang, cd.nugent}@ulster.ac.uk
[2] School of Computer Science and Engineering, South China University of Technology, Guangzhou 510006, China
wingng@ieee.org, jjzhangscut@gmail.com

Abstract. Human activity recognition is a crucial component of applications in the areas of pervasive computing in healthcare. Human activity recognition approaches which adopt a data-driven approach are challenged by handling uncertainty in the data. These uncertainties arise due to sensor unreliability, natural noise and variance introduced by those performing the underlying activities. In this paper we propose an approach to human activity recognition based on Radial Basis Function Neural Networks (RBFNN) trained via a minimization of Localized Generalization Error in an effort to minimize the effects of uncertainty in the data. The proposed approach minimizes the generalization error taking into consideration both the training error and the stochastic sensitivity measure, which subsequently results in an improved generalization capability and improved tolerance to the uncertainty in the data. The approached developed was evaluated using data collected from the IESim smart environment simulation tool. Eleven activities were performed in a simulated environment, with uncertainty in the data stemming from user variance in completing the activities and the sensor placements in the environment. Classification accuracy of 98.86% was achieved demonstrating that the proposed RBFNN approach is robust to minor differences in unseen samples, many of which are caused by data uncertainty, following training which offers good generalization capability.

Keywords: Human activity recognition · Data uncertainty · Localized generation error · Radial basis function neural network

1 Introduction

Human activity recognition (HAR) involves the automatic recognition of a user's activity in a smart environment using computational methods. HAR is a crucial component of applications in, for example, connected health, ambient assistive living

© Springer International Publishing AG 2017
S.F. Ochoa et al. (Eds.): UCAmI 2017, LNCS 10586, pp. 498–507, 2017.
DOI: 10.1007/978-3-319-67585-5_50

and pervasive computing in healthcare. At the core of the smart environment is the sensor technology. Sensors are used to capture the status of the environment, the movement of users and their interactions with the environment itself. User's activities are therefore reflected by low-level sensor activation data which subsequently provides the fundamental information for the modelling of human activities. HAR models can be used to recognize and interpret activities for the purposes of monitoring health and wellbeing in addition to identifying instances when assistance may be required. Modelling human activities in smart environment is, however, a complex problem which offers a number of key challenges. One of the main challenges is that data obtained from low-level sensors may be unreliable [1], due to sensor tolerances, implications based on battery usage, transmission errors, data management errors or in situations when the sensors are faulty, temperamental or have malfunctioned [2]. Incomplete data may also occur if sensor positioning within the environment precludes a full representation of user behaviour being captured. In addition to the issues surrounding sensor unreliability, users may perform the same activity in different ways which adds further challenges to the modelling process in the form inter-user variance. In a densely sensed environment, sensor activations which are irrelevant to the current activities could also be included in the data collection process. All of these situations are realistic circumstances which the HAR process needs to be resilient of.

For data-driven modelling approaches it is fundamental to be able to handle and accommodate the uncertainties in the data. It has been demonstrated in [3] that there is a strong correlation between the quality of the data and the performance of the HAR models derived from data-driven approaches. Although strategies can be put in place to pre-process the collected data, the processing time to undertake this can be both excessive and labor-intensive. This approach is therefore not necessarily always a viable option. In situations where the size of the activity data collection is small, due to, challenges with data collection and annotation and/or the low frequency of the activity execution, data-driven modelling approaches are compelled to make use of all the available data for the benefit of improved model performance, as the uncertain data samples still have the potential to provide (partially) useful information to the modelling process.

In an effort to address the problem of modelling activities from data with known uncertainties, we propose in this paper a Radial Basis Function Neural Network (RBFNN) model trained by the Localized Generalization Error Model (L-GEM) for the underlying HAR model. The proposed approach minimizes the generalization error by taking consideration of both the training error and the stochastic sensitivity measure, which results in a better generalization capability and improved tolerance to the uncertainty in the data. On one hand, neural networks trained via a minimization of only the training error may result in overfitting the data, that is, the network memorizes the training data and cannot predict well those unseen data with small changes to the training data. On the other hand, the Stochastic Sensitivity Measure (ST-SM) of a neural network provides a quantitative measure on the change of network outputs with respect to perturbations of network inputs. Given two neural networks with the same training error, one would prefer the one with smaller ST-SM value since it is not sensitive to the minor changes to the network inputs and therefore it can handle the uncertainty in the data to some extent. In the literature, the L-GEM approach has had success with its application to a range of different classifiers, for example, multilayer perceptron neural networks [4] and support vector machines [5]. In addition, the L-GEM approach has been proven to be effective to improve feature selection [6] and sample selection [7] problems. In this paper, we focus on the architecture selection for the RBFNN model in order to reach the minimized L-GEM value and its application to HAR modelling with datasets containing known uncertainty.

To facilitate the evaluation of the proposed approach the Open Data Initiative (ODI) [8] was availed of to provide a platform for the objective assessment and comparison of activity recognition solutions. The ODI environment supports the simulation and collection of data with uncertainty and hence can be used to support the evaluation of HAR approaches based on their capability to handle different types and degrees of uncertainties. In this paper, as a case study, we investigated the generalization of the HAR model based on the uncertainty caused by variation in user performance and incomplete data based on sensor placement in the environment.

The remainder of the paper is organized as follows. Section 2 presents the methodology of the proposed HAR approach on RBFNN trained via the minimization of the L-GEM. Section 3 introduces the experimental setup, evaluation results and discussion. It also introduces the IESim environment and the data collection process. Evaluation and results are discussed and comparisons are made with a number of HAR models. Section 4 concludes the paper with the potential opportunities for further systematic evaluations.

2   Methodology

In this section, we first introduce the concept of the L-GEM. Then we introduce the quantitative measure on the change of network outputs with respect to perturbations of network inputs by using the Stochastic Sensitivity Measure (ST-SM) with the RBFNN. Finally, we choose the architecture and the optimal parameters for the RBFNN which minimizes the L-GEM, as the selected output model.

2.1   Localized Generalization Error Model (L-GEM)

The upper bound of a classifier's generalization error can be defined by the L-GEM [3, 9], on unseen data samples which are similar to the training data. Unseen data which have low similarity to the training data are not relevant in the L-GEM approach. The generalization capability of a classifier on the samples from an untrained area is not considered to be meaningful and may even been seen as being counterproductive. The training error (R_{emp}) of a classifier is defined as follows:

$$R_{emp} = \frac{1}{N} \sum_{b=1}^{N} (F(x_b) - f(x_b))^2 \tag{1}$$

where $F(x_b), f(x_b)$ denotes the target output on the training sample x_b and the output of the classifier, respectively. N is the number of training samples in the dataset.

A Q-neighborhood is defined in (2) for a training sample x_b to include all unseen samples located near x_b:

$$S_Q(x_b) = \{x | x = x_b + \Delta x, |\Delta x_i| \leq Q, i = 1, 2, \ldots, n\} \tag{2}$$

where n and Δx_i denote the number of features and the perturbation of the ith input feature respectively. The Q-union (S_Q) is formed by the union of all Q-neighborhoods. The L-GEM then computes the upper bound of the generalization error of a given classifier for all unseen samples in S_Q.

For a given Q, the L-GEM is defined as follows:

$$R_{SM}(Q) = \int_{S_Q} (F(x) - f(x))^2 p(x) dx \tag{3}$$

where $p(x)$ denotes the unknown probability density function of x in S_Q.

By applying the Hoeffdings inequality, with probability $1 - \eta$, we have:

$$R_{SM}(Q) \leq \left(\sqrt{R_{emp}} + \sqrt{E_{S_Q}\left((\Delta y)^2\right)} + A \right)^2 + \varepsilon = R_{SM}^*(Q) \tag{4}$$

where $\varepsilon = B\sqrt{\ln \eta / (-2m)}$, A, B, and $E_{S_Q}\left((\Delta y)^2\right)$ denote the maximum output difference of the target outputs, the maximum possible value of the training error, and the stochastic sensitivity measure (ST-SM) of the output differences, respectively. $\sqrt{R_{emp}}$ is calculated using Eq. (1) for each output node. In general, $A = B = 1$ for classification with [0, 1] outputs. The ST-SM is defined as the expectation of the squared differences between outputs of the training samples and unseen samples within their Q-neighborhood ($\Delta y = f(x_b + \Delta x) - f(x_b)$):

$$E_{S_Q}\left((\Delta y)^2\right) = \frac{1}{m} \sum_{b=1}^{m} E\left[(f(x_b + \Delta x) - f(x_b))^2\right] \tag{5}$$

2.2 Stochastic Sensitivity Measure (ST-SM) for RBFNN

The RBFNN model is proposed for the HAR task given its advantage of fast training and its capability of universal approximation given enough hidden neurons. It has been proved that RBFNN with one hidden layer is capable of universal function approximation [17]. An RBFNN can be described as

$$f(x) = \sum_{j=1}^{M} w_j \exp\left(\frac{||x - u_j||^2}{-2v_j^2}\right) = \sum_{j=1}^{M} w_j \phi_j(x) \tag{6}$$

where M, w_j, u_j, and v_j denote the number of hidden neurons, the connection weight between the jth hidden neuron and the output neuron, the center vector and the width of the jth RBFNN hidden neuron, respectively.

The Stochastic Sensitivity Measure (ST-SM) of a neural network provides a quantitative measure on the change of network outputs with respect to perturbations of network inputs. Intuitively, it measures how sensitive the network output is to the input change. In [3, 9], both inputs and weights are not required to be independently identically distributed and allowed to have their own mean and variance. Moreover, perturbations to inputs and weights are allowed to be arbitrary. Hence, perturbed samples (x) can be considered as unseen samples located around the training samples (x_b). In this work, we assume that inputs are independent and not identically distributed while weight perturbations are not considered. So, the ith input feature has its own expectation μ_{x_i} and variance $\sigma_{x_i}^2$. The input perturbation of the ith input feature is a random variable having a uniform distribution with zero mean and a variance of $\sigma_{\Delta x_i}^2$. After training, centers and widths of the hidden neurons and connection weights are fixed.

Let u_{ji} denote the ith input feature of the center of the jth hidden RBF neuron $\left(u_j = (u_{j1}, \ldots, u_{jn})'\right)$, $p(\Delta x)$ denote the probability density function of the input perturbations which are uniformly distributed in the Q-neighborhood, i.e. $p(\Delta x) = 1/(2Q)^n$. For uniformly distributed input perturbations, we have $\sigma_{\Delta x_i}^2 = \frac{(2Q)^2}{12} = Q^2/3$. Theoretically, we do not restrict the magnitudes of input perturbations as long as the variance of the input perturbation $\left(\sigma_{\Delta x_i}^2\right)$ is finite. Nevertheless, uniform distribution is assumed here because all unseen samples should have an equal chance of occurrence without any prior knowledge on the distribution of unseen samples around the training samples.

By the law of large numbers, when the number of input features is not too low, $\phi_j(x)$ would have a log-normal distribution when n is not too small. Hence, the ST-SM of a RBRFNN ST-SM is given by [9]:

$$E_{S_Q}\left((\Delta y)^2\right) = \frac{1}{3}Q^2 \sum_{j=1}^{M} \gamma_j + \frac{0.2}{9}Q^4 n \sum_{j=1}^{M} \xi_j \tag{7}$$

where $\xi_i = \varphi_j/v_j^4$ and $\gamma_j = \varphi_j\left(\sum_{i=1}^{n}\left(\sigma_{x_i}^2 + (\mu_{x_i} - u_{ji})^2\right)/v_j^4\right)$. γ_j is defined by $\gamma_j = \varphi_j\left(\sum_{i=1}^{n}\left(\sigma_{x_i}^2 + (\mu_{x_i} - u_{ji})^2\right)/v_j^4\right)$. φ_j is defined by $\varphi_j = (w_j)^2 exp((Var(s_j)/2v_j^4) - (E(s_j)/v_j^2))$, where $E(\Delta)$ and $Var(\Delta)$ denotes the expectation operator and the variance operator, respectively, and s_j is given by $s_j = ||x - u_j^2||$.

In this study, each activity is pre-defined by a sequence of key tasks, which are captured by 21 sensors. The status of these sensors, activated or deactivated, form a 21-Dimensional feature vector which is then used to train the RBFNN.

2.3   Finding Optimal RBFNN Using R^*_{SM}

The ultimate goal of RBFNN training is to find the set of parameters such that the trained RBFNN yields the minimum generalization error. After fixing the number of hidden neurons (M), centers and widths of hidden neurons can be found by off-the-shelf k-means clustering while the connection weights are determined by a least square method after centers and widths are fixed. Therefore, the RBFNN training can be simplified to the problem of finding optimal M for RBFNN yielding the minimum L-GEM value (R^*_{SM}) among choices. In this section, we propose a new technique based on R^*_{SM} to find the optimal number of hidden neurons which makes use of the generalization capability of the RBFNN. By fixing Q, the optimization problem is defined as follows:

$$\min R^*_{SM}(Q) \tag{8}$$

For a given training dataset, a fixed Q defines a fixed Q-union around training samples. Therefore, the RBFNN yielding a smaller R^*_{SM} means a better generalization capability for unseen samples located in the Q-union. The Q value defines the maximum difference between unseen samples under consideration and the training samples. As Q increases, more samples are located within the Q-neighborhood which may lead to a larger $R^*_{SM}(Q)$ value since more dissimilar samples are included in the Q-union, and a classifier with a very large $R^*_{SM}(Q)$ upper bound may not be meaningful. Nevertheless, as Q decreases, a large portion of unseen samples may be located outside the Q-union, meaning that these samples are dissimilar to the training samples. In this case, one may consider revising the training data to include more such data and retrain the classifier, since one may not expect a classifier to perfectly classify unseen samples that are totally different from the training data. Usually $Q = 0.1$ which means a 10% maximum difference for input range [0, 1] yields a good performance. The Q value provides a geometric meaning given a dataset.

The optimization problem (8) is solved using the following algorithm.

(1) Start with M equals to the number of classes;
(2) Train an RBFNN with M hidden neurons;
(3) Compute the $R^*_{SM}(Q)$ value for the trained RBFNN;
(4) If $M < N$, $M = M + 1$ and go to step 2.

3   Experimental Setup and Results

In this Section, we briefly introduce the dataset for the evaluation. The results attained by the proposed RBFNN model is presented followed by the comparison and discussion with performance by other models previously considered within the remit of ODI.

3.1 IESim Environment and Data Collection

IESim is a simulation tool which can be used to produce a simulated sensorized environment to facilitate and capture user engagement [8]. The tool simulates the design and implementation of a real sensorized environment with multiple sensors positioned in the simulation environment and objects. User's engagement with the simulated environment is captured through use of an avatar. Relevant data from the user interaction is captured and stored in multiple formats to suit different requirements for differing data analytics modules. The dataset used for the evaluation of the proposed approach was generated from a study protocol with a designed simulated environment. The environment consists of five rooms with 21 sensors to capture a range of targeted activities being undertaken. Figure 1 provides the list of activities of interest and the layout for the simulation environment. A total number of eight users participated in the study for data collection on all the pre-defined activities and each user repeated the performance seven times each. A data set was generated from this with a total of 616 sensor activations.

Activity 1 – Go to Bed
Activity 2 – Use Toilet
Activity 3 – Watch TV
Activity 4 – Prepare Breakfast
Activity 5 – Take Shower
Activity 6 – Leave House
Activity 7 – Get Cold Drink
Activity 8 – Get Hot Drink
Activity 9 – Prepare Dinner
Activity 10 – Get Dressed
Activity 11 – Use Telephone

(a)

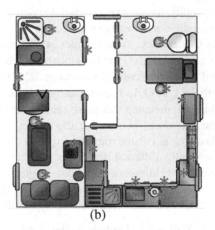

(b)

Fig. 1. (a) List of pre-defined activities (b) the simulation environment in IESim for data collection, where the red stars represent sensors placements [10].

The detailed proposal of the dataset used in the study can be found in [8]. The data collection contains uncertainty caused from a number of aspects [10]. These include cases of incorrect self-annotation on the data, the effects of which resulted in sensor events being assigned to either the previous or following activity which created uncertainty in the collected data sets. In addition, on a small number of occasions, participants skipped sub-tasks within the activities they were completing, which also had an effect on the quality of the data. In situations where a sensor with prolonged activation was utilized for a particular activity, the activation was sometimes incorrectly recorded in the performance of the following activity. Also, the data collected exhibited high variance in the patterns for the same activity between different users.

3.2 Evaluation Results and Discussion

The evaluation of the proposed approach was compared against two other Neural Network models, a Multi-Layered Perceptron (MLP) which achieved the best performance for HAR compared with a range of other models (as previously reported in [10]) and a Deep Neural Network [10] given its popularity and success in other application domains, including computer vision [11], speech recognition [12] and natural language processing [13] using the simulated data. In total, n = 308 data were generated where 220 were used for training and 88 for testing.

In the previous study [10], the MLP model achieved the highest classification accuracy of 97.72%, presented in Table 1, compared to other HAR models based on a fuzzy linguistic approach [14], a Dynamic Instance Activation (DIA) approach which is a generalized version of the Dynamic Rule Activation approach [15]. Experimental results in Table 1 show that the proposed RBFNN model trained by the L-GEM outperforms the MLP and the deep neural network. The potential of the deep neural network, unfortunately, has not been shown by its performance in this study. One of the fundamental factors to the success of deep learning approaches in general is the availability of large amounts of data for training. There are a large number of parameters to be learned in the given network as a result of the complexity of the network structure. The size of the training data ($n = 220$) could be insufficient for this deep neural network to achieve its optimal performance given the size of parameters required for training. The MLP model is trained well by minimizing only the training error which may lead to overfitting. In contrast, the RBFNN trained via the minimization of the L-GEM makes use of both the training error and the stochastic sensitivity measure. The trained RBFNN learns well from training samples (min. training error) and is not sensitive to change in inputs (min. ST-SM). There was only one misclassification made which was on the data of Activity 6 'Leave house' being misclassified as Activity 5 'Take shower'. As a result, the trained RBFNN has demonstrated that is robust to minor differences in future unseen samples with respect to training samples which leads to its good generalization capability.

Table 1. Classification accuracies of the different models on the supplied unseen test dataset.

Models	ANN	Deep NN	RBFNN_LGEM
Classification accuracy (%)	97.72	96.59	98.86

4 Conclusion and Future Work

Given the challenge of handling data uncertainty in HAR, this paper has demonstrated the importance of the generalization capacity of HAR models on their prediction performances. The RBFNN model minimizes the generalization error taking consideration of both the training error and the stochastic sensitivity measure, which results in better generalization capability and improved tolerance to the uncertainty in the data. The performance of the RBFNN model proposed is superior to a wide range of previous tested HAR approaches within the remit of the ODI. As a case study, the evaluation of the RBFNN model was evaluated on data uncertainty from a limited number of scenarios. In future work, the IESim environment will be utilized to further facilitate systematic evaluations of HAR models on handling and accommodating sensor uncertainties from faulty or malfunctioning sensors. In addition, the RBFNN model will be evaluated using other activity datasets in the literature.

Acknowledgements. This work was supported by both the Research Challenge Fund by Ulster University, the National Natural Science Foundation of China under Grant 61572201 and the Fundamental Research Funds for the Central Universities (2017ZD052). Invest Northern Ireland is acknowledged for partially supporting this project under the Competence Centre Programs Grant RD0513853 – Connected Health Innovation Centre.

References

1. Ranganathan, A., Al-Muhtadi, J., Campbell, R.H.: Reasoning about uncertain contexts in pervasive computing environments. IEEE Pervasive Comput. 3(2), 62–70 (2004)
2. Hong, X., Nugent, C., Mulvenna, M., McClean, S., Scotney, B., Devlin, S.: Evidential fusion of sensor data for activity recognition in smart homes. Pervasive Mobile Comput. 5(3), 236–252 (2009)
3. Nugent, C.D., Synnott, J., Gabrielli, C., Zhang, S., Espinilla, M., Calzada, A., Lundstrom, J., Cleland, I., Synnes, K., Hallberg, J., Spinsante, S.: Improving the quality of user generated data sets for activity recognition. In: Ubiquitous Computing and Ambient Intelligence: 10th International Conference, UCAmI 2016, Gran Canaria, Spain, 2016, Part II 10, pp. 104–110
4. Yeung, D.Y., Li, J.C., Ng, W.W.Y., Chan, P.P.K.: MLPNN training via a multiobjective optimization of training error and stochastic sensitivity. IEEE Trans. Neural Netw. Learn. Syst. 27(5), 978–992 (2016)
5. Sun, B.B., Ng, W.W.Y., Chan, P.P.K.: Improved sparse LSSVMs based on the localized generalization error model. Int. J. Mach. Learn. Cybern. (2016)
6. Ng, W.W.Y., Yeung, D.S., Firth, M., Tsang, E.C.C., Wang, X.Z.: Feature selection using localized generalization error for supervised classification problems using RBFNN. Pattern Recogn. 41(12), 3706–3719 (2008)
7. Ng, W.W.Y., Hu, J.J., Yeung, D.S., Yin, S.H., Roli, F.: Diversified sensitivity-based undersampling for imbalance classification problems. IEEE Trans. Cybernet. 45(11), 2402–2412 (2015)
8. Synnott, J., Chen, L., Nugent, C.D., Moore, G.: The creation of simulated activity datasets using a graphical intelligent environment simulation tool. In: Engineering in Medicine and Biology Society (EMBC), Chicago, IL, USA, pp. 4143–4146 (2014)
9. Yeung, D.S., Ng, W.W.Y., Wang, D.F., Tsang, E.C.C., Wang, X.Z.: Localized generalization error model and its application to architecture selection for radial basis function neural network. IEEE Trans. Neural Netw. 18(5), 1294–1305 (2007)
10. Synnott, J., Nugent, C.D., Zhang, S. Calzada, A., Cleland, I., Espinilla, M., Quero, J.M., Lundstrom, J.: Environment simulation for the promotion of the open data initiative. In: IEEE International Conference on Smart Computing (SMARTCOMP), St. Louis, Missouri, pp. 1–6 (2016)
11. Lee, H., Grosse, R., Ranganath, R., Ng, A.Y.: Convolutional deep belief networks for scalable unsupervised learning of hierarchical representations. In: Proceedings of the 26th International Conference on Machine Learning, Montreal, QC, Canada, pp. 609–616 (2009)

12. Hinton, G., Deng, L., Yu, D., Dahl, G.E., Mohamed, A.R., Jaitly, N., Senior, A., Vanhoucke, V., Nguyen, P., Sainath, T.N., Kingsbury, B.: Deep neural networks for acoustic modeling in speech recognition: the shared views of four research groups. IEEE Signal Process. Mag. **29**(6), 82–97 (2012)

13. Collobert, R., Weston, J.: A unified architecture for natural language processing: deep neural networks with multitask learning. In: Proceedings of the 25th International Conference on Machine learning, Helsinki, Finland, pp. 160–167 (2008)

14. Mikut, R., Jäkel, J., Gröll, L.: Interpretability issues in data-based learning of fuzzy systems. Fuzzy Sets Syst. **150**(2), 179–197 (2005)

15. Calzada, A., Liu, J., Wang, H., Kashyap, A.: A new dynamic rule activation method for extended belief rule-based systems. IEEE Trans. Knowl. Data Eng. **27**(4), 880–894 (2015)

16. Ordóñez, F.J., Roggen, D.: Deep convolutional and LSTM recurrent neural networks for multimodal wearable activity recognition. Sensors **16**(1), 115 (2016)

17. Park, J., Sandberg, I.W.: Universal approximation using radial-basis-function networks. Neural Comput. **3**(2), 246–257 (1991)

Formal Specification for Ambient Assisted Living Scenarios

Hubert Kenfack Ngankam[1]([✉]), Hélène Pigot[1], Marc Frappier[2],
Camila H. Oliveira[1], and Sylvain Giroux[1]

[1] Laboratoire Domus, Université de Sherbrooke,
Sherbrooke, Québec J1K 2R1, Canada
{Hubert.Kenfack.Ngankam,Helene.Pigot,Camila.oliveira,
Sylvain.Giroux}@usherbrooke.ca
[2] Laboratoire GRIL, Université de Sherbrooke,
Sherbrooke, Québec J1K 2R1, Canada
Marc.Frappier@usherbrooke.ca
https://www.usherbrooke.ca/domus/

Abstract. Formal specifications are used to prove software correctness in a critical system. Ambient Assisted Living (AAL) technologies require unambiguous and precise requirements as they provide critical services for home monitoring. Several AAL technologies have already been designed using scenario-driven approach. But most of them do not precise how to ensure the correctness and conformity of the scenario related to end-user specifications. The multidisciplinary requirements brought by the design team and the assistance to the elderly need a rigorous mechanism for validating and specifying assistance scenarios. In this article, we propose a formal specification approach for scenario construction in the context of AAL technologies. We explain how to instantiate any scenario from the modeled specification, and give some results obtained by using the Alloy language and its validation module. We present a case study applied to nighttime wandering scenario.

Keywords: Ambient Assisted Living · Ubiquitous computing · Formal specification · Scenario · Task model

1 Introduction

Ambient Intelligence refers to a vision of the future information society where smart application enables people and devices to interact together and with the environment. Following this approach, it becomes possible to develop a quiet and non-intrusive technology integrated into the environment to support assistance to aging in place. The home environment becomes smart and responsive to users through pervasive computing. **A**mbient **A**ssisted **L**iving (AAL) technologies allow people to perform activities of daily living despite cognitive and physical deficits occurring during aging. The development of assistance to help

© Springer International Publishing AG 2017
S.F. Ochoa et al. (Eds.): UCAmI 2017, LNCS 10586, pp. 508–519, 2017.
DOI: 10.1007/978-3-319-67585-5_51

elderly participating in their daily activities requires the user to be at the center of the assistance design.

In this context, the design of AAL technologies demands the involvement of all stakeholders for coping with several expertise. The user-centered design favors this involvement by allowing the end users and their relatives to express their needs, and the medical experts to precise how cognitive and physical deficits impact on the daily life activities. Expertise between medical staff and scientists are shared to determine the data to gather in the home and the assistance to provide for fostering autonomy. To cover all the needs expressed by the AAL technologies, the different experts need an iterative and inclusive process that allows each stage of the senior's assistance process to be expressed. Thus, an assistance scenario to the elderly describes the behaviors of the system, the user, the environment and the sequences of tasks performed by the user and the system to meet a goal.

This paper has a dual purpose:

1. To propose a scenario-driven multi-layered architecture to take into account the requirements of the multidisciplinary approach, which allows the construction of a precise scenario of assistance to the elderly in a user-centered design process.
2. To formalize the creation of assistance scenarios and validate their conformity by successive refinements whenever they change.

The use of the Alloy's Analyzer, modeling language allows to determine incremental simulations to check in logic clauses if specifications remain correct when scaling [1]. It helps to clarify the requirements of multidisciplinary approach and develop several assistance scenarios to satisfy these requirements. Finally, we applied this approach to develop several assistance scenarios to foster elderly autonomy.

The rest of this article is divided into six sections. Section 2 explores the related work done in AAL technologies and scenario-driven approaches. Section 3 describes the need for a formal specification model when using scenario-driven approach. Section 4 describes how to use Alloy language to design and validate scenarios to facilitate aging in place. Section 5 shows a concrete use of the implementation of the formal specifications applied to the nighttime wandering scenario and its representation in a hierarchical model. Section 6 concludes this document.

2 Related Work

AAL technologies are characterized by the fact that the profile of the assisted people evolves over time. Therefore, the chosen approach to build AAL technologies should be able to focus on semantic, be adaptive to elderly evolution and allow an iterative refinement of the specification. AAL technologies complexity and the critical aspects regarding the objectives and the user's fragilities require rigorous, precise and unambiguous approach to satisfy the needed assistance.

Several efforts have been made to ensure these constraints [4–8]. However, they do not offer user-centered management mechanisms, and they are little or badly understood by other members of the team.

The scenario-driven approach describes the different interactions of people and their activities. It emphasizes the description of a typical usage situation, the purpose, the actions and the objects concerned, and leaves aside the constraints related to the interface. It presents possible ways to use a system to accomplish some desired functions. It allows an interactive design of the system and rapid communication between several different actors. It is easier to write a story in the form of a script and to enrich it as new demands emerge. Hence, the scenario-driven and the use cases approaches are sometimes favored [3]. They offer the possibility for all team members to share the same level of understanding and to express their needs in a rigorous way. Generally, use cases are organized around a semi-formal method, UML [3]. UML has a well defined syntax that is easily readable by computer scientists, although less understandable by other specialists. The practice and understanding of UML go through a mandatory phase of learning the concepts of the language. This learning phase is not obvious for non-computer actors. Therefore, UML is not always the better choice for a user-centered multidisciplinary design process.

To address expertises issues, the assistance scenarios are expressed as a schema translated into formal specifications. A formal specification is a logical expression, in a formal language consisting of a collection of properties that some system should satisfy. To facilitate the reading of the scenarios, the different stakeholders share a common representation in a hierarchical form, where a scenario is made up of tasks and sub-tasks. The scenario-based approach increases the involvement of users and non-experts in the process of creating scenarios that meet the specifications of the elderly. As soon as a new need appears, it is taken into account in the scenario and validated by all the members of the team. The use of scenario-based approach reduces complexity by taking each aspect of the problem, decomposing them it into a task, and indicating for each task the constraints of satisfactions as preconditions, post-conditions or goal to be reached. The scenario-driven approach is more appropriate in the construction of cognitive assistance solutions. Writing scenarios for various perspectives (user, system and clinical) allows each stakeholder to express and represent various information, which meets the AAL requirements.

3   The Requirements of User-Centered Scenario-Based Approach in AAL

Most applications in AAL involve multiple stakeholders who participate in the design process for providing an expected assistance. They include computer scientists, ergonomists, engineers, home automation specialists, occupational therapists, gerontologists, nursing aides, caregivers and the elderly. Participatory and user-centered design is generally used to consider the requirements of each area of expertise [10]. In traditional AAL technologies only computer scientists access and control the specifications emerging from user needs as shown in Fig. 1. It is then difficult for the other stakeholders of the team to understand the new transformations following new needs emerging as the design process unfolds. This situation is likely to slow down treatments and to introduce a mistakes. Thus, a scenario-based approach is used to describe the provided assistance. This approach makes it possible to describe in a simple way the different stages, conditions, and tools necessary for the implementation of the desired assistance. It helps all stakeholders to better understand the requirements of each area of expertise. In addition, the use of a scenario-based approach reduces complexity in the design process by taking each aspect of the problem, decomposing it into a task, indicating for each task the constraints of satisfactions and accessibility. Insofar as it allows to focus on the main functional aspects of the assistance to be specified, the scenario-driven approach is more appropriate in the construction of cognitive assistance scenarios.

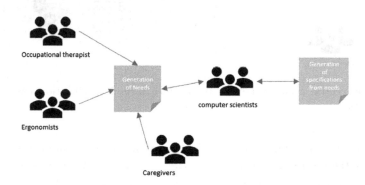

Fig. 1. Standard model to produce specifications based on user requirements

However, as stated in [9], although scenario-based approaches are becoming ubiquitous in systems analysis and design, they remain vague in definition and scope. Indeed, current practices in designing AAL technologies show a lack of structuring, managing, and developing process in how they will be used in diverse contexts. The use of formal specifications requires a rigorous approach to provide better understanding of the AAL technologies design for assistance in daily living activities. The following section shows the elements that characterize a scenario and the conditions for its construction.

3.1   Scenario Modeling Specification Requirements

This work proposes a user-centered approach in which all stakeholders share a common access to the description and transformation of the AAL requirements. In the proposed architecture the different stakeholders are organized around the representation of the scenario Sect. 3.1. All the stakeholders have access to add or modify a scenario. The underlying formal specifications ensure the validation and conformity of the evolution. Validation is a process used to comprehensively verify that the functional specifications of a given system remain consistent and do not lead to ambiguity. Conformity is defined here in terms of compliance with AAL technologies requirements (Fig. 2).

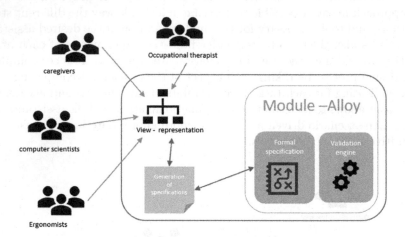

Fig. 2. User-centric scenario models to produce formal specification based on user requirements

The scenario modeling requires that the following constraints should be met to consider the requirements related to the satisfaction of the user needs:

Representation of knowledge: The scenario allows to share various expertises brought by the interdisciplinary team members. This non-technical knowledge is most often presented as a tree of actions to be done. Scenarios are iteratively constructed during a brainstorming session.

Federate the different stakeholders: Several sub objectives are met during the design process. The scenario approach allows each stakeholder to clearly specify and share the requirements while keeping in mind the final objective.

Stay focused: The scenario approach and its hierarchical representation help to focus on a specific task rather than a global view of the solution.

Concrete specification: Concrete hierarchical models representation are clearer, easier to understand than flat ones. The description of user assistance is easily expressed by instances corresponding to their needs. This approach makes it possible to move quickly from an abstract model to a concrete model and vice versa.

Complexity: A need can be translated into a basic set of tasks to be undertaken to satisfy the required assistance. Each task is analyzed individually during the process. This makes it possible to construct several sets of trees that can nest on the task to produce new scenarios.

To analyze and represent an assistance scenario, we rely on the **H**ierarchical **T**ask **A**nalysis (HTA) models. HTA was developed to overcome the limitation of the classical time-and-motion methods in analyzing complex non-repetitive cognitively loaded tasks [11]. Several studies show that these models can be adapted to the activities of daily living. The modeling and representation of a scenario is inspired on the **C**oncurrent **T**ask **T**ree (CTT) model [12], a support for developing and analyzing task models. Our formal specifications are based on the following definitions of a scenario.

1. A scenario is a tree decomposed into a goal(root), several tasks (internal nodes) and action (sheets).
2. The goal is the state of satisfaction to be achieved.
3. The tasks are the decomposition of the steps to be taken to achieve the goal.
4. A task may be decomposed into subtasks.
5. No decomposition into a single subtask is allowed.
6. Subtasks issued from the same parent are considered as siblings and are linked by an operator. The operator is specified by the parent.
7. Preconditions and postconditions are associated to a subtask.
8. A task can be performed by one or more users.
9. Decomposition ends when a subtask is considered as an elementary task.
10. An elementary task is considered as an action.
11. Each elementary task can be decomposed into physical and computer action, comprehensible by a program, or associated with a set of sensors or effectors.
12. The actions describe the interactions between the user and the objects in that location.

The following section describes how the various requirements of a scenario are written in formal specifications using Alloy.

4   Formal Scenario Specification Using Alloy

The approach of scenario-driven development is combined with an object-oriented logical language to formalize the definition of various needed assistance. The aim of our solution is to enable the stakeholders to understand the other members of the team during the design process. The approach provides specifications in accordance with the assistance needs, and guarantees, by formal validation, that each instance is accurate. Formal specifications are used for designing, validating, documenting, communicating, re-engineering, and reusing solutions [13]. A large number of tools have been designed to allow the verification of specifications. Among them we have chosen Alloy [1]. Alloy is a language that captures the essence of software abstractions simply and succinctly. It performs fully automatic analysis and can expose the subtlest flaws. Alloy was also chosen because, it produces an abstract model of a system, making it much easier to evolve, or expand in the future. Thus, Alloy can ensure that new modifications of a system are compatible with its original specification. It can be used before, during and between the design stage, and during the implementation stage.

4.1   Scenario Specification Using Alloy

An Alloy specification is based on signatures. A signature is similar to a class in object-oriented programming languages, as it declares a set of objects with their attributes. However, a signature does not contain methods. An Alloy specification is essentially a set of facts regarding objects of a signature. Figure 3 show the signatures of the specification of our scenario-driven approach. The keyword sig introduces the declaration of a signature.

```
module scenarios

sig User{}
sig Room{}
sig Furniture{}
sig Operator{}
sig Condition{}

enum TaskType {abstractTask, interactionTask, systemTask, userTask}

abstract sig Task{
    taskType : TaskType,
    user : set User,
    parent : lone CompositeTask,
    precondition : some Condition,
    postcondition : some Condition
}

sig CompositeTask extends Task{
    operator : one Operator
}
```

```
sig Action extends Task{
    room : one Room,
    furniture : set Furniture
}

one sig Goal extends CompositeTask {} {
    no parent
}

fact {
    // All tasks are reachable from Goal
    Task in Goal.*~parent
    // Action are not abstract
    not (abstractTask in Action.taskType)
    //No decomposition into one element is permitted
    all s: CompositeTask |  #(s.(~parent)) > 1 or  #(s.(~parent)) = 0
    //The goal is always an abstract type
    Goal.taskType = abstractTask
    //All tasks except Goal have a parent
    all s: Task-Goal | one s.parent
}

assert acyclic {
    // No cycle
    no s: Task | s in s.^(~parent)
}
```

Fig. 3. Formal specification and facts describing a scenario

Signatures User, Room, Furniture, Operator and Condition contain no attribute definition, meaning that they mainly serve to define basic types used in other signatures. A Task of a scenario is specified by an abstract signature from which a CompositeTask and an Action inherit. An action is distinguished from a subtask by the fact that rooms and furnitures are specified. The enum keyword introduces a signature TaskType and enumerates its elements. It allows us to define the type of attribute taskType of a task. The signature Goal, which inherits from CompositeTask, is decorated with keyword one; it indicates that it contains only one object. The value of attribute user of an object of Task is a set; that denotes the users involved in the task. Attribute parent defines that each task has at most one parent, as indicated with the keyword lone. The task Goal has no parent, as indicated by the constraint no parent. An attribute is represented in Alloy by a binary relation. For instance, attribute parent is a subset of the Cartesian product Task × CompositeTask. Alloy provides several operators on relations, like "~", which denotes the inverse of a relation.

4.2   Specifying Constraints on Signatures and Attributes Using Facts

Facts, introduced by the keyword fact, are constraints that must be satisfied by an *instance* of the specification, *i.e*, a set of values for the signatures and their attributes. Several facts have been defined to express the constraints to be respected by the scenario-driven approach as shown in Fig. 3. The first fact states that all tasks are reachable from the root of a scenario, which is given by task instance Goal. It is expressed using operator ".", which denotes the composition of two relations, and also stands for accessing the value of an attribute. Operator "* " denotes the reflexive-transitive closure of a binary relation. Thus, the expression "Goal.*~parent" denotes all tasks that can be reached from instance Goal using the inverse of the parent relation (*i.e*, the subtasks of a task). Keyword all denotes universal quantification of first-order logic. Operator "#" returns the cardinality of a set. Thus, the third fact in Fig. 3 states that each composite task has either no subtask or more than one subtask. Keyword one is a predicate that checks that a set contains only one element.

Facts validation

Finding an instance of a specification allows checking that the facts and constraints of a specification are consistent, *i.e*, there are no contradiction in the facts of the model. This amounts to finding an instance of the specification for which each fact holds. The command "run for n" search for the existence of an instance of the specification with at most n objects in each signature, which is called a *scope* in Alloy. The command "run for 1" command verifies that our scenario can be broken down into a single task: the root. The alloy analyzer finds this instance. The command run for 1 but exactly 3 Task tries to find an instance for at most 1 object in each signature except for signature Task, which must contain exactly 3 objects. This makes it possible to verify that there exists a scenario with 3 tasks, which is true. The command run for 1 but exactly 2 Task fails, because there should be no instance with exactly 2 tasks, since the Goal, when decomposed, must have either 0 subtask or more than 1, which makes at least 3 tasks when the Goal is decomposed.

4.3   Specification Validation Using Assertions

An assertion is a theorem that should be provable from the specification. Alloy proves assertion by analyzing all possible instances of a specification for a given scope. An assertion is a constraint that is intended to be valid for all possible cases in a scenario. For a given scenario, checking an assertion might yield counterexamples that represent cases in which the facts and declarations hold, but the assertion does not. Figure 3 shows one assertion, introduced by the keyword assert, which states that it must not occur any cycle in the parent relationship, using the transitive closure operator "^".

To validate the assertions, we instruct the analyzer to search for a counterexample in which the assertion is violated using command check on a given scope. Alloy then verifies all specification instances within the specified scope satisfying the facts. An assertion is valid up to that number of objects in the scope if no counterexample is found. However, it does not guarantee that the assertion is valid for any number of objects. In practice, specification faults are usually be uncovered using reasonably small scopes (this is called "the small scope hypothesis" in the Alloy community). The results presented in the Table 1 show the performances obtained for the assertions defined at the Fig. 3. By increasing the scope. Alloy translates the assertion into a large Boolean formula and uses a SAT solver to verify assertions. The Alloy Analyzer returns the number of variables and the number of clauses used in the Boolean translation of the Alloy model. For example, the command check with scope of 10 in the acyclic assertion identifies that 10,781 variables were used to generate 19,988 clauses in 1.8 min. The size of the Boolean formula to be solved grows exponentially with the scope. No counterexamples were found.

Table 1. Assertion performance test results

Scope	Acyclic		
	Vars	Clauses	T(ms)
3	713	1 083	18
5	2 212	19 988	41
10	10 781	19 988	109 320
15	28 545	54 266	1 226 549

5   Formal Specifications for Nighttime Wandering

5.1   Nighttime Wandering Problem

The Alloy model has been applied on a specific problem occurring among people with Alzheimer disease who suffer from nighttime Wandering. Wandering is qualified by movements without specific or apparent purpose but that are not entirely random [2]. It occurs mostly during night when elderly people with cognitive impairments walk around and confuse day and night. Several authors in the literature address this problem by proposing various night monitoring assistance solutions based on the person's profile [2,14,15]. The scenario-driven approach highlights four important aspects of nighttime wandering:

1. Identify the awakening of the person.
2. Accompany the elderly to satisfy its needs (toilet - kitchen - living room).
3. Calm and Relax the elderly if necessary.
4. Accompany the elderly back to bed.

5.2   Nighttime Wandering Representation

For a better readability of the scenario, we used a hierarchical representation of tasks based on the CTT model to display the different steps and tasks to be undertaken. This representation highlights the sequence of activities at the first level of the hierarchical tree of tasks. One of the advantages of this task model is the ability to reuse tasks that are defined in other scenario.

Figure 4 shows the hierarchical representation of the task organization for the nighttime wandering scenario. The four subtasks - **Get Out the Room; Assistance; Incentive to return to bed; Back in the room** are the ones that will be run to complete the scenario. Each subtask can be processed independently as is the case with the subtask prompt to return to sleep as illustrated by the section (b) in Fig. 4. This decomposition also applies to Subtasks like Get Out the Room; Toilet; Salon; Kitchen; Assist Person; Back in the room. An advantage of this decomposition is to avoid too many combinatorial variables generated to find the conditions of satisfiability. At the design stage, the decomposition is much more compact and facilitates the subdivision of the sub-problem and its representation.

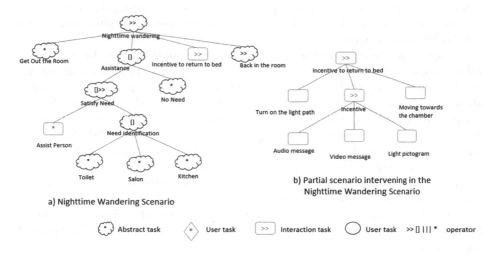

Fig. 4. Hierarchical nighttime wandering scenario

5.3   Formal Specification of the Nighttime Wandering

The nighttime wandering specifications have been checked on five different scopes As shown in Table 2. All subtasks including their decomposition are fully executed in the different scope. The results presented in the Table 2 show the performances obtained for the assertions defined in the nighttime wandering scenario by increasing the scope from 3 to 15. Example, for the scope 10, Alloy searches all possible combinations of at most 10 objects of each signature in 17,584 variables for a counterexample that violates the assertion in a total of 33,579 clauses. As no counterexample has been found the assertion may be valid in this scope.

6   Conclusion

We have presented a formal model for the description and design of scenarios in AAL. We have chosen a specification based on a logic and object-oriented

Table 2. Nighttime wandering specification results

Scope	Vars	Clause	T(ms)
3	14 061	26 231	56
4	14 291	26 563	55
5	14 521	26 895	43
10	17 584	33 579	57
15	35 330	69 051	116

notation. This approach has been chosen for three reasons: (1) enabling of reasoning about incremental and complex activities, (2) reducing the design cost, (3) offering description for analyzing a scenarios by using relational logic and a constraint solver approach.

Using a specification method in AAL scenarios makes it possible to involve all the stakeholders early in the design process while maintaining an important level of abstraction. It then supports the interdisciplinarity process and a multi-step validation by offering an appropriate expression of stakeholders needs. The results obtained for the assertions and the facts show that the proposed specifications are in accordance with the needs expressed by the stakeholders. The choice of scope and the number of clauses produced show that a wide range of cases has been considered.

The scenario-driven approach results obtained with the nighttime wandering make it possible to validate the proposed specifications. This scenario was chosen because of its complexity of design and wide involvement of various stakeholders. Several aspects of AAL technologies were addressed during the design phase of its scenario.

This formal specification will be extended to other Activities of Daily Living to provide reliable AAL technologies for fostering autonomy of the elderly. We found Alloy is helpful, although we believe that other specification languages like CSP and Event-B could generate high-level specifications that are much more understandable by all team members.

Acknowledgement. This research was funded by Canada Networks of Centres of Excellence (NCE) program, AGE-WELL.

References

1. Jackson, D.: Alloy: a lightweight object modelling notation. ACM Trans. Softw. Eng. Methodol. (TOSEM) **11**(2), 256–290 (2002)
2. Radziszewski, R., Ngankam, H., Pigot, H., Grégoire, V., Lorrain, D., Giroux, S.: An ambient assisted living nighttime wandering system for elderly. In: Proceedings of the 18th International Conference on Information Integration and Web-based Applications and Services (iiWAS2016), pp. 368–374. ACM (2016)
3. Snook, C., Butler, M.: UML-B: formal modeling and design aided by UML. ACM Trans. Softw. Eng. Methodol. (TOSEM) **15**(1), 92–122 (2006)
4. Otte, F.J.P., Saurer, B.R., Stork, W.: Unsupervised learning in ambient assisted living for pattern and anomaly detection: a survey. In: O'Grady, M.J., Vahdat-Nejad, H., Wolf, K.-H., Dragone, M., Ye, J., Röcker, C., O'Hare, G. (eds.) AmI 2013. CCIS, vol. 413, pp. 44–53. Springer, Cham (2013). doi:10.1007/978-3-319-04406-4_6
5. Perera, C., Zaslavsky, A., Christen, P., Georgakopoulos, D.: Context aware computing for the internet of things: a survey. IEEE Commun. Surv. Tutor. **16**(1), 414–454 (2014)
6. Cook, D.J., Song, W.: Ambient intelligence and wearable computing: sensors on the body, in the home, and beyond. J. Ambient Intell. Smart Environ. **1**(2), 83–86 (2009)
7. Cook, D.J., Augusto, J.C., Jakkula, V.R.: Review: ambient intelligence: technologies, applications, and opportunities. Pervasive Mob. Comput. **4**(5), 277–298 (2009)
8. Acampora, G., Cook, D.J., Rashidi, P., Vasilakos, A.V.: A survey on ambient intelligence in healthcare. Proc. IEEE **12**(101), 277–298 (2013)
9. Weidenhaupt, K., Pohl, K., Jarke, M., Haumer, P., Aachen, R.: Scenarios in system development: current practice. IEEE Softw. **15**(2), 34–45 (1998)
10. Verza, R., Carvalho, M.L., Battaglia, M.A., Uccelli, M.M.: An interdisciplinary approach to evaluating the need for assistive technology reduces equipment abandonment. Multiple Scler. J. **12**(1), 88–93 (2006)
11. Stanton, N.A.: Hierarchical task analysis: developments, applications, and extensions. Appl. Ergon. **1**(37), 55–79 (2006)
12. Mori, G., Fabio, P., Carmen, S.: CTTE: support for developing and analyzing task models for interactive system design. IEEE Trans. Softw. Eng. **28**(8), 797–813 (2002)
13. Lamsweerde, A.V.: Formal specification: a roadmap. In: Proceedings of the Conference on the Future of Software Engineering, pp. 147–159 (2000)
14. Radziszewski, R., Kenfack, N.H., Grégoire, V., et al.: Designing calm and non-intrusive ambient assisted living system for monitoring nighttime wanderings. Int. J. Pervasive Comput. Commun. **13**(2), 114–129 (2017)
15. Lai, C.K., Arthur, D.G.: Wandering behaviour in people with dementia. J. Adv. Nurs. **2**(44), 173–182 (2003)

Visitrack: A Pervasive Service for Monitoring the Social Activity of Older Adults Living at Home

Alonso Gaete[1], Francisco J. Gutierrez[1(✉)], Sergio F. Ochoa[1], Pablo Guerrero[1], and André Wyzykowski[2]

[1] Department of Computer Science, University of Chile, Beauchef 851, 3rd Floor, Santiago, Chile
{agaete,frgutier,sochoa,pguerrer}@dcc.uchile.cl
[2] Statistics and Informatics Department, Federal University of Santa Catarina, Campus Universitário Trindade, Cx.P. 476, Florianópolis, SC 88040-900, Brazil
abvwmc@gmail.com

Abstract. Advances in medical science allow people to live longer and more independently than some decades ago. However, this does not directly help older adults improve their mental wellbeing. Several studies show that elderly people usually suffer from some level of social isolation that negatively impacts on their physical and mental conditions. As a way to address such a problem, this paper presents Visitrack, a pervasive and unobtrusive service conceived to monitor the social activity of older adults living at home. Based on sensing data retrieved and processed by the system, it can take several actions. For instance, informing family members and friends about long periods with no social activity at the older adult's home. The proposed service has been evaluated through a controlled experimental study, obtaining highly accurate results.

Keywords: Older adults · Aging in place · Ambient assisted living · Monitoring · Social interaction · Empirical study

1 Introduction

Worldwide population is progressively getting older at a dramatic speed, given the current advances in health provision, technology support, and prosperous living conditions that extend the life expectancy of people. This aging phenomenon represents a challenge to the public social and health services of many developed and developing countries, mainly because of the costs and required effort to sustain the independent living of older adults. Over the last years, several studies have identified aging in place strategies as a potential solution to deal with this situation (e.g., [17, 24–26, 34]).

Aging in place is generally understood as the ability to live in one's own home and community safely, independently, and comfortably, regardless of age, income, or ability level. Typically, Ambient Assisted Living (AAL) technology is envisioned as a facilitator for improving the wellbeing of older adults and extending the period in which these people can live autonomously at their home.

Jointly with this tendency of improving the living conditions of older adults, it has appeared an antagonist tendency that reduces the time that family members have

© Springer International Publishing AG 2017
S.F. Ochoa et al. (Eds.): UCAmI 2017, LNCS 10586, pp. 520–530, 2017.
DOI: 10.1007/978-3-319-67585-5_52

available to devote to spare activities [20], such as interacting face-to-face with their older adults [16]. Several reasons justify this tendency; for instance: the need of women to work for ensuring the sustainability of their own family, an increase on the length of working shifts, and the desire to spend time in leisure activities.

Face-to-face interactions are a key factor that helps keep older adults emotionally up, physically active, and motivated [2]. In that respect, a low level of social interaction tends to produce depression and other mental health issues, particularly among older adults [10, 11], as well as a reduced life expectancy in this user group [18, 19, 27]. In other words, it does not make sense to try improving the wellbeing of older adults without considering social support as a fundamental aspect to address. Several researchers state that face-to-face social support is the cornerstone for the quality of human life [2, 6, 13, 21]. Therefore, addressing this concern results in technology with high impact in the quality of life and overall wellbeing of older adults. In particular, this turns critical for those people that have small social networks and spend long time periods at home, i.e., those at high risk of becoming socially isolated. Although the proportion of socially isolated older adults varies across different cultures and societies, it is clear that this is currently a global issue [8].

In order to address this challenge considering the needs of both older adults and other family members, this paper presents a pervasive service to monitor the face-to-face social activity conducted by older adults living independently at home. This information would allow the system to promote visits to the older adult when required, balance the load of performing these visits among family members, and keep a permanent diagnosis of the social connectedness of the older adult.

Identifying visits of family members and friends to the older adults is a highly valuable asset for addressing this challenge. However, accomplishing with this task is not trivial, since the acquired information must be accurate, reliable, objective, and recorded on time. Moreover, the monitoring process should non-intrusive, hopefully pervasive, secure, and consider privacy restrictions that limit technology adoption among older adults [15]. Although literature reports several proposals for in-home activity recognition targeted to older adults, most of them fail in simultaneously addressing all these quality requirements.

The monitoring service presented in this article, named Visitrack, addresses the stated requirements in order to extend the capabilities of the SocialConnector system [23]. Through a controlled experimental study, we evaluated the overall performance of Visitrack in a simulated setting under lab conditions. The obtained results have been highly accurate, both in terms of overall precision (90.5%) and recall (93.5%), as well as unobtrusive and useful for older adults and their family members.

The rest of the paper is structured as follows. Section 2 reviews related work. Section 3 describes Visitrack and presents its main functionality. Section 4 reports the conducted empirical evaluation and discusses the obtained results. Finally, Sect. 5 concludes and provides perspectives on future work.

2 Related Work

Monitoring incoming visits to the home of older adults is the first step of a larger endeavor aiming to provide effective social support in aging in place scenarios. While the problem of remote sensing and activity monitoring of older adults is not new in AAL, it has been strongly reliant on external hardware [9, 33].

On the one hand, previous attempts to provide in-home monitoring to older adults use ambient and wearable sensors to collect biomedical, physiological, and activity data in the form of a wireless network installed in or around the house, appliances, and furniture [3, 29]. On the other hand, devices like smartphones [7] and Microsoft Kinect [4, 28] have also proven useful for instrumenting pervasive monitoring of older adults.

McDuff et al. [22] followed a more holistic approach involving a multimodal sensor set-up for continuous logging of audio, visual, physiological and contextual data. Using a webcam, a Microsoft Kinect device, an ambient microphone, and an electro-dermal wrist sensor along a portable GPS carried by the user, the proposed system enabled user reflection on their affective state through an interactive interface.

Following a different line of reasoning, Fogarty et al. [14] through an in-home deployment trial reflected on trade-offs regarding instrumentation and quantity and quality of collected information. Similarly, Demiris et al. [12] state that older adults generally accept sensors and actuators once they are assimilated as being part of their surrounding environment. For instance, this could be the case of smart home systems or residence care facilities already equipped with sensor networks.

While valuable, prior research shows limitations with regard to the pervasiveness of these systems in line with the expectations of older adults about technology acceptance. Instrumenting a house is a challenge, since elderly people perceive this task as disruptive, difficult to achieve, and expensive. These concerns have been reported as being problematic to older adults, particularly in terms of technology adoption [15]. In that respect, Birnholtz and Jones-Rounds [5] state that aging in place schemas need to foster a sense of independence, while simultaneously enable monitoring and frequent interaction in an unobtrusive way. Vines et al. [31] emphasize that mediating the caregiving space of older adults with AAL technology does have an impact on the involved stakeholders, which goes beyond non-invasive sensing. Issues like explicit reassurance, information control, prompt feedback, and access to activity data all need to be addressed with regard to acceptance and adoption of assistive technologies.

As a first attempt to design a system for monitoring incoming visits at the home of an older adult, we initially rely on state-of-the-art algorithms for detecting and identifying people within a family network. Viola and Jones [32] conceived an object detection framework based on the sequential identification of image features through an iterative probabilistic approach. With proper training, this system works fairly well for detecting people faces under multiple lighting conditions and different levels of resolutions, even in the cases with a noisy training dataset. Although the obtained results from this approach seem promising for detecting faces in standalone images, it shows limitations in the case of properly recognizing people from a larger set, such as accurately identifying what family members visited an older adult over a long period of time.

In order to overcome this limitation, literature reports several classification models supporting people identification from a trained dataset of photos. This approach is commonly based on extracting particular features from the image—which varies between models—and comparing these features against the training dataset. For instance, Turk and Pentland [30] follow an approach based on principal component analysis to reduce the dimensionality of images and induce a classifier comparing the target image with those in the training set. Ahonen et al. [1] identify local binary pattern histograms to compare images and classify them following similitude measures, which displays fairly good results in practice according to a literature survey conducted by Zhao et al. [35].

Building upon these lines of research, our proposal explicitly address factors that contribute to improve technology acceptance by older adults, such as perceived usability, usefulness, availability, and ubiquity. Therefore, the odds for an effective in-home deployment and acceptance of Visitrack seem increased.

3   System Design

Visitrack was implemented as an extension—running in background—of the Social-Connector system [23]. The latter is a ubiquitous application that allows older adults to interact with other family members exchanging messages, family pictures, and through videoconferences (Fig. 1).

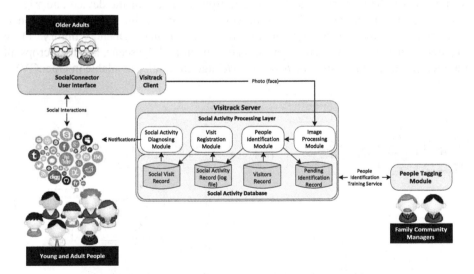

Fig. 1. Architecture of the physical environment

The service uses the frontal camera and the microphone of the tablet. When this application detects a person, it uploads a picture of his/her face to the server. Then, the server runs a process to recognize that face. Regardless of the result of such an operation, it records the visit in a log file that keeps the history of the social activity in that house.

If the face of the visitor is not recognized, family community managers can manually tag it using a particular software module. This new information is then used as input for future automatic face recognitions. The information about the social activity of the older adults can be periodically sent to particular family members, such as those acting as caregivers or monitors, as a way to making them aware about the social activity status of the older adult, deliver alerts, or try persuading other family members to visit the elderly person.

The system architecture shows data coupling among various components of the system; e.g., between the Visitrack client and the server, and also among the services provided by the server. This decoupling of the functionality (or data coupling) allows the system to evolve its components in a quite autonomous way. For instance, it is possible to reengineer the social activity diagnosis module (Fig. 1), without the need to change source code in the rest of the server components. The same happens if we decide to evolve the visit registration or people identification modules, which represents an advantage for the system.

4   Visitrack Client

This service uses the microphone of the tablet PC to capture samples of the environmental noise. If the detected sound intensity is over certain threshold, then the service assumes that a potential social activity is being conducted at home, so it runs the monitoring process. This starts by activating the frontal camera of the device and tries to detect a phace in the physical environment using video (Fig. 2). Such detection is performed using the *FaceRecognizer* algorithm available in the OpenCV library[1]. Once the algorithm detects a face, the service takes a picture of the scene, and then crops all the faces in the picture using the *haarcascade* algorithm (also available in OpenCV).

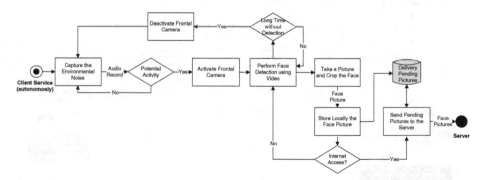

Fig. 2.   Information processing flow at the client side

Finally, once cropped, the faces are stored locally in the device, and then sent to the server via Internet. If the connection between the client and the server is not available, the face pictures are kept in the local storage until the communication link is

---

[1]   http://www.opencv.org/.

reestablished. In the server side there is a listener agent that is permanently waiting for new pictures.

4.1 Visitrack Server

When a picture with a face is received from the tablet, the system extracts its characteristics through the Image Processing Module (depicted in Fig. 1) that uses Local Binary Pattern Histograms [1]. Using the picture description, the People Identification Module intends to recognize the identity of the person by matching this description with those stored in the database of potential visitors for such a family (i.e., the Visitors Record). Figure 3 shows the information flow between each component of the Visitrack server application.

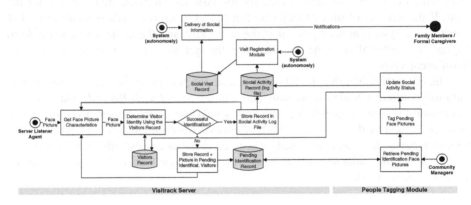

Fig. 3. Information processing flow at the server side

If the person in the new picture is identified, then such a picture is deleted and a record is added to the system log file (i.e., the Social Activity Record) alongside contextual metadata related to such a visit. In other case, the cropped photo is stored in the Pending Identification Record. At any time, as indicated with dashed lines in Fig. 3, the community managers can manually label these images, which triggers a reprocessing of the pending pictures and an updates all the records in the server in order to keep a coherent status of the Social Visits and Visitors Records. Using such a mechanism, the system is fed and retrained.

Periodically, the *Visit Registration Module* processes the system log file, determines the length and frequency of the visits, and stores such information in the *Social Visit Record*. The information of these visits can then be used by the system to keep informed, according to a set of rules, family members, community managers, and formal caregivers.

4.2 Visit Registration

Accurately determining the length of a visit is a challenge for the system, given that the video recording process only captures a part of the older adult's house. Therefore, locating strategically the camera helps increase the chance for effectively capturing a visit.

The visit registration process uses as input the stored information in the *Social Activity Record*, which corresponds to several triples ordered chronologically. Each triple has an ID that identifies the tablet PC, the ID of the person captured by the camera, and a timestamp indicating the instant in which such a picture was taken.

In order to determine the visits, the whole time period to be monitored is discretized using short time blocks (e.g., slots of 2 or 3 min), where each block has an ID. Then, the triples in the *Social Activity Record* are reviewed chronologically, where every time block that matches with a certain face capture is consequently labeled for each person. Multiples captures for the same time block are ignored.

Consecutive time blocks having the same person are defined as the *time range of the visit*, which includes a beginning time for the visit and an associated duration for the visit. If the number of time blocks between two consecutive visits is small (e.g., 1–4 blocks), the system assumes that it is the same visit and the camera was not able to capture the visitor all the time. In other case, the system assumes that they correspond to different visits.

The ID of the tablet PC, the ID of the visitor, the beginning time of the visit, and its duration conform a tuple that is maintained in the *Social Visit Record*. Although this information is coarse-grained, it is still highly valuable for the system given that it can be directly used by the system to decide when to deliver a notification, identify a target person to persuade or keep informed, or provide visual awareness information about the social status of the older adults. These latter mechanisms will be designed and evaluated as part of future work.

5   Evaluation Results

In order to assess the overall performance of Visitrack, we conducted a controlled experiment simulating three independent family meetings. Each meeting was held in a living room that was equipped with a tablet PC running a version of the SocialConnector system that embedded Visitrack. As hardware support, we used a tablet Samsung Galaxy Tab E, 9.6, running over WiFi.

In every scenario, participants were prompted to enter and leave the room simulating visits to an older adult. The authors kept independent records of who entered and left the room, and at what times. These notes then served to compute the ground truth for evaluating Visitrack. Each case scenario was individually and independently observed in time periods of 2 h, replicated over a period of two days.

As performance metrics, we computed the service *precision* (i.e., how many visits were effectively conducted with regard to the total number of those detected by the system), *recall* (i.e., how many visits were effectively detected by the system with regard to the total number of those performed by the study participants), and F_1 *score* (i.e., the harmonic mean between precision and recall, hence representing a balance measure). These metrics were selected because they are commonly used in information retrieval for evaluating the performance of classifier models. Table 1 reports the obtained results in the experiment.

Table 1. Performance of Visitrack in simulated family meetings

	Precision	Recall	F_1 score
Scenario 1	0.909	0.952	0.930
Scenario 2	0.906	0.935	0.920
Scenario 3	0.901	0.917	0.909

A 100% of the simulated visits were detected, even if they lasted less than ten seconds. If the person is in the capturing area of the camera during 2–3 s, and his/her face is in a frontal or semi-frontal position with regard the camera, the system is going to detect and record that visit. The *precision* shown in Table 1 is high, although the system identified as visit some situations that were not as such. However, these false detections can be identified and fixed by the family community managers using the *people tagging module* (Fig. 1). For instance, if the detected object (e.g., a mug) is recognized by the system as a face, then it is enough that such an object be labeled as "no person" in the pending identification record. Therefore, the system will iterate over all the pending visits and recalculate them with this new base of knowledge. Fixing these situations takes family community managers only a couple of minutes and allows the system to increase its detection precision to 100% of the visits.

Concerning the obtained *recall*, there were only some few short visits that were not recorded properly. In these cases, visits involved several people that were not recorded properly. Although most visitors were detected, some of them were missing. Finally, considering the *F₁ score*, we can see that the algorithm of visit detection not only is highly accurate but also reliable. The social information that it records is objective and is available to be used by the system once it arrives to the server. Therefore, it turns possible to make on-time decisions or deliver messages based upon this information. These are highly desirable quality attributes for this type of systems.

Given that the monitoring process ran in background, users were not really aware of the monitoring activity, which provided pervasiveness to the service. Both the information stored in the tablet and the server, as well as the data communicated to the server travelled through secure—encrypted—channels. This provides an important security level to the system.

On the other hand, only face pictures are stored and communicated from the tablet to the server, and those pictures are deleted once communicated to the server (in the case of the data stored in the tablet) or once the identity of the person has been established (in case of the server). Moreover, the information about the visits is aggregated to use only by the system, which provides some privacy protection to the visitors. Furthermore, given that all participants are relatives or friends of monitored older adults, and since the social interaction among them does not represent a taboo or something to negatively care about, this aspect was not an issue for the people participating in the evaluation process. Indeed, through informal observation on the process, study participants and older adults proved somewhat favorable to the installation of Visitrack in their own homes if they had the chance to do so. This will be formally evaluated through a controlled in-the-wild experiment as future work. Similarly, the quality attributes shown by the proposed monitoring service make us expect a contribution of it in other application domains, such as monitoring social activities of persons suffering autism, Asperger, or in the case of informal caregivers of chronically-ill patients or handicapped people.

6   Conclusions and Future Work

Aging in place is envisioned as an instrumental strategy to deal with the accelerated aging process experimented by the worldwide population over the last decades. This strategy usually requires technology—such as AAL systems—to support the daily living activities of older adults. In particular, a key need to address is the social support of elderly people within their close social networks. Particularly, literature acknowledges that face-to-face social support is the cornerstone for improving wellbeing and sustaining acceptable levels of quality of life [2, 6, 13, 21]. Therefore, it is important to consider this value when conceiving AAL systems targeted to support older adults living at home. However, this consideration is also constrained by quality requirements that are related to how older adults perceive and expect to accept domestic technology. In that respect, it turns equally important that social supporting solutions be accurate, non-intrusive, reliable, objective, and that they record and provide information on time with a particular focus on sustaining people's privacy.

Given that most of the solutions reported in the literature for monitoring social activities usually consider broader and less restrictive interaction scenarios, they are particularly not concerned by addressing the stated quality attributes. As a way to bridge this gap, the Visitrack service contributes with an alternative strategy to monitoring the social activity of older adults, with a particular emphasis on not disrupting the living and social ecosystems of elderly users.

This work also shows that an excessive instrumentation is not necessarily required to monitor complex ecosystems, without compromising pervasiveness, information accuracy, and privacy. Although the reported results are still preliminary, we expect this research helps positively impact the quality of life and wellbeing of older adults.

The next step in this research initiative includes replicating the evaluation study in real-life scenarios, by monitoring social activity directly at home. We also envisage to define decision rules to promote and balance the engagement of family members in providing face-to-face social support to their older adults.

Acknowledgments. This work has been partially supported by the Fondecyt Project (Chile), grant: 1150252. The work of Francisco J. Gutierrez has been supported by the Ph.D. Scholarship Program of Conicyt Chile (CONICYT-PCHA/Doctorado Nacional/2013-21130075).

References

1. Ahonen, T., Hadid, A., Pietikäinen, M.: Face Recognition with Local Binary Patterns. In: Pajdla, T., Matas, J. (eds.) ECCV 2004. LNCS, vol. 3021, pp. 469–481. Springer, Heidelberg (2004). doi:10.1007/978-3-540-24670-1_36
2. Albrecht, T.L., Burleson, B.R., Sarason, I.: Meaning and Methods in the Study of Communication and Social Support: An Introduction. Commun. Res. **19**(2), 149–153 (1992)
3. Atallah, L., Lo, B., Yang, G.-Z., Siegemund, F.: Wirelessly accessible sensor populations (WASP) for elderly care monitoring. In: Proceedings of the International Conference on Pervasive Computing Technologies for Healthcare (PervasiveHealth 2008). IEEE Press, New York (2008). doi:10.1109/PCTHEALTH.2008.4571011
4. Bieryla, K.A.: Xbox kinect training to improve clinical measures of balance in older adults: a pilot study. Aging Clin. Exp. Res. **28**(3), 451–457 (2016)
5. Birnholtz, J., Jones-Rounds, M.: Independence and interaction: understanding seniors' privacy and awareness needs for aging in place. In: Proceedings of the ACM SIGCHI Conference on Human Factors in Computing Systems (CHI 2010), pp. 143–152. ACM Press, New York (2010)
6. Braithwaite, D.O., Waldron, V.R., Finn, J.: Communication of social support in computer-mediated groups for people with disabilities. Health Commun. **11**(2), 123–151 (1999)
7. Castro, L.A., Favela, J., Quintana, E., Perez, M.: Behavioral data gathering for assessing functional status and health in older adults using mobile phones. Pers. Ubiquit. Comput. **19**(2), 379–391 (2015)
8. Cloutier-Fisher, D., Kobayashi, K., Smith, A.: The subjective dimension of social isolation: a qualitative investigation of older adults' experiences in small social support networks. J. Aging Stud. **25**(4), 407–414 (2011)
9. Cook, D.J., Das, S.K.: How smart are our environments? An updated look at the state of the art. Pervasive Mob. Comput. **3**, 53–73 (2007)
10. Cornwell, E.Y., Waite, L.J.: Social disconnectedness, perceived isolation, and health among older adults. J. Health Soc. Behav. **50**(1), 31–48 (2009)
11. Coyle, C.E., Dugan, E.: Social isolation, loneliness and health among older adults. J. Aging Health **24**(8), 1346–1363 (2012)
12. Demiris, G., Hensel, B.K., Skubic, M., Rantz, M.: Senior residents' perceived need of and preferences for "smart home" sensor technologies. Int. J. Technol. Assess. Health Care **24**(1), 120–124 (2008)
13. Dickson-Markman, F., Shern, D.L.: Social support and health in the elderly. J. Appl. Commun. Res. **18**(1), 49–63 (1990)
14. Fogarty, J., Au, C., Hudson, S.E.: Sensing from the basement: a feasibility study of unobtrusive and low-cost home activity recognition. In: Proceedings of the ACM Symposium on User Interface Software and Technology (UIST 2006), pp. 91–100. ACM Press, New York (2006)
15. Garg, V., Camp, L.J., Lorenzen-Huber, L., Shankar, K., Connelly, K.: Privacy concerns in assisted living technologies. Ann. Telecommun. **69**(1), 75–88 (2014)
16. Gutierrez, F.J., Ochoa, S.F.: Mom, I do have a family.: attitudes, agreements, and expectations on the interaction with chilean older adults. In: Proceedings of the ACM Conference on Computer-Supported Cooperative Work and Social Computing (CSCW 2016), pp. 1402–1411. ACM Press, New York (2016)
17. Gutierrez, F.J., Ochoa, S.F.: It takes at least two to Tango: understanding the cooperative nature of elderly caregiving in Latin America. In: Proceedings of the ACM Conference on Computer-Supported Cooperative Work and Social Computing (CSCW'17). ACM Press, New York, pp. 1618–1630 (2017)

18. Holt-Lunstad, J., Smith, T.B., Baker, M., Harris, T., Stephenson, D.: Loneliness and social isolation as risk factors for mortality: a meta-analytic review. Perspect. Psychol. Sci. **10**(2), 227–237 (2015)
19. Holwerda, T.J., Beekman, A.T., Deeg, D.J., Stek, M.L., van Tilburg, T.G., Visser, P.J., Schmand, B., Jonker, C., Schoevers, R.A.: Increased risk of mortality associated with social isolation in older men: only when feeling lonely? Results from the Amsterdam study of the elderly (AMSTEL). Psychol. Med. **42**(4), 843–853 (2012)
20. Ilies, R., Dimotakis, N., de Pater, I.E.: Psychological and physiological reactions to high workloads: implications for well-being. Pers. Psychol. **63**(2), 407–436 (2010)
21. LaRocca, M.A., Scogin, F.R.: The effect of social support on quality of life in older adults receiving cognitive behavioral therapy. Clin. Gerontol. **38**(2), 131–148 (2015)
22. McDuff, D., Karlson, A., Kapoor, A., Roseway, A., Czerwinski, M.: AffectAura: An Intelligent System for Emotional Memory. In: Proceedings of the ACM SIGCHI Conference on Human Factors in Computing Systems (CHI 2012), pp. 849–858 ACM Press, New York, (2012)
23. Muñoz, D., Gutierrez, F.J., Ochoa, S.F., Baloian, N.: SocialConnector: a ubiquitous system to ease the social interaction among family community members. Comput. Syst. Sci. Eng. **30**(1), 57–68 (2015)
24. Mynatt, E.D., Melenhorst, A.-S., Fisk, A.-D., Rogers, W.A.: Aware technologies for aging in place: understanding user needs and attitudes. IEEE Pervasive Comput. **3**(2), 36–41 (2004)
25. Procter, R., Greenhalgh, T., Wherton, J., Sugarhood, P., Rouncefield, M., Hinder, S.: The day-to-day co-production of ageing in place. Comput. Support. Coop. Work **23**(3), 245–267 (2014)
26. Rowan J., Mynatt, E.D.: Digital family portrait field trial: support for aging in place. In: Proceedings of the ACM SIGCHI Conference on Human Factors in Computing Systems (CHI'05). ACM Press, New York, pp. 521–530 (2005)
27. Steptoe, A., Shankar, A., Demakakos, P., Wardle, J.: Social isolation, loneliness, and all-cause mortality in older men and women. Proc. Natl. Acad. Sci. U.S.A. **110**(15), 5797–5801 (2013)
28. Stone, E.E., Skubic, M.: Fall detection in homes of older adults using the microsoft kinect. IEEE J Biomed Health Inform. **19**(1), 290–301 (2015)
29. Suryadevara, N.K., Mukhopadhyay, S.C., Wang, R., Rayudu, R.K.: Forecasting the behavior of an elderly using wireless sensors data in a smart home. Eng. Appl. Artif. Intell. **26**, 2641–2652 (2013)
30. Turk, M., Pentland, A.: Eigenfaces for recognition. J. Cogn. Neurosci. **3**(1), 71–86 (1991)
31. Vines, J., Lindsay, S., Pritchard, G.W., Lie, M., Greathead, D., Olivier, P., Brittain, K.: Making family care work: dependence, privacy and remote home monitoring telecare systems. In: Proceedings of the ACM International Joint Conference on Pervasive and Ubiquitous Computing (UbiComp'13). ACM Press, New York, pp. 607–616 (2013)
32. Viola, P., Jones, M.J.: Robust real-time face detection. Int. J. Comput. Vision **57**(2), 137–154 (2004)
33. Wagner, F., Basran, J., Dal Bello-Haas, V.: A review of monitoring technology for use with older adults. J. Geriatr. Phys. Ther. **35**(1), 28–34 (2012)
34. Wiles, J.L., Leibing, A., Guberman, N., Reeve, J., Allen, R.S.E.: The meaning of "aging in place" to older people. Gerontologist **52**(3), 357–366 (2012)
35. Zhao, W., Chellappa, R., Phillips, P., Rosenfeld, A.: Face Recognition: A Literature Survey. ACM Comput. Surv. **35**(4), 399–458 (2003)

Ad-hoc and Sensor Networks

Energy Efficient Rekeying Protocol for Wireless Sensor and Actor Networks

Nisha Hooda and Mayank Dave[✉]

Department of Computer Engineering, National Institute of Technology, Kurukshetra, India
nnisha040@gmail.com, mdave@nitkkr.ac.in

Abstract. Securing the information exchange between the network nodes is very important in wireless sensor and actor networks as actions taken by the actor nodes on the performance is dependent upon the sensed data. This paper proposes an energy-efficient rekeying protocol for WSANs named as energy-efficient hybrid key management protocol that assigns the key management responsibility to the actor nodes. The proposed protocol organizes network nodes into clusters and categorizes nodes into critical and non-critical nodes. It establishes unique pairwise keys only for pairs of active neighboring sensor nodes after analysis of the network traffic and minimizes the storage overhead. The protocol is distributed and is able to handle compromise of both critical and non-critical nodes. Simulation results show that the technique is highly energy-efficient and enhances the network lifetime.

Keywords: Wireless sensor and actor networks · Security · Energy efficient · Rekeying · Dynamic key management · Network lifetime

1 Introduction

Automation has become an inevitable component in human life. For instance, office buildings are often installed with fire alarms to perform automatic water sprinkling immediately whenever fire is detected. Sensors form the basic component of these systems. Due to such applications wireless sensor networks (WSNs) have gained high popularity in the recent years. However, to incorporate the automated nature into WSNs, wireless sensor and actor networks (WSANs) have been developed. A WSAN consists of several sensor nodes and small number of resource-rich actor nodes responsible for performing actions on the environment based on the sensed data [1, 2]. In this paper the terms actor and actuator are used interchangeably.

Cryptographic keys are used in a network for securing the information exchanged between any pair or group of nodes. Key management in any WSN or WSAN involves the establishment and maintenance of the cryptographic keys for securing the information exchange [3, 4]. In order to reduce the runtime processing and communication overhead in the resource-scarce sensor nodes, key pre-distribution has been widely adopted in WSNs. Key pre-distribution involves loading of keying material into the sensor nodes prior to deployment. The compromise of any sensor node discloses the keys to the adversaries and therefore, the keying information in the valid nodes needs

© Springer International Publishing AG 2017
S.F. Ochoa et al. (Eds.): UCAmI 2017, LNCS 10586, pp. 533–544, 2017.
DOI: 10.1007/978-3-319-67585-5_53

to be updated. Dynamic key management is the process of updating keys (rekeying) while the network is in operation.

Although numerous key management protocols have been proposed in the literature for WSNs, very few have focused on WSANs. This paper proposes a distributed and hybrid dynamic key management protocol for WSANs called as energy-efficient hybrid key management protocol (EEHKM).

The contribution of the proposed protocol is three-fold. Firstly, it organizes network nodes into clusters and assigns key management responsibility to multiple actor nodes lying within the proximity of that cluster. This way it avoids single point of failure problem as compared to the centralized protocols. Secondly, it classifies the network nodes into two categories: critical and non-critical nodes. Compromise of critical nodes is handled through on-demand rekeying within the cluster of the compromised node whereas compromise of any non-critical node is taken care by periodic rekeying. Finally, it reduces the storage requirement in each sensor node and establishes unique pair-wise keys only for active pairs of neighboring sensor nodes. This minimizes the size of key refresh messages and the number of pair-wise key establishment operations. Consequently, the energy consumption of the key management operations is minimized and the network lifetime is enhanced.

The rest of the paper is organized as follows: in Sect. 2 we discuss few hybrid key management protocols along with some of the basic protocols proposed in literature for WSNs. Section 3 explains the network architecture. Section 4 describes phases of the proposed protocol. Section 5 explains the way the proposed protocol works. In Sect. 6, we present the simulation results. Finally, we conclude the paper in Sect. 7.

2   Related Work

Several hybrid key management protocols have been proposed for WSNs. These protocols basically combine features of two or more of the basic protocols to produce more efficient key management protocols. Firstly, we discuss some of the basic key management protocols proposed for WSNs. Next, we discuss some of the efficient hybrid key management protocols proposed in the literature for WSNs.

The resource-limited nature of WSNs has led to an increased popularity of the symmetric key based key management protocols in WSNs. Additionally, in order to reduce the runtime processing overhead on the sensor nodes most of the basic protocols follow key pre-distribution. The most basic symmetric key pre-distribution based protocol termed as the master key-based scheme [5] loads a same key termed as the master key into all the network nodes. This master key is later used for securing the communication between the network nodes. However, the compromise of a single network node will lead to the compromise of the entire network making the protocol non-resilient against the node capture attacks.

Another basic protocol termed as the E-G scheme [6] loads a subset of keys (key ring) selected from a global key pool into each network node. This scheme allows any two neighboring nodes to establish secure communication if they share one or more keys. However, resilience of this scheme is low against the node capture attacks as a common key may have been used for securing multiple network links. In order to improve the resilience of this protocol against the node capture attacks, another robust key management protocol termed as the q-composite scheme was proposed [7]. This protocol allows any pair of neighboring nodes to establish pair-wise keys only if they share at least q keys. The pair-wise key is established by applying a hash function to the set of common keys existing between neighboring nodes. As a result, the resilience is improved as there is less possibility of same key being used for securing multiple network links.

The protocol proposed in [8] combines q-composite scheme with the polynomial pool-based key management scheme for secure communication. This protocol establishes pair-wise keys between any pair of network nodes using an intermediate node to enhance security. However, the storage requirement of this protocol remains high as each node needs to maintain both cryptographic keys as well as polynomials as the keying material.

Another hybrid key management protocol combines elliptic curve cryptography (ECC) with symmetric curve cryptography [9]. This protocol has chosen ECC as considering it to be the best option among the various asymmetric key management protocols in WSNs. The protocol considers a heterogeneous hierarchical network model in which network nodes are organized into clusters to achieve scalability. The results show that the protocol reduces communication overhead and storage requirement as compared to the E-G and q-composite schemes.

A hybrid energy-efficient key management protocol that combines static key management and dynamic key management to address the heterogeneous security requirements of WSNs is proposed in [10]. The protocol takes into account the fact that different levels of security may be desired in different parts of the network. The network nodes are organized into different sub networks and different levels of security is provided in different sub networks. The protocol uses static keys for low security sub networks and dynamic keys for high security sub networks.

An efficient hybrid key management protocol that combines public key cryptography technique with matrix-based approach has been proposed in [11] for heterogeneous WSNs. The protocol uses the concept of lower triangular, upper triangular and symmetric matrix for securing the group communication and the node-to-node communication. The communication between the base station and the cluster heads is secured using the ElGamal Public key encryption technique. The protocol avoids man-in-the-middle attack as the keys are loaded into the sensor nodes prior to deployment. The protocol achieves 100% node-to-node connectivity.

A hybrid key management protocol proposed for WSANs employs asymmetric key management for securing the communication occurring among the actor nodes and symmetric key management for securing the communication among the normal sensor nodes [12]. A storage-efficient dynamic key protocol called as sequence-base key management (SKM) for WSNs is proposed in [13]. The storage requirement of this protocol is very low as each node needs to maintain just two small pieces of information as the keying material. Each network link is secured by using a unique pair-wise key thereby making the protocol highly resilient against the node capture attacks.

In [14], an energy-efficient and traffic aware key management protocol (EETKM) is proposed for WSNs to establish pair-wise keys between those pairs of neighboring sensor nodes that are in the active state. This reduces the number of keys that need to be maintained by each sensor node. However, the storage requirement per node is still high as each node needs to maintain multiple keys. SKM establishes pair-wise keys for each pair of neighboring sensor nodes irrespective of the fact whether these nodes need to communicate with each other or not. Although EETKM establishes pair-wise keys only for active pair of neighboring sensor nodes, the storage overhead of EETKM is high as each sensor node needs to maintain multiple keys.

3   Network Architecture

In literature, mainly two architectures have been proposed for WSANs: semi-automated architecture and automated architecture. In semi-automated architecture, the sensor nodes forward the sensed data to the base station. The base station then assigns tasks to the actor nodes. On the other hand, in automated architecture, the sensor nodes forward the sensed data directly to the actor nodes. The actor nodes then collaborate with each other to perform actions on the environment. The response time of the automated architecture is much smaller as compared to the semi-automated architecture [2]. The proposed protocol EEHKM follows automated hierarchical network architecture as shown in Fig. 1.

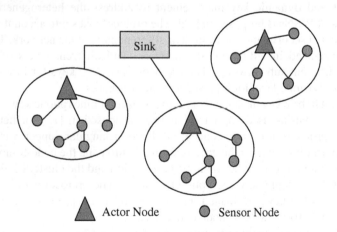

Fig. 1. Network Architecture.

EEHKM takes advantage of the resource-rich nature of the actor nodes (ANs) to minimize the overhead on the resource-scarce sensor nodes. The network nodes are organized into clusters and the responsibility of intra cluster key management is assigned to the ANs. For every event detected by the sensor nodes, the sensed information is passed to the actor nodes, which then take appropriate actions on the environment. In order to maintain the permanent logs, the actor nodes periodically forward collected data to the sink node. The interval after which the logs are forwarded by the actor nodes to the sink node is decided on the basis of criticality of the underlying WSN application. This interval is usually kept small for a critical application such as fire detection as compared to the less critical applications such as air quality monitoring.

4   Network Operation Phases of Proposed Protocol

This section explains details of different phases of operation of the proposed protocol.

4.1   Keying Material Pre-distribution

Similar to the SKM scheme [13], EEHKM also requires each network node to maintain two tiny pieces of information i.e. the first term of a numerical sequence and its recursive formula as its keying material. The recursive formula defines an infinite numerical sequence whereas the first term acts as the seed from which values of the sequence are generated by using the recursive formula. For instance, each node may be loaded with following pair:

$$\text{(First term, recursive formula)} = \left(3,\ 4u_n + 2\right)$$

In this example by using the first term 3, the sequence terms generated are 14, 58 and 234 and so on. These two pieces of information allows establishment of unique pair-wise keys between each pair of neighboring sensor nodes with little computation.

4.2   Pair-Wise Key Establishment

After nodes are deployed into the target region, the pair-wise keys are established only after the exchange of RTS/CTS frames by the underlying MAC protocol as in EETKM [14]. In this way, unique pair-wise keys are established only between those pairs of neighboring nodes that are active.

4.3   Initialization of Rekey Data Structures

The target region is divided into areas and each area is associated with at least one actor node. The actor node(s) assigned to any are responsible for performing two main tasks. First, informing other neighboring actor nodes and collaborating with them to take appropriate actions on the surroundings for any event reported by the sensor nodes belonging to their area. The second task performed by the actor node is generating new keying material and distributing it to the valid nodes of its associated area.

In the proposed protocol, the keying material update message is termed as KUPD. A unique identifier is assigned to each KUPD. Every network node maintains identifier of the most recently received KUPD message in a variable KUPD_ID. Any node on receiving a KUPD message compares the identifier of the received KUPD message with the value contained in its KUPD_ID variable. If the identifier of the newly received

KUPD message is one more than the value contained in its KUPD_ID variable, then the node forwards the received KUPD message to its valid neighboring nodes and updates the value maintained by it in the KUPD_ID variable. Otherwise, it concludes that it has already received, processed and forwarded the most recent KUPD message to all of its valid neighboring nodes. Thus, it will not forward the currently received update message to its neighboring nodes. This way the proposed protocol performs controlled flooding and reduces the communication overhead.

4.4 Key Material Refresh

The proposed EEHKM protocol is a distributed protocol as the key management responsibility is distributed among multiple actor nodes in contrast to SKM, which is a centralized protocol. Consequently, EEHKM avoids the single point of failure problem. Additionally, the time interval between the detection of any node compromise and the start of forwarding of key refresh messages is less for EEHKM as compared to SKM. This is due to the fact that SKM assigns the entire responsibility of key management to the base station. Due to this reason, in SKM, for every key refresh operation, the request messages must pass through a large number of network nodes before reaching the base station. The base station then sends the new keying material to the valid network nodes. On the other hand in EEHKM, the request messages need to propagate just to the associated actor nodes that are usually located at much smaller number of hops away as compared to the base station. These actor nodes then initiate the keying material update process.

5   Proposed Protocol

5.1   Overview

Each area of the network is assigned multiple actor nodes as being responsible for initiating keying material update on the compromise of any node belonging to its area. These actor nodes revoke the compromised node from the network through keying material update i.e. replacement of the old keying material with new keying material in all the valid network nodes.

EEHKM is a hybrid protocol. It combines the storage-efficiency of SKM with the traffic-awareness of EETKM to minimize the energy consumption of key management operations and enhance the network lifetime of WSANs. An actor node using EEHKM protocol is responsible for performing rekeying both periodically and on-demand in all the non-compromised nodes of its cluster. In this way, an actor node will maintain the symmetric keys that it shares with the nodes of its cluster. The periodic rekeying is done for the non-critical nodes. The on-demand rekeying is performed on the detection of compromise of the critical nodes [15]. EEHKM considers the following types of nodes as critical:

- Actor node: Actor nodes (AN) act on the environment based on what information they have collected or received. The compromise of any of the actor nodes will have a major impact on the network security as the actor nodes are responsible for performing rekeying. As a result actor nodes are considered as critical nodes in EEHKM.

- Cut-vertex node: The cut-vertex nodes are considered as critical nodes in EEHKM as compromise of any cut-vertex node partitions the network into segments thereby badly affecting the operation of multiple network nodes.
- Location: Any node that lies within one-hop distance of any actor node is considered as critical.
- Degree: Degree of the compromised node is above a certain threshold value, *th*. If below condition is true, then rekeying will be performed

$$c.Deg > th. \tag{1}$$

In the proposed protocol, this threshold is decided depending on the criticality of the underlying WSAN application i.e. the value of *th* for a critical WSAN application such as fire detection is less as compared to other less critical applications such as air quality monitoring.

5.2 Handling Compromise of a Critical Sensor Node and Actor Node Belonging to Area $Area_i$

The procedure for handling the compromise of critical member sensor nodes as defined in Algorithm 1. Table 1 lists the notations used by the proposed protocol.

Table 1. Notations used

Symbol	Meaning
$x.y$	Value of variable y maintained by node x
N_C	Number of currently compromised nodes
$x.Neg$	Identifiers of neighboring nodes of node x
$x.Deg$	Degree of node x
$x.Actornodes$	Actor nodes responsible for performing rekeying on the compromise of node x
M_j	jth sensor node
A_q	qth actor node
$PK(r, s)$	Pair-wise key used for securing the communication occurring between the nodes r and s

When a sensor node M_j is detected to be compromised, then $M_j.ActorNodes$ perform rekeying. Let $M_j.ActorNodes = \{A_1, A_2, A_3,..., A_p\}$. Each node checks whether the neighboring node is the compromised node or not. The update message KUPD is forwarded only to the valid neighboring nodes using the pair-wise keys shared with them.

Suppose nodes from A_1 to A_{p-1} have already failed i.e. unavailable to perform rekeying when M_j is detected to be compromised, then A_p is the first available actor node for handling the compromise of M_j. A_p generates the updated (new) keying material i.e. new pair of first term and recursive formula.

1. A_p then creates the KUPD message containing the new keying material and identifier of the compromised node and forwards the update message to its neighboring nodes using the pair-wise keys shared with them, except for the compromised node.
2. The neighbors of A_p also forward the same message to their neighbors using controlled flooding except for the neighboring compromised node and so on, until all the valid network nodes receive the update message.

Algorithm 1. HANDLE NODE COMPROMISE

1. A_p generates new keying material (KM).
2. A_p creates KUPD message.
3. $KUPD = KM \parallel KUPD_{ID} \parallel M_j;$
4.   for each neighNode $\in (A_p.Neg - M_j)$:
5. $S = PK(A_p, \text{neighNode})$;
6. $KUPD = E_S(KUPD)$; //encrypt update message using pair-wise key shared with the neighboring node.
7.   end for
8. A_p updates the value of $A_p.KUPD_{ID}$ with $KUPD$

---

6   Simulation Results

We evaluate performance of the proposed protocol EEHKM and compared it with two other dynamic key management protocols: SKM [13] and EETKM [14]. The network parameters used in simulation are shown in Table 2. Initially, each node is randomly pre-distributed with the first term and the recursive formula of a numerical sequence. The comparison of EEHKM with other existing protocols was based on the number of links rekeyed, energy consumption of key refresh operations and the network lifetime.

Table 2.   Simulation parameters

Parameter	Value
Area of deployment	500×500 m
Total number of network nodes	500
Total number of clusters	25
Number of actor nodes	25
Number of sensor nodes	475
Radio range of actor nodes	50 m
Radio range of sensor nodes	20 m

6.1 Number of Links Rekeyed

The network nodes are compromised in a random order and the number of network links that are rekeyed is counted. The results are shown in Fig. 2. It can be seen that the results are same for EEHKM and EETKM as in both these protocols only the active links i.e. the links that are used in some routing path are rekeyed. On the other hand in SKM, links between all the valid network nodes are rekeyed. Consequently, the rekeying overhead of EEHKM and EETKM is much less as compared to that of SKM. The relation between the number of links rekeyed in SKM, EETKM and EEHKM is shown in Eq. 2.

$$LR_{SKM} > LR_{EETKM} = LR_{EEHKM}. \tag{2}$$

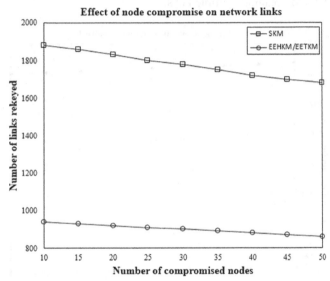

Fig. 2. Number of compromised nodes vs. number of links rekeyed.

6.2 Energy Consumption of Key Refresh Operations

Two main factors that affect the energy consumption of key refresh operations are the number of links rekeyed and the size of key refresh message. More the number of compromised sensor nodes more will be the number of links rekeyed during each key refresh operation. When the number of links that are rekeyed increases the energy consumption also increases. Further, in the proposed protocol EEHKM the size of the rekey message is reduced and therefore, the communication overhead and the energy consumption is least in EEHKM as compared to SKM and EETKM. Equation 3 shows the relation between the size of key refresh message in EEKHM, SKM and EETKM. We may obtain the relation between energy consumption, *EC* of key refresh operation in EEHKM, SKM and EETKM as shown in Eq. 4.

$$KUPD\_EETKM_{size} > KUPD\_SKM_{size} = KUPD\_EEHKM_{size}. \tag{3}$$

$$EC_{EETKM} > EC_{SKM} > ECEE_{HKM}. \tag{4}$$

Figure 3 shows the scenario when the number of active pair of neighboring sensor nodes is high and key refresh message size is large. It can be seen that the energy consumption is smallest in the case of EEHKM as the number of links rekeyed and key refresh message size is smallest in EEHKM in comparison to SKM and EETKM. We also observe that the energy consumption of EETKM is more as compared to the EEHKM and SKM schemes. This is due to the fact that the size of the key refresh message is more in EETKM as compared to EEHKM and SKM as each key refresh message in EETKM contains multiple keys.

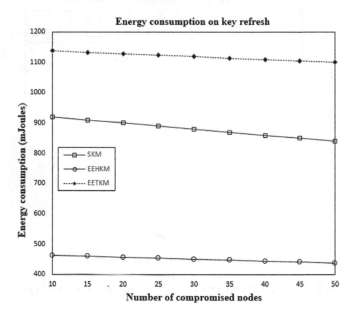

Fig. 3. Energy consumption of key refresh operations.

6.3   Network Lifetime

The lifetime of any WSAN is directly affected by energy consumption made by the key management strategy deployed in it. Higher the rate at which energy is consumed by any key management technique, smaller the duration the network survives and vice-versa. In the scenario where the number of active pair of neighboring sensor nodes is high and a large number of keys are maintained by each network node, the energy consumption of EETKM is higher as compared to that of SKM. Consequently, the network survives longer duration in SKM as compared to EETKM as shown in Fig. 4. When the number of compromised nodes increases, more and more key refresh operations are performed leading to increased energy consumption and reduced network lifetime. As the energy consumption of proposed EEHKM is

smallest in comparison to SKM and EETKM, the network survives the longest duration in EEHKM for any number of compromised nodes.

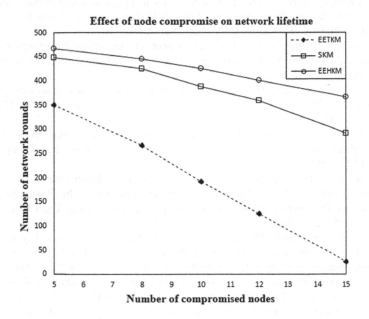

Fig. 4. Effect of node compromise on network lifetime.

7   Conclusion

A rekeying protocol that minimizes energy consumption is proposed in this paper for
WSANs. The proposed protocol assigns the responsibility of key management to
multiple network nodes and thus avoids single point of failure. It is highly resilient
against node capture attacks as each network link is secured using a unique pair-wise
key and compromise of any network node will affect only the direct links of that node.
The network lifetime of the WSAN is enhanced through reduction of the energy
consumption of key management operations. In future we may explore periodic rekeying
schemes in presence of compromise node to enhance the network lifetime.

References

1. Akyildiz, I.F., Kasimoglu, I.H.: Wireless sensor and actor networks: research challenges. Ad
   Hoc Netw. **2**(4), 351–367 (2004)
2. Heo, T., Kim, H., Doh, Y., Kim, K., Park, J., Kim, N., Jun, J., Ko, J.: Multi-tiered and
   distributed WSAN for cooperative indoors environment management. Mob. Inf. Syst. (2017).
   doi:10.1155/2017/6979178
3. Perrig, A., Stankovic, J., Wagner, D.: Security in wireless sensor networks. Commun. ACM
   47(6), 53–57 (2004)

4. He, X., Niedermeier, M., De Meer, H.: Dynamic key management in wireless sensor networks: a survey. J. Netw. Comput. Appl. **36**(2), 611–622 (2013)
5. Lai, B., Kim, S., Verbauwhede, I.: Scalable session key construction protocol for wireless sensor networks. In: Proceedings of IEEE Workshop on Large Scale Real Time and Embedded Systems (LARTES), IEEE Press, New York (2002)
6. Eschenauer, L., Gligor, V.D.: A key-management scheme for distributed sensor networks. In: Proceedings of 9th ACM Conference on Computer and Communications Security (CCS 2002), pp. 41–47 (2002)
7. Chan, H., Perrig, A., Song, D.: Random key predistribution schemes for sensor networks. In: Proceeding of 2003 IEEE Symposium on Security and Privacy, pp. 197–213. IEEE Press, New York (2003)
8. Mary Anita, E.A., Geetha, R., Kannan, E.: A novel hybrid key management scheme for establishing secure communication in wireless sensor networks. Wirel. Pers. Commun. **82**(3), 1419–1433 (2015)
9. Zhou, R., Yang, H.: A hybrid key management scheme for heterogeneous wireless sensor networks based on ECC and trivariate symmetric polynomial. In: Proceeding of 2011 International Conference on Uncertainty Reasoning and Knowledge Engineering (URKE), vol. 1, pp. 251–255 (2011)
10. Landstra, T., Zawodnick, M., Jagannathan, S.: Energy-efficient hybrid key management protocol for wireless sensor networks. In: Proceeding of 32nd IEEE Conference on Local Computer Networks (LCN 2007), pp. 1009–1016. IEEE Press, New York (2007)
11. Doraipandian, Manivannan, Rajapackiyam, Ezhilarasie, Neelamegam, P., Rai, Anuj Kumar: An Efficient and Hybrid Key Management Scheme for Three Tier Wireless Sensor Networks Using LU Matrix. In: Abraham, Ajith, Mauri, Jaime Lloret, Buford, John F., Suzuki, Junichi, Thampi, Sabu M. (eds.) ACC 2011. CCIS, vol. 192, pp. 111–121. Springer, Heidelberg (2011). doi:10.1007/978-3-642-22720-2_11
12. Lee, Y., Lee, S.: A new efficient key management protocol for wireless sensor and actor networks. Int. J. Comput. Sci. Inf. Secur. **6**(2), 15–22 (2009)
13. Messai, M.L., Seba, H., Aliouat, M.: A lightweight key management scheme for wireless sensor networks. J. Supercomput. **71**(12), 4400–4422 (2015)
14. Kousalya, C.G., Raja, J.: An energy efficient traffic-based key management scheme for wireless sensor networks. In: Proceeding of International Conference on Networking and Digital Society (ICNDS 2009), vol. 2, pp. 156–161. IEEE Press, New York (2009)
15. Ahlawat, P., Dave, M.: A hybrid approach for path vulnerability matrix on random key predistribution for wireless sensor networks. Wirel. Pers. Commun. **94**(4), 1–27 (2016)

Healing Partitioned Wireless Sensor Networks

Gaurav Kumar and Virender Ranga[✉]

Department of Computer Engineering,
National Institute of Technology, Kurukshetra, Haryana, India
gngauravnain@gmail.com, virender.ranga@nitkkr.ac.in

Abstract. Sensor nodes in wireless sensor networks are prone to failures because of their sensitiveness in the harsh surroundings. Sometimes, a failure of large scale nodes may occur in the deployed network and it converts connected network into disjoint segments called network partition problem. Therefore, a deployed application demands a continuous fault repairing mechanism to repair the lost connectivity. Deployment of additional relay node in damaged network is one of the best methods to restore the network operation. However, the relay node placement problem is shown to be an NP-hard problem. In this paper, we propose a swarm intelligence based solution to find the best locations of relay node placement in polynomial time. The simulation results show the performance gain of proposed solution over the state-of-the-art solutions.

Keywords: Connectivity · Relay node · Meta-heuristic · Swam intelligence

1 Introduction

In the recent years, a boost in the development of applications of wireless sensor networks (WSNs) has been observed. SNs have the power to sense, compute and transmit the data to other SNs or base station (BS) for further processing [1]. Sometimes, we deploy SN in such areas where recharge or replacement of the battery is impossible. Due to this type of applications, WSNs are prone to many types of failures such as hardware failure (unavailability of a power source, no coverage), natural disaster (volcano, flood, earthquake etc.) and explosion on the battlefield or coal mine. Therefore, it requires a special attention towards repair mechanisms for WSNs. A lot of work has been done to guarantee the normal functioning of all underlying operations. One of repairing mechanism is to connect different segmented parts of the disjoint network to provide inter-segment connectivity (partitions in WSN might be created due to large scale failures of SNs). This is a very well-known and well-researched problem of WSNs. A number of researchers find a different kind of solutions like (algorithmic based, approximation based, heuristic based) to restore lost connectivity in WSNs [2, 3]. With the help of additional SNs. However, SNs have smaller coverage and low connectivity. Therefore, we require a special type of node, i.e. relay node (RNs), to repair the disjoint partitioned network. RNs have larger battery power and longer coverage area compared to SNs. Relay node placement (RNP) requires advance knowledge about the communication range of SNs as well as RNs and working area of WSNs. The problem of placing RNs in the disjoint partitioned segments, to provide lost

© Springer International Publishing AG 2017
S.F. Ochoa et al. (Eds.): UCAmI 2017, LNCS 10586, pp. 545–557, 2017.
DOI: 10.1007/978-3-319-67585-5_54

connectivity in WSN, is called relay node placement problem (RNPP) [3, 4]. Our main objective is to place a minimum number of relay nodes and maintain lost connectivity among all segments. Some solutions have been proposed to minimize the number of required RNs. Nowadays, a new era of meta-heuristic based solutions are suggested to solve NP-hard or NP-complete problems because of their simplicity, flexibility and capability to solve complex problem in polynomial time [5]. Problem independence and randomness are two main features of any meta-heuristic based approach. These two features allow swam intelligence to search solutions both globally and locally. Global searching and local searching in solution space is called as exploration and exploitation, respectively. Till date, swarm intelligence (SI) like particle swarm optimization (PSO) [6], artificial bee colony (ABC) [7], ant colony optimization (ACO) [8], genetic algorithm (GA) [9] have been proposed to solve RNPP, but without considering network partition problem (NPP) in the network. We propose a novel solution, which minimizes the count of RNs in the network, by using a Grey wolf optimizer algorithm (GWO) [10]. As per our view, till date, no one has attempted to solve RNPP for segmented networks by using GWO. The remainder of the paper is organized as follows: Sect. 2 presents related works. Section 3 shows our proposed problem. Section 4 discusses the basis concept of GWO. Implementation of the proposed solution and the results of the simulations are shown in Sects. 5 and 6, respectively. Finally, Sect. 7 concludes the paper and discusses the future work.

2 Literature Review

In this section, we have shown a survey on previously attempted solutions for RNPP. RNPP techniques can be classified into four categories, i.e. (algorithmic-based, approximation based, heuristic based, swarm intelligence based) [2]. In this paper, we discuss only two of them (because of space constraint).

2.1 Swarm Intelligence Based Solutions

The authors of [6] have been implemented PSO to tackle the problem of RNPP in static hybrid networks. Particle swarm optimization is adopted with the integer planning problem to reduce the solution space. The results show that an optimal deployment of RNs largely improve energy efficiency and location of BS has a direct impact on results. Hashim [7] proposed an approach to increase the energy efficiency of WSN by deploying RNs using ABC. The key idea behind the usage of ABC is to optimize network parameter and extend the network lifetime with the minimum number of RNs. Kamal [8] jointly solve the problem of RNP and trajectory calculation for a mobile data collector (MDC) in hierarchical WSN using ACO SI. The proposed ACO based approach considers the model of traveling salesman problem (TSP). In [9], Azharuddin and Jana suggest an evolutionary GA-based technique of RNPP in hierarchical WSN. Initially, they consider a set of potential locations and seek to minimize RNs using GA based operations (crossover and mutation). Each potential location is considered as genes, which can hold two values 0 and 1. If a particular location is selected, it is marked as 1 otherwise 0. Performing efficient mutation and crossover with linear programming (LP) results in effective performance and generate optimized solutions.

2.2 Heuristic Solutions

Senel et al. [11] suggest an approach which places RNs towards the estimated center of mass of segmented area of the network. They did not consider the concept of minimum Steiner tree (MST), due to the creation of cut-vertex, which results in the partition of network again and again. Spider-web heuristic based approach [10] is considered to solve RNPP which guarantee inward placement of relays with better coverage and connectivity. In [12], Chen et al. proposed an approach for the application of WSN in wind farm monitoring. Their proposed approach strives to place RNs to connect sub-networks and get back inter-sub-network lost connectivity. The authors of [13] considered the working area as a grid with equal sized cells. Each segmented part of the network is represented by representative nodes. In [14] Bhattacharya et al. tackle the problem of placing RNs as well as BS, to get predefined performance objectives, which is called as multi-sink Steiner network minimum cost-Hop constraint (MSS-MCHC). The idea behind the placement of multiple sinks is to handle the network design scalability. Their proposed work includes a polynomial time approximation based algorithm (SmartSelect) which aims to minimize the cost of placing BSs and RNs. Based on the results of SmartSelect another heuristic algorithm is selected to improve the previous solution by destroying current one and explore solution space iteratively.

3 Problem Description

A flat structure of WSN is considered with random deployment of SNs. Initially, each SN is able to communicate with other SN using a wireless medium. The base station or sink node is established to observe the smooth working of the network. SNs transmit the sensed information using any predefined routing policy. When a number of SNs stops working due to their low battery power or damage their hardware due to an explosion on the battlefield, or any other issue, then segments are formed in the network. All these segments may not be able to transmit the useful information towards BS. Each segment holds a subset of SNs and the route to sink node may be disconnected. To tackle with this type of problem we suggest a meta-heuristic based approach to place RNs in the disconnected part of the network. Our problem can be defined as: *"WSN consists of a large number of tiny SNs. When any cut-vertex sensor node or any segmented group(s) of SNs is/are not reachable from sink node or from any other group, then the partition is formed. Network partitioning can be happened on a large scale, where a large number of SNs gets failed. Suppose N_{Seg} number of segments are created and each segment is represented by a single RN. Therefore, we have N_{Seg} number of points in the 2-D plane where the communication range of RN is considered as R. Our proposed solution address the problem of placing RNs in the damaged area to restore lost connectivity with a minimum count of RNs."*

4   The Grey Wolf Optimizer

Grey wolf optimizer (GWO) algorithm is a discrete nature swarm intelligence technique. It is inspired from the social and attacking behavior of grey wolves. Grey wolves are a special member of Candie family and prefer to live in a flock of size 5–12. The population of grey wolves is divided based upon a hierarchy. The one on the top of hierarchy dominates lower ones and so on.

The social hierarchy, shown in Fig. 1, is based on the dominance of wolves [10]. At the top of the hierarchy, a leader is present. The leader may be female or male, but the leader must have the ability to guide the group members. Wolves, at the top position of hierarchy, are called as alpha wolves (α). Alpha wolves have the privilege to make decisions and convey orders to all other group members. The second position in wolf social hierarchy is reserved for Beta wolves (β). Beta wolves take orders from alphas and convey the same to lower level members. Betas help alphas to make the decision about group management activities. In the case of unavailability of alphas, beta leads the other group members. At the third position, Delta wolves (δ) are present. Deltas follow the order of betas and alphas and give the order to omegas. Deltas have been assigned the role of, scout, hunter and they are the most experienced members of the family. They help another member during hunting and arrange food. Omega wolves (ω) available at the bottom of the hierarchy. Omegas follow the order given by the other wolves and acknowledge the same. Omegas are dominated by all others in the group of wolves. They get the food at last when all others have been finished. Grey wolves attack prey in a well-planned manner and forward gradually towards the location of prey. The same hunting procedure can be used to solve optimization problems. We also follow the same procedure to solve RNPP in an efficient manner. Grey wolves complete the hunting process in steps, which is shown below, suggested by [15].

Fig. 1.   Social hierarchy of gray wolves

- Trailing and tracking
- Surrounding the prey
- Aggress the prey

The mathematical modeling of hunting procedure [10] is shown in the next part of the paper. Our proposed algorithm uses the same concept to find an optimum location of RNs for a given set of representative nodes.

4.1 Surrounding the Prey

When the group of grey wolves encircles the prey, following mathematical model is used.

$$\vec{D} = \left| \vec{R} . \overrightarrow{L_P} (i) - \vec{L}(i) \right| \tag{1}$$

$$\vec{L}(i+1) = \overrightarrow{L_P} (i) - \vec{Q} . \vec{D} \tag{2}$$

In Eq. 1 and 2, $\vec{D}$ represent distance, $\vec{L}p$ and $\vec{L}$ denote the location vector of prey and wolf respectively, $\vec{R}$ and $\vec{Q}$ are coefficient vectors which helps to make a good surrounding for prey and i represents the iteration number. Next two equations are used to generate both coefficient vectors $\vec{R}$ and $\vec{Q}$.

$$\vec{R} = 2.\vec{r}1 \tag{3}$$

$$\vec{Q} = 2.\vec{q}\,\vec{r} - .\vec{q} \tag{4}$$

In Eqs. 3 and 4, $\vec{r}1$ and $\vec{r}2$ are random vectors in the range [0, 1] and $\vec{q}$ is decreased from value 2 to 0.

4.2 Aggress the Prey

Attacking or aggressing the prey requires establishing a specific model to apply GWO to solve optimization problems. In this section, we give a generalized modeling for alpha, beta, delta and omega based on the study of authors [10]. Mathematical modeling for alpha, beta, and delta are given as:

$$\overrightarrow{D_\alpha} = \left| \overrightarrow{R_1} . \overrightarrow{L_\alpha} - \vec{L} \right|, \overrightarrow{D_\beta} = \left| \overrightarrow{R_2} . \overrightarrow{L_\beta} - \vec{L} \right|, \overrightarrow{D_\delta} = \left| \overrightarrow{R_3} . \overrightarrow{L_\delta} - \vec{L} \right| \tag{5}$$

$$\overrightarrow{L_1} = \overrightarrow{L_\alpha} - \overrightarrow{Q_1} . \overrightarrow{D_\alpha}, \overrightarrow{L_2} = \overrightarrow{L_\beta} - \overrightarrow{Q_2} . \overrightarrow{D_\beta}, \overrightarrow{L_3} = \overrightarrow{L_\delta} - \overrightarrow{Q_3} . \overrightarrow{D_\delta}, \tag{6}$$

$$\vec{L}(i+1) = (\overrightarrow{L_1} + \overrightarrow{L_2} + \overrightarrow{L_3})/3 \tag{7}$$

The pseudo-code of GWO is shown below in Algorithm 1.

Algorithm 1. *Grey Wolf Optimizer Algorithm [10]*
1. **Procedure** *GWO(initial population)*
2. *Initialize population* $\vec{L}\alpha$ *(i = 1, 2,.........,n)*
3. *Initialize coefficient vectors* $\vec{q}$, $\vec{Q}$ *and* $\vec{R}$
4. $\vec{L_\alpha}$- *First best possible solution*
5. $\vec{L_\beta}$ - *Second best possible solution*
6. $\vec{L_\delta}$- *Third best possible solution*
7. **while** *(j <Max number of iterations)* **do**
8. **for** *each search agent* **do**
9. *Modify probable position of current search agent using equation 7*
10. **endfor**
11. *Modify vectors* $\vec{q}$, $\vec{Q}$ *and* $\vec{R}$
12. *Compute fitness of each search agents*
13. *Modify location vectors* $\vec{L_\alpha}$, $\vec{L_\beta}$, *and* $\vec{L_\delta}$
14. *j ← j + 1*
15. **endwhile**
16. **return** $\vec{L_\alpha}$ *Return the best solution*
17. **end** *procedure*

---

5 Our Proposed Solution

In this section, we have discussed our proposed solution based on the GWO. We have mapped our problem using mathematical model of GWO. Initially, the set of segments S act as a flock of Grey Wolves and used as input for GWO Algorithm 1. The output of GWO can be somewhere in the damaged region such as all wolves (segments) encircle the prey (potential RN) position. Our proposed idea strives to populate RNs inwards center of the damaged area and strives to restore inter-segment lost connectivity. Our proposed solution is divided into different phases. Each phase gradually populates RNs and restore the segmented disjoint network. All of the phases are listed below:

 i. Find the relative position of representative node
 ii. Neighbor discovery
 iii. Placed the RNs using GWO
 iv. Termination phase

For better understanding, we discussed our proposed solution with an example to demonstrate the working of different phases. Step-by-step and detailed explanation of the proposed solution is shown in the next subsections.

5.1   Find the Relative Position of Representative Node

The process of repairing lost connectivity is started with failures of a large scale of SNs. During the normal working of WSN, when BS recognizes a sudden decrease in the number of packets received, then it is considered by the BS that segmentation/partition has been occurred in the network. At this point of failure, there is a need to execute a RNPP algorithm to repair the lost connectivity of the network. In the first phase of our proposed solution, we find a relative position of the representative node. Every segment is denoted Segi where i is $0 \leq i \leq N_{Seg}$ and N_{Seg} is total number of segments in the network. For experimentation purpose, the whole segment is denoted as a single X-Y coordinate location. Figure 2 shows the seven disconnected segments where 2-D coordinate of all segments are shown as: Seg1: (39, 77), Seg2: (68, 58), Seg3: (47, 15), Seg4: (2, 65), Seg5: (41, 54), Seg6: (7, 71) and Seg7: (69, 5). The above locations are calculated in the real simulation. The X-Y location is used as representative node for respective segments. Throughout this work, we use Euclidean distance to find the smallest distance between any two points. The formula used to find the Euclidean distance is stated below in Eq. 8.

$$|p_1, p_2| = \sqrt{(x_1 - x_2)^2 + (y_1 - y_2)^2},\qquad(8)$$

where p_1 and p_2 represent two points, $|p_1, p_2|$ represents the Euclidean distance, and (x_1, y_1) and (x_2, y_2) are the X-Y coordinate of p_1 and p_2, respectively.

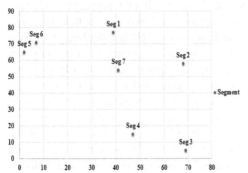

Fig. 2. Representative node of each segment is denoted by Segi

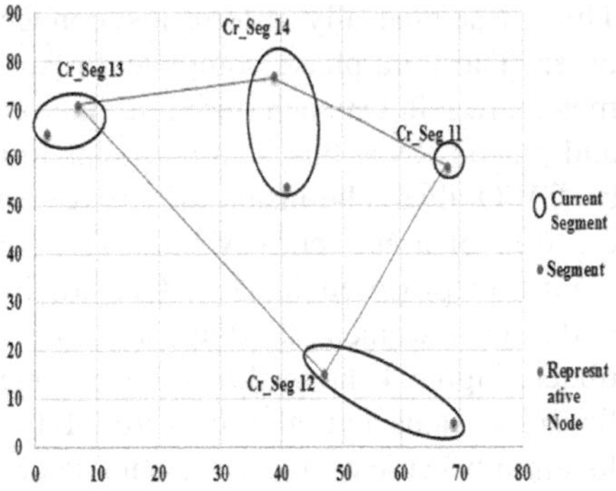

Fig. 3. Every segment join with its neighbor where Rr = 15 m

5.2   Neighbor Discovery

The second phase is suggested to find segments which are in the proximity of each other. Therefore, the proposed algorithm initiates the neighbor discovery process. This phase is executed for every disconnected segment. We assume that the representative node of every segment is an RN for the sake of simplicity. Due to this, it helps us to reduce the total number of calculations. To find neighboring segment Seg_n of segment Seg_i, it must satisfy equality $|Seg_i, Seg_n| \leq 2 * R$. The neighboring segments are shown in Fig. 4, where Seg_2 has no neighboring segment, therefore it is converted into segment Cr_Seg11, Seg_4 combines with Seg_3 and create segment Cr_Seg12, Seg_6 combines with Seg_5 and create segment Cr_Seg13, and Seg_1 combines with Seg_7 and create segment Cr_Seg14. Figure 3 also shows a convex hull generated over current representative nodes. The current round segments are denoted by Cr_Seg_{ij} where i shows the iteration number and j denotes the segment number.

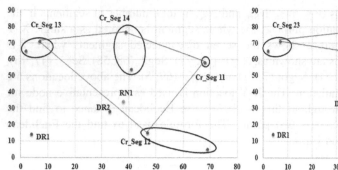

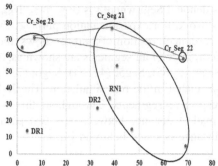

Fig. 4. First RN RN1 (38, 34) is placed

Fig. 5. Relay node RN1 connect two segments into single one

5.3   Placed the RNs Using GWO

This phase gradually restores lost connectivity and connect disjoint segments with each other. The third phase completes in several iterations until two or less than two segments are left. On each iteration, one optimized location of RN is calculated by GWO and placed RN at that location helps to restore connectivity. Optimized location given by GWO always be inside the convex hull. As current segments change, it leads to the creation of a new convex hull. The convex hull is generated using a Graham Scan algorithm proposed in [16]. Considering, one node as a representative for all other nodes in a segment. Further, a convex hull is shown over only these representative nodes. Figure 4 shows 3 new nodes, one is RN1 (38, 34) i.e. optimized location of the first relay node and other two are DR1 (4, 14) and DR2 (33, 28) denotes the discarded location because of, these are outside of convex hull. It is a side effect of meta-heuristic based solution of their random nature. This side effect can be removed with the help of the convex hull algorithm. Figure 5 shows how a relay node RN1 helps to restore lost inter-segment connectivity. Here, segment Cr_Seg12 connect with segment Cr_Seg14 and create segment Cr_Seg21.

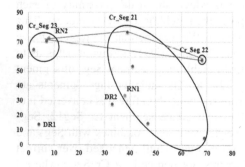

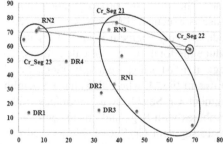

Fig. 6. Second RN RN2 (8, 73) is placed

Fig. 7. Third relay node RN3 (36, 72) is placed

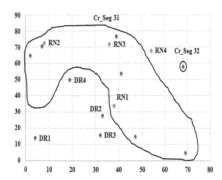

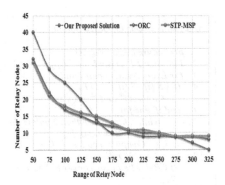

Fig. 8. Only two segments are left and Relay node RN4 (54, 68) is placed

Fig. 9. Comparison for varying range with number of segment is $N_{Seg} = 5$

Figure 6 is the outcome of the second iteration where one more relay node RN2 (8, 73) is placed. But this does not create a connection between any two segments. Relay node RN2 lies on the line of the respective convex hull. In the third iteration of the proposed algorithm, the location of third relay node RN3 (36, 72) is found using GWO. Figure 7 shows two more discarded location DR3 (32, 16) and DR4 (19, 50). Sometimes, GWO generates locations which are not so relevant. Therefore, we discarded this type of locations using convex hull.

5.4 Termination Phase

The last phase is the termination phase. Our proposed solution is terminated when two or less than two segments are left in the WSN. The termination condition is inspired by the feature of GWO, because it requires at least three sized population to optimize the result. Same is taken in our proposed solution. Figure 8 shows disjoint segments left after the placement of required relays. Further, last two segments are connected manually. The location of relays might be somewhere on the joining line of last two representative nodes. The required number of RN to connect last two segments is calculated with the help of equality $\frac{|p_1, p_2|}{2*R}$ where p_1 and p_2 are X-Y coordinates of last two segments. If only one segment is left, lost connectivity is restored successfully. The pseudo-code of our proposed solution is shown in Algorithm 2.

Algorithm 2. Our Proposed Solution

```
 1:  procedure (Area, N_Seg, R)
 2:  Initialize 2-D array S and N_Relay ← 0;
 3:  for Every segment pair i and j
 4:    if | S [i] , S [j] | ≤ 2 × R_r
 5:      Connect i^th and j^th segment
 6:  end if end for
 7:      while S have more than 2 points do
 8:          Initialize C_Relay [2] ;
 9:    CH ← Compute a convex hull over S
10:    C_Relay ← GWO (S) ;
11:    If CRelay lie inside convex hull CH
12:    N_Relay++ ;
13:    Initialize integer C Temp_Seg ← 0 ;
14:    Initialize and 2-D array Temp_Seg ;
15:    for i ← 0 to N_Seg
16:    if | S [i] , C_Relay | ≤ 2 × R_r
17:    Temp_Seg ← S[i];
18:    C_Temp_Seg + + ;
19:    end if end for
20:    if C_Temp_Seg == 0
21:    Create a new Segment with current relay.
22:    else if C_Temp_Seg == 1
23:    Add current relay to respective segment
24:    Else
25:    for all elements in Temp_Seg
26:    Join together
27:    S = S − Temp_Seg;
28:    end for end if
29:    end if end if
30:    end while
31:    if S have two point then
32:    Temp ← | S [0], S [1] | /(2 × R_r)
33:    N_Relay ← N_Relay + Temp
34:    end if
35:    return N_Relay
36:  end procedure
```

6   Comparison and Results Discussion

Here, we compare our proposed solution with other state-of-art approaches (ORC [13], STP-MSP [17]). The comparison and simulation results are an evidence of our work done. We have implemented our algorithm in JAVA environment. Our results show that proposed solution is outperformed others when the communication range is large. But due to the randomness of GWO, sometimes the performance of our proposed solution is degraded when transmission range is small. The comparison is done, on the basis of total number of RN counts required to restore lost connectivity.

Initially, we choose some simulation parameters which are listed in Table 1. The following parameters are used to evaluate the proposed solution: (a) Number of disjoint segments (N_{Seg}), (b) transmission range of relay node (R) and (c) total number of relay node (N_{Relay}). During simulations, we have taken 1000 m × 1000 m area having a varying number of disconnected networks. Number of segments may vary from 5 to 10

Table 1. Simulation parameters

Parameter	Value
Area	1000 m × 1000 m
Sensor nodes	100–500
Total number of partition	5–10
Communication range of RNs	50 m–325 m
Number of placed RNs	5–45

and count of RNs also varies with the number of segments. All simulation results have been taken into consideration after the average of 30 experiments. Therefore, it is a strong evidence to increase the confidence level about the proposed solution. ORC [13] and STP-MSP [17] is the baseline RNP approaches, choose for comparison.

6.1   Total Number of Relay Nodes

This metric is used to compare the effectiveness of the proposed approaches for comparison. Our main objective is to minimize the total number of relay nodes. In Fig. 9, we compare the results for varying communication range, but the number of segments is taken fixed i.e. 5. The transmission range of RN has a direct impact on the total count of RNs. The same scenario is depicted in Fig. 10 which shows the result of ORC, STP-MSP. This simulation shows the side effect of stochastic nature of GWO where our algorithm outputs more numbers of relays compared with others. In this, it has been observed that our proposed solution outperforms over ORC and STP-MSP in all cases if range of an RN is 200 m. The relationship between the number of segments and total RNs can be seen here also. The last simulation which we have conducted, is only for our proposed solution. We combine all three parameters (number of segments, communication range, the number of RNs) to show a scenario about the impact of the count of the segments on the final count of RNs. Figure 11 is a 3-D dimension of simulation where a clear view of the above said can be seen.

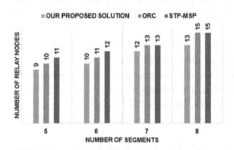

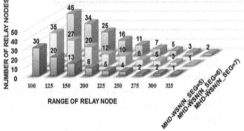

Fig. 10. Comparison for varying segments, where range of a relay node is R = 200 m

Fig. 11. Results of our proposed solution for varying number of segments

7 Conclusion and Future Work

WSNs have lots of applications in several scenarios, e.g. underwater, coal mine, battlefield, and forest) where the risk to human life is more. Therefore, the demand of WSNs increases for several real life applications. Further, the harsh surroundings become a problem for WSN, when the network is partitioned into several disjoint segments. At that time, there is a need to populate RNs which help to restore connectivity. To address this problem, we suggested a swarm intelligence based solution while considering GWO as a relevant SI to find the best positions of RNs. To reduce the impact stochastic nature of GWO, we embedded convex hull approach along with GWO while populating RNs inwards center of the damaged region. At last, we evaluate the performance gain of our proposed solution with some state-of-art solutions where we found good results. In the future, we check our proposed solution on the real test bed.

References

1. Ranga, V., Dave, M., Verma, A.K.: Network partitioning recovery mechanisms in WSANs: a survey. Wirel. Pers. Commun. **72**, 857–917 (2013)
2. Verma, A., Ranga, V., Angra, S.: Relay node placement techniques in wireless sensor networks. In: 2015 IEEE International Conference on Green Computing and Internet of Things (ICGCIoT), pp. 1384–1389 (2015)
3. Ranga, V., Dave, M., Verma, A.K.: Node stability aware energy efficient single node failure recovery approach for WSANs. Malays. J. Comput. Sci. **29**(2), 106–123 (2016)
4. Ranga, V., Dave, M., Verma, A.K.: A hybrid timer based single node failure recovery approach for WSANs. Wirel. Pers. Commun. **77**(3), 2155–2182 (2014)
5. Ranga, V., Dave, M., Verma, A.K.: Relay node placement to heal partitioned wireless sensor networks. Comput. Electr. Eng. **48**, 371–388 (2015)
6. Zhao, C., Chen, P.G.: Particle swarm optimization for optimal deployment of relay nodes in hybrid sensor networks. In: IEEE Congress on Evolutionary Computation. CEC 2007, pp. 3316–3320. IEEE, (2007)
7. Hashim, H.A., Ayinde, B.O., Abido, M.A.: Optimal placement of relay nodes in wireless sensor network using artificial bee colony algorithm. J. Netw. Comp. Appl. **64**, 239–248 (2016)
8. Kamal, K.R.: Ant colony optimization for jointly solving relay node placement and trajectory calculation in hierarchical wireless sensor networks (2014)
9. Azharuddin, M., Jana, P.K.: A ga-based approach for fault tolerant relay node placement in wireless sensor networks. In: 2015 Third International Conference on Computer, Communication, Control and Information Technology (C3IT), pp. 1–6. IEEE, (2015)
10. Mirjalili, S., Mirjalili, S.M., Lewis, A.: Grey wolf optimizer. Adv. Eng. Softw. **69**, 46–61 (2014)
11. Senel, F., Younis, M., Akkaya, K.: A robust relay node placement heuristic for structurally damaged wireless sensor networks. In: IEEE 34th Conference on Local Computer Networks. LCN 2009, pp. 633–640. IEEE, (2009)
12. Chen, Q., Hu, Y., Chen, Z., Grout, V., Zhang, D., Wang, H., Xing, H., Improved relay node placement algorithm for wireless sensor networks application in wind farm. In: 2013 IEEE International Conference on Smart Energy Grid Engineering (SEGE), pp. 1–6. IEEE, (2013)

13. Lee, S., Younis, M.: Optimized relay node placement for connecting disjoint wireless sensor networks. Comput. Netw. **56**(12), 2788–2804 (2012)
14. Bhattacharya, A., Rao, A., Naveen, K., Nishanth, P., Anand, S., Kumar, A.: Qos constrained optimal sink and relay placement in planned wireless sensor networks. In: 2014 International Conference on Signal Processing and Communications (SPCOM), pp. 1–5. IEEE, (2014)
15. Muro, C., Escobedo, R., Spector, L., Coppinger, R.: Wolf-pack (canis lupus) hunting strategies emerge from simple rules in computational simulations. Behav. Proc. **88**(3), 192–197 (2011)
16. Graham, R.L.: An efficient algorith for determining the convex hull of a finite planar set. Inf. Process. Lett **1**(4), 132–133 (1972)
17. Cheng, X., Du, D.-Z., Wang, L., Xu, B.: Relay sensor placement in wireless sensor networks. Wirel. Netw. **14**(3), 347–355 (2008)

Decentralized Authentication for Opportunistic Communications in Disaster Situations

Iván Santos-González[✉], Pino Caballero-Gil, Jezabel Molina-Gil,
and Alexandra Rivero-García

Department of Computer Engineering, University of La Laguna, Tenerife, Spain
{jsantosg,pcaballe,jmmolina,ariverog}@ull.edu.es

Abstract. This work presents a new secure system for deploying opportunistic communications for emergency management after any disaster in which network infrastructures have become collapsed or unavailable. This proposal uses different wireless technologies such as Bluetooth Low Energy, Wi-Fi Direct and LTE Direct to enable device-to-device communications between users through their smartphones. In this way, the system allows the deployment of decentralized communications in fragmented scenarios, what is essential for disaster relief applications. The general procedure of the proposed system is based on the use of chat rooms with possibility of real-time streaming. Two different types of chat rooms are defined: public chat rooms with open access for all registered and authenticated users, and private chat rooms that can be used by different authorized groups of people. The permissions required to use different chat room are established thanks to the use of a decentralized authentication scheme based on public keys and certificate graphs, where different trust levels can be applied. The proposed scheme includes also a decision protocol to choose the most appropriate communication technology in every moment, and a power saving protocol that minimizes the impact of the system on the device's battery consumption. The first results of field experiments made with a beta application developed for Android smartphones are promising.

1 Introduction

One of the worst consequences of many natural disasters is the interruption of communications due to the destruction or overloading of physical communication infrastructures. This communication interruption becomes a key issue for the people who are victims of a disaster because it could imply that they become totally isolated, and that the organizations responsible for the emergency response cannot do their job properly.

In recent years, several national and international research projects have proposed different solutions to deal with emergency situations. One of them is CRISYS project [1], based on the capacity to offer critic responses in the scope of the security and safety in emergency situations. Another related project is RESCUECELL [2], which uses smartphones in conjunction with an special kit to

© Springer International Publishing AG 2017
S.F. Ochoa et al. (Eds.): UCAmI 2017, LNCS 10586, pp. 558–569, 2017.
DOI: 10.1007/978-3-319-67585-5_55

locate smartphones after avalanches and earthquakes. Finally, TRADR project [3] combines humans and robots in mixed teams to offer assistance in emergency situations. The existence of these projects is a proof of the need for innovations to improve the assistance in emergency situations, so this topic can be considered an emerging and trending topic nowadays.

In most cases, disasters are unpredictable, so it is unrealistic to assume that then everybody will bring some special gadget. However, a gadget that everybody carries almost always is a smartphone because now these devices are used for many tasks, from calling and texting, to email, video viewing, Internet access, social media, geolocation, photography, etc. Thus, smartphones are used here for designing a new opportunistic communication system based on the combination of multiple wireless technologies, which can be applied in emergency situations where centralized network infrastructures are not available. Some previous works [4,5] have proposed the use of multiple technologies of mobile devices to build one-hop network through Device-to-Device (D2D) communications.

The proposal here presented combines different technologies, such as Bluetooth Low Energy (BLE) [6], Wi-Fi Direct [7] or LTE Direct [8], and the general procedure is based on the use of public chat rooms that can be accessed once registered and authenticated using asymmetric cryptography where distributed public key certification is faced through certificate certificate graphs [9]. On the other hand, in the proposed system it is expected that different authorities that have an indispensable role in emergencies, can use the system to access private chat rooms thanks to the use of secret keys shared in groups.

The present work is structured as follows. Section 2 describes a brief state of the art. The proposed system is defined in Sect. 3. Section 4 introduces the distributed authentication based on certificate graphs used in the proposal to improve security. Section 5 defines the decision protocol to select the technology. Section 6 describes the trust level scheme developed to ensure key transmission and system resistance. Finally, some conclusions and open issues close this paper.

2   Preliminaries

During the last years, different proposals have been presented in the field of communications in emergency situations. Some of them use a decentralised scheme like [10], but many of them have focused their systems on the use of the emergency call. This mode allows users to make an emergency call even when they do not have coverage to make phone calls to their contacts. To make this system works, the European Union imposed in 1991 its members states the use of the 112 number to make emergency calls. Moreover it imposed on mobile operators and mobile phone manufactures the adaptation of all their products so that, regardless of the mobile operator to which a user belongs, it allows him/her use the network infrastructure of any other operator to make emergency calls. This is the basis of the application Alpify [11], which allows users, through the emergency call system in cases where there is no Internet connection, to notify emergencies through SMS with georeferenced coordinates of their position to emergency services and a selected contact person. A problem that derives from the use of the emergency call system, is the need of availability of some network infrastructure for the correct operation of the application since it implies having coverage of at least one operator. In the situation proposed above, the initial hypothesis is that there is no coverage of any mobile operator because the network infrastructures are unusable or collapsed by a disaster, or do not exist because the users are in remote or difficult access places. In these cases, the use of any system based on communications using network infrastructures is not a feasible solution to the proposed problem. Moreover, the use of any system that needs a previous agreement between the company that develops the system and the different emergency services of every state of each country, implies difficulty to use them worldwide. In addition, centralized systems such as Alpify only notify emergency services and the previously selected contact person but, depending on where they are located, such contacts may be delayed until they reach the position of the person in a situation of emergency. Failure to contact the nearest people that could help in a faster way is a significant disadvantage of this type of systems compared to others, such as the one described here.

Other systems, such as [12], propose the use of a wireless technology known as Wi-Fi Direct, which, if there is no Internet connection, can be used to notify people within the coverage range. Their basis is to send an emergency message including the geolocated position of the sender, to other people in the range of Wi-Fi Direct. If a user that receives this message has an Internet connection, he/she notifies the emergency automatically to the emergency services. Otherwise, unless the message has been received before, the message is forwarded through a multi-hop system to every user nearby. This system implies an improvement compared to other systems than only use the emergency call, but has problems when the number of users with Wi-Fi Direct technology is small.

A different solution is based on the use of devices like laptops that are carried by emergency services, as in [13]. In that proposal the hypothesis is that the first units of the emergency services that arrive at the site deploy a Mobile Ad-hoc NETwork (MANET) based on Wi-Fi through the laptops they carry, creating a multi-hop ad-hoc network. Afterwards, a group communication system based on Peer-to-Peer is proposed, which admits services such as VoIP, Push-to-Talk, instant messaging, social networks, etc. Moreover, they propose the use of an information system to rescue people in earthquakes, which allows them to manage all the logistics necessary in this kind of catastrophe. One of the advantages offered by this type of solution is that the network is managed by specialized personnel who we suppose have prior learning, and restricted only to emergency services, preventing other users from accessing the network. However, people who have suffered the catastrophe, and might be isolated, remain isolated for as long as it takes emergency services to reach the catastrophe, which could be of vital importance. The system proposed in this paper tries to solve this situation of deprivation of aid through involving close people who, even though they could have suffered the disaster, maybe they would be able to help if necessary.

3   Proposed System

Communications in emergencies and/or natural disasters can be considered so far an unsolved problem because it has not yet been envisaged that communication systems should be able to operate without network infrastructures in exceptional cases. For this reason, this work proposes a new communication system for situations such as these, in which network infrastructures may be unavailable. This system uses different wireless technologies (BLE, Wi-Fi Direct and LTE Direct), regardless of the technology used at any moment, to establish communication with the users that are in the range of those technologies. The proposal works in the same way, regardless of which of the three communication technologies is available at any given time.

The new system gives users the ability to communicate directly with other users or use different chat rooms available for global group communication. Different chat rooms are available so that users can exchange messages and organize the help tasks in emergency situations, so that the performed tasks are stored for possible later review by other users. Public chat rooms can be used by all, but private chat rooms can be only used by people or groups of people with the corresponding permissions. A good example of the procedure of this system is the fact that some chat rooms are only available for emergency services such as firefighters, police, health personnel, etc. In this way, only people who belong to these groups and who have the necessary permissions, can access, read and answer messages from these private chat rooms.

In order to enable the system to work, all users store on their smartphones an encrypted copy of all chat rooms, including private chat rooms, in their states at the time of the last connection. Thus, when a device detects nearby devices, it establishes a communication, synchronizes its local copies with the most updated state, and, if the user has an Internet connection, synchronizes the local copies with the master copy stored on the central server.

After downloading the application, users can use the public chat room and to make direct communications through D2D with other users. If a user wants to access private chat rooms and has an Internet connection, he/she has to send a request to the server with the credentials of the affiliation group, and the administrator decides whether to grant access or not. Once the user is registered in the system, he/she receives from the central server a pair of public/private keys. When the administrator approves the membership of this user in some private groups, he/she receives the secret keys used to encrypt the chat rooms that correspond to these groups. If the user does not have an Internet connection, he/she can send a request to another user with the necessary trust level to run an authentication procedure on the system, as explained in Sect. 6. This is done this way because in emergency situations where usually there is no Internet connection, the application could be shared between users who only have public permission. In this way, authenticated users could authenticate others through an interactive strong identification scheme based on a challenge-response scheme with digital signature [14], without the need for any of them to have an Internet connection. Once a device has an Internet connection, it communicates with the server to inform about whether it has been authenticated or it has authenticated by/to other user, and then the server decides whether to revoke that authentication or not. The certification scheme is described in Sect. 4.

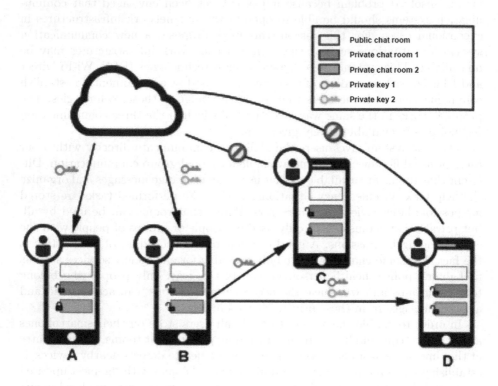

Fig. 1. Key sharing scheme

Every user is identified by his/her MAC or IMEI and his/her name in the application. Moreover, every chat room belongs to a group of users and nobody has access to a chat room if he/she does not belong to this group. Every group has a secret key, and the users can belong to several groups. By default, all users belong to the group with access, read and write permissions for public chat rooms. When a user is authenticated, he/she receives the secret keys of all existent chat rooms that he/she has permissions. In this way, users can read messages published in authorized chat rooms, including previously published messages. In synchronization cases, users cooperate with the system by forwarding the received messages and synchronizing their local copies and messages with the copies of other users and the central server, when connected to Internet, even though those users do not have the permissions of a determined group. Figure 1 shows the proposed key sharing scheme for the case of 4 users A, B, C and D who have access to the public chat room. The arrows represent a communication, and for this communication the users have to be connected. In the case of users A and B, both have Internet connection, and at the time of registration and authentication with the central server of the system, they receive from it their keys, and the keys corresponding to the chat rooms that they have access, which correspond in that example to one chat room for user A and two chat rooms for user B. Users C and D do not have Internet connection and therefore they have to register and authenticate through user B, and receive from him/her their keys and the keys that correspond to the chat rooms that they have access, which are in this example, one and two, respectively.

4   Offline Authentication

In case of no connection with the central server, the used authentication procedure is based on the distributed concept of certificate graph, which has been used in ad-hoc networks [15,16].

A certificate graph is a directed graph that represents public keys and certificates. In particular, every vertex u of this graph represents a network node with a pair of public/private keys, and every edge (u, v) represents a certificate associated with the public key of v, signed with the private key of u. In this graph, a sequence of certificates $\{(u, u_0), (u_0, u_1), ..., (u_m, v)\}$, where all vertices are different, is named chain of certificates from u to v. The length of the chain is the number of certificates in the chain, which in the previous case is $m + 2$.

Figure 2 shows the certificates stored in each node for a simple example.

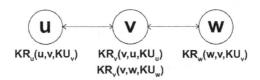

Fig. 2. Certificate graph example

Each device has an identification associated with its MAC or IMEI (n) that grants access to the chat rooms if it is updated. Moreover, each node has a pair of public and private keys (KU_n, KS_n) created in a centralized way by itself as well as its own certificate. This certificate is emitted by the CA and confirms that the public key is associated to the node because it is the only one that has the corresponding private key. The CA is responsible for maintaining the association between the ID and the keys, as well as the certificates $Cert_n = (KR_{CA}(KU_n), KU_{CA})$.

As commented in the previous section, every node is responsible for the registration of its pair of keys (KU_n, KS_n) in order to obtain the necessary certificate. Due to the environment in disaster situations, it is possible that some devices do not have direct connection to the CA, so they would have problems to obtain the certificate. However, according to the defined scenario, it is possible that the devices that have certificates can act as a Certification Authority for those devices which require certificates and cannot reach a CA.

Any node that has not been authenticated by the CA must follow the next steps to guarantee that it is a valid node. The node m without a valid certificate and no access to a certification authority, requires to connect with another device n who already belongs to the network. This node n has a certificate $Cert_n = (KR_{CA}(KU_n,), KU_{CA})$ because it already belongs to the network. Thus, it is responsible for acting as CA in front of the new node m. This node m cannot communicate with anybody because in order to establish a communications valid certificate is required. As explained in the previous section, the node m generates its pair of keys (KU_m, KR_m) and sends it to the node n for its certification. The node n certifies it with its private key certificated by the CA, being the new certificate of the node m $Cert_m = (KR_n(KU_m), (KR_{CA}(KU_n), KU_{CA}))$.

With this certificate, a message M signed with the private key of the node m, $KR_m(M)$ can be decrypted by any node of the network thanks to the certificate generated by n, which guarantees that it is a valid node. As can be seen, in this case a node x that receives this certificate can securely decrypt a message sent by m as it can check that the certificate it contains is valid. For this verification, it uses the public key of the node n, which was authenticated by the CA. Then, it knows that the node m has been authenticated by n. Therefore, this signature allows using the network through a challenge-response scheme with digital signature used for access control.

If a node x only has contact with the node m that was certified by the node n, the certificate generated by the node m for this node x corresponds to the next chain of certificates:

$$Cert_x = (KR_m(KU_x), (KR_n(KU_m), KU_n),$$

$$(KR_{AC}(KU_n), KU_{AC})$$

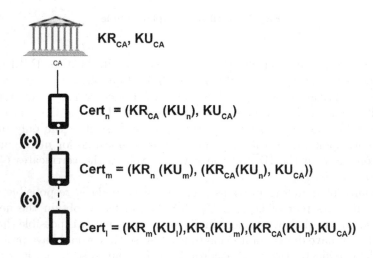

Fig. 3. Key certificate generation scheme

A message M signed by the node x, $KR_x(M)$ can be decrypted by every node of the network following the next steps.

1. KU_n is verified through KU_{AC} applied over $KR_{AC}(KU_n)$
2. KU_m is verified through KU_n applied over $KR_n, (KU_m)$
3. KU_x is verified through KU_m applied over $KR_m(KU_x)$
4. M is verified through KU_x applied over $KR_x(M)$

Therefore, thanks to the concepts of certificate graph and chain of certificates, the use of our application can been extended to possible disaster situations where many nodes are not registered and authenticated directly by the server and network infrastructures are not available (see Fig. 3).

5   Choice of Technology

In order to choose the specific technology to be used in each communication, an automatic decision protocol has been designed. This protocol allows users not to have to select the technology because it automatically chooses the most appropriate one for the communication in each moment. The developed protocol is based on different variables such as the number of peers found in the last successful attempts (established during a period defined by the user, which by default is 30 min), a parameter that depends on how recent are the last successful attempts, to prioritize the most recent attempts, and the consumption weight of each technology.

In the first use of the protocol, since no previous attempt exists, it is found which is the available technology that has the highest number of possible neighbour users. In the next attempts, the technology that produces the best results according to the aforementioned parameters is prioritized. Besides, after a number (defined by the user, and established by default as 10) of continued communications using the same technology, the system forces the attempt to use a different technology. On this way, we avoid that a technology that can be promising but in previous attempts has not been used, would not be marginalized. In particular, to choose the technology to be used in each moment, the formula $W = \frac{\sum_{i=1}^{10} i \cdot b \cdot N_i}{W_c}$ is used to compute the weight of each technology, W, where i represents each one of the last 10 attempts with that technology, the Boolean variable b indicates whether the technology was successfully used (1) or not (0) in the attempt i, N_i is the number of peers discovered in the attempt i with that technology, and W_c represents the consumption weight of that technology.

The consumption weight W_c has been computed for every technology after a consumption study based on a benchmark application for the BLE and Wi-Fi Direct technologies and assuming that the consumption of LTE Direct is similar that the one of BLE as it is described in [17]. The decision function to select a technology is defined after applying the above formula on each of the three considered technologies so that the technology that produces the highest result of the formula is the one to be used for the communication.

The battery consumption is an important aspect in all mobile and device to device applications as we can see in [18], but if there is a scope where this aspect is even more important is in the emergency situations. In this kind of situations we do not know how long it will take until help arrives. The duration of the battery of the smartphone could be of vital importance. To mitigate this problem, we propose a power saving protocol that decreases the battery consumption and improves the device useful life. This power saving protocol consists on the use of time frames when the system searches nearby devices or send data, and other time frames when the device is in power saving mode without sending or searching.

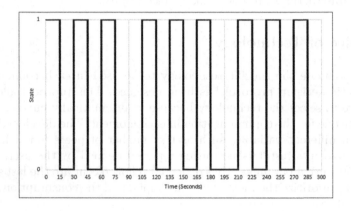

Fig. 4. Power saving protocol time frames

The system used in the beta implementation uses the Android platform, so the time is taken from the Internet time. According to the general procedure, the devices perform the search of nearby devices or send packages every 15 s during 3 iterations, then wait 30 s to do the next round of 3 iterations of 15 s, and so on. The use of this frame of 30 s is done to save energy, and synchronize with devices that could start the package sending or searching nearby devices in a different frame. Figure 4 shows the frame state in every moment. In the x axis, the time in seconds is represented while in the y axis the state, 1 or 0 depending whether the device is working or in power saving mode, is represented. The use of this power saving protocol produces a huge battery saving in comparison with the same system without any power saving protocol. Besides, the user experience and the success rate of communications do not decrease significantly because sending and searching operations have a time of few seconds to operate and they are not immediate. This difference in the power consumption is 55% less using the system without any power saving protocol than the system that uses the proposed power saving protocol. This measurement ensures that the use of the power saving protocol fulfills its mission and reduces the power consumption of the system more than a half, involving an important improvement in emergency situations where the smartphone battery life is very important.

6   Trust Levels

The trust of users in the proposed system is an important factor to have into account at the time of authenticating other users and passing them the credentials that are necessary to use the different chat rooms. For this reason, a trust level scheme has been developed.

The trust scheme is based on the fact that the generated certificate graph has different trust levels, whose maximum value corresponds to the certification authority. Besides, the nodes certificated directly by the CA have also high trust values because they have a direct or semi-direct connection with the CA.

We can see the trust graph as a tree where the different nodes are leaves of it. The trust of each node corresponds to the level of trust of the tree level to which it belongs, which decreases in every new level. In the beta implementation we considered that when we have 3 levels, the last level has lost the trust necessary to authenticate users as new system members. Thus, a dynamic decrease of trust is established with each new level until the level 3 is reached. To do this, each node stores the information about the number of nodes that had at the moment of its authentication in the initial level. The information about its actual level is not necessary to be stored because its calculation is trivial. Thus, depending on the number of nodes of each level and the level where each node is, a limitation for the number of nodes each node can certify exists. The maximum number of nodes of each level $k < 4$ can be calculated applying the formula $\prod_{i=0}^{k<4} \frac{N}{2^i}$, where N is the number of nodes directly certified by the certification authority. This formula is adapted to guarantee that in an extreme emergency situation where only few people are certified directly by the certification authority, the application can be used.

Figure 5 shows how trust decreases along with the different tree levels until the third level where it is not possible to authenticate new users. To the right of the image, we can see the number of nodes that can authenticate each node at each level. Each node stores the number of nodes directly certified by the CA. When a user has Internet connection, it can send its credentials to the CA, to be re-certified, so that he/she and his/her certified nodes go up in the hierarchy of the tree, producing a reorganization of the tree and an update of the number N, what produces that the number of nodes that can be certified by the nodes of lower levels increases, as can be also seen in Fig. 5.

The number N' is the number of nodes directly certified by the certification authority. According to the formula, when the calculation of nodes that can be certified results in a non integer, we round it to the superior integer number. Reorganizations of the tree allows that the system can increase the number of new certified nodes. An example of this happens when emergency personnel and victims go from the emergency environment to a non-emergency environment where they have Internet connection.

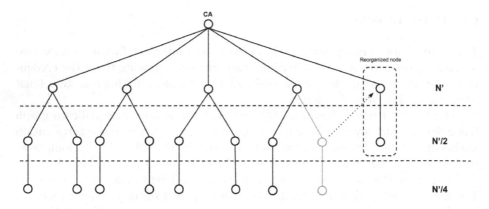

Fig. 5. Reorganized trust level scheme

7 Conclusions

This work proposes a communication system based on the combination of different wireless technologies, which is useful for situations in which a communication infrastructure cannot be used, such as disasters. The described system is based on the use of public chat rooms with open access for all registered and authenticated users, and private chat rooms that can be used by specific user groups such as emergency personnel. Apart from the authentication process based on asymmetric cryptography, chat rooms are protected with secret key encryption to allow users to cooperate in forwarding messages. In addition, new users can be registered in cases of unexpected emergencies, thanks to the proposed offline authentication based on certification through certificate graphs.

The proposal also includes an automatic technology decision system, based on a study of the battery consumption of the different technologies through a benchmark application over the Android system, which is the system for which a beta implementation has been developed. In addition, a power saving protocol has been developed that increases the efficiency of the proposed system.

This is part of a work in progress so several problems remain open. The security level of the developed application could be increased through its verification under different attacks and its testing in real disaster situations. Moreover, the proposed solution must be proved in a simulated disaster scenario with some nodes. Finally, new features could be added, such as voice communication or the possibility of sending files and/or videoconferencing.

Acknowledgements. This work has been partially supported by the grants TESIS2015010102, TESIS2015010106, IPT-2012-0585- 370000, RTC-2014-1648-8 y TEC2014-54110-R.

References

1. CRISYS: Critical response in security and safety emergencies. http://cordis. europa.eu/project/rcn/98623_en.pdf. Accessed 4 July
2. RESCUECELL: Using Cell Phone Detection TEchnology to Save Lives. http:// www.rescuecell.eu/. Accessed 4 July
3. TRADR: Long-Term Human-Robot Teaming for Robot-Assisted Disaster Response. http://www.tradr-project.eu. Accessed 4 July
4. Gandotra, P., Jha, R.K.: Device-to-device communication in cellular networks: a survey. J. Netw. Comput. Appl. **71**, 99–117 (2016)
5. Asadi, A., Wang, Q., Mancuso, V.: A survey on device-to-device communication in cellular networks. IEEE Commun. Surv. Tutorials **16**(4), 1801–1819 (2014)
6. Gomez, C., Oller, J., Paradells, J.: Overview and evaluation of bluetooth low energy: an emerging low-power wireless technology. Sensors **12**(9), 11734–11753 (2012)
7. Wi-Fi Direct, Wi-Fi Alliance. https://www.wi-fi.org/discover-wi-fi/wi-fi-direct. Accessed 4 July
8. Balraj, S.: LTE Direct Overview. Qualcomm Research, San Diego (2015)
9. Capkun, S., Buttyan, L., Hubaux, J.P.: Self-organized public-key management for mobile ad hoc networks. IEEE Trans. Mob. Comput. **2**(1), 52–64 (2003)
10. Seedorf, J., Gill, B., Kutscher, D., Schiller, B., Kohlweyer, D.: Fully decentralised authentication scheme for ICN in disaster scenarios. In: ACM International Conference on Information-Centric Networking, pp. 191–192 (2014)
11. Alpify. http://www.safe365.com/. Accessed 4 July
12. Santos-González, I., Rivero-García, A., Caballero-Gil, P., Hernández-Goya, C.: Alternative communication system for emergency situations. In: WEBIST, pp. 397–402 (2014)
13. Jang, H.C., Lien, Y.N., Tsai, T.C.: Rescue information system for earthquake disasters based on MANET emergency communication platform. In: ACM International Conference on Wireless Communications and Mobile Computing: Connecting the World Wirelessly, pp. 623–627 (2009)
14. Stallings, W.: Cryptography and Network Security: Principles and Practices. Pearson Education India (2006)
15. Yi, S., Kravets, R.: Composite key management for ad hoc networks. MobiQuitous **4**, 52–61 (2004)
16. Dahshan, H., Irvine, J.: A robust selforganized public key management for mobile ad hoc networks. Secur. Commun. Netw. **3**(1), 16–30 (2010)
17. Qualcomm Technologies. LTE Direct Always-on Device-toDevice Proximal Discovery. https://www.qualcomm.com/media/documents/files/lte-direct-always-on-device-to-device-proximal-discovery.pdf. Accessed 4 July
18. Yu, C.H., Tirkkonen, O., Doppler, K., Ribeiro, C.: Power optimization of device-to-device communication underlaying cellular communication. In: IEEE International Conference on Communications, pp. 1–5 (2009)

FLIHSBC: Fuzzy Logic and Improved Harmony Search Based Clustering Algorithm for Wireless Sensor Networks to Prolong the Network Lifetime

Deepika Agrawal[✉] and Sudhakar Pandey

Department of IT, National Institute of Technology Raipur, Raipur, India
deepika721@gmail.com, spandey96@gmail.com

Abstract. Wireless sensor networks (WSNs) is a rapidly growing technology. WSNs comprises of sensor nodes having limited energy as battery powers them. These batteries cannot be changed or recharged as they are operated in a harsh environment. Energy conservation mechanism should be developed. Through study, it is found that clustering is an approach for achieving energy efficiency. In this type of protocols, cluster heads (CH) are chosen among the sensor nodes and then clusters are formed by assigning non-cluster head to the nearest cluster head. Load balancing and the distribution of the cluster heads are the major drawbacks. To deal with the mentioned difficulties, a double optimization based on fuzzy logic approach and harmony search algorithm is proposed in this paper known as fuzzy logic and improved harmony search based clustering (FLIHSBC) algorithm. The proposed algorithm not only balances the energy consumption but also helps in maximizing the network lifetime. Simulation results proved that the proposed algorithm performs better in prolonging the lifetime of the sensor network.

Keywords: Wireless sensor networks · Energy optimization · Harmony search algorithm · Fuzzy logic · Clustering

1 Introduction

Wireless sensor networks have obtained substantial progress in the recent years. As, it becomes the core technology of the Internet of things (IoT), WSNs are extremely transforming the human lives. WSNs is even deployed in the harsh environment to perform the monitoring tasks periodically [1]. Both military and civilian scenarios are involved in the wide application of WSNs.

The sensor nodes in the WSNs have some constraints like limited battery life, transmission range, processing capability and memory. As the development of technology progresses, there is not any significant improvement in battery technology [2]. It is a bottleneck in the development of WSNs. So, maximizing the lifetime of the network will be a major research topic in present and in the future.

© Springer International Publishing AG 2017
S.F. Ochoa et al. (Eds.): UCAmI 2017, LNCS 10586, pp. 570–578, 2017.
DOI: 10.1007/978-3-319-67585-5_56

Designing of a clustering protocol that decreases the consumption of energy of the network is a key issue that needs to be solved. Clustering [3, 4] is a technique that is developed to decrease the consumption of the energy.

Nowadays, more researchers are trying to increase the network lifetime by the development of heuristic and meta-heuristic based clustering algorithms. Due to the uncertainty in the variable number and the strong constraints of the clustering problem in WSNs, it is appropriate to design clustering algorithm with meta-heuristics.

This paper tries to propose a clustering algorithm based on a meta-heuristic algorithm, namely, improved Harmony Search (HS) algorithm [5, 6] and fuzzy logic approach [7]. The proposed algorithm i.e., fuzzy logic and improved harmony search based clustering (FLIHSBC) algorithm is an energy efficient algorithm.

To evaluate the performance of the FLIHSBC algorithm, it is compared with one of the known algorithm from the literature, namely, HSA [8]. Results of the experiment prove that the FLIHSBC algorithm has better performance than another algorithm in all the scenarios. Thus, the FLIHSBC algorithm is a load balanced energy-efficient and scalable clustering algorithm.

The rest of the paper is structured as follows:

Section 2 describes the work done so far related to clustering with meta-heuristics techniques. Section 3 represents the assumptions made for the proposed algorithm and the energy model used. Section 4 illustrates the problem formulation and the proposed algorithm in detail. Section 5 states the experimental results of the proposed algorithm followed by conclusion.

2 Related Works

Low Energy Adaptive Clustering hierarchy (LEACH) [9] is one standard protocol in which cluster heads are chosen based on a probabilistic model. This protocol is very low in performance. It chooses cluster head randomly without considering residual energy or other factors. Here, selection of cluster head is done through random way. It is possible that the low energy node becomes the cluster head. To solve this issue, LEACH-Centralized (LEACH-C) [10], Energy Efficient Heterogeneous Clustering (EEHC) [11], Stable Election protocol (SEP) [12] are developed. LEACH-C considered residual energy for CH selection. EEHC and SEP are based on heterogeneous networks.

Nowadays, application of evolutionary algorithms in clustering has removed some of the stated difficulties [13]. The optimal cluster heads selection with high residual energy can be treated as a NP-hard problem [14]. Evolutionary algorithm uses trial and error method to obtain a solution of an optimization problem. Genetic Algorithm (GA) is the most common evolutionary algorithm and it is based on natural genetics. A GA based algorithm [15] is proposed for data routing in a WSNs with the use of relay nodes. The Roulette-wheel selection method is employed to select the individuals and the fitness function is defined. A critical node is selected from the relay nodes for mutation operation. This node dissipates maximum energy as it receives and transmits data.

A GAR based on GA is proposed [16] in which the distance from the relay node to the BS is minimized. Tournament selection is used to select the individuals. A novel differential evolution (DE) based algorithm for clustering is proposed [17]. This algorithm prevents the faster death of the fully loaded CHs and prolongs the network lifetime. Ant colony optimization (ACO) models the behavior of ants to find the food source. This method is used for multi-path routing [18] to prolong network lifetime for event based applications.

Particle swarm optimization (PSO) models the behavior of a flock of birds flying to resources and is used in LEACH based routing [19, 20]. A music based optimization method for clustering is proposed in [8] that consider energy and intra cluster distance to obtain optimal clusters. It has several flaws it does not balance load between nodes thus energy consumption is higher. Also, selection of tentative CHs is done by considering energy only.

The fuzzy logic approach in clustering is used to preserve energy. Several protocols used the fuzzy logic technique to maximize the lifetime of the network. Three parameters are used as a fuzzy variable namely, concentration, energy, and centrality [21]. These parameters elect CH based on fuzzy output 'chance'. A similar approach proposed is Cluster Head Election mechanism using Fuzzy logic (CHEF) [22]. Here residual energy and local distance are the fuzzy variables for CH selection.

3   Preliminaries

3.1   Assumptions

The following assumptions are made with respect to the network:

- Random deployment of nodes.
- The network is fixed in which all sensor nodes and the sink are static.
- All sensor nodes are homogeneous in nature, having equal initial energy.
- The radio channel is symmetric.
- All the sensor nodes are aware of their positions.
- Once deployed, left unattended.

3.2   Radio Energy Model

For calculation of the energy consumed in transmitting and receiving, our proposed protocol used first order radio model [23].

4   Problem Formulation and Proposed Solution

Since, sensor nodes are battery powered and cannot be replenished, hence, it is critical to balance the depletion of the energy in the network, to increase the lifetime of the sensor network. In this section, a new load balanced energy-efficient clustering algorithm for WSNs is proposed, the FLIHSBC algorithm, based on fuzzy logic and improved HS algorithm. First, clustering process of the proposed algorithm for WSNs is described. Next, Improved Harmony Search Algorithm is presented. Finally, the proposed algorithm i.e., FLIHSBC algorithm is presented.

4.1 Clustering Process of the Proposed Solution

The protocol's operation is divided into rounds. In each round, operation is partitioned in two phases: grouping of nodes into clusters i.e., cluster formation and data transmission.

In the cluster formation phase, CHs are selected and clusters are formed. Here, tentative CHs are elected through fuzzy logic. Two parameters are chosen for electing CHs. These are applied as an input in a fuzzy inference engine and output 'rank' is calculated. Fuzzy if-then rules are applied to calculate the rank. Within neighbors, nodes having higher rank are elected as a tentative CHs. Here, rank is calculated for each node and those having highest rank among neighbors will be elected as a tentative CHs.

The input variable should take the equivalent fuzzy linguistic value. The first input variable 'Distance_BS' has close, attainable, and far as the fuzzy linguistic values. Close and far have trapezoidal membership function while attainable follows triangular membership function. The second input variable 'Residual Energy' has less, average and surplus as the fuzzy linguistic values. Less and surplus follows trapezoidal membership function while average has triangular membership function.

The output variable 'rank' has nine fuzzy linguistic values. They are very low, low, rather low, medium low, medium, medium high, rather high, high, very high. Very low and very high have trapezoidal membership function while the others have a triangular membership function. Fuzzy inference Engine (FIS) fuzzifies the crisp input values into appropriate linguistic values. It uses the provided membership functions. Mamdani method is used to develop rules so that the fuzzified input variables are processed. From the combination of different linguistic values, a total of 9 rules are there as specified in Table 1.

Table 1. Fuzzy if-then rules

S. no.	Residual energy	Distance_BS	Rank
1.	Less	Far	Very low
2.	Less	Medium	Low
3.	Less	Close	Rather low
4.	Average	Far	Medium low
5.	Average	Medium	Medium
6.	Average	Close	Medium high
7.	Surplus	far	Rather high
8.	Surplus	Medium	High
9.	Surplus	Close	Very high

Center of area (CoA) method is applied to defuzzify the output linguistic variable into a crisp value. After completion of CHs selection, sensor nodes that are not elected as a CH will join the closest CHs. In the Data Transmission phase, first CHs collect the data from cluster members. Then, the data is aggregated and then the collected data is transmitted to the sink.

4.2 Harmony Search Algorithm

In the HSA, musicians seek for a perfect state of harmony. There is an objective function that either needs to be maximized or minimized. There are several steps include in a HSA-based approach. They are:

Step 1: Initialization of algorithm parameters and optimization problem

Here for the presented problem, consumption of energy in network is to be minimized. The objective function for the current problem is defined in next section. Harmony Memory Size is number of solution vectors in the Harmony Memory Matrix. For effectively use of the memory, the HSA adopts some parameters to improve the solution vector like Harmony Memory Considering Rate (HMCR), Pitch Adjusting Rate (PAR) and the maximum number of searches that are to be initialized.

Step 2: Initialization of the Harmony Memory (HM)

The initial HM comprises of a HMS number of solutions that is randomly generated for the considered problem. Index of the N number of cluster heads is the solution of the defined problem. Harmony Memory is represented by:

$$
HM = \begin{bmatrix} I_1^1 & I_2^1 & \cdots & I_k^1 \\ I_1^2 & I_2^2 & \cdots & I_k^2 \\ \vdots & \vdots & \ddots & \vdots \\ I_1^{HMS} & I_2^{HMS} & \cdots & I_k^{HMS} \end{bmatrix} \begin{bmatrix} F^1 \\ F^2 \\ \vdots \\ F^{HMS} \end{bmatrix}
$$

Each row denotes random solution for the formulated optimization problem. F^j represents the objective function value for each row of random solution.

Step 3: Improvising a new harmony from the initial Harmony Memory

Let's X'= $(x_1', \ldots, x_i', \ldots, x_n')$ is a new harmony generated based on two parameters, harmony memory considerations and pitch adjustments as per the requirements of clustering in WSNs. This is given by Eqs. (1) and (2).

$$
x_j' \leftarrow \begin{cases} x_j' \in HM \text{ with probability } HMCR \\ x_j' \in x_j \text{ with probability } (1 - HMCR) \end{cases} \tag{1}
$$

HMCR is defined in step 1 as the probability to select a new value from the HM members, and the probability to generate it randomly is defined by (1-HMCR). If x_j' is generated from the HM, then it should be further modified as per the Pitch Adjustment Rate (PAR). The probability of a candidate to be modified is defined by PAR and the probability of doing nothing is defined by (1-PAR) given by Eq. (2).

$$x'_j \leftarrow \begin{cases} x^n_j \in HM \text{ with probability } PAR \\ x'_j \text{ with probability } (1 - PAR) \end{cases} \tag{2}$$

Step 4: Updating the Harmony Memory

The objective function value is calculated for the newly generated Harmony Vector. If the calculated value is found better than the worst objective function value then a new harmony memory replaces the worst harmony memory.

Step 5: Go to step 3 until termination criterion is reached

When the termination criteria are reached, the best solution is selected. This best solution is the solution for the formulated optimization problem.

4.3 Proposed Algorithm

FLIHSBC algorithm is based on double optimization. First is done through fuzzy logic and second is done through Harmony Search Algorithm.

Tentative cluster-heads are chosen based on fuzzy logic as described in Sect. 4.1. After that, Sect. 4.2 is applied. Harmony Search Algorithm is applied to find the optimal number of cluster heads. The objective function which is used to find the optimum is given by Eq. (3).

$$Minimize f_{obj} = \alpha_1 * f_1 + \alpha_2 * f_2 + \alpha_3 * f_3 \tag{3}$$

where, $\alpha_1 + \alpha_2 + \alpha_3 = 1$, $\alpha_2 \geq (\alpha_1 + \alpha_3)$. Also, $0 < f_1, f_2, f_3 < 1$.

Lower the function value, better the CH selection. The different functions are f_1 is the Average distance from all neighbor nodes

$$f_1 = \sum_{j=1}^{m} \frac{1}{l_j} \left(\sum_{i=1}^{l_j} dis(CH_j, S_i) \right) \tag{4}$$

where, m = number of clusters and l_j = number of neighbors of jth cluster.
f_2 is the Average distance from the sink

$$f_2 = \sum_{j=1}^{m} \frac{1}{m} (dist(CH_j, BS)) \tag{5}$$

f_3 is the Energy Ratio

$$f_3 = \frac{\sum_{i=1}^{N} E(node_i)}{\sum_{j=1}^{m} E(CH_m)} \tag{6}$$

After the final CHs are chosen, nodes with the nearest distance to the CH will join the cluster. After the cluster creation, cluster members transmit the data to the CH and then from CH to the base station. The process of selection of clusters is repeated in every round. The information about the distance from the base station, residual energy and density are attached to the data packet during the transmission of data from node to their respective CH. With this information, best Cluster Heads are chosen. Cluster heads creates a Time Division Multiple Access (TDMA) schedule for cluster members. In this schedule only, respective cluster members transmit their data to the CH.

5   Results and Discussion

This section describes the results of the experiments of simulation. The simulations are performed in MATLAB. Six scenarios are randomly generated with varying number of nodes from 50 to 100 with an increment of 10 in each scenario. To prove the success of our FLIHSBC algorithm, the well-known Harmony Search Algorithm (HSA) [8] is used for comparison. For comparing the performances of the algorithms, two metrics are used for each scenario, namely, (a) Average of the remaining residual energy that represents the average of the remaining residual energy of all nodes. (b) The network lifetime that represents the number of rounds until the first node dies in the network. Table 2 depicts the simulation parameters. The result that is obtained is by taking the average of 15 simulation runs.

Table 2. Simulation parameters

Parameter	Value
Located area of nodes (m^2)	100 × 100
Locations of nodes	Randomly distributed and located
Location of sink	Center of the network (50,50)
Number of deployed nodes	50, 60, 70, 80, 90, 100
Initial energy	0.5 J
Eelec	50 nJ/bit
εamp	0.0010 pJ/bit/m4
Data aggregation energy EDA	5 nJ/bit

5.1   Average Remaining Residual Energy

Figure 1 shows the graph for the average remaining residual energy for different scenarios having different number of nodes. It can be seen from the Fig. 1 that the FLIHSBC algorithm has the higher residual energy, it means that the FLIHSBC algorithm consumes less energy. From Fig. 1, it is concluded that the FLIHSBC algorithm performs better in all the scenarios. It also states that the FLIHSBC algorithm saves more energy than HSA.

5.2   Network Lifetime

Balancing the consumption of energy has an impact on the lifetime of the network. It is an important criterion in energy efficiency in WSNs. The residual energy directly

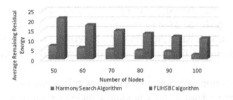

Fig. 1. Average Remaining Residual Energy

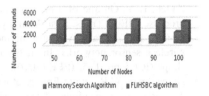

Fig. 2. Network lifetime

affects the network lifetime. The FLIHSBC algorithm gives best results in prolonging the lifetime of the network than HSA in all the scenarios as shown in Fig. 2.

6 Conclusion

In this paper, fuzzy logic based improved harmony search algorithm known as FLIHSBC algorithm is proposed. In FLIHSBC algorithm, whole network is divided into tentative clusters by fuzzy logic. Distance to Base Station, residual energy and density are taken as input parameters for fuzzy inference engine. Unlike the previous clustering protocol which is used for comparison which selects tentative CHs by considering only residual energy, FLIHSBC algorithm considers all the important parameters and elects appropriate CHs. After that, Harmony Search Algorithm is utilized to optimize the number of clusters formed. The objective function for Harmony Search Algorithm considers average distance from all neighbor nodes, average distance from the sink and the energy ratio. Through simulation results, it is shown that the FLIHSBC algorithm outperforms in preserving energy and thus maximizes the life span of the sensor network. The FLIHSBC algorithm balances the load in the network by considering the distance of node from the sink in the objective function of the HSA. In future, we will try to consider topological changes in the network by taking mobile nodes either sensor nodes or sink.

References

1. Akyildiz, I.F., et al.: Wireless sensor networks: a survey. Comput. Netw. **38**(4), 393–422 (2002)
2. Younis, O., et al.: Node clustering in wireless sensor networks: recent developments and deployment challenges. IEEE Netw. **20**, 20–25 (2006)
3. Abbasi, A.A., et al.: A survey on clustering algorithms for wireless sensor networks. Comput. Commun. **30**, 2826–2841 (2007)
4. Afsar, M.M., et al.: Clustering in sensor networks: a literature survey. J. Netw. Comput. Appl. **46**, 198–226 (2014)
5. Geem, Z.W., et al.: A new heuristic optimization algorithm: harmony search. Simulation **76** (28), 60–68 (2001)
6. Wang, L., et al.: An enhanced harmony search algorithm for assembly sequence planning. Int. J. Modell. Identif. Control **18**(1), 18–25 (2013)

7. Zadeh, L.A.: Outline of a new approach to the analysis of complex systems and decision processes. IEEE Trans. Syst. Man Cybern. SMC **3**, 28–44 (1973)
8. Hoang, D.C., et al.: A robust harmony search algorithm based clustering protocol for wireless sensor networks. In: IEEE International Conference on Communications Workshops (ICC), pp. 1–5. IEEE (2010).
9. Heinzelman, W.R., et al.: Energy-efficient communication protocol for wireless microsensor networks. In: Proceedings of the 33rd Annual Hawaii International Conference on System Sciences, 2002.
10. Heinzelman, W.B., et al.: An application-specific protocol architecture for wireless microsensor networks. IEEE Trans. Wirel. Commun. **1**, 660–670 (2002)
11. Younis, O., et al.: HEED: a hybrid, energy-efficient, distributed clustering approach for ad hoc sensor networks. IEEE Trans. Mob. Comput. **3**, 366–379 (2004)
12. Afsar, M.M., Tayarani Najaran, M.-H.: A novel energy-efficient and distance-based clustering approach for wireless sensor networks. In: Snášel, V., Krömer, P., Köppen, M., Schaefer, G. (eds.) Soft Computing in Industrial Applications. AISC, vol. 223, pp. 177–186. Springer, Cham (2014). doi:10.1007/978-3-319-00930-8_16
13. De Jong, K.: Evolutionary Computation: A Unified Approach. MIT Press, Cambridge (2006)
14. Latiff, N.M., et al.: Performance comparison of optimization algorithms for clustering in wireless sensor networks. In: MASS 2007, IEEE International Conference on Mobile Adhoc and Sensor Systems, pp. 1–4. IEEE (2007)
15. Bari, A., et al.: A genetic algorithm based approach for energy efficient routing in two-tiered sensor networks. Ad Hoc Netw. **7**(4), 665–676 (2009)
16. Gupta, S.K., Kuila, P., Jana, P.K.: GAR: an energy efficient GA-based routing for wireless sensor networks. In: Hota, C., Srimani, P.K. (eds.) ICDCIT 2013. LNCS, vol. 7753, pp. 267–277. Springer, Heidelberg (2013). doi:10.1007/978-3-642-36071-8_21
17. Pratyay, K., et al.: A novel differential evolution based clustering algorithm for wireless sensor networks. Appl. Soft Comput. **25**, 414–425 (2014)
18. Okdem, S., et al.: Routing in wireless sensor networks using an Ant Colony Optimization (ACO) router chip. Sensors **9**, 9–921 (2009)
19. Liang, Y., Yu, H.: PSO-based energy efficient gathering in sensor networks. In: Jia, X., Wu, J., He, Y. (eds.) MSN 2005. LNCS, vol. 3794, pp. 362–369. Springer, Heidelberg (2005). doi:10.1007/11599463_36
20. Latiff, N.M.A., et al.: Performance comparison of optimization algorithms for clustering in wireless sensor networks. IEEE International Conference on Mobile Adhoc and Sensor Systems, Pisa, pp. 1–4 (2007).
21. Gupta, I., et al.: Cluster-head election using fuzzy logic for wireless sensor networks. In: 3rd Annual Communication Networks and Services Research Conference (CNSR 2005), pp. 255–260 (2005)
22. Kim, J., et al.: CHEF: cluster head election mechanism using fuzzy logic in wireless sensor networks. In: 10th International Conference on Advanced Communication Technology, vol. 1, pp. 654–659 (2008)
23. Taheri, H., et al.: An energy-aware distributed clustering protocol in wireless sensor networks using fuzzy logic. AdHoc Netw. **10**(7), 1469–1481 (2012)

Supporting Real-Time Message Delivery in Disaster Relief Efforts: An Analytical Approach

Rodrigo M. Santos[1]([✉]), Javier Orozco[1], Sergio F. Ochoa[2], Roc Meseguer[3], and Daniel Mosse[4]

[1] Dpto. de Ing. Eléctrica y de Computadoras, UNS - IIIE, CONICET,
Bahía Blanca, Argentina
ierms@criba.edu.ar
[2] Universidad de Chile, Santiago, Chile
[3] Universitat Politècnica de Catalunya, Barcelona, Spain
[4] University of Pittsburgh, Pittsburgh, USA

Abstract. Several initiatives propose the use of opportunistic networks and heterogeneous devices to help overcome the communication and coordination limitations evidenced during first response activities in disaster relief scenarios. These solutions tend to create an Internet of Things ecosystem in which most components are mobile, autonomous and interact with other in a loosely-coupled fashion. Regardless the benefits provided by these infrastructures, the message delivery on them does not consider time constraints. This aspect is particularly relevant in this scenario since the time to conduct the first response activities is quite short, therefore they must be done quickly and coordinately. Trying to help address this challenge, this paper proposes a message propagation model for opportunistic networks that considers heterogeneous devices and guarantees the real-time behavior of the network by bounding the maximum delay for messages transmission. The message propagation is modeled using an analytical approach. Two different scheduling policies are used to analyze the model and their feasibility conditions are proved.

Keywords: Opportunistic networks · Real-time message delivery · Disaster relief scenarios · Mobile computing ecosystem

1 Introduction

Every year natural disasters hit urban areas and produce dramatic losses in terms of both, human life and damage to property. Example of these extreme events are earthquakes, tsunamis, wild fires, floods and volcano eruptions. Typically, the first 72 h after the event (known as the "golden relief time") are the most important ones, since after that the probability to find survivors is really low [17]. In order to address the first response, several teams are deployed in the field, which usually involve firemen, police officers, medical personnel, and military

© Springer International Publishing AG 2017
S.F. Ochoa et al. (Eds.): UCAmI 2017, LNCS 10586, pp. 579–590, 2017.
DOI: 10.1007/978-3-319-67585-5_57

units. Each team has a leader that coordinates the activities inside the team, with other team leaders, and also with an incident commander who is in charge of the operations in the field. In this scenario, it is very important to provide communication and coordination capabilities to the first responders.

When disasters strike, traditional communications collapse: telephone lines fall down and cell phone towers if not down are usually overloaded with messages and calls. Rescuers should use alternative communication channels. Usually, the interactions are done with VHF/UHF radio systems since it allows a quick deployment of the communication system, which is a mandatory requirement [10]. However, these systems have several shortcomings, such as limited number of channels, messages being overwritten by more powerful devices or mixed messages as transmitters are not well identified. Moreover, these radio systems are limited to support resilient network protocols and topologies, keep a multi-organizational coordination, and maintain information consistency [10]. Without an appropriate communication support, the decisions made by the incident commander and the team leaders are based only on their own experience, since no or little information is available to support such activity. Moreover, activities coordination becomes a challenge almost impossible to overcome. Given this situation, it is not surprising to see improvisation in the field [17], which usually impact negatively on the emergency response process, as observed in the Yarnell Hill Fire [6] and also in World Trade Center [11].

Many communication infrastructures have also been proposed to try deal with the need of a suitable (digital) communication; most of them are based on mobile ad hoc networks (MANETs) or opportunistic networks (OppNets), and mobile computing devices [1,5,7,16]. Recently, these infrastructures have been evolving toward the Internet of Thing (IoT) scenario, where many heterogeneous devices interconnected via MANETs or OppNets interact to provide information support and also additional communication and coordination capability to first responders [12,14]. The current availability of IoT-enabled devices can help increase the resilience of the communication in the field, by leveraging their spontaneous wireless networking capabilities while the conventional communication infrastructure is out of service [15].

In [17] the use of an opportunistic network for collaborative applications (like the one needed in the first hours after a natural disaster) is analyzed and the first concepts of time constraints are introduced. In [18] there is an analysis of real-time traffic for the case of FIFO scheduling at the gateway without priorities.

In [2] the authors analyze the stochastic performance of different routing strategies under different inter-meeting times distributions. The authors do not contemplate a real-time behavior as no deterministic guarantee is provided. Additionally, the use of mules has been proposed in previous works, as a way to keep the network resilient in case of node failures or to transport data in distributed networks that cover wide areas without communications infrastructure (or with limited connections among nodes). In [9] different techniques are proposed to determine the mules paths considering the geographic conditions and the infrastructure present. In [4] a trade-off analysis is presented to minimize the number of mules in the system, while guaranteeing throughput requirements on one side and the optimum path to cover the territory.

Regardless the usefulness of the previous works, they do not consider accomplishing with real-time restrictions for the message delivery. This requirement is mandatory in disaster relief efforts given the time constraints existing to conduct the first response activities during the golden relief time. In this sense, this proposal takes a step forward in order to try deal with a challenge that still remains open. The proposal also opens the door to the participation of IoT world in these solutions, since a wide variety of computing and sensing devices can become part of this ecosystem.

The main contribution of this paper is a bounded message propagation model for OppNets that involves IoT-enabled devices as nodes, and supports communication in the field during first responses. An analytical approach is used to represent the propagation model and the IoT-based communication infrastructure. Although the message delivery in OppNets is based on a best effort approach, it can be used in several real-time environments if certain conditions are met. The paper also introduces two message scheduling policies for these networks and computes the maximum delay for the message delivery. With this information, the feasibility of implementing a real-time OppNet is evaluated.

Next section describes the proposed model emphasizing in its role as facilitator of the message propagation in the disaster area. Section 3 shows the schedulability analysis of the proposed models. Section 4 presents an example, and Sect. 5 presents the conclusions and future work.

2   System Model

In a disaster relief scenario, the VHF radio systems used by first response teams although easy to use impose several limitations. In [13] some of the most important are explained. These are the impossibility to transmit digital information and the lack of enough channels for all the teams and the general coordination. An alternative to address these limitations is to use mobile phones, but after a disaster typically most infrastructure-based communication systems are damaged or collapsed. Therefore, we follow [1,5,7] to use OppNets built upon a multi-hop chain that transfers information from the command post to the teams in the field and back. As there are time restrictions, the transmissions have real-time characteristics. Message end-to-end delay should be predictable.

Figure 1 shows a general deployment of first response teams and the different actors involved in a disaster relief ecosystem. First response teams are typically coordinated by an incident commander (IC), who is located in the command post (in the field). From there, the IC assigns tasks and coordinates activities of the first responders. Each team has a *gateway*, i.e., a person/device who is in charge of coordinating activities with other teams. This node receives the information from its team members and transfers it to the command post. At the same time, it receives the orders and recommendations from the IC and transmits them to the team members.

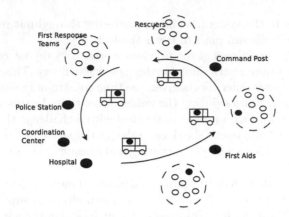

Fig. 1. Mules routing for emergency handling. Gateways are marked in black; small black circles are the gateways of the first response teams

Typically, the area in which teams are deployed is large, and the distance among the teams and also between them and the command post is too big to allow for a direct link. To cope with this problem, *mules* are introduced for transporting the messages in both directions. Mules can be implemented in different ways, for example with drones, motorcycles, cars (autonomous or not), or even bicycles [8]. The information flow in the system has four steps: $N \rightarrow G \rightarrow Mule \rightarrow G \rightarrow N$. Where N denotes a node and G is the gateway related to that node. We assume no gateway failures given that any node can take over the role of the gateway.

From a communications point of view, each team is independent of any other. That is, the communication being held inside a team has no influence on other teams, either because they are working at a different radio frequency channel or because they are so distant that their radios are not interfering with each other. Based on this, we can define the set of *gateways*: $\mathbf{\Gamma} = \{G_1, G_2, \ldots, G_n\}$. Each of the n Gateways is responsible for interchanging messages with the *mules* and the nodes. That is, *mules* only communicate with a node through a *gateway*. For each G_i there is a set of n_i nodes: $\mathbf{N}_{G_i} = \{N_{i_1}, N_{i_2}, \ldots, N_{i_n}\}$.

In real-time, system predictability is mandatory, as every possible situation should be contemplated to guarantee the deadlines. Although contention based protocols work well in the average, the back off algorithms introduce uncertainties at the transmission moment preventing their use in real-time communication systems. Time Division Multiple Access (TDMA) protocols are suitable for real-time operation as they are able to transmit messages in a predictable (bounded) time, since each node has access to a transmission slot periodically.

In TDMA schemes, time is considered to be slotted and the duration of one slot is considered as the unit of time. The duration of the slot is determined by the system designer and it involves parameters like the speed of the *mule* and the distance both in time and space between two consecutive *mules*.

Each node $N_{j_i} \in G_j$ has a set of μ_i messages to transmit, $M(N_{j_i}) = \{m_{ji1}, m_{ji2}, \ldots, m_{ji\mu_i}\}$. Moreover, three types of messages are considered in the system: periodic, sporadic and aperiodic. They are described by a tuple $m_{jih}\langle P_{jih}, C_{jih}, D_{jih}\rangle$, where P_{jih} is the period or minimum intergeneration time of the message, C_{jih} is the worst case time for transmitting a message and D_{jih} is the deadline. Both periodic and sporadic messages have to be received before their deadlines, while aperiodic messages have no real-time constraint. That is, deadlines associated with these messages are infinite and they have the lowest priority in the system; they are usually transmitted if there is time. Sporadic messages are aimed to handle emergency calls, such as imminent possible explosions or breakdowns. Once a node generates a periodic or sporadic message, it has to wait for the minimum time (specified by the period) to generate a new one of the same kind.

3   Real-Time Schedulability Analysis

In this section, message scheduling is analyzed from a real-time point of view. We determine that there are four scheduling stages: *nodes-gateways*, *gateways-mules*, *mules-gateways* and *gateways-nodes*. In what follows, for illustration, feasible conditions for each level are determined for two scheduling policies: First In First Out (FIFO) and Rate Monotonic (RM) [3].

The end-to-end worst case transmission time requires the analysis of each stage in the transmission process. Due to the real-time requirements, the scheduling in each stage is analyzed considering the worst case situation. Equation 1 establishes the end-to-end delay for a message m_i originated at *node* $i \in G_j$ and destined to node $h \in G_k$.

$$T_{\text{end\_to\_end},i} = T_{NG} + Wait_G + Wait_M + T_{GN} \tag{1}$$

where T_{NG} is the time required for the message to go from the node to the gateway; $Wait_G$ is the time the message spends in the gateway until it is completely uploaded to the mule; $Wait_M$ stands for the time the message is in the mule until it is received by the destination gateway; and T_{GN} is the time required for the message to go from the gateway to the destination node.

In Sect. 3.2 we will show how these variables are derived for FIFO and Rate Monotonic scheduling protocols, and shown in Eqs. 2 and 3.

3.1   Node-Gateway

For real-time messages, TDMA variants have been proposed [19]. TDMA reserves a slot in every frame for each node that needs to transmit. Node's clocks should be synchonized. The first response teams may have between 10 and 30 people [6], plus a set of sensors for a maximum of 40–50 nodes in a team.

Each node transmits in a fixed slot time, τ, in every frame T_f. The worst situation for a message in a node is to be generated just after its time slot. In that case, the node will have to wait for the next frame before being able to start to transmit the message. If message length C is greater than τ, a total of $T_f = \lceil C/\tau \rceil$ frames would be necessary.

If the node has several messages to transmit, different approaches can be considered. The simplest one is to assume a FIFO order; in that case, the worst case situation occurs when the message is the last one in the node's queue, MQ.

Lemma 1. *For a maximum of* $|MQ|$ *messages in a node, the worst case delay for a single node to transmit a message to a gateway with FIFO order is given by:*

$$T_{NG} = T_f \sum_{i=1}^{|MQ|} \left\lceil \frac{C_i}{\tau} \right\rceil \tag{2}$$

Note: we dropped the subindex reflecting the gateway and the node, because we are just analyzing the node delay, which is independent of the others.

In case that rate monotonic (RM) order is used for transmitting, each priority level has its queue, where messages wait for being transmitted. In that case, higher priority messages are always dispatched before lower priority ones. Typically, the number of priority levels is restricted for implementation details.

Lemma 2. *Equation 3 defines the delay to transmit a message from a single node to the gateway with rate monotonic ordering. Where* HP *denotes the set of higher priority messages.*

$$\min t \text{ s.t } t = T_f \sum_{i=1}^{|MQ|} \left\lceil \frac{C_i}{\tau} \right\rceil + \sum_{j \in HP} \left\lceil \frac{t}{T_j} \right\rceil T_f \left\lceil \frac{C_j}{\tau} \right\rceil \tag{3}$$

Within the first response team, the *gateway* is another *node* with its own time slice within the frame. Therefore, the previous analysis is valid for the reverse case in which messages are transmitted from the *gateway* to the *node*. In other words, the GN and NG delays can be analyzed jointly.

3.2   Gateway-Mule-Gateway

Once messages are queued in the gateway for transmission, the following two hops (gateway-mule and mule-gateway) are analyzed together, given their symmetry. The message exchange between the *mule* and the gateway can begin as soon as they get into communication range and continue until they lose contact. When the *mule* and the *gateway* are within transmission range, they will exchange messages in a full-duplex way. The number of messages that they can exchange is then only restricted by the time interval in which they are within range.

The period of the *mule*, P_{mu}, can then be seen as the sum of two time windows, $P_{mu} = B+W$, where B is the duration of the blind window (i.e., when a gateway cannot transmit to the *mule*), and W is the duration of the transmission window. P_{mu} represents the interval of time between two consecutive mules connecting to the gateway.

Let us assume that $\forall i\ C_i = C$, The interval of time in which the *mule* is within transmission range with the *gateway* is the transmission window, noted W. Thus, the number of messages ω uploaded to the *mule* by the *gateway* in the transmission window can be obtained from equation: $\omega = W/C$

The mules may have a queue for each gateway, so messages with destination nodes in the network of a particular gateway are enqueued there. The queuing capacity of a mule is equal to the number of messages that can be delivered during the transmission window. To guarantee that all the messages in the system are delivered by their deadlines, we have to ensure that enough mules are present for this, either by enlarging the transmission window or by incorporating more mules to the system. The number of mules in the system is notated ξ.

Mules start their trajectory at a certain gateway. This gateway has a privileged situation with respect to the others as it will always find an empty queue, while the following ones will have to wait for the arrival of a mule with an empty queue. This fact has to be considered when computing the set of messages that each gateway has to schedule. While the first gateway in the path only deals with the messages originated in its nodes, downstream gateways will have to consider their own messages and also those from the previous ones. Although these messages are not actually served by the gateway, they interfere with the transmission. The position within the path determines the priority in the same way a "daisy chain" arrangement does it.

The set of messages that gateway G_j has to deal with, is the union of all the messages from its nodes, plus all the messages generated in upstream gateways:

$$M(G_j) = \cup_{h=1}^{j-1} \cup_{i=1}^{n_h} \cup_{x=1}^{\mu_i} m_{hix} \tag{4}$$

where n_j is the number of nodes connected to gateway G_j and μ_i is the number of messages originating in node N_{j_i} of gateway G_j. The bandwidth required by the set of messages associated to gateway G_j is given by:

$$U_{M(G_j)} = \sum_{h=1}^{j} \sum_{i=1}^{n_j} \sum_{x=1}^{\mu_i} \frac{C_{hix}}{P_{hix}} \tag{5}$$

Lemma 3. *For a gateway G_j to be able to transmit its messages, the bandwidth demand for the set of messages associated to it should be:*

$$U_{M(G_j)} \le \xi \frac{W}{P_{mu}} \tag{6}$$

FIFO: The waiting time for a message in a FIFO queue in the gateway is a function of the number of messages Q, generated in the *gateway* G_j and the interference that upstream gateways G_1 to G_{j-1} may introduce.

Lemma 4. *Provided (6) is satisfied, the worst-case waiting time for a message arriving to the gateway G_j is given by:*

$$Wait_{G_j} = \mathtt{minimum} \ t \ \mathtt{s.t.} \ t = B + Q \cdot C + \left\lceil \frac{\sum_{h=1}^{j-1} \sum_{i=1}^{n_j} \sum_{x=1}^{\mu_i} \left\lceil \frac{t}{P_{hix}} \right\rceil C_{hix}}{\omega} \right\rceil P_{mu} \quad (7)$$

The time spent by messages in the mule is just the time used by the mule to reach the destination gateway, because once messages are uploaded to the mule, they will be delivered at the destination gateway. $Wait_{mu} = T_{trip}$.

Rate Monotonic: The use of rate monotonic priority order in the system is conditioned by the "daisy chain" disposition of the gateways. To avoid priority inversions that could eventually produce starvation in some gateways, the store-and-forward mechanism is used along the way. Like before, the mules queue length is equal to the amount of messages that can be uploaded to the mule while being in the transmission range of the gateway, ω.

Let us assume $\omega = 2$, there are three gateways, each one has a message and they are in reverse order of priority. Therefore, the first message has the lowest priority, but as it is the first in the "daisy chain" it is uploaded to the mule. In the second gateway, the medium priority message is uploaded. When the mule gets to the third gateway, the high priority message has to be uploaded to prevent a priority inversion, and the lowest priority message is exchanged by the highest priority one. To do this, the transmissions between the gateways and the mules are assumed to be full-duplex.

Like in the FIFO case, gateways downstream have to consider the interference of higher priority messages from upstream gateways. Note that the transmission order is not affected by the gateway position; it is only affected by the priority of messages, making the overall system fair.

Lemma 5. *Under Rate Monotonic order and subject to Eq. (6), a message m of priority π will have the worst case delay (in the gateway-mule-gateway path) given by:*

$$Wait_{G_j} = \mathtt{minimum} \ t \ \ \mathtt{s.t.} \ \ t = \sum_{\forall m \in \pi} C + B \left\lceil \frac{t}{P_{mu}} \right\rceil + \sum_{\forall \chi \in HP} \left\lceil \frac{t}{P_\chi} \right\rceil C \quad (8)$$

Mule Transport Time. In both cases, FIFO and RM, T_{trip} is the time spent by the message in the mule, which corresponds to the time the mule moves from the gateway where it got the message to the destination node, through its fixed path. Clearly, this is independent of the scheduling algorithm that is chosen and depends only on the technology used for the mules and other optimization criteria (e.g., saving fuel).

3.3   Scheduling Condition

Lemma 6. *An opportunistic network operating with mules and gateways implementing FIFO or RM order is schedulable if:*

$$\forall m_{ijh} \quad D_{ijh} \geq T_{\mathtt{end\_to\_end}, ijh} \quad (9)$$

4   Example

The following example shows the main characteristics of both FIFO and Rate Monotonic orderings at the *gateway* and how messages are delivered in each case by the *mule*. Let's suppose there are two *mules* in the system and that the round trip is $T_{rt} = 10$. The distance between the *mules* is 5, that is the period of the *mule* is $T_p = 5$. In the worst case, the blind window is $B = 3$ leaving only 2 slots for the transmission window, $W = 2$. It is assumed that all messages have the same length and that it is equal to the slot. The *gateways* have queue length $|MQ| = 3$. With these parameters, the *gateway* can transfer to the *mule* only two messages in each transmission window, $\omega = 2$. As the *mules* move around the ring in one direction, in the worst case, the destination is just upstream and almost a whole round is needed for the *mule* to reach it. As $W = 2$ and $T_{rt} = 10$, in the worst case the trip takes $T_{trip} = 8$ slots. Let the set of messages be: $M(G) = \{(6, 1, 40, 1), (6, 1, 40, 1), (15, 1, 100, 2)\}$. For the case of FIFO ordering all messages have the same priority and are put into the queue in order of arrival, for example m_1, m_2 and m_3. With Fixed Priorities, messages m_1 and m_2 have the highest priority in the *gateway* so they are transmitted whenever the *mule* is in range.

For the FIFO ordering, Fig. 2 shows the evolution of the message transmission from the *gateway* to the *mule*. Each message is represented in a different row and color while the *mule* is represented in the last one with two colors, grey for the blind window and white for the transmission one. Arrows indicate the instant at which the messages arrive to the *gateway*. As can be seen, messages arrive just after the transmission window finishes. With the arrival of a new *mule*, two messages are uploaded. In this case m_1 and m_2. The boxes in the messages rows indicate that the messages are uploaded to the *mule*. The worst case response time is given by Eq. 7.

For the case of RM ordering, there are two queues one for each priority. The worst case waiting time is given by Eq. 8, for messages (m_1, m_2) and m_3 is $t = 5$ and $t = 24$, respectively. In Fig. 3 the evolution of the messages transmissions are shown. Only at $t = 24$ in accordance with Eq. 8 message m_3 is able to get into the *mule*.

From the example, it is clear that RM benefits higher priority messages by delivering them first. However, as can be seen in Figs. 2 and 3 in both cases m_3 is dispatched and there is no backlog in the queue at the moment $t = 31$.

The traffic towards the *gateways* is restricted to 20% only for each *mule*. The network configuration and the time required for a *mule* to do a round-trip and the fact that there is only one going through a *gateway* each time, it is deduced that there are a maximum of two *mules*. So the maximum traffic in the network towards any *gateway* should not be greater than 40%. If all the messages in the *gateway* are transmitted towards only one *gateway* and considering that the demand is 36.7%, with the two *mules* mentioned it is enough to satisfy the demand.

Figures 4 and 5 show how both *mules* deliver the messages in destiny. Each *mule* is represented in a different row. In white, it is shown a previous message

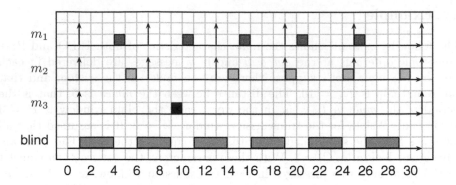

Fig. 2. FIFO ordering, m_1, m_2 and m_3, m_3 is able to get into the *mule* at $t = 9$.

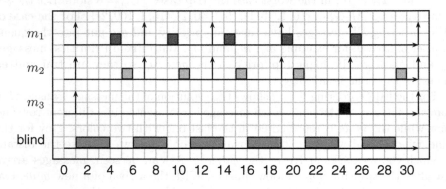

Fig. 3. RM ordering, m_1, m_2 and m_3, m_3 is able to get into the *mule* at $t = 24$

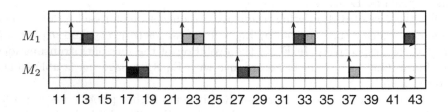

Fig. 4. m_1, m_2 and m_3. FIFO order in the *gateway*

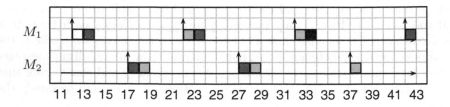

Fig. 5. m_1, m_2 and m_3. RM order in the *gateway*

that M_1 may have queued before m_1 and m_2. The temporal sequence is correlated with Figs. 2 and 3, as can be seen the destination of messages originated in the *gateway* are just prior to coming back so the *mule* needs to do almost a complete round-trip before delivering the first message. The example shows that it is possible to deliver all the messages with just two *mules*.

It is necessary to compute the schedulability of the network by computing the delays in the gateways by using Eqs. (10) and (11) for the FIFO and RM respectively.

$$T_{\text{end\_to\_end}} = NG + 9 + 19 + GN = NG + 28 + GN \tag{10}$$

$$
\begin{aligned}
T_{\text{end\_to\_end},m_1} &= NG + 5 + 19 + GN = NG + 24 + GN \\
T_{\text{end\_to\_end},m_2} &= NG + 5 + 19 + GN = NG + 24 + GN \\
T_{\text{end\_to\_end},m_3} &= NG + 24 + 19 + GN = NG + 43 + GN
\end{aligned} \tag{11}
$$

From the previous results it is clear that the system is schedulable if the delay in the transit of messages from the nodes to the *gateway* and the *gateway* to the nodes is less than: $NG + GN \leq D_i - T_{\text{end\_to\_end},i}$.

5   Conclusions and Future Work

In this paper a model for real-time communications among search and rescue teams and incident commander in disaster relief areas is proposed. A bounded message propagation model for OppNets that involves IoT-enabled devices as nodes, and supports communication in the field during first responses is introduced. Two scheduling policies were analyzed (FIFO and RM) in this context. While the first one facilitates the unrestricted information flow, the second one introduces priorities that guarantee that important messages arrive first to destination. Particularly, the analytic results show that the RM helps improve the response times of high priority messages, which usually are those that make a difference in disaster relief scenarios. These results provide predictability to real-time message propagation in an OppNet which is the main contribution of the paper.

Next steps in this initiative considers performing a proof-of-concept to verify the analytic results obtained based on the proposed model, and thus determine more accurately the impact of this proposal for both, the research community and the application domain.

Acknowledgments. This work was partially supported by the Spanish government (TIN2016-77836-C2-2-R).

References

1. Arimura, S., Uchida, N., Shibata, Y.: Self power supplied micro wireless ballooned network for disaster recovery. In: Advanced Information Networking and Applications Workshops (WAINA), pp. 255–260 (2013)
2. Boldrini, C., Conti, M., Passarella, A.: Performance modelling of opportunistic forwarding under heterogenous mobility. Comput. Commun. **48**, 56–70 (2014)

3. Cayssials, R., Orozco, J., Santos, J., Santos, R.: Rate monotonic scheduling of real-time control systems with the minimum number of priority levels. In: Proceedings of the 11th Euromicro Conference on Real-Time Systems, pp. 54–59 (1999)
4. Das, A., Mazumder, A., Sen, A., Mitton, N.: On mobile sensor data collection using data mules. In: Proceedings of Computing, Networking and Communications (ICNC), pp. 1–7 (2016)
5. Gomez, K., Goratti, L., Rasheed, T., Reynaud, L.: Enabling disaster-resilient 4G mobile communication networks. IEEE Commun. Mag. **52**(12), 66–73 (2014)
6. Hardy, K., Comfort, L.K.: Dynamic decision processes in complex, high-risk operations: The Yarnell hill fire, June 30 2013. Saf. Sci. Part A **71**, 39–47 (2015)
7. Herlich, M., Yamada, S.: Motivation for a step-by-step guide to set up wireless disaster recovery networks. In: Proceedings of Information and Communication Technologies for Disaster Management (ICT-DM), pp. 64–70 (2015)
8. Huang, C.M., Lan, K.c., Tsai, C.Z.: A survey of opportunistic networks. In: Advanced Information Networking and Applications - Workshops (WAINA), pp. 1672–1677. IEEE (2008)
9. Jain, G., Babu, S., Raj, R., Benson, K., Manoj, B., Venkatasubramanian, N.: On disaster information gathering in a complex shanty town terrain. In: Global Humanitarian Technology Conference-South Asia Satellite (GHTC-SAS), pp. 147–153 (2014)
10. Manoj, B.S., Baker, A.H.: Communication challenges in emergency response. Commun. ACM **50**(3), 51–53 (2007)
11. Mendonça, D.: Decision support for improvisation in response to extreme events: learning from the response to the 2001 world trade center attack. Decis. Support Syst. **43**(3), 952–967 (2007)
12. Monares, Á., Ochoa, S.F., Herskovic, V., Santos, R., Pino, J.A.: Modeling interactions in human-centric wireless sensor networks. In: Proceedings of Computer Supported Cooperative Work in Design (CSCWD), pp. 661–666 (2014)
13. Monares, Á., Ochoa, S.F., Pino, J.A., Herskovic, V., Rodriguez-Covili, J., Neyem, A.: Mobile computing in urban emergency situations: improving the support to firefighters in the field. Expert Syst. Appl. **38**(2), 1255–1267 (2011)
14. Monares, Á., Ochoa, S.F., Santos, R., Orozco, J., Meseguer, R.: Modeling IoT-based solutions using human-centric wireless sensor networks. Sensors **14**(9), 15687–15713 (2014)
15. Petersen, H., Baccelli, E., Wählisch, M., Schmidt, T.C., Schiller, J.: The role of the Internet of Things in network resilience. In: Giaffreda, R., Cagáňová, D., Li, Y., Riggio, R., Voisard, A. (eds.) IoT360 2014. LNICSSITE, vol. 151, pp. 283–296. Springer, Cham (2015). doi:10.1007/978-3-319-19743-2_39
16. Santos, R., Mosse, D., Znati, T., Comfort, L.: Design and implementation of a witness unit for opportunistic routing in tsunami alert scenarios. Saf. Sci. **90**, 75–83 (2015)
17. Santos, R., Ochoa, S.F.: Disseminating shared information in disaster relief efforts: a communication computable model. In: Proceedings of Systems, Man, and Cybernetics (SMC), pp. 3446–3451 (2011)
18. Santos, R., Orozco, J., Ochoa, S.F.: A real-time analysis approach in opportunistic networks. ACM SIGBED Rev. **8**(3), 40–43 (2011)
19. Yun, C., Lim, Y.K.: ASO-TDMA: ad-hoc self-organizing tdma protocol for ship-borne ad-hoc networks. EURASIP J. Wirel. Commun. Netw. **2012**(1), 1–13 (2012)

Flying Real-Time Network for Disaster Assistance

Rodrigo M. Santos[1]([✉]), Javier Orozco[1], Daniel Mosse[2], Vinicius Petrucci[3],
Sergio F. Ochoa[4], and Roc Meseguer[5]

[1] Dpto. de Ing. Eléctrica y de Computadoras, UNS - IIIE, CONICET,
Bahía Blanca, Argentina
ierms@criba.edu.ar
[2] University of Pittsburgh, Pittsburgh, USA
[3] Universidade Federal da Bahia, Salvador, Bahia, Brazil
[4] Universidad de Chile, Santiago, Chile
[5] Universitat Politècnica de Catalunya, Barcelona, Spain

Abstract. Landslides and large floods are serious natural disasters that
every year cause multiple deaths and loss in property around the world.
When these events occur in areas like the "favelas" or mountain regions
in coastal cities like Rio de Janeiro, the situation becomes critical as
buildings and infrastructures are not prepared to withstand them. Search
and rescue teams in such disaster areas need to rely on real-time communication, which often cannot be adequately provided by cell or radio
networks. In this paper, we argue that flying ad-hoc networks can provide the support needed in these scenarios and propose a new solution
towards that goal, termed Flying Witness Units. We make our case by
presenting real-time schedulability analysis of message delivery for a disaster scenario.

Keywords: UAVs · FANET · Real-time · Schedulability · Disaster management

1 Introduction

Every year natural disasters hit urban areas and produce dramatic losses in terms
of both, human life and damage to property. The more destructive incidents
(earthquakes, flash-floods, tsunamis and landslides) are characterized by their
sudden development without previous alert, while some natural disasters can be
detected earlier. In any case, once the incident happens, there are only a few
hours to rescue survivors. This period is called the *golden relief time* and lasts
up to 72 h [11]. Communication becomes the bottleneck for the search and rescue
(SAR) teams dealing with the disaster and they have real-time characteristics
and need to be reliable.

In 2011, in Rio de Janeiro, a large flood and landslides took place and almost
nine hundred people died, more than one thousand were injured, more than ten
thousand lost their houses and almost a hundred are still missed, according to

© Springer International Publishing AG 2017
S.F. Ochoa et al. (Eds.): UCAmI 2017, LNCS 10586, pp. 591–602, 2017.
DOI: 10.1007/978-3-319-67585-5_58

Rio de Janeiro State Civil Defense reports [18]. At that time, SAR teams were deployed in the area and, as with all such emergency incidents, SAR teams used both VHF and UHF radios as the primary means of communications, depending on local legislation. This has two main problems. First, such radios are not reliable given that there is no way to ensure that the message has been received properly or even that it has reached the destination. Second, it only transmits voice and no digital data such as maps/images. In some cases, the lack of information leads to critical decisions to be taken based on wrong information, as in the Yarnell Hill wild fire where 19 firemen were trapped by the fire and died.

In previous work, we have previously proposed the utilization of special devices named *witness units* (WUs) to provide support after a tsunami alert or event, helping move people to shelters, predefined according to Local Contingency Plans, where the wave will not reach. WUs are used to inform community leaders and passers of the best routes to the shelters [16]. WUs can be attached to street light poles (or other static resilient locations) and are connected to the disaster management center through a satellite network. WUs rely on standard Wi-Fi and provide access points (APs) for the human users. However, these units do not move, they are placed in fixed locations before the event occurs.

To adapt the network to unknown and dynamic environments, the concept of *mules* was previously introduced [14] to provide real-time guarantees to the message delivery between the SAR teams and the incident commander (IC) in the command post (CP). In this case, the members of each SAR team (including the leader) build a local ad-hoc network where the SAR leader is in charge of acting as gateway to the CP. Since there may be several hundred meters or even kilometers between a SAR team and the IC, a direct connection is typically not feasible. Thus, mules can be implemented with unmanned or manned vehicles that physically transport the information in digital format. Mules can move among all the different SAR teams exchanging (collecting and delivering) messages. It is possible to deployed in certain places nodes to act as bridges between two otherwise disconnected areas.

In this paper, we introduce the idea of deploying a network of flying witness units (or FWUs) through the use of UAVs or drones. In [5] drones or UAV are defined as any aircraft that is operated without the possibility of direct human intervention from within or on the aircraft. Drones come in many different sizes and shapes and are designed to primarily collect data to meet a multitude of different tasks and applications. The lack of an onboard pilot means drones exist in a variety of sizes, from microUAVs that can be held in the palm of your hand to large aircraft and airships that rival the size and power of traditional piloted craft. Drone models include fixed-wing aircraft, rotary-wing, tilt-rotor, ducted fan, and even airships. This variety of sizes and forms offers a dizzying array of options for organizations involved with disaster mitigation and relief.

The UAVs will act as mules and/or bridges to provide the required connectivity. The whole network can be seen as a FANET (Flying Ad-Hoc Network) [1]. While there have been recent efforts investigating FANETs, it remains a great challenge to design and deploy efficient network architectures comprised of UAVs.

Such deployed networks need to address the real-time behavior and feasibility analysis to meet timeliness of message delivery. The use of drones must be coordinated with Air Operations office as the Incident Command System (ICS) doctrine adopted by most First Response Agencies include the aerial support, so flight safety rules should be followed.

Contribution: This paper presents three contributions. The first one is the extension of the witness units to Flying Witness Units with capacity to store-and-forward information between SAR teams and IC. The second contribution is the computation of real-time feasibility conditions for this kind of networks where there is no end-to-end path available continuously. The analysis is done at the network layer. Finally, indications on the network deployment and how nodes should be distributed to have a predictable behavior in messages transmissions are presented.

Organization: The rest of the paper is organized in the following way. There is a large amount of bibliography about drones and their use for disaster relief and rescue support, in Sect. 2 some of the most important papers are commented. In Sect. 3 the system proposal is presented and the transmission model used is introduced. We also discuss the network deployment issue. In Sect. 4, the real-time model is presented for computing the feasibility conditions. Algorithms are presented and a brief example is developed. In Sect. 5 the proposal is discussed considering real constraints and finally in Sect. 6, conclusions are drawn.

2   Related Work

Previous research works have considered some kind of alternative/opportunistic networks for disaster assistance. A human-centric wireless sensor network was introduced in [11] to improve communication and coordination of critical information during search and rescue activities. While the added layer of human sensors can help input extra information into the network, the underlying deployed network is still necessary and an essential key to the success of the communication.

In [10] the authors proposed a human-centric approach to model IoT based solutions for man made incidents like train derailments, terrorist attacks in public places. The idea is in line with what is proposed in this paper although in the reference paper, the SAR teams used a MANET as the network paradigm.

The design of a Witness Unit (WU) device was proposed in [16] to provide rescuers with the necessary communication in an emergency area. A WU can use a satellite network for remotely connecting the rescuers to emergency command centers. A WU is statically placed ahead of time in a safe and suitable place to fully cover a determined rescue area, which limits this type of networks to known disaster locations (too expensive for scalability). While the proposal in [16] is attractive because of its simple architecture, a potential shortcoming is that WUs are site-specific and need to be statically placed in some predefined areas. This would require a priori knowledge regarding likely disasters in those areas and would demand network deployment efforts ahead of time.

In [2] the National Aeronautics and Space Administration (NASA) Glenn Research Center, presents the Unmanned Aircraft System (UAS) to select and test a communication technology for the UAS Control and Non-Payload Communications (CNPC) link. The authors evaluate the performance of several potential technologies for the CNPC link through detailed software simulations resulting LTE and 802.16 ranked as the top two.

The SMAVNET (Swarming Micro Air Vehicle Network) project at EPFL introduces a flying ad-hoc self-organizing network that uses swarming communication protocols to build an alternative wireless network for rescuers in emergency scenarios. They propose a kind of self-organizing mesh network, where the UAVs rely on multi-hop communications to better cover the operation area [8].

The full deployment of FANETs at large scale may be too intricate for the scenarios we are considering, given that it would require dealing with non-trivial decisions such as dynamic routing [12].

In [3] the authors claims that to date, there have been no practical solutions outside military applications, to immediately assist emergency disaster relief communication. In consequence, they propose an autonomous system to deploy UAV as the first phase disaster recovery communication network for wide-area relief. An automation algorithm control the deployment and positioning of a set of quadcopter UAVs based on a hexagonal pattern distribution using an open source MAVLink point-to-point communication protocol. The distributed execution of the algorithm is based on a centralized management of UAV cells through assigning the role of supernodes to some specific UAVs. The use of open-source solutions makes the system easily reproducible and accessible but, at the same time expose it to several ways of network attacks that require extensive protocol modifications and adds [9].

In this paper we propose a flying real-time ad-hoc network to provide support to SAR teams in disaster relief scenarios. We introduce a feasibility analysis based on the demand bound function and dividing the message propagation in different stages each one with a computed release time and deadline. To the best of the authors knowledge, this kind of analysis have not been done before for ad-hoc networks and particularly in the case of FANETs.

3   Proposed Network System

We argue that UAVs have several advantages as an alternative network system in a disaster environment. For example, UAV technology can reduce the risk assumed by a rescue crew and enhance its effectiveness while providing viewing angles that are impossible to obtain with other types of mules. The cost of UVAs is falling and their technological capabilities are increasing rapidly including: automated obstacle avoidance, route planning, point-to-point navigation using way-points and tracking points of interest. All these features facilitates and autonomous deployment of the network to provide the necessary connectivity among the different SAR teams.

UAVs may become the primary form of transportation for support technologies in disaster scenarios. Mostly used for video surveillance, in these cases UAVs equipped with data communication and software capabilities can share data in a collaborative architecture building an efficient FANET. They hold a great potential when their collected data is integrated to an existing geographic information system (GIS) and a crisis management protocol. As explained in Sect. 1, drones may have different sizes and flight autonomy. A proper distribution of them is necessary to provide the best network coverage in the disaster area and support the relief and rescue activities.

3.1   Flying Witness Units (FWU)

A FWU physically stores and transfers data from one location to another or eventually transmits the data to another FWU acting as bridge linking disconnected areas. Thus, a FWU needs to have enough computation power and lifetime to provide an access point to SAR teams, while acting as gateways to the IC in charge of the SAR operation. There are basically two kinds of FWU. The first one is used to support in direct contact the SAR team. In this case, each team counts with a dedicated FWU that follows it and is used as gateway to the challenged network. Although basically tied to the SAR team, the drone may move around to get full contact with the second group of FWU.

Figure 1 shows a possible deployment of the FWUs, implemented by UAVs. In the figure, the cell phones represent SAR team members, who communicate with the FWUs, that in turn communicate with other FWUs in the FANET, that deliver the message to the IC. An added value of the FANET is that, in addition to SAR teams, survivors will also have access to the network. In the case of survivors, the access to the network is limited to "listeners" so they can receive directives on how to proceed or in case of allowing the transmission of data, it will be through a special application so important information can be sent to the command post. In that case, survivors can receive information and eventually indicate their presence in the way of a very short identification message through the WiFi connection.

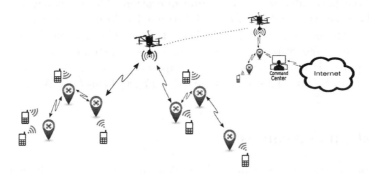

Fig. 1. Deployment of WU and two mobile UAV mules (aka FWU); SAR members are depicted by smartphones.

We envision the FWUs landing at certain spots (for more extensive message exchange, for dropping a WU dynamically, or simply for saving energy) and flying again following the movements of the SAR team. We also envision the FWUs being remotely controlled to start with, specially those carrying WUs to be deployed near SAR teams. Thereafter, truly autonomous behavior is the goal.

3.2 Network Deployment

Network deployment is a key issue in emergency situations. The communication network cannot be set-up ahead of time for two main reasons. First, some natural disasters (such as landslides) typically destroy most structures (mudslides also cover almost everything with mud). Second, it is not clear where one should deploy the new communications network ahead of time, given that it is impossible to predict where the disaster will occur[1]. Once the incident has taken place, the IC decides where the SAR teams should be deployed first to start the disaster relief activities and with each team a FWU is also deployed. These FWU will probably not been enough to cover the transmission range between the teams and the IC. Additional FWU should be used then in the form of bridges or mules to Only once the incident has taken place, are the proper locations to deploy the FWUs selected by the IC in the CP.

The network system proposed in this work is based on a FANET which is built with the FWUs that are associated to the SAR teams and those operating as mules and/or bridges. The communication between the SAR teams and the CP is performed in a hierarchical way. In the lowest level, the members of the SAR team transmit information to the closest FWU acting as gateway to the FANET.

The FANET is, from its operating point of view, an opportunistic network in which there is no stable path between any pair of nodes in the system [1]. In an emergency scenario, real-time messages have to be delivered before their deadlines [15] to be useful. For this to occur, it is necessary to have bounded end-to-end transmission delays so the worst-case can be compared with the deadline to verify the feasibility of the real-time operation. The challenge in this case is that the network delay cannot be determined beforehand as the topology is variable and there are variable physical constraints. This is typical schedulability analysis of real-time systems; our contribution is to extend this analysis for the case of opportunistic mixed networks, composed of mobile nodes, semi-fixed or fixed FWUs and an IC. This is what we call a *Flying Real-Time Network*, FRTN, as shown in Fig. 2.

4   Real-Time Analysis

We consider a set of periodic and independent messages sent by the nodes (SAR teams); for simplicity of presentation all messages have the same length, that

---
[1] There are exceptions, of course, such as a tsunami detection and warning systems in any town that is to be protected.

is, they have equal payloads. Formally, a message m_i originating in node i is described by the tuple $\langle C, P, r, D \rangle$, where C is the time required to transmit a message, P is the period, r is the release time, and D is the relative deadline. The absolute deadline is computed from the release time and relative deadline, $d = r + D$. For simplicity, we consider the time is divided in atomic units or slots. Events occur at the beginning of a slot. Time is noted $t = 0, 1, \ldots, n$.

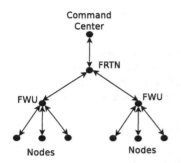

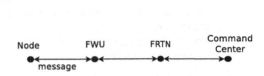

Fig. 2. Proposed network topology   **Fig. 3.** Message propagation pipeline

The proposed network has a tree structure with nodes exchanging messages with the FWU. The FWU interacts with the FRTN that is connected with the IC. Figure 2 shows a graph representing the network. Messages are generated in nodes and go through levels before reaching the IC. In the reverser path, a message sent by the IC should traverse the same levels to reach a SAR team. The transmission path can be seen as a "pipeline" where each stage/level can not process the message until it has been released by the previous one.

Figure 3 shows the propagation model for a message. Each stage in the transmission process requires a proper scheduling algorithm and for each level the real-time feasibility conditions should be verified for the system. Described in this way, we have to consider the moment in which the message arrives to intermediate nodes and the latest instant at which it should leave that node. Suppose there is one hop between the source and destination node. A message has a total delay of x slots if it is transmitted alone in the network and as soon as it arrives to the intermediate hop it is sent again. Suppose that the delay from the source to the intermediate node is y slots. If the message is release at $r = 0$, it is not possible for that message to arrive before $r = 0 + y$ to the intermediate node. The message should not leave the intermediate node after $D - x - y$ in order to arrive before its deadline to the destination node. In this way, the message should be processed in the intermediate node in at most $D - x - y - r$. We introduce the following notation to deal with the schedulability analysis in the intermediate nodes. For intermediate node j the release time of message i coming from node i is noted r_i^j, the deadline is noted D_i^j and the transmission time is noted C_i^j.

There are several scheduling algorithms. Among the most used we can mention Rate Monotonic (RM) and Earliest Deadline First (EDF). In the first case, priorities are assigned to messages based on the period, with shorter periods higher priorities. At each opportunity, the message with higher priority is dispatched. In the second case, the highest priority is given to the message with the closer deadline. In that way, whenever the node has the chance to transmit, it dispatches the message with the closest deadline. EDF can reach better utilization of the network. Even though a different policy can be employed at each hop in the path, for simplicity, we assume an EDF scheduling policy for all the stages.

For modifying the release times:

1. For any initial node of the precedence graph, set $r_i^* = r_i$.
2. Select a message m_i^j such that its release time has not been modified but the release times of all immediate predecessors m_i^h have been modified. If no such message exists, exit.
3. Set $r_i^j = \max[r_i, \max(r_i^h + C : m_i^h \prec m_i^j)]$.
4. Return to step 2

Algorithm 1. Chetto Algorithm for modifying release times

For modifying the deadlines:

1. For any terminal node of the precedence graph, set $d_i^* = d_i$
2. Select a message m_i such that its deadline has not been modified but the deadlines of all immediate successors m_k have been modified. If no such message exists, exit.
3. Set $d_i^j = \min[d_i, \min(d_i^k - C : m_j \prec m_k)]$.
4. Return to step 2

Algorithm 2. Chetto Algorithm for modifying deadlines

EDF is optimal for scheduling a set of independent periodic messages within a network. However, in the problem proposed here, the message should traverse several hops before reaching destination and in each hop, a scheduling policy is followed. This affects the independent condition as a message can not be dispatched from node j if it has not leave node i before. Thus, there is a dependency in the scheduling conditions of node j with respect to the scheduling conditions in node i. To overcome this problem, we adopt the Chetto algorithm [4] that transforms a set of precedence related messages in a set of independent ones. In this way, a message with one hop is transformed in *two independent messages* being sent by two nodes but with release and deadlines modified for each one of them. In this way, message m_i going through node j to node k is seen as two independent messages: m_i^i and m_i^j that have equal transmission time but different release times and deadlines. To accomplish this decoupling of the precedence relations, Chetto modifies the release times beginning from the first stage and the deadlines starting with the last one. Algorithms 1 and 2, present in pseudo-code the algorithms for modifying the release and deadlines respectively.

In our proposal, some drones are used as bridges so they are in a fix location while others actually transport the messages between two nodes. This, introduces a delay that is not related with the transmission rate or computation power of the processor but with the time needed by the UAV to transport the data between nodes i and j, Δt_{ij}. This delay can be considered constant and equal for every message between those two nodes. However, this delay affects the end-to-end transmission time and should be taken into account. The transport delay has to be subtracted from the deadline computed for that stage.

$$d_i^j = d_i^j - \Delta t_{ij} \tag{1}$$

Once the message transmission has been broken into different stages, the real-time feasibility test can be performed in each node of the "pipeline". To do this we use the demand bound function, $dbf(t_1, t_2)$, introduced in [17]. This test computes the worst-case work demand and compares it to the time available in the system for message transmissions. For each stage or intermediate node S_i, if the available time is greater than the messages demand, the system is feasible. We formalize the definition for the dbf function in the interval $[t_0, t_1]$ based on [17] in the following way:

Definition 1. *The demand function for stage S_i, denoted by $dbf_i(t_0, t_1)$, is the total time taken by all the instances of the messages going through S_i, having release time and deadline within $[t_0, t_1]$. For periodic messages, the demand function can be computed as follows:*

$$dbf_i(t_0, t_1) \stackrel{def}{=} \max(0, \sum_{m_h^i \in S_i} \left(\left\lfloor \frac{t_1 - d_h^i}{P_h} \right\rfloor - \left\lceil \frac{t_0 - r_h^i}{P_h} \right\rceil + 1 \right) C) \tag{2}$$

where d_h^i represents the modified deadline in stage j by Chetto algorithm and Eq. 1.

For any interval of length t, the $dbf(t_0, t_0 + t)$ is defined as the maximum possible demand in any interval of length t [17]:

$$dbf(t) \stackrel{def}{=} \max_{t_0} dbf(t_0, t_0 + t) \tag{3}$$

Finally, we introduce the necessary and sufficient feasibility condition for the system.

$$\forall S_i, \forall t dbf_{S_i}(t) \leq t \tag{4}$$

4.1 Computing the Condition

In the this example we show how the real-time condition is computed. Suppose a network is deployed after a landslide. Three different SAR teams are deployed in the area. Each team has 10 members and one FWU that acts as gateway to the FRTN, which is composed of a set of FWUs acting as mules for providing connectivity among teams and the IC. Each node within the SAR team generates a message report and sends it to the IC every five minutes. These messages are forwarded by the gateway to the FRTN as soon as possible. Assume that each message contains 250 KB (or 2 Mb) of data, voice or pictures, and the transmission link with the FWU is a 1 Mb/s wireless link. We assume the messages have a simultaneous release at instant zero. With this condition, each message requires 2 s to be transferred from the node to the FWU. With 10 nodes operating with a round robin scheme, the FWU receives all the messages within 20 s. In this case, $r_{i0} = 0$ for all m_i. Each message has two hops to reach the CP and an absolute deadline of 600 s. Let's suppose the flying time of the mules in the FRTN is 360 s. In the worst case, the flying mule require 60 s to deliver to the IC the 30 messages collected from the FWU associated to the SAR teams. With these constraints, the available time for transmission is just 180 s. Applying algorithms 2 and 1 to each message we have 180 s for the last relative deadline and 160 s for the first one.

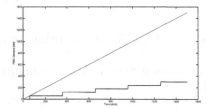

Fig. 4. FWU 10 messages. *Notes:* dbf in black and t bound in red. (Color figure online)

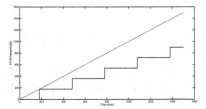

Fig. 5. FRTN 30 messages. *Notes:* dbf in black and t bound in red. (Color figure online)

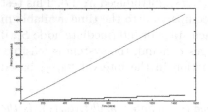

Fig. 6. FWU 30 messages. *Notes:* dbf in black and t bound in red. (Color figure online)

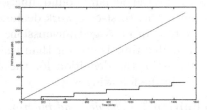

Fig. 7. FRTN 90 messages. *Notes:* dbf in black and t bound in red. (Color figure online)

Figures 4 and 5 present the *dbf* in the FWU and the FRTN respectively. In both cases, the load is quite light and more traffic is possible. Figures 6 and 7 show the *dbf* in both hops when the number of messages being forwarded are tripled and it shows that the system is still feasible. With all these considerations, the system still works within the real-time parameters proposed.

The previous example presents a very simple case with just a few elements in the network. When the FRTN is larger and the message has several hops before reaching the destination, additional problems like routing appear and should be considered at the moment of doing the real-time analysis.

5   Discussion

The network system proposed in this work is flexible and general enough to be applicable to support SAR activities in several natural disasters, such as landslides, floods, or earthquakes. The use of UAVs opens up the possibility of dynamically deploying a data network (FRTN) with the needed coverage in these disaster areas. The deployment of the FRTN with FWUs will depend on the characteristics of the disaster and the geographic features of the region.

There are several trade-offs to consider depending on the operational areas of each FWU responsible for storing and carrying data from one location to another. The problem of determining the best route design to deploy and position the FWUs is an open research question. One critical issue is that of variable data rate in wireless communication. The communication rate is much higher (up to 54 Mbit/s in 802.11g) when the FWUs are closer to each other, and much lower when the FWUs are far away (even lower than 1 Mbit/s in 802.11g) [13].

A FWU with a buffer of tens of megabytes flying at a speed of few tens of meters per second could deliver a network bandwidth over 1 Mbps, whereas a wireless direct link within a distance of few kilometers could deliver a much slower rate of a few tens of Kbps [6]. However, direct links can deliver a single message with low latency while a FWU may require a few minutes. The understanding of these trade-offs is key to benefit from the FWU network deployment [7].

We note that the FWUs should be deployed in such a way that the specific areas are covered with a satisfactory periodicity so as to effectively transfer the information from the SAR teams towards the CP. Real-time delivery of the messages can be best accomplished in cases where FWUs can work upon controlled mobility and predefined trajectories.

6   Conclusion and Future Work

In this paper we argue for the use of UAVs as a future network to provide communication support for SAR activities in situations of natural disasters, such as flood and landslides. For that, we designed a mixed flying ad-hoc network with teams of rescuers, witness units, and flying witness units (mobile and portable, even by a SAR Unit) to transmit messages from the field to the incident commander. We also provided an analysis to prove real-time guarantees on message transmissions in our proposed network. We show that real-time requirements can be met by decomposing the message delivery in multiple independent stages.

The next step in this research is to consider the message routing within the FRTN when a whole switching network is deployed to collect the information. This requires an important amount of UAV to provide the necessary connectivity and to reduce the amount of mules. The real-time analysis should include in that case congestion and energy considerations.

Acknowledgments. This work was partially supported by the Spanish government (TIN2016-77836-C2-2-R).

References

1. Bekmezci, İ., Sahingoz, O.K., Temel, Ş.: Flying ad-hoc networks (fanets): A survey. Ad Hoc Netw. **11**(3), 1254–1270 (2013)
2. Bretmersky, S.C., Bishop, W.D., Dailey, J.E., Chevalier, C.T.: Communications technology assessment for the unmanned aircraft system (UAS) control and non-payload communications (CNPC) link. Technical report, NASA (2014)
3. Bupe, P., Haddad, R., Rios-Gutierrez, F.: Relief and emergency communication network based on an autonomous decentralized UAV clustering network. In: SoutheastCon, pp. 1–8 (2015)
4. Chetto, H., Chetto, M.: Some results of the earliest deadline scheduling algorithm. IEEE Trans. Softw. Eng. **15**(10), 1261–1269 (1989)
5. Cross, A.R.: Drones for disaster response and relief operations. Technical report Red Cross (2015). http://www.issuelab.org/resources/21683/21683.pdf
6. Frew, E.W., Brown, T.X.: Networking issues for small unmanned aircraft systems. J. Intell. Robot. Syst. **54**(1–3), 21–37 (2009)
7. Henkel, D., Brown, T.X.: On controlled node mobility in delaytolerant networks of unmanned aerial vehicles. In: International Symposium on Advance Radio Technolgoies (ISART), pp. 7–9 (2006)
8. Jimenez-Pacheco, A., Bouhired, D., Gasser, Y., Zufferey, J.C., Floreano, D., Rimoldi, B.: Implementation of a wireless mesh network of ultra light mavs with dynamic routing. In: IEEE Globecom Workshops, pp. 1591–1596 (2012)
9. Marty, J.A.: Vulnerability analysis of the mavlink protocol for command and control of unmanned aircraft. Technical report, DTIC Document (2013)
10. Monares, Á., Ochoa, S.F., Santos, R., Orozco, J., Meseguer, R.: Modeling IoT-based solutions using human-centric wireless sensor networks. Sensors **14**(9), 15687–15713 (2014)
11. Ochoa, S.F., Santos, R.: Human-centric wireless sensor networks to improve information availability during urban search and rescue activities. Inf. Fus. **22**, 71–84 (2015)
12. Rosati, S., Krużelecki, K., Heitz, G., Floreano, D., Rimoldi, B.: Dynamic routing for flying Ad hoc networks. IEEE Trans. Vehicular Technol. **65**(3), 1690 1700 (2016)
13. Sahingoz, O.K.: Networking models in flying Ad-hoc networks (fanets): Concepts and challenges. J. Intell. Robot. Syst. **74**(1), 513–527 (2014)
14. Santos, R., Orozco, J., Ochoa, S., Meseguer, R., Mosse, D.: Supporting real-time message delivery in disaster relief efforts: an analytical approach. University of Pittsburgh, Technical report (2016)
15. Santos, R., Urriza, J., Santos, J., Orozco, J.: New methods for redistributing slack time in real-time systems: Applications and comparative evaluations. J. Syst. Softw. **69**(1–2), 115–128 (2004)
16. Santos, R., Mosse, D., Znati, T., Comfort, L.: Design and implementation of a witness unit for opportunistic routing in tsunami alert scenarios. Saf. Sci. **90**, 75–83 (2016)
17. Serreli, N., Lipari, G., Bini, E.: The demand bound function interface of distributed sporadic pipelines of tasks scheduled by edf. In: Euromicro Conference on Real-Time Systems (ECRTS), pp. 187–196 (2010)
18. Toro, J., de Moura, F.S., Pedroso, F.F., Marques, F.: Avaliacao de perdas e danos: Inundacoes e deslizamentos na regiao serrana do rio de janeiro. Technical report, World Bank (2012)

Human-Computer Interaction (HCI)

Effective User Stories are Affective

Pankaj Kamthan[1](✉) and Nazlie Shahmir[2]

[1] Concordia University, Montreal, Canada
kamthan@cse.concordia.ca
[2] WestJet Airlines Limited, Calgary, Canada
nshahmir@westjet.com

Abstract. The ever strengthening symbiosis between software and society calls for increasing attention on the emotions of the users in the engineering of software. In the context of agile software development, this paper proposes a preliminary framework for a user-centered and conceptual model-based process for engineering affective user stories, and illustrates a part of it by an example.

Keywords: Affective computing · Agile methodology · Conceptual modeling · Human-information interaction · Requirements engineering · User experience

1 Introduction

In the past decade or so, there has been a notable permeation of the agile methodologies in the development of interactive software systems. In interacting with these systems, a user can have different kinds of experiences. For example, certain interactions may engage, help, and delight a user, while others may bore, hinder, and/or disappoint. If an agile project team anticipates a positive user experience, then *user* and *affect* need to be *forethought*, and need to be essential concerns *throughout* the agile process. In particular, *agile requirements engineering* needs to be sensitive towards not only instrumental quality attributes (such as *utility* and *usability*), but also towards non-instrumental quality attributes (such as *motivation* and *emotion*). The purpose of this paper is to serve as a starting point towards such an endeavor.

The rest of the paper is organized as follows. In Sect. 2, background is provided and related work is highlighted. The conceptual models and, based on these models, a process, necessary for affective user story engineering, are introduced in Sect. 3. In Sect. 4, directions for future research are outlined. Finally, in Sect. 5, concluding remarks are given.

2 Background and Related Work

In this paper, emotion is considered one aspect of affect. The study of emotion has a long and rich history in human-computer interaction [1]. The apparent convergence in the past decade or so of software engineering, human-computer interaction, and marketing has led to consideration of emotion during software development also [2].

© Springer International Publishing AG 2017
S.F. Ochoa et al. (Eds.): UCAmI 2017, LNCS 10586, pp. 605–611, 2017.
DOI: 10.1007/978-3-319-67585-5_59

In recent years, the human affect factors have played an increasing role in 'conventional' requirements engineering. For example, a stimulus-perception-response model for experience-related requirements engineering has been proposed [3]; for measuring emotions of stakeholders involved in a requirements engineering process, an affect grid has been recommended [4]; a requirements engineering process oriented towards users' needs and motivations has been presented [5]; and in a requirements engineering process for emergency systems, emotional goals of the elderly have been included [6].

In agile methodologies, requirements engineering is usually scenario-oriented, and software requirements are usually expressed as either *user stories* or lightweight *use cases*. In this paper, the interest is exclusively in user stories, although some of the ideas apply to use cases as well. To date, there has been relatively less attention on the study of human affect factors in agile requirements engineering [7]. In particular, the prevalent models, such as C3 (Card, Conversation, Confirmation) and INVEST (Independent, Negotiable, Valuable, Estimatable, Small, Testable), for authoring effective, 'high-quality', user stories do not have any provision for affect [8].

3   A Preliminary Framework for Affective User Story Engineering

Figure 1 shows a compendium of interrelated conceptual models that are necessary for a rigorous baselining, comprehensive understanding, and systematic engineering of affective user stories. The directions in the graph indicate a 'depends-on' relationship.

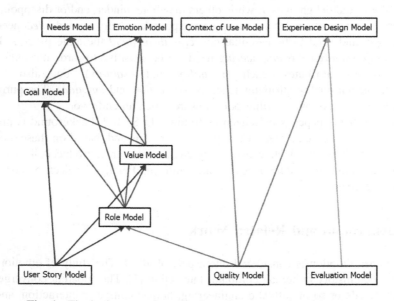

Fig. 1. The basic steps of an affective user story engineering process.

To improve communication among stakeholders, and to reduce the potential of lexical ambiguity, these conceptual models could be complemented by a *glossary*.

Figure 2 shows an abstraction of a nonlinear affective user story engineering process for a single arbitrary iteration of an agile process. This process is independent of any specific agile methodology, can be applied exhaustively to all iterations of an agile process, and includes the following steps, which can be repeated, as necessary:

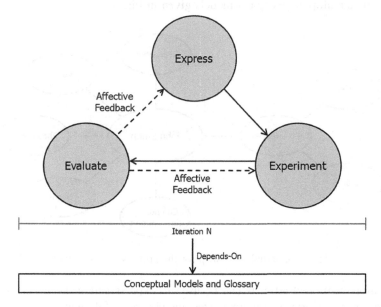

Fig. 2. The basic steps of an affective user story engineering process.

(1) **Express** a subset of user stories for a given iteration of an agile process. Each user story in this subset should include local and/or global constraints, as applicable, related to non-instrumental quality attributes. The acceptance criteria for each user story should include proper support for error handling.

(2) **Experiment** with the user stories by developing one or more user experience design (UXD) prototypes of different fidelity. These prototypes should be user-centered, could rely on (possibly) anthropomorphic metaphors with suitable affordances, and may reuse UXD knowledge, such as interaction design patterns. They should include proper support for error messages, as the responses by a software system to usage errors continue to be causes of consternation among the users [9].

(3) **Evaluate** the prototype (by involving actual users) for experience and affect. This, upon an analysis of the data obtained from ethnographic feedback (with information related to affect), may lead to a refinement of the user stories and/or the prototype (as indicated by dashed lines in Fig. 2).

3.1   Example

This example, meant for the purpose of illustration only, is about the development of a search functionality of a human resources information system (HRIS) at a University that allows students to seek possibilities for employment.

Figure 3 shows a part of the mind map of a primary persona for a student role and, based on it, Table 1 shows part of that persona for the same student role. Together, they operationalize multiple conceptual models given in Fig. 1.

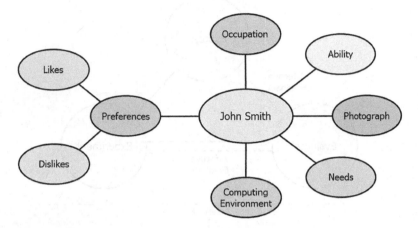

Fig. 3. A partial mind map for the primary persona, John.

The aforementioned artifacts can be used to express certain necessary and inter-related set of user stories of different sizes, including the following:

US-1.   A student can create a profile on HRIS to be able to search privately

US-2.   A student can use his/her OpenID to login to HRIS to avail himself/herself of employment opportunities.

US-3.   A student can access a textual or a graphical search interface to be able to search according to his/her preferences.

US-4.   A student can filter search results to be able to focus his/her search results.

US-5.   A student can adjust the number of search results presented at a time to be able to scroll through them easily.

US-6.   A student can download a job posting of his/her choice to be able to have access to at a later time.

US-7.   A student can save his/her search options to be able to return to them at a later time.

US-8.   A student can deactivate, temporarily or permanently, any unsolicited message prompts to be able to search undistracted.

The details of extrospection from sample users, the construction and representation of conceptual models, acceptance criteria and other metainformation related to the user stories, the UXD prototype, and error message design, are significant, but have been omitted due to consideration of space.

Table 1. A partial description of the primary persona, John, along with user story identifiers.

	John Smith, The Potential Graduate

. . .

Goal: To look for a job at a bank's financial services department.

. . .

- John likes using one set of login information in his personal interactions with all University information systems. **[US-1] [US-2]**
- He likes to be able to easily keep a copy of all the details of the job offers he may find interesting. **[US-6]**
- He likes all the job descriptions to have the same format so that he can compare them easily.

. . .

- John dislikes unsought advertisements. **[US-8]**
- He finds it difficult to remember the meaning of icons, and prefers text instead. **[US-3]**
- He gets distressed if the search results are irrelevant. **[US-4]**
- He finds simultaneously presented large amount of information to be overwhelming. **[US-5]**
- He finds it inconvenient to repeat his search and go through the results all over again. **[US-7]**

. . .

4   Directions for Future Research

The prospects for positive uses invariably also create the potential for negative uses. These negative uses could be identified and subsequently modeled as negative user stories [10]. For example, the following are a couple of negative user stories related to HRIS and to persona, John:

NUS-1.   A black hat hacker wants to send nocuous data in HTTP headers to gain unauthorized access to functionality and information.

NUS-2.   A spammer wants to post a message to disseminate unsolicited advertisement.

These negative user stories, if realized, not only pose security, privacy, and/or safety risks that can lead to (possibly irreparable) loss, but also lead to different kinds of emotional reactions, such as annoyance, anxiety, and/or anguish, from users, thereby forming an overall negative user experience. Thus, seeking ways of measuring and minimizing the impact of such negative uses is of research interest.

There are a number of areas that could benefit from conducting empirical studies in organizations with appropriate agile process maturity levels, including the following: (1) to assess the feasibility of an industrial deployment of the conceptual models and the proposed affective user story engineering process; and (2) to investigate the return on investment (ROI) in constructing the conceptual models, since constructing any artifact entails costs that needs to be justified against the anticipated benefits. In particular, investigating the interplay between affect and application software for specific domains, such as airline reservation, healthcare information, and learning management, is of special research interest.

5 Conclusion

If current surveys are any indicator, then the movement towards agile methodologies, the behavioral changes in people due to their reliance on software, and the role of affect in how software is perceived, acquired, and used, are only likely to increase. These can have long-term implications for any organization involved in software development, and therefore should not be ignored.

For continued success and longevity of projects, lasting economic sustainability, and being perceived as socially responsible, it is in the long-term strategic interest of an organization (1) to recognize affect as a 'first-class' concern in the engineering of its software systems; (2) to align its business model with people-oriented requirements engineering; and (3) to develop a culture that encourages an in-depth understanding of the mental, emotional, and physical states of users before, during, and after use of software systems. This, in the context of an agile project, means identifying, distilling, and modeling appropriate knowledge related to user and affect, and equipping the affective user story engineering process with such knowledge, as this paper has attempted to show.

References

1. Norman, D.A.: The Design of Everyday Things. Basic Books, New York (2013)
2. Kołakowska, A., Landowska, A., Szwoch, M., Szwoch, W., Wróbel, M.R.: Emotion recognition and its application in software engineering. In: The Sixth International Conference on Human System Interaction, Gdańsk, Poland, 6–8 June 2013
3. Callele, D., Neufeld, E., Schneider, K.: An introduction to experience requirements. In: The Eighteenth IEEE International Requirements Engineering Conference, Sydney, Australia, 27 September–1 October 2010 (2010)
4. Colomo-Palacios, R., Casado-Lumbreras, C., Soto-Acosta, P., García-Crespo, Á.: Using the affect grid to measure emotions in software requirements engineering. J. Univ. Comput. Sci. 17(9), 1281–1298 (2011)
5. Sutcliffe, A.: User-oriented requirements engineering. In: The Second IEEE International Workshop on Usability and Accessibility Focused Requirements Engineering, Karlskrona, Sweden, 25–25 Aug 2014
6. Miller, T., Pedell, S., Lopez-Lorca, A.A., Mendoza, A., Sterling, L., Keirnan, A.: Emotion-led modelling for people-oriented requirements engineering: the case study of emergency systems. J. Syst. Softw. 105, 54–71 (2015)
7. Schön, E.-M., Thomaschewski, J., Escalona, M.J.: Agile requirements engineering: a systematic literature review. Comput. Stand. Interfaces 49, 79–91 (2017)

8. Cohn, M.: User Stories Applied: For Agile Software Development. Addison-Wesley, Boston (2004)
9. Shariat, J., Saucier, C.S.: Tragic Design: The Impact of Bad Product Design and How to Fix It. O'Reilly Media (2017)
10. Kamthan, P., Shahmir, N.: A characterization of negative user stories. In: The Twenty Eighth International Conference on Software Engineering and Knowledge Engineering, Redwood City, USA, 1–3 July 2016

A Semantic Approach to Enrich User Experience in Museums Through Indoor Positioning

Jaime Duque Domingo[1]([⊠]), Carlos Cerrada[1], Enrique Valero[2], and J.A. Cerrada[1]

[1] Departamento de Ingeniería de Software y Sistemas Informáticos, UNED, ETSI Informática, C/Juan del Rosal, 16., 28040 Madrid, Spain
jaimeduque@amenofis.com
[2] School of Energy, Geoscience, Infrastructure and Society, Heriot-Watt University, Edinburgh EH14 4AS, UK

Abstract. This article presents a novel ontology aiming to connect an Indoor Positioning System (IPS) to Europeana, the European Union digital platform for cultural heritage. The main purpose of this system is to deliver information about Cultural Heritage Objects (CHO) to users navigating in museums, when they approach certain pieces of art. Although different semantic works have been previously published regarding the problem of finding optimal paths with IPS, the novelty of this work is the combination of indoor positioning and a semantic view of cultural objects. This ontology enriches the experience of users and offers a new way of enjoying art. The paper shows the effectiveness of the proposed ontology to connect a widely known database to a wireless positioning system. The potential of the developed method is shown using data obtained from the Royal Museums of Fine Arts of Belgium, one of the most important European art galleries, with more than six thousand master pieces listed in Europeana. Some experiments have been also carried out in the Old masters Museum, one of the constituent museums of the Royal Museums that is dedicated to European painters from the 15th to the 18th centuries.

Keywords: Indoor positioning · WPS · RGB-D sensors · WiFi positioning · *fingerprint* · *depth map* · OWL · Ontology · SPARQL · Ubiquitous computing · User experience · Europeana · Royal Museums of Fine Arts of Belgium

1 Introduction

Modern Indoor Positioning Systems (IPS) facilitates the interaction of users with the environment, estimating the position of people or objects inside a building [9]. This kind of systems can be useful in certain environments, where the location of users is considered as a trigger for different operations (e.g., enable or disable machines, open doors, information management ...).

© Springer International Publishing AG 2017
S.F. Ochoa et al. (Eds.): UCAmI 2017, LNCS 10586, pp. 612–623, 2017.
DOI: 10.1007/978-3-319-67585-5_60

This interaction between people and the environment involves a set of concepts, entities and the relationships among them, which are defined in the ontology. In this article, a novel ontology is presented aiming to connect a previously developed IPS [12] to Europeana.

Europeana [17] is the European Union's digital platform for cultural heritage, giving access to different types of content from different institutions. More than 3,000 institutions across Europe have contributed to Europeana. The collections let users explore Europe's cultural and scientific heritage from prehistory to the modern day. The digital objects in Europeana are stored in the cultural institution and are hosted on their networks. Europeana collects contextual information or metadata about items. The data.europeana.eu Linked Open Data pilot dataset contains open metadata on approximately 2.4 million texts, images, videos and sounds.

The rest of the paper is structured as follows: Sect. 2 explores previous works related to the techniques used in this article. In Sect. 3, the developed ontology is described, illustrating how it is linked to the positioning systems and how the navigation system works. Finally, Sect. 4 shows carried out experiments and Sect. 5 remarks the main features of the presented system and proposes future works.

2 Overview of Related Work

2.1 WPS and RGB-D Positioning

WiFi Positioning Systems (WPS) are mainly founded on the *fingerprinting* technique [19]. This technique creates a map of the environment recording, in each point, the received signal from a mobile phone (i.e., *Received Signal Strength Indication* (RSSI)). This map is used afterward to obtain the position of a user in real-time, comparing the values received from the user's portable device to those stored in the map.

One of the main advantages of WPS solutions with respect to similar technologies (e.g., RFID or Bluetooth) is the use of devices commonly installed in inhabited environments (i.e., routers), whereas other solutions require dedicated infrastructure. Also, WPS can be used to provide Internet access aiming to share information.

With respect to people and objects positioning, some technologies based on computer vision (e.g., RGB-D sensors) have been increasingly used to deliver more precise results, such as the method *Kinect Positioning System* (KPS), analyzed in [22]. A more complex solution is shown in [24], where the authors present an indoor human tracking application using two depth-cameras. More recently, in [26], authors proposed a model for merging Kinect trajectories. Using the global coordinates at the same time stamp, their system is able to determine the distance between two skeletons in order to discern between different users.

The developed IPS presented by our team in [12] combines two widely-known technologies: (WPS), extensively used in indoor positioning, and computer vision by means of RGB-D sensors. The trajectory of users is considered in both ways:

exploiting the WPS trajectory and the trajectory of the skeletons of the users in the *depth map*. The skeletons are obtained by means of the techniques presented in [6,27], where authors propose new algorithms to quickly and accurately predict 3D positions of body joints from depth images. The mentioned IPS is the base of the work presented in [13], where the system tracks the position of visitors in a museum.

2.2   Knowledge Engineering

In the field of computer science, an ontology [14,15] is the definition and classification of concepts and entities, and the relationships between them. Ontologies use entities in the universe of discourse (e.g., classes, relations, functions, or other objects) and formal axioms that constrain the interpretation and well-formed use of these terms. They can be represented in the W3C Web Ontology Language (OWL) [8], which is a Semantic Web language designed to represent knowledge about things, groups of things, and relations between them.

In the last decade, different approaches have been presented to deliver semantic views of the indoor navigation problem. In [28], authors propose an Indoor Navigation Ontology (INO), which supports the path searching and the presentation of tasks of a navigation system. More recently, an extended version of INO is used in [20], in which an augmented reality solution is also considered to provide a richer experience. Another approach for indoor routing was developed by [11], where authors propose a different ontology (ONALIN) that provides path searching for individuals with special needs and preferences. In [18], authors present a location-based service (LBS) to figure out the path between a starting point and a destination. This is based on an ontology that enriches the standard positioning since users can share, manage and query data semantically. OGC GeoSPARQL [7] offers support for representing and querying geospatial data on the Semantic Web. However, it is mostly prepared to represent geometry topology, like polygons, instead of being used as a tool for positioning purposes.

2.3   About Data in Europeana

Europeana is a project developed by the European Commission to incentive member states to digitalize and enhance digital preservation in Europe. The portal provides free access to a wide array of digital content. It allows in a simple but powerful way to find resources from all over Europe. It contains over 50 million records. These featured datasets represent over a million of the best, openly licensed, directly accessible media objects - books, photos, art, artifacts, audio clips and more. Europeana has several ways to retrieve data. Information can be obtained by REST API Standard over HTTP, which returns JSON data, or by Annotations REST API, which returns JSON-LD. Other possibilities include OAI-PMH Harvest data via the OAI-PMH protocol and Linked Open Data Queries retrieving data in SPARQL. Data can also be linked to external data sources, such as the Swedish cultural heritage aggregator, GeoNames, the GEMET thesaurus or DBPedia.

The use of an ontology in this system, in order to connect it to Europeana, facilitates a dynamic behavior, adding new functionalities in a simpler manner without modifying data models.

3   Analysis of the System

As mentioned in previous sections, the main purpose of this work is the development of an ontology that links an indoor positioning system to the Europeana database, aiming to deliver information about Cultural Heritage Objects (CHO) to museums' users, considering their location inside a building. This information about master pieces is retrieved from the database through SPARQL queries.

Even if this system could be applied in every museum in Europe whose works are stored in Europeana database, Royal Museums of Fine Arts of Belgium (Brussels, Belgium) has been chosen to illustrate this paper. Consider, for instance, the search for information about the famous painting of Rogier Van der Weyden "Déploration". After the corresponding SPARQL query, the information shown in Table 1 is provided.

Longitude and latitude coordinates of the Royal Museums can be easily retrieved. However, the position of the pieces inside the museum is not in Europeana. Therefore, it is needed to create another relation giving the precise room and position of a masterpiece to be used with the developed system. In order to do that, an ontology has been created.

Table 1. Result for the query of "Déploration"

CHO identifier	http://data.europeana.eu/proxy/provider/2048001/Athena_Plus_ProvidedCHO_KIK_IRPA_Brussels_Belgium_AP_10325768
Title	"Déploration"@fr
Creator	"Van der Weyden, Rogier"@fr
Date	"1441/1464"
Type	"tableau[peinture]"
Subject	"event"
Format	"peint"
Provenance	"Object: Musées Royaux des Beaux-Arts de Belgique, Bruxelles"
Provider	"AthenaPlus"
Dataprovider	"KIK-IRPA, Brussels (Belgium)"
mediaURL	http://balat.kikirpa.be/image/thumbnail/B117883.jpg

3.1   New Ontology for Obtaining the Position of a CHO

As previously mentioned, an ontology is composed of different elements. Classes provide an abstraction mechanism for grouping resources with similar characteristics. In this particular case, two OWL class identifiers have been predefined, namely the classes *Thing* and *Nothing*. The extension of *Thing* is the set of all individuals, whereas for *Nothing* it is the empty set. Consequently, every OWL class is a subclass of *Thing*, [8]. The individuals in the class extension are called the instances of the class. If a class is defined as a subclass, the set of individuals that accepts should be a subset of those individuals in the parent class.

OWL distinguishes two main categories of properties to be defined in an ontology: Object properties, which link individuals to individuals; and Datatype properties, which link individuals to data values.

Domain and range are axioms used in the inference process. Both are defined as built-in properties. A domain axiom (marked as green arrows in Fig. 1) links a property to a class description and asserts that the subjects of such property statements must belong to the class extension of the indicated class description. A range axiom (black arrows in Fig. 1) links a property to either a class description or a data range. This axiom asserts that the values of this property must belong to the class extension of the class description or to data values in the specified data range.

The ontology of Fig. 1 has been implemented. As shown, it delivers different types of information.

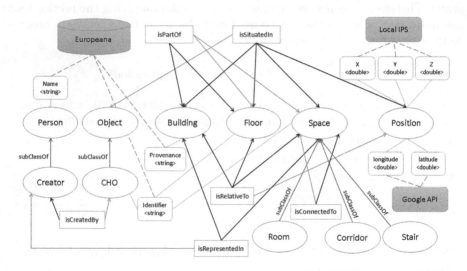

Fig. 1. Implemented ontology where domain and range axioms are marked as green and black arrows respectively. (Color figure online)

There are six general subclasses of *Thing*: *Person*, *Object*, *Building*, *Floor*, *Space* and *Position*. Also, *Creator* is a subclass of *Person*, *CHO* is a subclass of *Object*, and *Room*, *Corridor* and *Stair* are subclasses of *Space*.

Person refers to all kinds of individuals, but *Creator* just refers to the creators mainly retrieved from Europeana. The data property "Name" of type *<string>* accepts values as "Van der Weyden, Rogier". The class *Person* allows extending the system with other types of individuals: producers, owners, people represented in the CHO, etc.

Object refers to all kinds of objects that can be located inside a building: a computer or a table in a room, a screen or TV, a painting on a wall, etc.

The extension of the class *CHO* is composed of particular objects with an identifier to link with Europeana. The data property "Identifier" of type *<string>*, which is an identifier in Europeana, accepts values as shown in Table 1.

Building is the place related to the host institution. It has the data property "Provenance" of type *<string>* that accepts values as "Musées Royaux des Beaux-Arts de Belgique, Bruxelles".

Regarding spatial-related classes, the class *Floor* represents a floor of the building where there are several spaces (class *Space*). These spaces are represented by the subclasses *Room, Corridor,* and *Stair. Floor* and *Space* have also identifiers in order to know their particular names. For example, the room with identifier "70_Weyden" (as shown later in Fig. 3), is the one where the painting "Déploration" is exhibited. This room is part of the floor labeled as "Second floor".

Position is the class indicating the position (local or global) of an object. It contains three data properties "X", "Y", "Z", of type *<double>* that include a relative local position with respect to a space, a floor or a building. The other two data properties, "longitude" and "latitude", of type *<double>*, are not relative to a space, floor or building. These values are used for global positioning with Google APIs as will be explained later. Note that the system is flexible in terms of establishing relationships between spaces, floors or buildings and this can be modified according to particular cases.

Furthermore, it is worth mentioning several object properties, which link individuals to other individuals. The object property "isRelativeTo" indicates that an instance of the class *Position* is relative to an instance of the class *Building, Floor* or *Space*. It is subsequently relative to the subclasses *Room, Corridor,* and *Stair*. This property is used for local positioning, where the three data properties "X", "Y", "Z" are relative to a particular building, floor or space.

The object property "isPartOf" indicates the place where spaces or floors are located. For example, a room is part of a floor and also part of a building. Simultaneously, a floor is part of a building.

The property "isSituatedIn" makes reference to the place where an object is situated. For example, the painting "The Census at Bethlehem", of Pieter Bruegel the Elder, is an instance of the class *CHO* situated in the room with identifier "68_Bruegel" and also situated in the floor with identifier "Second floor". Subsequently, it is situated in the building with the provenance "Royal Museums of Fine Arts of Belgium".

The property "isConnectedTo" is used to obtain the optimal path between two spaces, as shown in the next sections. The rooms are connected to other rooms, corridors or stairs. As will be shown in Sect. 3.5, A* algorithm [16] has been used to find the shortest path between two rooms.

Finally, there are two object properties related to authors. The property "isCreatedBy" means that a CHO has been conceived by a creator. The CHO previously mentioned, which refers to "Déploration", was painted by the creator with the name "Van der Weyden". And the property "isRepresentedIn" indicates where author's artworks are displayed.

3.2   Linking an IPS with the Ontology

The presented ontology can be linked with two different classes of IPS: one of them based on global positioning and another one oriented to local positioning. The difference between them is whether the coordinates they return are global to the Earth or relative to a certain building, floor or space (usually rooms).

The local positioning systems are more precise in indoor environments. For this reason, it is better to use a global positioning system, like Google API, to identify whether the user is in a building, i.e., Royal Museums of Fine Arts of Belgium, Prado Museum or Louvre Museum. Then, the local IPS, as [12], is used for indoor positioning delivering precise coordinates.

Considering this combination of IPS, the proposed system figures out which is the nearest artwork with respect to the user, by filtering pieces situated at less than 5 meters and ordering them by distance. This distance is implemented by means of the Euclidean distance between the user position and the position of the artwork. The system implements an SPARQL query, which makes use of federated queries [23] to access to the remote SPARQL endpoint of Europeana.

The two mentioned types of IPS are explained in Sects. 3.3 and 3.4.

3.3   Estimating Position by Means of Google and Android APIs

Android provides an API in android.location [1] delivering the position of a user according three different methods: GPS, Cell-ID, and Wi-Fi. The system returns the position to a Location Listener object that invokes a method each time a new Location object is received. The determination of the best location, if there are several results from the different methods, is decided by means of parameters related to accuracy, speed, and battery-efficiency.

Google also provides a Location Services API [5]. According to the location Android API [2], Google Location Services API provides a more powerful and high-level framework, which automatically handles location providers, user's movement, and location accuracy. It also provides a method to establish fences surrounding a location and detection when the user is inside the area.

Finally, Google Maps Geolocation API [4] provides a web service by means of HTTPS and using POST. This service receives a list of cell towers and a list of WiFi routers, obtained by the client, with their respective signal strength. The service returns the location with longitude and latitude and the accuracy. The communications with the service are established using the JSON format.

The created ontology is flexible and able to assign a value of longitude and latitude to a position instance. Note that all the previously described systems return the user's location using longitude and latitude values. In order to combine Google APIs with the presented ontology, it is initially better to obtain the closer building to the user by means of Vincenty's formulae [29], used in geodesy to calculate the distance between two points on the surface of a spheroid. Later, it is possible to obtain the closest CHO by means of Haversine formula [21], method to calculate the distance between two locations in a simple way. It has an error because the radius of the sphere is not the same in all parts of the Earth. When two locations are close, it is possible to use a medium radio of 6371 Km with minor error.

Some libraries like [10] or embedded Javascript [30] allow extending SPARQL functionalities. The ldodds:Distance function calculates the distance between two geographic coordinates based on longitude and latitude.

3.4   Estimating Position by Means of Depth Maps and WiFi Networks

A generalized version of the previous work [12] has been used for indoor positioning purposes. The proposed system is used for obtaining the identification and the user's position in a scenario composed of different rooms where there are several people carrying smartphones. Two or more RGB-D sensors are situated in each room for obtaining the coordinates of users by means of their skeletons. The skeletons are obtained with the technique presented in [6,27], where authors propose new algorithms to quickly and accurately predict 3D positions of bodies from depth images.

Users, or visitors in the case of museums, carry smartphones that establish a connection to some accessible network. These smartphones obtain RSSI data and synchronously send them to a central web server. Simultaneously, this central web server obtains body information from different RGB-D sensors.

Figure 2 illustrates this system. Several users can be seen with their corresponding paths at certain time stamps. This system requires at least two RGB-D sensors in each room and all users need the application running. Eight WiFi access points (i.e., routers) have to be accessible in the entire scenario to obtain good WPS positioning.

The used SPARQL query obtains the nearest artwork with respect to the user. It filters pieces situated in a range of 5 meters. The query makes use of federated queries [23] to access to the remote SPARQL endpoint of Europeana and makes use of AQR functions [25] to calculate Euclidean distances. Note that a SPARQL Jena server [3] has been created to support the ontology.

3.5   Obtaining Optimal Path Between Two Rooms

The presented ontology has been also prepared for obtaining the best path between two rooms. As can be seen in Fig. 1, rooms are connected to other rooms, corridors or stairs. A* algorithm [16] has been used to find the shortest path between two rooms, which are considered as nodes in a graph. Users can

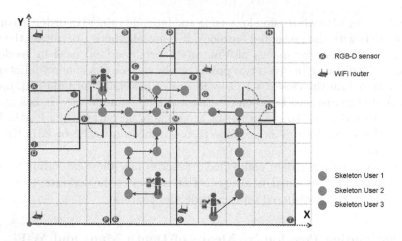

Fig. 2. Skeleton trajectories in a running example of the IPS developed. Twenty RGB-D sensors are deployed in the scenario.

select a CHO in the catalog and the system calculates the optimal path from their current position.

In Fig. 3, an A* algorithm returns the optimal path to go from the room "David", where Jacques-Louis David's painting "Marat Assassiné" is located, to the room "70_Weyden", where users can find Weyden's painting "Déploration".

The rooms are subclasses of *Space*, and in Fig. 3, the link between them is the object property "isConnectedTo", shown in the previous ontology.

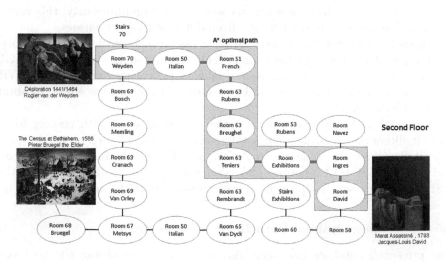

Fig. 3. Obtaining optimal path between two rooms

4   Experiments

Aiming to test the proposed ontology, an experiment has been designed and carried out in the Royal Museum of Fine Arts of Belgium. This experiment consisted of two stages, as detailed in the following.

First, a user walked around the museum, registering the location of each painting linked to Europeana by means of an Android application which has been developed for this purpose (see Fig. 4a) and installed in smartphones. The position of each masterpiece is delivered by the Google API and stored in the database. Note that this process is only performed once, and it does not need to be repeated at least paintings are relocated inside the museum. Four paintings were chosen and their positions registered in the database.

Later, a different user navigated through the rooms, retrieving information from Europeana with the mentioned application installed in his cellphone. The 4 studied paintings were visited 5 times each, delivering the application the correct information every time the user was in a range of 5 meters. Figure 4b shows an example where the system is detecting the masterpiece "The Census at Bethlehem" by Pieter Bruegel.

(a) Android application   (b) Detecting painting

Fig. 4. Experiments developed using Google Location Services API.

5   Results and Conclusions

This article presents a new ontology for connecting a previously developed Indoor Positioning System (IPS) and Europeana, the EU digital platform for cultural heritage. As shown, the proposed ontology can be used in a museum for enhancing the user experience, by inferring knowledge about cultural heritage objects.

The article also explains an option to obtain the optimal path between the position of the user and a painting in the museum based on the A* algorithm.

In order to test the developed ontology, some experiment has been carried out, taking advantage of the Google Location API. Even though data from the ontology was correctly retrieved and the position of users was properly obtained by means of data from cell towers and WiFi networks, the installation of more WiFi access points could improve the positioning.

Future works include the testing of the mentioned IPS system (combining RGB-D sensors and WPS), together with the solution presented in this paper, in a museum environment.

Acknowledgments. This work has been developed with the help of the research projects DPI2013-44776-R and DPI2016-77677-P of MICINN. It also belongs to the activities carried out within the framework of the research network CAM RoboCity2030 S2013/MIT-2748 of Comunidad de Madrid.

References

1. Android Location API. Android Developers Application Programming Interface. http://developer.android.com/reference/android/location/package-summary.html
2. Android Location Strategies. Android Developers Application Programming Interface. http://developer.android.com/guide/topics/location/strategies.html
3. Apache Jena Server. Apache. http://jena.apache.org
4. Google Maps Geolocation API. Google Maps Application Programming Interface. http://developers.google.com/maps/documentation/geolocation/intro
5. Google Play Services Location APIs. Google Play Services Application Programming Interface. http://developer.android.com/training/location/retrieve-current.html
6. Barmpoutis, A.: Tensor body: real-time reconstruction of the human body and avatar synthesis from RGB-D. IEEE Trans. Cybern. **43**(5), 1347–1356 (2013)
7. Consortium, O.G., et al.: Ogc geosparql-a geographic query language for RDF Data. OGC Candidate Implementation Standard 2 (2012)
8. Consortium, W.W.W., et al.: Owl 2 web ontology language document overview (2012)
9. Deak, G., Curran, K., Condell, J.: A survey of active and passive indoor localisation systems. Comput. Commun. **35**(16), 1939–1954 (2012)
10. Dodds, L.: Sparql geo extensions (2006)
11. Dudas, P.M., Ghafourian, M., Karimi, H.A.: ONALIN: ontology and algorithm for indoor routing. In: Tenth International Conference on Mobile Data Management: Systems, Services and Middleware, MDM 2009, pp. 720–725. IEEE (2009)
12. Duque Domingo, J., Cerrada, C., Valero, E., Cerrada, J.: Indoor positioning system using depth maps and wireless networks. J. Sens. **2016** (2016)
13. Duque-Domingo, J., Herrera, P.J., Valero, E., Cerrada, C.: Deciphering egyptian hieroglyphs: towards a new strategy for navigation in museums. Sensors **17**(3), 589 (2017)
14. Gruber, T.R.: Toward principles for the design of ontologies used for knowledge sharing. Int. J. Hum. Comput. Stud. **43**(5–6), 907–928 (1995)
15. Guber, T.: A translational approach to portable ontologies. Knowl. Acquisit. **5**(2), 199–229 (1993)
16. Hart, P.E., Nilsson, N.J., Raphael, B.: A formal basis for the heuristic determination of minimum cost paths. IEEE Trans. Syst. Sci. Cybern. **4**(2), 100–107 (1968)

17. Isaac, A., Haslhofer, B.: Europeana linked open data (data.europeana.eu). Semant. Web **4**(3), 291–297 (2013)
18. Lee, K., Lee, J., Kwan, M.P.: Location-based service using ontology-based semantic queries: a study with a focus on indoor activities in a university context. Comput. Environ. Urban Syst. **62**, 41–52 (2017)
19. Liu, W., Chen, Y., Xiong, Y., Sun, L., Zhu, H.: Optimization of sampling cell size for fingerprint positioning. Int. J. Distrib. Sens. Netw. **2014** (2014)
20. Matuszka, T., Gombos, G., Kiss, A.: A new approach for indoor navigation using semantic webtechnologies and augmented reality. In: Shumaker, R. (ed.) VAMR 2013. LNCS, vol. 8021, pp. 202–210. Springer, Heidelberg (2013). doi:10.1007/978-3-642-39405-8_24
21. de Mendoza, J., et al.: Memoria sobre algunos métodos nuevos de calcular la longitud por las distancias lunares: y aplicación de su teórica a la solución de otros problemas de navegación. En la Imprenta real (1795)
22. Nakano, Y., Izutsu, K., Tajitsu, K., Kai, K., Tatsumi, T.: Kinect positioning system (kps) and its potential applications. In: International Conference on Indoor Positioning and Indoor Navigation, vol. 13, p. 15 (2012)
23. Prud'hommeaux, E., Buil-Aranda, C., et al.: SPARQL 1.1 federated query. W3C Recommendation 21 (2013)
24. Saputra, M.R.U., Widyawan, W., Putra, G.D., Santosa, P.I.: Indoor human tracking application using multiple depth-cameras. In: 2012 International Conference on Advanced Computer Science and Information Systems (ICACSIS), pp. 307–312. IEEE (2012)
25. Seaborne, A.: ARQ-A SPARQL Processor for Jena. Obtained through the Internet (2010). http://jena.sourceforge.net/ARQ
26. Sevrin, L., Noury, N., Abouchi, N., Jumel, F., Massot, B., Saraydaryan, J.: Characterization of a multi-user indoor positioning system based on low cost depth vision (kinect) for monitoring human activity in a smart home. In: 2015 37th Annual International Conference of the IEEE Engineering in Medicine and Biology Society (EMBC), pp. 5003–5007. IEEE (2015)
27. Shotton, J., Sharp, T., Kipman, A., Fitzgibbon, A., Finocchio, M., Blake, A., Cook, M., Moore, R.: Real-time human pose recognition in parts from single depth images. Commun. ACM **56**(1), 116–124 (2013)
28. Tsetsos, V., Anagnostopoulos, C., Kikiras, P., Hasiotis, P., Hadjiefthymiades, S.: A human-centered semantic navigation system for indoor environments. In: Proceedings of the International Conference on Pervasive Services, ICPS 2005, pp. 146–155. IEEE (2005)
29. Vincenty, T.: Direct and inverse solutions of geodesics on the ellipsoid with application of nested equations. Surv. Rev. **23**(176), 88–93 (1975)
30. Williams, G.: Extensible SPARQL functions with embedded Javascript. In: SFSW (2007)

Model-Driven Context Management
for Self-adaptive User Interfaces

Enes Yigitbas[(✉)], Silas Grün, Stefan Sauer, and Gregor Engels

s-lab - Software Quality Lab, Paderborn University,
Zukunftsmeile 1, 33102 Paderborn, Germany
{enes.yigitbas,gruensil,sauer,engels}@upb.de

Abstract. The user interfaces (UIs) of interactive systems become increasingly complex since many heterogeneous and dynamically changing context-of-use parameters regarding user profile, platform, and usage environment have to be supported. Self-adaptive UIs have been promoted as a solution for context variability due to their ability to automatically adapt to the context-of-use at runtime. Context modeling and context management are important prerequisites for supporting self-adaptive UIs, but introduce additional complexity since context information has to be captured using sensors from heterogeneous sources and dynamic context changes have to be monitored to enable UI adaptation at runtime. To overcome the complex and cumbersome task of context management, we present a model-driven approach for developing a flexible context manager supporting self-adaptive UIs. Our approach consists of a new context modeling language, named ContextML, for specification of various context-of-use situations. Based on the specified context model, our approach enables automatic generation of context services for monitoring context-of-use parameters. The benefit of our approach is demonstrated by a case study, where generated context services provide context information and trigger the adaptation of UIs for a university library web application.

Keywords: Model-driven UI development · Self-adaptive UIs · Context-awareness · Context management

1   Introduction

Acceptance and usability of a user interface is highly influenced by its context-of-use, which is defined in terms of the user, platform, and environment [1]. As todays user interfaces of interactive systems become increasingly complex since many heterogeneous contexts of use have to be supported, it is no longer sufficient to provide a single one-size-fits-all user interface. Building multiple UIs for the same functionality due to context variability is also difficult since context changes can lead to the combinatorial explosion of the number of possible adaptations and there is a high cost incurred by manually developing multiple versions of the UI [2].

© Springer International Publishing AG 2017
S.F. Ochoa et al. (Eds.): UCAmI 2017, LNCS 10586, pp. 624–635, 2017.
DOI: 10.1007/978-3-319-67585-5_61

In recent research, self-adaptive UIs have been promoted as a solution for context variability due to their ability to automatically adapt to the context-of-use at runtime [2]. A key goal behind self-adaptive UIs is plasticity denoting a UI's ability to preserve its usability despite dynamically changing context-of-use parameters [3]. In our previous work [4], we presented a model-driven development approach for self-adaptive UIs, but special attention is required for context management due to the complexity of capturing context information through various sensors from heterogeneous sources and monitoring dynamically changing context-of-use parameters. In detail, the following challenges have to be addressed to integrate context management aspects into model-driven development of self-adaptive UIs:

- *C1: Specification of contextual parameters:* A modeling language is required for specifying different contexts-of-use. That means, different contextual situations that can occur during usage of the UI should be modeled. With the help of this language, developers should be able to separately specify needed context sensor services that should be included in their customized context manager.
- *C2: Generation of context sensor services:* Based on the specified context-of-use model, code for the required context services need to be generated for monitoring context information and triggering the adaptation at runtime.
- *C3: Execution of context services and runtime monitoring:* For supporting runtime monitoring of dynamic context changes, the generated context services should observe the context sensors and provide context information data.

To address the above described challenges, our solution idea is based on the integration of model-driven UI development and adaptation with model-driven context management. Therefore, we introduce a new modeling language, called ContextML, that supports the specification of various context situations. Based on the specified context model, different context services are generated that make use of existing sensor libraries to monitor contextual parameters. We show, how generated context services are integrated in our UI framework for triggering and executing UI adaptations at runtime.

The remaining sections of the paper are organized as follows: Sect. 2 presents our Model-Driven Context Management Framework (MCMF). In Sect. 3, we present the implementation of our approach. Section 4 shows the benefit and usefulness of our approach based on a case study. Related work is presented in Sect. 5 and finally Sect. 6 concludes the paper and gives an outlook on future work.

2   Model-Driven Context Management Framework

Our approach, solving the before stated challenges, is a Model-driven Context Management Framework that is depicted in Fig. 1. It is sectioned in three development phases. In the following, we will give a brief overview of the whole

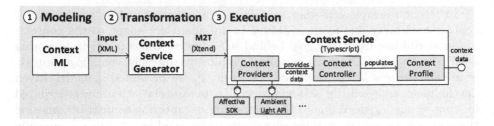

Fig. 1. Mode-driven Context Management Framework

framework. Technical details regarding modeling and implementation are discussed in the subsequent sections.

The first phase of the framework is the creation of a context model at design time. For this, we introduce the context modeling language *ContextML*. It allows to define a set of context properties and the needed context provider interfaces to capture the relevant context information. These interfaces are later on referenced as *Context Providers*. For example, the environmental light condition of our context-of-use can be captured by using a provided *Ambient Light API*. Also the types of these properties and their behavior, in terms of data updating, has to be defined. In our example, ambient light is monitored as current light-level, and it shall be updated as soon as a change is detected (event-triggered). This model is automatically saved as an XML file for better processability.

After finishing the context modeling phase, the context model specified in *ContextML* serves as an input for the *Context Service Generator* in the second phase. The latter creates an executable code for the *Context Service* with a Model-To-Text-Transformation (M2T), based on code fragments in form of Angular[1] code. The generator consists of several sub-generators, which are described in detail later on.

The last phase comprises the *Context Service* at runtime, whose components are created in the previous generation step. The before defined providers and the *Context Profile* are directly derived from the defined model. In the providers we can insert code to access information supported by APIs or libraries for JavaScript. In our case, Ambient Light API[2] and Affectiva SDK[3] are shown as examples for sensing context information data through sensors. The observed context information is pushed to the *Context Controller*, which connects the providers with the *Context Profile*. There, the data is stored and offered to external systems or components, which can use the context information for different purposes like UI self-adaptation.

---

[1] https://angular.io.

[2] https://www.w3.org/TR/ambient-light/.

[3] https://github.com/Affectiva.

3 Implementation

In this section we describe the implementation of our Model-Driven Context Management Framework in detail.

3.1 ContextML

The first challenge addressed in our approach was the specification of contextual parameters. To support a holistic modeling of contextual parameters, we introduce a new modeling language *ContextML* that is designed conform to the *Context Metamodel* depicted in Fig. 2.

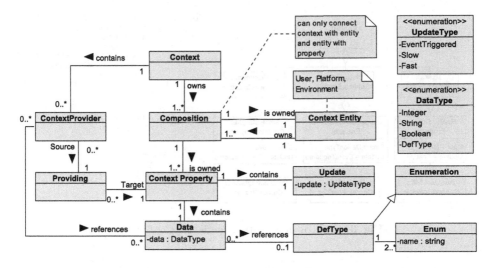

Fig. 2. Context metamodel

The root element and central class of the metamodel is the class *Context* that connects all parts of the model. The *Context Entities* are categories for tracked context data and are further refined by *Context Properties*, which allow a concrete specification of the triplet *User*, *Platform* and *Environment*. The *Context Properties* are containers for the concrete context data and connect it with meta information, which is important for the connection of the generated elements. It covers the used data type and the update type. The latter is the way the single data set shall be updated. This can be *"Fast"* (every 5 s), *"Slow"* (every 100 s) or *"EventTriggered"*, which is as soon as the context information changes. Moreover, the reference to the desired *Context Provider* is saved, which is the before mentioned source of context information. The *DataType* can be a standard type like *Integer*, *String* or *Boolean*, but also a user defined type is supported by a *DefType*. This is an enumeration, which contains *Enums*, which include a selection of different states of that type. The metamodel is designed for a broad scope of context modeling aspects and allows adding more *entities*, *properties*, *data types*, and other *provider*.

An example of a context model excerpt specified based on this metamodel is depicted in Fig. 3. It shows a set of possible context entities. For illustrating the context modeling language, exemplary entities which contain some exemplary context properties are shown. This model snippet will also be used to demonstrate the generation process. Based on the metamodel, we also created a textual language for *ContextML* using Xtext[4], which provides an Eclipse plugin. It allows an easy modeling of the context, due to error highlighting and code completion. That way the required programming knowledge and error potential is reduced. An example is displayed on the right side of Fig. 3.

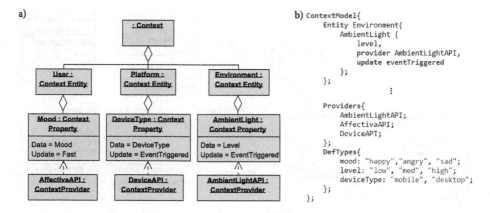

Fig. 3. Excerpt of a context model in *ContextML*

After saving the model file an XML file is generated automatically, which serves as an input for the *Context Service Generator*.

3.2   Context Service Generator

In this section, we describe the process of generating *Context Services* represented as Angular code in form of Typescript. The generation is based on the XML file of the previously mentioned context model.

The structure of the generator for the *Context Service* is shown in Fig. 4. It has a main generator that splits the generation into four kinds of files that will be generated. Our *Context Service Generator* is a template-based code generator that is implemented with *Xtend*[5].

First, the *ContextServiceGenerator* invokes the *ContextControllerGenerator* which generates the main Angular service that connects and controls all the

---

[4] https://eclipse.org/Xtext/.
[5] http://www.eclipse.org/xtend/.

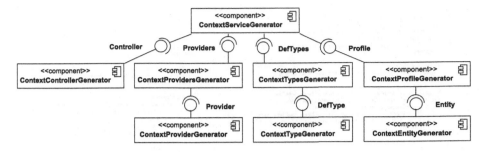

Fig. 4. Component diagram of Context Service Generator

other parts. The generated *Context Controller* contains *subscriptions* to *subjects*, which push changed data automatically to the subscriber based on the *rxjs observer pattern*[6]. Furthermore, it contains timers for the properties which are not updated in an event-based manner.

The *ContextProvidersGenerator* invokes the *ContextProviderGenerator* for each provider that is listed in the context model. This creates a folder with all provider files. Each contains standard imports and used *DefTypes*. The business logic code for controlling and managing of sensor sources, like APIs or libraries has to be inserted manually. This is due to the very individual structure of numerous interfaces. Those can be fairly easy to use, like standard HTML5 APIs[7], but can be individual and more complex as well, like the Affectiva SDK for emotion recognition. In our case study we have already implemented some exemplary Context Providers.

The *ContextTypesGenerator* invokes similar to the *ContextProvidersGenerator* the *ContextTypeGenerator* for each user definded *DefType*. This creates a folder with type files, that are imported by the providers. Each file contains the *Enums* defined in the context model.

The last generator component is the *ContextProfileGenerator* that creates a central context data profile file and invokes the *ContextEntityGenerator* for each declared entity in the context model. This creates a file for each entity which contains all the defined properties and the corresponding *getter* and *setter* methods.

An example for the generation of a *Context Provider* is depicted in Fig. 5. The code excerpt depicted in Fig. 5(a) represents the Xtend template for generating specific context providers to capture context information through sensor libraries. In Fig. 5(b) the generated code for the *AmbientLight* provider is illustrated. The code of the generated context provider is responsible for monitoring the environmental lighting condition at runtime by using the *AmbientLightAPI*.

---

[6] https://github.com/Reactive-Extensions/RxJS.
[7] https://www.w3.org/2009/dap/.

```
a) 1  '''
   2   import { Injectable } from '@angular/core';
   3   import { Observable } from 'rxjs';
   4   import { BehaviorSubject } from 'rxjs/Rx';
   5   «FOR type: typeList»
   6     import { «type» } from '../types/«type»';
   7   «ENDFOR»
   8
   9   @Injectable()
  10   export class «providerName.toFirstUpper»Service {
  11
  12     «FOR prop: propertyList»
  13       «var propName = prop.getNamedItem("name")»
  14       «var propType = prop.getNamedItem("type")»
  15       private «propName»: «propType»;
  16       private _«propName»Subject: BehaviorSubject<«propType»> ...
  17       public «propName»Subject: Observable<«propType»> =    ...
  18     «ENDFOR»
  19
  20     constructor(){
  21
  22     }
  23
  24     «FOR prop: propertyList»
  25       «var propName = prop.getNamedItem("name")»
  26       get«propName.toFirstUpper»(){
  27         this._«propName»Subject.next(this.«propName»);
  28       }
  29     «ENDFOR»
  30   }
  31  '''
```

```
b) 1  import { Injectable } from '@angular/core';
   2  import { Observable } from 'rxjs';
   3  import { BehaviorSubject } from 'rxjs/Rx';
   4  import { Level } from '../types/Level';
   5
   6  @Injectable()
   7  export class AmbientLightAPI {
   8
   9    private ambientLight: Level;
  10    private _ambientLightSubject: BehaviorSubject<Level> ...
  11    public ambientLightSubject: Observable<Level> ...
  12
  13    constructor(){
  14      window.addEventListener('devicelight', event => {
  15        var html = document.getElementsByTagName('html')[0];
  16        if (event.value > 300) {
  17          this.ambientLight = 2;
  18        }else if(event.value > 100){
  19          this.ambientLight = 1;
  20        }else{
  21          this.ambientLight = 0;
  22        }
  23        this.getAmbientLight();
  24      });
  25    }
  26
  27    getAmbientLight(){
  28      this._ambientLightSubject.next(this.ambientLight);
  29    }
  30  }
```

Fig. 5. Xtend template excerpt for ContextProviderGenerator (a) and its generated code (b)

3.3   Context Service

At runtime, the generated *Context Service* works as a background service, that can be used by any web application based on the *Angular* framework. A runtime system overview is depicted in Fig. 6. Depending on the defined update type of the context properties, the context providers either access the information event-based or triggered by the timer of the *Context Controller*. Through the subjects of the observer pattern, new data is directly pushed to the subscriptions of the controller. At the same time, the corresponding property is updated in the context profile. Based on the provided context information data through the *Context Service*, an *Adaptation Service* is able to dynamically monitor context information and trigger adaptation mechanisms, for instance to adapt a *Final UI*.

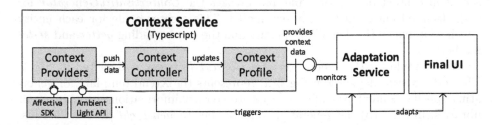

Fig. 6. Communication within the Context Service at runtime

4   Case Study

For illustrating the benefit of our Model-Driven Context Management Framework, we present a case study where our framework is applied in the context of self-adaptive user interfaces. Based on our framework, we specified a context-of-use model and generated various context services that support the monitoring of contextual parameters. The observed context information and occurring context changes were provided to the adaptation service of a self-adaptive UI. Based on the provided context information, the adaptation service was able to adapt the UI at runtime, that means it reacted to context-of-use changes by automatically changing layout, navigation or task-feature set of the UI [4]. In the following the case study and the application of our generated context services in the context of self-adaptive UIs is explained in more detail.

The case study setting is based on an example scenario which is derived from the university library management domain (see Fig. 7). The scenario setting is a library web application for universities which is called "LibSoft". LibSoft provides core library management functionality like searching, reserving and lending books. LibSoft's UI can be accessed by heterogeneous users and user roles (like student or staff member) through a broad range of networked interaction devices (e.g. smartphones, tablets, terminals etc.) which are used in various environmental contexts (e.g. brightness, loudness, while moving etc.). Depending on the situation, users are able to access their library services where, when and how it suits them best. For example, if the user wants to pursue a self-determined cross-channel book lending process, she can begin an interaction using one channel (search and reserve a book with her laptop at home), modify the transaction on her way using a mobile channel, and finalize the book lending process at the university library via self-check-out terminal or at the staff desk. In the described example scenario, each channel has its own special context-of-use and eventually the contextual parameters regarding user, platform and environment can dynamically change. Figure 8 shows such a context-of-use (CoU) change from CoU2 to CoU4 (compare Fig. 7). The depicted context-of-use object model excerpts in Fig. 8 illustrate how different contextual parameters regarding user, platform and environment can change. Therefore, it is important to continuously monitor the context-of-use parameters and react to possible changes by automatically adapting the UI for the new context-of-use situation.

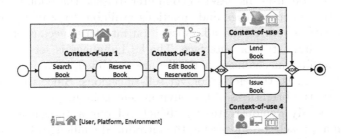

Fig. 7. Example scenario: UIs in dynamically changing context-of-use situations.

Already a small set of contextual parameters can highly influence the UI since lots of context situations can occur if the context-of-use parameters dynamically

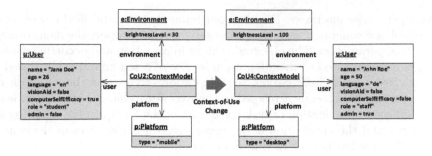

Fig. 8. Context-of-use object model excerpts

change. The generated context services based on our framework were able to continuously monitor the context information data. Furthermore the generated context services were able to detect changes in contextual parameters and notified the adaptation service of the self-adaptive UI to apply adaptation mechanisms.

The interplay between the generated context services and the existing adaptation approach resulted in self-adaptive UIs that are aware of their context-of-use. Screenshots of the resulting self-adaptive UI are depicted in Fig. 9. According to the monitored context information for CoU2, the layout for the UI is optimized for a mobile device used in a darker environment, because the user Jane is editing her book reservation while travelling to the library and it is already quite dark outside (see left side of Fig. 9). Also, the UI is adapted to the user properties by enabling access to the functions and navigation available to students. The UI language is set to English as it is preferred by the user Jane. Since Jane is recognized as a self-efficacious user with the application, she gets extended functionalities, like a more complex search and filter mechanism for the list view of the books. When the context changes from CoU2 to CoU4, the generated self-adaptive UI adapts itself automatically to the new contextual parameters. In this case, the staff members view on a desktop device with a wider and brighter layout is shown, displaying the list of reserved books, because in CoU4 a staff member, John Roe, uses his desktop computer to issue the book to Jane. Additionally, to the functionalities and functions available to staff members, John is provided with a link to the administration interface, because he is granted access to the administration interface. The UI Language is set to German and the search and filter mechanisms of the list are simplified, because he just started using LibSoft and is, therefore, not yet self-efficacious. Since the location is a well-lit library, the brightness of the environment is high.

The case study demonstrates the benefit of our approach and showcases our solution approach for addressing the introduced challenges C1-C3. Through the separate specification of context models, relevant context services that are needed for monitoring context information are generated in a comfortable and automated way. The case study also shows how generated context services can be coupled with adaptation services for example to realize self-adaptive UIs. Beside that, it is conceivable that our framework and generated context services can be also applied for other adaptation purposes in other domains.

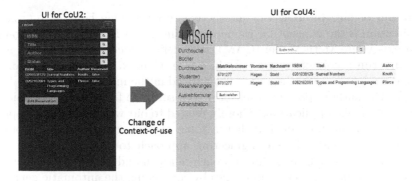

Fig. 9. UI adaptation according to different contexts-of-use

5 Related Work

Various approaches in the area of context-aware computing were presented in the past years. We briefly present a selection of works that focus on context-aware applications based on models.

An important architecture for building context-aware applications was already presented by Dey et al. [5]. They developed a context toolkit that enables rapid prototyping of context-aware applications. The architecture of their context toolkit consists of sensors to collect context information, widgets to encapsulate the contextual information and provide methods to access the information, as well as interpreters to transform the context information into high-level formats that are easier to handle. Beside this approach, various other frameworks like WildCAT or JCAF were introduced to support the development of context-aware applications. Both, WildCAT [6] and JCAF [7] are frameworks based on the programming language Java and they support context management by allowing the definition of a dynamic data model to represent the execution context for several application domains. In addition, they offer a programming interface to discover, interpret and monitor the events occurring in an execution context and record every change occurring in the context model. Similar to these frameworks, Costa [8] presents an architecture based on the Event-Control-Action paradigm that is composed of three components: context processor, controller and action performer. The context processor component captures context information from the user's environment, performs context reasoning and generates context and situation events. The controller component observes events from context processors, monitors condition rules and triggers actions on action performer when the condition is satisfied. A systematic and methodological approach for developing context-aware systems is presented in [9]. In this paper, the authors present a model-based approach that addresses the development of context-aware applications from both the theoretical and practical perspectives.

While before mentioned approaches consider context management for a broad spectrum of applications areas, there are also specific approaches that deal with context management and context modeling specifically for supporting the adaptation of user interfaces of interactive systems. One holistic approach in this direction is the conceptual framework named TriPlet [10]. TriPlet contains a Context-Aware Meta-Model (CAM), that defines concepts required to implement and run a context-aware user interface. Context modeling and context-awareness related approaches were also applied in the mobile context. In [11] for example, the authors present a sensor-driven software framework for rapid prototyping of mobile applications. Closely related to our work is also the approach [12], where the authors deal with the topic of context-aware self-adaptation. They present a model-driven engineering approach to generate context-aware self-adaptation mechanisms. Our approach relies on and extends existing model-driven context management approaches by supporting the automatic generation of context services to monitor and detect context information changes. Although we showed the feasibility and usefulness of our context services in the context of self-adaptive UIs, it is possible to extend our framework through new sensor sources and context entities and therefore conceivable to apply it in various other application scenarios.

6   Conclusion and Outlook

In this paper, we present a model-driven context management framework. The framework consists of a novel context modeling language, named ContextML, that supports modeling of various context-of-use situations. Based on the specified context model, our framework enables the automatic generation of context services for monitoring context-of-use parameters at runtime. The benefit of our approach is illustrated based on a case study where generated context services are applied in the context of self-adaptive UIs. The case study shows how generated context services can be coupled with an adaptation service to provide context information data and trigger adaptation mechanisms at runtime. This allows runtime UI adaptation realized by an automatic reaction to dynamically changing context-of-use parameters like user profile, platform, and usage environment.

In ongoing research, we investigate how additional context information properties can be automatically monitored and captured by context sensors to be used for further adaptation scenarios. Further research will also cover the application of our framework for other adaptation purposes in other domains.

Acknowledgement. This work is based on "KoMoS", a project of the "it's OWL" Leading-Edge Cluster, partially funded by the German Federal Ministry of Education and Research (BMBF).

References

1. Calvary, G., Coutaz, J., Thevenin, D., Limbourg, Q., Bouillon, L., Vanderdonckt, J.: A unifying reference framework for multi-target user interfaces. Interact. Comput. **15**, 289–308 (2003)
2. Akiki, P.A., Bandara, A.K., Yu, Y.: Adaptive model-driven user interface development systems. ACM Comput. Surv. **47**(1), 64:1–64:33 (2014)
3. Coutaz, J.: User interface plasticity: model driven engineering to the limit! In: Proceedings of the 2nd ACM SIGCHI Symposium on Engineering Interactive Computing Systems, pp. 1–8. ACM (2010)
4. Yigitbas, E., Stahl, H., Sauer, S., Engels, G.: Self-adaptive UIs: integrated model-driven development of UIs and their adaptations. In: Anjorin, A., Espinoza, H. (eds.) ECMFA 2017. LNCS, vol. 10376, pp. 126–141. Springer, Cham (2017). doi:10.1007/978-3-319-61482-3_8. https://cs.uni-paderborn.de/fileadmin/informatik/fg/dbis/Publikationen/2017/ECMFA.pdf
5. Dey, A.K., Abowd, G.D., Salber, D.: A conceptual framework and a toolkit for supporting the rapid prototyping of context-aware applications. Hum. Comput. Interact. **16**(2), 97–166 (2001)
6. David, P.-C., Ledoux, T.: WildCAT: a generic framework for context-aware applications. In: Proceedings of the 3rd International Workshop on Middleware for Pervasive and Ad-Hoc Computing (MPAC 2005), pp. 1–7. ACM, New York (2005)
7. Bardram, J.E.: The Java Context Awareness Framework (JCAF) – a service infrastructure and programming framework for context-aware applications. In: Gellersen, H.-W., Want, R., Schmidt, A. (eds.) Pervasive 2005. LNCS, vol. 3468, pp. 98–115. Springer, Heidelberg (2005). doi:10.1007/11428572_7
8. Costa, P.D.: Architectural support for context-aware applications: from context models to services platforms. Ph.D. thesis, University of Twente (2007)
9. Jaouadi, I., Ben Djemaa, R., Ben-Abdallah, H.: A model-driven development approach for context-aware systems. Softw. Syst. Model. (2016)
10. Motti, V.G., Vanderdonckt, J.: A computational framework for context-aware adaptation of user interfaces. In: IEEE Seventh International Conference on Research Challenges in Information Science (RCIS), pp. 1–12 (2013)
11. Gamecho, B., Gardeazabal, L., Abascal, J.: A sensor-driven framework for rapid prototyping of mobile applications using a context-aware approach. In: García, C.R., Caballero-Gil, P., Burmester, M., Quesada-Arencibia, A. (eds.) UCAmI 2016. LNCS, vol. 10069, pp. 469–480. Springer, Cham (2016). doi:10.1007/978-3-319-48746-5_48
12. Ruiz-López, T., Rodríguez-Domínguez, C., Rodríguez, M.J., Ochoa, S.F., Garrido, J.L.: Context-aware self-adaptations: from requirements specification to code generation. In: Urzaiz, G., Ochoa, S.F., Bravo, J., Chen, L.L., Oliveira, J. (eds.) UCAmI 2013. LNCS, vol. 8276, pp. 46–53. Springer, Cham (2013). doi:10.1007/978-3-319-03176-7_7

Human-Computer Interaction Task Classification via Visual-Based Input Modalities

Anas Samara[✉], Leo Galway, Raymond Bond, and Hui Wang

School of Computing, Computer Science Research Institute, Ulster University,
Belfast BT37 0QB, UK
samara-a@ulster.ac.uk, {l.galway,rb.bond,h.wang}@ulster.ac.uk

Abstract. Enhancing computers with the facility to perceive and recognise the user feelings and abilities, as well as aspects related to the task, becomes a key element for the creation of Intelligent Human-Computer Interaction. Many studies have focused on predicting users' cognitive and affective states and other human factors, such as usability and user experience, to achieve high quality interaction. However, there is a need for another approach that will empower computers to perceive more about the task that is being conducted by the users. This paper presents a study that explores user-driven task-based classification, whereby the classification algorithm used features from visual-based input modalities, i.e. facial expression via webcam, and eye gaze behaviour via eye-tracker. Within the experiments presented herein, the dataset employed by the model comprises four different computer-based tasks. Correspondingly, using a Support Vector Machine-based classifier, the average classification accuracy achieved across 42 subjects is 85.52% when utilising facial-based features as an input feature vector, and an average accuracy of 49.65% when using eye gaze-based features. Furthermore, using a combination of both types of features achieved an average classification accuracy of 87.63%.

Keywords: Task classification · Visual-based input modalities · Intelligent HCI

1 Introduction

Human-Computer Interaction (HCI) researchers utilise different methodologies to improve the interaction between users and computer systems. Accordingly, there are endeavours to endow computers with logical reasoning abilities about the user in order to provide more intelligent interaction [2,9,12]. Also, achieving an intelligent and adaptive form of HCI depends on the software application (i.e. the user interface), and the domain in which the software is being employed, together with other constraints related to the interface functions, and task characteristics and requirements [12]. Subsequently, the system becomes able to provide error-tolerant operations as well as providing system state diagnosis to support human decision making [2]. Therefore, a more robust integration

© Springer International Publishing AG 2017
S.F. Ochoa et al. (Eds.): UCAmI 2017, LNCS 10586, pp. 636–642, 2017.
DOI: 10.1007/978-3-319-67585-5_62

between humans and computers may be obtained, resulting in the achievement of reliable HCI, where the systems have the ability to make suitable adaptation in relation to contextual information about both the task and the user's affective and cognitive states [9].

Therefore, as one of the steps towards implementing an intelligent HCI, this work investigates the use of visual-based input modalities in order to capture the nature of tasks that a user is undertaking. Four categories of computer usage, which represent the most used interfaces for ordinary computer users, have been employed within the experiments carried out. To this end, a number of supervised classification experiments have been carried out and reported within this work.

In the next section of this paper an overview of the visual-based input channels used, including facial and eye tracking-based features, is presented. This is followed by a brief discussion of the methodology employed within the investigations, whereby details of the data acquisition protocol are presented, along with details of the methods of feature extraction and feature vector representation that have been used. The final section presents the results obtained and provides a discussion of both the results and future potential work.

2   Background

Facial expressions are considered as one of the most relevant features that can provide an indication about a user's emotional state. Subsequently, features extracted from facial expressions are utilised due to their ease of use, improved accuracy and the unobtrusive nature of the data acquisition [10]. On the other hand, many research studies have reported that tracking eye gaze behaviour using different measurements can reflect the performance of users. For instance, pupil dilation is strongly correlated with mental workload [8]. Additionally, measurements that relate to eye movement within a HCI context can provide useful information about attention, such as the use of *fixations* which represent the moments that user's eyes are relatively stationary on a specific object, and *saccades*, which represent eye movements between *fixations* [11]. Consequently, eye gaze metrics have been exploited in information visualisation analysis, as presented in the work given in [14]. Further studies have identified and exploited the differences in eye gaze patterns across different visualising techniques [4]. Moreover, eye gaze pattern is used to identify the nature of the user task as presented in [7], in which the authors showed that the pattern of eye movement does change across different categories of tasks including: Reading, Mathematical Reasoning, Searching and Object Manipulation. Subsequently, the aim of the work presented herein is to explore the relationship between the category of software application in use and the associated physiological measurements, in particular visual-based channels including facial expressions and eye gaze metrics.

3   Methodology

The quantitative analysis presented within this paper uses the classification accuracy obtained from a supervised machine learning approach as a measure of the relationship between features extracted from visual-based inputs and the computer task (i.e. user interface) that is being performed. Consequently, the primary components of the methodology used are presented within the following subsections.

3.1   Data Acquisition: Participants and Tasks

In total, 42 participants comprising staff and students at Ulster University took part in the study. During the study, four sessions were recorded for each participant, whereby in each session the participant undertook a different designated computer-based task that selected according to most common computer usage, as given in [3]. Consequently, the categories of tasks selected are: (T1) Operating System Task, where the participant was asked to perform ordinary administrative tasks with the Windows operating system, such as changing background, changing screen saver, adding a predefined input keyboard language, and changing time zone; (T2) Online Shopping Task, where the participant was asked to search for a Tablet-PC with a specified set of properties; (T3) Excel Spreadsheet Manipulation Task, where the participant was asked to manipulate an existing spreadsheet in order to insert a new record, sort the data in ascending order, use an aggregation function, and create a line graph from the data; (T4) Entertainment Game-based Task, where the participant was asked to play a variation of the Pacman arcade game with the purpose of achieving the highest possible score within 3 min. For each session, a task should be completed within the given time limit, and whilst each participant was carrying out the requested task, a video of the upper part of the participant was recorded using a typical webcam, and the eye gaze tracked using an Eye-Tribe tracker.

3.2   Facial-Based Feature Extraction

The various facial-based features are typically based on the location of the face components. Consequently, the *"Chehra"* facial landmark detector is used to locate the location of the eyes, eyebrows, nose and mouth [1]. These points are subsequently employed in order to extract a distance-based feature vector comprised of the Euclidean-distance between points as described in [13]. The resulting distance-based feature vectors generated were then used as input vector within the classification process, as will be discussed later.

3.3   Eye Gaze-Based Feature Extraction

Using an infrared light emitting eye tracker, several measurements from eye gaze tracking can be acquired and employed within a feature vector. Indeed, the features utilised for task classification presented herein were based on a number of statistical metrics, calculated from the eye gaze tracking measurements acquired during the tasks.

Statistical Metrics: The following statistical functions were applied to the measurements from eye gaze data samples acquired within a window of one second length (i.e. for 30 samples captured per second):

1. Summation *(sum)*: where values within the window are added sequentially

$$sum = \sum_{i=0}^{n} X_i$$

2. Mean (μ): represents the average of the measurement values of the window

$$\mu = \frac{1}{N} \sum_{i=0}^{n} X_i$$

3. Standard Deviation (σ): represents the dispersion (i.e. variation) of the measurement values within the window

$$\sigma = \sqrt{\frac{1}{N} \sum_{i=0}^{n} (X_i - \mu)^2}$$

Eye Gaze Tracking Measurements: Eye gaze tracking produces many measurements for each eye separately, which are used in the statistical functions previously described. Correspondingly, the eye tracking features utilised are based on the study given in the work of Steichen et al. [14]:

1. *Fixations Number:* the number of eye fixations detected during the window
2. *Fixations Rate:* the rate of eye fixation samples with regard to the total number of samples during the window
3. *Pupil Size:* the size of the pupil given in arbitrary units
4. *Saccade Length:* the distance between two fixations
5. *Absolute Saccade Angle:* the angle between a saccade and the x-axis
6. *Relative Saccade Angle:* the angle between two consecutive saccades

3.4 Combination of Facial-Based and Eye Gaze-Based Features

The extracted features from the facial expressions were combined with features populated from eye gaze measurements, i.e. the concatenation of the facial-based feature vector (comprising 1176 features) with the eye gaze-based feature vector (comprising 26 features). Subsequently, the resultant vector that represents the fusion of facial-based and eye gaze-based features contained a total of 1202 features.

3.5 Machine Learning Technique Used for Classification

For both input channels, after the features have been extracted and represented, as previously described, they were used as predictors and the corresponding task label used as a target class for the supervised machine learning classifier. Accordingly, the extracted features were classified using a prediction model trained using 10-fold cross validation. A specific type of Support Vector Machine (SVM) was employed, namely the C-Support Vector with linear kernel shipped with the online SVM library [5,6]. Moreover, lower and upper bounds of the confidence interval were calculated using a 95% confidence level.

4   Experimental Results

As previously mentioned, evaluation of the classifier used during the experiments, employed classification accuracy as the primary metric. Table 1 reports the average classification accuracy using the facial-based, the eye gaze-based, and the combination-based feature vectors. As shown, the combination of facial and eye gaze-based features achieved the highest classification accuracy of 87.63%.

Table 1. Average classification accuracy across all subjects

Feature vector type	Classification accuracy	
	Average	Standard deviation
Facial-based	85.52% ± 0.38	6.57
Eye gaze-based	49.65% ± 0.55	10.76
Combination-based	87.63% ± 0.38	6.61

Moreover, Fig. 1 shows the classification accuracy for each individual participant using the different predictor vectors. As may be observed in Fig. 1, facial-based feature vector produced a higher classification accuracy across all participants, with an overall average classification accuracy of 85.52%, than the feature vector comprised of eye gaze-based features, which produced an average classification accuracy of 49.65%, as previously given in Table 1. However, the highest average classification accuracy, 87.63%, was obtained using a combination of both facial and eye gaze-based features within the feature vector. From the results obtained it is clear that a combination of both types of features produces a marginally improved classification accuracy. In some cases, as may be observed in Fig. 1, facial-based feature vectors yielded similar and slightly better accuracies for some participants.

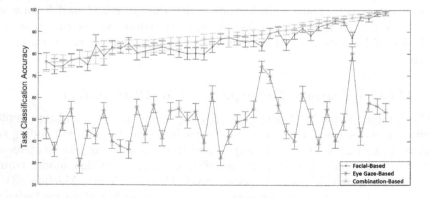

Fig. 1. Task classification accuracy of the 42 subjects. The results sorted in ascending order of the combination feature accuracy

5   Conclusion and Future Work

This paper presented an HCI data collection study, together with the subsequent results and analysis, for the purpose of computer-based task classification. Within the investigations presented, classification accuracy was used as an evaluation metric. The results obtained show that facial-based features achieve higher classification accuracy than the eye gaze-based features. Consequently, this would suggest that facial features potentially provide a more systematic pattern than eye features when different user interfaces are used. Moreover, the results show that in the majority of cases, combining facial-based features with eye gaze-based features potentially improves task classification. In future, this work will be expanded to exploit other input channels for the purpose of modelling the user's affective and cognitive states. Along with the embodiment of real-time information about the task being conducted, it is anticipated that such a rich feature vector will facilitate more accurate task classification and subsequent development of a more intelligent form of HCI.

References

1. Asthana, A., Zafeiriou, S., Cheng, S., Pantic, M.: Incremental face alignment in the wild. In: Proceedings of the IEEE Computer Society Conference on Computer Vision and Pattern Recognition, pp. 1859–1866 (2014)
2. Balint, L.: Adaptive interfaces for human-computer interaction: a colorful spectrum of present and future options. In: 1995 IEEE International Conference on Systems, Man and Cybernetics, vol. 1 (1995)
3. Beauvisage, T.: Computer usage in daily life. In: Proceedings of the 27th International Conference on Human Factors in Computing Systems CHI 2009, p. 575 (2009)
4. Blascheck, T., Kurzhals, K., Raschke, M., Burch, M., Weiskopf, D., Ertl, T.: State-of-the-art of visualization for eye tracking data. In: Eurographics Conference on Visualization (EuroVis), pp. 1–20 (2014)
5. Chang, C.C., Lin, C.J.: LIBSVM - A Library for Support Vector Machines (2001)
6. EL-Manzalawy, Y.: WLSVM (2005). http://www.cs.iastate.edu/~yasser/wlsvm/
7. Iqbal, S.T., Bailey, B.P.: Using eye gaze patterns to identify user tasks. In: The Grace Hopper Celebration of Women in Computing, p. 6 (2004)
8. Iqbal, S.T., Zheng, X.S., Bailey, B.P.: Task-evoked pupillary response to mental workload in human-computer interaction. In: Extended Abstracts of the 2004 Conference on Human Factors and Computing Systems, CHI 2004, p. 1477 (2004)
9. Karray, F., Alemzadeh, M., Saleh, J.A., Arab, M.N.: Human-computer interaction: overview on state of the art. Int. J. Smart Sens. Intell. Syst. 1, 137–159 (2008)
10. Lanatà, A., Valenza, G., Scilingo, E.P.: Eye gaze patterns in emotional pictures. J. Ambient Intell. Humaniz. Comput. 4, 705–715 (2013)
11. Poole, A., Ball, L.J.: Eye tracking in human-computer interaction and usability research: current status and future prospects. In: Encyclopedia of Human-Computer Interaction, pp. 211–219 (2005)
12. Saffer, D.: Designing for Interaction: Creating Innovative Applications and Devices Voices that Matter. New Riders, San Francisco (2009)

13. Samara, A., Galway, L., Bond, R., Wang, H.: Sensing affective states using facial expression analysis. In: García, C.R., Caballero-Gil, P., Burmester, M., Quesada-Arencibia, A. (eds.) UCAmI 2016. LNCS, vol. 10069, pp. 341–352. Springer, Cham (2016). doi:10.1007/978-3-319-48746-5_35
14. Steichen, B., Conati, C., Carenini, G.: Inferring visualization task properties, user performance, and user cognitive abilities from eye gaze data. TIIS **4**(2), 11:1–11:29 (2014)

Towards Human-Centric Interfaces for Decision Making Support in Geriatric Centers

Luis A. Castro[1(✉)], Amanda Tapia[1], Cynthia B. Perez[1], and Jessica Beltrán-Márquez[2]

[1] Sonora Institute of Technology (ITSON), Ciudad Obregon, Mexico
luis.castro@acm.org, amanda.tapiaz7@gmail.com,
cynthia.perez@itson.edu.mx
[2] CONACYT-CITEDI-IPN, Tijuana, Mexico
jbeltran@citedi.mx

Abstract. Older adults can suffer from neurodegenerative diseases, which can make them dependent on family members or trained personnel in geriatric centers. In this work, we aimed at identifying the main information elements needed for decision making in geriatric centers. We present the results of a qualitative study using grounded theory as the analytic lens for a contextual study carried out with workers of a geriatric center. The main contribution of this paper is a set of information elements that are needed for different types of decisions taken at a geriatric center. The results of this work can be used for designing better interfaces for the decision making support in geriatric centers.

Keywords: Human-centric interface · Older adults · Caregivers · Decision making support

1 Introduction

Older adults who suffer from chronic illness or neurodegenerative conditions may not be able to carry out several activities of daily life (ADL). Many of them are assisted by professional caregivers or family members who help them thrive. Although family members often volunteer as caregivers, there are institutions that can provide specialized care by physicians, psychologists, and nurses. These institutions are often residences, where older adults live, or community-dwelling adults who spend a few hours a day in the institution or geriatric center (GC).

In many developing regions, including Mexico, geriatric centers do not have much technology providing support to their internal processes. In such institutions in Mexico, instead of using technology, it is commonplace to take notes and jot down several observed behaviors of older adults or assessments. These data happens to be essential for assessing the progress of the older adult. However, although important, these notes can often become a liability for the institution due to shifts, personnel turnover, workload stress, and health care [1]. That is, in the case of a critical event, GCs do not have enough information to prove that the provided care was appropriate, let alone to determine that the decisions made were the right calls. Also, in many cases the number of older adults is greater than the number of caregivers, leading to constant overwork.

© Springer International Publishing AG 2017
S.F. Ochoa et al. (Eds.): UCAmI 2017, LNCS 10586, pp. 643–654, 2017.
DOI: 10.1007/978-3-319-67585-5_63

Then, GC's caregivers constantly maintain record of activities carried out by residents, since it is one of the main ways of keeping track of events. Even if these data are a valuable resource, generally, the follow-up of these notes is complex due to personal turnover or shifts. This makes it difficult for clinicians to make decisions regarding attention and care [1].

In this regard, human-centric interfaces can be of great help as a support in the decision making process pertaining to clinical or non-clinical decisions. Decision making can be regarded as a cognitive process in which an individual selects among a set of alternatives, yielding to reinforcing a belief or a course of action. In some occupations, such as in health care, decision making is critical, and are subject to strict regulations and accountability. In fact, a set of medical guidelines have been created as a way to guide decisions and criteria during medical practice in specific areas of healthcare (Visit https://www.guideline.gov/).

In this context, interfaces that can provide support in decision making processes can be of great help for healthcare professionals. Those said tools can turn instrumental in understanding patient data [2]. In particular, they can be fundamental for presenting relevant information to doctors, nurses, family members, or a community [2–6]. In this work, we aim at identifying information elements that can be useful for decision making in GCs. In particular, our ultimate goal is crafting design guidelines that can be useful for developers interested in providing human-centric interfaces. For this, we carried out a qualitative study with professionals who work regularly with older adults. Our results provide a framework for understanding what information elements are taken into account when making clinical and non-clinical decisions in a GC.

2   Related Work

In the medical field, an extensive use of data generated from multiple sources is becoming commonplace, which is used to support, and make sense, of the decision making processes [7]. In particular, in the healthcare domain, these sources can be readings from medical devices [4], manual annotations by medical staff regarding the patients [8], lab results [9], or patients' behavioral data provided by self-report or family members.

Clinical practices have increasingly focused on analyzing digitalized patient data for developing decision support systems [10, 11]. There is a growing need for storing and organizing patient data to contribute with the constant assessment of clinical cases or studies [12]. A valid concern related to how to present, design, or implement information in an effective way, so that the user's activities can be effectively supported [7]. For example, in [13], the authors present the critical factors for designing information technologies and communication technologies (ICT) to support Type 1 diabetes management. The findings pointed toward developing ICTs' design insights for teenagers' auto management and commitment of informal caregivers [13]. Finally, some other works have been developed in which they integrate healthcare knowledge [14]. As such, decision support systems in health care are not new [10, 15, 16], however, previous works usually place particular emphasis on clinical decision making for physicians.

Although the literature for decision support systems in healthcare is extensive, to the best of our knowledge, this is one of the first works aimed at highlighting the information elements that are needed for decision making at a geriatric center, particularly in Mexico. These information elements can be the building blocks of appropriate human-centric interfaces that be used for supporting clinical or non-clinical decision making in geriatric centers. In particular, we present a study involving a geriatric center where technology uptake has been historically slow.

3   Methods

In this section, we present the methods related to the qualitative study as well as a description of the GC and the participants:

The Geriatric Center (GC) and Informants
The GC where we mainly carried out this work is a non-for-profit, privately-funded geriatric center for patients diagnosed with dementia. It counts with 14 full-time employees, which includes 9 clinicians, 2 kitchen workers, 1 manager, 1 financial administrator, and 1 janitress. In addition, there are a number of volunteers who are usually family members or university students.

The GC provides attention to approximately 30–35 patients per month. Patients who apply for admission at the center undergo a pre-admission screening and baseline testing by the clinicians for eligibility. Although the center is privately funded, it charges family members an undisclosed fee for its services.

The GC is located in a mid-size city of approximately 400,000 inhabitants in Northwest Mexico. Physically, the premises were originally a social interest house, but it now includes the following spaces: a gym, a workout area, a patio for home-grown vegetables, rest areas, appropriate toilets, an infirmary, a kitchen, administrative offices, and a meeting room. It is fully gated, with a double check security point for safety, where visitors much register, and where family members meet and greet with the GC staff before leaving their family members for the day.

Table 1. Demographics of our informants

ID	Role	Gender	Age	Exp. (years)	Main work
I-1	Psychologist	F	30	4	Geriatric center
I-2	Physiotherapist	F	45	9	Geriatric center
I-3	Nurse	F	55	25	Hospital
I-4	Nutritionist	F	22	1	Geriatric center
I-5	Nurse	F	23	0.5	Geriatric center
I-6	Psychologist	M	24	3	Geriatric center
I-7	Nurse	F	26	2	Hospital
I-8	Caregiver	F	46	19	Residence
I-9	Caregiver	F	35	15	Residence
I-10	Manager	F	40	15	Hospital

Our informants (see Table 1) work regularly with older adults as part of their professional practice. They were mainly recruited from the aforementioned GC, and professionals who work at hospitals, who also volunteer at older adult residences.

Data Collection and Analysis

We carried out 10 semi-structured interviews. Interviews lasted in average 45 min each. All interviews were audio recorded and verbatim transcribed for their posterior analysis. The interview protocol consisted of 23 questions and involved the topics related to the activities carried out by adults, information management practices, health care, and decision making in the institution. For this work, only 7 interviews were considered since 3 of them (I-8, I-9, I-10) did not provide useful information regarding decision making in the GC.

Our analysis aimed at uncovering current practices in the geriatric center in terms of decision making, which includes processes, actors, information needs, and timing. The findings of this work will be ultimately used for designing appropriate human-centric interfaces for decision making support in geriatric centers. We used Grounded Theory [17] for the data analysis. Grounded theory is a technique for systematic analysis of qualitative data, to uncover patterns and topics that are recurrent throughout the data. The coding process was carried out as follows: One author coded two interviews (open coding). Then, those codes were refined by two of the authors, and posteriorly used to code the rest of the interviews until saturation was reached. Then, axial and selective coding was iteratively carried out by two authors.

4   Results: Decision Making in the GC

After a result of the analysis, we identified four elements that are the building blocks of the geriatric center under study (see Fig. 1):

1. **Quality of service management.** This element involves the development and refinement of business processes related to maintaining quality of service. This is pivotal to the center since it is a non-for-profit, privately-funded institution.
2. **Attention and health care management.** This element involves all the processes that are related to attention and health care of patients in the center. They are carried out by professionals of health care.
3. **Health care data management.** Policies and practices related management of data related to patients and their clinical assessments.
4. **Coordination and communication process.** Policies, practices, and processes related to maintain coordination among different shifts or roles of the GC's personnel, which have a direct influence on the patient's care.

Within those elements, there were identified two main set of decision making processes that have an influence on the center's operations, and which is precisely the focus of this work: (a) decision making in attention and health care, and (b) decision making for management. We next describe these two processes, which are related to how data and information are created, collected, managed, and ultimately used for decision making.

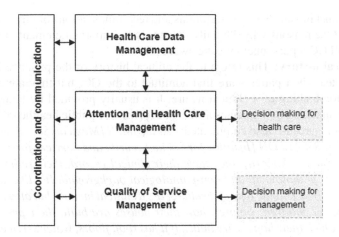

Fig. 1. Identified GC's elements and decision making

4.1 Decision Making for Health Care

This process, which is part of the Attention and Health Care Management block (Fig. 1), includes a set of factors that are taken into account when making decisions of clinical nature. There are primarily five factors that have an influence in clinical decision making in the GC, which are fundamentally records from clinical assessments and observations as well as therapy planning about patients.

Figure 2 shows the factors that influence decision making during attention and care in the GC under study. As seen, some of them relate to clinical data and others to observations or information of other kind that is needed for decision making. In fact, those factors can be grouped into three main classes: on-site clinical factors, off-site clinical factors, and management factors. We next explain each of them:

− **Off-site clinical factors:** These may refer to factors that pertain to health care, although they are not necessarily directly in charge of the GC, but they certainly need to be made aware of. These usually involve changes made by a physician or health care institutes such as changes in medication, diagnoses, and the like. In addition, it also involves incidents that happen when family members are in change of patients such as falls, sleep deprivation, food intake, and so forth.
  • **Daily registry:** This refers to a registry (i.e., logbook) that is updated every day as the patient arrives to the GC. It may be information provided by the family members such as sleep deprivation, or incidents/events that happened while at home. In addition, it also involves annotations by the physical therapists who record relevant information regarding the physical shape of the patient (e.g., lack of strength). In this regard, I-3 commented: *"Anything that happens such as a fall, [bone] fracture, sprain. In what refers to my physical area [her area of expertise], if I know that [the patient] fell, then I asked 'what did the doctor say?', about the prescription and indications. I make a copy and attach it."* Here, I-3 is commenting on the importance of what the doctor outside the GC may say about the patient. Since the GC is not a registered primary care institution, the GC

personnel must rely on prescriptions and recommendations of physicians. This is one of the reasons why the daily registry is an important element of information that all GC's personnel must be aware of.

- **Clinical history:** This refers to the clinical history of the patients. It is usually collected when patients are first admitted to the GC, but they are essential for decision making of a clinical nature. It is usually provided by family members and maintained by clinicians affiliated to private or public healthcare institutions. In this regard, I-3 also commented: *"At the IMSS [Mexican Social Security Institute] or ISSSTESON [Institute for Social Security and Services for State Workers in the State of Sonora], they have their clinical record, their [clinical] history. They are pathological and non-pathological background. It's like having all, in general, [like] name, type of dwelling. It's a clinical history, but also their habitat, number of children, siblings, how their houses are built, the types of materials [with which their houses are built], if it has roof, floors, water service, electricity, sewage, all that. It provides a general picture of that history, and the pathological ones, [they] give an idea of the types of environmental effects. Also, [it provides an idea of] what could have triggered the disease. For instance, the dietary habits, physical activity. All that help us consider certain type of risks."* This aspect is also important to have all those information elements at hand, particularly when a decision is about to be made.

- **On-site clinical factors:** These refer to factors that pertain to the core of the activities carried out in the GC. They are carried out by health care professionals such as physicians, nurses, physical therapists or psychologists. They can be classified into two: Observations and Clinical assessment.

  - **Observations:** This refers to data that is captured by GC staff who work directly with the patients such as nurses. Some of these data involve annotating behaviors, symptoms, last prescription, and information that may lead to better clinical decision making. Finally, it also involves annotations made by the nurses such as vital sings readings. For instance, I-7 commented: *"I introduce myself and ask the family member how he or she passed the night. You also make the patient tells you about it, talk it out, while you are assessing him or her. He or she thinks you are having a conversation but you are [in fact] assessing him or her. We measure her or his vital signs like the arterial tension, cardiac frequency, respiratory frequency, we use the Evans scale for pain assessment, but that's just the beginning. Then, we see what's been indicated [by the physician]."* In this case, I-7 works primarily for a hospital but she is assigned to the geriatric ward. The way she 'assesses' her patients is not uncommon among the GC's personnel, since many use this informal approach to make them feel more comfortable. Still, although important for the quality of care, capturing many of these observations can be challenging due to the nature of her work. Although this information element is important for better clinical assessment, it may prove challenging if data annotation or collection tools are not that adequate.

  - **Clinical assessment:** This refers to regular assessment carried by clinicians in the GC to measure the progress of the patients. Therapy compliance plans are designed, and then, progress is measured on a regular basis. In this center, they are carried out every four months, and use standard clinical instruments for measurement ranging from physiological, cognitive, to social. Regarding this, I-2 stated: *"For the four-month assessment, that's when I reflect on everything… the patient had a fall, he or he was like this, he or she had a fall two months ago. It is documented in an evaluation. That's the way it is carried out: such a date had a fall, the indication was this, or the doctor recommended this and that."* Although not stated by I-2, it is important to mention that in this center they, all of the areas involved, make the assessment in a 2-week period, and then get together to discuss the assessment in a multi-disciplinary fashion. According to their own accounts, this is an important practice for them, since it helps provide with the necessary information from all partied involved, in case critical decisions have to be made. This assessment is important since it is used to classify patients in terms of the stage they are in.

– **Management factors:** These refer to factors that, although important for decision making, may not directly involve activities of a clinical nature. Some of them refer to supervising the compliance of the work plans of the caregivers, so they can provide a progress report to family members. Also, it involves the coordination and communication processes among caregivers.

  • **Therapy compliance plan:** These refer to the compliance plan of physical, psychological, and clinical nature. In addition, it also involves a nutrition plan. The execution of these plans is then paramount for understanding the progress of patients. It is also important to make the necessary adjustment of these plans. In this regard, I-2 commented: *"I have a list [of patients] that are being assigned day to day. I [also] have a weekly intervention plan. The adult goes to the gym three times a week for 25 to 30 min, depending on their issue. [also] I daily have 12 to 13 personalized adults with a physical profile, and we work out on the priorities."* This plan is a bit of information that is important for certain decisions that have to be made by the administration of the GC, particularly when it comes to evaluating performance of caregivers, as well as better understanding the workload. This aspect seems to be particularly important, as some caregivers expressed that some extra 'hands' are needed.

  • **Coordination and communication:** This process is usually held during regular meetings between caregivers, including all the personnel related to health care and attention. In these sessions, comments are shared about the patients, so they can all be in the loop. It is during these sessions that critical decisions regarding health care are taken. It also involves communication with family members regarding the patient care as well as informal debriefing meeting where extraordinary events regarding patients are shared. Although regular meetings are crucial, informal debriefing among caregivers and family members seem to be decisive as information sharing can be limited or deficient. In this regard, I-4 expressed: *"Family members are really busy some times and do not inform us about everything. Some of them [do], but some others don't. There are exceptions, like they change the medication, and do not inform is. That's why one has to keep an eye on the patient, in the changes of behavior or something."* In this sense, regular meetings among caregivers are expected, and they are professionals who know what information can be relevant to share. This may not be the case of all family members, who may disregard information that can be otherwise important.

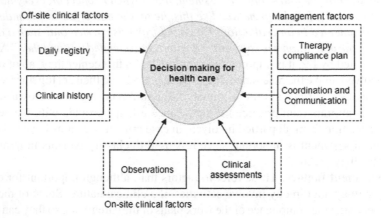

Fig. 2. Factors influencing decision making for health care in the GC

4.2 Decision Making for Management

For management, decision making seems to be more complex since there are several factors involved. Also, there are some inputs and outputs that are expected, and they are fundamental for the institute. Decision making for management (see Fig. 3) involves taking decisions that have to do with operations, planning, and financial resources for operation.

- **Inputs:** These refer to the elements needed for decision making for management. It usually involves different types of information needed for decision making.
  - **Type of information:** These usually refer to the types of information generated from the different areas of care: physical therapy, psychological therapy, and clinical care. In addition, some information is also obtained from the four-month assessment, and the medical history of the patient.
- **Factors:** These refer to the factors that have some effect on decision making for management. Generally, they refer to needs and requirements by clients, caregivers, and the appropriate environment for geriatric care. Also, it involves a high-quality data in the registry. Third, it involves managerial practices of supervision in which they can make sure of teamwork and feedback among caregivers.
  - **Needs:** They refer to the needs that are identified through frequent care of patients. Some of them refer to the needs expressed by their clients (i.e., family members), caregivers in terms of materials and tools needed for carrying out their work, and, finally, to the needs identified in the geriatric center for enabling spaces that can fulfill the needs of clients and patients. Regarding the needs of infrastructure, I-6 commented: *"Before, this place was not here. The place grew around here. The center was much smaller. I think there was demand, which is a good thing, and still is growing. It's a bit complicated because of the space we used to have. Maybe*

because of the [increased] number of older adults. The personnel... we feel that we are short of two or three more personnel... to provide a better service to adults because at times I have to directly be with 13 adults. It's a bit complicated and a lot of burden..." As such, the GC is an organization that needs to fulfill the needs of its clients, patients, but also those of their personnel for providing adequate care. In this sense, some of the decisions to be made by the management have to take into account aspects that can ultimately relate to the kind of service that is being provided to patients.

- **Registry:** It is fundamental that the registry is up-to-date. Even more, making sure that the information is valid and complete is important for decision making. This is essential for critical decision making, as commented by I-1: *"If they change some medication, and at times it [the registry] is not updated or there is no registry because the family member [for instance] do not let us know if medication doses was increased."* In this sense, the management has to make sure that the information they are collecting for the registry is up-to-date, correct, and valid. Many of their managerial decisions have to be made considering this aspect, since is the basis for making the right decisions.
- **Supervision:** Supervision related to the managerial practices needed to help run the GC. This is important since decisions have to be made that contribute to achieving the goals of the GC, as well as fulfilling the needs of clients and patients. It also relates to supervising the behavior of adults on and off the GC, for which family members have an important role.
- **Demand and social impact:** This factor helps determine the type of impact that the GC is having upon the community in which is located. In some way, as mentioned by some of our informants, this factor is reflected in the number of applications made by clients to be, as well as the fulfillment of the needs in the environment. This is important as it leads to the mission of the organization as such. Then, some decisions made by the administration go in this direction.
- **Outputs:** These refer to the outputs generated by the decision making process for management.
  - **Goals:** It refers to the goals stated by the GC in terms of fulfilling the needs of adequate care for the community.
  - **Quality of service:** This refers to the quality of service that the GC aims at providing to their patients.
  - **Multidisciplinary approach:** One of the goals of the GC is offering a multidisciplinary care approach to patients, which involves multidisciplinary sessions for decision making.

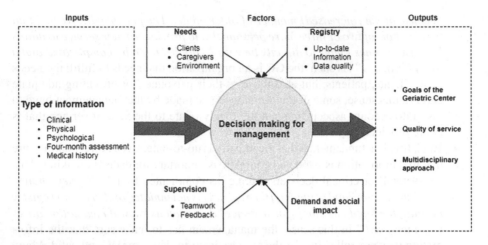

Fig. 3. Inputs, factors, and outputs related to decision making for management

5 Discussion

The purpose of this study was to understand the information elements needed for deci-sion making in the GC. We also aimed at gaining insights into the design of adequate interfaces for decision making. Results from this study unraveled two broad categories for decision making –health care, and management–, which are deeply entrenched between each other. Among these, some of the emerging topics, directly related to deci-sion making, include (a) clinical information elements on and off the GC, (b) therapy compliance plan, (c) identification of patient needs, and those of caregivers for providing adequate care, and (d) timely, quality data. Design considerations based on these topics, and directly linked to decision making are next presented:

Design Considerations for Interfaces for Decision Makers in Geriatric Centers

– Inclusion of primary caregiver's accounts. The interfaces must consider the inclusion of reports by family members. As continually reported by our informants, considering this information is paramount for making the right calls, or adjusting the therapy plan for the older adult due to unexpected events (i.e., falls).
– Collaborative nature of work. Understand the collaborative nature such as this one, in which managerial and clinical practices influence each other. Different points of view must come to a common understanding before taking final decisions.
– Identify a finite set of important decisions. This will enable the identification of adequate information elements that are needed for particular decisions, and the stake-holders that are involved in them. Interfaces should consider those decisions since some involve aggregated data from several months, and these types of decisions that merit careful consideration.
– Customization. The interfaces must account not only for individual differences among patients (i.e., disease stage), but also for the different roles and agenda of

decision makers. In many cases, workers operate at different levels of care, in different areas of the geriatric center.
- Collective vs individual decisions. Critical decisions are made in full consensus among all the disciplines involved in the older adults care. Other decisions such as adjusting a physical therapy may be made individually.

Design Considerations for Decision Support Systems in Emergent Regions

- Technology uptake low. Technology uptake such as information systems has been historically low in small GCs such as the one presented in this paper. This is particularly true of countries such as Mexico, which can derive in challenges such as delayed decision making. This may yield low-quality data derived from paper-based records, since data could be incomplete, unclear, invalid, or inaccurate.
- Process-driven data capture. Business processes must be taken into account for designing appropriate interfaces for capturing data. Supervising roles must ensure data quality such as those quality assurance departments found in manufacture.
- Automatic monitoring of behaviors. Sensors could help report and monitor –perhaps automatically– behaviors and occurrences on and off the GC.

Limitations
There was the potential selection bias, by having only one male as an informant. A more representative sample could help provide more comprehensive design insights.

6 Conclusions

Following a qualitative study approach, we unraveled some elements that are related to decision making for health care and management in a geriatric center. Although limited, we believe that this work helps shed some light into the issues that are related to decision making in a GC with similar characteristics. In this work, we provided valuable insights into the elements that need to be considered for appropriate interfaces that can help make decisions. Future work includes designing an interface that can be used by stakeholders when making collaborative decisions in a GC.

Acknowledgements. This work was partially funded by National Council for Science and Technology (CONACYT) in Mexico with a scholarship provided to the second author. We thank our informants for their support.

References

1. Soto-Mendoza, V., Garcia-Macias, J.A.: Lessons learned from a long-running assistive system for geriatric care. In: Pecchia, L., et al. (eds.) International Workshop on Ambient Assisted Living (IWAAL 2014), pp. 83–90. Switzerland, Springer, Cham (2014)
2. Le, T., et al.: Health providers' perceptions of novel approaches to visualizing integrated health information. Methods Inf. Med. **52**(3), 250–258 (2013)

3. Amri, S., Ltifi, H., Ayed, M.B.: Towards an intelligent evaluation method of medical data visualizations. In: 15th International Conference on Intelligent Systems Design and Applications (ISDA 2015), Marrakesh, IEEE (2015)
4. Görges, M., Westenskow, D.R., Markewitz, B.A.: Evaluation of an integrated intensive care unit monitoring display by critical care fellow physicians. J. Clin. Monit. Comput. 26(6), 429–436 (2012)
5. Bock, C., et al.: Engaging older adults in the visualization of sensor data facilitated by an open platform for connected devices. Technol. Health Care 24(4), 541–550 (2016)
6. Placer County Department of Health and Human Services: Be Well Placer: Community Dashboard (2017). http://www.placerdashboard.org/
7. Sedig, K., Parsons, P.: Interaction design for complex cognitive activities with visual representations: a pattern-based approach. AIS Trans. Hum. Comput. Interact. 5(2), 84–133 (2013)
8. Soto-Mendoza, V., et al.: Design of a predictive scheduling system to improve assisted living services for elders. ACM Trans. Intell. Syst. Technol. (TIST) 6(4), 53 (2015)
9. Tang, P.C., et al.: Personal health records: definitions, benefits, and strategies for overcoming barriers to adoption. J. Am. Med. Inform. Assoc. 13(2), 121–126 (2006)
10. Kawamoto, K., et al.: Improving clinical practice using clinical decision support systems: a systematic review of trials to identify features critical to success. BMJ 330(7494), 765 (2005)
11. Musen, M.A., Middleton, B., Greenes, R.A.: Clinical decision-support systems. In: Shortliffe, E.H., Cimino, J.J. (eds.) Biomedical Informatics. Springer, London (2014). doi: 10.1007/978-1-4471-4474-8_22
12. Zillner, S., et al.: Semantic visualization of patient information. In: 21st IEEE International Symposium on Computer-Based Medical Systems (CBMS 2008), Jyväskylä, IEEE (2008)
13. Bedrossian, J., et al.: Critical design factors for information technology supporting type 1 diabetes management. In: Systems and Information Engineering Design Symposium (SIEDS 2016), Charlottesville, IEEE (2016)
14. Nasiri, S., Fathi, M.: Toward an integrated e-health based on acquired healthcare knowledge. In: Middle East Conference on Biomedical Engineering (MECBME 2014), Doha, IEEE (2014)
15. Hunt, D.L., et al.: Effects of computer-based clinical decision support systems on physician performance and patient outcomes: a systematic review. JAMA 280(15), 1339–1346 (1998)
16. Miller, R.A.: Medical diagnostic decision support systems—past, present, and future. J. Am. Med. Inform. Assoc. 1(1), 8–27 (1994)
17. Corbin, J., Strauss, A.: Basics of Qualitative Research: Techniques and Procedures for Developing Grounded Theory. Sage, Thousand Oaks (2008)

StraightenUp: Implementation and Evaluation of a Spine Posture Wearable

Gabriela Cajamarca[1] , Iyubanit Rodríguez[1] , Valeria Herskovic[1(✉)] ,
and Mauricio Campos[2]

[1] Department of Computer Science, Pontificia Universidad Católica de Chile,
Santiago, Chile
{mgcajamarca,iyubanit,vherskovic}@uc.cl
[2] School of Medicine, Pontificia Universidad Católica de Chile, Santiago, Chile
macampos@med.puc.cl

Abstract. Human posture and activity levels are indicators for assessing health and quality of life. Maintaining improper posture for an extended period of time can lead to health issues, e.g. improper alignment of the vertebrae and accelerated degenerative disc. This, in turn, can be the cause of back pain, neurological deterioration, deformity, and cosmetic issues. Some wearable prototypes have been proposed for spine posture monitoring, however, there has not been enough consideration for the users' experience with these devices, to understand which characteristics are central to acceptance and long-term use. This paper presents a prototype of a low-cost spine posture wearable, along with its preliminary evaluation, which aims both to confirm that the wearable can measure spine posture and to evaluate user experience with this device. The results show that the wearable was comfortable, causing a sensation of security, and that feedback to users would be needed to help improve posture. Further work is required to make sure the device is easy to put on and remove, and discreet enough to be worn in public.

1 Introduction

Human posture and activity levels are indicators for assessing health and quality of life. This type of information may be monitored remotely [1]. Information such as the number of walking steps per day, and the curvature of the spine, may be used to help users improve posture and activity levels. Maintaining improper posture for prolonged time can result in pain and discomfort [2], which can disrupt health, daily activities and family life [3].

Some portable computing devices have been proposed to measure posture and trunk motions, e.g. a lumbopelvic motion monitor [4], a system of dynamic monitoring and orthopaedic imaging [5], and textile sensors for upper body postures [6]. These wearable devices are sometimes voluminous and visible to others. User experience, user requirements, cultural context, and aesthetics must be considered as a central factor when designing wearable devices. Therefore, further study is needed, not only to properly and accurately monitor these conditions,

© Springer International Publishing AG 2017
S.F. Ochoa et al. (Eds.): UCAmI 2017, LNCS 10586, pp. 655–665, 2017.
DOI: 10.1007/978-3-319-67585-5_64

but also to understand how to provide a positive user experience. This paper aims to focus on understanding factors that affect user experience with these wearables. To accomplish this goal, we designed, implemented and evaluated a low-cost wearable device to monitor spine inclination. This device measures angles in the sagittal plane continuously in real-time by using three 3-axis accelerometers placed along on a wearable device. Thirty participants tested the prototype to evaluate its usability and design.

This paper is organized as follows: first, we discuss related work, regarding how spine posture has been monitored and research on user experience regarding wearable devices. Then, we present the design and implementation of our device, called *StraightenUp*. The fourth section describes the evaluation of the device, followed by our results and conclusions.

2   Related Work

2.1   Monitoring Spine Posture

The systems for measuring human postures, especially related to the torso, have been classified based on the position of the sensors (transmitter) and the sources (receiver), as follows. Systems may be *outside-in*, when the sources are on the body, but the sensors are elsewhere (e.g. movement is tracked through cameras), *inside-out*, when the sensors on the body, but the sources are elsewhere (e.g. accelerometer-based systems), *inside-in*, when both sensors and sources are on the body (usually used as wearables for longer-term use), or *outside-out*, when both sensors and sources are not on the user's body (e.g. x-rays) [7].

Some systems that can be used for dynamic monitoring of the spine are portable devices that are embedded with accelerometer, gyroscope, and GPS, which have proven to be effective and are gaining popularity [8]. The characteristics which have made them successful are their small size, low cost, and integration capabilities [9].

Activity recognition may be used to improve patient care, or to understand behavioral changes for healthy users [10]. For instance, a mobility monitoring system for older adults that used two accelerometers (one on the trunk and the other on the thigh) and a small data-logger, was used to distinguish between static and dynamic activities, and to detect sitting, standing and lying activities [11]. A portable smart garment, designed specifically for posture monitoring, was used to monitor trunk postures during daily activities, finding that it may help improve kyphosis (forward rounding of the back) [12].

There are several approaches and initiatives that seek to monitor postures through technology; however, most research has focused on the technology (accuracy, sensitivity and specificity) itself [13]. Our work aims to consider the technological factors as on par with the user experience factors; i.e., we consider that just as important as being able to accurately monitor posture, is how the user experiences the monitoring device.

2.2   User Experience with Wearable Technologies

The rapid advances and innovations in mobile, ubiquitous and pervasive computing have changed how users and designers perceive and employ these technologies. For example, the quantified self movement [14] has pushed for technologies that monitor every aspect of users' lives, through mobile and wearable technologies - and many users have started using popular wearables to track information about their lives (e.g. FitBit, Misfit, Apple Watch, Garmin Wearables).

The most important factor in the acceptance of wearables is their usefulness [15]. Other factors such as ease of use, usability, quality and connectivity affect use rates [16], but few research has focused on the factors that affect user behavior and adoption [17].

3   StraightenUp: A Wearable Device to Monitor Spine Inclination

We designed and implemented a wearable device to monitor spine inclination. This device continuously measures the angle in the sagittal plane in real-time by using three 3-axis accelerometers (LilyPad Accelerometer ADXL335) placed on a modified back support brace. This data is sent to the computer (see Fig. 1).

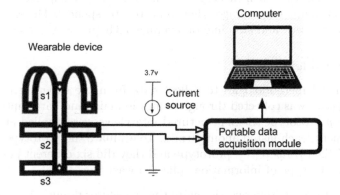

Fig. 1. Scheme for monitoring spine inclination

The modified back support brace was built out of several back support and pregnancy support belts, to be adjustable (through velcro straps) and fit tightly to the body, to minimize differences in orientation between the sensors (sewn on the brace) and the user's body. The three sensors were attached to the brace on the upper trunk, central trunk and lower trunk (see Fig. 2). The sensors were connected by cable to a data acquisition system using Arduino Leonardo (ATmega32U4 microcontroller with built-in USB), Bluetooth module HC-05 and a 1000 mAh battery. These components were put into a small, 3D-printed box, to be carried by the subjects (or stuck on the side of the brace with velcro).

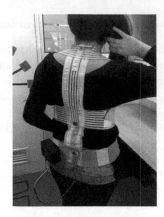

Fig. 2. StraightenUp: end result of brace with sensors, and controller box

4 Methodology

4.1 Participants

Our participants were 30 higher education students (7 women and 23 men). The weight of participants ranged from 43 to 106 kgs (average: 68.5), and their height ranged from 1.51 to 1.83 m (average: 1.68). 14 of the participants reported they suffered back pain. On average, they reported to spend 9.4 h per day sitting (min $= 4$, max $= 14$), and standing on average 3.3 h (min $= 1$, max $= 8$).

4.2 Data Collection

We used mixed methodologies to collect data from the experiment. Quantitative information was collected through a questionnaire and data captured by the *StraightenUp* prototype. Semi-structured interviews were applied at the end of the experiment, each lasted about 10 min. To evaluate the prototype the participants used the *StraightenUp* prototype and they did six different positions with their body. The type of information collected was:

1. AttrakDiff is a 28-item questionnaire that measures pragmatic manipulation, hedonic stimulation, hedonic identification and attraction of software products [18]. We used the English version and online questionnaire [19].
2. *StraightenUp* prototype collected information from the three accelerometers for each position performed by the participant. In total six positions were executed.
3. Audio recordings from the interviews.

4.3 Experiment

The experiment was performed during April 2017 in Santiago, Chile. For the experiment, the participants first read and signed an informed consent form. Then, the experiment was carried out in two phases:

Phase I: At this stage participants wore the prototype on the upper body (trunk). Then, participants were instructed to assume the different postures. Each posture lasted for approx 20 s (50 measurements were taken during that period) in a predefined sequence of six positions in the sagittal plane: back, straight and rigid, straight and relaxed, tilted in 60°, tilted in 30° and tilted as low as possible (see Fig. 3). This sequence was selected to test the precision and accuracy of the sensors, as the measurements from the device could be compared to a known standard. In each position, the participant had his/her back straight and his/her eyes facing the front. The angles and positions were marked on the wall for reference.

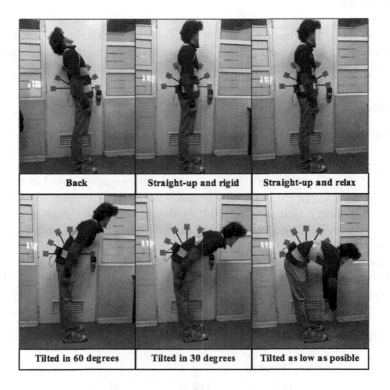

Fig. 3. Evaluation of *StraightenUp* with six positions.

Phase II: In the second part the AttrakDiff questionnaire was applied to assess the usability and the design of the prototype. For this, participants completed the online questionnaire. Finally, an interview was done to know the participant's opinion about *StraightenUp*. The interview focused on knowing: (1) the aspects that the user liked or disliked about the prototype, (2) situations or moments where the participants would use the prototype, and (3) what improvements they recommended to the prototype.

4.4 Analysis

The data obtained from the accelerometers were analyzed by descriptive statistics, for which the R program was used [20]. For the analysis of the data collected from the AttrakDiff questionnaire we used the results obtained from the AttrakDiff site [19]. We also used thematic analysis to code and analyze the data [21] of interviews, which were recorded and transcribed. Each interview was assigned a code (P1 to P30). Some quotes from participants are provided in the results (translated from Spanish).

5 Results

In this section, first we discuss the results from StraightenUp for posture classification. Then, we perform qualitative analysis of the individual interviews, and finally we discuss the user experience results.

5.1 Body Posture Classification

Influence of sensor position: An analysis of the positions of individual sensors showed that the data distribution for the back, tilted in 60 and 30°, and tilted as low as possible (flexion) are more strongly grouped (see Table 1). On the other hand, for the rigid and relaxed positions, the sensor located in the middle part of the back (s2 in Fig. 1) produced more variable measurements. We believe that the variability that occurs in s2 is due to the body type and build of the participants, leading s2 to be tilted at different angles for each participant. However, this does not necessarily mean that measurements from s2 are incorrect or not useful. The sensor located in the upper part of the back (s1 in Fig. 1) is affected by orientation errors caused by the movements of the head for the back and flexion/low tilted positions.

Table 1. Descriptive Statistics (M = mean, SD = standard deviation)

Postures	Sensors					
	s1		s2		s3	
	M	SD	M	SD	M	SD
Back	−56.62	14.92	49.32	57.38	−47.36	52.27
Rigid	−45.72	5.27	−36.68	70.37	−60.26	28.92
Relax	−42.94	4.38	−29.00	78.41	−60.88	29.33
60°	−20.24	6.52	−59.51	5.73	−48.35	11.83
60°	−4.96	9.45	−33.82	15.81	−35.07	12.66
Flexion	11.78	24.27	−0.62	17.04	−13.37	14.71

Influence of type of posture: We input the data collected by the prototype into the Weka software[1] to assess whether the sensors were accurate enough to automatically classify a measurement into one of the six body postures. To assess the performance of the classifier we used a set of 9000 instances collected from 30 participants with 50 data points for each posture. Using all three sensors, 99.5% of instances were classified correctly. Given the variability of data that occurred in s2, we also removed it from the analysis, finding that the rate of classification decreased to 97.5%, so we decided to keep data from all three sensors. The confusion matrix in Table 2 shows that the results had high precision, with very few instances of missclassified information. There was a minor amount of confusion between the classes rigid, relax and back only. This confusion is due to the fact that the three postures (back, rigid and relax) are highly similar. This relatively consistent pattern indicates that the statistical classification model is robust and capable of discriminating accurately between six body postures.

Table 2. Confusion matrix for global sagittal alignment classification

	Back	Rigid	Relax	60°	30°	Flexion	TP Rate %	Precision %
Back	1490	6	3	0	0	0	99.3%	99.7%
Rigid	2	1485	13	0	0	0	99%	99.1%
Relax	2	7	1491	0	0	0	99.4%	98.9%
60°	0	0	0	1496	4	0	99.7%	99.9%
30°	0	0	0	1	1498	1	99.9%	99.7%
Flexion	0	0	0	0	0	1500	100%	99.6%

5.2 Analysis of Individual Interviews

1. *Perception of device:* Overall, all participants liked the wearable concept and found it useful and practical. They described the overall interaction with the StraightenUp wearable as very comfortable, and liked that it is like a garment and fits the body, causing a sensation of security: "I liked the fit very much [...] it gave me a sensation of security, that's what I felt". Most participants stated that it was difficult to put on because of the number of straps: "It's comfortable but I think you'd need help putting it on - I can't imagine putting it on myself, I wouldn't know how to use it on my own". They also suggested that you could conceal the box by reducing the size "The box that is on the back should be smaller, otherwise I think that if you sat down, having a box on the back would be uncomfortable".

2. *Motivation of use:* Participants agreed that the information provided by the device can improve posture habits and reduce discomfort in the spine. "For example, I'm trying to remember all the time that I have to fix my posture to

---

[1] Weka, available at: http://www.cs.waikato.ac.nz/ml/weka.

reduce the pain I feel. If there was something that could help me do that, it would be good". A participant stated that he would not like to use the device because of its appearance: "Generally, because of aesthetic concerns, I think body awareness could be improved in less artificial ways".

3. *Frequency of use:* About the appropriate place to use the device all participants stated that they would like to use it in the office (workplace) during the hours they are sitting. "The time I'm at work basically, since I spend so much time sitting and that is when I have more pain, then I would use it when I'm at work".

4. *Device expectations:* All participants stated that a feedback signal is needed to alert if they are using bad posture "It should give me feedback, when I'm slouching I would clearly prefer if it warned me". About half of the participants would prefer that the alert be a vibration in the device "It should simply vibrate and warn you without having to communicate with the cellphone necessarily", while the others prefer to receive notifications in their cell phone "Send me a notification to my cellphone, everyone is always carrying their cellphone".

5.3   User Experience Results

Overall, AttrakDiff scores were generally favorable, i.e. the overall user experience of StraightenUp was rated as positive (although there is still much room for improvement). In all four dimensions, StraightenUp was rated as moderately good, with best ratings in attractiveness (ATT; M 0.92), pragmatic quality (PQ; M 0.89) and hedonic quality - stimulation (HQ-S; M 0.89). The weakest score was in the hedonic quality - identity (HQ-I, M 0.49) category, which means that StraightenUp is perceived as a non-presentable device, i.e. it does not have the appearance of a finished product. Figure 4 shows a diagram of the mean values on a scale of −3 to 3. Overall, the results show that users feel StraightenUp would be useful, but that presentation must be improved.

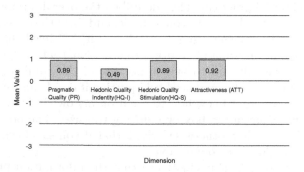

Fig. 4. AttrakDiff mean values for each category

5.4   Discussion

Testing of StraightenUp revealed its ability to distinguish between the following positions: back, rigid, relaxed, tilted in 60° , tilted in 30° and flexion with a high degree of accuracy. Some studies [22,23] indicate that the performance of these systems differs for many reasons, such as the different ways of evaluating, the number and type of sensors used, the location and attachment of the sensors to the body, and the number of the recognized postures. In our case, the possible positions were classified accurately, although they were very discrete, that is, further testing must be done to assess to what degree we could detect smaller shifts in the angle the back is tilted, for example.

Our results agreed with previous research stating that wearable devices should be discreet and not voluminous. There is still a necessity for wearable devices and prototypes that can integrate more seamlessly with users' lives and aesthetics.

Our experiment suggests that one of the possible factors that hinder the adoption of wearables is the difficulty of putting on and taking off the device. Some previous researchers [24] have detected this inconvenience and have tried to solve it. They have used a modular design in smart garments showing that this design has great potential for precision and comfort to make the system useful in context and accepted by its users. Another indicator for the adoption of wearables has to do with the perceived utility of these devices [25]. Most participants indicated that the use of alerts in the body (trunk) in real time may be a technique that helps improve posture habits. In this sense Ribeiro [26] points out that the provision of a constant postural feedback influences the postural behavior. This could generate a greater adhesion of these devices.

The participants of this experiment were healthy people with spinal discomfort (since they spend a large part of the day sitting down). Other back issues (e.g. deformation of the spine, sagittal balance) will need further testing with the particular demographic that is suffering from those medical conditions.

6   Conclusion

The experience of using a device that classifies real-time human postures detected with three triaxial accelerometers attached to the trunk was positive. The evaluation was performed through an online questionnaire (quantitative data) and individual interviews (qualitative data) that were complemented to give greater meaning to these results by providing a better understanding of the feelings and attitudes towards the device of the participants. Results indicated that StraightenUp was comfortable to use and could potentially be useful for controlling spinal posture by receiving real-time postural alerts. Future steps are aimed at improving and evaluating the experience of using the portable device in a clinical context to support the diagnosis of sagittal imbalance in elderly patients suffering from chronic pain due to deformation of the spine.

Acknowledgments. This project was supported partially by CONICYT-PCHA/ Doctorado Nacional/2014-63140077, CONICIT and MICIT Costa Rica PhD scholarship grant, Universidad de Costa Rica and CONICYT/FONDECYT N°1150365 (Chile).

References

1. Lewis, J.S., Valentine, R.E.: Clinical measurement of the thoracic kyphosis: a study of the intra-rater reliability in subjects with and without shoulder pain. BMC Musculoskelet. Disord. **11**(1), 39 (2010)
2. Varshney, U.: Pervasive healthcare and wireless health monitoring. Mob. Netw. Appl. **12**(2–3), 113–127 (2007)
3. Gureje, O., Von Korff, M., Simon, G.E., Gater, R.: Persistent pain and well-being: a world health organization study in primary care. JAMA **280**(2), 147–151 (1998)
4. Ribeiro, D.C., Sole, G., Abbott, J.H., Milosavljevic, S.: The effectiveness of a lumbopelvic monitor and feedback device to change postural behavior: a feasibility randomized controlled trial. J. Orthop. Sports Phys. Ther. **44**(9), 702–711 (2014). PMID: 25098195
5. Farra, N., El-Sayed, B., Moacdieh, N., Hajj, H., Hajj, Z., Haidar, R.: A mobile sensing and imaging system for real-time monitoring of spine health. J. Med. Imaging Health Inform. **1**(3), 238–245 (2011)
6. Harms, H., Amft, O., Tröster, G., Roggen, D.: Smash: A distributed sensing and processing garment for the classification of upper body postures. In: Proceedings of the ICST 3rd International Conference on Body Area Networks, BodyNets 2008, pp. 22:1–22:8. ICST (Institute for Computer Sciences, Social-Informatics and Telecommunications Engineering), Brussels, Belgium (2008)
7. Saggio, G., Sbernini, L.: New scenarios in human trunk posture measurements for clinical applications. In: 2011 IEEE International Symposium on Medical Measurements and Applications, pp. 13–17, May 2011
8. Zheng, Y., Wong, W.K., Guan, X., Trost, S.: Physical activity recognition from accelerometer data using a multi-scale ensemble method. In: Proceedings of the Twenty-Seventh AAAI Conference on Artificial Intelligence, AAAI 2013, pp. 1575–1581. AAAI (2013)
9. Walsh, M., O'Flynn, B., O'Mathuna, C., Hickey, A., Kellett, J.: Correlating average cumulative movement and barthel index in acute elderly care. In: O'Grady, M.J., Vahdat-Nejad, H., Wolf, K.-H., Dragone, M., Ye, J., Röcker, C., O'Hare, G. (eds.) AmI 2013. CCIS, vol. 413, pp. 54–63. Springer, Cham (2013). doi:10.1007/ 978-3-319-04406-4_7
10. Atallah, L., Lo, B., King, R., Yang, G.Z.: Sensor placement for activity detection using wearable accelerometers. In: 2010 International Conference on Body Sensor Networks, pp. 24–29, June 2010
11. Lyons, G., Culhane, K., Hilton, D., Grace, P., Lyons, D.: A description of an accelerometer-based mobility monitoring technique. Med. Eng. Phys. **27**(6), 497–504 (2005)
12. Lou, E., Lam, G.C., Hill, D.L., Wong, M.S.: Development of a smart garment to reduce kyphosis during daily living. Med. Biol. Eng. Comput. **50**(11), 1147–1154 (2012)
13. Peetoom, K.K.B., Lexis, M.A.S., Joore, M., Dirksen, C.D., Witte, L.P.D.: Literature review on monitoring technologies and their outcomes in independently living elderly people. Disabil. Rehab. Assist. Technol. **10**(4), 271–294 (2015)

14. Swan, M.: The quantified self: Fundamental disruption in big data science and biological discovery. Big Data **1**(2), 85–99 (2013)
15. Gao, Y., Li, H., Luo, Y.: An empirical study of wearable technology acceptance in healthcare. Ind. Manag. Data Syst. **115**(9), 1704–1723 (2015)
16. Moon, B.C., Chang, H.: Technology acceptance and adoption of innovative smartphone uses among hospital employees. Healthc. Inform. Res. **20**(10), 304–312 (2014)
17. Kim, S.H.: Moderating effects of job relevance and experience on mobile wireless technology acceptance: adoption of a smartphone by individuals. Inform. Manag. **45**(6), 387–393 (2008)
18. Isleifsdottir, J., Larusdottir, M.: Measuring the user experience of a task oriented software. In: Proceedings of the International Workshop on Meaningful Measures: Valid Useful User Experience Measurement, Reykjavik, Iceland, vol. 8, pp. 97–101, June 2008
19. Attrakdiff: Attrakdiff. http://www.attrakdiff.de. Accessed 30 Mar 2017
20. Consortium, R: Take control of your r code (2016). https://www.rstudio.com/products/rstudio/download/
21. Braun, V., Clarke, V.: Using thematic analysis in psychology. Qual. Res. Psychol. **3**(2), 77101 (2006)
22. Gjoreski, H., Lustrek, M., Gams, M.: Accelerometer placement for posture recognition and fall detection. In: 2011 Seventh International Conference on Intelligent Environments, pp. 47–54, July 2011
23. Bayat, A., Pomplun, M., Tran, D.A.: A study on human activity recognition using accelerometer data from smartphones. Procedia Comput. Sci. **34**, 450–457 (2014)
24. Wang, Q., Chen, W., Markopoulos, P.: Smart garment design for rehabilitation. In: Fardoun, H.M., R. Penichet, V.M., Alghazzawi, D.M. (eds.) REHAB 2014. CCIS, vol. 515, pp. 260–269. Springer, Heidelberg (2015). doi:10.1007/978-3-662-48645-0_22
25. Beech, R., Roberts, D.: Assistive technology and older people. SCIE website - briefing paper, August 2008
26. Ribeiro, D.C., Milosavljevic, S., Abbott, J.H.: Effectiveness of a lumbopelvic monitor and feedback device to change postural behaviour: a protocol for the elf cluster randomised controlled trial. BMJ Open **7**(1), e015568 (2017)

Haptic Mobile Augmented Reality System for the Treatment of Phobia of Small Animals in Teenagers

Cristina Ramírez-Fernández[1,2(✉)], Alberto L. Morán[2], Eloísa García-Canseco[2], Victoria Meza-Kubo[2], Edgar Barreras[2], Octavio Valenzuela[2], and Netzahualcóyotl Hernández[3]

[1] Instituto Tecnológico de Ensenada, Ensenada, Mexico
[2] Facultad de Ciencias, Universidad Autónoma de Baja California, Ensenada, México
{cristina_ramirez,alberto.moran,eloisa.garcia,mmeza,ebarrera, al331047}@uabc.edu.mx
[3] Centro de Investigación Científica y de Educación Superior de Ensenada, Ensenada, México
hcruz@cicese.mx

Abstract. Some of the fears of small animals present in childhood are maintained and cause significant discomfort until the adolescent stage, even causing phobias. A treatment used in the traditional therapy of phobias is the live exposure to the object of fear, however one of the problems with this treatment is patient resistance and eventual therapy abandonment. The use of intelligent environments is an alternative that allows to support the therapy through the virtual, gradual and controlled exposure of the patient to the animal to which s/he is afraid. In this research, we present the design, development and evaluation of a haptic mobile augmented reality system for the treatment of small animals phobia using the TPAD haptic device. The proposed haptic system includes features that allow (i) diagnosing the level of phobia of small animals, (ii) self-adjusting the phobia treatment using support vector machines, and (iii) user progress statistics based on the estimated stress level and time touching the screen. A usability and performance evaluation of the system with 14 teenagers, suggests that the haptic system is perceived as useful and usable, while providing an effective and accessible way to treat the patient and to adjust the therapy challenge level.

Keywords: Phobia treatment · Haptic mobile augmented reality · Teenagers

1 Introduction

Smart environments and increased use of mobile technologies have created new opportunities for interaction for adolescents [1]. According to epidemiological evidence, 12.5% of the general population has a phobia of small animals, with 5% being adolescents [2]. Individuals with animal phobia typically experience an increase in physiological arousal in anticipation of or during exposure to the animal, and often demonstrate a fainting or near-fainting response that affects their daily living [3]. For the treatment of phobia there are behavioral and cognitive behavioral treatments, which are variants of the exposure technique. This exposure technique is applied more gradually and less

© Springer International Publishing AG 2017
S.F. Ochoa et al. (Eds.): UCAmI 2017, LNCS 10586, pp. 666–676, 2017.
DOI: 10.1007/978-3-319-67585-5_65

aversively through the technique of systematic desensitization in vivo, forced practice and participant modeling [4].

However, in the exposure technique, not all patients benefit from this treatment, because it involves live exposure with the animal to which they are afraid, which encourages many patients to abandon treatment because they feel threatened [3]. This way, in recent years several alternative technological solutions have served to treat phobia through intelligent environments that allow for therapy implementation. In these settings the patients interact gradually and in a controlled way with the animal, e.g. [4, 5]. Thus, the use of the technologies allows to approach the patient without exposing it directly with the real animal [6].

For example, the use of augmented reality (AR), which is a branch of virtual reality (VR), has been shown to be effective in treating phobia [7]. With augmented virtual reality information is integrated in 3D in a real environment in real-time [8]. In addition, augmented reality allows changes in the animal's characteristics to adapt the patient's exposure to the animal [7]. However, most live exposure treatments that use technology, focus on desktop applications that miss the availability and accessibility of mobile technologies [9, 10].

In this paper we propose, implement and evaluate PhobyTherapy, a haptic mobile augmented reality system for the treatment of small animal phobia. PhobyTherapy uses the TPAD Phone [11–14]; using the TPAD Phone when you run your finger over something with texture like a wood table or a porcelain pot on the screen, you can feel the microscopic pattern tugging on your skin [14]. The TPAD can recreate the patterns with detail finer than the pixels on your screen. In this work, the TPAD Phone is used as a haptic device to provide tactile stimulus to the user when interacting with the animal. In the system, the user first sets the challenge level of the exercise based on a diagnosis of his/her phobia. Second, the user interacts with the animal s/he is afraid of by getting multimodal (i.e. visual, auditory, haptic) feedback. In addition, the challenge level of each exercise is adjusted using an adaptation module based on the user's performance according to the time s/he touched the animal in the screen and the movement (tremor) of his/her hand.

The main contribution of this research is a haptic mobile augmented reality tool that allows the experts to objectively adapt, execute and monitor the progress of the patient's therapy. A preliminary evaluation suggests that PhobyTherapy is perceived as a usable, useful and accessible tool that provides multisensory stimuli through the successive approach therapy method for the treatment of small animal phobia.

2   Related Work

In the literature, several approaches are presented for the treatment of small animal phobia using virtual reality. The main results of those investigations indicate that virtual reality exposure is an effective treatment for specific phobias and can be useful as a therapeutic tool for several psychological disorders. In addition, the use of a VR system provides some advantages in terms of patient-therapist communication and a more controlled and secure interaction with the animal [15], however its use is capable of inducing anxiety in the participants [5]. For instance, [6] proposes an AR system for the treatment of specific phobia (cockroaches and spiders) using a head-mounted display and VR goggles. In addition, in [9] an AR system was developed on a mobile phone for the treatment of cockroach phobia, where the main results indicate that the use of the game reduced the level of fear and avoidance before a "one-session" AR exposure treatment. Additionally, in virtual environments or AR systems the user interacts or visualizes the animal s/he is afraid of by means of devices such as projective augmented reality systems, haptic devices (e.g. Novint Falcon) or head-mounted displays [15–18]. Despite these contributions, none of them combines mobile technology with AR and multisensory feedback (i.e. visual, auditory, haptic). This work proposes an AR, mobile and haptic application that in addition to being accessible, gradually controls the user's treatment in an individualized way.

3   Contextual Study and Design Insights

Firstly, a contextual study was carried out at a local Rehabilitation Center where two psychologists, who have more than 10 years of experience, attend approximately 120 patients per year. In this study, semi-structured questionnaires were applied to understand how the traditional psychological therapy applied in the treatment of small animal phobia is conducted. In addition, a participatory design focus group session was conducted with experts to generate system design ideas to be developed using the TPAD phone haptic device [11]. Secondly, a diagnostic experiment was conducted in a secondary school where 120 third grade adolescents (age mean ± std: 14.77 ± 0.49 years, 66 males, 54 females) participated in determining the animals to be included in the system. In the experiment, the Personality Inventory (PID-5-BF, 4 point-scale) for DSM-V for child age 11-17 [3] was used to identify if any of the adolescents had any degree of phobia to the animals mentioned in the applied survey (see Fig. 1).

Fig. 1. Survey and diagnosis with adolescents to determine the 5 main animals they fear and their possible level of phobia.

As a result, we obtained the requirements to create a system where the user could interact with the small animal. The recommendations of the experts were as follows: (i) determine the level of phobia of the user based on the results of the Personality Inventory (PID-5-BF) questionnaire for DSM-V for child age 11–17 [3]; (ii) after the initial diagnosis, the animal interaction scenarios need to have different levels of difficulty according to the diagnosis of the user; (iii) at the end of the interaction with the scenario, the system must be self-configured based on the user's performance to adapt the approach level to the animal; and (iv) the system must provide feedback to the user in a positive way so that s/he knows his/her performance through messages or graphs that are easy to understand. Regarding the survey applied, we identified 74 animals that are feared, being the five top ones: the spider, the snake, the cockroach, the mouse or rat, and the scorpion (see Fig. 2). Finally, psychologists analyzed the responses generated by the adolescents and determined that 77 of them have different levels of phobia towards the 5 animals identified (5 severe, 29 moderate and 43 mild).

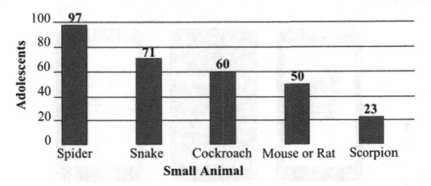

Fig. 2. The 5 top animals to which the 120 surveyed adolescents are afraid of.

4   System Development

The application was developed using the Eclipse IDE with the SDK java language and the Andar library for augmented reality in the Android platform [19]. Its design was informed with the expert-generated recommendations and it includes the three most feared small animals (i.e. spider, snake and cockroach) as identified in the survey applied to the adolescents. Also, two metrics were included to adapt the performance of the treatment; the first one is the time that the user interacts with the animal when touching the screen of the TPAD phone to feel its texture, and the second is the level of stress detected through measuring the movement (tremor) of the hand while holding the TPAD phone. To measure hand tremor we used the accelerometer sensor with a sampling frequency based on [20], which argued that tremor usually has a maximum frequency of 7 Hz, thus, in accordance with the Niquist's theorem the sampling frequency should be at least of 14 Hz. Our sampling frequency was 50 Hz, ensuring the sampling frequency required and providing a fruitful dataset for analysis.

The resulting system is PhobyTherapy, which consists of four main components: diagnostic (calibration), therapy execution, augmented feedback and progress statistics. In the diagnosis or calibration of the application, the user selects an animal with which s/he wants to perform the treatment, and in the first interaction s/he responds a survey (i.e. PID-5-BF [4]) that allows him/her to obtain the appropriate scenario based on his/her phobia level. During therapy execution, the user interacts with the virtual animal and receives visual, auditory and haptic feedback (touching the TPAD phone screen allows the user to perceive the texture of the animal). The interaction depends on the level of phobia detected in the diagnosis, divided into three levels of challenge: (i) image of a playful animal in 2D (for severe phobia), (ii) image of a real animal in 2D (for moderate phobia), and (iii) 3D augmented reality animal (for mild phobia, see Fig. 3a). In addition, Fig. 3b presents an example of the augmented feedback provided (i.e., you can do it, well done, good, very good, excellent) depending on the user's performance i.e. the time the user touched the animal in the screen and the level of perceived stress. Finally, Fig. 3c depicts an example of the user's progress statistics according to the SVM module results.

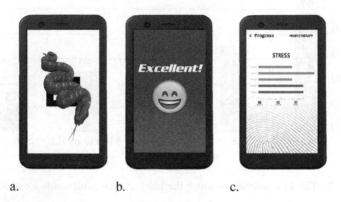

a.   b.   c.

Fig. 3. PhobyTherapy: (a) 3D augmented animal (for mild phobia), (b) example of the augmented feedback provided, and (c) user's progress statistics.

5   System Evaluation

First Evaluation: Quality of the Animal's Skin Texture Perception. We conducted three evaluations in an iterative way; in the first evaluation a pilot experiment was carried out to determine the quality of the animal's texture when touching the screen of the TPAD phone [11]. In the experiment participants were blindfolded and randomly touched 5 textures (one for each animal). Then they answered a questionnaire (5-point Likert scale) to provide their perception of similarity of the haptic skin texture used in the system with respect to the skin of a real animal (i.e. none, little, regular, similar, very similar). In this first evaluation, 32 subjects (age mean ± std: 24.06 ± 13.68 years, 7 males, 25 females) determined the quality of the textures of the animals to be used in the system (Fig. 4). The results suggest that on average the spider, mouse and cockroach textures were similar to the real animals (4.3/5, 4.2/5, 4.4/5 respectively), while the snake and scorpion were very similar (4.9/5 and 4.8/5).

Fig. 4. A participant touching the animal's skin textures on the TPAD haptic phone and answering the questionnaire assisted by one of the researchers.

Second Evaluation: Participants' Stress Perception Levels. In this evaluation, the data obtained from the adolescents diagnosed with phobia were collected. The data were taken in 4-s intervals to determinate stress perception, as these have been reported as suitable for studying accelerometer data regarding tremor events [21, 22]. We classified the obtained data using SVM (Support Vector Machines). Stimulus materials consisted of 20 images of several varieties of the animals the participants have phobia to, as used in other studies [22]. All pictures were similar in size, contrast, and complexity. Distribution of pattern overlay was randomly distributed along each animal's category (see Fig. 5). In addition, participants observed each picture through a horizontal inclination on the TPAD phone's haptic screen. The stress level was measured based on the perception of global stress [23], which evaluates perceived stress according to threatening situations. Participants classified their stress level using a five-point stress scale [24]. Each picture was shown during 4 s [25] followed by the Visual Analog Scale (VAS). Finally, participants reported their conditions by indicating their perception of stress based on the VAS after observing each picture: calm, bugs me, makes me nervous, could upset me, disturbed.

Fig. 5. Example of overlay stimuli. Pattern overlay is 25% each, starting from 0 to 100%, which represent a distribution of intense level of stimuli, from intense to not intense; respectively

In this evaluation, participants were 44 of the 77 adolescents (age mean ± std: 14.65 ± 0.51 years, 24 males, 20 females) diagnosed by experts with some degree of phobia. Data analysis indicates that our participants expressed significantly different phobia levels among each other. Some of them varied they tremor reaction according to each level of stimuli presented, whereas, others did not reflect any change in their tremor (see the results of participant 2 in Fig. 6). Finally, each data collected was calculated in a linear acceleration of 4-second data segments. Each participant training data fulfilled 20 samples with the respective stress perception as reported by the participant. Cross-validation shows a variety of precision, which fluctuates from 70 to 90% with an arithmetic mean of 81.76% for all our participants.

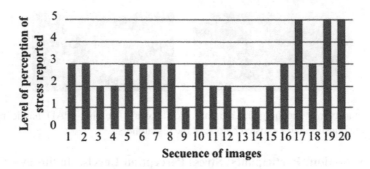

Fig. 6. Example of stress perception for collected data session of participant 2, which represent non-variety for images stimuli. Bars represent the percentage of stimuli reaction settled. Lines represent the stress perception reported by the participant.

Third Evaluation: System Usability and Participants' Performance. Participants were adolescents diagnosed with phobia. They signed a consent form and agreed to be videotaped during the experiment. Test predictions were: (1) the usability perception of the system is high, and (2) the performance of the participants is better at the end of the interactions with each animal. The evaluation procedure consisted of a welcome message, initial explanation, on-entry questionnaire, explanation about how to conduct the exercise, treatment, and on-exit questionnaire. In total there were two treatment sessions for each participant; the selection of the animal for each of them was randomly assigned according to his/her diagnostic of phobia (e.g. spider, cockroach, snake).

At the beginning of each session, the participant was instructed to select the randomly assigned animal, answer the diagnostic survey and interact four times with that animal (with 1 min rest periods between each interaction). In the execution of the therapy, the participant held the TPAD phone haptic device with one hand and interacted with the animal to see it, listen to it and touch its texture with the other hand as long as possible. At the end of the interaction, the participant obtained a feedback (i.e. you can do it, well done, good, very good, excellent) according to his/her performance based on the time during which s/he touched the texture of the animal and his/her calculated stress level. Finally, the System Usability Scale (SUS) [26] and Technology Acceptance Model (TAM) [27] questionnaires (5-point Likert scale) were applied.

Participants were 14 adolescents (age mean ± std: 14.54 ± 0.84 years, 7 males, 7 females) diagnosed with phobia. There were 28 therapy sessions in total (2 for each participant), where 10 participants were randomly assigned to interact with the spider, 11 with the snake, and 7 with the cockroach. All participants stated that they have a daily contact with technology and that they have their own mobile phone. In addition, none of the participants were under small animal phobia treatment (see Fig. 7).

a.   b.

Fig. 7. (a) A participant conducting the phobia treatment using the PhobyTherapy application; (b) participant responding the SUS [26] and TAM questionnaires [27].

Regarding ease of use, the application was perceived as easy to use (median 4.5/5), easy to operate (median 4.8/5) and easy to learn (median 4.9/5). Participants noted that the incremental way of listening, seeing and feeling the animal encouraged them to interact with it, i.e. as a cartoon (playful in 2D, pleasant sound), as in real life (2D photo, real sound) and with motion (augmented reality in 3D, real sound). In addition, participants indicated that they liked to know their progress through positive feedback and progress statistics. Regarding usefulness, the application was perceived as useful for psychological treatment (median 4.9/5). Regarding intention of use, most participants declared that they would use it if they had it available at their home (median 4.8/5), as it is easy to interact with it and to operate it. In addition, 71.14% of the participants showed their interest in using the system for an extended period to treat their fear of these animals and see if there is a transfer to their activities of daily living. However, two participants diagnosed with severe phobia, mentioned that they were about to faint when using the application. These comments suggest that PhobyTherapy can be used as a supportive tool for moderate or mild phobia treatment. However, those participants who are diagnosed with severe phobia should use the application in a controlled setting under the supervision of an expert in psychological therapy.

Regarding the performance of the 10 participants that were randomly assigned to conduct phobia therapy with the spider, 2 were diagnosed as suffering from severe phobia (P5, P8), 6 as moderate and 2 as mild. Figure 8 shows the results of the intervention suggesting that 50% of the participants improved their performance, while 2 participants in all four interactions had an excellent result (P1, P9). However, the two participants diagnosed with severe phobia did not show improvement (see Fig. 8).

Similarly, for the 11 participants that were randomly assigned to conduct phobia therapy with the snake, 6 were diagnosed as suffering from moderate phobia and 5 as mild. The results show evidence that 90.9% of the participants improved their performance and that only participant P1 decreased his/her performance in the last interaction (i.e. obtained well done). Also, for the 7 participants that were randomly assigned to conduct phobia therapy with the cockroach, 3 were diagnosed as suffering from moderate phobia and 4 as mild. The results of the intervention suggest that 71.42% of participants improved their performance. In addition, participant P9 obtained excellent in all interactions, however participant P10 diminished his/her performance at the end of the four interactions.

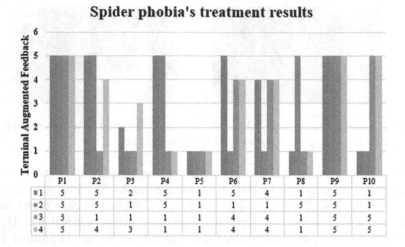

Fig. 8. Spider phobia's treatment results (i.e., 1 = you can do it, 2 = well done, 3 = good, 4 = very good, and 5 = excellent) on the four interactions.

Finally, the participants' usability and performance results were analyzed by the experts who showed their interest in using the tool with patients who are currently under treatment. In addition, the experts suggested that the accessibility of the tool could strengthen the implementation and follow-up of treatment at home, as well as compliance with the therapy program. In particular, the experts considered that the haptic feature that allows the patient to interact with the animal by touch is a novel feature that should be calibrated for each patient.

6   Conclusions and Future Work

This article presents a mobile augmented reality tool with haptic feedback developed based on a context study, focus group and analysis of the population to whom it is addressed. The results of the preliminary evaluation with adolescents diagnosed with small animal phobia suggest that PhobyTherapy is perceived as useful and easy to use, and participants expressed a high intention to use it. In addition, the results show evidence that participants improved their performance in treatment by increasing the time they touched the animal, and decreasing their stress according to the perceived movement (tremor) of their hand. However, participants diagnosed with severe phobia did not show improvement. In spite of this, as participants were not exposed live directly to the actual animal, that made it possible for them to complete the evaluation. Therefore, our results suggest that, like the solutions found in related work (e.g. [15–17]), these tools can be used in controlled settings under the supervision of experts for patients diagnosed with severe phobia.

As future work, we will include different intensities of haptic feedback to analyze if it has an impact on the treatment, besides adding different positions that the phone can have when the user interacts with it in the training of the SVM. Also, we plan to conduct an evaluation for a longer period with 71.14% of the adolescents who participated in the preliminary evaluation, as they are interested in continuing with the treatment. Our plan is to include more participants (adolescents and experts) to strengthen the aspects observed, and determining if the use of PhobyTherapy generates benefits from a clinical point of view.

References

1. Microsoft Corporation: Being Human: Human-Computer Interaction in the Year 2020. Microsoft Research Ltd., Cambridge (2008)
2. Merckelbach, H., De Jong, P.J., Muris, P., Van Den Hout, M.A.: The etiology of specific phobias: a review. Clin. Psychol. Rev. **16**, 337–361 (1996)
3. American Psychiatric Association: Diagnostic and Statistical Manual of Mental Disorders. American Psychiatric Association, Arlington (2013)
4. Quero, S., Nebot, S., Rasal, P., Bretón-lópez, J., Baños, R.M., Botella, C.: Las Tecnologías de la Información y la Comunicación en el Tratamiento de la Fobia a Animales Pequeños en la Infancia. Behav. Psychol. **22**, 255–274 (2014)
5. Bretón-López, J., Quero, S., Botella, C., García-Palacios, A., Baños, R., Alcañiz, M.: An augmented reality system validation for the treatment of cockroach phobia. Cyberpsychol. Behav. Soc. Netw. **13**, 705–710 (2010)
6. Botella, C., Pérez-Ara, M.Á., Bretón-López, J., Quero, S., García-Palacios, A., Baños, R.M.: In Vivo versus augmented reality exposure in the treatment of small animal phobia: a randomized controlled trial. PLoS ONE. **11**, 1–23 (2016)
7. Alice, I., Giglioli, C., Pallavicini, F., Pedroli, E., Serino, S., Riva, G., Chicchi Giglioli, I.A., Pallavicini, F., Pedroli, E., Serino, S., Riva, G.: Augmented reality?: a brand new challenge for the assessment and treatment of psychological disorders. Comput. Math. Methods Med. **2015**, 1–12 (2015)
8. Lee, B.K.: Augmented reality in education and training. Tech Trends. **56**, 13–22 (2012)
9. Botella, C., Breton-López, J., Quero, S., Baños, R.M., García-Palacios, A., Zaragoza, I., Alcaniz, M.: Treating cockroach phobia using a serious game on a mobile phone and augmented reality exposure: a single case study. Comput. Human Behav. **27**, 217–227 (2011)
10. de Sá, M., Churchill, E.: Mobile augmented reality: a design perspective. In: Huang, W. (ed.) Human Factors in Augmented Reality Environments, pp. 139–164. Springer, New York (2012)
11. Mullenbach, J., Shultz, C., Colgate, J.E., Piper, A.M.: Exploring Affective Communication Through Variable-Friction Surface Haptics. In: CHI 2014 (2014)
12. Jin, S., Mullenbach, J., Shultz, C., Colgate, J., Piper, A.: OS-Level Surface Haptics for Touch-Screen Accessibility. In: ASSETS 2014 Proceedings of the 16th International ACM SIGACCESS Conference on Computers & Accesibility. pp. 315–316 (2010)
13. Mullenbach, J., Shultz, C., Piper, A.M., Peshkin, M., Colgate, J.E.: Surface haptic interactions with a TPad tablet. In: Proceedings of the Adjunct Publication, 26th Annual ACM Symposium on User Interface Software and Technology – UIST 2013 Adjun, pp. 7–8 (2013).
14. Tangible, H.: TPAD Phone. http://www.thetpadphone.com/.
15. Wrzesien, M., Botella, C., Bretón-López, J., del Río González, E., Burkhardt, J.-M., Alcañiz, M., Pérez-Ara, M.Á.: Treating small animal phobias using a projective-augmented reality system: a single-case study. Comput. Hum. Behav. **49**, 343–353 (2015)
16. Juan, M.C., Alcañiz, M., Monserrat, C., Botella, C., Baños, R., Guerrero, B.: Using augmented reality to treat phobias. IEEE Comput. Graph. Appl. **25**(6), 31–37 (2005)

17. Cavrag, M., Larivière, G., Cretu, A.: Interaction with Virtual Spiders for Eliciting Disgust in the Treatment of Phobias. In: IEEE International Symposium on Haptic, Audio and Visual Environments and Games, HAVE 2014 (2014).

18. Rinck, M., Koene, M., Telli, S., Moerman-van den Brink, W., Verhoeven, B., Becker, E.S.: The time course of location-avoidance learning in fear of spiders. Cogn. Emot. **30**, 1–14 (2015)

19. Sood, R.: Pro Android Augmented Reality. Springer, New York (2012)

20. Sama, A., Perez-Lopez, C., Romagosa, J.: Dyskinesia and motor state detection in Parkinson's disease patients with a single movement sensor. In: 2012 Annual International Conference of the IEEE on Engineering in Medicine and Biology Society (EMBC), pp. 1194–1197 (2012).

21. Narayanan, M.R., Redmond, S.J.: Longitudinal falls-risk estimulation using triaxal accelerometry. IEEE Trans. Biomed. Eng. **57**, 534–541 (2010)

22. Kolassa, I.T., Musial, F., Mohr, A., Trippe, R.H., Milther, W.: Electrophysiological correlates of treat processing in spider phobics. Psychophysiology **42**, 520–530 (2005)

23. Cohen, S., Williamson, G.: The Social Psychology Of Health: Claremont Symposium on Applied Social Psychology. Wiley, New York (1998)

24. Dunn, K., Curtis, M.: Incredible 5 Point Scale: The Significantly Improved and Expanded, Assisting Students in Understanding Social Interactions and Controlling Their Emotional Responses, 2nd edn. AAPC Publishing, Kansas (2012)

25. Stark, R., Walter, B., Schienle, A., Vaitl, D.: Psychophysiological correlates of disgust and disgust sensitivity. J. Psychophysiol. **19**, 50–60 (2005)

26. Brooke, J.: SUS-A quick and dirty usability scale. Usabil. Eval. Ind. **189**, 194 (1996)

27. Davis, F.: Perceived usefulness, perceived ease of use, and user acceptance of information technology. MIS Q. **13**, 319–340 (1989)

Semi-autonomous Conversational Robot to Deal with Problematic Behaviors from People with Dementia

Dagoberto Cruz-Sandoval[✉] and Jesús Favela

Computer Science Department, CICESE, Ensenada, Mexico
dagoberto@cicese.edu.mx, favela@cicese.mx

Abstract. Conversing with an older adult who suffers from dementia is challenging. There are frequent disruptions due to loss of attention, errors in interpretation, and low motivation from the person with dementia. We aim to develop a conversational robot that could assist people with dementia and their caregivers address problematic behaviors such as anxiety and depression. As an initial step in this direction we have designed a semiautonomous conversational agent. The agent is capable of participating in simple conversations with the coordination of a human operator to be perceived as an engaging speaker. We present the requirements of the semiautonomous conversational robot, and describe Eva, a prototype implemented to address these requirements. An evaluation conducted with eight caregivers of people with dementia show that the robot was perceived as an autonomous agent that could engage in a long conversation with fluidity.

Keywords: Socially assistive robot · Conversational agent · People with dementia · Problematic behaviors

1 Introduction

The prevalence of dementia including Alzheimer's disease is expected to increase as the aging population continues to grow [1]. People with dementia experience troubles with memory and orientation which create concern about the individual's safety and ability to look after themselves [2]. Moreover, a person with dementia (PwD) experiences behavioral and psychological symptoms, such as anxiety or aggression that can put her, or her caregivers, at risk [3]. This dependence on others may lead to caregiver burden, psychological issues, physical health problems and increased stress for the caregiver and the family because the person who suffers from dementia demands a significant amount of surveillance [4].

Non-pharmacological interventions aim at reducing the incidence of problematic behaviors, to ultimately stimulate definite changes in behavioral patterns in PwD and their caregivers. Recent advances in social robotics have stimulated research on the use of robots to support this type of interventions. Social Assistive Robot (SAR) systems have been used to assist interventions based on companionship and social interaction [5, 6], physical and mental activity [7], and activities of daily living [8]. The application of SARs in the care of people with dementia is a field with ample opportunities for further research [9].

© Springer International Publishing AG 2017
S.F. Ochoa et al. (Eds.): UCAmI 2017, LNCS 10586, pp. 677–688, 2017.
DOI: 10.1007/978-3-319-67585-5_66

We aim at assisting caregivers who might experience difficulties providing effective assistance to a PwD 24/7 with the design of a robot that enacts strategies for effective social interaction. This robot could be used to ameliorate problematic symptoms of dementia and lessen caregiver burden. To achieve this long-term goal, we first conducted a contextual and qualitative study to discover and understand needs and opportunities to manage problematic behaviors [10]. We found that the main social interaction strategy – to deal with problematic behaviors such as depression, anxiety, and aggression - is to enact a personalized conversation with the residents. Caregivers often use this strategy to calm, distract, and relax the residents. Thus, we envision an autonomous SAR that can enact a conversation customized to the personality and preferences of each PwD.

In this work, we present to Eva, a semi-autonomous conversational agent. We present the requirements that informed the robot design that combines the autonomous features of Eva and a platform that allows a human operator to seamlessly handle disruptions during an interaction. We present results of a preliminary evaluation with the aim to find if the robot is successfully perceived as an autonomous agent and to gather data to inform and improve our prototype.

2   Requirements for a Semi-autonomous Conversational Robot for People with Dementia

A study was conducted to elicit requirements for a semi-autonomous conversational robot for people with dementia. It included interviews with caregivers, observations in a residence for PwD, and results of a study of an intervention with a robotic pet [reference]. We next describe the main requirements.

2.1   Mechanism for Handling Disruptions

Robot and operator should be coordinated to create a seamless interaction with the user. So that the user perceives that it is interacting with one entity. This implies controlling delays of the interventions, avoiding contradictions and avoiding concurrent interventions. Whit this kind of mechanism, we can conduct studies using the Wizard and Oz model - a human-centric method that uses real technology in a real environment [11], to inform new aspects and requirements for our prototype.

2.2   Multimodal Operation of the Robot

We propose the use of voice as the main communication interface with the robot since conversation is a proven strategy to relax and comfort PwD. Furthermore, it is a natural form of interaction that represents little or no challenge to many people who suffer dementia. However, the caregivers should have a quick and smooth way to interrupt an interaction that could trigger a negative response from the PwD. Thus, our solution must allow multimodal interfaces (in addition to the voice) to operate the robot. We propose the use of a mobile or wearable system to use gestures to operate basic features (interrupt interaction, turn on/off microphone).

2.3   Activities to Interact with a Person with Dementia

The Alzheimer's Association has published guidelines for activities aimed at stimulating PwD [12]. Many of these activities are based on verbal communication. These activities include: inviting the person to tell you more when he or she talks about a recent memory; telling jokes; completing famous sayings; listening to favorite music; ask the person about his favorite hobby (or her family, sports hero, favorite pet, cities). Thus, our prototype should implement one or more of these activities to stimulate the PwD during the interaction.

2.4   Behaviors to Get the Attention of the User

Lack of interest in socializing is a common behavior on a PwD. Maintaining the PwD engaged during an interaction is challenging. Thus, our prototype must have diverse strategies to (re)engage a PwD into the interaction. These strategies could include behaviors to catch the interest of the PwD such as movements or expressions of emotion.

3   Eva: A Semi-autonomous Conversational Robot

Eva addresses the requirements discussed above and implements non-pharmacological interventions such as cognitive games and music therapy. Eva is able to recognize natural language to trigger an activity or interaction, also Eva can communicate with the user through speech.

Eva can function autonomously or be controlled by a human operator using a console. The autonomous features refer to those activities when Eva can interpret the user utterance into an intent and trigger an action. The autonomous activities supported by Eva include telling time and date, triggering smalltalk, telling jokes, playing word games, such as completing sayings, and playing songs or videos. A human operator can interrupt or trigger these autonomous features as well as control emotions exhibited by the robot via animated eyes. While our long-term objective is to design a fully autonomous conversational agent, its current semi-autonomous implementation is meant to conduct a formative evaluations with potential users and to elicit new requirements.

3.1   Eva's Architecture

Eva's architecture is embedded in a Raspberry PI board. We used Raspberry PI because it allows to install tools and resources over an operating system; also, it offers a stable way to get/set resources to the cloud. In addition, we employ sensors (microphone) and actuators (speaker, servomotors) connected to the board, and a smartphone to display Eva's eyes (see Fig. 1), to display emotion.

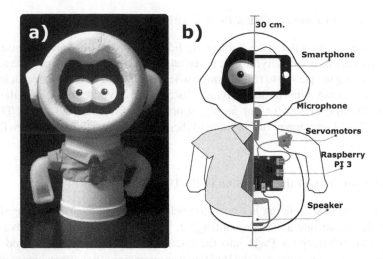

Fig. 1. (a) The robot Eva, (b) Eva's hardware components.

The software components of Eva have been developed using NodeJS,[1] a JavaScript runtime, to manage hardware components and run services to allow remote connections to control robot Eva (see Fig. 2).

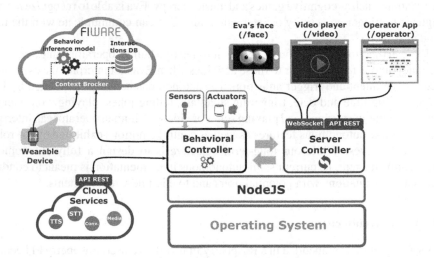

Fig. 2. Architecture of the robot Eva

Eva's architecture has two main components called controllers. The behavioral controller is responsible for managing hardware components. Thus, the behavioral controller processes audio inputs/outputs from the user and motor movements. Moreover, this controller manages requests and responses to the cognitive services (speech

---

[1] https://nodejs.org/.

to text and text to speech), media (music and video) services, and conversational platform. The second controller, called server controller, is responsible for running an HTTP server to allow remote connections. Based on a REST architecture, the server controller implements services to process a request by a remote client (operator app) and generate responses to one or all clients (operator app, face interface, and video interface). The controllers communicate with each other. Thus, if a remote client (operator app) request certain behavior from Eva (personalized utterance, facial expression); the server controller processes the request and communicates to the behavioral controller which manages the HW components and cloud services to trigger a specific behavior from Eva. Furthermore, this communication allows sending information from the behavioral controller to the remote clients via the server controller.

3.2 Behavioral Controller

Hardware components are managed by the behavioral controller. Hence, this controller works at a low-level of the architecture to access the hardware directly. The behavioral controller captures and processes an audio input from the microphone, plays an audio with Eva's response on the speaker, and activates the servomotor to shake Eva's arm. The behavioral controller uses cognitive services from the cloud to implement the main process of Eva - to understand and respond to a certain utterance from the user. Hence, the behavioral controller requests and manages responses from cloud services. We used three cognitive services: Speech-to-Text (STT) powered by Google Cloud Speech API[2], Text-to-Speech (TTS) powered by IBM Watson[3], and a conversational platform powered by API.AI[4]. Besides, the behavioral controller requests to API Google Music to gather information about songs and videos.

Moreover, the behavioral controller can respond to information obtained from a Fiware[5] cloud, were two additional modules reside. First, a behavior inference model which uses raw data gathered from a wearable device used by a user (PwD or operator) to infer the presence of a problematic behavior, such as anxiety, or to detect gestures used by the operator to control Eva. A second module stores all interactions with the robot to build a log of each interaction. All data will be managed by Fiware Context Broker to allocate data to the appropriate module for processing.

3.3 Server Controller

Eva is not fully autonomous. Breakdowns can appear during the interaction; thus, we provide a mechanism to deal with these disruptions to enact a seamless interaction with the user. For this purpose, we implemented a web server on Eva which can allow remote connections to operate Eva's features. Furthermore, the web server is used to share information to complement behavior and features of the robot.

---

[2] https://cloud.google.com/speech/.
[3] https://www.ibm.com/watson/developercloud/text-to-speech.html.
[4] https://api.ai/.
[5] https://www.fiware.org/.

We developed the server controller based on MVC (model, view, controller) model and the REST architecture. Thereby, the server controller runs an HTTP server to allow remote connections from the clients which can request and obtain information from Eva. Three clients with different purposes were developed to enable a connection to the controller server.

Eva's face. If a client access via a web browser Eva's face route (/face), the controller server renders a view whose main feature is to display a 3D animation of Eva's eyes. Based on Three.js[6], this view displays Eva's emotions. Animations for seven emotions (i.e. neutral, thinking, sadness, love, surprise, happiness, and fear) were implemented. The server controller, via a WebSocket, can send a signal to this client to display an animation. Thus, an operator can control the emotions displayed by Eva.

Video player. The robot Eva can display a video on an external screen. If a client accesses the video player route (/video), the server controller renders a video player view. Via a WebSocket, the server controller sends video information (video ID) to the client to play the video via a YouTube page.

Operator app. Our proposal is a mechanism to make an intervention when a disruption appears during the interaction with Eva. Thus, via the web browser, the operator can access the operator app (/operator) to manage and control behaviors and features from Eva. The operator app use front-end technologies (AngularJS[7]) to enable a communication to the server controller - which in turn communicates with the behavioral controller - via a REST API. Using the operator app, the user-operator can enable robot features to enact an Eva behavior. Furthermore, the server controller sends information about actions from Eva.

The operator app (see Fig. 3) includes the following modules to control the robot Eva, and display information about the interaction:

1. **Microphone settings.** The robot operator can enable/disable the microphone. This allows the operator to choose what Eva can "hear".
2. **Disruption alerts.** When the robot Eva does not process an utterance from the user, the server controller communicates to operator app the information of the disruption. Hence, the operator can enact actions to help Eva recover from the disruption and continue the interaction.
3. **Logs panel.** This panel displays the events during the interaction. Autonomous actions by Eva (color blue) such as what it heard, what it said, and what it did. Actions deployed by the operator (color red) such as deployed emotions, personalized speeches, and songs chosen. Finally, interpretation of the input user utterances (color gray).
4. **Personalized utterances.** Using this feature, the operator can send a personalized phrase to the server controller, thus Eva will speak this utterance to the user. Moreover, we defined a set of predefined utterances for Eva; with a mouse-click, the operator can choose and send any of these predefined speeches.
5. **Emotions**. During the interaction, the operator can enable any animation to emulate an emotion in Eva. The operator app sends the information to the server controller,

---

[6] https://threejs.org/.
[7] https://angularjs.org/.

then the server sends a signal to Eva's face client to display the emotion on the smartphone screen.

6. **Trigger the autonomous activities.** The operator can trigger an autonomous activity from Eva. Thus, the operator can initiate smalltalk, a game to complete sayings, or tell jokes.

7. **Media control.** When Eva plays a song or video requested by the user, the operator can pause or stop the resource from the operator app. The operator can combine the music and utterances from Eva to enrich the interaction. Furthermore, the operator can search a specific song, artist or video; and sends the information to the server controller for Eva to play the song.

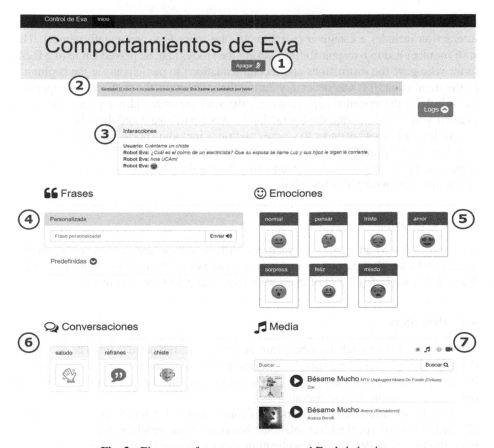

Fig. 3. Elements of operator app to control Eva's behavior.

4 Preliminary Evaluation

While our long-term goal is to enact robot-based interventions to deal with problematic behaviors, as an initial step in this direction, we aim to test the feasibility of this technology being adopted by a PwD.

We conducted a preliminary study to validate our approach - combining the autonomous features of Eva and the platform designed to handle disruptions during the interaction. Our aim was to find if the robot is successfully perceived as an autonomous agent. Besides, we expected to gather data to inform and improve our prototype. For this study, we recruited caregivers from a geriatric residence. We consider that a caregiver has a better understanding of behaviors and needs from a PwD. In such way, the caregiver's perception can give us reliable information about an interaction with the Eva by our target users.

4.1 Setup

For our study, we used a setup in which participants interacted with Eva. The cycle of interaction includes a caregiver (participant), the robot Eva, and a staff member. The staff member had two responsibilities during the study; first, he played a role of a facilitator who gave the instructions and recommendations to participants at the beginning of the interaction; if it was necessary during the interaction, the staff member operated the robot via the operator app. However, the staff member did not participate in an explicit way (speak) during the interaction between participant and the robot.

All interactions were under the same conditions including place, duration, and terms of interaction. Participants interacted with the robot Eva in an office at the geriatric residence where they work. Participants sited facing the robot. All session lasted 5 min. All interactions were video recorded.

4.2 Participants

A sample of $N = 8$ participants was recruited. All participants are caregivers at a geriatric residence located in Ensenada, Mexico. Their age ranged from 21 to 33 years ($M = 28$, $SD = 4.03$), while 5 (62.5%) of them were female and 3 (37.5%) were male.

4.3 Procedure

First, the facilitator (staff member) introduces Eva to the participant. The facilitator explains Eva's features and describes how to trigger each feature. Moreover, the facilitator warns the participant about Eva's limitations, but he does not say anything regarding a possible remote operation.

After being introduced to Eva and her features, the facilitator exposes the long-term aim of Eva - help to deal with problematic behaviors from people with dementia. Moreover, the facilitator describes an application scenario where Eva plays music, tells jokes and engages the user in games, such as completing sayings, to distract a resident who is experiencing anxiety. Finally, the facilitator invites the participant to have an open interaction with Eva during 5 min.

Eva begins and finishes the interaction. Once the interaction has begun, the staff member becomes the robot operator, while sitting out of the field of vision from the participant.

Only when an alert of disruption appears in the operator app, the operator can manage Eva's features to avoid a breakdown in the interaction. But, the operator has the freedom to trigger the emotions in Eva' face - by for example reproducing an expression of happiness in the robot eyes when the participant is laughs.

5 Instruments

Our main aim was to find if robot Eva is successfully perceived as an autonomous agent. Thus, the focus of our study was in measuring the user perception of the social abilities and social presence of the robot. This will help us to obtain information to work on features that increase the users' sense of social presence. For this, we used quantitative and qualitative techniques for data gathering and analysis. Our quantitative analysis, is based on the model proposed by Heerink et al. [13] for the investigation of social abilities and social presence of Eva. The qualitative analyses was based on the observation and open comments made by participants.

6 Quantitative Results

We used four constructs of the model proposed by Heerink et al. Perceived Enjoyment (PENJ), Perceived Ease of Use (PEOU), Perceived Sociability (PS), and Social Presence (SP) were used to assess the social abilities of the robot Eva.

After the interaction session, each participant answered a questionnaire related to these constructs. PENJ, PEOU, and PS constructs were measured by five items, while SP was measured with four items. Participants replied to these statements on a Likert-type scale (I agree ... 1 = not at all/5 = completely).

We calculated Cronbach's alpha to test the construct reliability. A solid construct would have an alpha of Cronbach at least 0.7 [14]. PENJ ($\alpha C = 0.856$), PS ($\alpha C = 0.715$), and SP ($\alpha C = 0.702$) were reliable, while PEOU ($\alpha C = 0.494$) was not reliable (see Table 1). There were no anomalies in data.

Table 1. Descriptive statistics for each construct.

	Min.	Max.	Mean	Std. dev.
Perceived enjoyment (PENJ)	11.00	21.00	17.50	3.51
Perceived ease of use (PEOU)	16.00	24.00	20.50	2.61
Perceived sociability (PS)	12.00	18.00	15.75	2.19
Social presence (SP)	9.00	23.00	15.63	4.50

With these constructs, we were able to test 2 of 7 hypotheses proposed by Heerink et al.

H1. Perceived Enjoyment is influenced by Social Presence.

H2. Social Presence is influenced by Perceived Sociability.

We tested these hypotheses with correlations (strictly explorative) because a regression analysis demands preferably at least 20 participants for each construct [13].

A positive correlation between constructs within the hypotheses could be confirmed using Pearson correlation scores (see Fig. 4). For H1, there was a positive Pearson correlation = 0.55 between PENJ and SP; for H2; there was a positive Pearson correlation = 0.69 between SP and PS.

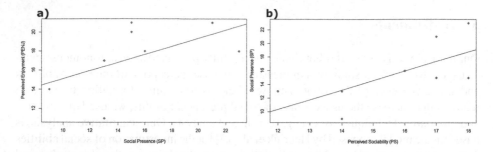

Fig. 4. Correlation diagrams (a) between PENJ and SP; (b) between SP and PS.

These correlations only show that these variables are related, but it does not establish their causality. A regression analysis is an appropriate method to test these hypotheses, but the number of participants was small to do this.

6.1   Qualitative Results

After the quantitative questionnaire, we asked a couple of open questions to the participants: (1) What do you think about Eva? (2) Do you think that Eva can enact an interaction with a PwD?. The transcript of these questions and recorded videos were analyzed by an open coding scheme to identify information and opportunities to improve the design and behavior of Eva.

During the interaction, the facial expression of Eva was controlled by an operator. All the participants had a positive reaction to these emotions. Laughs and positive comments were the most common reactions from participants.

"[Laughs] Eva! What does it mean that face [love]? Do you like this song?" [**P3. P = Participant**].

"Eva, what are you thinking? Why do you move your eyes [thinking]?" [**P8**].

"I like your eyes so much [Laughs]." [**P4**].

That provided evidence that the facial expressions used by Eva created rapport with the users.

Eva's embodiment was a recurrent theme during the study.

"You are a girl, aren't you? then, why are you wearing a shirt and tie? You need a dress or something like that" [**P5**].

"She [Eva] is cute, but her eyes are so big. Those big eyes can be a problem with the residents [elderly people] because they do not like to be looked at directly" [**P7**].

Other participants gave us their opinion about the utterances used by Eva.

"She [Eva] must use more affective terms during the interaction. We [caregivers] use a lot of this kind of words during our interactions with elderly people with dementia" [**P2**].

Two participants gave additional suggestions regarding the strategy of Eva could follow to interact with a PwD.

"Many residents [elderly people with dementia] yell us things like What are you doing here? And why do you look at me? How will Eva manage that behavior?" **[P2]**.

"The interaction is ok. Eva is the main actor in the interaction. But, the main actor should be the person with dementia. I think Eva must listen more and talk less." **[P6]**.

During the study, none of the participants expressed doubts or questions about the autonomy of Eva. Thus, we assume that all participants experience a seamless interaction with Eva. Moreover, we interpret that participants perceived a fully autonomous robot.

7 Conclusions and Future Work

We introduced Eva, a semi-autonomous conversational robot. Our long-term goal is for Eva to enact interventions to assist with problematic behaviors exhibited by PwD. This work represents an initial step to achieve this goal. Combining the autonomous features of Eva and a platform to handle disruptions during an interaction, we conducted a preliminary evaluation with a group of caregivers.

Results from this evaluation show that the robot was perceived as an autonomous agent that could engage in an interaction with fluidity. Furthermore, caregiver's opinion represents opportunities and challenges to improve our prototype. In addition, the evaluation informed the design of our next prototype in the following ways:

Autonomous emotions: Displaying emotions proved important during the interactions with the caregivers. However, an operator triggered this animation in Eva. Thus, we face the challenge of developing an automatic mechanism to trigger emotions.

Features runtime: Searching and playing a song requested by the user takes a few seconds in which the conversation is interrupted. We will address this by having Eva maintain the conversation while it becomes ready to reproduce the song.

Caregivers suggestions: The caregivers interact day-by-day with people with dementia. Hence, we need more information by them. As the short-term aim, we will conduct a focus group to obtain data to inform and improve our prototype.

Acknowledgment. This work was partially supported by grant 723174 (SmartSDK project) from the Horizon 2020 EU program and CONACYT.

References

1. Prince, M., Bryce, R., Albanese, E., Wimo, A., Ribeiro, W., Ferri, C.P.: The global prevalence of dementia: a systematic review and metaanalysis. Alzheimers Dement. **9**, 63–75.e2 (2013)
2. Ferri, C.P., Prince, M., Brayne, C., Brodaty, H., Fratiglioni, L., Ganguli, M., Hall, K., Hasegawa, K., Hendrie, H., Huang, Y., Jorm, A., Mathers, C., Menezes, P.R., Rimmer, E., Scazufca, M.: Alzheimer's disease international: global prevalence of dementia: a Delphi consensus study. Lancet **366**, 2112–2117 (2005)
3. Sadowsky, C.H., Galvin, J.E.: Guidelines for the management of cognitive and behavioral problems in dementia. J. Am. Board. Fam. Med. **25**, 350–366 (2012)

4. Ory, M.G., Hoffman, R.R., Yee, J.L., Tennstedt, S., Schulz, R.: Prevalence and impact of caregiving: a detailed comparison between dementia and nondementia caregivers. Gerontologist. **39**, 177–185 (1999)
5. Shibata, T.: An overview of human interactive robots for psychological enrichment. Proc. IEEE **92**, 1749–1758 (2004)
6. Shibata, T.: Therapeutic seal robot as biofeedback medical device: qualitative and quantitative evaluations of robot therapy in dementia care. Proc. IEEE **100**, 2527–2538 (2012)
7. Rudzicz, F., Wang, R., Begum, M., Mihailidis, A.: Speech interaction with personal assistive robots supporting aging at home for individuals with Alzheimer's disease. ACM Trans. Access. Comput. **7**, 1–22 (2015)
8. McColl, D., Louie, W.Y.G., Nejat, G.: Brian 2.1: a socially assistive robot for the elderly and cognitively impaired. IEEE Robot. Autom. Mag. **20**, 74–83 (2013)
9. Nestorov, N., Stone, E., Lehane, P., Eibrand, R.: Aspects of socially assistive robots design for dementia care. In: Proceedings - IEEE Symposium on Computer-Based Medical Systems. pp. 396–400. IEEE (2014)
10. Cruz-Sandoval, D., Favela, J.: Human-robot interaction to deal with problematic behaviors from people with dementia. In: Proceedings of the 10th EAI International Conference on Pervasive Computing Technologies for Healthcare. ACM (2016)
11. Steinfeld, A., Jenkins, O.C., Scassellati, B.: The oz of wizard. In: Proceedings of the 4th ACM/IEEE International Conference on Human Robot Interaction - (HRI 2009), p. 101. ACM Press, New York (2009)
12. Alzheimer's Association: Living with alzheimers: 101 Activities. http://www.alz.org/living_with_alzheimers_101_activities.asp
13. Heerink, M., Krose, B., Evers, V., Wielinga, B.: Measuring acceptance of an assistive social robot: a suggested toolkit. In: RO-MAN 2009 - The 18th IEEE International Symposium on Robot and Human Interactive Communication, pp. 528–533. IEEE (2009)
14. Nunnaly, J.C., Bernstein, I.H.: Psychometric Theory. McGraw-Hill, New York (1978)

Multiplatform Career Guidance System Using IBM Watson, Google Home and Telegram

A User Experience and Usability Evaluation

Daniel Calvo[1,2(✉)], Luis Quesada[1], Gustavo López[1],
and Luis A. Guerrero[1]

[1] University of Costa Rica, San José, Costa Rica
{daniel.calvomarin, luis.quesada, gustavo.lopez_h,
guerreroblanco}@ucr.ac.cr
[2] Samtec Smart Platform Group, New Albany, IN, USA

Abstract. Even with the availability of several tests to provide clarity in choosing our career path, the decision remains a tough one to undertake. Most of the available tests are either monotonous, resulting in a tedious effort to go through them entirely, or are just plain boring. In this paper, however, we present a new and different approach to career guidance systems. We use Google home as a speech-based interface and Telegram as a text-based interface to generate a conversation between the users and a bot for career guidance. The idea is to provide an easy and friendly interface with an interactive user experience while gathering the required data to provide career guidance. To evaluate the system, we used the University of Costa Rica's Computer Science and Informatics Department scenario. In this scenario, students must decide between three possible emphases: Software Engineering, Information Technologies, and Computer Science. A usability and user experience evaluation of the system was performed with the participation of 72 freshmen.

Keywords: Career guidance · IBM Watson · Personality traits · Google home · Conversational interface · Telegram

1 Introduction

Career guidance is a complex task that has a high impact on the life of people undergoing a career selection process. Career guidance includes informing, advising, assessing characteristics, teaching to enable, networking, managing, mentoring and interviewing to extract information about a person [1]. Moreover, career guidance is a process that requires the involvement of multiple people and can't be effectively carried out by a single guidance practitioner [2].

For many years, companies and researchers have developed career guidance tools based mostly on online surveys or traditional computer-based interfaces. These tools, however, are usually used for self-assessment and are an add-on to the much bigger process of career guidance.

© Springer International Publishing AG 2017
S.F. Ochoa et al. (Eds.): UCAmI 2017, LNCS 10586, pp. 689–700, 2017.
DOI: 10.1007/978-3-319-67585-5_67

In this paper, we present a career guidance system, focused on the IT domain (i.e., helps to select between software engineering (SE), computer science (CS), and information technologies (IT) management), which uses Google Home and Telegram to extract information from the user to create an assay and with it perform an analytical comparison of personalities using IBM Watson personality models.

The focus of this research emerged due to the separation of the CS career at the University of Costa Rica (UCR) into three different emphases. In order to test our career guidance system, we used three profiles based on those three academic emphases.

The system was built using model driven development and API.AI, a development tool that allows creating natural language conversations and provides a processing engine to easy the creation of the dialogues [3].

The system user experience was evaluated with the help of seventy-two incoming Computer Science students and the results were promising.

This document is structured as follows: Sect. 2 shows related work, Sect. 3 describes the proposed systems, Sect. 4 explains how the system works, Sect. 5 describes the evaluation and the results, and Sect. 6 includes conclusions and future work.

2 Related Work

Different technological approaches have been explored to support the career guidance process. This section describes some of those efforts.

Games are an interesting way to engage and extract information from people starting their studies [4–6].

In their work, Shi and Shih [4] use a current version of the Holland Codes [7] to define career paths. Their game is based on interactive fiction and simulation. The goal of the game is for users to understand the occupational characteristics and difficulties to provide a comprehensive understanding and ultimately help them improve their career decisions.

Dunwell et al. propose a similar approach in [5] that consists of a serious game with elements that promote professional development, decision making and understanding the dynamic nature of the job market. Authors, however, do not describe the theory used for the development of the tool.

Waypass, proposed by Garcia et al. [6], uses a different approach to gaming. It provides an experience using scenarios and storytelling to motivate users. Their proposal is based on the self-determination theory [8] and uses concepts such as auto-discovery, inspiration, transformation, and exploration to guide the user through the career selection path.

Other, simpler approaches have also been implemented, for instance [9] proposes L4All, a system that aims to support the exploration of experiences, so to reflect on them while making decisions. It uses different categories including educational, occupational and personal. The goal of this system is to find the qualifications of an individual in a domain of expertise to determine if it fits the user.

Other systems are more focused on the career guidance method than the user experience method, which involves the overall usability of the system. For instance, [10, 11] delve in how to use big data tools and fuzzy logic to facilitate goal alignment and generate career path recommendations.

Other works, such as [12], focus on comparisons of performance over classification algorithms applied to vocational orientation (i.e., focused on the machine learning part of the problem). Moreover, clustering algorithms have been applied to classify students based on the likeliness of their profile with other students that already picked a career [13]. Expert systems have also been developed for vocational decisions [14].

Similar works, to the one presented in this paper have also been performed. For instance [15] presents a computational platform that makes psychometric questions for about 40 min, and then generates an analysis that is sent as a report to the student through email. The report includes personality analysis, aptitudes, skills, motivations, and preferences. The authors describe that this analysis is made through an artificial intelligence engine capable of getting conclusions as a professional would.

Our approach differs to the projects presented in this section by two main characteristics. The first one is that our development is based on natural user interfaces using a chat-like communication or conversation (speech). The second one is that the evaluation is focused on usability and user experience rather than the technical part of the issue. This approach is based on engaging the young participants and determining their satisfaction levels while using the system.

3   System Overview

This section describes the system, its component, and technologies applied to it. This includes the user interface, the proxy service (API.AI) used for communication and dialogue computation, and the personality evaluator (IBM Watson). Figure 1 shows a graphical system overview including all these components.

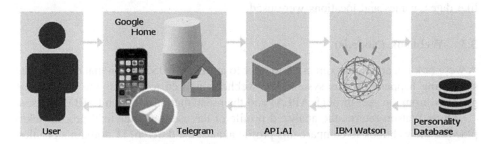

Fig. 1. System architecture and software used

3.1   User Interfaces

The idea behind this project was to create a natural and intuitive way to conduct a conversation that would allow the extraction of an assay, which could be compared with others stored in our database. To achieve that, we built natural interactions, simulating a human conversation using Google Home (speech interface) and Telegram (text interface). Telegram was used in a chat-like format.

Google Home

Google Home is a voice activated speaker manufactured and commercialized by Google [16]. It runs a version of Google Assistant, an intelligent personal assistant designed to allow conversational usage [17]. Google Assistant uses a natural language user interface to answer questions, make recommendations, and perform actions by delegating requests to a set of services. Moreover, it delivers information to users predicting their requirements.

Some of the promotional commands for Google Assistant include: "Ok Google, Remind me to pick up a birthday card", "Ok Google, Book me a table for 6 at Quartino for 8:30", "Ok Google, Who invented sushi?" [17].

In this project, Google Home is used to interact using voice with the user. A set of questions are asked and the results computed and transcribed to be processed.

Telegram

Telegram is an instant messaging service that allows users to exchange texts, photos, videos, stickers, audios, and files. Telegram has developed clients for mobile devices and other operative systems in traditional PCs [18]. The reason to use Telegram is because it allows third-party developers to create bots. These bots can perform different activities, such as simulating a conversation. In this project, a bot is used to simulate a conversation with the user and asked the required information to perform a personality analysis.

3.2 Natural Language Interface (API.AI)

In this project, API.AI was used to develop a bot that generates the dialog using natural language, which is deployed in both Google Home and Telegram. API.AI is capable of recognizing entities and intents inside a text and transform it into actionable data [3].

A set of 18 intents were added to the career guider agent. Recognition of entities like dates, names and locations were used.

3.3 Webhook (Node.js)

A webhook is a common expression to refer to an HTTP POST action that occurs when something happens. In this system, the webhook is used to process the information gathered from the user through API.AI and then send that information to IBM Watson.

Once Watson returns the analyzed profile of the user, an analytical process takes place in the webhook to compare this profile against the different IT domain's profiles. This in turn, defines the most similar profile between a user and an IT domain.

3.4 Fulfillment Service (IBM Watson Personality Models)

The core of this system is the personality model provided by IBM Watson [19]. Watson is an artificial intelligence system capable of several functions such as processing data in natural language or performing recognition patterns, with many more uses. In this project, we are using the Personality Insights provided by Watson.

Each time a user interacts with the bot, it transcribes the conversation into text that is then compiled at the end of the session. Later, the gathered text is sent to IBM Watson to execute the personality analysis. In total fifty-two traits of a personality are retrieved by Watson Personality Insights service.

3.5 Personality Database

The records of this database are in the form of summarized outputs of the Watson personality analysis. Ten profiles of each IT domain under study were gathered from the internet, and the personality evaluation was performed using the about me section in their professional blogs. For each domain, the fifty-two traits of each profile were summarized along with their partners inside the domain to generate a representative profile.

4   System Functionality and Performed Analysis

This section describes the performed analysis and explains how the system works when the components are assembled.

4.1   Providing Career Guidance

As it was described before, the system is available in two platforms: speech-based (using Google Home) and text-based (using Telegram).

To offer a personalized and good user experience, the bot asks the users for their name and a brief introduction about themselves. The dialog consists of a set of open-ended questions made by the bot.

The idea behind the dialog is to encourage the user to provide information with relatively long answers (i.e., avoiding yes/no answers).

The bot can recognize the contexts of the conversation and handle the dialog accordingly. Once all the questions are answered, the analysis is performed and the results are shown.

The result is a description of the user's personality and a recommendation of the domain that would best suit the user according to their personality. An output example is:

> *Daniel, your profile analysis is ready. According to my professional lecture of yourself, the career path that I advise you is: **Computer Science**.*
>
> *This is your profile summary: You are shrewd. You are energetic: you enjoy a fast-paced, busy schedule with many activities. You are philosophical: you are open and intrigued by new ideas and love exploring them. You are authority-challenging: you prefer to challenge authority and traditional values to help bring about positive changes.*
>
> *Your choices are driven by a desire for discovery. You are relatively unconcerned with both tradition and taking pleasure in life. You care more about making your own path than following what others have done. And you prefer activities with a purpose greater than just personal enjoyment.*

4.2   Performed Analysis

This section describes the IT domains profiles, characteristics and how users' personality was analyzed to propose a recommendation.

Computer Science and Informatics School Career Paths Personality Traits
A general overview of the big five personality traits for each IT domain is shown in Table 1. On the other hand, Table 2 details which are the most different traits of each IT domain.

Table 1. IT Domain profiles with the five main personality traits' percentile values.

Personality trait	Software Engineering	Computer Science	Information Technologies
Openness	87.1%	79.5%	90.3%
Conscientiousness	50.9%	54.0%	49.8%
Extraversion	30.7%	15.5%	44.1%
Agreeableness	8.8%	6.8%	7.6%
Emotional range	61.1%	65.0%	66.3%

Table 2. Most different traits between IT domains. Computer Science as CS, Information Technologies as IT and Software Engineering as SE.

Personality trait	Domain	Direction	Detail
Practicality	CS	Less	Have a desire to get the job done, a desire for skill and efficiency, which can include physical expression and experience
Liberty	CS	Less	Have a desire for fashion and new things, as well as the need for an escape
Altruism	IT	Most	Find that helping others is genuinely rewarding, that doing things for others is a form of self-fulfillment rather than self-sacrifice
Openness to change	CS	Less	Emphasize independent action, thought, and feeling, as well as a readiness for new experiences
Challenge	SE	Less	Have an urge to achieve, to succeed, and to take on challenges

According to the analysis and summary performed by Watson over our personality database, we have concluded that computer scientists are on average skeptical and inner-directed. On the other hand, software engineers represent a shrewd and inner-directed profile. Finally, the information technologists showed to have a shrewd profile.

For Watson, our mean found was that the computer scientist is independent, the software engineer is trusting of others and the information technologist is energetic.

A common quality of all the profiles is to be authority-challenging and philosophical. Also for Watson, all the profiles tend to be unconcerned with both taking pleasure in life or tradition, they prefer to make their own path rather than follow what others have done.

Analyzing Users' Personality

One could say that any user could use Watson tools to get their profile analysis and make a comparison between his profile and other profiles. To make an objective comparison, however, we decided to use the Euclidean distance to find the nearest profile in a multidimensional space. Equation 1 shows how this distance is calculated [20].

$$(p,q) = d(q,p) = \sqrt{\sum_{i=1}^{n} (q_i - p_i)^2} \tag{1}$$

The distance between the user profile p and every profile q is calculated. At the end, the nearest profile is selected and showed as the system's recommendation.

By using this method, we are getting a pseudo-ranking of recommendations, something that is useful if we would like to extend this system to a broader scope.

5 Evaluation

The evaluation of this project is focused on the user experience. Even though the career paths are very important, several studies have delved into this topic, therefore, we will focus on the usability and overall user experience.

5.1 Procedure

Seventy-two freshmen of the CS School at UCR tested the application. As they represent the real target of the application, their assessment of the user experience is the closest to the real perception users will have.

At the evaluation moment, Google Home only supported English. To test both experiences we asked English spoken students to test the Google Home bot. The rest of the students tested the bot trough the messaging app. The length of the interaction between the students and the bot was on average less than 12 min. Once the interaction ended, the students filled an evaluation of usability and user experience survey.

The main source of questions for the survey used in this work is the System Usability Scale [21]. The survey included the following questions:

Close-ended questions
- I think that I would like to use this system frequently
- I found the system unnecessarily complex
- I thought the system was easy to use
- I think that I would need the support of a technical person to be able to use this system
- I found the various functions in this system were well integrated
- I thought there was too much inconsistency in this system
- I would imagine that most people would learn to use this system very quickly
- I found the system very cumbersome to use
- I felt very confident using the system
- I needed to learn a lot of things before I could get going with this system

- I felt the system is exciting
- I felt the system is innovative
- I felt the system is motivating
- I felt the system is attractive
- I would recommend the usage of this system to my friends

Open-ended questions
- What is the main goal of the system?
- What do you like least about the system?
- What do you like the most about the system?

Describe the system with 3 words
In a range from 1 to 10, how do you evaluate the system?
What career path you want to follow?
What career path did the system recommend you?

6   Results

This section presents the results of the evaluation performed. The results include responses to the System Usability Scale questionnaire and the rest of the questions asked. One of the main question asked was: What is the main goal of the system? No information regarding this was provided before the evaluation. Figure 2 shows the main results for this question.

In Fig. 2, the response with more support by the participants was to support a career choice, we believe that this response is associated with a guide more than a recommendation. The second response was to define the career path, we interpret this as a recommendation (i.e., the system decides for the user). The third response in significance was to analyze user personality. Other responses in less significance were combined into one category. They included: to gather information, to help in complex tasks, to talk, and to get a conclusion for a future decision.

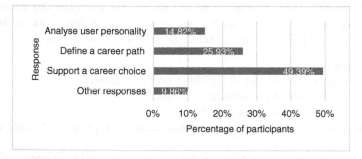

Fig. 2. Responses of participants to the question: What is the main goal of the system?

The responses to the System Usability Scale questionnaire were overall positive. Participants strongly agreed with the easy to use system and they also commented that it was easy to learn. Even though the participants agreed that the system is not complex

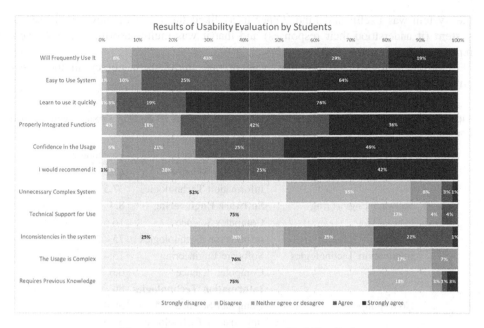

Fig. 3. Responses to the System Usability Scale.

and does not require any previous knowledge, it still, however, was found to have some inconsistencies during the sessions. Figure 3 shows the results of this part of the survey.

Another question was: What do you like least about the system? The main response here was that participants did not like the personality analysis (27.78% of the respondents).

The top usability issue reported by 9.72% of the respondents was that the speech-based system cut their voice when they were talking. Other users (6.94%) only reported that the system had bugs.

Focused on the conversation and the main goal of the system, 9.72% did not like the questions asked by the bot. Another group of users (2.78%) did not like that the system required long answers, and 4.78% did not like the extension of the session.

Some other issues reported by the participants include: the system changed the context of the questions, the analysis of the responses was inadequate, the system was monotonous, and the system was too formal. Moreover, they did not like that they weren't allowed to extend their responses once the question was asked and the first response was given. All these issues correspond to 38.28% of the respondents.

In contrast to the 'What do you like least about the system question,' we also asked, what do you like the most about the system? The top answers to this question included: easy to use (20%), questions from the tutor (15%), the interface (12.5%), the naturality (10%), and that the system was intuitive (4%).

Other participants responded that they liked the fast response, the results and that the system was coherent. They also liked that the interaction was in real time and that the system was useful and kind. Other users liked the fact that they could use the system (it understood their responses) and that it was multiplatform. These answers represent 38.5% of the total responses.

Even though this was not the focus of this study, the accuracy in the career guidance is depicted in Table 3.

Table 3. System accuracy results based on students desired IT domain versus recommended domain.

Student's personal preference	Proposed emphasis	Percentage
Computer Science	**Computer Science**	**62.5**
	Information Technologies	37.5
Software Engineering	**Software Engineering**	**8.4**
	Computer Science	16.6
	Information Technologies	75
Information Technologies	Software Engineering	13.4
	Computer Science	6.6
	Information Technologies	**80**
No response	Computer Science	36.4
	Information Technologies	63.6

The total accuracy was 40%. The specific accuracy for IT is 92.3%, for CS is 62.5%, and for SE 8.33%.

Results show that 58.82% of the time, IT path was recommended, CS was recommended 20.59% and SE just 5.88%. More detail is provided on this in the conclusions section.

7 Conclusion and Future Work

The undergraduate CS curriculum at UCR offers three career paths. We developed a career path advisor using tools provided by Watson. In addition, we evaluated a speech-based version using Google Home and a text-based version using Telegram. The evaluation was focused on user experience.

The results allowed us to conclude that the system is usable and generates a good user experience. From our point of view, this tool will help users to get more engaged in the process of choosing a career path. Moreover, the students were comfortable interacting with the system. Most of them agreed or strongly agreed to recommend it. The participants were also able to correctly identify the system's purpose.

One of the most disliked attributes of the system was the extent of the conversation, as the users perceived it as a long process. This attribute is not directly related to the system usability. Therefore, the interaction between CS students and bots (based on speech or text) supported by artificial intelligence provides a satisfying experience.

The students chatted naturally using both interfaces. Eighty-nine percent of the students agreed and strongly agreed about how easy was to use the system. Ninety-five percent learned to use it quickly. This experience should inspire the exploration of novel means of interaction between people and systems.

Furthermore, our system uses a personality database component to perform a profile analysis using Watson. Although the personality database was not directly assessed, the results were accepted by the students (only 27.78% of the participants expressed that they did not like the personality analysis). The personality database could be enhanced to get more accurate profiles.

Data concerning the accuracy of the system was taken although it was out of the scope of this study; It was done to have a base for future work. A 36.1% of accuracy is not at all satisfactory. Moreover, based on data there could exist a bias of the system to select Information Technologies path.

Given the characteristics of the information, we conclude that the SE profile had some issues, hence was not recommended properly.

In the future, we would like to test different decision backends to improve the performance of our current profile matcher. Moreover, a longitudinal study could be conducted to learn about how the career path recommendation varies over time.

As a reference to future work, a combination of these new interfaces and traditional mechanisms for career guidance could be evaluated to determine if a more natural interface affects the results of automatic career guidance systems.

Since the division of the CS emphases has taken place only this year, it is a premature problem. We would like to gather data related to the decisions made by students that participated in the test, to know the proper metrics required to measure the performance of career path recommendation systems directed to CS School students at the UCR.

Acknowledgment. This work was partially supported by Centro de Investigaciones en Tecnologías de la Información y Comunicación (CITIC), Escuela de Ciencias de la Computación e Informática (ECCI) both at Universidad de Costa Rica. Grants No. 834-B6-178, PID-CI-1233-2016 and 326-B6-357, and by Samtec Smart Platform Group.

References

1. Ford, G.: Guidance for Adults: Harnessing Partnership Potential. Careers Research and Advisory Centre, Cambridge (2001)
2. Haug, E.H., Plant, P.: Research-based knowledge: researchers' contribution to evidence-based practice and policy making in career guidance. Int. J. Educ. Vocat. Guidance **16**, 137–152 (2016)
3. API.AI. API.AI. https://api.ai/
4. Shi, Y.-R., Shih, J.-L.: Game-based career guidance systems design concept. In: 2012 IEEE Fourth International Conference on Digital Game and Intelligent Toy Enhanced Learning, pp. 187–191 (2012)
5. Dunwell, I., et al.: MeTycoon: a game-based approach to career guidance. In: 2013 5th International Conference on Games and Virtual Worlds for Serious Applications (VS-GAMES), pp. 1–6 (2013)

6. Garcia, O., Serra, J., Membrives, J., Juarez, J.J.: Waypass: a gamified self-knowledge quest for teenagers. In: 2016 8th International Conference on Games and Virtual Worlds for Serious Applications (VS-GAMES), pp. 1–4 (2016)
7. Nauta, M.M.: The development, evolution, and status of Hollands theory of vocational personalities: reflections and future directions for counseling psychology. J. Couns. Psychol. **57**, 11–22 (2010)
8. Ryan, R.M., Deci, E.L.: Self-determination theory and the facilitation of intrinsic motivation, social development, and well-being. Am. Psychol. **55**, 68–78 (2000)
9. Poulovassilis, A., Selmer, P., Wood, P.T.: Flexible querying of lifelong learner metadata. IEEE Trans. Learn. Technol. **5**, 117–129 (2012)
10. Cazier, J.A., Green, J.A.: Life coach: using big data and analytics to facilitate the attainment of life goals. In: 2016 49th Hawaii International Conference on System Sciences (HICSS), pp. 1000–1008 (2016)
11. Razak, T.R., Hashim, M.A., Noor, N.M., Halim, I.H.A., Shamsul, F.F.S.: Career path recommendation system for UiTM Perlis students using fuzzy logic. In: 2014 5th International Conference on Intelligent and Advanced Systems (ICIAS), pp. 1–5 (2014)
12. Bulbul, H.I., Unsal, Ö.: Comparison of classification techniques used in machine learning as applied on vocational guidance data. In: 2011 10th International Conference on Machine Learning and Applications and Workshops, vol. 2, pp. 298–301 (2011)
13. Haji, E.E., Mani, A.A., Harzli, M.E.: A pairing individual-trades system, using KNN method: the educational and vocational guidance as a case study. In: 2014 Third IEEE International Colloquium in Information Science and Technology (CIST), pp. 74–79 (2014)
14. El Haji, E., Azmani, A., El Harzli, M.: Expert system design for educational and vocational guidance, using a multi-agent system. In: 2014 International Conference on Multimedia Computing and Systems (ICMCS), pp. 1018–1024 (2014)
15. Yannakoudakis, H., Yannakoudakis, E.J.: The architecture of the ARISTON expert system for vocational counselling. In: 2015 International Conference on Industrial Engineering and Operations Management (IEOM), pp. 1–6 (2015)
16. Google: Google Home. Home by you. Help by Google (2017)
17. Google: Google Assistant (2017)
18. Telegram: Telegram: a new era of messaging (2017)
19. IBM: Do your best work with Watson (2017)
20. Deza, E., Deza, M.M.: Encyclopedia of Distances. Springer, Berlin (2009)
21. Brooke, J.: Usability Evaluation in Industry. CRC Press, Boca Raton (1996)

Sustainability

GreenSoul: An IoT Platform for Empowering Users' Energy Efficiency in Public Buildings

Diego Casado-Mansilla[1]([✉]), I. Moschos[3], Oihane Kamara-Esteban[2], A. Tsolakis[3], Cruz E. Borges[2], S. Krinidis[3], Diego López-de-Ipiña[1], and D. Tzovaras[3]

[1] DeustoTech INTERNET, University of Deusto, 48007 Bilbao, Spain
{dcasado,dipina}@deusto.es

[2] DeustoTech ENERGY, Fundación Deusto, University of Deusto, 48007 Bilbao, Spain
{oihane.esteban,cruz.borges}@deusto.es

[3] IT Institute CERTH, Center of Research & Technology Hellas, Thermi, Thessaloniki, Greece
{imoschos,tsolakis,krinidis,dimitrios.tzovaras}@iti.gr

Abstract. The GreenSoul (GS) framework aims to provide a low-cost energy-efficient Information and Communications Technology (ICT) platform which seamlessly augments a traditional public-use building with a set of assets (apps, interactive interfaces, device adaptors, smart meters and a Decision Support Engine), which mediate in the interactions of users with their environments and the energy consuming devices or systems present in them. GreenSoul envisions public use buildings as ecosystems of GreenSoul-ed devices which cooperate with other devices, standard Smart Meters and, very importantly, with eco-educated and eco-aware users to minimize the unnecessary energy consumption. GS architecture is supported by a socio-economic behavioural model, which aids on behaviour understanding to turn energy consuming devices into active pro-sustainability agents that manifest to their surrounding users how well or badly they are being manipulated (energy-wise), offer tips about how to use them more efficiently and even adapt their own functioning to avoid energy waste.

Keywords: IoT framework · Sustainability · Energy-efficiency · Internet-of-things · Edge computing · Semantic interoperability

1 Introduction

On 25th October 2012, the EU adopted the Directive 2012/27/EU on energy efficiency (known as the Energy Efficiency Directive [1]), a significant milestone in promoting EU energy efficiency objectives. Specifically, the EU 20-20-20 by 2020 energy target commands *(a)* a reduction of the greenhouse gas emissions by 20% compared to 1990, *(b)* to increase the share of renewable energy sources in energy consumption to 20% and *(c)* a 20% increase in energy efficiency. On 2016, the Commission proposed an update including a new 30% energy efficiency target for 2030.

© Springer International Publishing AG 2017
S.F. Ochoa et al. (Eds.): UCAmI 2017, LNCS 10586, pp. 703–714, 2017.
DOI: 10.1007/978-3-319-67585-5_68

The GreenSoul (GS) project[1] aims to surpass the objectives of energy efficiency targets imposed from the EU with an ICT platform empowered by a novel socio-economic and behavioural model. This model aims at guiding and aiding more eco-aware practices on people, devices and buildings. Specifically, the key contribution of GreenSoul will be to transform both the energy consumption practices of workers of public buildings and the operation mode of the energy consuming devices that they interact with (e.g. coffee-makers, PCs, printers, etc.) at their working environments. GS's view is that it is possible to surpass EU targets providing a true technological collaboration among people (employees), devices of private and collective use and buildings.

The need for this multi-level and collaborative approach is two-fold. On the one side, it lays on the growing issue of misusing energy consuming devices and systems in buildings, as one of the main sources of unnecessary energy consumption. Notably, they account for 40% of energy end-use in the EU [2] and making them more efficient is, therefore, paramount. On the other side, households have already been targeted success-fully either by the academia and public administrations. However, public buildings or buildings of public use still demand more attention. In this scenario, the overall goal of this work is to present the conceptual architecture of the GS platform.

2 Related Work

Many factors influence consumer behaviour and practices. Technological developments, considerations of the general economic situation, age, social norms, belief systems and cultural traits, marketing strategies: all play an important role in defining what we consider a normal way of life. On the one hand, a recent research suggests that consumer preferences change over time [5], and consequently the focus should shift from the consumer behaviour *per se* (which tends to imply emphasis on individual or group pref-erences) to how different consumption practices take hold in the society. On the other hand, there are different ways to deliver feedback and expect an appropriate reaction to them as reviewed in [6] and meta-analysed in [7, 8]. However, the key lies in combining different measures to achieve substantial energy savings up to 20% [15].

Research on energy efficiency points to the fact that the link between measures, i.e. a wider deployment of Smart Meters, and behaviour analytics is crucially important because there is evidence to suggest that technical interventions alone have lower impact and are more cost-ineffective if carried out in isolation, i.e. without any accompanying program designed to encourage behaviour change [6]. In this context, research into behavioural change [9] aims to identify the educational, social, psychological and economic drivers underlying energy consumption patterns, and to define and evaluate measures – such as policy initiatives and incentive systems – that may influence those patterns in desired ways. With regards to public buildings, an additional problem is that their tenants, employees or visitors do not have the same awareness and motivations regarding energy consumption as they may have in their homes. Workers are usually unaware of the actual electricity bill of their organisation and about how their often

---

[1] http://www.greensoul-h2020.eu.

unconscious misuse of appliances is contributing towards increasing energy consumption and thus CO_2 emissions. Indeed, a report surveying the buildings sector across nine countries [10] recognised the role of occupant behaviour as having 'as much impact on energy consumption as the efficiency of equipment'.

GS resembles some previously reported architectures which follow the edge computing paradigm [16] and feature similar aspects as the GS framework [3, 4].

3 GreenSoul Solution Architecture

The architecture proposed for this project is divided into three layers according to its physical deployment as can be observed in Fig. 1: (1) *Device Layer*; (2) *Building Layer*; and (3) *Cloud Layer*. Each of these layers and the components and modules behind them are described in this section. The communication interfaces, protocols and databases selected, and interdependencies among the devised GS architecture components are also detailed. An overview of the GS components is listed below.

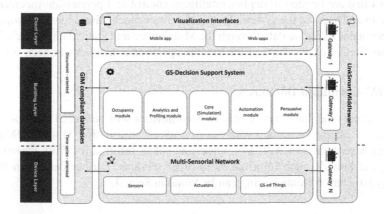

Fig. 1. GreenSoul Reference Architecture

3.1 Multi-sensorial Network

Various sensors are installed inside the building premises and monitor raw data regarding current building operation (e.g. energy consumption or occupancy). Dedicated Device Managers (software) collect and pre-process these data and transforms them in GIM-compliant event messages. This information is spread to the upper layers of GS architecture through the Middleware. Actuators are also utilized in order to facilitate load control mechanisms within pilot buildings, when such actions are necessary.

Additional components are the GS-ed Things and GS adaptors which are described in Sect. 5. These are new electronic devices developed in the context of the GreenSoul attach-able to appliances or electrical equipment of collective use at pilot's buildings (e.g. printers, coffee-makers, outlets or power strips). The purpose of such adaptors is to optimise usage of the mentioned appliances and electrical equipment.

3.2 Middleware

The interoperability needs, derived mostly from the variety of sensors, actuators and software systems installed, are tackled in the GreenSoul architecture by a well-known Internet of Things (IoT) middleware called LinkSmart[2] (right side of Fig. 1). Its main function is to facilitate seamless integration of GS-ed devices and legacy sensors infrastructure with GS software applications. LinkSmart includes a Device Manager component that provides the capabilities for heterogeneous devices virtualization through a common interface, for easier access to the lower Device Layer, independently of the technology used. Besides, through the Event Manager component, it provides a publish/subscribe service, for enabling events-based communication, i.e. enabling publishing and distribution to those components which have subscribed to receive them.

3.3 Decision Support System

The GreenSoul Decision Support Engine includes the set of instructions and algorithmic processes that are needed to deploy intelligent control and persuasion mechanisms to the devices and users in the system. In order for these mechanisms to work properly, the GS DSS obtains dynamic data through the Middleware and static data through the GIM Database. Further explanation of the module operation is available at Sect. 6.1.

3.4 GIM-Compliant Databases

Static and real-time information from GS-ed devices will be stored in non-relational databases which are compliant with the GreenSoul Information Model (GIM). These databases have their own APIs to connect and gather information from various GS-ed devices and provide such information to other services. Further details on the GIM ontology structure for data storing can be found in Sect. 4.

3.5 Visualization Interfaces

The components of the Cloud layer provide enriched graphical representation of energy-related data both in terms of individual and group-based device use, as well as a distribution channel for the persuasion messages from GreenSoul solution. Access to such information will be provided through all web-enabled devices (PC's, tablets, smartphones etc.). Energy-consumption data captured, stored and processed, per device and user, is accessible from these interfaces towards providing a user-friendly portal to analyse and display required information for educational and informative purposes, on devices that are being accessed daily in conformity with agreed behavioural change and modification processes and protocols in buildings where GreenSoul is deployed.

---

[2] http://www.linksmart.eu/.

4 GIM Information Modelling and Information Collection

A common information model is essential when interconnection between heterogeneous resources is required. GIM introduces a shared vocabulary of well-defined entities, attributes and objects that provide interoperability through different information sharing protocols and make information in-between various GS components easily accessible. Both static and dynamic data are translated and presented in an understandable and uniform way, so as to be used from all GS components.

Static information includes constant contextual data that have been modelled in a GIM compliant manner to describe elements such as the building architectural map, devices location, sensors and so on. Furthermore, dynamic aspects related to the building are also included, containing among others, energy consumption, indoor environmental information, occupancy, and users' interactions with the building's assets. All that information is supported by a hybrid storage repository within the GIM by employing both InfluxDB and MongoDB for handling time-dependent information and large amounts of static and historical events (document-dependent) respectively.

Access to such data under a robust and unobtrusive, yet fast and complete manner is achieved through a RESTful-based application programming interface (API) that allows through a series of services over HTTP to insert, updated, delete and retrieve stored knowledge.

The definition of GIM has been produced in the form of XML schemas [11], which is one of the most widely-used formats for sharing structured information. More specifically, it provides a globally acceptable language for transmission of energy-related information. Another advantage is that semantics stemming from XML schemas can be easily translated in various ontologies (i.e. RDF/XML) through simple XSL transformations. The high level architecture of GIM is depicted in Fig. 2.

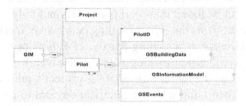

Fig. 2. High-level GIM schema

The two core elements of this architecture are the *GSInformationModel* entity and the *Event* entity, both described in Fig. 3. The former includes objects related to static information such as the building systems, sensors, devices, users, persuasion strategies, settings, etc. The latter, specifies objects regarding dynamic information, such as sensors' obtained measurements, updated evaluated data, selection of an optimised persuasive strategy for certain groups of workers and so on.

Fig. 3. GIM: Information model and event entities

GIM modelling was conceived having in mind the interoperability. This is the reason why open and well-known standards were included to cover several components of the final GS Data model. Specifically, parts of gbXML[3] are utilized to facilitate the building shell modelling (construction/material/windows etc.) and environmental context elements (weather, campus structure around the building etc.). Also, obXML [12] protocol is used to model occupants' behaviour inside the building, which is derived from the Drivers-Needs-Actions-Systems (DNAS) modelling framework.

According to the application and in alignment with the interoperable GIM approach, there are additional variables/modes for persuasion mechanisms for energy efficiency improvement that are already partially integrated and that can be further improved.

5   GreenSoul-ed Things

A set of everyday electrical devices of collective use will be selected from the pilot sites (especially those with a high-energy consumption rate) to attach adaptors to them that transform them into GreenSoul-ed Things (GS-ed Things). These adaptors enhance the bare equipment that can be found in a workplace with not only local intelligence and remote actuations mechanisms but also providing persuasive interfaces to interact with their users in the environments, enabling the use of Edge/Fog-computing techniques [13] for a more effective decision making where and when it is needed. According to the analysis carried out on the initial phases of the project's pilot sites (see Table 1 for a short description of them), the selected electrical devices to be enriched are coffee-makers, elevators, printers, desk's power strips, lighting and HVAC systems. As can be observed, these devices are used at three different levels: *individual* (desk's power strips), group or *work-team*-level (coffee-makers and printers), and *building-level* (lighting, HVAC system and elevators).

GS-ed Things fulfil a two-fold purpose: *(a)* provide users with feedback through physical and ambient cues that help them understand and learn how to optimise their interaction with the augmented devices and systems in an energy-wise manner and *(b)* ensure remote controllability to enable convenient energy-modes and practices, e.g. remote switching off/on, reaching ideal temperatures, and so forth as per the device decision trees' tables.

---

[3] http://www.gbxml.org/.

Table 1. Pilot scenarios for the GreenSoul framework.

Pilot	Max. num. of occupants	Country
Institute of Cartography of Andalusia	~200	Seville, Spain
IT of the University of Deusto.	92	Bilbao, Spain
Pilea-Hortiatis Municipality Hall	25	Thessaloniki, Greece
Haywards Heath	22	Sussex, UK
Allia Ltd	~300	Cambridge, UK
Energy & Innovation Centre	12	Weiz, Austria

GS-ed Things are composed of several Open Source Hardware and Software components which enable them to connect directly to the LinkSmart middleware through HTTP operations. GS-ed Things feature Internet connection, so they can be directly accessed from everywhere through LinkSmart, being their resources exposed following RESTful principles. Furthermore, adaptors attached to everyday things provide embedded current sensors to measure energy consumption, helping to monitor the current operational status of the appliances that they are connected to.

6   GreenSoul Decision Support System (DSS)

6.1   Main Control Algorithm

DSS supports a set of operations for monitoring and control the building assets (e.g. lights, HVAC, appliances, etc). The main goal is to maximize energy efficiency while respecting occupants' comfort.

The overall flow diagram of the DSS operation is depicted in Fig. 4. The building is divided into lighting zones (including one or more sets of lights) and thermal zones (including one or more HVAC units) based on topology and usage. Appliances, such as monitors and printers, are also considered as a separate category. The purpose of this module is to calculate the most energy efficient states of the system, while requiring minimum comfort sacrifice from the end-users; for each lighting/thermal zone, the optimal operational state of lighting and HVAC devices is computed respectively.

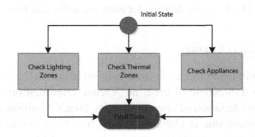

Fig. 4. Overall flow diagram of the DSS operation

The aforementioned process can be seen in more detail in Fig. 5. At first, the module receives the current occupancy status from the occupancy extraction mechanism [14] in order to decide its next actions. If the zone is empty, the system automatically turns off any lights that are on. The same stands true for the HVAC systems, but only after checking the occupancy prediction [17] for the next minutes. In the case when there are people in the zone, the system resides on the analytics engine to evaluate occupants' visual/thermal comfort. More specifically, current environmental data are obtained from the multi-sensorial network (luminance measurements for lighting, indoor air, temperature and humidity for HVAC). These values, along with contextual data related with the specific zone (profiles of users, building spatial information etc.) are used to extract an initial estimation of the preferable comfort value for each zone. Then, previous end-users' corrective actions on defining their preferable luminance/temperature settings are taken into account in order to re-calculate the *comfort threshold* (mean of visual/thermal comfort) of the zone that users consider as acceptable.

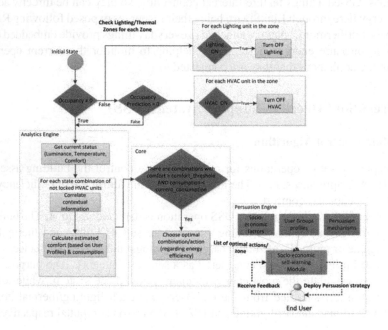

Fig. 5. Flow diagram for each visual/thermal zone

6.2   Core (Simulation) Engine

In a later stage, the core DSS engine simulates various states of the system devices, while respecting the comfort threshold of the zone. Various combinations of operation modes are examined (e.g. combination of open light units, blinds' position etc.) and ultimately, the most energy efficient one is chosen. Finally, having calculated the corresponding increase/decrease in luminance/temperature which should be derived by each light/HVAC unit, the relative *setpoints* can be sent to the Persuasion Engine.

6.3   Persuasion Engine

The Persuasion Engine has been designed to implement a novel socio-economic self-learning module, which would be able to estimate the best persuasion strategy to be deployed per each cluster of users. The module achieves this by receiving the list of actions per device and zone from the CoreEngine and collecting socio-economic factors (e.g. age, preferences, etc.) and persuasion techniques that have already been identified and stored in the GIM database. Then, it assigns weighted factors to these criteria in order to match user profiles against their corresponding strategies. Eventually, a stochastic and self-learning mechanism is adopted (through a Reinforcement Learning algorithm); the user receives the deployed persuasion strategy and either responds successfully or chooses to ignore it. This success status feedback causes the engine to re-evaluate its selected strategy and achieve better future results.

7   Use Cases

The use case scenarios introduced in this section are focused on the application of the GreenSoul framework in multiple tertiary non-controllable environments (see Table 1) towards controlling and leading end-users' energy consumption. By providing a "greener" education through the proper messages and incentives, enriched with effective persuasion and motivation mechanisms adapted to the users' profiles, occupants' energy-related awareness is expected to rise to levels that will have (in)direct impact to the building's consumption. It is our ultimate goal to affect and promote a change in the behaviour of the people who populate shared spaces in public buildings, which can be rather cumbersome since currently eco-friendly behaviours are based entirely on individual belief and effort, and the link between actions and results, regarding energy consumption, is not always very clear.

Energy, social and financial related human behaviour models are formulated for each pilot premises taking into consideration behavioural aspects such as age, education, family, eco-awareness and so on, combined with information extracted by the equipment installed (i.e. smart meters) filtered through static data already modelled in GIM (i.e. positioning – gbXML, devices and assets), offering a multi-parameter analysis that provides the proper weights for two aspects: (a) creating the comfort level inputs for the DSS, and (b) assign incentive strategies to the proper building population.

Namely, two specific uses cases that can best describe the added-value offered by the GreenSoul solution are described in the following sections: a Lighting and an HVAC scenarios as mappings to the GS-architecture.

7.1   Lighting Scenario

Eve, Maria and Roger work together in the same office, located in building fully equipped with blinds, lights, and an HVAC system that keeps the temperature of the room at the desired level. At noon, they decide to turn off the HVAC and open the windows so that fresh air circulates inside the office. By the end of the day, Maria is the last person to leave the office. She has closed the windows but has forgotten to switch off the lights. After 1 min she is informed through an application on her Smartphone that she has forgotten the lights on. The application tries to convince Maria through persuasion techniques to return back and switch off the lights. There is a time-limit of 10 min set by the application, in order for Maria to react as soon as possible. Finally, Maria gets convinced to return back and switch the lights off.

Within this scenario, the GreenSoul Device Network would be composed of the light bulbs, LEDs lamps, corridor lights, energy smart meters, blinds, sensors (presence, motion entry/exit). Data such as the number of persons in the room and the amount of irradiance are constantly sent to the LinkSmart middleware. The DSS receives the data from the middleware and sends information to the room occupants through visual prompts to make people aware about their real-time actions by displaying indoor irradiance conditions inside the office, giving energy advice to the users regarding the use of lights in each room, displaying notifications for lighting misuse through applications on the users' PCs or mobile phones, or providing data about the quantity of energy that can be saved by just decreasing temperature some degrees through the thermostat. The ultimate purpose is to persuade users to follow a more energy efficient behaviour. In addition, the DSS can directly actuate over the lighting units, by turning them off when needed. Figure 6 shows how the components of the Lighting Scenario are mapped to the Greensoul architecture.

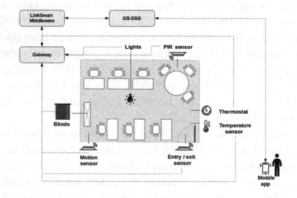

Fig. 6. Mapping of the Lighting Scenario to the GS architecture

7.2 HVAC Scenario

Similarly to the first use case scenario, the HVAC scenario follows a slightly different approach, mainly due to thermal inertia.

Giannis, Nick and Steve work together in the same office, located in a remote building fully equipped with a HVAC system that keeps the temperature of the room at the desired level, and various sensors for measuring required real-time data (e.g. temperature, humidity, consumption, etc). It is a sunny summer day and the office is rather hot, therefore they close the windows and turn on the HVAC to lower the temperature of the room. At noon, they decide to go for lunch but they usually forget to turn off or raise the temperature set point of the HVAC system. However, based on knowledge extracted by the GS behavioural models, the system after anticipating such behaviour, issues a message saying that if they are gone for more than 15', they should turn off the HVAC or raise the set point for two degrees if they are going to be back in less than that. The application tries to convince Giannis and Nick (that are more fond of such tactics) by explaining the reasons behind the two different actions as well as the merits, through appropriate persuasion techniques. If there is no response from them, a second message is sent, as in the lighting scenario case. Finally, Giannis regulates the set point to a higher temperature and thus reducing the HVAC power consumption.

The components and methods used within this scenario are similar to the previous description (see Sect. 7.1), utilising only different kind of real-time information and decision making logic. Furthermore, as already explained, the GreenSoul Behavioural models provide the necessary information for selecting the optimal time and user for applying the persuasion techniques.

8   Conclusions and Future Work

In this paper an innovative ICT architecture has been presented following the Edge Computing paradigm to foster behavioural change towards a more lenient use of primary energy resources in a building of public use. To this end, the architecture consists of three layers that loosely resemble their physical localization: the device layer, the building layer and the cloud layer. The main innovation resides in the presence of the GreenSould-ed devices. These devices will be the cornerstone to retrieve process and foster behavioural change in an autonomous and resilient way. Finally, two use cases have been described and mapped to the aforementioned architecture. This paper only covers the overall architecture without taking into consideration the best option to develop its components. In this sense, the following steps will include an in depth analysis of different middleware options, including not only technical aspects (like performance) but also social ones (ease of use or community friendliness). Furthermore we envisage to develop a comparison between different algorithmic strategies to create the forecasting module and the DSS.

Acknowledgement. This scientific paper has been supported by the H2020 project GreenSoul. The project received funding from the European Union's Horizon 2020 research and innovation programme under grant agreement No 696129.

References

1. Directive 2012/27/EU of the European Parliament and of the Council of 25 October 2012 on energy efficiency, amending Directives 2009/125/EC and 2010/30/EU and repealing Directives 2004/8/EC and 2006/32/EC Text with EEA relevance. OJ L 315, 14.11.2012, pp. 1–56 (2012). http://eur-lex.europa.eu/legal-content/EN/TXT/?uri=CELEX:32012L0027
2. Directive 2010/31/EU of the European Parliament and of the Council of 19 May 2010 on the energy performance of buildings. OJ L 153 of 18.6.2010, pp. 13–35 (2010). http://eur-zlex.europa.eu/legal-content/EN/TXT/?uri=celex:32010L0031

3. Vega-Barbas, M., Casado-Mansilla, D., Valero, M.A., López-de-Ipina, D., Bravo, J., Flórez, F.: Smart spaces and smart objects interoperability architecture (S3OiA). In: 2012 Sixth International Conference on Innovative Mobile and Internet Services in Ubiquitous Computing (IMIS), pp. 725–730. IEEE (2012)

4. Kamara-Esteban, O., Pijoan, A., Alonso-Vicario, A., Borges, C.E.: On-demand energy monitoring and response architecture in a ubiquitous world. Pers. Ubiquitous Comput. **21**, 1–15 (2017)

5. Simmins, J.J.: The impact of PAP 8 on the Common Information Model (CIM). In: Smart Grid, Power Systems Conference and Exposition (PSCE) (2011)

6. EEA: Achieving energy efficiency through behaviour change: what does it take?. ISSN 1725–2237, EEA Technical report No 5/2013 (2013)

7. Delmas, M.A., Fischlein, M., Asensio, O.I.: Information strategies and energy conservation behavior: a meta-analysis of experimental studies from 1975 to 2012. Energy Policy **61**, 729–739 (2013)

8. Osbaldiston, R., Schott, J.P.: Environmental sustainability and behavioral science: meta-analysis of proenvironmental behavior experiments. Environ. Behav. **44**, 257–299 (2012)

9. Department of Energy & Climate Change: An introduction to thinking about "'energy behaviour': a multi model approach", gov.uk (2011)

10. Breukelman, M.: Energy efficiency in buildings: business realities and opportunities. In: World Business Council for Sustainable Development WBCSD (2008)

11. DeVos S., Widergren, E., Zhu, J.: XML for CIM Model Exchange. In 22nd IEEE Power Eng. Soc. Int. Conf. on Power Industry Comp. App., PICA 2001. pp. 31–37 (2001)

12. Turner, W., Hong, T.: A technical framework to describe occupant behaviour for building energy simulations. In BECC Conference Sacramento (2013)

13. Bonomi, F., Milito, R., Zhu, J., Addepalli, S.: Fog computing and its role in the internet of things. In Proceedings of the first edition of the MCC workshop on mobile cloud computing (pp. 13–16). ACM (2012)

14. Zikos, S., Tsolakis, A., Meskos, D., Tryferidis, A., Tzovaras, D.: Conditional Random Fields-based approach for real-time building occupancy estimation with multi-sensory networks. Autom. Constr. **68**, 128–145 (2016)

15. Casado-Mansilla, D., Lopez-de-Armentia, J., Garaizar, P., López-de-Ipiña, D.: To switch off the coffee-maker or not: that is the question to be energy-efficient at work. In CHI' 14 Extended Abstracts on Human Factors in Computing Systems, pp. 2425–2430. ACM (2014)

16. Garcia Lopez, P., Montresor, A., Epema, D., Datta, A., Higashino, T., Iamnitchi, A., Riviere, E.: Edge-centric computing: vision and challenges. ACM SIGCOMM Comput. Commun. Rev. **45**(5), 37–42 (2015)

17. Adamopoulou, A.A., Tryferidis, A.M., Tzovaras, D.K.: A context-aware method for building occupancy prediction. Energy Build. **110**, 229–244 (2016)

Machine Learning for Prediction of Frost Episodes in the Maule Region of Chile

Patricia Möller-Acuña, Roberto Ahumada-García,
and José Antonio Reyes-Suárez[✉]

Facultad de Ingeniería, Universidad de Talca, Talca, Chile
{pmoller,jareyes}@utalca.cl, robertoahumadagarcia@gmail.com

Abstract. Frosts are one of the main risks faced by farmers during the winter and spring seasons. These events can cause significant damage to diverse types of crops. In Chile, these frost generates significant losses in the agricultural production sector, causing crop losses of an entire year and compromising the income of the following year, especially fruit and wine makers. In this work we developed a prediction model based on historical agrometeorological information able to predict efficiently and up to 12 h earlier the occurrence of a frost event in the Maule Region of Chile. Various algorithms and machine learning methods were evaluated, we found that Random Forest exhibits the best results overall. The results obtained in the frost prediction reach over (90%) of efficiency in most of the evaluated scenarios.

Keywords: Frost episodes · Machine learning · Prediction · Agrometeorological

1 Introduction

One of the most risky climatic variable farmers deal yearly is winter and spring frosts. When the air temperature takes values equal or less than zero degrees we are talking about the "frost" phenomenon. The cold sensitivity of a plant depends on its state of development, being the most vulnerable phenological states flowering and fruit setting [1, 2]. According to the literature we can identify two types of frost: (i) The advective frosts are generally associated to the passage of a cold front with invasion of masses of air at low temperatures [3], causing in general severe damages; (ii) Radiation frosts are produced by the cooling of the lower layers of the atmosphere. Several studies related to the frequency and effects of frost conditions in the agriculture have been exhibited worldwide during last years [4], which shows the importance of assessing the occurrence of frost episodes. It has been reported that economic losses due frost episodes in agriculture of the Maule Region in Chile raises between US$ 600 and US$ 900 million yearly. The volume of fruit exported decreases by 15–20%. Meanwhile the negative impact on the employment of seasonal agricultural workers is estimated to generate a decrease close to 20% [5]. Frost protection techniques

© Springer International Publishing AG 2017
S.F. Ochoa et al. (Eds.): UCAmI 2017, LNCS 10586, pp. 715–720, 2017.
DOI: 10.1007/978-3-319-67585-5_69

are normally divided into indirect and direct methods or passive and active methods[6]. Machine learning is a branch of artificial intelligence in which methods developed through a computer are able to learn based on previous experience. Currently the predictability of frost events depends to a large extent on temperature forecasts based on general predictive models [7]. In these cases, an hour-by-hour (or even shorter time-scale) prediction of the estimated average temperature is carried out for each zone of interest. There are numerous recent studies reported in the literature, where artificial intelligence models are used to develop models to predict extreme weather conditions [4]. In particular, the prediction of low temperature events these highlight the difficulty of traditional models, based on general regression techniques, to predict extreme events [8]. This article presents a frost prediction model using local historical agro climatological information. This model is able to predict efficiently and with up to 12 h in advance the occurrence of a frost event.

1.1 Characterization of Frost Eepisodes

In this article we focus in areas located in the VII Maule Region - Chile, including Molina, San Rafael, Pencahue, Colbún, Longavi, San Javier, Yerbas Buenas and Curicó. These zones are commonly affected by frost events, causing severe damage to the region's agriculture productivity year by year. On each of these areas an automatic weather station (AWS) is operating and recording climatic variables hourly. This data is publicly available including temperature, humidity, radiation and wind speed and direction among others. In order to group and identify the different frost events, we performed a characterization of these events for the period 2010–2016 on each one of the zones previously identified. The number of frost episodes recorded in these areas are variable, between 120 and 180 events on different areas analyzed. We consider that a frost episode occurs when the temperature recorded on any of de AWS analyzed was less than or equal to 0°C. During the period 2010–2016, an average of 168 frosts episodes where registered on the AWSs studied. The average intensity of these frost events was -2.3°C. On the other hand, the average duration of the registered frosts are approximately 4 h and 30 min. It is observed that about 70% of the frost events recorded. Finally, when analyzing the start time of the different frost episodes recorded in the AWS analyzed, it can be seen that about 90% of all the frost episodes recorded occurs between 00:00 am and 7:00 am. In general the frost does not present a clear behavior that is possible to describe adequately with the variables before mentioned. Although there are certain trends in frequency, duration and intensity of recorded events, it is not possible to find a clear and simple relation to predict the occurrence of a new frost event. This shows the complexity associated with the frost phenomenon. This motivates the research developed in this work, associated to train and evaluate models of prediction of frost events using machine learning techniques, which allow to integrate new variables.

2   Predictive Model

In a first stage we focused on generating a data set to be used in the process of developing a prediction model of frost events. For this we take as a basis the frost events, which correspond to the "Class 1" of our problem (Frost). In the same way, we took records of the days when no frost was recorded, forming a data set corresponding to the "Class 2" of our problem (Non-Frost) that occurred between the months of May and August in the period 2010–2016 in each of the stations studied. Each of these examples from our reference set was characterized with attributes or descriptors associated with: temperature, relative humidity, solar radiation, dew point, wind speed and direction. It should be mentioned that each of these descriptors corresponds to measurements made and recorded every 15 min by each AWS during the period 2010–2016. This information was debugged and deposited in a local database that is available for consultation at the following link http://appsbio.utalca.cl/fia/. The different examples of Frost and Non-Frost considered in the reference set are then characterized by a vector of attributes associated with the above mentioned descriptors. In this case, the information recorded in each AWS for each case was considered during the interval of 9 hours prior to the delivery of the frost forecast, from 06:00 to 12:00 h. Given the reference set previously described, we evaluated several classification methods as Naive Bayes [9], Random-Forest, Decision Trees and SVM. All of which were implemented in the programming language R. Each model was evaluated for each one of the AWSs, to perform the different evaluations we obtained performance rates that help us to determine how well each model performed the predictive task. The performance of each predicted model was estimated using a Leave One-Out Cross Validation procedure (LOOCV). Where a model is trained using all but one example, then use that reserved example to test or evaluate the trained model. This process is performed for each of the examples in the training set. From the results obtained in LOOCV the following performance measures were obtained for this problem: (i) Overall efficiency (OE) of the model, which corresponds to the overall success rate of the prediction. (ii) Undetected Frost Rate (UFR), which corresponds to percentage or rate of frost events that were not detected by the model. (iii) False Alerts (FA) rate, which corresponds to percentage or rate of non-frost events predicted incorrectly.

2.1   Prediction Results for Frost Events in the Maule Region of Chile

Evaluation of the Model Period 2010–2016 in the Different AWSs Studied

Several techniques and modeling strategies were evaluated in order to generate the most robust prediction model for the proposed task, this corresponds "to predict the occurrence of a frost event for the locality in each AWS using agro-climatology information of each reference AWS". Observing the composition of examples of the reference set in all AWSs clearly shows an imbalance of classes where the minority class (examples of Frost) is in a ratio close to 1: 4 with respect to the majority class (examples of NO-Frost). This situation generates a problem in the performance obtained by the different classification models evaluated. In all cases, UFR values (undetected frost rate) are obtained over 30%, even reaching values of up to 60% in the case of Naive Bayes. All of this is associated with the error of the minority class, clearly indicating the effect of the imbalance of classes on the performance of the trained models.To address this situation we used the methodology called SMOTE (an acronym for Synthetic Minority Oversampling Technique), which is an algorithm used to increase the sensitivity of a classifier to the minority class. This occurs through the generation of synthetic data from actual data, using the average attributes of a combination of various examples of the class that is unbalanced [10]. A balancing optimization process was performed between the classes of this problem in order to find the precise amount of artificial examples necessary to obtain good performance indicators in the models generated. This was done using a standard procedure available in R to balance training set. The results of the evaluation of the different classification methods evaluated exhibits that Random Forest methods significantly outperforms the rest of Machine Learning algorithms also evaluated for this task (results not showed here). The performance results for the Random Forest approach is showed in Table 1, where the values for OE, UFR and FA were obtained for each one of the AWSs analyzed.

Table 1. Performance of Random Forest method for prediction of frost episodes for each AWS of the Maule Region of Chile. Measured as OE (%), UFR (%) and FA (%).

AWS	OE (%)	UFR (%)	FA (%)
3 esquinas - Molina	95	6	5
Lontue - Molina	96	5	4
San Rafael - San Rafael	8	3	2
San Pedro -Pencahue	92	9	8
Colbún - Colbún	94	7	6
Longavi Norte - Longavi	97	5	3
Longavi Sur - Longavi	95	7	5
San Javier - San Javier	93	7	7
Yerbas Buenas - Yerbas Buenas	91	9	8
Tutuquen - Curico	93	7	7

Evaluation of the Model by Seasons

Based on the Random-Forest method that gave better results in the previous stage, a second performance evaluation strategy of this model was developed. For this, it was considered to test the performance of each prediction model (for each AWS) on all the records of the reference set of any one year, whose data were not used to train the model prediction. This scenario also takes into account that there is a significant variability in agro-climatological information recorded year after year, for example in terms of average temperatures, rainfall, which is reflected in other variables such as humidity, wind, etc. The results of the seasonal evaluation for each AWS are presented in Table 2. The results obtained show that the performance obtained by the Random-Forest method in this new evaluation scenario decreases significantly with respect to the previous case. This is undoubtedly due to the temporality effect that exists in the climate and is represented in this new scenario of evaluation. However, in this new scenario, Random-Forest continues to deliver significantly better results than the other classification methods evaluated. It is also seen that in most of the seasons evaluated in the different AWSs, performances measured as OE over 80%, representing a significant improvement in the errors of this type reported with traditional methods of temperature prediction, and those are accepted by the farming community as an acceptable and useful result. From Table 2 it can be observed that in particular the year 2011 was a more complex season to predict compared to the other seasons. This is explained by the characterization of the frosts of that year presented atypical conditions, with low temperature averages and a dry year in general. It is possible to think that the Frost and Non-Frost records of the 2011 season may be affecting the performance of the prediction model for the other seasons.

Table 2. Seasonal performance of the Random Forest method for prediction of frost episodes for each AWS of the Maule Region of Chile between the years 2010 - 2016. Measured as OE (%)

AWS	Overall efficiency (%)						
	2010	2011	2012	2013	2014	2015	2016
3 esquinas - Molina	93	83	92	93	89	90	91
Lontue - Molina	91	80	87	84	89	90	90
San Rafael - San Rafael	97	90	96	96	97	97	98
San Pedro -Pencahue	91	82	93	93	89	92	93
Colbún - Colbún	92	81	94	90	91	95	89
Longavi Norte - Longavi	94	91	90	93	89	90	94
Longavi Sur - Longavi	90	89	92	91	87	92	93
San Javier - San Javier	92	85	89	93	91	86	93
Yerbas Buenas - Yerbas Buenas	90	79	81	81	84	85	87
Tutuquen - Curico	94	82	94	92	92	90	94

3   Conclusion and Future Work

Frosts recorded in historical data show devastating effects for agriculture in south-central Chile. This paper presents the development of a prediction model of frost episodes based on meteorological information and machine learning techniques. Several machine learning methods were evaluated for this task, finding that the Random-Forest classification algorithm gave the best results in the different scenarios and conditions evaluated for Frozen and Non-Frozen records in the period 2010–2016 of the different AWSs studied in the Maule Region - Chile. However, it is important to mention that it is necessary to study area by area separately, according to the results obtained. This indicates that this algorithm is better adapted to the conditions proposed in the problem of this work, associated with "predicting the occurrence of a frost event using agroclimatological information". The developed model reaches an efficiency close to (90%) efficiency, being able to predict up to 12 h in advance the occurrence of a frost episode. This work therefore gives conclusive results as to whether it is possible to generate an early prediction model of frost events based on historical agro-meteorological information. It is worth mentioning that this corresponds to an initial work in this subject, and it is therefore necessary to validate the methodology presented with records associated with other meteorological stations and in different geographic areas of the country, to give generality to the proposed model. Additionally we are in the stage of development of predictive models associated with inferring the start time, intensity and duration presented by the frost events studied here.

References

1. Levitt, J.: Responses of Plants to Environmental Stresses. Chilling, Freezing and High Temperature Stresses, vol. 1, 2nd edn. Academic Press Inc., New York (1980)
2. Sakai, A., Larcher, W.: Frost Survival of Plants. Responses and Adaptation to Freezing Stress, vol. 2. Springer-Verlag, Berlin (1987)
3. Snyder, R., Paw, U., Thompson, J.: Passive frost protection of trees and vines. University of California DANR Leaflet N° 21429 (1987)
4. Giarolla, A., Chou, S.C., Faria, R.: Evaluation of the occurence of agricultural frost in state of Parana, Brazil, generated by a regional forecast model. Geophysical Research Abstracts. In: EGU2013-1943, vol. 15 (2013)
5. Odepa: Estudio: Efecto heladas de septiembre en frutales y hortalizas entre la Región de Coquimbo y la del Maule. Estudio encargado por la Oficina de Estudios y Políticas Agrarias (Odepa) del Ministerio de Agricultura (2013)
6. Kalma, J., Laug, G., Caprio, J., Hamer, P.: Advances in Bioclimatology. The Bioclimatology of Frost. Springer-Verlag, Berlin (1992). 144 pages
7. Bagdonas, A., Georg, J. Gerber, J.: Techniques of frost prediction and methods of frost and cold protection. World Meteorological Organization Technical Note, No. 157. Geneva, Switzerland (1978). 160 pages
8. Sallis, P., Jarur, M., Trujillo, M.: Frost prediction characteristics and classification using computational neural networks. In: Köppen, M., Kasabov, N., Coghill, G. (eds.) ICONIP 2008. LNCS, vol. 5506, pp. 1211–1220. Springer, Heidelberg (2009). doi:10.1007/978-3-642-02490-0_147
9. Rish, I.: An empirical study of the naive Bayes classifier. In: JCAI Workshop on Empirical Methods in AI (1997)
10. Chawla, N.V., Bowyer, K.W., Hall, L.O., Kegelmeyer, W.P.: SMOTE: Synthetic minority over-sampling technique. J. Artif. Intell. Res. **16**, 321–357 (2002). http://doi.org/10.1613/jair.953

Temperature and Humidity Dependence for Household- and City-Wide Electricity Demand Prediction in Managua, Nicaragua

Stephen Suffian[1(✉)], Diego Ponce de Leon Barido[2], and Pritpal Singh[1]

[1] Villanova University, Villanova, PA 19085, USA
ssuffian@villanova.edu
[2] University of California Berkeley, Berkeley, CA 94720, USA

Abstract. Hourly electrical energy demand predictions improve grid reliability, stability, and minimize costs by maintaining system frequency and optimizing unit commitment and economic dispatch. Weather data, specifically ambient temperature and humidity, is commonly used as a predictor for demand. This paper utilizes the data from a recent demand response and behavioral energy efficiency pilot in Managua, Nicaragua in order to evaluate the relationship between household temperature and demand data, city-wide temperature and demand data, and the potential for utilizing household-level data to predict city-wide demand. Results from this paper indicate that temperature and humidity data can help to inform both household-level and city-wide prediction of electricity demand. Further, the available household level data was found to have a limited relationship with city-wide demand.

Keywords: Electrical energy demand prediction · Support vector regression · Random forests

1 Introduction

Hourly electrical energy demand predictions improve grid reliability, stability, and minimize costs by maintaining system frequency and optimizing unit commitment and economic dispatch. Grid operators seek to match aggregate electricity demand with system supply at all times, and therefore must predict demand ahead of time in order to ensure that certain power plants are prepared to generate in a way that minimizes system cost. Prediction error negatively impacts the grid in several ways. If not properly managed, it can impact system frequency and damage grid equipment and customer appliances. Fast ramping power plants, which typically have a higher generation cost, must be utilized to address the error, leading to increased wholesale electricity prices. Prediction on the aggregate level has been thoroughly researched, most recently with a resurgence of papers using a variety of machine learning approaches such as autoregressive integrated moving average (ARIMA) [1], multiple linear regression (MLR) [2], support vector regression (SVR) [3], and random forest regressions (RFR) [4]. These approaches improve prediction accuracy by relying on the added complexity of the

© Springer International Publishing AG 2017
S.F. Ochoa et al. (Eds.): UCAmI 2017, LNCS 10586, pp. 721–727, 2017.
DOI: 10.1007/978-3-319-67585-5_70

model to seek out more informative patterns in the data and achieve greater accuracy. The rising use of variable renewable energy sources such as wind and solar inject additional uncertainty into the power grid, requiring more sophisticated and more accurate prediction. Improved wind [5] and solar [6] prediction methods, as well as energy storage mechanisms, are being researched and implemented to address these issues. Recent work has also been conducted using smart-meter data to inform demand prediction [7].

With the rise of internet of things (IoT) and information communication technology (ICT) devices, there is an opportunity to employ low-cost sensor networks to incorporate new data sources in prediction models. This is particularly pertinent for countries that have not yet invested in smart metering infrastructure and are experiencing significant electricity demand growth because it offers a low-cost method of accessing valuable data to enhance demand prediction.

This paper uses household and city-wide level data to improve electrical energy demand prediction for Managua, Nicaragua. Nicaragua has been following an aggressive program to increase the percentage of renewable energy contribution to its power generation mix. Since 2015, at times the country has exceeded 50% generation by renewables with a goal of reaching 90% renewable generation by 2020 [8]. In tropical regions of the world, such as Central America, temperature and humidity impact the energy required of cooling loads such as refrigeration and air conditioning. For this reason, the relationship between temperature/humidity and demand may be even more closely tied than in cooler climates.

The goals of this paper are to evaluate the utility of temperature and humidity for household-level demand prediction, and to evaluate the utility of personal weather station data and household level demand data for improving city-wide prediction. Results from MLR, SVR, and RFR are compared for each prediction. The results can further inform demand prediction on a national level, as Managua comprises approximately 45% of total national electrical energy demand. Previous work has shown improvements to national-level demand prediction, with machine learning approaches offering up to 21% reductions in prediction error from the dispatch center's approach [9]. Improved prediction can lead to improved system stability, reduced electricity costs, and provide opportunities for greater renewable energy generation.

2   Methodology

2.1   Data Collection

A variety of data sources were used in this analysis. Household data came from a 60-person behavioral energy efficiency and demand response study conducted in Managua from June 2015-December 2016 [10]. In that study, electricity demand data from 20 homes and small businesses was collected and was used in this analysis. Private weather station data came from a Davis Vantage Vue weather station connected to a Raspberry Pi running *weeWX*, an open source weather software. This weather station was installed above an office in Managua and recorded temperature and humidity data at 30 min intervals from June 1st, 2015 to December 5th, 2016. Public weather data came from WorldWeatherOnline's historical weather API, which offers temperature and humidity data from the Augusto C. Sandino International Airport in Managua, Nicaragua at 3-hour intervals. Finally, demand data for the city of Managua is available on Nicaragua's Load Dispatch Center website (www.cndc.org.ni). All data was resampled to an hourly frequency. Public weather data was up-sampled through a linear interpolation of temperature and humidity. Analysis was conducted in Python 2.7 on an HP Envy dv6 notebook with 8 GB memory running Ubuntu 16.04. The scikit-learn 0.18.1 python library was used for all regression models.

2.2 Household Level

The household analysis seeks to find whether temperature and humidity data collected within the house, as well as similar outdoor data, can inform better hour-ahead household level demand prediction. The features used for prediction were: 'Pri-T/H': time-lagged temperature and humidity data from the private weather station, 'WWO T/H': time-lagged WorldWeatherOnline temperature and humidity, 'In T/H': indoor temperature and humidity, and 'D': time-lagged indoor electricity demand. Time-lags of 1–25 h were included in each model, leading to a total of 120 features.

Eight separate collections of features were used: (1) 'Pri-T/H', (2) 'WWO T/H', (3) 'In T/H', (4) 'Pri-T/H', 'In-T/H', and 'WWO T/H' titled 'All T/H', (5) 'D', (6) 'D' and 'In T/H' titled 'D + In', (7) 'D', 'Pri-Th', and 'WWO T/H' titled 'D + Out', (8) all features titled 'All'.

After evaluating the r-squared values of different features sets, regressions were constructed for prediction, using the first 50% for training and rest for evaluation. Prediction using MLR was then compared to a similar approach using SVR as well as RFR. For the SVR, a hyper-parameter search using a random sample of data split between training and test yielded optimal performance with a radial-basis function kernel with C = 1000, gamma = 10e−6, and epsilon = .0001.

2.3 City-Wide Level

The city-wide analysis used the previously described weather data as well as Managua demand data to conduct hour-ahead demand prediction. The same variables were used as in the household level analysis, with the addition of feature set 'CD': city-wide demand data. For this analysis, four feature collections were compared: (1) 'Pri-T/H' and 'WWO T/H', (2) 'CD', (3) 'CD' and 'WWO T/H' (4) 'CD' and 'Pri T/H', and 'CD', (5) 'CD', 'Pri T/H', and 'WWO T/H' titled 'All'.

The use of household demand data to inform city-wide prediction was also explored. Limitations in the household-level dataset prevented the data from being directly compared to the other approaches. However, 6 households contained data that could be merged with the Managua electricity demand data to allow for prediction. Each household contained slightly different time ranges, so each model containing both household and city-wide data was compared against models constructed during those time ranges using only city-wide data.

3 Results and Discussion

3.1 Household Level

Figure 1 displays a boxplot containing r-squared values from models built for each household at each hour. Each box indicates a different subset of features used in the regression model. This plot indicates that while most of the variance can be described by lagged power, the inclusion of outdoor and indoor temperature and humidity data raises the mean r-squared value from (.64) to (.84).

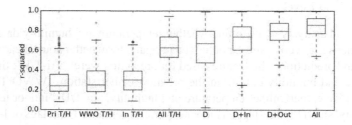

Fig. 1. R-squared values with different feature subsets

While on average, lagged household energy demand explains a greater amount of the variance than temperature/humidity, a subset of houses have r-squared values for temperature/humidity that are similar or even greater than for demand, as can be seen in Fig. 2. This indicates that certain households are well-correlated with temperature and humidity, which may be due to the appliances in a home resulting in different levels of electricity demand. For example, households with multiple refrigerators may have their demand better correlated with temperature and humidity.

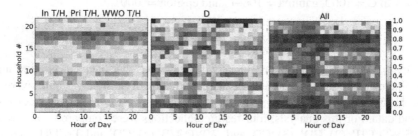

Fig. 2. R-squared values of regressions with different subset of features used

Figure 3 describes the results of hour-ahead household demand prediction. For all models, the best results used all available data. The SVR achieved the best results, with an average of 20.7%. Mean Absolute Percent Error (MAPE). The MLR showed the greatest increase in performance when using all data as opposed to only a subset. The SVR and RFR both appear to have more heavily relied on the demand data for prediction. In the case of the RFR, it appears that there was overfitting when the temperature/humidity data was incorporated, or that the predictions were close enough that the difference was due to the random selection of trees used in each model. The temperature and humidity data provides a noticeable improvement for both the MLR (MAPE decreased by 24%) and SVR models (MAPE decreased by 2.3%).

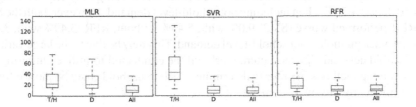

Fig. 3. MAPE values for household demand prediction with different feature sets

Issues with data quality limited the analysis, as many of the sensors in the households had extended data gaps. Further, communication errors within the system may have led to outliers in the dataset. Future work will look into methods of more advanced data cleaning and sampling, in order to provide better results.

3.2 City-Wide Level

Table 1 shows the results of the MLR, SVR, and RFRs for predicting city-wide demand in Managua. Overall, the SVR achieves the best results, with a MAPE of 2.99% when using only publicly available weather data in addition to city-wide demand data.

Table 1. MAPE for hour-ahead city demand prediction using different feature sets

Model type	Included variables				
	WWO + Pri T/H	CD	CD + Pri T/H	CD + WWO T/H	All
MLR	7.44%	3.98%	4.01%	3.87%	3.86%
SVR	13.06%	3.06%	3.07%	2.99%	3.04%
RFR	5.86%	3.13%	3.21%	3.27%	3.1%

Improvements in prediction when using weather data indicate the value of incorporating low-cost sensor-level data. For the SVR, using only time-lagged city demand data, a 3.06% MAPE was achieved, which translates to 6.9 MWh of Mean Absolute Error. When also incorporating publicly available weather data, a 2.99% MAPE was achieved, which translates to 6.7 MWh of Mean Absolute Error. The accumulation of this hourly difference in error (.2 MWh) over the course of a year yields 73 MWh. This indicates a small but promising improvement in accuracy, especially considering the weather data was linearly interpolated to hourly samples from 3-hour samples.

The private weather station didn't improve accuracy, possibly due to its location. It was installed only 5 meters above the ground in a residential compound and may have encountered a strong heat island effect, with the mean temperature of the station being 1.2 °F greater than that from the public weather data that comes from the airport outside of town. Future work will evaluate the benefits of having weather stations in several locations across the city where demand is highest.

The use of household level demand data to inform city-wide prediction led to mixed results. The mean MAPE for MLR improved from 4.41% using only city-wide lagged demand data to 4.27% when including household-level demand. However, both the SVR and RFR performed worse (SVR: 9.0% with, 5.45% without, RFR: 3.49% with, 3.41% without) when including household-level demand. This may be due to the large variation in household demand signals. Future work will be conducted to utilize clustering and other sampling methods in order to determine which households may be most informative for predicting city-wide demand.

4 Conclusion

This work evaluated the use of temperature, humidity, and consumption data on household-level and city-wide electrical energy demand prediction. MLRs, SVRs, and RFRs were used with to evaluate the value of this data for demand prediction. Results show that the use of temperature and humidity data improves prediction models both on the household and city-wide level. In both cases, SVRs were found to be the best model type. The available household level demand was found to show a limited relationship to city-wide demand, although additional data collection, improved sampling, and the use of clustering could lead to a stronger relationship for the future. Low-cost sensor-level data can help inform demand prediction both on a household and city-wide level. Improved prediction can lead to improved system stability, reduced electricity costs, and provide opportunities for greater renewable energy generation.

References

1. Leaa, C.-M., Ko, C.-N.: Short-term load forecasting using lifting scheme and ARIMA models. Expert Syst. Appl. **38**(5), 5902–5911 (2011)
2. Amral, N., Ozveren, C., King, D.: Short term load forecasting using multiple linear regression. In: 42nd International Universities Power Engineering Conference, Brighton, UK (2007)
3. Wang, B., Leng, X., Zahng, X.H., Shan, C.H., Cong, Z.: Application profiles of support vector machine in short-term load forecasting. Proc. CSU-EPSA **23**(4), 115–121 (2011)
4. Lahouar, A., Siama, J.B.H.: Day-ahead load forecast using random forest and expert input selection. Energy Convers. Manage. **103**, 1040–1051 (2015)
5. Tascikaraoglu, A., Uzunoglu, M.: A review of combined approaches for prediction of short-term wind speed and power. Renew. Sust. Energy Rev. **34**, 243–254 (2014)
6. Yadav, K., Chandel, S.S.: Solar radiation prediction using artificial neural network techniques: a review. Renew. Sust. Energy Rev. **33**, 772–781 (2014)
7. Quilumba, F.L., Lee, W.-J., Huang, H., Wang, D.Y., Szabados, R.L.: Using smart meter data to improve the accuracy of intraday load forecasting considering customer behavior similarities. IEEE Trans. Smart Grid **6**(2), 911–918 (2014)
8. Estrategia y Negocios, Nicaragua quiere tener 90% de energyas renovables en 2020, 29 4 (2015)

9. Suffian, S., de Leon Barido, D.P., Ingalhalikar, M., Singh P.: Increasing grid flexibility through improved electricity demand prediction in nicaragua. In: International Conference on Machine and Learning Applications, Miami (2015)
10. de Leon Barido, D.P., Suffian, S., Rosa, J., Brewer, E., Kammen, D.M.: Enabling Micro-level Demand-Side Grid Flexibility in Resource Constrained Environments. ACM, New York (2017)

Special Session on Socio-Cognitive and Affective Computing

A Distributed Tool to Perform Dynamic Therapies for Social Cognitive Deficit Through Avatars

Mario García-Sánchez🆔, Miguel A. Teruel$^{(\boxtimes)}$🆔, Elena Navarro🆔,
Pascual González🆔, and Antonio Fernández-Caballero🆔

LoUISE Research Group, Computing Systems Department,
University of Castilla – La Mancha, Albacete, Spain
Mario.Garcia17@alu.uclm.es, miguel@dsi.uclm.es,
{Elena.Navarro,Pascual.Gonzalez,Antonio.Fdez}@uclm.es

Abstract. Patients suffering from Social Cognition Deficits have difficulties when trying to understand its interlocutor emotional status. In order to contribute to the treatment of this deficit, we have developed a distributed application to offer remote therapies and using the concept of *avatars*. By using this application, therapist embody avatars that convey their emotions, voices and gestures. Therefore, this application enables patient to recognize the avatars emotions which, in turn, are controlled by the therapist. For this aim, a distributed software has been developed along with different devices such as a Kinect v2 for motion tracking and a facial expression analyzer. Unity has been used for the development of this application to make this type of remote therapy possible.

Keywords: Social cognitive deficit · Therapy · Rehabilitation · Distributed architecture · Emotions

1 Introduction

One of the key features that distinguish humans from other living beings is their ability to interact with their peers. To facilitate such interaction, emotion recognition becomes critical as it helps us to adapt not only our conversation but also even our corporal behavior. This indicates that suffering from *Social Cognition Deficits* can be very disabling for any person. According to Harvey and Penn [1], social cognition "is a set of cognitive processes applied to the recognition, understanding, accurate processing, and effective use of social cues in real-world situations". Therefore, social cognition deficit hinders people abilities to become social beings. Some authors, such as Zwieten et al. [2], have even related them to antisocial behaviors that put individual at risk for criminality, substance dependence, etc. Moreover, these deficits are unfortunately frequent because people with different diseases, such as schizophrenia [3], autism spectrum [4] or attention-deficit/hyperactivity disorder (ADHD) [5]. Therefore, the development of solutions that facilitate the treatment of people suffering from these deficits emerges as a clear need.

© Springer International Publishing AG 2017
S.F. Ochoa et al. (Eds.): UCAmI 2017, LNCS 10586, pp. 731–741, 2017.
DOI: 10.1007/978-3-319-67585-5_71

Considering that humans exploit both their voice and body movements to communicate with their peers our proposal is to offer people suffering from Social Cognition Deficits with an application that guide them in the process of learning to recognize such emotions. This application has been designed exploiting virtual avatars that are controlled by specialists to convey specific emotions to patients. These avatars are shown to the patients in a virtual reality environment, so that specialists are controlling continuously the environment surrounding the patients and, thus, how the treatment is offered to them. Moreover, in order to facilitate specialists' interaction, a training process is carried out to detect which facial expression are used by the specialists to convey a specific emotion. This application also features support to modulate specialists' voice according to avatars' gender as well as to detect patients' movements that are used to control avatars' interaction. Finally, we would like to highlight that this application has not been developed from scratch but integrating different proposals in order to speed up the development process.

This paper is organized as follows. After this introduction, Sect. 2 presents some works related with the one presented here. Next, Sect. 3 describes the architecture to visualize emotions and body gestures through avatars. After that, Sect. 4 illustrates a case study to show how the architecture is put into practice. Finally, Sect. 5 draws our conclusions a future works.

2 Emotion Recognition

Emotions play a relevant role in human relationship and enable people to respond adaptively to threats and opportunities found in the environment. Thus, the inability of certain persons to recognize or express these emotions may be critical, and could contribute to their social dysfunctions. There are several collectives where this problem represents a serious challenge. For example, people with psychiatric disorder, such as schizophrenia [3] or autism spectrum [4], or those that suffer acquired brain injury (ABI) [6] after an accident, a stroke, etc., are one of the most relevant groups affected by this problem.

One of the main strategies to recognize an emotion is taking into account some physiological signal that individuals display as a reaction to an emotion. For this aim, the *human face* plays a fundamental role in emotion recognition. As Calvo and Nummenmaa stated [7], facial expressions of emotion involve a physical component of morphological changes of a face and an affective component conveying information about the expresser's internal feelings. This relevance of facial expression in emotion recognition has been used in several studies that allow recognize a human emotion by analyzing an individual's face [8]. Other studies try to define learning strategies to avoid the lack the emotion recognition capability of certain individuals [9]. This relevance of facial expression in emotion recognition has led to use static photos showing a specific emotion as one of the most frequently used therapies. However, real world is not static but dynamic, so one of the main criticisms to the use of static images is the low ecological validity of its use [10]. Thus, it is relevant to include not only static images but also dynamic ones to improve the learning process.

Moreover, although the face is a very relevant mirror of an emotion, there are other stimuli that enable to improve the emotion recognition task. As Keltner et al. [11] noticed, emotional expression is a multimodal phenomenon so that, in addition to facial muscle movements, there are other ways to express an emotion. For example, vocalizations, respiration, movements of the arms and hands, head movements or other gesture could be used to recognize an emotion. Thus, in the learning process of emotion recognition it is relevant to take into account this multidimensional aspect of emotional expression.

Thus, taking into account the dynamic and multidimensional nature of emotion expression, we have created a tool that enables therapists to put into practice ad hoc emotional recognition learning therapies adapted to the features of each patient.

3 A Distributed Architecture for Conveying Emotions and Body Gestures Through Avatars

The main goal of this work is to present an architecture to convey the voice, facial expressions and body movements of a user (e.g. a therapist, physician, patient, etc.) by means of an avatar so that he may interact remotely with another user. In this sense, such avatar will be able to reproduce the user's emotions. Moreover, it is worth noting that the avatars to be used in this architecture are created and fully personalized by using Adobe Fuse[1]. This software enables us to create 3D avatars from scratch by customizing more than 280 attributes. Moreover, this software has been chosen because it enables us to generate humanlike avatars, thus improving the chances of acceptance of the avatars by the user [12]. The proposed architecture is illustrated in Fig. 1, where it can be seen how the different user's input stimulus are conveyed by means of the avatar. More specifically, this architecture consists of the following layers:

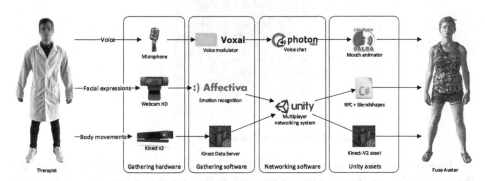

Fig. 1. Hardware and software architecture to convey voice, facial expressions and body movement by means of a Fuse avatar

---

[1] Adobe Fuse CC: http://www.adobe.com/products/fuse.html.

- *Gathering hardware*: First, the therapist's side of this distributed application will gather his/her movements, face and raw voice by using several hardware devices.
- *Gathering software*: Once the previous stimuli have been gathered, a software layer will process them in order to obtain the therapist's movements, emotions and modulated voice (aimed ad adapting it to the avatars age and gender as it will be explained in Sect. 3.1).
- *Networking software*: With the previous processed stimuli ready to be sent, a networking layer will transmit them to the patient's side application by using cloud network services to transmit both data and voice.
- *Unity assets*: Finally, the patient's application will implement several Unity assets [13] which will transform the data received through the network into the avatar's expressions, movements and voice.

In the following subsections, the mechanisms developed to express each one of those input stimuli are detailed. Thus, Sect. 3.1 will deal with the voice modulation and transmission, Sect. 3.2 will explain the recognition of emotions and finally, Sect. 3.3 will describe the gathering and transmission process for the therapist movements.

3.1 Voice

User's voice is gathered through a microphone and modified in real-time by using a voice modulation software[2]. Thanks to this voice modulator, it is possible to adapt the user's voice to the avatar's gender and age as needed (see Fig. 2). Since the avatar is run as a Unity-based application, in order to transmit the modulated voice stream, Photon voice[3] is used since it is integrated with Unity (Fig. 1).

Fig. 2. Modulator configuration for old woman voice

Finally, once the voice reaches the remote computer, it is not only played, but also the avatars lips are synced with the received audio stream. For this aim, a Unity asset named SALSA[4] is used. Thanks to this asset, the avatars eyes are moved randomly, thus creating a more human-like face.

---

[2] Voxal Voice Changer: http://www.nchsoftware.com/voicechanger.

[3] Photon Voice: https://www.photonengine.com/en-US/voice/.

[4] SALSA with RandomEyes: http://crazyminnowstudio.com/unity-3d/lip-sync-salsa/.

Fig. 3. Emotion recognition trainer application

3.2 Facial Expression

In order to make the avatar displays the user's emotions, we start by recording his/her face by using a high definition camera and recognize 7 different emotions (anger, contempt, disgust, fear, joy, sadness and surprise). This emotion recognition is performed by using Affectiva [14], which is integrated with Unity by using its own SDK. Aiming at improving the emotion recognition, a training software was developed to adjust such recognition for each user. Figure 4 shows the trainer application asking a user (left side) to imitate a target face (right side) for the recognition of joy emotion.

Fig. 4. Fuse avatar showing a mild (left) and a strong (right) happiness emotion

Once an emotion has been recognized, it is sent through the Unity UNET network[5] by means of Remote Procedure Calls (RPC). A script running in the avatar's computer executes a RPC every time a new emotion is recognized that alters the avatar's blendshapes [15]. It is worth noting that such emotions are considered as strong or mild

---

[5] Unity UNET: https://docs.unity3d.com/Manual/UNetOverview.html.

emotions. In order words, depending of the intensity of the user's facial expression, the avatar will show a strong or mild emotion (Fig. 4).

3.3   Body Movements

The avatar is required to replicate user's movements. Therefore, to gather such movements, a Kinect v2 device is used [16]. Nevertheless, the problem here is that the gathered user's skeleton must be synced though the network. To address this issue, it was decided to use an out-of-the-box solution.

More specifically, we use Kinect Data Server[6] in order to gather the user's movements and send it through UNET to the client (see Fig. 5). Such client will feature a different Unity asset[7] able to get data Kinect Data Server, thus creating a VRNP-like [17] client-server system. Finally, this Unity asset processes the received body movements making the Fuse avatar replicate them.

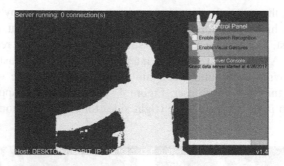

Fig. 5. Kinect Data Server detecting a user

4   A Distributed Application to Perform Dynamic Therapies for Social Cognitive Deficit Through Avatars

Once the distributed architecture has been shown, this section presents the distributed tool for social cognition deficit treatment [1] that has been developed. The goal of this system is to help patients suffering from social cognitive deficit, who has difficulties recognizing the emotional status of his/her interlocutor. Therefore, they interact with an avatar which is remotely controlled by a therapist in order to try to recognize the avatars emotions. In the following, the applications used by the therapist and the patients are explained.

---

[6] Kinect v2 Examples with MS-SDK: http://www.assetstore.unity3d.com/en/#!/content/18708.

[7] Kinect v2 VR Examples: http://www.assetstore.unity3d.com/en/#!/content/61376.

4.1   Patient's Application

This application is used by patients suffering from social cognitive deficit to interact with his/her therapist remotely. In order to make this interaction more immersive, patients use a Virtual Reality (VR) headset featuring eye-tracking[8]. This VR interaction style also enables patients to "feel" presence of other individuals. Therefore, specialists can take advantage of this facility to modify their position regarding the patient, thus making him/her feel under more or less pressure. Moreover, since we are using an eye-tracking-enabled headset, it is possible to know where the patient is looking while performing the therapy. This information can be useful for therapists, thus making them aware if the patient is really looking at the avatar [18].

Fig. 6. Patient's view when interacting with the therapist's avatar

As aforementioned, the goal of this system is to facilitate patient may recognize avatars' emotions. Therefore, the interaction of the patient with the therapist is made basically by means of voices. As an example, the therapist could ask the patient "what emotion am I showing right now?" and the patient will try to guess such emotion afterwards. Figure 6 shows a screenshot of the patient's application where it can be seen an avatar controlled remotely by a therapist.

Finally, it is worth noting that the client application will also send a video stream of the patient to the therapist. However, since the patient will be using a headset, therapist will not see the patient's whole face. However, the video stream can be used to record the session and to analyze the patient's body movements later on.

4.2   Therapist's Application

On the contrary to the patient's application, therapists do not use a VR headset to interact. In this case, therapist emotions, voice and movements are gathered by using the elements shown in the architecture illustrated in Sect. 3 (see Fig. 1). Therefore, this

---

[8] FOVE 0: https://www.getfove.com/.

application uses a Kinect v2 device with Kinect Data Server to gather his/her movements which, in turn, are replicated by his/avatar.

Besides, a RGB camera captures the therapist face in order to recognize the therapist's emotions and apply them to the avatar. Finally, his/her voice is also recorded and sent to the patient's computer once it has been modulated to fit the avatar's gender and age.

In spite of the emotion, movement and voice recognition features of this application, the therapist may enable or disable them, as needed. For instance, regarding the emotions, the therapist can choose between making the avatar show the recognize emotion or just choosing which emotion it will show among 13 different possibilities, namely, 6 mild emotions, 6 strong emotions and a neutral one (see Fig. 7).

Fig. 7. Therapist's view when interacting with a remote patient

Regarding the movement recognition, it is possible to convey the gathered movements to the avatar or just make it play a standard idle animation. Moreover, the avatar can walk around the virtual therapist's office. This is done either by recognizing the therapist position by using Kinect or just moving it by using a computer keyboard. In the event that the latter option is selected, the avatar would play a standard walking animation instead of reproducing therapist actual steps. Finally, the therapist can also enable or disable the transmission of his/her voice.

Figure 7 shows the interface of this application where the panel at the bottom may be used to enable/disable the recognition and transmission of facial expressions, body movements (gestures and walking), and voice. This panel also enables the therapist to manually establish the avatar's expression instead of using the recognized one. Moreover, at the top-left corner, a video stream of the patient is shown, thus enabling the therapist to watch the remote patient. Finally, the interface also shows both the avatars of the therapist and the so that the former may be aware of its avatar position regarding the patient's [18]. However, the patient's avatar is always static, used only as a reference of the patient's location in the virtual therapist's office.

5 Conclusions and Future Work

Social cognitive deficits [1] is frequent in patients affected by schizophrenia [3], autism spectrum [4] or acquired brain injury (ABI) [6]. Patients suffering from these deficits are unable to understand the emotion status of their interlocutors. Therefore, such patients have social interaction problems derived from this problem.

In this work, we are proposing a distributed system to perform remote rehabilitation therapies [19] for social cognitive deficit. This system enables therapists to embody avatars that interact with the affected patients. For this aim, this system gathers therapist's emotions, voice and movements that are conveyed to the avatar's. In this sense, the therapist interacts with the patient through the avatar to present him different emotions. However, therapist may also choose avatars movements and emotions, instead of using his/her own ones. Besides, patients interact with this system by using a VR headset in order to have a more immersive experience. Thus, the therapy consists in representing emotions through the avatar that have to be recognized by the.

To make this system possible, a distributed software and hardware architecture has been used. By using the devices identified on this architecture, voice, emotions and body movements of the therapist are gathered and sent to the avatar. For voice, a modulator is used in order to adapt it to the avatar's gender and age. As far as the emotions are concerned, a facial expressions recognition software is used to recognize 13 different emotions (6 strong, 6 mild and one neutral). Finally, a Kinect v2 will be used to gather the user's movements.

As a future work, it is planned to create a therapies editor that will enable the therapist to create a session script that will be automatically played by the avatar. This will facilitate that therapists will not be required to be connected to the system. Thus, a voice recognition software will be added to our architecture, aimed at recognizing the patient's voice. Hence, it will be possible to verify if such patient has recognized the avatar's emotion correctly. Thanks to this automated recognition, the therapist will be able to create dynamic session scripts based on the correctness of the emotion recognitions, thus increasing or decreasing the difficulty of the session.

Finally, the application features 6 predefined avatars. As another future work, it is being considered the possibility of creating a different application that will import a custom Fuse avatar into our system. This avatar will be adapted to the specific needs of the patients. This personalization will be especially relevant for those suffering from schizophrenia, so that they will be able to visualize their auditory hallucinations.

Acknowledgements. This work was partially supported by Spanish Ministry of Economy, Industry and Competitiveness, State Research Agency/European Regional Development Fund under EmoBioFeedback (DPI2016-80894-R), HA-SYMBIOSIS (TIN2015-72931-EXP) and Vi-SMARt (TIN2016-79100-R) Grants. We would also want to thank Rumen Filkov for providing us with his Kinect assets for Unity.

References

1. Harvey, P.D., Penn, D.: Social cognition: the key factor predicting social outcome in people with schizophrenia? Psychiatry (Edgmont) **7**, 41–44 (2010)
2. van Zwieten, A., Meyer, J., Hermens, D.F., Hickie, I.B., Hawes, D.J., Glozier, N., Naismith, S.L., Scott, E.M., Lee, R.S.C., Guastella, A.J.: Social cognition deficits and psychopathic traits in young people seeking mental health treatment. PLoS ONE **8**, e67753 (2013)
3. Gottesman, I.I.: Schizophrenia Genesis: The Origins of Madness. WH Freeman/Times Books/Henry Holt & Co, New York (1991)
4. Baron-Cohen, S., Wheelwright, S., Skinner, R., Martin, J., Clubley, E.: The autism-spectrum quotient (AQ): evidence from asperger syndrome/high-functioning autism, malesand females, scientists and mathematicians. J. Autism Dev. Disord. **31**, 5–17 (2001)
5. Teruel, M.A., Navarro, E., Romero, D., García, M., Fernández-Caballero, A., González, P.: An innovative tool to create neurofeedback games for ADHD treatment. In: Ferrández, J.M., Álvarez-Sánchez, J.R., de la Paz, F., Toledo Moreo, J., Adeli, H. (eds.) Natural and Artificial Computation for Biomedicine and Neuroscience, pp. 183–192. Springer International Publishing, Switzerland (2017). doi:10.1007/978-3-319-59740-9_18
6. Rosenberg, H., McDonald, S., Dethier, M., Kessels, R.P.C., Westbrook, R.F.: Facial emotion recognition deficits following moderate-severe traumatic brain injury (TBI): re-examining the valence effect and the role of emotion intensity. J. Int. Neuropsychol. Soc. **20**, 994–1003 (2014)
7. Calvo, M.G., Nummenmaa, L.: Perceptual and affective mechanisms in facial expression recognition: an integrative review. Cogn. Emot. **30**, 1081–1106 (2016)
8. Fernández-Caballero, A., Martínez-Rodrigo, A., Pastor, J.M., Castillo, J.C., Lozano-Monasor, E., López, M.T., Zangróniz, R., Latorre, J.M., Fernández-Sotos, A.: Smart environment architecture for emotion detection and regulation. J. Biomed. Inf. **64**, 55–73 (2016)
9. Calvo, M.G., Nummenmaa, L.: Perceptual and affective mechanisms in facial expression recognition: An integrative review. Cogn. Emot. **30**, 1081–1106 (2016)
10. Garrido, M.V., Lopes, D., Prada, M., Rodrigues, D., Jerónimo, R., Mourão, R.P.: The many faces of a face: comparing stills and videos of facial expressions in eight dimensions (SAVE database). Behav. Res. Methods. (2016)
11. Keltner, D., Cordaro, D.T.: Understanding multimodal emotional expressions: recent advances in basic emotion theory. In: Fernández-Dols, J.-M., Russel, J.A. (eds.) The Science fo Facial Expresion. Oxford University Press, Oxford (2017)
12. Mori, M., MacDorman, K., Kageki, N.: The uncanny valley [from the field]. IEEE Robot. Autom. Mag. **19**, 98–100 (2012)
13. Menard, M., Wagstaff, B.: Game Development with Unity. Cengage Learning, Boston (2014)
14. McDuff, D., Mahmoud, A., Mavadati, M., Amr, M., Turcot, J., Kaliouby, R. el: AFFDEX SDK: a cross-platform real-time multi-face expression recognition toolkit. In: 2016 CHI Conference Extended Abstracts on Human Factors in Computing Systems (CHI EA 2016), pp. 3723–3726. ACM Press, Santa Clara, USA (2016)
15. Lewis, J.P., Anjyo, K.: Direct manipulation blendshapes. IEEE Comput. Graph. Appl. **30**, 42–50 (2010)
16. Lachat, E., Macher, H., Mittet, M.A., Landes, T., Grussenmeyer, P.: First experiences with Kinect v2 sensor for close range 3D modelling. Int. Arch. Photogramm. Remote Sens. Spat. Inf. Sci. **40**, 93 (2015)

17. Taylor, R.M., Hudson, T.C., Seeger, A., Weber, H., Juliano, J., Helser, A.T.: VRPN: a device-independent, network-transparent VR peripheral system. In: ACM Symposium on Virtual Reality Software and Technology (VRST 2001) p. 55. ACM Press, Baniff, Canada (2001)
18. Teruel, M.A., Navarro, E., González, P.: Towards an awareness interpretation for physical and cognitive rehabilitation systems. In: García, C.R., Caballero-Gil, P., Burmester, M., Quesada-Arencibia, A. (eds.) Ubiquitous Computing and Ambient Intelligence, pp. 121–132. Springer International Publishing, Switzerland (2016). doi:10.1007/978-3-319-48746-5_13
19. Teruel, M.A., Navarro, E., González, P.: Exploiting awareness for the development of collaborative rehabilitation systems. Mob. Inf. Syst. J. (2017, in press)

Human-Avatar Symbiosis in Cognitive Cybertherapies: Proof of Concept for Auditory Verbal Hallucinations

Antonio Fernández-Caballero[1,2,5(✉)], Patricia Fernández-Sotos[3,5],
Elena Navarro[1,2,5], Pascual González[1,2,5], Jorge J. Ricarte[4], Laura Ros[4],
José M. Latorre[4], and Roberto Rodríguez-Jiménez[3,5]

[1] Instituto de Investigación en Informática de Albacete,
Universidad de Castilla-La Mancha, 02071 Albacete, Spain
antonio.fdez@uclm.es
[2] Departamento de Sistemas Informáticos, Universidad de Castilla-La Mancha,
02071 Albacete, Spain
[3] Instituto de Investigación Hospital 12 de Octubre (i+12),
Avda. de Córdoba s/n, 28041 Madrid, Spain
[4] Facultad de Medicina de Albacete, Universidad de Castilla-La Mancha,
02071 Albacete, Spain
[5] Centro de Investigación Biomédica en Red, Salud Mental (CIBERSAM),
Avda. Monforte de Lemos 3-5, 29029 Madrid, Spain

Abstract. Schizophrenia, a health and social problem of enormous importance and cost, is a serious mental disorder that has defied researchers for many years. Virtual and augmented reality (VR/AR) is proving to be a powerful experimental tool to study such complex cognitive processes. But there are no VR/AR tools for the systematic treatment of schizophrenia. Avatars do not incorporate adaptation, learning and evolution able to produce natural communication and interaction with humans. To significantly advance the state of art, it is proposed to supplement VR/AR with brain-computer interfaces (BCI) based on obtaining electrical brain signals. The project "Human-avatar symbiosis in cognitive cybertherapies: Proof of concept for auditory verbal hallucinations" assesses whether, through the complementary use of VR/AR and BCI, it is possible to achieve human-machine symbiosis (between a patient who hears voices and "his/her" avatar), which would provide an unforeseen advance. It relies on automatic adaptation, learning and evolution over BDI (beliefs-desires-intentions) models, proper of the intelligent agency paradigm inspired in social behaviour. The proof of concept will show if the proposal is an alternative/complement to conventional therapies of auditory verbal hallucinations and can guide the patient from a negative socio-emotional behaviour toward successful social situations.

Keywords: Human-avatar symbiosis · Virtual reality · Augmented reality · Brain-computer interfaces · Auditory verbal hallucinations

© Springer International Publishing AG 2017
S.F. Ochoa et al. (Eds.): UCAmI 2017, LNCS 10586, pp. 742–753, 2017.
DOI: 10.1007/978-3-319-67585-5_72

1   Introduction

Schizophrenia is a serious mental disorder that has been a challenge for researchers and human understanding for many years. In fact, schizophrenia is a health and social problem of great importance and economic cost. Based on traditional postulates, such as delusions or hallucinations are a primary symptom of schizophrenia that can not be addressed [1], the neuropsychological treatment of schizophrenia has been a subject forgotten until recently. Fortunately, scepticism about the neuropsychiatric/neuropsychological treatments of schizophrenia symptoms has been disappearing, mainly due to three factors:

- First, the emergence of more evidence on the fact that cognitive, social and neurological factors are involved in schizophrenic disorder, so that the symptoms can be understood and modified.
- Second, the low or null efficacy of neuroleptic drugs for the treatment of schizophrenia, despite their chronic administration and side effects such as drowsiness or weight gain. It is estimated that at least one in two patients leaves medication [2]. In addition, between 20 and 60% of patients are non-responders to drug treatment [3]. The effect of neuroleptics, compared to placebo, is only found in a mid-range [4]. In a recent longitudinal study carried out over 20 years, it was observed that more than 70% of patients receiving antipsychotic drug treatment continued to show symptoms [5].
- Third, increased studies showing a clear efficacy of cognitive cut-off therapies, such as training in cognition and social interaction, cognitive-behavioural therapy for psychotic disorders or metacognitive training [6].

These factors highlight the need for a cognitive and social approach that allows the implementation of socio-cognitive treatments. As shown in Fig. 1, the treatment of auditory hallucinations combines medication and psychotherapy. Unfortunately, it has been proven that the achievements of this approach are currently still scarce.

There is an increase of studies that connect the appearance of symptoms with neurological deficits that are activated in situations of social interaction. For example, the appearance of schizophrenia symptoms is associated with the activation of some brain areas (the most studied so far is the lateral prefrontal cortex) when facing challenging social situations or where there is a perception of evaluation (e.g. [7]). Thus, clarification of the interaction between environmental/social and neurological mechanisms through novel integrative approaches offers a wide range of opportunities for therapy and prevention of schizophrenia in patients (for example, [8]). In this sense, it is expected that studies using cognitive neurotechnologies could shed light on certain high-level cognitive functions present or absent in psychiatric patients with auditory verbal hallucinations (AVH).

This paper introduces a novel project in line with the previous objective to help patients suffering AVH.

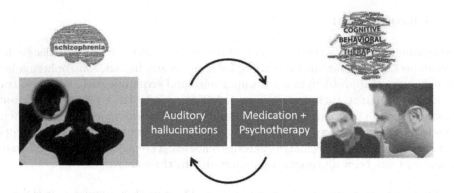

Fig. 1. Currently, auditory hallucinations are treated by psychotherapists with poor clinical success

2 Human-Machine Symbiosis as Alternative Cybertherapy in Auditory Verbal Hallucinations

The project "Human-avatar symbiosis in cognitive cybertherapies: Proof of concept for auditory verbal hallucinations" aims to show that human-machine symbiosis (here, between patient and avatar) is a novel exploratory and breakthrough pathway of cognitive computer-mediated treatment. This symbiosis is based on virtual and augmented reality (VR/AR) and computer-brain interfaces (BCI). It is guided by psychotherapists and capable of offering an alternative/complement to conventional therapies. This way, it is meant to make a qualitative leap toward a substantial improvement of auditory hallucinations. This alternative, nowadays unthinkable by traditional methods, consists in guiding the patient to social situations of success. The project aims to collect a novel and emerging idea that is not yet mature, but which can radically transform research in certain areas of mental health.

Today, virtual reality (VR) technologies have already proven to be promising supplements in psychotherapy. In fact, VR is a technology with potential benefit in rehabilitation assessment, treatment and research [9]. Virtual realities allow users to interact in real-time with three-dimensional computer-generated environments [10,11]. They allow the creation of ecologically valid stimulus environments, thus offering clinical assessment and rehabilitation options not present in traditional methods. The fact that VR applications simulate real experiences and provoke emotions, including physiological symptoms such as sweating or nausea, highlights their potential to complement conventional therapies. For users to experience virtual environments as real, two conditions are required: immersion and presence. Immersion describes a state in which the user's self-awareness diminishes due to his/her increasing participation in the virtual environment. The feeling of being physically immersed gives rise to a sense of presence, which includes the perception of the environment as real [12,13]. On the other hand, people seem to experience a strong sense of control in VR [14]. Moreover, another technology that has greatly advanced in recent years is augmented reality (AR). AR describes the overlapping of virtual elements in the real world. Therefore, people have a visualisation of the real world and virtual elements at the same time [15]. Research on the use of VR and AR technologies in psychotherapy has mainly focused on behavioural therapy and has demonstrated to be effective in the treatment of certain phobias [16].

On the other hand, symbiosis is defined as "a close and prolonged association between two or more organisms of different species that benefits each member". Until now, human-machine symbiosis is being applied timidly in the medical sciences as a way to improve quality of life. In the present case, symbiosis is mainly aimed at benefiting the patient in his/her improvement of mental illness through interaction with a personal avatar. However, the avatar also benefits from the symbiotic interaction, as it advances in its knowledge of the patient throughout its entire useful life. Human-machine symbiosis is related to various cognitive neurotechnologies such as neuroelectronics, particularly when considering brain-computer interfaces (BCI) technologies. The main objectives of the human-machine symbiosis are: (1) to allow computers to facilitate logical thinking since they now facilitate the solution of formulated problems, and (2) to allow humans and computers to cooperate in decision-making and control of complex situations without inflexible dependence of predetermined programs [17].

We believe that the clarification of neural and social mechanisms of interaction, through the use of electroencephalography (EEG) registers (here, through signals obtained from BCI low-cost devices) during social functioning in virtual environments, offers a great opportunity for the creation of effective therapies for the healing of auditory hallucinations and even their prevention. This proposal includes the analysis of the neural processes present to the pathological social interactions of schizophrenia and their relation with electric cerebral activation in the form of feedback. In this way it will be possible to better understand certain high-level cognitive functions, such as the formation of knowledge and belief, reasoning and decision making, emotion, interaction and communication.

Finally, a genuine human-machine symbiosis is not viable without continuous adaptation, learning and evolution of the machine (in this case, the avatar). We propose to use the paradigm of intelligent agents given their pronounced character of autonomous and flexible behaviour [18,19], which means that such systems are capable of acting in an independent and autonomous manner in a social environment in order to achieve their design objectives. The beliefs-desires-intentions (BDI) model of the agency approximates this type of behaviour by means of two related theories about the philosophical concept of intentionality. (a) Intentional systems are defined as entities that are subject to desires and other propositional attitudes, and (b) the theory of practical reasoning is a common-sense psychological framework for understanding ourselves and others, based on beliefs, desires and intentions.

Figure 2 shows the path we consider worth exploring towards the achievement of a new paradigm in the cybertreatment of this mental disorder. Figure 2a shows what we have come to call "patient-hallucination interaction". This is

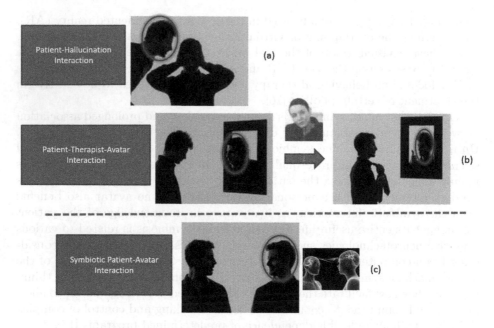

Fig. 2. Evolving to symbiotic human-avatar interaction

the situation that must be treated by specialists. It also shows that the patient is totally at the mercy of his/her own auditory hallucinations. In turn, Fig. 2b represents the still incipient current state of the issue in cognitive cyberterapies associated with the disease. In fact, some recent work (e.g. [20]) is demonstrating the viability and importance of avatars (fully controlled by therapists) in VR/AR environments.

This step has been denominated "patient-therapist-avatar interaction". The avatar interacts with the patient through the therapist's control. Finally, the proposal is graphically reflected in Fig. 2c. The goal is also to achieve an authentic symbiotic patient-avatar interaction in a VR/AR environment, but now the avatar is totally and absolutely conformed to the image of his/her patient, having evolved in a BDI-based model of interaction (see Fig. 2b) with the therapists involved in the treatment of the schizophrenic patient.

3   Current Picture of the Problem

3.1   Virtual/Augmented Reality and Simulated Test of Social Interaction

Psychiatric disorders are not only manifested in a social context, but the environment and the interactions of each day also cause mental disorder. Mental health and social life are closely related as shown by the high frequency of social deficits of psychiatric patients and the greater presence of psychiatric disorders in people exposed to adverse social environments. For example, childhood sexual abuse and parental neglect is a clear risk factor for serious mental illness such as borderline personality disorder and schizophrenia.

The design of VR/AR instruments can be a powerful experimental tool for the study of complex cognitive processes that occur in situations of social interaction. Normally, therapeutic intervention occurs in a very socially restricted environment (therapist and patient), so the testing and extrapolation to social situations of the therapies learned from the therapist is very limited.

Although there are some studies that support the ecological validity of VR/AR for various rehabilitating aspects of schizophrenia, such as assessing cognitive flexibility in situations of daily living experiences [21], such as improvement of social skills in the face of role-playing [22], improvement of social cognition [23], or motivation for work reinsertion [24], still there are no VR/AR tools available for the systematic treatment of schizophrenia, despite their great potential. However, they are increasingly being accepted and demanded by mental health professionals, so they should soon complement the work of therapeutic intervention in patients with schizophrenia, especially in aspects such as treatment of auditory verbal hallucinations.

There are already timid contributions that explore the benefits of VR/AR in the treatment of hallucinations, but do not have sufficient methodological rigour. For example, in a brief experiment, in which feedback errors were manipulated, delusional ideas associated with the distortion of reality were improved [25]. From an ethical point of view, reproducing the auditory hallucinations in the patient for treatment with VR does not produce effects on physical activation or anxiety [26].

In addition, virtual environments offer the advantage of giving the participant total control over the virtual situation, thus reducing any anxiety situa-

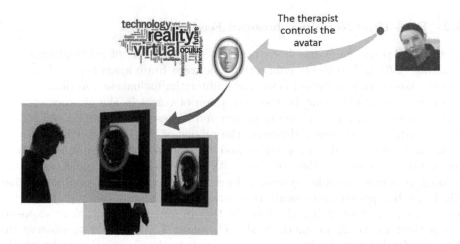

Fig. 3. The state-of-the-art already allows the therapist to control avatars in a non-immersive VR reality environment. But the avatar has no adaptation capability

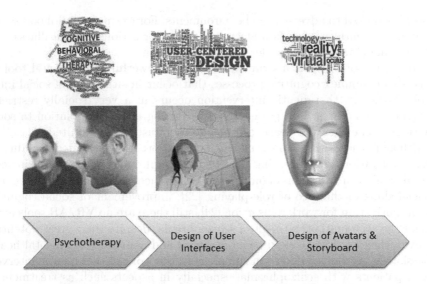

Fig. 4. The human-avatar symbiotic interaction proposal is based on the information collected by the therapist during psychotherapy sessions with the patient. The therapist uses a tool for the design of avatars and scripts (from the patient's description of his/her mental idea of the voices). User interfaces are designed to facilitate the therapist's descriptive work

tion. As a summary, it can be affirmed that firm steps are already being taken nowadays towards the control of avatars by psychotherapists in virtual environments. But, as shown in Fig. 3, in today's systems there is no presence of adaptation/learning/automatic customisation of avatars to the patients' needs.

3.2   Real-Time Neuropsychosocial Feedback

In the last years, EEG has been used for the diagnosis of schizophrenia (for example, [27]) and to locate connectivity between brain areas involved in more specific aspects of schizophrenia such as auditory hallucinations. Auditory verbal hallucinations (AVH), that is, the perception of voices in the absence of auditory stimulus, is a very limiting symptom and is present between 50 and 80% of people with schizophrenia. However, the origins of AVH are still inconsistent, even after having used neuroimaging and electrophysiology techniques. In fact, the central mechanism that produces AVH involves not a single sense, but belongs to a more complex system of interaction. It should be emphasised that EEG can be applied more easily than other neuroimaging methods since it is less invasive, not requiring the introduction of ionising radiation or exposing the patient to strong magnetic fields. Therefore, EEG is used to observe the connectivity between brain areas from changes in the electrical signal with the advantage of less invasiveness and better adaptability to portable/mobile devices.

It is also important to note that simple localisation of structural and functional dysfunctions is insufficient to explain the complex psychopathology of schizophrenia. For this reason, new models postulate that the symptoms of schizophrenia may be due to a failure in the integration of the activity of different neural circuits or hypothesise of the lack of neuronal connectivity [28]. Brain-computer interfaces based on obtaining real-time brain electrical (EEG) signals could allow patients to achieve brain self-regulation through neurological feedback.

4   A New and Alternative Proposal of Auditory Verbal Hallucinations Cybertherapy

Currently, the cognitive and behavioural treatment of auditory hallucinations in patients suffering schizophrenia consists of maintaining face-to-face sessions to treat hallucinations and dosing medication (see Fig. 1). However, we are convinced that a cybertherapy based on human-avatar symbiotic interaction will take us beyond the mere attempt to solve a cognitive and behavioural problem. The evolution proposed is to bring together several disciplines to build a truly intelligent artificial cognitive system. This project seeks to better understand the brain of schizophrenic patients in order to treat their mental disease more satisfactorily.

Figure 4 is intended to detail the general approach of this proposal. In first place, the patient-avatar symbiotic interaction proposal is based on an automated collection of psychotherapy sessions between therapist and patient. These valuable conversations make it possible to describe extensively the patient's auditory hallucinations. The system to be developed will feature a user-centred interface tool to design:

1. The avatars designed by the patient, which will represent the characters described as hallucinations.
2. The scripts (or possible courses) needed by the therapist to guide the conversations with the patient through avatars, in order to deal with auditory hallucinations.
3. The VR/AR environments in which the experiments between the avatars and the patient will be carried out.

Once the VR/AR environments and the personalised avatars have been designed, depending on the patient's auditory hallucinations, the system is prepared for a first stage in which the therapist controls the conversations of the avatars with the patient. It follows the pre-designed pathways of different scripts established from the classic treatment sessions. This first stage is fundamental in the future patient-avatar symbiosis. Figure 5 represents the ideas that underlie this stage.

As already mentioned, the psychotherapist controls the avatar according to the possible scripts depending on the patient's reactions in this VR/AR environment. Simultaneously, the avatar evolves from the beliefs, desires and intentions

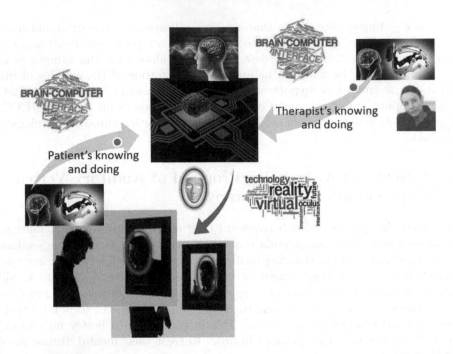

Fig. 5. The avatar runs the therapist's script in a VR/AR environment. Meanwhile, BCI interfaces capture the knowledge and intentions of patient and therapist. The avatar adapts by learning from the human mind's signals

of both therapist and patient by using BCI techniques. In this way, the avatar's "brain" conforms to the reality and needs of the patient's socio-affective relationship, while collecting the psychotherapist's know-how (knowledge and professional experience). This continuous learning/adaptation of the avatar in different sessions will incrementally forge the human-avatar symbiotic interaction. As previously discussed, the adaptation and evolution of the avatar is based on learning theories of the intelligent agents paradigm, and more specifically from the BDI model. In this case, the orientation to follow is as described next:

– Beliefs represent information about the world (here, the world of auditory hallucinations). In this proposal, the avatar agent assumes the beliefs of both patient and therapist. Beliefs are disputed by the avatar based on the brain activity of patient and therapist.
– Desires, also known as goals, correspond to the tasks assigned to the agent. The avatar agent assumes the therapist's wishes, while learning from the patient's reactions and constant new goals. All this is captured neurally to direct the patient to a positive socio-affective state.
– Intentions are action sequences that an agent must perform. All intention is implemented as a stack of plan instances. In our case, intentions incorporate the scripts that the psychotherapist has been able to design from the therapy

sessions with the patient. These scripts will change throughout the entire neurofeedback process.
– Plans. BDI agents typically have a predefined set of plans. But, in this case, the plans are shaped according to the brain activity captured and analysed in real-time.

Finally, the goal outlined in the project described is reached. As shown in Fig. 6, symbiotic interaction is now a certainty. In a VR/AR reality environment, during its daily life, the avatar knows perfectly the needs of "his/her" patient. Evidently, this proposal remains always under the supervision of psychotherapists in order to show if the proposed techniques of symbiotic human-machine interaction can offer a new cognitive cybertherapy capable of offering a complement/alternative to conventional therapies. This would make a qualitative leap towards a substantial improvement in schizophrenic patients with auditory hallucinations, as avatars lead the patient to social situations of success.

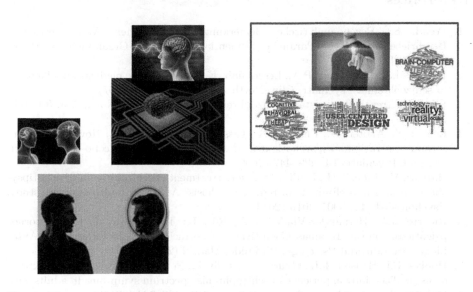

Fig. 6. The symbiotic interaction between human and avatar is now possible, thanks to the fact that the avatar perfectly complements the patient's needs to surpass the auditory hallucinations

5   Conclusions

This paper has introduced the "Human-avatar symbiosis in cognitive cybertherapies: Proof of concept for auditory verbal hallucinations" project. The overall objective of the project is to evaluate whether it is possible to achieve an actual human-machine symbiosis (between a patient who hears voices and "his/her" avatar) through the combined use of virtual and augmented reality, and brain-computer interfaces technologies.

The team members of this project foresee a yet non evaluable advance in the treatment of auditory verbal hallucinations in schizophrenic patients. The proposal also relies on automatic machine adaptation, learning and evolution over beliefs-desires-intentions models, proper of the intelligent agency paradigm inspired in social behaviour. The proof of concept resulting from the project should show if the proposal is an alternative/complement to conventional therapies of auditory verbal hallucinations and can guide the patient from a negative socio-emotional behaviour toward successful social situations.

Acknowledgements. This work was partially supported by Spanish Ministerio de Economía, Industria y Competitividad, Agencia Estatal de Investigación (AEI)/European Regional Development Fund under HA-SYMBIOSIS (TIN2015-72931-EXP) grant.

References

1. Freud, S.: Psychoanalytische Bemerkungen über einen Autobiographisch Beschriebenen Fall von Paranoia (Dementia paranoides). Gesammelte Werke **8**, 240–320 (1911)
2. Byerly, M.J., Nakonezny, P.A., Lescouflair, E.: Antipsychotic medication adherence in schizophrenia. Psychiatr. Clin. North Am. **30**, 437–452 (2007)
3. Elkis, H.: Treatment-resistant schizophrenia. Psychiatr. Clin. North Am. **30**, 511–533 (2007)
4. Leucht, S., Arbter, D., Engel, R.R., Kissling, W., Davis, J.M.: How effective are second- generation antipsychotic drugs? A meta-analysis of placebo-controlled trials. Mol. Psychiatr. **14**, 429–447 (2009)
5. Harrow, M., Jobe, T.H., Faull, R.N.: Does treatment of schizophrenia with antipsychotic medications eliminate or reduce psychosis? A 20-year multi-follow-up study. Psychol. Med. **44**, 3007–3016 (2014)
6. Ricarte, J.J., Hernández-Viadel, J.V., Ros, L.: Tratamiento de los trastornos psicóticos. Nuevas Terapias Cognitivas y Aportaciones de la Experiencia Autobiográfica. Editorial Psicología Pirámide, Madrid (2014)
7. Hooker, C.I., Benson, T.L., Gyurak, A., Tully, L.: Neural activity to positive expressions predicts daily experience of schizophrenia-spectrum symptoms in adults with high social anhedonia. J. Abnorm. Psychol. **123**, 190–204 (2014)
8. Krabbendam, L., Hooker, C.L., Aleman, A.: Neural effects of the social environment. Schizophr. Bull. **40**, 248–251 (2014)
9. Schultheis, M.T., Rizzo, A.A.: The application of virtual reality technology in rehabilitation. Rehabil. Psychol. **46**, 296 (2001)
10. Segal, R., Bhatia, M., Drapeau, M.: Therapists' perception of benefits and costs of using virtual reality treatments. Cyberpsychol. Behav. SoC. Netw. **14**, 29–34 (2011)
11. Rodríguez, A., Rey, B., Clemente, M., Wrzesien, M., Alcañiz, M.: Assessing brain activations associated with emotional regulation during virtual reality mood induction procedures. Expert Sys. Appl. **42**, 1699–1709 (2015)
12. Martinez, J., Garcia, A.S., Oliver, M., Molina, J.P., González, P.: Identifying 3D geometric shapes with a vibrotactile glove. IEEE Comput. Graph. Appl. **99** (2014). doi:10.1109/MCG.2014.81

13. Martínez, J., García, A.S., Oliver, M., Molina, J.P., González, P.: VITAKI: a vibrotactile prototyping toolkit for virtual reality and video games. Int. J. Hum. Comput. Interact. **30**, 855–871 (2014)
14. Hobbs, C.N., Kreiner, D.N., Honeycutt, M.W., Hinds, R.M., Brockman, C.J.: The illusion of control in a virtual reality setting. North Am. J. Psychol. **123**, 551–564 (2010)
15. Botella, C.M., Juan, M.X., Baños, R.M., Alcañiz, M., Guillén, V., Rey, B.: Mixing realities? An application of augmented reality for the treatment of cockroach phobia. Cyberpsychol. Behav. **8**, 216–217 (2005)
16. Eichenberg, C.: Application of "virtual realities" in psychotherapy: possibilities, limitations and effectiveness. In: Virtual Reality, Chap. 22. InTech (2011)
17. Licklider, J.C.R.: Man-computer symbiosis. IRE Trans. Hum. Fact. Electron. **1**, 4–11 (1960)
18. Gascueña, J.M., Navarro, E., Fernández-Caballero, A.: Model-driven engineering techniques for the development of multi-agent systems. Eng. Appl. Artif. Intell. **25**, 159–173 (2012)
19. Pavón, J., Gómez-Sanz, J., Fernández-Caballero, A., Valencia-Jiménez, J.J.: Development of intelligent multisensor surveillance systems with agents. Robot. Auton. Syst. **55**, 892–903 (2007)
20. Ruse, S.A., Harvey, P.D., Davis, V.G., Atkins, A.S., Fox, K.H., Keefe, R.S.E.: Virtual reality functional capacity assessment in schizophrenia: preliminary data regarding feasibility and correlations with cognitive and functional capacity performance. Schizophr. Res. Cogn. **1**, e21–e26 (2014)
21. Han, K.: Assessment of cognitive flexibility in real life using virtual reality: a comparison of healthy individuals and schizophrenia patients. Comput. Biol. Med. **42**, 841–847 (2012)
22. Park, K., Ku, J., Choi, S., Jang, G., Park, J.: A virtual reality application in role-plays of social skills training for schizophrenia: a randomized, controlled trial. Psychiatr. Res. **189**, 166–172 (2011)
23. Peyroux, E., Franck, N.: RC2S: a cognitive remediation program to improve social cognition in schizophrenia and related disorders. Front. Hum. Neurosci. **8**, 400 (2014)
24. Tsang, M.M., Man, D.W.: A virtual reality-based vocational training system (VRVTS) for people with schizophrenia in vocational rehabilitation. Schizophr. Res. **144**, 51–62 (2013)
25. Moritz, S., Voigt, M., Köther, U., Leighton, L., Kjahili, B., Babur, Z., Jungclaussen, D., Veckenstedt, R., Grzella, K.: Can virtual reality reduce reality distortion? Impact of performance feedback on symptom change in schizophrenia patients. J. Behav. Ther. Exp. Psychiatr. **45**, 267–271 (2014)
26. Stinson, K., Valmaggia, L.R., Antley, A., Slater, M., Freeman, D.: Cognitive triggers of auditory hallucinations: an experimental investigation. J. Behav. Ther. Exp. Psychiatr. **41**, 179–184 (2010)
27. Zhao, Q., Hu, B., Liu, L., Ratcliffe, M., Peng, H., Zhai, J., Li, L., Shi, Q., Liu, Q., Qi, Y.: An EEG based nonlinearity analysis method for schizophrenia diagnosis. In: 9th IASTED International Conference on Biomedical Engineering, pp. 136–142 (2012)
28. Ruiz, S., Birbaumer, N., Sitaram, R.: Abnormal neural connectivity in schizophrenia and fMRI-brain-computer interface as a potential therapeutic approach. Front. Psychiatr. **4**, 17 (2013)

Nonlinear Methodologies Applied to Automatic Recognition of Emotions: An EEG Review

Beatriz García-Martínez[1], Arturo Martínez-Rodrigo[1]([⊠]), Raúl Alcaraz[1],
Antonio Fernández-Caballero[2], and Pascual González[2]

[1] Instituto de Tecnologías Audiovisuales, Universidad de Castilla-La Mancha,
16071 Cuenca, Spain
Arturo.Martinez@uclm.es
[2] Instituto de Investigación en Informática de Albacete,
Universidad de Castilla-La Mancha, 02071 Albacete, Spain

Abstract. Development of algorithms for automatic detection of emotions is essential to improve affective skills of human-computer interfaces. In the literature, a wide variety of linear methodologies have been applied with the aim of defining the brain's performance under different emotional states. Nevertheless, recent findings have demonstrated the nonlinear and dynamic behavior of the brain. Thus, the use of nonlinear analysis techniques has notably increased, reporting promising results with respect to traditional linear methods. In this sense, this work presents a review of the latest advances in the field, exploring the main nonlinear metrics used for emotion recognition from EEG recordings.

Keywords: Emotion recognition · Complexity · Regularity · Predictability · Connectivity patterns

1 Introduction

Emotions are essential in human experiences since they influence in cognition, perception and daily tasks like learning, communication and rational decision-making [11]. Although emotions are basic in human interaction processes, human-machine interfaces (HMIs) are still not able to properly identify human emotional states and execute actions according to those feelings [56]. In a technological society in which HMIs are being increasingly applied in countless fields like medicine [45], computer games [9] or digital society [62], there is an urgent need of developing automatic systems able to correctly interpret human emotions. In this sense, the affective computing science [50] is mainly focused on the development and improvement of algorithms for emotions recognition, thus endowing affective systems of emotional intelligence [17,41].

In any case, quantifying an emotion is not a simple task. One of the main reasons is the fact that there are no standard models for the definition of emotional states [63]. Hence, in the literature there is a wide variety of theories for discrete emotion classification. Those emotional models vary from Ekman's six

© Springer International Publishing AG 2017
S.F. Ochoa et al. (Eds.): UCAmI 2017, LNCS 10586, pp. 754–765, 2017.
DOI: 10.1007/978-3-319-67585-5_73

basic emotions (happiness, sadness, surprise, disgust, anger and fear) [14], to those in which dozens of emotional states are defined (a total of fifty-five different emotional states were defined by the HUMAINE project) [59]. Nonetheless, the model presented by Russell is nowadays one of the most extended [57]. This two-dimensional model distributes all emotions in two dimensions called valence (pleasantness or unpleasantness) and arousal (calmness or excitement). Locations of emotions within this model are according to their level of these two dimensions.

Emotions have been traditionally identified by means of facial gestures and vocal expressions [7, 38]. Nevertheless, those physical features are not universally accepted since social and cultural aspects may influence on the way emotions are expressed in each part of the world [58]. For this reason, emotion recognition studies have focused on the assessment of physiological signals, which present different levels of activation for distinct emotional states [40]. Furthermore, physiological variables have demonstrated to follow a similar behavior independently of social and environmental factors, thus they can be universally accepted [63]. In this sense, electrocardiogram (ECG), electromyogram (EMG) or electro-dermal activity (EDA) have been widely studied under different emotional conditions. However, the most promising physiological variable is the electroencephalogram (EEG), since it reflects the first response to an external stimulus while the rest of variables are secondary effects of the brain's processes [26].

Traditionally, EEG recordings have been studied from a linear point of view, using linear algorithms based on statistical parameters and frequency characteristics of the signals [26]. However, some works have recently demonstrated a complex performance of the brain dynamics, suggesting that nonlinear analysis methodologies are more suitable than linear techniques for a better assessment of the underlying processes contained within EEG time series [8]. For this reason, the application of nonlinear metrics for EEG signals analysis has notably increased in the last years for the study of diseases like Alzheimer, Parkinson, epilepsy, depression or schizophrenia, among others [54].

In the present paper, nonlinear metrics are classified according to the algorithm used for the characterization of the nonlinearity of a temporal signal [2]. In this sense, indexes of evaluation of dimensional complexity (see Sect. 2.1) are based on the analysis of the evolution of correlation and temporal properties of a signal. Other metrics focus on the quantification of regularity and degree of chaos of finite time series (see Sect. 2.2). On the other hand, measurements of predictability can be provided with different symbolic metrics (see Sect. 2.3). Finally, it is also possible to detect functional connectivity patterns between different brain regions (as described in Sect. 2.4).

2   Nonlinear Feature Extraction from EEG Recordings

The basic principle of nonlinear techniques for time series analysis is the quantification of the intrinsic patterns generated by the chaotic dynamics of a complex system [16]. Currently, a wide number of algorithms for nonlinear signal assessment can be found in literature. Those metrics can be classified into four different groups, depending on their computation methods for nonlinearity evaluation.

2.1   Correlation and Dimensional Complexity Metrics

These methodologies allow to evaluate nonlinearity features of a time series by a thorough study of correlation properties directly in the time domain, where the signal is considered a geometric object [15]. It is the case of fractal algorithms, which focus on the time-evolutionary features and correlation properties for dynamic temporal signal characterization. Fractal dimension (FD) metrics analyze temporal ordering of time series by means of the quantification of the non-integer or fractional dimension that a geometric object occupies in the Euclidean space [16].

In the emotion recognition field, FD algorithms have been extensively used. For instance, Hatamikia and Nasrabadi [20] computed Katz and Petrosian's algorithms to detect four emotions corresponding to the four quadrants of the valence-arousal space (HAHV - high arousal, high valence; HALV - high arousal, low valence; LAHV - low arousal, high valence; LALV - low arousal, low valence). The combination of these two FD methods with other nonlinear metrics reported a classification accuracy around 70%. In another work, Sourina and Liu reported similar accuracy results using Higuchi and box-counting FD methods to discern between positive, negative and neutral feelings [60]. In the case of Lan et al. [31], Higuchi's FD was combined with spectral and statistical parameters to distinguish between happiness, pleasantness, fear and fright. Furthermore, multifractal FD algorithms have also been considered given the strong complexity and multiscalar nature of the brain. Hence, Lui and Sourina [37] demonstrated the effectiveness of multifractal Higuchi FD for discerning between more than two emotional states. In this sense, they achieved a maximum accuracy of 85.83% for two emotions, and 54.58% for eight emotions (happy, surprised, satisfied, protected, angry, frightened, unconcerned and sad) [37].

Detrended fluctuation analysis (DFA) has also been applied in emotion recognition processes. DFA is based on the quantification and evaluation of fluctuations in a non-stationary temporal signal to distinguish between internal and external causes of fluctuations of a complex system [47]. For this purpose, a scaling factor α is used as a self-similarity parameter that represents the main correlation features of the signal. In the literature, DFA has been used in combination with linear and nonlinear indexes for emotional states detection with EEG recordings. For example, Yuvaraj et al. [65] combined DFA with FD and spectral features to study the brain's performance of subjects with Parkinson's disease under six different emotional states (the six Ekman's basic emotions). However, results of DFA and FD were slightly lower than those reported by some linear metrics. Nevertheless, given the high complexity of the neural system, DFA has also been computed in its multifractal form with the aim of improving the results reported by single DFA. In this sense, Paul et al. [48] applied several multifractal DFA algorithms and different classifiers to recognize positive and negative feelings, reporting a classification rate of 84.5% for positive emotions and 82.5% for negative emotions.

All FD and DFA metrics previously described can be computed directly from time series, thus reducing the computational complexity of those indexes. Nevertheless, other methodologies require a reconstruction of the phase space of the time series to be analyzed, being a reconstructed phase space valid if any state of the dynamical system under study can be defined at any point [28]. Hence, a temporal signal is transformed into a geometric object or *attractor* in a state. The reconstruction of the phase space is made according to the Taken's delay embedding theorem, which asserts that an attractor can be reconstructed from a time delayed embedded space preserving the topological properties of the original time series [16].

One of the most used methods for reconstructed phase spaces characterization and measurement of dimensional complexity of a dynamic system is the correlation dimension (CD). This index is based on the assessment of the attractor's dimensionality by means of the quantification of the self-similarity of its points in the phase space [28]. To calculate the CD of a signal, the correlation sum of the temporal sequence (i.e., the number of points in the reconstructed space closer than a threshold r) is firstly computed [28]. Then, CD value corresponds to the line fitting slope in the log-log plot of the correlation sum as a function of r.

Numerous recent works have reported interesting results of the application of CD on EEG recordings for discerning between a group of emotional states. For instance, Peng *et al.* [49] combined CD with other linear and nonlinear features to assess chronic stress of mothers of children with mental retardation and mothers of healthy children. Apart from demonstrating the considerable effectiveness of nonlinear methods with respect to linear techniques, results reported an increase of CD for stress group in comparison with controls [49]. In addition, Khalili and Moradi [29] computed the CD of EEG signals and other physiological parameters to discern between positive, negative and rest states. Results highlighted the reliability and efficiency of EEG over other peripheral signals to detect emotions [29]. Furthermore, Hoseingholizade *et al.* [21] claimed that positive and negative stimuli produced a decrease of CD in frontal, temporal and parietal brain regions with respect to rest states. That could be translated into a more active implication of those areas when facing emotional situations, either positive or negative [21].

Finally, Hurst exponent (HE) has been also widely used to extract correlation properties of temporal signals. HE is based on the estimation of statistical self-similarity and correlation features of fractal time series by evaluating the asymptotic behavior and the recurrence rate of similar patterns at different scales in the reconstructed phase space [6,16]. In emotions recognition research field, Wang *et al.* [64] applied HE together with spectral, wavelet, and nonlinear features to discern between positive and negative states. Nevertheless, results derived from nonlinear methods were slightly lower in this case than those extracted from linear analysis techniques.

2.2   Regularity Metrics

Regularity of a time series can be defined as the degree of stability or chaos of the corresponding geometric attractor. More repetitiveness of patterns in a time series derives in a high level of regularity, while non-repetitive and disordered signals are considered strongly irregular. A well-known measure of regularity of a time series is entropy, which quantifies the disorder or rate of information contained within a temporal signal [28]. There is a wide variety of algorithms for entropy computation. For instance, approximate entropy (ApEn) assigns a non-negative number with higher values for completely irregular signals and lower levels for time series with many repetitive patterns [51]. ApEn is computed as the logarithmic likelihood that two sequences that match for m points (within a tolerance r) will also match for $m + 1$ points with the same tolerance r. Nevertheless, this algorithm considers each pattern matches itself, which influences on the entropy result obtained. As a solution, an improvement of ApEn called sample entropy (SampEn) was introduced [53]. SampEn excludes self-matches from the calculations so that the final entropy result is independent of the selected pattern length [53]. Furthermore, a new improvement called quadratic SampEn (QSampEn) estimates the regularity of a time series with an algorithm insensitive to the selection of threshold r by adding the term $\ln(2r)$ to SampEn equation [30].

In the literature, many works have studied the suitability of these regularity-based entropy metrics for emotions recognition. Indeed, most of these works have outperformed the results previously obtained for identification of emotional states with other linear and nonlinear indexes. It is the case of García-Martínez et al. [19], who demonstrated that QSampEn was the first single metric to correctly discern between calm and negative stress states. Furthermore, only two EEG channels from left frontal and right parietal areas were necessary to reach a classification accuracy over 75% [19]. In the same work, SampEn was also calculated, although it reported a slightly lower discriminant ability than QSampEn [19]. ApEn and SampEn have also been calculated to detect depression [52], positive and negative states [23], high and low levels of arousal and valence [27], and emotions in the four quadrants of the arousal-valence space [55].

However, it has been previously commented on the multiscale nature of physiological signals. In this sense, multiscale entropy (MEn) can be a useful tool to calculate the regularity of time series in multiple time scales. This method consists of computing and averaging independent entropy values for each time scale, commonly considering consecutive and non-overlapped samples [12]. With this algorithm, Li et al. [35] reported an accuracy of 70% when discerning between different emotional states. Nevertheless, an improvement of 12% was obtained by means of the empirical mode decomposition (EMD) of the original time series [35]. EMD is a time-frequency technique based on the Hilbert-Huang transformation used for non-stationary signals analysis [66]. Hence, all EEG channels were decomposed into intrinsic mode functions (IMF) on which SampEn was then computed. In this sense, Zhang et al. [66] applied EMD to discern between the four quadrants of the arousal-valence space with a discriminant power around

95%. Similarly, Mert and Akan [43] used multivariate EMD with SampEn and Shannon entropy (ShEn) from IMFs to identify emotions with high and low levels of valence and arousal.

2.3   Predictability and Symbolic Metrics

Predictability of nonlinear systems depends on the stability and deterministic temporal evolution of the time series dynamics. To this respect, Lyapunov exponents (LE) are well-known indexes for predictability quantification by means of the characterization of the trajectories in the reconstructed phase space [28]. In this sense, the exponential convergence or divergence of the trajectories with respect to the initial point informs about the degree of predictability or chaos of the system. An exponentially fast increase of divergence of the trajectories corresponds to a higher level of unpredictability, and it is represented with positive exponents. A multidimensional system presents one LE for each scale, but in many occasions only the largest Lyapunov exponent (LLE) is enough to characterize the system.

This metric has been applied in a variety of studies reporting interesting results in emotional states detection with EEG signals. With a combination of LLE and other nonlinear methods, Hosseini et al. [22] showed an accuracy over 80% to discern between calm and stress states. Furthermore, EEG signals reported better results than the rest of peripheral recordings in this work [22]. Similarly, Hosseinifard et al. [24] combined LLE and other nonlinear features with machine learning algorithms, reaching a discriminant ability around 90%. On the other hand, Acar et al. [1] reported the existence of considerable differences in LLE values for subjects under three emotional states, namely happiness, sadness and fear.

Symbolic methodologies base their performance in a transformation of the original time series into discrete symbols that are grouped in sequences or words according to their temporal order [47]. Hence, the word length template has to be previously defined and it has to be moved along the signal one step each time to form new sequences. A thorough analysis of these symbolic patterns with different techniques is the key to obtain valuable information of the underlying dynamic processes in those time series.

In addition, symbolic time series can also be analyzed with entropy metrics able to assess temporal relationships among samples contained within a sequence. For example, common Shannon entropy (ShEn) has been computed in emotions recognition context to detect excitement, happiness, sadness and hatred [3]. Murugappan et al. [46] also compared the performance of ShEn with linear techniques to discern between five emotions (disgust, happy, surprise, fear and neutral). Results of ShEn were around 83% of accuracy, outperforming those reported by linear methods [46]. Another interesting symbolic metric is permutation entropy (PerEn), which evaluates the ordering of the data of a sequence in a fast and noise-robust manner [5]. This metric was used by Li et al. [34] to detect states of excitement and fear with a discriminant ability around 80%. However, PerEn only considers the order of the data in a pattern, ignoring the amplitudes of the samples in the sequence. Thus, a new approach called amplitude-aware permutation entropy (AAPE) was developed as an improvement of PerEn's algorithm [4]. García-Martínez *et al.* [18] has recently computed the predictability-based metrics PerEn and AAPE with the regularity-based QSampEn to discern between calm and distress emotional states. The combination of only two channels (left parietal P3 from AAPE and right parietal P4 from QSampEn) showed a classification accuracy over 80%, also demonstrating the complementarity of regularity and predictability-based entropy measures [18].

Furthermore, Lempel and Ziv proposed a symbolic algorithm for evaluation of time series randomness called Lempel-Ziv complexity (LZC) [33]. This technique converts a time series into a binary sequence and quantifies the different patterns in the signal and their temporal occurrence rate. High values of LZC represent high levels of complexity of a word sequence. The effectiveness of this technique has been demonstrated by Chen *et al.* [10], reporting a discriminatory ability of about 80% for identification of different emotions only using a single index in a simple classification model. On the other hand, Akar *et al.* [2] studied the EEG processes of patients with major depression under different emotional conditions. In this sense, LZC and other nonlinear methodologies were computed, demonstrating a highlighting ability of LZC when discerning between depression patients and healthy controls [2].

2.4   Functional Connectivity Metrics

Dynamic systems, such as the brain, are characterized by a strong stochasticity and complex coordinated interconnections of all areas contained within the whole system. Hence, it is also necessary to study the possible connections among brain lobes instead of just developing algorithms for single-electrode level assessment. In this sense, functional connectivity evaluates the relation between brain regions in the search of functional patterns, ignoring the existence of anatomical corticocortical connections between those areas [61]. Functional connectivity can be measured by means of a variety of algorithms mainly based on the quantification of correlation, coherence, and phase and magnitude synchronization [32]. Correlation gives information about the similarity of two time series, with high levels of correlation corresponding to higher similarity. On the other hand, coherence measures the similarity of two signals (exactly as correlation does) as a function of frequency. One of the most used algorithms for coherence estimation is the magnitude squared coherence (MSC), which evaluates and compares the power spectral density of two different EEG channels [25]. Finally, phase and magnitude synchronization metrics assess the differences in phase and magnitude between two EEG electrodes.

In the literature, several works have searched for precise functional patterns associated with specific emotional states. In this context, Lee and Hsieh [32] studied correlation, coherence and phase synchronization to discern between positive, negative and neutral emotional states. Their study reported a better performance of phase synchronization over the rest of metrics, and a higher amount of synchronization for positive emotions [32]. Martini *et al.* [42] also studied synchronization features of EEG signals under unpleasant and neutral emotional states. In addition, Miskovic and Schmidt [44] evaluated coherence and synchronization patterns to discern between pleasant, unpleasant and neutral stimuli. Jadhav *et al.* [25] applied MSC to identify four emotions (happy, sad, angry and relax) in a group of students before and after 8 weeks of meditation. In that work, the power of meditation for regulating the level of arousal triggered by each emotional state was demonstrated [25]. MSC was also applied by Daly *et al.* [13] to assess the effects of musical stimuli with emotional content. A very recent EEG-based work has also studied the influence of musical parameter timing on brain areas [39]. Finally, Li *et al.* [36] measured coherence patterns of subjects under different emotional conditions, reporting a higher coherence in the case of negative emotions.

3   Conclusions

This state-of-the-art review has demonstrated the suitability of nonlinear analysis methodologies for emotion recognition with brain activity recordings. Indeed, most of the research works which apply those nonlinear techniques have reported results that notably outperform the discriminant power of traditional linear metrics. All the aforementioned analysis methodologies evaluate the complexity of temporal signals from different perspectives. Hence, their combination would lead to an improvement of the results. Nevertheless, in the literature there are dozens of nonlinear metrics that have not been applied yet in emotions recognition context. For this reason, it would be interesting to study other techniques that could provide new insights about the dynamics of the underlying processes developed in the brain under different emotions. In this sense, it would be possible to endow affective computing systems with emotional intelligence and capability for properly interacting with humans from an emotional point of view.

Acknowledgments. This work was partially supported by Spanish Ministerio de Economía, Industria y Competitividad, Agencia Estatal de Investigación (AEI)/ European Regional Development Fund under Vi-SMARt (TIN2016-79100-R), HA-SYMBIOSIS (TIN2015-72931-EXP) and EmoBioFeedback (DPI2016-80894-R) grants. Beatriz García-Martínez holds the FPU16/03740 scholarship from Spanish Ministerio de Educación, Cultura y Deporte.

References

1. Acar, S., Saraoglu, H., Akar, A.: Feature extraction for EEG-based emotion prediction applications through chaotic analysis. Turkey National Biomedical Engineering Meeting (2015)
2. Akar, S.A., Kara, S., Agambayev, S., Bilgiç, V.: Nonlinear analysis of EEGs of patients with major depression during different emotional states. Comput. Biol. Med. **67**, 49–60 (2015)
3. Aravind, E., Deepak, S., Sudheer, A.: EEG-based emotion recognition using statistical measures and auto-regressive modeling. In: International Conference on Computational Intellegence & Communication Technology, pp. 587–591 (2015)

4. Azami, H., Escudero, J.: Amplitude-aware permutation entropy: illustration in spike detection and signal segmentation. Comput. Methods Programs Biomed. **128**, 40–51 (2016)
5. Bandt, C., Pompe, B.: Permutation entropy: a natural complexity measure for time series. Phys. Rev. Lett. **88**(17), 174102 (2002)
6. Blythe, D.A.J., Haufe, S., Müller, K.R., Nikulin, V.V.: The effect of linear mixing in the EEG on Hurst exponent estimation. Neuroimage **99**, 377–87 (2014)
7. Calvo, R.A., D'Mello, S.K.: Affect detection: an interdisciplinary review of models, methods, and their applications. IEEE Trans. Affect. Comput. **1**(1), 18–37 (2010)
8. Cao, Y., Cai, L., Wang, J., Wang, R., Yu, H., Cao, Y., Liu, J.: Characterization of complexity in the electroencephalograph activity of Alzheimer's disease based on fuzzy entropy. Chaos **25**(8), 083116 (2015)
9. Chanel, G., Rebetez, C., Bétrancourt, M., Pun, T.: Emotion assessment from physiological signals for adaptation of game difficulty. IEEE Trans. Syst. Man Cybern. Part A **41**(6), 1052–1063 (2011)
10. Chen, D., Han, N., Chen, J., Guo, H.: Novel algorithm for measuring the complexity of electroencephalographic signals in emotion recognition. J. Med. Imaging Health Inform. **7**(1), 203–2010 (2017)
11. Coan, J.A., Allen, J.J.B.: Handbook of Emotion Elicitation and Assessment. Oxford University Press, Oxford (2007)
12. Costa, M., Goldberger, A.L., Peng, C.K.: Multiscale entropy analysis of biological signals. Phys. Rev. E Stat. Nonlin. Soft Matter Phys. **71**(2 Pt 1), 021906 (2005)
13. Daly, I., Malik, A., Hwang, F., Roesch, E., Weaver, J., Kirke, A., Williams, D., Miranda, E., Nasuto, S.J.: Neural correlates of emotional responses to music: an EEG study. Neurosci. Lett. **573**, 52–57 (2014)
14. Ekman, P.: An argument for basic emotions. Cogn. Emot. **6**(3–4), 169–200 (1992)
15. Esteller, R., Vachtsevanos, G., Echauz, J., Litt, B.: A comparison of waveform fractal dimension algorithms. IEEE Trans. Circ. Syst. I Fundam. Theory Appl. **48**(2), 177–183 (2001)
16. Faust, O., Bairy, M.G.: Nonlinear analysis of physiological signals: a review. J. Mech. Med. Biol. **12**(4), 124005 (2012)
17. Fernández-Caballero, A., Martínez-Rodrigo, A., Pastor, J.M., Castillo, J.C., Lozano-Monasor, E., López, M.T., Zangróniz, R., Latorre, J.M., Fernández-Sotos, A.: Smart environment architecture for emotion detection and regulation. J. Biomed. Inform. **64**, 55–73 (2016)
18. García-Martínez, B., Martínez-Rodrigo, A., Zangróniz, R., Pastor, J.M., Alcaraz, R.: Symbolic analysis of brain dynamics detects negative stress. Entropy **19**(5), 196 (2017)
19. García-Martínez, B., Martínez-Rodrigo, A., Zangróniz Cantabrana, R., Pastor García, J., Alcaraz, R.: Application of entropy-based metrics to identify emotional distress from electroencephalographic recordings. Entropy **18**(6), 221 (2016)
20. Hatamikia, S., Nasrabadi, A.: Recognition of emotional states induced by music videos based on nonlinear feature extraction and SOM classification. In: 21st Iranian Conference on Biomedical Engineering (ICBME), pp. 333–337. IEEE (2014)
21. Hoseingholizade, S., Golpaygani, M.R.H., Monfared, A.S.: Studying emotions through nonlinear processing of EEG. Procedia Soc. Behav. Sci. **32**, 163–169 (2012)
22. Hosseini, S.A., Khalilzadeh, M.A., Changiz, S.: Emotional stress recognition system for affective computing based on bio-signals. J. Biol. Syst. **18**, 101–114 (2010)
23. Hosseini, S.A., Naghibi-Sistani, M.B.: Emotion recognition method using entropy analysis of EEG signals. Int. J. Image Graph. Sig. Process. **3**(5), 30 (2011)

24. Hosseinifard, B., Moradi, M.H., Rostami, R.: Classifying depression patients and normal subjects using machine learning techniques and nonlinear features from EEG signal. Comput. Methods Progr. Biomed. **109**(3), 339–345 (2013)
25. Jadhav, N., Manthalkar, R., Joshi, Y.: Effect of meditation on emotional response: an EEG-based study. Biomed. Signal Process. Control **34**, 101–113 (2017)
26. Jenke, R., Peer, A., Buss, M.: Feature extraction and selection for emotion recognition from EEG. IEEE Trans. Affect. Comput. **5**(3), 327–339 (2014)
27. Jie, X., Cao, R., Li, L.: Emotion recognition based on the sample entropy of EEG. Biomed. Mater. Eng. **24**(1), 1185–92 (2014)
28. Kantz, H., Schreiber, T.: Nonlinear Time Series Analysis. Cambrigde University Press, Cambrigde (2003)
29. Khalili, Z., Moradi, M.: Emotion recognition system using brain and peripherical signals: using correlation dimension to improve the results of EEG. In: International Conference on Neural Networks, pp. 1571–1575 (2009)
30. Lake, D.E., Moorman, J.R.: Accurate estimation of entropy in very short physiological time series: the problem of atrial fibrillation detection in implanted ventricular devices. Am. J. Physiol. Heart Circ. Physiol. **300**(1), H319–25 (2011)
31. Lan, Z., Sourina, O., Wang, L., Liu, Y.: Real-time EEG-based emotion monitoring using stable features. Vis. Comput. **32**, 347–358 (2016)
32. Lee, Y.Y., Hsieh, S.: Classifying different emotional states by means of EEG-based functional connectivity patterns. PLoS ONE **9**(4), e95415 (2014)
33. Lempel, A., Ziv, J.: On the complexity of finite sequences. IEEE Trans. Inf. Theory **22**(1), 75–81 (1976)
34. Li, X., Qi, X., Tian, Y., Sun, X., Fran, M., Cai, E.: Application of the feature extraction based on combination of permutation entropy and multi-fractal index to emotion recognition. Chin. High Technol. Lett. **26**(7), 617–624 (2016)
35. Li, X., Xie, J., Hou, Y., Wang, J.: An improved multiscale entropy algorithm and its performance analysis in extraction of emotion EEG features. Chin. High Technol. Lett. **25**(10), 865–870 (2015)
36. Li, Y., Cao, D., Wei, L., Tang, Y., Wang, J.: Abnormal functional connectivity of EEG gamma band in patients with depression during emotional face processing. Clin. Neurophysiol. **126**(11), 2078–2089 (2015)
37. Liu, Y., Sourina, O.: EEG-based subject-dependent emotion recognition algorithm using fractal dimension. In: IEEE International Conference on Systems, Man and Cybernetics, pp. 3166–3171 (2014)
38. Lozano-Monasor, E., López, M.T., Vigo-Bustos, F., Fernández-Caballero, A.: Facial expression recognition in ageing adults: from lab to ambient assisted living. J. Ambient Intell. Humanized Comput. **8**, 567–578 (2017)
39. Martínez-Rodrigo, A., Fernández-Sotos, A., Latorre, J.M., Moncho-Bogani, J., Fernández-Caballero, A.: Neural correlates of phrase rhythm: an EEG study of bipartite vs. rondo sonata form. Front. Neuroinform. **11**, 29 (2017)
40. Martínez-Rodrigo, A., Zangróniz, R., Pastor, J.M., Fernández-Caballero, A.: Arousal level classification in the ageing adult by measuring electrodermal skin conductivity. In: Bravo, J., Hervás, R., Villarreal, V. (eds.) AmIHEALTH 2015. LNCS, vol. 9456, pp. 213–223. Springer, Cham (2015). doi:10.1007/978-3-319-26508-7_21
41. Martínez-Rodrigo, A., Zangróniz, R., Pastor, J.M., Sokolova, M.V.: Arousal level classification of the aging adult from electro-dermal activity: from hardware development to software architecture. Pervasive Mob. Comput. **34**, 46–59 (2017)

42. Martini, N., Menicucci, D., Sebastiani, L., Bedini, R., Pingitore, A., Vanello, N., Milanesi, M., Landini, L., Gemignani, A.: The dynamics of EEG gamma responses to unpleasant visual stimuli: from local activity to functional connectivity. NeuroImage **60**(2), 922–932 (2012)
43. Mert, A., Akan, A.: Emotion recognition from EEG signals by using multivariate empirical mode decomposition. Pattern Anal. Appl. (2016)
44. Miskovic, V., Schmidt, L.A.: Cross-regional cortical synchronization during affective image viewing. Brain Res. **1362**, 102–111 (2010)
45. Mitchell, A.J., Lord, K., Slattery, J., Grainger, L., Symonds, P.: How feasible is implementation of distress screening by cancer clinicians in routine clinical care? Cancer **118**(24), 6260–9 (2012)
46. Murugappan, M., Nagarajan, R., Yaacob, S.: Combining spatial filtering and wavelet transform for classifying human emotions using EEG signals. J. Med. Biol. Eng. **31**(1), 45–51 (2011)
47. Paraschiv-Ionescu, A., Buchser, E., Rutschmann, B., Aminian, K.: Nonlinear analysis of human physical activity patterns in health and disease. Phys. Rev. E Stat. Nonlin. Soft Matter Phys. **77**(2 Pt 1), 021913 (2008)
48. Paul, S., Mazumder, N., Ghosh, P., Tibarewala, D., Vimalarini, G.: EEG-based emotion recognition system using MFDFA as feature extractor. In: International Conference on Robotics, Automation, Control and Embedded Systems (2015)
49. Peng, H., Hu, B., Zheng, F., Fan, D., Zhao, W., Chen, X., Yang, Y., Cai, Q.: A method of identifying chronic stress by EEG. Pers. Ubiquit. Comput. **17**(7), 1341–1347 (2013)
50. Picard, R.W.: Affective computing (1995)
51. Pincus, S.M.: Approximate entropy as a measure of system complexity. Proc. Natl. Acad. Sci. USA **88**(6), 2297–301 (1991)
52. Puthankattil, S.D., Joseph, P.K.: Analysis of EEG signals using wavelet entropy and approximate entropy: a case study on depression patients. Int. J. Med. Health Biomed. Pharm. Eng. **8**(7), 420–424 (2014)
53. Richman, J.S., Moorman, J.R.: Physiological time-series analysis using approximate entropy and sample entropy. Am. J. Physiol. Heart Circ. Physiol. **278**(6), H2039–49 (2000)
54. Rodríguez-Bermúdez, G., Garcia-Laencina, P.J.: Analysis of EEG signals using nonlinear dynamics and chaos: a review. Appl. Math. Inf. Sci. **9**(5), 2309 (2015)
55. Rui, C., Li, L., Junjie, C.: Comparative study of approximate entropy and sample entropy in EEG data analysis. Biothecnol. Indian J. **7**(11), 493–498 (2013)
56. Rukavina, S., Gruss, S., Hoffmann, H., Tan, J.W., Walter, S., Traue, H.C.: Affective computing and the impact of gender and age. PLoS ONE **11**(3), e0150584 (2016)
57. Russell, J.A.: A circumplex model of affect. J. Pers. Soc. Psychol. **39**(6), 1161–1178 (1980)
58. Russell, J.A., Bachorowski, J.A., Fernandez-Dols, J.M.: Facial and vocal expressions of emotion. Ann. Rev. Psychol. **54**, 329–49 (2003)
59. Schröder, M., Cowie, R.: Towards emotion-sensitive multimodal interfaces: the challenge of the European network of excellence HUMAINE. In: Adapting the Interaction Style to Affective Factors Workshop in conjunction with User Modeling (2005)
60. Sourina, O., Liu, Y.: A fractal-based algorithm of emotion recognition from EEG using arousal-valence model. In: Proceeding of the International Conference on Bio-Inspired Systems and Signal Processing, pp. 209–214 (2011)

61. Sporns, O., Tononi, G., Edelman, G.M.: Theoretical neuroanatomy: relating anatomical and functional connectivity in graphs and cortical connection matrices. Cereb. Cortex 10(2), 127–141 (2000)
62. Tadic, B., Gligorijevic, V., Mitrovic, M., Suvakov, M.: Co-evolutionary mechanisms of emotional bursts in online social dynamics and networks. Entropy 15(12), 5084–5120 (2013)
63. Valenza, G., Lanata, A., Scilingo, E.P.: The role of nonlinear dynamics in affective valence and arousal recognition. IEEE Trans. Affect. Comput. 3(2), 237–249 (2012)
64. Wang, X., Nie, D., Lu, B.: Emotional state classification from EEG data using machine learning approach. Neurocomputing 129, 94–106 (2014)
65. Yuvaraj, R., Murugappan, M., Ibrahim, N.M., Sundaraj, K., Omar, M.I., Mohamad, K., Palaniappan, R.: Optimal set of EEG features for emotional state classification and trajectory visualization in Parkinson's disease. Int. J. Psychophysiol. 94(3), 482–95 (2014)
66. Zhang, Y., Ji, X., Zhang, S.: An approach to EEG-based emotion recognition using combined feature extraction method. Neurosci. Lett. 633, 152–157 (2016)

Study of Electroencephalographic Signal Regularity for Automatic Emotion Recognition

Arturo Martínez-Rodrigo[1]([✉]), Beatriz García-Martínez[1], Raúl Alcaraz[1], Antonio Fernández-Caballero[2], and Pascual González[2]

[1] Instituto de Tecnologías Audiovisuales, Universidad de Castilla-La Mancha, 16071 Cuenca, Spain
Arturo.Martinez@uclm.es
[2] Instituto de Investigación en Informática de Albacete, Universidad de Castilla-La Mancha, 02071 Albacete, Spain

Abstract. Nowadays, emotional intelligence plays a key role in improving human-machine interaction (HMI). The main objective of HMI is to fill the gap between human emotional states and the reaction of a computer in accordance with this feeling. However, there is a lack of mathematical emotional models to implement affective computing systems into real applications. Consequently, this paper explores the properties of the nonlinear methodology based on Quadratic Sample Entropy (QSE) for the recognition of different emotional subspaces. Precisely, 665 segments of 32-channel electroencephalographic recordings from 32 subjects elicited with different emotional stimuli have been analyzed to validate the proposed model. Results conclude that QSE is a promising feature to be taken into account. Indeed, this metric has reported a discriminant ability around 72% using a support vector machine classifier. This result is comparable with the outcomes reported by other more complex methodologies which use multi-parametric analysis.

Keywords: Electroencephalography · Emotions · Physiological computing · Nonlinear · Quadratic Sample Entropy

1 Introduction

Nowadays, affective computing (AC) has become the main field of research that enables intelligent systems to recognize, feel, infer and interpret human emotions [21,29]. Indeed, AC plays a key role in human-machine interaction since computers are unable to interpret emotional information from humans [18]. Thus, AC emerged with the aim of recognizing emotions from different human activities in order to take the most adequate response as consequence of a given stimulus (e.g. [6,10,11]). Acquiring emotional information, processing the discretized data and reacting adequately are important parts in this kind of system. In this regard, computational models are required to accomplish the task. Indeed, emotion-aware computing builds emotional interactions between human and computer by developing computational models. These models are based on

© Springer International Publishing AG 2017
S.F. Ochoa et al. (Eds.): UCAmI 2017, LNCS 10586, pp. 766–777, 2017.
DOI: 10.1007/978-3-319-67585-5_74

the various sensor-captured information which are used to build a computing system with the capability of perception and interpretation of humans' emotion, as well as providing humanized responses [35]. Consequently, the detection and analysis of humans' emotions are key in the development of affective models [7].

1.1 Bio-Inspired Methodologies

In the literature, a wide range of technologies and methodologies have been used for emotional information acquisition and recognition. Most of them are based on speech processing and facial recognition. These bio-inspired technologies, based on physical features, are known as traditional methods in the scientific literature. On the one hand, speech processing approaches are mainly focused on the analysis and processing of different acoustic features such as intensity or tone [37]. On the other hand, facial recognition proposals are based on the analysis and processing of facial expressions and gesture interpretation [4] which are often linked to a specific emotion. However, both facial recognition and speech analysis may introduce uncertainty into the emotional model. Indeed, the same gesture or sound may have different meanings depending on cultural aspects, social status, gender or age, among other confounding factors [17]. Moreover, gesture expressions are usually complemented by body expressions, which may reinforce or even change the meaning of a gesture. Similarly, it is important to remark that, occasionally, people tend to hide their true emotions, because they want to be accepted in certain social contexts, or they even want to prevent from being discriminated in certain social collectives [13].

1.2 Physiological Computing

Considering the previous drawbacks from bio-inspired methodologies, a new trend has gained special relevance in the last years. Thus, physiological computing (PC) emerges with the aim of recognizing emotional states from assessing the several physiological variables and bio-potentials captured from the human's body [38]. Indeed, the same stimulus may affect people differently, given that emotional states depend on the personality, disposition, motivation, or even phobias or traumas occurred in the past. Nevertheless, regardless of the subjects, neuro-physiological researchers agree that feeling an emotion leads to changes in physiological activity [27]. From an anatomical point of view, the physiological variations caused when feeling an emotion produce alterations in the arousal of the central nervous system (CNS) with different levels of depth, depending on the nature of emotion [8]. In this regard, the CNS reacts on the peripheral nervous system (PNS) and, consequently on the sympathetic and parasympathetic nervous system, leading to physiological reactions that can be measured and quantified. Unlike traditional methods, physiological reactions can not be avoided or feigned.

According to PC, different physiological variables can be used to assess the emotional state. Some of the most widely used are electro-dermal activity (EDA), heart rate variability (HRV), electromyography (EMG) and physical activity

(PA), among others (e.g. [22,23,36]). All these physiological variables are somehow linked to the CNS throughout the sympathetic and parasympathetic components and, therefore, they are capable of measuring the physiological changes produced in our body when facing a stimulus. Nevertheless, the use of certain physiological signals could be more adequate depending on the type of emotion to be recognized. For instance, it has been reported that EDA and EMG are exclusively linked with sympathetic component and, therefore, with the level of alert [22,24]. On the other hand, HRV seems to be related to the parasympathetic components of the PNS, but it is highly influenced by other confounding variables like exercise, heart disease or allergic reactions [2]. Considering these factors, different multi-parametric studies have been performed in order to cover the maximum possible emotional spectrum [36].

In the last years, the study of brain activity by means of electroencephalography (EEG) recordings has gained a significant interest in the building of emotional models. The main reason is that cognitive processes are firstly originated on our brain, and then they are transmitted throughout the CNS to the rest of physiological variables [16]. Taking this into account, it seems more pertinent to directly measure on the source of emotional processes, rather than on secondary physiological variables originated by different processes produced in our brain. However, it is important to consider that the study of EEG requires an intensification of the signal processing methods due to the multi-modal behavior inherent to EEG (up to 128 channels in the standard 10–20 system) and the low signal-to-noise ratio of EEG recordings. Nevertheless, recent advances in micro-controllers of ultra low power consumption, boosted by the emerging technologies in the Internet of Things, have led to miniaturized and faster devices with an increasing memory and processing capability [3].

1.3   Emotion Models

To find a standard procedure for detecting and quantifying an emotion is not an easy task. One of the main reasons is that a gold standard on the definition of emotions does not exist [36]. Consequently, a number of models and theories to classify emotional states can be found in the literature. Thus, models of emotions range from those trying to classify a few discrete emotions [9] to those which define dozens of emotional states [34]. Nevertheless, the model proposed by Russell in the 80's is the most used to date [32]. It is a two-dimensional model which considers that all possible emotions can be defined by means of valence (pleasantness - displeasure) and arousal (activated - deactivated) axes. Therefore, several emotions can be simply mapped onto the valence–arousal space [14]. In this regard, it is usual to explore the four emotional quadrants bounded by a two-dimensional cognitive emotional representation (see, for instance, [14,18,25]); that is, Low Arousal–Low Valence (LALV), High Arousal–Low Valence (HALV), Low Arousal–High Valence (LAHV), and High Arousal–High Valence (HAHV). Traditionally, these models have been quantified by means of linear techniques, for instance using evoked potentials or frequency bands decomposition, among other methodologies [17]. However, recent studies have shown that addressing the emotion recognition issue from a nonlinear point of view may reveal hidden relevant information, not discovered until now [12]. In this regard, it is interesting to remark that the brain presents a really complex and heterogeneous performance, which makes its behavior far from being considered linear [5]. Moreover, the nonlinearity of the brain is introduced even at cellular level, since the dynamic behavior of individual neurons is governed by threshold and saturation phenomena [1].

Considering the need to assess new emotional classification models from a nonlinear point of view, this study tries to evaluate the capability of nonlinear regularity metrics in recognition of four emotional quadrants. For this purpose, Quadratic Sample Entropy (QSE) is used. Then, the performance of this metric, computed on each EEG channel is assessed using a reduction selection method based on principal component analysis (PCA) and a support vector machine (SVM) classifier. The rest of this study is summarized as follows. Section 2 describes the study population, data acquisition, data preprocessing and nonlinear metric calculation. Section 3 presents the results and finally, Sect. 4 discusses the results and provides some final conclusions.

2   Methods

2.1   Study Population

EEG recordings from the Database for Emotion Analysis using Physiological Signals (DEAP) [18] were analyzed in this study. These signals were acquired by means of a Biosemi ActiveTwo device during an experiment of emotional elicitation with audiovisual stimuli. Thus, a set of 32 healthy volunteers (19 to 37 years old; mean of 26.9 years; 50% men) visualized forty videos with emotional content, each with a length of one minute. Therefore, a total of 1280 recordings from a broad variety of affective states were registered. After each video, levels of valence and arousal, subjectively perceived by each participant were also collected through self-assessment manikins (SAM) [26]. More detailed information about the DEAP database can be found in [18].

Considering that stimuli were selected to induce responses throughout the whole range of emotions, the recordings in the four quadrants of the valence–arousal space were selected in this study, i.e. LALV (sad, depress, sentimental), HALV (distress, hate, shock), LAHV (cheerful, happy, lovely) and HAHV (fun, exciting, joy). They were selected according to previous works that also deal with automatic identification of discrete emotions [14]. Thus, the group of LALV was formed by 127 recordings rated with levels of valence lower than 4 and arousal lower than 4. Similarly, the group of HALV was formed by 157 recordings rated with levels of valence lower than 4 and arousal higher than 6. Moreover, the group of LAHV was formed by 106 recordings rated with levels of valence higher than 6 and arousal lower than 4. Finally, the group of HAHV was formed by 275 recordings rated with levels of valence higher than 6 and arousal higher than 6. Thus, a total of 665 recordings were finally analyzed. In Fig. 1 a distribution of samples and their location throughout the valence–arousal axis can be found, together with the rest of recordings excluded from this study.

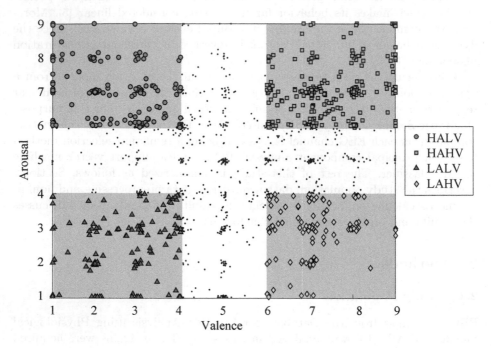

Fig. 1. Distribution of the recordings contained by the DEAP dataset within the valence–arousal space. The EEG recordings chosen for this study are clearly highlighted

2.2 Preprocessing Applied to the EEG Recordings

The EEG recordings were registered at a sample frequency of 512 Hz in order to acquire the EEG signals from 32 electrodes distributed on the scalp, according to the standardized 10–20 system (see Fig. 2). As in previous works (e.g. [12,18]), the last 30 second-length interval from each recording was selected for its analysis. Each recording was initially referenced to the mean of all electrodes [18]. Thereafter, forward/backward high-pass (3 Hz cut-off frequency) and low-pass (45 Hz cut-off frequency) filtering approaches were used to remove baseline and power-line interferences [18]. Note that this preprocessing preserves the most interesting frequency band in the EEG [33]. Next, contamination from electrical activity of other physiological systems (e.g., eyes, heart, and so on), as well as technical artifacts like electrode-pops, were reduced by making use of independent component analysis (ICA) [33]. Thus, independent components were obtained from the EEG signals and, then, visually revised to remove those containing noise and interferences. Nonetheless, other artifacts like EMG and other interferences causing a high-amplitude noise could not be eliminated with ICA. Moreover, EMG artifacts are the most difficult ones to eliminate, because of the overlapping of their spectrum with EEG frequency range, specially with β (14 – 29 Hz) and γ (30 – 45 Hz) bands [15]. As a solution, EEG segments from reconstructed signals with too high-frequency noise were interpolated from adjacent electrodes [30].

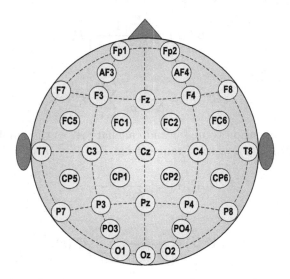

Fig. 2. International 10–20 system for electrode placement used in this work

2.3 Quadratic Sample Entropy

Sample Entropy (*SampEn*) examines a time series for similar epochs and assigns a non-negative number to the sequence, with larger values corresponding to more irregularity in the data [31]. Two input parameters, a run length m and a tolerance window r, must be specified for *SampEn* to be computed. $SampEn(m, r, N)$, being N the length of the time series, is the negative logarithm of the conditional probability that two sequences similar for m points remain similar at the next point, where self-matches are not included in calculating the probability. Thus, a lower value of *SampEn* also indicates more self-similarity in the time series.

Formally, given N data points from a time series $\{x(n)\} = x(1), x(2), \ldots, x(N)$, *SampEn* is defined as follows [31]:

1. Form vector sequences of size m, $\mathbf{X}_m(1), \ldots, \mathbf{X}_m(N - m + 1)$, defined by $\mathbf{X}_m(i) = \{x(i), x(i+1), \ldots, x(i+m-1)\}$, for $1 \leq i \leq N - m$. These vectors represent m consecutive x values, starting with the ith point.

2. Define the distance between vectors $\mathbf{X}_m(i)$ and $\mathbf{X}_m(j)$, $d[\mathbf{X}_m(i), \mathbf{X}_m(j)]$, as the absolute maximum difference between their scalar components:

$$d[\mathbf{X}_m(i), \mathbf{X}_m(j)] = \max_{k=0,\ldots,m-1} \left(|x(i+k) - x(j+k)| \right). \tag{1}$$

3. For a given $\mathbf{X}_m(i)$, count the number of j ($1 \le j \le N - m$, $j \ne i$), denoted as B_i, such that the distance between $\mathbf{X}_m(i)$ and $\mathbf{X}_m(j)$ is less than or equal to r. Then, for $1 \le i \le N - m$:

$$B_i^m(r) = \frac{1}{N-m-1} B_i. \tag{2}$$

4. Define $B^m(r)$ as:

$$B^m(r) = \frac{1}{N-m} \sum_{i=1}^{N-m} B_i^m(r). \tag{3}$$

5. Increase the dimension to $m+1$ and calculate A_i as the number of $\mathbf{X}_{m+1}(i)$ within r of $\mathbf{X}_{m+1}(j)$, where j ranges from 1 to $N - m$ ($j \ne i$). Then, $A_i^m(r)$ is defined as:

$$A_i^m(r) = \frac{1}{N-m-1} A_i. \tag{4}$$

6. Set $A^m(r)$ as:

$$A^m(r) = \frac{1}{N-m} \sum_{i=1}^{N-m} A_i^m(r). \tag{5}$$

Thus, $B^m(r)$ is the probability that two sequences will match for m points, whereas $A^m(r)$ is the probability that two sequences will match for $m+1$ points. Finally, $SampEn$ is defined as:

$$SampEn(m,r) = \lim_{N \to \infty} \left\{ -\ln \left[\frac{A^m(r)}{B^m(r)} \right] \right\}, \tag{6}$$

which is estimated by the statistic:

$$SampEn(m,r,N) = -\ln \left[\frac{A^m(r)}{B^m(r)} \right]. \tag{7}$$

Although m and r are critical in determining the outcome of $SampEn$, no guidelines exist for optimizing their values. In principle, accuracy and confidence of the entropy estimate improve as the number of length matches m increases. The number of matches are increased by choosing small m (short templates) and large r (wide tolerance). However, penalties appear when too relaxed criteria are used [28]. For smaller r values, poor conditional probability estimates are achieved, while for larger r values, too much detailed system information is lost and $SampEn$ tends to zero for all processes. To avoid a significant noise contribution on $SampEn$ computation, one must choose r larger than most of the noise [28]. A slight modification of $SampEn$ to do it more insensitive to the r

selection is the named *Quadratic SampEn* (QSE) [19]. This new measure allows to vary r as needed to achieve confident estimates of the conditional probability and is defined as

$$QSE(m, r, N) = SampEn(m, n, r) + \ln(2r). \qquad (8)$$

3 Experimental Results

QSE was computed for non-overlapped EEG segments of $N = 640$ samples (5 s EEG segment times 128 samples per second). Then, the final values of entropy were computed as the mean of six consecutive segments. In this regard, values of $m = 2$ and $r = 0.2$ were used as input parameters for the QSE calculation. In order to quantify the statistical significance of EEG channels, an ANalysis Of VAriance (ANOVA) was performed. Firstly, a ShaphiroWilks test corroborated that data distribution was normal and homocedastic. Then, ANOVA was computed for all the channels, resulting a total of 23 out of 32 significant EEG channels ($\rho < 0.05$). In this regard, the most relevant channels were parietals P3 ($\rho = 8.12 \times 10^{-10}$) and P4 ($\rho = 6.32 \times 10^{-8}$), right central-parietals CP2 ($\rho = 1.38 \times 10^{-4}$) and CP6 ($\rho = 6.93 \times 10^{-5}$) and left frontal-central FC2 ($\rho = 9.01 \times 10^{-7}$).

In order to take advantage of the complementary information from the different EEG channels, the global classification performance was assessed using an SVM classifier, with Gaussian kernel and a scaling factor of 0.35. Nevertheless, given the high amount of EEG information, some methodology for selection process or dimensionality reduction had to be performed before carrying out the classification. Indeed, it is possible that different variables are measuring the same driving principle within a system. Consequently, it is possible to reduce the variables by taking advantage of redundant information. In this study, PCA was computed for the sake of reducing the quantity of information involved in the study. Thus, components were added until the sum of the variances reached a 95%, conforming a model with 14 orthogonal features computed from the 32 EEG channels. This model reached a global correctness of 72.5%, where the specific true positive and false negative rates for each emotional subspace can be observed through the confusion matrix shown in Fig. 3.

As it can be observed, HAHV (happy) reached the highest true positive rate with an accuracy of 90%, where only 7% was misclassified as HALV (distress) and 3% was misclassified as LALV (sad, depressed). Then, the emotional subspace HALV (distress) reached a notable correctness of 68%, where 20% of recordings were misclassified as HAHV and 10% and 2% as LALV and LAHV, respectively. Finally, both LAHV and LALV achieved a similar performance with 58% and 53% of the samples correctly classified, misclassifying a total of 42% and 47% of the samples from each group, respectively. It is interesting to highlight that 20% of recordings were misclassified as HALV during LALV classification.

4   Discussion and Conclusions

In this study, a new predictive model for emotion classification has been proposed. To perform the experiments, a nonlinear metric based on QSE has been used to assess the degree of regularity from EEG signals. Although this metric has been used previously to classify the calm–distress tandem [12], to the best of our knowledge, this is the first time that QSE is used to discern among different emotional quadrants in Russell's emotional model.

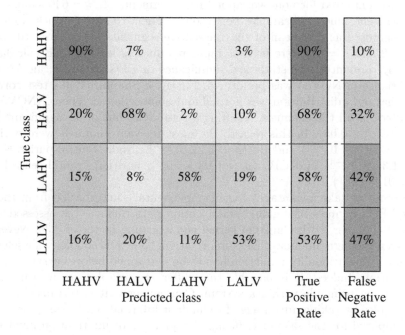

Fig. 3. Confusion matrix for the four groups under study, namely HAHV, LAHV, HALV and LALV, when using an SVM classifier

It is worth noting that not many studies can be found in the literature addressing the emotion detection and classification challenge from an EEG point of view. Furthermore, comparison among works should be considered with caution, since small variations on the methodology or samples included in the analysis may result in very different outcomes. In this regard, Koelstra et al. [18] achieved a global accuracy of 62% and 57% for both arousal and valence axes, respectively. Although they used the same database, a linear methodology was applied in the analysis. Concretely, they analyzed the EEG recordings by means of frequency band decomposition [18]. Moreover, Hatamikia et al. [14] used different nonlinear methodologies as approximate entropy, spectral entropy, Katzs fractal dimension and Petrosians fractal dimension to characterize the EEG signals contained in the DEAP database. They achieved 55.15% correctness when classifying four emotional classes of valence and arousal levels, and using a hierarchical model containing two different classifiers. In addition, Yi-Hun et al. [20] used a new nonlinear methodology based on the kernel eigen-emotion pattern and an SVM classifier, achieving 73.42% and 73.57% in valence–arousal dimensions, respectively. Nevertheless, only seven participants were enrolled in that study, where a different visual database was used. Finally, Mert and Akan [25] used a complex empirical mode decomposition method to analyze nonlinear and nonstationary time series, achieving a correctness of 51% and 67% for the arousal and valence dimensions, respectively.

Taking these results into consideration, it can be concluded that our proposal has obtained comparable results to other existing works in the scientific literature, although computing exclusively QSE on the EEG signals. Even when the global correctness of our model is a bit higher, the model proposed could be considered unbalanced due to the disparity of performance among the different emotional states. Indeed, while emotional subspace HAHV achieved a correctness of 90%, the rest of quadrants are below 70%. Nevertheless, it is important to remark that this study only introduces an exploratory analysis and consequently, further actions should be conducted in order to improve the model and its performance. In this regard, a more precise analysis should be accomplished to detect which EEG channels are contributing more significantly to emotion detection, thus leading to more efficient models as well as to the reduction of the processing load.

Acknowledgments. This work was partially supported by Spanish Ministerio de Economía, Industria y Competitividad, Agencia Estatal de Investigación (AEI) / European Regional Development Fund under HA-SYMBIOSIS (TIN2015-72931-EXP), ViSMARt (TIN2016-79100-R) and EmoBioFeedback (DPI2016-80894-R) grants. Beatriz García-Martínez holds the FPU16/03740 scholarship from Spanish Ministerio de Educación, Cultura y Deporte.

References

1. Abásolo, D., Hornero, R., Gómez, C., García, M., López, M.: Analysis of EEG background activity in alzheimer's disease patients with lempel-ziv complexity and central tendency measure. Med. Eng. Phys. **28**(4), 315–322 (2006)
2. Acharya, U.R., Joseph, K.P., Kannathal, N., Lim, C.M., Suri, J.S.: Heart rate variability: a review. Med. Biol. Eng. Comput. **44**(12), 1031–1051 (2006)
3. Al-Fuqaha, A., Guizani, M., Mohammadi, M., Aledhari, M., Ayyash, M.: Internet of things: a survey on enabling technologies, protocols, and applications. IEEE Commun. Surv. Tutorials **17**(4), 2347–2376 (2015)
4. Calvo, R.A., D'Mello, S.: Affect detection: an interdisciplinary review of models, methods, and their applications. IEEE Trans. Affect. Comput. **1**(1), 18–37 (2010)
5. Cao, Y., Cai, L., Wang, J., Wang, R., Yu, H., Cao, Y., Liu, J.: Characterization of complexity in the electroencephalograph activity of alzheimer's disease based on fuzzy entropy. Chaos **25**(8), 083116 (2015)
6. Castillo, J.C., Castro-González, Á., Fernández-Caballero, A., Latorre, J.M., Pastor, J.M., Fernández-Sotos, A., Salichs, M.A.: Software architecture for smart emotion recognition and regulation of the ageing adult. Cogn. Comput. **8**(2), 357–367 (2016)

7. Castillo, J.C., Fernández-Caballero, A., Castro-González, Á., Salichs, M.A., López, M.T.: A framework for recognizing and regulating emotions in the elderly. In: Pecchia, L., Chen, L.L., Nugent, C., Bravo, J. (eds.) IWAAL 2014. LNCS, vol. 8868, pp. 320–327. Springer, Cham (2014). doi:10.1007/978-3-319-13105-4_46

8. Colibazzi, T., Posner, J., Wang, Z., Gorman, D., Gerber, A., Yu, S., Zhu, H., Kangarlu, A., Duan, Y., Russell, J.A., et al.: Neural systems subserving valence and arousal during the experience of induced emotions. Emotion 10(3), 377 (2010)

9. Ekman, P.: An argument for basic emotions. Cogn. Emot. 6(3–4), 169–200 (1992)

10. Castillo, J.C., Fernández-Caballero, A., Castro-González, Á., Salichs, M.A., López, M.T.: A framework for recognizing and regulating emotions in the elderly. In: Pecchia, L., Chen, L.L., Nugent, C., Bravo, J. (eds.) IWAAL 2014. LNCS, vol. 8868, pp. 320–327. Springer, Cham (2014). doi:10.1007/978-3-319-13105-4_46

11. Fernández-Caballero, A., Martínez-Rodrigo, A., Pastor, J.M., Castillo, J.C., Lozano-Monasor, E., López, M.T., Zangróniz, R., Latorre, J.M., Fernández-Sotos, A.: Smart environment architecture for emotion detection and regulation. J. Biomed. Inform. 64, 55–73 (2016)

12. García-Martínez, B., Martínez-Rodrigo, A., Zangróniz Cantabrana, R., Pastor García, J., Alcaraz, R.: Application of entropy-based metrics to identify emotional distress from electroencephalographic recordings. Entropy 18(6), 221 (2016)

13. Gomes, M., Oliveira, T., Silva, F., Carneiro, D., Novais, P.: Establishing the relationship between personality traits and stress in an intelligent environment. In: Ali, M., Pan, J.-S., Chen, S.-M., Horng, M.-F. (eds.) IEA/AIE 2014. LNCS, vol. 8482, pp. 378–387. Springer, Cham (2014). doi:10.1007/978-3-319-07467-2_40

14. Hatamikia, S., Nasrabadi, A.: Recognition of emotional states induced by music videos based on nonlinear feature extraction and som classification. In: 21th Iranian Conference on Biomedical Engineering (ICBME), pp. 333–337. IEEE (2014)

15. Jadhav, P., Shanamugan, D., Chourasia, A., Ghole, A., Acharyya, A., Naik, G.: Automated detection and correction of eye blink and muscular artefacts in EEG signal for analysis of autism spectrum disorder. In: Engineering in Medicine and Biology Society (EMBC), 2014 36th Annual International Conference of the IEEE, pp. 1881–1884. IEEE (2014)

16. Jenke, R., Peer, A., Buss, M.: Feature extraction and selection for emotion recognition from EEG. IEEE Trans. Affect. Comput. 5(3), 327–339 (2014)

17. Kim, M.K., Kim, M., Oh, E., Kim, S.P.: A review on the computational methods for emotional state estimation from the human EEG. Comput. Math. Methods Med. 2013, 573734 (2013)

18. Koelstra, S., Muhl, C., Soleymani, M., Lee, J.S., Yazdani, A., Ebrahimi, T., Pun, T., Nijholt, A., Patras, I.: Deap: a database for emotion analysis using physiological signals. IEEE Trans. Affect. Comput. 3(1), 18–31 (2012)

19. Lake, D.E., Moorman, J.R.: Accurate estimation of entropy in very short physiological time series: the problem of atrial fibrillation detection in implanted ventricular devices. Am. J. Physiol. Heart Circ. Physiol. 300(1), H319–H325 (2011)

20. Liu, Y.H., Wu, C.T., Kao, Y.H., Chen, Y.T.: Single-trial EEG-based emotion recognition using kernel eigen-emotion pattern and adaptive support vector machine. In: Engineering in Medicine and Biology Society (EMBC), 2013 35th Annual International Conference of the IEEEm, pp. 4306–4309. IEEE (2013)

21. Lozano-Monasor, E., López, M.T., Vigo-Bustos, F., Fernández-Caballero, A.: Facial expression recognition in ageing adults: from lab to ambient assisted living. J. Ambient Intell. Humanized Comput. 8, 1–12 (2017)

22. Martínez-Rodrigo, A., Zangróniz, R., Pastor, J.M., Fernández-Caballero, A.: Arousal level classification in the ageing adult by measuring electrodermal skin conductivity. In: Bravo, J., Hervás, R., Villarreal, V. (eds.) AmIHEALTH 2015. LNCS, vol. 9456, pp. 213–223. Springer, Cham (2015). doi:10.1007/978-3-319-26508-7_21

23. Martínez-Rodrigo, A., Zangróniz, R., Pastor, J.M., Sokolova, M.V.: Arousal level classification of the aging adult from electro-dermal activity: from hardware development to software architecture. Pervasive Mob. Comput. 34, 46–59 (2017)

24. Mauss, I.B., Robinson, M.D.: Measures of emotion: a review. Cogn. Emot. 23(2), 209–237 (2009)

25. Mert, A., Akan, A.: Emotion recognition from EEG signals by using multivariate empirical mode decomposition. Pattern Anal. Appl (2016)

26. Morris, J.D.: Observations SAM: the Self-Assessment Manikin - An efficient cross-cultural measurement of emotional response. J. Advertising Res. 35(6), 63–68 (1995)

27. Nasoz, F., Lisetti, C.L., Alvarez, K., Finkelstein, N.: Emotion recognition from physiological signals for user modeling of affect. In: Proceedings of the 3rd Workshop on Affective and Attitude User Modelling, Pittsburgh, PA, USA (2003)

28. Pincus, S.M.: Approximate entropy as a measure of system complexity. Proc. Nat. Acad. Sci. USA 88(6), 2297–2301 (1991)

29. Poria, S., Cambria, E., Bajpai, R., Hussain, A.: A review of affective computing: from unimodal analysis to multimodal fusion. Inf. Fusion 37, 98–125 (2017)

30. Reis, P.M., Hebenstreit, F., Gabsteiger, F., von Tscharner, V., Lochmann, M.: Methodological aspects of EEG and body dynamics measurements during motion. In: Towards a New Cognitive Neuroscience: Modeling Natural Brain Dynamics, p. 9 (2014)

31. Richman, J.S., Moorman, J.R.: Physiological time-series analysis using approximate entropy and sample entropy. Am. J. Physiol. Heart Circ. Physiol. 278(6), H2039–H2049 (2000)

32. Russell, J.A.: A circumplex model of affect. J. Pers. Soc. Psychol. 39(6), 1161–1178 (1980)

33. Sanei, S.: Adaptive Processing of Brain Signals. Wiley, Oxford (2013)

34. Schröder, M., Cowie, R.: Towards emotion-sensitive multimodal interfaces: The challenge of the european network of excellence humaine. In: Adapting the Interaction Style to Affective Factors Workshop in Conjunction with User Modeling (2005)

35. Tao, J., Tan, T.: Affective computing: a review. In: Tao, J., Tan, T., Picard, R.W. (eds.) ACII 2005. LNCS, vol. 3784, pp. 981–995. Springer, Heidelberg (2005). doi:10.1007/11573548_125

36. Valenza, G., Lanata, A., Scilingo, E.P.: The role of nonlinear dynamics in affective valence and arousal recognition. IEEE Trans. Affect. Comput. 3(2), 237–249 (2012)

37. Ververidis, D., Kotropoulos, C.: Emotional speech recognition: Resources, features, and methods. Speech Commun. 48(9), 1162–1181 (2006)

38. Wagner, J., Kim, J., André, E.: From physiological signals to emotions: implementing and comparing selected methods for feature extraction and classification. In: IEEE International Conference on Multimedia and Expo, ICME 2005, pp. 940–943. IEEE (2005)

User Mood Detection in a Social Network Messenger Based on Facial Cues

Payam Jome Yazdian[1] and Hadi Moradi[1,2(✉)]

[1] School of ECE, University of Tehran, North Karegar Street,
1439957131 Tehran, Iran
{pjyazdian,moradih}@ut.ac.ir
[2] Intelligent Systems Research Institute, SKKU, Suwon, South Korea

Abstract. In this paper, we propose a mood detection approach which is crucial for human-computer and human-human interaction. In the proposed method, the facial emotional changes are observed through a camera while users use a social network messenger. The advantage of this approach, over the previously proposed approaches, is in its natural setup in which people facially express their feelings, while they read and interact in the social network. This setup eliminates the need for artificial stimulus since social networks are normally filled with different stimulus. The proposed approach is implemented on the Telegram social media messenger. The results show good performance in determining the mood of users. A very promising usage of the proposed approach is in helping human-human relation by providing the mood of one person to another person before an encounter.

Keywords: Mood · Emotion · Mood detection · Emotional · Facial expression features · Face · Affective · Computing · Human Computer Interaction (HCI)

1 Introduction

Recently, there have been efforts to integrate emotional intelligence into computers and robots. Emotional intelligence requires two capabilities: the ability to recognize emotions and the ability to express or employ them. As an application of emotional intelligence, the effectiveness of an online advertisement, which depends on the emotion and mood of the user, depends on recognizing and expressing emotions. A user in a good mood may easily be convinced to buy an item or pay for a trip while a user in bad mood may easily reject an advertisement for buying an item. For a user in bad mood, extra efforts are needed to convince him/her and targeted advertisement becomes more important. Consequently, several studies have proposed methods to recognize affective states, such as emotion [1] and mood [2, 3], of users for Human-Computer Interaction [4]. On the other hand, there are researchers proposed methods to show body expression [5] and facial expression [6].

Since mood and emotion may be confused, it is important to determine mood. Mood represents the non-reflective feeling state that influences affects [7]. Furthermore, it can influence our motivation and behavior [8]. For instance, people in good mood, feel better and more satisfied with their life while people in bad mood think less

© Springer International Publishing AG 2017
S.F. Ochoa et al. (Eds.): UCAmI 2017, LNCS 10586, pp. 778–788, 2017.
DOI: 10.1007/978-3-319-67585-5_75

positive about their life [9]. More precisely, mood can impact the way that people perceive the world and react to the stimulus. It should be noted that the mood term has been loosely used to address emotion in several literatures.

Generally, mood is represented in two main categories: good vs. bad. On the other hand, happy, cheerful, glum, irritable, excited, relaxed, calm, bored, weary, gloomy and sad are other categories of mood states discussed in the literature. It should be noted that people may not be always aware of their mood state until their attention is drawn to it. Furthermore, we always experience one kind of mood at a time with no sharp change in our mood [10].

Although there have been several studies for emotion detection, using facial expression [11], body gesture [12], speech signals [13], and even reflected wireless signal from body [14], there are few studies done on mood detection. For instance, standard input device keystroke [15] and mouse movement pattern [16] are used to determine a user's mood state. Also psychological questionnaire, e.g. AD-ACL [17], and physiological assessment, such as skin conductance [18], are other proposed methods to measure mood.

In this paper, we have proposed an applicable and reliable method to determine mood using visual inputs. The approach is based on the fact that emotions are affected by mood state [19]. The advantage of the proposed method, compared to the previously proposed by Hashemian et al. [2], is in its natural setting. The first approach proposed by Hashemian et al. [2] needs long term observation to determine mood while their second proposed approach [20] needs artificial stimulus to determine mood. Finally, beside the detected emotions over time, the approach uses facial features such as lip press and nose wrinkle to better determine mood. The approach has been implemented and tested with good accuracy.

2 Related Works

Mood and emotion are closely related while they are distinct phenomena. Mood and emotion are different in structural properties such as clarity, duration, and stability. Also they have different subjective context [21]. In psychology, mood is assessed using questionnaires and check list [22]. However, these approaches are time consuming and language-cultural dependent. To handle this shortcoming, pictorial assessment was proposed in which pictures are used instead of words. To cite an instances, SAM [23] is an example of mood evaluation method which is time consuming, not user friendly, and impractical for online applications.

In 2003, MIT Media lab designed a robot, named Kismet, which behaved adapted to the person interacting with it. Kismet [6] could detect affective intent state through tone of voice. After an interaction, the system could determine affects in two short and long term to model emotion and mood, respectively.

Thrasher et al. [24] considered upper body postural features to detect mood. They used mood induction via 8 min music, during two happy and sad sessions. Their study proved that certain mood states, could be detected considering certain body postures.

In Katsimerou et al. [25] presented a model to map from punctual facial emotion to mood. They proposed a simple model which uses the mean of emotions as a principle feature to determine mood. They proposed a more complex model in which discount factor is used as a memory to adapt smoothly over time. The proposed model achieves up to 62% accuracy detecting mood in four mood classes.

The most similar research to ours is the study done by Katsimerou et al. [26] in which they employed actors to play different moods. Then they determined several features from facial expressions to determine users' mood.

Our proposed approach is based on Hashemian et al. [2] approach in which several facial emotional features can be used to determine mood of a person. In [20], Hashemian et al. proposed an inductive approach by intentionally changing the emotions with aid of showing selected funny clips to their subjects. The advantage of this approach is in its shorter period of time needed to determine mood compared to their first approach [2]. Their first proposed approach, which is called the non-inductive approach, needs to take samples over an adequate period of time to determine mood based on changes in emotions. In the best case they classified neutral and good mood with 91.1% accuracy without emotion induction. Also, they reached 91.5% correct classification rate for good vs. bad mood by emotion induction

In this paper, we propose an approach to detect users' mood based on facial emotional features, which is similar to Hashemian et al. works [2, 20]. However, our method is unobtrusive, culture-independent, and applicable in real world settings. This approach has been implemented to detect mood throughout routine smartphone usage without any change in users' activities. The proposed approach is advantageous to the approaches which need to get the body posture, such as the work by Thrasher et al. [24], since getting the full body posture is not easy while people may not be willing to show their full body posture at certain times. It should be noted that we purposefully separate facial emotional features from other emotional features, such as vocal emotional features, to highlight the source of detecting information.

3   The Proposed Approach

This research is initiated based on Thayer's [27] claim that mood can change our outlook. Sirota et al. investigated the effect of mood on zygomatic and corrugator activities as well [28]. Likewise, Ekman found depression and euphoria are shown in facial signals [29]. Consequently, it is expected that if someone shows positive emotions several times in a day, he/she might be in a good mood. Also, if a person shows negative emotions throughout a period of time, then the person is probably experiencing a bad mood. Figure 1 shows a sample facial emotional expression which shows different moods while different emotions are shown. As it can be seen, the facial-emotional changes over time have been treated as signals.

As mentioned earlier, our proposed approach is based on the approaches proposed by Hashemian et al. [2, 20]. However, we further evaluated the emotional features suitable to determine mood. More importantly, the approach uses the built-in emotion stimulation in social networks, which makes the emotions change more rapidly. In other words, in this approach we do not intentionally induce or stimulate emotions and use the naturally built-in emotion induction, available in reading posts and viewing video clips, to determine mood. Since people frequently use social networks, such as

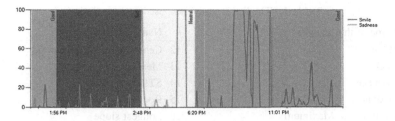

Fig. 1. A user's emotional signals sample. Blue signal represents smile and orange signal is sadness. Highlighted boundaries represent mood in which green is good mood, white is neutral and red is bad mood. These are determined by the user. (Color figure online)

Telegram, the proposed approach can receive great amount of data over time to detect mood.

In this approach, we use the front camera of tablets or smartphones to determine the emotions of users automatically in real-time. The users were asked to report their mood every 30 min to label the data. The 30-minutes interval is used since mood is fairly stable over short period of times and may change each hour or so [30].

The labeled data is used to train a classifier and select best features for mood detection. Table 1 shows the features initially suggested for mood detection in the proposed approach. There are total of 29 feature classes that can be applied on time and frequency domains. It should be noted that there are five features under the ith feature class, i.e. feature class number 9. Furthermore, feature classes 5th, 6th, and 10th, actually represent two distinct features each.

The proposed features are extracted for the six basic emotions, introduced by Ekman et al. [31]. Furthermore, six available expressions, i.e. smile, lip press, lip pucker, smirk, nose wrinkle, and mouth open, were considered in the feature extraction process, with total of 348 features in time and frequency domains. It's worth to mention that we have omitted the facial expressions of the upper half of the face since these have less contribution in mood detection compared to the lower half of the face. After evaluating these emotional features, with the aid of sequential forward selection method, three of them, i.e. fear, disgust, and surprise, were eliminated entirely. Thus, 174 features remained in the frequency and time domains, for further evaluation. Also, 5 expressions were eliminated from the features leaving only 58 facial expression features to be evaluated. Then, a second round of feature selection were performed in which 11 features (Table 2) were selected out of these 232 features.

Interestingly, smile-based features, which is a facial expression, had the highest classification impact over all the selected features. In other words, this sub-feature of Joy has better effect in correctly determining mood of a person than Joy itself.

A look at the features in Table 2 suggests that there are justifications for the selection of these features. For instance, the median of smile signal values should be higher in people in good mood with respect to people in bad mood. In other words, people in good mood smile more frequently with wide-spread values compared to people in bad mood. Also, the average distance between smile peaks should be lower in people in good mood compared the ones in a bad mood since people in good mood

Table 1. The list of initial proposed feature classes

#	Name of the features	#	Name of the features
1	Mean	12	Center value of largest bin
2	STD	13	Mean of derivative
3	Variance	14	STD of derivative
4	Median	15	Root mean of derivative
5	Minimum & Maximum	16	Longest slope
6	Lower & upper quartile	17	Number of peaks
7	Skewness	18	Average peaks distance
8	Kurtosis	19	Distance between two maximal peaks
9	i^{th} percentiles[a]; i $\in$ {1, 25, 50, 75, 95}	20	Power spectrum
10	Inter quantile & inter percentile	21	area under signal
11	Largest bin portion in frequency histogram	21	Signal energy

aThe p^{th} **percentile** is a value so that roughly **p**% of the data are smaller and (100−**p**)% of the data are larger.

Table 2. The 11 best features for mood detection.

Rank	Signal	Feature
1	Smile	Minimum
2		Median
3		Inter quartile (75–50)
4		Largest bin with respect to all
5	Sad	Average distance between peaks
6		Median
7		Percentile 95th
8		Percentile 95th
9	Joy	Average distance between peaks
10	Anger	STD
11	Smile	Maximum frequency in the Fourier transform

tend to show higher intensity smile compared to people in bad mood. This is also true for the average distance between peaks of joy. On the other hand, the higher the STandard Deviation (STD) of anger, the wider the spread of anger that should happen in people in bad mood.

Finally, derivative features, e.g. longer and shortest ascending/descending slope, are used to evaluate how much a person welcomes a specific emotion according to his/her mood. A person in a good mood is probably impressionable at positive contents which may result into a steep increasing slope in the smile signal.

4 Implementation

The proposed approach is implemented on the Telegram messenger [32] which is widely used in Iran, with over 20 million users. We designed a background service, running simultaneously with the telegram messenger on the Android platform, to do all the data collection and processing. To be able to recognize emotions while users using Telegram, the typical version of Telegram is modified to activate the front camera of the Android device and process facial features. The customized version of Telegram is called "UTTelegram" which have been distributed to the participants in the study. The emotions are recognized using the free version of Affectiva© SDK [33]. The following data are collected and sent to the server for further processing: (a) the recognized emotions by Affectiva©, (b) the watched contents' features such as starting time, finish played video's time, and the video's message ID, (c) a self-reported mood state is collected through a questionnaire which pops up every 30 min.

During the data collection and test, the participants were informed about the study's purpose, using an information letter. To protect the privacy of subjects and to maintain the confidentiality of the identifiable data, no image is stored for future processing. Instead, we used Affectiva© SDK to process video streams in real-time and only store the detected emotional states and facial expression features. Storing the emotional and facial expressions rather than actual video streams helps to reduce the size of data greatly which is necessary to reduce the data stored and transferred over the network. We processed 5 frames per second to reduce the data size while it would not affect our mood detection approach. The collected data during a day is sent to our server automatically every 24 h. The general structure of the proposed system is shown in Fig. 2.

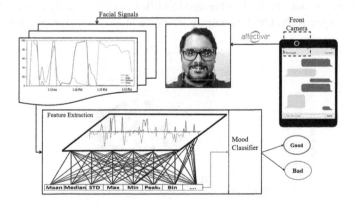

Fig. 2. The general structure of our proposed approach

5 Result and Discussion

Sixteen subjects, including 11 males and 5 females, participated in the study over 3 months with over 105 h of data. The subjects were not asked to do any specific task. They were supposed to normally use their messenger.

In this study, we have focused on discriminating good and bad mood since neutral mood has a large overlap with the other two moods which causes difficulty discriminating these three moods from each other. It can be easily seen in Fig. 3 that the neutral mood is scattered all over the data and it cannot be discriminated in such condition. It should be noted that a large part of data did not show any specific emotion or high ranked expression. In other words, we eliminated the data which did not show emotions since they do not provide needed information to determine mood. This is equivalent to consider only the moments in which a user is stimulated by a social network content. Particularly, while a subject is using his device without any sensible emotion, he/she has put on a neutral mask and practically these frames have no useful information for classification into good or bad moods. Although this is not completely and generally true, eliminating these cases has been beneficial for us in the current phase of the research.

To analyze the data, Weka© data mining software [34] was used. Table 3 shows the classification results for True Positive (TP) for good, bad, and both cases moods. It should be mentioned that the all-males classification was performed with higher accuracy. This can be due to the fact that males and females have different models which show their psychological difference in expressing facial emotional features [35]. However, we haven't enough data from female participants to perform valid classification in this group separately. Also, it should be noted that after non-sensible emotion elimination, the number of bad mood cases were much lower than the good mood cases. This could be the result of less detection accuracy rate in negative emotions and expressions in facial analyzer component. Thus, it can be expected to have lower classification accuracy for bad moods compared to the good moods.

Figure 3 illustrates a sample of data distribution for three features related to the smile facial expression. In detail, blue and red filled circles are truly clustered good and bad moods, respectively. On the contrary, stars are incorrectly clustered samples which

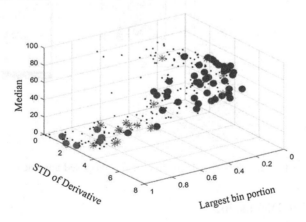

Fig. 3. Scatter plot of the clustered samples in high ranked features, i.e. median of smile, STD of derivative of smile and the largest bin portion. Circles are clustered truly in which red is bad and blue is good mood. Stars show incorrect clustered. Black dots are the neutral mood class. (Color figure online)

Table 3. The 11 best features for mood detection.

Rank	Signal	Feature
1	Smile	Minimum
2		Median
3		Inter quartile (75–50)
4		Largest bin with respect to all
5		Average distance between peaks
6	Sad	Median
7		Percentile 95th
8		Percentile 95th
9	Joy	Average distance between peaks
10	Anger	STD
11	Smile	Maximum frequency in the Fourier transform

are actually belonged to their own color clusters. Additionally, black dots are neutral mood samples which have significant overlap with other moods.

After feature selection we used decision tree J48 classifier [36] with 7 fold leave-one-out. Due to lack of huge dataset, we picked decision tree classifier which can also overcome the imbalance samples per classes. In each ten iterative steps, the classifier has chosen distinct part of all six parts of data as the test set and the remaining as the training set. Finally, we calculated the correct classification rate in each iteration and reported the results in Table 3. Table 4 shows confusion matrix for the good and bad mood and Table 5 shows the classification results.

Table 4. The classification results for True Positive (TP) of bad, good, and average moods.

Group name	Bad mood TP	Good mood TP	Average TP
All-population	0.591	0.912	0.833
Only Males	0.773	0.980	0.915

Table 5. Confusion matrix

Detected	Actual	
	Bad mood	Good mood
Bad mood	17	5
Good mood	1	45

One of the interesting observations in our study is that people in bad mood use Telegram messenger more than the people in good mood (Fig. 4). This may suggest that people in bad mood need more companionship than people in good mood which shows the importance of developing socially intelligent systems. As a matter of fact, our experiment suggests that people in bad mood pretend to be neutral to avoid their

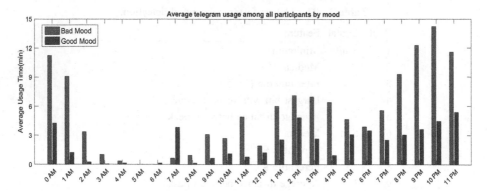

Fig. 4. The distribution of Telegram usage based on bad and good mood throughout days.

feelings. Regarding this fact, our bad mood samples in which participants express feelings are less than good ones.

6 Conclusion

In this paper, we presented an approach for detecting mood based on facial emotional and facial features. Six features from smile, three features from sadness, and one features from angry and joy signals were selected which are useful for determining mood with at least 83% accuracy. The advantage of the developed method is in its usefulness in natural settings. The proposed approach can be used for better human-human interaction by detecting the mood of a person and sending it to another person who would be in an encounter with the first person in near future.

As far as we know, there is no recent work assessed mood in such a natural setting. Furthermore, our proposed approach has better accuracy compared to the proposed approaches in [2] and [20] with no need for emotion induction. This is because the proposed approach, uses the natural emotion induction incorporated in the messengers such as Telegram.

The future work would focus more on collecting more data to generalize the model with more data. Also, more information, such as personality type, other facial expressions, and facial action units, would be used to better perform mood detection. Finally, the content of media on the social network would be further analyzed to incorporate this information into the classification process (Table 6).

Table 6. Classification results

TP Rate	FP Rate	Precision	Recall	F-Measure	ROC Area	Class
0.773	0.020	0.944	0.773	0.850	0.805	Bad
0.980	0.227	0.906	0.980	0.941	0.805	Good
0.915	0.163	0.918	0.915	0.913	0.805	Average

Acknowledgments. This research is partially funded by Cognitive Sciences and Technologies Council (COGC) of Iran. The authors like to thank all the participants in this study.

References

1. Sebe, N., Cohen, I., Gevers, T., Huang, T.S.: Emotion recognition based on joint visual and audio cues. In: 18th International Conference on Pattern Recognition (ICPR 2006), pp. 1136–1139 (2006)
2. Hashemian, M., Nikoukaran, A., Moradi, H., Mirian, M.S., Tehrani-Doost, M.: Determining mood using emotional features
3. Katsimerou, C., Heynderickx, I., Redi, J.A.: Predicting mood from punctual emotion annotations on videos. IEEE Trans. Affect. Comput. **6**(2), 179–192 (2015)
4. Jaimes, A., Sebe, N.: Multimodal human–computer interaction: a survey. Comput. Vis. Image Underst. **108**, 116–134 (2007)
5. Zecca, M., Mizoguchi, Y., Endo, K., Iida, F., Kawabata, Y., Endo, N., Itoh, K., Takanishi, A.: Whole body emotion expressions for KOBIAN humanoid robot—preliminary experiments with different emotional patterns. In: RO-MAN 2009—The 18th IEEE International Symposium on Robot and Human Interactive Communication, pp. 381–386. IEEE (2009)
6. Breazeal, C.: Emotion and sociable humanoid robots. Int. J. Hum. Comput. Stud. **59**, 119–155 (2003)
7. Russell, J.A.: Core affect and the psychological construction of emotion. Psychol. Rev. **110**, 145–172 (2003)
8. Kelley, S.W., Hoffman, K.D.: An investigation of positive affect, prosocial behaviors and service quality. J. Retail. **73**, 407–427 (1997)
9. Forgas, J.P., Bower, G.H.: Mood effects on person-perception judgments. J. Pers. Soc. Psychol. **53**, 53–60 (1987)
10. Hanjalic, A., Xu, L.-Q.: Affective video content representation and modeling. IEEE Trans. Multimed. **7**, 143–154 (2005)
11. Cohen, I., Sebe, N., Garg, A., Chen, L.S., Huang, T.S.: Facial expression recognition from video sequences: temporal and static modeling. Comput. Vis. Image Underst. **91**, 160–187 (2003)
12. Kleinsmith, A., Bianchi-Berthouze, N.: Affective body expression perception and recognition: a survey. IEEE Trans. Affect. Comput. **4**, 15–33 (2013)
13. El Ayadi, M., Kamel, M.S., Karray, F.: Survey on speech emotion recognition: features, classification schemes, and databases. Pattern Recognit. **44**, 572–587 (2011)
14. Zhao, M., Adib, F., Katabi, D.: Emotion recognition using wireless signals. In: Proceedings of the 22nd Annual International Conference on Mobile Computing and Networking, pp. 95–108 (2016)
15. Kolakowska, A.: A review of emotion recognition methods based on keystroke dynamics and mouse movements. In: 2013 6th International Conference on Human System Interactions (HSI), IEEE, pp. 548–555 (2013)
16. Zimmermann, P., Guttormsen, S., Danuser, B., Gomez, P.: Affective computing—a rationale for measuring mood with mouse and keyboard. Int. J. Occup. Saf. Ergon. **9**, 539–551 (2003)
17. Thayer, R.E.: Measurement of activation through self-report. Psychol. Rep. **20**, 663–678 (1967)
18. Picard, R.W., Scheirer, J.: The galvactivator: a glove that senses and communicates skin conductivity. In: 9th International Conference on Human-Computer Interaction (2001)

19. Ekman, P., Davidson, R.J.: The Nature of Emotion: Fundamental Questions. Oxford University Press, New York (1994)
20. Hashemian, M., Moradi, H., Mirian, M.S., Tehrani-Doost, M.: Determining mood via emotions observed in face by induction. In: 2014 2nd RSI/ISM International Conference on Robotics and Mechatronics (ICRoM 2014), pp. 717–722 (2014)
21. Beedie, C., Terry, P., Lane, A.: Distinctions between emotion and mood. Cognit. Emot. **19**, 847–878 (2005)
22. Thayer, R.E.: The Biopsychology of Mood and Arousal. Oxford University Press, New York (1989)
23. Bradley, M.M., Lang, P.J.: Measuring emotion: the self-assessment manikin and the semantic differential. J. Behav. Ther. Exp. Psychiatry **25**, 49–59 (1994)
24. Thrasher, M., Van der Zwaag, M.D., Bianchi-Berthouze, N., Westerink, J.H.D.M.: Mood recognition based on upper body posture and movement features. In: D'Mello, S., Graesser, A., Schuller, B., Martin, J.-C. (eds.) ACII 2011. LNCS, vol. 6974, pp. 377–386. Springer, Heidelberg (2011). doi:10.1007/978-3-642-24600-5_41
25. Katsimerou, C., Redi, J.A., Heynderickx, I.: A Computational Model for Mood Recognition, pp. 122–133. Blackwell, Oxford (2014)
26. Katsimerou, C., Redi, J.A.: Neural Prediction of the User' S Mood from Visual Input (2013)
27. Thayer, R.: The Origin of Everyday Moods. Oxford University Press, Oxford (1996)
28. Sirota, A.D., Schwartz, G.E., Kristeller, J.L.: Facial muscle activity during induced mood stales: differential growth and carry-over of elated versus depressed patterns. Psychophysiology **24**, 691–699 (1987)
29. Ekman, P., Friesen, W.V.: Unmasking the Face: A Guide to Recognizing Emotions from Facial Clues. Ishk, Los Altos (2003)
30. Parkinson, B.: Changing Moods: The Psychology of Mood and Mood Regulation. Addison-Wesley Longman Limited, Boston (1996)
31. Ekman, P., Friesen, W.: V: measuring facial movement with the facial action coding system. Emot. Hum. Face **2**, 178–211 (1982)
32. Durov, N., Durov, P.: Telegram messenger (2013)
33. Mcduff, D.: AFFDEX SDK : a cross-platform real- time multi-face expression recognition toolkit. In: Proceedings of the 2016 CHI Conference Extended Abstracts on Human Factors in Computing Systems, pp. 3723–3726 (2016)
34. Hall, M., Frank, E., Holmes, G., Pfahringer, B., Reutemann, P., Witten, I.H.: The WEKA data mining software: an update. ACM SIGKDD Explor. Newsl. **11**, 10–18 (2009)
35. Morris, J.A., Feldman, D.C.: The dimensions, antecedents, and consequences of emotional labor. Acad. Manag. Rev. **21**, 986–1010 (1996)
36. Salzberg, S.L.: C4. 5: Programs for machine learning by J. Ross Quinlan. Morgan Kaufmann Publishers, Inc., 1993. Mach. Learn. **16**, 235–240 (1994)

3D Kinect-Based Gaze Region Estimation in a Driving Simulator

D. González-Ortega$^{(\boxtimes)}$, J. González-Díaz, F.J. Díaz-Pernas, M. Martínez-Zarzuela, and M. Antón-Rodríguez

Department of Signal Theory, Communications and Telematics Engineering, Telecommunications Engineering School, University of Valladolid, Valladolid, Spain
{davgon,pacper,marmar,mirant}@tel.uva.es,
julian.gonzalez.diaz.95@gmail.com

Abstract. In this paper, we present a 3D Kinect-based gaze region estimation module to add gaze pattern information in a driving simulator. Gaze region is estimated using only face orientation cues, similarly to other previous approaches in the literature. An initial user-based calibration stage is included in our approach. The module is able to detect the region, out of 7 in which the driving scene was divided, that a driver is gazing on route every processed frame. 8 people tested the module, which achieved an accuracy of 88.23%. The information provided by the gaze estimation module enriches the driving simulator data and makes it possible a multimodal driving performance analysis.

Keywords: 3D computer vision · Kinect device · Face tracking · Gaze estimation · Driving simulator · Confusion matrix

1 Introduction

Event simulation is increasingly being used in many different areas. Simulators can speed up the process of acquisition of basic abilities and are configured as tools of great learning and research capacity. Particularly, driving simulators make possible the learning and re-education of drivers through the inclusion of varied routes and traffic situations that can compromise safety. Moreover, driving simulators can store data that can be analyzed to study the different aspects that play a role on traffic safety and the shortage in driving abilities that can lead to traffic dangerous situations.

We developed a driving simulator with varied routes (urban and interurban) and traffic events to analyze the driving safety level. The simulator can show in real time and store in files for further processing, not only information about the vehicle (position, speed, rpm (revolutions per minute), gear, and fuel consumption) but also the committed traffic violations.

Another important aspect to measure driver allocation of attention is the gaze location and patterns [1]. Research studies of drivers have used measures of fixation and gaze frequency and length to emphasize driver information processing, search, capacity, and requirements. Novice drivers adjust their visual search strategies to the environment situation less effectively than experienced drivers, gazing more often to the immediate

© Springer International Publishing AG 2017
S.F. Ochoa et al. (Eds.): UCAmI 2017, LNCS 10586, pp. 789–795, 2017.
DOI: 10.1007/978-3-319-67585-5_76

surroundings, and relying less on peripheral vision for vehicle control. There is a relationship between the visual search strategies of novice drivers and their underdeveloped vehicle skills and less spare attentional capacity than experienced drivers [2].

Gaze estimation methods, particularly in the field of driving monitoring, consider both eye and head orientation or only head orientation [3]. Although by using eye and head orientation cues, detailed gaze direction can be estimated, eye orientation cannot always be measured in vehicular environments due to, for instance, a large head rotation or illumination variations between day and night. All of these factors cause degradation of eye detection algorithms [3]. Coarse gaze direction can be obtained by using only head orientation since a driver's effective visual field is limited and, usually, a person moves the head to a comfortable position before orienting the eye. This coarse gaze direction can be adequate for Forward Collision Warning (FCW) systems, which do not require a detailed gaze direction to reduce false warnings [4].

Kinect sensor add-on for the Xbox 360 video game platform, which emerged at the end of 2010, interprets the 3D information of the scene obtained through infrared structured light that is read by a standard CMOS sensor. It is a low-cost alternative to 2D cameras that present problems difficult to address, such as occlusions between human body parts, range of motions, and drastic illumination and environmental changes. Since its commercial launch, many developers and researchers have used the Kinect device in their work, in different areas, e.g. head-pose and facial expression tracking, hand gesture recognition, human activity recognition, and healthcare applications [5].

Jafari and Ziou [6] presented a method for gaze estimation under normal head movement. While head position and orientation are acquired by Kinect, they obtained eye direction by a supplementary PTZ (Pan-Tilt-Zoom) camera. Fridman et al. [7] presented a method to estimate driver gaze region using a 2D camera with information about only head position and not eye position. Their approach focused on the head as the cue for classifying broad regions of eye movement to provide a method for real-time driver state estimation while providing a more feasible method for assessing driver behavior in experimental setting. They showed that even small shifts in facial configuration are sufficiently distinct for a classifier to accurately disambiguate head pose into one out of 6 driver gaze regions.

We developed a Kinect-based gaze region estimation module and integrated it in a driving simulator to enrich the information obtained by the simulator for further analysis. The module is able to extract the region that the driver is gazing each processed frame after an initial calibration stage. The module was tested with 8 people while driving in the simulator on the same route with satisfactory results.

The rest of the paper is organized as follows. Section 2 describes the developed 3D Kinect-based gaze region estimation module that we integrated in a driving simulator. Experimental results with eight people are presented in Sect. 3. Finally, Sect. 4 draws the main conclusions about the presented work.

2   3D Kinect-Based Gaze Region Estimation Module Integrated

We aimed to integrate a gaze region estimation module in a driving simulator that we had already developed. The driving simulator includes different scenarios and traffic situations interesting to analyze the safety level of the drivers in the experiments. The driver has to react to all the situations adequately to ensure safety. The simulator stores a lot of data from the driver vehicle on each route such as position, speed, rpm, gear, and fuel consumption. The simulator was developed with the Unity game engine and the 3D modeling programs Blender and 3ds Max. It can be executed in an off-the-shelf computer and a low-cost device such as the Logitech G27. The simulator allows to analyze the driving style of different people taking into account their reactions to the traffic situations they have to face and their outcomes. It also allows the awareness-raising and the learning of safe driving techniques.

The joint analysis of the gaze patterns, driving styles, and safety level of drivers can identify the visual search strategies that lead to the safest driving. Moreover, the training on these visual search strategies included in the simulator can improve visual search skills in drivers of varied age and experience as stated by [8].

We have adopted the 3D Kinect device to estimate the gaze region in each processed frame. We have used the Kinect for Windows SDK and the Face Tracking SDK for Kinect for Windows in the driving simulator Unity project to integrate a module in our simulator to achieve Kinect-based face tracking and gaze region estimation from it.

When a user is in front of the Kinect device, the module achieves face tracking through the extraction of a large number of facial points. If these points are joined forming triangles, the 3D facial mesh is built. The module tracks robustly the face in frontal and non-frontal positions. From those facial points, three rotation angles are obtained: yaw, pitch, and roll, as shown in [9]. Yaw is the face rotation around the vertical axis, pitch is the face rotation around the side-to-side axis, and roll is the face rotation around the front-to-back axis.

We are going to estimate the gaze region through the face position as some methods mentioned in Sect. 1. From experimental results, we discarded the roll angle because it does not provide relevant information regarding the driver's face position when he or she is gazing the different regions in which we have divided the simulator scene.

The yaw and pitch angles initially range from 0 to 360° increasing rightwards and upwards. We have subtracted 360° to the value of yaw and pitch if they range from 180 to 360°. This way, they range from −180 to 180°. The pitch angle has a positive value if the face is looking up the ceiling and has a negative value if the face is looking down the floor. The yaw angle has a positive value if the face is turned towards the right shoulder and it has a negative value if the face is turned towards the left shoulder. Although absolute values near 90° are difficult to track, the range of values for a person driving in the simulator are much smaller and then precisely obtained by the Kinect. The simulator scene is projected onto a big screen of dimensions 260 × 195 cm. We have divided the screen in 7 representative regions: (1) straight ahead, (2) speedometer, (3) rear-view mirror, (4) left mirror and left door glass, (5) steering wheel with another speedometer, (6) rpm meter and gear indicator, and (7) right part of the dashboard, as shown in Fig. 1. It was very important to take a good decision about the number of scene regions as it is necessary to distinguish among all the regions that the driver is going to gaze for a different purpose but taking into account that the larger the number of regions is, the worse the gaze region estimation performance is.

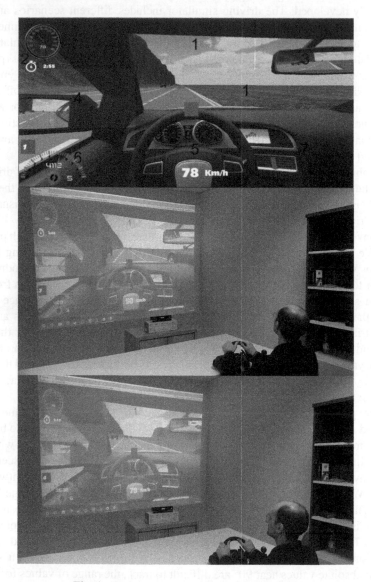

Fig. 1. Simulator scenes. (Color figure online)

3 Experimental Results

We evaluated the gaze region estimation module over an 8-driver dataset. Each driver made the same route in our driving simulator in the research laboratory. The 7 regions of interest of the scene were colored differently and identified with a printed number without compromising the driving performance. After the initial calibration stage in which each driver had to gaze 5 different points on the screen, he or she had to drive on the route and had to say out loud the number of the region that was gazing at every time a red square appeared in the middle of the screen. That red square appeared every 4 s on the screen during the simulation route. On the bottom left part of the screen below the left mirror, the region detected by the module is written so that we wrote it down each pair of regions for a processed frame: the actual region that the driver is gazing and the region detected by the module. Figure 1 shows simulator scenes with the 7 considered regions and the number of the region detected by the gaze region estimation module printed in white below the left mirror.

We obtained 2923 pairs of regions in the experiments, with approximately 365 pairs per driver. From these data, we obtained the confusion matrix for the 7-region gaze region estimation problem as shown in Fig. 2. The row dimension is indexed by the actual regions the drivers were gazing and the column dimension is indexed by the detected regions given by the gaze estimation module. As one can suppose, the drivers gazed some regions much more frequently than others. The most observed region by far was "straight ahead" (1), followed by three regions with similar frequencies among them: "left mirror and left door glass" (4), "rear-view mirror" (3), and steering wheel with another speedometer (5). The global accuracy including all the regions was 88.23%. All the regions except the "rear-view mirror" had an accuracy larger than 83%. The "rear-view mirror" had an accuracy of 67.54%. It can be explained by the fact that the

		Detected region						
		1	2	3	4	5	6	7
Actual region	1	1539 (93.61%)	6 (0.36%)	9 (0.55%)	5 (0.30%)	82 (4.99%)	0 (0.00%)	3 (0.18%)
	2	1 (0.93%)	103 (96.26%)	0 (0.00%)	3 (2.80%)	0 (0.00%)	0 (0.00%)	0 (0.00%)
	3	111 (32.46%)	0 (0.00%)	231 (67.54%)	0 (0.00%)	0 (0.00%)	0 (0.00%)	0 (0.00%)
	4	18 (4.65%)	38 (9.82%)	0 (0.00%)	323 (83.46%)	2 (0.52%)	6 (1.55%)	0 (0.00%)
	5	44 (15.07%)	0 (0.00%)	0 (0.00%)	0 (0.00%)	246 (84.25%)	0 (0.00%)	2 (0.68%)
	6	0 (0.00%)	0 (0.00%)	0 (0.00%)	9 (9.68%)	3 (3.23%)	81 (87.10%)	0 (0.00%)
	7	2 (3.45%)	0 (0.00%)	0 (0.00%)	0 (0.00%)	0 (0.00%)	0 (0.00%)	56 (96.55%)

Fig. 2. Confusion matrix for the 7-region classification problem. The 7 regions are mentioned in Sect. 2 and represented in Fig. 1. (Color figure online)

drivers may gaze the border part of this region frequently, which may erroneously be taken by a part of region 1 by the gaze estimation module.

Fridman et al. [7] also used a camera to estimate driver gaze region with only information about face position and divided the scene in 6 regions (quite similar to our 7 regions) although there are differences with our approach. For instance, they used a 2D camera placed on 2 vehicles on a real route. They obtained an accuracy of 65% (lower than our 88.23%) with a user-based model comparable to our method as we used a user calibration stage. They increased the accuracy to 92.5% only computing the regions detected with high confidence by their systems. This way, it cannot be comparable to our system as ours computes all the detected regions.

4 Conclusions

In this paper, we have presented a gaze region estimation module integrated in a driving simulator with a view to storing and analyzing the regions that drivers are gazing on route. This information can give insight into the gaze patterns of the driver and correlate them with the driving style and traffic safety.

A low-cost 3D camera as Kinect is used to fulfil gaze region estimation through only face orientation cues. 8 people took part in the experiments to test the module. A global accuracy of 88.23% was achieved, which is adequate to add the gaze region data in the driving simulation studies. As every person moves the head differently towards he or she wants to gaze, the module has a user-based calibration stage. In this calibration, the person has to gaze five different points in the screen. The calibration could include more points particularly in the border among the scene regions to adapt the module more precisely.

The driving simulator with the information provided by the validated gaze region estimation stands out as a powerful tool to achieve multimodal robust driving monitoring analysis.

Acknowledgments. This work was partially supported by the Movilidad Investigadores UVA-Banco Santander 2017 Scheme and by the National Department of Traffic (DGT), which belongs to the Spanish Ministry of the Interior, under Project SPIP2017-02257.

References

1. Hakamies-Blomqvist, L., Mynttinen, S., Backman, M., Mikkonen, V.: Age-related differences in driving: are older drivers more serial? Int. J. Behav. Dev. **23**(3), 575–589 (1999)
2. McKnight, A.J., McKnight, A.S.: Young novice drivers: careless or clueless? Accid. Anal. Prev. **35**(6), 921–925 (2003)
3. Hansen, D.W., Ji, Q.: In the eye of the beholder: A survey of models for eyes and gaze. IEEE Trans. Pattern Anal. Mach. Intell. **32**(3), 478–500 (2010)
4. Lee, S.J., Jo, J., Jung, H.G., Park, K.R., Kim, J.: Real-time gaze estimator based on driver's head orientation for forward collision warning system. IEEE Trans. Intell. Transp. Syst. **12**(1), 254–267 (2011)
5. Zhang, Z.: Microsoft kinect sensor and its effect. IEEE Multimed. **19**(2), 4–10 (2012)

6. Jafari, R., Ziou, D.: Gaze estimation using Kinect/PTZ camera. In: Proceedings of the IEEE International Symposium on Robotic and Sensors Environments (ROSE), pp. 13–18 (2012)
7. Fridman, L., Langhans, P., Lee, J., Reimer, B.: Driver gaze region estimation without use of eye movement. IEEE Intell. Syst. 31(3), 49–56 (2016)
8. Pradhan, A.K., Hammel, K.R., Deramus, R., Pollatsek, A., Noyce, D.A., Fisher, D.L.: Using eye movements to evaluate effects of driver age on risk perception in a driving simulator. Hum. Factors 47(4), 840–852 (2005)
9. Face tracking. Kinect for Windows. https://msdn.microsoft.com/en-us/library/jj130970.aspx. Accessed May 2017

An Emotional Expression Monitoring Tool for Facial Videos

Indrani Mandal[(✉)], Terry Ferguson, Gabriel De Pace, and Kunal Mankodiya

University of Rhode Island, Kingston, RI 02881, USA
indrani_mandal@my.uri.edu

Abstract. The proliferation of mobile devices and the ubiquitous nature of cameras today serve to increase the importance of Emotionally Aware Computational Devices. We present a tool to help clinicians and mental health professionals to monitor and assess patients by providing an automated appraisal of a patient's mood as determined from facial expressions. The App takes video as input from a patient and creates an annotated, configurable record for the clinician as output accessible from mobile devices, Internet or IoT devices.

1 Introduction

64% of Americans own a Smart phone and rely on it for accessing online services and information. 62% of Americans use a Smart phone to look up a health condition [20]. Smart phones are more powerful than ever. They are fully equipped with audio, video recording abilities and Internet, besides placing calls. Our goal is to harness the power of Smart phones and the Internet to improve access to mental health care.

Mental health is becoming increasingly important as we seek to better understand and help those who have been diagnosed and are working to overcome mental health issues. One way to allow the medical community to have increased access to a high-fidelity record of a patient's state is via a hand-held device and medical record residing in the cloud.

The contribution of this paper is to propose a novel framework for using automated emotion detection from videos in the wild to track patient emotional state over time to assist in clinician diagnosis and follow-up of treatments for Depression.

Computer Vision techniques have merged with machine learning techniques giving us Convolutional Neural Networks that outperform traditional Computer Vision methods [4] at the individual level since each human expresses facial emotions differently and uniquely. If improved, it will become possible to make this technique available to people at risk of mental disorders who could then seek medical treatment at the early stages. Three main factors contributing to significant performance improvements are:

1. Efficient methods for training deep artificial neural networks [19]
2. Availability of affordable high performance computational units like GPU(s)

© Springer International Publishing AG 2017
S.F. Ochoa et al. (Eds.): UCAmI 2017, LNCS 10586, pp. 796–807, 2017.
DOI: 10.1007/978-3-319-67585-5_77

3. Availability of data-sets like MMI, KDEF, DISFA and CK+ with labeled training data.

In recent years, convolutional neural networks (CNNs) have gained popularity in object and expression recognition [11]. CNNs allow us to manipulate realistic data sets with larger images. In this study we have used CNN models to detect happiness, neutral and negative emotions including sadness, anger, disgust, surprise and fear which we label as 'other' expressed by people's faces. Figure 1 depicts the human emotional states used in this study.

Fig. 1. Primary human emotional states from the KDEF Dataset: Surprise, Sad, Neutral, Happy, Disgust, Anger and Fear

2   Background

A good summary of Human Emotional Recognition efforts can be found in a recent article by Barros et al. [2] Several fields including neuroscience, psychology and computer science have been working on the problem of Recognizing Human Emotions from facial and other features for decades.

Ekman and Friesen [9] determined that facial expressions expressing the following six emotions: angry, disgust, fear, happy, sad and surprise are consistent across race and culture. Neutral can be added to this list. These expressions are generated by the contraction of muscles in the face, and these changes can be tracked and measured. The Facial Action Coding System (FACS) (and later EMFACS - Emotional Facial Action Coding System) was developed for just this purpose and has become a standard in the field, used as it is here in the openface library. Measurement Units called Action Units (AUs) were extracted from areas of the face and their method sought to link templates of AUs to the six emotions.

In the 1990's emotions were determined to improve human interaction with computers and robots [17], including a robot assisting in diagnosis of mental stress [21]. These early systems relied on the tone of the user's voice. Later systems combined expressive modalities, voice tone, body posture and facial expressions [7,10]. Studies went on to show the validity of this approach, detecting its analog in the human brain. Human brains also incorporate information from past experience [1].

With the formal introduction of Convolutional Neural Networks in 1998 [12], they were applied to the emotion recognition problem in 2002. Machine Learning techniques such as CNNs and Support Vector Machines now show the most promise in this area of research.

3   Related Work

Mankodiya et al. [15] have used Facial Landmark Tracking in a sequence of video frames to calculate the emotional engagement level of the user. The group had used CSIRO Face Analysis SDK (CFAS) which provides a set of components that extract facial geometry from video to measure facial dynamics.

Jaiswal et al. [11], have analyzed three facial features: (a) face shape, (b) appearance and (c) dynamics. They have noted that automatic facial AU recognition involves the analysis of these three features for best results. Each of the three facial features are considered an important source of information for the modeling of facial AU detectors. AU recognition models with high accuracy can be obtained by learning all three features collectively.

Kahou et al. [8] has reported the use of Recurrent Neural Networks with conjunction with Convolutional neural networks to recognize emotions. RNNs use continuous valued hidden layers to propagate information over a sequence. This combination architecture is especially good for detection of emotion in the wild. The hybrid architecture of Convolutional and Recurrent Networks has outperformed the solo CNNs.

Bartlett et al. [3] have compared different machine learning techniques like AdaBoost, Linear Discriminant analysis and Support Vector Machines (SVMs) to automatic facial expression recognition processes.

Burkert et al. [5], have used Convolutional Neural Networks to recognize facial expression. The architecture does not rely on traditional hand-crafted extraction of features but learns the features automatically through the data set used to train the network which requires the least manual interface.

Byeon et al. [6] have proposed work on video based emotion recognition. A three dimensional Convolutional Neural Network was developed that uses five consecutive video frames as input.

Sèbastien Ouellet [18] has reported real time recognition of emotion using Deep Convolutional Network architecture. The network was trained on 1.2 million images from ImageNet to extract features from the images. The model used a seven layer architecture consisting of five convolutional layers, two fully connected layers and one logistic regression layer in addition.

Barros et al. [2] has designed a Multichannel Convolutional Neural Network (MCCNN) model to extract features from visual stimuli. They feed a continuous stream of frames as the input to the model which outputs a label for an emotional state.

4   Dataset

The KDEF and DISFA data sets were used for this study. The KDEF data set was used for model accuracy testing. The DISFA dataset was used as sample patient video to create the calendar.

4.1 KDEF Dataset

The Karolinska Directed Emotional Faces (KDEF) data set consists of 4900 colored facial photographs of men and women expressing 7 primary human emotions [14]. The emotions photographed were Happy, Sad, Surprised, Angry, Disgust, Fear and Neutral. The material was developed in 1998 by Daniel Lundqvist, Anders Flykt and Professor Arne Öhman at Karolinska Institutet, Department of Clinical Neuroscience, Section of Psychology, Stockholm, Sweden (Fig. 2).

Fig. 2. KDEF Data Set

4.2 DISFA Dataset

The Denver Intensity of Spontaneous Facial Expressions (DISFA) is a non-pose facial expression dataset. The dataset consists of facial stereo videos of 27 volunteers, 15 males and 12 females of differing age and race. Facial videos of the subjects were recorded while they reacted to a four-minute emotive video stimulus [16]. Each video contains 4845 frames captured at 20 frames per second (Fig. 3).

Fig. 3. Frames extracted from DISFA dataset

5 Proposed Approach

There have been many apps or devices to help us monitor our physical health, find doctors, and remind us of appointments. There has not been an app or

Internet of Things (IoT) device to help us manage our psychological state or treatment for conditions such as depression.

This study proposes a prototype to address this issue as shown in Fig. 4. The patient keeps a video journal by recording a frontal facial video. The video is captured using a cell phone or web camera and uploaded to the Cloud for processing. The video is then analyzed for emotions and a calender is generated. The calender keeps track of the raw video, sequence of emotions expressed in the video and then displays a pie chart containing the percentage of happy, neutral and negative emotions like sad, anger, disgust or fear for each day of recording.

The calendar keeps a record of the patient's mood over time, thereby making it feasible for a mental health care provider to access and track a patient's progress reliably between visits. The health care providers don't have to rely on a patient's memory.

To simulate this model, video from the DISFA dataset was used. Subjects were recorded while they were responding to various emotional stimuli.

The results of G. Levi and T. Hassner reported in Recognition in the Wild via Convolutional Neural Networks [13] have been replicated on KDEF and DISFA datasets as part of emotion recognition processing.

Levi and Hassner pre-processes the images by converting them to gray scale and cropping the images to a target region of the face. They also assume the faces are in-plane aligned.

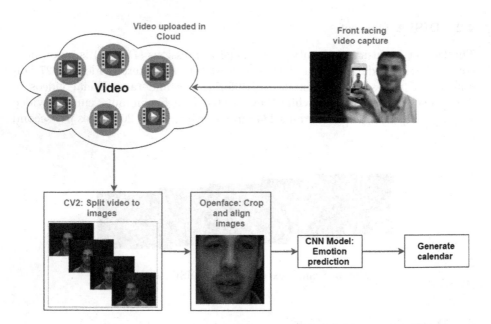

Fig. 4. Work flow of the App starts with the patient capturing a video of himself which is uploaded to the cloud for further processing. The videos are split into frames and a label for each frame is generated by the model. The model labels are stored in a calendar that is accessible by mobile devices.

6   Depression Management App Workflow

The following steps outline the anticipated steps that are taken to work with the Depression Management App once it is prescribed by the Clinician.

6.1   Video Captured

The client (patient) uses a device such as a mobile phone or other camera to capture video of his face. A clinician could direct the patient to discuss his feelings, respond to a question, or could simply be instructed to make a short video using the App (Depression Management Tool).

6.2   Cloud Upload

The App then uploads the video to the Server which resides in the Cloud. The time stamp of the video file is recorded so in the case of a delay before uploading the accuracy of timing will be maintained. The Cloud is needed for availability and for storage since the size and number of files can get large.

The Cloud is well-documented. For our purposes we are discussing a Server or Servers that have access to a large amount of storage able to keep many video files and many more image files along with databases for each patient's analyzed collection of files. The Servers will also process video files as they are uploaded and lastly must be able to process the requests for data and transmit them to the requesting devices.

6.3   Pre-processing: Frame Isolation

Each video is first pre-processed by having the individual frames extracted to standard images. OpenCV is a well-known, open-source library and is used for this step. Assuming a three minute video at thirty frames per second will generate upwards of 9k images, it is possible to down-sample the number of frames, as fewer frames are needed to capture emotions.

6.4   Pre-processing: Cropping

We have used OpenFace to preprocess the images. OpenFace allows us to define 3 target features we want to extract and put a bounding box centered around these features.

The networks trained by Levi and Hassner required 256 by 256 pixel images as input. OpenFace was used to create a bounding box of size 256 by 256 pixels around the target features. The Openface library makes use of a neural network to detect the face in the image, and set the cropping boundaries.

The FACS system provides us with the set of landmarks or points on the face which are measured to determine and quantify changes in expression. The landmarks used were outer corner of the left eye, outer corner of right eye and the tip of the nose. To indicate the facial landmarks that should be used, Openface uses numerical codes as specified in the API. The ones we selected are Outer Eyes and Nose [36, 45, 33], right eye landmark, left eye landmark and nose landmark indices respectively.

Once the landmarks were identified, OpenFace network cropped the image to produce target area of the face.

6.5   Emotion Detection Model

Each of the faces isolated in the image frames is then input to the Emotion Detection Model. The model gives as output the emotion detected from one of the categories. Since each frame is independent, this step can be done in parallel.

Levi and Hassner obtained a pre-trained model that was originally trained on CASIA recognition data-set used for object classification networks [13]. The pre-trained network was trained on human faces depicting emotions to learn relevant features of emotion recognition. Oversampling of the training data was done to provide better age and gender classification. The models were trained using Caffe framework.

The Convolutional Neural Network used in the pretrained model has 5 convolutional layers, 7 RELU layers, 1 norm1 layer, 3 pooling followed by 3 fully connected layers, 2 dropout layers and 1 Softmax layer for classification.

The convolutional layer consists of a set of filters or kernels that can learn features [12]. Each filter convolves across the height and width of the image (input volume) during the forward pass. The first layers act as edge detectors by differentiating between outlines and borders. The edge detector layers pick up low level features like lines by differentiating between contrasts.

The mid level features like curves are picked up by the convolutional layers following the layers extracting low level features. The high level features are captured by the deeper layers. They represent shape, orientation, position and image transformation [2].

Hence the network learns the specific filters that find the most likeness with the input image which represents a specific kind of feature at some location in the input image.

The RELU layer applies a function to the output of the convolutional layers to produce the activation layer.

The activation maps of all the filters that are stacked along the depth of the network dimension to form the complete output volume of a layer. Convolutional networks feature spatial correlation by enforcing local connectivity between neurons from adjacent layers.

Pooling is used to downsize an activation layer to a desired size. Pooling is done by using filters of compatible size and stride. MAX pooling was used for the model used in this study.

Fully connected layers are used for high-level reasoning. Neurons in a fully connected layer are fully connected to all activations in the previous layer like regular Neural Networks. Their activations can hence be computed with a matrix multiplication followed by a bias offset.

Dropout layers are used to turn off random neurons in order to reduce the chance of overfitting. The Dropout layers are connected between the fully connected layers.

The loss layer specifies how the network training penalizes the deviation between the predicted and true labels and is the last layer in the network. Various loss functions appropriate for different tasks may be used there. Softmax loss used in the model is used for predicting a single class of K mutually exclusive classes.

Hence we see as the depth of the network increases, the convolutional layer produces features with higher complexity. The network can be fine tuned to correctly classify into target features by increasing the number of learning layers.

6.6   Aggregating the Data

The output of the model is the detected emotion from that particular frame and this is matched up with the time stamp of the input image and stored on the Server. This is the minimal database, but can also contain a notes field for the client and another for the user (clinician). The database is stored on a cloud Server where it is available to be queried.

6.7   Displaying the Data

The App provides an interface for the user (clinician) to specify what data is needed for display, including dates of interest and the level of detail from hourly, daily, weekly, monthly or yearly. The Server then examines the database for the specified dates and prepares the data according to the choice made so it can be sent to the App. For example, if daily was selected, then the Server considers all the records for each requested day and aggregates the emotional data by percentage of each emotion detected, and sends this back to the App for display. For March 15th it may be that 30% of the detected emotions were happy, 55% were neutral and 15% sad. It is the task of the App to display this

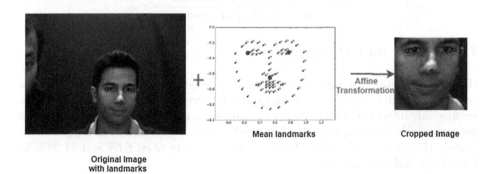

Original Image with landmarks   **Mean landmarks**   **Cropped Image**

Fig. 5. Openface landmarks used to identify a face in the picture and crop out the target region

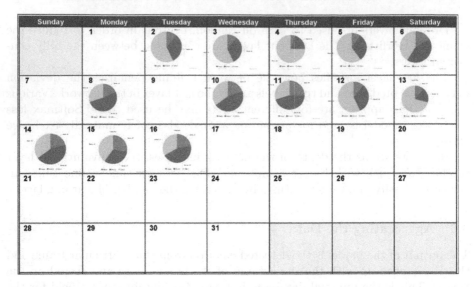

Fig. 6. Model Calendar of a patient that can be accessed by the clinician as well as the patient on mobile devices and the Internet. The pie chart shows the percentage of happy, neutral and 'other' emotions like sadness, fear, anger or disgust

(simplified, smaller) data set as requested by the user. These displays may take the form of a calendar with a pie chart for each day representing the proportion of each emotion, or a line graph of emotion vs. time for the selected duration (Fig. 6).

6.8 Performance

The accuracy of a model is determined by testing it on data on which that model has not been trained. The accuracy is calculated as the difference between the predicted level and the actual level.

$$err = \frac{\text{number of mistakes}}{\text{total number of observations}}$$

7 Results and Discussion

Happiness and neutral emotions were easy to detect and displayed a higher accuracy of prediction while disgust and sadness were hardest to predict. However, we are only interested in measuring happiness and neutral emotions correctly as we assume that an emotionally disturbed person would not show signs of happiness. Happiness and neutral have an accuracy rate of 84.69% and 87.33% for faces from different angles.

Table 1 shows (that) the overall accuracy of emotion prediction improves when frontal facial images are used as in Table 2. Table 2 shows (that) the accuracy of happiness prediction jumps from 87.69% to 95.92%. The overall accuracy

Table 1. Confusion matrix of Emotional state predictions from video frames taken at multiple angles including total Accuracy for each feature.

Emotion	Angry	Disgust	Fear	Happy	Neutral	Sad	Surprise	Total	Accuracy (%)
Angry	33	48	4	4	194	8	3	294	11.22
Disgust	116	41	0	26	100	10	0	293	13.99
Fear	23	7	31	32	133	21	47	294	10.54
Happy	16	11	0	249	17	1	0	294	84.69
Neutral	9	11	5	0	255	10	2	292	87.33
Sad	10	21	4	5	227	21	2	290	7.24
Surprise	7	8	20	11	123	11	107	287	37.28

Table 2. Confusion matrix of Emotional state predictions from frontal video frames including total Accuracy for each feature.

Emotion	Angry	Disgust	Fear	Happy	Neutral	Sad	Surprise	Total	Accuracy (%)
Angry	16	3	2	2	68	6	1	98	16.33
Disgust	50	12	0	10	20	6	0	98	12.24
Fear	11	1	19	14	14	7	32	98	19.39
Happy	4	0	0	94	0	0	0	98	95.92
Neutral	3	0	3	0	84	7	1	292	85.71
Sad	2	0	2	5	72	14	1	97	14.43
Surprise	1	1	10	5	4	1	75	97	77.32

of the model is 36.04% when faces from different angles are used, compared to 45.91% when frontal faces are used for prediction.

Figure 5 shows cropping the face to the targeted region using facial landmarks drastically improves the accuracy of prediction. The model trained by Levi and Hassner looks at a 126 by 126 pixel region at the center of the input picture. If the target region containing a facial landmark is not present in the 126 by 126 pixel region, the accuracy deteriorates.

8   Conclusions and Future Work

Applications of this research attempt to increase accessibility and reduce barriers to obtaining mental health care and increase successful monitoring of mental health issues. The App would assist health care providers with easy and reliable patient condition tracking at the click of a button.

The prototype could be improved in many ways. Each of the processing steps could be examined and improved independently. The next step is to improve the accuracy and capability of the emotion detection module. There are other models already trained and these could be compared to our current results. We plan to train our own model and tune the model to recognize every emotion with greater accuracy.

Deploying a working prototype to a clinical trial for some months then gathering feedback would be the next concrete step.

References

1. Adolphs, R.: Neural systems for recognizing emotion. Curr. Opin. Neurobiol. **12**(2), 169–177 (2002)
2. Barros, P., Jirak, D., Weber, C., Wermter, S.: Multimodal emotional state recognition using sequence-dependent deep hierarchical features. Neural Netw. **72**, 140–151 (2015)
3. Bartlett, M.S., Littlewort, G., Frank, M., Lainscsek, C., Fasel, I., Movellan, J.: Recognizing facial expression: machine learning and application to spontaneous behavior. In: 2005 IEEE Computer Society Conference on Computer Vision and Pattern Recognition (CVPR 2005), vol. 2, pp. 568–573. IEEE (2005)
4. Bengio, Y.: Learning deep architectures for AI. Found. Trends ® Mach. Learn. **2**(1), 1–127 (2009)
5. Burkert, P., Trier, F., Afzal, M.Z., Dengel, A., Liwicki, M.: Dexpression: deep convolutional neural network for expression recognition. arXiv preprint arXiv:1509.05371 (2015)
6. Byeon, Y.H., Kwak, K.C.: Facial expression recognition using 3D convolutional neural network. Int. J. Adv. Comput. Sci. Appl. **5**(12), 1–8 (2014)
7. Chen, S., Tian, Y., Liu, Q., Metaxas, D.N.: Recognizing expressions from face and body gesture by temporal normalized motion and appearance features. Image Vis. Comput. **31**(2), 175–185 (2013). Affect Analysis in Continuous Input. http://www.sciencedirect.com/science/article/pii/S0262885612001023
8. Ebrahimi Kahou, S., Michalski, V., Konda, K., Memisevic, R., Pal, C.: Recurrent neural networks for emotion recognition in video. In: Proceedings of the 2015 ACM on International Conference on Multimodal Interaction, pp. 467–474. ACM (2015)
9. Ekman, P., Friesen, W.: Constants across cultures in the face and emotion. J. Pers. Soc. Psychol. **17**(2), 124–129 (1971)
10. Gunes, H., Piccardi, M.: Automatic temporal segment detection and affect recognition from face and body display. IEEE Trans. Syst. Man Cybern. Part B Cybern. **39**(1), 64–84 (2009)
11. Jaiswal, S., Valstar, M.: Deep learning the dynamic appearance and shape of facial action units. In: 2016 IEEE Winter Conference on Applications of Computer Vision (WACV), pp. 1–8. IEEE (2016)
12. LeCun, Y., Bottou, L., Bengio, Y., Haffner, P.: Gradient-based learning applied to document recognition. Proc. IEEE **86**(11), 2278–2324 (1998)
13. Levi, G., Hassner, T.: Emotion recognition in the wild via convolutional neural networks and mapped binary patterns. In: Proceedings of the 2015 ACM on International Conference on Multimodal Interaction, ICMI 2015, pp. 503–510. ACM, New York (2015). http://doi.acm.org/10.1145/2818346.2830587
14. Lunqvist D., F.A., Öhman A.: The Karolinska Directed Emotional Faces - KDEF CD ROM from Department of Clincal Neuroscience (1998)

15. Mankodiya, K., Sharma, V., Martins, R., Pande, I., Jain, S., Ryan, N., Gandhi, R.: Understanding user's emotional engagement to the contents on a smartphone display: psychiatric prospective. In: 2013 IEEE 10th International Conference on and 10th International Conference on Autonomic and Trusted Computing (UIC/ATC) Ubiquitous Intelligence and Computing, pp. 631–637. IEEE (2013)

16. Mavadati, S.M., Mahoor, M.H., Bartlett, K., Trinh, P., Cohn, J.F.: DISFA: a spontaneous facial action intensity database. IEEE Trans. Affect. Comput. **4**(2), 151–160 (2013)

17. Morishima, S., Harashima, H.: Facial expression synthesis based on natural voice for virtual face-to-face communication with machine. In: 1993 IEEE Virtual reality annual international symposium, pp. 486–491. IEEE (1993)

18. Ouellet, S.: Real-time emotion recognition for gaming using deep convolutional network features. arXiv preprint arXiv:1408.3750 (2014)

19. Schmidhuber, J.: Deep learning in neural networks: an overview. Neural Netw. **61**, 85–117 (2015)

20. Smith, A.: US smartphone use in 2015. http://www.pewinternet.org/2015/04/01/us-smartphone-use-in-2015/

21. Tokuno, S., Tsumatori, G., Shono, S., Takei, E., Suzuki, G., Yamamoto, T., Mituyoshi, S., Shimura, M.: Usage of emotion recognition in military health care. In: Defense Science Research Conference and Expo (DSR), pp. 1–5. IEEE (2011)

Evaluation of an Affective Wearable Tool for the Transmission of Affection Gestures Between Geographically Separated Loved Ones

Flor B. Montañez[✉], Alberto L. Morán, Victoria Meza-Kubo,
and Eloísa García-Canseco

Facultad de Ciencias, UABC, Universidad de Baja California, Ensenada, Mexico
{flor.montaez,alberto.moran,mmeza,eloisa.garcia}@uabc.edu.mx

Abstract. This paper presents the design, development and preliminary evaluation of an affective wearable device for the transmission of affection gestures between grandparents and grandchildren who are geographically separated. A preliminary evaluation of the device with 33 subjects showed that it is possible to evoke affection gestures. Moreover, such gestures of affection can be tuned in such a way to appear to be real, in order to allow a closer and constant relationship between geographically separated loved ones.

Keywords: Affective wearable computing · Transmission of affection gestures · Grandparent-grandchild relation

1 Introduction

According to the migration and remittances yearbook (2016), Mexico is among the countries with the highest migration rates in the world, involving almost 12 million people [1]. Family separation is one of the highest costs migrants and their families face, affecting in particular the family ties between grandparents and grandchildren. To keep in touch and prevent the relationship from being lost, grandparents and grandchildren use either telephony services or multimedia services such as e-mails, chats or video calls as means of communication [2]. When grandparents establish communication with their grandchildren, they seek to transmit affection to the extent that technology allows. For example, they send kisses and hugs through different gestures, sounds and changes in tone of voice.

Affective wearable computing is defined as a garment system equipped with sensors and instruments that allow the recognition, transmission and interpretation of affective patterns of the wearer [3]. The development of affective wearable computing devices enables the possibility to reproduce the feelings of affection with no delay as realistic as possible, and to maintain a closer and constant relationship between geographically separated loved ones [4–6]. In this work we present a preliminary evaluation of an affective wearable computing prototype that reproduces four affection gestures (i.e. hugging, kissing, tickling in the abdomen and tapping on the shoulder), to assert the

© Springer International Publishing AG 2017
S.F. Ochoa et al. (Eds.): UCAmI 2017, LNCS 10586, pp. 808–813, 2017.
DOI: 10.1007/978-3-319-67585-5_78

fidelity with which the gesture representations evoke the respective affection gestures and the usability perception of the device by the participants.

2 Preliminary Evaluation of an Affective Wearable Device

In order to obtain the perception of use of the proposed device, a preliminary evaluation study was conducted. In this study, subjects are intended to evoke the sensations reproduced by the device as affection gestures.

Device Description. The function of the device is the transmission and evocation of affection gestures between grandparents and grandchildren who are separated geographically, aiming at stimulating the feeling of closeness and family bonding. In its current inception, the device is used between two geographically separated users, a sender and a receiver. The sender, as the name implies, is responsible for generating and issuing the affection gestures, while the receiver is responsible for receiving and interpreting them. In this study, the sender is simulated with a computerized environment that allows selecting the affection gestures to be used (see Fig. 1(a)), and it has a wearable client application (see Fig. 1(b)) that reproduces the affection gestures sent from the sender application. The prototype currently implements four affection gestures: hugging, kissing, tickling in the abdomen and tapping on the shoulder. For its operation, it is necessary to establish a connection between them to allow communication. Figure 1 shows the current architecture of the device.

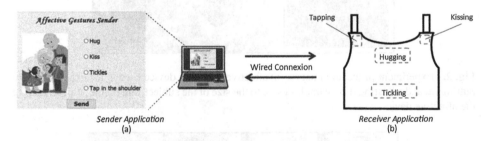

Fig. 1. System architecture, a sender application and a wearable computing vest receiver.

Study Participants. The experiment involved 33 undergraduate students from different careers; 16 from a public university and 17 from a technological institute. Their average age was 20.5 years (SD 1.78), 24 were men and 13 women.

Independent Variable. There was a single independent variable, affection gestures, with four possible values: hugging, kissing, tickling in the abdomen and tapping on the shoulder.

Dependent Variable. We have considered a single dependent variable: Evocation of feelings of affection gestures. This measures whether the subjects were able to relate the perceived stimulus to the actual corresponding affection gesture.

Hypothesis. The sensations that reproduce the device are able to evoke affection gestures regardless of whether they are of different type, namely kissing, hugging, tickling and tapping.

Procedure. The experiment was carried out in a controlled laboratory environment, applying to each individual subject the following steps:

The first step was to put on the wearable device (vest), as shown in Fig. 2. We also explained them that during the development of the experiment they could feel some patterns of vibration, pressure or sounds from it; without explaining that they intended to reproduce affection gestures. Later, the four affection gestures (see Fig. 3) were applied to each subject. At the end of each application of affection gestures, a couple of questions were asked to the subject with the intention of identifying if s/he perceived something and if this evoked to him/her an affection gesture, and in this case, which one. At the end of the experiment, each subject answered an on-exit survey to measure the usability perception and the level of evocation with which the affection gestures were perceived. To provide the subjects with information during their filling the survey, they were explained that the intention of the device was to reproduce an affection gesture and to evoke it in them, mentioning the gestures without indicating in which area of the body each one was reproduced to avoid influencing their responses in the survey.

Fig. 2. Experiment procedure images, (a) affective wearable device used in the experiment, (b) putting on and adjusting the wearable device to the size of the subject, and (c) the subject wearing the affective device.

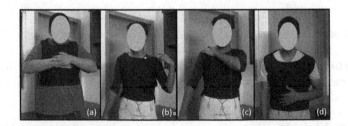

Fig. 3. Location were the 4 affection gestures were provided by the affective wearable device: (a) hugging, represented with slight pressure on the chest, through an air bag, which was inflated by an air pump; (b) kissing, reproduced with the sound of a kiss through a speaker placed on the left shoulder; (c) tapping on the shoulder, reproduced with a sequence of two vibrations on the right shoulder through a mini vibrator motor; and (d) tickling in the abdomen, reproduced with a sequence of vibrations using 2 mini vibrator motors placed in the abdomen.

3   Results

The objective of the experiment was to determine if using the developed device it was possible to evoke the sensations of the intended affection gestures. Table 1 shows a summary of the results of the experiment for each affection gesture. The hugging and the kissing affection gestures evoked such affection gestures 57.57% (57/99) and 53.53% (53/99) of the times, respectively; while the tickling and tapping gestures evoked such affection gestures 19.19% (19/99) and 3.03% (3/99) of the time, respectively.

Table 1. Results obtained from the experiment for evocation of the affection gestures reproduced by the wearable device.

Affection gesture	YES	NO
Hugging	57	29
Kissing	53	46
Tickling	19	73
Tapping	3	85

In order to test the hypothesis, the obtained data were analyzed with a Kruskal-Wallis test. The result obtained was an approximate value of $p = 0.0001$, which results in rejecting the hypothesis. Therefore, it can be said that there is a significant difference between the evocations that the device reproduces in its four variants.

Also, Table 2 shows the results obtained from the Questionnaire for User Interaction Satisfaction (QUIS) that each subject answered regarding their perception of use of the evaluated device. Each subject rated the four affection gestures with a 5-point Likert scale, where 0 = None, 1 = Little, 2 = Real enough, 3 = Real and 4 = Very real.

Table 2. Results from the QUIS on-exit questionnaire.

	Hugging	Kissing	Tickling	Tapping
None	9.09%	12.12%	18.18%	30.30%
Little	18.18%	12.12%	27.27%	24.24%
Real enough	33.33%	15.15%	18.18%	21.21%
Real	36.36%	24.24%	30.30%	18.18%
Very real	3.03%	36.36%	6.06%	6.06%

4   Discussion

In interpreting the data in Table 2, it can be seen that the affection gesture best perceived by the participants was the kissing gesture, which was perceived by 25 out of 33 subjects (75.7%) as real enough, real or very real. A possible explanation for this could be that it was reproduced in an auditory way, and that it was easier to perceive and identify a sound rather than as a gesture [7].

Regarding the perception of the affection gestures, the best perceived one was the hugging gesture, which was perceived by 24 subjects out of 33 (72.7%) as sufficiently real, real or very real. For the tickling gesture, 18 subjects out of 33 (54.5%) perceived it as sufficiently real, real or very real. Finally, in the case of the tapping gesture, only 15 subjects out of 33 (45.4%) perceived it as sufficiently real, real or very real, being this gesture the least well perceived by the group of subjects.

A possible explanation for the hugging being the most well perceived affection gesture is that it was represented in the device with a pressure on the chest, while the tickling in the abdomen and the tapping on the shoulder gestures were through vibrations. In addition, according to the literature, the torso is an area that has a large number of mechanoreceptors and is particularly sensitive to changes in pressure exerted on it [8]. Therefore, a possible recommendation from this result would be to redesign the way in which the tickling and the tapping gestures are represented in the wearable device in order to make them more noticeable.

In addition, [9] establishes that the affection gestures that grandparents most want to transmit to their grandchildren are hugs and kisses, which for grandchildren are the most meaningful affective behaviors from grandparents. This could be another reason why the hugging and kissing affection gestures were the ones that were most perceived by the subjects when evoking the sensation of having received a hug or a kiss.

5   Conclusions and Future Work

From this study, it was found that it is possible to perceive and/or evoke affection gestures with the developed prototype. In addition, of the four affection gestures reproduced by the device, the participants identified that receiving a hug or a kiss were the most well perceived and/or evoked gestures. This was possibly due to the way they were designed and implemented in the device and to their affective meaning to the subjects. Also, the tickles in the abdomen and a tap on the shoulder affection gestures were least perceived and/or evoked by participants. This was possibly due to the way they were designed and implemented in the device, and were perceived as not sufficiently resembling to the actual affection gestures.

Therefore, we can conclude that it was possible to transmit affection gestures using the affective wearable computing device proposed to be used by grandparents and grandchildren who are geographically separated. Also, it is necessary that the tickling and tapping affection gestures be redesigned and re-implemented to resemble more closely to the actual ones, so that subjects can perceive them and/or evoke them more appropriately. Finally, it should be considered that there are affection gestures with greater affective meaning than others. These can be taken as feedback to improve future affective wearable computing prototypes for this task.

As future work, we intend to improve the design and implementation of the affection gestures that were less perceived and/or evoked (tickling and tapping) by participants, in order to bring them to resemble closer to the actual ones. Likewise, it is proposed to re-implement the device so that the sender is able to receive affection gestures through a second affective wearable computing device and the receiver can emit affection gestures from the proposed device, allowing affective feedback from both sides. We are also working on a second version of the wearable device which will use Bluetooth and a Smartphone for connectivity and processing, with the aim of making it actually mobile and improving its reach.

References

1. Consejo Nacional de Población; BBVA-Research.: Anuario de Migración y Remesas, México 2016, Fundación BBVA Bancomer. https://www.fundacionbbvabancomer.org/nota.aspx? nota=53a24ffc-380d-4620-8d8448046e9d98eb&tit=Anuario-de-Migracion-y-Remesa (2016). Accedido el 15 de Marzo de 2017
2. Harwood, J.: Communication media use in the grandparent-grandchild relationship. J. Commun. **50**(4), 56–78 (2000)
3. Picard, R.W., Healey, J.: Affective wearable's. Pers. Technol. **1**(4), 231–240 (1997)
4. Rosella, F., Genz, R.: U.S. Patent Application No. 11/515,690 (2006)
5. Mueller, F.F., Vetere, F., Gibbs, M.R., Kjeldskov, J., Pedell, S., Howard, S.: Hug over a distance. In: CHI 2005 Extended Abstracts on Human Factors in Computing Systems, pp. 1673–1676 (2005)
6. Teh, J.K., Tsai, Z., Koh, J.T., Cheok, A.D.: Mobile implementation and user evaluation of the Huggy Pajama system. In: Haptics Symposium (HAPTICS), 2012 IEEE, pp. 471–478 (2012)
7. Gescheider, G.A.: Some comparisons between touch and hearing. IEEE Trans. Man-Mach. Syst. **11**(1), 28–35 (1970)
8. Jones, L.A., Nakamura, M., Lockyer, B.: Development of a tactile vest. In: Proceedings 12th International Symposium on Haptic Interfaces for Virtual Environment and Teleoperator Systems, HAPTICS 2004, pp. 82–89 (2004)
9. Mansson, D.H.: A qualitative analysis of grandparents' expressions of affection for their young adult grandchildren. North Am. J. Psychol. **14**(2), 207–219 (2012)

Special Session on AmI Systems and Machine Learning

Autism Screening Using an Intelligent Toy Car

Hadi Moradi[1,2(✉)], Sorour E. Amiri[4], Rozhina Ghanavi[1], Babak Nadjar Aarabi[1], and Hamid-Reaza Pouretemad[3]

[1] School of ECE, University of Tehran, North Karegar Street, Tehran, Iran
{moradih,rghanavi,araabi}@ut.ac.ir
[2] Intelligent Systems Research Institute, SKKU, Suwon, South Korea
[3] Shahid Beheshti University, Tehran, Iran
[4] Computer Science Department, Virginia Tech, Blacksburg, VA, USA
esorour@vt.edu

Abstract. The number of cases reported with Autism Spectrum disorder (ASD), as a developmental disorder, has increased sharply in recent decades. Early diagnosis of ASD in children is essential for proper treatment and intervention. The difficulties in early detection of autism encouraged the authors to design a novel intelligent toy car for autism screening. The toy car is equipped with an accelerometer, which records a subject's usage behavior in terms of accelerations in three dimensions. A set of features, consisting of forty-four movement characteristics, has been extracted which can be used to discriminate between children with autism and normal children. The intelligent toy car has been tested on 25 children with autism and 25 normal children as the test and control groups respectively. Support Vector Machine (SVM) is used to distinguish between the children with autism and other children. The system has 85% correct classification rate, 93% sensitivity and 76% specificity. The results are the same for boys and girls indicating the possible widespread use of this system among all children.

Keywords: Autism spectrum disorder (ASD) · Motor movement · Intelligent toy · Machine learning

1 Introduction

Autism Spectrum Disorders [1] (ASDs) are developmental disorders, with signs in early ages of an individual's life. They have a great number of symptoms, which may differ in each individual. One of the most important issues and symptoms in people with autism is their difficulty and lack of social activities and interaction with others. As an example, inability to make eye contact is a well-known symptom of ASDs [2]. In addition, a great percentage of individuals with ASD have restricted areas of interests and show stereotypical and repetitive behavior [2–4].

Despite the severe impacts that this disorder can have on the life of an individual, treatment at early stages of his/her life can be very effective. In other word, it can reduce, the impacts of the disorder severely [4–8]. Consequently, it is essential to detect ASDs at early ages of the life of children with autism for efficient treatment. Nevertheless, in many countries and especially in developing ones, the small number of experts available

© Springer International Publishing AG 2017
S.F. Ochoa et al. (Eds.): UCAmI 2017, LNCS 10586, pp. 817–827, 2017.
DOI: 10.1007/978-3-319-67585-5_79

to diagnose autism prevents early diagnosis and treatment. Furthermore, the lack of general knowledge about autism and possible negligence of parents makes it harder to detect autism at its early stages in children with autism. On the other hand, recent evidences show a significant increase in autism especially in countries such as the US in which the ratio of autism in 70s and 80s was 1 in 10000 while it was 1 in 68 in 2010. Therefore, there is a great need to design and develop automatic methods for autism screening, which do not require an expert's full diagnosis. Such systems can play the role of early warning systems to warn parents and caregivers for further screening and evaluation.

That is why there has been much research focused on developing methods that can assist in the initial screening of autism. For instance, there have been many studies applying different biomarkers to detect children with autism. A few of them apply genetic science for autism detection [9–12]. Shen et al. [9] reported evidence suggesting that genetic factors have a great contribution in the development of ASDs. They propose a clinical genetic test, which includes Karyotype, fragile X testing, and CMA all together. In 2009, Wang et al. [10] published their findings on the relation of suscepti-bility to ASDs and strong association signals detected on specific genes. Vorstman et al. [11] explain the abnormalities in genetic structures in autistic and schizophrenic patients. Veenstra-VanderWeele et al. [12] work, is a comprehensive article on the effects of genetic abnormalities in ASDs. In another study [13], Momeni et al. showed blood-based biomarkers can be used to detect ASDs. They diagnose ASDs by profiling the blood plasma of the subjects. They reported that the peptide pattern of children with autism is significantly different from non-autistic ones. They also investigated the relation between the symptoms of ASDs and different peptide patterns. In their study, an experi-ment that can profile the peptide using only 3-ml of blood is proposed. Results of the analysis of the blood samples of 28 children with autism and 30 non-autistic ones between 3–12 years old demonstrated 86% sensitivity and 77% specificity.

In a few studies, Electroencephalography (EEG) was utilized as a distinctive biomarker for autism diagnosis [14–16]. Sheikhani et al. [14] used Quantitative EEG (QEEG) signals of 17 children with autism and 11 non-autistic ones between 6 to 11 years old. By using statistical approaches, their best distinction level is 96.4%. Kamel et al. [15] used average Fast Fourier Transform (FFT) and Related Fisher Linear Discriminant (RFLD) of EEG signals to detect autism. Their data sample consists of 15 children from 10 to 11 years old. The average correct rate is 92%. William Bosl et al. [16] suggest that as a neuro-developmental disorder, ASDs must show brain abnormal-ities before the behavior symptoms appear. They designed a method, which analyzes the EEG signals of individuals and finds their abnormalities as a biomarker to diagnose the high risk of ASD. The participants' ages were between 6 to 24 months, 46 infants with high risk of ASDs and 33 infants in control group. Their results were achieved for children between 9–12 months old with 80% accuracy of detection. Other notable studies apply computer science and machine learning for automatic ASD detection [17–20]. For instance, there are researchers used image and vision processing technologies to detects ASD. Perego et al. [17] applied action detection methods to autism diagnosis. They analyzed upper limb movements like reach-and-throw, considering the fact that these movements are milestones in child development. They use infrared cameras and markers on designated parts of a subject's body to record movements. Their selected features include time spent for each part to perform the whole action and amount of adjustment movements. Finally Support Vector Machine (SVM) [21] was used to classify subjects based on their movements. Subjects include 10 normal children with average age of 41.6 (±9.23) months and 10 children with autism with average age of 41.44 (±16.07) months. Min and Tewfik [18] developed a method to automatically recognize autism by detecting repetitive and self-injurious behaviors. Using wearable sensors to record the body movement, they analyzed the recorded data of 4 children. They used Linear Prediction Coding (LPC) to classify repetitive movements. The recall rate of detecting self-injurious behaviors, flapping and rocking are 95.5%, 93.5%, and 95.5% respectively. Xu et al. [19] tried to screen autism in natural conditions by analyzing differences of vocal patterns between autistic, language delayed and normal developing children by applying a novel system, named LENA (Language ENvironment Analysis). Their subjects were between 8 months to 48 months old, 106 children in typically developed group, 49 children in language-delayed group and 77 children in autistic group. Recorded data was collected from 2006 to 2009 and the achieved accuracy is 85% to 90%. Kannappan et al. [20] used a Fuzzy Cognitive Map (FCM) to detects and predict the ASDs. FCM combines the advantages of fuzzy logic and neural networks. Their main goal was to propose a method of predicting the severity of autism with the help of non-linear Hebbian unsupervised learning algorithm and FCM.

All of the aforementioned diagnosis methods require extensive knowledge of autism symptoms, which necessitate parents to consult experts. In the absence of such measures, the detection of autism is delayed for at least few years. Furthermore, many of these approaches need high cost and complicated devices and tools which are not widely available. Finally, a few of these studies, such as LENA, have not been officially supported or widely referenced.

In this paper, we present an automatic method to detect children with autism with high probability of having ASDs in a natural environment without the presence of any expert. If the results of detection show a great chance of being autistic, parents are notified to consult a specialist for more thorough checking. Since children with autism, especially those under 6 years old, tend to spend a great amount of time playing with toys, it is more likely for an autistic child to show distinctive patterns and symptoms of ASD playing with a toy. From all ASD symptoms, the repetitive and stereotypical movements in long durations are most probable to show themselves in using a toy. It worth mentioning that the number of autistic males is 5 to 6 times more than autistic females [3, 22]. That is why an off-the-shelf toy car is used to have better chance of being used by children with autism. We developed an intelligent toy car through which a child is monitored and his/her pattern of toy movement is analyzed.

2   Subjects and Methods

The children with autism in CTAD were diagnosed using DSM-IV criteria [1] and confirmed by two independent experts. Furthermore, GARS test and ADI-R questionnaire were used in the diagnosis procedure, which is accepted in Europe and USA/Canada [23, 24].

The control group was chosen from a kindergarten, located near CTAD in Tehran, Iran. All children in the control group had developed normally and did not have any developmental or mental disorders. They were tested between May 2012 and December 2012.

Data pertaining to 6 children with autism and 7 normal children are omitted because of the short test time or interruptions at the middle of the test and unreliable recorded data. As shown in Table 1, the ratio of the number of males to the number of females and ages of participants in two groups do not have any significant differences.

Table 1. Details of participants

Gender		ASD	Controls
Male	Number	21	16
	Mean (s.d.)	4.763 (1.037)	5.250 (0.774)
	Median (range)	4.75 (3.5–7)	5.25 (4–6)
Female	Number	4	9
	Mean (s.d.)	4.800 (1.254)	4.56 (0.347)
	Median (range)	4.5 (4–7)	4.5 (4–5)
Total	Number	25	25
	Mean (s.d.)	4.77 (1.03)	5.02 (0.73)

3   The Intelligent Toy Car Design

In the first version of the car, a Wii remote [25] was embedded in the toy car to record the movements. The Wii remote, or Wiimote in short, has a 3-axis Micro Electro Mechanical System (MEMS) ADXL330 accelerometer, which measures the instantaneous acceleration with a minimum full-scale range of ± 3.6 g [26]. As previous studies show that children with autism are more interested in playing with toys that have blinking lights, moving parts, or sound [27], a set of flashing LEDs are embedded on the roof of the toy car to make it more attractive for children with autism (Fig. 1(b)).

In the first version of the car, the acceleration data collected by the Wiimote is sent over to a computer using Bluetooth connection. The data is collected and can be viewed in a Graphical User Interface (GUI) designed for this purpose (Fig. 1(c)) or stored for further processing in a file (Fig. 1(d)). In the new version of the car the Wiimote, which was bulky and limited, was replaced by an ESP8266 board equipped with ADXL345 accelerometer. The use of ESP8266, which is an Internet Of Things (IOT) module, gives the ability of using various communications methods. The circuit is capable of high speed data sampling with a Node MCU and a WiFi-module (Fig. 2(b)). Data collected by this circuit was sent over a WiFi connection to an Android phone (Fig. 2(a)). The

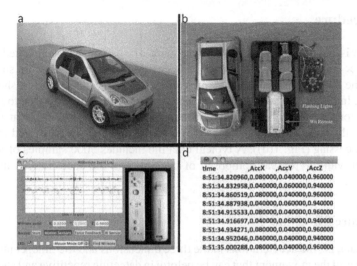

Fig. 1. (a) and (b) show the toy car with the embedded Wii Remote and flashing light. (c) A view of User Interface of the Acceleration recorder application. (d) A sample of the saved data from a participant's actions.

data which is collected and can be viewed in a GUI on an Android phone trough an application which has been developed. The data would be sent to a server for further processing and analysis. The collected data would be used to improve classification rate.

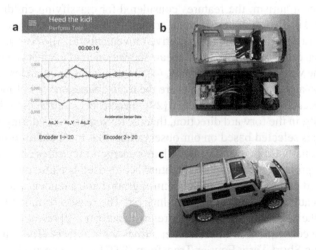

Fig. 2. (a) The new version of toy car's Android application. (b) The toy car with the embedded circuit, consists of ESP 8266 IOT module. (c) The second version of intelligent toy car.

4   Procedure

The toy car is given to each participant to play with. The participants were tested in approximately 3×3 meters rooms, in which only the system operator and the subject were present. The test and data recordings were continued as long as the subjects show interest in playing. In practice, on average the subjects played five minutes with the toy car.

The recorded data in the computer, from each subject, includes instantaneous accelerations in the three dimensions (Fig. 1(c)) and the time, which are stored in a file for further processing (Fig. 1(d)). A typical data file includes 5000 samples of a subject's interaction with the toy car composed of the time and the accelerations in the three dimensions.

4.1   Feature Extraction

The raw data, i.e. the accelerations in the three dimensions and the time, contain important features of the movement that can be helpful in detecting repetitive and stereotypical motor movements. A set of these features can form a feature vector representing the movement features and can be used to distinguish children with autism from normal ones. This feature vector can be used instead of the large and varying size raw data. Determining a suitable feature set for a special application for classification, such as classifying the children with autism, requires an insight into the application's field [21]. Here, the extracted feature vector must contain important properties of movement, which would be helpful in detecting repetitive and stereotypical movements. Based on the knowledge about autism, the features considered for classifying children with autism are categorized in the following six main groups: (1) the play time to measure the perseverance of a participant in doing a repetitive movements, (2) the correlation of accelerations between each two axes, (3) the mean and variance of each acceleration direction to measure the variability of movements, (4) the dominant frequencies of each acceleration direction and their power to measure the main characteristics of movements [28], (5) the total acceleration signals' energy [29] in each acceleration direction, and (6) the number of jolts, in the forward direction, that the toy experiences during a test. The fifth feature group is selected based on our observations that most children with autism like to play in a spatially limited space and with less energetic activities compared to children in the control group. The last selected feature is proposed because our numerous observations showed that children from the control group have a tendency to jolt the toy car, children with autism did not show such interest. The reason of this difference may be attributed to the cognitive deficit in children with autism [30] resulting in their inability to predict the consequences of their interactions with objects. The number of jolts is extracted using Short Term Fourier Transform (STFT) [31] approach.

4.2   Constructing a Classifier

Recognizing distinctive movement patterns between autistic and normal groups is possible after extracting the feature vector from each sample. The samples are divided into train and test groups. The train group, consisting of 80% of all the samples, is used to train the classifier and determine the proper threshold for an accurate classifier. In the next step the data from the test group, i.e. the remaining 20% of the samples, is used to measure the accuracy of the designed classifier.

A Support Vector Machine (SVM) classifier, with soft margin and polynomial kernel, is used for the classification purpose [32]. The classic version of SVM is a linear classifier, which divides the subjects into two separate groups. The goal is to determine a hyperplane that can classify all the training samples. However, as can be seen in Fig. 3(d), such a hyperplane may not be unique [32]. The main goal in SVM classifier is to find the best hyperplane, which has the maximum distance from each class of subjects reducing the error probability [21, 32]. In general, the two classes are not linearly separable or samples belong to more than two groups. Consequently, the multi class non-linear version of SVM classifier is used.

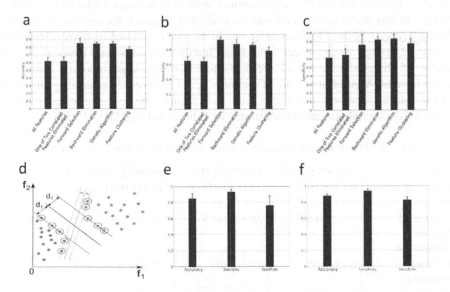

Fig. 3. (a), (b) and (c) The best accuracy, sensitivity, and specificity achieved by classifier with different feature selection methods respectively. (d) An example of two linearly separable groups of samples by two different hyperplanes. (e) The best accuracy, sensitivity and specificity achieved by all samples, i.e. males and females together. (f) The best result achieved by male.

4.3 Validation the Classifier

As a typical approach in improving the classification, K-fold cross validation is used to improve the reliability of the results and generalize them to an independent data [33]. K-fold cross validation method divides all samples into K separate folds (In this study K = 5). Each time the classifier algorithm is executed, it uses one-fold of samples in the testing phase and the remaining folds are used in the training phase. This process is performed K times using different folds. By averaging all achieved results, the Correct

Classification Rate (CCR), True Positive rate (TP rate or sensitivity) and True Negative rate (TN rate or specificity) are calculated.

4.4   Feature Selection

Although the features were introduced based on possible relation to the movement characteristics of children with autism, however, there are many overlapping features or there are features that did not show their importance in our study. There could be two reasons for the latter case: (a) the ratio of the number of features, i.e. forty-four features, to the number of participants is large which makes it too large for the algorithm to find an optimal classifier for these features, (b) these features are not capable of separating children with autism from normal ones. Consequently, it is necessary to find the best subset of features that can provide maximum separation between the autistic and normal groups. In this study, several methods are evaluated to reduce the number of features in the feature vector, i.e.: (1) eliminating one of the two correlated features of the feature vector, (2) using forward selection to determine the most important features, (3) using backward elimination on the feature vector to remove the least important features, (4) using Genetic Algorithm to find an optimum set of features (5) clustering all features and selecting a representative feature from each cluster. The results of feature selection, using different methods, are demonstrated in Table 2 and Fig. 3(a), (b) and (c).

Table 2.   The result of the classifiers with different feature conditioning methods.

Method	Accuracy (s.d.)	Sensitivity (s.d.)	Specificity (s.d.)	# of features
Complete feature set	0.624 (0.043)	0.651 (0.054)	0.612 (0.087)	44
Correlated feature elimination	0.616 (0.053)	0.637 (0.058)	0.643 (0.071)	31
Forward selection	0.85 (0.06)	0.93 (0.03)	0.76 (0.12)	5
Backward elimination	0.84 (0.024)	0.87 (0.016)	0.82 (0.04)	8
Genetic algorithm	0.842 (0.030)	0.864 (0.037)	0.832 (0.051)	18
Feature clustering	0.768 (0.035)	0.779 (0.048)	0.776 (0.058)	10

It must be noted that since this intelligent toy is planned to be used as an early warning system, and the costs of not detecting children with autism is more than false detection of normal children, we have aimed to maximize the Sensitivity while the Correct Classification Rate (CCR) and Specificity are maintained at acceptable values. However, it has been suggested to maximize specificity to avoid alarming parents and making them nervous about their children. In such a case, the training can be aimed at maximizing specificity.

5   Results

In Table 2 the results of classification with different feature sets, which were selected by various feature selection methods, are shown. As can be seen in Table 2, the accuracy (0.85 ± 0.06) and sensitivity (0.93 ± 0.03) belong to the feature set provided by forward selection method, which includes features like the number of jolts in forward direction, dominant frequency in X direction as well as Y direction and total energy of acceleration signals in Y and Z directions. But the best specificity (0.83) is achieved by the feature set that belongs to the genetic algorithm. Note that the achieved feature set by forward selection method was used to examine only male samples. Figure 3(e) and (f) show that no significant difference between the results of the two classifications, i.e. classification of males and females, exists. Thus, the independence of the results from the gender of the samples can be deducted.

6   Discussion

The design and successful use of the intelligent toy car suggests that using technology can ease the screening of children with autism and reduce the cost. On the other hand, it is needed to do further tests and increase the accuracy of such systems to increase the confidence in using technology for autism screening. One way to increase the accuracy of such system is to consider further autism symptoms and try to recognize them using technology. Consequently, we have added two shaft encoders on each of the car's shaft. By adding the shaft encoders, we expected that the discrimination rate can be improved since further symptoms can be evaluated and used for separating children with autism from other children. We have a proof of concept that children with autism play with car's wheels much more than normal children. The output of these two encoders and the accelerometer would be fused together to improve the classification rate. To ease the use of the system, an Android application has been developed that connects to the car and records the data. The data is sent to a server for further processing. Collecting data over internet allows us to improve the classification rate by receiving further data. The application provides simple statistical usage data for parents and would report possible existence of autism to parents.

Finally, it should be mentioned that we like to call this system as an early warning system rather than a screening system. The final screening should be performed by an expert after a warning is given to parents or caregivers.

7   Conclusion

In this paper the design of a novel automated ASD early warning system based on off-the-shelf equipment is discussed. Due to the importance of determining the best features capable of classifying children with autism, different approaches were used to choose most efficient subset of features that result in maximum specificity, sensitivity and correct classification rate. The 44 features suggested initially gave 65.1% sensitivity, 61.2% specificity and 62.4% CCR. After using the presented feature selection methods

(Elimination of correlated features, forward selection, backward elimination, genetic algorithm, and feature clustering) sensitivity, specificity, and CCR were increased respectively to 93%, 76%, and 85%. The result of the classifier for only male samples shows the independency of the result from the gender of participants.

The current ongoing study is focused on fusing the data from shaft encoders, implemented on the car, with the accelerometer data to increase the accuracy of discrimination. Finally, the system would be implemented as part of a screening room in which multiple technologies would be used to provide better and more reliable screening.

Acknowledgments. This research is partially funded by Cognitive Sciences and Technologies Council (COGC) of Iran. The authors would like to thank the Center for the Treatment of Autistic Disorders (CTAD) and Vista kindergarten for their support to perform experiments.

References

1. American Psychiatric Association: Task Force on DSMIV. Diagnostic and Statistical Manual of Mental Disorders: DSM-IV-TR. American Psychiatric Publishing, Inc, Washington, DC (2000)
2. Reznick, J.S., Baranek, G.T., Reavis, S., Watson, L.R., Crais, E.R.: A parent-report instrument for identifying one-year-olds at risk for an eventual diagnosis of autism: the first year inventory. J. Autism Dev. Disord. **37**, 1691–1710 (2007)
3. Baron-Cohen, S.: Autism and Asperger Syndrome. Oxford University Press, Oxford (2008)
4. Bryson, S.E., Rogers, S.J., Fombonne, E.: Autism spectrum disorders: early detection, intervention, education, and psychopharmacological management (2003). http://www.ncbi.nlm.nih.gov/pubmed/14574826
5. Ospina, M.B., Seida, J.K., Clark, B., Karkhaneh, M., Hartling, L., Tjosvold, L., Vandermeer, B., Smith, V.: Behavioural and developmental interventions for autism spectrum disorder: a clinical systematic review (2008). http://www.ncbi.nlm.nih.gov/pubmed/19015734
6. Levy, S.E., Mandell, D.S., Schultz, R.T.: Autism. Lancet **374**, 1627–1638 (2009)
7. Dawson, G., Osterling, J.: The Effectiveness of Early Intervention. Paul H. Brookes, Baltimore (1997)
8. Charman, T., Baird, G.: Practitioner review: diagnosis of autism spectrum disorder in 2- and 3-year-old children (2002). http://www.ncbi.nlm.nih.gov/pubmed/11944873
9. Shen, Y., Dies, K.A., Holm, I.A., Bridgemohan, C., Sobeih, M.M., Caronna, E.B., Miller, K.J., Frazier, J.A., Silverstein, I., Picker, J., et al.: Clinical genetic testing for patients with autism spectrum disorders. Pediatrics **125**, e727–e735 (2010)
10. Wang, K., Zhang, H., Ma, D., Bucan, M., Glessner, J.T., Abrahams, B.S., Salyakina, D., Imielinski, M., Bradfield, J.P., Sleiman, P.M.A., et al.: Common genetic variants on 5p14. 1 associate with autism spectrum disorders. Nature **459**, 528–533 (2009)
11. Vorstman, J.A.S., Staal, W.G., Van Daalen, E., Van Engeland, H., Hochstenbach, P.F.R., Franke, L.: Identification of novel autism candidate regions through analysis of reported cytogenetic abnormalities associated with autism. Mol. Psychiatry **11**, 18–28 (2005)
12. Veenstra-VanderWeele, J., Christian, S.L., Cook Jr., E.H.: Autism as a paradigmatic complex genetic disorder. Annu. Rev. Genom. Hum. Genet. **5**, 379–405 (2004)
13. Momeni, N., Bergquist, J., Brudin, L., Behnia, F., Sivberg, B., Joghataei, M.T., Persson, B.L.: A novel blood-based biomarker for detection of autism spectrum disorders. Transl. Psychiatry **2**, e91 (2012)

14. Sheikhani, A., Behnam, H., Mohammadi, M.R., Noroozian, M., Mohammadi, M.: Detection of abnormalities for diagnosing of children with autism disorders using of quantitative electroencephalography analysis. J. Med. Syst. **36**, 957–963 (2012)

15. Kamel, M.I., Alhaddad, M.J., Malibary, H.M., Thabit, K., Dahlwi, F., Alsaggaf, E.A., Hadi, A.A.: EEG based autism diagnosis using regularized Fisher linear discriminant analysis. Int. J. Image Graph. Signal Process. **4**, 35 (2012)

16. Bosl, W., Tierney, A., Tager-flusberg, H., Nelson, C.: EEG complexity as a biomarker for autism spectrum disorder risk. BMC Med. **9**, 18 (2011)

17. Perego, P., Forti, S., Crippa, A., Valli, A., Reni, G.: Reach and throw movement analysis with support vector machines in early diagnosis of autism. In: Annual International Conference of the IEEE Engineering in Medicine and Biology Society (EMBC), pp. 2555–2558 (2009)

18. Min, C.H., Tewfik, A.H.: Automatic characterization and detection of behavioral patterns using linear predictive coding of accelerometer sensor data. In: Annual International Conference of the IEEE Engineering in Medicine and Biology Society (EMBC), pp. 220–223 (2010)

19. Xu, D., Gilkerson, J., Richards, J., Yapanel, U., Gray, S.: Child vocalization composition as discriminant information for automatic autism detection. In: Annual International Conference of the IEEE Engineering in Medicine and Biology Society (EMBC), pp. 2518–2522 (2009)

20. Kannappan, A., Tamilarasi, A., Papageorgiou, E.I.: Analyzing the performance of fuzzy cognitive maps with non-linear hebbian learning algorithm in predicting autistic disorder. Expert Syst. Appl. **38**, 1282–1292 (2011)

21. Duda, R.O., Hart, P.E., Stork, D.G.: Pattern Classification. Wiley-Interscience, Hoboken (2012)

22. Newschaffer, C.J., Croen, L.A., Daniels, J., Giarelli, E., Grether, J.K., Levy, S.E., Mandell, D.S., Miller, L.A., Pinto-Martin, J., Reaven, J., et al.: The epidemiology of autism spectrum disorders*. Annu. Rev. Public Health **28**, 235–258 (2007)

23. Gilliam, J.E.: Gilliam Asperger's Disorder Scale (GADS). Pro-Ed, Austin, TX (2001)

24. Lord, C., Rutter, M., Le Couteur, A.: Disorders, autism diagnostic interview-revised: a revised version of a diagnostic interview for caregivers of individuals with possible pervasive developmental. J. Autism Dev. Disord. **24**, 659–685 (1994)

25. Wii Official Site. http://www.nintendo.com/wii/what-is-wii

26. A. Devices: ADXL330 Small, Low Power, 3-Axis\pm2 g iMEMS Accelerometer. Data Sheet), Rev. PrA, pp. 1–8 (2005)

27. Sautter, R.A., LeBlanc, L.A., Gillett, J.N.: Using free operant preference assessments to select toys for free play between children with autism and siblings. Res. Autism Spectr. Disord. **2**, 17–27 (2008)

28. Burrus, C.S.: Fast Fourier Transforms. Connexions, Rice University, Houston (2008)

29. Shmaliy, Y.: Continuous-Time Signals. Springer, New York (2006)

30. Baron-Cohen, S.: Autism: the empathizing-systemizing (E-S) theory. Ann. N. Y. Acad. Sci. **1156**, 68–80 (2009)

31. Allen, J.B.: Short term spectral analysis, synthesis, and modification by discrete {Fourier} transform. In: IEEE Trans Acoust. Speech, Signal Process. ASSP-25, pp. 235–238 (1977)

32. Theodoridis, S.: Pattern Recognition, 2nd edn. Academic Press an imprint of Elsevier Science (2003). ISBN:0-12-685875-6

33. Kohavi, R., et al.: A study of cross-validation and bootstrap for accuracy estimation and model selection. In: International Joint Conference on Artificial Intelligence, pp. 1137–1145 (1995)

Daily Routines Inference Based on Location History

Sergio Salomón[1]($\boxtimes$), Cristina Tîrnăucă[2], Rafael Duque[2],
and José Luis Montaña[2]

[1] Axpe Consulting Cantabria S.L., CDTUC,
Fase A, Planta 1, Local 108-111 Avenida de Los Castros S/N,
39005 Santander, Spain
ssalomong@axpecantabria.com
[2] Departamento de Matemáticas, Estadística Y Computación,
Universidad de Cantabria,
Avenida de Los Castros S/N, 39005 Santander, Spain
{cristina.tirnauca,rafael.duque,joseluis.montana}@unican.es

Abstract. The huge amount of location tracker data generated by electronic devices makes them an ideal source of information for detecting trends and behaviors in their users' lives. Learning these patterns is very important for recommender systems or applications targeted at behavior prediction. In this work we show how user location history can be processed in order to extract the most relevant visited locations and to model the user's profile through a weighted finite automaton, a probabilistic graphical structure that is able to handle locations and temporal context compactly. Our condensed representation gives access to the user's routines and can play an important role in recommender systems.

Keywords: Geolocation · User profiles · Weighted finite automaton · Pattern mining · Ubiquitous computing

1 Introduction

The geolocation consists in the estimation of the geographic location of an object. This task usually generates a pair of latitude and longitude coordinates, but it may also involve other variables like altitude, timestamp or real-world location labels (establishment name, street address, zone, country, etc.). Nowadays, most of the electronic devices like mobile phones, tablets, wearable computers or vehicles perform this job implicitly. In addition, a great number of social networks allow its users to register their location - running trails, geotagged photos or travel logs - and sometimes it does not require an explicit interaction either. This form of computation is known as Ubiquitous Computing [8], where the interaction occurs anytime, everywhere and with any computer device, including everyday objects like a watch or a pair of glasses. The geolocation on this context produces a big amount of data that could be analyzed to obtain movement

© Springer International Publishing AG 2017
S.F. Ochoa et al. (Eds.): UCAmI 2017, LNCS 10586, pp. 828–839, 2017.
DOI: 10.1007/978-3-319-67585-5_80

patterns, fitness records, traffic statistics or travel trends. It also has applications in non-technological fields, like the study of wildlife behavior or migratory processes.

Within the Ubiquitous Computing field, the unsupervised construction of user profiles from data (*profiling* [2]) is a well-known problem with applications such as behavior prediction and recommender systems. The user interaction records can be used to extract information about correlations and patterns in the habits and preferences of those users, and they can further be employed to model and represent any given user. We focus on the task of profiling from geolocation user records. This type of data involves specific data handling and data analysis tasks, like the identification of points of interest in the geolocation records and the search of significant patterns on the temporal context. Once the profiles are obtained, they can be used to describe the user movement or to generate automatic recommendations of places to visit.

In this paper, we propose an approach to generate user description profiles from trajectories through the building of probabilistic graphical models. First, we identify the frequently visited locations and the likelihood distributions of transitions between locations over time. Second, we use those distributions to build a weighted finite automaton that represents user patterns in a probabilistic manner. Finally, we extract descriptive text in natural language for each user in the system. With this framework, we get an easy-to-visualize generative model that can be fed as input to a recommender system, and a human readable description of the user.

The paper is structured as follows. In Sect. 2, we highlight the relevant contributions in trajectory data mining and the related work for profiling users based on trajectories. Section 3 describes our approach for the formulated problem. In Sect. 4, our method is tested on a dataset to analyze its performance. Finally, in Sect. 5 we present some conclusions and further work ideas.

2   Related Work

The spatio-temporal traces, or *trajectories*, could be considered as time series and manipulated accordingly. However, this data type motivated the emergence of a new research topic called *trajectory data mining* (TDM), with domain-specific algorithms designed for working with this kind of data. In [11], Zheng reviews several of the tasks involved in TDM: data preprocessing, data management (storing trajectories, creating good indexing systems, retrieving relevant information, etc.), handling uncertainty (missing or noisy data), pattern mining, classification and anomalies detection. The same paper also presents different ways of representing trajectories: graphs, matrices and tensors. The specific difficulties in preprocessing trajectories are: the noise filtering on coordinate points and estimation of real values; the identification of points belonging to same locations or areas; the compression of big sized trajectories; the segmentation of trajectories in subtrajectories; the matching of the coordinates to real-world locations like street addresses and roads; and the uncertainty introduced by sampling points with long time separations.

First, there are a few approaches for the detection of *stay points*, geographic regions where the user stayed for a while. Giannotti and Nanni [1] propose the computation of popular regions through a grid-based method with point-density thresholds and a neighborhood function. Karli and Saygin [5] eliminate high speed (or sparse) points from the trajectories and extract important places with density clustering (DBSCAN) over different time intervals. Li et al. [6] propose an algorithm that uses time and distance thresholds to identify stationary segments and compute stay points for a user trajectory. Ye et al. [9] extracts the significant places of a user location history applying the previous algorithm and next a density-based clustering method (OPTICS) to group found points into the same stationary zones. Yuan et al. [10] detect parking places in taxis trajectories by using a similar method, and they include a test phase of the threshold algorithm with a supervised model to improve the identification precision before applying clustering.

The strategies used for mining sequential patterns are very similar to the classic ones for association rules, but they also take into account the time information. Giannotti and Nanni [1] extract trajectory patterns above a support boundary from temporal annotated sequences and grid-based popular regions. Ye et al. [9] first compute non-temporal patterns through hybrid tree projection, item skipping and frequent itemsets (Closet+ method) and frequent closed subsequences (CloSpan method), and then extract temporal-aware patterns with different time granularity via geometric approximations. After this process, association rules are generated from conditional patterns.

For the user profiling problem, a user can be represented simply as a set of patterns or association rules (extracted through the above mentioned techniques), or as a more sophisticated structure that captures the particularities of the user's characteristics and behavior. As an example of the second case, Hung et al. [3] model the user via probabilistic suffix trees to measure the user similarity and discover user communities. Li et al. [6] use a semantic hierarchical graph, but for the representation of the location history and not the user's routines, to allow the comparison of trajectories and the similarity calculation. In [7], the user interactions are modeled with a weighted finite automaton, without including specific geolocation information in this construction. We continue this approach, defining a framework to model geolocation data with a weighted finite automaton that also considers temporal information.

3   Extraction of User Profiles

The problem we address is the extraction of user profiles from their location history. Therefore, we can assume that a first preprocessing step in which the records are filtered by user id is already performed, and from this point forward, our methodology is presented for logged trajectories of a single user. Furthermore, each trajectory will correspond to one calendar day, and they are listed in chronological order.

The trajectory π^j of a user in a given day ($j \in \{1, \ldots, L\}$) is represented as a sequence of chronological-ordered points $\pi^j = [p_1^j, \cdots, p_{m_j}^j]$, each p_i^j being a three-dimensional vector containing the geographical coordinates (latitude and longitude) and the timestamp indicating the time (hour:minute:second) when that particular GPS (Global Positioning System) location was recorded. We will refer to its components by $p_i^j.lat$, $p_i^j.lon$ and $p_i^j.ts$, respectively.

3.1 Stay Points

The first step in our methodology is the transformation of these trajectories into sequences of visited locations of interest, or *stay points*. This will significantly reduce their size without loosing any relevant information. The stay points are geographical regions where the user stayed for a while. Thus, in comparison with a raw GPS point, these spots carry some meaning: it can be a workplace, a restaurant, a mall, etc. The algorithm we use was introduced in [6] and it is described in Fig. 1 for the sake of completeness. It takes as input a list of GPS points (a trajectory), a distance limit and a time limit, and it produces a list of stay points, each of them having latitude and longitude coordinates, an *arrival* timestamp and a *leaving* timestamp. Roughly, if a user spent more than *timeLim* minutes within a distance of *distLim* meters, that region is considered a stay point. The reader is referred to [6] for a discussion about the relevance of using this approached as compared to others.

1: **procedure** STAYPOINTSDETECTION($[p_1, \ldots, p_m]$, *distLim*, *timeLim*)
2:     *staypoints* $:= \emptyset$
3:     $i := 1$
4:     **while** $i < m$ **do**
5:       $j := i + 1$
6:       **while** $j <= m$ **do**
7:         $dist := distance((p_i.lat, p_i.lon), (p_j.lat, p_j.lon))$
8:         **if** $dist > distLim$ **then**
9:           $tspan := p_j.ts - p_i.ts$
10:          **if** $tspan > timeLim$ **then**
11:            $lat := \frac{p_i.lat + \ldots + p_{j-1}.lat}{j-i}$
12:            $lon := \frac{p_i.lon + \ldots + p_{j-1}.lon}{j-i}$
13:            Add $(lat, lon, p_i.ts, p_{j-1}.ts)$ to *staypoints*
14:          **end if**
15:          $i := j$
16:          break
17:        **end if**
18:        $j := j + 1$
19:      **end while**
20:      $i := i + 1$
21:    **end while**
22:    return *staypoints*
23: **end procedure**

Fig. 1. Stay points detection algorithm

The distance between points is calculated with the haversine formula

$$r * 2 * \arcsin \left(\sqrt{\sin^2 \frac{lat_2 - lat_1}{2} + \cos(lat_1) * \cos(lat_2) * \sin^2 \frac{lon_2 - lon_1}{2}} \right) \quad (1)$$

where (lat_1, lon_1) and (lat_2, lon_2) are the coordinates in radians of the two geographical points and r is the radius of the earth (6371 for kilometers and 3956 for miles).

After applying the State Point Detection Algorithm to all trajectories of a user, each $\pi^j = [p_1^j, \ldots, p_{m_j}^j]$ becomes $sp^j = [s_1^j, \ldots, s_{n_j}^j]$, with each s_i^j a four-dimensional vector with the following components $(s_i^j.lat, s_i^j.lon, s_i^j.arv, s_i^j.lev)$.

3.2 Regions of Interest

In a second phase, we propose to substitute multiple entries of the same stay point with a discrete label that identifies a certain region of interest. The reason for this is that the same stay point may have a slightly different set of coordinates each day (just imagine strolling through a park: each day the person may have different routes, but the region of interest should only be one). To this end, we apply a density-based clustering method (DBSCAN) on the spatial features (latitude and longitude) of the set of computed stay points. Because of this, stay points very close in space are assigned the same cluster. DBSCAN needs two parameters: the minimum number of points in a cluster and the maximum distance radius to search for points which should be within the same cluster (this may vary depending on the application and available data). The distance between points is again computed with the haversine formula of Eq. (1) (note that most implementations of DBSCAN use by default the Euclidean distance). We keep the count of stay points inside each cluster for model visualization purposes, since it can be seen as an approximation of the number of visits to each region.

As a result of applying the DBSCAN algorithm, the set $SP = \bigcup_{j=1}^{L} sp^j$ of all stay points of a given user will be partitioned into k clusters $C_1, \ldots, C_k$. Moreover, we denote by c_i the centroid of cluster C_i and by r_i its radius, with i in $\{1, \ldots, k\}$.

$$c_i = \left(\frac{\sum_{s \in C_i} s.lat}{|C_i|}, \frac{\sum_{s \in C_i} s.lon}{|C_i|} \right)$$

$$r_i = \max_{s \in C_i} distance(c_i, (s.lat, s.lon))$$

3.3 User Profiles

As we want to extract patterns in the daily behavior, the trajectories must be segmented based on the time interval of the day. This segmentation can be done using at least three different strategies: fixed values (e.g., one interval per hour of the day), by means of data distribution (e.g., computing percentiles to have intervals with an equally distributed number of records) or by means of the data density (e.g., using a partition-based clustering algorithm). In Example 1 we show how this three approaches could lead to very different segmentations.

Example 1. Let us assume that we want to have three time intervals and that the timestamps recorded for one user in one particular day are 10:00, 11:00, 15:00, 21:00, 22:00 and 23:00. Then the three different approaches mentioned above will result in three distinct intervals (see Fig. 2).

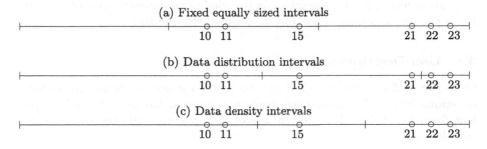

Fig. 2. Different ways of choosing intervals

In this work we opt for the first method, leaving the other two possibilities as further research topics. Thus, we set $\mathcal{I} = [I_1, \ldots, I_H]$ to be a partition of the $[0:00:00, 23:59:59]$ range into H intervals of equal length. Then, we compute the counts of each possible transition from a stay point in cluster C to a stay point in cluster C' with the following formula.

$$count_l(C, C') = |\{(j, i) \mid s_i^j \in C, s_{i+1}^j \in C', s_i^j.lev, s_{i+1}^j.arv \in I_l\}|$$

Then, one can use these counts to model a user's profile with a weighted finite automaton $\mathcal{M} = (in, out, \{W_l\}_{l \in \{1, \ldots, H\}})$ over the alphabet $\{1, \ldots, H\}$ with k states $C_1, \ldots, C_k$, in which the matrices of weights are defined as follows.

$\forall C, C' \in \{C_1, \ldots, C_k\}:$

$$W_l(C, C') = \frac{count_l(C, C') + \alpha}{\sum_{l' \in \{1, \ldots, H\}} \sum_{j \in \{1, \ldots, k\}} (count_{l'}(C, C_j) + \alpha)}$$

$$= \frac{count_l(C, C') + \alpha}{\alpha k H + \sum_{l' \in \{1, \ldots, H\}} \sum_{j \in \{1, \ldots, k\}} count_{l'}(C, C_j)}$$

The value $W_l(C, C')$ represents the likelihood of going from a point in C to a point in C' in a given time interval I_l. In the above formula, Laplace smoothing was used to avoid having many zeros when the collection of records is small. If enough data is available, the value of α can be set to zero.

The *in* and *out* functions can be used to compute the "typical" first and last stay points in the user's trajectories. Each of these will have an associated likelihood as weight, defined with the next formulas.

$$in(C_i) = \frac{|\{j \in \{1, \ldots, L\} \mid s_1^j \in C_i\}|}{L}$$

$$out(C_i) = \frac{|\{j \in \{1, \ldots, L\} \mid s_{n_j}^j \in C_i\}|}{L}$$

This weighted finite automaton $\mathcal{M}$ is a condensed representation of the activity of the user spanning a possibly very wide period of time.

3.4   User Description

Once the profile is computed, it can be used to generate the answer to many questions by simply translating them from natural language to their equivalent formula. We list here just a few of them, along with the corresponding translation.

Q1: Where is the user more likely to be in the time instance t? (list the first x more probable places)

A1: Sort the list of pairs $[(c_j, \sum_{i \in \{1, \ldots, k\}} W_l(C_i, C_j))]_{j \in \{1, \ldots, k\}}$ in descending order by the value of the second element in each pair, where l is chosen such that $t \in I_l$. Output the first x elements.

Q2: Where is the user more likely to go next if we know that in the time instance t his geographical coordinates are (lat, lon)? (list the first x more probable places)

A2: Let l be such that $t \in I_l$ and consider the set

$$PC = \{i \in \{1, \ldots, k\} \mid distance(c_i, (lat, lon)) \leq r_i\}$$

If PC is not empty, sort the list of pairs $[(c_j, W_l(C_i, C_j))]_{i \in PC, j \in \{1, \ldots, k\}}$ in descending order by the value of the second element in each pair. Output the first x elements. Note that this should be done avoiding possible duplicates (e.g., if there exists i_1, i_2 in PC such that both $W_l(C_{i_1}, C_j)$ and $W_l(C_{i_2}, C_j)$ make it to the top x most probable next locations, that particular j should be counted only once).

On the other hand, if $PC = \emptyset$, then one could extend the search to I_{l-1} and I_{l+1}, or consider the closest centroid while the distance is within a reasonable range (if the given coordinates are for a location in New York, it does not make any sense to search for the next place to visit while in Hong Kong, even if this is the closest location for which records do exist).

Q3: Which are the time intervals in which the user is most active? (list the first x of them)

A3: Let $Act(l) := \sum_{i \in \{1,...,k\}} \sum_{j \in \{1,...,k\}} W_l(C_i, C_j)$, for all l in $\{1, \ldots, H\}$. Sort the list of pairs $[(l, Act(l))]_{l \in \{1,...,H\}}$ in descending order by the value of the second element in each pair. Output the first x elements.

Q4: Which are the time intervals in which the user is never active? (if any)

A4: Output all l in $\{1, \ldots, H\}$ such that $Act(l) = 0.0$ (for this particular question, the smoothing parameter α must be set to zero).

Q5: Which is the most probable region in which the user would start their day?

A5: Sort the list of triples $[(c_j, r_j, in(C_j))]_{j \in \{1,...,k\}}$ in descending order by the value of the third element in each triple. Output the first x elements.

Q6: Which is the most probable region in which the user would end their day?

A6: Sort the list of triples $[(c_j, r_j, out(C_j))]_{j \in \{1,...,k\}}$ in descending order by the value of the third element in each triple. Output the first x elements.

The same set of questions can be addressed by imposing further conditions regarding some particular day of the week. For example, the fifth question can be modified into "Which is the most probable region in which the user would start their Sunday?". These questions cannot be directly answered by using the weighted finite automaton $\mathcal{M}$. Nevertheless, a simple filtering of the initial set $\{\pi^1, \ldots, \pi^L\}$ of trajectories by selecting only those days that are Sundays would solve this problem. The same strategy would work if we want to differentiate between weekdays and weekends, working days and bank holidays, or between different months of the year.

And although one can think of many other questions that can be answered by this condensed representation of a user's life (the records can often span many years), there are other aspects that are inevitably lost. For instance, if we want to know which is most probable sequence $A \rightarrow B \rightarrow C$ while being at location A in the time instance t, the only possibility (get B the most probable next location while being in A, and C the most probable next location while being in B) could return rather unexpected results (see Example 2 below).

Example 2. Let us assume that we have only one time interval and $L = 10$ (ten days with available records). In four of these days, the user would go from A to B and next from B to D. In the other six days, the user would go from E to B and from B to C. The corresponding weighted finite automaton would list B as the most probable next location while being in A (with probability 1), and C as the most probable next location while being in B (with probability 0.6). Therefore, the recommended route would be $A \rightarrow B \rightarrow C$ (although this never happened!), while the right answer should be $A \rightarrow B \rightarrow D$.

4   Experimentation

We test the method we proposed over a public dataset of GPS trajectories. The data used is the Geolife GPS trajectory dataset [12] from the Urban Computing group of Microsoft Research Asia. This dataset provides 18670 trajectories, with over 24 million points, from 182 users over 5 years. It contains latitude, longitude, altitude and timestamp variables. Due to the high levels of noise, we discard the altitude feature in our experimentation. The data is distributed over 30 cities of China and some cities of USA and Europe, but most of the records are located in Beijing. As it is explained in its user guide, this repository was obtained from GPS loggers and GPS phones with different sampling rates. Our intention in this case study is to learn the routines of these users.

Although we applied the proposed methodology to the whole set of users, apart from presenting some statistical information (see Table 1), we report on the results obtained for one particular user, randomly chosen (user 35).

Table 1. Dataset statistics

	Min	Max	Mean	Median	User 35
Number of available days (L)	1	1245	58.43	19	56
Number of initial points ($M := \sum_{j=1}^{L} m_j$)	17	2158884	136701	35182	312042
Number of stay points ($N := \sum_{j=1}^{L} n_j$)	0	3703	273.69	67	905
Number of clusters (k)	0	214	13.87	5	19
Compression ratio N/M	0.0	0.0714	0.0074	0.0024	0.0029
Compression ratio k/N	0.0	0.2	0.0602	0.0588	0.02

In Fig. 3 we present the whole trajectory for this user and the set of all its stay points (computed for each day with distance and time thresholds of 35 m and 5 min respectively).

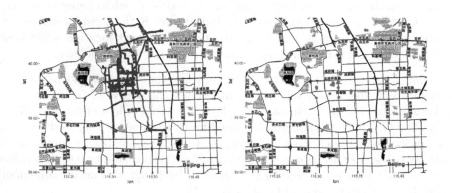

Fig. 3. User 35 trajectory (left) and stay points (right)

Thanks to the street map on which the trajectories and the stay points were displayed, one can visualize the effect of the StayPointDetection Algorithm.

Namely, the algorithm successfully removed the GPS points recorded while in transit. Moreover, hundreds of similar but not identical locations are mapped to only one stay point (for this particular user, most of the entries are five seconds apart, so one hour of staying in the office would produce 1200 entries in the dataset). After this step, the DBSCAN algorithm is performed to obtain clusters of stay points that are within a 100 m radius. The minimum size for a cluster is set to three (it is reasonable to consider regions that only appear once or twice in a two months time frame to be irrelevant to the user's habits). This parameter is probably the most problematic to set for a heterogeneous collection of users. Ideally, its value should be variable and should depend on the number of days in the location history.

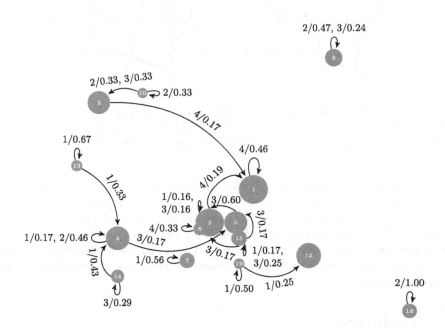

Fig. 4. Weighted automaton for user 35

In order to build its weighted finite automaton $\mathcal{M}$, we set H, the number of intervals, to 8. In Fig. 4 we show the states of a visually enhanced version of $\mathcal{M}$: the position of each state corresponds to its geographical location and the radius is proportional to the size of the cluster. For a better readability, only the more significant transitions (with likelihoods higher than 0.15) and relevant regions of interest (with at least five stay points) are graphically depicted in the figure.

As we argued in Sect. 3.4, this condensed representation gives many insights on the user's routines. For example, his home and workplace are probably somewhere inside C_1 and C_3, since they are by far the most visited places. And because the *in* and *out* values of C_3 are very close to one, it means that it must be the user's home. Also, one may compute the likelihood of visiting a certain place during the first time interval of the day (for instance) and output the most probable next locations (see Fig. 5-left). Note that if we condition the search by fixing the actual location (for example, if we know that the user's actual location is somewhere in C_3), the result might be different (see Fig. 5-right).

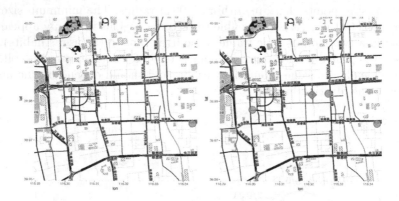

Fig. 5. Next probable locations for the first interval, with or without knowing the actual position; each of the three more probable states are marked by a circle, and the actual location, if known, is represented by a diamond (see the right-hand side map)

Regarding the activity rates of different intervals, we can observe that very little activity (if any) is detected in the 5–8 intervals. A possible explanation could be that the GPS is using GMT time instead of local time (for Beijing, GMT+8). Under this assumption, the user is mostly inactive from 8pm to 8am local time (no activity at all from 23pm to 5am), and the peak interval is from 8am to 11am (going to work), followed closely by the third interval: 2pm to 5pm (returning home).

5   Conclusions

The prevalent GPS technology in our daily lives is, on one hand, a valuable source of information about our routines and life style preferences. On the other hand, this huge quantity of data makes it difficult to extract relevant and useful information. In this work, we show how an automatic transformation of those millions of records into a reasonably small-sized, easy to build and interpret, weighted finite automaton can ease this information extraction task. As long as GPS-logging is user-authorized and the resulting output is used legally, this can be a precious input to recommender systems. The weighted finite automaton is able to estimate a probability distribution over all locations visited by a user and each time interval (something which would be difficult to achieve with traditional methods or even with other probabilistic graphical models such as Bayes Nets or Markov Chains). It remains to see how to adapt this strategy to an online learning setting, in which states and transitions could be created and updated as more information is recorded (new data could come in stream). Also, as future work, we intend to enhance this automaton with other semantic information in order to enable tagging each location with its corresponding label (library, cinema, supermarket, school, gas station, restaurant, etc.).

Acknowledgments. The authors gratefully acknowledge the financial support from the project TI16-IN-007 of SODERCAN and project PAC::LFO (MTM2014-55262-P) of Ministerio de Ciencia e Innovación (MICINN), Spain. The geographic maps included in this paper were plotted using the *ggmap* R package [4].

References

1. Giannotti, F., Nanni, M., Pinelli, F., Pedreschi, D.: Trajectory pattern mining. In: Proceedings of the 13th ACM SIGKDD International Conference on Knowledge Discovery and Data Mining, KDD 2007, pp. 330–339. ACM, New York (2007)
2. Hildebrandt, M.: Defining profiling: a new type of knowledge? In: Hildebrandt, M., Gutwirth, S. (eds.) Profiling the European Citizen. Springer, Dordrecht (2008). doi:10.1007/978-1-4020-6914-7_2
3. Hung, C.C., Chang, C.W., Peng, W.C.: Mining trajectory profiles for discovering user communities. In: Proceedings of the 2009 International Workshop on Location Based Social Networks, LBSN 2009, pp. 1–8. ACM, New York (2009)
4. Kahle, D., Wickham, H.: ggmap: spatial visualization with ggplot2. R J. **5**(1), 144–161 (2013)
5. Karli, S., Saygin, Y.: Mining periodic patterns in spatio-temporal sequences at different time granularities. Intell. Data Anal. **13**(2), 301–335 (2009)
6. Li, Q., Zheng, Y., Xie, X., Chen, Y., Liu, W., Ma, W.Y.: Mining user similarity based on location history. In: Proceedings of the 16th ACM SIGSPATIAL International Conference on Advances in Geographic Information Systems, GIS 2008, pp. 34: 1–34: 10. ACM, New York (2008)
7. Tîrnăucă, C., Duque, R., Montaña, J.L.: Automatic generation of user interaction models. In: García, C.R., Caballero-Gil, P., Burmester, M., Quesada-Arencibia, A. (eds.) UCAmI 2016. LNCS, vol. 10069, pp. 406–418. Springer, Cham (2016). doi:10.1007/978-3-319-48746-5_42
8. Weiser, M.: The computer for the 21st century. In: Baecker, R.M., Grudin, J., Buxton, W.A.S., Greenberg, S. (eds.) Human-computer Interaction: toward the year 2000, pp. 933–940. Morgan Kaufmann Publishers Inc., San Francisco (1995)
9. Ye, Y., Zheng, Y., Chen, Y., Feng, J., Xie, X.: Mining individual life pattern based on location history. In: Proceedings - IEEE International Conference on Mobile Data Management, pp. 1–10 (2009)
10. Yuan, J., Zheng, Y., Zhang, L., Xie, X., Sun, G.: Where to find my next passenger. In: Proceedings of the 13th International Conference on Ubiquitous Computing, UbiComp 2011, pp. 109–118. ACM, New York (2011)
11. Zheng, Y.: Trajectory data mining: an overview. ACM Trans. Intell. Syst. Technol. **6**(3), 29: 1–29: 41 (2015)
12. Zheng, Y., Li, Q., Chen, Y., Xie, X., Ma, W.Y.: Understanding mobility based on gps data. In: Proceedings of the 10th International Conference on Ubiquitous Computing, UbiComp 2008, pp. 312–321. ACM, New York (2008)

Distributed Unsupervised Clustering for Outlier Analysis in the Biggest Milky Way Survey: ESA Gaia Mission

Daniel Garabato[1]([⊠]), Carlos Dafonte[1], Marco A. Álvarez[1],
and Minia Manteiga[2]

[1] Departamentos de Tecnologìas de la Informaciòn y las Comunicaciones,
Universidade da Coruña (UDC), Elviña, 15071 A Coruña, Spain
`daniel.garabato@udc.es`
[2] Departamentos de Ciencias de la Navegación y de la Tierra,
Universidade da Coruña (UDC), Paseo de Ronda 51, 15011 A Coruña, Spain

Abstract. The Gaia mission (ESA) is collecting huge amounts of information about the objects that populate our Galaxy and beyond. Such data must be processed and analyzed before being released, and this work is carried out by the Data Processing and Analysis Consortium (DPAC) through several work packages. One of these packages is Outlier Analysis, devoted to the study, by means of unsupervised clustering, of all the objects that cannot be fitted into any of the existent models. An algorithm based on optimized Self-Organized Maps (SOM) is proposed and implemented for taking advantage of distributed computing platforms, such as the MapReduce paradigm for Apache Hadoop and Apache Spark. Finally, the processing times of the sequential implementation of the algorithm is compared to the Hadoop and Spark based ones.

Keywords: Computational Astrophysics · Fast Self-Organized Maps · Parallel computing · Map-reduce · Apache Hadoop · Apache Spark · Remote sensing

1   Introduction

Nowadays, we are facing the era of Big Data and many applications have to deal with huge volumes of data, including their storage, management, and analysis. Such an analysis implies that vast amounts of data have to be processed in order to extract some knowledge, and it cannot be done anymore using traditional software packages that run on a single machine, typically the scientist's computer or laptop. It will require a migration towards Data Mining applications, which are designed to run distributed among several machines arranged in a cluster, taking advantage of the underlying computation power.

This is the case of some astronomical surveys, such as the Gaia mission, where the on-board spacecraft instruments gather hundreds of Gigabytes that need to

© Springer International Publishing AG 2017
S.F. Ochoa et al. (Eds.): UCAmI 2017, LNCS 10586, pp. 840–852, 2017.
DOI: 10.1007/978-3-319-67585-5_81

be processed by the scientific community. This paper presents an optimized Self-Organized Map (SOM) [16] algorithm designed using a distributed approach based on MapReduce [15,26], so that it can be computed on enormous datasets. In order to measure the performance of the algorithm, it is applied to the analysis of outlier sources in the Gaia mission.

Gaia is the cornerstone mission of the European Space Agency (ESA) and it aims to provide the most precise census of the Milky Way, that is approximately a 1% of the objects in our Galaxy, allowing to study its composition, formation, and evolution [6,23]. Since its launch in December 2013, the spacecraft has been gathering at around 36 GB of data per day, which will result in the order of a Petabyte after its five years of routine operations, becoming a challenge in the Computational Astrophysics field. In order to process and analyze such an amount of data, ESA established the Data Processing and Analysis Consortium (DPAC), an international scientific network responsible for preparing the data releases. In September 2016 the first one was delivered to the astronomical community [10,11], including some preliminary astrometry; whereas the final catalog is foreseen for around 2023, and will be populated with the entire observations, as well as the data analysis produced by DPAC.

DPAC is organized in a hierarchy of different working packages (WP), that are devoted to specific tasks within the processing effort. This paper is framed in the Outlier Analysis (OA WP), which is a part of the Astrophysical Parameters Inference System (APSIS) [2,17,19,20] and the Catalog Access. OA is aimed at analyzing, by means of unsupervised Artificial Intelligence techniques and using spectrophotometric data, all the sources that cannot be successfully classified into any of the well known astronomical classes (Stars, Quasars, Galaxies, etc.) by the main classification package (DSC, Discrete Source Classifier) [22]. These outlier sources are expected to be at around a 10% of the whole Gaia dataset ($\sim 10^8$ sources, ~ 100 GB). It provides an accurate analysis in order to help the scientists to understand and unveil their nature according to the Gaia source types considered so far: stars, white dwarfs, ultra cool dwarfs, quasars, galaxies, and planetary nebulae. Since stars is the most popular category it aims at identifying sub-types [17].

Analyzing outliers is always an arduous task, since it implies dealing with unknown or damaged objects, whose available information may not be accurate at all, and the high dimensionality of the data makes the process even more complex. Dimensionality reduction and clustering are the most popular techniques to tackle such an issue. On the one hand, dimensionality reduction techniques pretend to simplify the original dataset by reducing the number of variables under consideration without losing too much information, which leads to faster analysis of the data. There are some frequently used algorithms such as Principal Component Analysis (PCA) [14] or Linear Discriminant Analysis (LDA) [7]. On the other hand, clustering is aimed at grouping the data according to their inner nature into a number of clusters or groups. Many clustering algorithms are available, however, no one can be regarded as a general problem solver: an algorithm suitable for a certain task, may not be suitable for another or it may not be the most appropriate one; it must be carefully studied and selected [27].

In particular, SOM [16] are a type of Artificial Neural Network (ANN) intended for clustering, as well as dimensionality reduction at the same time, which fits really well the main goal of OA: unsupervised classification. The SOM projects the input data into a number of groups or clusters, usually arranged in a two-dimensional (or three-dimensional) lattice. Every object that is under analysis is assigned to one cluster, and each cluster has a representative (prototype) which stands for all the sources that are associated with such a cluster. These prototypes are mutated over an iterative process called learning or training, in which they are progressively adapted to fit the input data. There are many different variants of the learning algorithms introduced by Kohonen in 1982 [16], such as the one proposed by us in [5] to deal with non numerical data.

The work presented in this paper makes use of the traditional Kohonen's algorithm, slightly modified as it will be described in Sect. 3, because the OA module needs, by its requirements and specifications within APSIS, to use unsupervised Artificial Intelligence (AI) techniques, as well as this algorithm was found to perform really well in Astronomy [8,9,18].

The paper is organized as follows: Sect. 2 presents the Gaia dataset that will be used to test the distributed SOM algorithm proposed in Sect. 3; Sect. 4 introduces a visualization tool used to explore astronomical SOMs; In Sect. 5 the performance measured for the different distributed implementations, as well as the sequential baseline, are compared; Finally, in Sect. 6 some conclusions are extracted and future developments are proposed.

2   Testing Dataset

The first Gaia Data Release was published in September 2016, however, it only contains some basic astrometry and no photometry (or spectroscopy) was delivered at all. It is expected that, in the upcoming data releases, the information about the sources will be widely increased, until the whole Gaia catalog is published. Because OA needs to use spectrophotometric data to classify the sources to a Gaia source-type, it cannot be tested using the available information, so a semi-empirical dataset will be used instead. Such a dataset is based on the ground survey SDSS DR7 [24] and it is composed of 10125 spectroscopic observation classified as *unknown* by the SDSS spectroscopic classification pipeline (faint objects, incomplete spectra, etc.), which have already been studied in [8]. These sources have been transformed into the Gaia Blue and Red Photometer (BP/RP) format (Fig. 1a) by means of the Gaia Object Generator [13].

2.1   Preprocesing

It is well known that applying a good preprocessing to the data before presenting them to a clustering technique can significantly enhance its performance. Hence, since it was the preprocessing which empirically offered a better performance, the data presented above in Sect. 2 will be transformed as follows (Fig. 1):

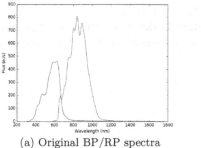
(a) Original BP/RP spectra

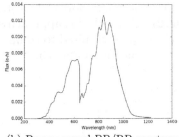
(b) Preprocessed BP/RP spectrum

Fig. 1. BP/RP spectra preprocessing.

1. Firstly, we remove the pixels that lie in the extremes of both BP and RP spectra, since they correspond to the low signal-to-noise ratio (SNR) pixels of the satellite's payload CDD and they may not be reliable at all.
2. The resulting BP and RP spectra are joined into a single spectrum, removing the overlapping region to avoid redundant wavelengths, and interpolating those points where there is no information or the information is wrong (i.e. missing values, negative flux, etc.).
3. In order to avoid interstellar reddening, we applied a correction based on Cardelli extinction model [4].
4. The resulting spectrum is scaled to determine its area to 1 unit:

$$F_i' = \frac{F_i}{\sum_{i \in S}(F_i)} \tag{1}$$

where F_i is the flux of a spectrum in band i and S represents the bands of the spectrum. This allows us to compare objects with different brightness (magnitudes) by their spectra using similarity distance functions, such as the Euclidean distance.

3   Distributing the SOM Learning Algorithm

The vast amounts of data led us to implement a parallel design of the Kohonen's algorithm [16]. At this point, it must be taken into account that the online algorithm is not suitable for a parallel implementation because it performs a observation-by-observation processing within one iteration and the prototypes are updated for each observation, whereas the batch algorithm processes all the observations within one iteration and then the prototypes are updated, allowing for parallelization at iteration level [12]. Hence, the batch algorithm is the unique choice. Additionally, the batch algorithm does not take into account the order of the input observations, becoming more stable than the online one. In order to speed up the algorithm, we decided to use an optimization version of the algorithm, called FastSOM, which looks for the winner within the immediate neighborhood of the previous winner once a number of iterations have succeed and the SOM becomes more or less stable, instead of searching within the whole map (Fig. 2). Although this approach slightly decreases the overall performance, the execution times required to compute are considerably reduced, so it is worth implementing such an approach.

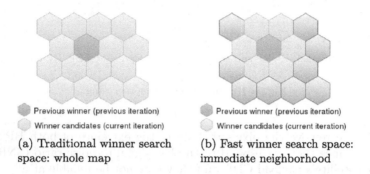

(a) Traditional winner search   (b) Fast winner search space:
space: whole map   immediate neighborhood

Fig. 2. Winner search spaces

This algorithm was parallelized using Apache Hadoop/Spark, since these are the software frameworks chosen by Gaia DPAC to process their data. Map-Reduce is a distributed programming model that allows to spread the workload over a cluster of machines by defining two tasks: (a) the map task divides the input data into small chunks (key/value pairs) that are processed independently producing a (potentially different) key/value pair output for each one; and (b) the reduce task gathers the outputs produced by the map tasks grouped and sorted by key, processing each group individually. These tasks must be appropriately defined and designed according to the algorithm, as well as the driver, which manages the map/reduce tasks and gathers the final results.

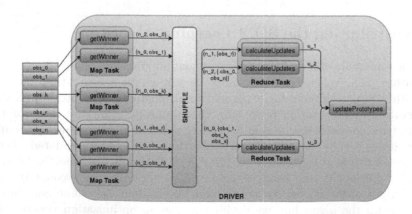

Fig. 3. Map-Reduce design for Self-Organized Maps.

Regarding the Map-Reduce design of the SOM, the map task determines the winner cluster for each input observation (preprocessed spectrum), whereas the reduce task computes partial updates for the cluster's prototypes, as it can be observed in Fig. 3. The *shuffle* box represents the process of grouping and sorting by key the outputs of the map tasks, typically implemented by the underlying framework. Such a design is implemented as follows:

Apache Hadoop: The SOM algorithm is implemented just using the map/reduce procedures available in such a framework. On the other hand, the driver performs a sequential merge of the partial prototype updates.

Apache Spark: The map task is implemented using the available map procedure. However, the reduce task is implemented using a workaround by means of a combiner procedure. Additionally, instead of using a sequential approach to merge the partial prototype updates, a Spark reduce procedure is used. This implementation is actually proposed to be included as a Gaia DPAC Catalog Access data mining tool available for the public community, so that users can analyze their own subsets of Gaia data.

3.1   Actual SOM Implementation for OA

The implementations discussed above in Sect. 3 are valid for a pure Apache Hadoop or Apache Spark framework. However, all the APSIS modules of Gaia DPAC, including OA, must be implemented using an abstraction of the Apache Hadoop framework called SAGA [3].

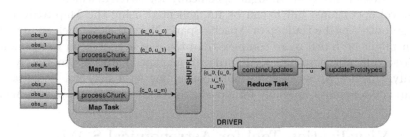

Fig. 4. Alternative Map-Reduce design for Self-Organized Maps in SAGA.

Due to SAGA requirements and constraints, the proposed distributed design is not feasible at all, and an alternative one has been developed, as it can be observed in Fig. 4. Basically, the map task is now responsible for determining the winner cluster and computing the partial prototype updates, however, it works over a chunk of the input observations, instead of a single one. Then, a reduce task is used to combine the partial prototype updates calculated for each chunk. This combination procedure is quite heavy in terms of memory, so, depending on the number of chunks, a multi-level hierarchy of combiners may be used to

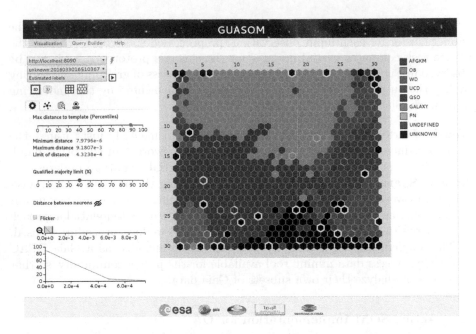

Fig. 5. Screenshot with estimated Gaia labels for SDSS semi-empirical dataset.

overcome such an issue. Finally, the merge procedure is analogous to the one exposed in the previous design.

This design has been thought specifically for SAGA, which provides some high-level operations, but it can be implemented using the Map-Reduce paradigm in both Apache Hadoop or Apache Spark. Nevertheless, such an implementation might be much more complex than the one described in Sect. 3, since it requires to handle data directly in order to manage chunks appropriately. Additionally, this design is rather memory consuming so it may not be suitable for certain environments, specially for Apache Spark which tries to work in memory.

4   A Visualization Tool for Astronomical SOMs

The data processed by the SOM should be further analyzed by experts on the domain of application, in this case astronomers or astrophysicists. A web-based visualization tool called GUASOM has been developed so that they can easily explore OA SOM maps, and it will be published along with the Data Releases. It can provide different SOM representations, from the classical *hits* or *umatrix* visualizations to new and more specific ones:

Gaia labels: Displays the distribution of astronomical classes among all the SOM clusters, according to the predominant class, determined by performing template matching to a reference set of well-known Gaia sources (Fig. 5).

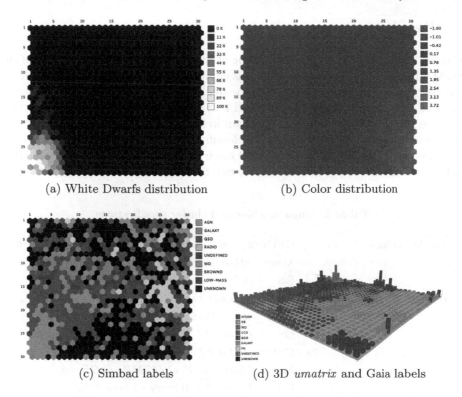

(a) White Dwarfs distribution   (b) Color distribution

(c) Simbad labels   (d) 3D *umatrix* and Gaia labels

Fig. 6. Specialized views

Category distribution: This visualization allows to represent which clusters may contain sources of a certain type according to their labels (Fig. 6a).

Color distribution: It represents the ordering of the map according to the colors of the stars that activate each cluster (Fig. 6b).

Simbad labels: This is a domain specific representation, and it shows the most probable astronomical class associated with each cluster according to an offline cross-match performed on the Simbad generalist database [25] in which the sources related to each cluster were searched (Fig. 6c).

Three-dimensional representations: They provide an enriched visualization by combining two of any of the ones discussed above, such as the *umatrix* and the Gaia labels distribution which can be observed in Fig. 6d.

This application can provide many other features, such as cluster exploration in order to analyze the content of each cluster, cross-match with external catalogs (i.e. Simbad [25]) or communication with external astronomical tools (i.e. Topcat, Vaex, etc.). More information about GUASOM can be found in [1].

5   Results

Firstly, although it is not the main topic of this paper, the scientific results of the SOM will be briefly addressed when it is computed over the SDSS semi-empirical dataset presented in Sect. 2. Despite the quality of the objects contained by this dataset, the SOM is quite well ordered and similar sources are placed together in close regions of the map, as it is shown in Fig. 5. However, at around a 15% of the sources could not be successfully classified because either they didn't fitted into any class (*unknown*) or they fitted more than one class (*undefined*). Further details about the study of this dataset can be found in [8].

Table 1. Single machine and cluster specifications.

Single machine		CPUs	*2 × Intel Xeon CPU X5660 @ 2.80 GHz × 6*
		Mem.	*32 GB DDR3 @ 1333 MHz (8 GB × 4)*
		OS	*Debian 8.6 Jessie - 3.16.0-4-amd64*
Hadoop/Spark cluster	2×	CPUs	*2 × Intel Xeon CPU E5420 @ 2.50GHz × 4*
		Mem.	*24 GB DDR2 @ 667 MHz (4 GB × 6)*
		OS	*Debian 7.7 Wheezy - Linux 3.2.0-4-amd64*
	2×	CPUs	*2 × Intel Xeon CPU E5472 @ 3.00 GHz × 4*
		Mem.	*32 GB DDR2 @ 667 MHz (4 GB × 8)*
		OS	*Debian 7.7 Wheezy - Linux 3.2.0-4-amd64*
	1×	CPUs	*2 × Intel Xeon CPU X5550 @ 2.67 GHz × 4*
		Mem.	*24 GB DDR3 @ 1333 MHz (4 GB × 6)*
		OS	*Debian 7.7 Wheezy - Linux 3.2.0-4-amd64*

Now, setting aside the scientific results offered by the SOM, it is necessary to analyze the time performances achieved by the different algorithm implementations. Hence, it is necessary to describe the environment in which the tests were carried out. Table 1 shows the physical features of the machines used to ran the tests, being all of them under the same Java version: *Oracle Java 1.7.0_72*.

Once the scenario has been arranged, the execution times obtained over two hundred iterations for the sequential and distributed versions of the SOM are compared in Table 2 and Fig. 7. It can be observed that the Spark implementation is much more faster than the others, even for small datasets, which may experience some overhead due to initialization and communications among the nodes. This is exactly what is happening to the Hadoop implementation, so the execution times for this version when the dataset is fairly small are greater than the sequential ones. The main difference between Hadoop and Spark is that Hadoop stores intermediate data to the file system, so they must be written and read many times, whereas Spark works with the data in memory. However, when the size of the dataset becomes larger enough (more than a million objects), it

Table 2. Time measurements for the different implementations (hours).

		10 k	50 k	100 k	500 k	1 M	10 M	100 M
Sequential	Regular	10.8	53.8	107.1	538.8	1076.7	11067.1	1117775.7[a]
	Fast	2.8	14.0	27.7	140.5	280.8	2899.0	281028.8[a]
Hadoop	Regular	13.8	36.8	41.4	45.1	48.7	560.5	6446.5
	Fast	5.3	11.8	13.1	15.7	22.0	171.9	1678.5
Spark	Regular	1.5	2.6	4.6	20.1	39.3	375.7	4604.6
	Fast	0.7	1.3	2.1	8.5	16.5	156.4	1735.5

[a]These values were estimated based on times for the initial iterations.

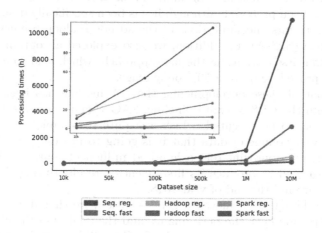

Fig. 7. Comparative of execution times (hours).

can be observed that the sequential approach becomes unfeasible, while the distributed approaches scale reasonably.

According to these measurements, the OA module would run on the whole outlier dataset detected by DSC in approximately two months using our small Hadoop cluster. Nevertheless, we have noticed that the usage of a newer Java version highly improved the performance of the algorithm, obtaining execution times much faster than the previous versions of Java.

Regarding SAGA, although it was not possible to measure times on the operations platforms yet, due to the established schedule (OA will start to operate during the next operations cycle, third data release), however, it was successfully run in the pre-integration platform. The Hadoop cluster used for running SAGA is composed of several machines with hundreds of cores, so the processing times are expected to be much faster than in our cluster (a couple of weeks), even though SAGA is expected to ad a 10% of overhead with respect to a pure Hadoop due to the framework managements tasks.

6   Conclusions and Future Work

This article addresses the analysis of astronomical data by means of Self-Organized Maps (SOM), applied to outlier classification (OA) over enormous datasets collected by the Gaia mission. Additionally, a visualization tool for astronomical SOMs, which will be a part of the Gaia catalog software, has been commented briefly in order to explore the SOM results.

To this purpose, two distributed versions of the SOM algorithm have been implemented, one for Apache Hadoop and the other one for Apache Spark, and they have been found to scale appropriately (specially the Spark one) for huge datasets, such as the Gaia one. In addition, an alternative Map-Reduce implementation has been proposed, although it has been specifically designed to overcome the constraints and limitations of the ad-hoc Hadoop framework used by such a pipeline (SAGA). In addition, we also explored an optimization of the SOM algorithm itself, by using the fast approach, which lead to a speed up of the training procedure up to a 50% on average.

As a result of these developments, the OA module has been successfully integrated into the CU8 software pipeline, SAGA, and it is expected to take a couple of weeks to be executed, which are quite reasonable times taking into account the vast volume of data that it is going to process (10% of the whole Gaia dataset, i.e. approximately a hundred million of sources, 100 GB). This module is expected to produce its first scientific results during the third Gaia data release, around the end of year 2018.

Finally, although we achieved a good solution, we should continue looking forward to upgrade both the performance and the quality of the algorithm. We also expect that the overhead caused by SAGA will be significantly reduced in the upcoming SAGA implementations, so that it will speed up the execution of the OA module. Additionally, we are already working on new SOM algorithm optimizations to improve its performance, such as a very promising GPU/CPU mixed computing version based on Nvidia CUDA [21]. Currently, GPU computing is not supported by SAGA, but this paradigm is suitable for both Apache Spark and Apache Hadoop.

Acknowledgements. This work was supported by the Spanish *FEDER* through Grants ESP2016-80079-C2-2-R, and ESP2014-55996-C2-2-R.

References

1. Álvarez, M.A., Dafonte, C., Garabato, D., Manteiga, M.: Analysis and knowledge discovery by means of Self-Organizing Maps for Gaia data releases. In: Hirose, A., Ozawa, S., Doya, K., Ikeda, K., Lee, M., Liu, D. (eds.) ICONIP 2016. LNCS, vol. 9950, pp. 137–144. Springer, Cham (2016). doi:10.1007/978-3-319-46681-1_17
2. Bailer-Jones, C.A.L., et al.: The Gaia astrophysical parameters inference system (Apsis). Pre-launch description. Astron. Astrophys. **559**, A74 (2013)
3. Brunet, P., Montmorry, A., Frezouls, B.: Big data challenges, an insight into the GAIA Hadoop solution. In: SpaceOps Conferences, AIAA, June 2012

4. Cardelli, J.A., Clayton, G.C., Mathis, J.S.: The relationship between infrared, optical, and ultraviolet extinction. Astrophys. J. **345**, 245–256 (1989)
5. del Coso, C., Fustes, D., Dafonte, C., Nóvoa, F.J., Rodríguez-Pedreira, J.M., Arcay, B.: Mixing numerical and categorical data in a Self-Organizing Map by means of frequency neurons. Appl. Soft Comput. **36**, 246–254 (2015)
6. de Bruijne, J.H.J.: Science performance of Gaia, ESA's space-astrometry mission. Astrophys. Space Sci. **341**, 31–41 (2012)
7. Fisher, R.A.: The use of multiple measurements in taxonomic problems. Ann. Eugenics **7**(7), 179–188 (1936)
8. Fustes, D., Manteiga, M., Dafonte, C., Arcay, B., Ulla, A., Smith, K., Borrachero, R., Sordo, R.: An approach to the analysis of SDSS spectroscopic outliers based on Self-Organizing Maps: designing the outlier analysis software package for the next Gaia survey. Astron. Astrophys. **559**, A7 (2013)
9. Fustes, D., Dafonte, C., Arcay, B., Manteiga, M., Smith, K., Vallenari, A., Luri, X.: SOM ensemble for unsupervised outlier analysis. Application to outlier identification in the Gaia astronomical survey. ESWA **40**(5), 1530–1541 (2013)
10. Collaboration, G., Brown, A.G.A., Vallenari, A., Prusti, T., de Bruijne, J.H.J., Mignard, F., Drimmel, R., Babusiaux, C., Bailer-Jones, C.A.L., Bastian, U., et al.: Gaia data release 1. Summary of the astrometric, photometric, and survey properties. Astron. Astrophys. **595**, A2 (2016)
11. Collaboration, G., Prusti, T., de Bruijne, J.H.J., Brown, A.G.A., Vallenari, A., Babusiaux, C., Bailer-Jones, C.A.L., Bastian, U., Biermann, M., Evans, D.W., et al.: The Gaia mission. Astron. Astrophys. **595**, A1 (2016)
12. Garabato, D., Dafonte, C., Manteiga, M., Fustes, D., Álvarez, M.A., Varela, B.A.: A distributed learning algorithm for Self-Organizing Maps intended for outlier analysis in the GAIA - ESA mission. In: IFSA-EUSFLAT (2015)
13. Isasi, Y., Figueras, F., Luri, X., Robin, A.C.: GUMS & GOG: simulating the universe for Gaia. Astrophys. Space Sci. Proc. **14**, 415 (2010)
14. Jolliffe, I.: Principal Component Analysis. Springer, New York (2002)
15. Karau, H., Konwinski, A., Wendell, P., Zaharia, M.: Learning Spark: Lightning-Fast Big Data Analytics, 1st edn. O'Reilly Media Inc., Sebastopol (2015)
16. Kohonen, T.: Self-organized formation of topologically correct feature maps. Biol. Cybern. **43**(1), 59–69 (1982)
17. Manteiga, M., Carricajo, I., Rodríguez, A., Dafonte, C., Arcay, B.: Starmind: a fuzzy logic knowledge-based system for the automated classification of stars in the MK system. Astron. J. **137**(2), 3245–3253 (2009)
18. Naim, A., Ratnatunga, K.U., Griffiths, R.E.: Galaxy morphology without classification: Self-Organizing Maps. ArXiv Astrophysics e-prints, April 1997
19. Ordóñez, D., Dafonte, C., Arcay, B., Manteiga, M.: HSC: a multi-resolution clustering strategy in Self-Organizing Maps applied to astronomical observations. Appl. Soft Comput. J. **12**(1), 204–215 (2012)
20. Ordóñez-Blanco, D., Arcay, B., Dafonte, C., Manteiga, M., Ulla, A.: Object classification and outliers analysis in the forthcoming Gaia mission. Lect. Notes Essays Astrophys. **4**, 97–102 (2010)
21. Sanders, J., Kandrot, E.: CUDA by Example: An Introduction to General-Purpose GPU Programming, 1st edn. Addison-Wesley Professional, Reading (2010)
22. Smith, K.W.: The discrete source classifier in Gaia-Apsis, p. 239 (2012)
23. Torra, J., Gaia Group: Gaia: the challenge begins. In: Highlights of Spanish Astrophysics VII, pp. 82–94, May 2013

24. Tsalmantza, P., et al.: A semi-empirical library of galaxy spectra for Gaia classification based on SDSS data and PÉGASE models. Astron. Astrophys. **537**, A42 (2012)
25. Wenger, M., et al.: The SIMBAD astronomical database: the CDS reference database for astronomical objects. Astron. Astrophys., Suppl. Ser. **143**(1), 9–22 (2000)
26. White, T.: Hadoop: The Definitive Guide. O'Reilly Media Inc., Sebastopol (2015)
27. Xu, R., Wunsch, D.: Survey of clustering algorithms. IEEE Trans. Neural Netw. **16**(3), 645–678 (2005)

Opinion Dissemination Computational Model

María Teresa Signes Pont[1]([⊠]), Higinio Mora[1],
Antonio Cortés Castillo[2], and Mario Nieto Hidalgo[1]

[1] Department of Computer Science Technology,
University of Alicante, Alicante, Spain
{teresa, hmora, mnieto}@dtic.ua.es
[2] Department of Computer Science, University of Panama,
Panama City, Panama
antonio.cortes@up.ac.pa

Abstract. The dissemination of opinions is a very important phenomenon in modern societies because it shapes politics, policies and then guides the evolution of societies in the future. The scheme is very simple: an opinion is transmitted by a leader to other people in his (her) neighborhood. People can be convinced or not and so, in turn, they convey their updated opinion (or their previous one) to their neighbors. This paper presents a computational framework based on a set binary local rules that have the capability to model the transmission of opinion between neighbors. Several neighborhood types are considered, such as 4- and 8-neighbours and knight (chess) neighbors. Different behavioral patterns are analyzed in relation to rule type, neighborhood type, and leader type.

Keywords: System dynamics · Opinion dissemination · Neighborhood rules · Complexity · Behavioral pattern

1 Introduction

Nowadays, the dissemination of opinions is a very important phenomenon because it shapes politics, policies and then guides the evolution of societies in the future. The rise of the media and social networks [1–4] is responsible of the huge spread of users interventions related to social issues such as fashions, collective decision making, rumors, expansion of ideologies and propagation of cultural items that are immediately shared, updated and forwarded by people [5]. Opinion dynamics has motivated a lot of research in different fields such as mathematics, physics, and computer sciences. Some models depict the situation as a graph interconnecting individuals that perform a combination of their own opinions with those of their neighbors, so that a consensus is reached depending on the connectivity of the graph [6]. On the contrary, bounded confidence models are used when people do not reach a consensus but accept other opinions when they are sufficiently close to their own opinion. These models generate cluster formation [7]. From a mathematical standpoint, we can discern between two main approaches: the interacting particle systems where the agents occupy discrete states and their relationships are simple rules between them or the crowd behavior models that are depicted by means of differential equations to implement the average

© Springer International Publishing AG 2017
S.F. Ochoa et al. (Eds.): UCAmI 2017, LNCS 10586, pp. 853–858, 2017.
DOI: 10.1007/978-3-319-67585-5_82

behavior of the system as a whole. Both approaches can be specified in order to meet the features of a real scenario. The former can be specified by contact processes [8, 9], voter models or majority opinion models [10], the latter by schools of fish, flocks of birds, pedestrian movements in streets and vehicular traffic [11, 12]. In this paper we present a computational model of opinion dissemination based on a set of elementary neighbor rules that define the spatial interaction between individuals that are placed on a grid. The individual state can be "1" or "0", depending on his (her) agreement or disagreement with a concrete item propagated by a leader. In this model, each initial process of opinion dissemination needs only one individual to spread. The paper is structured in four parts. Following the introduction Sect. 2 presents a detailed explanation of the computational model. Section 3 is devoted to present some examples. Section 4 summarizes and presents concluding remarks as well as future work.

2 Background of the Dissemination Model

The model presented in this paper is based on previous work. References [13, 14] provide an approach to the dynamics of infectious diseases expansion which aims to establish a link between traditional simulation of the Susceptible-Infectious (SI) and Susceptible-Infectious-Recovered (SIR) models based on ordinary differential equations (ODE), and a very simple method based on both connectivity between people and elementary binary rules that define the result of these contacts. The present research shares part of these premises as far as we consider opinion dissemination as an infectious disease expansion in a population for computational concerns: the Susceptible group represents society and the Infected group is composed of people belonging to this society that have been convinced by an opinion coming from a leader. Let's consider a $n \times n$ grid. The n^2 cells stand for the population in a concrete society. The state space for the cell is $\{1, 0\}$; these values represent the agreement/disagreement of people related to the spreading of an opinion. The capability of an opinion to spread among people is modelled by both a local interaction rule between cells and a connectivity pattern. The cell values update according to the local rules over time and the connectivity between cells is defined as a neighborhood relationship. We define a local interaction by a rule R. See Eq. (1).

$$R : \{0, 1\} \times \{0, 1\} \rightarrow \{0, 1\}$$
$$(x,y) \rightarrow R(x,y) = a_i$$

(1)

$a_i \in \{0, 1\}$; $i \in [0, 3]$; $R(0, 0) = a_3$, $R(0, 1) = a_1$, $R(1, 0) = a_2$, $R(1, 1) = a_0$

So we can define $2^4 = 16$ different local rules depending of the values of the sequence $a_3 \, a_2 \, a_1 \, a_0$. Let m stand for the number of a particular rule, R_m. This number has binary representation, that is to say $m = a_3 \, a_2 \, a_1 \, a_0$, $m \in [0, 2^4-1]$. As an example, we consider $m = 7$ so, $a_3 = 0$; $a_2 = 1$; $a_1 = 1$ and $a_0 = 1$. Connectivity is defined by a neighborhood relationship on the grid. In this paper we consider three types of neighborhood relationship. The Von Neumann neighborhood is composed of a central cell and its four adjacent cells (4-neighbours, horizontal and vertical connection). The Moore neighborhood is composed of a central cell and the eight cells surrounding it

(8-neighbours, horizontal, vertical and diagonal connection). Finally, the knight neighborhood follows the "L" pattern, i.e. moving two squares horizontally then one square vertically, or moving one square horizontally then two squares vertically. As an example, Fig. 1. shows the effect of rule R_7 for the three different neighborhood types. We assume that the leader cell value is "1" and the cells update over time when they contact with it, depending of the neighborhood type. The blue color is used to show the dissemination of the value "1" among the population of "0" at $t = 1$. The rules are characterized by their dissemination effect (See Table 1).

0	0	0	0	0
0	0	0	0	0
0	0	1	0	0
0	0	0	0	0
0	0	0	0	0

$t = 0$ (red)

0	0	0	0	0
0	0	1	0	0
0	1	1	1	0
0	0	1	0	0
0	0	0	0	0

$t = 1$(blue) (V.N)

0	0	0	0	0
0	1	1	1	0
0	1	1	1	0
0	1	1	1	0
0	0	0	0	0

$t = 1$ (blue) (M)

0	1	0	1	0
1	0	0	0	1
0	0	1	0	0
1	0	0	0	1
0	1	0	1	0

$t = 1$ (blue) (k)

Fig. 1. Behavioral pattern of dissemination provided by R_7 at $t = 1$, in relation to different connectivity relationships (Von Neumann, Moore and knight neighborhoods)

We consider that a leader cell with an initial "1" value has a *successful spreading* among its neighbors when $R_m (1, 0) = 1$ and $R_m (1, 1) = 1$ (the rules R_5, R_7, R_{13} and R_{15} are able to do it). On the contrary, $R_m (1, 0) = 0$ and $R_m (1, 1) = 0$ are considered as an *unsuccessful spreading* of value "1", as done by the rules R_0, R_1, R_4 and R_5. We consider there is *no spreading* when no changes are triggered by the leader cell, and *swapping* when the interaction of the leader cell triggers a change of the value of its neighbours. After the leader cell acts at t, the neighbour cells in turn are leader cells that do the same on their neighbours, at $t + 1$.

3   Cases Study

We analyze different cases of dissemination effects. Figure 2 shows the behavioural pattern of dissemination of the leader cell "0" combined with rule R_{14} in a 5×5 grid for the Moore neighbourhood, when the population cells is "1". The pattern results in an alternate concentric square rings region of "0" and "1". We only can observe changes in the grid for even values of the time. R_{14} provides both an unsuccessful spreading of the leader value "0" in a population of "1" cells and a swapping triggered by the values "1" over the "1" neighbors. Figure 3 shows the graphic representation of the inversion of the trend.

Figure 4 shows the behavioural pattern of dissemination of leader cell "1" combined with rule R_9 in a 5×5 grid for the knight neighborhood when the population cells is "0". Here the pattern results in an alternate concentric diamond shaped rings of "0" and "1". We only can observe changes in the grid for even values of the time. R_9 provides both a no spreading of the leader value "1" in a population of "0" cells and a swapping triggered by the values "0" over the "0 s". Figure 5 shows the graphic representation of the consensus.

Table 1. The behavioural pattern of dissemination of the rules.

Leader cell	Neighbor cell				
		0	0	1	Rule	Behavioral pattern
		0	0	R_0 R_1 R_4 R_5	Successful spreading of "0"
		0	1	R_0 R_2 R_6 R_7	No spreading of "0"
		1	0	R_8 R_9 R_{12} R_{13}	Swapping
		1	1	R_{10} R_{11} R_{14} R_{15}	Unsuccessful spreading of "0"
	1	0	0	R_0 R_2 R_8 R_{10}	Unsuccessful spreading of "1"
		0	1	R_1 R_3 R_9 R_{11}	No spreading of "1"
		1	0	R_4 R_6 R_{12} R_{14}	Swapping
		1	1	R_5 R_7 R_{13} R_{15}	Successful spreading of "1"

1 1 1 1 1	1 1 1 1 1	0 0 0 0 0
1 1 1 1 1	1 1 1 1 1	0 1 1 1 0
1 1 0 1 1	1 1 0 1 1	0 1 0 1 0
1 1 1 1 1	1 1 1 1 1	0 1 1 1 0
1 1 1 1 1	1 1 1 1 1	0 0 0 0 0
t = 0 (red)	t = 1 (blue)	t = 2 (green)

t	"0"	"1"	New agreements
0	1	24	0
1	1	24	0
2	17	8	16

Fig. 2. Behavioural pattern of dissemination of leader cell "0" combined with rule R_{14} (5 × 5 grid, Moore neighborhood, population cells "1")

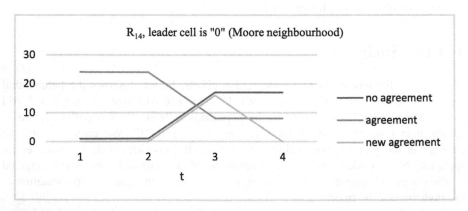

Fig. 3. Graphic representation of the spreading effect (inversion of the trend) of rule R_{14}, (Moore neighbourhood, 5 × 5 grid and leader cell "0").

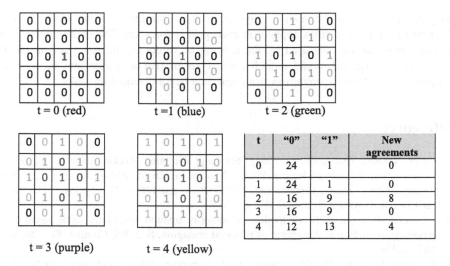

Fig. 4. The behavioural pattern of dissemination of leader cell "1" combined with rule R_9 (5 × 5 grid, knight neighborhood, population cells "0")

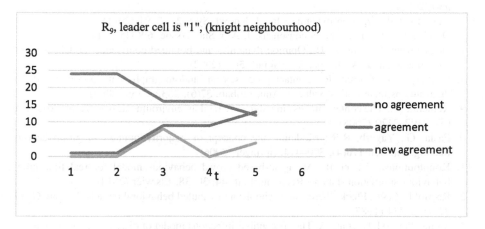

Fig. 5. Graphic representation of the spreading effect (consensus) of rule R_9 (knight neighbourhood, 5 × 5 grid and leader cells "1").

4   Conclusions and Future Work

The present research allows to draw some qualitative conclusions. Our model has the capability to characterize the spreading of an opinion in a population depending on the local rule, the neighborhood type and the leader cell state. When the spreading occurs, the dissemination can be total or partial, with inversion of the trend or with consensus, and the speed of the dissemination process is variable depending on the leader's initial state. Some improvements to the model can be suggested right now. Opinion dissemination can be thought as a more fuzzy process that overcomes the two states space assigned to each cell in the model. A layer structure of similar two state cells grids, with different dissemination rules applied on each grid is foreseen. The fuzzy effect of the dissemination can be measured by the column of values of the same cell in all the layers. This framework could model a wider set of real scenarios and be used for dissemination patterns recognition from real data beyond modeling tasks.

References

1. Guan, Xiaolan, Zhang, Zhenji, Zhang, Shugang: Evolution Mechanism of the Ecological Dissemination System of Internet Public Opinion. In: Zhang, Zhenji, Shen, Zuojun Max, Zhang, Juliang, Zhang, Runtong (eds.) LISS 2014, pp. 1769–1776. Springer, Heidelberg (2015). doi:10.1007/978-3-662-43871-8_255
2. Alvarez-Galvez, J.: Network models of minority opinion spreading: using agent-based modeling to study possible scenarios of social contagion. Soc. Sci. Comput. Rev. **34**, 567–581 (2016)
3. Kenneth, J., et al.: On the coevolution of stereotype, culture, and social relationships: an agent-based model. Soc. Sci. Comput. Rev. **32**, 295–311 (2013)
4. O'Sullivan, D.: Changing neighborhoods-neighborhoods changing. A framework for spatially explicit agent-based models of social systems. Sociol. Methods Res. **37**(4), 498–530 (2009)
5. Xia, H., et al.: Opinion dynamics. Int. J. Knowl. Syst. **2**, 72–91 (2011)
6. De Groot, M.H.: Reaching a consensus. J. Am. Stat. Assoc. **69**(345), 118–121 (1974)
7. Hegselmann, R., Krause, U.: Opinion dynamics and bounded confidence models, analysis, and simulation. J. Artif. Soc. Soc. Simul. **5**(3) (2002)
8. Chatterjee, S., Durrett, R.: Contact processes on random graphs with power law decree distributions have critical value 0. Ann. Probab. **37**(6), 2332–2356 (2009)
9. Remenik, D.: The contact process in a dynamic random environment. Ann. Appl. Probab. **18**(6), 2392–2420 (2008)
10. Pasia, G., Yagerb, R.R.: Modeling the concept of majority opinion in group decision making. Inf. Sci. **176**(4), 390–414, Springer (2006)
11. Kountouriotisa, V., et al.: An agent-based crowd behaviour model for real time crowd behaviour simulation. Pattern Recognit. Lett. **44**, 30–38, Elsevier (2014)
12. Reynolds, C.W.: Flocks, herds, and schools: a distributed behavioral model. Comput. Graph. **21**(4), 25–34 (1987)
13. Signes Pont, M.T., et al.: A. The susceptible-infectious model of disease expansion analyzed under the scope of connectivity and neighbor rules. In: Second International Conference on Computer Science, Information Technology and Applications Proceedings, pp. 1–10, Zürick (2017)
14. Signes Pont, M.T., et al.: The susceptible-infectious-recovered (SIR) model of disease expansion: a new approach. In: Proceeding of 17th Conference on Mathematical Modelling in Engineering & Human Behaviour (2017)

Author Index